DUNGEONS & DRAGONS®

PLAYER'S HANDBOOK

Core Rulebook I v.3.5

Based on the original DUNGEONS & DRAGONS game
created by E. Gary Gygax and Dave Arneson.

U.S., CANADA,
ASIA, PACIFIC, & LATIN AMERICA
Wizards of the Coast, Inc.
P.O. Box 707
Renton WA 98057-0707
QUESTIONS? 1-800-324-6496

EUROPEAN HEADQUARTERS
Wizards of the Coast, Belgium
T Hofsveld 6d
1702 Groot-Bijgaarden
Belgium
+322- 467- 3360

620-17542-001-EN   9 8 7 6 5 4 3 2
First Printing: July 2003

Visit our website at www.wizards.com/dnd

CREDITS

PLAYER'S HANDBOOK DESIGN
Jonathan Tweet

PLAYER'S HANDBOOK D&D DESIGN TEAM
Monte Cook, Jonathan Tweet,
Skip Williams

ADDITIONAL DESIGN
Peter Adkison, Richard Baker

EDITORS
Julia Martin, John Rateliff

EDITORIAL ASSISTANCE
David Noonan, Jeff Quick,
Penny Williams

MANAGING EDITOR
Kim Mohan

CORE D&D CREATIVE DIRECTOR
Ed Stark

DIRECTOR OF RPG R&D
Bill Slavicsek

VISUAL CREATIVE DIRECTOR
Jon Schindehette

ART DIRECTOR
Dawn Murin

D&D CONCEPTUAL ARTISTS
Todd Lockwood, Sam Wood

D&D LOGO DESIGN
Matt Adelsperger, Sherry Floyd

COVER ART
Henry Higginbotham

INTERIOR ARTISTS
Lars Grant-West, Scott Fischer,
John Foster, Todd Lockwood,
David Martin, Arnie Swekel, Sam Wood

GRAPHIC DESIGNERS
Sean Glenn, Sherry Floyd, Dawn Murin

TYPOGRAPHER
Nancy Walker

CARTOGRAPHER
Todd Gamble

PHOTOGRAPHER
Craig Cudnohufsky

BRAND MANAGER
Ryan Dancey

CATEGORY MANAGER
Keith Strohm

PROJECT MANAGERS
Larry Weiner, Josh Fischer

DIGI-TECH SPECIALIST
Joe Fernandez

PRODUCTION MANAGER
Chas DeLong

SPECIAL THANKS
Cindi Rice, Jim Lin, Richard Garfield,
Skaff Elias, Andrew Finch,
Jefferson L. Dunlap

PLAYER'S HANDBOOK REVISION
Andy Collins

D&D REVISION TEAM
Rich Baker, Andy Collins, David Noonan,
Rich Redman, Skip Williams

ADDITIONAL DEVELOPMENT
Bill Slavicsek, Ed Stark

PROOFREADERS
Bill McQuillan, Penny Williams

MANAGING EDITOR
Kim Mohan

CORE D&D CREATIVE DIRECTOR
Ed Stark

DIRECTOR OF RPG R&D
Bill Slavicsek

ART DIRECTOR
Dawn Murin

COVER ART
Henry Higginbotham

INTERIOR ARTISTS
Lars Grant-West, Scott Fischer,
John Foster, Jeremy Jarvis,
Todd Lockwood, David Martin,
Wayne Reynolds, Arnie Swekel, Sam Wood

GRAPHIC DESIGNER
Dawn Murin

CARTOGRAPHER
Todd Gamble

GRAPHIC PRODUCTION SPECIALISTS
Angelika Lokotz, Carmen Cheung

PHOTOGRAPHER
Craig Cudnohufsky

VICE PRESIDENT OF PUBLISHING
Mary Kirchoff

CATEGORY MANAGER
Anthony Valterra

PROJECT MANAGERS
Martin Durham

PRODUCTION MANAGER
Chas DeLong

OTHER R&D CONTRIBUTORS
Paul Barclay, Michele Carter, Bruce
Cordell, Mike Donais, David
Eckelberry, Skaff Elias, Andrew Finch,
Rob Heinsoo, Gwendolyn F.M. Kestrel,
Christopher Perkins, Charles Ryan,
Jonathan Tweet, Jennifer Clarke
Wilkes, James Wyatt

SPECIAL THANKS
Mary Elizabeth Allen, Stephen Radney-
McFarland, Liz Schuh, Andy Smith,
Alex Weitz

Contents

Introduction

This is the DUNGEONS & DRAGONS® Roleplaying Game, the game that defines the genre and has set the standard for fantasy roleplaying for more than 30 years.

D&D® is a game of your imagination in which you participate in thrilling adventures and dangerous quests by taking on the role of a hero—a character you create. Your character might be a strong fighter or a clever rogue, a devout cleric or a powerful wizard. With a few trusted allies at your side, you explore ruins and monster-filled dungeons in search of treasure. The game offers endless possibilities and a multitude of choices—more choices than even the most sophisticated computer game, because you can do whatever you can imagine.

THE D&D GAME

The D&D game is a fantasy game of your imagination. It's part acting, part storytelling, part social interaction, part war game, and part dice rolling. You and your friends create characters that develop and grow with each adventure they complete. One player is the Dungeon Master (DM). The DM controls the monsters and enemies, narrates the action, referees the game, and sets up the adventures. Together, the Dungeon Master and the players make the game come alive.

This *Player's Handbook* has all the rules players need to create characters, select equipment, and engage in combat with a variety of supernatural and mythical foes.

The *Dungeon Master's Guide*, available separately, provides the DM with advice, guidelines, and everything he or she needs to create challenges, adventures, and full-fledged D&D campaigns, including sections on prestige classes, magic items, and character rewards.

The *Monster Manual*, available separately, contains material that players and DMs alike will find useful. With hundreds of monsters to populate all levels of dungeons, this tome also includes monster creation rules, information on playing monsters as characters, details on monster tactics, and powered-up versions of standard creatures.

Together, these three volumes comprise the core rules for the DUNGEONS & DRAGONS game.

THREE DIMENSIONS

The DUNGEONS & DRAGONS game is a game of imagination, but it is also a game of tactics and strategy. Miniatures and a battle grid provide the best way to visualize the action. Miniatures, representing characters and monsters in the game, can be purchased from most hobby shops. The *Dungeon Master's Guide* includes a paper battle grid. More durable versions may be purchased separately.

The game assumes the use of miniatures and a battle grid, and the rules are written from this perspective.

CHARACTERS

Your characters star in the adventures you play, just like the heroes of a book or movie. As a player, you create a character using the rules in this book. Your character might be a savage barbarian from the frozen wastes or a clever rogue with a quick wit and a quicker blade. You might be a deadly archer trained in survival techniques or a wizard who has mastered the arcane arts. As your character participates in adventures, he or she gains experience and becomes more powerful.

ADVENTURES

Your character is an adventurer, a hero who sets out on epic quests for fortune and glory. Other characters join your adventuring party to explore dungeons and battle monsters such as the terrible dragon or the carnivorous troll. These quests unfold as stories created by the actions your characters perform and the situations your DM presents.

A DUNGEONS & DRAGONS adventure features plenty of action, exciting combat, terrifying monsters, epic challenges, and all kinds of mysteries to uncover. What lies at the heart of the dungeon? What waits around the next corner or behind the next door? Playing the roles of your characters, you and your friends face the dangers and explore a world of medieval fantasy.

One adventure might play out in a single game session; another might stretch across several sessions of play. A session lasts as long as you and your friends want to play, from a couple of hours to an all-day affair. The game can be stopped at any time and picked up wherever you left off when everyone gets back together.

Every adventure is different, every quest unique. Your character might explore ancient ruins guarded by devious traps or loot the tomb of a long-forgotten wizard. You might sneak into a castle to spy on an enemy or face the life-draining touch of an undead creature. Anything is possible in a DUNGEONS & DRAGONS game, and your character can try to do anything you can imagine.

PLAYING THE GAME

DUNGEONS & DRAGONS uses a core mechanic to resolve all actions in the game. This central game rule keeps play fast and intuitive.

The Core Mechanic: Whenever you attempt an action that has some chance of failure, you roll a twenty-sided die (d20). To determine if your character succeeds at a task (such as attacking a monster or using a skill), you do this:

WHY A REVISION?

The new DUNGEONS & DRAGONS game debuted in 2000. In the three years since the d20 Game System energized the RPG industry, we've gathered tons of data on how the game is being played. We consider D&D to be a living game that constantly evolves as it is played.

We've gathered feedback from as many people who have played D&D as we could. We've talked to you at conventions, examined countless message boards devoted to the game, and collected information from a variety of customer-response outlets including our customer service department. We used all this data to retool the game from the ground up and incorporate everyone's suggestions. We listened to what you had to say, and we responded enthusiastically to improve the game and this product.

If this is your first experience with D&D, we welcome you to a wonderful world of adventure and imagination. If you used the prior version of

this book, rest assured that this revision is a testament to our dedication to continuous product improvement. We've updated errata, clarified rules, and made the game even better than it was. But also rest assured that this is an upgrade of the d20 System, not a new edition of the game. This revision is compatible with all existing products, and those products can be used with the revision with only minor adjustments.

What's new in the revised *Player's Handbook*? We've increased the number of feats and spells to choose from, and we've added new class features to the barbarian, bard, druid, monk, ranger, and sorcerer. The entire book has been polished and refined, all in response to your feedback and to reflect the way the game is actually being played. We've streamlined some rules, expanded others. We've overhauled skills and spells.

Take a look, play the game. We think you'll like how everything turned out.

- Roll a d20.
- Add any relevant modifiers.
- Compare the result to a target number.

If the result equals or exceeds the target number (set by the DM or given in the rules), your character succeeds. If the result is lower than the target number, you fail.

THE RULES

Important: You don't have to memorize this book to play the game. Once you understand the basics, start playing! Use this book as a reference during play. When in doubt, stick to the basics, keep playing, and have fun.

One part of the book you may end up referring to frequently, at least for a while, is the glossary that begins on page 304. Here's where you'll find definitions of the terms we use in the rules and information on how a character is affected by certain conditions (such as being stunned). If you come across a term you're not familiar with and you want to know more, look it up in the glossary (and also check the index, of course).

WHAT YOU NEED TO PLAY

Your group needs these items to play D&D.

- The *Player's Handbook, Dungeon Master's Guide,* and *Monster Manual* revised core rulebooks. (All players might want to have their own copies of the books.)
- A copy of the character sheet at the back of this book for each player.
- A battle grid. The *Dungeon Master's Guide* contains one.
- Miniatures to represent each character and the monsters that challenge them.
- A set of dice for each player. A set of dice includes at least one four-sided die (d4), four six-sided dice (d6), one eight-sided die (d8), two ten-sided dice (d10), one twelve-sided die (d12), and one twenty-sided die (d20).
- Pencils, scrap paper, and graph paper to keep notes and to map the locations your characters will explore.

DICE

We describe dice rolls with expressions such as "3d4+3," which means "roll three four-sided dice and add 3" (resulting in a number between 6 and 15). The first number tells you how many dice to roll (adding the results together). The number immediately after the "d" tells you the type of die to use. Any number after that indicates a quantity that is added or subtracted from the result. Some examples include:

1d8: One eight-sided die, generating a number from 1 to 8. This is the amount of damage a longsword deals.

1d8+2: One eight-sided die plus 2, generating a number from 3 to 10. A character with a +2 Strength bonus deals this amount of damage when using a longsword.

2d4+2: Two four-sided dice plus 2, resulting in a number from 4 to 10. This is the amount of damage a 3rd-level wizard deals with a *magic missile* spell.

d%: Percentile dice work a little differently. You generate a number between 1 and 100 by rolling two different-colored ten-sided dice. One color (designated before you roll) is the tens digit. The other is the ones digit. Rolls of 7 and 1, for example, give you a result of 71. Two 0s represent 100. Some percentile dice show the tens digit in tens (00, 10, 20, etc.) and the ones digit in ones (0, 1, 2, etc.). In this case, a roll of 70 and 1 is 71, and 00 and 0 is 100.

Important! Not every action requires a die roll. Roll dice in combat and other dramatic situations when success is never a certainty.

The d20 is used to determine whether or not your character succeeds at an action. The other dice are used to determine what happens after you succeed.

Players should roll dice openly so that everyone can see the re-sults. The DM may make some rolls in secret to build suspense and maintain mystery.

WHAT CHARACTERS CAN DO

A character can try to do anything you can imagine, just as long as it fits the scene the DM describes. Depending on the situation, your character might want to listen at a door, search an area, bargain with a shopkeeper, talk to an ally, jump across a pit, move, use an item, or attack an opponent.

Characters accomplish tasks by making skill checks, ability checks, or attack rolls, using the core mechanic.

Skill Checks

To make a skill check, roll a d20 and add your character's skill modifier. Compare the result to the Difficulty Class (DC) of the task at hand.

An unopposed skill check's success depends on your result compared to a DC set by the DM or the skill's description (see Chapter 4).

An opposed skill check's success depends on your result compared to the result of the character opposing your action. The opponent's check might be made using the same skill or a different skill, as set forth in the skill's description.

Ability Checks

Ability checks are used when a character doesn't have any ranks in a skill and tries to use that skill untrained. (Some skills, however, can't be used untrained.)

Ability checks are also used to determine success when no skill applies.

To make an ability check, roll a d20 and add your character's modifier for the appropriate ability.

Attack Rolls

To attack an opponent, roll a d20 and add your character's attack bonus. If the result equals or exceeds the opponent's Armor Class (AC), the attack succeeds.

On a successful attack, roll the dice indicated for the weapon you used to determine how much damage your attack deals.

Damage reduces hit points (hp). When all of a character's hit points are gone, the character falls unconscious and is dying. (See Chapter 8: Combat for details.)

A critical hit deals more damage. If you roll a natural 20 on an attack roll, you threaten a critical hit. Roll again to confirm it. If the second attack roll is successful, then the critical hit is confirmed and you deal more damage (see page 140 for more information).

THE COMBAT ROUND

Combat is played in rounds. Each round represents 6 seconds in the game world, regardless of how long it takes to play out the round. Combat starts with initiative checks to determine the order of play for the entire battle. There are three types of actions: standard actions, move actions, and full-round actions. In a round, you can do one of these four things: Take a standard action and then a move action; take a move action and then a standard action; take two move actions; or perform a full-round action. (See Chapter 8: Combat for details.)

THE PLAYER'S ROLE

As a player, you use this handbook to create and run a character. Your character is an adventurer, part of a team that regularly delves into dungeons and battles monsters. Play wherever everyone feels comfortable and there's a place to set the battle grid and miniatures, roll the dice, and spread out your books and character sheets.

The DM sets each scene and describes the action. It's your job to decide what your character is like, how he or she relates to the other adventurers, and act accordingly. You can play a serious paladin or a wisecracking rogue, a reckless barbarian or a cautious wizard. With your character in mind, respond to each situation as it comes up. Sometimes combat is called for, but other situations might be solved through magic, negotiation, or judicious skill use.

Also consider how you respond. Do you narrate your character's action ("Tordek moves to the doorway and attacks the bugbear") or speak as your character ("I move to the doorway and take a mighty swing at the monster")? Either method is fine, and you can even vary your approach to match the situation.

D&D is a social experience as well as an imaginative one. Be creative, be daring, and be true to your character . . . and most of all, have fun!

CHARACTER CREATION

Review Chapters 1 through 5, then follow these steps to create a 1st-level character. You need a photocopy of the character sheet, a pencil, scrap paper, and four 6-sided dice.

CHECK WITH YOUR DUNGEON MASTER

Your DM may have house rules or campaign standards that vary from these rules. You should also find out what the other players have created so that your character fits into the group.

ROLL ABILITY SCORES

Roll your character's six ability scores. Determine each score by rolling four six-sided dice, ignoring the lowest die roll, and totaling the other three. Record your six results on scrap paper.

See Chapter 1 (beginning on the next page) for more details.

CHOOSE YOUR CLASS AND RACE

Choose your class and race at the same time, because some races are better suited to certain classes. The classes, detailed in Chapter 3, are barbarian, bard, cleric, druid, fighter, monk, paladin, ranger, rogue, sorcerer, and wizard. Each class description includes a "Races" section that provides some advice.

The races, described in Chapter 2, are human, dwarf, elf, gnome, halfling, half-elf, and half-orc.

Write your class and race selections on your character sheet.

ASSIGN AND ADJUST ABILITY SCORES

Now that you know your character's class and race, take the ability scores you rolled earlier and assign each to one of the six abilities: Strength, Dexterity, Constitution, Intelligence, Wisdom, and Charisma. Adjust these scores up or down, according to your race, as indicated on Table 2–1: Racial Ability Adjustments (page 12).

Put high scores in abilities that support your class selection. Each class description includes an "Abilities" section that provides some advice.

For each ability score, record the character's modifier, as indicated on Table 1–1: Ability Modifiers and Bonus Spells (page 8). Ability modifiers adjust many die rolls in the game, including attack rolls, damage rolls, skill checks, and saving throws.

Record your adjusted ability scores and their modifiers on your character sheet.

REVIEW THE STARTING PACKAGE

There is at least one starting package at the end of each class description. Look at your class's starting package. It offers a fast way to complete the next several steps of character creation. If you like the feat, skills, and equipment listed there, record this information on your character sheet. Otherwise, use this information as a guide and make your own decisions.

RECORD RACIAL AND CLASS FEATURES

Your character's race and class provide certain features. Most of these are automatic, but some involve making choices and thinking

ahead about upcoming character creation steps. Feel free to look ahead or to backtrack and do something over if you need to.

SELECT SKILLS

Your character's class and Intelligence modifier determine how many skill points you have to buy skills (see page 62).

Skills are measured in ranks. Each rank adds +1 to skill checks made using a specific skill.

At 1st level, you can buy as many as 4 ranks in a class skill (a skill on your class's list of class skills) for 4 skill points, or as many as 2 ranks in a cross-class skill (a skill from another class's list of class skills) for the same cost. (You get more out of purchasing class skills.)

Buying skills goes faster if you spend 4 skill points (your maximum) on every skill you buy, as we've done in the starting packages.

Once you've selected your skills, determine the skill modifier for each one. To do this, add the skill ranks to the ability modifier associated with the skill and record it on your character sheet.

Table 4–2: Skills (page 63) lists all skills in the game and indicates which skills are class skills for which classes.

SELECT A FEAT

Each 1st-level character starts with one feat. Table 5–1: Feats (page 90) lists all feats, their prerequisites (if any), and a brief description.

REVIEW DESCRIPTION CHAPTER

Look over Chapter 6: Description. It helps you detail your character. You can handle this now or wait until later.

SELECT EQUIPMENT

Use the equipment from your class's starting package, or randomly determine your starting gold (see page 111) and buy your own gear piece by piece, using the information in Chapter 7: Equipment.

RECORD COMBAT NUMBERS

Determine these statistics and record them on your character sheet.

Hit Points: Your hit points (hp) determine how hard your character is to kill. At 1st level, wizards and sorcerers get 4 hp; rogues and bards get 6 hp; clerics, druids, monks, and rangers get 8 hp; fighters and paladins get 10 hp; and barbarians get 12 hp. To this number, add your character's Constitution modifier.

Armor Class: Your Armor Class (AC) determines how hard your character is to hit. Add the following numbers together to get your AC: 10 + your armor bonus + your shield bonus + your size modifier + your Dexterity modifier.

Initiative: Your character's initiative modifier equals your Dexterity modifier. The Improved Initiative feat provides an additional modifier if you selected it.

Attack Bonuses: Your class determines your base attack bonus. To determine your melee attack bonus for when you get into close-combat fights, add your Strength modifier to your base attack bonus. To determine your ranged attack bonus for when you attack from a distance, add your Dexterity modifier to your base attack bonus.

Saving Throws: Your class determines your base saving throw bonuses. To these numbers, add your Constitution modifier to get your Fortitude save, your Dexterity modifier to get your Reflex save, and your Wisdom modifier to get your Will save.

DETAILS, DETAILS, DETAILS

Now choose a name for your character, determine the character's gender, choose an alignment, decide the character's age and appearance, and so on. Chapter 6: Description can help with this.

There's no need to develop your character completely. With your DM's permission, you can always add or even change details as you play and get a better feel for your character.

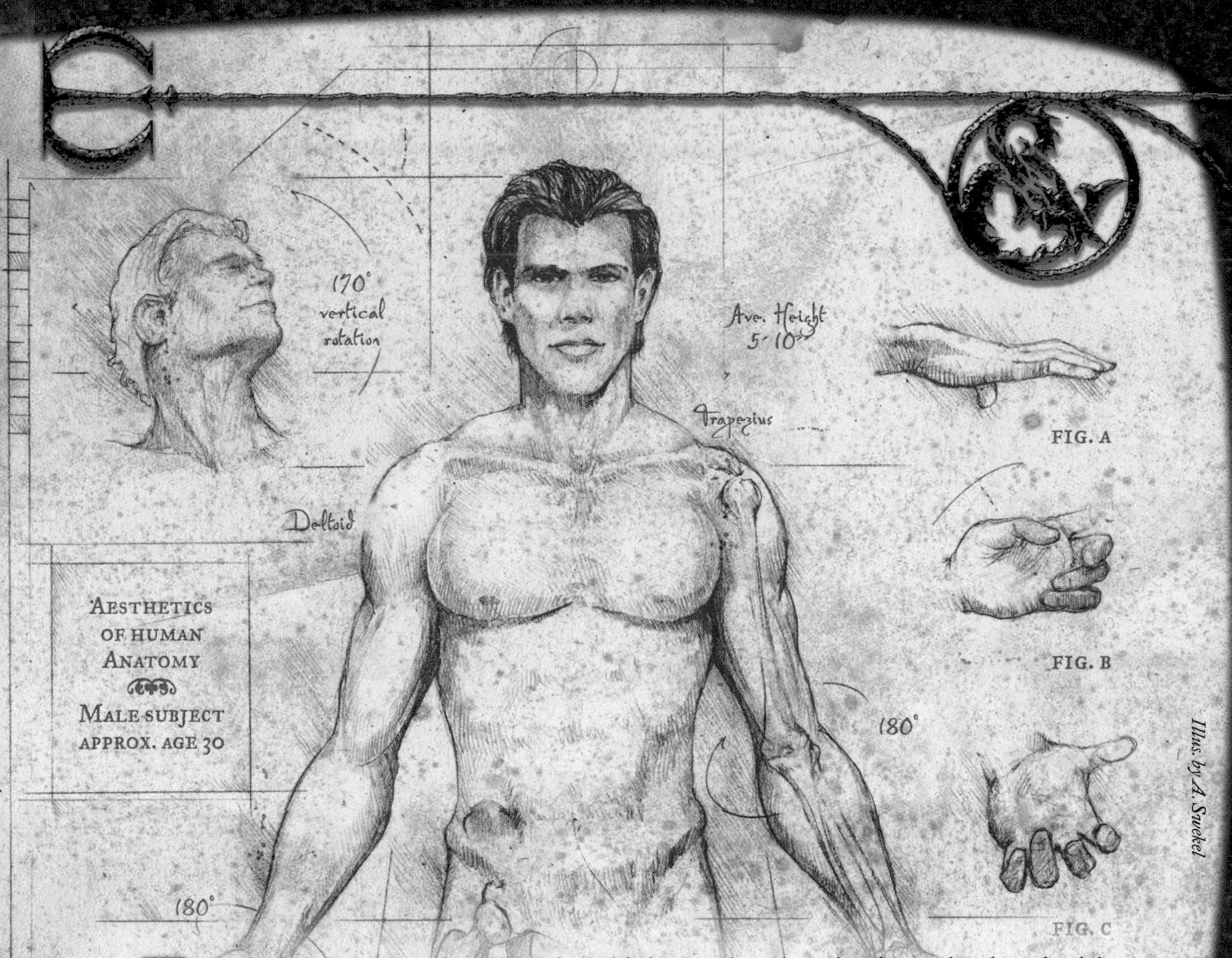

Illus. by A. Snekel

AESTHETICS OF HUMAN ANATOMY

MALE SUBJECT APPROX. AGE 30

170° vertical rotation

Ave. Height 5'10"

Trapezius

Deltoid

FIG. A

FIG. B

180°

180°

FIG. C

90°

Just about every die roll you make is going to be modified based on your character's abilities. A tough character has a better chance of surviving a wyvern's poison sting. A perceptive character is more likely to notice bugbears sneaking up from behind. A stupid character is not as likely to find a secret door that leads to a hidden treasure chamber. Your ability scores tell you what your modifiers are for rolls such as these.

Your character has six abilities: Strength (abbreviated Str), Dexterity (Dex), Constitution (Con), Intelligence (Int), Wisdom (Wis), and Charisma (Cha). Each of your character's above-average abilities gives you a benefit on certain die rolls, and each below-average ability gives you a disadvantage on other die rolls. When creating your character, you roll your scores randomly, assign them to the abilities as you like, and raise and lower them according to the character's race. Later, you can increase them as your character advances in experience.

ABILITY SCORES

To create an ability score for your character, roll four six-sided dice (4d6). Disregard the lowest die roll and total the three highest ones. The result is a number between 3 (horrible) and 18 (tremendous). The average ability score for a typical commoner is 10 or 11, but your character is not typical. The most common ability scores for player characters (PCs) are 12 and 13. (That's right, the average player character is above average.)

Make this roll six times, recording each result on a piece of paper. Once you have six scores, assign each score to one of the six abilities. At this step, you need to know what kind of person your character is going to be, including his or her race and class, in order to know how best to distribute the ability scores. Choosing a race other than human or half-elf causes some of these ability scores to change (see Table 2–1: Racial Ability Adjustments, page 12).

ABILITY MODIFIERS

Each ability, after changes made because of race, has a modifier ranging from –5 to +5. Table 1–1: Ability Modifiers and Bonus Spells (on the next page) shows the modifier for each score. It also shows bonus spells, which you'll need to know about if your character is a spellcaster.

The modifier is the number you apply to the die roll when your character tries to do something related to that ability. For instance, you apply your character's Strength modifier to your roll when he or she tries to hit someone with a sword. You also use the modifier with some numbers that aren't die rolls—for example, you apply your character's Dexterity modifier to his or her Armor Class (AC). A positive modifier is called a bonus, and a negative modifier is called a penalty.

ABILITIES AND SPELLCASTERS

The ability that governs bonus spells (see Chapter 3: Classes) depends on what type of spellcaster your character is: Intelligence for wizards; Wisdom for clerics, druids, paladins, and rangers; or Charisma for sorcerers and bards. In addition to having a high ability score, a spellcaster must be of high enough class level to be able to cast spells of a given spell level. (See the class descriptions in Chapter 3 for details.) For instance, the wizard Mialee has an Intelligence

TABLE 1–1: ABILITY MODIFIERS AND BONUS SPELLS

Score	Modifier	0	1st	2nd	3rd	4th	5th	6th	7th	8th	9th
1	−5	Can't cast spells tied to this ability									
2–3	−4	Can't cast spells tied to this ability									
4–5	−3	Can't cast spells tied to this ability									
6–7	−2	Can't cast spells tied to this ability									
8–9	−1	Can't cast spells tied to this ability									
10–11	0	—	—	—	—	—	—	—	—	—	—
12–13	+1	—	1	—	—	—	—	—	—	—	—
14–15	+2	—	1	1	—	—	—	—	—	—	—
16–17	+3	—	1	1	1	—	—	—	—	—	—
18–19	+4	—	1	1	1	1	—	—	—	—	—
20–21	+5	—	2	1	1	1	1	—	—	—	—
22–23	+6	—	2	2	1	1	1	1	—	—	—
24–25	+7	—	2	2	2	1	1	1	1	—	—
26–27	+8	—	2	2	2	2	1	1	1	1	—
28–29	+9	—	3	2	2	2	2	1	1	1	1
30–31	+10	—	3	3	2	2	2	2	1	1	1
32–33	+11	—	3	3	3	2	2	2	2	1	1
34–35	+12	—	3	3	3	3	2	2	2	2	1
36–37	+13	—	4	3	3	3	3	2	2	2	2
38–39	+14	—	4	4	3	3	3	3	2	2	2
40–41	+15	—	4	4	4	3	3	3	3	2	2
42–43	+16	—	4	4	4	4	3	3	3	3	2
44–45	+17	—	5	4	4	4	4	3	3	3	3
etc....											

Column group heading: Bonus Spells (by Spell Level)

score of 15, so she's smart enough to get one bonus 1st-level spell and one bonus 2nd-level spell. (She will not actually get the bonus 2nd-level spell until she is a 3rd-level wizard, since that's the minimum level a wizard must be to cast 2nd-level spells.)

If your character's ability score is 9 or lower, you can't cast spells tied to that ability. For example, if Mialee's Intelligence score dropped to 9 because of a poison that reduces intellect, she would not be able to cast even her simplest spells until cured.

REROLLING

If your scores are too low, you may scrap them and roll all six scores again. Your scores are considered too low if the sum of your modifiers (before adjustments because of race) is 0 or lower, or if your highest score is 13 or lower.

THE ABILITIES

Each ability partially describes your character and affects some of his or her actions.

The description of each ability includes a list of races and creatures along with their average scores in that ability. (Not every creature has a score in every ability, as you'll see when you look at the lists that follow.) These scores are for an average, young adult creature of the indicated race or kind, such as a dwarf tax collector, a halfling merchant, or an unexceptional gnoll. An adventurer—say, a dwarf fighter or a gnoll ranger—probably has better scores, at least in the abilities that matter most to that character, and player characters are above average overall.

STRENGTH (STR)

Strength measures your character's muscle and physical power. This ability is especially important for fighters, barbarians, paladins, rangers, and monks because it helps them prevail in combat. Strength also limits the amount of equipment your character can carry (see Chapter 9: Adventuring).

You apply your character's Strength modifier to:
- Melee attack rolls.
- Damage rolls when using a melee weapon or a thrown weapon (including a sling). (*Exceptions:* Off-hand attacks receive only one-half the character's Strength bonus, while two-handed attacks receive one and a half times the Strength bonus. A Strength penalty, but not a bonus, applies to attacks made with a bow that is not a composite bow.)
- Climb, Jump, and Swim checks. These are the skills that have Strength as their key ability.
- Strength checks (for breaking down doors and the like).

AVERAGE STRENGTH SCORES

Example Race or Creature Kind	Average Strength	Average Modifier
Allip, shadow, will-o'-wisp	—	—
Lantern archon, bat, toad	1	−5
Rat swarm	2	−4
Stirge, monkey, Tiny monstrous spider	3	−4
Grig, Small monstrous centipede	4–5	−3
Hawk, cockatrice, pixie	6–7	−2
Quasit, badger	8–9	−1
Human, beholder, dire rat	10–11	+0
Mind flayer, dog, pony, ghoul	12–13	+1
Gnoll, dire badger, baboon, manta ray	14–15	+2
Black pudding, choker, Large shark	16–17	+3
Centaur, displacer beast, minotaur	18–19	+4
Ape, ogre, flesh golem, gorgon	20–21	+5
Fire giant, triceratops, elephant	30–31	+10
Great wyrm gold dragon	46–47	+18

DEXTERITY (DEX)

Dexterity measures hand-eye coordination, agility, reflexes, and balance. This ability is the most important one for rogues, but it's also high on the list for characters who typically wear light or medium armor (rangers and barbarians) or no armor at all (monks, wizards, and sorcerers), and for anyone who wants to be a skilled archer.

You apply your character's Dexterity modifier to:
- Ranged attack rolls, including those for attacks made with bows, crossbows, throwing axes, and other ranged weapons.
- Armor Class (AC), provided that the character can react to the attack.
- Reflex saving throws, for avoiding fireballs and other attacks that you can escape by moving quickly.

- Balance, Escape Artist, Hide, Move Silently, Open Lock, Ride, Sleight of Hand, Tumble, and Use Rope checks. These are the skills that have Dexterity as their key ability.

AVERAGE DEXTERITY SCORES

Example Race or Creature Kind	Average Dexterity	Average Modifier
Shrieker (fungus)	—	—
Gelatinous cube (ooze)	1	−5
Colossal animated object	4–5	−3
Purple worm, ogre zombie	6–7	−2
Ogre, basilisk, fire giant, tendriculos	8–9	−1
Human, triton, boar, giant fire beetle	10–11	+0
Bugbear, lammasu, hobgoblin	12–13	+1
Displacer beast, hieracosphinx	14–15	+2
Blink dog, wraith, lion, octopus	16–17	+3
Astral deva (angel), ethereal filcher	18–19	+4
Arrowhawk, bone devil	20–21	+5
Elder air elemental	32–33	+11

CONSTITUTION (CON)

Constitution represents your character's health and stamina. A Constitution bonus increases a character's hit points, so the ability is important for all classes.

You apply your character's Constitution modifier to:
- Each roll of a Hit Die (though a penalty can never drop a result below 1—that is, a character always gains at least 1 hit point each time he or she advances in level).
- Fortitude saving throws, for resisting poison and similar threats.
- Concentration checks. Concentration is a skill, important to spellcasters, that has Constitution as its key ability.

If a character's Constitution score changes enough to alter his or her Constitution modifier, the character's hit points also increase or decrease accordingly.

AVERAGE CONSTITUTION SCORES

Example Race or Creature Kind	Average Constitution	Average Modifier
Ghoul, mummy, shadow	—	—
Centipede swarm, locust swarm	8–9	−1
Human, imp, dire weasel, grick	10–11	+0
Rust monster, medusa, otyugh, nymph	12–13	+1
Light horse, merfolk, troglodyte	14–15	+2
Tiger, chimera, assassin vine	16–17	+3
Polar bear, gargoyle, umber hulk	18–19	+4
Elephant, aboleth, tyrannosaurus	20–21	+5
The tarrasque	35	+12

INTELLIGENCE (INT)

Intelligence determines how well your character learns and reasons. This ability is important for wizards because it affects how many spells they can cast, how hard their spells are to resist, and how powerful their spells can be. It's also important for any character who wants to have a wide assortment of skills.

You apply your character's Intelligence modifier to:
- The number of languages your character knows at the start of the game.
- The number of skill points gained each level. (But your character always gets at least 1 skill point per level.)
- Appraise, Craft, Decipher Script, Disable Device, Forgery, Knowledge, Search, and Spellcraft checks. These are the skills that have Intelligence as their key ability.

A wizard gains bonus spells based on her Intelligence score. The minimum Intelligence score needed to cast a wizard spell is 10 + the spell's level.

An animal has an Intelligence score of 1 or 2. A creature of humanlike intelligence has a score of at least 3.

AVERAGE INTELLIGENCE SCORES

Example Race or Creature Kind	Average Intelligence	Average Modifier
Zombie, golem, ochre jelly	—	—
Carrion crawler, purple worm, camel	1	−5
Tiger, hydra, dog, horse	2	−4
Gray render, tendriculos, rast	3	−4
Otyugh, griffon, displacer beast	4–5	−3
Troll, hell hound, ogre, yrthak	6–7	−2
Troglodyte, centaur, gnoll	8–9	−1
Human, bugbear, wight, night hag	10–11	+0
Dragon turtle, cloud giant, lamia	12–13	+1
Invisible stalker, wraith, will-o'-wisp	14–15	+2
Beholder, succubus, trumpet archon	16–17	+3
Mind flayer, death slaad, nightwing	18–19	+4
Kraken, titan, nightcrawler	20–21	+5
Great wyrm gold dragon	32–33	+11

WISDOM (WIS)

Wisdom describes a character's willpower, common sense, perception, and intuition. While Intelligence represents one's ability to analyze information, Wisdom represents being in tune with and aware of one's surroundings. An "absentminded professor" has low Wisdom and high Intelligence. A simpleton (low Intelligence) might still have great insight (high Wisdom). Wisdom is the most important ability for clerics and druids, and it is also important for paladins and rangers. If you want your character to have acute senses, put a high score in Wisdom. Every creature has a Wisdom score.

You apply your character's Wisdom modifier to:
- Will saving throws (for negating the effect of charm person and other spells).
- Heal, Listen, Profession, Sense Motive, Spot, and Survival checks. These are the skills that have Wisdom as their key ability.

Clerics, druids, paladins, and rangers get bonus spells based on their Wisdom scores. The minimum Wisdom score needed to cast a cleric, druid, paladin, or ranger spell is 10 + the spell's level.

AVERAGE WISDOM SCORES

Example Race or Creature Kind	Average Wisdom	Average Modifier
Gelatinous cube (ooze), animated object	1	−5
Shrieker (fungus)	2	−4
Red slaad, githyanki	6–7	−2
Purple worm, grimlock, troll	8–9	−1
Human, lizardfolk, phantom fungus	10–11	+0
Owlbear, hyena, shadow, remorhaz	12–13	+1
Wraith, owl, giant praying mantis	14–15	+2
Devourer, lillend, androsphinx	16–17	+3
Couatl, erinyes devil, guardian naga	18–19	+4
Unicorn, storm giant	20–21	+5
Great wyrm gold dragon	32–33	+11

CHARISMA (CHA)

Charisma measures a character's force of personality, persuasiveness, personal magnetism, ability to lead, and physical attractiveness. This ability represents actual strength of personality, not merely how one is perceived by others in a social setting. Charisma is most important for paladins, sorcerers, and bards. It is also important for clerics, since it affects their ability to turn undead. Every creature has a Charisma score.

You apply your character's Charisma modifier to:
- Bluff, Diplomacy, Disguise, Gather Information, Handle Animal, Intimidate, Perform, and Use Magic Device checks. These are the skills that have Charisma as their key ability.
- Checks that represent attempts to influence others.

- Turning checks for clerics and paladins attempting to turn zombies, vampires, and other undead.

Sorcerers and bards get bonus spells based on their Charisma scores. The minimum Charisma score needed to cast a sorcerer or bard spell is 10 + the spell's level.

AVERAGE CHARISMA SCORES

Example Race or Creature Kind	Average Charisma	Average Modifier
Zombie, golem, shrieker (fungus)	1	−5
Spider, crocodile, lizard, rhinoceros	2	−4
Tendriculos, octopus	3	−4
Dire rat, weasel, chuul, donkey	4–5	−3
Badger, troll, giant fire beetle, bear	6–7	−2
Gnoll, dire boar, manticore, gorgon	8–9	−1
Human, wolverine, dretch (demon)	10–11	0
Treant, roper, doppelganger, night hag	12–13	+1
Storm giant, barghest, medusa	14–15	+2
Ogre mage, pixie, harpy, achaierai	16–17	+3
Greater barghest, nixie	18–19	+4
Astral deva (angel), kraken	20–21	+5
Great wyrm gold dragon	32–33	+11

EXAMPLE OF GENERATING AND ASSIGNING ABILITY SCORES

Monte wants to create a new character. He rolls four six-sided dice (4d6) and gets 5, 4, 4, and 1. Ignoring the lowest roll (1), he records the result on scratch paper: 13. He rolls the dice five more times and gets these six scores: 13, 10, 15, 12, 8, and 14. Monte decides to play a strong, tough dwarf fighter. Now he assigns his scores to abilities.

Strength gets the highest score, 15. His character has a +2 Strength bonus that will serve him well in combat.

Constitution gets the next highest score, 14. The dwarf's +2 racial bonus to Constitution (see Table 2–1: Racial Ability Adjustments, page 12) improves his Constitution score to 16, which gives him a +3 modifier. This bonus gives the character more hit points and better Fortitude saving throws.

Monte puts his lowest score, 8, into Charisma. The dwarf's −2 racial penalty to Charisma (see Table 2–1) reduces his Charisma score to 6, for a −2 penalty.

Monte has two bonus-range scores left (13 and 12), plus an average score (10). Dexterity gets the 13 (+1 bonus), which helps with ranged weapon attacks and with Reflex saving throws. (Monte's also thinking ahead. A Dexterity score of 13 qualifies his character for the Dodge feat—see Table 5–1: Feats, page 90).

Wisdom gets the 12 (+1 bonus). The Wisdom bonus helps with perception skills, such as Spot and Listen (see Table 4–2: Skills, page 63), as well as with Will saving throws.

Intelligence gets the 10 (no bonus or penalty). An average Intelligence isn't bad for a fighter.

Monte records his character's race, class, ability scores, and ability modifiers on his character sheet.

CHANGING ABILITY SCORES

Over time, the ability scores your character starts with can change. Ability scores can increase with no limit. Points at which ability changes occur include the following:

- Add 1 point to any score upon attaining 4th level and at every fourth level your character attains thereafter (8th, 12th, 16th, and 20th level).
- Many spells and magical effects temporarily increase or decrease ability scores. The *ray of enfeeblement* spell reduces a creature's Strength, and the *bull's strength* spell increases it. Sometimes a spell hampers a character, reducing his or her ability score. A character trapped by an *entangle* spell, for example, acts as if his or her Dexterity were 4 points lower than it really is.
- Several magic items improve ability scores as long as the character is using them. For example, *gloves of Dexterity* improve the wearer's Dexterity score. (Magic items are described in the *Dungeon Master's Guide*.) Note that a magic item of this type can't change an ability score by more than +6.
- Some rare magic items can boost an ability score permanently, as can a *wish* spell. Such an increase is called an inherent bonus. An ability score can't have an inherent bonus of more than +5.
- Poisons, diseases, and other effects can temporarily harm an ability (ability damage). Ability points lost to damage return on their own at a rate of 1 point per day for each damaged ability.
- Some effects drain abilities, resulting in a permanent loss (ability drain). Points lost this way don't return on their own, but they can be regained with spells, such as *restoration*.
- As a character ages, some ability scores go up and others go down. See Table 6–5: Aging Effects (page 109).

When an ability score changes, all attributes associated with that score change accordingly. For example, when Mialee becomes a 4th-level wizard, she decides to increase her Intelligence score to 16. That score gives her a 3rd-level bonus spell (which she'll pick up upon attaining 5th level, when she becomes able to cast 3rd-level spells), and it also increases the number of skill points she gets per level from 4 to 5 (2 per level for her class, plus another 3 per level from her Intelligence bonus). As a new 4th-level character, she can get the skill points immediately after raising her Intelligence, so she'll get 5 points for attaining 4th level in the wizard class. She does not retroactively get additional points for her previous levels (that is, skill points she would have gained if she had had an Intelligence score of 16 starting at 1st level).

INTELLIGENCE, WISDOM, AND CHARISMA

You can use your character's Intelligence, Wisdom, and Charisma scores to guide you in roleplaying your character. Here is some background (just guidelines) about what these scores can mean.

A smart character (one with high Intelligence) is curious, knowledgeable, and prone to using big words. A character with a high Intelligence but low Wisdom may be smart but absentminded, or knowledgeable but lacking in common sense. A character with high Intelligence but low Charisma may be a know-it-all or a reclusive scholar. A smart character lacking in both Wisdom and Charisma may put her foot in her mouth often.

A character with low Intelligence mispronounces and misuses words, has trouble following directions, or fails to get the joke.

A character with high Wisdom may be sensible, serene, "in tune," alert, or centered. A character with high Wisdom but low Intelligence may be aware, but simple. A character with high Wisdom but low

Charisma knows enough to speak carefully and may become an advisor (or "power behind the throne") rather than a leader. The wise character lacking in both Intelligence and Charisma is uncouth and unsophisticated.

A character with a low Wisdom score may be rash, imprudent, irresponsible, or "out of it."

A character with high Charisma may be attractive, striking, personable, and confident. A character with high Charisma but low Intelligence can usually pass herself off as knowledgeable, until she meets a true expert. A charismatic character with low Wisdom may be popular, but she doesn't know who her real friends are. A charismatic character lacking in both Intelligence and Wisdom is likely to be shallow and unaware of others' feelings.

A character with low Charisma may be reserved, gruff, rude, fawning, or simply nondescript.

FIG. A

FIG. B

FIG. C

FIG. D

FIG. E

FIG. F

FIG. G

Illus. by A. Swekel

CHAPTER TWO — RACES

he elven woods are home to the elves and their allies. Not many dwarves or half-orcs live there. In turn, elves, humans, halflings, and half-orcs are hard to find in underground dwarven cities. And while nonhumans may travel through the human countryside, most country folk are humans. In the big cities, however, the promise of power and profit brings together people of all the common races: humans, dwarves, elves, gnomes, half-elves, half-orcs, and halflings.

CHOOSING A RACE

After you roll your ability scores and before you write them on your character sheet, choose your character's race. At the same time, you should choose a class, since race affects how well a character can do in each class. Once you know your character's race and class, assign your ability score rolls to particular abilities, alter those abilities according to race, and continue detailing your character.

You can play a character of any race and class combination, but certain races do better pursuing certain careers. Halflings, for example, can be fighters, but their small size and special features make them better as rogues.

Your character's race gives you plenty of cues as to what sort of person he or she is, how he or she feels about characters of other races, and what his or her motivations might be. Remember, however, that these descriptions apply only to the majority of each race's members. In each race, some individuals diverge from the norm, and your character could be one of these. Don't let a description of a race keep you from detailing your character as you like.

RACIAL CHARACTERISTICS

Your character's race determines some of his or her qualities.

ABILITY ADJUSTMENTS

Find your character's race on Table 2–1: Racial Ability Adjustments (see the next page) and apply the adjustments you see there to your character's ability scores. If these changes put your score above 18 or below 3, that's okay, except in the case of Intelligence, which does not go below 3 for characters. (If your half-orc character would have an adjusted Intelligence of 1 or 2, make it 3 instead.)

For example, Lidda, a halfling, has a +2 racial bonus on her Dexterity score and a –2 racial penalty on her Strength score. Knowing this, her player puts her best score rolled (15) in Dexterity so that it will increase to 17. She doesn't want a Strength penalty, so she puts an above-average score (12) in Strength. Her Strength score drops to 10, which carries neither a bonus nor a penalty.

FAVORED CLASS

Each race's favored class is also given on Table 2–1: Racial Ability Adjustments. A character's favored class doesn't count against him or her when determining experience point penalties for multiclassing (see XP for Multiclass Characters, page 60).

For example, as a halfling rogue, Lidda can add a second class later on (becoming a multiclass character) without worrying about an XP penalty, because rogue is the favored class for halflings.

11

Illus. by T. Lockwood

Human Half-Orc Half-Elf Dwarf Elf Gnome Halfling

TABLE 2–1: RACIAL ABILITY ADJUSTMENTS

Race	Ability Adjustments	Favored Class
Human	None	Any
Dwarf	+2 Constitution, –2 Charisma	Fighter
Elf	+2 Dexterity, –2 Constitution	Wizard
Gnome	+2 Constitution, –2 Strength	Bard
Half-elf	None	Any
Half-orc	+2 Strength, –2 Intelligence[1], –2 Charisma	Barbarian
Halfling	+2 Dexterity, –2 Strength	Rogue

1 A half-orc's starting Intelligence score is always at least 3. If this adjustment would lower the character's score to 1 or 2, his score is nevertheless 3.

RACE AND LANGUAGES

In a big city, visitors can hear all manner of languages being spoken. Dwarves haggle over gems in Dwarven, elf sages engage in learned debates in Elven, and preachers call out prayers in Celestial. The language heard most, however, is Common, a tongue shared by all who take part in the culture at large. With all these languages in use, it is easy for people to learn other languages, and adventurers often speak several tongues.

All characters know how to speak Common. A dwarf, elf, gnome, half-elf, half-orc, or halfling also speaks a racial language, as appropriate. A smart character (one who had an Intelligence bonus at 1st level) speaks other languages as well, one extra language per point of Intelligence bonus as a starting character. Select your character's bonus languages (if any) from the list found in his or her race's description later in this chapter.

Literacy: Any character except a barbarian can read and write all the languages he or she speaks. (A barbarian can become literate by spending skill points; see Illiteracy, page 25.)

Class-Related Languages: Clerics, druids, and wizards can choose certain languages as bonus languages even if they're not on the lists found in the race descriptions. These class-related languages are as follows:

Cleric: Abyssal, Celestial, Infernal.
Druid: Sylvan.
Wizard: Draconic.

HUMANS

Most humans are the descendants of pioneers, conquerors, traders, travelers, refugees, and other people on the move. As a result, human lands are home to a mix of people—physically, culturally, religiously, and politically different. Hardy or fine, light-skinned or dark, showy or austere, primitive or civilized, devout or impious, humans run the gamut.

Personality: Humans are the most adaptable, flexible, and ambitious people among the common races. They are diverse in their tastes, morals, customs, and habits. Others accuse them of having little respect for history, but it's only natural that humans, with their relatively short life spans and constantly changing cultures, would have a shorter collective memory than dwarves, elves, gnomes, or halflings.

Physical Description: Humans typically stand from 5 feet to a little over 6 feet tall and weigh from 125 to 250 pounds, with men noticeably taller and heavier than women. Thanks to their penchant for migration and conquest, and to their short life spans, humans are more physically diverse than other common races. Their skin shades range from nearly black to very pale, their hair from black to blond (curly, kinky, or straight), and their facial hair (for men) from sparse to thick. Plenty of humans have a dash of nonhuman blood, and they may demonstrate hints of elf, orc, or other lineages. Members of this race are often ostentatious or

Illus. by T. Lockwood

Human · Half-Orc · Gnome · Halfling · Dwarf · Half-Elf · Elf

unorthodox in their grooming and dress, sporting unusual hairstyles, fanciful clothes, tattoos, body piercings, and the like. Humans have short life spans, reaching adulthood at about age 15 and rarely living even a single century.

Relations: Just as readily as they mix with each other, humans mix with members of other races, among which they are known as "everyone's second-best friends." Humans serve as ambassadors, diplomats, magistrates, merchants, and functionaries of all kinds.

Alignment: Humans tend toward no particular alignment, not even neutrality. The best and the worst are found among them.

Human Lands: Human lands are usually in flux, with new ideas, social changes, innovations, and new leaders constantly coming to the fore. Members of longer-lived races find human culture exciting but eventually a little wearying or even bewildering.

Since humans lead such short lives, their leaders are all young compared to the political, religious, and military leaders among the other races. Even where individual humans are conservative traditionalists, human institutions change with the generations, adapting and evolving faster than parallel institutions among the elves, dwarves, gnomes, and halflings. Individually and as a group, humans are adaptable opportunists, and they stay on top of changing political dynamics.

Human lands generally include relatively large numbers of nonhumans (compared, for instance, to the number of nondwarves who live in dwarven lands).

Religion: Unlike members of the other common races, humans do not have a chief racial deity. Pelor, the sun god, is the most commonly worshiped deity in human lands, but he can claim nothing like the central place that the dwarves give Moradin or the elves give Corellon Larethian in their respective pantheons. Some humans are the most ardent and zealous adherents of a given religion, while others are the most impious people around.

Language: Humans speak Common. They typically learn other languages as well, including obscure ones, and they are fond of sprinkling their speech with words borrowed from other tongues: Orc curses, Elven musical expressions, Dwarven military phrases, and so on.

Names: Human names vary greatly. Without a unifying deity to give them a touchstone for their culture, and with such a fast breeding cycle, humans mutate socially at a fast rate. Human culture, therefore, is more diverse than other cultures, and no human names are truly typical. Some human parents give their children dwarven or elven names (pronounced more or less correctly).

Adventurers: Human adventurers are the most audacious, daring, and ambitious members of an audacious, daring, and ambitious race. A human can earn glory in the eyes of her fellows by amassing power, wealth, and fame. Humans, more than other people, champion causes rather than territories or groups.

HUMAN RACIAL TRAITS

- **Medium:** As Medium creatures, humans have no special bonuses or penalties due to their size.
- Human base land speed is 30 feet.
- 1 extra feat at 1st level, because humans are quick to master specialized tasks and varied in their talents. See Chapter 5: Feats.
- 4 extra skill points at 1st level and 1 extra skill point at each additional level, since humans are versatile and capable. (The 4 skill points at 1st level are added on as a bonus, not multiplied in; see Chapter 4: Skills.)
- **Automatic Language:** Common. **Bonus Languages:** Any (other than secret languages, such as Druidic). See other racial lists for common languages or the Speak Language skill (page 82) for a more comprehensive list. Humans mingle with all kinds of other folk and thus can learn any language found in an area.

Illus. by T. Lockwood

- Favored Class: Any. When determining whether a multiclass human takes an experience point penalty, her highest-level class does not count. (See XP for Multiclass Characters, page 60.)

DWARVES

Dwarves are known for their skill in warfare, their ability to withstand physical and magical punishment, their knowledge of the earth's secrets, their hard work, and their capacity for drinking ale. Their mysterious kingdoms, carved out from the insides of mountains, are renowned for the marvelous treasures that they produce as gifts or for trade.

Personality: Dwarves are slow to laugh or jest and suspicious of strangers, but they are generous to those few who earn their trust. Dwarves value gold, gems, jewelry, and art objects made with these precious materials, and they have been known to succumb to greed. They fight neither recklessly nor timidly, but with careful courage and tenacity. Their sense of justice is strong, but at its worst it can turn into a thirst for vengeance. Among gnomes, who get along famously with dwarves, a mild oath is "If I'm lying, may I cross a dwarf."

Physical Description: Dwarves stand only 4 to 4-1/2 feet tall, but they are so broad and compact that they are, on average, almost as heavy as humans. Dwarf men are slightly taller and noticeably heavier than dwarf women. Dwarves' skin is typically deep tan or light brown, and their eyes are dark. Their hair is usually black, gray, or brown, and worn long. Dwarf men value their beards highly and groom them very carefully. Dwarves favor simple styles for their hair, beards, and clothes. Dwarves are considered adults at about age 40, and they can live to be more than 400 years old.

Relations: Dwarves get along fine with gnomes, and passably with humans, half-elves, and halflings. Dwarves say, "The difference between an acquaintance and a friend is about a hundred years." Humans, with their short life spans, have a hard time forging truly strong bonds with dwarves. The best dwarf–human friendship is often between a human and a dwarf who liked the human's parents and grandparents. Dwarves fail to appreciate elves' subtlety and art, regarding elves as unpredictable, fickle, and flighty. Still, elves and dwarves have, through the ages, found common cause in battles against orcs, goblins, and gnolls. Through many such joint campaigns, the elves have earned the dwarves' grudging respect. Dwarves mistrust half-orcs in general, and the feeling is mutual. Luckily, dwarves are fair-minded, and they grant individual half-orcs the opportunity to prove themselves.

Alignment: Dwarves are usually lawful, and they tend toward good. Adventuring dwarves are less likely to fit the common mold, however, since they're more likely to be those who did not fit perfectly into dwarven society.

Dwarven Lands: Dwarven kingdoms usually lie deep beneath the stony faces of mountains, where the dwarves mine gems and precious metals and forge items of wonder. Trustworthy members of other races are welcome in such settlements, though some parts of these lands are off limits even to them. Whatever wealth the dwarves can't find in their mountains, they gain through trade. Dwarves dislike water travel, so enterprising humans frequently handle trade in dwarven goods when travel is along a water route.

Dwarves in human lands are typically mercenaries, weaponsmiths, armorsmiths, jewelers, and artisans. Dwarf bodyguards are renowned for their courage and loyalty, and they are well rewarded for their virtues.

Religion: The chief deity of the dwarves is Moradin, the Soul Forger. He is the creator of the dwarves, and he expects his followers to work for the betterment of the dwarf race.

Language: Dwarves speak Dwarven, which has its own runic script. Dwarven literature is marked by comprehensive histories of kingdoms and wars through the millennia. The Dwarven alphabet is also used (with minor variations) for the Gnome, Giant, Goblin, Orc, and Terran languages. Dwarves often speak the languages of their friends (humans and gnomes) and enemies. Some also learn Terran, the strange language of earth-based creatures such as xorns.

Names: A dwarf's name is granted to him by his clan elder, in accordance with tradition. Every proper dwarven name has been used and reused down through the generations. A dwarf's name is not his own. It belongs to his clan. If he misuses it or brings shame to it, his clan will strip him of it. A dwarf stripped of his name is forbidden by dwarven law to use any dwarven name in its place.

Male Names: Barendd, Brottor, Eberk, Einkil, Oskar, Rurik, Taklinn, Tordek, Traubon, Ulfgar, Veit.

Female Names: Artin, Audhild, Dagnal, Diesa, Gunnloda, Hlin, Ilde, Liftrasa, Sannl, Torgga.

Clan Names: Balderk, Dankil, Gorunn, Holderhek, Loderr, Lutgehr, Rumnaheim, Strakeln, Torunn, Ungart.

Adventurers: A dwarf adventurer may be motivated by crusading zeal, a love of excitement, or simple greed. As long as his accomplishments bring honor to his clan, his deeds earn him respect and status. Defeating giants and claiming powerful magic weapons are sure ways for a dwarf to earn the respect of other dwarves.

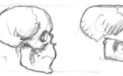

Human Skull *Dwarf Skull*

DWARF RACIAL TRAITS

- +2 Constitution, –2 Charisma: Dwarves are stout and tough but tend to be gruff and reserved.
- Medium: As Medium creatures, dwarves have no special bonuses or penalties due to their size.
- Dwarf base land speed is 20 feet. However, dwarves can move at this speed even when wearing medium or heavy armor or when carrying a medium or heavy load (unlike other creatures, whose speed is reduced in such situations).
- Darkvision: Dwarves can see in the dark up to 60 feet. Darkvision is black and white only, but it is otherwise like normal sight, and dwarves can function just fine with no light at all.

- Stonecunning: This ability grants a dwarf a +2 racial bonus on Search checks to notice unusual stonework, such as sliding walls, stonework traps, new construction (even when built to match the old), unsafe stone surfaces, shaky stone ceilings, and the like. Something that isn't stone but that is disguised as stone also counts as unusual stonework. A dwarf who merely comes within 10 feet of unusual stonework can make a Search check as if he were actively searching, and a dwarf can use the Search skill to find stonework traps as a rogue can. A dwarf can also intuit depth, sensing his approximate depth underground as naturally as a human can sense which way is up. Dwarves have a sixth sense about stonework, an innate ability that they get plenty of opportunity to practice and hone in their underground homes.
- Weapon Familiarity: Dwarves may treat dwarven waraxes and dwarven urgroshes (see Chapter 7: Equipment) as martial weapons, rather than exotic weapons.
- Stability: Dwarves are exceptionally stable on their feet. A dwarf gains a +4 bonus on ability checks made to resist being bull rushed or tripped when standing on the ground (but not when climbing, flying, riding, or otherwise not standing firmly on the ground).
- +2 racial bonus on saving throws against poison: Dwarves are hardy and resistant to toxins.
- +2 racial bonus on saving throws against spells and spell-like effects: Dwarves have an innate resistance to magic spells.
- +1 racial bonus on attack rolls against orcs (including half-orcs) and goblinoids (including goblins, hobgoblins, and bugbears): Dwarves are trained in the special combat techniques that allow them to fight their common enemies more effectively.
- +4 dodge bonus to Armor Class against monsters of the giant type (such as ogres, trolls, and hill giants): This bonus represents special training that dwarves undergo, during which they learn tricks that previous generations developed in their battles with giants. Any time a creature loses its Dexterity bonus (if any) to Armor Class, such as when it's caught flat-footed, it loses its dodge bonus, too. The *Monster Manual* has information on which creatures are of the giant type.
- +2 racial bonus on Appraise checks that are related to stone or metal items: Dwarves are familiar with valuable items of all kinds, especially those made of stone or metal.
- +2 racial bonus on Craft checks that are related to stone or metal: Dwarves are especially capable with stonework and metalwork.
- Automatic Languages: Common and Dwarven. Bonus Languages: Giant, Gnome, Goblin, Orc, Terran, and Undercommon. Dwarves are familiar with the languages of their enemies and of their subterranean allies.
- Favored Class: Fighter. A multiclass dwarf's fighter class does not count when determining whether he takes an experience point penalty for multiclassing (see XP for Multiclass Characters, page 60). Dwarven culture extols the virtues of battle, and the vocation comes easily to dwarves.

ELVES

Elves mingle freely in human lands, always welcome yet never at home there. They are well known for their poetry, dance, song, lore, and magical arts. Elves favor things of natural and simple beauty. When danger threatens their woodland homes, however, elves reveal a more martial side, demonstrating skill with sword, bow, and battle strategy.

Personality: Elves are more often amused than excited, and more likely to be curious than greedy. With such a long life span, they tend to keep a broad perspective on events, remaining aloof and unfazed by petty happenstance. When pursuing a goal, however, whether an adventurous mission or learning a new skill or art, they can be focused and relentless. They are slow to make friends and enemies, and even slower to forget them. They reply to petty insults with disdain and to serious insults with vengeance.

Physical Description: Elves are short and slim, standing about 4-1/2 to 5-1/2 feet tall and typically weighing 95 to 135 pounds, with elf men the same height as and only marginally heavier than elf women. They are graceful but frail. They tend to be pale-skinned and dark-haired, with deep green eyes. Elves have no facial or body hair. They prefer simple, comfortable clothes, especially in pastel blues and greens, and they enjoy simple yet elegant jewelry. Elves possess unearthly grace and fine features. Many humans and members of other races find them hauntingly beautiful. An elf reaches adulthood at about 110 years of age and can live to be more than 700 years old.

Elves do not sleep, as members of the other common races do. Instead, an elf meditates in a deep trance for 4 hours a day. An elf resting in this fashion gains the same benefit that a human does from 8 hours of sleep. While meditating, an elf dreams, though these dreams are actually mental exercises that have become reflexive through years of practice. The Common word for an elf's meditation is "trance," as in "four hours of trance."

Relations: Elves consider humans rather unrefined, halflings a bit staid, gnomes somewhat trivial, and dwarves not at all fun. They look on half-elves with some degree of pity, and they regard half-orcs with unrelenting suspicion. While haughty, elves are not particular the way halflings and dwarves can be, and they are generally pleasant and gracious even to those who fall short of elven standards (a category that encompasses just about everybody who's not an elf).

Alignment: Since elves love freedom, variety, and self-expression, they lean strongly toward the gentler aspects of chaos. Generally, they value and protect others' freedom as well as their own, and they are more often good than not.

Elven Lands: Most elves live in woodland clans numbering less than two hundred souls. Their well-hidden villages blend into the trees, doing little harm to the forest. They hunt game, gather food, and grow vegetables, and their skill and magic allow them to support themselves amply without the need for clearing and plowing land. Their contact with outsiders is usually limited, though some few elves make a good living trading finely worked elven clothes and crafts for the metals that elves have no interest in mining.

Elves encountered in human lands are commonly wandering minstrels, favored artists, or sages. Human nobles compete for the services of elf instructors, who teach swordplay to their children.

Religion: Above all others, elves worship Corellon Larethian, the Protector and Preserver of life. Elven myth holds that it was from his blood, shed in battles with Gruumsh, the god of the orcs, that the elves first arose. Corellon is a patron of magical study, arts, dance, and poetry, as well as a powerful warrior god.

Language: Elves speak a fluid language of subtle intonations and intricate grammar. While Elven literature is rich and varied, it is the language's songs and poems that are most famous. Many bards learn Elven so they can add Elven ballads to their repertoires. Others simply memorize Elven songs by sound. The Elven script, as flowing as the spoken word, also serves as the script for Sylvan, the language of dryads and pixies, for Aquan, the language of water-based creatures, and for Undercommon, the language of drow and other subterranean creatures.

Names: When an elf declares herself an adult, usually some time after her hundredth birthday, she also selects a name. Those who knew her as a youngster may or may not continue to call her by her "child name," and she may or may not care. An elf's adult name is a unique creation, though it may reflect the names of those she admires or the names of others in her family. In addition, she bears her family name. Family names are combinations of regular Elven words; some elves traveling among humans translate their family names into Common, while others use the Elven version.

Illus. by T. Lockwood

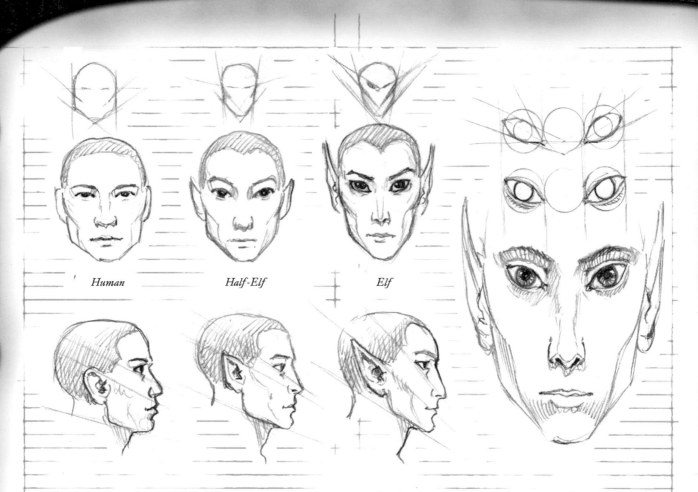

Human *Half-Elf* *Elf*

Male Names: Aramil, Aust, Enialis, Heian, Himo, Ivellios, Laucian, Quarion, Soveliss, Thamior, Tharivol.

Female Names: Anastrianna, Antinua, Drusilia, Felosial, Ielenia, Lia, Mialee, Qillathe, Silaqui, Vadania, Valanthe, Xanaphia.

Family Names (Common Translations): Amastacia (Starflower), Amakiir (Gemflower), Galanodel (Moonwhisper), Holimion (Diamonddew), Liadon (Silverfrond), Meliamne (Oakenheel), Naïlo (Nightbreeze), Siannodel (Moonbrook), Ilphukiir (Gemblossom), Xiloscient (Goldpetal).

Adventurers: Elves take up adventuring out of wanderlust. Life among humans moves at a pace that elves dislike: regimented from day to day but changing from decade to decade. Elves among humans, therefore, find careers that allow them to wander freely and set their own pace. Elves also enjoy demonstrating their prowess with the sword and bow or gaining greater magical powers, and adventuring allows them to do so. Good elves may also be rebels or crusaders.

ELF RACIAL TRAITS

- +2 Dexterity, –2 Constitution: Elves are graceful but frail. An elf's grace makes her naturally better at stealth and archery.
- Medium: As Medium creatures, elves have no special bonuses or penalties due to their size.
- Elf base land speed is 30 feet.
- Immunity to magic sleep effects, and a +2 racial saving throw bonus against enchantment spells or effects.
- Low-Light Vision: An elf can see twice as far as a human in starlight, moonlight, torchlight, and similar conditions of poor illumination. She retains the ability to distinguish color and detail under these conditions.
- Weapon Proficiency: Elves receive the Martial Weapon Proficiency feats for the longsword, rapier, longbow (including composite longbow), and shortbow (including composite

shortbow) as bonus feats. Elves esteem the arts of swordplay and archery, so all elves are familiar with these weapons.
- +2 racial bonus on Listen, Search, and Spot checks. An elf who merely passes within 5 feet of a secret or concealed door is entitled to a Search check to notice it as if she were actively looking for it. An elf's senses are so keen that she practically has a sixth sense about hidden portals.
- Automatic Languages: Common and Elven. Bonus Languages: Draconic, Gnoll, Gnome, Goblin, Orc, and Sylvan. Elves commonly know the languages of their enemies and of their friends, as well as Draconic, the language commonly found in ancient tomes of secret knowledge.
- Favored Class: Wizard. A multiclass elf's wizard class does not count when determining whether she takes an experience point penalty for multiclassing (see XP for Multiclass Characters, page 60). Wizardry comes naturally to elves—indeed, they sometimes claim to have invented it, and fighter/wizards are especially common among them.

GNOMES

Gnomes are welcome everywhere as technicians, alchemists, and inventors. Despite the demand for their skills, most gnomes prefer to remain among their own kind, living in comfortable burrows beneath rolling, wooded hills where animals abound.

Personality: Gnomes adore animals, beautiful gems, and jokes of all kinds. Members of this race have a great sense of humor, and while they love puns, jokes, and games, they also relish tricks—the more intricate the better. They apply the same dedication to more practical arts, such as engineering, as they do to their pranks.

Gnomes are inquisitive. They love to find things out by personal experience. At times they're even reckless. Their curiosity makes them skilled engineers, since they are always trying new ways to build things. Sometimes a gnome pulls a prank just to see how the people involved will react.

Physical Description: Gnomes stand about 3 to 3-1/2 feet tall and weigh 40 to 45 pounds. Their skin ranges from dark tan to woody brown, their hair is fair, and their eyes can be any shade of blue. Gnome males prefer short, carefully trimmed beards. Gnomes generally wear leather or earth tones, and they decorate their clothes with intricate stitching or fine jewelry. Gnomes reach adulthood at about age 40, and they typically live about 350 years, though some can live almost 500 years.

Relations: Gnomes get along well with dwarves, who share their love of precious objects, their curiosity about mechanical devices, and their hatred of goblins and giants. They enjoy the company of halflings, especially those who are easygoing enough to put up with pranks and jests. Most gnomes are a little suspicious of the taller races—humans, elves, half-elves, and half-orcs—but they are rarely hostile or malicious.

Alignment: Gnomes are most often good. Those who tend toward law are sages, engineers, researchers, scholars, investigators, or consultants. Those who tend toward chaos are minstrels, tricksters, wanderers, or fanciful jewelers. Gnomes are good-hearted, and even the tricksters among them are more playful than vicious. Evil gnomes are as rare as they are frightening.

Gnome Lands: Gnomes make their homes in hilly, wooded lands. They live underground but get more fresh air than dwarves do, enjoying the natural, living world on the surface whenever they can. Their homes are well hidden by both clever construction and illusions. Those who come to visit and are welcome are ushered into the bright, warm burrows. Those who are not welcome never find the burrows in the first place.

Gnomes who settle in human lands are commonly gemcutters, mechanics, sages, or tutors. Some human families retain gnome tutors. During his life, a gnome tutor can teach several generations of a single human family.

Religion: The chief gnome god is Garl Glittergold, the Watchful Protector. His clerics teach that gnomes are to cherish and support their communities. Pranks are seen as ways to lighten spirits and to keep gnomes humble, not as ways for pranksters to triumph over those they trick.

Language: The Gnome language, which uses the Dwarven script, is renowned for its technical treatises and its catalogs of knowledge about the natural world. Human herbalists, naturalists, and engineers commonly learn Gnome in order to read the best books on their topics of study.

Names: Gnomes love names, and most have half a dozen or so. As a gnome grows up, his mother gives him a name, his father gives him a name, his clan elder gives him a name, his aunts and uncles give him names, and he gains nicknames from just about anyone. Gnome names are typically variants on the names of ancestors or distant relatives, though some are purely new inventions. When dealing with humans and others who are rather "stuffy" about names, a gnome learns to act as if he has no more than three names: a personal name, a clan name, and a nickname. When deciding which of his several names to use among humans, a gnome generally chooses the one that's the most fun to say. Gnome clan names are combinations of common Gnome words, and gnomes almost always translate them into Common when in human lands (or into Elven when in elven lands, and so on).

Male Names: Boddynock, Dimble, Fonkin, Gimble, Glim, Gerbo, Jebeddo, Namfoodle, Roondar, Seebo, Zook.

Female Names: Bimpnottin, Caramip, Duvamil, Ellywick, Ellyjobell, Loopmottin, Mardnab, Roywyn, Shamil, Waywocket.

Clan Names: Beren, Daergel, Folkor, Garrick, Nackle, Murnig, Ningel, Raulnor, Scheppen, Turen.

Nicknames: Aleslosh, Ashhearth, Badger, Cloak, Doublelock, Filchbatter, Fnipper, Oneshoe, Sparklegem, Stumbleduck.

Adventurers: Gnomes are curious and impulsive. They may take up adventuring as a way to see the world or for the love of exploring. Lawful gnomes may adventure to set things right and to protect the innocent, demonstrating the same sense of duty toward society as a whole that gnomes generally exhibit toward their own enclaves. As lovers of gems and other fine items, some gnomes take to adventuring as a quick, if dangerous, path to wealth. Depending on his relations to his home clan, an adventuring gnome may be seen as a vagabond or even as something of a traitor (for abandoning clan responsibilities).

GNOME RACIAL TRAITS

- **+2 Constitution, –2 Strength:** Like dwarves, gnomes are tough, but they are small and therefore not as strong as larger humanoids.
- **Small:** As a Small creature, a gnome gains a +1 size bonus to Armor Class, a +1 size bonus on attack rolls, and a +4 size bonus on Hide checks, but he uses smaller weapons than humans use, and his lifting and carrying limits are three-quarters of those of a Medium character.
- Gnome base land speed is 20 feet.
- **Low-Light Vision:** A gnome can see twice as far as a human in starlight, moonlight, torchlight, and similar conditions of poor illumination. He retains the ability to distinguish color and detail under these conditions.
- **Weapon Familiarity:** Gnomes may treat gnome hooked hammers (see page 118) as martial weapons rather than exotic weapons.
- +2 racial bonus on saving throws against illusions: Gnomes are innately familiar with illusions of all kinds.
- Add +1 to the Difficulty Class for all saving throws against illusion spells cast by gnomes. Their innate familiarity with these effects make their illusions more difficult to see through. This adjustment stacks with those from similar effects, such as the Spell Focus feat.
- +1 racial bonus on attack rolls against kobolds and goblinoids (including goblins, hobgoblins, and bugbears): Gnomes battle these creatures frequently and practice special techniques for fighting them.
- +4 dodge bonus to Armor Class against monsters of the giant type (such as ogres, trolls, and hill giants): This bonus represents special training that gnomes undergo, during which they learn tricks that previous generations developed in their battles with giants. Any time a creature loses its Dexterity bonus (if any) to Armor Class, such as when it's caught flat-footed, it loses its dodge bonus, too. The *Monster Manual* has information on which creatures are of the giant type.
- +2 racial bonus on Listen checks: Gnomes have keen ears.
- +2 racial bonus on Craft (alchemy) checks: A gnome's sensitive nose allows him to monitor alchemical processes by smell.
- **Automatic Languages:** Common and Gnome. **Bonus Languages:** Draconic, Dwarven, Elven, Giant, Goblin, and Orc. Gnomes deal more with elves and dwarves than elves and dwarves deal with one another, and they learn the languages of their enemies (kobolds, giants, goblins, and orcs) as well. In addition, a gnome can speak with a burrowing mammal (a badger, fox, rabbit, or the like, see below). This ability is innate to gnomes. See the *speak with animals* spell description, page 281.
- **Spell-Like Abilities:** 1/day—*speak with animals* (burrowing mammal only, duration 1 minute). A gnome with a Charisma score of at least 10 also has the following spell-like abilities: 1/day—*dancing lights, ghost sound, prestidigitation.* Caster level 1st; save DC 10 + gnome's Cha modifier + spell level. See the spell descriptions on pages 216, 235, and 264, respectively.
- **Favored Class:** Bard. A multiclass gnome's bard class does not count when determining whether he takes an experience point penalty (see XP for Multiclass Characters, page 60).

HALF-ELVES

Humans and elves sometimes wed, the elf attracted to the human's energy and the human to the elf's grace. These marriages end quickly as elves count years because a human's life is so brief, but they leave an enduring legacy—half-elf children.

The life of a half-elf can be hard. If raised by elves, the half-elf seems to grow with astounding speed, reaching maturity within two decades. The half-elf becomes an adult long before she has had time to learn the intricacies of elven art and culture, or even grammar. She leaves behind her childhood friends, becoming physically an adult but culturally still a child by elven standards. Typically, she leaves her elven home, which is no longer familiar, and finds her way among humans.

If, on the other hand, she is raised by humans, the half-elf finds herself different from her peers: more aloof, more sensitive, less ambitious, and slower to mature. Some half-elves try to fit in among humans, while others find their identities in their differences. Most find places for themselves in human lands, but some feel like outsiders all their lives.

Personality: Most half-elves have the curiosity, inventiveness, and ambition of the human parent, along with the refined senses, love of nature, and artistic tastes of the elf parent.

Physical Description: To humans, half-elves look like elves. To elves, they look like humans—indeed, elves call them half-humans. Half-elf height ranges from under 5 feet to about 6 feet tall, and weight usually ranges from 100 to 180 pounds. Half-elf men are taller and heavier than half-elf women, but the difference is less pronounced than that found among humans. Half-elves are paler, fairer, and smoother-skinned than their human parents, but their actual skin tone, hair color, and other details vary just as human features do. Half-elves' eyes are green, just as are those of their elf parents. A half-elf reaches adulthood at age 20 and can live to be more than 180 years old.

Most half-elves are the children of human–elf pairings. Some, however, are the children of parents who themselves are partly human and partly elf. Some of these "second generation" half-elves have humanlike eyes, but most still have green eyes.

Relations: Half-elves do well among both elves and humans, and they also get along well with dwarves, gnomes, and halflings. They have elven grace without elven aloofness and human energy without human boorishness. They make excellent ambassadors and go-betweens (except between elves and humans, since each side suspects the half-elf of favoring the other). In human lands where elves are distant or not on friendly terms with other races, however, half-elves are viewed with suspicion.

Some half-elves show a marked disfavor toward half-orcs. Perhaps the similarity between themselves and half-orcs (a partly human lineage) makes these half-elves uncomfortable.

Alignment: Half-elves share the chaotic bent of their elven heritage, but, like humans, they tend toward both good and evil in equal proportion. Like elves, they value personal freedom and creative expression, demonstrating neither love of leaders nor desire for followers. They chafe at rules, resent others' demands, and sometimes prove unreliable, or at least unpredictable.

Half-Elven Lands: Half-elves have no lands of their own, though they are welcome in human cities and elven forests. In large cities, half-elves sometimes form small communities of their own.

Religion: Half-elves raised among elves follow elven deities, principally Corellon Larethian (god of the elves). Those raised among humans often follow Ehlonna (goddess of the woodlands).

Language: Half-elves speak the languages they are born to, Common and Elven. Half-elves are slightly clumsy with the intricate Elven language, though only elves notice, and even so half-elves do better than nonelves.

Names: Half-elves use either human or elven naming conventions. Ironically, a half-elf raised among humans is often given an elven name in honor of her heritage, just as a half-elf raised among elves often takes a human name.

Adventurers: Half-elves find themselves drawn to strange careers and unusual company. Taking up the life of an adventurer comes easily to many of them. Like elves, they are driven by wanderlust.

HALF-ELF RACIAL TRAITS

- **Medium:** As Medium creatures, half-elves have no special bonuses or penalties due to their size.
- Half-elf base land speed is 30 feet.
- Immunity to *sleep* spells and similar magical effects, and a +2 racial bonus on saving throws against enchantment spells or effects.
- **Low-Light Vision:** A half-elf can see twice as far as a human in starlight, moonlight, torchlight, and similar conditions of poor illumination. She retains the ability to distinguish color and detail under these conditions.
- +1 racial bonus on Listen, Search, and Spot checks: A half-elf does not have the elf's ability to notice secret doors simply by passing near them. Half-elves have keen senses, but not as keen as those of an elf.
- +2 racial bonus on Diplomacy and Gather Information checks: Half-elves get along naturally with all people.
- **Elven Blood:** For all effects related to race, a half-elf is considered an elf. Half-elves, for example, are just as vulnerable to special effects that affect elves as their elf ancestors are, and they can use magic items that are only usable by elves. (See the *Monster Manual* for more information about elves, and the *Dungeon Master's Guide* for more on magic items.)
- **Automatic Languages:** Common and Elven. Bonus Languages: Any (other than secret languages, such as Druidic). Half-elves have all the versatility and broad (if shallow) experience that humans have.
- **Favored Class:** Any. When determining whether a multiclass half-elf takes an experience point penalty, her highest-level class does not count (see XP for Multiclass Characters, page 60).

HALF-ORCS

In the wild frontiers, tribes of human and orc barbarians live in uneasy balance, fighting in times of war and trading in times of peace. Half-orcs who are born in the frontier may live with either human or orc parents, but they are nevertheless exposed to both cultures. Some, for whatever reason, leave their homeland and travel to civilized lands, bringing with them the tenacity, courage, and combat prowess that they developed in the wilds.

Personality: Half-orcs tend to be short-tempered and sullen. They would rather act than ponder and would rather fight than argue. Those who are successful, however, are the ones with enough self-control to live in a civilized land, not the crazy ones.

Half-orcs love simple pleasures such as feasting, drinking, boasting, singing, wrestling, drumming, and wild dancing. Refined enjoyments such as poetry, courtly dancing, and philosophy are lost on them. At the right sort of party, a half-orc is an asset. At the duchess's grand ball, he's a liability.

Physical Description: Half-orcs stand between 6 and 7 feet tall and usually weigh between 180 and 250 pounds. A half-orc's grayish pigmentation, sloping forehead, jutting jaw, prominent teeth, and coarse body hair make his lineage plain for all to see.

Orcs like scars. They regard battle scars as tokens of pride and ornamental scars as things of beauty. Any half-orc who has lived among or near orcs has scars, whether they are marks of shame indicating servitude and identifying the half-orc's former owner, or marks of pride recounting conquests and high status. Such a half-orc living among humans may either display or hide his scars, depending on his attitude toward them.

Half-orcs mature a little faster than humans and age noticeably faster. They reach adulthood at age 14, and few live longer than 75 years.

Relations: Because orcs are the sworn enemies of dwarves and elves, half-orcs can have a rough time with members of these races. For that matter, orcs aren't exactly on good terms with humans, halflings, or gnomes, either. Each half-orc finds a way to gain acceptance from those who hate or fear his orc cousins. Some half-orcs are reserved, trying not to draw attention to themselves. A few demonstrate piety and good-heartedness as publicly as they can (whether or not such demonstrations are genuine). Others simply try to be so tough that others have no choice but to accept them.

Alignment: Half-orcs inherit a tendency toward chaos from their orc parents, but, like their human parents, they favor good and evil in equal proportions. Half-orcs raised among orcs and willing to live out their lives with them are usually the evil ones.

Half-Orc Lands: Half-orcs have no lands of their own, but they most often live among orcs. Of the other races, humans are the ones most likely to accept half-orcs, and half-orcs almost always live in human lands when not living among orc tribes.

Religion: Like orcs, many half-orcs worship Gruumsh, the chief orc god and the archenemy of Corellon Larethian, god of the elves. While Gruumsh is evil, half-orc barbarians and fighters may worship him as a war god even if they are not evil themselves. Worshipers of Gruumsh who are tired of explaining themselves, or who don't want to give humans a reason to distrust them, simply don't make their religion public knowledge. Half-orcs who want to solidify their connection to their human heritage, on the other hand, follow human gods, and they may be outspoken in their shows of piety.

Language: Orc, which has no alphabet of its own, uses Dwarven script on the rare occasions when someone writes something down. Orc writing turns up most frequently in graffiti.

Names: A half-orc typically chooses a name that helps him make the impression that he wants to make. If he wants to fit in among humans, he chooses a human name. If he wants to intimidate others, he chooses a guttural orc name. A half-orc who has been raised entirely by humans has a human given name, but he may choose another name once he's away from his hometown. Some half-orcs, of course, aren't quite bright enough to choose a name this carefully.

Orc Male Names: Dench, Feng, Gell, Henk, Holg, Imsh, Keth, Krusk, Ront, Shump, Thokk.

Orc Female Names: Baggi, Emen, Engong, Myev, Neega, Ovak, Ownka, Shautha, Vola, Volen.

Adventurers: Half-orcs living among humans are drawn almost invariably toward violent careers in which they can put their strength to good use. Frequently shunned from polite company, half-orcs often find acceptance and friendship among adventurers, many of whom are fellow wanderers and outsiders.

HALF-ORC RACIAL TRAITS

- **+2 Strength, –2 Intelligence, –2 Charisma:** Half-orcs are strong, but their orc lineage makes them dull and crude.
- **Medium:** As Medium creatures, half-orcs have no special bonuses or penalties due to their size.
- Half-orc base land speed is 30 feet.
- **Darkvision:** Half-orcs (and orcs) can see in the dark up to 60 feet. Darkvision is black and white only, but it is otherwise like normal sight, and half-orcs can function just fine with no light at all.
- **Orc Blood:** For all effects related to race, a half-orc is considered an orc. Half-orcs, for example, are just as vulnerable to special effects that affect orcs as their orc ancestors are, and they can use magic items that are only usable by orcs. (See the *Monster Manual* for more information about orcs, and the *Dungeon Master's Guide* for more on magic items.)
- **Automatic Languages:** Common and Orc. Bonus Languages: Draconic, Giant, Gnoll, Goblin, and Abyssal. Smart half-orcs (who are rare) may know the languages of their allies or rivals.
- **Favored Class:** Barbarian. A multiclass half-orc's barbarian class does not count when determining whether he takes an experience point penalty (see XP for Multiclass Characters, page 60). Ferocity runs in a half-orc's veins.

HALFLINGS

Halflings are clever, capable opportunists. Halfling individuals and clans find room for themselves wherever they can. Often they are strangers and wanderers, and others react to them with suspicion or curiosity. Depending on the clan, halflings might be reliable, hard-working (if clannish) citizens, or they might be thieves just waiting for the opportunity to make a big score and disappear in the dead of night. Regardless, halflings are cunning, resourceful survivors.

Personality: Halflings prefer trouble to boredom. They are notoriously curious. Relying on their ability to survive or escape danger, they demonstrate a daring that many larger people can't match.

Halfling clans are nomadic, wandering wherever circumstance and curiosity take them. Halflings enjoy wealth and the pleasures it can bring, and they tend to spend gold as quickly as they acquire it.

Halflings are also famous collectors. While more orthodox halflings may collect weapons, books, or jewelry, some collect such objects as the hides of wild beasts—or even the beasts themselves. Wealthy halflings sometimes commission adventurers to retrieve exotic items to complete their collections.

Physical Description: Halflings stand about 3 feet tall and usually weigh between 30 and 35 pounds. Their skin is ruddy, and their hair is black and straight. They have brown or black eyes. Halfling men often have long sideburns, but beards are rare among them and mustaches are almost unseen. They like to wear simple, comfortable, and practical clothes. A halfling reaches adulthood at the age of 20 and generally lives into the middle of her second century.

Relations: Halflings try to get along with everyone else. They are adept at fitting into a community of humans, dwarves, elves, or gnomes and making themselves valuable and welcome. Since

Illus. by T. Lockwood

Illus. by T. Lockwood

human society changes faster than the societies of the longer-lived races, it is human society that most frequently offers halflings opportunities to exploit, so halflings are most often found in or around human lands.

Alignment: Halflings tend to be neutral. While they are comfortable with change (a chaotic trait), they also tend to rely on intangible constants, such as clan ties and personal honor (a lawful trait).

Halfling Lands: Halflings have no lands of their own. Instead, they live in the lands of other races, where they can benefit from whatever resources those areas have to offer. Halflings often form tight-knit communities in human or dwarven cities. While they work readily with others, they often make friends only among their own kind. Halflings also settle into secluded places where they set up self-reliant villages. Halfling communities, however, are known for picking up and moving en masse to some place that offers a new opportunity, such as a new mine that has just opened, or to a land where a devastating war has made skilled workers hard to find. If these opportunities are temporary, the community may pick up and move again once the opportunity is gone, or once a better one presents itself. Some halfling communities, on the other hand, take to traveling as a way of life, driving wagons or guiding boats from place to place and maintaining no permanent home.

Religion: The chief halfling deity is Yondalla, the Blessed One, protector of the halflings. Yondalla promises blessings and protection to those who heed her guidance, defend their clans, and cherish their families. Halflings also recognize countless lesser gods, who rule over individual villages, forests, rivers, lakes, and so on. The halflings pay homage to these deities to ensure safe journeys as they travel from place to place.

Language: Halflings speak their own language, which uses the Common script. They write very little in their own language, so, unlike dwarves, elves, and gnomes, they don't have a rich body of written work. The halfling oral tradition, however, is very strong. While the Halfling language isn't secret, halflings are loath to share it with others. Almost all halflings speak Common, since they use it to deal with the people in whose lands they are living or through which they are traveling.

Names: A halfling has a given name, a family name, and possibly a nickname. It would seem that family names are nothing more than nicknames that stuck so well they have been passed down through the generations.

Male Names: Alton, Beau, Cade, Eldon, Garret, Lyle, Milo, Osborn, Roscoe, Wellby.

Female Names: Amaryllis, Charmaine, Cora, Euphemia, Jillian, Lavinia, Lidda, Merla, Portia, Seraphina, Verna.

Family Names: Brushgather, Goodbarrel, Greenbottle, Highhill, Hilltopple, Leagallow, Tealeaf, Thorngage, Tosscobble, Underbough.

Adventurers: Halflings often set out on their own to make their way in the world. Halfling adventurers are typically looking for a way to use their skills to gain wealth or status. The distinction between a halfling adventurer and a halfling out on her own looking for "a big score" can get blurry. For a halfling, adventuring is less of a career than an opportunity. While halfling opportunism can sometimes look like larceny or fraud to others, a halfling adventurer who learns to trust her fellows is worthy of trust in return.

HALFLING RACIAL TRAITS

- **+2 Dexterity, −2 Strength:** Halflings are quick, agile, and good with ranged weapons, but they are small and therefore not as strong as other humanoids.
- **Small:** As a Small creature, a halfling gains a +1 size bonus to Armor Class, a +1 size bonus on attack rolls, and a +4 size bonus on Hide checks, but she uses smaller weapons than humans use, and her lifting and carrying limits are three-quarters of those of a Medium character.
- Halfling base land speed is 20 feet.
- **+2 racial bonus on Climb, Jump, and Move Silently checks:** Halflings are agile, surefooted, and athletic.
- **+1 racial bonus on all saving throws:** Halflings are surprisingly capable of avoiding mishaps.
- **+2 morale bonus on saving throws against fear:** This bonus stacks with the halfling's +1 bonus on saving throws in general.
- **+1 racial bonus on attack rolls with thrown weapons and slings:** Throwing and slinging stones is a universal sport among halflings, and they develop especially good aim.
- **+2 racial bonus on Listen checks:** Halflings have keen ears.
- **Automatic Languages:** Common and Halfling. **Bonus Languages:** Dwarven, Elven, Gnome, Goblin, and Orc. Smart halflings learn the languages of their friends and enemies.
- **Favored Class:** Rogue. A multiclass halfling's rogue class does not count when determining whether she takes an experience point penalty for multiclassing (see XP for Multiclass Characters, page 60). Halflings have long had to rely on stealth, wit, and skill, and the vocation of rogue comes naturally to them.

SMALL CHARACTERS

A Small character gets a +1 size bonus to Armor Class, a +1 size bonus on attack rolls, and a +4 size bonus on Hide checks. The bonus on attacks results from the fact that it's really relative size that matters in determining attack chances. It's no harder for a halfling to hit another halfling than it is for a human to hit another human, because the attacking halfling's bonus on attack rolls counteracts the defending halfling's bonus to Armor Class. Likewise, a halfling has an easy time hitting a human, just as a human has an easy time hitting an ogre, and an ogre has an easy time hitting a giant.

A Small character's carrying capacity is three-quarters of that of a Medium character (see Bigger and Smaller Creatures, page 162).

A Small character generally moves about two-thirds as fast as a Medium character.

A Small character must use smaller weapons than a Medium character (see Weapon Size, page 113).

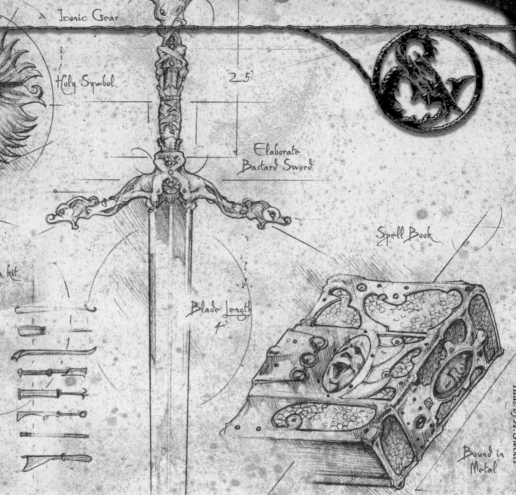

Illus. by A. Swekel

Labels on illustration: A Iconic Gear · Holy Symbol · 2.5' · Elaborate Bastard Sword · 8" · Example provided is of Pelor · Open kit · Blade Length 4' · Spell Book · Bound in Metal · Thieves' Picks and Tools

dventurers seek gold, glory, justice, fame, power, knowledge, or maybe some other goal—perhaps noble or perhaps base. Each chooses a different way to attain those goals, from brutal combat power, to mighty magic, to subtle skills. Some adventurers prevail and grow in experience, wealth, and power. Others die.

Your character's class is his or her profession or vocation. It determines what he or she is able to do: combat prowess, magical ability, skills, and more. Class is probably the first choice you make about your character—just ahead of race, or perhaps in conjunction with that decision. The class you choose determines where you should best place your character's ability scores and suggests which races are best to support that class choice.

THE CLASSES

The eleven classes, in the order they're presented in this chapter, are as follows:

Barbarian: A ferocious warrior who uses fury and instinct to bring down foes.

Bard: A performer whose music works magic—a wanderer, a tale-teller, and a jack-of-all trades.

Cleric: A master of divine magic and a capable warrior as well.

Druid: One who draws energy from the natural world to cast divine spells and gain strange magical powers.

Fighter: A warrior with exceptional combat capability and unequaled skill with weapons.

Monk: A martial artist whose unarmed strikes hit fast and hard—a master of exotic powers.

Paladin: A champion of justice and destroyer of evil, protected and strengthened by an array of divine powers.

Ranger: A cunning, skilled warrior of the wilderness.

Rogue: A tricky, skillful scout and spy who wins the battle by stealth rather than brute force.

Sorcerer: A spellcaster with inborn magical ability.

Wizard: A potent spellcaster schooled in the arcane arts.

Class Name Abbreviations: Class names are abbreviated as follows: barbarian Bbn; bard Brd; cleric Clr; druid Drd; fighter Ftr; monk Mnk; paladin Pal; ranger Rgr; rogue Rog; sorcerer Sor; wizard Wiz.

THE MULTICLASS CHARACTER

As your character advances in level, he or she may add new classes. Adding a new class gives the character a broader range of abilities, but all advancement in the new class is at the expense of advancement in the character's other class or classes. A wizard, for example, might become a combination wizard/fighter. Adding the fighter class would give her proficiency in more weapons, better Fortitude saving throws, and so on, but it would also mean that she doesn't gain new wizard abilities when she adds this second class and thus is not as powerful a wizard as she otherwise would have become if she had chosen to continue advancing as a wizard. Rules for creating and advancing multiclass characters can be found at the end of this chapter.

CLASS AND LEVEL BONUSES

An attack roll, saving throw, or skill check is a combination of three numbers, each representing a different factor: a random factor (the number you roll on a d20), a number representing the character's innate abilities (the ability modifier), and a bonus representing the character's experience and training. This third factor depends, either directly or indirectly, on the character's class and level. Table 3–1: Base Save and Base Attack Bonuses (see below) summarizes the figures for this third factor when it applies to base save bonuses and base attack bonuses.

Base Save Bonus: The two numbers given in this column on Table 3–1 apply to saving throws. Whether a character uses the first (good) bonus or the second (poor) bonus depends on his or her class and the type of saving throw being attempted. For example, fighters get the lower bonus on Reflex and Will saves and the higher bonus on Fortitude saves, while rogues get the lower bonus on Fortitude and Will saves and the higher bonus on Reflex saves. Monks are equally good at all three types of saving throws. See each class's description to find out which bonus applies to which category of saves. If a character has more than one class (see Multiclass Characters, page 59), the base save bonuses for each class are cumulative.

Base Attack Bonus: On an attack roll, apply the bonus from the appropriate column on Table 3–1 according to the class to which the character belongs. Whether a character uses the first (good) base attack bonus, the second (average) base attack bonus, or the third (poor) base attack bonus depends on his or her class. Barbarians, fighters, paladins, and rangers have a good base attack bonus, so they use the first Base Attack Bonus column. Clerics, druids, monks, and rogues have an average base attack bonus, so they use the second column. Sorcerers and wizards have a poor base attack bonus, so they use the third column. Numbers after a slash indicate additional attacks at reduced bonuses: "+12/+7/+2" means three attacks per round, with an attack bonus of +12 for the first attack, +7 for the second, and +2 for the third. Any modifiers on attack rolls apply to all these attacks normally, but bonuses do not grant extra attacks. For example, when Lidda the halfling rogue is 2nd level, she has a base attack bonus of +1. With a thrown weapon, she adds her Dexterity bonus (+3), her size bonus (+1), and a racial bonus (+1) for a total of +6. Even though a +6 base attack bonus would grant an additional attack at +1, raising that number to +6 via ability, racial, size, weapon, or other bonuses doesn't grant Lidda an additional attack. If a character has more than one class (see Multiclass Characters, page 59), the base attack bonuses for each class are cumulative.

LEVEL-DEPENDENT BENEFITS

In addition to attack bonuses and saving throw bonuses, all characters gain other benefits from advancing in level. Table 3–2: Experience and Level-Dependent Benefits summarizes these additional benefits.

XP: This column on Table 3–2 shows the experience point total needed to attain a given character level—that is, the total of all the character's levels in classes. (A character's level in a class is called his or her class level.) For any character (including a multiclass one), XP determines overall character level, not individual class levels.

Class Skill Max Ranks: The maximum number of ranks a character can have in a class skill is equal to his or her character level + 3. A class skill is a skill frequently associated with a particular class—for example, Spellcraft is a class skill for wizards. Class skills are given in each class description in this chapter (see also Table 4–2: Skills, page 63, for more information on skills).

Cross-Class Skill Max Ranks: For cross-class skills (skills not associated with a character's class), the maximum number of ranks a character can have is one-half the maximum for a class skill. For example, at 1st level a wizard could have 2 ranks in Move Silently (typically associated with rogues, and on that class's list of class skills), but no more. These 2 ranks in a cross-class skill would cost the wizard 4 skill points, whereas the same 4 points would buy 4 ranks in a wizard class skill, such as Spellcraft. The half ranks (1/2) indicated on Table 3–2 don't improve skill checks. They simply represent partial purchase of the next skill rank and indicate that the character is training to improve that skill.

Feats: Every character gains one feat at 1st level and another at every level divisible by three (3rd, 6th, 9th, 12th, 15th, and 18th level). These feats are in addition to any bonus feats granted as class features (see the class descriptions later in this chapter) and the bonus feat granted to all humans. See Chapter 5: Feats for more information about feats.

Ability Score Increases: Upon attaining any level divisible by four (4th, 8th, 12th, 16th, and 20th level), a character increases one of his or her ability scores by 1 point. The player chooses which ability score to improve. For example, a sorcerer with a starting Charisma of 16 might increase this to 17 at 4th level. At 8th level, the same character might increase his Charisma score again (from 17 to 18) or could choose to improve some other ability instead. The ability improvement is permanent.

TABLE 3–1: BASE SAVE AND BASE ATTACK BONUSES

Class Level	Base Save Bonus (Good)	Base Save Bonus (Poor)	Base Attack Bonus (Good)	Base Attack Bonus (Average)	Base Attack Bonus (Poor)
1st	+2	+0	+1	+0	+0
2nd	+3	+0	+2	+1	+1
3rd	+3	+1	+3	+2	+1
4th	+4	+1	+4	+3	+2
5th	+4	+1	+5	+3	+2
6th	+5	+2	+6/+1	+4	+3
7th	+5	+2	+7/+2	+5	+3
8th	+6	+2	+8/+3	+6/+1	+4
9th	+6	+3	+9/+4	+6/+1	+4
10th	+7	+3	+10/+5	+7/+2	+5
11th	+7	+3	+11/+6/+1	+8/+3	+5
12th	+8	+4	+12/+7/+2	+9/+4	+6/+1
13th	+8	+4	+13/+8/+3	+9/+4	+6/+1
14th	+9	+4	+14/+9/+4	+10/+5	+7/+2
15th	+9	+5	+15/+10/+5	+11/+6/+1	+7/+2
16th	+10	+5	+16/+11/+6/+1	+12/+7/+2	+8/+3
17th	+10	+5	+17/+12/+7/+2	+12/+7/+2	+8/+3
18th	+11	+6	+18/+13/+8/+3	+13/+8/+3	+9/+4
19th	+11	+6	+19/+14/+9/+4	+14/+9/+4	+9/+4
20th	+12	+6	+20/+15/+10/+5	+15/+10/+5	+10/+5

TABLE 3–2: EXPERIENCE AND LEVEL-DEPENDENT BENEFITS

Character Level	XP	Class Skill Max Ranks	Cross-Class Skill Max Ranks	Feats	Ability Score Increases
1st	0	4	2	1st	—
2nd	1,000	5	2-1/2	—	—
3rd	3,000	6	3	2nd	—
4th	6,000	7	3-1/2	—	1st
5th	10,000	8	4	—	—
6th	15,000	9	4-1/2	3rd	—
7th	21,000	10	5	—	—
8th	28,000	11	5-1/2	—	2nd
9th	36,000	12	6	4th	—
10th	45,000	13	6-1/2	—	—
11th	55,000	14	7	—	—
12th	66,000	15	7-1/2	5th	3rd
13th	78,000	16	8	—	—
14th	91,000	17	8-1/2	—	—
15th	105,000	18	9	6th	—
16th	120,000	19	9-1/2	—	4th
17th	136,000	20	10	—	—
18th	153,000	21	10-1/2	7th	—
19th	171,000	22	11	—	—
20th	190,000	23	11-1/2	—	5th

For multiclass characters, feats and ability score increases are gained according to character level, not class level. Thus, a 3rd-level wizard/1st-level fighter is a 4th-level character overall and eligible for her first ability score boost.

CLASS DESCRIPTIONS

The rest of this chapter, up to the section on multiclass characters, describes the character classes in alphabetical order. Each description begins with a general discussion in "game world" terms, the sort of description that characters in the game world could understand and the way such a character might describe himself or herself. This information is followed by brief advice on such a character's typical role in a group of adventurers. These descriptions are general; individual members of a class may differ in their attitudes, outlooks, and other aspects.

GAME RULE INFORMATION

Following the general class description comes game rule information. Not all of the following categories apply to every class.

Abilities: The Abilities entry tells you which abilities are most important for a character of that class. Players are welcome to "play against type," but a typical character of that class will have his or her highest ability scores where they'll do the most good (or, in game world terms, be attracted to the class that most suits his or her talents or for which he or she is best qualified).

Alignment: A few classes restrict a character's possible alignments. For example, a bard must have a nonlawful alignment. An entry of "Any" means that characters of this class are not restricted in alignment.

Hit Die: The type of Hit Die used by characters of the class determines the number of hit points gained per level.

HD Type	Class
d4	Sorcerer, wizard
d6	Bard, rogue
d8	Cleric, druid, monk, ranger
d10	Fighter, paladin
d12	Barbarian

A character rolls one Hit Die each time he or she gains a new level, then applies any Constitution modifier to the roll and adds the result to his or her hit point total. Thus, a character has the same number of Hit Dice as levels. For his or her first Hit Die, a 1st-level character gets the maximum hit points rather than rolling (although Constitution modifiers, positive or negative, still apply).

For example, Vadania gets a d8 Hit Die because she's a druid. At 1st level, she gets 8 hit points instead of rolling. Since she has a Constitution score of 13, she applies a +1 bonus, raising her hit points to 9. When she reaches 2nd level (and every level thereafter), Vadania's player rolls a d8, adds 1 (for her Constitution bonus), and then adds the total to Vadania's hit points.

If your character has a Constitution penalty and gets a result of 0 or lower after the penalty is applied to the Hit Die roll, ignore the roll and add 1 to your character's hit point total anyway. It is not possible to lose hit points (or not receive any) when gaining a level, even for a character with a rotten Constitution score.

Class Table: This table details how a character improves as he or she gains levels in the class. Some of this material is repeated from Table 3–1: Base Save and Base Attack Bonuses, but with more detail on how the numbers apply to that class. Class tables typically include the following information.

Level: The character's level in that class.

Base Attack Bonus: The character's base attack bonus and number of attacks.

Fort Save: The base save bonus on Fortitude saving throws. The character's Constitution modifier also applies.

Ref Save: The base save bonus on Reflex saving throws. The character's Dexterity modifier also applies.

Will Save: The base save bonus on Will saving throws. The character's Wisdom modifier also applies.

Special: Level-dependent class abilities, each explained in the Class Features section that follows.

Spells per Day: How many spells of each spell level the character can cast each day. If the entry is "—" for a given level of spell, the character may not cast any spells of that level. If the entry is "0," the character may cast spells of that level only if he or she is entitled to bonus spells because of a high ability score tied to spellcasting. (Bonus spells for wizards are based on Intelligence; bonus spells for clerics, druids, paladins, and rangers are based on Wisdom; and bonus spells for sorcerers and bards are based on Charisma. See Table 1–1: Ability Modifiers and Bonus Spells, page 8.) If the entry is a number other than 0, the character may cast that many spells plus any bonus spells each day.

A character can always choose to prepare a lower-level spell to fill a higher-level spell slot (see Spell Slots, page 178).

Class Skills: This section of a class description gives the class's list of class skills, the number of skill points the character starts with at 1st level, and the number of skill points gained each level thereafter. A character gets some number of skill points at each level depending on the class in question, such as 6 for a ranger or 8 for a rogue. To this number, apply the character's Intelligence modifier (and 1 bonus point, if the character is human) to determine the total skill points gained each level (but always at least 1 skill point per level, even for a character with an Intelligence penalty). A 1st-level character starts with four times this number of skill points. Since the maximum ranks in a class skill for a character is character level + 3, at 1st level you can buy as many as 4 ranks in any class skill, at a cost of 1 skill point per rank.

For example, Vadania is a half-elf druid, so she gets 4 skill points per level. She has a +1 Intelligence modifier, so that goes up to 5 skill points per level. At 1st level, she gets four times that amount, or 20 skill points. Her maximum rank for a class skill at 1st level is 4, so she could, for example, divvy up her 20 points among five class skills with 4 ranks each. (It's more useful to have a higher score in a few skills than a lower score in many.)

You can also buy skills from other classes' skill lists, but each skill point buys only 1/2 rank in these cross-class skills, and you can buy only half the maximum ranks a class skill would have (thus, the maximum rank for a cross-class skill at 1st level is 2).

Lars Grant-West

Class Features: Special characteristics of the class. When applicable, this section also mentions restrictions and disadvantages of the class. Class features include some or all of the following.

Weapon and Armor Proficiency: This section details which weapons and armor types the character is proficient with. Regardless of training, cumbersome armor interferes with certain skills (such as Climb) and with the casting of most arcane spells. Characters can become proficient with other weapon or armor types by acquiring the appropriate Armor Proficiency (light, medium, heavy), Shield Proficiency, and Weapon Proficiency (exotic, martial, or simple) feats. (See Chapter 5: Feats.)

Spells: Wizards, sorcerers, clerics, druids, and bards use spells. Fighters, barbarians, rogues, and monks do not. Paladins and rangers gain the ability to use spells at 4th level.

Other Features: Each class has certain unique capabilities. Some, such as the rogue, have few; others, such as the monk, have many.

Some abilities are supernatural or spell-like. Using a spell-like ability is essentially like casting a spell (but without components; see Components, page 174), and it provokes attacks of opportunity. Using a supernatural ability is not like casting a spell. (See Chapter 8: Combat, especially Attacks of Opportunity, page 137, and Use Special Ability, page 142.)

Ex-Members: If, for some reason, a character is forced to give up this class, these are the rules for what happens. Unless otherwise noted in a class description, an ex-member of a class retains any weapon and armor proficiencies he or she has gained.

Starting Package: This section provides suggested feats, skills, equipment, and other details for a 1st-level character of this class. You can ignore this information and create a character from scratch, or use the package as is for your first character (simply copy the details onto your character sheet), or take some portions of the package (such as equipment) and choose other details (such as skills) yourself. Dungeon Masters can also use these packages to quickly create 1st-level nonplayer characters.

The starting packages assume that you spend 4 skill points on every skill you start with (so as to excel in a few things rather than dabble in many). The skill table in each package presents the skills in order of probable importance to the character.

Each starting package is associated with a race. The packages do not take into account racial traits, so be sure to note your character's racial traits (described in Chapter 2: Races), including ability modifiers and bonuses on skill checks. The package also does not list all class features, so note your character's class features as well.

Gear for a character means adventuring gear, not clothes. Assume that your character owns at least one outfit of normal clothes. Pick any one of the following clothing outfits (see Clothing in Chapter 7: Equipment) for free: artisan's outfit, entertainer's outfit, explorer's outfit, monk's outfit, peasant's outfit, scholar's outfit, or traveler's outfit.

BARBARIAN

From the frozen wastes of the north and the hellish jungles of the south come brave, even reckless, warriors. Civilized people call them barbarians or berserkers and suspect them of mayhem, impiety, and atrocities. These "barbarians," however, have proven their mettle and their value to those who would be their allies. To enemies who underestimated them, they have proved their cunning, resourcefulness, persistence, and mercilessness.

Adventures: Adventuring is the best chance barbarians have of finding a place in a civilized society. They're not well suited to the monotony of guard duty or other mundane tasks. Barbarians also have no trouble with the dangers, the uncertainties, and the wandering that adventuring involves. They may adventure to defeat hated enemies. They also have a noted distaste for that which they consider unnatural, including undead, demons, and devils.

Characteristics: The barbarian is an excellent warrior. Where the fighter's skill in combat comes from training and discipline, however, the barbarian has a powerful rage. While in this berserk fury, he becomes stronger and tougher, better able to defeat his foes and withstand their attacks. These rages leave him winded, and he has the energy for only a few such spectacular displays per day, but those few rages are usually sufficient. He is at home in the wild, and he runs at great speed.

Alignment: Barbarians are never lawful. They may be honorable, but at heart they are wild. This wildness is their strength, and it could not live in a lawful soul. At best, barbarians of chaotic alignment are free and expressive. At worst, they are thoughtlessly destructive.

Religion: Some barbarians distrust established religions and prefer an intuitive, natural relationship to the cosmos over formal worship. Others devote themselves to powerful deities, such as Kord (god of strength), Obad-Hai (god of nature), or Erythnul (god of slaughter). A barbarian is capable of fierce devotion to his god.

Background: Barbarians come from uncivilized lands or from barbaric tribes on the outskirts of civilization. A barbarian adventurer may have been lured to the settled lands by the promise of riches, may have escaped after being captured in his homeland and sold into "civilized" slavery, may have been recruited as a soldier, or may have been driven out of his homeland by invaders. Barbarians share no bond with each other unless they come from the same tribe or land. In fact, they think of themselves not as barbarians but as warriors.

Races: Human barbarians come from the distant wild lands on the edge of civilization. Most half-orc barbarians lived among orcs before abandoning them for human lands. Dwarf barbarians are rare, usually hailing from dwarven kingdoms that have fallen into barbarism as a result of recurrent war with goblinoids, orcs, and giants. Barbarians of other races are very rare.

Among the brutal humanoids, barbarians are more common than fighters. Orcs and ogres are especially likely to be barbarians.

Other Classes: As people of the wild, barbarians are most comfortable in the company of rangers, druids, and clerics of nature deities, such as Obad-Hai or Ehlonna. Many barbarians admire the talents and spontaneity of bards, and some are enthusiastic lovers of music. Barbarians don't trust that which they don't understand, and that includes wizardry, which they call "book magic." They find sorcerers more understandable than wizards, but maybe that's just because sorcerers tend to be more charismatic. Monks, with their studied, practiced, deliberate approach to combat, sometimes have a hard time seeing eye to eye with barbarians, but members of these classes aren't necessarily hostile to each other. Barbarians have no special attitude toward fighters, paladins, clerics, or rogues.

Role: A barbarian's typical primary role in a group of adventurers is as a front-line combat specialist. No other character can match his sheer toughness. He can also serve as a good scout, thanks to his speed, skill selection, and trap sense.

GAME RULE INFORMATION

Barbarians have the following game statistics.

Abilities: Strength is important for barbarians because of its role in combat, and several barbarian class skills are based on Strength. Dexterity is also useful to barbarians, especially those who wear light armor. Wisdom is also important for several of the barbarian's class skills. A high Constitution score lets a barbarian rage longer (and live longer, because it gives him more hit points).

Alignment: Any nonlawful.

Hit Die: d12.

Class Skills

The barbarian's class skills (and the key ability for each skill) are Climb (Str), Craft (Int), Handle Animal (Cha), Intimidate (Cha), Jump (Str), Listen (Wis), Ride (Dex), Survival (Wis), and Swim (Str). See Chapter 4: Skills for skill descriptions.

Skill Points at 1st Level: (4 + Int modifier) × 4.

Skill Points at Each Additional Level: 4 + Int modifier.

Class Features

All of the following are class features of the barbarian.

Weapon and Armor Proficiency: A barbarian is proficient with all simple and martial weapons, light armor, medium armor, and shields (except tower shields).

Fast Movement (Ex): A barbarian's land speed is faster than the norm for his race by +10 feet. This benefit applies only when he is wearing no armor, light armor, or medium armor and not carrying a heavy load. Apply this bonus before modifying the barbarian's speed because of any load carried or armor worn. For example, a human barbarian has a speed of 40 feet, rather than 30 feet, when wearing light or no armor. When wearing medium armor or carrying a medium load, his speed drops to 30 feet. A halfling barbarian has a speed of 30 feet, rather than 20 feet, in light or no armor. When wearing medium armor or carrying a medium load, his speed drops to 20 feet.

Illiteracy: Barbarians are the only characters who do not automatically know how to read and write. A barbarian may spend 2 skill points to gain the ability to read and write all languages he is able to speak.

A barbarian who gains a level in any other class automatically gains literacy. Any other character who gains a barbarian level does not lose the literacy he or she already had.

Rage (Ex): A barbarian can fly into a screaming blood frenzy a certain number of times per day. In a rage, a barbarian gains phenomenal strength and durability but becomes reckless and less able to defend himself. He temporarily gains a +4 bonus to Strength, a +4 bonus to Constitution, and a +2 morale bonus on Will saves, but he takes a –2 penalty to Armor Class.

Krusk

The increase in Constitution increases the barbarian's hit points by 2 points per level, but these hit points go away at the end of the rage when his Constitution score drops back to normal. (These extra hit points are not lost first the way temporary hit points are; see Temporary Hit Points, page 146.) While raging, a barbarian cannot use any Charisma-, Dexterity-, or Intelligence-based skills (except for Balance, Escape Artist, Intimidate, and Ride), the Concentration skill, or any abilities that require patience or concentration, nor can he cast spells or activate magic items that require a command word, a spell trigger (such as a wand), or spell completion (such as a scroll) to function. He can use any feat he has except Combat Expertise, item creation feats, and metamagic feats. A fit of rage lasts for a number of rounds equal to 3 + the character's (newly improved) Constitution modifier. A barbarian may prematurely end his rage. At the end of the rage, the barbarian loses the rage modifiers and restrictions and becomes fatigued (–2 penalty to Strength, –2 penalty to Dexterity, can't charge or run) for the duration of the current encounter (unless he is a 17th-level barbarian, at which point this limitation no longer applies; see below).

A barbarian can fly into a rage only once per encounter. At 1st level he can use his rage ability once per day. At 4th level and every four levels thereafter, he can use it one additional time per day (to a maximum of six times per day at 20th level). Entering a rage takes no time itself, but a barbarian can do it only during his action (see Initiative, page 136), not in response to someone else's action. A barbarian can't, for example, fly into a rage when

TABLE 3–3: THE BARBARIAN

Level	Base Attack Bonus	Fort Save	Ref Save	Will Save	Special
1st	+1	+2	+0	+0	Fast movement, illiteracy, rage 1/day
2nd	+2	+3	+0	+0	Uncanny dodge
3rd	+3	+3	+1	+1	Trap sense +1
4th	+4	+4	+1	+1	Rage 2/day
5th	+5	+4	+1	+1	Improved uncanny dodge
6th	+6/+1	+5	+2	+2	Trap sense +2
7th	+7/+2	+5	+2	+2	Damage reduction 1/—
8th	+8/+3	+6	+2	+2	Rage 3/day
9th	+9/+4	+6	+3	+3	Trap sense +3
10th	+10/+5	+7	+3	+3	Damage reduction 2/—
11th	+11/+6/+1	+7	+3	+3	Greater rage
12th	+12/+7/+2	+8	+4	+4	Rage 4/day, trap sense +4
13th	+13/+8/+3	+8	+4	+4	Damage reduction 3/—
14th	+14/+9/+4	+9	+4	+4	Indomitable will
15th	+15/+10/+5	+9	+5	+5	Trap sense +5
16th	+16/+11/+6/+1	+10	+5	+5	Damage reduction 4/—, rage 5/day
17th	+17/+12/+7/+2	+10	+5	+5	Tireless rage
18th	+18/+13/+8/+3	+11	+6	+6	Trap sense +6
19th	+19/+14/+9/+4	+11	+6	+6	Damage reduction 5/—
20th	+20/+15/+10/+5	+12	+6	+6	Mighty rage, rage 6/day

struck down by an arrow in order to get the extra hit points from the increased Constitution, although the extra hit points would be of benefit if he had gone into a rage earlier in the round, *before* the arrow struck.

Uncanny Dodge (Ex): At 2nd level, a barbarian gains the ability to react to danger before his senses would normally allow him to do so. He retains his Dexterity bonus to AC (if any) even if he is caught flat-footed or struck by an invisible attacker. However, he still loses his Dexterity bonus to AC if immobilized.

If a barbarian already has uncanny dodge from a different class (a barbarian with at least four levels of rogue, for example), he automatically gains improved uncanny dodge (see below) instead.

Trap Sense (Ex): Starting at 3rd level, a barbarian has an intuitive sense that alerts him to danger from traps, giving him a +1 bonus on Reflex saves made to avoid traps and a +1 dodge bonus to AC against attacks made by traps. These bonuses rise by +1 every three barbarian levels thereafter (6th, 9th, 12th, 15th, and 18th level). Trap sense bonuses gained from multiple classes stack.

Improved Uncanny Dodge (Ex): At 5th level and higher, a barbarian can no longer be flanked; he can react to opponents on opposite sides of him as easily as he can react to a single attacker. This defense denies a rogue the ability to sneak attack the barbarian by flanking him, unless the attacker has at least four more rogue levels than the target has barbarian levels.

If a character already has uncanny dodge (see above) from a second class, the character automatically gains improved uncanny dodge instead, and the levels from the classes that grant uncanny dodge stack to determine the minimum level a rogue must be to flank the character.

Damage Reduction (Ex): At 7th level, a barbarian gains the ability to shrug off some amount of injury from each blow or attack. Subtract 1 from the damage the barbarian takes each time he is dealt damage from a weapon or a natural attack. At 10th level, and every three barbarian levels thereafter (13th, 16th, and 19th level), this damage reduction rises by 1 point. Damage reduction can reduce damage to 0 but not below 0.

Greater Rage (Ex): At 11th level, a barbarian's bonuses to Strength and Constitution during his rage each increase to +6, and his morale bonus on Will saves increases to +3. The penalty to AC remains at −2.

Indomitable Will (Ex): While in a rage, a barbarian of 14th level or higher gains a +4 bonus on Will saves to resist enchantment spells. This bonus stacks with all other modifiers, including the morale bonus on Will saves he also receives during his rage.

Tireless Rage (Ex): At 17th level and higher, a barbarian no longer becomes fatigued at the end of his rage.

Mighty Rage (Ex): At 20th level, a barbarian's bonuses to Strength and Constitution during his rage each increase to +8, and his morale bonus on Will saves increases to +4. The penalty to AC remains at −2.

Ex-Barbarians

A barbarian who becomes lawful loses the ability to rage and cannot gain more levels as a barbarian. He retains all the other benefits of the class (damage reduction, fast movement, trap sense, and uncanny dodge).

Half-Orc Barbarian Starting Package

Armor: Studded leather (+3 AC, armor check penalty −1, speed 40 ft., 20 lb.).

Weapons: Greataxe (1d12, crit ×3, 12 lb., two-handed, slashing).

Shortbow (1d6, crit ×3, range inc. 60 ft., 2 lb., piercing).

Dagger (1d4, crit 19–20/×2, range inc. 10 ft., 1 lb., light, piercing).

Skill Selection: Pick a number of skills equal to 4 + Int modifier.

Skill	Ranks	Ability	Armor Check Penalty
Climb	4	Str	−1
Survival	4	Wis	—
Listen	4	Wis	—
Jump	4	Str	−1
Swim	4	Str	−2
Ride	4	Dex	—
Intimidate	4	Cha	—
Spot (cc)	2	Wis	—

Feat: Weapon Focus (greataxe).

Gear: Backpack with waterskin, one day's trail rations, bedroll, sack, and flint and steel. Quiver with 20 arrows.

Gold: 2d4 gp.

BARD

It is said that music has a special magic, and the bard proves that saying true. Wandering across the land, gathering lore, telling stories, working magic with his music, and living on the gratitude of his audience—such is the life of a bard. When chance or opportunity draws them into a conflict, bards serve as diplomats, negotiators, messengers, scouts, and spies.

A bard's magic comes from the heart. If his heart is good, a bard brings hope and courage to the downtrodden and uses his tricks, music, and magic to thwart the schemes of evildoers. If the nobles of the land are corrupt, the good bard is an enemy of the state, cunningly evading capture and raising the spirits of the oppressed. But music can spring from an evil heart as well. Evil bards forego blatant violence in favor of manipulation, holding sway over the hearts and minds of others and taking what enraptured audiences "willingly" give.

Adventures: Bards see adventures as opportunities to learn. They practice their many skills and abilities, and they especially relish the opportunity to enter a long-forgotten tomb, to discover ancient works of magic, to decipher old tomes, to travel to strange places, to encounter exotic creatures, and to learn new songs and stories. Bards love to accompany heroes (and villains), joining their entourage to witness their deeds firsthand—a bard who can tell a marvelous story from personal experience earns renown among his fellows. Indeed, after telling so many stories about heroes doing mighty deeds, many bards take these themes to heart and assume heroic roles themselves.

Characteristics: A bard brings forth magic from his soul, not from a book. He can cast only a small number of spells, but he can do so without selecting or preparing them in advance. His magic emphasizes charms and illusions over the more dramatic evocation spells that wizards and sorcerers often use.

In addition to spells, a bard works magic with his music and poetry. He can encourage allies, hold his audiences rapt, and counter magical effects that rely on speech or sound.

Bards have some of the skills that rogues have, although bards are not as focused on skill mastery as rogues are. A bard listens to stories as well as telling them, of course, so he has a vast knowledge of local events and noteworthy items.

Alignment: Bards are wanderers, guided by whim and intuition rather than by tradition or law. The spontaneous talent, magic, and lifestyle of the bard are incompatible with a lawful alignment.

Religion: Bards revere Fharlanghn (god of roads). They sometimes camp near his wayside shrines, hoping to earn some coin from the travelers who stop to leave offerings for the god. Many bards, even those who are not elves, worship Corellon Larethian, god of the elves and patron of poetry and music. Many good bards are partial to Pelor (god of the sun), believing that he watches over them in their travels. Bards given to chaos and occasional larceny favor Olidammara (god of thieves). Those who have turned to evil ways are known to worship Erythnul (god of slaughter), though few admit to it. In any event, bards spend so much time on the road that, while they may be devoted to a deity, they are rarely devoted to any particular temple.

Background: An apprentice bard learns his skills from a single experienced bard, whom he follows and serves until he is ready to strike out on his own. Many bards were once young runaways or orphans, befriended by wandering bards who became their mentors. Since bards occasionally congregate in informal "colleges," the apprentice bard may meet many of the more prominent bards in the area. Still, a bard has no strong allegiance to bards as a whole. In fact, some are highly competitive with other bards, jealous of their reputations and defensive about their territories.

Races: Bards are commonly human, gnome, elf, or half-elf. Humans take well to the wandering life and adapt easily to new lands and customs. Gnomes have a sense of humor and trickery that lends itself to a bardic career. Elves are talented in music and magic, so the career of the bard comes naturally to them. A bard's wandering ways suit many half-elves, who often feel like strangers even when at home. Half-orcs, even those raised among humans, find themselves ill suited to the demands of a bard's career. There are no bardic traditions among dwarves or halflings, though occasional individuals of these races find teachers to train them in the ways of the bard.

Bards are exceedingly rare among the savage humanoids, except among centaurs. Centaur bards sometimes train the children of humans or other humanoids.

Gimble

Other Classes: A bard works well with companions of other classes. He often serves as the spokesman of the party, using his social skills for the party's benefit. In a party without a wizard or sorcerer, the bard contributes his magic. In a party without a rogue, he uses his skills. A bard is curious about the ways of more focused or dedicated adventurers, so he often tries to pick up pointers from fighters, sorcerers, and rogues.

Role: The bard is perhaps the ultimate generalist. In most adventuring groups, he works best in a supporting role. He can't usually match the stealth of the ranger or the rogue, the spellcasting power of the cleric or the wizard, or the combat prowess of the barbarian or the fighter. However, he makes all the other characters better at what they do, and he can often fill in for another character when needed. For a typical group of four characters, the bard is perhaps the most useful fifth character to consider adding, and he can make a great team leader.

GAME RULE INFORMATION

Bards have the following game statistics.

Abilities: Charisma determines how powerful a spell a bard can cast, how many spells he can cast per day, and how

Illus. by W. Reynolds

TABLE 3–4: THE BARD

Level	Base Attack Bonus	Fort Save	Ref Save	Will Save	Special	Spells per Day 0	1st	2nd	3rd	4th	5th	6th
1st	+0	+0	+2	+2	Bardic music, bardic knowledge, countersong, *fascinate*, inspire courage +1	2	—	—	—	—	—	—
2nd	+1	+0	+3	+3		3	0	—	—	—	—	—
3rd	+2	+1	+3	+3	Inspire competence	3	1	—	—	—	—	—
4th	+3	+1	+4	+4		3	2	0	—	—	—	—
5th	+3	+1	+4	+4		3	3	1	—	—	—	—
6th	+4	+2	+5	+5	*Suggestion*	3	3	2	—	—	—	—
7th	+5	+2	+5	+5		3	3	2	0	—	—	—
8th	+6/+1	+2	+6	+6	Inspire courage +2	3	3	3	1	—	—	—
9th	+6/+1	+3	+6	+6	Inspire greatness	3	3	3	2	—	—	—
10th	+7/+2	+3	+7	+7		3	3	3	2	0	—	—
11th	+8/+3	+3	+7	+7		3	3	3	3	1	—	—
12th	+9/+4	+4	+8	+8	*Song of freedom*	3	3	3	3	2	—	—
13th	+9/+4	+4	+8	+8		3	3	3	3	2	0	—
14th	+10/+5	+4	+9	+9	Inspire courage +3	4	3	3	3	3	1	—
15th	+11/+6/+1	+5	+9	+9	Inspire heroics	4	4	3	3	3	2	—
16th	+12/+7/+2	+5	+10	+10		4	4	4	3	3	2	0
17th	+12/+7/+2	+5	+10	+10		4	4	4	4	3	3	1
18th	+13/+8/+3	+6	+11	+11	*Mass suggestion*	4	4	4	4	4	3	2
19th	+14/+9/+4	+6	+11	+11		4	4	4	4	4	4	3
20th	+15/+10/+5	+6	+12	+12	Inspire courage +4	4	4	4	4	4	4	4

hard those spells are to resist (see Spells, below). Charisma, Dexterity, and Intelligence are important for many of the bard's class skills.

Alignment: Any nonlawful.

Hit Die: d6.

Class Skills

The bard's class skills (and the key ability for each skill) are Appraise (Int), Balance (Dex), Bluff (Cha), Climb (Str), Concentration (Con), Craft (Int), Decipher Script (Int), Diplomacy (Cha), Disguise (Cha), Escape Artist (Dex), Gather Information (Cha), Hide (Dex), Jump (Str), Knowledge (all skills, taken individually) (Int), Listen (Wis), Move Silently (Dex), Perform (Cha), Profession (Wis), Sense Motive (Wis), Sleight of Hand (Dex), Speak Language (n/a), Spellcraft (Int), Swim (Str), Tumble (Dex), and Use Magic Device (Cha). See Chapter 4: Skills for skill descriptions.

Skill Points at 1st Level: (6 + Int modifier) × 4.

Skill Points at Each Additional Level: 6 + Int modifier.

Class Features

All of the following are class features of the bard.

Weapon and Armor Proficiency: A bard is proficient with all simple weapons, plus the longsword, rapier, sap, short sword, shortbow, and whip. Bards are proficient with light armor and shields (except tower shields).

Because the somatic components required for bard spells are relatively simple, a bard can cast bard spells while wearing light armor without incurring the normal arcane spell failure chance. However, like any other arcane spellcaster, a bard wearing medium or heavy armor or using a shield incurs a chance of arcane spell failure if the spell in question has a somatic component (most do). A multiclass bard still incurs the normal arcane spell failure chance for arcane spells received from other classes.

TABLE 3–5: BARD SPELLS KNOWN

Level	0	1st	2nd	3rd	4th	5th	6th
				Spells Known			
1st	4	—	—	—	—	—	—
2nd	5	2[1]	—	—	—	—	—
3rd	6	3	—	—	—	—	—
4th	6	3	2[1]	—	—	—	—
5th	6	4	3	—	—	—	—
6th	6	4	3	—	—	—	—
7th	6	4	4	2[1]	—	—	—
8th	6	4	4	3	—	—	—
9th	6	4	4	3	—	—	—
10th	6	4	4	4	2[1]	—	—
11th	6	4	4	4	3	—	—
12th	6	4	4	4	3	—	—
13th	6	4	4	4	4	2[1]	—
14th	6	4	4	4	4	3	—
15th	6	4	4	4	4	3	—
16th	6	5	4	4	4	4	2[1]
17th	6	5	5	4	4	4	3
18th	6	5	5	5	4	4	3
19th	6	5	5	5	5	4	4
20th	6	5	5	5	5	5	4

1 Provided the bard has a high enough Charisma score to have a bonus spell of this level.

Spells: A bard casts arcane spells (the same type of spells available to sorcerers and wizards), which are drawn from the bard spell list (page 181). He can cast any spell he knows without preparing it ahead of time, the way a wizard or cleric must (see below). Every bard spell has a verbal component (singing, reciting, or music).

To learn or cast a spell, a bard must have a Charisma score equal to at least 10 + the spell level (Cha 10 for 0-level spells, Cha 11 for

1st-level spells, and so forth). The Difficulty Class for a saving throw against a bard's spell is 10 + the spell level + the bard's Charisma modifier.

Like other spellcasters, a bard can cast only a certain number of spells of each spell level per day. His base daily spell allotment is given on Table 3–4: The Bard. In addition, he receives bonus spells per day if he has a high Charisma score (see Table 1–1: Ability Modifiers and Bonus Spells, page 8). When Table 3–4 indicates that the bard gets 0 spells per day of a given spell level (for instance, 1st-level spells for a 2nd-level bard), he gains only the bonus spells he would be entitled to based on his Charisma score for that spell level.

The bard's selection of spells is extremely limited. A bard begins play knowing four 0-level spells (also called cantrips) of your choice. At most new bard levels, he gains one or more new spells, as indicated on Table 3–5: Bard Spells Known. (Unlike spells per day, the number of spells a bard knows is not affected by his Charisma score; the numbers on Table 3–5 are fixed.)

Upon reaching 5th level, and at every third bard level after that (8th, 11th, and so on), a bard can choose to learn a new spell in place of one he already knows. In effect, the bard "loses" the old spell in exchange for the new one. The new spell's level must be the same as that of the spell being exchanged, and it must be at least two levels lower than the highest-level bard spell the bard can cast. For instance, upon reaching 5th level, a bard could trade in a single 0-level spell (two spell levels below the highest-level bard spell he can cast, which is 2nd) for a different 0-level spell. At 8th level, he could trade in a single 0-level or 1st-level spell (since he now can cast 3rd-level bard spells) for a different spell of the same level. A bard may swap only a single spell at any given level, and must choose whether or not to swap the spell at the same time that he gains new spells known for the level.

As noted above, a bard need not prepare his spells in advance. He can cast any spell he knows at any time, assuming he has not yet used up his allotment of spells per day for the spell's level. For example, at 1st level, Gimble the bard can cast two 0-level spells per day for being 1st level (see Table 3–4: The Bard). However, he knows four 0-level spells: *detect magic, ghost sound, light,* and *read magic* (see Table 3–5: Bard Spells Known). Thus, on any given day, he can cast some combination of those four spells a total of two times. He does not have to decide ahead of time which spells he'll cast.

Bardic Knowledge: A bard picks up a lot of stray knowledge while wandering the land and learning stories from other bards. He may make a special bardic knowledge check with a bonus equal to his bard level + his Intelligence modifier to see whether he knows some relevant information about local notable people, legendary items, or noteworthy places. (If the bard has 5 or more ranks in Knowledge (history), he gains a +2 bonus on this check.)

DC	Type of Knowledge	Examples
10	Common, known by at least a substantial minority of the local population.	A local mayor's reputation for drinking; common legends about a powerful place of mystery.
20	Uncommon but available, known by only a few people in the area.	A local priest's shady past; legends about a powerful magic item.
25	Obscure, known by few, hard to come by.	A knight's family history; legends about a minor place of mystery or magic item.
30	Extremely obscure, known by very few, possibly forgotten by most who once knew it, possibly known only by those who don't understand the significance of the knowledge.	A mighty wizard's childhood nickname; the history of a petty magic item.

A successful bardic knowledge check will not reveal the powers of a magic item but may give a hint as to its general function. A bard may not take 10 or take 20 on this check; this sort of knowledge is essentially random. The DM can determine the Difficulty Class of the check by referring to the table above.

Bardic Music: Once per day per bard level, a bard can use his song or poetics to produce magical effects on those around him (usually including himself, if desired). While these abilities fall under the category of bardic music and the descriptions discuss singing or playing instruments, they can all be activated by reciting poetry, chanting, singing lyrical songs, singing melodies (fa-la-la, and so forth), whistling, playing an instrument, or playing an instrument in combination with some spoken performance. Each ability requires both a minimum bard level and a minimum number of ranks in the Perform skill to qualify; if a bard does not have the required number of ranks in at least one Perform skill, he does not gain the bardic music ability until he acquires the needed ranks.

Starting a bardic music effect is a standard action. Some bardic music abilities require concentration, which means the bard must take a standard action each round to maintain the ability. Even while using bardic music that doesn't require concentration, a bard cannot cast spells, activate magic items by spell completion (such as scrolls), or activate magic items by magic word (such as wands). Just as for casting a spell with a verbal component (see Components, page 174), a deaf bard has a 20% chance to fail when attempting to use bardic music. If he fails, the attempt still counts against his daily limit.

Countersong (Su): A bard with 3 or more ranks in a Perform skill can use his music or poetics to counter magical effects that depend on sound (but not spells that simply have verbal components). Each round of the countersong, he makes a Perform check. Any creature within 30 feet of the bard (including the bard himself) that is affected by a sonic or language-dependent magical attack (such as a *sound burst* or *command* spell) may use the bard's Perform check result in place of its saving throw if, after the saving throw is rolled, the Perform check result proves to be higher. If a creature within range of the countersong is already under the effect of a noninstantaneous sonic or language-dependent magical attack, it gains another saving throw against the effect each round it hears the countersong, but it must use the bard's Perform check result for the save. Countersong has no effect against effects that don't allow saves. The bard may keep up the countersong for 10 rounds.

Fascinate (Sp): A bard with 3 or more ranks in a Perform skill can use his music or poetics to cause one or more creatures to become fascinated with him. Each creature to be fascinated must be within 90 feet, able to see and hear the bard, and able to pay attention to him. The bard must also be able to see the creature. The distraction of a nearby combat or other dangers prevents the ability from working. For every three levels a bard attains beyond 1st, he can target one additional creature with a single use of this ability (two at 4th level, three at 7th level, and so on).

To use the ability, a bard makes a Perform check. His check result is the DC for each affected creature's Will save against the effect. If a creature's saving throw succeeds, the bard cannot attempt to fascinate that creature again for 24 hours. If its saving throw fails, the creature sits quietly and listens to the song, taking no other actions, for as long as the bard continues to play and concentrate (up to a maximum of 1 round per bard level). While fascinated, a target takes a –4 penalty on skill checks made as reactions, such as Listen and Spot checks. Any potential threat, such as an ally of the bard approaching the fascinated creature, requires the bard to make another Perform check and allows the creature a new saving throw against a DC equal to the new Perform check result. Any obvious threat, such as someone drawing a weapon, casting a spell, or aiming a ranged weapon at the target, automatically breaks the effect. *Fascinate* is an enchantment (compulsion), mind-affecting ability.

Inspire Courage (Su): A bard with 3 or more ranks in a Perform skill can use song or poetics to inspire courage in his allies (including himself), bolstering them against fear and improving their combat abilities. To be affected, an ally must be able to hear the bard sing. The effect lasts for as long as the ally hears the bard sing and for 5 rounds thereafter. An affected ally receives a +1 morale bonus on saving throws against charm and fear effects and a +1 morale bonus on attack and weapon damage rolls. At 8th level, and every six bard levels thereafter, this bonus increases by 1 (+2 at 8th, +3 at 14th, and +4 at 20th). Inspire courage is a mind-affecting ability.

Inspire Competence (Su): A bard of 3rd level or higher with 6 or more ranks in a Perform skill can use his music or poetics to help an ally succeed at a task. The ally must be within 30 feet and able to see and hear the bard. The bard must also be able to see the ally. Depending on the task that the ally has at hand, the bard may use his bardic music to lift the ally's spirits, to help him or her focus mentally, or in some other way. The ally gets a +2 competence bonus on skill checks with a particular skill as long as he or she continues to hear the bard's music. The DM may rule that certain uses of this ability are infeasible—chanting to make a rogue move more quietly, for example, is self-defeating. The effect lasts as long as the bard concentrates, up to a maximum of 2 minutes. A bard can't inspire competence in himself. Inspire competence is a mind-affecting ability.

Suggestion (Sp): A bard of 6th level or higher with 9 or more ranks in a Perform skill can make a *suggestion* (as the spell) to a creature that he has already fascinated (see above). Using this ability does not break the bard's concentration on the *fascinate* effect, nor does it allow a second saving throw against the *fascinate* effect. Making a *suggestion* doesn't count against a bard's daily limit on bardic music performances. A Will saving throw (DC 10 + 1/2 bard's level + bard's Cha modifier) negates the effect. This ability affects only a single creature (but see *mass suggestion*, below). *Suggestion* is an enchantment (compulsion), mind-affecting, language-dependent ability.

Inspire Greatness (Su): A bard of 9th level or higher with 12 or more ranks in a Perform skill can use music or poetics to inspire greatness in himself or a single willing ally within 30 feet, granting him or her extra fighting capability. For every three levels a bard attains beyond 9th, he can target one additional ally with a single use of this ability (two at 12th level, three at 15th, four at 18th). To inspire greatness, a bard must sing and an ally must hear him sing. The effect lasts for as long as the ally hears the bard sing and for 5 rounds thereafter. A creature inspired with greatness gains 2 bonus Hit Dice (d10s), the commensurate number of temporary hit points (apply the target's Constitution modifier, if any, to these bonus Hit Dice), a +2 competence bonus on attack rolls, and a +1 competence bonus on Fortitude saves. The bonus Hit Dice count as regular Hit Dice for determining the effect of spells such as *sleep*. Inspire greatness is a mind-affecting ability.

Song of Freedom (Sp): A bard of 12th level or higher with 15 or more ranks in a Perform skill can use music or poetics to create an effect equivalent to the *break enchantment* spell (caster level equals the character's bard level). Using this ability requires 1 minute of uninterrupted concentration and music, and it functions on a single target within 30 feet. A bard can't use *song of freedom* on himself.

Inspire Heroics (Su): A bard of 15th level or higher with 18 or more ranks in a Perform skill can use music or poetics to inspire tremendous heroism in himself or a single willing ally within 30 feet, allowing that creature to fight bravely even against overwhelming odds. For every three bard levels the character attains beyond 15th, he can inspire heroics in one additional creature. To inspire heroics, a bard must sing and an ally must hear the bard sing for a full round. A creature so inspired gains a +4 morale bonus on saving throws and a +4 dodge bonus to AC. The effect lasts for as long as the ally hears the bard sing and for up to 5 rounds thereafter. Inspire heroics is a mind-affecting ability.

Mass Suggestion (Sp): This ability functions like *suggestion*, above, except that a bard of 18th level or higher with 21 or more ranks in a Perform skill can make the *suggestion* simultaneously to any number of creatures that he has already fascinated (see above). *Mass suggestion* is an enchantment (compulsion), mind-affecting, language-dependent ability.

Ex-Bards

A bard who becomes lawful in alignment cannot progress in levels as a bard, though he retains all his bard abilities.

Gnome Bard Starting Package

Armor: Studded leather (+3 AC, armor check penalty –1, arcane spell failure chance n/a, speed 20 ft., 10 lb.).

Weapons: Longsword (1d6, crit 19–20/×2, 2 lb., one-handed, slashing).

Light crossbow (1d6, crit 19–20/×2, range inc. 80 ft., 2 lb., piercing).

Skill Selection: Pick a number of skills equal to 6 + Int modifier.

Skill	Ranks	Ability	Armor Check Penalty
Perform (string instruments)	4	Cha	—
Spellcraft	4	Int	—
Use Magic Device	4	Cha	—
Gather Information	4	Cha	—
Listen	4	Wis	—
Decipher Script	4	Int	—
Diplomacy	4	Cha	—
Knowledge (any one)	4	Int	—
Sleight of Hand	4	Dex	–1
Disguise	4	Cha	—

Feat: If Dexterity is 13 or higher, Dodge; if Dexterity is 12 or lower, Improved Initiative instead.

Spells Known: 0 level—*detect magic, ghost sound, light, read magic.*

Gear: Backpack with waterskin, one day's trail rations, bedroll, sack, and flint and steel. Three torches. Case with 10 crossbow bolts. Lute (common). Spell component pouch.

Gold: 2d4 gp.

CLERIC

The handiwork of the gods is everywhere—in places of natural beauty, in mighty crusades, in soaring temples, and in the hearts of worshipers. Like people, gods run the gamut from benevolent to malicious, reserved to intrusive, simple to inscrutable. The gods, however, work mostly through intermediaries—their clerics. Good clerics heal, protect, and avenge. Evil clerics pillage, destroy, and sabotage. A cleric uses the power of his god to make the god's will manifest. And if a cleric uses his god's power to improve his own lot, that's to be expected, too.

Adventures: Ideally, a cleric's adventures support his god's causes, at least in a general way. A good cleric, for example, helps those in need. If, through noble acts, he can improve the reputation of his god or temple, that's even better. An evil cleric seeks to increase his own power and that of his deity, so that others will respect and fear both.

Clerics sometimes receive orders, or at least suggestions, from their ecclesiastical superiors, directing them to undertake missions for the church. The clerics and their companions are compensated fairly for these missions, and the church may be especially generous with the casting of needed spells or divine magic items as payment.

Of course, clerics are people, too, and they may have any or all of the more common motivations for adventuring.

Characteristics: Clerics are masters of divine magic, which is especially good at healing. Even an inexperienced cleric can bring people back from the brink of death, and an experienced cleric can bring back people who have crossed over that brink.

As channelers of divine energy, clerics can affect undead creatures. A good cleric can turn away or even destroy undead; an evil cleric can bring such creatures under his control.

Clerics have some combat training. They can use simple weapons, and they are trained in the use of armor, since armor does not interfere with divine spells the way it does with arcane spells.

Alignment: Like the gods they serve, clerics can be of any alignment. Because people more readily worship good deities than neutral or evil ones, there are more good than evil clerics. Clerics also tend toward law instead of chaos, since lawful religions tend to be more structured and better able to recruit and train clerics than chaotic ones.

Typically, a cleric is the same alignment as his deity, though some clerics are one step away from their respective deities in alignment. For example, most clerics of Heironeous, the god of valor (who is lawful good), are lawful good, but some are lawful neutral or neutral good. Additionally, a cleric may not be neutral (that is, neutral on both the good–evil axis and the lawful–chaotic axis) unless his deity is also neutral.

Religion: Every reasonably well-known deity has clerics devoted to him or her, so clerics can be of any religion. The deity most commonly worshiped by human clerics in civilized lands is Pelor (god of the sun). The majority of nonhuman clerics are devoted to the chief god of the appropriate racial pantheon. Most clerics are officially ordained members of religious organizations, commonly called churches. Each has sworn to uphold the ideals of his church.

Some clerics devote themselves not to a god but to a cause or a source of divine power. These characters wield magic the way clerics devoted to individual gods do, but they are not associated with any religious institution or any particular practice of worship. A cleric devoted to good and law, for example, may be on friendly terms with the clerics of lawful and good deities and may extol the virtues of a good and lawful life, but he is not a functionary in a church hierarchy.

Background: Most clerics join their churches as young adults, though some are devoted to a god's service from a young age, and a few feel the call later in life. While some clerics are tightly bound to their churches' activities on a daily basis, others have more freedom to conduct their lives as they please, so long as they do so in accordance with their gods' wishes.

Clerics of a given religion are all supposed to get along, though schisms within a church are often more bitter than conflicts between religions. Clerics who share some basic ideals, such as goodness or lawfulness, may find common cause with each other and see themselves as part of an order or body that supersedes any given religion. Clerics of opposed goals, however, are sworn enemies. In civilized lands, open warfare between religions occurs only during civil wars and similar social upheavals, but vicious politicking between opposing churches is common.

Races: All the common races are represented in this class, since the need for religion and divine magic is universal. The clerics of most races, however, are too focused on their religious duties to undertake an adventurer's life. Crusading, adventuring clerics most often come from the human and dwarf races.

Among the savage humanoids, clerics are less common. The exception is troglodytes, who take well to divine magic and are often led by priests who make a practice of sacrificing and devouring captives.

Other Classes: In an adventuring party, the cleric is everybody's friend and often the glue that holds the party together. As the one who can channel divine energy, a cleric is a capable healer, and adventurers of every class appreciate being put back together after they've taken some hard knocks. Clerics sometimes clash with druids, since druids represent an older, more primal relationship between the mortal and the divine. Mostly, though, the religion of a cleric determines how he gets along with others. A cleric of Olidammara (god of thieves) gets along fine with rogues and ne'er-do-wells, for example, while a cleric of Heironeous (god of valor) rankles at such company.

Role: The cleric serves as a typical group's primary healer, diviner, and defensive specialist. He can hold his own in a fight but usually isn't well served by charging to the front of combat. The cleric's domains and spell selection can greatly affect his role as well.

GAME RULE INFORMATION

Clerics have the following game statistics.

Abilities: Wisdom determines how powerful a spell a cleric can cast, how many spells he can cast per day, and how hard those spells are to resist (see Spells, below). A high Constitution score improves a cleric's hit points, and a high Charisma score improves his ability to turn undead.

Alignment: A cleric's alignment must be within one step of his deity's (that is, it may be one step away on either the lawful–chaotic axis or the good–evil axis, but not both). Exceptions are the clerics of St. Cuthbert (a lawful neutral deity), who may choose only between lawful good and lawful neutral for their alignment. A cleric may not be neutral unless his deity's alignment is also neutral.

Hit Die: d8.

Jozan

Class Skills

The cleric's class skills (and the key ability for each skill) are Concentration (Con), Craft (Int), Diplomacy (Cha), Heal (Wis), Knowledge (arcana) (Int), Knowledge (history) (Int), Knowledge (religion) (Int), Knowledge (the planes) (Int), Profession (Wis), and Spellcraft (Int). See Chapter 4: Skills for skill descriptions.

Domains and Class Skills: A cleric who chooses the Animal or Plant domain adds Knowledge (nature) (Int) to the cleric class skills listed above. A cleric who chooses the Knowledge domain adds all Knowledge (Int) skills to the list. A cleric who chooses the Travel domain adds Survival (Wis) to the list. A cleric who chooses the Trickery domain adds Bluff (Cha), Disguise (Cha), and Hide (Dex) to the list. See Deity, Domains, and Domain Spells, below, for more information.

Skill Points at 1st Level: (2 + Int modifier) × 4.

Skill Points at Each Additional Level: 2 + Int modifier.

Class Features

All of the following are class features of the cleric.

Weapon and Armor Proficiency: Clerics are proficient with all simple weapons, with all types of armor (light, medium, and heavy), and with shields (except tower shields).

Every deity has a favored weapon (see Deities, page 106), and his or her clerics consider it a point of pride to wield that weapon. A cleric who chooses the War domain receives the Weapon Focus feat related to that weapon as a bonus feat. He also receives the appropriate Martial Weapon Proficiency feat as a bonus feat, if the weapon falls into that category. See Chapter 5: Feats for details.

TABLE 3–6: THE CLERIC

Level	Base Attack Bonus	Fort Save	Ref Save	Will Save	Special	Spells per Day[1]									
						0	1st	2nd	3rd	4th	5th	6th	7th	8th	9th
1st	+0	+2	+0	+2	Turn or rebuke undead	3	1+1	—	—	—	—	—	—	—	—
2nd	+1	+3	+0	+3		4	2+1	—	—	—	—	—	—	—	—
3rd	+2	+3	+1	+3		4	2+1	1+1	—	—	—	—	—	—	—
4th	+3	+4	+1	+4		5	3+1	2+1	—	—	—	—	—	—	—
5th	+3	+4	+1	+4		5	3+1	2+1	1+1	—	—	—	—	—	—
6th	+4	+5	+2	+5		5	3+1	3+1	2+1	—	—	—	—	—	—
7th	+5	+5	+2	+5		6	4+1	3+1	2+1	1+1	—	—	—	—	—
8th	+6/+1	+6	+2	+6		6	4+1	3+1	3+1	2+1	—	—	—	—	—
9th	+6/+1	+6	+3	+6		6	4+1	4+1	3+1	2+1	1+1	—	—	—	—
10th	+7/+2	+7	+3	+7		6	4+1	4+1	3+1	3+1	2+1	—	—	—	—
11th	+8/+3	+7	+3	+7		6	5+1	4+1	4+1	3+1	2+1	1+1	—	—	—
12th	+9/+4	+8	+4	+8		6	5+1	4+1	4+1	3+1	3+1	2+1	—	—	—
13th	+9/+4	+8	+4	+8		6	5+1	5+1	4+1	4+1	3+1	2+1	1+1	—	—
14th	+10/+5	+9	+4	+9		6	5+1	5+1	4+1	4+1	3+1	3+1	2+1	—	—
15th	+11/+6/+1	+9	+5	+9		6	5+1	5+1	5+1	4+1	4+1	3+1	2+1	1+1	—
16th	+12/+7/+2	+10	+5	+10		6	5+1	5+1	5+1	4+1	4+1	3+1	3+1	2+1	—
17th	+12/+7/+2	+10	+5	+10		6	5+1	5+1	5+1	5+1	4+1	4+1	3+1	2+1	1+1
18th	+13/+8/+3	+11	+6	+11		6	5+1	5+1	5+1	5+1	4+1	4+1	3+1	3+1	2+1
19th	+14/+9/+4	+11	+6	+11		6	5+1	5+1	5+1	5+1	5+1	4+1	4+1	3+1	3+1
20th	+15/+10/+5	+12	+6	+12		6	5+1	5+1	5+1	5+1	5+1	4+1	4+1	4+1	4+1

1 In addition to the stated number of spells per day for 1st- through 9th-level spells, a cleric gets a domain spell for each spell level, starting at 1st. The "+1" in the entries on this table represents that spell. Domain spells are in addition to any bonus spells the cleric may receive for having a high Wisdom score.

TABLE 3–7: DEITIES

Deity	Alignment	Domains	Typical Worshipers
Heironeous, god of valor	Lawful good	Good, Law, War	Paladins, fighters, monks
Moradin, god of the dwarves	Lawful good	Earth, Good, Law, Protection	Dwarves
Yondalla, goddess of the halflings	Lawful good	Good, Law, Protection	Halflings
Ehlonna, goddess of the woodlands	Neutral good	Animal, Good, Plant, Sun	Elves, gnomes, half-elves, halflings, rangers, druids
Garl Glittergold, god of the gnomes	Neutral good	Good, Protection, Trickery	Gnomes
Pelor, god of the sun	Neutral good	Good, Healing, Strength, Sun	Rangers, bards
Corellon Larethian, god of the elves	Chaotic good	Chaos, Good, Protection, War	Elves, half-elves, bards
Kord, god of strength	Chaotic good	Chaos, Good, Luck, Strength	Fighters, barbarians, rogues, athletes
Wee Jas, goddess of death and magic	Lawful neutral	Death, Law, Magic	Wizards, necromancers, sorcerers
St. Cuthbert, god of retribution	Lawful neutral	Destruction, Law, Protection, Strength	Fighters, monks, soldiers
Boccob, god of magic	Neutral	Knowledge, Magic, Trickery	Wizards, sorcerers, sages
Fharlanghn, god of roads	Neutral	Luck, Protection, Travel	Bards, adventurers, merchants
Obad-Hai, god of nature	Neutral	Air, Animal, Earth, Fire, Plant, Water	Druids, barbarians, rangers
Olidammara, god of thieves	Chaotic neutral	Chaos, Luck, Trickery	Rogues, bards, thieves
Hextor, god of tyranny	Lawful evil	Destruction, Evil, Law, War	Evil fighters, monks
Nerull, god of death	Neutral evil	Death, Evil, Trickery	Evil necromancers, rogues
Vecna, god of secrets	Neutral evil	Evil, Knowledge, Magic	Evil wizards, sorcerers, rogues, spies
Erythnul, god of slaughter	Chaotic evil	Chaos, Evil, Trickery, War	Evil fighters, barbarians, rogues
Gruumsh, god of the orcs	Chaotic evil	Chaos, Evil, Strength, War	Half-orcs, orcs

Aura (Ex): A cleric of a chaotic, evil, good, or lawful deity has a particularly powerful aura corresponding to the deity's alignment (see the *detect evil* spell for details). Clerics who don't worship a specific deity but choose the Chaotic, Evil, Good, or Lawful domain have a similarly powerful aura of the corresponding alignment.

Spells: A cleric casts divine spells (the same type of spells available to the druid, paladin, and ranger), which are drawn from the cleric spell list (page 183). However, his alignment may restrict him from casting certain spells opposed to his moral or ethical beliefs; see Chaotic, Evil, Good, and Lawful Spells, below. A cleric must choose and prepare his spells in advance (see below).

To prepare or cast a spell, a cleric must have a Wisdom score equal to at least 10 + the spell level (Wis 10 for 0-level spells, Wis 11 for 1st-level spells, and so forth). The Difficulty Class for a saving throw against a cleric's spell is 10 + the spell level + the cleric's Wisdom modifier.

Like other spellcasters, a cleric can cast only a certain number of spells of each spell level per day. His base daily spell allotment is given on Table 3–6: The Cleric. In addition, he receives bonus spells per day if he has a high Wisdom score (see Table 1–1: Ability Modifiers and Bonus Spells, page 8). A cleric also gets one domain spell of each spell level he can cast, starting at 1st level. When a cleric prepares a spell in a domain spell slot, it must come from one of his two domains (see Deities, Domains, and Domain Spells, below, for details).

Clerics do not acquire their spells from books or scrolls, nor do they prepare them through study. Instead, they meditate or pray for their spells, receiving them through their own strength of faith or as divine inspiration. Each cleric must choose a time at which he must spend 1 hour each day in quiet contemplation or supplication to regain his daily allotment of spells. Typically, this hour is at dawn or noon for good clerics and at dusk or midnight for evil ones. Time spent resting has no effect on whether a cleric can prepare spells. A cleric may prepare and cast any spell on the cleric spell list (page 183), provided that he can cast spells of that level, but he must choose which spells to prepare during his daily meditation.

Deity, Domains, and Domain Spells: Choose a deity for your cleric. Sample deities are listed on Table 3–7: Deities and described on pages 106–108. The cleric's deity influences his alignment, what magic he can perform, his values, and how others see him. You may also choose for your cleric to have no deity.

If the typical worshipers of a deity include the members of a race, a cleric must be of the indicated race to choose that deity as his own. (The god may have occasional worshipers of other races, but not clerics.)

When you have chosen an alignment and a deity for your cleric, choose two domains from among those given on Table 3–7 for the deity. While the clerics of a particular religion are united in their reverence for their deity, each cleric emphasizes different aspects of the deity's interests. You can select an alignment domain (Chaos, Evil, Good, or Law) for your cleric only if his alignment matches that domain.

If your cleric is not devoted to a particular deity, you still select two domains to represent his spiritual inclinations and abilities. The restriction on alignment domains still applies.

Each domain gives your cleric access to a domain spell at each spell level he can cast, from 1st on up, as well as a granted power. Your cleric gets the granted powers of both the domains selected. With access to two domain spells at a given spell level, a cleric prepares one or the other each day in his domain spell slot. If a domain spell is not on the cleric spell list (page 183), a cleric can prepare it only in his domain spell slot. Domain spells and granted powers are given in Cleric Domains, pages 185–189.

For example, Jozan is a 1st-level cleric of Pelor. He chooses Good and Healing (from Pelor's domain options) as his two domains. He gets the granted powers of both his selected domains. The Good domain allows him to cast all spells with the good descriptor at +1 caster level (as if he were one level higher as a cleric) as a granted power, and it gives him access to *protection from evil* as a 1st-level domain spell. The Healing domain allows him to cast all healing subschool spells of the conjuration school at +1 caster level as a granted power, and it gives him access to *cure light wounds* as a 1st-level domain spell. When Jozan prepares his spells, he gets one 1st-level spell for being a 1st-level cleric, one bonus 1st-level spell for having a high Wisdom score (15), and one 1st-level domain spell. The domain spell must be one of the two to which he has access, either *protection from evil* or *cure light wounds*.

Spontaneous Casting: A good cleric (or a neutral cleric of a good deity) can channel stored spell energy into healing spells that the cleric did not prepare ahead of time. The cleric can "lose" any prepared spell that is not a domain spell in order to cast any *cure* spell of the same spell level or lower (a *cure* spell is any spell with "cure" in its name). For example, a good cleric who has prepared *command* (a 1st-level spell) may lose *command* in order to cast *cure light wounds* (also a 1st-level spell). Clerics of good deities can cast *cure* spells in this way because they are especially proficient at wielding positive energy.

An evil cleric (or a neutral cleric of an evil deity), on the other hand, can't convert prepared spells to *cure* spells but can convert them to *inflict* spells (an *inflict* spell is one with "inflict" in its name). Such clerics are especially proficient at wielding negative energy.

A cleric who is neither good nor evil and whose deity is neither good nor evil can convert spells to either *cure* spells or *inflict* spells (player's choice), depending on whether the cleric is more proficient at wielding positive or negative energy. Once the player makes this choice, it cannot be reversed. This choice also determines whether the cleric turns or commands undead (see below). *Exceptions:* All lawful neutral clerics of Wee Jas (goddess of death and magic) convert prepared spells to *inflict* spells, not *cure* spells. All clerics of St. Cuthbert (god of retribution) and all nonevil clerics of Obad-Hai (god of nature) convert prepared spells to *cure* spells, not *inflict* spells.

Chaotic, Evil, Good, and Lawful Spells: A cleric can't cast spells of an alignment opposed to his own or his deity's (if he has one). For example, a good cleric (or a neutral cleric of a good deity) cannot cast evil spells. Spells associated with particular alignments are indicated by the chaos, evil, good, and law descriptors in their spell descriptions (see Chapter 11: Spells).

Turn or Rebuke Undead (Su): Any cleric, regardless of alignment, has the power to affect undead creatures (such as skeletons, zombies, ghosts, and vampires) by channeling the power of his faith through his holy (or unholy) symbol (see Turn or Rebuke Undead, page 159).

A good cleric (or a neutral cleric who worships a good deity) can turn or destroy undead creatures. An evil cleric (or a neutral cleric who worships an evil deity) instead rebukes or commands such creatures, forcing them to cower in awe of his power. If your character is a neutral cleric of a neutral deity, you must choose whether his turning ability functions as that of a good cleric or an evil cleric. Once you make this choice, it cannot be reversed. This decision also determines whether the cleric can cast spontaneous *cure* or *inflict* spells (see above). *Exceptions:* All lawful neutral clerics of Wee Jas (goddess of death and magic) rebuke or command undead. All clerics of St. Cuthbert (god of retribution) and all nonevil clerics of Obad-Hai (god of nature) turn or destroy undead.

A cleric may attempt to turn undead a number of times per day equal to 3 + his Charisma modifier. A cleric with 5 or more ranks in Knowledge (religion) gets a +2 bonus on turning checks against undead.

Bonus Languages: A cleric's bonus language options include Celestial, Abyssal, and Infernal (the languages of good, chaotic evil, and lawful evil outsiders, respectively). These choices are in addition to the bonus languages available to the character because of his race (see Race and Languages, page 12, and the Speak Language skill, page 82).

Ex-Clerics

A cleric who grossly violates the code of conduct required by his god (generally by acting in ways opposed to the god's alignment or purposes) loses all spells and class features, except for armor and shield proficiencies and proficiency with simple weapons. He cannot thereafter gain levels as a cleric of that god until he atones (see the *atonement* spell description, page 201).

Human Cleric Starting Package

Armor: Scale mail (+4 AC, armor check penalty –4, speed 20 ft., 30 lb.).

Heavy wooden shield (+2 AC, armor check penalty –2, 10 lb.).

Weapons: Heavy mace (1d8, crit ×2, 8 lb., one-handed, bludgeoning).

Light crossbow (1d8, crit 19–20/×2, range inc. 80 ft., 4 lb., piercing).

Skill Selection: Pick a number of skills equal to 3 + Int modifier.

Skill	Ranks	Ability	Armor Check Penalty
Spellcraft	4	Int	—
Concentration	4	Con	—
Heal	4	Wis	—
Knowledge (religion)	4	Int	—
Diplomacy	4	Cha	—
Gather Information (cc)	2	Cha	—
Listen (cc)	2	Wis	—

Feat: Scribe Scroll.

Bonus Feat: Alertness.

Deity/Domains: Pelor/Good and Healing.

Gear: Backpack with waterskin, one day's trail rations, bedroll, sack, and flint and steel. Case with 10 crossbow bolts. Wooden holy symbol (sun disc of Pelor). Three torches.

Gold: 1d4 gp.

DRUID

The fury of a storm, the gentle strength of the morning sun, the cunning of the fox, the power of the bear—all these and more are at the druid's command. The druid, however, claims no mastery over nature. That claim, she says, is the empty boast of a city dweller. The druid gains her power not by ruling nature but by being at one with it. To trespassers in a druid's sacred grove, and to those who feel her wrath, the distinction is overly fine.

Adventures: Druids adventure to gain knowledge (especially about animals and plants unfamiliar to them) and power. Sometimes their superiors call on their services. Druids may also bring their power to bear against those who threaten what they love, which more often includes ancient stands of trees or trackless mountains than people. While druids accept that which is horrific or cruel in nature, they hate that which is unnatural, including aberrations (such as beholders and carrion crawlers) and undead (such as zombies and vampires). Druids sometimes lead raids against such creatures, especially when they encroach on the druids' territory.

Characteristics: Druids cast divine spells much the same way clerics do, though most get their spells from the power of nature rather than from deities. Their spells are oriented toward nature and animals. In addition to spells, druids gain an increasing array of magical powers, including the ability to take the shapes of animals, as they advance in level.

The armor of a druid is restricted by traditional oaths to the items noted in Weapon and Armor Proficiency (below). All other armor is prohibited. Though a druid could learn to wear full plate, putting it on would violate her oath and suppress her druidic powers.

Druids avoid carrying much worked metal with them because it interferes with the pure and primal nature that they attempt to embody.

Alignment: Druids, in keeping with nature's ultimate indifference, must maintain at least some measure of dispassion. As such, they must be neutral on at least one alignment axis (chaotic–lawful or good–evil), if not both. Just as nature encompasses such dichotomies as life and death, beauty and horror, and peace and violence, so two druids can manifest different or even opposite alignments (neutral good and neutral evil, for instance) and still be part of the druidic tradition.

Religion: A druid reveres nature above all. She gains her magical powers either from the force of nature itself or from a nature deity. The typical druid pursues a mystic spirituality of transcendent union with nature rather than devoting herself to a divine entity. Still, some druids revere or at least respect either Obad-Hai (god of nature) or Ehlonna (goddess of the woodlands).

Background: Though their organization is invisible to most outsiders, who consider druids to be loners, druids are actually part of a society that spans the land, ignoring political borders. A prospective druid is inducted into this society through secret rituals involving tests that not all survive. Only after achieving some level of competence is the druid allowed to strike out on her own.

All druids are nominally members of this druidic society, though some individuals are so isolated that they have never seen any high-ranking members of the society or participated in druidic gatherings. All druids recognize each other as brothers and sisters. Like true creatures of the wilderness, however, druids sometimes compete with or even prey on each other.

A druid may be expected to perform services for higher-ranking druids, though proper payment is tendered for such assignments. Likewise, a lower-ranking druid may appeal for aid from her higher-ranking comrades in exchange for a fair price in coin or service.

Druids may live in small towns, but they always spend a good portion of their time in wild areas. Even large cities surrounded by cultivated land as far as the eye can see often have druid groves nearby—small, wild refuges where druids live and which they protect fiercely. Near coastal cities, such refuges may be nearby islands, where the druids can find the isolation they need.

Races: Elves and gnomes have an affinity for natural lands and often become druids. Humans and half-elves also frequently adopt this path, and druids are particularly common among savage humans. Dwarves, halflings, and half-orcs are rarely druids.

Few from among the brutal humanoids are inducted into druidic society, though gnolls have a fair contingent of evil druids among them. Gnoll druids are accepted, though perhaps not welcomed, by druids of other races.

Vadania

Other Classes: The druid shares with rangers and many barbarians a reverence for nature and a familiarity with natural lands. She doesn't much understand the urban mannerisms typical of a rogue, and she finds arcane magic disruptive and slightly distasteful. The typical druid also dislikes the paladin's devotion to abstract ideals instead of "the real world." Druids, however, are nothing if not accepting of diversity, and they take little offense at other characters, even those very different from them.

Role: The druid enjoys extraordinary versatility. Though she lacks the sheer healing power of the cleric, she makes up for it with additional offensive power, thanks to her spell selection and wild shape ability. A druid backed up by another secondary healer (such as a paladin) can prove extremely valuable to a group of adventurers. Her animal companion also provides valuable melee combat support.

GAME RULE INFORMATION

Druids have the following game statistics.

Abilities: Wisdom determines how powerful a spell a druid can cast, how many spells she can cast per day, and how hard those spells are to resist. To cast a spell, a druid must have a Wisdom score of 10 + the spell's level. A druid gets bonus spells based on

Wisdom. The Difficulty Class of a saving throw against a druid's spell is 10 + the spell's level + the druid's Wisdom modifier.

Since a druid wears only light or medium armor, a high Dexterity score greatly improves her defensive ability.

Alignment: Neutral good, lawful neutral, neutral, chaotic neutral, or neutral evil.

Hit Die: d8.

Class Skills

The druid's class skills (and the key ability for each skill) are Concentration (Con), Craft (Int), Diplomacy (Cha), Handle Animal (Cha), Heal (Wis), Knowledge (nature) (Int), Listen (Wis), Profession (Wis), Ride (Dex), Spellcraft (Int), Spot (Wis), Survival (Wis), and Swim (Str). See Chapter 4: Skills for skill descriptions.

Skill Points at 1st Level: (4 + Int modifier) × 4.

Skill Points at Each Additional Level: 4 + Int modifier.

Class Features

All of the following are class features of the druid.

Weapon and Armor Proficiency: Druids are proficient with the following weapons: club, dagger, dart, quarterstaff, scimitar, sickle, shortspear, sling, and spear. They are also proficient with all natural attacks (claw, bite, and so forth) of any form they assume with wild shape (see below). Druids are proficient with light and medium armor but are prohibited from wearing metal armor; thus, they may wear only padded, leather, or hide armor. (A druid may also wear wooden armor that has been altered by the *ironwood* spell so that it functions as though it were steel. See the *ironwood* spell description, page 246.) Druids are proficient with shields (except tower shields) but must use only wooden ones.

A druid who wears prohibited armor or carries a prohibited shield is unable to cast druid spells or use any of her supernatural or spell-like class abilities while doing so and for 24 hours thereafter.

Spells: A druid casts divine spells (the same type of spells available to the cleric, paladin, and ranger), which are drawn from the druid spell list (page 189). Her alignment may restrict her from casting certain spells opposed to her moral or ethical beliefs; see Chaotic, Evil, Good, and Lawful Spells, below. A druid must choose and prepare her spells in advance (see below).

To prepare or cast a spell, the druid must have a Wisdom score equal to at least 10 + the spell level (Wis 10 for 0-level spells, Wis 11 for 1st-level spells, and so forth). The Difficulty Class for a saving throw against a druid's spell is 10 + the spell level + the druid's Wisdom modifier.

Like other spellcasters, a druid can cast only a certain number of spells of each spell level per day. Her base daily spell allotment is given on Table 3–8: The Druid. In addition, she receives bonus spells per day if she has a high Wisdom score (see Table 1–1: Ability Modifiers and Bonus Spells, page 8). She does not have access to any domain spells or granted powers, as a cleric does.

TABLE 3–8: THE DRUID

Level	Base Attack Bonus	Fort Save	Ref Save	Will Save	Special	Spells per Day 0	1st	2nd	3rd	4th	5th	6th	7th	8th	9th
1st	+0	+2	+0	+2	Animal companion, nature sense, wild empathy	3	1	—	—	—	—	—	—	—	—
2nd	+1	+3	+0	+3	Woodland stride	4	2	—	—	—	—	—	—	—	—
3rd	+2	+3	+1	+3	Trackless step	4	2	1	—	—	—	—	—	—	—
4th	+3	+4	+1	+4	Resist nature's lure	5	3	2	—	—	—	—	—	—	—
5th	+3	+4	+1	+4	Wild shape (1/day)	5	3	2	1	—	—	—	—	—	—
6th	+4	+5	+2	+5	Wild shape (2/day)	5	3	3	2	—	—	—	—	—	—
7th	+5	+5	+2	+5	Wild shape (3/day)	6	4	3	2	1	—	—	—	—	—
8th	+6/+1	+6	+2	+6	Wild shape (Large)	6	4	3	3	2	—	—	—	—	—
9th	+6/+1	+6	+3	+6	Venom immunity	6	4	4	3	2	1	—	—	—	—
10th	+7/+2	+7	+3	+7	Wild shape (4/day)	6	4	4	3	3	2	—	—	—	—
11th	+8/+3	+7	+3	+7	Wild shape (Tiny)	6	5	4	4	3	2	1	—	—	—
12th	+9/+4	+8	+4	+8	Wild shape (plant)	6	5	4	4	3	3	2	—	—	—
13th	+9/+4	+8	+4	+8	A thousand faces	6	5	5	4	4	3	2	1	—	—
14th	+10/+5	+9	+4	+9	Wild shape (5/day)	6	5	5	4	4	3	3	2	—	—
15th	+11/+6/+1	+9	+5	+9	Timeless body, wild shape (Huge)	6	5	5	5	4	4	3	2	1	—
16th	+12/+7/+2	+10	+5	+10	Wild shape (elemental 1/day)	6	5	5	5	4	4	3	3	2	—
17th	+12/+7/+2	+10	+5	+10		6	5	5	5	5	4	4	3	2	1
18th	+13/+8/+3	+11	+6	+11	Wild shape (6/day, elemental 2/day)	6	5	5	5	5	4	4	3	3	2
19th	+14/+9/+4	+11	+6	+11		6	5	5	5	5	5	4	4	3	3
20th	+15/+10/+5	+12	+6	+12	Wild shape (elemental 3/day, Huge elemental)	6	5	5	5	5	5	4	4	4	4

A druid prepares and casts spells the way a cleric does, though she cannot lose a prepared spell to cast a *cure* spell in its place (but see Spontaneous Casting, below). A druid may prepare and cast any spell on the druid spell list (page 189), provided that she can cast spells of that level, but she must choose which spells to prepare during her daily meditation.

Spontaneous Casting: A druid can channel stored spell energy into summoning spells that she hasn't prepared ahead of time. She can "lose" a prepared spell in order to cast any *summon nature's ally* spell of the same level or lower. For example, a druid who has prepared *repel vermin* (a 4th-level spell) may lose *repel vermin* in order to cast *summon nature's ally IV* (also a 4th-level spell).

Chaotic, Evil, Good, and Lawful Spells: A druid can't cast spells of an alignment opposed to her own or her deity's (if she has one). For example, a neutral good druid cannot cast evil spells. Spells associated with particular alignments are indicated by the chaos, evil, good, and law descriptors in their spell descriptions (see Chapter 11: Spells).

Bonus Languages: A druid's bonus language options include Sylvan, the language of woodland creatures. This choice is in addition to the bonus languages available to the character because of her race (see Race and Languages, page 12, and the Speak Language skill, page 82).

A druid also knows Druidic, a secret language known only to druids, which she learns upon becoming a 1st-level druid. Druidic is a free language for a druid; that is, she knows it in addition to her regular allotment of languages and it doesn't take up a language slot. Druids are forbidden to teach this language to nondruids. Druidic has its own alphabet.

Animal Companion (Ex): A druid may begin play with an animal companion selected from the following list: badger, camel, dire rat, dog, riding dog, eagle, hawk, horse (light or heavy), owl, pony, snake (Small or Medium viper), or wolf. If the DM's campaign takes place wholly or partly in an aquatic environment, the DM may add the following creatures to the druid's list of options: crocodile, porpoise, Medium shark, and squid. This animal is a loyal companion that accompanies the druid on her adventures as appropriate for its kind.

A 1st-level druid's companion is completely typical for its kind except as noted in the sidebar on page 36. As a druid advances in level, the animal's power increases as shown on the table in the sidebar.

If a druid releases her companion from service, she may gain a new one by performing a ceremony requiring 24 uninterrupted hours of prayer. This ceremony can also replace an animal companion that has perished.

A druid of 4th level or higher may select from alternative lists of animals (see the sidebar). Should she select an animal companion from one of these alternative lists, the creature gains abilities as if the character's druid level were lower than it actually is. Subtract the value indicated in the appropriate list header from the character's druid level and compare the result with the druid level entry on the table in the sidebar to determine the animal companion's powers. (If this adjustment would reduce the druid's effective level to 0 or lower, she can't have that animal as a companion.) For example, a 6th-level druid could select a leopard as an animal companion. The leopard would have characteristics and special abilities as if the druid were 3rd level (taking into account the –3 adjustment) instead of 6th level.

Nature Sense (Ex): A druid gains a +2 bonus on Knowledge (nature) and Survival checks.

Wild Empathy (Ex): A druid can use body language, vocalizations, and demeanor to improve the attitude of an animal (such as a bear or a monitor lizard). This ability functions just like a Diplomacy check made to improve the attitude of a person (see Chapter 4: Skills). The druid rolls 1d20 and adds her druid level and her Charisma modifier to determine the wild empathy check result. The typical domestic animal has a starting attitude of indifferent, while wild animals are usually unfriendly.

To use wild empathy, the druid and the animal must be able to study each other, which means that they must be within 30 feet of one another under normal conditions. Generally, influencing an animal in this way takes 1 minute but, as with influencing people, it might take more or less time.

A druid can also use this ability to influence a magical beast with an Intelligence score of 1 or 2 (such as a basilisk or a girallon), but she takes a –4 penalty on the check.

Woodland Stride (Ex): Starting at 2nd level, a druid may move through any sort of undergrowth (such as natural thorns, briars, overgrown areas, and similar terrain) at her normal speed and without taking damage or suffering any other impairment. However, thorns, briars, and overgrown areas that have been magically manipulated to impede motion still affect her.

Trackless Step (Ex): Starting at 3rd level, a druid leaves no trail in natural surroundings and cannot be tracked. She may choose to leave a trail if so desired.

THE DRUID'S ANIMAL COMPANION

A druid's animal companion is different from a normal animal of its kind in many ways. The companion is treated as a magical beast, not an animal, for the purpose of all effects that depend on its type (though it retains an animal's HD, base attack bonus, saves, skill points, and feats). It is superior to a normal animal of its kind and has special powers, as described below.

Class Level	Bonus HD	Natural Armor Adj.	Str/Dex Adj.	Bonus Tricks	Special
1st–2nd	+0	+0	+0	1	Link, share spells
3rd–5th	+2	+2	+1	2	Evasion
6th–8th	+4	+4	+2	3	Devotion
9th–11th	+6	+6	+3	4	Multiattack
12th–14th	+8	+8	+4	5	
15th–17th	+10	+10	+5	6	Improved evasion
18th–20th	+12	+12	+6	7	

Animal Companion Basics: Use the base statistics for a creature of the companion's kind, as given in the *Monster Manual*, but make the following changes.

Class Level: The character's druid level. The druid's class levels stack with levels of any other classes that are entitled to an animal companion (such as the ranger) for the purpose of determining the companion's abilities and the alternative lists available to the character.

Bonus HD: Extra eight-sided (d8) Hit Dice, each of which gains a Constitution modifier, as normal. Remember that extra Hit Dice improve the animal companion's base attack and base save bonuses. An animal companion's base attack bonus is the same as that of a druid of a level equal to the animal's HD. An animal companion has good Fortitude and Reflex saves (treat it as a character whose level equals the animal's HD). An animal companion gains additional skill points and feats for bonus HD as normal for advancing a monster's Hit Dice (see the *Monster Manual*).

Natural Armor Adj.: The number noted here is an improvement to the animal companion's existing natural armor bonus.

Str/Dex Adj.: Add this value to the animal companion's Strength and Dexterity scores.

Bonus Tricks: The value given in this column is the total number of "bonus" tricks that the animal knows in addition to any that the druid might choose to teach it (see the Handle Animal skill, page 74). These bonus tricks don't require any training time or Handle Animal checks, and they don't count against the normal limit of tricks known by the animal. The druid selects these bonus tricks, and once selected, they can't be changed.

Link (Ex): A druid can handle her animal companion as a free action, or push it as a move action, even if she doesn't have any ranks in the Handle Animal skill. The druid gains a +4 circumstance bonus on all wild empathy checks and Handle Animal checks made regarding an animal companion.

Share Spells (Ex): At the druid's option, she may have any spell (but not any spell-like ability) she casts upon herself also affect her animal companion. The animal companion must be within 5 feet of her at the time of casting to receive the benefit. If the spell or effect has a duration other than instantaneous, it stops affecting the animal companion if the companion moves farther than 5 feet away and will not affect the animal again, even if it returns to the druid before the duration expires. Additionally, the druid may cast a spell with a target of "You" on her animal companion (as a touch range spell) instead of on herself. A druid and her animal companion can share spells even if the spells normally do not affect creatures of the companion's type (animal).

Evasion (Ex): If an animal companion is subjected to an attack that normally allows a Reflex saving throw for half damage, it takes no damage if it makes a successful saving throw.

Devotion (Ex): An animal companion's devotion to its master is so complete that it gains a +4 morale bonus on Will saves against enchantment spells and effects.

Multiattack: An animal companion gains Multiattack as a bonus feat if it has three or more natural attacks (see the *Monster Manual* for details on this feat) and does not already have that feat. If it does not have the requisite three or more natural attacks, the animal companion instead gains a second attack with its primary natural weapon, albeit at a –5 penalty.

Improved Evasion (Ex): When subjected to an attack that normally allows a Reflex saving throw for half damage, an animal companion takes no damage if it makes a successful saving throw and only half damage if the saving throw fails.

ALTERNATIVE ANIMAL COMPANIONS

As explained in the text on page 35, a druid of sufficiently high level can select her animal companion from one of the following lists, applying the indicated adjustment to the druid's level (in parentheses) for purposes of determining the companion's characteristics and special abilities.

4th Level or Higher (Level –3)

Ape (animal)	Dire weasel
Bear, black (animal)	Leopard (animal)
Bison (animal)	Lizard, monitor (animal)
Boar (animal)	Shark, Large[1] (animal)
Cheetah (animal)	Snake, constrictor (animal)
Crocodile (animal)[1]	Snake, Large viper (animal)
Dire badger	Wolverine (animal)
Dire bat	

7th Level or Higher (Level –6)

Bear, brown (animal)	Dire wolverine
Crocodile, giant (animal)	Elasmosaurus[1] (dinosaur)
Deinonychus (dinosaur)	Lion (animal)
Dire ape	Rhinoceros (animal)
Dire boar	Snake, Huge viper (animal)
Dire wolf	Tiger (animal)

10th Level or Higher (Level –9)

Bear, polar (animal)	Shark, Huge[1] (animal)
Dire lion	Snake, giant constrictor (animal)
Megaraptor (dinosaur)	Whale, orca[1] (animal)

13th Level or Higher (Level –12)

Dire bear	Elephant (animal)
Octopus, giant[1] (animal)	

16th Level or Higher (Level –15)

Dire shark[1]	Triceratops (dinosaur)
Dire tiger	Tyrannosaurus (dinosaur)
Squid, giant[1] (animal)	

1 Available only in an aquatic environment.

Resist Nature's Lure (Ex): Starting at 4th level, a druid gains a +4 bonus on saving throws against the spell-like abilities of fey (such as dryads, pixies, and sprites).

Wild Shape (Su): At 5th level, a druid gains the ability to turn herself into any Small or Medium animal and back again once per day. Her options for new forms include all creatures with the animal type (see the *Monster Manual*). This ability functions like the *polymorph* spell, except as noted here. The effect lasts for 1 hour per druid level, or until she changes back. Changing form (to animal or back) is a standard action and doesn't provoke an attack of opportunity.

The form chosen must be that of an animal the druid is familiar with. For example, a druid who has never been outside a temperate forest could not become a polar bear.

A druid loses her ability to speak while in animal form because she is limited to the sounds that a normal, untrained animal can make, but she can communicate normally with other animals of the same general grouping as her new form. (The normal sound a wild parrot makes is a squawk, so changing to this form does not permit speech.)

A druid can use this ability more times per day at 6th, 7th, 10th, 14th, and 18th level, as noted on Table 3–8: The Druid. In addition, she gains the ability to take the shape of a Large animal at 8th level, a Tiny animal at 11th level, and a Huge animal at 15th level. The new form's Hit Dice can't exceed the character's druid level. For instance, a druid can't take the form of a dire bear (a Large creature that always has at least 12 HD) until 12th level, even though she can begin taking Large forms at 8th level.

At 12th level, a druid becomes able to use wild shape to change into a plant creature, such as a shambling mound, with the same size restrictions as for animal forms. (A druid can't use this ability to take the form of a plant that isn't a creature, such as a tree or a rose bush.)

At 16th level, a druid becomes able to use wild shape to change into a Small, Medium, or Large elemental (air, earth, fire, or water) once per day. These elemental forms are in addition to her normal wild shape usage. In addition to the normal effects of wild shape, the druid gains all the elemental's extraordinary, supernatural, and spell-like abilities. She also gains the elemental's feats for as long as she maintains the wild shape, but she retains her own creature type (humanoid, in most cases).

At 18th level, a druid becomes able to assume elemental form twice per day, and at 20th level she can do so three times per day. At 20th level, a druid may use this wild shape ability to change into a Huge elemental.

Venom Immunity (Ex): At 9th level, a druid gains immunity to all poisons.

A Thousand Faces (Su): At 13th level, a druid gains the ability to change her appearance at will, as if using the *alter self* spell (page 197), but only while in her normal form.

Timeless Body (Ex): After attaining 15th level, a druid no longer takes ability score penalties for aging (see Table 6–5: Aging Effects, page 109) and cannot be magically aged. Any penalties she may have already incurred, however, remain in place. Bonuses still accrue, and the druid still dies of old age when her time is up.

Ex-Druids

A druid who ceases to revere nature, changes to a prohibited alignment, or teaches the Druidic language to a nondruid loses all spells and druid abilities (including her animal companion, but not including weapon, armor, and shield proficiencies). She cannot thereafter gain levels as a druid until she atones (see the *atonement* spell description, page 201).

Half-Elf Druid Starting Package

Armor: Hide (+3 AC, armor check penalty –3, speed 20 ft., 25 lb.).

Heavy wooden shield (+2 AC, armor check penalty –2, 10 lb.).

Weapons: Scimitar (1d6, crit 18–20/×2, 4 lb., one-handed, slashing).

Club (oaken cudgel): (1d6, crit ×2, 10 ft., 3 lb., one-handed, bludgeoning).

Sling (1d4, crit ×2, range inc. 50 ft., 0 lb., Medium, bludgeoning).

Skill Selection: Pick a number of skills equal to 4 + Int modifier.

Skill	Ranks	Ability	Armor Check Penalty
Spellcraft	4	Int	—
Concentration	4	Con	—
Survival	4	Wis	—
Heal	4	Wis	—
Handle Animal	4	Cha	—
Knowledge (nature)	4	Int	—
Listen	4	Wis	—
Spot	4	Wis	—

Feat: Scribe Scroll.

Gear: Backpack with waterskin, one day's trail rations, bedroll, sack, and flint and steel. Pouch with 10 sling bullets. Holly and mistletoe. Three torches.

Animal Companion: Wolf (see the *Monster Manual* for details).

Gold: 1d6 gp.

Tordek

LOCKWOOD

FIGHTER

The questing knight, the conquering overlord, the king's champion, the elite foot soldier, the hardened mercenary, and the bandit king—all are fighters. Fighters can be stalwart defenders of those in need, cruel marauders, or gutsy adventurers. Some are among the land's best souls, willing to face death for the greater good. Others are among the worst, with no qualms about killing for private gain, or even for sport. Fighters who are not actively adventuring may be soldiers, guards, bodyguards, champions, or criminal enforcers. An adventuring fighter might call himself a warrior, a mercenary, a thug, or simply an adventurer.

Adventures: Most fighters see adventures, raids, and dangerous missions as their jobs. Some have patrons who pay them regularly. Others prefer to live like prospectors, taking great risks in hopes of the big haul. Some fighters are more civic-minded and use their combat skills to protect endangered people who cannot defend themselves. Whatever their initial motivations, however, fighters often wind up living for the thrill of combat and adventure.

Characteristics: Of all the classes, the fighter has the best all-around fighting capabilities (hence the name). Fighters are familiar with all the standard weapons and armors. In addition to general fighting prowess, each fighter develops particular specialties of his own. A given fighter may be especially capable with certain weapons; another might be trained to execute specific fancy maneuvers. As fighters gain experience, they get more opportunities to develop their fighting skills. Thanks to their focus on combat maneuvers, they can master the most difficult ones relatively quickly.

Alignment: Fighters may be of any alignment. Good fighters are often crusading types who seek out and fight evil. Lawful fighters may be champions who protect the land and its people. Chaotic fighters may be wandering mercenaries. Evil fighters tend to be bullies and petty villains who simply take what they want by brute force.

Religion: Fighters often worship Heironeous (god of valor), Kord (god of strength), St. Cuthbert (god of retribution), Hextor (god of tyranny), or Erythnul (god of slaughter). A fighter may style himself as a crusader in the service of his god, or he may just want someone to pray to before putting his life on the line yet another time.

Background: Fighters come to their profession in many ways. Most have had formal training in a noble's army or at least in the local militia. Some have trained in formal academies. Others are self-taught—unpolished but well tested. A fighter may have taken up the sword as a way to escape the limits of life on the farm, or he may be following a proud family tradition. Fighters share no special identity. They do not see themselves as a group or brotherhood. Those who hail from a particular academy, mercenary company, or lord's regiment, however, share a certain camaraderie.

Races: Human fighters are usually veterans of some military service, typically from mundane parents. Dwarf fighters are commonly former members of the well-trained strike teams that protect the underground dwarven kingdoms. They are typically members of warrior families that can trace their lineages back for millennia, and they may have rivalries or alliances with other dwarf fighters of a different lineage. Elf fighters are typically skilled with the longsword. They are proud of their ability at swordplay and eager to demonstrate or test it. Half-orc fighters are often self-taught outcasts who have achieved enough skill to earn recognition and something akin to respect. Gnome and halfling fighters usually stay in their own communities as part of the area militia rather than adventuring. Half-elves are rarely fighters, but they may take up swordplay in honor of the elven tradition.

Among the brutal humanoids, few can manage the discipline it takes to be a true fighter. The militaristic hobgoblins, however, produce quite a number of strong and skilled fighters.

Other Classes: The fighter excels in a straight fight, but he relies on others for magical support, healing, and scouting. On a team, it is his job to man the front lines, protect the other party members, and bring the tough opponents down. Fighters might not understand the arcane ways of wizards or share the faith of clerics, but they recognize the value of teamwork.

Role: In most adventuring parties, the fighter serves as a melee combatant, charging into the fray while his comrades support him with spells, ranged attacks, and other effects. Fighters who favor

ranged combat can prove very deadly, though without other melee support, they can find themselves in front-line combat more often than they might prefer.

Regdar

GAME RULE INFORMATION
Fighters have the following game statistics.

Abilities: Strength is especially important for fighters because it improves their melee attack and damage rolls. Constitution is important for giving fighters lots of hit points, which they need in their many battles. Dexterity is important for fighters who want to be good archers or who want access to certain Dexterity-oriented feats, but the heavy armor that fighters usually wear reduces the benefit of a very high Dexterity score.

Alignment: Any.

Hit Die: d10.

Class Skills
The fighter's class skills (and the key ability for each skill) are Climb (Str), Craft (Int), Handle Animal (Cha), Intimidate (Cha), Jump (Str), Ride (Dex), and Swim (Str). See Chapter 4: Skills for skill descriptions.

Skill Points at 1st Level: (2 + Int modifier) × 4.

Skill Points at Each Additional Level: 2 + Int modifier.

Class Features
All of the following are class features of the fighter.

Weapon and Armor Proficiency: A fighter is proficient with all simple and martial weapons and with all armor (heavy, medium, and light) and shields (including tower shields).

Bonus Feats: At 1st level, a fighter gets a bonus combat-oriented feat in addition to the feat that any 1st-level character gets and the bonus feat granted to a human character. The fighter gains an additional bonus feat at 2nd level and every two fighter levels thereafter (4th, 6th, 8th, 10th, 12th, 14th, 16th, 18th, and 20th). These bonus feats must be drawn from the feats noted as fighter bonus feats on Table 5–1: Feats (page 90). A fighter must still meet all prerequisites for a bonus feat, including ability score and base attack bonus minimums. (See Chapter 5: Feats for descriptions of feats and their prerequisites.)

These bonus feats are in addition to the feat that a character of any class gets every three levels (see Table 3–2: Experience and Level-Dependent Benefits, page 22). A fighter is not limited to the list of fighter bonus feats when choosing these feats.

Dwarf Fighter Starting Package
Armor: Scale mail (+4 AC, armor check penalty –4, speed 20 ft., 30 lb.).

Heavy wooden shield (+2 AC, armor check penalty –2, 10 lb.)

Weapons: Dwarven waraxe (1d10, crit ×3, 8 lb., one-handed, slashing).

Shortbow (1d6, crit ×3, range inc. 60 ft., 2 lb., piercing).

Skill Selection: Pick a number of skills equal to 2 + Int modifier.

TABLE 3–9: THE FIGHTER

Level	Base Attack Bonus	Fort Save	Ref Save	Will Save	Special
1st	+1	+2	+0	+0	Bonus feat
2nd	+2	+3	+0	+0	Bonus feat
3rd	+3	+3	+1	+1	
4th	+4	+4	+1	+1	Bonus feat
5th	+5	+4	+1	+1	
6th	+6/+1	+5	+2	+2	Bonus feat
7th	+7/+2	+5	+2	+2	
8th	+8/+3	+6	+2	+2	Bonus feat
9th	+9/+4	+6	+3	+3	
10th	+10/+5	+7	+3	+3	Bonus feat
11th	+11/+6/+1	+7	+3	+3	
12th	+12/+7/+2	+8	+4	+4	Bonus feat
13th	+13/+8/+3	+8	+4	+4	
14th	+14/+9/+4	+9	+4	+4	Bonus feat
15th	+15/+10/+5	+9	+5	+5	
16th	+16/+11/+6/+1	+10	+5	+5	Bonus feat
17th	+17/+12/+7/+2	+10	+5	+5	
18th	+18/+13/+8/+3	+11	+6	+6	Bonus feat
19th	+19/+14/+9/+4	+11	+6	+6	
20th	+20/+15/+10/+5	+12	+6	+6	Bonus feat

Skill	Ranks	Ability	Armor Check Penalty
Climb	4	Str	–6
Jump	4	Str	–6
Ride	4	Dex	—
Swim	4	Str	–12
Intimidate	4	Cha	—
Listen (cc)	2	Wis	—
Search (cc)	2	Int	—
Spot (cc)	2	Wis	—

Feat: Weapon Focus (dwarven waraxe).

Bonus Feat (Fighter): If Strength is 13 or higher, Power Attack; if Strength is 12 or lower, Improved Initiative instead.

Gear: Backpack with waterskin, one day's trail rations, bedroll, sack, flint and steel, quiver with 20 arrows.

Gold: 4d4 gp.

Human Fighter Starting Package

Armor: Scale mail (+4 AC, armor check penalty –4, speed 20 ft., 30 lb.).

Weapons: Greatsword (2d6, crit 19–20/×2, 8 lb., two-handed, slashing).

Shortbow (1d6, crit ×3, 60 ft., 2 lb., piercing).

Skill Selection: Pick a number of skills equal to 3 + Int modifier.

Skill	Ranks	Ability	Armor Check Penalty
Climb	4	Str	–4
Jump	4	Str	–4
Ride	4	Dex	—
Swim	4	Str	–8
Intimidate	4	Cha	—
Listen (cc)	2	Wis	—
Search (cc)	2	Int	—
Spot (cc)	2	Wis	—

Feat: Weapon Focus (greatsword).

Bonus Feat (Fighter): If Strength is 13 or higher, Power Attack; if Strength is 12 or lower, Improved Initiative instead.

Bonus Feat (Human): Blind-Fight.

Gear: Backpack with waterskin, one day's trail rations, bedroll, sack, flint and steel, quiver with twenty arrows.

Gold: 2d4 gp.

MONK

Dotted across the landscape are monasteries—small, walled cloisters inhabited by monks who pursue personal perfection through action as well as contemplation. They train themselves to be versatile warriors skilled at fighting without weapons or armor. The inhabitants of monasteries headed by good masters serve as protectors of the people. Ready for battle even when barefoot and dressed in peasant clothes, monks can travel unnoticed among the populace, catching bandits, warlords, and corrupt nobles unawares. In contrast, the residents of monasteries headed by evil masters rule the surrounding lands through fear, as an evil warlord and his entourage might. Evil monks make ideal spies, infiltrators, and assassins.

An individual monk is unlikely to care passionately about championing commoners or amassing wealth. She cares primarily for the perfection of her art and, thereby, her personal perfection. Her goal is to achieve a state that is beyond the mortal realm.

Adventures: A monk approaches an adventure as if it were a personal test. While not prone to showing off, monks are willing to try their skills against whatever obstacles confront them. They are not greedy for material wealth, but they eagerly seek that which can help them perfect their art.

Characteristics: The key feature of the monk is her ability to fight unarmed and unarmored. Thanks to her rigorous training, she can strike as hard as if she were armed and strike faster than a warrior with a sword.

Though a monk casts no spells, she has a magic of her own. She channels a subtle energy, called *ki*, which allows her to perform amazing feats. The monk's best-known feat is her ability to stun an opponent with an unarmed blow. A monk also has a preternatural awareness that allows her to dodge an attack even if she is not consciously aware of it.

As a monk gains experience and power, her mundane and *ki*-oriented abilities grow, giving her more and more power over herself and, sometimes, over others.

Alignment: A monk's training requires strict discipline. Only those who are lawful at heart are capable of undertaking it.

Religion: A monk's training is her spiritual path. She is inner-directed and capable of a private, mystic connection to the spiritual world, so she needs neither clerics nor gods. Certain lawful gods, however, may appeal to monks, who may meditate on those gods' likenesses and attempt to emulate their deeds. The three most likely candidates for a monk's devotion are Heironeous (god of valor), St. Cuthbert (god of retribution), and Hextor (god of tyranny).

Background: A monk typically trains in a monastery. Most monks were children when they joined the monastery, sent to live there when their parents died, when there wasn't enough food to support them, or in return for some kindness that the monastery had performed for the family. Life in the monastery is so focused that by the time a monk sets off on her own, she feels little connection to her former family or village.

In larger cities, master monks have set up monk schools to teach their arts to those who are interested and worthy. The monks who study at these academies often see their rural cousins from the monasteries as backward.

A monk may feel a deep connection to her monastery or school, to the monk who taught her, to the lineage into which she was trained, or to all of these. Some monks, however, have no sense of connection other than to their own path of personal development.

Monks recognize each other as a select group set apart from the rest of the populace. They may feel kinship, but they also love to compete with each other to see whose *ki* is strongest.

Races: Monasteries are found primarily among humans, who have incorporated them into their ever-evolving culture. Thus, many monks are humans, and many more are half-orcs and half-elves who live among humans. Elves are capable of single-minded, long-term devotion to an interest, art, or discipline, and some of them leave the forests to become monks. The monk tradition is alien to dwarf and gnome culture, and halflings typically have too mobile a lifestyle to commit themselves to a monastery, so dwarves, gnomes, and halflings very rarely become monks.

The savage humanoids do not have the stable social structure that allows monk training, but the occasional orphaned or abandoned child from some humanoid tribe winds up in a civilized monastery or is adopted by a wandering master. The evil subterranean elves known as the drow have a small but successful monk tradition.

Other Classes: Monks sometimes seem distant because they often have neither motivation nor skills in common with members of other classes. Monks do, however, work well with the support of others, and they usually prove themselves reliable companions.

Role: The monk functions best as an opportunistic combatant, using her speed to get into and out of combat quickly rather than engaging in prolonged melees. She also makes an excellent scout, particularly if she focuses her skill selection on stealth.

GAME RULE INFORMATION

Monks have the following game statistics.

Abilities: Wisdom powers the monk's special offensive and defensive capabilities. Dexterity provides an unarmored monk with a better defense and with bonuses to some class skills. Strength helps a monk's unarmed combat ability.

Alignment: Any lawful.

Hit Die: d8.

Class Skills

The monk's class skills (and the key ability for each skill) are Balance (Dex), Climb (Str), Concentration (Con), Craft (Int), Diplomacy (Cha), Escape Artist (Dex), Hide (Dex), Jump (Str), Knowledge (arcana) (Int), Knowledge (religion) (Int), Listen (Wis), Move Silently (Dex), Perform (Cha), Profession (Wis), Sense Motive (Wis), Spot (Wis), Swim (Str), and Tumble (Dex). See Chapter 4: Skills for skill descriptions.

Skill Points at 1st Level: (4 + Int modifier) × 4.

Skill Points at Each Additional Level: 4 + Int modifier.

Class Features

All of the following are class features of the monk.

Weapon and Armor Proficiency: Monks are proficient with certain basic peasant weapons and some special weapons that are part of monk training. The weapons with which a monk is proficient are club, crossbow (light or heavy), dagger, handaxe, javelin, kama, nunchaku, quarterstaff, sai, shuriken, siangham, and sling. (See Chapter 7: Equipment for descriptions of these weapons.) Monks are not proficient with any armor or shields—in fact, many of the monk's special powers require unfettered movement. When wearing armor, using a shield, or carrying a medium or heavy load, a monk loses her AC bonus, as well as her fast movement and flurry of blows abilities.

AC Bonus (Ex): A monk is highly trained at dodging blows, and she has a sixth sense that lets her avoid even unanticipated attacks. When unarmored and unencumbered, the monk adds her Wisdom bonus (if any) to her AC. In addition, a monk gains a +1 bonus to AC at 5th level. This bonus increases by 1 for every five monk levels thereafter (+2 at 10th, +3 at 15th, and +4 at 20th level).

These bonuses to AC apply even against touch attacks or when the monk is flat-footed. She loses these bonuses when she is immobilized or helpless, when she wears any armor, when she carries a shield, or when she carries a medium or heavy load.

Flurry of Blows (Ex): When unarmored, a monk may strike with a flurry of blows at the expense of accuracy. When doing so, she may make one extra attack in a round at her highest base attack bonus, but this attack takes a −2 penalty, as does each other attack made that round. The resulting modified base attack bonuses are shown in the Flurry of Blows Attack Bonus column on Table 3–10: The Monk. This penalty applies for 1 round, so it also affects attacks of opportunity the monk might make before her next action. When a monk reaches 5th level, the penalty lessens to −1, and at 9th level it disappears. A monk must use a full attack action (see page 143) to strike with a flurry of blows.

When using flurry of blows, a monk may attack only with unarmed strikes or with special monk weapons (kama, nunchaku, quarterstaff, sai, shuriken, and siangham). She may attack with unarmed strikes and special monk weapons interchangeably as

TABLE 3–10: THE MONK

Level	Base Attack Bonus	Fort Save	Ref Save	Will Save	Special	Flurry of Blows Attack Bonus	Unarmed Damage[1]	AC Bonus	Unarmored Speed Bonus
1st	+0	+2	+2	+2	Bonus feat, flurry of blows, unarmed strike	−2/−2	1d6	+0	+0 ft.
2nd	+1	+3	+3	+3	Bonus feat, evasion	−1/−1	1d6	+0	+0 ft.
3rd	+2	+3	+3	+3	Still mind	+0/+0	1d6	+0	+10 ft.
4th	+3	+4	+4	+4	*Ki* strike (magic), slow fall 20 ft.	+1/+1	1d8	+0	+10 ft.
5th	+3	+4	+4	+4	Purity of body	+2/+2	1d8	+1	+10 ft.
6th	+4	+5	+5	+5	Bonus feat, slow fall 30 ft.	+3/+3	1d8	+1	+20 ft.
7th	+5	+5	+5	+5	Wholeness of body	+4/+4	1d8	+1	+20 ft.
8th	+6/+1	+6	+6	+6	Slow fall 40 ft.	+5/+5/+0	1d10	+1	+20 ft.
9th	+6/+1	+6	+6	+6	Improved evasion	+6/+6/+1	1d10	+1	+30 ft.
10th	+7/+2	+7	+7	+7	*Ki* strike (lawful), slow fall 50 ft.	+7/+7/+2	1d10	+2	+30 ft.
11th	+8/+3	+7	+7	+7	Diamond body, greater flurry	+8/+8/+8/+3	1d10	+2	+30 ft.
12th	+9/+4	+8	+8	+8	Abundant step, slow fall 60 ft.	+9/+9/+9/+4	2d6	+2	+40 ft.
13th	+9/+4	+8	+8	+8	Diamond soul	+9/+9/+9/+4	2d6	+2	+40 ft.
14th	+10/+5	+9	+9	+9	Slow fall 70 ft.	+10/+10/+10/+5	2d6	+2	+40 ft.
15th	+11/+6/+1	+9	+9	+9	Quivering palm	+11/+11/+11/+6/+1	2d6	+3	+50 ft.
16th	+12/+7/+2	+10	+10	+10	*Ki* strike (adamantine), slow fall 80 ft.	+12/+12/+12/+7/+2	2d8	+3	+50 ft.
17th	+12/+7/+2	+10	+10	+10	Timeless body, tongue of the sun and moon	+12/+12/+12/+7/+2	2d8	+3	+50 ft.
18th	+13/+8/+3	+11	+11	+11	Slow fall 90 ft.	+13/+13/+13/+8/+3	2d8	+3	+60 ft.
19th	+14/+9/+4	+11	+11	+11	Empty body	+14/+14/+14/+9/+4	2d8	+3	+60 ft.
20th	+15/+10/+5	+12	+12	+12	Perfect self, slow fall any distance	+15/+15/+15/+10/+5	2d10	+4	+60 ft.

1 The value shown is for Medium monks. See Table 3–11: Small or Large Monk Unarmed Damage for Small or Large monks.

desired. For example, at 6th level, the monk Ember could make one attack with her unarmed strike at an attack bonus of +3 and one attack with a special monk weapon at an attack bonus of +3. When using weapons as part of a flurry of blows, a monk applies her Strength bonus (not Str bonus × 1-1/2 or × 1/2) to her damage rolls for all successful attacks, whether she wields a weapon in one or both hands. The monk can't use any weapon other than a special monk weapon as part of a flurry of blows.

In the case of the quarterstaff, each end counts as a separate weapon for the purpose of using the flurry of blows ability. Even though the quarterstaff requires two hands to use, a monk may still intersperse unarmed strikes with quarterstaff strikes, assuming that she has enough attacks in her flurry of blows routine to do so. For example, an 8th-level monk could make two attacks with the quarterstaff (one with each end) at a +5 attack bonus and one with an unarmed strike at a +0 attack bonus, or she could attack with one end of the quarterstaff and one unarmed strike each at a +5 attack bonus, and with the other end of the quarterstaff at a +0 attack bonus, or she could attack with one end of the quarterstaff and one unarmed strike at a +5 attack bonus each, and with the other end of the quarterstaff at a +0 attack bonus. She cannot, however, wield any other weapon at the same time that she uses a quarterstaff.

Ember

When a monk reaches 11th level, her flurry of blows ability improves. In addition to the standard single extra attack she gets from flurry of blows, she gets a second extra attack at her full base attack bonus.

Unarmed Strike: Monks are highly trained in fighting unarmed, giving them considerable advantages when doing so. At 1st level, a monk gains Improved Unarmed Strike as a bonus feat. A monk's attacks may be with either fist interchangeably or even from elbows, knees, and feet. This means that a monk may even make unarmed strikes with her hands full. There is no such thing as an off-hand attack for a monk striking unarmed. A monk may thus apply her full Strength bonus on damage rolls for all her unarmed strikes.

Usually a monk's unarmed strikes deal lethal damage, but she can choose to deal nonlethal damage instead with no penalty on her attack roll. She has the same choice to deal lethal or nonlethal damage while grappling (see page 156).

A monk's unarmed strike is treated both as a manufactured weapon and a natural weapon for the purpose of spells and effects that enhance or improve either manufactured weapons or natural weapons (such as the *magic fang* and *magic weapon* spells).

A monk also deals more damage with her unarmed strikes than a normal person would, as shown on Table 3–10: The Monk. The unarmed damage on Table 3–10 is for Medium monks. A Small monk deals less damage than the amount given there with her unarmed attacks, while a Large monk deals more damage; see Table 3–11: Small or Large Monk Unarmed Damage.

TABLE 3–11: SMALL OR LARGE MONK UNARMED DAMAGE

Level	Damage (Small Monk)	Damage (Large Monk)
1st–3rd	1d4	1d8
4th–7th	1d6	2d6
8th–11th	1d8	2d8
12th–15th	1d10	3d6
16th–19th	2d6	3d8
20th	2d8	4d8

Bonus Feat: At 1st level, a monk may select either Improved Grapple or Stunning Fist as a bonus feat. At 2nd level, she may select either Combat Reflexes or Deflect Arrows as a bonus feat. At 6th level, she may select either Improved Disarm or Improved Trip as a bonus feat. (See Chapter 5: Feats for descriptions.) A monk need not have any of the prerequisites normally required for these feats to select them.

Evasion (Ex): A monk of 2nd level or higher can avoid even magical and unusual attacks with great agility. If she makes a successful Reflex saving throw against an attack that normally deals half damage on a successful save (such as a red dragon's fiery breath or a *fireball*), she instead takes no damage. Evasion can be used only if a monk is wearing light armor or no armor. A helpless monk (such as one who is unconscious or paralyzed) does not gain the benefit of evasion.

Fast Movement (Ex): At 3rd level, a monk gains an enhancement bonus to her speed, as shown on Table 3–10. A monk in armor (even light armor) or carrying a medium or heavy load loses this extra speed.

Still Mind (Ex): A monk of 3rd level or higher gains a +2 bonus on saving throws against spells and effects from the school of enchantment, since her meditation and training improve her resistance to mind-affecting attacks.

Ki Strike (Su): At 4th level, a monk's unarmed attacks are empowered with *ki*. Her unarmed attacks are treated as magic weapons for the purpose of dealing damage to creatures with damage reduction (see Damage Reduction, page 291 of the *Dungeon Master's Guide*). Ki strike improves with the character's monk level. At 10th level, her unarmed attacks are also treated as lawful weapons for the purpose of dealing damage to creatures with damage reduction. At 16th level, her unarmed attacks are treated as adamantine weapons for the purpose of dealing damage to creatures with damage reduction and bypassing hardness (see Smashing an Object, page 165).

Slow Fall (Ex): At 4th level or higher, a monk within arm's reach of a wall can use it to slow her descent. When first using this ability, she takes damage as if the fall were 20 feet shorter than it actually is. The monk's ability to slow her fall (that is, to reduce the effective distance of the fall when next to a wall) improves with her monk level until at 20th level she can use a nearby wall to slow her descent and fall any distance without harm. See the Special column on Table 3–10 for details.

Purity of Body (Ex): At 5th level, a monk gains control over her body's immune system. She gains immunity to all diseases except for supernatural and magical diseases (such as mummy rot and lycanthropy).

LOCKWOOD

Wholeness of Body (Su): At 7th level or higher, a monk can heal her own wounds. She can heal a number of hit points of damage equal to twice her current monk level each day, and she can spread this healing out among several uses.

Improved Evasion (Ex): At 9th level, a monk's evasion ability improves. She still takes no damage on a successful Reflex saving throw against attacks such as a dragon's breath weapon or a *fireball*, but henceforth she takes only half damage on a failed save. A helpless monk (such as one who is unconscious or paralyzed) does not gain the benefit of improved evasion.

Diamond Body (Su): At 11th level, a monk is in such firm control of her own metabolism that she gains immunity to poisons of all kinds.

Abundant Step (Su): At 12th level or higher, a monk can slip magically between spaces, as if using the spell *dimension door*, once per day. Her caster level for this effect is one-half her monk level (rounded down).

Diamond Soul (Ex): At 13th level, a monk gains spell resistance equal to her current monk level + 10. In order to affect the monk with a spell, a spellcaster must get a result on a caster level check (1d20 + caster level; see Spell Resistance, page 177) that equals or exceeds the monk's spell resistance.

Quivering Palm (Su): Starting at 15th level, a monk can set up vibrations within the body of another creature that can thereafter be fatal if the monk so desires. She can use this quivering palm attack once a week, and she must announce her intent before making her attack roll. Constructs, oozes, plants, undead, incorporeal creatures, and creatures immune to critical hits cannot be affected. Otherwise, if the monk strikes successfully and the target takes damage from the blow, the quivering palm attack succeeds. Thereafter the monk can try to slay the victim at any later time, as long as the attempt is made within a number of days equal to her monk level. To make such an attempt, the monk merely wills the target to die (a free action), and unless the target makes a Fortitude saving throw (DC 10 + 1/2 the monk's level + the monk's Wis modifier), it dies. If the saving throw is successful, the target is no longer in danger from that particular quivering palm attack, but it may still be affected by another one at a later time.

Timeless Body (Ex): Upon attaining 17th level, a monk no longer takes penalties to her ability scores for aging and cannot be magically aged. Any such penalties that she has already taken, however, remain in place. Bonuses still accrue, and the monk still dies of old age when her time is up.

Tongue of the Sun and Moon (Ex): A monk of 17th level or higher can speak with any living creature.

Empty Body (Su): At 19th level, a monk gains the ability to assume an ethereal state for 1 round per monk level per day, as though using the spell *etherealness*. She may go ethereal on a number of different occasions during any single day, as long as the total number of rounds spent in an ethereal state does not exceed her monk level.

Perfect Self: At 20th level, a monk has tuned her body with skill and quasi-magical abilities to the point that she becomes a magical creature. She is forevermore treated as an outsider (an extraplanar creature) rather than as a humanoid for the purpose of spells and magical effects. For instance, charm person does not affect her. Additionally, the monk gains damage reduction 10/magic, which allows her to ignore (instantly regenerate) the first 10 points of damage from any attack made by a nonmagical weapon or by any natural attack made by a creature that doesn't have similar damage reduction (see Damage Reduction, page 291 of the *Dungeon Master's Guide*). Unlike other outsiders, the monk can still be brought back from the dead as if she were a member of her previous creature type.

Ex-Monks

A monk who becomes nonlawful cannot gain new levels as a monk but retains all monk abilities.

Like a member of any other class, a monk may be a multiclass character, but multiclass monks face a special restriction. A monk who gains a new class or (if already multiclass) raises another class by a level may never again raise her monk level, though she retains all her monk abilities.

Human Monk Starting Package

Armor: None (speed 30 ft.).

Weapons: Quarterstaff (1d6/1d6, crit ×2, 4 lb., two-handed, bludgeoning).

Sling (1d4, crit ×2, range inc. 50 ft., 0 lb., bludgeoning).

Skill Selection: Pick a number of skills equal to 5 + Int modifier.

Skill	Ranks	Ability	Armor Check Penalty
Listen	4	Wis	—
Climb	4	Str	0
Move Silently	4	Dex	0
Tumble	4	Dex	0
Jump	4	Str	0
Escape Artist	4	Dex	0
Hide	4	Dex	0
Swim	4	Str	0
Balance	4	Dex	0

Feat: If Dexterity is 13 or higher, Dodge; if Dexterity is 12 or lower, Improved Initiative instead.

Bonus Feat: If Dexterity is 13 or higher, Mobility; if Dexterity is 12 or lower, Blind-Fight instead.

Gear: Backpack with waterskin, one day's trail rations, bedroll, sack, and flint and steel. Three torches. Pouch with 10 sling bullets.

Gold: 2d4 gp.

PALADIN

The compassion to pursue good, the will to uphold law, and the power to defeat evil—these are the three weapons of the paladin. Few have the purity and devotion that it takes to walk the paladin's path, but those few are rewarded with the power to protect, to heal, and to smite. In a land of scheming wizards, unholy priests, bloodthirsty dragons, and infernal fiends, the paladin is the final hope that cannot be extinguished.

Adventures: Paladins take their adventures seriously and have a penchant for referring to them as quests. Even a mundane mission is, in the heart of the paladin, a personal test—an opportunity to demonstrate bravery, to develop martial skills, to learn tactics, and to find ways to do good. Still, the paladin really comes into her own when leading a mighty campaign against evil, not when merely looting ruins.

Characteristics: Divine power protects the paladin and gives her special powers. It wards off harm, protects her from disease, lets her heal herself, and guards her heart against fear. A paladin can also direct this power to help others, healing their wounds or curing diseases. Finally, a paladin can use this power to destroy evil. Even a novice paladin can detect evil, and more experienced paladins can smite evil foes and turn away undead. In addition, this power draws a mighty steed to the paladin and imbues that mount with strength, intelligence, and magical protection.

Alignment: Paladins must be lawful good, and they lose their divine powers if they deviate from that alignment. Additionally, paladins swear to follow a code of conduct that is in line with lawfulness and goodness.

Religion: A paladin need not devote herself to a single deity—devotion to righteousness is enough. Those paladins who do align themselves with particular religions prefer Heironeous (god of valor) over all others, but some paladins follow Pelor (god of the sun). Paladins devoted to a god are scrupulous in observing religious duties and are welcome in every associated temple.

Background: No one ever chooses to be a paladin. Becoming a paladin is answering a call, accepting one's destiny. No one, no matter how diligent, can become a paladin through practice. The nature is either within one or not, and it is not possible to gain the paladin's nature by any act of will. It is possible, however, to fail to recognize one's own potential, or to deny one's destiny. Occasionally, one who is called to be a paladin denies that call and pursues some other life instead.

Most paladins do answer the call and begin training as adolescents. Typically, they become squires or assistants to experienced paladins, train for years, and finally set off on their own to further the causes of good and law. Other paladins find their calling later in life, after having pursued some other career. All paladins, regardless of background, recognize in each other an eternal bond that transcends culture, race, and even religion. Any two paladins, even from opposite sides of the world, consider themselves comrades.

Races: Humans, with their ambitious souls, make great paladins. Half-elves, who often have human ambition, may also find themselves called into service as paladins. Dwarves are sometimes paladins, but becoming a paladin may be hard on a dwarf because it means putting

the duties of the paladin's life before duties to family, clan, and king. Elf paladins are few, and they tend to follow quests that take them far and wide because their lawful bent puts them out of synch with life among the elves. Members of the other common races rarely hear the call to become paladins.

Among the savage humanoids, paladins are all but unheard of.

Other Classes: Even though paladins are in some ways set apart from others, they eagerly team up with those whose skills and capabilities complement their own. They work well with good and lawful clerics, and they appreciate working with anyone who is brave, honest, and committed to good. While they cannot abide evil acts by their companions, they are otherwise willing to work with a variety of people quite different from themselves. Charismatic, trustworthy, and well respected, the paladin makes a fine leader for a team.

Role: The paladin's chief role in most groups is as a melee combatant, but she contributes other useful support as well. She makes a good secondary healer, and her high Charisma opens up fine leadership opportunities.

GAME RULE INFORMATION

Paladins have the following game statistics.

Abilities: Charisma enhances a paladin's healing power, self-protective capabilities, and undead turning ability. Strength is important for her because of its role in combat. A Wisdom score of 14 or higher is required to get access to the most powerful paladin spells, and a score of 11 or higher is required to cast any paladin spells at all.

Alignment: Lawful good.

Hit Die: d10.

Alhandra

TABLE 3–12: THE PALADIN

Level	Base Attack Bonus	Fort Save	Ref Save	Will Save	Special	1st	2nd	3rd	4th
1st	+1	+2	+0	+0	Aura of good, *detect evil*, smite evil 1/day	—			
2nd	+2	+3	+0	+0	Divine grace, lay on hands	—	—	—	—
3rd	+3	+3	+1	+1	Aura of courage, divine health	—	—	—	—
4th	+4	+4	+1	+1	Turn undead	0	—	—	—
5th	+5	+4	+1	+1	Smite evil 2/day, special mount	0	—	—	—
6th	+6/+1	+5	+2	+2	*Remove disease* 1/week	1	—	—	—
7th	+7/+2	+5	+2	+2		1	—	—	—
8th	+8/+3	+6	+2	+2		1	0	—	—
9th	+9/+4	+6	+3	+3	*Remove disease* 2/week	1	0	—	—
10th	+10/+5	+7	+3	+3	Smite evil 3/day	1	1	—	—
11th	+11/+6/+1	+7	+3	+3		1	1	0	—
12th	+12/+7/+2	+8	+4	+4	*Remove disease* 3/week	1	1	1	—
13th	+13/+8/+3	+8	+4	+4		1	1	1	—
14th	+14/+9/+4	+9	+4	+4		2	1	1	0
15th	+15/+10/+5	+9	+5	+5	*Remove disease* 4/week, smite evil 4/day	2	1	1	1
16th	+16/+11/+6/+1	+10	+5	+5		2	2	1	1
17th	+17/+12/+7/+2	+10	+5	+5		2	2	2	1
18th	+18/+13/+8/+3	+11	+6	+6	*Remove disease* 5/week	3	2	2	1
19th	+19/+14/+9/+4	+11	+6	+6		3	3	3	2
20th	+20/+15/+10/+5	+12	+6	+6	Smite evil 5/day	3	3	3	3

Class Skills

The paladin's class skills (and the key ability for each skill) are Concentration (Con), Craft (Int), Diplomacy (Cha), Handle Animal (Cha), Heal (Wis), Knowledge (nobility and royalty) (Int), Knowledge (religion) (Int), Profession (Wis), Ride (Dex), and Sense Motive (Wis). See Chapter 4: Skills for skill descriptions.

Skill Points at 1st Level: (2 + Int modifier) × 4.

Skill Points at Each Additional Level: 2 + Int modifier.

Class Features

All of the following are class features of the paladin.

Weapon and Armor Proficiency: Paladins are proficient with all simple and martial weapons, with all types of armor (heavy, medium, and light), and with shields (except tower shields).

Aura of Good (Ex): The power of a paladin's aura of good (see the *detect good* spell) is equal to her paladin level, just like the aura of a cleric of a good deity.

Detect Evil (Sp): At will, a paladin can use *detect evil*, as the spell.

Smite Evil (Su): Once per day, a paladin may attempt to smite evil with one normal melee attack. She adds her Charisma bonus (if any) to her attack roll and deals 1 extra point of damage per paladin level. For example, a 13th-level paladin armed with a longsword would deal 1d8+13 points of damage, plus any additional bonuses for high Strength or magical effects that would normally apply. If the paladin accidentally smites a creature that is not evil, the smite has no effect, but the ability is still used up for that day.

At 5th level, and at every five levels thereafter, the paladin may smite evil one additional time per day, as indicated on Table 3–12: The Paladin, to a maximum of five times per day at 20th level.

Divine Grace (Su): At 2nd level, a paladin gains a bonus equal to her Charisma bonus (if any) on all saving throws.

Lay on Hands (Su): Beginning at 2nd level, a paladin with a Charisma score of 12 or higher can heal wounds (her own or those of others) by touch. Each day she can heal a total number of hit points of damage equal to her paladin level × her Charisma bonus. For example, a 7th-level paladin with a 16 Charisma (+3 bonus) can heal 21 points of damage per day. A paladin may choose to divide her healing among multiple recipients, and she doesn't have to use it all at once. Using lay on hands is a standard action.

Alternatively, a paladin can use any or all of this healing power to deal damage to undead creatures. Using lay on hands in this way requires a successful melee touch attack and doesn't provoke an attack of opportunity. The paladin decides how many of her daily allotment of points to use as damage after successfully touching an undead creature.

Aura of Courage (Su): Beginning at 3rd level, a paladin is immune to fear (magical or otherwise). Each ally within 10 feet of her gains a +4 morale bonus on saving throws against fear effects. This ability functions while the paladin is conscious, but not if she is unconscious or dead.

Divine Health (Ex): At 3rd level, a paladin gains immunity to all diseases, including supernatural and magical diseases (such as mummy rot and lycanthropy).

Turn Undead (Su): When a paladin reaches 4th level, she gains the supernatural ability to turn undead. She may use this ability a number of times per day equal to 3 + her Charisma modifier. She turns undead as a cleric of three levels lower would. (See Turn or Rebuke Undead, page 159.)

Spells: Beginning at 4th level, a paladin gains the ability to cast a small number of divine spells (the same type of spells available to the cleric, druid, and ranger), which are drawn from the paladin spell list (page 191). A paladin must choose and prepare her spells in advance.

To prepare or cast a spell, a paladin must have a Wisdom score equal to at least 10 + the spell level (Wis 11 for 1st-level spells, Wis 12 for 2nd-level spells, and so forth). The Difficulty Class for a saving throw against a paladin's spell is 10 + the spell level + the paladin's Wisdom modifier.

Like other spellcasters, a paladin can cast only a certain number of spells of each spell level per day. Her base daily spell allotment is given on Table 3–12: The Paladin. In addition, she receives bonus spells per day if she has a high Wisdom score (see Table 1–1: Ability Modifiers and Bonus Spells, page 8). When Table 3–12 indicates that the paladin gets 0 spells per day of a given spell level (for instance, 1st-level spells for a 4th-level paladin), she gains only the bonus spells she would be entitled to based on her Wisdom score for that spell level The paladin does not have access to any domain spells or granted powers, as a cleric does.

A paladin prepares and casts spells the way a cleric does, though she cannot lose a prepared spell to spontaneously cast a *cure* spell in its place. A paladin may prepare and cast any spell on the paladin spell list (page 191), provided that she can cast spells of that level, but she must choose which spells to prepare during her daily meditation.

Through 3rd level, a paladin has no caster level. At 4th level and higher, her caster level is one-half her paladin level.

Special Mount (Sp): Upon reaching 5th level, a paladin gains the service of an unusually intelligent, strong, and loyal steed to serve her in her crusade against evil (see the sidebar). This mount is usually a heavy warhorse (for a Medium paladin) or a warpony (for a Small paladin).

Once per day, as a full-round action, a paladin may magically call her mount from the celestial realms in which it resides. The mount immediately appears adjacent to the paladin and remains for 2 hours per paladin level; it may be dismissed at any time as a free action. The mount is the same creature each time it is summoned, though the paladin may release a particular mount from service (if it has grown too old to join her crusade, for instance). Each time the mount is called, it appears in full health, regardless of any damage it may have taken previously. The mount also appears wearing or carrying any gear it had when it was last dismissed (including barding, saddle, saddlebags, and the like). Calling a mount is a conjuration (calling) effect.

Should the paladin's mount die, it immediately disappears, leaving behind any equipment it was carrying. The paladin may not summon another mount for thirty days or until she gains a paladin level, whichever comes first, even if the mount is somehow returned from the dead. During this thirty-day period, the paladin takes a –1 penalty on attack and weapon damage rolls.

Remove Disease (Sp): At 6th level, a paladin can produce a *remove disease* effect, as the spell, once per week. She can use this ability one additional time per week for every three levels after 6th (twice per week at 9th, three times at 12th, and so forth).

Code of Conduct: A paladin must be of lawful good alignment and loses all class abilities if she ever willingly commits an evil act. Additionally, a paladin's code requires that she respect legitimate authority, act with honor (not lying, not cheating, not using poison, and so forth), help those in need (provided they do not use the help for evil or chaotic ends), and punish those who harm or threaten innocents.

Associates: While she may adventure with characters of any good or neutral alignment, a paladin will never knowingly associate with evil characters, nor will she continue an association with someone who consistently offends her moral code. A paladin may accept only henchmen, followers, or cohorts who are lawful good.

Ex-Paladins

A paladin who ceases to be lawful good, who willfully commits an evil act, or who grossly violates the code of conduct loses all paladin spells and abilities (including the service of the paladin's mount, but not weapon, armor, and shield proficiencies). She may not progress any farther in levels as a paladin. She regains her abilities and advancement potential if she atones for her violations (see the *atonement* spell description, page 201), as appropriate.

Like a member of any other class, a paladin may be a multiclass character, but multiclass paladins face a special restriction. A paladin who gains a level in any class other than paladin may never again raise her paladin level, though she retains all her paladin abilities. The path of the paladin requires a constant heart. If a character adopts this class, she must pursue it to the exclusion of all other careers. Once she has turned off the path, she may never return.

THE PALADIN'S MOUNT

The paladin's mount is is superior to a normal mount of its kind and has special powers, as described below. The standard mount for a Medium paladin is a heavy warhorse, and the standard mount for a Small paladin is a warpony (see below for statistics). Your DM may work with you to select another kind of mount, such as a riding dog (for a halfling paladin) or a Large shark (for a paladin in an aquatic campaign). A paladin's mount is treated as a magical beast, not an animal, for the purpose of all effects that depend on its type (though it retains an animal's HD, base attack bonus, saves, skill points, and feats).

Paladin Level	Bonus HD	Natural Armor Adj.	Str Adj.	Int	Special
5th–7th	+2	+4	+1	6	Empathic link, improved evasion, share spells, share saving throws
8th–10th	+4	+6	+2	7	Improved speed
11th–14th	+6	+8	+3	8	*Command* creatures of its kind
15th–20th	+8	+10	+4	9	Spell resistance

Paladin's Mount Basics: Use the base statistics for a creature of the mount's kind, as given in the *Monster Manual*, but make changes to take into account the attributes and characteristics summarized on the table and described below.

Bonus HD: Extra eight-sided (d8) Hit Dice, each of which gains a Constitution modifier, as normal. Extra Hit Dice improve the mount's base attack and base save bonuses. A special mount's base attack bonus is equal to that of a cleric of a level equal to the mount's HD. A mount has good Fortitude and Reflex saves (treat it as a character whose level equals the animal's HD). The mount gains additional skill points or feats for bonus HD as normal for advancing a monster's Hit Dice (see the *Monster Manual*).

Natural Armor Adj.: The number on the table is an improvement to the mount's existing natural armor bonus. It represents the preternatural toughness of a paladin's mount.

Str Adj.: Add this figure to the mount's Strength score.

Int: The mount's Intelligence score.

Empathic Link (Su): The paladin has an empathic link with her mount out to a distance of up to 1 mile. The paladin cannot see through the mount's eyes, but they can communicate empathically. Note that even intelligent mounts see the world differently from humans, so misunderstandings are always possible.

Because of this empathic link, the paladin has the same connection to an item or place that her mount does, just as with a master and his familiar (see Familiars, page 52).

Improved Evasion (Ex): When subjected to an attack that normally allows a Reflex saving throw for half damage, a mount takes no damage if it makes a successful saving throw and half damage if the saving throw fails.

Share Spells: At the paladin's option, she may have any spell (but not any spell-like ability) she casts on herself also affect her mount.

The mount must be within 5 feet at the time of casting to receive the benefit. If the spell or effect has a duration other than instantaneous, it stops affecting the mount if it moves farther than 5 feet away and will not affect the mount again even if it returns to the paladin before the duration expires. Additionally, the paladin may cast a spell with a target of "You" on her mount (as a touch range spell) instead of on herself. A paladin and her mount can share spells even if the spells normally do not affect creatures of the mount's type (magical beast).

Share Saving Throws: For each of its saving throws, the mount uses its own base save bonus or the paladin's, whichever is higher. The mount applies its own ability modifiers to saves, and it doesn't share any other bonuses on saves that the master might have (such as from magic items or feats).

Improved Speed (Ex): The mount's speed increases by 10 feet.

Command (Sp): Once per day per two paladin levels of its master, a mount can use this ability to command other any normal animal of approximately the same kind as itself (for warhorses and warponies, this category includes donkeys, mules, and ponies), as long as the target creature has fewer Hit Dice than the mount. This ability functions like the *command* spell, but the mount must make a DC 21 Concentration check to succeed if it's being ridden at the time (in combat, for instance). If the check fails, the ability does not work that time, but it still counts against the mount's daily uses. Each target may attempt a Will save (DC 10 + 1/2 paladin's level + paladin's Cha modifier) to negate the effect.

Spell Resistance (Ex): A mount's spell resistance equals its master's paladin level + 5. To affect the mount with a spell, a spellcaster must get a result on a caster level check (1d20 + caster level; see Spell Resistance, page 177) that equals or exceeds the mount's spell resistance.

SAMPLE PALADIN'S MOUNTS

The statistics below are for normal creatures of the appropriate kinds; they do not include the modifications given on the table above.

Heavy Warhorse: CR 2; Large animal; HD 4d8+12; hp 30; Init +1; Spd 50 ft.; AC 14, touch 10, flat-footed 13; Base Atk +3; Grp +11; Atk +6 melee (1d6+4, hoof); Full Atk +6/+6 melee (1d6+4, 2 hooves) and +1 melee (1d4+2, bite); Space/Reach 10 ft./5 ft.; SQ low-light vision, scent; SV Fort +7, Ref +5, Will +2; Str 18, Dex 13, Con 17, Int 2, Wis 13, Cha 6.

Skills and Feats: Jump +12, Listen +5, Spot +4; Endurance, Run.

Warpony: CR 1/3; Medium animal; HD 2d8+4; hp 13; Init +1; Spd 40 ft.; AC 13, touch 11, flat-footed 12; Base Atk +1; Grp +3; Atk +3 melee (1d3+2, hoof); Full Atk +3/+3 melee (1d3+2, 2 hooves); Space/Reach 5 ft./5 ft.; SQ low-light vision, scent; SV Fort +5, Ref +4, Will +0; Str 15, Dex 13, Con 14, Int 2, Wis 11, Cha 4.

Skills and Feats: Jump +6, Listen +5, Spot +5; Endurance.

See page 85 of the *Dungeon Master's Guide* for information on how to read a creature's statistics block.

Skill	Ranks	Ability	Armor Check Penalty
Heal	4	Wis	—
Ride	4	Dex	—
Diplomacy	4	Cha	—
Spot (cc)	2	Wis	—
Listen (cc)	2	Wis	—
Climb (cc)	2	Str	–6
Search (cc)	2	Int	—

Feat: Weapon Focus (longsword).
Bonus Feat: Improved Initiative.
Gear: Backpack with waterskin, one day's trail rations, bedroll, sack, flint and steel. Hooded lantern, three pints of oil. Quiver with 20 arrows. Wooden holy symbol (fist of Heironeous, god of valor).
Gold: 6d4 gp.

RANGER

The forests and hills are home to fierce and cunning creatures, such as blood-thirsty owlbears and malicious dis-placer beasts. But more cunning and powerful than these monsters is the ranger, a skilled hunter and stalker. He knows the woods as if they were his home (as indeed they are), and he knows his prey in deadly detail.

Adventures: A ranger often accepts the role of protector, aiding those who live in or travel through the woods. In addition, a ranger carries grudges against certain types of crea-tures and looks for opportunities to find and destroy them. He may also adven-ture for all the reasons that a fighter does.

Characteristics: A ranger can use a variety of weapons and is quite capable in combat. His skills allow him to survive in the wilderness, to find his prey, and to avoid detection. He also has special knowledge about

Soveliss

certain types of creatures, which makes it easier for him to find and defeat such foes. Finally, an experienced ranger has such a tie to nature that he can actually draw upon natural power to cast divine spells, much as a druid does.

Alignment: Rangers can be of any alignment. Most are good, and such rangers usually function as protectors of the wild areas. In this role, a ranger seeks out and destroys or drives off evil creatures that threaten the wilderness. Good rangers also pro-tect those who travel through the wilder-ness, serving sometimes as guides and sometimes as unseen guardians. Most rangers are also chaotic, preferring to follow the ebb and flow of nature or of their own hearts instead of rigid rules. Evil rangers, though rare, are much to be feared. They revel in nature's thoughtless cruelty and seek to emulate her most fearsome predators. They gain divine spells just as good rangers do, for nature her-self is indifferent to good and evil.

Religion: Though a ranger gains his divine spells from the power of nature, he like anyone else may worship a chosen deity. Ehlonna (goddess of the wood-lands) and Obad-Hai (god of nature) are the most common deities revered by rangers, though some prefer more mar-tial deities.

Background: Some rangers gained their training as part of special military teams, but most learned their skills from solitary masters who accepted them as stu-dents and assistants. The rangers of a partic-ular master may count themselves as cohorts, or they may be rivals for the status of best student and thus rightful heir to their master's fame.

Races: Elves often choose the ranger's path. They are at home in the woods, and they have the grace to move stealthily. Half-elves who feel their elf parent's connection to the woods are also likely to adopt this class.

TABLE 3–13: THE RANGER

Level	Base Attack Bonus	Fort Save	Ref Save	Will Save	Special	Spells per Day 1st	2nd	3rd	4th
1st	+1	+2	+2	+0	1st favored enemy, Track, wild empathy	—	—	—	—
2nd	+2	+3	+3	+0	Combat style	—	—	—	—
3rd	+3	+3	+3	+1	Endurance	—	—	—	—
4th	+4	+4	+4	+1	Animal companion	0	—	—	—
5th	+5	+4	+4	+1	2nd favored enemy	0	—	—	—
6th	+6/+1	+5	+5	+2	Improved combat style	1	—	—	—
7th	+7/+2	+5	+5	+2	Woodland stride	1	—	—	—
8th	+8/+3	+6	+6	+2	Swift tracker	1	0	—	—
9th	+9/+4	+6	+6	+3	Evasion	1	0	—	—
10th	+10/+5	+7	+7	+3	3rd favored enemy	1	1	—	—
11th	+11/+6/+1	+7	+7	+3	Combat style mastery	1	1	0	—
12th	+12/+7/+2	+8	+8	+4		1	1	1	—
13th	+13/+8/+3	+8	+8	+4	Camouflage	1	1	1	—
14th	+14/+9/+4	+9	+9	+4		2	1	1	0
15th	+15/+10/+5	+9	+9	+5	4th favored enemy	2	1	1	1
16th	+16/+11/+6/+1	+10	+10	+5		2	2	1	1
17th	+17/+12/+7/+2	+10	+10	+5	Hide in plain sight	2	2	2	1
18th	+18/+13/+8/+3	+11	+11	+6		3	2	2	1
19th	+19/+14/+9/+4	+11	+11	+6		3	3	3	2
20th	+20/+15/+10/+5	+12	+12	+6	5th favored enemy	3	3	3	3

Humans are often rangers as well, being adaptable enough to learn their way around the woods even if it doesn't come naturally to them. Half-orcs may find the ranger's life more comfortable than life among cruel and taunting humans (or orcs). Gnome rangers are more common than gnome fighters, but still they tend to remain in their own lands rather than adventure among "the big people." Dwarf rangers are rare, but they can be quite effective. Instead of living in the surface wilderness, they are at home in the endless caverns beneath the earth. Here they hunt down and destroy the enemies of dwarvenkind with the relentless precision for which dwarves are known. Dwarf rangers are often known as cavers. Halfling rangers are highly respected for their ability to help communities of halflings prosper as they pursue their nomadic lifestyle.

Among the savage humanoids, only gnolls are commonly rangers, using their skills to slyly stalk their prey.

Classes: Rangers get along well with druids and to some extent with barbarians. They are known to bicker with paladins, mostly because they often share goals but differ in style, tactics, approach, philosophy, and esthetics. Since rangers don't often look to other people for support or friendship, they find it easy to tolerate people who are quite different from themselves, such as bookish wizards and preachy clerics. They just don't care enough to get upset about others' differences.

Role: The ranger's best role is that of a scout and secondary combatant. Without the heavy armor of the fighter or the staying power of the barbarian, the ranger should focus on opportunistic and ranged attacks. Most rangers use their animal companions as sentries, scouts, or to assist them in melee combat.

GAME RULE INFORMATION

Rangers have the following game statistics.

Abilities: Dexterity is important for a ranger both because he tends to wear light armor and because several ranger skills are based on that ability. Strength is important because rangers frequently get involved in combat. Several ranger skills are based on Wisdom, and a Wisdom score of 14 or higher is required to get access to the most powerful ranger spells. A Wisdom score of 11 or higher is required to cast any ranger spells at all. One of the ranger's trademark skills, his ability to track foes, is based on Wisdom.

Alignment: Any.

Hit Die: d8.

Class Skills

The ranger's class skills (and the key ability for each skill) are Climb (Str), Concentration (Con), Craft (Int), Handle Animal (Cha), Heal (Wis), Hide (Dex), Jump (Str), Knowledge (dungeoneering) (Int), Knowledge (geography) (Int), Knowledge (nature) (Int), Listen (Wis), Move Silently (Dex), Profession (Wis), Ride (Dex), Search (Int), Spot (Wis), Survival (Wis), Swim (Str), and Use Rope (Dex). See Chapter 4: Skills for skill descriptions.

Skill Points at 1st Level: (6 + Int modifier) × 4.

Skill Points at Each Additional Level: 6 + Int modifier.

Class Features

All of the following are class features of the ranger.

Weapon and Armor Proficiency: A ranger is proficient with all simple and martial weapons, and with light armor and shields (except tower shields).

Favored Enemy (Ex): At 1st level, a ranger may select a type of creature from among those given on Table 3–14: Ranger Favored Enemies. Due to his extensive study of his chosen type of foe and training in the proper techniques for combating such creatures, the ranger gains a +2 bonus on Bluff, Listen, Sense Motive, Spot, and Survival checks when using these skills against creatures of this type. Likewise, he gets a +2 bonus on weapon damage rolls against such creatures.

At 5th level and every five levels thereafter (10th, 15th, and 20th level), the ranger may select an additional favored enemy from those given on the table. In addition, at each such interval, the bonus against any one favored enemy (including the one just selected, if so desired) increases by 2. For example, a 5th-level ranger has two favored enemies; against one he gains a +4 bonus on Bluff, Listen, Sense Motive, Spot, and Survival checks and weapon damage rolls, and against the other he has a +2 bonus. At 10th level, he has three favored enemies, and he gains an additional +2 bonus, which he can allocate to the bonus against any one of his three favored enemies. Thus, his bonuses could be either +4, +4, +2 or +6, +2, +2.

If the ranger chooses humanoids or outsiders as a favored enemy, he must also choose an associated subtype, as indicated on the table. If a specific creature falls into more than one category of favored enemy (for instance, devils are both evil outsiders and lawful outsiders), the ranger's bonuses do not stack; he simply uses whichever bonus is higher. See the *Monster Manual* for more information on types of creatures.

TABLE 3–14: RANGER FAVORED ENEMIES

Type (Subtype)	Examples
Aberration	beholder
Animal	bear
Construct	golem
Dragon	black dragon
Elemental	invisible stalker
Fey	dryad
Giant	ogre
Humanoid (aquatic)	merfolk
Humanoid (dwarf)	dwarf
Humanoid (elf)	elf
Humanoid (goblinoid)	hobgoblin
Humanoid (gnoll)	gnoll
Humanoid (gnome)	gnome
Humanoid (halfling)	halfling
Humanoid (human)	human
Humanoid (orc)	orc
Humanoid (reptilian)	kobold
Magical beast	displacer beast
Monstrous humanoid	minotaur
Ooze	gelatinous cube
Outsider (air)	arrowhawk
Outsider (chaotic)	demon
Outsider (earth)	xorn
Outsider (evil)	devil
Outsider (fire)	salamander
Outsider (good)	angel
Outsider (lawful)	formian
Outsider (native)	tiefling
Outsider (water)	tojanida
Plant	shambling mound
Undead	zombie
Vermin	monstrous spider

Track: A ranger gains Track (see page 101) as a bonus feat.

Wild Empathy (Ex): A ranger can use body language, vocalizations, and demeanor to improve the attitude of an animal (such as a bear or a monitor lizard). This ability functions just like a Diplomacy check to improve the attitude of a person (see page 72). The ranger rolls 1d20 and adds his ranger level and his Charisma bonus to determine the wild empathy check result. The typical domestic animal has a starting attitude of indifferent, while wild animals are usually unfriendly.

To use wild empathy, the ranger and the animal must be able to study each other, which means that they must be within 30 feet of one another under normal visibility conditions. Generally, influencing an animal in this way takes 1 minute, but, as with influencing people, it might take more or less time.

The ranger can also use this ability to influence a magical beast with an Intelligence score of 1 or 2 (such as a basilisk or a girallon), but he takes a –4 penalty on the check.

Combat Style (Ex): At 2nd level, a ranger must select one of two combat styles to pursue: archery or two-weapon combat. This choice affects the character's class features but does not restrict his selection of feats or special abilities in any way.

If the ranger selects archery, he is treated as having the Rapid Shot feat, even if he does not have the normal prerequisites for that feat.

If the ranger selects two-weapon combat, he is treated as having the Two-Weapon Fighting feat, even if he does not have the normal prerequisites for that feat.

The benefits of the ranger's chosen style apply only when he wears light or no armor. He loses all benefits of his combat style when wearing medium or heavy armor.

Endurance: A ranger gains Endurance (see page 93) as a bonus feat at 3rd level.

Animal Companion (Ex): At 4th level, a ranger gains an animal companion selected from the following list: badger, camel, dire rat, dog, riding dog, eagle, hawk, horse (light or heavy), owl, pony, snake (Small or Medium viper), or wolf. If the DM's campaign takes place wholly or partly in an aquatic environment, the DM may add the following creatures to the ranger's list of options: crocodile, porpoise, Medium shark, and squid. This animal is a loyal companion that accompanies the ranger on his adventures as appropriate for its kind. (For instance, an aquatic creature can't adventure with a ranger on land and shouldn't be selected by a nonaquatic character without extenuating circumstances). In most cases, the animal companion functions as a mount, sentry, scout, or hunting animal, rather than as a protector.

This ability functions like the druid ability of the same name (see page 35), except that the ranger's effective druid level is one-half his ranger level. For example, the animal companion of a 4th-level ranger would be the equivalent of a 2nd-level druid's animal companion. A ranger may select from the alternative lists of animal companions just as a druid can, though again his effective druid level is half his ranger level. Thus, he must be at least an 8th-level ranger to select from the druid's list of 4th-level animal companions, and if he chooses one of those animals, his effective druid level would be reduced by 3, to 1st level. Like a druid, a ranger cannot select an alternative animal if the choice would reduce his effective druid level below 1st.

Spells: Beginning at 4th level, a ranger gains the ability to cast a small number of divine spells (the same type of spells available to the cleric, druid, and paladin), which are drawn from the ranger spell list (page 191). A ranger must choose and prepare his spells in advance (see below).

To prepare or cast a spell, a ranger must have a Wisdom score equal to at least 10 + the spell level (Wis 11 for 1st-level spells, Wis 12 for 2nd-level spells, and so forth). The Difficulty Class for a saving throw against a ranger's spell is 10 + the spell level + the ranger's Wisdom modifier.

Like other spellcasters, a ranger can cast only a certain number of spells of each spell level per day. His base daily spell allotment is given on Table 3–13: The Ranger. In addition, he receives bonus spells per day if he has a high Wisdom score (see Table 1–1: Ability Modifiers and Bonus Spells, page 8). When Table 3–13 indicates that the ranger gets 0 spells per day of a given spell level (for instance, 1st-level spells for a 4th-level ranger), he gains only the bonus spells he would be entitled to based on his Wisdom score for that spell level. The ranger does not have access to any domain spells or granted powers, as a cleric does.

A ranger prepares and casts spells the way a cleric does, though he cannot lose a prepared spell to cast a *cure* spell in its place. A ranger may prepare and cast any spell on the ranger spell list, provided that he can cast spells of that level, but he must choose which spells to prepare during his daily meditation.

Through 3rd level, a ranger has no caster level. At 4th level and higher, his caster level is one-half his ranger level.

Improved Combat Style (Ex): At 6th level, a ranger's aptitude in his chosen combat style (archery or two-weapon combat) improves. If he selected archery at 2nd level, he is treated as having the Manyshot feat (page 97), even if he does not have the normal prerequisites for that feat.

If the ranger selected two-weapon combat at 2nd level, he is treated as having the Improved Two-Weapon Fighting feat (page 96), even if he does not have the normal prerequisites for that feat.

As before, the benefits of the ranger's chosen style apply only when he wears light or no armor. He loses all benefits of his combat style when wearing medium or heavy armor.

Woodland Stride (Ex): Starting at 7th level, a ranger may move through any sort of undergrowth (such as natural thorns, briars, overgrown areas, and similar terrain) at his normal speed and without taking damage or suffering any other impairment. However, thorns, briars, and overgrown areas that are enchanted or magically manipulated to impede motion still affect him.

Swift Tracker (Ex): Beginning at 8th level, a ranger can move at his normal speed while following tracks without taking the normal –5 penalty. He takes only a –10 penalty (instead of the normal –20) when moving at up to twice normal speed while tracking.

Evasion (Ex): At 9th level, a ranger can avoid even magical and unusual attacks with great agility. If he makes a successful Reflex saving throw against an attack that normally deals half damage on a successful save (such as a red dragon's fiery breath or a *fireball*), he instead takes no damage. Evasion can be used only if the ranger is wearing light armor or no armor. A helpless ranger (such as one who is unconscious or paralyzed) does not gain the benefit of evasion.

Combat Style Mastery (Ex): At 11th level, a ranger's aptitude in his chosen combat style (archery or two-weapon combat) improves again. If he selected archery at 2nd level, he is treated as having the Improved Precise Shot feat (page 96), even if he does not have the normal prerequisites for that feat.

If the ranger selected two-weapon combat at 2nd level, he is treated as having the Greater Two-Weapon Fighting feat (page 95), even if he does not have the normal prerequisites for that feat.

As before, the benefits of the ranger's chosen style apply only when he wears light or no armor. He loses all benefits of his combat style when wearing medium or heavy armor.

Camouflage (Ex): A ranger of 13th level or higher can use the Hide skill in any sort of natural terrain, even if the terrain doesn't grant cover or concealment.

Hide in Plain Sight (Ex): While in any sort of natural terrain, a ranger of 17th level or higher can use the Hide skill even while being observed.

Elf Ranger Starting Package

Armor: Studded leather (+3 AC, armor check penalty –1, speed 30 ft., 20 lb.).

Weapons: Longsword (1d8, crit 19–20/×2, 4 lb., one-handed, slashing).

Short sword, off hand (1d6, crit 19–20/×2, 2 lb., light, piercing).

Note: When striking with both swords, the ranger takes a –4 penalty with his longsword and a –8 penalty with his short sword. If he has a Strength bonus, add only one-half of it to his damage roll with the short sword, which is in his off hand, but add the full Strength bonus to his damage roll with the longsword.

Longbow (1d8, crit ×3, range inc. 100 ft., 3 lb., piercing).

Skill Selection: Pick a number of skills equal to 6 + Int modifier.

Skill	Ranks	Ability	Armor Check Penalty
Survival	4	Wis	—
Hide	4	Dex	−1
Move Silently	4	Dex	−1
Listen	4	Wis	—
Spot	4	Wis	—
Knowledge (nature)	4	Int	—
Climb	4	Str	−1
Heal	4	Wis	—
Swim	4	Str	−2
Search	4	Int	—

Feat: Point Blank Shot.

Favored Enemy: Magical beast.

Gear: Backpack with waterskin, one day's trail rations, bedroll, sack, and flint and steel. Three torches. Quiver with 20 arrows.

Gold: 2d4 gp.

ROGUE

Rogues have little in common with one another. Some are stealthy thieves. Others are silver-tongued tricksters. Still others are scouts, infiltrators, spies, diplomats, or thugs. What they do share is versatility, adaptability, and resourcefulness. In general, rogues are skilled at getting what others don't want them to get: entrance into a locked treasure vault, safe passage past a deadly trap, secret battle plans, a guard's trust, or some random person's pocket money.

Adventures: Rogues adventure for the same reason they do most other things: to get what they can get. Some are after loot; others want experience. Some crave fame; others seek infamy. Quite a few also enjoy a challenge. Figuring out how to thwart a trap or avoid an alarm is great fun for many rogues.

Characteristics: Rogues are highly skilled, and they can concentrate on developing any of several categories of skills. While not equal to members of many other classes in combat, a rogue knows how to hit where it hurts, and she can dish out a lot of damage with a sneak attack.

Rogues have a sixth sense when it comes to avoiding danger. Experienced rogues develop mystical powers and skills as they master the arts of stealth, evasion, and sneak attacks. In addition, while not capable of casting spells on their own, rogues can "fake it" well enough to cast spells from scrolls, activate wands, and use just about any other magic item.

Alignment: Rogues follow opportunities, not ideals. Though they are more likely to be chaotic than lawful, they are a diverse bunch, so they may be of any alignment.

Religion: Although they are not renowned for their piety, most rogues revere Olidammara (god of thieves). Evil rogues might secretly worship Nerull (god of death) or Erythnul (god of slaughter). Since rogues are so diverse, however, many of them worship other deities, or none at all.

Background: Some rogues are officially inducted into an organized fellowship of rogues or "guild of thieves." Some are self-taught; others learned their skills from independent mentors. Often, an experienced rogue needs an assistant for scams, second-story jobs, or just for watching her back. She recruits a likely youngster, who then learns the skills of the trade on the job. Eventually the trainee is ready to move on, perhaps because the mentor has run afoul of the law, or perhaps because the trainee has double-crossed her mentor and needs some "space."

Rogues do not see each other as fellows unless they happen to be members of the same guild or students of the same mentor. In fact, rogues trust other rogues less than they trust anyone else. They're no fools.

Races: Adaptable and often unprincipled, humans take to the rogue's life with ease. Halflings, elves, and half-elves also find themselves well suited to the demands of this career. Dwarf and gnome rogues, while less common, are renowned as experts with locks and traps. Half-orc rogues tend toward thuggery.

Rogues are common among brutal humanoids, especially goblins and bugbears. Rogues who learn their arts in savage lands, however, generally don't have much experience with complex mechanisms such as traps and locks.

Other Classes: Rogues love and hate working with members of other classes. They excel when protected by warriors and supported by spellcasters. There are plenty of times, however, that they wish everyone else was as quiet, guileful, and patient as they. Rogues are particularly wary of paladins, so they endeavor to prove themselves useful when contact with paladins is unavoidable.

Role: The rogue's role in a group can vary dramatically based on her skill selection—from charismatic con artist to cunning burglar to agile combatant—but most rogues share certain aspects. They aren't capable of prolonged melee combat, so they focus on opportunistic sneak attacks or ranged attacks. The rogue's stealth and her trapfinding ability make her one of the best scouts in the game.

TABLE 3–15: THE ROGUE

Level	Base Attack Bonus	Fort Save	Ref Save	Will Save	Special
1st	+0	+0	+2	+0	Sneak attack +1d6, trapfinding
2nd	+1	+0	+3	+0	Evasion
3rd	+2	+1	+3	+1	Sneak attack +2d6, trap sense +1
4th	+3	+1	+4	+1	Uncanny dodge
5th	+3	+1	+4	+1	Sneak attack +3d6
6th	+4	+2	+5	+2	Trap sense +2
7th	+5	+2	+5	+2	Sneak attack +4d6
8th	+6/+1	+2	+6	+2	Improved uncanny dodge
9th	+6/+1	+3	+6	+3	Sneak attack +5d6, trap sense +3
10th	+7/+2	+3	+7	+3	Special ability
11th	+8/+3	+3	+7	+3	Sneak attack +6d6
12th	+9/+4	+4	+8	+4	Trap sense +4
13th	+9/+4	+4	+8	+4	Sneak attack +7d6, special ability
14th	+10/+5	+4	+9	+4	—
15th	+11/+6/+1	+5	+9	+5	Sneak attack +8d6, trap sense +5
16th	+12/+7/+2	+5	+10	+5	Special ability
17th	+12/+7/+2	+5	+10	+5	Sneak attack +9d6
18th	+13/+8/+3	+6	+11	+6	Trap sense +6
19th	+14/+9/+4	+6	+11	+6	Sneak attack +10d6, special ability
20th	+15/+10/+5	+6	+12	+6	—

GAME RULE INFORMATION

Rogues have the following game statistics.

Abilities: Dexterity provides extra protection for the lightly armored rogue. Dexterity, Intelligence, and Wisdom are important for many of the rogue's skills. A high Intelligence score also gives the rogue extra skill points, which can be used to expand her repertoire.

Alignment: Any.

Hit Die: d6.

Class Skills

The rogue's class skills (and the key ability for each skill) are Appraise (Int), Balance (Dex), Bluff (Cha), Climb (Str), Craft (Int), Decipher Script (Int), Diplomacy (Cha), Disable Device (Int), Disguise (Cha), Escape Artist (Dex), Forgery (Int), Gather Information (Cha), Hide (Dex), Intimidate (Cha), Jump (Str), Knowledge (local) (Int), Listen (Wis), Move Silently (Dex), Open Lock (Dex), Perform (Cha), Profession (Wis), Search (Int), Sense Motive (Wis), Sleight of Hand (Dex), Spot (Wis), Swim (Str), Tumble (Dex), Use Magic Device (Cha), and Use Rope (Dex). See Chapter 4: Skills for skill descriptions.

Skill Points at 1st Level: (8 + Int modifier) × 4.

Skill Points at Each Additional Level: 8 + Int modifier.

Class Features

All of the following are class features of the rogue.

Weapon and Armor Proficiency: Rogues are proficient with all simple weapons, plus the hand crossbow, rapier, shortbow, and short sword. Rogues are proficient with light armor, but not with shields.

Sneak Attack: If a rogue can catch an opponent when he is unable to defend himself effectively from her attack, she can strike a vital spot for extra damage. Basically, the rogue's attack deals extra damage any time her target would be denied a Dexterity bonus to AC (whether the target actually has a Dexterity bonus or not), or when the rogue flanks her target. This extra damage is 1d6 at 1st level, and it increases by 1d6 every two rogue levels thereafter. Should the rogue score a critical hit with a sneak attack, this extra damage is not multiplied. (See Table 8–5: Attack Roll Modifiers and Table 8–6: Armor Class Modifiers, page 151, for combat situations in which the rogue flanks an opponent or the opponent loses his Dexterity bonus to AC.)

Ranged attacks can count as sneak attacks only if the target is within 30 feet. A rogue can't strike with deadly accuracy from beyond that range.

With a sap (blackjack) or an unarmed strike, a rogue can make a sneak attack that deals nonlethal damage instead of lethal damage. She cannot use a weapon that deals lethal damage to deal nonlethal damage in a sneak attack, not even with the usual –4 penalty, because she must make optimal use of her weapon in order to execute a sneak attack. (See Nonlethal Damage, page 146.)

A rogue can sneak attack only living creatures with discernible anatomies—undead, constructs, oozes, plants, and incorporeal creatures lack vital areas to attack. Any creature that is immune to critical hits is not vulnerable to sneak attacks. The rogue must be

Lidda

able to see the target well enough to pick out a vital spot and must be able to reach such a spot. A rogue cannot sneak attack while striking a creature with concealment (see page 152) or striking the limbs of a creature whose vitals are beyond reach.

Trapfinding: Rogues (and only rogues) can use the Search skill to locate traps when the task has a Difficulty Class higher than 20. Finding a nonmagical trap has a DC of at least 20, or higher if it is well hidden. Finding a magic trap has a DC of 25 + the level of the spell used to create it.

Rogues (and only rogues) can use the Disable Device skill to disarm magic traps. A magic trap generally has a DC of 25 + the level of the spell used to create it.

A rogue who beats a trap's DC by 10 or more with a Disable Device check can study a trap, figure out how it works, and bypass it (with her party) without disarming it.

Evasion (Ex): At 2nd level and higher, a rogue can avoid even magical and unusual attacks with great agility. If she makes a successful Reflex saving throw against an attack that normally deals half damage on a successful save (such as a red dragon's fiery breath or a *fireball*), she instead takes no damage. Evasion can be used only if the rogue is wearing light armor or no armor. A helpless rogue (such as one who is unconscious or paralyzed) does not gain the benefit of evasion.

Trap Sense (Ex): At 3rd level, a rogue gains an intuitive sense that alerts her to danger from traps, giving her a +1 bonus on Reflex saves made to avoid traps and a +1 dodge bonus to AC against attacks made by traps. These bonuses rise to +2 when the rogue reaches 6th level, to +3 when she reaches 9th level, to +4 when she reaches 12th level, to +5 at 15th, and to +6 at 18th level. Trap sense bonuses gained from multiple classes stack.

Uncanny Dodge (Ex): Starting at 4th level, a rogue can react to danger before her senses would normally allow her to do so. She retains her Dexterity bonus to AC (if any) even if she is caught flat-footed or struck by an invisible attacker. However, she still loses her Dexterity bonus to AC if immobilized.

If a rogue already has uncanny dodge from a different class (a rogue with at least two levels of barbarian, for example), she automatically gains improved uncanny dodge (see below) instead.

Improved Uncanny Dodge (Ex): A rogue of 8th level or higher can no longer be flanked; she can react to opponents on opposite sides of her as easily as she can react to a single attacker. This defense denies another rogue the ability to sneak attack the character by flanking her, unless the attacker has at least four more rogue levels than the target does.

If a character already has uncanny dodge (see above) from a second class, the character automatically gains improved uncanny dodge instead, and the levels from the classes that grant uncanny dodge stack to determine the minimum rogue level required to flank the character.

Special Abilities: On attaining 10th level, and at every three levels thereafter (13th, 16th, and 19th), a rogue gains a special ability of her choice from among the following options.

Crippling Strike (Ex): A rogue with this ability can sneak attack opponents with such precision that her blows weaken and hamper them. An opponent damaged by one of her sneak attacks also takes 2 points of Strength damage. Ability points lost to damage return on their own at the rate of 1 point per day for each damaged ability.

Defensive Roll (Ex): The rogue can roll with a potentially lethal blow to take less damage from it than she otherwise would. Once per day, when she would be reduced to 0 or fewer hit points by damage in combat (from a weapon or other blow, not a spell or special ability), the rogue can attempt to roll with the damage. To use this ability, the rogue must attempt a Reflex saving throw (DC = damage dealt). If the save succeeds, she takes only half damage from the blow; if it fails, she takes full damage. She must be aware of the attack and able to react to it in order to execute her defensive roll—if she is denied her Dexterity bonus to AC, she can't use this ability. Since this effect would not normally allow a character to make a Reflex save for half damage, the rogue's evasion ability does not apply to the defensive roll.

Improved Evasion (Ex): This ability works like evasion, except that while the rogue still takes no damage on a successful Reflex saving throw against attacks such as a dragon's breath weapon or a *fireball*, henceforth she henceforth takes only half damage on a failed save. A helpless rogue (such as one who is unconscious or paralyzed) does not gain the benefit of improved evasion.

Opportunist (Ex): Once per round, the rogue can make an attack of opportunity against an opponent who has just been struck for damage in melee by another character. This attack counts as the rogue's attack of opportunity for that round. Even a rogue with the Combat Reflexes feat can't use the opportunist ability more than once per round.

Skill Mastery: The rogue becomes so certain in the use of certain skills that she can use them reliably even under adverse conditions. Upon gaining this ability, she selects a number of skills equal to 3 + her Intelligence modifier. When making a skill check with one of these skills, she may take 10 even if stress and distractions would normally prevent her from doing so. A rogue may gain this special ability multiple times, selecting additional skills for it to apply to each time.

Slippery Mind (Ex): This ability represents the rogue's ability to wriggle free from magical effects that would otherwise control or compel her. If a rogue with slippery mind is affected by an enchantment spell or effect and fails her saving throw, she can attempt it again 1 round later at the same DC. She gets only this one extra chance to succeed on her saving throw.

Feat: A rogue may gain a bonus feat in place of a special ability.

Halfling Rogue Starting Package

Armor: Leather (+2 AC, speed 20 ft., 7-1/2 lb.).

Weapons: Short sword (1d4, crit 19–20/×2, 1 lb., light, piercing).

Light crossbow (1d6, crit 19–20/×2, range inc. 80 ft., 2 lb., piercing).

Dagger (1d3, crit 19–20/×2, range inc. 10 ft., 1/2 lb., light, piercing).

Skill Selection: Pick a number of skills equal to 8 + Int modifier.

Skill	Ranks	Ability	Armor Check Penalty
Move Silently	4	Dex	0
Hide	4	Dex	0
Spot	4	Wis	—
Listen	4	Wis	—
Search	4	Int	—
Disable Device	4	Int	—
Open Lock	4	Dex	—
Climb	4	Str	0
Use Magic Device	4	Cha	—
Sleight of Hand	4	Dex	0
Decipher Script	4	Int	—
Bluff	4	Cha	—
Intimidate	4	Cha	—

Feat: Improved Initiative.

Gear: Backpack with waterskin, one day's trail rations, bedroll, sack, and flint and steel. Thieves' tools. Hooded lantern and three pints of oil. Case with 10 crossbow bolts.

Gold: 4d4 gp.

Hennet

SORCERER

Sorcerers create magic the way a poet creates poems, with inborn talent honed by practice. They have no books, no mentors, no theories—just raw power that they direct at will. Some sorcerers claim that the blood of dragons courses through their veins. That claim may be true in some cases—it is common knowledge that certain powerful dragons can take humanoid form and even have humanoid lovers, and it's difficult to prove that a given sorcerer does not have a dragon ancestor. It's true that sorcerers often have striking good looks, usually with a touch of the exotic that hints at an unusual heritage. Others hold that the claim is either an unsubstantiated boast on the part of certain sorcerers or envious gossip on the part of those who lack the sorcerer's gift.

Adventures: The typical sorcerer adventures in order to improve his abilities. Only by testing his limits can he surpass them. A sorcerer's power is inborn—part of his soul. Developing this power is a quest in itself for many sorcerers, regardless of how they wish to use their power.

Some good sorcerers are driven by the need to prove themselves. Marked as different by their power, they seek to win places in society and to prove themselves to others. Evil sorcerers also feel themselves set apart from others—apart and above. They adventure to gain power over those they look down upon.

TABLE 3–16: THE SORCERER

Level	Base Attack Bonus	Fort Save	Ref Save	Will Save	Special	Spells per Day									
						0	1st	2nd	3rd	4th	5th	6th	7th	8th	9th
1st	+0	+0	+0	+2	Summon familiar	5	3	—	—	—	—	—	—	—	—
2nd	+1	+0	+0	+3		6	4	—	—	—	—	—	—	—	—
3rd	+1	+1	+1	+3		6	5	—	—	—	—	—	—	—	—
4th	+2	+1	+1	+4		6	6	3	—	—	—	—	—	—	—
5th	+2	+1	+1	+4		6	6	4	—	—	—	—	—	—	—
6th	+3	+2	+2	+5		6	6	5	3	—	—	—	—	—	—
7th	+3	+2	+2	+5		6	6	6	4	—	—	—	—	—	—
8th	+4	+2	+2	+6		6	6	6	5	3	—	—	—	—	—
9th	+4	+3	+3	+6		6	6	6	6	4	—	—	—	—	—
10th	+5	+3	+3	+7		6	6	6	6	5	3	—	—	—	—
11th	+5	+3	+3	+7		6	6	6	6	6	4	—	—	—	—
12th	+6/+1	+4	+4	+8		6	6	6	6	6	5	3	—	—	—
13th	+6/+1	+4	+4	+8		6	6	6	6	6	6	4	—	—	—
14th	+7/+2	+4	+4	+9		6	6	6	6	6	6	5	3	—	—
15th	+7/+2	+5	+5	+9		6	6	6	6	6	6	6	4	—	—
16th	+8/+3	+5	+5	+10		6	6	6	6	6	6	6	5	3	—
17th	+8/+3	+5	+5	+10		6	6	6	6	6	6	6	6	4	—
18th	+9/+4	+6	+6	+11		6	6	6	6	6	6	6	6	5	3
19th	+9/+4	+6	+6	+11		6	6	6	6	6	6	6	6	6	4
20th	+10/+5	+6	+6	+12		6	6	6	6	6	6	6	6	6	6

Characteristics: Sorcerers cast spells through innate power rather than through careful training and study. Their magic is intuitive rather than logical. Sorcerers know fewer spells than wizards do and acquire powerful spells more slowly than wizards, but they can cast spells more often and have no need to select and prepare their spells ahead of time. Sorcerers do not specialize in certain schools of magic the way wizards sometimes do.

FAMILIARS

Familiars are magically linked to their masters. In some sense, the familiar and the master are practically one being. That's why, for example, the master can cast a personal range spell on a familiar even though he can normally cast such a spell only on himself. A familiar is a normal animal that gains new powers and becomes a magical beast when summoned to service by a sorcerer or wizard. It retains the appearance, Hit Dice, base attack bonus, base save bonuses, skills, and feats of the normal animal it once was, but it is treated as a magical beast instead of an animal for the purpose of any effect that depends on its type. Only a normal, unmodified animal may become a familiar. Thus, a druid/sorcerer can't use her animal companion as a familiar.

A familiar also grants special abilities to its master (a sorcerer or wizard), as given on the table below. These special abilities apply only when the master and familiar are within 1 mile of each other.

Levels of different classes that are entitled to familiars (such as sorcerer and wizard) stack for the purpose of determining any familiar abilities that depend on the master's level.

Familiar	Special
Bat	Master gains a +3 bonus on Listen checks
Cat	Master gains a +3 bonus on Move Silently checks
Hawk	Master gains a +3 bonus on Spot checks in bright light
Lizard	Master gains a +3 bonus on Climb checks
Owl	Master gains a +3 bonus on Spot checks in shadows
Rat	Master gains a +2 bonus on Fortitude saves
Raven[1]	Master gains a +3 bonus on Appraise checks
Snake[2]	Master gains a +3 bonus on Bluff checks
Toad	Master gains +3 hit points
Weasel	Master gains a +2 bonus on Reflex saves

1 A raven familiar can speak one language of its master's choice as a supernatural ability.

2 Tiny viper.

Familiar Basics: Use the basic statistics for a creature of the familiar's kind, as given in the *Monster Manual*, but make the following changes:

Hit Dice: For the purpose of effects related to number of Hit Dice, use the master's character level or the familiar's normal HD total, whichever is higher.

Hit Points: The familiar has one-half the master's total hit points (not including temporary hit points), rounded down, regardless of its actual Hit Dice. For example, at 2nd level, Hennet has 9 hit points, so his familiar has 4.

Attacks: Use the master's base attack bonus, as calculated from all his classes. Use the familiar's Dexterity or Strength modifier, whichever is greater, to get the familiar's melee attack bonus with natural weapons. Damage equals that of a normal creature of the familiar's kind.

Saving Throws: For each saving throw, use either the familiar's base save bonus (Fortitude +2, Reflex +2, Will +0) or the master's (as calculated from all his classes), whichever is better. The familiar uses its own ability modifiers to saves, and it doesn't share any of the other bonuses that the master might have on saves (from magic items or feats, for example).

Skills: For each skill in which either the master or the familiar has ranks, use either the normal skill ranks for an animal of that type or the master's skill ranks, whichever are better. In either case, the familiar uses its own ability modifiers. Regardless of a familiar's total skill modifiers, some skills (such as Craft) may remain beyond the familiar's ability to use.

Familiar Ability Descriptions: All familiars have special abilities (or impart abilities to their masters) depending on the master's combined level in classes that grant familiars, as shown on the table below. The abilities given on the table are cumulative.

Natural Armor Adj.: The number noted here is an improvement to the familiar's existing natural armor bonus. It represents the preternatural toughness of a spellcaster's familiar.

Since sorcerers gain their powers without undergoing the years of rigorous study that wizards go through, they don't have the background of arcane knowledge than most wizards have. However, they do have more time to learn fighting skills, and they are proficient with simple weapons.

Alignment: For a sorcerer, magic is an intuitive art, not a science. Sorcery favors the free, chaotic, creative spirit over the disciplined mind, so sorcerers tend slightly toward chaos over law.

Religion: Some sorcerers favor Boccob (god of magic), while others revere Wee Jas (goddess of death and magic). However, many sorcerers follow other deities, or none at all. (Wizards typically learn to follow Boccob or Wee Jas from their mentors, but most sorcerers are self-taught, with no master to induct them into a religion.)

Background: Sorcerers develop rudimentary powers at puberty. Their first spells are incomplete, spontaneous, uncontrolled, and sometimes dangerous. A household with a budding sorcerer in it may be troubled by strange sounds or lights, which can create the impression that the place is haunted. Eventually, the young sorcerer understands the power that he has been wielding unintentionally. From that point on, he can begin practicing and improving his powers.

Sometimes a sorcerer is fortunate enough to come under the care of an older, more experienced sorcerer, someone who can help him understand and use his new powers. More often, however, sorcerers are on their own, feared by erstwhile friends and misunderstood by family.

Sorcerers have no sense of identity as a group. Unlike wizards, they gain little by sharing their knowledge and have no strong incentive to work together.

Races: Most sorcerers are humans or half-elves, but the innate talent for sorcery is unpredictable, and it can show up in any of the common races.

Arcane spellcasters from savage lands or from among the brutal humanoids are more likely to be sorcerers than wizards. Kobolds are especially likely to take up this path, and they are fierce, if inarticulate, proponents of the "blood of the dragons" theory.

Other Classes: Sorcerers find that they have the most in common with members of other largely self-taught classes, such as druids and rogues. They sometimes find themselves at odds with members of the more disciplined classes, such as paladins and monks. Since they cast the same spells as wizards but do so in a different way, they sometimes find themselves in competition with wizards.

Role: A sorcerer tends to define his role based on his spell selection. A sorcerer who focuses on damage-dealing spells becomes a center of the party's offensive power. Another may rely on more subtle magics, such as charms and illusions, and thus take a quieter role. A party with a sorcerer should strongly consider including a second spellcaster, such as a bard, cleric, druid, or even a wizard, to make up for the sorcerer's lack of versatility. Since a sorcerer often has a powerful presence that gives him a way with people, he may serve as the "face" for an adventuring party, negotiating, bargaining, and speaking for others. The sorcerer's spells often help him sway others or gain information, so he makes an excellent spy or diplomat for an adventuring group.

Int: The familiar's Intelligence score. Familiars are as smart as people, though not necessarily as smart as smart people.

Alertness (Ex): The presence of the familiar sharpens its master's senses. While a familiar is within arm's reach, the master gains the Alertness feat (page 89).

Improved Evasion (Ex): When subjected to an attack that normally allows a Reflex saving throw for half damage, a familiar takes no damage if it makes a successful saving throw and half damage even if the saving throw fails.

Share Spells: At the master's option, he may have any spell (but not any spell-like ability) he casts on himself also affect his familiar. The familiar must be within 5 feet at the time of casting to receive the benefit. If the spell or effect has a duration other than instantaneous, it stops affecting the familiar if it moves farther than 5 feet away and will not affect the familiar again even if it returns to the master before the duration expires. Additionally, the master may cast a spell with a target of "You" on his familiar (as a touch range spell) instead of on himself. A master and his familiar can share spells even if the spells normally do not affect creatures of the familiar's type (magical beast).

Empathic Link (Su): The master has an empathic link with his familiar out to a distance of up to 1 mile. The master cannot see through the familiar's eyes, but they can communicate empathically. Because of the limited nature of the link, only general emotional content (such as fear, hunger, happiness, curiosity) can be communicated. Note that the low Intelligence of a low-level master's familiar limits what the creature is able to communicate or understand, and even intelligent familiars see the world differently from humans, so misunderstandings are always possible.

Because of this empathic link, the master has the same connection to an item or place that his familiar does. For instance, if his familiar has seen a room, the master can teleport into that room as if he has seen it too.

Deliver Touch Spells (Su): If the master is 3rd level or higher, a familiar can deliver touch spells for him. If the master and the familiar are in contact at the time the master casts a touch spell, he can designate his familiar as the "toucher." The familiar can then deliver the touch spell just as the master could. As usual, if the master casts another spell before the touch is delivered, the touch spell dissipates.

Speak with Master (Ex): If the master is 5th level or higher, a familiar and the master can communicate verbally as if they were using a common language. Other creatures do not understand the communication without magical help.

Speak with Animals of Its Kind (Ex): If the master is 7th level or higher, a familiar can communicate with animals of approximately the same kind as itself (including dire varieties): bats with bats, rats with rodents, cats with felines, hawks and owls and ravens with birds, lizards and snakes with reptiles, toads with amphibians, weasels with similar creatures of the family Mustelidae (weasels, minks, polecats, ermines, skunks, wolverines, and badgers). Such communication is limited by the intelligence of the conversing creatures.

Spell Resistance (Ex): If the master is 11th level or higher, a familiar gains spell resistance equal to the master's level + 5. To affect the familiar with a spell, another spellcaster must get a result on a caster level check (1d20 + caster level; see Spell Resistance, page 177) that equals or exceeds the familiar's spell resistance.

Scry on Familiar (Sp): If the master is 13th level or higher, he may scry on his familiar (as if casting the *scrying* spell) once per day.

Master Class Level	Natural Armor Adj.	Int	Special
1st–2nd	+1	6	Alertness, improved evasion, share spells, empathic link
3rd–4th	+2	7	Deliver touch spells
5th–6th	+3	8	Speak with master
7th–8th	+4	9	Speak with animals of its kind
9th–10th	+5	10	—
11th–12th	+6	11	Spell resistance
13th–14th	+7	12	*Scry* on familiar
15th–16th	+8	13	—
17th–18th	+9	14	—
19th–20th	+10	15	—

GAME RULE INFORMATION

Sorcerers have the following game statistics.

Abilities: Charisma determines how powerful a spell a sorcerer can cast, how many spells he can cast per day, and how hard those spells are to resist (see Spells, below). Like a wizard, a sorcerer benefits from high Dexterity and Constitution scores.

Alignment: Any.

Hit Die: d4.

Class Skills

The sorcerer's class skills (and the key ability for each skill) are Bluff (Cha), Concentration (Con), Craft (Int), Knowledge (arcana) (Int), Profession (Wis), and Spellcraft (Int). See Chapter 4: Skills for skill descriptions.

Skill Points at 1st Level: (2 + Int modifier) × 4.

Skill Points at Each Additional Level: 2 + Int modifier.

TABLE 3–17: SORCERER SPELLS KNOWN

Level	0	1st	2nd	3rd	4th	5th	6th	7th	8th	9th
1st	4	2	—	—	—	—	—	—	—	—
2nd	5	2	—	—	—	—	—	—	—	—
3rd	5	3	—	—	—	—	—	—	—	—
4th	6	3	1	—	—	—	—	—	—	—
5th	6	4	2	—	—	—	—	—	—	—
6th	7	4	2	1	—	—	—	—	—	—
7th	7	5	3	2	—	—	—	—	—	—
8th	8	5	3	2	1	—	—	—	—	—
9th	8	5	4	3	2	—	—	—	—	—
10th	9	5	4	3	2	1	—	—	—	—
11th	9	5	5	4	3	2	—	—	—	—
12th	9	5	5	4	3	2	1	—	—	—
13th	9	5	5	4	4	3	2	—	—	—
14th	9	5	5	4	4	3	2	1	—	—
15th	9	5	5	4	4	4	3	2	—	—
16th	9	5	5	4	4	4	3	2	1	—
17th	9	5	5	4	4	4	3	3	2	—
18th	9	5	5	4	4	4	3	3	2	1
19th	9	5	5	4	4	4	3	3	3	2
20th	9	5	5	4	4	4	3	3	3	3

Class Features

All of the following are class features of the sorcerer.

Weapon and Armor Proficiency: Sorcerers are proficient with all simple weapons. They are not proficient with any type of armor or shield. Armor of any type interferes with a sorcerer's arcane gestures, which can cause his spells with somatic components to fail.

Spells: A sorcerer casts arcane spells (the same type of spells available to bards and wizards), which are drawn primarily from the sorcerer/wizard spell list (page 192). He can cast any spell he knows without preparing it ahead of time, the way a wizard or a cleric must (see below).

To learn or cast a spell, a sorcerer must have a Charisma score equal to at least 10 + the spell level (Cha 10 for 0-level spells, Cha 11 for 1st-level spells, and so forth). The Difficulty Class for a saving throw against a sorcerer's spell is 10 + the spell level + the sorcerer's Charisma modifier.

Like other spellcasters, a sorcerer can cast only a certain number of spells of each spell level per day. His base daily spell allotment is given on Table 3–16: The Sorcerer. In addition, he receives bonus spells per day if he has a high Charisma score (see Table 1–1: Ability Modifiers and Bonus Spells, page 8).

A sorcerer's selection of spells is extremely limited. A sorcerer begins play knowing four 0-level spells (also called cantrips) and two 1st-level spells of your choice. At each new sorcerer level, he gains one or more new spells, as indicated on Table 3–17: Sorcerer

Spells Known. (Unlike spells per day, the number of spells a sorcerer knows is not affected by his Charisma score; the numbers on Table 3–17 are fixed.) These new spells can be common spells chosen from the sorcerer/wizard spell list (page 192), or they can be unusual spells that the sorcerer has gained some understanding of by study. For example, a sorcerer with a scroll or spellbook detailing an unusual sorcerer/wizard spell (one not on the sorcerer/wizard spell list in this book) could select that spell as one of his new spells for attaining a new level, provided that it is of the right spell level. The sorcerer can't use this method of spell acquisition to learn spells at a faster rate, however.

Upon reaching 4th-level sorcerer level after that (6th, 8th, and so on), a sorcerer can choose to learn a new spell in place of one he already knows. In effect, the sorcerer "loses" the old spell in exchange for the new one. The new spell's level must be the same as that of the spell being exchanged, and it must be at least two levels lower than the highest-level sorcerer spell the sorcerer can cast. For instance, upon reaching 4th level, a sorcerer could trade in a single 0-level spell (two spell levels below the highest-level sorcerer spell he can cast, which is 2nd) for a different 0-level spell. At 6th level, he could trade in a single 0-level or 1st-level spell (since he now can cast 3rd-level sorcerer spells) for a different spell of the same level. A sorcerer may swap only a single spell at any given level, and must choose whether or not to swap the spell at the same time that he gains new spells known for the level.

Unlike a wizard or a cleric, a sorcerer need not prepare his spells in advance. He can cast any spell he knows at any time, assuming he has not yet used up his spells per day for that spell level. For example, at 1st level, the sorcerer Hennet can cast four 1st-level spells per day—three for being 1st level (see Table 3–16: The Sorcerer), plus one thanks to his Charisma score of 15 (see Table 1–1: Ability Modifiers and Bonus Spells, page 8). However, he knows only two 1st-level spells: *magic missile* and *sleep* (see Table 3–17: Sorcerer Spells Known). Thus, on any given day, he can cast some combination of the two spells a total of four times. He does not have to decide ahead of time which spells he'll cast.

Familiar: A sorcerer can obtain a familiar. Doing so takes 24 hours and uses up magical materials that cost 100 gp. A familiar is a magical beast that resembles a small animal and is unusually tough and intelligent. The creature serves as a companion and servant.

The sorcerer chooses the kind of familiar he gets. As the sorcerer advances in level, his familiar also increases in power.

If the familiar dies or is dismissed by the sorcerer, the sorcerer must attempt a DC 15 Fortitude saving throw. Failure means he loses 200 experience points per sorcerer level; success reduces the loss to one-half that amount. However, a sorcerer's experience point total can never go below 0 as the result of a familiar's demise or dismissal. For example, suppose that Hennet is a 3rd-level sorcerer with 3,230 XP when his owl familiar is killed by a bugbear. Hennet makes a successful saving throw, so he loses 300 XP, dropping him below 3,000 XP and back to 2nd level (see the *Dungeon Master's Guide* for rules for losing levels). A slain or dismissed familiar cannot be replaced for a year and day. A slain familiar can be raised from the dead just as a character can be, and it does not lose a level or a Constitution point when this happy event occurs.

A character with more than one class that grants a familiar may have only one familiar at a time.

Human Sorcerer Starting Package

Armor: None (speed 30 ft.).

Weapons: Shortspear (1d6, crit ×2, range inc. 20 ft., 3 lb., one-handed, piercing).

Light crossbow (1d8, crit 19–20/×2, range inc. 80 ft., 4 lb., piercing).

Skill Selection: Pick a number of skills equal to 3 + Int modifier.

Skill	Ranks	Ability	Armor Check Penalty
Spellcraft	4	Int	—
Concentration	4	Con	—
Knowledge (arcana)	4	Int	—
Bluff	4	Cha	—
Gather Information (cc)	2	Cha	—
Diplomacy (cc)	2	Cha	—
Hide (cc)	2	Dex	0
Move Silently (cc)	2	Dex	0

Feat: Toughness.

Bonus Feat: Combat Casting.

Spells Known: 0-level spells—*detect magic, ghost sound, light, read magic.*

1st-level spells—*magic missile, sleep.*

Gear: Backpack with waterskin, one day's trail rations, bedroll, sack, and flint and steel. Hooded lantern, five pints of oil. Spell component pouch. Case with 10 crossbow bolts.

Gold: 3d4 gp.

WIZARD

A few unintelligible words and fleeting gestures carry more power than a battleaxe, when they are the words and gestures of a wizard. These simple acts make magic seem easy, but they only hint at the time the wizard must spend poring over her spellbook preparing each spell for casting, and the years before that spent in apprenticeship to learn the arts of magic.

Wizards depend on intensive study to create their magic. They examine musty old tomes, debate magical theory with their peers, and practice minor magics whenever they can. For a wizard, magic is not a talent but a difficult, rewarding art.

Adventures: Wizards conduct their adventures with caution and forethought. When prepared, they can use their spells to devastating effect. When caught by surprise, they are vulnerable. They seek knowledge, power, and the resources to conduct their studies. They may also have any of the noble or ignoble motivations that other adventurers have.

Characteristics: The wizard's strength is her spells. Everything else is secondary. She learns new spells as she experiments and grows in experience, and she can also learn them from other wizards. In addition to learning new spells, a wizard can, over time,

learn to manipulate her spells so they go farther, work better, or are improved in some other way.

Some wizards prefer to specialize in a certain type of magic. Specialization makes a wizard more powerful in her chosen field, but it denies her access to some of the spells that lie outside that field. (See School Specialization, page 57.)

Like a sorcerer, a wizard can call a familiar—a small, magical animal companion that serves her. For some wizards, their familiars are their only true friends.

Alignment: Overall, wizards show a slight tendency toward law over chaos because the study of magic rewards those who are disciplined. Illusionists and transmuters, however, are masters of deception and change, respectively. They favor chaos over law.

Religion: Wizards commonly revere Boccob (god of magic). Some, especially necromancers or simply more misanthropic wizards, prefer Wee Jas (goddess of death and magic). Evil necromancers are known to worship Nerull (god of death). Wizards in general are more devoted to their studies than to their spiritual sides.

Background: Wizards recognize each other as comrades or rivals. Even wizards from very different cultures or magical traditions have much in common because they all conform to the same laws of magic. Unlike fighters or rogues, wizards see themselves as members of a distinct, if diverse, group. In civilized lands where they study in academies, schools, or guilds, wizards also identify themselves and others according to membership in these formal organizations. But while a guild magician may look down her nose at a rustic wizard who learned his arts from a doddering hermit, she nevertheless can't deny the rustic's identity as a wizard.

Races: Humans take to magic for any of various reasons: curiosity, ambition, lust for power, or just personal inclination. Human wizards tend to be practical innovators, creating new spells or using old spells creatively.

Elves are enthralled by magic, and many of them become wizards for love of the art. Elf wizards see themselves as artists, and they hold magic in high regard as a wondrous mystery, as opposed to the more pragmatic human wizards, who see magic more as a set of tools or tricks.

Illusion magic comes so simply to gnomes that becoming an illusionist is just natural for the brighter and more talented ones. Gnome wizards who don't specialize in the school of illusion are rare, but they don't suffer under any special stigma.

TABLE 3–18: THE WIZARD

Level	Base Attack Bonus	Fort Save	Ref Save	Will Save	Special	0	1st	2nd	3rd	4th	5th	6th	7th	8th	9th
1st	+0	+0	+0	+2	Summon familiar, Scribe Scroll	3	1	—	—	—	—	—	—	—	—
2nd	+1	+0	+0	+3		4	2	—	—	—	—	—	—	—	—
3rd	+1	+1	+1	+3		4	2	1	—	—	—	—	—	—	—
4th	+2	+1	+1	+4		4	3	2	—	—	—	—	—	—	—
5th	+2	+1	+1	+4	Bonus feat	4	3	2	1	—	—	—	—	—	—
6th	+3	+2	+2	+5		4	3	3	2	—	—	—	—	—	—
7th	+3	+2	+2	+5		4	4	3	2	1	—	—	—	—	—
8th	+4	+2	+2	+6		4	4	3	3	2	—	—	—	—	—
9th	+4	+3	+3	+6		4	4	4	3	2	1	—	—	—	—
10th	+5	+3	+3	+7	Bonus feat	4	4	4	3	3	2	—	—	—	—
11th	+5	+3	+3	+7		4	4	4	4	3	2	1	—	—	—
12th	+6/+1	+4	+4	+8		4	4	4	4	3	3	2	—	—	—
13th	+6/+1	+4	+4	+8		4	4	4	4	4	3	2	1	—	—
14th	+7/+2	+4	+4	+9		4	4	4	4	4	3	3	2	—	—
15th	+7/+2	+5	+5	+9	Bonus feat	4	4	4	4	4	4	3	2	1	—
16th	+8/+3	+5	+5	+10		4	4	4	4	4	4	3	3	2	—
17th	+8/+3	+5	+5	+10		4	4	4	4	4	4	4	3	2	1
18th	+9/+4	+6	+6	+11		4	4	4	4	4	4	4	3	3	2
19th	+9/+4	+6	+6	+11		4	4	4	4	4	4	4	4	3	3
20th	+10/+5	+6	+6	+12	Bonus feat	4	4	4	4	4	4	4	4	4	4

Half-elf wizards feel both the elf's attraction to magic and the human's drive to conquer and understand. Some of the most powerful wizards are half-elves.

Dwarf and halfling wizards are rare because their societies don't encourage the study of magic. Half-orc wizards are rare because few half-orcs have the brains necessary for wizardry.

Drow (evil subterranean elves) often take up wizardry, but wizards are quite rare among the savage humanoids.

Other Classes: Wizards prefer to work with members of other classes. They love to cast their spells from behind strong fighters, to "magic up" rogues and send them out to scout, and to rely on the divine healing of clerics. They may find members of certain classes (such as sorcerers, rogues, and bards) to be not quite serious enough, but they're not judgmental.

Role: The wizard's role depends somewhat on her spell selection, but most wizards share certain similarities in function. They are among the most offensively minded of the spellcasting classes, with a broad range of options available for neutralizing enemies. Some wizards provide great support to their comrades by way of their spells, while others may focus on divination or other facets of wizardry.

GAME RULE INFORMATION

Wizards have the following game statistics.

Abilities: Intelligence determines how powerful a spell a wizard can cast, how many spells she can cast, and how hard those spells are to resist (see Spells, below). A high Dexterity score is helpful for a wizard, who typically wears little or no armor, because it provides her with a bonus to Armor Class. A good Constitution score gives a wizard extra hit points, a resource that she is otherwise very low on.

Alignment: Any.

Hit Die: d4.

Mialee

Class Skills

The wizard's class skills (and the key ability for each skill) are Concentration (Con), Craft (Int), Decipher Script (Int), Knowledge (all skills, taken individually) (Int), Profession (Wis), and Spellcraft (Int). See Chapter 4: Skills for skill descriptions.

Skill Points at 1st Level: (2 + Int modifier) × 4.

Skill Points at Each Additional Level: 2 + Int modifier.

Class Features

All of the following are class features of the wizard.

Weapon and Armor Proficiency: Wizards are proficient with the club, dagger, heavy crossbow, light crossbow, and quarterstaff, but not with any type of armor or shield. Armor of any type interferes with a wizard's movements, which can cause her spells with somatic components to fail.

Spells: A wizard casts arcane spells (the same type of spells available to sorcerers and bards), which are drawn from the sorcerer/wizard spell list (page 192). A wizard must choose and prepare her spells ahead of time (see below).

To learn, prepare, or cast a spell, the wizard must have an Intelligence score equal to at least 10 + the spell level (Int 10 for 0-level spells, Int 11 for 1st-level spells, and so forth). The Difficulty Class for a saving throw against a wizard's spell is 10 + the spell level + the wizard's Intelligence modifier.

Like other spellcasters, a wizard can cast only a certain number of spells of each spell level per day. Her base daily spell allotment is given on Table 3–18: The Wizard. In addition, she receives bonus spells per day if she has a high Intelligence score (see Table 1–1: Ability Modifiers and Bonus Spells, page 8).

ARCANE SPELLS AND ARMOR

Wizards and sorcerers do not know how to wear armor effectively. If desired, they can wear armor anyway (though they'll be clumsy in it), or they can gain training in the proper use of armor (with the various Armor Proficiency feats—light, medium, and heavy—and the Shield Proficiency feat), or they can multiclass to add a class that grants them armor proficiency (see Multiclass Characters later in this chapter). Even if a wizard or sorcerer is wearing armor with which he or she is proficient, however, it might still interfere with spellcasting.

Most characters have a difficult time casting arcane spells while wearing armor or carrying shields (see Arcane Spell Failure, page 122). The armor restricts the complicated gestures that they must make while casting any spell that has a somatic component (most do). To find the arcane spell failure chance for a wizard or sorcerer wearing a certain type of armor, see Table 7–6: Armor and Shields (page 123).

By contrast, bards not only know how to wear light armor effectively, but they can also ignore the arcane spell failure chance for such armor. However, they too wear heavier armor ineffectively and must either learn to wear heavier armor via the appropriate Armor Proficiency feat (medium or heavy) or add a class (such as fighter) that grants them such proficiency as a class feature. A bard wearing armor heavier than light or using any type of shield incurs the normal arcane spell failure chance, even if he becomes proficient with that armor.

If a spell doesn't have a somatic component, an arcane spellcaster can cast it with no problem while wearing armor. Such spells can also be cast even if the caster's hands are bound or if he or she is grappling (although Concentration checks still apply normally). Also, the metamagic feat Still Spell allows a spellcaster to prepare or cast a spell at one spell level higher than normal without the somatic component. This also provides a way to cast a spell while wearing armor without risking arcane spell failure. See Chapter 5: Feats for more about metamagic feats such as Still Spell.

Unlike a bard or sorcerer, a wizard may know any number of spells (see Writing a New Spell into a Spellbook, page 179). She must choose and prepare her spells ahead of time by getting a good night's sleep and spending 1 hour studying her spellbook. While studying, the wizard decides which spells to prepare (see Preparing Wizard Spells, page 177).

Bonus Languages: A wizard may substitute Draconic for one of the bonus languages available to the character because of her race (see Chapter 2: Races). Many ancient tomes of magic are written in Draconic, and apprentice wizards often learn it as part of their studies.

Familiar: A wizard can obtain a familiar in exactly the same manner as a sorcerer can. See the sorcerer description and the accompanying Familiars sidebar for details.

Scribe Scroll: At 1st level, a wizard gains Scribe Scroll as a bonus feat. This feat enables her to create magic scrolls (see Scribe Scroll, page 99, and Creating Magic Items, page 282 of the *Dungeon Master's Guide*).

Bonus Feats: At 5th, 10th, 15th, and 20th level, a wizard gains a bonus feat. At each such opportunity, she can choose a metamagic feat, an item creation feat, or Spell Mastery. The wizard must still meet all prerequisites for a bonus feat, including caster level minimums. (See Chapter 5 for descriptions of feats and their prerequisites.)

These bonus feats are in addition to the feat that a character of any class gets every three levels (as given on Table

Nebin [gnome illusionist]

3–2: Experience and Level-Dependent Benefits, page 22). The wizard is not limited to the categories of item creation feats, metamagic feats, or Spell Mastery when choosing these feats.

Spellbooks: A wizard must study her spellbook each day to prepare her spells (see Preparing Wizard Spells, page 177). She cannot prepare any spell not recorded in her spellbook, except for *read magic*, which all wizards can prepare from memory.

A wizard begins play with a spellbook containing all 0-level wizard spells (except those from her prohibited school or schools, if any; see School Specialization, page 57) plus three 1st-level spells of your choice. For each point of Intelligence bonus the wizard has (see Table 1–1: Ability Modifiers and Bonus Spells, page 8), the spellbook holds one additional 1st-level spell of your choice. At each new wizard level, she gains two new spells of any spell level or levels that she can cast (based on her new wizard level) for her spellbook. For example, when a wizard attains 5th level, she can cast 3rd-level spells. At this point, she can add two new 3rd-level spells to her spellbook, or one 2nd-level spell and one 3rd-level spell, or any combination of two spells between 1st and 3rd level. At any time, a wizard can also add spells found in other wizards' spellbooks to her own (see Adding Spells to a Wizard's Spellbook, page 178).

SCHOOL SPECIALIZATION

A school is one of eight groupings of spells, each defined by a common theme, such as illusion or necromancy. If desired, a wizard may specialize in one school of magic (see below). Specialization allows a wizard to cast extra spells from her chosen school, but she then never learns to cast spells from some other schools. Essentially, the wizard gains exceptional mastery over a single school by neglecting the study of other schools.

A specialist wizard can prepare one additional spell of her specialty school per spell level each day. She also gains a +2 bonus on Spellcraft checks to learn the spells of her chosen school (see Adding Spells to a Wizard's Spellbook, page 178).

The wizard must choose whether to specialize and, if she does so, choose her specialty at 1st level. At this time, she must also give up two other schools of magic (unless she chooses to specialize in divination; see below), which become her prohibited schools. For instance, if she chooses to specialize in conjuration, she might decide to give up enchantment and necromancy, or evocation and transmutation. A wizard can never give up divination to fulfill this requirement. Spells of the prohibited school or schools are not available to the wizard, and she can't even cast such spells from scrolls or fire them from wands. She may not change either her specialization or her prohibited schools later.

The eight schools of arcane magic are abjuration, conjuration, divination, enchantment, evocation, illusion, necromancy, and trans-

mutation. Spells that do not fall into any of these schools are called universal spells.

Abjuration: Spells that protect, block, or banish. An abjuration specialist is called an abjurer.

Conjuration: Spells that bring creatures or materials to the caster. A conjuration specialist is called a conjurer.

Divination: Spells that reveal information. A divination specialist is called a diviner. Unlike the other specialists, a diviner must give up only one other school.

Enchantment: Spells that imbue the recipient with some property or grant the caster power over another being. An enchantment specialist is called an enchanter.

Evocation: Spells that manipulate energy or create something from nothing. An evocation specialist is called an evoker.

Illusion: Spells that alter perception or create false images. An illusion specialist is called an illusionist.

Necromancy: Spells that manipulate, create, or destroy life or life force. A necromancy specialist is called a necromancer.

Transmutation: Spells that transform the recipient physically or change its properties in a more subtle way. A transmutation specialist is called a transmuter.

Universal: Not a school, but a category for spells that all wizards can learn. A wizard cannot select universal as a specialty school or as a prohibited school. Only a limited number of spells fall into this category.

Elf Wizard Starting Package

Armor: None (speed 30 ft.).

Weapons: Quarterstaff (1d6/1d6, crit ×2, 4 lb., two-handed, bludgeoning).

Light crossbow (1d8, crit 19–20/×2, range inc. 80 ft., 4 lb., piercing).

Skill Selection: Pick a number of skills equal to 2 + Int modifier.

Skill	Ranks	Ability	Armor Check Penalty
Spellcraft	4	Int	—
Concentration	4	Con	—
Knowledge (arcana)	4	Int	—
Decipher Script	4	Int	—
Hide (cc)	2	Dex	0
Move Silently (cc)	2	Dex	0
Search (cc)	2	Int	—
Spot (cc)	2	Wis	—

Feat: Toughness.

School Specialization: None.

Spellbook: All 0-level spells, plus *charm person, summon monster I,* and *sleep,* plus one of these spells of your choice per point of Intelligence bonus (if any): *cause fear, color spray, magic missile,* and *silent image.*

Gear: Backpack with waterskin, one day's trail rations, bedroll, sack, and flint and steel. Ten candles, map case, three pages of parchment, ink, inkpen. Spell component pouch, spellbook. Case with 10 crossbow bolts.

Gold: 3d6 gp.

EXPERIENCE AND LEVELS

Experience points (XP) measure how much your character has learned and how much he or she has grown in personal power. Your character earns XP by defeating monsters and other opponents. The DM assigns XP to the characters at the end of each adventure based on what they have accomplished. Characters accumulate XP from one adventure to another. When a character earns enough XP, he or she attains a new character level (see Table 3–2: Experience and Level-Dependent Benefits, page 22).

Advancing a Level: When your character's XP total reaches at least the minimum XP needed for a new character level (see Table 3–2), he or she "goes up a level." For example, when Tordek obtains 1,000 or more XP, he becomes a 2nd-level character. As soon as he accumulates a total of 3,000 XP or higher (2,000 more than he had when he gained 2nd level), he reaches 3rd level. Going up a level provides the character with several immediate benefits (see below).

A character can advance only one level at a time. If, for some extraordinary reason, a character's XP reward from a single adventure would be enough to advance two or more levels at once, he or she instead advances one level and gains just enough XP to be 1 XP short of the next level. Any excess experience points are not retained. For example, if Tordek has 5,000 XP (1,000 points short of 4th level) and gains 6,000 more, he would normally be at 11,000 XP—enough for 5th level. Instead, he attains 4th level, and his XP total stands at 9,999.

Training and Practice: Characters spend time between adventures training, studying, or otherwise practicing their skills. This work consolidates what they learn on adventures and keeps them in top form. If, for some reason, a character can't practice or train for an extended time, the DM may reduce XP awards or even cause the character to lose experience points.

LEVEL ADVANCEMENT

Each character class description includes a table that shows how the class features and statistics increase as a member of that class advances in level. When your character attains a new level, make these changes.

1. Choose Class: A typical character has only one class, and when he or she attains a new level, it is a new level in that class. If your character has more than one class or wants to acquire a new class, you choose which class goes up one level. The other class or classes stay at the previous level. (See Multiclass Characters, page 59.)

2. Base Attack Bonus: The base attack bonus for fighters, barbarians, rangers, and paladins increases by 1 every level. The base attack bonus for other characters increases at a slower rate. If your character's base attack bonus changes, record it on your character sheet.

3. Base Save Bonuses: Like base attack bonuses, base save bonuses improve at varying rates as characters increase in level. Check your character's base save bonuses for the class that has advanced in level to see if any of them have increased by 1. Some base save bonuses increase at every even-numbered level; others increase at every level divisible by three.

4. Ability Score: If your character has just attained 4th, 8th, 12th, 16th, or 20th character level, choose one of his or her ability scores and raise it by 1 point. (It's okay for a score to go above 18.) It's the overall character level, not the class level, that counts for this adjustment.

If your character's Constitution modifier increases by 1 (see Table 1–1: Ability Modifiers and Bonus Spells, page 8), add +1 to his or her hit point total for every character level below the one just attained. For example, if you raise your character's Constitution from 11 to 12 at 4th level, he or she gets +3 hit points (one each for 1st, 2nd, and 3rd levels). Add these points before rolling for hit points (the next step).

5. Hit Points: Roll a Hit Die, add your character's Constitution modifier, and add the total roll to his or her hit points. Even if the character has a Constitution penalty and the roll was so low as to yield a result of 0 or fewer hit points, always add at least 1 hit point upon gaining a new level.

6. Skill Points: Each character gains skill points to spend on skills as detailed in the appropriate class description. For class skills, each skill point buys 1 rank, and a character's maximum rank in the skill is his or her character level + 3. For cross-class skills, each skill point only buys 1/2 rank, and the maximum rank in the skill is one-half that of a class skill (don't round up or down). See Table 3–2: Experience and Level-Dependent Benefits, page 22.

If you have been "maxing out" a skill (putting as many skill points into it as possible), you don't have to worry about calculating your maximum rank with it. At each new level, you can always assign 1 skill point—and just 1—to any skill that you're maxing out. (If it's a cross-class skill, this point buys 1/2 rank.)

Remember that you buy skills based on the class you have advanced in, so that only those skills given as class skills for that class can be purchased as class skills for this level, regardless of what other classes you may have levels in.

Your character's Intelligence modifier affects the number of skill points he or she gets at each level (see Table 1–1: Ability Modifiers and Bonus Spells, page 8). This rule represents an intelligent character's ability to learn faster over time. Use your character's current Intelligence score, including all permanent changes (such as inherent bonuses, ability drains, or an Intelligence increase gained at step 4, above) but not any temporary changes (such as ability damage, or enhancement bonuses gained from spells or magic items, such as a *headband of intellect*), to determine the number of skill points you gain.

7. **Feats:** Upon attaining 3rd level and at every third level thereafter (6th, 9th, 12th, 15th, and 18th level), the character gains one feat of your choice (see Table 5–1: Feats, page 90). The character must meet any prerequisites for the feat in order to select it. As with ability score increases, it is the overall character level, not the class level, that determines when a character gets a new feat.

8. **Spells:** Spellcasting characters gain the ability to cast more spells as they advance in levels. Each class description for a spellcasting class includes a Spells per Day section (on the class table) that shows the base number of spells (without bonus spells for high ability scores) of a given spell level that a character can cast at each class level. See your character's class description in this chapter for details.

9. **Class Features:** Check your character's class description in this chapter for any new capabilities your character may receive. Many characters gain special attacks or new special powers as they advance in levels.

MULTICLASS CHARACTERS

A character may add new classes as he or she progresses in level, thus becoming a multiclass character. The class abilities from a character's different classes combine to determine a multiclass character's overall abilities. Multiclassing improves a character's versatility at the expense of focus.

CLASS AND LEVEL FEATURES

As a general rule, the abilities of a multiclass character are the sum of the abilities of each of the character's classes.

Level: "Character level" is a character's total number of levels. It is used to determine when feats and ability score boosts are gained, as noted on Table 3–2: Experience and Level-Dependent Benefits (page 22).

"Class level" is a character's level in a particular class. For a character whose levels are all in the same class, character level and class level are the same.

Hit Points: A character gains hit points from each class as his or her class level increases, adding the new hit points to the previous total. For example, Lidda the halfling began as a rogue and attained 4th level, then added levels of wizard at her next two level advancements. As a 4th-level rogue/2nd-level wizard, her total hit points are 6 + 1d6 + 1d6 + 1d6 + 1d4 + 1d4.

Base Attack Bonus: Add the base attack bonuses acquired for each class to get the character's base attack bonus. A resulting value of +6 or higher provides the character with multiple attacks. Find the character's base attack bonus on Table 3–1: Base Save and Base Attack Bonuses (page 22) to see how many additional attacks the character gets and at what bonuses. For instance, a 6th-level rogue/4th-level wizard would have a base attack bonus of +6 (+4 for the rogue class and +2 for the wizard class). A base attack bonus of +6 allows a second attack with a bonus of +1 (given as +6/+1 on Table 3–1), even though neither the +4 from the rogue levels nor the +2 from the wizard levels normally allows an extra attack.

Saving Throws: Add the base save bonuses for each class together. A 7th-level rogue/4th-level wizard has a +3 base save bonus on Fortitude saving throws (+2 as a 7th-level rogue and +1 as a 4th-level wizard), a +6 on Reflex saving throws (+5 and +1), and a +6 on Will saving throws (+2 and +4).

Skills: If a skill is a class skill for any of a multiclass character's classes, then character level determines a skill's maximum rank. (The maximum rank for a class skill is 3 + character level.)

If a skill is not a class skill for any of a multiclass character's classes, the maximum rank for that skill is one-half the maximum for a class skill.

For example, a 7th-level rogue/4th-level wizard (an 11th-level character) can have as many as 14 ranks in any skill that is a class skill for rogues or wizards. That same character can have as many as 7 ranks in any skill that is not a class skill for rogues or wizards.

Class Features: A multiclass character gets all the class features of all his or her classes but must also suffer the consequences of the special restrictions of all his or her classes. (*Exception:* A character who acquires the barbarian class does not become illiterate.) Some class features don't work well with the skills or class features of other classes. For example, although rogues are proficient with light armor, a rogue/wizard still has an arcane spell failure chance if wearing armor.

In the special case of turning undead, both clerics and experienced paladins have the same ability. If the character's paladin level is 4th or higher, her effective turning level is her cleric level plus her paladin level minus 3. Thus, a 5th-level paladin/4th-level cleric turns undead as a 6th-level cleric.

In the special case of uncanny dodge, both experienced barbarians and experienced rogues have the same ability. When a barbarian/rogue would gain uncanny dodge a second time (for her second class), she instead gains improved uncanny dodge, if she does not already have it. Her barbarian and rogue levels stack to determine the rogue level an attacker needs to flank her. For example, a 2nd-level barbarian/4th-level rogue could only be flanked by a rogue of at least 10th level.

In the special case of obtaining a familiar, both wizards and sorcerers have the same ability. A sorcerer/wizard stacks his sorcerer and wizard levels to determine the familiar's natural armor, Intelligence score, and special abilities.

Feats: A multiclass character gains a feat every three character levels, regardless of individual class level (see Table 3–2: Experience and Level-Dependent Benefits, page 22).

Ability Increases: A multiclass character increases one ability score by 1 point every four character levels, regardless of individual class level (see Table 3–2: Experience and Level-Dependent Benefits, page 22).

Spells: The character gains spells from all of his or her spellcasting classes. Thus, an experienced ranger/druid may have access to the spell *protection from elements* both as a ranger and as a druid. Since the spell's effect is based on the class level of the caster, the player must keep track of whether the character is preparing and casting *protection from elements* as a ranger or as a druid.

ADDING A SECOND CLASS

When a character with one class gains a level, he or she may choose to increase the level of his or her current class or pick up a new class at 1st level. (A character can't gain 1st level in the same class more than once, even if this would allow him or her to select different class features, such as a different set of domains for a cleric.) The DM may restrict the choices available based on the way he or she handles classes, skills, experience, and training. For instance, the character may need to find a tutor to teach him or her the ways of the new class. Additionally, the DM may require the player to declare what class the character is "working on" before he or she makes the jump to the next level, so the character has time to practice new skills.

The character gains the 1st-level base attack bonus, base save bonuses, class skills, weapon proficiencies, armor and shield proficiencies, spells, other class features of the new class, hit points of the appropriate Hit Die type, and the new class's number of skill points gained at each additional level (not that number × 4, as is the case for a 1st-level character).

Picking up a new class is not exactly the same as starting a character in that class. Some of the benefits a 1st-level character gains (such as four times the usual number of skill points) represent the advantage of training while the character was young and fresh, with lots of time to practice. When picking up a new class, a character does not receive the following starting benefits given to characters who begin their careers in that class.

- Maximum hit points from the first Hit Die.
- Quadruple the per-level skill points.
- Starting equipment.
- Starting gold.

ADVANCING A LEVEL

A multiclass character who attains a new level either increases one of his or her current class levels by one or picks up a new class at 1st level.

When a multiclass character advances a level in a current class, he or she gets all the standard benefits that a character normally receives for attaining that level in that class: more hit points, possible bonuses on attack rolls, Armor Class, and saving throws (depending on the class and the new level), possible new class features (as defined by the class), possible new spells, and new skill points.

Skill points must be spent according to the class that the multiclass character just advanced in (see Table 4–1: Skill Points per Level, page 62). Skills purchased from Table 4–2: Skills are purchased at the cost appropriate for that class.

Rules for characters beyond 20th level (including multiclass characters beyond 20th level) are covered in the *Dungeon Master's Guide*.

XP FOR MULTICLASS CHARACTERS

Developing and maintaining skills and abilities in more than one class is a demanding process. Depending on a character's class levels and race, he or she might or might not take an XP penalty.

Even Levels: If your multiclass character's classes are nearly the same level (all within one class level of each other), then he or she can balance the needs of the multiple classes without penalty. For instance, a 4th-level wizard/3rd-level rogue takes no penalty, nor does a 2nd-level fighter/2nd-level wizard/3rd-level rogue.

Uneven Levels: If any two of your multiclass character's classes are two or more levels apart, the strain of developing and maintaining different skills at different levels takes its toll. Your multiclass character takes a –20% penalty to XP for each class that is not within one level of his or her highest-level class. These penalties apply from the moment the character adds a class or raises a class's level too high. For instance, a 4th-level wizard/3rd-level rogue gets no penalty, but if that character raises his wizard level to 5th, then he takes the –20% penalty from that point on until his levels were nearly even again.

Races and Multiclass XP: A favored class (see the individual race entries in Chapter 2: Races) does not count against the character for purposes of the –20% penalty to XP. In such cases, calculate the XP penalty as if the character did not have that class. For instance, Bergwin is an 11th-level gnome character (a 9th-level rogue/2nd-level bard). He takes no penalty to his XP because he has only one nonfavored class. (Bard is favored for gnomes.) Suppose he then attains 12th level and adds 1st level as a fighter to his classes, becoming a 9th-level rogue/2nd-level bard/1st-level fighter. He then takes a –20% penalty on future XP he earns because his fighter level is so much lower than his rogue level. Were he awarded 1,200 XP for an adventure, he would receive only 80% of that amount, or 960 XP. If he thereafter rose to 13th level and picked up a fourth class (by adding

1st-level cleric, for example), he would take a –40% XP penalty from then on.

As a second example, consider a dwarf 7th-level fighter/2nd-level cleric. This character takes no penalty because his fighter class is favored for dwarves and thus not counted when determining whether his classes are even. Nor does he take any penalty for adding 1st-level rogue to the mix, since his cleric and rogue classes are only one level apart. In this case, cleric counts as the character's highest class.

A human's or half-elf's highest-level class is always considered his or her favored class.

HOW MULTICLASSING WORKS

Lidda, a 4th-level halfling rogue, decides to expand her repertoire by learning some wizardry. She locates a mentor who teaches her the ways of a wizard, and she spends a lot of time looking over the shoulder of Mialee, her party's wizard, while the latter prepares her spells each morning. When Lidda amasses 10,000 XP, she becomes a 5th-level character. Instead of becoming a 5th-level rogue, however, she becomes a 4th-level rogue/1st-level wizard. Now, instead of gaining the benefits of attaining a new level as a rogue, she gains the benefits of a 1st-level wizard. She gains a wizard's Hit Die (d4), a 1st-level wizard's +2 bonus on Will saves, and 4 skill points (2 for one wizard level +2 for the Intelligence bonus derived from her Intelligence score of 14) that she can spend as a wizard. These benefits are added to the scores she already had as a rogue. Her base attack bonus, Reflex save bonus, and Fortitude save bonus do not increase because these numbers are +0 for a 1st-level wizard. She gains a 1st-level wizard's beginning spellbook and spells per day. Her rogue skills and sneak attack capability, however, do not improve. She could spend some of her 4 skill points to improve her rogue skills, but, since they would be treated as cross-class skills for a wizard, these skill points would each buy only one-half rank. (The exceptions are any Craft or Profession skills she may have, since Craft and Profession are class skills for both the rogue and the wizard.)

On reaching 15,000 XP, she becomes a 6th-level character. She decides she'd like to continue along the wizard path, so she increases her wizard level instead of her rogue level. Again she gains the wizard's benefits for attaining a new level rather than the rogue's. As a 2nd-level wizard, she gains another d4 Hit Die, her base attack bonus and base Will save bonus each go up by +1, she gains 4 more skill points, and she can now prepare another 0-level spell and another 1st-level spell each day (as noted on Table 3–18: The Wizard). Additionally, as a 6th-level character overall, she gets her third feat (see Table 3–2: Experience and Level-Dependent Benefits, page 22).

At this point, Lidda is a 6th-level character: a 4th-level rogue/2nd-level wizard. She casts spells as a 2nd-level wizard does, and she sneak attacks as a 4th-level rogue does. Her combat skill is a little better than a 4th-level rogue's would be, because she has learned something about fighting during her time as a wizard. (Her base attack bonus went up by +1 when she became a 2nd-level wizard.) Her base Reflex save bonus is +4 (+4 from her rogue class and +0 from her wizard class), better than a 6th-level wizard's but not as good as a 6th-level rogue's. Her base Will save bonus is +4 (+1 from her rogue class and +3 from her wizard class), better than a 6th-level rogue's but not as good as a 6th-level wizard's.

At each new level, Lidda must decide whether to increase her rogue level or her wizard level. Of course, if she really wants to have diverse abilities, she could even acquire a third class— maybe fighter.

Illus. by A. Swekel

L idda the rogue can walk quietly up to a door, put her ear to it, and hear the troglodyte priest on the other side casting a spell on his pet crocodile. If Jozan the cleric were to try the same thing, he'd probably make so much noise that the troglodyte would hear him. Jozan could, however, identify the spell that the evil priest is casting. Actions such as these rely on the skills that characters have (in this case, Move Silently, Listen, and Spellcraft).

SKILLS SUMMARY

A character's skills represent a variety of abilities. As a character advances in level, he or she gets better at using some or all of her skills.

Getting Skills: A character gets a base allotment of 2, 4, 6, or 8 skill points for each new level, depending on the class to which that level was added. If the character gaining his or her 1st character level overall (that is, gaining his or her first level in any class), add his or her Intelligence modifier to the base skill point allotment for the class and multiply the total by four; then add an extra 4 points if the character is human.

If you buy a class skill (such as Listen for a rogue or Spellcraft for a cleric), your character gets 1 rank (equal to a +1 bonus on checks with that skill) for each skill point. If you buy other classes' skills (cross-class skills), you get 1/2 rank per skill point. Your maximum rank in a class skill is your character level + 3. Your maximum rank in a cross-class skill is one-half of this number (do not round up or down).

Using Skills: To make a skill check, roll:

1d20 + skill modifier
(Skill modifier = skill rank + ability modifier
+ miscellaneous modifiers)

This roll works just like an attack roll or a saving throw—the higher the roll, the better. Either you're trying to match or exceed a certain Difficulty Class (DC), or you're trying to beat another character's check result. For instance, to sneak quietly past a guard, Lidda needs to beat the guard's Listen check result with her own Move Silently check result.

Skill Ranks: A character's number of ranks in a skill is based on how many skill points a character has invested in a skill. Many skills can be used even if the character has no ranks in them; doing this is called making an untrained skill check.

Ability Modifier: The ability modifier used in a skill check is the modifier for the skill's key ability (the ability associated with the skill's use). The key ability of each skill is noted in its description and on Table 4–2: Skills.

Miscellaneous Modifiers: Miscellaneous modifiers include racial bonuses, armor check penalties, and bonuses provided by feats, among others.

ACQUIRING SKILL RANKS

Ranks indicate how much training or experience your character has with a given skill. Each of his or her skills has a rank, ranging from 0 (for a skill in which your character has no training at all) to a number equal to 3 + character level (for a character who has increased a skill to its maximum rank). When making a skill check, you add your character's skill ranks to the roll as part of the skill modifier, so the more ranks you have, the higher your skill check result will be.

Ranks tell you how proficient you are and reflect your training in a given skill. In general, while anyone can get a lucky roll, a character with, say, 10 ranks in a given skill has a higher degree of training and expertise in that skill than a character with 9 ranks or fewer.

The class starting packages in Chapter 3 provide an easy way to select 1st-level skills, because they assume that you max out (increase to maximum rank) each skill you buy and because they provide a shorter list from which to choose. Although selecting skills from a starting package feels very different from buying them rank by rank, your character winds up spending the same number of skill points no matter which way you select 1st-level skills.

The Skills paragraph on page 59 covers the skill acquisition rules for multiclass characters.

TABLE 4–1: SKILL POINTS PER LEVEL

Class	1st-Level Skill Points[1]	Higher-Level Skill Points[2]
Barbarian	(4 + Int modifier) × 4	4 + Int modifier
Bard	(6 + Int modifier) × 4	6 + Int modifier
Cleric	(2 + Int modifier) × 4	2 + Int modifier
Druid	(4 + Int modifier) × 4	4 + Int modifier
Fighter	(2 + Int modifier) × 4	2 + Int modifier
Monk	(4 + Int modifier) × 4	4 + Int modifier
Paladin	(2 + Int modifier) × 4	2 + Int modifier
Ranger	(6 + Int modifier) × 4	6 + Int modifier
Rogue	(8 + Int modifier) × 4	8 + Int modifier
Sorcerer	(2 + Int modifier) × 4	2 + Int modifier
Wizard	(2 + Int modifier) × 4	2 + Int modifier

1 Humans add +4 to this total at 1st level.
2 Humans add +1 each level.

ACQUIRING SKILLS AT 1ST LEVEL

Follow these steps to pick skills for your 1st-level character:

1. Determine the number of skill points your character gets. This number depends on his or her class and Intelligence modifier, as shown on Table 4–1: Skill Points per Level. For example, Lidda is a 1st-level halfling rogue with an Intelligence score of 14 (+2 Int modifier). At the start of play, she has 40 skill points to spend (8 + 2 = 10; 10 × 4 = 40).

A character gets at least 4 skill points (1 × 4 = 4) at 1st level, even if he or she has an Intelligence penalty.

A human gets 4 extra skill points as a 1st-level character. A human character with the same class and Intelligence modifier as Lidda would have 44 skill points at the start of play.

2. Spend the skill points. Each skill point you spend on a class skill gets you 1 rank in that skill. Class skills are the skills found on your character's class skill list. Each skill point you spend on a

cross-class skill gets your character 1/2 rank in that skill. Cross-class skills are skills not found on your character's class skill list. (Half ranks do not improve your skill check, but two 1/2 ranks make 1 rank.) Your maximum rank in a class skill is 4. In a cross-class skill, it's 2.

Table 4–2: Skills shows all the skills and indicates which are class skills and which are cross-class skills for each class.

Spend all your skill points. You can't save them to spend later.

SKILLS AT HIGHER LEVELS

When your character attains a new level, follow these steps to gain new skills and improve those he or she already has.

1. Determine the number of skill points your character gets. See Table 4–1: Skill Points per Level.

A character gets at least 1 skill point at each new level, even if he or she has an Intelligence penalty.

A human gets 1 extra skill point per level.

2. You can improve any class skill that you've previously maxed out by 1 rank or any cross-class skill that you've previously maxed out by 1/2 rank.

3. If you have not maxed out a skill, you can spend extra skill points on it and increase its rank further.

First, find out what your character's maximum rank in that skill is. If it's a class skill, the maximum rank is the character's new level + 3. If it's a cross-class skill, the maximum rank is half of that number (do not round up or down).

You may spend the number of skill points it takes to max out the skill, provided that you have that many skill points to spend.

4. If you want to pick up a new skill for your character, you can spend skill points equal to his or her character level + 3. These skill points buy 1 rank each if the new skill is a class skill or 1/2 rank each if it's a cross-class skill.

Regardless of whether a skill is purchased as a class skill or a cross-class skill, if it is a class skill for any of your classes, your maximum rank equals your total character level + 3.

USING SKILLS

When your character uses a skill, you make a skill check to see how well he or she does. The higher the result of the skill check, the better. Based on the circumstances, your result must match or beat a particular number (a DC or the result of an opposed skill check) for the check to be successful. The harder the task, the higher the number you need to roll.

Circumstances can affect your check. A character who is free to work without distractions can make a careful attempt and avoid simple mistakes. A character who has lots of time can try over and over again, thereby assuring the best outcome. If others help, the character may succeed where otherwise he or she would fail.

CHARACTER SKILLS

When you create your character, you will probably only be able to purchase ranks in a handful of skills. It may not seem as though you have as many skills as real people do—but the skills on your character sheet don't actually define everything your character can do.

Your character may have solid familiarity with many skills, without having the actual training that grants skill ranks. Knowing how to strum a few chords on a lute or clamber over a low fence doesn't really mean you have ranks in Perform or Climb. Ranks in those skills represent training beyond everyday use—the ability to impress an audience with a wide repertoire of songs on the lute, or to successfully scale a 100-foot-high cliff face.

So how do normal people get through life without ranks in a lot of skills? For starters, remember that not every use of a skill

requires a skill check. Performing routine tasks in normal situations is generally so easy that no check is required. And when a check might be called for, the DC of most mundane tasks rarely exceeds 10, let alone 15. In day-to-day life, when you don't have enemies breathing down your neck and your life depending on success, you can take your time and do things right—making it easy, even without any ranks in the requisite skill, to succeed (see Checks without Rolls, page 65).

You're always welcome to assume that your character is familiar with—even good at, as far as everyday tasks go—many skills beyond those for which you actually gain ranks. The skills you buy ranks in, however, are those with which you have truly heroic potential.

TABLE 4–2: SKILLS

Skill	Bbn	Brd	Clr	Drd	Ftr	Mnk	Pal	Rgr	Rog	Sor	Wiz	Untrained	Key Ability
Appraise	cc	C	cc	cc	cc	cc	cc	cc	C	cc	cc	Yes	Int
Balance	cc	C	cc	cc	cc	C	cc	cc	C	cc	cc	Yes	Dex[1]
Bluff	cc	C	cc	cc	cc	cc	cc	cc	C	C	cc	Yes	Cha
Climb	C	C	cc	cc	C	C	cc	C	C	cc	cc	Yes	Str[1]
Concentration	cc	C	C	C	cc	C	C	C	cc	C	C	Yes	Con
Craft	C	C	C	C	C	C	C	C	C	C	C	Yes	Int
Decipher Script	cc	C	cc	cc	cc	cc	cc	cc	C	cc	C	No	Int
Diplomacy	cc	C	C	C	cc	C	C	cc	cc	cc	cc	Yes	Cha
Disable Device	cc	cc	cc	cc	cc	cc	cc	cc	C	cc	cc	No	Int
Disguise	cc	C	cc	cc	cc	cc	cc	cc	C	cc	cc	Yes	Cha
Escape Artist	cc	C	cc	cc	cc	C	cc	cc	C	cc	cc	Yes	Dex[1]
Forgery	cc	cc	cc	cc	cc	cc	cc	cc	C	cc	cc	Yes	Int
Gather Information	cc	C	cc	cc	cc	cc	cc	cc	C	cc	cc	Yes	Cha
Handle Animal	C	cc	cc	C	C	cc	C	C	cc	cc	cc	No	Cha
Heal	cc	cc	C	C	cc	cc	C	C	cc	cc	cc	Yes	Wis
Hide	cc	C	cc	cc	cc	C	cc	C	C	cc	cc	Yes	Dex[1]
Intimidate	C	cc	cc	cc	C	cc	cc	cc	C	cc	cc	Yes	Cha
Jump	C	C	cc	cc	C	C	cc	C	C	cc	cc	Yes	Str[1]
Knowledge (arcana)	cc	C	C	cc	cc	C	cc	cc	cc	C	C	No	Int
Knowledge (architecture and engineering)	cc	C	cc	cc	cc	cc	cc	cc	cc	cc	C	No	Int
Knowledge (dungeoneering)	cc	C	cc	cc	cc	cc	cc	C	cc	cc	C	No	Int
Knowledge (geography)	cc	C	cc	cc	cc	cc	cc	C	cc	cc	C	No	Int
Knowledge (history)	cc	C	C	cc	cc	cc	cc	cc	cc	cc	C	No	Int
Knowledge (local)	cc	C	cc	cc	cc	cc	cc	cc	C	cc	C	No	Int
Knowledge (nature)	cc	C	cc	C	cc	cc	cc	C	cc	cc	C	No	Int
Knowledge (nobility and royalty)	cc	C	cc	cc	cc	cc	C	cc	cc	cc	C	No	Int
Knowledge (religion)	cc	C	C	cc	cc	C	C	cc	cc	cc	C	No	Int
Knowledge (the planes)	cc	C	C	cc	cc	cc	cc	cc	cc	cc	C	No	Int
Listen	C	C	cc	C	cc	C	cc	C	C	cc	cc	Yes	Wis
Move Silently	cc	C	cc	cc	cc	C	cc	C	C	cc	cc	Yes	Dex[1]
Open Lock	cc	cc	cc	cc	cc	cc	cc	cc	C	cc	cc	No	Dex
Perform	cc	C	cc	cc	cc	C	cc	cc	C	cc	cc	Yes	Cha
Profession	cc	C	C	C	cc	C	C	C	C	C	C	No	Wis
Ride	C	cc	cc	C	C	cc	C	C	cc	cc	cc	Yes	Dex
Search	cc	cc	cc	cc	cc	cc	cc	cc	C	C	cc	Yes	Int
Sense Motive	cc	C	cc	cc	cc	C	C	cc	C	cc	cc	Yes	Wis
Sleight of Hand	cc	C	cc	cc	cc	cc	cc	cc	C	cc	cc	No	Dex[1]
Speak Language	cc	C	cc	cc	cc	cc	cc	cc	cc	cc	cc	No	None
Spellcraft	cc	C	C	C	cc	cc	cc	cc	cc	C	C	No	Int
Spot	cc	cc	cc	C	cc	C	cc	C	C	cc	cc	Yes	Wis
Survival	C	cc	cc	C	cc	cc	cc	C	cc	cc	cc	Yes	Wis
Swim	C	C	cc	C	C	C	cc	C	C	cc	cc	Yes	Str[2]
Tumble	cc	C	cc	cc	cc	C	cc	cc	C	cc	cc	No	Dex[1]
Use Magic Device	cc	C	cc	cc	cc	cc	cc	cc	C	cc	cc	No	Cha
Use Rope	cc	cc	cc	cc	cc	cc	cc	C	C	cc	cc	Yes	Dex

1 Armor check penalty applies to checks.
2 Double the normal armor check penalty applies to checks.

SKILL CHECKS

A skill check takes into account a character's training (skill rank), natural talent (ability modifier), and luck (the die roll). It may also take into account his or her race's knack for doing certain things (racial bonus) or what armor he or she is wearing (armor check penalty), or a certain feat the character possesses, among other things. For instance, a character who has the Skill Focus feat (page 100) related to a certain skill gets a +3 bonus on all checks involving that skill.

To make a skill check, roll 1d20 and add your character's skill modifier for that skill. The skill modifier incorporates the character's ranks in that skill and the ability modifier for that skill's key ability, plus any other miscellaneous modifiers that may apply, including racial bonuses and armor check penalties. The higher the result, the better. Unlike with attack rolls and saving throws, a natural roll of 20 on the d20 is not an automatic success, and a natural roll of 1 is not an automatic failure.

Difficulty Class

Some checks are made against a Difficulty Class (DC). The DC is a number set by the DM (using the skill rules as a guideline) that you must score as a result on your skill check in order to succeed. For example, climbing the outer wall of a ruined tower may have a DC of 15. For your character to climb the wall, you must get a result of 15 or better on a Climb check. A Climb check is 1d20 + Climb ranks (if any) + Strength modifier + any other modifiers that apply. Table 4–3: Difficulty Class Examples shows some example DCs for skill checks.

TABLE 4–3: DIFFICULTY CLASS EXAMPLES

Difficulty (DC)	Example (Skill Used)
Very easy (0)	Notice something large in plain sight (Spot)
Easy (5)	Climb a knotted rope (Climb)
Average (10)	Hear an approaching guard (Listen)
Tough (15)	Rig a wagon wheel to fall off (Disable Device)
Challenging (20)	Swim in stormy water (Swim)
Formidable (25)	Open an average lock (Open Lock)
Heroic (30)	Leap across a 30-foot chasm (Jump)
Nearly impossible (40)	Track a squad of orcs across hard ground after 24 hours of rainfall (Survival)

Opposed Checks

An opposed check is a check whose success or failure is determined by comparing the check result to another character's check result. In an opposed check, the higher result succeeds, while the lower result fails. In case of a tie, the higher skill modifier wins. If these scores are the same, roll again to break the tie.

For example, to sneak up on someone, you make a Move Silently check. Anyone who might hear you can make a Listen check to react to your presence. For the opponent to hear you, his or her Listen check result must equal or exceed your Move Silently check result.

TABLE 4–4: EXAMPLE OPPOSED CHECKS

Task	Skill (Key Ability)	Opposing Skill (Key Ability)
Con someone	Bluff (Cha)	Sense Motive (Wis)
Pretend to be someone else	Disguise (Cha)	Spot (Wis)
Create a false map	Forgery (Int)	Forgery (Int)
Hide from someone	Hide (Dex)	Spot (Wis)
Make a bully back down	Intimidate (Cha)	Special[1]
Sneak up on someone	Move Silently (Dex)	Listen (Wis)
Steal a coin pouch	Sleight of Hand (Dex)	Spot (Wis)
Tie a prisoner securely	Use Rope (Dex)	Escape Artist (Dex)

1 An Intimidate check is opposed by the target's level check, not a skill check. See the Intimidate skill description, page 76, for more information.

Trying Again

In general, you can try a skill check again if you fail, and you can keep trying indefinitely. Some skills, however, have consequences of failure that must be taken into account. A few skills are virtually useless once a check has failed on an attempt to accomplish a particular task. For most skills, when a character has succeeded once at a given task, additional successes are meaningless.

For example, if Lidda the rogue misses an Open Lock check, she can try again and keep trying. If, however, a trap in the lock goes off if she misses an Open Lock check by 5 or more, then failure has its own penalties.

Similarly, if Lidda misses a Climb check, she can keep trying, but if she misses by 5 or more, she falls (after which she can get up and try again).

If Tordek has negative hit points and is dying, Lidda can make an untrained Heal check to make him stable. If the check fails, Tordek probably loses another hit point, but Lidda can try again in the next round.

If a skill carries no penalties for failure, you can take 20 and assume that you go at it long enough to eventually succeed eventually (see Checks without Rolls, page 65).

Untrained Skill Checks

Generally, if your character attempts to use a skill he or she does not possess, you make a skill check as normal. The skill modifier doesn't have a skill rank added in because the character has no ranks in the skill. Any other applicable modifiers, such as the modifier for the skill's key ability, are applied to the check.

Many skills can be used only by someone who is trained in them. If you don't have Spellcraft, for example, you just don't know enough about magic even to attempt to identify a spell, regardless of your class, ability scores, or experience level. Skills that cannot be used untrained are indicated by a "No" in the Untrained column on Table 4–2: Skills.

For example, Krusk the barbarian's 4 ranks in Climb make his Climb check results 4 points higher than they otherwise would be, but even Gimble the bard, with no Climb ranks, can make a Climb check because Climb can be used untrained. Gimble has a skill modifier of –1 (+0 for his Strength, –1 for armor), but he can give it a try. However, Gimble's ranks in Use Magic Device let him do something that he otherwise couldn't do at all—namely, use a magic item as if he had a particular spell on his class spell list that he actually doesn't have. Krusk, with no ranks in the skill, can't make a Use Magic Device check even at a penalty because Use Magic Device can't be used untrained.

Favorable and Unfavorable Conditions

Some situations may make a skill easier or harder to use, resulting in a bonus or penalty to the skill modifier for a skill check or a change to the DC of the skill check. It's one thing for Krusk, with his Survival skill, to hunt down enough food to eat while he's camping for the day in the middle of a lush forest, but foraging for food while traveling across barren desert is an entirely different matter.

The DM can alter the chance of success in four ways to take into account exceptional circumstances.

1. Give the skill user a +2 circumstance bonus to represent conditions that improve performance, such as having the perfect tool for the job, getting help from another character (see Combining Skill Attempts, page 65), or possessing unusually accurate information.

2. Give the skill user a –2 circumstance penalty to represent conditions that hamper performance, such as being forced to use improvised tools or having misleading information.

3. Reduce the DC by 2 to represent circumstances that make the task easier, such as having a friendly audience or doing work that can be subpar.

4. Increase the DC by 2 to represent circumstances that make the task harder, such as having an uncooperative audience or doing work that must be flawless.

Conditions that affect your character's ability to perform the skill change the skill modifier. Conditions that modify how well the character has to perform the skill to succeed change the DC. A bonus to the skill modifier and a reduction in the check's DC have the same result: They create a better chance of success. But they represent different circumstances, and sometimes that difference is important.

ACCESS TO SKILLS

The rules assume that a character can find a way to learn any skill. For instance, if Jozan wants to learn Profession (sailor), nothing in the rules exists to stop him. However, the DM is in charge of the world and makes all the decisions about where one can learn certain skills and where one can't. While Jozan is living in a desert, for example, the DM can decide that he has no way of learning to be a sailor. It's up to the DM to say whether a character can learn a given skill in a given setting.

For example, Gimble the bard wants to entertain a band of dwarves who are staying at the same inn where he and his party are staying. Before playing his lute, Gimble listens to the dwarves' drinking songs so he can judge their mood. Doing so improves his performance, giving him a +2 circumstance bonus on his check. His player rolls a 5 and adds +9 for his skill modifier (4 ranks, +3 Charisma modifier, and +2 for his impromptu research). His check result is 14. The DM sets the base DC at 15. However, the dwarves are in a good mood because they have recently won a skirmish with orc bandits, so the DM reduces the DC to 13. (Gimble's performance isn't better just because the dwarves are in a good mood, so Gimble doesn't get a bonus to add to his skill modifier. Instead, the DC goes down.) The leader of the dwarven band, however, has heard that a gnome spy works for the bandits, and he's suspicious of Gimble. The DC to entertain him is higher than normal: 17 instead of 15. Gimble's skill check result (14) is high enough to entertain the dwarves (DC 13) but not their leader (DC 17). The dwarves applaud Gimble and offer to buy him drinks, but their leader eyes him suspiciously.

Time and Skill Checks

Using a skill might take a round, take no time, or take several rounds or even longer. Most skill uses are standard actions, move actions, or full-round actions. Types of actions define how long activities take to perform within the framework of a combat round (6 seconds) and how movement is treated with respect to the activity (see Action Types, page 138). Some skill checks are instant and represent reactions to an event, or are included as part of an action. These skill checks are not actions. Other skill checks represent part of movement. The distance you jump when making a Jump check, for example, is part of your movement. Each skill description specifies the time required to make a check.

Practically Impossible Tasks

Sometimes you want to do something that seems practically impossible. In general, a task considered practically impossible has a DC of 40, 60, or even higher (or it carries a modifier of +20 or more to the DC).

Practically impossible tasks are hard to delineate ahead of time. They're the accomplishments that represent incredible, almost logic-defying skill and luck. Picking a lock by giving it a single, swift kick might entail a +20 modifier to the DC; swimming up a waterfall could require a Swim check against DC 80; and balancing on a fragile tree branch might have a DC of 90.

The DM decides what is actually impossible and what is merely practically impossible. Characters with very high skill modifiers are capable of accomplishing incredible, almost unbelievable tasks, just as characters with very high combat bonuses are.

Checks without Rolls

A skill check represents an attempt to accomplish some goal, usually while under some sort of time pressure or distraction. Sometimes, though, a character can use a skill under more favorable conditions and eliminate the luck factor.

Taking 10: When your character is not being threatened or distracted, you may choose to take 10. Instead of rolling 1d20 for the skill check, calculate your result as if you had rolled a 10. For many routine tasks, taking 10 makes them automatically successful. Distractions or threats (such as combat) make it impossible for a character to take 10. In most cases, taking 10 is purely a safety measure—you know (or expect) that an average roll will succeed but fear that a poor roll might fail, so you elect to settle for the average roll (a 10). Taking 10 is especially useful in situations where a particularly high roll wouldn't help (such as using Climb to ascend a knotted rope, or using Heal to give a wounded PC long-term care).

For example, Krusk the barbarian has a Climb skill modifier of +6 (4 ranks, +3 Strength modifier, −1 penalty for wearing studded leather armor). The steep, rocky slope he's climbing has a Climb DC of 10. With a little care, he can take 10 and succeed automatically. But partway up the slope, a goblin scout begins pelting him with sling stones. Krusk needs to make a Climb check to get up to the goblin, and this time he can't simply take 10. If his player rolls 4 or higher on 1d20, he succeeds.

Taking 20: When you have plenty of time (generally 2 minutes for a skill that can normally be checked in 1 round, one full-round action, or one standard action), you are faced with no threats or distractions, and the skill being attempted carries no penalties for failure, you can take 20. In other words, eventually you will get a 20 on 1d20 if you roll enough times. Instead of rolling 1d20 for the skill check, just calculate your result as if you had rolled a 20. Taking 20 means you are trying until you get it right, and it assumes that you fail many times before succeeding. Taking 20 takes twenty times as long as making a single check would take. Since taking 20 assumes that the character will fail many times before succeeding, if you did attempt to take 20 on a skill that carries penalties for failure (for instance, a Disable Device check to disarm a trap), your character would automatically incur those penalties before he or she could complete the task (in this case, the character would most likely set off the trap). Common "take 20" skills include Escape Artist, Open Lock, and Search.

For example, Krusk comes to a cliff face. He attempts to take 10, for a result of 16 (10 plus his +6 skill modifier), but the DC is 20, and the DM tells him that he fails to make progress up the cliff. (His check result is at least high enough that he does not fall.) Krusk cannot take 20 because there is a penalty associated with failure (falling, in this case). He can try over and over, and eventually he may succeed, but he might fall one or more times in the process. Later, Krusk finds a cave in the cliff and searches it. The DM sees in the Search skill description that each 5-foot-square area takes a full-round action to search, and she secretly assigns a DC of 15 to the attempt. She estimates that the floors, walls, and ceiling of the cave make up about ten 5-foot squares, so she tells Krusk's player that it takes 1 minute (10 rounds) to search the whole cave. Krusk's player gets a result of 12 on 1d20, adds no skill ranks because Krusk doesn't have the Search skill, and adds −1 because that is Krusk's Intelligence modifier. His roll fails. Now the player declares that Krusk is going to search the cavern high and low, taking as long as it takes. The DM takes the original time of 1 minute and multiplies it by 20, for 20 minutes. That's how long it takes for Krusk to search the whole cave in exacting detail. Now Krusk's player treats his roll as if it were 20, for a result of 19. That's good enough to beat the DC of 15, and Krusk finds an old bronze key under a loose rock.

Ability Checks and Caster Level Checks: The normal take 10 and take 20 rules apply for ability checks. Neither rule applies to caster level checks (such as when casting *dispel magic* or attempting to overcome spell resistance).

COMBINING SKILL ATTEMPTS

When more than one character tries the same skill at the same time and for the same purpose, their efforts may overlap.

Individual Events

Often, several characters attempt some action and each succeeds or fails independently.

For example, Krusk and each of his friends needs to climb a slope if they're all to get to the top. Regardless of Krusk's roll, the other characters need successful checks, too. Every character makes a skill check.

Aid Another

You can help another character achieve success on his or her skill check by making the same kind of skill check in a cooperative effort. If you roll a 10 or higher on your check, the character you are helping gets a +2 bonus to his or her check, as per the rule for favorable conditions. (You can't take 10 on a skill check to aid another.) In many cases, a character's help won't be beneficial, or only a limited number of characters can help at once. The DM limits cooperation as he or she sees fit for the given conditions.

For instance, if Krusk has been badly wounded and is dying, Jozan can try a Heal check to keep him from losing more hit points. One other character can help Jozan. If the other character makes a Heal check against DC 10, then Jozan gets a +2 circumstance bonus on the Heal check he makes to help Krusk. The DM rules that two characters couldn't help Jozan at the same time because a third person would just get in the way.

In cases where the skill restricts who can achieve certain results (such as with Disable Device, Search, and Survival), you can't aid another to grant a bonus to a task that your character couldn't achieve alone. For instance, a character who doesn't have the trapfinding class feature can't use Search to help a rogue find a magic trap, since the helper couldn't attempt to find the magic trap on his own.

Skill Synergy

It's possible for a character to have two skills that work well together, such as someone with both Jump and Tumble. In general, having 5 or more ranks in one skill gives the character a +2 bonus on skill checks with each of its synergistic skills, as noted in the skill description and on Table 4–5: Skill Synergies. In some cases, this bonus applies only to specific uses of the skill in question, and not to all checks. Some skills provide benefits on other checks made by a character, such as those checks required to use certain class features.

TABLE 4–5: SKILL SYNERGIES

5 or more ranks in . . .	Gives a +2 bonus on . . .
Bluff	Diplomacy checks
Bluff	Disguise checks to act in character
Bluff	Intimidate checks
Bluff	Sleight of Hand checks
Craft	related Appraise checks
Decipher Script	Use Magic Device checks involving scrolls
Escape Artist	Use Rope checks involving bindings
Handle Animal	Ride checks
Handle Animal	wild empathy checks (class feature)
Jump	Tumble checks
Knowledge	
(arcana)	Spellcraft checks
(architecture and engineering)	Search checks involving secret doors and similar compartments
(dungeoneering)	Survival checks when underground
(geography)	Survival checks to keep from getting lost or for avoiding hazards
(history)	bardic knowledge checks (class feature)
(local)	Gather Information checks
(nature)	Survival checks in aboveground natural environments
(nobility and royalty)	Diplomacy checks
(religion)	checks to turn or rebuke undead (class feature)
(the planes)	Survival checks when on other planes
Search	Survival checks when following tracks
Sense Motive	Diplomacy checks
Spellcraft	Use Magic Device checks involving scrolls
Survival	Knowledge (nature) checks
Tumble	Balance checks
Tumble	Jump checks
Use Magic Device	Spellcraft checks to decipher spells on scrolls
Use Rope	Climb checks involving climbing ropes
Use Rope	Escape Artist checks involving ropes

Your DM may limit certain synergies if desired, or he may add more synergies for specific situations.

ABILITY CHECKS

Sometimes a character tries to do something to which no specific skill really applies. In these cases, you make an ability check. An ability check is a roll of 1d20 plus the appropriate ability modifier. Essentially, you're making an untrained skill check. The DM assigns a Difficulty Class, or sets up an opposed check when two characters are engaged in a contest using one ability score or another. The initiative check in combat, for example, is essentially a Dexterity check. The character who rolls highest goes first.

In some cases, an action is a straight test of one's ability with no luck involved. Just as you wouldn't make a height check to see who is taller, you don't make a Strength check to see who is stronger. When two characters arm wrestle, for example, the stronger character simply wins. In the case of identical scores, roll a die.

TABLE 4–6: EXAMPLE ABILITY CHECKS

Task	Key Ability
Breaking open a jammed or locked door[1]	Strength
Threading a needle	Dexterity
Holding one's breath	Constitution
Navigating a maze	Intelligence
Recognizing a stranger you've seen before	Wisdom
Getting oneself singled out in a crowd	Charisma

1 See page 165 for information on breaking down doors and smashing objects.

SKILL DESCRIPTIONS

This section describes each skill, including common uses and typical modifiers. Characters can sometimes use skills for purposes other than those noted here. For example, you might be able to impress a bunch of riders by making a Ride check.

Here is the format for skill descriptions.

SKILL NAME

The skill name line includes (in addition to the name of the skill) the following information.

Key Ability: The abbreviation of the ability whose modifier applies to the skill check. *Exception:* Speak Language has "None" as its key ability because the use of this skill does not require a check.

Trained Only: If this notation is included in the skill name line, you must have at least 1 rank in the skill to use it. If it is omitted, the skill can be used untrained (with a rank of 0). If any special notes apply to trained or untrained use, they are covered in the Untrained section (see below).

Armor Check Penalty: If this notation is included in the skill name line, an armor check penalty applies (when appropriate) to checks using this skill. If this entry is absent, an armor check penalty does not apply.

The skill name line is followed by a general description of what using the skill represents. After the description are a few other types of information:

Check: What a character ("you" in the skill description) can do with a successful skill check and the check's DC.

Action: The type of action using the skill requires, or the amount of time required for a check.

Try Again: Any conditions that apply to successive attempts to use the skill successfully. If the skill doesn't allow you to attempt the same task more than once, or if failure carries an inherent penalty (such as with the Climb skill), you can't take 20. If this paragraph is omitted, the skill can be retried without any inherent penalty, other than the additional time required.

Special: Any extra facts that apply to the skill, such as special effects deriving from its use or bonuses that certain characters receive because of class, feat choices, or race.

Synergy: Some skills grant a bonus to the use of one or more other skills because of a synergistic effect. This entry, when present, indicates what bonuses this skill may grant or receive because of such synergies. See Table 4–5 for a complete list of bonuses granted by synergy between skills (or between a skill and a class feature).

Restriction: The full utility of certain skills is restricted to characters of certain classes or characters who possess certain feats. This entry indicates whether any such restrictions exist for the skill.

Untrained: This entry indicates what a character without at least 1 rank in the skill can do with it. If this entry doesn't appear, it means that the skill functions normally for untrained characters (if it can be used untrained) or that an untrained character can't attempt checks with this skill (for skills that are designated as "Trained Only").

APPRAISE (INT)

Use this skill to tell an antique from old junk, a sword that's old and fancy from an elven heirloom, and high-quality jewelry from cheap stuff made to look good.

Check: You can appraise common or well-known objects with a DC 12 Appraise check. Failure means that you estimate the value at 50% to 150% of its actual value. The DM secretly rolls 2d6+3, multiplies the result by 10%, multiplies the actual value by that percentage, then tells you the resulting value for the item. (For a common or well-known item, your chance of estimating the value within 10% is fairly high even if you fail the check—in such a case, you made a lucky guess.)

Appraising a rare or exotic item requires a successful check against DC 15, 20, or higher. If the check is successful, you estimate the value correctly; failure means you cannot estimate the item's value.

A magnifying glass (page 130) gives you a +2 circumstance bonus on Appraise checks involving any item that is small or highly detailed, such as a gem. A merchant's scale (page 130) gives you a +2 circumstance bonus on Appraise checks involving any items that are valued by weight, including anything made of precious metals. These bonuses stack.

Action: Appraising an item takes 1 minute (ten consecutive full-round actions).

Try Again: No. You cannot try again on the same object, regardless of success.

Special: A dwarf gets a +2 racial bonus on Appraise checks that are related to stone or metal items because dwarves are familiar with valuable items of all kinds (especially those made of stone or metal).

The master of a raven familiar (see the Familiars sidebar, page 52) gains a +3 bonus on Appraise checks.

A character with the Diligent feat gets a +2 bonus on Appraise checks.

Synergy: If you have 5 ranks in any Craft skill, you gain a +2 bonus on Appraise checks related to items made with that Craft skill (see Craft, page 70).

Untrained: For common items, failure on an untrained check means no estimate. For rare items, success means an estimate of 50% to 150% (2d6+3 times 10%).

BALANCE (DEX; ARMOR CHECK PENALTY)

You can keep your balance while walking on a tightrope, a narrow beam, a slippery ledge, or an uneven floor.

Check: You can walk on a precarious surface. A successful check lets you move at half your speed along the surface for 1 round. A failure by 4 or less means you can't move for 1 round. A failure by 5 or more means you fall. The difficulty varies with the surface, as follows:

Narrow Surface	Balance DC[1]	Difficult Surface	Balance DC[1]
7–12 inches wide	10	Uneven flagstone	10[2]
2–6 inches wide	15	Hewn stone floor	10[2]
Less than 2 inches wide	20	Sloped or angled floor	10[2]

1 Add modifiers from Narrow Surface Modifiers, below, as appropriate.
2 Only if running or charging. Failure by 4 or less means the character can't run or charge, but may otherwise act normally.

Narrow Surface Modifiers

Surface	DC Modifier[1]
Lightly obstructed (scree, light rubble)	+2
Severely obstructed (natural cavern floor, dense rubble)	+5
Lightly slippery (wet floor)	+2
Severely slippery (ice sheet)	+5
Sloped or angled	+2

1 Add the appropriate modifier to the Balance DC of a narrow surface. These modifiers stack.

Being Attacked while Balancing: You are considered flat-footed while balancing, since you can't move to avoid a blow, and thus you lose your Dexterity bonus to AC (if any). If you have 5 or more ranks in Balance, you aren't considered flat-footed while balancing. If you take damage while balancing, you must make another Balance check against the same DC to remain standing.

Accelerated Movement: You can try to walk across a precarious surface more quickly than normal. If you accept a –5 penalty, you can move your full speed as a move action. (Moving twice your speed in a round requires two Balance checks, one for each move action used.) You may also accept this penalty in order to charge across a precarious surface; charging requires one Balance check for each multiple of your speed (or fraction thereof) that you charge.

Action: None. A Balance check doesn't require an action; it is made as part of another action or as a reaction to a situation.

Special: If you have the Agile feat, you get a +2 bonus on Balance checks.

Synergy: If you have 5 or more ranks in Tumble, you get a +2 bonus on Balance checks.

BLUFF (CHA)

You can make the outrageous or the untrue seem plausible, or use doublespeak or innuendo to deliver a secret message to another character. The skill encompasses acting, conning, fast talking, misdirection, prevarication, and misleading body language. Use a bluff to sow temporary confusion, get someone to turn and look where you point, or simply look innocuous.

Check: A Bluff check is opposed by the target's Sense Motive check. See the accompanying table for examples of different kinds of bluffs and the modifier to the target's Sense Motive check for each one.

BLUFF EXAMPLES

Example Circumstances	Sense Motive Modifier
The target wants to believe you.	−5
"These emeralds aren't stolen. I'm just desperate for coin right now, so I'm offering them to you cheap."	
The bluff is believable and doesn't affect the target much.	+0
"I don't know what you're talking about, sir. I'm just a simple peasant girl here for the fair."	
The bluff is a little hard to believe or puts the target at some risk.	+5
"You orcs want to fight? I'll take you all on myself. I don't need my friends' help. Just don't get your blood all over my new surcoat."	
The bluff is hard to believe or puts the target at significant risk.	+10
"This diadem doesn't belong to the duchess. It just looks like hers. Trust me, I wouldn't sell you jewelry that would get you hanged, would I?"	
The bluff is way out there, almost too incredible to consider.	+20
"You might find this hard to believe, but I'm actually a lammasu who's been polymorphed into halfling form by an evil sorcerer. You know we lammasus are trustworthy, so you can believe me."	

Favorable and unfavorable circumstances weigh heavily on the outcome of a bluff. Two circumstances can weigh against you: The bluff is hard to believe, or the action that the target is asked to take goes against its self-interest, nature, personality, orders, or the like. If it's important, the DM can distinguish between a bluff that fails because the target doesn't believe it and one that fails because it just asks too much of the target. For instance, if the target gets a +10 bonus on its Sense Motive check because the bluff demands something risky, and the Sense Motive check succeeds by 10 or less, then the target didn't so much see through the bluff as prove reluctant to go along with it. A target that succeeds by 11 or more has seen through the bluff (and would have done so even if that bluff had not entailed any demand).

A successful Bluff check indicates that the target reacts as you wish, at least for a short time (usually 1 round or less) or believes something that you want it to believe. Bluff, however, is not a *suggestion* spell. For example, you could use a bluff to put a shopkeeper off guard by saying that his shoes are untied. At best, such a bluff would make the shopkeeper glance down at his shoes. It would not cause him to ignore you and fiddle with his shoes.

A bluff requires interaction between you and the target. Creatures unaware of you cannot be bluffed.

Feinting in Combat: You can also use Bluff to mislead an opponent in melee combat (so that it can't dodge your next attack effectively). To feint, make a Bluff check opposed by your target's Sense Motive check, but in this case, the target may add its base attack bonus to the roll along with any other applicable modifiers. If your Bluff check result exceeds this special Sense Motive check result, your target is denied its Dexterity bonus to AC (if any) for the next melee attack you make against it. This attack must be made on or before your next turn.

Feinting in this way against a nonhumanoid is difficult because it's harder to read a strange creature's body language; you take a −4 penalty on your Bluff check. Against a creature of animal Intelligence (1 or 2) it's even harder; you take a −8 penalty. Against a non-intelligent creature, it's impossible.

Feinting in combat does not provoke an attack of opportunity.

Creating a Diversion to Hide: You can use the Bluff skill to help you hide. A successful Bluff check gives you the momentary diversion you need to attempt a Hide check while people are aware of you. This usage does not provoke an attack of opportunity.

Delivering a Secret Message: You can use Bluff to get a message across to another character without others understanding it. Two rogues, for example, might seem to be talking about bakery goods when they're really planning how to break into the evil wizard's laboratory. The DC is 15 for simple messages, or 20 for complex messages, especially those that rely on getting across new information. Failure by 4 or less means you can't get the message across. Failure by 5 or more means that some false information has been implied or inferred. Anyone listening to the exchange can make a Sense Motive check opposed by the Bluff check you made to transmit in order to intercept your message (see Sense Motive, page 81).

Action: Varies. A Bluff check made as part of general interaction always takes at least 1 round (and is at least a full-round action), but it can take much longer if you try something elaborate. A Bluff check made to feint in combat or create a diversion to hide is a standard action. A Bluff check made to deliver a secret message doesn't take an action; it is part of normal communication. However, the DM may limit the amount of information you can convey in a single round.

Try Again: Varies. Generally, a failed Bluff check in social interaction makes the target too suspicious for you to try again in the same circumstances, but you may retry freely on Bluff checks made to feint in combat. Retries are also allowed when you are trying to send a message, but you may attempt such a retry only once per round. Each retry carries the same chance of miscommunication.

Special: A ranger gains a bonus on Bluff checks when using this skill against a favored enemy (see page 47).

The master of a snake familiar (see the Familiars sidebar, page 52) gains a +3 bonus on Bluff checks.

If you have the Persuasive feat, you get a +2 bonus on Bluff checks.

Synergy: If you have 5 or more ranks in Bluff, you get a

Krusk helps Jozan climb the cliff.

+2 bonus on Diplomacy, Intimidate, and Sleight of Hand checks, as well as on Disguise checks made when you know you're being observed and you try to act in character.

CLIMB (STR; ARMOR CHECK PENALTY)

Use this skill to scale a cliff, to get to the window on the second story of a wizard's tower, or to climb out of a pit after falling through a trapdoor.

Check: With a successful Climb check, you can advance up, down, or across a slope, a wall, or some other steep incline (or even a ceiling with handholds) at one-quarter your normal speed. A slope is considered to be any incline at an angle measuring less than 60 degrees; a wall is any incline at an angle measuring 60 degrees or more.

A Climb check that fails by 4 or less means that you make no progress, and one that fails by 5 or more means that you fall from whatever height you have already attained.

A climber's kit (page 130) gives you a +2 circumstance bonus on Climb checks.

The DC of the check depends on the conditions of the climb. Compare the task with those on the following table to determine an appropriate DC.

Climb DC	Example Surface or Activity
0	A slope too steep to walk up, or a knotted rope with a wall to brace against.
5	A rope with a wall to brace against, or a knotted rope, or a rope affected by the *rope trick* spell.
10	A surface with ledges to hold on to and stand on, such as a very rough wall or a ship's rigging.
15	Any surface with adequate handholds and footholds (natural or artificial), such as a very rough natural rock surface or a tree, or an unknotted rope, or pulling yourself up when dangling by your hands.
20	An uneven surface with some narrow handholds and footholds, such as a typical wall in a dungeon or ruins.
25	A rough surface, such as a natural rock wall or a brick wall.
25	An overhang or ceiling with handholds but no footholds.
—	A perfectly smooth, flat, vertical surface cannot be climbed.

Climb DC Modifier[1]	Example Surface or Activity
−10	Climbing a chimney (artificial or natural) or other location where you can brace against two opposite walls (reduces DC by 10).
−5	Climbing a corner where you can brace against perpendicular walls (reduces DC by 5).
+5	Surface is slippery (increases DC by 5).

1 These modifiers are cumulative; use any that apply.

You need both hands free to climb, but you may cling to a wall with one hand while you cast a spell or take some other action that requires only one hand. While climbing, you can't move to avoid a blow, so you lose your Dexterity bonus to AC (if any). You also can't use a shield while climbing.

Any time you take damage while climbing, make a Climb check against the DC of the slope or wall. Failure means you fall from your current height and sustain the appropriate falling damage. (The *Dungeon Master's Guide* has information on falling damage.)

Accelerated Climbing: You try to climb more quickly than normal. By accepting a −5 penalty, you can move half your speed (instead of one-quarter your speed).

Making Your Own Handholds and Footholds: You can make your own handholds and footholds by pounding pitons into a wall.

Doing so takes 1 minute per piton, and one piton is needed per 3 feet of distance. As with any surface that offers handholds and footholds, a wall with pitons in it has a DC of 15. In the same way, a climber with a handaxe or similar implement can cut handholds in an ice wall.

Catching Yourself When Falling: It's practically impossible to catch yourself on a wall while falling. Make a Climb check (DC = wall's DC + 20) to do so. It's much easier to catch yourself on a slope (DC = slope's DC + 10).

Catching a Falling Character While Climbing: If someone climbing above you or adjacent to you falls, you can attempt to catch the falling character if he or she is within your reach. Doing so requires a successful melee touch attack against the falling character (though he or she can voluntarily forego any Dexterity bonus to AC if desired). If you hit, you must immediately attempt a Climb check (DC = wall's DC + 10). Success indicates that you catch the falling character, but his or her total weight, including equipment, cannot exceed your heavy load limit or you automatically fall. If you fail your Climb check by 4 or less, you fail to stop the character's fall but don't lose your grip on the wall. If you fail by 5 or more, you fail to stop the character's fall and begin falling as well.

Action: Climbing is part of movement, so it's generally part of a move action (and may be combined with other types of movement in a move action). Each move action that includes any climbing requires a separate Climb check. Catching yourself or another falling character doesn't take an action.

Special: You can use a rope to haul a character upward (or lower a character) through sheer strength. You can lift double your maximum load (see page 162) in this manner.

A halfling has a +2 racial bonus on Climb checks because halflings are agile and surefooted.

The master of a lizard familiar (see the Familiars sidebar, page 52) gains a +3 bonus on Climb checks.

If you have the Athletic feat, you get a +2 bonus on Climb checks.

A creature with a climb speed (such as a monstrous spider, or a character under the effect of a *spider climb* spell) has a +8 racial bonus on all Climb checks. The creature must make a Climb check to climb any wall or slope with a DC higher than 0, but it always can choose to take 10 (see Checks without Rolls, page 65), even if rushed or threatened while climbing. If a creature with a climb speed chooses an accelerated climb (see above), it moves at double its climb speed (or at its land speed, whichever is slower) and makes a single Climb check at a −5 penalty. Such a creature retains its Dexterity bonus to Armor Class (if any) while climbing, and opponents get no special bonus to their attacks against it. It cannot, however, use the run action while climbing.

Synergy: If you have 5 or more ranks in Use Rope, you get a +2 bonus on Climb checks made to climb a rope, a knotted rope, or a rope-and-wall combination.

CONCENTRATION (CON)

You are particularly good at focusing your mind.

Check: You must make a Concentration check whenever you might potentially be distracted (by taking damage, by harsh weather, and so on) while engaged in some action that requires your full attention. Such actions include casting a spell, concentrating on an active spell (such as *detect magic*), directing a spell (such as *spiritual weapon*), using a spell-like ability (such as a paladin's *remove disease* ability), or using a skill that would provoke an attack of opportunity (such as Disable Device, Heal, Open Lock, and Use Rope, among others). In general, if an action wouldn't normally provoke an attack of opportunity, you need not make a Concentration check to avoid being distracted.

If the Concentration check succeeds, you may continue with the action as normal. If the check fails, the action automatically fails and is wasted. If you were in the process of casting a spell, the spell is lost (see Cast a Spell, page 140). If you were concentrating on an active spell, the spell ends as if you had ceased concentrating on it. If you were directing a spell, the direction fails but the spell remains active. If you were using a spell-like ability, that use of the ability is lost. A skill use also fails, and in some cases a failed skill check may have other ramifications as well.

The table below summarizes various types of distractions that cause you to make a Concentration check. If the distraction occurs while you are trying to cast a spell, you must add the level of the spell you are trying to cast to the appropriate Concentration DC. (See Concentration, page 170, for more information.) If more than one type of distraction is present, make a check for each one; any failed Concentration check indicates that the task is not completed.

Concentration DC[1]	Distraction
10 + damage dealt	Damaged during the action.[2]
10 + half of continuous damage last dealt	Taking continuous damage during the action.[3]
Distracting spell's save DC	Distracted by nondamaging spell.[4]
10	Vigorous motion (on a moving mount, taking a bouncy wagon ride, in a small boat in rough water, belowdecks in a storm-tossed ship).
15	Violent motion (on a galloping horse, taking a very rough wagon ride, in a small boat in rapids, on the deck of a storm-tossed ship).
20	Extraordinarily violent motion (earthquake).
15	Entangled.
20	Grappling or pinned. (You can cast only spells without somatic components for which you have any required material component in hand.)
5	Weather is a high wind carrying blinding rain or sleet.
10	Weather is wind-driven hail, dust, or debris.
Distracting spell's save DC	Weather caused by a spell, such as *storm of vengeance*.[4]

1 If you are trying to cast, concentrate on, or direct a spell when the distraction occurs, add the level of the spell to the indicated DC.

2 Such as during the casting of a spell with a casting time of 1 round or more, or the execution of an activity that takes more than a single full-round action (such as Disable Device). Also, damage stemming from an attack of opportunity or readied attack made in response to the spell being cast (for spells with a casting time of 1 action) or the action being taken (for activities requiring no more than a full-round action). (See also Distracting Spellcasters, page 160.)

3 Such as from *Melf's acid arrow*.

4 If the spell allows no save, use the save DC it would have if it did allow a save.

Action: None. Making a Concentration check doesn't take an action; it is either a free action (when attempted reactively) or part of another action (when attempted actively).

Try Again: Yes, though a success doesn't cancel the effect of a previous failure, such as the loss of a spell you were casting or the disruption of a spell you were concentrating on.

Special: You can use Concentration to cast a spell, use a spell-like ability, or use a skill defensively, so as to avoid attacks of opportunity altogether. This doesn't apply to other actions that might provoke attacks of opportunity (such as movement or loading a crossbow). The DC of the check is 15 (plus the spell's level, if casting a spell or using a spell-like ability defensively). If the Concentration check succeeds, you may attempt the action normally without provoking any attacks of opportunity. A successful Concentration check still doesn't allow you to take 10 on another check if you are in a stressful situation; you must make the check normally. If the Concentration check fails, the related action also automatically fails (with any appropriate ramifications), and the action is wasted, just as if your concentration had been disrupted by a distraction.

A character with the Combat Casting feat gets a +4 bonus on Concentration checks made to cast a spell or use a spell-like ability while on the defensive (see page 140) or while grappling or pinned.

CRAFT (INT)

You are trained in a craft, trade, or art, such as alchemy, armorsmithing, basketweaving, bookbinding, bowmaking, blacksmithing, calligraphy, carpentry, cobbling, gemcutting, leatherworking, locksmithing, painting, pottery, sculpting, shipmaking, stonemasonry, trapmaking, weaponsmithing, or weaving.

Like Knowledge, Perform, and Profession, Craft is actually a number of separate skills. For instance, you could have the skill Craft (carpentry). Your ranks in that skill don't affect any Craft (pottery) or Craft (leatherworking) checks you might make. You could have several Craft skills, each with its own ranks, each purchased as a separate skill.

A Craft skill is specifically focused on creating something. If nothing is created by the endeavor, it probably falls under the heading of a Profession skill (page 80).

Check: You can practice your trade and make a decent living, earning about half your check result in gold pieces per week of dedicated work. You know how to use the tools of your trade, how to perform the craft's daily tasks, how to supervise untrained helpers, and how to handle common problems. (Untrained laborers and assistants earn an average of 1 silver piece per day.)

The basic function of the Craft skill, however, is to allow you to make an item of the appropriate type. The DC depends on the complexity of the item to be created. The DC, your check results, and the price of the item determine how long it takes to make a particular item. The item's finished price also determines the cost of raw materials. (In the game world, it is the skill level required, the time required, and the raw materials required that determine an item's price. That's why the item's price and the Craft DC are used to determine how long it takes to make the item and the cost of the raw materials.)

In some cases, the *fabricate* spell (page 229) can be used to achieve the results of a Craft check with no actual check involved. However, you must make an appropriate Craft check when using the spell to make articles requiring a high degree of craftsmanship (jewelry, swords, glass, crystal, and so forth).

A successful Craft check related to woodworking in conjunction with the casting of the *ironwood* spell (page 246) enables you to make wooden items that have the strength of steel.

When casting the spell *minor creation* (page 253), you must succeed on an appropriate Craft check to make a complex item. For instance, a successful Craft (bowmaking) check might be required to make straight arrow shafts.

All crafts require artisan's tools (page 129) to give the best chance of success. If improvised tools are used, the check is made with a –2 circumstance penalty. On the other hand, masterwork artisan's tools provide a +2 circumstance bonus on the check.

To determine how much time and money it takes to make an item, follow these steps.

1. Find the item's price in Chapter 7: Equipment of this book or in the *Dungeon Master's Guide*, or have the DM set the price for an item not otherwise described. Put the price in silver pieces (1 gp = 10 sp).

2. Find the DC from the table below, or have the DM set one.

3. Pay one-third of the item's price for the cost of raw materials.

4. Make an appropriate Craft check representing one week's work.

If the check succeeds, multiply your check result by the DC. If the result × the DC equals the price of the item in sp, then you have completed the item. (If the result × the DC equals double or triple the price of the item in silver pieces, then you've completed the task in one-half or one-third of the time. Other multiples of the DC reduce the time in the same manner.) If the result × the DC doesn't equal the price, then it represents the progress you've made this week. Record the result and make a new Craft check for the next week. Each week, you make more progress until your total reaches the price of the item in silver pieces.

If you fail a check by 4 or less, you make no progress this week. If you fail by 5 or more, you ruin half the raw materials and have to pay half the original raw material cost again.

Progress by the Day: You can make checks by the day instead of by the week. In this case your progress (check result × DC) is in copper pieces instead of silver pieces.

Creating Masterwork Items: You can make a masterwork item—a weapon, suit of armor, shield, or tool that conveys a bonus on its use through its exceptional craftsmanship, not through being magical. To create a masterwork item, you create the masterwork component as if it were a separate item in addition to the standard item. The masterwork component has its own price (300 gp for a weapon or 150 gp for a suit of armor or a shield) and a Craft DC of 20. Once both the standard component and the masterwork component are completed, the masterwork item is finished. *Note:* The cost you pay for the masterwork component is one-third of the given amount, just as it is for the cost in raw materials.

Repairing Items: Generally, you can repair an item by making checks against the same DC that it took to make the item in the first place. The cost of repairing an item is one-fifth of the item's price.

When you use the Craft skill to make a particular sort of item, the DC for checks involving the creation of that item are typically as given on the following table.

Item	Craft Skill	Craft DC
Acid	Alchemy[1]	15
Alchemist's fire, smokestick, or tindertwig	Alchemy[1]	20
Antitoxin, sunrod, tanglefoot bag, or thunderstone	Alchemy[1]	25
Armor or shield	Armorsmithing	10 + AC bonus
Longbow or shortbow	Bowmaking	12
Composite longbow or composite shortbow	Bowmaking	15
Composite longbow or composite shortbow with high strength rating	Bowmaking	15 + (2 × rating)
Crossbow	Weaponsmithing	15
Simple melee or thrown weapon	Weaponsmithing	12
Martial melee or thrown weapon	Weaponsmithing	15
Exotic melee or thrown weapon	Weaponsmithing	18
Mechanical trap	Trapmaking	Varies[2]
Very simple item (wooden spoon)	Varies	5
Typical item (iron pot)	Varies	10
High-quality item (bell)	Varies	15
Complex or superior item (lock)	Varies	20

1 You must be a spellcaster to craft any of these items.
2 Chapter 3 of the *Dungeon Master's Guide* contains a set of rules for how to construct traps.

Action: Does not apply. Craft checks are made by the day or week (see above).

Try Again: Yes, but each time you miss by 5 or more, you ruin half the raw materials and have to pay half the original raw material cost again.

Special: A dwarf has a +2 racial bonus on Craft checks that are related to stone or metal, because dwarves are especially capable with stonework and metalwork.

A gnome has a +2 racial bonus on Craft (alchemy) checks because gnomes have sensitive noses.

You may voluntarily add +10 to the indicated DC to craft an item. This allows you to create the item more quickly (since you'll be multiplying this higher DC by your Craft check result to determine progress). You must decide whether to increase the DC before you make each weekly or daily check.

To make an item using Craft (alchemy), you must have alchemical equipment and be a spellcaster. If you are working in a city, you can buy what you need as part of the raw materials cost to make the item, but alchemical equipment is difficult or impossible to come by in some places. Purchasing and maintaining an alchemist's lab (page 129) grants a +2 circumstance bonus on Craft (alchemy) checks because you have the perfect tools for the job, but it does not affect the cost of any items made using the skill.

Synergy: If you have 5 ranks in a Craft skill, you get a +2 bonus on Appraise checks related to items made with that Craft skill.

DECIPHER SCRIPT (INT; TRAINED ONLY)

Use this skill to piece together the meaning of ancient runes carved into the wall of an abandoned temple, to get the gist of an intercepted letter written in the Infernal language, to follow the directions on a treasure map written in a forgotten alphabet, or to interpret the mysterious glyphs painted on a cave wall.

Check: You can decipher writing in an unfamiliar language or a message written in an incomplete or archaic form. The base DC is 20 for the simplest messages, 25 for standard texts, and 30 or higher for intricate, exotic, or very old writing.

If the check succeeds, you understand the general content of a piece of writing about one page long (or the equivalent). If the check fails, the DM makes a DC 5 Wisdom check for you to see if you avoid drawing a false conclusion about the text. (Success means that you do not draw a false conclusion; failure means that you do.)

The DM secretly makes both the Decipher Script check and (if necessary) the Wisdom check, so that you can't tell whether the conclusion you draw is true or false.

Action: Deciphering the equivalent of a single page of script takes 1 minute (ten consecutive full-round actions).

Try Again: No.

Special: A character with the Diligent feat gets a +2 bonus on Decipher Script checks.

Synergy: If you have 5 or more ranks in Decipher Script, you get a +2 bonus on Use Magic Device checks involving scrolls.

DIPLOMACY (CHA)

Use this skill to persuade the chamberlain to let you see the king, to negotiate peace between feuding barbarian tribes, or to convince the ogre mages that have captured you that they should ransom you back to your friends instead of twisting your limbs off one by one. Diplomacy involves etiquette, social grace, tact, subtlety, and a way with words. A skilled character knows the formal and informal rules of conduct, social expectations, proper forms of address, and so on. This skill represents the ability to give others the right impression of yourself, to negotiate effectively, and to influence others.

Check: You can change the attitudes of others (nonplayer characters) with a successful Diplomacy check; see the Influencing NPC Attitudes sidebar, below, for basic DCs. (The *Dungeon Master's Guide* has more information on influencing NPCs.) In negotiations, participants roll opposed Diplomacy checks, and the winner gains the advantage. Opposed checks also resolve situations when two advocates or diplomats plead opposite cases in a hearing before a third party.

Action: Changing others' attitudes with Diplomacy generally takes at least 1 full minute (10 consecutive full-round actions). In some situations, this time requirement may greatly increase. A rushed Diplomacy check (such as an attempt to head off a fight between two angry warriors) can be made as a full-round action, but you take a –10 penalty on the check.

Try Again: Optional, but not recommended because retries usually do not work. Even if the initial Diplomacy check succeeds, the other character can be persuaded only so far, and a retry may do more harm than good. If the initial check fails, the other character has probably become more firmly committed to his position, and a retry is futile.

Special: A half-elf has a +2 racial bonus on Diplomacy checks, thanks to her ability to relate well to others.

If you have the Negotiator feat, you get a +2 bonus on Diplomacy checks.

Synergy: If you have 5 or more ranks in Bluff, Knowledge (nobility and royalty), or Sense Motive, you get a +2 bonus on Diplomacy checks.

DISABLE DEVICE (INT; TRAINED ONLY)

Use this skill to disarm a trap, jam a lock (in either the open or closed position), or rig a wagon wheel to fall off. You can examine a fairly simple or fairly small mechanical device and disable it. The effort requires at least a simple tool of the appropriate sort (a pick, pry bar, saw, file, or the like). Attempting a Disable Device check without a set of thieves' tools (page 130) imposes a –2 circumstance penalty on the check, even if a simple tool is employed. The use of masterwork thieves' tools provides a +2 circumstance bonus on the check.

Check: Your DM makes the Disable Device check for you secretly, so that you don't necessarily know whether you've succeeded. The DC depends on how tricky the device is. Disabling (or rigging or jamming) a fairly simple device has a DC of 10; more intricate and complex devices have higher DCs.

If the check succeeds, you disable the device. If it fails by 4 or less, you have failed but can try again. If you fail by 5 or more, something goes wrong. If the device is a trap, you spring it. If you're attempting some sort of sabotage, you think the device is disabled, but it still works normally.

You also can rig simple devices such as saddles or wagon wheels to work normally for a while and then fail or fall off some time later (usually after 1d4 rounds or minutes of use).

Device	Time	Disable Device DC[1]	Example
Simple	1 round	10	Jam a lock
Tricky	1d4 rounds	15	Sabotage a wagon wheel
Difficult	2d4 rounds	20	Disarm a trap, reset a trap
Wicked	2d4 rounds	25	Disarm a complex trap, cleverly sabotage a clockwork device

1 If you attempt to leave behind no trace of your tampering, add 5 to the DC.

Action: The amount of time needed to make a Disable Device check depends on the task, as noted above. Disabling a simple device takes 1 round and is a full-round action. An intricate or complex device requires 1d4 or 2d4 rounds.

Try Again: Varies. You can retry if you have missed the check by 4 or less, though you must be aware that you have failed in order to try again.

Special: If you have the Nimble Fingers feat, you get a +2 bonus on Disable Device checks.

A rogue who beats a trap's DC by 10 or more can study the trap, figure out how it works, and bypass it (along with her companions) without disarming it.

Restriction: Rogues (and other characters with the trapfinding class feature) can disarm magic traps. A magic trap generally has a DC of 25 + the spell level of the magic used to create it. For instance, disarming a trap set by the casting of *explosive runes* has a DC of 28 because *explosive runes* is a 3rd-level spell.

The spells *fire trap, glyph of warding, symbol,* and *teleportation circle* also create traps that a rogue can disarm with a successful Disable Device check. *Spike growth* and *spike stones,* however, create magic traps against which Disable Device checks do not succeed. See the individual spell descriptions in Chapter 11: Spells for details.

DISGUISE (CHA)

Use this skill to change your own appearance or someone else's. The effort requires at least a few props, some makeup, and some time. The use of a disguise kit (page 130) provides a +2 circumstance bonus on a Disguise check. A disguise can include an apparent change of height or weight amounting to no more than one-tenth of the original.

You can also use Disguise to impersonate people, either individuals or types. For example, you might, with little or no actual disguise, make yourself seem like a traveler even if you're a local.

Check: Your Disguise check result determines how good the disguise is, and it is opposed by others' Spot check results. If you don't draw any attention to yourself, others do not get to make Spot checks. If you come to the attention of people who are suspicious (such as a guard who is watching commoners walking through a city gate), the DM can assume that such observers are taking 10 on their Spot checks.

You get only one Disguise check per use of the skill, even if several people are making Spot checks against it. Your DM makes your Disguise check secretly, so that you can't be sure how good the result is.

The effectiveness of your disguise depends in part on how much you're attempting to change your appearance.

INFLUENCING NPC ATTITUDES

Use the table below to determine the effectiveness of Diplomacy checks (or Charisma checks) made to influence the attitude of a nonplayer character, or wild empathy checks made to influence the attitude of an animal or magical beast. The *Dungeon Master's Guide* has more information on NPC attitudes.

For example, if a character encounters a nonplayer character whose initial attitude is hostile, that character needs to get a result of 20 or higher on a Diplomacy check (or Charisma check) to change that NPC's attitude. On any result less than 20, the NPC's attitude is unchanged. On a result of 20 to 24, the NPC's attitude improves to unfriendly.

Initial Attitude	Hostile	Unfriendly	Indifferent	Friendly	Helpful
Hostile	Less than 20	20	25	35	50
Unfriendly	Less than 5	5	15	25	40
Indifferent	—	Less than 1	1	15	30
Friendly	—	—	Less than 1	1	20
Helpful	—	—	—	Less than 1	1

New Attitude (DC to achieve)

Attitude	Means	Possible Actions
Hostile	Will take risks to hurt you	Attack, interfere, berate, flee
Unfriendly	Wishes you ill	Mislead, gossip, avoid, watch suspiciously, insult
Indifferent	Doesn't much care	Socially expected interaction
Friendly	Wishes you well	Chat, advise, offer limited help, advocate
Helpful	Will take risks to help you	Protect, back up, heal, aid

Disguise	Disguise Check Modifier
Minor details only	+5
Disguised as different gender[1]	–2
Disguised as different race[1]	–2
Disguised as different age category[1]	–2[2]

1 These modifiers are cumulative; use any that apply.
2 Per step of difference between your actual age category and your disguised age category. The steps are: young (younger than adulthood), adulthood, middle age, old, and venerable.

If you are impersonating a particular individual, those who know what that person looks like get a bonus on their Spot checks according to the table below. Furthermore, they are automatically considered to be suspicious of you, so opposed checks are always called for.

Familiarity	Viewer's Spot Check Bonus
Recognizes on sight	+4
Friends or associates	+6
Close friends	+8
Intimate	+10

Usually, an individual makes a Spot check to see through your disguise immediately upon meeting you and each hour thereafter. If you casually meet many different creatures, each for a short time, check once per day or hour, using an average Spot modifier for the group. For example, if you are trying to pass for a merchant at a bazaar, the DM can make one Spot check per hour for the people you encounter, using a +1 bonus on the check to represent the average for the crowd (most people with no Spot ranks and a few with good Spot modifiers).

Action: Creating a disguise requires 1d3×10 minutes of work.

Try Again: Yes. You may try to redo a failed disguise, but once others know that a disguise was attempted, they'll be more suspicious.

Special: Magic that alters your form, such as *alter self, disguise self, polymorph,* or *shapechange,* grants you a +10 bonus on Disguise checks (see the individual spell descriptions in Chapter 11: Spells). You must succeed on a Disguise check with a +10 bonus to duplicate the appearance of a specific individual using the *veil* spell. Divination magic that allows people to see through illusions (such as *true seeing*) does not penetrate a mundane disguise, but it can negate the magical component of a magically enhanced one.

You must make a Disguise check when you cast a *simulacrum* spell (page 279) to determine how good the likeness is.

If you have the Deceptive feat, you get a +2 bonus on Disguise checks.

Synergy: If you have 5 or more ranks in Bluff, you get a +2 bonus on Disguise checks when you know that you're being observed and you try to act in character.

ESCAPE ARTIST (DEX; ARMOR CHECK PENALTY)

Use this skill to slip out of bonds or manacles, wriggle through tight spaces, or escape the grip of a monster that grapples you.

Check: The table below gives the DCs to escape various forms of restraints.

Ropes: Your Escape Artist check is opposed by the binder's Use Rope check. Since it's easier to tie someone up than to escape from being tied up, the binder gets a +10 bonus on his or her check.

Manacles and Masterwork Manacles: The DC for manacles is set by their construction.

Tight Space: The DC noted on the table is for getting through a space where your head fits but your shoulders don't. If the space is long, such as a chimney, the DM may call for multiple checks. You can't get through a space that your head does not fit through.

Grappler: You can make an Escape Artist check opposed by your enemy's grapple check to get out of a grapple or out of a pinned condition (so that you're only grappling). See Escape from Grapple under If You're Grappling, page 156.

Restraint	Escape Artist DC
Ropes	Binder's Use Rope check at +10
Net, *animate rope* spell, *command plants* spell, *control plants* spell, or *entangle* spell	20
Snare spell	23
Manacles	30
Tight space	30
Masterwork manacles	35
Grappler	Grappler's grapple check result

Action: Making an Escape Artist check to escape from rope bindings, manacles, or other restraints (except a grappler) requires 1 minute of work. Escaping from a net or an *animate rope, command plants, control plants,* or *entangle* spell is a full-round action. Escaping from a grapple or pin is a standard action. Squeezing through a tight space takes at least 1 minute, maybe longer, depending on how long the space is.

Try Again: Varies. You can make another check after a failed check if you're squeezing your way through a tight space, making multiple checks. If the situation permits, you can make additional checks, or even take 20, as long as you're not being actively opposed.

Special: If you have the Agile feat, you get a +2 bonus on Escape Artist checks.

Synergy: If you have 5 or more ranks in Escape Artist, you get a +2 bonus on Use Rope checks to bind someone.

If you have 5 or more ranks in Use Rope, you get a +2 bonus on Escape Artist checks when escaping from rope bonds.

OTHER WAYS TO BEAT A TRAP

It's possible to ruin many traps without making a Disable Device check.

Ranged Attack Traps: Once a trap's location is known, the obvious way to ruin it is to smash the mechanism—assuming the mechanism can be accessed. Failing that, it's possible to plug up the holes from which the projectiles emerge. Doing this prevents the trap from firing unless its ammunition does enough damage to break through the plugs.

Melee Attack Traps: These devices can be thwarted by smashing the mechanism or blocking the weapons, as noted above. Alternatively, if a character studies the trap as it triggers, he might be able to time his dodges just right to avoid damage. A character who is doing nothing but studying a trap when it first goes off gains a +4 dodge bonus against its attacks if it is triggered again within the next minute.

Pits: Disabling a pit trap generally ruins only the trapdoor, making it an uncovered pit. Filling in the pit or building a makeshift bridge across it is an application of manual labor, not the Disable Device skill. Characters could neutralize any spikes at the bottom of a pit by attacking them—they break just as daggers do.

Magic Traps: *Dispel magic* helps here. Someone who succeeds on a caster level check against the level of the trap's creator suppresses the trap for 1d4 rounds. This works only with a targeted *dispel magic,* not the area version (see the spell description, page 223).

Traps are discussed in greater detail in Chapter 3 of the *Dungeon Master's Guide.*

FORGERY (INT)

Use this skill to fake a written order from the duchess instructing a jailer to release prisoners, to create an authentic-looking treasure map, or to detect forgeries that others try to pass off.

Check: Forgery requires writing materials appropriate to the document being forged, enough light or sufficient visual acuity to see the details of what you're writing, wax for seals (if appropriate), and some time. To forge a document on which the handwriting is not specific to a person (military orders, a government decree, a business ledger, or the like), you need only to have seen a similar document before, and you gain a +8 bonus on your check. To forge a signature, you need an autograph of that person to copy, and you gain a +4 bonus on the check. To forge a longer document written in the hand of some particular person, a large sample of that person's handwriting is needed.

Your DM makes your Forgery check secretly, so that you're not sure how good your forgery is. As with Disguise, you don't even need to make a check until someone examines the work. Your Forgery check is opposed by the Forgery check of the person who examines the document to check its authenticity. The examiner gains modifiers on his or her check if any of the conditions on the table below exist.

Condition	Reader's Forgery Check Modifier
Type of document unknown to reader	–2
Type of document somewhat known to reader	+0
Type of document well known to reader	+2
Handwriting not known to reader	–2
Handwriting somewhat known to reader	+0
Handwriting intimately known to reader	+2
Reader only casually reviews the document	–2

A document that contradicts procedure, orders, or previous knowledge, or one that requires sacrifice on the part of the person checking the document can increase that character's suspicion (and thus create favorable circumstances for the checker's opposing Forgery check).

Action: Forging a very short and simple document takes about 1 minute. A longer or more complex document takes 1d4 minutes per page.

Try Again: Usually, no. A retry is never possible after a particular reader detects a particular forgery. But the document created by the forger might still fool someone else. The result of a Forgery check for a particular document must be used for every instance of a different reader examining the document. No reader can attempt to detect a particular forgery more than once; if that one opposed check goes in favor of the forger, then the reader can't try using his own skill again, even if he's suspicious about the document.

Special: If you have the Deceitful feat, you get a +2 bonus on Forgery checks.

Restriction: Forgery is language-dependent; thus, to forge documents and detect forgeries, you must be able to read and write the language in question. A barbarian can't learn the Forgery skill unless he has learned to read and write.

GATHER INFORMATION (CHA)

Use this skill for making contacts in an area, finding out local gossip, rumormongering, and collecting general information.

Check: An evening's time, a few gold pieces for buying drinks and making friends, and a DC 10 Gather Information check get you a general idea of a city's major news items, assuming there are no obvious reasons why the information would be withheld. (Such reasons might include racial enmity—if you are an elf hanging out in an orc city, for example—or your inability to speak the local language.) The higher your check result, the better the information.

If you want to find out about a specific rumor ("Which way to the ruined temple of Erythnul?") or a specific item ("What can you tell me about that pretty sword the captain of the guard walks around with?"), or obtain a map, or do something else along those lines, the DC for the check is 15 to 25, or even higher.

Action: A typical Gather Information check takes 1d4+1 hours.

Try Again: Yes, but it takes time for each check. Furthermore, you may draw attention to yourself if you repeatedly pursue a certain type of information.

Special: A half-elf has a +2 racial bonus on Gather Information checks, thanks to her ability to relate well to others.

If you have the Investigator feat, you get a +2 bonus on Gather Information checks.

Synergy: If you have 5 or more ranks in Knowledge (local), you get a +2 bonus on Gather Information checks.

HANDLE ANIMAL (CHA; TRAINED ONLY)

Use this skill to drive a team of horses pulling a wagon over rough terrain, to teach a dog to guard, or to teach a tyrannosaurus to "speak" on your command.

Check: The DC depends on what you are trying to do.

Task	Handle Animal DC
Handle an animal	10
"Push" an animal	25
Teach an animal a trick	15 or 20[1]
Train an animal for a general purpose	15 or 20[1]
Rear a wild animal	15 + HD of animal

1 See the specific trick or purpose below.

General Purpose	DC	General Purpose	DC
Combat riding	20	Hunting	20
Fighting	20	Performance	15
Guarding	20	Riding	15
Heavy labor	15		

Handle an Animal: This task involves commanding an animal to perform a task or trick that it knows. For instance, to command a trained attack dog to attack a foe requires a DC 10 Handle Animal check. If the animal is wounded or has taken any nonlethal damage or ability score damage, the DC increases by 2. If your check succeeds, the animal performs the task or trick on its next action.

"Push" an Animal: To push an animal means to get it to perform a task or trick that it doesn't know but is physically capable of performing. This category also covers making an animal perform a forced march or forcing it to hustle for more than 1 hour between sleep cycles (see Chapter 9: Adventuring). If the animal is wounded or has taken any nonlethal damage or ability score damage, the DC increases by 2. If your check succeeds, the animal performs the task or trick on its next action.

Teach an Animal a Trick: You can teach an animal a specific trick with one week of work and a successful Handle Animal check against the indicated DC. An animal with an Intelligence score of 1 (such as a snake or a shark) can learn a maximum of three tricks, while an animal with an Intelligence score of 2 (such as a dog or a horse) can learn a maximum of six tricks. Possible tricks (and their associated DCs) include, but are not necessarily limited to, the following.

Attack (DC 20): The animal attacks apparent enemies. You may point to a particular creature that you wish the animal to attack, and it will comply if able. Normally, an animal will attack only humanoids, monstrous humanoids, giants, or other animals. Teaching an animal to attack all creatures (including such unnatural creatures as undead and aberrations) counts as two tricks.

Come (DC 15): The animal comes to you, even if it normally would not do so (following you onto a boat, for example).

Defend (DC 20): The animal defends you (or is ready to defend you if no threat is present), even without any command being given. Alternatively, you can command the animal to defend a specific other character.

Down (DC 15): The animal breaks off from combat or otherwise backs down. An animal that doesn't know this trick continues to fight until it must flee (due to injury, a fear effect, or the like) or its opponent is defeated.

Fetch (DC 15): The animal goes and gets something. If you do not point out a specific item, the animal fetches some random object.

Guard (DC 20): The animal stays in place and prevents others from approaching.

Heel (DC 15): The animal follows you closely, even to places where it normally wouldn't go.

Perform (DC 15): The animal performs a variety of simple tricks, such as sitting up, rolling over, roaring or barking, and so on.

Seek (DC 15): The animal moves into an area and looks around for anything that is obviously alive or animate.

Stay (DC 15): The animal stays in place, waiting for you to return. It does not challenge other creatures that come by, though it still defends itself if it needs to.

Track (DC 20): The animal tracks the scent presented to it. (This requires the animal to have the scent ability; see the *Monster Manual* for details.)

Work (DC 15): The animal pulls or pushes a medium or heavy load.

Train an Animal for a Purpose: Rather than teaching an animal individual tricks, you can simply train it for a general purpose. Essentially, an animal's purpose represents a preselected set of known tricks that fit into a common scheme, such as guarding or heavy labor. The animal must meet all the normal prerequisites for all tricks included in the training package. If the package includes more than three tricks, the animal must have an Intelligence score of 2.

An animal can be trained for only one general purpose, though if the creature is capable of learning additional tricks (above and beyond those included in its general purpose), it may do so. Training an animal for a purpose requires fewer checks than teaching individual tricks does, but no less time. At your DM's option, you may be able to train an animal for a purpose that isn't mentioned here.

Combat Riding (DC 20): An animal trained to bear a rider into combat knows the tricks attack, come, defend, down, guard, and heel. Training an animal for combat riding takes six weeks. You may also "upgrade" an animal trained for riding to one trained for combat riding by spending three weeks and making a successful DC 20 Handle Animal check. The new general purpose and tricks completely replace the animal's previous purpose and any tricks it once knew. Warhorses and riding dogs (see the *Monster Manual*) are already trained to bear riders into combat, and they don't require any additional training for this purpose.

Fighting (DC 20): An animal trained to engage in combat knows the tricks attack, down, and stay. Training an animal for fighting takes three weeks.

Guarding (DC 20): An animal trained to guard knows the tricks attack, defend, down, and guard. Training an animal for guarding takes four weeks.

Heavy Labor (DC 15): An animal trained for heavy labor knows the tricks come and work. Training an animal for heavy labor takes two weeks.

Hunting (DC 20): An animal trained for hunting knows the tricks attack, down, fetch, heel, seek, and track. Training an animal for hunting takes six weeks.

Performance (DC 15): An animal trained for performance knows the tricks come, fetch, heel, perform, and stay. Training an animal for performance takes five weeks.

Riding (DC 15): An animal trained to bear a rider knows the tricks come, heel, and stay. Training an animal for riding takes three weeks.

Rear a Wild Animal: To rear an animal means to raise a wild creature from infancy so that it becomes domesticated. A handler can rear as many as three creatures of the same kind at once. A successfully domesticated animal can be taught tricks at the same time it's being raised, or it can be taught as a domesticated animal later.

Action: Varies. Handling an animal is a move action, while pushing an animal is a full-round action. (A druid or ranger can handle her animal companion as a free action or push it as a move action.) For tasks with specific time frames noted above, you must spend half this time (at the rate of 3 hours per day per animal being handled) working toward completion of the task before you attempt the Handle Animal check. If the check fails, your attempt to teach, rear, or train the animal fails and you need not complete the teaching, rearing, or training time. If the check succeeds, you must invest the remainder of the time to complete the teaching, rearing, or training. If the time is interrupted or the task is not followed through to completion, the attempt to teach, rear, or train the animal automatically fails.

Try Again: Yes, except for rearing an animal.

Special: You can use this skill on a creature with an Intelligence score of 1 or 2 that is not an animal, but the DC of any such check increases by 5. Such creatures have the same limit on tricks known as animals do. The *Monster Manual* provides information on teaching or training other kinds of creatures as appropriate.

A druid or ranger gains a +4 circumstance bonus on Handle Animal checks involving her animal companion. In addition, a druid's or ranger's animal companion knows one or more bonus tricks, which don't count against the normal limit on tricks known and don't require any training time or Handle Animal checks to teach.

If you have the Animal Affinity feat, you get a +2 bonus on Handle Animal checks.

Synergy: If you have 5 or more ranks in Handle Animal, you get a +2 bonus on Ride checks and wild empathy checks.

Untrained: If you have no ranks in Handle Animal, you can use a Charisma check to handle and push domestic animals, but you can't teach, rear, or train animals. A druid or ranger with no ranks in Handle Animal can use a Charisma check to handle and push her animal companion, but she can't teach, rear, or train other nondomestic animals.

HEAL (WIS)

Use this skill to keep a badly wounded friend from dying, to help others recover faster from wounds, to keep your friend from succumbing to a wyvern's poison sting, or to treat disease.

Check: The DC and effect depend on the task you attempt.

Task	Heal DC
First aid	15
Long-term care	15
Treat wound from caltrop, *spike growth*, or *spike stones*	15
Treat poison	Poison's save DC
Treat disease	Disease's save DC

First Aid: You usually use first aid to save a dying character. If a character has negative hit points and is losing hit points (at the rate of 1 per round, 1 per hour, or 1 per day), you can make him or her stable. A stable character regains no hit points but stops losing them. (See Dying, page 145.)

Long-Term Care: Providing long-term care means treating a wounded person for a day or more. If your Heal check is successful, the patient recovers hit points or ability score points (lost to ability damage) at twice the normal rate: 2 hit points per level for a full 8 hours of rest in a day, or 4 hit points per level for each full day of complete rest; 2 ability score points for a full 8 hours of rest in a day, or 4 ability score points for each full day of complete rest. You can tend as many as six patients at a time. You need a few items and supplies (bandages, salves, and so on) that are easy to come by in settled lands.

Giving long-term care counts as light activity for the healer. You cannot give long-term care to yourself.

Treat Wound from Caltrop, Spike Growth, or Spike Stones: A creature wounded by stepping on a caltrop moves at one-half normal speed. A successful Heal check removes this movement penalty.

A creature wounded by a *spike growth* or *spike stones* spell must succeed on a Reflex save or take injuries that reduce his speed by one-third. Another character can remove this penalty by taking 10 minutes to dress the victim's injuries and succeeding on a Heal check against the spell's save DC.

Treat Poison: To treat poison means to tend a single character who has been poisoned and who is going to take more damage from the poison (or suffer some other effect). Every time the poisoned character makes a saving throw against the poison, you make a Heal check. The poisoned character uses your check result or his or her saving throw, whichever is higher.

Treat Disease: To treat a disease means to tend a single diseased character. Every time he or she makes a saving throw against disease effects, you make a Heal check. The diseased character uses your check result or his or her saving throw, whichever is higher.

Action: Providing first aid, treating a wound, or treating poison is a standard action. Treating a disease or tending a creature wounded by a *spike growth* or *spike stones* spell takes 10 minutes of work. Providing long-term care requires 8 hours of light activity.

Try Again: Varies. Generally speaking, you can't try a Heal check again without proof of the original check's failure. For instance, until a poisoned character makes a saving throw against the poisoned wound you've treated, you can't know whether your Heal check was successful or not, so you can't retry the check. You can always retry a check to provide first aid, assuming the target of the previous attempt is still alive.

Special: A character with the Self-Sufficient feat gets a +2 bonus on Heal checks.

A healer's kit (page 130) gives you a +2 circumstance bonus on Heal checks.

HIDE (DEX; ARMOR CHECK PENALTY)

Use this skill to sink back into the shadows and proceed unseen, to approach a wizard's tower under cover of brush, or to tail someone through a busy street without being noticed.

Check: Your Hide check is opposed by the Spot check of anyone who might see you. You can move up to one-half your normal speed and hide at no penalty. When moving at a speed greater than one-half but less than your normal speed, you take a –5 penalty. It's practically impossible (–20 penalty) to hide while attacking, running or charging.

For example, Lidda has a speed of 20 feet. If she doesn't want to take a penalty on her Hide check, she can move only 10 feet as a move action (up to a maximum of 20 feet in a round).

A creature larger or smaller than Medium takes a size bonus or penalty on Hide checks depending on its size category: Fine +16, Diminutive +12, Tiny +8, Small +4, Large –4, Huge –8, Gargantuan –12, Colossal –16.

You need cover or concealment (see pages 150–152) in order to attempt a Hide check. Total cover or total concealment usually (but not always; see Special, below) obviates the need for a Hide check, since nothing can see you anyway.

If people are observing you, even casually, you can't hide. You can run around a corner or behind cover so that you're out of sight and then hide, but the others then know at least where you went. If your observers are momentarily distracted (such as by a Bluff check; see below), though, you can attempt to hide. While the others turn their attention from you, you can attempt a Hide check if you can get to a hiding place of some kind. (As a general guideline, the hiding place has to be within 1 foot per rank you have in Hide.) This check, however, is made at a –10 penalty because you have to move fast.

Sniping: If you've already successfully hidden at least 10 feet from your target, you can make one ranged attack, then immediately hide again. You take a –20 penalty on your Hide check to conceal yourself after the shot.

Creating a Diversion to Hide: You can use Bluff (page 67) to help you hide. A successful Bluff check can give you the momentary diversion you need to attempt a Hide check while people are aware of you.

Action: Usually none. Normally, you make a Hide check as part of movement, so it doesn't take a separate action. However, hiding immediately after a ranged attack (see Sniping, above) is a move action.

Special: If you are invisible, you gain a +40 bonus on Hide checks if you are immobile, or a +20 bonus on Hide checks if you're moving.

If you have the Stealthy feat, you get a +2 bonus on Hide checks.

A 13th-level ranger can attempt a Hide check in any sort of natural terrain, even if it doesn't grant cover or concealment. A 17th-level ranger can do this even while being observed (see page 48).

INTIMIDATE (CHA)

Use this skill to get a bully to back down, to frighten an opponent, or to make a prisoner give you the information you want. Intimidation includes verbal threats and body language.

Check: You can change another's behavior with a successful check. Your Intimidate check is opposed by the target's modified level check (1d20 + character level or Hit Dice + target's Wisdom bonus [if any] + target's modifiers on saves against fear). If you beat your target's check result, you may treat the target as friendly, but only for the purpose of actions taken while it remains intimidated. (That is, the target retains its normal attitude, but will chat, advise, offer limited help, or advocate on your behalf while intimidated. See the Diplomacy skill, above, for additional details.) The effect lasts as long as the target remains in your presence, and for 1d6×10 minutes afterward. After this time, the target's default attitude toward you shifts to unfriendly (or, if normally unfriendly, to hostile).

If you fail the check by 5 or more, the target provides you with incorrect or useless information, or otherwise frustrates your efforts.

Demoralize Opponent: You can also use Intimidate to weaken an opponent's resolve in combat. To do so, make an Intimidate check opposed by the target's modified level check (see above). If you win, the target becomes shaken for 1 round. A shaken character takes a –2 penalty on attack rolls, ability checks, and saving throws. You can intimidate only an opponent that you threaten in melee combat and that can see you.

Action: Varies. Changing another's behavior requires 1 minute of interaction. Intimidating an opponent in combat is a standard action.

Try Again: Optional, but not recommended because retries usually do not work. Even if the initial check succeeds, the other character can be intimidated only so far, and a retry doesn't help. If the initial check fails, the other character has probably become more firmly resolved to resist the intimidator, and a retry is futile.

Special: You gain a +4 bonus on your Intimidate check for every size category that you are larger than your target. Conversely, you take a –4 penalty on your Intimidate check for every size category that you are smaller than your target.

A character immune to fear (such as a paladin of 3rd level or higher) can't be intimidated, nor can nonintelligent creatures.

If you have the Persuasive feat, you get a +2 bonus on Intimidate checks.

Synergy: If you have 5 or more ranks in Bluff, you get a +2 bonus on Intimidate checks.

JUMP (STR; ARMOR CHECK PENALTY)

Use this skill to leap over pits, vault low fences, or reach a tree's lowest branches.

Check: The DC and the distance you can cover vary according to the type of jump you are attempting (see below).

Your Jump check is modified by your speed. If your speed is 30 feet (the speed of an unarmored human), then no modifier based on speed applies to the check. If your speed is less than 30 feet, you take a –6 penalty for every 10 feet of speed less than 30 feet. If your speed is greater than 30 feet, you gain a +4 bonus for every 10 feet beyond 30 feet. For instance, if you have a speed of 20 feet, you take a –6 penalty on your Jump checks. If, on the other hand, your speed is 50 feet, you gain a +8 bonus.

All Jump DCs given here assume that you get a running start, which requires that you move at least 20 feet in a straight line before attempting the jump. If you do not get a running start, the DC for the jump is doubled.

Distance moved by jumping is counted against your normal maximum movement in a round. For example, Krusk has a speed of 40 feet. If he moves 30 feet, then jumps across a 10-foot-wide chasm, he's then moved 40 feet total, so that's his move action.

If you have ranks in Jump and you succeed on a Jump check, you land on your feet (when appropriate). If you attempt a Jump check untrained, you land prone unless you beat the DC by 5 or more.

Long Jump: A long jump is a horizontal jump, made across a gap like a chasm or stream. At the midpoint of the jump, you attain a vertical height equal to one-quarter of the horizontal distance. The DC for the jump is equal to the distance jumped (in feet). For example, a 10-foot-wide pit requires a DC 10 Jump check to cross.

If your check succeeds, you land on your feet at the far end. If you fail the check by less than 5, you don't clear the distance, but you can make a DC 15 Reflex save to grab the far edge of the gap. You end your movement grasping the far edge. If that leaves you dangling over a chasm or gap, getting up requires a move action and a DC 15 Climb check.

Long Jump Distance	Jump DC[1]
5 feet	5
10 feet	10
15 feet	15
20 feet	20
25 feet	25
30 feet	30

1 Requires a 20-foot running start. Without a running start, double the DC.

High Jump: A high jump is a vertical leap made to reach a ledge high above or to grasp something overhead, such as a tree limb. The DC is equal to 4 times the distance to be cleared. For example, the DC for a high jump to land atop a 3-foot-high ledge is 12 (3 × 4).

If you jumped up to grab something, a successful check indicates that you reached the desired height. If you wish to pull yourself up, you can do so with a move action and a DC 15 Climb check. If you fail the Jump check, you do not reach the height, and you land on your feet in the same spot from which you jumped. As with a long jump, the DC is doubled if you do not get a running start of at least 20 feet.

High Jump Distance[1]	Jump DC[2]
1 foot	4
2 feet	8
3 feet	12
4 feet	16
5 feet	20
6 feet	24
7 feet	28
8 feet	32

1 Not including vertical reach; see below.
2 Requires a 20-foot running start. Without a running start, double the DC.

Obviously, the difficulty of reaching a given height varies according to the size of the character or creature. The maximum vertical reach (height the creature can reach without jumping) for an average creature of a given size is shown on the table below. (As a Medium creature, a typical human can reach 8 feet without jumping.) Quadrupedal creatures (such as horses) don't have the same vertical reach as a bipedal creature; treat them as being one size category smaller.

Creature Size	Vertical Reach
Colossal	128 ft.
Gargantuan	64 ft.
Huge	32 ft.
Large	16 ft.
Medium	8 ft.
Small	4 ft.
Tiny	2 ft.
Diminutive	1 ft.
Fine	1/2 ft.

Hop Up: You can jump up onto an object as tall as your waist, such as a table or small boulder, with a DC 10 Jump check. Doing so counts as 10 feet of movement, so if your speed is 30 feet, you could move 20 feet, then hop up onto a counter. You do not need to get a running start to hop up, so the DC is not doubled if you do not get a running start.

Jumping Down: If you intentionally jump from a height, you take less damage than you would if you just fell. The DC to jump down from a height is 15. You do not have to get a running start to jump down, so the DC is not doubled if you do not get a running start.

If you succeed on the check, you take falling damage as if you had dropped 10 fewer feet than you actually did. Thus, if you jump down a from height of just 10 feet, you take no damage. If you jump down from a height of 20 feet, you take damage as if you had fallen 10 feet.

Action: None. A Jump check is included in your movement, so it is part of a move action. If you run out of movement mid-jump, your next action (either on this turn or, if necessary, on your next turn) must be a move action to complete the jump.

Special: Effects that increase your movement also increase your jumping distance, since your check is modified by your speed.

If you have the Run feat, you get a +4 bonus on Jump checks for any jumps made after a running start.

A halfling has a +2 racial bonus on Jump checks because halflings are agile and athletic.

If you have the Acrobatic feat, you get a +2 bonus on Jump checks.

Synergy: If you have 5 or more ranks in Tumble, you get a +2 bonus on Jump checks.

If you have 5 or more ranks in Jump, you get a +2 bonus on Tumble checks.

KNOWLEDGE (INT; TRAINED ONLY)

Like the Craft and Profession skills, Knowledge actually encompasses a number of unrelated skills. Knowledge represents a study of some body of lore, possibly an academic or even scientific discipline. Below are listed typical fields of study. With your DM's approval, you can invent new areas of knowledge.

- Arcana (ancient mysteries, magic traditions, arcane symbols, cryptic phrases, constructs, dragons, magical beasts)
- Architecture and engineering (buildings, aqueducts, bridges, fortifications)
- Dungeoneering (aberrations, caverns, oozes, spelunking)
- Geography (lands, terrain, climate, people)
- History (royalty, wars, colonies, migrations, founding of cities)
- Local (legends, personalities, inhabitants, laws, customs, traditions, humanoids)
- Nature (animals, fey, giants, monstrous humanoids, plants, seasons and cycles, weather, vermin)
- Nobility and royalty (lineages, heraldry, family trees, mottoes, personalities)
- Religion (gods and goddesses, mythic history, ecclesiastic tradition, holy symbols, undead)
- The planes (the Inner Planes, the Outer Planes, the Astral Plane, the Ethereal Plane, outsiders, elementals, magic related to the planes)

Check: Answering a question within your field of study has a DC of 10 (for really easy questions), 15 (for basic questions), or 20 to 30 (for really tough questions).

In many cases, you can use this skill to identify monsters and their special powers or vulnerabilities. In general, the DC of such a check equals 10 + the monster's HD. A successful check allows you to remember a bit of useful information about that monster. For every 5 points by which your check result exceeds the DC, the DM can give another piece of useful information.

Action: Usually none. In most cases, making a Knowledge check doesn't take an action—you simply know the answer or you don't.

Try Again: No. The check represents what you know, and thinking about a topic a second time doesn't let you know something that you never learned in the first place.

Synergy: If you have 5 or more ranks in Knowledge (arcana), you get a +2 bonus on Spellcraft checks.

If you have 5 or more ranks in Knowledge (architecture and engineering), you get a +2 bonus on Search checks made to find secret doors or hidden compartments.

If you have 5 or more ranks in Knowledge (geography), you get a +2 bonus on Survival checks made to keep from getting lost or to avoid natural hazards.

If you have 5 or more ranks in Knowledge (history), you get a +2 bonus on bardic knowledge checks (see page 28).

If you have 5 or more ranks in Knowledge (local), you get a +2 bonus on Gather Information checks.

If you have 5 or more ranks in Knowledge (nature), you get a +2 bonus on Survival checks made in aboveground natural environments (aquatic, desert, forest, hill, marsh, mountains, or plains).

If you have 5 or more ranks in Knowledge (nobility and royalty), you get a +2 bonus on Diplomacy checks.

If you have 5 or more ranks in Knowledge (religion), you get a +2 bonus on turning checks against undead (see page 159).

If you have 5 or more ranks in Knowledge (the planes), you get a +2 bonus on Survival checks made while on other planes.

If you have 5 or more ranks in Knowledge (dungeoneering), you get a +2 bonus on Survival checks made while underground.

If you have 5 or more ranks in Survival, you get a +2 bonus on Knowledge (nature) checks.

Untrained: An untrained Knowledge check is simply an Intelligence check. Without actual training, you know only common knowledge (DC 10 or lower).

LISTEN (WIS)

Use this skill to hear approaching enemies, to detect someone sneaking up on you from behind, or to eavesdrop on someone else's conversation.

Check: Your Listen check is either made against a DC that reflects how quiet the noise is that you might hear, or it is opposed by your target's Move Silently check.

Your DM may decide to make the Listen check for you, so that you don't know whether not hearing anything means that nothing is there, or that you failed the check.

Listen DC	Sound
–10	A battle
0	People talking[1]
5	A person in medium armor walking at a slow pace (10 ft./round) trying not to make any noise.
10	An unarmored person walking at a slow pace (15 ft./round) trying not to make any noise
15	A 1st-level rogue using Move Silently to sneak past the listener
15	People whispering[1]
19	A cat stalking
30	An owl gliding in for a kill

[1] If you beat the DC by 10 or more, you can make out what's being said, assuming that you understand the language.

Listen DC Modifier	Condition
+5	Through a door
+15	Through a stone wall
–1	Per 10 feet of distance
–5	Listener distracted

In the case of people trying to be quiet, the DCs given on the table could be replaced by Move Silently checks, in which case the indi-

PLAYER KNOWLEDGE VERSUS CHARACTER KNOWLEDGE

It's pretty simple to measure a character's knowledge of things the player doesn't know. That's what a Knowledge skill check represents—for instance, the player of a character with many ranks in Knowledge (geography) isn't required to memorize all the geographical data about the campaign world to use his character's skill ranks.

The opposite case, however, is harder to adjudicate cleanly. What happens when a player knows something that his or her character does not have any reason to know? For instance, while most veteran players know that black dragons breathe acid, it's entirely likely that most inexperienced characters don't know that fact.

Generally speaking, it's impossible to separate completely your personal knowledge (also called player knowledge) from your character's knowledge. Ultimately, the decision on how (or if) to divide player knowledge from character knowledge must be made between the players and the DM. Some DMs encourage knowledgeable players to use their experience to help their characters succeed. Others prefer that characters display only the knowledge represented by their skill ranks and other game statistics. Most fall somewhere between those two extremes.

If in doubt, ask your DM how he or she prefers to handle such situations. The *Dungeon Master's Guide* has more information on this topic.

cated DC would be their average check result (or close to it). For instance, the DC 19 noted on the table for a cat stalking means that an average cat has a +9 bonus on Move Silently checks. Assuming an average roll of 10 on 1d20, its Move Silently check result would be 19.

Action: Varies. Every time you have a chance to hear something in a reactive manner (such as when someone makes a noise or you move into a new area), you can make a Listen check without using an action. Trying to hear something you failed to hear previously is a move action.

Try Again: Yes. You can try to hear something that you failed to hear previously with no penalty.

Special: When several characters are listening to the same thing, the DM can make a single 1d20 roll and use it for all the individuals' Listen checks.

A fascinated creature takes a –4 penalty on Listen checks made as reactions.

If you have the Alertness feat, you get a +2 bonus on Listen checks.

A ranger gains a bonus on Listen checks when using this skill against a favored enemy (see page 47).

An elf, gnome, or halfling has a +2 racial bonus on Listen checks, thanks to the keen ears with which members of those races are blessed.

A half-elf has a +1 racial bonus on Listen checks. Her hearing is good because of her elven heritage, but not as keen as that of a full elf.

A sleeping character may make Listen checks at a –10 penalty. A successful check awakens the sleeper.

MOVE SILENTLY (DEX; ARMOR CHECK PENALTY)

You can use this skill to sneak up behind an enemy or to slink away without being noticed.

Check: Your Move Silently check is opposed by the Listen check of anyone who might hear you. You can move up to one-half your normal speed at no penalty. When moving at a speed greater than one-half but less than your full speed, you take a –5 penalty. It's practically impossible (–20 penalty) to move silently while running or charging.

Noisy surfaces, such as bogs or undergrowth, are tough to move silently across. When you try to sneak across such a surface, you take a penalty on your Move Silently check as indicated below.

Surface	Check Modifier
Noisy (scree, shallow or deep bog, undergrowth, dense rubble)	–2
Very noisy (dense undergrowth, deep snow)	–5

Action: None. A Move Silently check is included in your movement or other activity, so it is part of another action.

Special: The master of a cat familiar (see the Familiars sidebar, page 52) gains a +3 bonus on Move Silently checks.

A halfling has a +2 racial bonus on Move Silently checks because halflings are nimble.

If you have the Stealthy feat, you get a +2 bonus on Move Silently checks.

OPEN LOCK (DEX; TRAINED ONLY)

You can pick padlocks, finesse combination locks, and solve puzzle locks. The effort requires at least a simple tool of the appropriate sort (a pick, pry bar, blank key, wire, or the like). Attempting an Open Lock check without a set of thieves' tools (page 130) imposes a –2 circumstance penalty on the check, even if a simple tool is employed. If you use masterwork thieves' tools, you gain a +2 circumstance bonus on the check.

Check: The DC for opening a lock varies from 20 to 40, depending on the quality of the lock, as given on the table below.

Lock	DC	Lock	DC
Very simple lock	20	Good lock	30
Average lock	25	Amazing lock	40

Action: Opening a lock is a full-round action.

Special: If you have the Nimble Fingers feat, you get a +2 bonus on Open Lock checks.

Untrained: You cannot pick locks untrained, but you might successfully force them open (see Smashing an Object, page 165).

PERFORM (CHA)

You are skilled in a type of artistic expression, which may encompass a variety of specific methods, and you know how to put on a show.

Like Craft, Knowledge, and Profession, Perform is actually a number of separate skills. For instance, you could have the skill Perform (act). Your ranks in that skill don't affect any checks you happen to make for Perform (oratory) or Perform (string instruments). You could have several Perform skills, each with its own ranks, each purchased as a separate skill.

Each of the nine categories of the Perform skill includes a variety of methods, instruments, or techniques, a small list of which is provided for each category below. The DM is free to expand any of these categories with additional methods, instruments, or techniques, as appropriate for his or her campaign.
- Act (comedy, drama, mime)
- Comedy (buffoonery, limericks, joke-telling)
- Dance (ballet, waltz, jig)
- Keyboard instruments (harpsichord, piano, pipe organ)
- Oratory (epic, ode, storytelling)
- Percussion instruments (bells, chimes, drums, gong)
- String instruments (fiddle, harp, lute, mandolin)
- Wind instruments (flute, pan pipes, recorder, shawm, trumpet)
- Sing (ballad, chant, melody)

Check: You can impress audiences with your talent and skill.

Perform DC	Performance
10	Routine performance. Trying to earn money by playing in public is essentially begging. You can earn 1d10 cp/day.
15	Enjoyable performance. In a prosperous city, you can earn 1d10 sp/day.
20	Great performance. In a prosperous city, you can earn 3d10 sp/day. In time, you may be invited to join a professional troupe and may develop a regional reputation.
25	Memorable performance. In a prosperous city, you can earn 1d6 gp/day. In time, you may come to the attention of noble patrons and develop a national reputation.
30	Extraordinary performance. In a prosperous city, you can earn 3d6 gp/day. In time, you may draw attention from distant potential patrons, or even from extraplanar beings.

A masterwork musical instrument (page 130) gives you a +2 circumstance bonus on Perform checks that involve its use.

Action: Varies. Trying to earn money by playing in public requires anywhere from an evening's work to a full day's performance, at the DM's discretion. The bard's special Perform-based abilities are described in that class's description (page 29).

Try Again: Yes. Retries are allowed, but they don't negate previous failures, and an audience that has been unimpressed in the past is likely to be prejudiced against future performances. (Increase the DC by 2 for each previous failure.)

Special: A bard must have at least 3 ranks in a Perform skill to inspire courage in his allies, or to use his countersong or his *fascinate* ability. A bard needs 6 ranks in a Perform skill to inspire competence, 9 ranks to use his *suggestion* ability, 12 ranks to inspire greatness, 15 ranks to use his *song of freedom* ability, 18 ranks to inspire heroics, and 21 ranks to use his *mass suggestion* ability. See Bardic Music in the bard class description, page 29.

In addition to using the Perform skill, you can entertain people with sleight of hand, tumbling, tightrope walking, and spells (especially illusions).

PROFESSION (WIS; TRAINED ONLY)

You are trained in a livelihood or a professional role, such as apothecary, boater, bookkeeper, brewer, cook, driver, farmer, fisher, guide, herbalist, herder, hunter, innkeeper, lumberjack, miller, miner, porter, rancher, sailor, scribe, siege engineer, stablehand, tanner, teamster, woodcutter, or the like.

Like Craft, Knowledge, and Perform, Profession is actually a number of separate skills. For instance, you could have the skill Profession (cook). Your ranks in that skill don't affect any Profession (miller) or Profession (miner) checks you might make. You could have several Profession skills, each with its own ranks, each purchased as a separate skill.

While a Craft skill represents ability in creating or making an item, a Profession skill represents an aptitude in a vocation requiring a broader range of less specific knowledge. To draw a modern analogy, if an occupation is a service industry, it's probably a Profession skill. If it's in the manufacturing sector, it's probably a Craft skill.

Check: You can practice your trade and make a decent living, earning about half your Profession check result in gold pieces per week of dedicated work. You know how to use the tools of your trade, how to perform the profession's daily tasks, how to supervise helpers, and how to handle common problems. For example, a sailor knows how to tie several basic knots, how to tend and repair sails, and how to stand a deck watch at sea. The DM sets DCs for specialized tasks.

Action: Not applicable. A single check generally represents a week of work.

Try Again: Varies. An attempt to use a Profession skill to earn an income cannot be retried. You are stuck with whatever weekly wage your check result brought you. Another check may be made after a week to determine a new income for the next period of time. An attempt to accomplish some specific task can usually be retried.

Untrained: Untrained laborers and assistants (that is, characters without any ranks in Profession) earn an average of 1 silver piece per day.

RIDE (DEX)

You can ride a mount, be it a horse, riding dog, griffon, dragon, or some other kind of creature suited for riding. If you attempt to ride a creature that is ill suited as a mount (such as most bipedal creatures), you take a –5 penalty on your Ride checks.

Check: Typical riding actions don't require checks. You can saddle, mount, ride, and dismount from a mount without a problem. The following tasks do require checks.

Task	Ride DC	Task	Ride DC
Guide with knees	5	Leap	15
Stay in saddle	5	Spur mount	15
Fight with warhorse	10	Control mount in battle	20
Cover	15	Fast mount or dismount	20[1]
Soft fall	15		
1 Armor check penalty applies.			

Guide with Knees: You can react instantly to guide your mount with your knees so that you can use both hands in combat. Make your Ride check at the start of your turn. If you fail, you can use only one hand this round because you need to use the other to control your mount.

Stay in Saddle: You can react instantly to try to avoid falling when your mount rears or bolts unexpectedly or when you take damage. This usage does not take an action.

Fight with Warhorse: If you direct your war-trained mount to attack in battle, you can still make your own attack or attacks normally. This usage is a free action.

Cover: You can react instantly to drop down and hang alongside your mount, using it as cover. You can't attack or cast spells while using your mount as cover. If you fail your Ride check, you don't get the cover benefit. This usage does not take an action.

Soft Fall: You can react instantly to try to take no damage when you fall off a mount—when it is killed or when it falls, for example. If you fail your Ride check, you take 1d6 points of falling damage. This usage does not take an action.

Leap: You can get your mount to leap obstacles as part of its movement. Use your Ride modifier or the mount's Jump modifier, whichever is lower, to see how far the creature can jump. If you fail your Ride check, you fall off the mount when it leaps and take the appropriate falling damage (at least 1d6 points). This usage does not take an action, but is part of the mount's movement.

Spur Mount: You can spur your mount to greater speed with a move action. A successful Ride check increases the mount's speed by 10 feet for 1 round but deals 1 point of damage to the creature. You can use this ability every round, but each consecutive round of additional speed deals twice as much damage to the mount as the previous round (2 points, 4 points, 8 points, and so on).

Control Mount in Battle: As a move action, you can attempt to control a light horse, pony, heavy horse, or other mount not trained for combat riding while in battle. If you fail the Ride check, you can do nothing else in that round. You do not need to roll for warhorses or warponies.

Fast Mount or Dismount: You can attempt to mount or dismount from a mount of up to one size category larger than yourself as a free action, provided that you still have a move action available that round. If you fail the Ride check, mounting or dismounting is a move action. You can't use fast mount or dismount on a mount more than one size category larger than yourself.

Action: Varies. Mounting or dismounting normally is a move action. Other checks are a move action, a free action, or no action at all, as noted above.

Special: If you are riding bareback, you take a –5 penalty on Ride checks.

If your mount has a military saddle (page 132), you get a +2 circumstance bonus on Ride checks related to staying in the saddle.

The Ride skill is a prerequisite for the feats Mounted Archery, Mounted Combat, Ride-By Attack, Spirited Charge, Trample. See the appropriate feat descriptions in Chapter 5: Feats for details.

If you have the Animal Affinity feat, you get a +2 bonus on Ride checks.

Synergy: If you have 5 or more ranks in Handle Animal, you get a +2 bonus on Ride checks.

SEARCH (INT)

You can find secret doors, simple traps, hidden compartments, and other details not readily apparent. The Spot skill lets you notice something, such as a hiding rogue. The Search skill lets a character discern some small detail or irregularity through active effort.

Search does not allow you to find complex traps unless you are a rogue (see Restriction, below).

Check: You generally must be within 10 feet of the object or surface to be searched. The table below gives DCs for typical tasks involving the Search skill.

Task	Search DC
Ransack a chest full of junk to find a certain item	10
Notice a typical secret door or a simple trap	20
Find a difficult nonmagical trap (rogue only)[1]	21 or higher
Find a magic trap (rogue only)[1]	25 + level of spell used to create trap
Notice a well-hidden secret door	30
Find a footprint	Varies[2]

1 Dwarves (even if they are not rogues) can use Search to find traps built into or out of stone.

2 A successful Search check can find a footprint or similar sign of a creature's passage, but it won't let you find or follow a trail. See the Track feat for the appropriate DC.

Action: It takes a full-round action to search a 5-foot-by-5-foot area or a volume of goods 5 feet on a side.

Special: An elf has a +2 racial bonus on Search checks, and a half-elf has a +1 racial bonus. An elf (but not a half-elf) who simply passes within 5 feet of a secret or concealed door can make a Search check to find that door.

If you have the Investigator feat, you get a +2 bonus on Search checks.

The spells *explosive runes, fire trap, glyph of warding, symbol,* and *teleportation circle* create magic traps that a rogue can find by making a successful Search check and then can attempt to disarm by using Disable Device. Identifying the location of a *snare* spell has a DC of 23. *Spike growth* and *spike stones* create magic traps that can be found using Search, but against which Disable Device checks do not succeed. See the individual spell descriptions in Chapter 11: Spells for details.

Active abjuration spells within 10 feet of each other for 24 hours or more create barely visible energy fluctuations. These fluctuations give you a +4 bonus on Search checks to locate such abjuration spells.

Synergy: If you have 5 or more ranks in Search, you get a +2 bonus on Survival checks to find or follow tracks.

If you have 5 or more ranks in Knowledge (architecture and engineering), you get a +2 bonus on Search checks to find secret doors or hidden compartments.

Restriction: While anyone can use Search to find a trap whose DC is 20 or lower, only a rogue can use Search to locate traps with higher DCs. (*Exception:* The spell *find traps* temporarily enables a cleric to use the Search skill as if he were a rogue.)

A dwarf, even one who is not a rogue, can use the Search skill to find a difficult trap (one with a DC higher than 20) if the trap is built into or out of stone. He gains a +2 racial bonus on the Search check from his stonecunning ability.

SENSE MOTIVE (WIS)

Use this skill to tell when someone is bluffing you, to discern hidden messages in conversations, or to sense when someone is being magically influenced. This skill represents sensitivity to the body language, speech habits, and mannerisms of others.

Check: A successful check lets you avoid being bluffed (see the Bluff skill, page 67). You can also use this skill to determine when "something is up" (that is, something odd is going on) or to assess someone's trustworthiness. Your DM may decide to make your Sense Motive check secretly, so that you don't necessarily know whether you were successful.

Task	Sense Motive DC
Hunch	20
Sense enchantment	25 or 15
Discern secret message	Varies

Hunch: This use of the skill involves making a gut assessment of the social situation. You can get the feeling from another's behavior that something is wrong, such as when you're talking to an impostor. Alternatively, you can get the feeling that someone is trustworthy.

Sense Enchantment: You can tell that someone's behavior is being influenced by an enchantment effect (by definition, a mind-affecting effect), such as *charm person,* even if that person isn't aware of it. The usual DC is 25, but if the target is dominated (see *dominate person* in Chapter 11: Spells), the DC is only 15 because of the limited range of the target's activities.

Discern Secret Message: You may use Sense Motive to detect that a hidden message is being transmitted via the Bluff skill. In this case, your Sense Motive check is opposed by the Bluff check of the character transmitting the message. For each piece of information relating to the message that you are missing, you take a –2 penalty on your Sense Motive check. For example, if you eavesdrop on people planning to assassinate a visiting diplomat, you take a –2 penalty on your check if you don't know about the diplomat. If you succeed by 4 or less, you know that something hidden is being communicated, but you can't learn anything specific about its content. If you beat the DC by 5 or more, you intercept and understand the message. If you fail by 4 or less, you don't detect any hidden communication. If you fail by 5 or more, you infer some false information.

Action: Trying to gain information with Sense Motive generally takes at least 1 minute, and you could spend a whole evening trying to get a sense of the people around you.

Try Again: No, though you may make a Sense Motive check for each Bluff check made against you.

Special: A ranger gains a bonus on Sense Motive checks when using this skill against a favored enemy (see page 47).

If you have the Negotiator feat, you get a +2 bonus on Sense Motive checks.

Synergy: If you have 5 or more ranks in Sense Motive, you get a +2 bonus on Diplomacy checks.

SLEIGHT OF HAND (DEX; TRAINED ONLY; ARMOR CHECK PENALTY)

You can cut or lift a purse and hide it on your person, palm an unattended object, hide a light weapon in your clothing, or perform some feat of legerdemain with an object no larger than a hat or a loaf of bread.

Check: A DC 10 Sleight of Hand check lets you palm a coin-sized, unattended object. Performing a minor feat of legerdemain, such as making a coin disappear, also has a DC of 10 unless an observer is determined to note where the item went.

When you use this skill under close observation, your skill check is opposed by the observer's Spot check. The observer's success doesn't prevent you from performing the action, just from doing it unnoticed.

You can hide a small object (including a light weapon, such as a handaxe, or an easily concealed ranged weapon, such as a dart, sling, or hand crossbow) on your body. Your Sleight of Hand check is opposed by the Spot check of anyone observing you or the Search check of anyone frisking you. In the latter case, the searcher gains a +4 bonus on the Search check, since it's generally easier to find such an object than to hide it. A dagger is easier to hide than most light weapons, and grants you a +2 bonus on your Sleight of Hand check to conceal it. An extraordinarily small object, such as a coin, shuriken, or ring, grants you a +4 bonus on your Sleight of Hand check to conceal it, and heavy or baggy clothing (such as a cloak) grants you a +2 bonus on the check. Drawing a hidden weapon is a standard action and doesn't provoke an attack of opportunity.

If you try to take something from another creature, you must make a DC 20 Sleight of Hand check to obtain it. The opponent makes a Spot check to detect the attempt, opposed by the same Sleight of Hand check result you achieved when you tried to grab the item. An opponent who succeeds on this check notices the attempt, regardless of whether you got the item.

You can also use Sleight of Hand to entertain an audience as though you were using the Perform skill. In such a case, your "act" encompasses elements of legerdemain, juggling, and the like.

Sleight of Hand

DC	Task
10	Palm a coin-sized object, make a coin disappear
20	Lift a small object from a person

Action: Any Sleight of Hand check normally is a standard action. However, you may perform a Sleight of Hand check as a free action by taking a –20 penalty on the check.

Try Again: Yes, but after an initial failure, a second Sleight of Hand attempt against the same target (or while you are being watched by the same observer who noticed your previous attempt) increases the DC for the task by 10.

Special: If you have the Deft Hands feat, you get a +2 bonus on Sleight of Hand checks.

Synergy: If you have 5 or more ranks in Bluff, you get a +2 bonus on Sleight of Hand checks.

Untrained: An untrained Sleight of Hand check is simply a Dexterity check. Without actual training, you can't succeed on any Sleight of Hand check with a DC higher than 10, except for hiding an object on your body.

SPEAK LANGUAGE (NONE; TRAINED ONLY)

Language	Typical Speakers	Alphabet
Abyssal	Demons, chaotic evil outsiders	Infernal
Aquan	Water-based creatures	Elven
Auran	Air-based creatures	Draconic
Celestial	Good outsiders	Celestial
Common	Humans, halflings, half-elves, half-orcs	Common
Draconic	Kobolds, troglodytes, lizardfolk, dragons	Draconic
Druidic	Druids (only)	Druidic
Dwarven	Dwarves	Dwarven
Elven	Elves	Elven
Giant	Ogres, giants	Dwarven
Gnome	Gnomes	Dwarven
Goblin	Goblins, hobgoblins, bugbears	Dwarven
Gnoll	Gnolls	Common
Halfling	Halflings	Common
Ignan	Fire-based creatures	Draconic
Infernal	Devils, lawful evil outsiders	Infernal
Orc	Orcs	Dwarven
Sylvan	Dryads, brownies, leprechauns	Elven
Terran	Xorns and other earth-based creatures	Dwarven
Undercommon	Drow, mind flayers	Elven

Common languages and their alphabets are summarized on the table above.

Action: Not applicable.

Try Again: Not applicable. There are no Speak Language checks to fail.

The Speak Language skill doesn't work like other skills. Languages work as follows.

- You start at 1st level knowing one or two languages (based on your race), plus an additional number of languages equal to your starting Intelligence bonus (see Chapter 2: Races).
- You can purchase Speak Language just like any other skill, but instead of buying a rank in it, you choose a new language that you can speak.
- You don't make Speak Language checks. You either know a language or you don't.
- A literate character (anyone but a barbarian who has not spent skill points to become literate) can read and write any language she speaks. Each language has an alphabet, though sometimes several spoken languages share a single alphabet.

SPELLCRAFT (INT; TRAINED ONLY)

Use this skill to identify spells as they are cast or spells already in place.

Spellcraft DC	Task
13	When using *read magic*, identify a *glyph of warding*. No action required.
15 + spell level	Identify a spell being cast. (You must see or hear the spell's verbal or somatic components.) No action required. No retry.
15 + spell level	Learn a spell from a spellbook or scroll (wizard only). No retry for that spell until you gain at least 1 rank in Spellcraft (even if you find another source to try to learn the spell from). Requires 8 hours.
15 + spell level	Prepare a spell from a borrowed spellbook (wizard only). One try per day. No extra time required.
15 + spell level	When casting *detect magic*, determine the school of magic involved in the aura of a single item or creature you can see. (If the aura is not a spell effect, the DC is 15 + one-half caster level.) No action required.
19	When using *read magic*, identify a *symbol*. No action required.
20 + spell level	Identify a spell that's already in place and in effect. You must be able to see or detect the effects of the spell. No action required. No retry.
20 + spell level	Identify materials created or shaped by magic, such as noting that an iron wall is the result of a *wall of iron* spell. No action required. No retry.
20 + spell level	Decipher a written spell (such as a scroll) without using *read magic*. One try per day. Requires a full-round action.
25 + spell level	After rolling a saving throw against a spell targeted on you, determine what that spell was. No action required. No retry.
25	Identify a potion. Requires 1 minute. No retry.
20	Draw a diagram to allow *dimensional anchor* to be cast on a *magic circle* spell. Requires 10 minutes. No retry. The DM makes this check.
30 or higher	Understand a strange or unique magical effect, such as the effects of a magic stream. Time required varies. No retry.

Check: You can identify spells and magic effects. The DCs for Spellcraft checks relating to various tasks are summarized on the table above.

Action: Varies, as noted above.

Try Again: See above.

Special: If you are a specialist wizard, you get a +2 bonus on Spellcraft checks when dealing with a spell or effect from your specialty school. You take a –5 penalty when dealing with a spell or effect from a prohibited school (and some tasks, such as learning a prohibited spell, are just impossible).

If you have the Magical Aptitude feat, you get a +2 bonus on Spellcraft checks.

Synergy: If you have 5 or more ranks in Knowledge (arcana), you get a +2 bonus on Spellcraft checks.

If you have 5 or more ranks in Use Magic Device, you get a +2 bonus on Spellcraft checks to decipher spells on scrolls.

If you have 5 or more ranks in Spellcraft, you get a +2 bonus on Use Magic Device checks related to scrolls.

Additionally, certain spells allow you to gain information about magic, provided that you make a successful Spellcraft check as detailed in the spell description. (For example, see the *detect magic* spell, page 219.)

SPOT (WIS)

Use this skill to notice bandits waiting in ambush, to see a rogue lurking in the alley, to see through a disguise, to read lips, or to see the monstrous centipede in the pile of trash.

Check: The Spot skill is used primarily to detect characters or creatures who are hiding. Typically, your Spot check is opposed by the Hide check of the creature trying not to be seen. Sometimes a creature isn't intentionally hiding but is still difficult to see, so a successful Spot check is necessary to notice it.

A Spot check result higher than 20 generally lets you become aware of an invisible creature near you, though you can't actually see it.

Spot is also used to detect someone in disguise (see the Disguise skill, page 72), and to read lips when you can't hear or understand what someone is saying.

The Dungeon Master may call for Spot checks to determine the distance at which an encounter begins. A penalty applies on such checks, depending on the distance between the two individuals or groups, and an additional penalty may apply if the character making the Spot check is distracted (not concentrating on being observant).

Condition	Penalty
Per 10 feet of distance	–1
Spotter distracted	–5

Read Lips: To understand what someone is saying by reading lips, you must be within 30 feet of the speaker, be able to see him or her speak, and understand the speaker's language. (This use of the skill is language-dependent.) The base DC is 15, but it increases for complex speech or an inarticulate speaker. You must maintain a line of sight to the lips being read.

If your Spot check succeeds, you can understand the general content of a minute's worth of speaking, but you usually still miss certain details. If the check fails by 4 or less, you can't read the speaker's lips. If the check fails by 5 or more, you draw some incorrect conclusion about the speech. Your DM rolls your check secretly in this case, so that you don't know whether you succeeded or missed by 5.

Action: Varies. Every time you have a chance to spot something in a reactive manner (for example, when someone tries to sneak past you while hidden, or you move into a new area), you can make a Spot check without using an action. Trying to spot something you failed to see previously is a move action. To read lips, you must concentrate for a full minute before making a Spot check, and you

can't perform any other action (other than moving at up to half speed) during this minute.

Try Again: Yes. You can try to spot something that you failed to see previously at no penalty. You can attempt to read lips once per minute.

Special: A fascinated creature takes a –4 penalty on Spot checks made as reactions.

If you have the Alertness feat, you get a +2 bonus on Spot checks.

A ranger gains a bonus on Spot checks when using this skill against a favored enemy (see page 47).

An elf has a +2 racial bonus on Spot checks because elves have keen senses.

A half-elf has a +1 racial bonus on Spot checks. Her eyesight is good because of her elven heritage, but not as keen as that of a full elf.

The master of a hawk familiar (see the Familiars sidebar, page 52) gains a +3 bonus on Spot checks in daylight or other lighted areas.

The master of an owl familiar (see the Familiars sidebar, page 52) gains a +3 bonus on Spot checks in shadowy or other darkened areas.

SURVIVAL (WIS)

Use this skill to follow tracks, hunt wild game, guide a party safely through frozen wastelands, identify signs that owlbears live nearby, predict the weather, or avoid quicksand and other natural hazards.

Check: You can keep yourself and others safe and fed in the wild. The table below gives the DCs for various tasks that require Survival checks.

Survival does not allow you to follow difficult tracks unless you are a ranger or have the Track feat (see the Restriction section below).

Survival DC	Task
10	Get along in the wild. Move up to one-half your overland speed while hunting and foraging (no food or water supplies needed). You can provide food and water for one other person for every 2 points by which your check result exceeds 10.
15	Gain a +2 bonus on all Fortitude saves against severe weather while moving up to one-half your overland speed, or gain a +4 bonus if you remain stationary. You may grant the same bonus to one other character for every 1 point by which your Survival check result exceeds 15.
15	Keep from getting lost or avoid natural hazards, such as quicksand.
15	Predict the weather up to 24 hours in advance. For every 5 points by which your Survival check result exceeds 15, you can predict the weather for one additional day in advance.
Varies	Follow tracks (see the Track feat).

Action: Varies. A single Survival check may represent activity over the course of hours or a full day. A Survival check made to find tracks is at least a full-round action, and it may take even longer at the DM's discretion.

Try Again: Varies. For getting along in the wild or for gaining the Fortitude save bonus noted in the table above, you make a Survival check once every 24 hours. The result of that check applies until the next check is made. To avoid getting lost or avoid natural hazards, you make a Survival check whenever the situation calls for one. Retries to avoid getting lost in a specific situation or to avoid a specific natural hazard are not allowed. For finding tracks, you can retry a failed check after 1 hour (outdoors) or 10 minutes (indoors) of searching.

Restriction: While anyone can use Survival to find tracks (regardless of the DC), or to follow tracks when the DC for the task is 10 or lower, only a ranger (or a character with the Track feat; see page 101) can use Survival to follow tracks when the task has a higher DC.

Special: If you have 5 or more ranks in Survival, you can automatically determine where true north lies in relation to yourself.

A ranger gains a bonus on Survival checks when using this skill to find or follow the tracks of a favored enemy (see page 47).

If you have the Self-Sufficient feat, you get a +2 bonus on Survival checks.

Synergy: If you have 5 or more ranks in Survival, you get a +2 bonus on Knowledge (nature) checks.

If you have 5 or more ranks in Knowledge (dungeoneering), you get a +2 bonus on Survival checks made while underground.

If you have 5 or more ranks in Knowledge (nature), you get a +2 bonus on Survival checks in aboveground natural environments (aquatic, desert, forest, hill, marsh, mountains, and plains).

If you have 5 or more ranks in Knowledge (geography), you get a +2 bonus on Survival checks made to keep from getting lost or to avoid natural hazards.

If you have 5 or more ranks in Knowledge (the planes), you get a +2 bonus on Survival checks made while on other planes.

If you have 5 or more ranks in Search, you get a +2 bonus on Survival checks to find or follow tracks.

SWIM (STR; ARMOR CHECK PENALTY)

Using this skill, a land-based creature can swim, dive, navigate underwater obstacles, and so on.

Check: Make a Swim check once per round while you are in the water. Success means you may swim at up to one-half your speed (as a full-round action) or at one-quarter your speed (as a move action). If you fail by 4 or less, you make no progress through the water. If you fail by 5 or more, you go underwater.

If you are underwater, either because you failed a Swim check or because you are swimming underwater intentionally, you must hold your breath. You can hold your breath for a number of rounds equal to your Constitution score, but only if you do nothing other than take move actions or free actions. If you take a standard action or a full-round action (such as making an attack), the remainder of the duration for which you can hold your breath is reduced by 1 round. (Effectively, a character in combat can hold his or her breath only half as long as normal.) After that period of time, you must make a DC 10 Constitution check every round to continue holding your breath. Each round, the DC for that check increases by 1. If you fail the Constitution check, you begin to drown (see Suffocation and Drowning in the *Dungeon Master's Guide*).

The DC for the Swim check depends on the water, as given on the table below.

Water	Swim DC
Calm water	10
Rough water	15
Stormy water	20[1]

1 You can't take 10 on a Swim check in stormy water, even if you aren't otherwise being threatened or distracted.

Each hour that you swim, you must make a DC 20 Swim check or take 1d6 points of nonlethal damage from fatigue.

Action: A successful Swim check allows you to swim one-quarter of your speed as a move action or one-half your speed as a full-round action.

Special: Swim checks are subject to double the normal armor check penalty and encumbrance penalty (see pages 123 and 162). For instance, full plate incurs a –12 penalty on Swim checks instead of –6.

If you have the Athletic feat, you get a +2 bonus on Swim checks.

If you have the Endurance feat, you get a +4 bonus on Swim checks made to avoid taking nonlethal damage from fatigue.

A creature with a swim speed can move through water at its indicated speed without making Swim checks. It gains a +8 racial bonus on any Swim check to perform a special action or avoid a hazard. The creature always can choose to take 10 on a Swim check, even if distracted or endangered when swimming. Such a creature can use the run action while swimming, provided that it swims in a straight line.

TUMBLE (DEX; TRAINED ONLY; ARMOR CHECK PENALTY)

You can dive, roll, somersault, flip, and so on. You can't use this skill if your speed has been reduced by armor, excess equipment, or loot (see Table 9–2: Carrying Loads, page 162).

Check: You can land softly when you fall or tumble past opponents. You can also tumble to entertain an audience (as though using the Perform skill). The DCs for various tasks involving the Tumble skill are given on the table below.

Tumble DC	Task
15	Treat a fall as if it were 10 feet shorter than it really is when determining damage.
15	Tumble at one-half speed as part of normal movement, provoking no attacks of opportunity while doing so. Failure means you provoke attacks of opportunity normally. Check separately for each opponent you move past, in the order in which you pass them (player's choice of order in case of a tie). Each additional enemy after the first adds +2 to the Tumble DC.
25	Tumble at one-half speed through an area occupied by an enemy (over, under, or around the opponent) as part of normal movement, provoking no attacks of opportunity while doing so. Failure means you stop before entering the enemy-occupied area and provoke an attack of opportunity from that enemy. Check separately for each opponent. Each additional enemy after the first adds +2 to the Tumble DC.

Obstructed or otherwise treacherous surfaces, such as natural cavern floors or undergrowth, are tough to tumble through. The DC for any Tumble check made to tumble into such a square is modified as indicated below.

Surface Is . . .	DC Modifier
Lightly obstructed (scree, light rubble, shallow bog[1], undergrowth)	+2
Severely obstructed (natural cavern floor, dense rubble, dense undergrowth)	+5
Lightly slippery (wet floor)	+2
Severely slippery (ice sheet)	+5
Sloped or angled	+2

1 Tumbling is impossible in a deep bog.

Accelerated Tumbling: You try to tumble past or through enemies more quickly than normal. By accepting a –10 penalty on your Tumble checks, you can move at your full speed instead of one-half your speed.

Action: Not applicable. Tumbling is part of movement, so a Tumble check is part of a move action.

Try Again: Usually no. An audience, once it has judged a tumbler as an uninteresting performer, is not receptive to repeat performances. You can try to reduce damage from a fall as an instant reaction only once per fall.

Special: If you have 5 or more ranks in Tumble, you gain a +3 dodge bonus to AC when fighting defensively instead of the usual +2 dodge bonus to AC (see Fighting Defensively, page 140).

If you have 5 or more ranks in Tumble, you gain a +6 dodge bonus to AC when executing the total defense standard action instead of the usual +4 dodge bonus to AC (see Total Defense, page 142).

If you have the Acrobatic feat, you get a +2 bonus on Tumble checks.

Synergy: If you have 5 or more ranks in Tumble, you get a +2 bonus on Balance and Jump checks.

If you have 5 or more ranks in Jump, you get a +2 bonus on Tumble checks.

USE MAGIC DEVICE
(CHA; TRAINED ONLY)

Use this skill to activate magic devices, including scrolls and wands, that you could not otherwise activate.

Check: You can use this skill to read a spell or to activate a magic item. Use Magic Device lets you use a magic item as if you had the spell ability or class features of another class, as if you were a different race, or as if you were of a different alignment.

You make a Use Magic Device check each time you activate a device such as a wand. If you are using the check to emulate an alignment or some other quality in an ongoing manner (to emulate a neutral evil alignment in order to keep yourself from being damaged by a *book of vile darkness* you are carrying when you are not evil, for example), you need to make the relevant Use Magic Device check once per hour.

You must consciously choose which requirement to emulate. That is, you must know what you are trying to emulate when you make a Use Magic Device check for that purpose. The DCs for various tasks involving Use Magic Device checks are summarized on the table below.

Lidda finds that using a magic device can be risky.

Activate Blindly: Some magic items are activated by special words, thoughts, or actions. You can activate such an item as if you were using the activation word, thought, or action, even when you're not and even if you don't know it. You do have to perform some equivalent activity in order to make the check. That is, you must speak, wave the item around, or otherwise attempt to get it to activate. You get a special +2 bonus on your Use Magic Device check if you've activated the item in question at least once before.

If you fail by 9 or less, you can't activate the device. If you fail by 10 or more, you suffer a mishap. A mishap means that magical energy gets released but it doesn't do what you wanted it to do. The DM determines the result of a mishap, as with scroll mishaps. The default mishaps are that the item affects the wrong target or that uncontrolled magical energy is released, dealing 2d6 points of damage to you. This mishap is in addition to the chance for a mishap that you normally run when you cast a spell from a scroll that you could not otherwise cast yourself (see the *Dungeon Master's Guide*).

Decipher a Written Spell: This usage works just like deciphering a written spell with the Spellcraft skill, except that the DC is 5 points higher. Deciphering a written spell requires 1 minute of concentration.

Emulate an Ability Score: To cast a spell from a scroll, you need a high score in the appropriate ability (Intelligence for wizard spells, Wisdom for divine spells, or Charisma for sorcerer or bard spells). Your effective ability score (appropriate to the class you're emulating when you try to cast the spell from the scroll) is your Use Magic Device check result minus 15. If you already have a high enough score in the appropriate ability, you don't need to make this check.

Emulate an Alignment: Some magic items have positive or negative effects based on the user's alignment. Use Magic Device lets you use these items as if you were of an alignment of your choice. For example, a *book of vile darkness* damages nonevil characters who touch it. With a successful Use Magic Device check, Lidda could emulate an evil alignment so that she could handle a *book of vile darkness* safely. You can emulate only one alignment at a time.

Task	Use Magic Device DC
Activate blindly	25
Decipher a written spell	25 + spell level
Use a scroll	20 + caster level
Use a wand	20
Emulate a class feature	20
Emulate an ability score	See text
Emulate a race	25
Emulate an alignment	30

Illus. by J. Foster

Emulate a Class Feature: Sometimes you need to use a class feature to activate a magic item. In this case, your effective level in the emulated class equals your Use Magic Device check result minus 20. For example, Lidda finds a magic chalice that turns regular water into holy water when a cleric or an experienced paladin channels positive energy into it as if turning undead. She attempts to activate the item by emulating the cleric's undead turning ability. Her effective cleric level is her check result minus 20. Since a cleric can turn undead at 1st level, she needs a Use Magic Device check result of 21 or higher to succeed.

This skill does not let you actually use the class feature of another class. It just lets you activate items as if you had that class feature.

If the class whose feature you are emulating has an alignment requirement, you must meet it, either honestly or by emulating an appropriate alignment with a separate Use Magic Device check (see above).

Emulate a Race: Some magic items work only for members of certain races, or work better for members of those races. You can use such an item as if you were a race of your choice. For example, Lidda, a halfling, could attempt to use a *dwarven thrower* (see page 226 of the *Dungeon Master's Guide*) as if she were a dwarf. If she failed her Use Magic Device check, the hammer would work for her as it normally would for a halfling, but if she succeeded, it would work for her as if she were a dwarf. You can emulate only one race at a time.

Use a Scroll: If you are casting a spell from a scroll, you have to decipher it first. Normally, to cast a spell from a scroll, you must have the scroll's spell on your class spell list. Use Magic Device allows you to use a scroll as if you had a particular spell on your class spell list. The DC is equal to 20 + the caster level of the spell you are trying to cast from the scroll. For instance, to cast *web* (a 2nd-level wizard spell) from a scroll, you would need a Use Magic Device check result of 23 or better, since the minimum caster level for *web* is 3rd level. See the *Dungeon Master's Guide* for more information on scrolls.

In addition, casting a spell from a scroll requires a minimum score (10 + spell level) in the appropriate ability. If you don't have a sufficient score in that ability, you must emulate the ability score with a separate Use Magic Device check (see above).

This use of the skill also applies to other spell completion magic items. The *Dungeon Master's Guide* has more information on such items.

Use a Wand: Normally, to use a wand, you must have the wand's spell on your class spell list. This use of the skill allows you to use a wand as if you had a particular spell on your class spell list.

This use of the skill also applies to other spell trigger magic items, such as staffs. The *Dungeon Master's Guide* has more information on such items.

Action: None. The Use Magic Device check is made as part of the action (if any) required to activate the magic item. (See Activate Magic Item, page 142, and the *Dungeon Master's Guide* for discussions of how magic items are normally activated.)

Try Again: Yes, but if you ever roll a natural 1 while attempting to activate an item and you fail, then you can't try to activate that item again for 24 hours.

Special: You cannot take 10 with this skill.

You can't aid another on Use Magic Device checks. Only the user of the item may attempt such a check.

If you have the Magical Aptitude feat, you get a +2 bonus on Use Magic Device checks.

Synergy: If you have 5 or more ranks in Spellcraft, you get a +2 bonus on Use Magic Device checks related to scrolls.

If you have 5 or more ranks in Decipher Script, you get a +2 bonus on Use Magic Device checks related to scrolls.

If you have 5 or more ranks in Use Magic Device, you get a +2 bonus to Spellcraft checks made to decipher spells on scrolls.

USE ROPE (DEX)

With this skill, you can make firm knots, undo tricky knots, and bind prisoners with ropes.

Check: Most tasks with a rope are relatively simple. The DCs for various tasks utilizing this skill are summarized on the table below.

Use Rope DC	Task
10	Tie a firm knot
10[1]	Secure a grappling hook
15	Tie a special knot, such as one that slips, slides slowly, or loosens with a tug
15	Tie a rope around yourself one-handed
15	Splice two ropes together
Varies	Bind a character

1 Add 2 to the DC for every 10 feet the hook is thrown; see below.

Secure a Grappling Hook: Securing a grappling hook requires a Use Rope check (DC 10, +2 for every 10 feet of distance the grappling hook is thrown, to a maximum DC of 20 at 50 feet). Failure by 4 or less indicates that the hook fails to catch and falls, allowing you to try again. Failure by 5 or more indicates that the grappling hook initially holds, but comes loose after 1d4 rounds of supporting weight. Your DM should make this check secretly, so that you don't know whether the rope will hold your weight.

Bind a Character: When you bind another character with a rope, any Escape Artist check that the bound character makes is opposed by your Use Rope check. You get a +10 bonus on this check because it is easier to bind someone than to escape from bonds. You don't even make your Use Rope check until someone tries to escape.

Action: Varies. Throwing a grappling hook is a standard action that provokes an attack of opportunity. Tying a knot, tying a special knot, or tying a rope around yourself one-handed is a full-round action that provokes an attack of opportunity. Splicing two ropes together takes 5 minutes. Binding a character takes 1 minute.

Special: A silk rope (page 127) gives you a +2 circumstance bonus on Use Rope checks. If you cast an *animate rope* spell on a rope, you get a +2 circumstance bonus on any Use Rope checks you make when using that rope. These bonuses stack.

If you have the Deft Hands feat, you get a +2 bonus on Use Rope checks.

Synergy: If you have 5 or more ranks in Use Rope, you get a +2 bonus on Climb checks made to climb a rope, a knotted rope, or a rope-and-wall combination.

If you have 5 or more ranks in Use Rope, you get a +2 bonus on Escape Artist checks when escaping from rope bonds.

If you have 5 or more ranks in Escape Artist, you get a +2 bonus on checks made to bind someone.

Fig. B

Clock works
set off snares

Skill

Stand
poison
thi

A feat is a special feature that either gives your character a new capability or improves one that he or she already has. For example, Lidda (a halfling rogue) chooses to start with the Improved Initiative feat at 1st level. That feat gives her a +4 bonus on her initiative checks. At 3rd level (see Table 3–2: Experience and Level-Dependent Benefits, page 22), she gains a new feat and chooses Dodge. This feat allows her to avoid the attacks of an opponent she selects by improving her Armor Class against that opponent.

Unlike a skill, a feat has no ranks. A character either has a feat or does not.

ACQUIRING FEATS

Unlike skills, feats are not bought with points. A player simply chooses them for his or her character. Each character gets one feat upon creation. At 3rd level and every three levels thereafter (6th, 9th, 12th, 15th, and 18th level), he or she gains another feat (see Table 3–2: Experience and Level-Dependent Benefits, page 22). Feats are gained according to character level, regardless of individual class levels.

Additionally, members of some classes get bonus feats as class features. These feats may be chosen from special lists (see Fighter Bonus Feats, below, and the individual class descriptions in Chapter 3 for details).

A human character also gets a bonus feat at 1st level, chosen by the player. This bonus feat can be any feat for which the character qualifies.

PREREQUISITES

Some feats have prerequisites. Your character must have the indicated ability score, class feature, feat, skill, base attack bonus, or other quality designated in order to select or use that feat. A character can gain a feat at the same level at which he or she gains the prerequisite. For example, at 3rd level, Krusk, a half-orc barbarian, could spend 1 skill point on the Ride skill (gaining his first rank in Ride) and select the Mounted Combat feat at the same time.

A character can't use a feat if he or she has lost a prerequisite. For example, if your character's Strength drops below 13 because of a *ray of enfeeblement* spell, he or she can't use the Power Attack feat until the prerequisite is once again met.

TYPES OF FEATS

Some feats are general, meaning that no special rules govern them as a group. Others are item creation feats, which allow spellcasters to create magic items of all sorts. A metamagic feat lets a spellcaster prepare and cast a spell with greater effect, albeit as if the spell were a higher spell level than it actually is.

FIGHTER BONUS FEATS

Fighters gain bonus feats selected from a subset of the feat list presented in Table 5–1 (page 90). Any feat designated as a fighter feat can be selected as a fighter's bonus feat. This designation does not restrict characters of other classes from selecting these feats, assuming that they meet any prerequisites.

87

A. Acid spray is pumped by the clock works

ITEM CREATION FEATS

Spellcasters can use their personal power to create lasting magic items. Doing so, however, is draining. A spellcaster must put a little of himself or herself into every magic item he or she creates.

An item creation feat lets a spellcaster create a magic item of a certain type. Regardless of the type of items they involve, the various item creation feats all have certain features in common.

XP Cost: Power and energy that the spellcaster would normally keep is expended when making a magic item. The XP cost equals 1/25 of the cost of the item in gold pieces (see the *Dungeon Master's Guide* for item costs). A character cannot spend so much XP on an item that he or she loses a level. However, upon gaining enough XP to attain a new level, he or she can immediately expend XP on creating an item rather than keeping the XP to advance a level.

Raw Materials Cost: Creating a magic item requires costly components, most of which are consumed in the process. The cost of these materials equals one-half the cost of the item.

For example, at 12th level Mialee the wizard gains the feat Forge Ring, and she creates a *ring of protection +3*. The cost of the ring is 18,000 gp, so it costs her 720 XP plus 9,000 gp to make.

Using an item creation feat also requires access to a laboratory or magical workshop, special tools, and so on. A character generally has access to what he or she needs unless unusual circumstances apply (if the character is traveling far from home, for instance).

Time: The time to create a magic item depends on the feat and the cost of the item. The minimum time is one day.

Item Cost: Brew Potion, Craft Wand, and Scribe Scroll create items that directly reproduce spell effects, and the power of these items depends on their caster level—that is, a spell from such an item has the power it would have if cast by a spellcaster of that level. A *wand of fireball* at caster level 8th, for example, would create *fireballs* that deal 8d6 points of damage and have a range of 720 feet. The price of these items (and thus the XP cost and the cost of the raw materials) also depends on the caster level. The caster level must be high enough that the spellcaster creating the item can cast the spell at that level. To find the final price in each case, multiply the caster level by the spell level, then multiply the result by a constant, as shown below:

Scrolls: Base price = spell level × caster level × 25 gp.
Potions: Base price = spell level × caster level × 50 gp.
Wands: Base price = spell level × caster level × 750 gp.

A 0-level spell is considered to have a spell level of 1/2 for the purpose of this calculation.

Extra Costs: Any potion, scroll, or wand that stores a spell with a costly material component or an XP cost also carries a commensurate cost. For potions and scrolls, the creator must expend the material component or pay the XP cost when creating the item. For a wand, the creator must expend fifty copies of the material component or pay fifty times the XP cost.

Some magic items similarly incur extra costs in material components or XP, as noted in their descriptions. For example, a *ring of three wishes* costs 15,000 XP in addition to its normal price (as many XP as it costs to cast *wish* three times).

METAMAGIC FEATS

As a spellcaster's knowledge of magic grows, she can learn to cast spells in ways slightly different from the ways in which the spells were originally designed or learned. For example, a spellcaster can learn to cast a spell without having to say its verbal component, to cast a spell for greater effect, or even to cast it with nothing but a moment's thought. Preparing and casting a spell in such a way is harder than normal but, thanks to metamagic feats, at least it is possible.

For instance, at 3rd level, Mialee chooses to gain Silent Spell, the feat that allows her to cast a spell without its verbal component. The cost of doing so, however, is that in preparing the spell,

she must use up a spell slot one spell level higher than the spell actually is. Thus, if she prepares *charm person* as a silent spell, it takes up one of her 2nd-level spell slots. It is still only a 1st-level spell, so the DC for the Will save against it does not go up. Mialee cannot prepare a 2nd-level spell as a silent spell because she would have to prepare it as a 3rd-level spell, and she can't use 3rd-level spell slots until she reaches 5th level.

Wizards and Divine Spellcasters: Wizards and divine spellcasters (clerics, druids, paladins, and rangers) must prepare their spells in advance. During preparation, the character chooses which spells to prepare with metamagic feats (and thus which ones take up higher-level spell slots than normal).

Sorcerers and Bards: Sorcerers and bards choose spells as they cast them. They can choose when they cast their spells whether to apply their metamagic feats to improve them. As with other spellcasters, the improved spell uses up a higher-level spell slot. But because the sorcerer or bard has not prepared the spell in a metamagic form in advance, he must apply the metamagic feat on the spot. Therefore, such a character must also take more time to cast a metamagic spell (one enhanced by a metamagic feat) than he does to cast a regular spell. If the spell's normal casting time is 1 action, casting a metamagic version is a full-round action for a sorcerer or bard. (This isn't the same as a 1-round casting time, as described under Cast a Spell, page 143.) For a spell with a longer casting time, it takes an extra full-round action to cast the spell.

Spontaneous Casting and Metamagic Feats: A cleric spontaneously casting a *cure* or *inflict* spell can cast a metamagic version of it instead. For instance, an 11th-level cleric can swap out a prepared 6th-level spell to cast an empowered *cure critical wounds* spell. Extra time is also required in this case. Casting a 1-action metamagic spell spontaneously is a full-round action, and a spell with a longer casting time takes an extra full-round action to cast.

Effects of Metamagic Feats on a Spell: In all ways, a metamagic spell operates at its original spell level, even though it is prepared and cast as a higher-level spell. Saving throw modifications are not changed unless stated otherwise in the feat description. The modifications made by these feats only apply to spells cast directly by the feat user. A spellcaster can't use a metamagic feat to alter a spell being cast from a wand, scroll, or other device.

Metamagic feats that eliminate components of a spell (such as Silent Spell and Still Spell) don't eliminate the attack of opportunity provoked by casting a spell while threatened. However, casting a spell modified by Quicken Spell does not provoke an attack of opportunity.

Metamagic feats cannot be used with all spells. See the specific feat descriptions for the spells that a particular feat can't modify.

Multiple Metamagic Feats on a Spell: A spellcaster can apply multiple metamagic feats to a single spell. Changes to its level are cumulative. A silent, stilled version of *charm person*, for example, would be prepared and cast as a 3rd-level spell (a 1st-level spell, increased by one spell level for each of the metamagic feats). You can't apply the same metamagic feat more than once to a single spell (for instance, you can't cast a twice-empowered *magic missile* to get +100% damage).

Magic Items and Metamagic Spells: With the right item creation feat, you can store a metamagic version of a spell in a scroll, potion, or wand. Level limits for potions and wands apply to the spell's higher spell level (after the application of the metamagic feat). A character doesn't need the metamagic feat to activate an item storing a metamagic version of a spell.

Counterspelling Metamagic Spells: Whether or not a spell has been enhanced by a metamagic feat does not affect its vulnerability to counterspelling or its ability to counterspell another spell (see Counterspells, page 170).

FEAT DESCRIPTIONS

Here is the format for feat descriptions.

FEAT NAME [TYPE OF FEAT]

Description of what the feat does or represents in plain language.

Prerequisite: A minimum ability score, another feat or feats, a minimum base attack bonus, a minimum number of ranks in one or more skills, or a class level that a character must have in order to acquire this feat. This entry is absent if a feat has no prerequisite. A feat may have more than one prerequisite.

Benefit: What the feat enables the character ("you" in the feat description) to do. If a character has the same feat more than once, its benefits do not stack unless indicated otherwise in the description. In general, having a feat twice is the same as having it once.

Normal: What a character who does not have this feat is limited to or restricted from doing. If not having the feat causes no particular drawback, this entry is absent.

Special: Additional facts about the feat that may be helpful when you decide whether to acquire the feat.

ACROBATIC [GENERAL]

You have excellent body awareness and coordination.

Benefit: You get a +2 bonus on all Jump checks and Tumble checks.

AGILE [GENERAL]

You are particularly flexible and poised.

Benefit: You get a +2 bonus on all Balance checks and Escape Artist checks.

ALERTNESS [GENERAL]

You have finely tuned senses.

Benefit: You get a +2 bonus on all Listen checks and Spot checks.

Special: The master of a familiar (see the Familiars sidebar, page 52) gains the benefit of the Alertness feat whenever the familiar is within arm's reach.

ANIMAL AFFINITY [GENERAL]

You are good with animals.

Benefit: You get a +2 bonus on all Handle Animal checks and Ride checks.

ARMOR PROFICIENCY (HEAVY) [GENERAL]

You are proficient with heavy armor (see Table 7–6: Armor and Shields, page 123).

Prerequisites: Armor Proficiency (light), Armor Proficiency (medium).

Benefit: See Armor Proficiency (light).

Normal: See Armor Proficiency (light).

Special: Fighters, paladins, and clerics automatically have Armor Proficiency (heavy) as a bonus feat. They need not select it.

ARMOR PROFICIENCY (LIGHT) [GENERAL]

You are proficient with light armor (see Table 7–6: Armor and Shields, page 123).

Benefit: When you wear a type of armor with which you are proficient, the armor check penalty for that armor applies only to Balance, Climb, Escape Artist, Hide, Jump, Move Silently, Pick Pocket, and Tumble checks.

Normal: A character who is wearing armor with which she is not proficient applies its armor check penalty to attack rolls and to all skill checks that involve moving, including Ride.

Special: All characters except wizards, sorcerers, and monks automatically have Armor Proficiency (light) as a bonus feat. They need not select it.

ARMOR PROFICIENCY (MEDIUM) [GENERAL]

You are proficient with medium armor (see Table 7–6: Armor and Shields, page 123).

Prerequisite: Armor Proficiency (light).

Benefit: See Armor Proficiency (light).

Normal: See Armor Proficiency (light).

Special: Fighters, barbarians, paladins, clerics, druids, and bards automatically have Armor Proficiency (medium) as a bonus feat. They need not select it.

ATHLETIC [GENERAL]

You have a knack for athletic endeavors.

Benefit: You get a +2 bonus on all Climb checks and Swim checks.

AUGMENT SUMMONING [GENERAL]

Your summoned creatures are more powerful than normal.

Prerequisite: Spell Focus (conjuration).

Benefit: Each creature you conjure with any *summon* spell gains a +4 enhancement bonus to Strength and Constitution for the duration of the spell that summoned it.

BLIND-FIGHT [GENERAL]

You know how to fight in melee without being able to see your foes.

Benefit: In melee, every time you miss because of concealment, you can reroll your miss chance percentile roll one time to see if you actually hit (see Concealment, page 152).

An invisible attacker gets no advantages related to hitting you in melee. That is, you don't lose your Dexterity bonus to Armor Class, and the attacker doesn't get the usual +2 bonus for being invisible (see Table 8–5: Attack Roll Modifiers and Table 8–6: Armor Class Modifiers, page 151). The invisible attacker's bonuses do still apply for ranged attacks, however.

You take only half the usual penalty to speed for being unable to see. Darkness and poor visibility in general reduces your speed to three-quarters normal, instead of one-half (see Table 9–4: Hampered Movement, page 163).

Normal: Regular attack roll modifiers for invisible attackers trying to hit you (see Table 8–5: Attack Roll Modifiers, page 151) apply, and you lose your Dexterity bonus to AC. The speed reduction for darkness and poor visibility (see Table 9–4: Hampered Movement, page 163) also applies.

Special: The Blind-Fight feat is of no use against a character who is the subject of a *blink* spell (see page 206).

A fighter may select Blind-Fight as one of his fighter bonus feats (see page 38).

BREW POTION [ITEM CREATION]

You can create potions, which carry spells within themselves. See the *Dungeon Master's Guide* for rules on potions.

Prerequisite: Caster level 3rd.

Benefit: You can create a potion of any 3rd-level or lower spell that you know and that targets one or more creatures. Brewing a potion takes one day. When you create a potion, you set the caster level, which must be sufficient to cast the spell in question and no higher than your own level. The base price of a potion is its spell level × its caster level × 50 gp. To brew a potion, you must spend 1/25 this base price in XP and use up raw materials costing one-half this base price.

When you create a potion, you make any choices that you would normally make when casting the spell. Whoever drinks the potion is the target of the spell.

Any potion that stores a spell with a costly material component or an XP cost also carries a commensurate cost. In addition to the costs derived from the base price, you must expend the material component or pay the XP when creating the potion.

TABLE 5–1: FEATS

General Feats	Prerequisites	Benefit
Acrobatic	—	+2 bonus on Jump and Tumble checks
Agile	—	+2 bonus on Balance and Escape Artist checks
Alertness	—	+2 bonus on Listen and Spot checks
Animal Affinity	—	+2 bonus on Handle Animal and Ride checks
Armor Proficiency (light)	—	No armor check penalty on attack rolls
Armor Proficiency (medium)	Armor Proficiency (light)	No armor check penalty on attack rolls
Armor Proficiency (heavy)	Armor Proficiency (medium)	No armor check penalty on attack rolls
Athletic	—	+2 bonus on Climb and Swim checks
Augment Summoning	Spell Focus (conjuration)	Summoned creatures gain +4 Str, +4 Con
Blind-Fight[1]	—	Reroll miss chance for concealment
Combat Casting	—	+4 bonus on Concentration checks for defensive casting
Combat Expertise[1]	Int 13	Trade attack bonus for AC (max 5 points)
Improved Disarm[1]	Combat Expertise	+4 bonus on disarm attempts; no attack of opportunity
Improved Feint[1]	Combat Expertise	Feint in combat as move action
Improved Trip[1]	Combat Expertise	+4 bonus on trip attempts; no attack of opportunity
Whirlwind Attack[1]	Dex 13, Combat Expertise, Dodge, Mobility, Spring Attack, base attack bonus +4	One melee attack against each opponent within reach
Combat Reflexes[1]	—	Additional attacks of opportunity
Deceitful	—	+2 bonus on Disguise and Forgery checks
Deft Hands	—	+2 bonus on Sleight of Hand and Use Rope checks
Diligent	—	+2 bonus on Appraise and Decipher Script checks
Dodge[1]	Dex 13	+1 dodge bonus to AC against selected target
Mobility[1]	Dodge	+4 dodge bonus to AC against some attacks of opportunity
Spring Attack[1]	Mobility, base attack bonus +4	Move before and after melee attack
Endurance	—	+4 bonus on checks or saves to resist nonlethal damage
Diehard	Endurance	Remain conscious at –1 to –9 hp
Eschew Materials	—	Cast spells without material components
Exotic Weapon Proficiency[1,2]	Base attack bonus +1	No penalty on attacks with specific exotic weapon
Extra Turning[3]	Ability to turn or rebuke creatures	Can turn or rebuke 4 more times per day
Great Fortitude	—	+2 bonus on Fortitude saves
Improved Counterspell	—	Counterspell with spell of same school
Improved Critical[1,2]	Proficiency with weapon, base attack bonus +8	Double threat range of weapon
Improved Initiative[1]	—	+4 bonus on initiative checks
Improved Turning	Ability to turn or rebuke creatures	+1 level for turning checks
Improved Unarmed Strike[1]	—	Considered armed even when unarmed
Improved Grapple[1]	Dex 13, Improved Unarmed Strike	+4 bonus on grapple checks; no attack of opportunity
Deflect Arrows[1]	Dex 13, Improved Unarmed Strike	Deflect one ranged attack per round
Snatch Arrows[1]	Dex 15, Deflect Arrows, Improved Unarmed Strike	Catch a deflected ranged attack
Stunning Fist[1]	Dex 13, Wis 13, Improved Unarmed Strike, base attack bonus +8	Stun opponent with unarmed strike
Investigator	—	+2 bonus on Gather Information and Search checks
Iron Will	—	+2 bonus on Will saves
Leadership	Character level 6th	Attract cohort and followers
Lightning Reflexes	—	+2 bonus on Reflex saves
Magical Aptitude	—	+2 bonus on Spellcraft and Use Magic Device checks
Martial Weapon Proficiency[2]	—	No penalty on attacks with specific martial weapon
Mounted Combat[1]	Ride 1 rank	Negate hits on mount with Ride check
Mounted Archery[1]	Mounted Combat	Half penalty for ranged attacks while mounted
Ride-By Attack[1]	Mounted Combat	Move before and after a mounted charge
Spirited Charge[1]	Mounted Combat, Ride-By Attack	Double damage with mounted charge
Trample[1]	Mounted Combat	Target cannot avoid mounted overrun
Natural Spell	Wis 13, Ability to use wild shape	Cast spells while in wild shape
Negotiator	—	+2 bonus on Diplomacy and Sense Motive checks
Nimble Fingers	—	+2 bonus on Disable Device and Open Lock checks
Persuasive	—	+2 bonus on Bluff checks and Intimidate checks
Point Blank Shot[1]	—	+1 bonus on ranged attack and damage within 30 ft.
Far Shot[1]	Point Blank Shot	Increase range increment by 50% or 100%
Precise Shot[1]	Point Blank Shot	No –4 penalty for shooting into melee
Rapid Shot[1]	Dex 13, Point Blank Shot	One extra ranged attack each round
Manyshot[1]	Dex 17, Point Blank Shot, Rapid Shot, base attack bonus +6	Shoot two or more arrows simultaneously
Shot on the Run[1]	Dex 13, Dodge, Mobility, Point Blank Shot, base attack bonus +4	Move before and after ranged attack
Improved Precise Shot[1]	Dex 19, Point Blank Shot, Precise Shot, base attack bonus +11	Ignore less than total cover/concealment on ranged attacks

Feat	Prerequisites	Benefit
Power Attack[1]	Str 13	Trade attack bonus for damage (up to base attack bonus)
Cleave[1]	Power Attack	Extra melee attack after dropping target
Great Cleave[1]	Cleave, Power Attack, base attack bonus +4	No limit to cleave attacks each round
Improved Bull Rush[1]	Power Attack	+4 bonus on bull rush attempts; no attack of opportunity
Improved Overrun[1]	Power Attack	+4 bonus on overrun attempts; no attack of opportunity
Improved Sunder[1]	Power Attack	+4 bonus on sunder attempts; no attack of opportunity
Quick Draw[1]	Base attack bonus +1	Draw weapon as free action
Rapid Reload[1]	Weapon Proficiency with crossbow	Reload crossbow more quickly
Run	—	Run at 5 times normal speed, +4 bonus on Jump checks made after a running start
Self-Sufficient	—	+2 bonus on Heal and Survival checks
Shield Proficiency	—	No armor check penalty on attack rolls
Improved Shield Bash[1]	Shield Proficiency	Retain shield bonus to AC when shield bashing
Tower Shield Proficiency	Shield Proficiency	No armor check penalty on attack rolls
Simple Weapon Proficiency	—	No −4 penalty on attack rolls with simple weapons
Skill Focus[2]	—	+3 bonus on checks with selected skill
Spell Focus[2]	—	+1 bonus on save DCs against specific school of magic
Greater Spell Focus[2]	—	+1 bonus on save DCs against specific school of magic
Spell Mastery[2]	Wizard level 1st	Can prepare some spells without spellbook
Spell Penetration	—	+2 bonus on caster level checks to defeat spell resistance
Greater Spell Penetration	Spell Penetration	+4 to caster level checks to defeat spell resistance
Stealthy	—	+2 bonus on Hide and Move Silently checks
Toughness[3]	—	+3 hit points
Track	—	Use Survival skill to track
Two-Weapon Fighting[1]	Dex 15	Reduce two-weapon fighting penalties by 2
Two-Weapon Defense[1]	Two-Weapon Fighting	Off-hand weapon grants +1 shield bonus to AC
Improved Two-Weapon Fighting[1]	Dex 17, Two-Weapon Fighting, base attack bonus +6	Gain second off-hand attack
Greater Two-Weapon Fighting[1]	Dex 19, Improved Two-Weapon Fighting, Two-Weapon Fighting, base attack bonus +11	Gain third off-hand attack
Weapon Finesse[1, 2]	Proficiency with weapon, base attack bonus +1	Use Dex modifier instead of Str modifier on attack rolls with light melee weapons
Weapon Focus[1, 2]	Proficiency with weapon, base attack bonus +1	+1 bonus on attack rolls with selected weapon
Weapon Specialization[1, 2]	Proficiency with weapon, Weapon Focus with weapon, fighter level 4th	+2 bonus on damage rolls with selected weapon
Greater Weapon Focus[1, 2]	Proficiency with weapon, Weapon Focus with weapon, fighter level 8th	+2 bonus on attack rolls with selected weapon
Greater Weapon Specialization[1, 2]	Proficiency with weapon, Greater Weapon Focus with weapon, Weapon Focus with weapon, Weapon Specialization with weapon, fighter level 12th	+4 bonus on damage rolls with selected weapon

Item Creation Feats	Prerequisites	Benefit
Brew Potion	Caster level 3rd	Create magic potions
Craft Magic Arms and Armor	Caster level 5th	Create magic weapons, armor, and shields
Craft Rod	Caster level 9th	Create magic rods
Craft Staff	Caster level 12th	Create magic staffs
Craft Wand	Caster level 5th	Create magic wands
Craft Wondrous Item	Caster level 3rd	Create magic wondrous items
Forge Ring	Caster level 12th	Create magic rings
Scribe Scroll	Caster level 1st	Create magic scrolls

Metamagic Feats	Prerequisites	Benefit
Empower Spell	—	Increase spell's variable, numeric effects by 50%
Enlarge Spell	—	Double spell's range
Extend Spell	—	Double spell's duration
Heighten Spell	—	Cast spells as higher level
Maximize Spell	—	Maximize spell's variable, numeric effects
Quicken Spell	—	Cast spells as free action
Silent Spell	—	Cast spells without verbal components
Still Spell	—	Cast spells without somatic components
Widen Spell	—	Double spell's area

1 A fighter may select this feat as one of his fighter bonus feats.

2 You can gain this feat multiple times. Its effects do not stack. Each time you take the feat, it applies to a new weapon, skill, school of magic, or selection of spells.

3 You can gain this feat multiple times. Its effects stack.

CLEAVE [GENERAL]

You can follow through with powerful blows.

Prerequisites: Str 13, Power Attack.

Benefit: If you deal a creature enough damage to make it drop (typically by dropping it to below 0 hit points or killing it), you get an immediate, extra melee attack against another creature within reach. You cannot take a 5-foot step before making this extra attack. The extra attack is with the same weapon and at the same bonus as the attack that dropped the previous creature. You can use this ability once per round.

Special: A fighter may select Cleave as one of his fighter bonus feats (see page 38).

COMBAT CASTING [GENERAL]

You are adept at casting spells in combat.

Benefit: You get a +4 bonus on Concentration checks made to cast a spell or use a spell-like ability while on the defensive (see Casting on the Defensive, page 140) or while you are grappling or pinned.

COMBAT EXPERTISE [GENERAL]

You are trained at using your combat skill for defense as well as offense.

Prerequisite: Int 13.

Benefit: When you use the attack action or the full attack action in melee, you can take a penalty of as much as –5 on your attack roll and add the same number (+5 or less) as a dodge bonus to your Armor Class. This number may not exceed your base attack bonus. The changes to attack rolls and Armor Class last until your next action.

Normal: A character without the Combat Expertise feat can fight defensively while using the attack or full attack action to take a –4 penalty on attack rolls and gain a +2 dodge bonus to Armor Class.

Special: A fighter may select Combat Expertise as one of his fighter bonus feats (see page 38).

COMBAT REFLEXES [GENERAL]

You can respond quickly and repeatedly to opponents who let their defenses down.

Benefit: When foes leave themselves open, you may make a number of additional attacks of opportunity equal to your Dexterity bonus. For example, a fighter with a Dexterity of 15 can make a total of three attacks of opportunity in 1 round—the one attack of opportunity any character is entitled to, plus two more because of his +2 Dexterity bonus. If four goblins move out of the character's threatened squares, he can make one attack of opportunity each against three of the four. You can still make only one attack of opportunity per opportunity.

With this feat, you may also make attacks of opportunity while flat-footed.

Normal: A character without this feat can make only one attack of opportunity per round and can't make attacks of opportunity while flat-footed.

Special: The Combat Reflexes feat does not allow a rogue to use her opportunist ability (see page 51) more than once per round.

A fighter may select Combat Reflexes as one of his fighter bonus feats (see page 38).

A monk may select Combat Reflexes as a bonus feat at 2nd level.

CRAFT MAGIC ARMS AND ARMOR
[ITEM CREATION]

You can create magic weapons, armor, and shields.

Prerequisite: Caster level 5th.

Benefit: You can create any magic weapon, armor, or shield whose prerequisites you meet (see the *Dungeon Master's Guide* for prerequisites and other information on these items). Enhancing a weapon, suit of armor, or shield takes one day for each 1,000 gp in the price of its magical features. To enhance a weapon, suit of armor, or shield, you must spend 1/25 of its features' total price in XP and use up raw materials costing one-half of this total price.

The weapon, armor, or shield to be enhanced must be a masterwork item that you provide. Its cost is not included in the above cost.

You can also mend a broken magic weapon, suit of armor, or shield if it is one that you could make. Doing so costs half the XP, half the raw materials, and half the time it would take to craft that item in the first place.

CRAFT ROD [ITEM CREATION]

You can create magic rods, which have varied magical effects.

Prerequisite: Caster level 9th.

Benefit: You can create any rod whose prerequisites you meet (see the *Dungeon Master's Guide* for prerequisites and other information on rods). Crafting a rod takes one day for each 1,000 gp in its base price. To craft a rod, you must spend 1/25 of its base price in XP and use up raw materials costing one-half of its base price.

Some rods incur extra costs in material components or XP, as noted in their descriptions. These costs are in addition to those derived from the rod's base price.

CRAFT STAFF [ITEM CREATION]

You can create magic staffs, each of which has multiple magical effects.

Prerequisite: Caster level 12th.

Benefit: You can create any staff whose prerequisites you meet (see the *Dungeon Master's Guide* for prerequisites and other information on staffs). Crafting a staff takes one day for each 1,000 gp in its base price. To craft a staff, you must spend 1/25 of its base price in XP and use up raw materials costing one-half of its base price. A newly created staff has 50 charges.

Some staffs incur extra costs in material components or XP, as noted in their descriptions. These costs are in addition to those derived from the staff's base price.

Lidda dodges the ray of a spell cast by an evil cleric.

CRAFT WAND [ITEM CREATION]

You can create wands, which hold spells (see the *Dungeon Master's Guide* for rules on wands).

Prerequisite: Caster level 5th.

Benefit: You can create a wand of any 4th-level or lower spell that you know. Crafting a wand takes one day for each 1,000 gp in its base price. The base price of a wand is its caster level × the spell level × 750 gp. To craft a wand, you must spend 1/25 of this base price in XP and use up raw materials costing one-half of this base price. A newly created wand has 50 charges.

Any wand that stores a spell with a costly material component or an XP cost also carries a commensurate cost. In addition to the cost derived from the base price, you must expend fifty copies of the material component or pay fifty times the XP cost.

CRAFT WONDROUS ITEM [ITEM CREATION]

You can create a wide variety of magic items, such as a *crystal ball* or a *flying carpet*.

Prerequisite: Caster level 3rd.

Benefit: You can create any wondrous item whose prerequisites you meet (see the *Dungeon Master's Guide* for prerequisites and other information on wondrous items). Enchanting a wondrous item takes one day for each 1,000 gp in its price. To enchant a wondrous item, you must spend 1/25 of the item's price in XP and use up raw materials costing half of this price.

You can also mend a broken wondrous item if it is one that you could make. Doing so costs half the XP, half the raw materials, and half the time it would take to craft that item in the first place.

Some wondrous items incur extra costs in material components or XP, as noted in their descriptions. These costs are in addition to those derived from the item's base price. You must pay such a cost to create an item or to mend a broken one.

DECEITFUL [GENERAL]
You have a knack for disguising the truth.

Benefit: You get a +2 bonus on all Disguise checks and Forgery checks.

DEFLECT ARROWS [GENERAL]
You can deflect incoming arrows, as well as crossbow bolts, spears, and other projectile or thrown weapons.

Prerequisites: Dex 13, Improved Unarmed Strike.

Benefit: You must have at least one hand free (holding nothing) to use this feat. Once per round when you would normally be hit with a ranged weapon, you may deflect it so that you take no damage from it. You must be aware of the attack and not flat-footed. Attempting to deflect a ranged weapon doesn't count as an action. Unusually massive ranged weapons, such as boulders hurled by giants, and ranged attacks generated by spell effects, such as *Melf's acid arrow*, can't be deflected.

Special: A monk may select Deflect Arrows as a bonus feat at 2nd level, even if she does not meet the prerequisites.

A fighter may select Deflect Arrows as one of his fighter bonus feats (see page 38).

DEFT HANDS [GENERAL]
You have exceptional manual dexterity.

Benefit: You get a +2 bonus on all Sleight of Hand checks and Use Rope checks.

DIEHARD [GENERAL]
You can remain conscious after attacks that would fell others.

Prerequisite: Endurance.

Benefit: When reduced to between –1 and –9 hit points, you automatically become stable. You don't have to roll d% to see if you lose 1 hit point each round.

When reduced to negative hit points, you may choose to act as if you were disabled, rather than dying. You must make this decision as soon as you are reduced to negative hit points (even if it isn't your turn). If you do not choose to act as if you were disabled, you immediately fall unconscious.

When using this feat, you can take either a single move or standard action each turn, but not both, and you cannot take a full-round action. You can take a move action without further injuring yourself, but if you perform any standard action (or any other action the DM deems as strenuous, including some free actions, such as casting a quickened spell) you take 1 point of damage after completing the act. If you reach –10 hit points, you immediately die.

Normal: A character without this feat who is reduced to between –1 and –9 hit points is unconscious and dying, as described in Chapter 8: Combat.

DILIGENT [GENERAL]
Your meticulousness allows you to analyze minute details that others miss.

Benefit: You get a +2 bonus on all Appraise checks and Decipher Script checks.

DODGE [GENERAL]
You are adept at dodging blows.

Prerequisite: Dex 13.

Benefit: During your action, you designate an opponent and receive a +1 dodge bonus to Armor Class against attacks from that opponent. You can select a new opponent on any action.

A condition that makes you lose your Dexterity bonus to Armor Class (if any) also makes you lose dodge bonuses. Also, dodge bonuses (such as this one and a dwarf's racial bonus on dodge attempts against giants) stack with each other, unlike most other types of bonuses.

Special: A fighter may select Dodge as one of his fighter bonus feats (see page 38).

EMPOWER SPELL [METAMAGIC]
You can cast spells to greater effect.

Benefit: All variable, numeric effects of an empowered spell are increased by one-half. An empowered spell deals half again as much damage as normal, cures half again as many hit points, affects half again as many targets, and so forth, as appropriate. For example, an empowered *magic missile* deals 1-1/2 times its normal damage (roll 1d4+1 and multiply the result by 1-1/2 for each missile). Saving throws and opposed rolls (such as the one you make when you cast *dispel magic*) are not affected, nor are spells without random variables. An empowered spell uses up a spell slot two levels higher than the spell's actual level.

ENDURANCE [GENERAL]
You are capable of amazing feats of stamina.

Benefit: You gain a +4 bonus on the following checks and saves: Swim checks made to resist nonlethal damage (see page 84), Constitution checks made to continue running (see page 144), Constitution checks made to avoid nonlethal damage from a forced march (see page 164), Constitution checks made to hold your breath (see page 84), Constitution checks made to avoid nonlethal damage from starvation or thirst (see page 304 of the *Dungeon Master's Guide*), Fortitude saves made to avoid nonlethal damage from hot or cold environments (see pages 302 and 303 of the *Dungeon Master's Guide*), and Fortitude saves made to resist damage from suffocation (see page 304 of the *Dungeon Master's Guide*). Also, you may sleep in light or medium armor without becoming fatigued.

Normal: A character without this feat who sleeps in medium or heavier armor is automatically fatigued the next day.

Special: A ranger automatically gains Endurance as a bonus feat at 3rd level (see page 48). He need not select it.

Illus. by J. Foster

ENLARGE SPELL [METAMAGIC]

You can cast spells farther than normal.

Benefit: You can alter a spell with a range of close, medium, or long to increase its range by 100%. An enlarged spell with a range of close now has a range of 50 ft. + 5 ft./level, while medium-range spells have a range of 200 ft. + 20 ft./level and long-range spells have a range of 800 ft. + 80 ft./level. An enlarged spell uses up a spell slot one level higher than the spell's actual level.

Spells whose ranges are not defined by distance, as well as spells whose ranges are not close, medium, or long, do not have increased ranges.

ESCHEW MATERIALS [GENERAL]

You can cast spells without relying on material components.

Benefit: You can cast any spell that has a material component costing 1 gp or less without needing that component. (The casting of the spell still provokes attacks of opportunity as normal.) If the spell requires a material component that costs more than 1 gp, you must have the material component at hand to cast the spell, just as normal.

EXOTIC WEAPON PROFICIENCY [GENERAL]

Choose a type of exotic weapon, such as dire flail or shuriken (see Table 7–5: Weapons, page 116, for a list of exotic weapons). You understand how to use that type of exotic weapon in combat.

Prerequisite: Base attack bonus +1 (plus Str 13 for bastard sword or dwarven waraxe).

Benefit: You make attack rolls with the weapon normally.

Normal: A character who uses a weapon with which he or she is not proficient takes a –4 penalty on attack rolls.

Special: You can gain Exotic Weapon Proficiency multiple times. Each time you take the feat, it applies to a new type of exotic weapon. Proficiency with the bastard sword or the dwarven waraxe has an additional prerequisite of Str 13.

A fighter may select Exotic Weapon Proficiency as one of his fighter bonus feats (see page 38).

EXTEND SPELL [METAMAGIC]

You can cast spells that last longer than normal.

Benefit: An extended spell lasts twice as long as normal. A spell with a duration of concentration, instantaneous, or permanent is not affected by this feat. An extended spell uses up a spell slot one level higher than the spell's actual level.

EXTRA TURNING [GENERAL]

You can turn or rebuke creatures more often than normal.

Prerequisite: Ability to turn or rebuke creatures.

Benefit: Each time you take this feat, you can use your abil-ity to turn or rebuke creatures four more times per day than normal.

If you have the ability to turn or rebuke more than one kind of creature (such as a good-aligned cleric with access to the Fire domain, who can turn undead and water creatures and can also rebuke fire creatures), each of your turning or rebuking abilities gains four additional uses per day.

Normal: Without this feat, a character can typically turn or rebuke undead (or other creatures) a number of times per day equal to 3 + his or her Charisma modifier.

Special: You can gain Extra Turning multiple times. Its effects stack. Each time you take the feat, you can use each of your turning or rebuking abilities four additional times per day.

FAR SHOT [GENERAL]

You can get greater distance out of a ranged weapon.

Prerequisite: Point Blank Shot.

Benefit: When you use a projectile weapon, such as a bow, its range increment increases by one-half (multiply by 1-1/2). When you use a thrown weapon, its range increment is doubled.

Special: A fighter may select Far Shot as one of his fighter bonus feats (see page 38).

FORGE RING [ITEM CREATION]

You can create magic rings, which have varied magical effects.

Prerequisite: Caster level 12th.

Benefit: You can create any ring whose prerequisites you meet (see the *Dungeon Master's Guide* for prerequisites and other infor-mation on rings). Crafting a ring takes one day for each 1,000 gp in its base price. To craft a ring, you must spend 1/25 of its base price in XP and use up raw materials costing one-half of its base price.

You can also mend a broken ring if it is one that you could make. Doing so costs half the XP, half the raw materials, and half the time it would take to forge that ring in the first place.

Some magic rings incur extra costs in material components or XP, as noted in their descriptions. For example, a *ring of three wishes* costs 15,000 XP in addition to costs derived from its base price (as many XP as it costs to cast *wish* three times). You must pay such a cost to forge such a ring or to mend a broken one.

GREAT CLEAVE [GENERAL]

You can wield a melee weapon with such power that you can strike multiple times when you fell your foes.

Prerequisites: Str 13, Cleave, Power Attack, base attack bonus +4.

Benefit: This feat works like Cleave, except that there is no limit to the number of times you can use it per round.

Special: A fighter may select Great Cleave as one of his fighter bonus feats (see page 38).

GREAT FORTITUDE [GENERAL]

You are tougher than normal.

Benefit: You get a +2 bonus on all Fortitude saving throws.

GREATER SPELL FOCUS [GENERAL]

Choose a school of magic to which you already have applied the Spell Focus feat. Your spells of that school are now even more potent than before.

Benefit: Add +1 to the Difficulty Class for all saving throws against spells from the school of magic you select. This bonus stacks with the bonus from Spell Focus.

Special: You can gain this feat multiple times. Its effects do not stack. Each time you take the feat, it applies to a new school of magic to which you already have applied the Spell Focus feat.

GREATER SPELL PENETRATION [GENERAL]

Your spells are remarkably potent, breaking through spell resist-ance more readily than normal.

Prerequisite: Spell Penetration.

Benefit: You get a +2 bonus on caster level checks (1d20 + caster level) made to overcome a creature's spell resistance. This bonus stacks with the one from Spell Penetration (see page 100).

GREATER TWO-WEAPON FIGHTING [GENERAL]

You are a master at fighting two-handed.

Prerequisites: Dex 19, Improved Two-Weapon Fighting, Two-Weapon Fighting, base attack bonus +11.

Benefit: You get a third attack with your off-hand weapon, albeit at a –10 penalty.

Special: A fighter may select Greater Two-Weapon Fighting as one of his fighter bonus feats (see page 38).

An 11th-level ranger who has chosen the two-weapon combat style is treated as having Greater Two-Weapon Fighting, even if he does not have the prerequisites for it, but only when he is wearing light or no armor (see page 48).

GREATER WEAPON FOCUS [GENERAL]

Choose one type of weapon, such as greataxe, for which you have already selected Weapon Focus. You can also choose unarmed strike or grapple as your weapon for purposes of this feat. You are especially good at using this weapon.

Prerequisites: Proficiency with selected weapon, Weapon Focus with selected weapon, fighter level 8th.

Benefit: You gain a +1 bonus on all attack rolls you make using the selected weapon. This bonus stacks with other bonuses on attack rolls, including the one from Weapon Focus (see below).

Special: You can gain Greater Weapon Focus multiple times. Its effects do not stack. Each time you take the feat, it applies to a new type of weapon.

A fighter must have Greater Weapon Focus with a given weapon to gain the Greater Weapon Specialization feat for that weapon.

A fighter may select Greater Weapon Focus as one of his fighter bonus feats (see page 38).

GREATER WEAPON SPECIALIZATION [GENERAL]

Choose one type of weapon, such as greataxe, for which you have already selected Weapon Specialization. You can also choose unarmed strike or grapple as your weapon for purposes of this feat. You deal extra damage when using this weapon.

Prerequisites: Proficiency with selected weapon, Greater Weapon Focus with selected weapon, Weapon Focus with selected weapon, Weapon Specialization with selected weapon, fighter level 12th.

Benefit: You gain a +2 bonus on all damage rolls you make using the selected weapon. This bonus stacks with other bonuses on damage rolls, including the one from Weapon Specialization (see below).

Special: You can gain Greater Weapon Specialization multiple times. Its effects do not stack. Each time you take the feat, it applies to a new type of weapon.

A fighter may select Greater Weapon Specialization as one of his fighter bonus feats (see page 38).

HEIGHTEN SPELL [METAMAGIC]

You can cast a spell as if it were a higher-level spell than it actually is.

Benefit: A heightened spell has a higher spell level than normal (up to a maximum of 9th level). Unlike other metamagic feats, Heighten Spell actually increases the effective level of the spell that it modifies. All effects dependent on spell level (such as saving throw DCs and ability to penetrate a *lesser globe of invulnerability*) are calculated according to the heightened level. The heightened spell is as difficult to prepare and cast as a spell of its effective level. For example, a cleric could prepare *hold person* as a 4th-level

spell (instead of a 2nd-level spell), and it would in all ways be treated as a 4th-level spell.

IMPROVED BULL RUSH [GENERAL]

You know how to push opponents back.

Prerequisites: Str 13, Power Attack.

Benefit: When you perform a bull rush (page 154), you do not provoke an attack of opportunity from the defender. You also gain a +4 bonus on the opposed Strength check you make to push back the defender.

Special: A fighter may select Improved Bull Rush as one of his fighter bonus feats (see page 38).

IMPROVED COUNTERSPELL [GENERAL]

You understand the nuances of magic to such an extent that you can counter your opponent's spells with great efficiency.

Benefit: When counterspelling, you may use a spell of the same school that is one or more spell levels higher than the target spell.

Normal: Without this feat, you may counter a spell only with the same spell or with a spell specifically designated as countering the target spell.

IMPROVED CRITICAL [GENERAL]

Choose one type of weapon, such as longsword or greataxe. With that weapon, you know how to hit where it hurts.

Prerequisite: Proficient with weapon, base attack bonus +8.

Benefit: When using the weapon you selected, your threat range is doubled. For example, a longsword usually threatens a critical hit on a roll of 19–20 (two numbers). If a character using a longsword has Improved Critical (longsword), the threat range becomes 17–20 (four numbers).

Special: You can gain Improved Critical multiple times. The effects do not stack. Each time you take the feat, it applies to a new type of weapon.

This effect doesn't stack with any other effect that expands the threat range of a weapon (such as the *keen edge* spell).

A fighter may select Improved Critical as one of his fighter bonus feats (see page 38).

IMPROVED DISARM [GENERAL]

You know how to disarm opponents in melee combat.

Prerequisites: Int 13, Combat Expertise.

Benefit: You do not provoke an attack of opportunity when you attempt to disarm an opponent, nor does the opponent have a chance to disarm you. You also gain a +4 bonus on the opposed attack roll you make to disarm your opponent.

Normal: See the normal disarm rules, page 155.

Special: A fighter may select Improved Disarm as one of his fighter bonus feats (see page 38).

A monk may select Improved Disarm as a bonus feat at 6th level, even if she does not meet the prerequisites.

IMPROVED FEINT [GENERAL]

You are skilled at misdirecting your opponent's attention in combat.

Prerequisites: Int 13, Combat Expertise.

Benefit: You can make a Bluff check to feint in combat as a move action.

Normal: Feinting in combat is a standard action.

A fighter may select Improved Feint as one of his fighter bonus feats (see page 38).

IMPROVED GRAPPLE [GENERAL]

You are skilled at grappling opponents.

Prerequisites: Dex 13, Improved Unarmed Strike.

Benefit: You do not provoke an attack of opportunity when you make a touch attack to start a grapple. You also gain a +4 bonus on all grapple checks, regardless of whether you started the grapple.

Normal: Without this feat, you provoke an attack of opportunity when you make a touch attack to start a grapple.

Special: A fighter may select Improved Grapple as one of his fighter bonus feats (see page 38).

A monk may select Improved Grapple as a bonus feat at 1st level, even if she does not meet the prerequisites.

IMPROVED INITIATIVE [GENERAL]

You can react more quickly than normal in a fight.

Benefit: You get a +4 bonus on initiative checks.

Special: A fighter may select Improved Initiative as one of his fighter bonus feats (see page 38).

IMPROVED OVERRUN [GENERAL]

You are skilled at knocking down opponents.

Prerequisites: Str 13, Power Attack.

Benefit: When you attempt to overrun an opponent, the target may not choose to avoid you. You also gain a +4 bonus on your Strength check to knock down your opponent.

Normal: Without this feat, the target of an overrun can choose to avoid you or to block you.

Special: A fighter may select Improved Overrun as one of his fighter bonus feats (see page 38).

IMPROVED PRECISE SHOT [GENERAL]

Your ranged attacks can ignore the effects of cover or concealment.

Prerequisites: Dex 19, Point Blank Shot, Precise Shot, base attack bonus +11.

Benefit: Your ranged attacks ignore the AC bonus granted to targets by anything less than total cover, and the miss chance granted to targets by anything less than total concealment. Total cover and total concealment provide their normal benefits against your ranged attacks.

In addition, when you shoot or throw ranged weapons at a grappling opponent, you automatically strike at the opponent you have chosen.

Normal: See pages 150–152 for rules on the effects of cover and concealment. Without this feat, a character who shoots or throws a ranged weapon at a target involved in a grapple must roll randomly to see which grappling combatant the attack strikes.

Special: A fighter may select Improved Precise Shot as one of his fighter bonus feats (see page 38).

An 11th-level ranger who has chosen the archery combat style is treated as having Improved Precise Shot, even if he does not have the prerequisites for it, but only when he is wearing light or no armor (see page 48).

IMPROVED SHIELD BASH [GENERAL]

You can bash with a shield while retaining its shield bonus to your Armor Class.

Prerequisite: Shield Proficiency.

Benefit: When you perform a shield bash, you may still apply the shield's shield bonus to your AC.

Normal: Without this feat, a character who performs a shield bash loses the shield's shield bonus to AC until his or her next turn.

Special: A fighter may select Improved Shield Bash as one of his fighter bonus feats (see page 38).

IMPROVED SUNDER [GENERAL]

You are skilled at attacking your opponents' weapons and shields, as well as other objects.

Prerequisites: Str 13, Power Attack.

Benefit: When you strike at an object held or carried by an opponent (such as a weapon or shield), you do not provoke an attack of opportunity (see Sunder, page 158).

You also gain a +4 bonus on any attack roll made to attack an object held or carried by another character.

Normal: Without this feat, you provoke an attack of opportunity when you strike at an object held or carried by another character.

Special: A fighter may select Improved Sunder as one of his fighter bonus feats (see page 38).

IMPROVED TRIP [GENERAL]

You are trained not only in tripping opponents safely but also in following through with an attack.

Prerequisites: Int 13, Combat Expertise.

Benefit: You do not provoke an attack of opportunity when you attempt to trip an opponent while you are unarmed. You also gain a +4 bonus on your Strength check to trip your opponent.

If you trip an opponent in melee combat, you immediately get a melee attack against that opponent as if you hadn't used your attack for the trip attempt. For example, at 11th level, Tordek gets three attacks at bonuses of +11, +6, and +1. In the current round, he attempts to trip his opponent. His first attempt fails (using up his first attack). His second attempt succeeds, and he immediately makes a melee attack against his opponent with a bonus of +6. Finally, he takes his last attack at a bonus of +1.

Normal: Without this feat, you provoke an attack of opportunity when you attempt to trip an opponent while you are unarmed. See Trip, page 158.

Special: At 6th level, a monk may select Improved Trip as a bonus feat, even if she does not have the prerequisites.

A fighter may select Improved Trip as one of his fighter bonus feats (see page 38).

IMPROVED TURNING [GENERAL]

Your turning or rebuking attempts are more powerful than normal.

Prerequisite: Ability to turn or rebuke creatures.

Benefit: You turn or rebuke creatures as if you were one level higher than you are in the class that grants you the ability.

IMPROVED TWO-WEAPON FIGHTING [GENERAL]

You are an expert in fighting two-handed.

Prerequisites: Dex 17, Two-Weapon Fighting, base attack bonus +6.

Benefit: In addition to the standard single extra attack you get with an off-hand weapon, you get a second attack with it, albeit at a –5 penalty (see Table 8–10, page 160).

Normal: Without this feat, you can only get a single extra attack with an off-hand weapon.

Special: A fighter may select Improved Two-Weapon Fighting as one of his fighter bonus feats (see page 38).

A 6th-level ranger who has chosen the two-weapon combat style is treated as having Improved Two-Weapon Fighting, even if he does not have the prerequisites for it, but only when he is wearing light or no armor (see page 48).

IMPROVED UNARMED STRIKE [GENERAL]

You are skilled at fighting while unarmed.

Benefit: You are considered to be armed even when unarmed—that is, you do not provoke attacks or opportunity from armed opponents when you attack them while unarmed. However, you still get an attack of opportunity against any opponent who makes an unarmed attack on you.

In addition, your unarmed strikes can deal lethal or nonlethal damage, at your option.

Normal: Without this feat, you are considered unarmed when attacking with an unarmed strike, and you can deal only nonlethal damage with such an attack.

Special: A monk automatically gains Improved Unarmed Strike as a bonus feat at 1st level. She need not select it.

A fighter may select Improved Unarmed Strike as one of his fighter bonus feats (see page 38).

INVESTIGATOR [GENERAL]

You have a knack for finding information.

Benefit: You get a +2 bonus on all Gather Information checks and Search checks.

IRON WILL [GENERAL]

You have a stronger will than normal.

Benefit: You get a +2 bonus on all Will saving throws.

LEADERSHIP [GENERAL]

You are the sort of person others want to follow, and you have done some work attempting to recruit cohorts and followers.

Prerequisite: Character level 6th.

Benefit: You can attract loyal companions and devoted followers, subordinates who assist you. Your DM has information on what sort of cohort and how many followers you can recruit.

Attacking with two arrows, thanks to the Manyshot feat

Special: Check with your DM before selecting this feat, and work with your DM to determine an appropriate cohort and followers for your character (the *Dungeon Master's Guide* has more information on cohorts and followers).

LIGHTNING REFLEXES [GENERAL]

You have faster than normal reflexes.

Benefit: You get a +2 bonus on all Reflex saving throws.

MAGICAL APTITUDE [GENERAL]

You have a knack for magical endeavors.

Benefit: You get a +2 bonus on all Spellcraft checks and Use Magic Device checks.

MANYSHOT [GENERAL]

You can fire multiple arrows simultaneously against a nearby target.

Prerequisites: Dex 17, Point Blank Shot, Rapid Shot, base attack bonus +6

Benefit: As a standard action, you may fire two arrows at a single opponent within 30 feet. Both arrows use the same attack roll (with a –4 penalty) to determine success and deal damage normally (but see Special).

For every five points of base attack bonus you have above +6, you may add one additional arrow to this attack, to a maximum of four arrows at a base attack bonus of +16. However, each arrow after the second adds a cumulative –2 penalty on the attack roll (for a total penalty of –6 for three arrows and –8 for four).

Damage reduction and other resistances apply separately against each arrow fired.

Special: Regardless of the number of arrows you fire, you apply precision-based damage (such as sneak attack damage) only once. If you score a critical hit, only the first arrow fired deals critical damage; all others deal regular damage.

A fighter may select Manyshot as one of his fighter bonus feats (see page 38).

A 6th-level ranger who has chosen the archery combat style is treated as having Manyshot even if he does not have the prerequisites for it, but only when he is wearing light or no armor (see page 48).

MARTIAL WEAPON PROFICIENCY [GENERAL]

Choose a type of martial weapon, such as a longbow (see Table 7–5: Weapons, page 116, for a list of martial weapons). You understand how to use that type of martial weapon in combat.

Use this feat to expand the list of weapons with which you are proficient beyond the basic list in your class description.

Benefit: You make attack rolls with the selected weapon normally.

Normal: When using a weapon with which you are not proficient, you take a –4 penalty on attack rolls.

Special: Barbarians, fighters, paladins, and rangers are proficient with all martial weapons. They need not select this feat.

You can gain Martial Weapon Proficiency multiple times. Each time you take the feat, it applies to a new type of weapon.

A cleric who chooses the War domain automatically gains the Martial Weapon Proficiency feat related to his deity's favored weapon as a bonus feat, if the weapon is a martial one. He need not select it.

A sorcerer or wizard who casts the spell *Tenser's transformation* on himself or herself gains proficiency with all martial weapons for the duration of the spell.

MAXIMIZE SPELL [METAMAGIC]

You can cast spells to maximum effect.

Benefit: All variable, numeric effects of a spell modified by this feat are maximized. A maximized spell deals maximum damage, cures the maximum number of hit points, affects the maximum number of targets, etc., as appropriate. For example, a maximized *fireball* deals 6 points of damage per caster level (up to a maximum of 60 points of damage at 10th caster level). Saving throws and opposed rolls (such as the one you make when you cast *dispel magic*) are not affected, nor are spells without random variables. A maximized spell uses up a spell slot three levels higher than the spell's actual level.

Illus. by J. Jarvis

An empowered, maximized spell gains the separate benefits of each feat: the maximum result plus one-half the normally rolled result. An empowered, maximized *fireball* cast by a 15th-level wizard deals points of damage equal to 60 plus one-half of 10d6.

MOBILITY [GENERAL]
You are skilled at dodging past opponents and avoiding blows.

Prerequisites: Dex 13, Dodge.

Benefit: You get a +4 dodge bonus to Armor Class against attacks of opportunity caused when you move out of or within a threatened area. A condition that makes you lose your Dexterity bonus to Armor Class (if any) also makes you lose dodge bonuses. Dodge bonuses (such as this one and a dwarf's racial bonus on dodge attempts against giants) stack with each other, unlike most types of bonuses.

Special: A fighter may select Mobility as one of his fighter bonus feats (see page 38).

MOUNTED ARCHERY [GENERAL]
You are skilled at using ranged weapons while mounted.

Prerequisites: Ride 1 rank, Mounted Combat.

Benefit: The penalty you take when using a ranged weapon while mounted is halved: –2 instead of –4 if your mount is taking a double move, and –4 instead of –8 if your mount is running (see Mounted Combat, page 157).

Special: A fighter may select Mounted Archery as one of his fighter bonus feats (see page 38).

MOUNTED COMBAT [GENERAL]
You are skilled in mounted combat.

Prerequisite: Ride 1 rank.

Benefit: Once per round when your mount is hit in combat, you may attempt a Ride check (as a reaction) to negate the hit. The hit is negated if your Ride check result is greater than the opponent's attack roll. (Essentially, the Ride check result becomes the mount's Armor Class if it's higher than the mount's regular AC.)

Special: A fighter may select Mounted Combat as one of his fighter bonus feats (see page 38).

NATURAL SPELL [GENERAL]
You can cast spells while in a wild shape.

Prerequisites: Wis 13, wild shape ability.

Benefit: You can complete the verbal and somatic components of spells while in a wild shape. For example, while in the form of a hawk, you could substitute screeches and gestures with your talons for the normal verbal and somatic components of a spell. You can also use any material components or focuses you possess, even if such items are melded within your current form. This feat does not permit the use of magic items while you are in a form that could not ordinarily use them, and you do not gain the ability to speak while in a wild shape.

NEGOTIATOR [GENERAL]
You are good at gauging and swaying attitudes.

Benefit: You get a +2 bonus on all Diplomacy checks and Sense Motive checks.

NIMBLE FINGERS [GENERAL]
You are adept at manipulating small, delicate objects.

Benefit: You get a +2 bonus on all Disable Device checks and Open Lock checks.

PERSUASIVE [GENERAL]
You have a way with words and body language.

Benefit: You get a +2 bonus on all Bluff checks and Intimidate checks.

POINT BLANK SHOT [GENERAL]
You are skilled at making well-placed shots with ranged weapons at close range.

Benefit: You get a +1 bonus on attack and damage rolls with ranged weapons at ranges of up to 30 feet.

Special: A fighter may select Point Blank Shot as one of his fighter bonus feats (see page 38).

POWER ATTACK [GENERAL]
You can make exceptionally powerful melee attacks.

Prerequisite: Str 13.

Benefit: On your action, before making attack rolls for a round, you may choose to subtract a number from all melee attack rolls and add the same number to all melee damage rolls. This number may not exceed your base attack bonus. The penalty on attacks and bonus on damage apply until your next turn.

Special: If you attack with a two-handed weapon, or with a one-handed weapon wielded in two hands, instead add twice the number subtracted from your attack rolls. You can't add the bonus from Power Attack to the damage dealt with a light weapon (except with unarmed strikes or natural weapon attacks), even though the penalty on attack rolls still applies. (Normally, you treat a double weapon as a one-handed weapon and a light weapon. If you choose to use a double weapon like a two-handed weapon, attacking with only one end of it in a round, you treat it as a two-handed weapon.)

A fighter may select Power Attack as one of his fighter bonus feats (see page 38).

PRECISE SHOT [GENERAL]
You are skilled at timing and aiming ranged attacks.

Prerequisite: Point Blank Shot.

Benefit: You can shoot or throw ranged weapons at an opponent engaged in melee without taking the standard –4 penalty on your attack roll (see Shooting or Throwing into a Melee, page 140).

Special: A fighter may select Precise Shot as one of his fighter bonus feats (see page 38).

QUICK DRAW [GENERAL]
You can draw weapons with startling speed.

Prerequisite: Base attack bonus +1.

Benefit: You can draw a weapon as a free action instead of as a move action. You can draw a hidden weapon (see the Sleight of Hand skill, page 81) as a move action.

A character who has selected this feat may throw weapons at his full normal rate of attacks (much like a character with a bow).

Normal: Without this feat, you may draw a weapon as a move action, or (if your base attack bonus is +1 or higher) as a free action as part of movement (see page 142). Without this feat, you can draw a hidden weapon as a standard action.

Special: A fighter may select Quick Draw as one of his fighter bonus feats (see page 38).

QUICKEN SPELL [METAMAGIC]
You can cast a spell with a moment's thought.

Benefit: Casting a quickened spell is a free action. You can perform another action, even casting another spell, in the same round as you cast a quickened spell. You may cast only one quickened spell per round. A spell whose casting time is more than 1 full-round action cannot be quickened. A quickened spell uses up a spell slot four levels higher than the spell's actual level. Casting a quickened spell doesn't provoke an attack of opportunity.

Special: This feat can't be applied to any spell cast spontaneously (including sorcerer spells, bard spells, and cleric or druid spells cast spontaneously), since applying a metamagic feat to a spontaneously cast spell automatically increases the casting time to a full-round action.

RAPID RELOAD [GENERAL]

Choose a type of crossbow (hand, light, or heavy). You can reload a crossbow of that type more quickly than normal.

Prerequisite: Weapon Proficiency (crossbow type chosen).

Benefit: The time required for you to reload your chosen type of crossbow is reduced to a free action (for a hand or light crossbow) or a move action (for a heavy crossbow). Reloading a crossbow still provokes an attack of opportunity.

If you have selected this feat for hand crossbow or light crossbow, you may fire that weapon as many times in a full attack action as you could attack if you were using a bow.

Normal: A character without this feat needs a move action to reload a hand or light crossbow, or a full-round action to reload a heavy crossbow.

Special: You can gain Rapid Reload multiple times. Each time you take the feat, it applies to a new type of crossbow.

A fighter may select Rapid Reload as one of his fighter bonus feats (see page 38).

RAPID SHOT [GENERAL]

You can use ranged weapons with exceptional speed.

Prerequisites: Dex 13, Point Blank Shot.

Benefit: You can get one extra attack per round with a ranged weapon. The attack is at your highest base attack bonus, but each attack you make in that round (the extra one and the normal ones) takes a −2 penalty. You must use the full attack action (see page 143) to use this feat.

Special: A fighter may select Rapid Shot as one of his fighter bonus feats (see page 38).

A 2nd-level ranger who has chosen the archery combat style is treated as having Rapid Shot, even if he does not have the prerequisites for it, but only when he is wearing light or no armor (see page 48).

RIDE-BY ATTACK [GENERAL]

You are skilled at making fast attacks from your mount.

Prerequisites: Ride 1 rank, Mounted Combat.

Benefit: When you are mounted and use the charge action, you may move and attack as if with a standard charge and then move again (continuing the straight line of the charge). Your total movement for the round can't exceed double your mounted speed. You and your mount do not provoke an attack of opportunity from the opponent that you attack.

Special: A fighter may select Ride-By Attack as one of his fighter bonus feats (see page 38).

RUN [GENERAL]

You are fleet of foot.

Benefit: When running, you move five times your normal speed (if wearing light or no armor and carrying no more than a light load) or four times your speed (if wearing medium or heavy armor or carrying a medium or heavy load). If you make a jump after a running start (see the Jump skill description, page 77), you gain a +4 bonus on your Jump check. While running, you retain your Dexterity bonus to AC.

Normal: You move four times your speed while running (if wearing light or no armor and carrying no more than a light load) or three times your speed (if wearing medium or heavy armor or carrying a medium or heavy load), and you lose your Dexterity bonus to AC.

SCRIBE SCROLL [ITEM CREATION]

You can create scrolls, from which you or another a spellcaster can cast the scribed spells. See the *Dungeon Master's Guide* for rules on scrolls.

Prerequisite: Caster level 1st.

Benefit: You can create a scroll of any spell that you know. Scribing a scroll takes one day for each 1,000 gp in its base price. The base price of a scroll is its spell level × its caster level × 25 gp. To scribe a scroll, you must spend 1/25 of this base price in XP and use up raw materials costing one-half of this base price.

Any scroll that stores a spell with a costly material component or an XP cost also carries a commensurate cost. In addition to the costs

Mialee casts a spell from a scroll she scribed.

derived from the base price, you must expend the material component or pay the XP when scribing the scroll.

SELF-SUFFICIENT [GENERAL]

You can take care of yourself in harsh environments and situations.

Benefit: You get a +2 bonus on all Heal checks and Survival checks.

SHIELD PROFICIENCY [GENERAL]

You are proficient with bucklers, small shields, and large shields.

Benefit: You can use a shield and take only the standard penalties (see Table 7–6: Armor and Shields, page 123).

Normal: When you are using a shield with which you are not proficient, you take the shield's armor check penalty on attack rolls and on all skill checks that involve moving, including Ride checks.

Special: Barbarians, bards, clerics, druids, fighters, paladins, and rangers automatically have Shield Proficiency as a bonus feat. They need not select it.

SHOT ON THE RUN [GENERAL]

You are highly trained in skirmish ranged weapon tactics.

Prerequisites: Dex 13, Dodge, Mobility, Point Blank Shot, base attack bonus +4.

Benefit: When using the attack action with a ranged weapon, you can move both before and after the attack, provided that your total distance moved is not greater than your speed.

Special: A fighter may select Shot on the Run as one of his fighter bonus feats (see page 38).

SILENT SPELL [METAMAGIC]

You can cast spells silently.

Benefit: A silent spell can be cast with no verbal components. Spells without verbal components are not affected. A silent spell uses up a spell slot one level higher than the spell's actual level.

Special: Bard spells cannot be enhanced by this metamagic feat.

SIMPLE WEAPON PROFICIENCY [GENERAL]

You understand how to use all types of simple weapons in combat (see Table 7–5: Weapons, page 116, for a list of simple weapons).

Benefit: You make attack rolls with simple weapons normally.

Normal: When using a weapon with which you are not proficient, you take a −4 penalty on attack rolls.

Special: All characters except for druids, monks, rogues, and wizards are automatically proficient with all simple weapons. They need not select this feat.

A sorcerer or wizard who casts the spell *Tenser's transformation* on himself or herself gains proficiency with all simple weapons for the duration of the spell.

SKILL FOCUS [GENERAL]

Choose a skill, such as Move Silently. You have a special knack with that skill.

Benefit: You get a +3 bonus on all checks involving that skill.

Special: You can gain this feat multiple times. Its effects do not stack. Each time you take the feat, it applies to a new skill.

SNATCH ARROWS [GENERAL]

You are adept at grabbing incoming arrows, as well as crossbow bolts, spears, and other projectile or thrown weapons.

Prerequisites: Dex 15, Deflect Arrows, Improved Unarmed Strike.

Benefit: When using the Deflect Arrows feat (page 93), you may catch the weapon instead of just deflecting it. Thrown weapons, such as spears or axes, can immediately be thrown back at the original attacker (even though it isn't your turn) or kept for later use.

You must have at least one hand free (holding nothing) to use this feat.

Special: A fighter may select Snatch Arrows as one of his fighter bonus feats (see page 38).

SPELL FOCUS [GENERAL]

Choose a school of magic, such as illusion. Your spells of that school are more potent than normal.

Benefit: Add +1 to the Difficulty Class for all saving throws against spells from the school of magic you select.

Special: You can gain this feat multiple times. Its effects do not stack. Each time you take the feat, it applies to a new school of magic.

SPELL MASTERY [SPECIAL]

You are so intimately familiar with certain spells that you don't need a spellbook to prepare them anymore.

Prerequisite: Wizard level 1st.

Benefit: Each time you take this feat, choose a number of spells equal to your Intelligence modifier that you already know. From that point on, you can prepare these spells without referring to a spellbook.

Normal: Without this feat, you must use a spellbook to prepare all your spells, except *read magic*.

SPELL PENETRATION [GENERAL]

Your spells are especially potent, breaking through spell resistance more readily than normal.

Benefit: You get a +2 bonus on caster level checks (1d20 + caster level) made to overcome a creature's spell resistance.

SPIRITED CHARGE [GENERAL]

You are trained at making a devastating mounted charge.

Prerequisites: Ride 1 rank, Mounted Combat, Ride-By Attack.

Benefit: When mounted and using the charge action, you deal double damage with a melee weapon (or triple damage with a lance).

Special: A fighter may select Spirited Charge as one of his fighter bonus feats (see page 38).

SPRING ATTACK [GENERAL]

You are trained in fast melee attacks and fancy footwork.

Prerequisites: Dex 13, Dodge, Mobility, base attack bonus +4.

Benefit: When using the attack action with a melee weapon, you can move both before and after the attack, provided that your total distance moved is not greater than your speed. Moving in this way does not provoke an attack of opportunity from the defender you attack, though it might provoke attacks of opportunity from other creatures, if appropriate. You can't use this feat if you are wearing heavy armor.

You must move at least 5 feet both before and after you make your attack in order to utilize the benefits of Spring Attack.

Special: A fighter may select Spring Attack as one of his fighter bonus feats (see page 38).

STEALTHY [GENERAL]
You are particularly good at avoiding notice.

Benefit: You get a +2 bonus on all Hide checks and Move Silently checks.

STILL SPELL [METAMAGIC]
You can cast spells without gestures.

Benefit: A stilled spell can be cast with no somatic components. Spells without somatic components are not affected. A stilled spell uses up a spell slot one level higher than the spell's actual level.

STUNNING FIST [GENERAL]
You know how to strike opponents in vulnerable areas.

Prerequisites: Dex 13, Wis 13, Improved Unarmed Strike, base attack bonus +8.

Benefit: You must declare that you are using this feat before you make your attack roll (thus, a failed attack roll ruins the attempt). Stunning Fist forces a foe damaged by your unarmed attack to make a Fortitude saving throw (DC 10 + 1/2 your character level + your Wis modifier), in addition to dealing damage normally. A defender who fails this saving throw is stunned for 1 round (until just before your next action). A stunned character can't act, loses any Dexterity bonus to AC, and takes a –2 penalty to AC. You may attempt a stunning attack once per day for every four levels you have attained (but see Special), and no more than once per round. Constructs, oozes, plants, undead, incorporeal creatures, and creatures immune to critical hits cannot be stunned.

Special: A monk may select Stunning Fist as a bonus feat at 1st level, even if she does not meet the prerequisites. A monk who selects this feat may attempt a stunning attack a number of times per day equal to her monk level, plus one more time per day for every four levels she has in classes other than monk.

A fighter may select Stunning Fist as one of his fighter bonus feats (see page 38).

TOUGHNESS [GENERAL]
You are tougher than normal.

Benefit: You gain +3 hit points.

Special: A character may gain this feat multiple times. Its effects stack.

TOWER SHIELD PROFICIENCY [GENERAL]
You are proficient with tower shields.

Prerequisite: Shield Proficiency.

Benefit: You can use a tower shield and suffer only the standard penalties (see Table 7–6: Armor and Shields, page 123).

Normal: A character who is using a shield with which he or she is not proficient takes the shield's armor check penalty on attack rolls and on all skill checks that involve moving, including Ride.

Special: Fighters automatically have Tower Shield Proficiency as a bonus feat. They need not select it.

TRACK [GENERAL]
You can follow the trails of creatures and characters across most types of terrain.

Benefit: To find tracks or to follow them for 1 mile requires a successful Survival check. You must make another Survival check every time the tracks become difficult to follow, such as when other tracks cross them or when the tracks backtrack and diverge.

You move at half your normal speed (or at your normal speed with a –5 penalty on the check, or at up to twice your normal speed with a –20 penalty on the check). The DC depends on the surface and the prevailing conditions, as given on the table below:

Surface	Survival DC	Surface	Survival DC
Very soft ground	5	Firm ground	15
Soft ground	10	Hard ground	20

Very Soft Ground: Any surface (fresh snow, thick dust, wet mud) that holds deep, clear impressions of footprints.

Soft Ground: Any surface soft enough to yield to pressure, but firmer than wet mud or fresh snow, in which a creature leaves frequent but shallow footprints.

Firm Ground: Most normal outdoor surfaces (such as lawns, fields, woods, and the like) or exceptionally soft or dirty indoor surfaces (thick rugs and very dirty or dusty floors). The creature might leave some traces (broken branches or tufts of hair), but it leaves only occasional or partial footprints.

Hard Ground: Any surface that doesn't hold footprints at all, such as bare rock or an indoor floor. Most streambeds fall into this category, since any footprints left behind are obscured or washed away. The creature leaves only traces (scuff marks or displaced pebbles).

Several modifiers may apply to the Survival check, as given on the table below.

Condition	Survival DC Modifier
Every three creatures in the group being tracked	–1
Size of creature or creatures being tracked:[1]	
Fine	+8
Diminutive	+4
Tiny	+2
Small	+1
Medium	+0
Large	–1
Huge	–2
Gargantuan	–4
Colossal	–8
Every 24 hours since the trail was made	+1
Every hour of rain since the trail was made	+1
Fresh snow cover since the trail was made	+10
Poor visibility:[2]	
Overcast or moonless night	+6
Moonlight	+3
Fog or precipitation	+3
Tracked party hides trail (and moves at half speed)	+5

1 For a group of mixed sizes, apply only the modifier for the largest size category.

2 Apply only the largest modifier from this category.

If you fail a Survival check, you can retry after 1 hour (outdoors) or 10 minutes (indoors) of searching.

Normal: Without this feat, you can use the Survival skill to find tracks, but you can follow them only if the DC for the task is 10 or lower. Alternatively, you can use the Search skill to find a footprint or similar sign of a creature's passage using the DCs given above, but you can't use Search to follow tracks, even if someone else has already found them.

Special: A ranger automatically has Track as a bonus feat. He need not select it.

This feat does not allow you to find or follow the tracks made by a subject of a *pass without trace* spell.

TRAMPLE [GENERAL]
You are trained in using your mount to knock down opponents.

Prerequisites: Ride 1 rank, Mounted Combat.

Benefit: When you attempt to overrun an opponent while mounted, your target may not choose to avoid you. Your mount may make one hoof attack against any target you knock down, gaining the standard +4 bonus on attack rolls against prone targets (see Overrun, page 157).

Special: A fighter may select Trample as one of his fighter bonus feats (see page 38).

TWO-WEAPON DEFENSE [GENERAL]

Your two-weapon fighting style bolsters your defense as well as your offense.

Prerequisites: Dex 15, Two-Weapon Fighting.

Benefit: When wielding a double weapon or two weapons (not including natural weapons or unarmed strikes), you gain a +1 shield bonus to your AC.

When you are fighting defensively or using the total defense action, this shield bonus increases to +2.

Special: A fighter may select Two-Weapon Defense as one of his fighter bonus feats (see page 38).

TWO-WEAPON FIGHTING [GENERAL]

You can fight with a weapon in each hand. You can make one extra attack each round with the second weapon.

Prerequisite: Dex 15.

Benefit: Your penalties on attack rolls for fighting with two weapons are reduced. The penalty for your primary hand lessens by 2 and the one for your off hand lessens by 6.

Normal: See Two-Weapon Fighting, page 160, and Table 8–10: Two-Weapon Fighting Penalties, page 160.

Special: A 2nd-level ranger who has chosen the two-weapon combat style is treated as having Two-Weapon Fighting, even if he does not have the prerequisite for it, but only when he is wearing light or no armor (see page 48).

A fighter may select Two-Weapon Fighting as one of his fighter bonus feats (see page 38).

WEAPON FINESSE [GENERAL]

You are especially skilled at using weapons that can benefit as much from Dexterity as from Strength.

Prerequisite: Base attack bonus +1.

Benefit: With a light weapon, rapier, whip, or spiked chain made for a creature of your size category, you may use your Dexterity modifier instead of your Strength modifier on attack rolls. If you carry a shield, its armor check penalty applies to your attack rolls.

Special: A fighter may select Weapon Finesse as one of his fighter bonus feats (see page 38).

Natural weapons are always considered light weapons.

WEAPON FOCUS [GENERAL]

Choose one type of weapon, such as greataxe. You can also choose unarmed strike or grapple (or ray, if you are a spellcaster) as your weapon for purposes of this feat. You are especially good at using this weapon. (If you have chosen ray, you are especially good with rays, such as the one produced by the *ray of frost* spell.)

Prerequisites: Proficiency with selected weapon, base attack bonus +1.

Benefit: You gain a +1 bonus on all attack rolls you make using the selected weapon.

Special: You can gain this feat multiple times. Its effects do not stack. Each time you take the feat, it applies to a new type of weapon.

A fighter may select Weapon Focus as one of his fighter bonus feats (see page 38). He must have Weapon Focus with a weapon to gain the Weapon Specialization feat for that weapon.

WEAPON SPECIALIZATION [GENERAL]

Choose one type of weapon, such as greataxe, for which you have already selected the Weapon Focus feat. You can also choose unarmed strike or grapple as your weapon for purposes of this feat. You deal extra damage when using this weapon.

Prerequisites: Proficiency with selected weapon, Weapon Focus with selected weapon, fighter level 4th.

Benefit: You gain a +2 bonus on all damage rolls you make using the selected weapon.

Special: You can gain this feat multiple times. Its effects do not stack. Each time you take the feat, it applies to a new type of weapon.

A fighter may select Weapon Specialization as one of his fighter bonus feats (see page 38).

WHIRLWIND ATTACK [GENERAL]

You can strike nearby opponents in an amazing, spinning attack.

Prerequisites: Dex 13, Int 13, Combat Expertise, Dodge, Mobility, Spring Attack, base attack bonus +4.

Benefit: When you use the full attack action, you can give up your regular attacks and instead make one melee attack at your full base attack bonus against each opponent within reach.

When you use the Whirlwind Attack feat, you also forfeit any bonus or extra attacks granted by other feats or abilities (such as the Cleave feat or the *haste* spell).

Special: A fighter may select Whirlwind Attack as one of his fighter bonus feats (see page 38).

WIDEN SPELL [METAMAGIC]

You can increase the area of your spells.

Benefit: You can alter a burst, emanation, line, or spread-shaped spell to increase its area. Any numeric measurements of the spell's area increase by 100%. For example, a *fireball* spell (which normally produces a 20-foot-radius spread) that is widened now fills a 40-foot-radius spread. A widened spell uses up a spell slot three levels higher than the spell's actual level.

Spells that do not have an area of one of these four sorts are not affected by this feat.

FIG. A

FIG. B

FIG. C

FIG. D

FIG. E

FIG. F

Ehlonna — A

Iuz — B

Heironeous — C

int Cuthbert — D

Olidammara — E

Rao — F

Obad-Hai — G

Wastri

Incabulos

Baccob

Procan

Tharizdun

Vecna

FIG. M

Illus. by A. Swekel

What does your character look like? How old is she? What sort of first impression does she make? When she prays, what deity or deities does she call on, if any? What led her to become an adventurer?

This chapter helps you establish your character's identity by creating details that make her more lifelike, like a main character in a novel or a movie. For many players, the action lies here, in defining a character as a person to be roleplayed.

When you first play a character, it's fine to leave the details sketchy. As you play the character over time, you will get a better sense of who you want her to be. You will develop her details in much the same way that an author develops a character over several drafts of a novel or over several novels in a series.

This chapter covers alignment (a character's place in the struggle between good and evil), religion (a character's deity or deities), vital statistics (name, gender, age, and so on), and personal description.

ALIGNMENT

In the temple of Pelor is an ancient tome. When the temple recruits adventurers for its most sensitive and important quests, each one who wants to participate must kiss the book. Those who are evil in their hearts are blasted by holy power, and even those who are neither good nor evil are stunned. Only those who are good can kiss the tome without harm and are trusted with the temple's most important work. Good and evil are not philosophical concepts in the D&D game. They are the forces that define the cosmos.

Devils in human guise stalk the land, tempting people toward evil. Holy clerics use the power of good to protect worshipers. Devotees of evil gods bring ruin on innocents to win the favor of their deities, while trusting that rewards await them in the afterlife. Crusading paladins fearlessly confront evildoers, knowing that this short life is nothing worth clinging to. Warlords turn to whichever supernatural power will help them conquer, and proxies for good and evil gods promise rewards in return for the warlords' oaths of obedience.

A creature's general moral and personal attitudes are represented by its alignment: lawful good, neutral good, chaotic good, lawful neutral, neutral, chaotic neutral, lawful evil, neutral evil, or chaotic evil. (See Table 6–1: Creature, Race, and Class Alignments, on the next page, for examples of which creatures, races, and classes favor which alignments.)

Choose an alignment for your character, using his or her race and class as a guide. Most player characters are good or neutral rather than evil. In general, evil alignments are for villains and monsters.

Alignment is a tool for developing your character's identity. It is not a straitjacket for restricting your character. Each alignment represents a broad range of personality types or personal philosophies, so two lawful good characters can still be quite different from each other. In addition, few people are completely consistent. A lawful good character may have a greedy streak that occasionally tempts him to take something or hoard something he has, even if that's not lawful or good behavior. People are also not consistent from day to day. A good character can lose his temper, a neutral character can be inspired to perform a noble act, and so on.

EXAMPLES

OF HOLY SYMBOLS

FIG. K

Choosing an alignment for your character means stating your intent to play that character a certain way. If your character acts in a way more appropriate to another alignment, the DM may decide that his alignment has changed to match his actions.

TYPICAL ALIGNMENTS

Creatures and members of classes shown in *italic type* on Table 6–1 are always of the indicated alignment. Except for paladins, they are born into that alignment. It is inherent, part of their nature. Usually, a creature with an inherent alignment has some connection (through ancestry, history, or magic) to the Outer Planes or is a magical beast.

For other creatures, races, and classes, the indicated alignment on Table 6–1 is the typical or most common one. Normal sentient creatures can be of any alignment. They may have inherent tendencies toward a particular alignment, but individuals can vary from this norm. Depending on the type of creature, these tendencies may be stronger or weaker. For example, kobolds and beholders are usually lawful evil, but kobolds display more variation in alignment than beholders because their inborn alignment tendency isn't as strong. Also, sentient creatures have cultural tendencies that usually reinforce alignment tendencies. For example, orcs tend to be chaotic evil, and their culture tends to produce chaotic evil members. A human raised among orcs is more likely than normal to be chaotic evil, while an orc raised among humans is less likely to be so.

TABLE 6–1: CREATURE, RACE, AND CLASS ALIGNMENTS

Lawful Good	Neutral Good	Chaotic Good
Archons	*Guardinals*	*Eladrins*
Gold dragons	Gnomes	Copper dragons
Lammasus	Centaurs	*Unicorns*
Dwarves	Giant eagles	Elves
Paladins	*Pseudodragons*	Rangers

Lawful Neutral	Neutral	Chaotic Neutral
Monks	*Animals*	Half-elves
Wizards	Halflings	Half-orcs
Formians	Humans	Barbarians
Azers	Lizardfolk	Bards
	Druids	Rogues

Lawful Evil	Neutral Evil	Chaotic Evil
Devils	Drow	*Demons*
Blue dragons	Goblins	Red dragons
Beholders	*Allips*	Vampires
Ogre mages	Ettercaps	*Troglodytes*
Hobgoblins	*Devourers*	Gnolls
Kobolds		Ogres
		Orcs

GOOD VS. EVIL

Good characters and creatures protect innocent life. Evil characters and creatures debase or destroy innocent life, whether for fun or profit.

"Good" implies altruism, respect for life, and a concern for the dignity of sentient beings. Good characters make personal sacrifices to help others.

"Evil" implies hurting, oppressing, and killing others. Some evil creatures simply have no compassion for others and kill without qualms if doing so is convenient. Others actively pursue evil, killing for sport or out of duty to some evil deity or master.

People who are neutral with respect to good and evil have compunctions against killing the innocent but lack the commitment to make sacrifices to protect or help others. Neutral people are committed to others by personal relationships. A neutral person may sacrifice himself to protect his family or even his homeland, but he would not do so for strangers who are not related to him.

Being good or evil can be a conscious choice, as with the paladin who attempts to live up to her ideals or the evil cleric who causes pain and terror to emulate his god. For most people, though, being good or evil is an attitude that one recognizes but does not choose. Being neutral on the good–evil axis usually represents a lack of commitment one way or the other, but for some it represents a positive commitment to a balanced view. While acknowledging that good and evil are objective states, not just opinions, these folk maintain that a balance between the two is the proper place for people, or at least for them.

Animals and other creatures incapable of moral action are neutral rather than good or evil. Even deadly vipers and tigers that eat people are neutral because they lack the capacity for morally right or wrong behavior.

LAW VS. CHAOS

Lawful characters tell the truth, keep their word, respect authority, honor tradition, and judge those who fall short of their duties. Chaotic characters follow their consciences, resent being told what to do, favor new ideas over tradition, and do what they promise if they feel like it.

"Law" implies honor, trustworthiness, obedience to authority, and reliability. On the downside, lawfulness can include close-mindedness, reactionary adherence to tradition, judgmentalness, and a lack of adaptability. Those who consciously promote lawfulness say that only lawful behavior creates a society in which people can depend on each other and make the right decisions in full confidence that others will act as they should.

"Chaos" implies freedom, adaptability, and flexibility. On the downside, chaos can include recklessness, resentment toward legitimate authority, arbitrary actions, and irresponsibility. Those who promote chaotic behavior say that only unfettered personal freedom allows people to express themselves fully and lets society benefit from the potential that its individuals have within them.

Someone who is neutral with respect to law and chaos has a normal respect for authority and feels neither a compulsion to obey nor a compulsion to rebel. She is honest but can be tempted into lying or deceiving others.

Devotion to law or chaos may be a conscious choice, but more often it is a personality trait that is recognized rather than being chosen. Neutrality on the lawful–chaotic axis is usually simply a middle state, a state of not feeling compelled toward one side or the other. Some few such neutrals, however, espouse neutrality as superior to law or chaos, regarding each as an extreme with its own blind spots and drawbacks.

Animals and other creatures incapable of moral action are neutral. Dogs may be obedient and cats free-spirited, but they do not have the moral capacity to be truly lawful or chaotic.

THE NINE ALIGNMENTS

Nine distinct alignments define all the possible combinations of the lawful–chaotic axis with the good–evil axis. Each alignment description below depicts a typical character of that alignment. Remember that individuals vary from this norm, and that a given character may act more or less in accord with his or her alignment from day to day. Use these descriptions as guidelines, not as scripts.

The first six alignments, lawful good through chaotic neutral, are the standard alignments for player characters. The three evil alignments are for monsters and villains.

Lawful Good, "Crusader": A lawful good character acts as a good person is expected or required to act. She combines a commitment to oppose evil with the discipline to fight relentlessly. She tells the truth, keeps her word, helps those in need, and speaks out against injustice. A lawful good character hates to see the guilty go unpunished. Alhandra, a paladin who fights evil without mercy and protects the innocent without hesitation, is lawful good.

Lawful good is the best alignment you can be because it combines honor and compassion.

Neutral Good, "Benefactor": A neutral good character does the best that a good person can do. He is devoted to helping others. He works with kings and magistrates but does not feel beholden to them. Jozan, a cleric who helps others according to their needs, is neutral good.

Neutral good is the best alignment you can be because it means doing what is good without bias for or against order.

Chaotic Good, "Rebel": A chaotic good character acts as his conscience directs him with little regard for what others expect of him. He makes his own way, but he's kind and benevolent. He believes in goodness and right but has little use for laws and regulations. He hates it when people try to intimidate others and tell them what to do. He follows his own moral compass, which, although good, may not agree with that of society. Soveliss, a ranger who waylays the evil baron's tax collectors, is chaotic good.

Chaotic good is the best alignment you can be because it combines a good heart with a free spirit.

Lawful Neutral, "Judge": A lawful neutral character acts as law, tradition, or a personal code directs her. Order and organization are paramount to her. She may believe in personal order and live by a code or standard, or she may believe in order for all and favor a strong, organized government. Ember, a monk who follows her discipline without being swayed either by the demands of those in need or by the temptations of evil, is lawful neutral.

Lawful neutral is the best alignment you can be because it means you are reliable and honorable without being a zealot.

Neutral, "Undecided": A neutral character does what seems to be a good idea. She doesn't feel strongly one way or the other when it comes to good vs. evil or law vs. chaos. Most neutral characters exhibit a lack of conviction or bias rather than a commitment to neutrality. Such a character thinks of good as better than evil—after all, she would rather have good neighbors and rulers than evil ones. Still, she's not personally committed to upholding good in any abstract or universal way. Mialee, a wizard who devotes herself to her art and is bored by the semantics of moral debate, is neutral.

Some neutral characters, on the other hand, commit themselves philosophically to neutrality. They see good, evil, law, and chaos as prejudices and dangerous extremes. They advocate the middle way of neutrality as the best, most balanced road in the long run.

Neutral is the best alignment you can be because it means you act naturally, without prejudice or compulsion.

Chaotic Neutral, "Free Spirit": A chaotic neutral character follows his whims. He is an individualist first and last. He values his own liberty but doesn't strive to protect others' freedom. He avoids authority, resents restrictions, and challenges traditions. A chaotic neutral character does not intentionally disrupt organizations as part of a campaign of anarchy. To do so, he would have to be motivated either by good (and a desire to liberate others) or evil (and a desire to make those different from himself suffer). A chaotic neutral character may be unpredictable, but his behavior is not totally random. He is not as likely to jump off a bridge as to cross it. Gimble, a bard who wanders the land living by his wits, is chaotic neutral.

Chaotic neutral is the best alignment you can be because it represents true freedom from both society's restrictions and a do-gooder's zeal.

Lawful Evil, "Dominator": A lawful evil villain methodically takes what he wants within the limits of his code of conduct without regard for whom it hurts. He cares about tradition, loyalty, and order but not about freedom, dignity, or life. He plays by the rules but without mercy or compassion. He is comfortable in a hierarchy and would like to rule, but is willing to serve. He condemns others not according to their actions but according to race, religion, homeland, or social rank. He is loath to break laws or promises. This reluctance comes partly from his nature and partly because he depends on order to protect himself from those who oppose him on moral grounds. Some lawful evil villains have particular taboos, such as not killing in cold blood (but having underlings do it) or not letting children come to harm (if it can be helped). They imagine that these compunctions put them above unprincipled villains. The scheming baron who expands his power and exploits his people is lawful evil.

Some lawful evil people and creatures commit themselves to evil with a zeal like that of a crusader committed to good. Beyond being willing to hurt others for their own ends, they take pleasure in spreading evil as an end unto itself. They may also see doing evil as part of a duty to an evil deity or master.

Lawful evil is sometimes called "diabolical," because devils are the epitome of lawful evil.

Devis

Illus. by J. Foster

Illus. by S. Wood

Lawful evil is the most dangerous alignment because it represents methodical, intentional, and frequently successful evil.

Neutral Evil, "Malefactor": A neutral evil villain does whatever she can get away with. She is out for herself, pure and simple. She sheds no tears for those she kills, whether for profit, sport, or convenience. She has no love of order and holds no illusion that following laws, traditions, or codes would make her any better or more noble. On the other hand, she doesn't have the restless nature or love of conflict that a chaotic evil villain has. The criminal who robs and murders to get what she wants is neutral evil.

Some neutral evil villains hold up evil as an ideal, committing evil for its own sake. Most often, such villains are devoted to evil deities or secret societies.

Neutral evil is the most dangerous alignment because it represents pure evil without honor and without variation.

Chaotic Evil, "Destroyer": A chaotic evil character does whatever his greed, hatred, and lust for destruction drive him to do. He is hot-tempered, vicious, arbitrarily violent, and unpredictable. If he is simply out for whatever he can get, he is ruthless and brutal. If he is committed to the spread of evil and chaos, he is even worse. Thankfully, his plans are haphazard, and any groups he joins or forms are poorly organized. Typically, chaotic evil people can be made to work together only by force, and their leader lasts only as long as he can thwart attempts to topple or assassinate him. The demented sorcerer pursuing mad schemes of vengeance and havoc is chaotic evil.

Chaotic evil is sometimes called "demonic" because demons are the epitome of chaotic evil.

Chaotic evil is the most dangerous alignment because it represents the destruction not only of beauty and life but also of the order on which beauty and life depend.

RELIGION

The gods are many. A few, such as Pelor (god of the sun), have grand temples that sponsor mighty processions through the streets on high holy days. Others, such as Erythnul (god of slaughter), have temples only in hidden places or evil lands. While the gods most strongly make their presence felt through their clerics, they also have lay followers who more or less attempt to live up to their deities' standards. The typical person has a deity whom he considers to be his patron. Still, it is only prudent to be respectful toward and even pray to other deities when the time is right. Before setting out on a journey, a follower of Pelor might leave a small sacrifice at a wayside shrine to Fharlanghn (god of roads) to improve his chances of having a safe journey. As long as one's own deity is not at odds with the others in such an act of piety, such simple practices are common. In times of tribulation, however, some people recite dark prayers to evil deities. Such prayers are best muttered under one's breath, lest others overhear.

Deities rule the various aspects of human existence: good and evil, law and chaos, life and death, knowledge and nature. In addition, various nonhuman races have racial deities of their own (see Table 6–2: Deities by Race). A character may not be a cleric of a racial deity unless he is of the right race, but he may worship such a deity and live according to that deity's guidance. For a deity who is not tied to a particular race (such as Pelor), a cleric's race is not an issue.

Deities of certain kinds of monsters are identified in the *Monster Manual*. Many more deities than those described here or mentioned in the *Monster Manual* also exist.

Your character may or may not have a patron deity. If you want him or her to have one, consider first the deities most appropriate to the character's race, class, and alignment (see Table 6–2: Deities by Race and Table 6–3: Deities by Class). If a cleric chooses a deity, which one he selects influences his capabilities. Players with cleric characters should refer to Deity, Domains, and Domain Spells, page 32, before picking a deity, though the information below describing the various gods and goddesses can help them make a decision.

TABLE 6–2: DEITIES BY RACE

Race	Deities
Human	By class and alignment
Dwarf	Moradin or by class and alignment
Elf	Corellon Larethian, Ehlonna, or by class and alignment
Gnome	Garl Glittergold, Ehlonna, or by class and alignment
Half-elf	Corellon Larethian, Ehlonna, or by class and alignment
Half-orc	Gruumsh or by class and alignment
Halfling	Yondalla, Ehlonna, or by class and alignment

TABLE 6–3: DEITIES BY CLASS

Class	Deities (Alignment)
Barbarian	Kord (CG), Obad-Hai (N), Erythnul (CE)
Bard	Pelor (NG), Fharlanghn (N), Olidammara (CN)
Cleric	Any
Druid	Obad-Hai (N)
Fighter	Heironeous (LG), Kord (CG), St. Cuthbert (LN), Hextor (LE), Erythnul (CE)
Illusionist	Boccob (N)
Necromancer	Wee Jas (LN), Nerull (NE)
Monk	Heironeous (LG), St. Cuthbert, (LN), Hextor (LE)
Paladin	Heironeous (LG)
Ranger	Ehlonna (NG), Obad-Hai (N)
Rogue	Olidammara (CN), Nerull (NE), Vecna (NE), Erythnul (CE)
Sorcerer	Wee Jas (LN), Boccob (N), Vecna (NE)
Wizard	Wee Jas (LN), Boccob (N), Vecna (NE)

DEITIES

Across the world, people and creatures worship a great number of varied deities. Those described here are the deities most often worshiped among the common races, by adventurers, and by villains. Each entry includes the deity's name, role, alignment, titles he or she is known by, and a general description. These deities' holy (or unholy) symbols are shown accompanying their descriptions. (See Table 3–7: Deities, page 32, for a summary of the most common deities, their alignments, the domains they are associated with, and their typical worshipers.)

Boccob

The god of magic, Boccob, is neutral. His titles include the Uncaring, Lord of All Magics, and Archmage of the Deities. Boccob is a distant deity who promotes no special agenda in the world of mortals. As a god of magic and knowledge, he is worshiped by wizards, sorcerers, and sages. The domains he is associated with are Knowledge, Magic, and Trickery. The quarterstaff is his favored weapon.

Corellon Larethian

The god of the elves, Corellon Larethian, is chaotic good. He is known as the Creator of the Elves, the Protector, Protector and Preserver of Life, and Ruler of All Elves. Corellon Larethian is the creator and protector of the elf race. He governs those things held in highest esteem among elves, such as magic, music, arts, crafts, poetry, and warfare. Elves, half-elves, and bards worship him. The domains he is associated with are Chaos, Good, Protection, and War. His favored weapon is the longsword. Gruumsh is his nemesis, and it is because of Corellon's battle prowess that Gruumsh is called "One-Eye."

Ehlonna

Ehlonna, the goddess of the woodlands, is neutral good. Her most commonly encountered title is Ehlonna of the Forests. Ehlonna watches over all good people who live in the forest, love the woodlands, or make their livelihood there. She is pictured sometimes as an elf and sometimes as a human. She is especially close to elves, gnomes, half-elves, and halflings. She is also worshiped by rangers and some druids. The domains she is associated with are Animal, Good, Plant, and Sun. Her favored weapon is the longbow.

Erythnul

The god of slaughter, Erythnul, is chaotic evil. His title is the Many. Erythnul delights in panic and slaughter. In civilized lands, his followers (including evil fighters, barbarians, and rogues) form small, criminal cults. In savage lands, evil barbarians, gnolls, bugbears, ogres, and trolls commonly worship him. The domains he is associated with are Chaos, Evil, Trickery, and War. His favored weapon is a morningstar with a blunt stone head.

Fharlanghn

Fharlanghn, the god of roads, is neutral. His title is Dweller on the Horizon. Fharlanghn's wayside shrines are common on well-used roads, for he is the deity of travel, roads, distance, and horizons. Bards, other wandering adventurers, and merchants favor Fharlanghn. The domains he is associated with are Luck, Protection, and Travel. The quarterstaff is his favored weapon.

Garl Glittergold

The god of the gnomes, Garl Glittergold, is neutral good. He is known as the Joker, the Watchful Protector, the Priceless Gem, and the Sparkling Wit. Garl Glittergold discovered the gnomes and led them into the world. Since then, he has been their protector. He governs humor, wit, gemcutting, and jewelrymaking. The domains he is associated with are Good, Protection, and Trickery. Garl's favored weapon is the battleaxe. He is renowned for the jokes and pranks he pulls on other deities, though not all his victims laugh off his jests. Garl once collapsed the cavern of Kurtulmak, the god of the kobolds. Since then, the two deities have been sworn enemies.

Gruumsh

Gruumsh, chief god of the orcs, is chaotic evil. His titles are One-Eye and He-Who-Never-Sleeps. Gruumsh calls on his followers to be strong, to cull the weak from their numbers, and to take all the territory that Gruumsh thinks is rightfully theirs (which is almost everything). The domains he is associated with are Chaos, Evil, Strength, and War. Gruumsh's favored weapon is the spear. He harbors a special hatred for Corellon Larethian, Moradin, and their followers. In ages past, Corellon Larethian put out Gruumsh's left eye in a fight.

Heironeous

The god of valor, Heironeous, is lawful good. His title is the Invincible. Heironeous promotes justice, valor, chivalry, and honor. The domains he is associated with are Good, Law, and War. His favored weapon is the longsword, and he is worshiped by paladins, good fighters, and good monks. His archenemy is Hextor, his half-brother.

Hextor

The god of tyranny, Hextor, is lawful evil. His titles are Champion of Evil, Herald of Hell, and Scourge of Battle. Hextor is the six-armed god of war, conflict, and destruction. Hextor's worshipers include evil fighters and monks. The domains he is associated with are Destruction, Evil, Law, and War. His favored weapon is the flail. He sends his followers to commit evil, and their special purpose is to overthrow the followers of his half-brother Heironeous wherever they are found.

Kord

Kord, the god of strength, is chaotic good. He is known as the Brawler. Kord is the patron of athletes, especially wrestlers. His worshipers include good fighters, barbarians, and rogues. The domains he is associated with are Chaos, Good, Luck, and Strength. Kord's favored weapon is the greatsword.

Moradin

The god of the dwarves, Moradin, is lawful good. His titles include the Soul Forger, Dwarffather, the All-Father, and the Creator. Moradin forged the first dwarves out of metal and gems and breathed life into them. He governs the arts and sciences of the dwarves: smithing, metalworking, engineering, and war. The domains he is associated with are Earth, Good, Law, and Protection. His favored weapon is the warhammer.

Illus. by S. Wood

Nerull

The god of death, Nerull, is neutral evil. He is known as the Reaper, the Foe of All Good, Hater of Life, Bringer of Darkness, King of All Gloom, and Reaper of Flesh. Nerull is the patron of those who seek the greatest evil for their own enjoyment or gain. The domains he is associated with are Death, Evil, and Trickery. His worshipers, who include evil necromancers and rogues, depict him as an almost skeletal cloaked figure who bears a scythe, his favored weapon.

Obad-Hai

Obad-Hai, the god of nature, is neutral. He is known as the Shalm. Obad-Hai rules nature and the wilderness, and he is a friend to all who live in harmony with the natural world. Barbarians, rangers, and druids sometimes worship him. The domains he is associated with are Air, Animal, Earth, Fire, Plant, and Water. Because Obad-Hai strictly adheres to neutrality, he is a rival of Ehlonna. Obad-Hai plays a shalm (a double-reed woodwind musical instrument, also spelled "shawm") and takes his title from this instrument. His favored weapon is the quarterstaff.

Olidammara

The god of rogues, Olidammara, is chaotic neutral. His title is the Laughing Rogue. Olidammara delights in wine, women, and song. He is a vagabond, a prankster, and a master of disguise. His temples are few, but many people are willing to raise a glass in his honor. Rogues and bards are frequently among his worshipers. The domains he is associated with are Chaos, Luck, and Trickery. The rapier is his favored weapon.

Pelor

Pelor, god of the sun, is neutral good. His title is the Shining One. Pelor is the creator of many good things, a supporter of those in need, and an adversary of all that is evil. He is the most commonly worshiped deity among ordinary humans, and his priests are well received wherever they go. Rangers and bards are found among his worshipers. The domains he is associated with are Good, Healing, Strength, and Sun. The mace is his favored weapon.

St. Cuthbert

The god of retribution, St. Cuthbert, is lawful neutral. He is known as St. Cuthbert of the Cudgel. St. Cuthbert exacts revenge and just punishment on those who transgress the law. Because evil creatures more commonly and flagrantly violate laws than good creatures do, St. Cuthbert favors good over evil, though he is not good himself. (His clerics cannot be evil.) The domains he is associated with are Destruction, Law, Protection, and Strength. His favored weapon is the mace.

Vecna

Vecna, the god of secrets, is neutral evil. He is known as the Maimed Lord, the Whispered One, and the Master of All That Is Secret and Hidden. Vecna rules that which is not meant to be known and that which people wish to keep secret. The domains he is associated with are Evil, Knowledge, and Magic. He usually appears as a lich who is missing his left hand and left eye. He lost his hand and eye in a fight with his traitorous lieutenant, Kas. Vecna's favored weapon is the dagger.

Wee Jas

Wee Jas, the goddess of death and magic, is lawful neutral. Her titles are Witch Goddess, Ruby Sorceress, Stern Lady, and Death's Guardian. Wee Jas is a demanding goddess who expects obedience from her followers. Her temples are few and far between, but she counts many powerful sorcerers and wizards (especially necromancers) among her worshipers. The domains she is associated with are Death, Law, and Magic. Her favored weapon is the dagger.

Yondalla

The goddess of the halflings, Yondalla, is lawful good. Her titles include the Protector and Provider, the Nurturing Matriarch, and the Blessed One. Yondalla is the creator and protector of the halfling race. She espouses harmony among halflings and stalwart defense against their enemies. Her followers hope to lead safe, prosperous lives by following her guidance. The domains she is associated with are Good, Law, and Protection. The short sword is her favored weapon.

VITAL STATISTICS

This section offers advice as you determine your character's name, gender, age, height, and weight. Start with some idea of your character's background and personality, and use that idea to help you add the details that bring him or her to life.

NAME

Invent or choose a name that fits your character's race and class. Chapter 2: Races contains some examples of elf, dwarf, halfling, gnome, and orc names (and thus half-elf and half-orc names, too). A name is a great way for you to start thinking about your character's background. For instance, a dwarf's name might be the name of a great dwarf hero, and your character may be striving to live up to his name. Alternatively, the name could be that of an infamous coward, and the character could be bent on proving that he is not like his namesake.

GENDER

Your character can be either male or female.

AGE

You can choose or randomly generate your character's age. If you choose it, it must be at least the minimum age for the character's race and class (see Table 6–4: Random Starting Ages). Your character's minimum starting age is the adulthood age of his or her race plus the number of dice indicated in the entry corresponding to the character's race and class on Table 6-4: Random Starting Ages. For example, an elf ranger must be at least 116 years old (adulthood age 110 plus 6, because the entry for an elf ranger is +6d6).

Alternatively, refer to Table 6–4: Random Starting Ages and roll dice to determine how old your character is. An elf ranger's randomly generated starting age, for example, is 110+6d6 years.

TABLE 6–4: RANDOM STARTING AGES

Race	Adulthood	Barbarian Rogue Sorcerer	Bard Fighter Paladin Ranger	Cleric Druid Monk Wizard
Human	15 years	+1d4	+1d6	+2d6
Dwarf	40 years	+3d6	+5d6	+7d6
Elf	110 years	+4d6	+6d6	+10d6
Gnome	40 years	+4d6	+6d6	+9d6
Half-elf	20 years	+1d6	+2d6	+3d6
Half-orc	14 years	+1d4	+1d6	+2d6
Halfling	20 years	+2d4	+3d6	+4d6

With age, a character's physical ability scores decrease and his or her mental ability scores increase (see Table 6–5: Aging Effects). The effects of each aging step are cumulative. However, none of a character's ability scores can be reduced below 1 in this way.

For example, when a human reaches 35 years of age, his Strength, Dexterity, and Constitution scores each drop 1 point, while his Intelligence, Wisdom, and Charisma scores each increase by 1 point. When he becomes 53 years old, his physical ability scores all drop an additional 2 points, while his mental ability scores increase by 1 again. So far he has lost a total of 3 points from his Strength, Constitution, and Dexterity scores and gained a total of 2 points to his Wisdom, Intelligence, and Charisma scores because of the effects of aging.

When a character reaches venerable age, the DM secretly rolls his or her maximum age, which is the number from the Venerable column on Table 6–5: Aging Effects plus the result of the dice roll indicated on the Maximum Age column on that table, and records the result, which the player does not know. A character who reaches his or her maximum age dies of old age at some time during the following year, as determined by the DM.

The maximum ages on Table 6–5 are for player characters. Most people in the world at large die from pestilence, accidents, infections, or violence before getting to venerable age.

TABLE 6–5: AGING EFFECTS

Race	Middle Age[1]	Old[2]	Venerable[3]	Maximum Age
Human	35 years	53 years	70 years	+2d20 years
Dwarf	125 years	188 years	250 years	+2d% years
Elf	175 years	263 years	350 years	+4d% years
Gnome	100 years	150 years	200 years	+3d% years
Half-elf	62 years	93 years	125 years	+3d20 years
Half-orc	30 years	45 years	60 years	+2d10 years
Halfling	50 years	75 years	100 years	+5d20 years

1 At middle age, –1 to Str, Dex, and Con; +1 to Int, Wis, and Cha.
2 At old age, –2 to Str, Dex, and Con; +1 to Int, Wis, and Cha.
3 At venerable age, –3 to Str, Dex, and Con; +1 to Int, Wis, and Cha.

HEIGHT AND WEIGHT

Choose your character's height and weight from the ranges mentioned in the appropriate race description (see Chapter 2) or from the ranges found on Table 6–6: Random Height and Weight. Think about what your character's abilities might say about his or her height and weight. A weak but agile character may be thin. A strong and tough character may be tall or just heavy.

Alternatively, roll randomly for your character's height and weight on Table 6–6: Random Height and Weight. The dice roll given in the Height Modifier column determines the character's extra height beyond the base height. That same number multiplied by the dice roll or quantity given in the Weight Modifier column determines the character's extra weight beyond the base weight. For example, Tordek (a male dwarf) has a height of 3 feet 9 inches plus 2d4 inches. Monte rolls 2d4 and gets a result of 6, so Tordek stands 4 feet 3 inches tall. Then Monte uses that same roll, 6, and multiplies it by 2d6 pounds. His 2d6 roll is 9, so Tordek weighs an extra 54 pounds (6 × 9) on top of his base 130 pounds, for a total of 184 pounds.

TABLE 6–6: RANDOM HEIGHT AND WEIGHT

Race	Base Height	Height Modifier	Base Weight	Weight Modifier
Human, male	4′10″	+2d10	120 lb.	× (2d4) lb.
Human, female	4′5″	+2d10	85 lb.	× (2d4) lb.
Dwarf, male	3′9″	+2d4	130 lb.	× (2d6) lb.
Dwarf, female	3′7″	+2d4	100 lb.	× (2d6) lb.
Elf, male	4′5″	+2d6	85 lb.	× (1d6) lb.
Elf, female	4′5″	+2d6	80 lb.	× (1d6) lb.
Gnome, male	3′0″	+2d4	40 lb.	× 1 lb.
Gnome, female	2′10″	+2d4	35 lb.	× 1 lb.
Half-elf, male	4′7″	+2d8	100 lb.	× (2d4) lb.
Half-elf, female	4′5″	+2d8	80 lb.	× (2d4) lb.
Half-orc, male	4′10″	+2d12	150 lb.	× (2d6) lb.
Half-orc, female	4′5″	+2d12	110 lb.	× (2d6) lb.
Halfling, male	2′8″	+2d4	30 lb.	× 1 lb.
Halfling, female	2′6″	+2d4	25 lb.	× 1 lb.

Illus. by T. Lockwood

LOOKS, PERSONALITY, AND BACKGROUND

You can detail your character to any degree you like. As you play the character, you will probably come up with more details you will want to add.

LOOKS

Decide what your character looks like using the descriptions of the various races in Chapter 2 as a starting point. Characters with high Charisma scores tend to be better looking than those with low Charisma scores, though a character with high Charisma could have strange looks that give him or her a sort of exotic beauty.

Your character can be right- or left-handed.

You can use your character's looks to tell something about his or her personality and background. For example:

- Krusk the half-orc is missing part of an ear and bears many scars that are the result of the violent life he led among the orcs that raised him. He keeps claws and fangs from beasts he has killed on a necklace.
- Alhandra the paladin has the hand of Heironeous branded on the inside of her forearm to show her devotion to him.
- Hennet the sorcerer wears an eclectic, makeshift outfit that is different from day to day, suggesting his chaotic nature.

PERSONALITY

Decide how your character acts, what she likes, what she wants out of life, what scares her, and what makes her angry. Race and alignment are good places to start when thinking about your character's personality, but they are bad places to stop. Make your lawful good dwarf (or whatever) different from every other lawful good dwarf.

A handy trick for making an interesting personality for your character is including some sort of conflict in her nature. For example, Tordek is lawful, but he's a little greedy, too. He may be tempted to steal occasionally if he can justify it to himself.

Your character's personality can change over time. Just because you decide some basic facts about your character's personality upon creation doesn't mean you need to abide by those facts as if they were holy writ. Let your character grow and evolve the way real people do.

BACKGROUND

Decide what your character's life has been like up until now. Here are a few questions to get you thinking.

- How did he decide to be an adventurer?
- How did he acquire his class? A fighter, for example, might have been in the militia, he may come from a family of soldiers, he may have trained in a martial school, or he may be a self-taught warrior.
- How did he get his starting equipment? Did he assemble it piece by piece over time? Was it a parting gift from a parent or mentor? Do any of his personal items have special significance to him?
- What's the worst thing that's ever happened to him?
- What's the best thing that's ever happened to him?
- Does he stay in contact with his family? What do his relatives think of him?

Naull

CUSTOMIZING YOUR CHARACTER

The rules for creating your character provide a common ground for players, but you can tweak the rules to make your character unique. Any substantive changes, however, must be approved by the DM.

Race: The rules for a character of a given race apply to most but not all people of that race. For example, you could create a dwarf descended from outcasts who have been exiled from dwarven society. Your dwarf would have grown up among humans. He would have the inborn qualities of a dwarf (better Constitution, worse Charisma, darkvision, and resistance to poison and spells) but not the cultural features (stonecunning, attack bonuses against goblinoids and orcs, dodge bonus against giants, bonuses on Appraise and Craft checks that relate to stone or metal, fighter as favored class, and perhaps even knowledge of the Dwarven language). You could probably talk your DM into giving your character some special bonuses to balance the loss of the cultural features.

Class: Some classes already give you plenty of room to customize your character. With your DM's approval, however, you could change some of your character's class features. For instance, if you want a fighter who used to work for the thieves' guild as an enforcer but who is now trying to become a legitimate bodyguard, he could be proficient only with the weapons and armor available to rogues, have 4 skill points per level instead of 2, and access to Bluff and Sense Motive as class skills. Otherwise, he would be a regular fighter.

Skills and Feats: You can call your skills, feats, and class features whatever your character would call them. Lidda, the halfling rogue, talks about "footpaddin'" rather than about "moving silently," so her player writes "Footpaddin'" down on her character sheet to stand for the Move Silently skill. Ember, the monk, calls her Move Silently skill "Rice Paper Walk."

You might also think of other skills that your character ought to have. Your DM has guidelines (in the *Dungeon Master's Guide*) for creating new skills.

Equipment: Your equipment can look the way you want it to look to match your character's style. One wizard's quarterstaff might be a plain, straight length of wood, while another wizard's is gnarled, twisted, and engraved with mystic runes.

Your character might have some items that aren't on the equipment lists (see Chapter 7). Agree with your DM on what a new item would do and how much it would cost, and then your character can have it.

Sometimes you see a weapon in a movie or read about one in a book, and you want your character to use that weapon. If it's not on the weapon list in Chapter 7, try to find a weapon on the list that seems equivalent. A katana (samurai sword), for example, is not on the weapon list, but you could equip your character with a katana and just treat it like a masterwork bastard sword.

Water Skin

Piton

Small Pouch

Rock Hammer

Back Pack

Climbing Gloves

Shovel

Illus. by A. Swekel

Grappler

In the marketplace of a big city, armorsmiths and weapon-smiths offer a wide variety of arms and armor for those with the gold to buy them. Here you can find practical, sturdy swords and perhaps a few elven blades of exceptional quality. Alchemists sell acid, alchemist's fire, and smokesticks for those who want something flashier than a trusty blade. Wizards (or, more likely, their brokers) even sell magic scrolls, wands, weapons, and other items.

This chapter covers the mundane and exotic merchandise that characters may want to purchase and how to go about doing so. (Magic items are covered in the *Dungeon Master's Guide*.)

EQUIPPING A CHARACTER

A beginning character generally has enough wealth to start out with the basics: some weapons, some armor suitable to his or her class (if any), and some miscellaneous gear. As the character undertakes adventures and amasses loot, he or she can afford bigger and better gear. At first, however, the options are limited by the character's budget.

STARTING PACKAGES

Each class has a starting package that provides default equipment (as well as default skills, a default feat, and so forth). If you equip your character with the default equipment, you can customize these packages a little by swapping in some equipment of your choice for the indicated equipment. Trades like this are fine as long as the value of the equipment you swap in isn't higher than the value of the equipment given in the package.

EQUIPMENT A LA CARTE

If you don't want to take the standard package for your character's class, you can instead purchase weapons, armor, and miscellaneous equipment item by item. You begin with a random number of gold pieces that is determined by your character's class, and then you decide how to spend it (see Table 7–1: Random Starting Gold). Alternatively, your DM can assign average starting gold for each character, as indicated on Table 7–1.

Table 7–1: Random Starting Gold

Class	Amount (average)	Class	Amount (average)
Barbarian	4d4 × 10 (100 gp)	Paladin	6d4 × 10 (150 gp)
Bard	4d4 × 10 (100 gp)	Ranger	6d4 × 10 (150 gp)
Cleric	5d4 × 10 (125 gp)	Rogue	5d4 × 10 (125 gp)
Druid	2d4 × 10 (50 gp)	Sorcerer	3d4 × 10 (75 gp)
Fighter	6d4 × 10 (150 gp)	Wizard	3d4 × 10 (75 gp)
Monk	5d4 (12 gp, 5 sp)		

Note that buying beginning equipment this way is an abstraction. Your character doesn't walk into a store with handfuls of gold and buy every item one by one. Rather, these items may have come the character's way as gifts from family, equipment from patrons, gear granted during military service, swag gained through duplicity, and so on.

Assume your character owns at least one outfit of normal clothes. Pick any one of the following clothing outfits for free: artisan's outfit, entertainer's outfit, explorer's outfit, monk's outfit, peasant's outfit, scholar's outfit, or traveler's outfit. (See Clothing, page 131.)

AVAILABILITY

All the items described in this chapter are assumed to be available to PCs with the wherewithal to buy them. Many of these items are very expensive and rare. You won't find them on the rack at a store in a town. But a character with the coin to buy an expensive item can usually connect with a seller and get a desired item.

If you want to buy something not described in this chapter, the general rule is that a character can buy anything that costs as much as 3,000 gp. Buying a more expensive item, such as a +2 *longsword*, means going to a big city where rare items are for sale, making a special deal with someone who makes or can provide the item, or paying a premium price to a merchant who makes a special effort to get what the character wants.

Depending on where in the fantasy world the character is, it might be possible to buy more expensive items without a problem, or it might be more difficult to do so. In a small town, for example, it's practically impossible to find someone who can make a suit of full plate armor. The DM determines what is and is not available depending on how he or she runs the world and where the characters are in it.

WEALTH AND MONEY

Adventurers are in the small group of people who regularly buy things with coins. Members of the peasantry trade mostly in goods, bartering for what they need and paying taxes in grain and cheese. Members of the nobility trade mostly in legal rights, such as the rights to a mine, a port, or farmland, or they trade in gold bars, measuring gold by the pound rather than by the coin.

COINS

The most common coin that adventurers use is the gold piece (gp). With 1 gold piece, a character can buy a belt pouch, 50 feet of hempen rope, or a goat. A skilled (but not exceptional) artisan can earn 1 gold piece a day. The gold piece is the standard unit of measure for wealth. When merchants discuss deals that involve goods or services worth hundreds or thousands of gold pieces, the transactions don't usually involve the exchange of that many individual coins. Rather, the gold piece is a standard measure of value, and the actual exchange is in gold bars, letters of credit, or valuable goods.

The most prevalent coin among commoners is the silver piece (sp). A gold piece is worth 10 silver pieces. A silver piece buys a laborer's work for a day, a common lamp, or a poor meal of bread, baked turnips, onions, and water.

Each silver piece is worth 10 copper pieces (cp). A single copper piece buys a candle, a torch, or a piece of chalk. Copper pieces are common among laborers and beggars.

In addition to copper, silver, and gold coins, which people use daily, merchants also recognize platinum pieces (pp), which are each worth 10 gp. These coins are not in common circulation, but adventurers occasionally find them as part of ancient treasure hoards.

The standard coin weighs about a third of an ounce (fifty to the pound). It is the exact size of the coin pictured in the illustration on page 168.

TABLE 7–2: COINS

		Exchange Value			
		CP	SP	GP	PP
Copper piece (cp)	=	1	1/10	1/100	1/1,000
Silver piece (sp)	=	10	1	1/10	1/100
Gold piece (gp)	=	100	10	1	1/10
Platinum piece (pp)	=	1,000	100	10	1

WEALTH OTHER THAN COINS

Most wealth is not in coins. It is livestock, grain, land, rights to collect taxes, or rights to resources (such as a mine or a forest). Gems and jewelry can also serve as portable wealth.

Trade

Guilds, nobles, and royalty regulate trade. Chartered companies are granted rights to dam rivers in order to provide power for mills, to conduct trade along certain routes, to send merchant ships to various ports, or to buy or sell specific goods. Guilds set prices for the goods or services that they control, and determine who may or may not offer those goods and services. Merchants commonly exchange trade goods without using currency. As a means of comparison, some trade goods are detailed on Table 7–3: Trade Goods.

TABLE 7–3: TRADE GOODS

Cost	Item
1 cp	One pound of wheat
2 cp	One pound of flour, or one chicken
1 sp	One pound of iron
5 sp	One pound of tobacco or copper
1 gp	One pound of cinnamon, or one goat
2 gp	One pound of ginger or pepper, or one sheep
3 gp	One pig
4 gp	One square yard of linen
5 gp	One pound of salt or silver
10 gp	One square yard of silk, or one cow
15 gp	One pound of saffron or cloves, or one ox
50 gp	One pound of gold
500 gp	One pound of platinum

SELLING LOOT

In general, a character can sell something for half its listed price. Characters who want to upgrade to better armor or weaponry, for example, can sell their old equipment for half price.

Trade goods are the exception to the half-price rule. A trade good, in this sense, is a valuable good that can be easily exchanged almost as if it were cash itself. Wheat, flour, cloth, gems, jewelry, art objects, and valuable metals are trade goods, and merchants often trade in them directly without using currency (see Table 7–3: Trade Goods). Obviously, merchants can sell these goods for slightly more than they pay for them, but the difference is small enough that you don't have to worry about it.

WEAPONS

A character's weapons help determine how capable he or she is in a variety of combat situations. See Table 7–5: Weapons for the characteristics of various weapons.

WEAPON CATEGORIES

Weapons are grouped into several interlocking sets of categories. These categories pertain to what training is needed to become proficient in a weapon's use (simple, martial, or exotic), the weapon's usefulness either in close combat (melee) or at a distance (ranged, which includes both thrown and projectile weapons), its relative encumbrance (light, one-handed, or two-handed), and its size (Small, Medium, or Large).

Simple, Martial, and Exotic Weapons: Anybody but a druid, monk, rogue, or wizard is proficient with all simple weapons. Barbarians, fighters, paladins, and rangers are proficient with all simple and all martial weapons. Characters of other classes are proficient with an assortment of mainly simple weapons and possibly also some martial or even exotic weapons. A character who uses a weapon with which he or she is not proficient takes a –4 penalty on attack rolls.

Melee and Ranged Weapons: Melee weapons are used for making melee attacks, though some of them can be thrown as well. Ranged weapons are thrown weapons or projectile weapons that are not effective in melee.

Reach Weapons: Glaives, guisarmes, lances, longspears, ranseurs, spiked chains, and whips are reach weapons. A reach weapon is a melee weapon that allows its wielder to strike at targets that aren't adjacent to him or her. Most reach weapons described in this chapter double the wielder's natural reach, meaning that a typical Small or Medium wielder of such a weapon can attack a creature 10 feet away, but not a creature in an adjacent square. A typical Large character wielding a reach weapon of the appropriate size can attack a creature 15 or 20 feet away, but not adjacent creatures or creatures up to 10 feet away.

Double Weapons: Dire flails, dwarven urgroshes, gnome hooked hammers, orc double axes, quarterstaffs, and two-bladed swords are double weapons. A character can fight with both ends of a double weapon as if fighting with two weapons, but he or she incurs all the normal attack penalties associated with two-weapon combat, just as though the character were wielding a one-handed weapon and a light weapon (see Two-Weapon Fighting, page 160). The character can also choose to use a double weapon two-handed, attacking with only one end of it; most wizards who wield quarterstaffs use them in this way. A creature wielding a double weapon in one hand (such as a human wielding a Small two-bladed sword) can't use it as a double weapon—only one end of the weapon can be used in any given round.

Thrown Weapons: Daggers, clubs, shortspears, spears, darts, javelins, throwing axes, light hammers, tridents, shuriken, and nets are thrown weapons. The wielder applies his or her Strength modifier to damage dealt by thrown weapons (except for splash weapons, such as a vial of acid; see Throw Splash Weapon, page 158).

It is possible to throw a weapon that isn't designed to be thrown (that is, a melee weapon that doesn't have a numeric entry in the Range Increment column on Table 7–5), but a character who does so takes a –4 penalty on the attack roll. Throwing a light or one-handed weapon is a standard action, while throwing a two-handed weapon is a full-round action. Regardless of the type of weapon, such an attack scores a threat (a possible critical hit) only on a natural roll of 20 and deals double damage on a critical hit. Such a weapon has a range increment of 10 feet.

Projectile Weapons: Light crossbows, slings, heavy crossbows, shortbows, composite shortbows, longbows, composite longbows, hand crossbows, and repeating crossbows are projectile weapons. Most projectile weapons require two hands to use (see specific weapon descriptions later in this chapter). A character gets no Strength bonus on damage rolls with a projectile weapon unless it's a specially built composite shortbow, specially built composite longbow, or sling. If the character has a penalty for low Strength, apply it to damage rolls when he or she uses a bow or a sling.

Ammunition: Projectile weapons use ammunition: arrows (for bows), bolts (for crossbows), or sling bullets (for slings). When using a bow, a character can draw ammunition as a free action; crossbows and slings require an action for reloading. Generally speaking, ammunition that hits its target is destroyed or rendered useless, while normal ammunition that misses has a 50% chance of being destroyed or lost.

Although they are thrown weapons, shuriken are treated as ammunition for the purposes of drawing them, crafting masterwork or otherwise special versions of them (see Masterwork Weapons, below), and what happens to them after they are thrown.

Light, One-Handed, and Two-Handed Melee Weapons: This designation is a measure of how much effort it takes to wield a weapon in combat. It indicates whether a melee weapon, when wielded by a character of the weapon's size category, is considered a light weapon, a one-handed weapon, or a two-handed weapon.

Light: A light weapon is easier to use in one's off hand than a one-handed weapon is, and it can be used while grappling. A light weapon is used in one hand. Add the wielder's Strength bonus (if any) to damage rolls for melee attacks with a light weapon if it's used in the primary hand, or one-half the wielder's Strength bonus

if it's used in the off hand. Using two hands to wield a light weapon gives no advantage on damage; the Strength bonus applies as though the weapon were held in the wielder's primary hand only.

An unarmed strike is always considered a light weapon.

One-Handed: A one-handed weapon can be used in either the primary hand or the off hand. Add the wielder's Strength bonus to damage rolls for melee attacks with a one-handed weapon if it's used in the primary hand, or 1/2 his or her Strength bonus if it's used in the off hand. If a one-handed weapon is wielded with two hands during melee combat, add 1-1/2 times the character's Strength bonus to damage rolls.

Two-Handed: Two hands are required to use a two-handed melee weapon effectively. Apply 1-1/2 times the character's Strength bonus to damage rolls for melee attacks with such a weapon.

Weapon Size: Every weapon has a size category, such as Small, Medium, or Large. This designation indicates the size of the creature for which the weapon was designed. A Small greatsword is a greatsword designed for a Small creature, such as a halfling. A Medium longsword is a longsword designed for a Medium creature, such as an elf. A Large shortbow is a shortbow designed for a Large creature, such as an ogre.

A weapon's size category isn't the same as its size as an object. A Medium dagger (one sized for a Medium character), for instance, is a Tiny object (see Table 9–10: Size and Armor Class of Objects, page 166). Instead, a weapon's size category is keyed to the size of the intended wielder. In general, a light weapon (such as a dagger) is an object two size categories smaller than the wielder, a one-handed weapon (such as a longsword) is an object one size category smaller than the wielder, and a two-handed weapon (such as a greatsword) is an object of the same size category as the wielder.

Inappropriately Sized Weapons: A creature can't make optimum use of a weapon that isn't properly sized for it. A cumulative –2 penalty applies on attack rolls for each size category of difference between the size of its intended wielder and the size of its actual wielder. Thus, a human wielding a Small dagger takes a –2 penalty on attack rolls (one size category different), and an ogre wielding a Small longsword takes a –4 penalty (two size categories different). If the creature isn't proficient with the weapon (a wizard attempting to wield a Small battleaxe, for instance), a –4 nonproficiency penalty also applies.

The measure of how much effort it takes to use a weapon (whether the weapon is designated as a light, one-handed, or two-handed weapon for a particular wielder) is altered by one step for each size category of difference between the wielder's size and the size of the creature for which the weapon was designed. For instance, a Small greatsword (a two-handed weapon for a Small creature) is considered a one-handed weapon for a Medium creature, or a light weapon for a Large creature. Conversely, a Large dagger (a light weapon for a Large creature) is considered a one-handed weapon for a Medium creature, or a two-handed weapon for a Small creature. If a weapon's designation would be changed to something other than light, one-handed, or two-handed by this alteration, the creature can't wield the weapon at all.

Improvised Weapons: Sometimes objects not crafted to be weapons nonetheless see use in combat—people fight with anything from broken bottles to chair legs to thrown mugs. Because such objects are not designed for this use, any creature that uses one in combat is considered to be nonproficient with it and takes a –4 penalty on attack rolls made with that object. To determine the size category and appropriate damage for an improvised weapon, the DM should compare its relative size and damage potential to the weapon list to find a reasonable match. For instance, a table leg is similar to a club, while a broken bottle is similar to a dagger. An improvised weapon scores a threat (a possible critical hit) on a natural roll of 20 and deals double damage on a critical hit. An improvised thrown weapon has a range increment of 10 feet.

WEAPON QUALITIES

The weapon a character uses says something about who he or she is. You probably want to equip your character with both a melee weapon and a ranged weapon. If you can't afford both your melee weapon of choice and your ranged weapon of choice, decide which is more important to the character.

What kind of weapon you select determines how your character can choose to wield it (with one hand or two) and how much damage he or she can deal with it. A two-handed weapon deals more damage than a one-handed weapon, but wielding a two-handed weapon prevents the wielder from using a shield, so that's a trade-off.

The number of weapons your character is proficient with depends on his or her class and race. A character can also become proficient with additional weapons by selecting the right feats. See Exotic Weapon Proficiency (page 94), Martial Weapon Proficiency (page 97), and Simple Weapon Proficiency (page 100).

A better weapon is usually more expensive than an inferior one, but more expensive doesn't always mean better. For instance, a rapier is more expensive than a longsword. For a dexterous rogue with the Weapon Finesse feat, a rapier is a terrific weapon. For a typical fighter, a longsword is better.

When selecting your character's weapons, keep in mind the following factors (given as column headings on Table 7–5).

Cost: This value is the weapon's cost in gold pieces (gp) or silver pieces (sp). The cost includes miscellaneous gear that goes with the weapon, such as a scabbard for a sword or a quiver for arrows. This cost is the same for a Small or Medium version of the weapon. A Large version costs twice the listed price.

Damage: The Damage columns give the damage dealt by the weapon on a successful hit. The column labeled "Dmg (S)" is for Small weapons, such as those typically wielded by a gnome or halfling. The column labeled "Dmg (M)" is for Medium weapons, such as those typically wielded by a dwarf, elf, half-elf, half-orc, or human. If two damage ranges are given, such as "1d6/1d6" for the quarterstaff, then the weapon is a double weapon (see Double Weapons, above, and Two-Weapon Fighting, page 160). Use the second damage figure given for the double weapon's extra attack.

Table 7–4: Tiny and Large Weapon Damage gives weapon damage values for weapons of those sizes. For instance, a Tiny longsword (such as might be wielded by a halfling or gnome fighter under the effect of a *reduce person* spell) deals 1d4 points of damage, while a Large greataxe (wielded by a half-orc barbarian under the effect of an *enlarge person* spell) deals 3d6 points of damage. The *Dungeon Master's Guide* has more information on weapons and combat for creatures smaller than Small and larger than Medium.

TABLE 7–4: TINY AND LARGE WEAPON DAMAGE

Medium Weapon Damage	Tiny Weapon Damage	Large Weapon Damage
1d2	—	1d3
1d3	1	1d4
1d4	1d2	1d6
1d6	1d3	1d8
1d8	1d4	2d6
1d10	1d6	2d8
1d12	1d8	3d6
2d4	1d4	2d6
2d6	1d8	3d6
2d8	1d10	3d8
2d10	2d6	4d8

Critical: The entry in this column notes how the weapon is used with the rules for critical hits. When your character scores a critical hit, roll the damage two, three, or four times, as indicated by its critical multiplier (using all applicable modifiers on each roll), and add all the results together.

Exception: Extra damage over and above a weapon's normal damage, such as that dealt by a sneak attack or the special ability of a flaming sword, is not multiplied when you score a critical hit.

×2: The weapon deals double damage on a critical hit.

×3: The weapon deals triple damage on a critical hit.

×3/×4: One head of this double weapon deals triple damage on a critical hit. The other head deals quadruple damage on a critical hit.

×4: The weapon deals quadruple damage on a critical hit.

19–20/×2: The weapon scores a threat (a possible critical hit) on a natural roll of 19 or 20 (instead of just 20) and deals double damage on a critical hit. (The weapon has a threat range of 19–20.)

18–20/×2: The weapon scores a threat on a natural roll of 18, 19, or 20 (instead of just 20) and deals double damage on a critical hit. (The weapon has a threat range of 18–20.)

19–20/×2: The weapon scores a threat (a possible critical hit) on a natural roll of 19 or 20 (instead of just 20) and deals double damage on a critical hit. (The weapon has a threat range of 19–20.)

18–20/×2: The weapon scores a threat on a natural roll of 18, 19, or 20 (instead of just 20) and deals double damage on a critical hit. (The weapon has a threat range of 18–20.)

Range Increment: Any attack at less than this distance is not penalized for range, so an arrow from a shortbow (range increment 60 feet) can strike at an enemy 59 feet away or closer with no penalty. However, each full range increment imposes a cumulative –2 penalty on the attack roll. A shortbow archer firing at a target 200 feet away takes a –6 penalty on the attack roll (–2 × 3, because 200 feet is at least three range increments but not four). A thrown weapon, such as a throwing axe, has a maximum range of five range increments. A projectile weapon, such as a bow, can shoot out to ten range increments.

Weight: This column gives the weight of a Medium version of the weapon. Halve this number for Small weapons, and double it for Large weapons.

Type: Weapons are classified according to the type of damage they deal: bludgeoning, piercing, or slashing. Some monsters may be resistant or immune to attacks from certain types of weapons. For example, a skeleton takes less damage from slashing weapons and piercing weapons.

Some weapons deal damage of multiple types (for example, the morningstar, which deals both bludgeoning and piercing damage). If a weapon is of two types, the damage it deals is not half one type and half another; all of it is both types. Therefore, a creature would have to be immune to both types of damage to ignore any of the damage from such a weapon.

In other cases, a weapon can deal either of two types of damage (such as the dagger, which can deal either piercing or slashing damage). In a situation when the damage type is significant, the wielder can choose which type of damage to deal with such a weapon.

Special: Some weapons have special features. See the weapon descriptions for details.

WEAPON DESCRIPTIONS

The weapons found on Table 7–5: Weapons are described below, along with any special options the wielder ("you") has for their use. Splash weapons are described under Special Substances and Items, page 128.

Arrows: An arrow used as a melee weapon is treated as a light improvised weapon (–4 penalty on attack rolls) and deals damage as a dagger of its size (critical multiplier ×2). Arrows come in a leather quiver that holds 20 arrows. An arrow that hits its target is destroyed; one that misses has a 50% chance of being destroyed or lost.

Axe, Throwing: A throwing axe is lighter than a handaxe and balanced for throwing. Gnome fighters often use throwing axes for both melee and ranged attacks.

Axe, Orc Double: An orc double axe is a double weapon. You can fight with it as if fighting with two weapons, but if you do, you incur all the normal attack penalties associated with fighting with two weapons, just as if you were using a one-handed weapon and a light weapon (see Two-Weapon Fighting, page 160). As its name suggests, it is most often found in the hands of powerful orc fighters. A creature wielding an orc double axe in one hand can't use it as a double weapon—only one end of the weapon can be used in any given round.

Battleaxe: The battleaxe is the most common melee weapon among dwarves.

Bolas: A set of bolas consists of two or three heavy wooden spheres connected by lengths of cord. Because the bolas can wrap around an enemy's leg or other limb, you can use this weapon to make a ranged trip attack against an opponent. You can't be tripped during your own trip attempt when using a set of bolas.

Bolts: A crossbow bolt used as a melee weapon is treated as a light improvised weapon (–4 penalty on attack rolls) and deals damage as a dagger of its size (crit ×2). Bolts come in a wooden case that holds 10 bolts (or 5, for a repeating crossbow). A bolt that hits its target is destroyed; one that misses has a 50% chance of being destroyed or lost.

Bullets, Sling: Bullets are lead spheres, much heavier than stones of the same size. They come in a leather pouch that holds 10 bullets. A bullet that hits its target is destroyed; one that misses has a 50% chance of being destroyed or lost.

Chain, Spiked: A spiked chain has reach, so you can strike opponents 10 feet away with it. In addition, unlike most other weapons with reach, it can be used against an adjacent foe.

Because the chain can wrap around an enemy's leg or other limb, you can make trip attacks with it. If you are tripped during your own trip attempt, you can drop the chain to avoid being tripped.

When using a spiked chain, you get a +2 bonus on opposed attack rolls made to disarm an opponent (including the roll to avoid being disarmed if such an attempt fails).

You can use the Weapon Finesse feat (page 102) to apply your Dexterity modifier instead of your Strength modifier to attack rolls with a spiked chain sized for you, even though it isn't a light weapon for you.

Club: A wooden club is so easy to find and fashion that it has no cost.

Crossbow, Hand: This exotic weapon is common among rogues and others who favor stealth over power. You can draw a hand crossbow back by hand. Loading a hand crossbow is a move action that provokes attacks of opportunity.

You can shoot, but not load, a hand crossbow with one hand at no penalty. You can shoot a hand crossbow with each hand, but you take a penalty on attack rolls as if attacking with two light weapons (see Table 8–10: Two-Weapon Fighting Penalties, page 160).

Crossbow, Heavy: You draw a heavy crossbow back by turning a small winch. Loading a heavy crossbow is a full-round action that provokes attacks of opportunity.

Normally, operating a heavy crossbow requires two hands. However, you can shoot, but not load, a heavy crossbow with one hand at a –4 penalty on attack rolls. You can shoot a heavy crossbow with each hand, but you take a penalty on attack rolls as if attacking with two one-handed weapons (see Table 8–10: Two-Weapon Fighting Penalties, page 160). This penalty is cumulative with the penalty for one-handed firing.

Crossbow, Light: You draw a light crossbow back by pulling a lever. Loading a light crossbow is a move action that provokes attacks of opportunity.

Normally, operating a light crossbow requires two hands.

Illus. by L. Grant-West

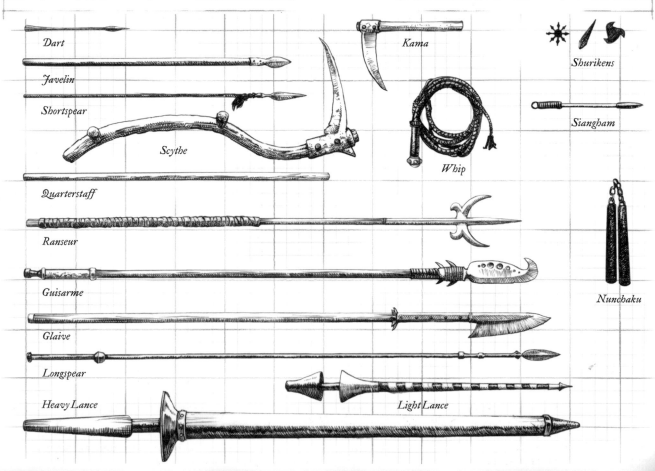

Dart

Javelin

Shortspear

Scythe

Quarterstaff

Ranseur

Guisarme

Glaive

Longspear

Heavy Lance

Kama

Whip

Light Lance

Shurikens

Siangham

Nunchaku

However, you can shoot, but not load, a light crossbow with one hand at a −2 penalty on attack rolls. You can shoot a light crossbow with each hand, but you take a penalty on attack rolls as if attacking with two light weapons (see Table 8–10: Two-Weapon Fighting Penalties, page 160). This penalty is cumulative with the penalty for one-handed firing.

Crossbow, Repeating: The repeating crossbow (whether heavy or light) holds 5 crossbow bolts. As long as it holds bolts, you can reload it by pulling the reloading lever (a free action). Loading a new case of 5 bolts is a full-round action that provokes attacks of opportunity.

You can fire a repeating crossbow with one hand or fire a repeating crossbow in each hand in the same manner as you would a normal crossbow of the same size. However, you must fire the weapon with two hands in order to use the reloading lever, and you must use two hands to load a new case of bolts.

Dagger: The dagger is a common secondary weapon. You get a +2 bonus on Sleight of Hand checks made to conceal a dagger on your body (see the Sleight of Hand skill, page 81).

Dagger, Punching: This dagger puts more force from your punch behind it, making it capable of deadly strikes.

Dart: A dart is the size of a large arrow and has a weighted head. Essentially, it is a small javelin.

TABLE 7–5: WEAPONS

Simple Weapons	Cost	Dmg (S)	Dmg (M)	Critical	Range Increment	Weight[1]	Type[2]
Unarmed Attacks							
Gauntlet	2 gp	1d2	1d3	×2	—	1 lb.	Bludgeoning
Unarmed strike	—	1d2[3]	1d3[3]	×2	—	—	Bludgeoning
Light Melee Weapons							
Dagger	2 gp	1d3	1d4	19–20/×2	10 ft.	1 lb.	Piercing or slashing
Dagger, punching	2 gp	1d3	1d4	×3	—	1 lb.	Piercing
Gauntlet, spiked	5 gp	1d3	1d4	×2	—	1 lb.	Piercing
Mace, light	5 gp	1d4	1d6	×2	—	4 lb.	Bludgeoning
Sickle	6 gp	1d4	1d6	×2	—	2 lb.	Slashing
One-Handed Melee Weapons							
Club	—	1d4	1d6	×2	10 ft.	3 lb.	Bludgeoning
Mace, heavy	12 gp	1d6	1d8	×2	—	8 lb.	Bludgeoning
Morningstar	8 gp	1d6	1d8	×2	—	6 lb.	Bludgeoning and piercing
Shortspear	1 gp	1d4	1d6	×2	20 ft.	3 lb.	Piercing
Two-Handed Melee Weapons							
Longspear[4]	5 gp	1d6	1d8	×3	—	9 lb.	Piercing
Quarterstaff[5]	—	1d4/1d4	1d6/1d6	×2	—	4 lb.	Bludgeoning
Spear	2 gp	1d6	1d8	×3	20 ft.	6 lb.	Piercing
Ranged Weapons							
Crossbow, heavy	50 gp	1d8	1d10	19–20/×2	120 ft.	8 lb.	Piercing
Bolts, crossbow (10)	1 gp	—	—	—	—	1 lb.	—
Crossbow, light	35 gp	1d6	1d8	19–20/×2	80 ft.	4 lb.	Piercing
Bolts, crossbow (10)	1 gp	—	—	—	—	1 lb.	—
Dart	5 sp	1d3	1d4	×2	20 ft.	1/2 lb.	Piercing
Javelin	1 gp	1d4	1d6	×2	30 ft.	2 lb.	Piercing
Sling	—	1d3	1d4	×2	50 ft.	0 lb.	Bludgeoning
Bullets, sling (10)	1 sp	—	—	—	—	5 lb.	

Martial Weapons	Cost	Dmg (S)	Dmg (M)	Critical	Range Increment	Weight[1]	Type[2]
Light Melee Weapons							
Axe, throwing	8 gp	1d4	1d6	×2	10 ft.	2 lb.	Slashing
Hammer, light	1 gp	1d3	1d4	×2	20 ft.	2 lb.	Bludgeoning
Handaxe	6 gp	1d4	1d6	×3	—	3 lb.	Slashing
Kukri	8 gp	1d3	1d4	18–20/×2	—	2 lb.	Slashing
Pick, light	4 gp	1d3	1d4	×4	—	3 lb.	Piercing
Sap	1 gp	1d4[3]	1d6[3]	×2	—	2 lb.	Bludgeoning
Shield, light	special	1d2	1d3	×2	—	special	Bludgeoning
Spiked armor	special	1d4	1d6	×2	—	special	Piercing
Spiked shield, light	special	1d3	1d4	×2	—	special	Piercing
Sword, short	10 gp	1d4	1d6	19–20/×2	—	2 lb.	Piercing
One-Handed Melee Weapons							
Battleaxe	10 gp	1d6	1d8	×3	—	6 lb.	Slashing
Flail	8 gp	1d6	1d8	×2	—	5 lb.	Bludgeoning
Longsword	15 gp	1d6	1d8	19–20/×2	—	4 lb.	Slashing
Pick, heavy	8 gp	1d4	1d6	×4	—	6 lb.	Piercing
Rapier	20 gp	1d4	1d6	18–20/×2	—	2 lb.	Piercing
Scimitar	15 gp	1d4	1d6	18–20/×2	—	4 lb.	Slashing
Shield, heavy	special	1d3	1d4	×2	—	special	Bludgeoning
Spiked shield, heavy	special	1d4	1d6	×2	—	special	Piercing
Trident	15 gp	1d6	1d8	×2	10 ft.	4 lb.	Piercing
Warhammer	12 gp	1d6	1d8	×3	—	5 lb.	Bludgeoning

Falchion: This sword, which is essentially a two-handed scimitar, has a curve that gives it the effect of a keener edge.

Flail, Dire: A dire flail is a double weapon. You can fight with it as if fighting with two weapons, but if you do, you incur all the normal attack penalties associated with fighting with two weapons, just as if you were using a one-handed weapon and a light weapon (see Two-Weapon Fighting, page 160). A creature wielding a dire flail in one hand can't use it as a double weapon—only one end of the weapon can be used in any given round.

When using a dire flail, you get a +2 bonus on opposed attack rolls made to disarm an enemy (including the opposed attack roll to avoid being disarmed if such an attempt fails).

You can also use this weapon to make trip attacks. If you are tripped during your own trip attempt, you can drop the dire flail to avoid being tripped.

Flail or Heavy Flail: With a flail, you get a +2 bonus on opposed attack rolls made to disarm an enemy (including the roll to avoid being disarmed if such an attempt fails).

You can also use this weapon to make trip attacks. If you are tripped during your own trip attempt, you can drop the flail to avoid being tripped.

Gauntlet: This metal glove protects your hands and lets you

Two-Handed Melee Weapons							
Falchion	75 gp	1d6	2d4	18–20/×2	—	8 lb.	Slashing
Glaive[4]	8 gp	1d8	1d10	×3	—	10 lb.	Slashing
Greataxe	20 gp	1d10	1d12	×3	—	12 lb.	Slashing
Greatclub	5 gp	1d8	1d10	×2	—	8 lb.	Bludgeoning
Flail, heavy	15 gp	1d8	1d10	19–20/×2	—	10 lb.	Bludgeoning
Greatsword	50 gp	1d10	2d6	19–20/×2	—	8 lb.	Slashing
Guisarme[4]	9 gp	1d6	2d4	×3	—	12 lb.	Slashing
Halberd	10 gp	1d8	1d10	×3	—	12 lb.	Piercing or slashing
Lance[4]	10 gp	1d6	1d8	×3	—	10 lb.	Piercing
Ranseur[4]	10 gp	1d6	2d4	×3	—	12 lb.	Piercing
Scythe	18 gp	1d6	2d4	×4	—	10 lb.	Piercing or slashing
Ranged Weapons							
Longbow	75 gp	1d6	1d8	×3	100 ft.	3 lb.	Piercing
Arrows (20)	1 gp	—	—	—	—	3 lb.	—
Longbow, composite	100 gp	1d6	1d8	×3	110 ft.	3 lb.	Piercing
Arrows (20)	1 gp	—	—	—	—	3 lb.	—
Shortbow	30 gp	1d4	1d6	×3	60 ft.	2 lb.	Piercing
Arrows (20)	1 gp	—	—	—	—	3 lb.	—
Shortbow, composite	75 gp	1d4	1d6	×3	70 ft.	2 lb.	Piercing
Arrows (20)	1 gp	—	—	—	—	3 lb.	—

Exotic Weapons	Cost	Dmg (S)	Dmg (M)	Critical	Range Increment	Weight[1]	Type[2]
Light Melee Weapons							
Kama	2 gp	1d4	1d6	×2	—	2 lb.	Slashing
Nunchaku	2 gp	1d4	1d6	×2	—	2 lb.	Bludgeoning
Sai	1 gp	1d3	1d4	×2	10 ft.	1 lb.	Bludgeoning
Siangham	3 gp	1d4	1d6	×2	—	1 lb.	Piercing
One-Handed Melee Weapons							
Sword, bastard	35 gp	1d8	1d10	19–20/×2	—	6 lb.	Slashing
Waraxe, dwarven	30 gp	1d8	1d10	×3	—	8 lb.	Slashing
Whip[4]	1 gp	1d2[3]	1d3[3]	×2	—	2 lb.	Slashing
Two-Handed Melee Weapons							
Axe, orc double[5]	60 gp	1d6/1d6	1d8/1d8	×3	—	15 lb.	Slashing
Chain, spiked[4]	25 gp	1d6	2d4	×2	—	10 lb.	Piercing
Flail, dire[5]	90 gp	1d6/1d6	1d8/1d8	×2	—	10 lb.	Bludgeoning
Hammer, gnome hooked[5]	20 gp	1d6/1d4	1d8/1d6	×3/×4	—	6 lb.	Bludgeoning and piercing
Sword, two-bladed[5]	100 gp	1d6/1d6	1d8/1d8	19–20/×2	—	10 lb.	Slashing
Urgrosh, dwarven[5]	50 gp	1d6/1d4	1d8/1d6	×3	—	12 lb.	Slashing or piercing
Ranged Weapons							
Bolas	5 gp	1d3[3]	1d4[3]	×2	10 ft.	2 lb.	Bludgeoning
Crossbow, hand	100 gp	1d3	1d4	19–20/×2	30 ft.	2 lb.	Piercing
Bolts (10)	1 gp	—	—	—	—	1 lb.	—
Crossbow, repeating heavy	400 gp	1d8	1d10	19–20/×2	120 ft.	12 lb.	Piercing
Bolts (5)	1 gp	—	—	—	—	1 lb.	—
Crossbow, repeating light	250 gp	1d6	1d8	19–20/×2	80 ft.	6 lb.	Piercing
Bolts (5)	1 gp	—	—	—	—	1 lb.	—
Net	20 gp	—	—	—	10 ft.	6 lb.	—
Shuriken (5)	1 gp	1	1d2	×2	10 ft.	1/2 lb.	Piercing

1 Weight figures are for Medium weapons. A Small weapon weighs half as much, and a Large weapon weighs twice as much.

2 When two types are given, the weapon is both types if the entry specifies "and," or either type (player's choice at time of attack) if the entry specifies "or."

3 The weapon deals nonlethal damage rather than lethal damage.

4 Reach weapon.

5 Double weapon.

deal lethal damage rather than nonlethal damage with unarmed strikes. A strike with a gauntlet is otherwise considered an unarmed attack. The cost and weight given are for a single gauntlet. Medium and heavy armors (except breastplate) come with gauntlets.

Gauntlet, Spiked: Your opponent cannot use a disarm action to disarm you of spiked gauntlets. The cost and weight given are for a single gauntlet. An attack with a spiked gauntlet is considered an armed attack.

Glaive: A glaive has reach. You can strike opponents 10 feet away with it, but you can't use it against an adjacent foe.

Greataxe: This big, heavy axe is a favorite of barbarians and anybody else who wants the capability to deal out incredible damage.

Greatclub: A greatclub is a two-handed version of a regular club. It is often studded with nails or spikes or ringed by bands of iron.

Greatsword: Adventurers recognize the greatsword as one of the best melee weapons available. It's reliable and powerful.

Guisarme: A guisarme has reach. You can strike opponents 10 feet away with it, but you can't use it against an adjacent foe.

Because of a guisarme's curved blade, you can also use it to make trip attacks. If you are tripped during your own trip attempt, you can drop the guisarme to avoid being tripped.

Halberd: Normally, you strike with a halberd's axe head, but the spike on the end is useful against charging opponents. If you use a ready action to set a halberd against a charge, you deal double damage on a successful hit against a charging character.

You can use the hook on the back of a halberd to make trip attacks. If you are tripped during your own trip attempt, you can drop the halberd to avoid being tripped.

Hammer, Gnome Hooked: A gnome hooked hammer is a double weapon. You can fight with it as if fighting with two weapons, but if you do, you incur all the normal attack penalties associated with fighting with two weapons, just as if you were using a one-handed weapon and a light weapon (see Two-Weapon Fighting, page 160). The hammer's blunt head is a bludgeoning weapon that deals 1d6 points of damage (crit ×3). Its hook is a piercing weapon that deals 1d4 points of damage (crit ×4). You can use either head as the primary weapon. The other head is the off-hand weapon. A creature wielding a gnome hooked hammer in one hand can't use it as a double weapon—only one end of the weapon can be used in any given round.

You can use the hook on a gnome hooked hammer to make trip attacks. If you are tripped during your own trip attempt, you can drop the gnome hooked hammer to avoid being tripped.

Gnomes treat gnome hooked hammers as martial weapons.

Hammer, Light: This is a small sledge light enough to throw. It is favored by dwarves.

Handaxe: Dwarves favor these axes as off-hand weapons.

Javelin: This weapon is a light, flexible spear intended for throwing. You can use it in melee, but not well. Since it is not designed for melee, you are treated as nonproficient with it and take a –4 penalty on attack rolls if you use it as a melee weapon.

Kama: The kama is a special monk weapon. This designation gives a monk (see Chapter 3: Classes) wielding a kama special options.

Because of a kama's shape, you can use it to make trip attacks. If you are tripped during your own trip attempt, you can drop the kama to avoid being tripped.

Kukri: This heavy, curved knife has its sharp edge on the inside of the curve.

Lance: A lance deals double damage when used from the back of a charging mount. It has reach, so you can strike opponents 10 feet away with it, but you can't use it against an adjacent foe.

While mounted, you can wield a lance with one hand.

Longbow: You need at least two hands to use a bow, regardless

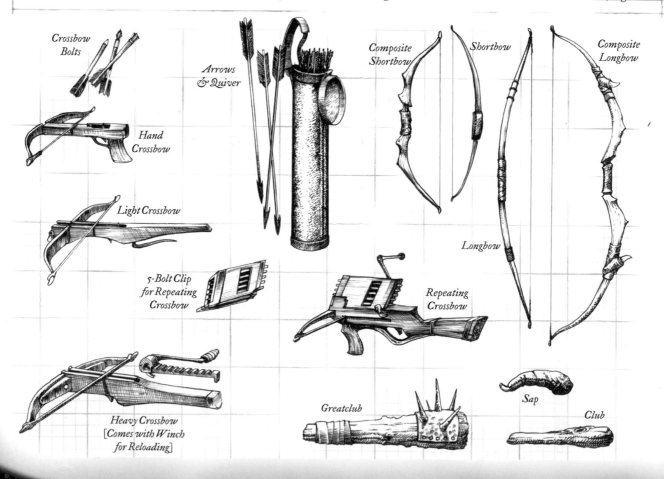

Crossbow Bolts

Hand Crossbow

Arrows & Quiver

Composite Shortbow

Shortbow

Composite Longbow

Light Crossbow

5-Bolt Clip for Repeating Crossbow

Repeating Crossbow

Longbow

Heavy Crossbow [Comes with Winch for Reloading]

Greatclub

Sap

Club

of its size. A longbow is too unwieldy to use while you are mounted. If you have a penalty for low Strength, apply it to damage rolls when you use a longbow. If you have a bonus for high Strength, you can apply it to damage rolls when you use a composite longbow (see below) but not a regular longbow.

Longbow, Composite: You need at least two hands to use a bow, regardless of its size. You can use a composite longbow while mounted. Composite bows are made from laminated horn, wood, or bone and built with a recurve, meaning that the bow remains bow-shaped even when unstrung. All composite bows are made with a particular strength rating (that is, each requires a minimum Strength modifier to use with proficiency). If your Strength bonus is less than the strength rating of the composite bow, you can't effectively use it, so you take a –2 penalty on attacks with it. The default composite longbow requires a Strength modifier of +0 or higher to use with proficiency. A composite longbow can be made with a high strength rating (representing an especially heavy pull) to take advantage of an above-average Strength score; this feature allows you to add your Strength bonus to damage, up to the maximum bonus indicated for the bow. Each point of Strength bonus granted by the bow adds 100 gp to its cost. For instance, a composite longbow (+1 Str bonus) costs 200 gp, while a composite longbow (+4 Str bonus) costs 500 gp.

For example, Tordek has a +2 Strength bonus. With a regular composite longbow, he gets no modifier on damage rolls. For 200 gp, he can buy a composite longbow (+1 Str bonus), which lets him add +1 to his damage rolls. For 300 gp, he can buy one that lets him add his entire +2 Strength bonus. Even if he paid 400 gp for a composite longbow (+3 Str bonus), he would still get only a +2 bonus on damage rolls and takes a –2 penalty on attacks with it because his Strength is insufficient to use the weapon to best advantage. The bow can't grant him a higher bonus than he already has.

For purposes of weapon proficiency and similar feats, a composite longbow is treated as if it were a longbow. Thus, if you have Weapon Focus (longbow), that feat applies both to longbows and composite longbows.

Longspear: A longspear has reach. You can strike opponents 10 feet away with it, but you can't use it against an adjacent foe. If you use a ready action to set a longspear against a charge, you deal double damage on a successful hit against a charging character.

Longsword: This classic, straight blade is the weapon of knighthood and valor. It is a favorite weapon of many paladins.

Mace, Heavy or Light: A mace is made of metal, even the haft, which makes it quite heavy and very hard to break.

Morningstar: This simple weapon combines the impact of a club with the piercing force of spikes.

Net: A fighting net has small barbs in the weave and a trailing rope to control netted opponents. You use it to entangle enemies.

When you throw a net, you make a ranged touch attack against your target. A net's maximum range is 10 feet. If you hit, the target is entangled. An entangled creature takes a –2 penalty on attack rolls and a –4 penalty on Dexterity, can move at only half speed, and cannot charge or run. If you control the trailing rope by succeeding on an opposed Strength check while holding it, the entangled creature can move only within the limits that the rope allows. If the entangled creature attempts to cast a spell, it must make a DC 15 Concentration check or be unable to cast the spell.

An entangled creature can escape with a DC 20 Escape Artist check (a full-round action). The net has 5 hit points and can be burst with a DC 25 Strength check (also a full-round action).

A net is useful only against creatures within one size category of you. For instance, a Small character wielding a net can entangle Tiny, Small, or Medium creatures.

A net must be folded to be thrown effectively. The first time you throw your net in a fight, you make a normal ranged touch attack

Illus. by L. Grant-West

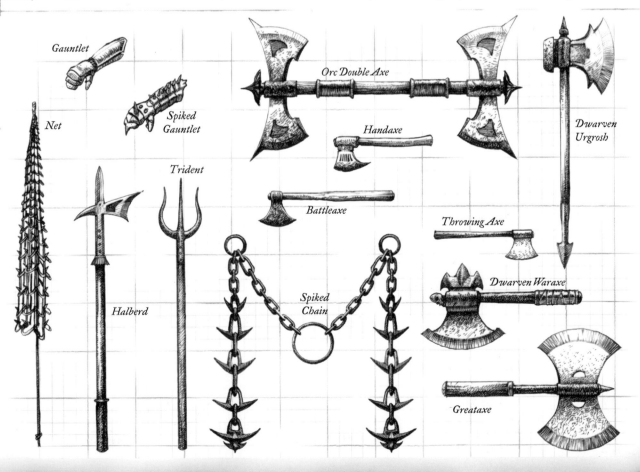

Gauntlet

Spiked Gauntlet

Orc Double Axe

Handaxe

Dwarven Urgrosh

Net

Trident

Battleaxe

Throwing Axe

Dwarven Waraxe

Halberd

Spiked Chain

Greataxe

roll. After the net is unfolded, you take a –4 penalty on attack rolls with it. It takes 2 rounds for a proficient user to fold a net and twice that long for a nonproficient one to do so.

Nunchaku: The nunchaku is a special monk weapon This designation gives a monk wielding a nunchaku special options. With a nunchaku, you get a +2 bonus on opposed attack rolls made to disarm an enemy (including the roll to avoid being disarmed if such an attempt fails).

Pick, Heavy or Light: A pick is designed to concentrate the force of its blow on a small area. A light or heavy pick resembles a miner's pick but is specifically designed for war.

Quarterstaff: The quarterstaff is the favorite weapon of many characters, from travelers, peasants, and merchants to monks, rangers, and wizards. A quarterstaff is a double weapon. You can fight with it as if fighting with two weapons, but if you do, you incur all the normal attack penalties associated with fighting with two weapons, just as if you were using a one-handed weapon and a light weapon (see Two-Weapon Fightng, page 160). You can also strike with either end singly, a fact that allows you to take full advantage of openings in your opponent's defenses. A creature wielding a quarterstaff in one hand can't use it as a double weapon—only one end of the weapon can be used in any given round.

The quarterstaff is a special monk weapon. This designation gives a monk (see Chapter 3: Classes) wielding a quarterstaff special options.

Ranseur: A ranseur has reach. You can strike opponents 10 feet away with it, but you can't use it against an adjacent foe.

With a ranseur, you get a +2 bonus on opposed attack rolls made to disarm an opponent (including the roll to avoid being disarmed if such an attempt fails).

Rapier: You can use the Weapon Finesse feat (page 102) to apply your Dexterity modifier instead of your Strength modifier to attack rolls with a rapier sized for you, even though it isn't a light weapon for you. You can't wield a rapier in two hands in order to apply 1-1/2 times your Strength bonus to damage.

Sai: A sai's pronglike extrusions are designed to help catch and disarm opponents' weapons. With a sai, you get a +4 bonus on opposed attack rolls made to disarm an enemy (including the roll to avoid being disarmed if such an attempt fails).

The sai is a special monk weapon. This designation gives a monk (see Chapter 3: Classes) wielding a sai special options.

Sap: A sap comes in handy when you want to knock an opponent out instead of killing it.

Scimitar: The curve on this blade gives it the effect of a keener edge.

Scythe: While it resembles the standard farm implement of the same name, this scythe is balanced and strengthened for war. The design of the scythe focuses tremendous force on the sharp point, as well as allowing devastating slashes with the blade edge.

Because of a scythe's shape, you can also use it to make trip attacks. If you are tripped during your own trip attempt, you can drop the scythe to avoid being tripped.

Shield, Heavy or Light: You can bash with a shield instead of using it for defense. See Armor, later in this chapter.

Shortbow: You need at least two hands to use a bow, regardless of its size. You can use a shortbow while mounted. If you have a penalty for low Strength, apply it to damage rolls when you use a shortbow. If you have a bonus for high Strength, you can apply it to damage rolls when you use a composite shortbow (see below) but not a regular shortbow.

Shortbow, Composite: You need at least two hands to use a bow, regardless of its size. You can use a composite shortbow while mounted. Composite bows are made from laminated horn, wood, or bone and built with a recurve, meaning that the bow remains bow-shaped even when unstrung. All composite bows are made

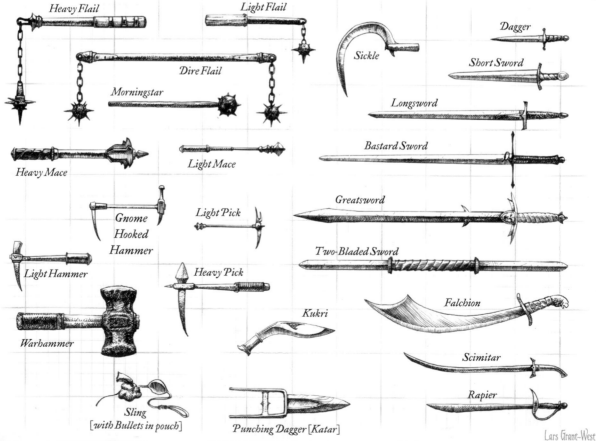

Heavy Flail
Light Flail
Dire Flail
Morningstar
Heavy Mace
Light Mace
Gnome Hooked Hammer
Light Pick
Light Hammer
Heavy Pick
Warhammer
Sling [with Bullets in pouch]
Punching Dagger [Katar]
Sickle
Dagger
Short Sword
Longsword
Bastard Sword
Greatsword
Two-Bladed Sword
Kukri
Falchion
Scimitar
Rapier

Lars Grant-West

with a particular strength rating (that is, each requires a minimum Strength modifier to use with proficiency). If your Strength bonus is lower than the strength rating of the composite bow, you can't effectively use it, so you take a –2 penalty on attacks with it. The default composite shortbow requires a Strength modifier of +0 or higher to use with proficiency. A composite shortbow can be made with a high strength rating (representing an especially heavy pull) to take advantage of an above-average Strength score; this feature allows you to add your Strength bonus to damage, up to the maximum bonus indicated for the bow. Each point of Strength bonus granted by the bow adds 75 gp to its cost. For instance, a composite shortbow (+1 Str bonus) costs 150 gp, while a composite shortbow (+4 Str bonus) costs 375 gp.

For example, Tordek has a +2 Strength bonus. With a regular composite shortbow, he gets no modifier on damage rolls. For 150 gp, he can buy a composite shortbow (+1 Str bonus), which lets him add +1 to his damage rolls. For 225 gp, he can buy one that lets him add his entire +2 Strength bonus. Even if he paid 300 gp for a composite shortbow (+3 Str bonus), he would still get only a +2 bonus on damage rolls and takes a –2 penalty to use it because his Strength is insufficient to use the weapon to best advantage. The bow can't grant him a higher bonus than he already has.

For purposes of weapon proficiency and similar feats, a composite shortbow is treated as if it were a shortbow. Thus, if you have Weapon Focus (shortbow), that feat applies both to shortbows and composite shortbows.

Shortspear: A shortspear is small enough to wield one-handed. It may also be thrown.

Shuriken: A shuriken is a special monk weapon. This designation gives a monk (see Chapter 3: Classes) wielding shuriken special options. A shuriken can't be used as a melee weapon.

Although they are thrown weapons, shuriken are treated as ammunition for the purposes of drawing them, crafting masterwork or otherwise special versions of them (see Masterwork Weapons, below), and what happens to them after they are thrown.

Siangham: The siangham is a special monk weapon. This designation gives a monk (see Chapter 3: Classes) wielding a siangham special options.

Sickle: This weapon is like a farmer's sickle, but it is strengthened for use as a weapon. It is favored by druids and by anyone who wants a weapon that might be overlooked by guards.

Because of a sickle's shape, you can also use it to make trip attacks. If you are tripped during your own trip attempt, you can drop the sickle to avoid being tripped.

Sling: A sling hurls lead bullets. It doesn't shoot as far as a crossbow, nor is it as powerful as a bow, but it's cheap and easy to improvise from common materials. Druids and halflings favor slings. Your Strength modifier applies to damage rolls when you use a sling, just as it does for thrown weapons. You can fire, but not load, a sling with one hand. Loading a sling is a move action that requires two hands and provokes attacks of opportunity.

You can hurl ordinary stones with a sling, but stones are not as dense or as round as bullets. Thus, such an attack deals damage as if the weapon were designed for a creature one size category smaller than you (for instance, 1d3 instead of 1d4, or 1d2 instead of 1d3), and you take a –1 penalty on attack rolls.

Spear: One of the simplest weapons in existence, the spear is favored by druids and sorcerers. It can be thrown. If you use a ready action to set a spear against a charge, you deal double damage on a successful hit against a charging character.

Spiked Armor: You can outfit your armor with spikes, which can deal damage in a grapple or as a separate attack. See Armor, later in this chapter.

Spiked Shield, Heavy or Light: You can bash with a spiked shield instead of using it for defense. See Armor, later in this chapter.

Strike, Unarmed: A Medium character deals 1d3 points of nonlethal damage with an unarmed strike, which may be a punch, kick, head butt, or other type of attack. A Small character deals 1d2 points of nonlethal damage. A monk or any character with the Improved Unarmed Strike feat can deal lethal or nonlethal damage with unarmed strikes, at her option. The damage from an unarmed strike is considered weapon damage for the purposes of effects that give you a bonus on weapon damage rolls.

An unarmed strike is always considered a light weapon. Therefore, you can use the Weapon Finesse feat (page 102) to apply your Dexterity modifier instead of your Strength modifier to attack rolls with an unarmed strike.

Sword, Bastard: Bastard swords are also known as hand-and-a-half swords. A bastard sword is too large to use in one hand without special training; thus, it is an exotic weapon. A character can use a bastard sword two-handed as a martial weapon.

Sword, Short: This sword is popular as an off-hand weapon.

Sword, Two-Bladed: A two-bladed sword is a double weapon. You can fight with it as if fighting with two weapons, but if you do, you incur all the normal attack penalties associated with fighting with two weapons, just as if you were using a one-handed weapon and a light weapon (see Two-Weapon Fighting, page 160). A creature wielding a two-bladed sword in one hand can't use it as a double weapon—only one end of the weapon can be used in any given round.

Trident: This three-tined piercing weapon can be thrown just as a shortspear or spear can be, but its range increment is shorter because it's not as aerodynamic as those other weapons. If you use a ready action to set a trident against a charge, you deal double damage on a successful hit against a charging character.

Urgrosh, Dwarven: A dwarven urgrosh is a double weapon. You can fight with it as if fighting with two weapons, but if you do, you incur all the normal attack penalties associated with fighting with two weapons, just as if you were using a one-handed weapon and a light weapon (see Two-Weapon Fighting, page 160). The urgrosh's axe head is a slashing weapon that deals 1d8 points of damage. Its spear head is a piercing weapon that deals 1d6 points of damage. You can use either head as the primary weapon. The other is the off-hand weapon. A creature wielding a dwarven urgrosh in one hand can't use it as a double weapon—only one end of the weapon can be used in any given round.

If you use a ready action to set an urgrosh against a charge, you deal double damage if you score a hit against a charging character. If you use an urgrosh against a charging character, the spear head is the part of the weapon that deals damage.

An urgrosh is also called a spear-axe. Dwarves treat dwarven urgroshes as martial weapons.

Waraxe, Dwarven: A dwarven waraxe is too large to use in one hand without special training; thus, it is an exotic weapon. A Medium character can use a dwarven waraxe two-handed as a martial weapon, or a Large creature can use it one-handed in the same way. A dwarf treats a dwarven waraxe as a martial weapon even when using it in one hand.

Warhammer: This weapon, favored by dwarves, is a one-handed sledge or maul with a large, heavy head.

Whip: A whip deals nonlethal damage. It deals no damage to any creature with an armor bonus of +1 or higher or a natural armor bonus of +3 or higher. The whip is treated as a melee weapon with 15-foot reach, though you don't threaten the area into which you can make an attack. In addition, unlike most other weapons with reach, you can use it against foes anywhere within your reach (including adjacent foes).

Using a whip provokes an attack of opportunity, just as if you had used a ranged weapon.

Because a whip can wrap around an enemy's leg or other limb, you can make trip attacks with it. If you are tripped during your own trip attempt, you can drop the whip to avoid being tripped.

When using a whip, you get a +2 bonus on opposed attack rolls made to disarm an opponent (including the roll to keep from being disarmed if the attack fails).

You can use the Weapon Finesse feat (page 102) to apply your Dexterity modifier instead of your Strength modifier to attack rolls with a whip sized for you, even though it isn't a light weapon for you.

MASTERWORK WEAPONS

A masterwork weapon is a finely crafted version of a normal weapon. Wielding it provides a +1 enhancement bonus on attack rolls.

You can't add the masterwork quality to a weapon after it is created; it must be crafted as a masterwork weapon (see the Craft skill, page 70). The masterwork quality adds 300 gp to the cost of a normal weapon (or 6 gp to the cost of a single unit of ammunition, such as an arrow). For example, a masterwork bastard sword costs 335 gp, while a set of 10 masterwork arrows costs 70 gp. Adding the masterwork quality to a double weapon costs twice the normal increase (+600 gp).

Masterwork ammunition is damaged (effectively destroyed) when used. The enhancement bonus of masterwork ammunition does not stack with any enhancement bonus of the projectile weapon firing it.

All magic weapons are automatically considered to be of masterwork quality. The enhancement bonus granted by the masterwork quality doesn't stack with the enhancement bonus provided by the weapon's magic.

Even though some types of armor and shields (such as spiked shields) can be used as weapons, you can't create a masterwork version of such an item that confers an enhancement bonus on attack rolls. Instead, masterwork armor and shields have lessened armor check penalties (see Masterwork Armor, page 126).

ARMOR

Your armor protects you in combat, but it can also slow you down. See Table 7–6: Armor and Shields for the list of armors available. The information given on this table is for armor sized for Medium creatures. The time it takes to get into or out of armor depends on its type (see Table 7–7: Donning Armor).

ARMOR QUALITIES

Armor isn't the only fashion statement a character can make, but it's a big one. In addition, depending on class, a character may be proficient with all, some, or no armors, including shields. To wear heavier armor effectively, a character can select the Armor Proficiency feats (page 89), but most classes are automatically proficient with the armors that work best for them.

Armor and shields can take damage from some types of attacks (see Sunder, page 158, and Smashing an Object, page 165).

When selecting your character's armor, keep in mind the following factors (given as column headings on Table 7–6: Armor and Shields).

Cost: The cost of the armor for Small or Medium humanoid creatures. See the Armor for Unusual Creatures sidebar for armor prices for other creatures.

Armor/Shield Bonus: Each armor grants an armor bonus to AC, while shields grant a shield bonus to AC. This number represents the protective value of the armor or shield. The armor bonus from a suit of armor doesn't stack with other effects or items that grant an armor bonus, such as the *mage armor* spell or *bracers of armor*. Similarly, the shield bonus from a shield doesn't stack with other effects that grant a shield bonus, such as the *shield* spell.

Maximum Dex Bonus: This number is the maximum Dexterity bonus to AC that this type of armor allows. Heavier armors limit mobility, reducing the wearer's ability to dodge blows. For example, chainmail permits a maximum Dexterity bonus of +2. A character with a Dexterity score of 18 normally gains a +4 bonus to AC, but wearing chainmail drops that bonus to +2. Such a character's final Armor Class would be 17 (10 base + 5 armor bonus + 2 Dex bonus = 17), assuming he has no other modifiers. This restriction doesn't affect any other Dexterity-related abilities (such as Reflex saves and skill checks).

Even if a character's Dexterity bonus to AC drops to 0 because of armor, this situation does not count as losing a Dexterity bonus to AC. For example, a rogue can't sneak attack a character just because he or she is wearing half-plate.

Your character's encumbrance (the amount of gear he or she carries) may also restrict the maximum Dexterity bonus that can be applied to his or her Armor Class; see Encumbrance by Armor, page 161, for details.

Shields: Shields do not affect a character's maximum Dexterity bonus.

Armor Check Penalty: Any armor heavier than leather hurts a character's ability to use some skills. An armor check penalty number is the penalty that applies to Balance, Climb, Escape Artist, Hide, Jump, Move Silently, Sleight of Hand, and Tumble checks by a character wearing a certain kind of armor. Double the normal armor check penalty is applied to Swim checks. Some characters don't much care about the armor check penalty, but others do. The barbarian, in particular, faces a trade-off between heavier armor and better skill check results. A character's encumbrance (the amount of gear carried, including armor) may also apply an armor check penalty; see Encumbrance by Armor, page 161, for details.

Shields: If a character is wearing armor and using a shield, both armor check penalties apply.

Nonproficient with Armor Worn: A character who wears armor and/or uses a shield with which he or she is not proficient takes the armor's (and/or shield's) armor check penalty on attack rolls and on all Strength-based and Dexterity-based ability and skill checks. The penalty for nonproficiency with armor stacks with the penalty for nonproficiency with shields.

Sleeping in Armor: A character who sleeps in medium or heavy armor is automatically fatigued the next day. He or she takes a –2 penalty on Strength and Dexterity and can't charge or run. Sleeping in light armor does not cause fatigue.

Arcane Spell Failure: Armor interferes with the gestures that a spellcaster must make to cast an arcane spell that has a somatic component. Arcane spellcasters face the possibility of arcane spell failure if they're wearing armor, so wizards and sorcerers usually don't do so. Bards can wear light armor without incurring any arcane spell failure chance for their bard spells.

Casting an Arcane Spell in Armor: A character who casts an arcane spell while wearing armor must usually make an arcane spell failure roll. The number in the Arcane Spell Failure Chance column on Table 7–6 is the chance that the spell fails and is ruined. If the spell lacks a somatic component, however, it can be cast with no chance of arcane spell failure.

Shields: If a character is wearing armor and using a shield, add the two numbers together to get a single arcane spell failure chance.

Speed: Medium or heavy armor slows the wearer down. It's better to be slow and alive than to be quick and dead, but don't neglect to give speed some thought. The number on Table 7–6 is the character's speed while wearing the armor. Humans, elves, half-elves, and half-orcs have an unencumbered speed of 30 feet. They use the first column. Dwarves, gnomes, and halflings have an unencumbered speed of 20 feet. They use the second column. Remember, however, that a dwarf's land speed remains 20 feet even in medium or heavy armor or when carrying a medium or heavy load.

Shields: Shields do not affect a character's speed.

Weight: This column gives the weight of the armor sized for a Medium wearer. Armor fitted for Small characters weighs half as much, and armor for Large characters weighs twice as much.

TABLE 7–6: ARMOR AND SHIELDS

Armor	Cost	Armor/Shield Bonus	Maximum Dex Bonus	Armor Check Penalty	Arcane Spell Failure Chance	Speed (30 ft.)	Speed (20 ft.)	Weight[1]
Light armor								
Padded	5 gp	+1	+8	0	5%	30 ft.	20 ft.	10 lb.
Leather	10 gp	+2	+6	0	10%	30 ft.	20 ft.	15 lb.
Studded leather	25 gp	+3	+5	–1	15%	30 ft.	20 ft.	20 lb.
Chain shirt	100 gp	+4	+4	–2	20%	30 ft.	20 ft.	25 lb.
Medium armor								
Hide	15 gp	+3	+4	–3	20%	20 ft.	15 ft.	25 lb.
Scale mail	50 gp	+4	+3	–4	25%	20 ft.	15 ft.	30 lb.
Chainmail	150 gp	+5	+2	–5	30%	20 ft.	15 ft.	40 lb.
Breastplate	200 gp	+5	+3	–4	25%	20 ft.	15 ft.	30 lb.
Heavy armor								
Splint mail	200 gp	+6	+0	–7	40%	20 ft.[2]	15 ft.[2]	45 lb.
Banded mail	250 gp	+6	+1	–6	35%	20 ft.[2]	15 ft.[2]	35 lb.
Half-plate	600 gp	+7	+0	–7	40%	20 ft.[2]	15 ft.[2]	50 lb.
Full plate	1,500 gp	+8	+1	–6	35%	20 ft.[2]	15 ft.[2]	50 lb.
Shields								
Buckler	15 gp	+1	—	–1	5%	—	—	5 lb.
Shield, light wooden	3 gp	+1	—	–1	5%	—	—	5 lb.
Shield, light steel	9 gp	+1	—	–1	5%	—	—	6 lb.
Shield, heavy wooden	7 gp	+2	—	–2	15%	—	—	10 lb.
Shield, heavy steel	20 gp	+2	—	–2	15%	—	—	15 lb.
Shield, tower	30 gp	+4[3]	+2	–10	50%	—	—	45 lb.
Extras								
Armor spikes	+50 gp	—	—	—	—	—	—	+10 lb.
Gauntlet, locked	8 gp	—	—	Special	[4]	—	—	+5 lb.
Shield spikes	+10 gp	—	—	—	—	—	—	+5 lb.

1 Weight figures are for armor sized to fit Medium characters. Armor fitted for Small characters weighs half as much, and armor fitted for Large characters weighs twice as much.

2 When running in heavy armor, you move only triple your speed, not quadruple.

3 A tower shield can instead grant you cover. See the description.

4 Hand not free to cast spells.

GETTING INTO AND OUT OF ARMOR

The time required to don armor depends on its type; see Table 7–7: Donning Armor.

Don: This column on Table 7–7 tells how long it takes a character to put the armor on. (One minute is 10 rounds.) Readying (strapping on) a shield is only a move action.

Don Hastily: This column tells how long it takes to put the armor on in a hurry. The armor check penalty and armor bonus for hastily donned armor are each 1 point worse than normal. For example, if Tordek donned his scale mail hastily, it would take him

1 minute (10 rounds), the armor would provide only a +3 bonus to his AC (instead of +4), and his armor check penalty would be –5 (instead of –4).

Remove: This column tells how long it takes to get the armor off (important to know if the wearer is suddenly submerged; see the drowning rules in the *Dungeon Master's Guide*). Loosing a shield (removing it from the arm and dropping it) is only a move action.

ARMOR FOR UNUSUAL CREATURES

Armor and shields for unusually big creatures, unusually little creatures, and nonhumanoid creatures have different costs and weights from those given on Table 7–6: Armor and Shields. Refer to the appropriate line on the table below and apply the multipliers to cost and weight for the armor type in question.

Size	Humanoid Cost	Humanoid Weight	Nonhumanoid Cost	Nonhumanoid Weight
Tiny or smaller[1]	×1/2	×1/10	×1	×1/10
Small	×1	×1/2	×2	×1/2
Medium	×1	×1	×2	×1
Large	×2	×2	×4	×2
Huge	×4	×5	×8	×5
Gargantuan	×8	×8	×16	×8
Colossal	×16	×12	×32	×12

1 Divide armor bonus by 2.

TABLE 7–7: DONNING ARMOR

Armor Type	Don	Don Hastily	Remove
Shield (any)	1 move action	n/a	1 move action
Padded, leather, hide, studded leather, or chain shirt	1 minute	5 rounds	1 minute[1]
Breastplate, scale mail, chainmail, banded mail, or splint mail	4 minutes[1]	1 minute	1 minute[1]
Half-plate or full plate	4 minutes[2]	4 minutes[1]	1d4+1 minutes[1]

1 If the character has some help, cut this time in half. A single character doing nothing else can help one or two adjacent characters. Two characters can't help each other don armor at the same time.

2 The wearer must have help to don this armor. Without help, it can be donned only hastily.

ARMOR DESCRIPTIONS

The types of armor found on Table 7–6: Armor and Shields are described below (in alphabetical order), along with any special benefits they confer on the wearer ("you").

Armor Spikes: You can have spikes added to your armor, which allow you to deal extra piercing damage (see Table 7–5: Weapons) on a successful grapple attack. The spikes count as a martial weapon. If you are not proficient with them, you take a –4 penalty on grapple checks when you try to use them. You can also make a regular melee attack (or off-hand attack) with the spikes, and they count as a light weapon in this case. (You can't also make an attack with armor spikes if you have already made an attack with another off-hand weapon, and vice versa.)

An enhancement bonus to a suit of armor does not improve the spikes' effectiveness, but the spikes can be made into magic weapons in their own right.

Banded Mail: This armor is made of overlapping strips of metal sewn to a backing of leather and chainmail. The strips cover vulnerable areas, while the chain and leather protect the joints and provide freedom of movement. Straps and buckles distribute the weight evenly. The suit includes gauntlets.

Breastplate: A breastplate covers your front and your back. It comes with a helmet and greaves (plates to cover your lower legs). A light suit or skirt of studded leather beneath the breastplate protects your limbs without restricting movement much.

Buckler: This small metal shield is worn strapped to your forearm. You can use a bow or crossbow without penalty while carrying it. You can also use your shield arm to wield a weapon (whether you are using an off-hand weapon or using your off hand to help wield a two-handed weapon), but you take a –1 penalty on attack rolls while doing so because of the extra weight on your arm. This penalty stacks with those that may apply for fighting with your off hand and for fighting with two weapons. In any case, if you use a weapon in your off hand, you don't get the buckler's AC bonus for the rest of the round.

You can't bash someone with a buckler.

Chain Shirt: A chain shirt protects your torso while leaving your limbs free and mobile. It includes a layer of quilted fabric worn underneath to prevent chafing and to cushion the impact of blows. A chain shirt comes with a steel cap.

Chainmail: This armor is made of interlocking metal rings. It includes a layer of quilted fabric worn underneath to prevent chafing and to cushion the impact of blows. Several layers of mail are hung over vital areas. Most of the armor's weight hangs from the shoulders, making chainmail uncomfortable to wear for long periods of time. The suit includes gauntlets.

Full Plate: This armor consists of shaped and fitted metal plates riveted and interlocked to cover the entire body. The suit includes gauntlets, heavy leather boots, a visored helmet, and a thick layer of padding that is worn underneath the armor. Buckles and straps distribute the weight over the body, so full plate hampers movement less than splint mail even though splint is lighter. Each suit of full plate must be individually fitted to its owner by a master armorsmith, although a captured suit can be resized to fit a new owner at a cost of 200 to 800 (2d4×100) gold pieces.

Full plate armor is also known as field plate.

Gauntlet, Locked: This armored gauntlet has small chains and braces that allow the wearer to attach a weapon to the gauntlet so that it cannot be dropped easily. It provides a +10 bonus on any roll made to keep from being disarmed in combat. Removing a weapon from a locked gauntlet or attaching a weapon to a locked gauntlet is a full-round action that provokes attacks of opportunity. The price given is for a single locked gauntlet. The weight given applies only if you're wearing a breastplate, light armor, or no armor. Otherwise, the locked gauntlet replaces a gauntlet you already have as part of the armor.

While the gauntlet is locked, you can't use the hand wearing it for casting spells or employing skills. (You can still cast spells with somatic components, provided that your other hand is free.)

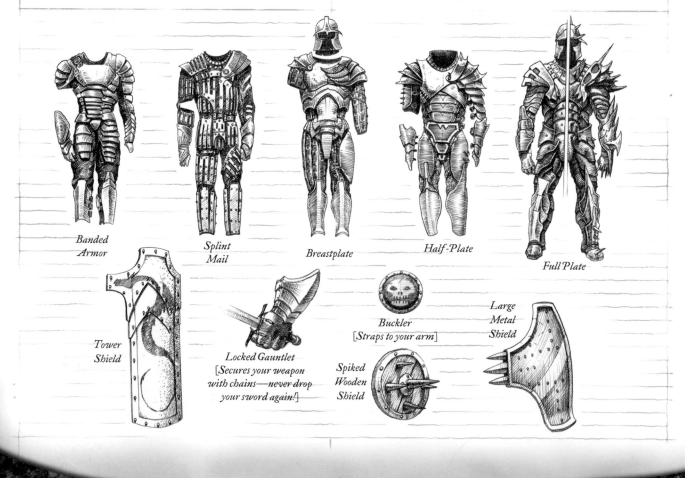

Banded Armor

Splint Mail

Breastplate

Half-Plate

Full Plate

Tower Shield

Locked Gauntlet
[Secures your weapon with chains—never drop your sword again!]

Spiked Wooden Shield

Buckler
[Straps to your arm]

Large Metal Shield

Like a normal gauntlet, a locked gauntlet lets you deal lethal damage rather than nonlethal damage with an unarmed strike.

Half-Plate: This armor is a combination of chainmail with metal plates (breastplate, epaulettes, elbow guards, gauntlets, tasses, and greaves) covering vital areas. Buckles and straps hold the whole suit together and distribute the weight, but the armor still hangs more loosely than full plate. The suit includes gauntlets.

Hide: This armor is prepared from multiple layers of leather and animal hides. It is stiff and hard to move in. Druids, who wear only nonmetallic armor, favor hide.

Leather: The breastplate and shoulder protectors of this armor are made of leather that has been stiffened by boiling in oil. The rest of the armor is made of softer and more flexible leather.

Padded: Padded armor features quilted layers of cloth and batting. It gets hot quickly and can become foul with sweat, grime, lice, and fleas.

Scale Mail: This armor consists of a coat and leggings (and perhaps a separate skirt) of leather covered with overlapping pieces of metal, much like the scales of a fish. The suit includes gauntlets.

Shield, Heavy, Wooden or Steel: You strap a shield to your forearm and grip it with your hand. A heavy shield is so heavy that you can't use your shield hand for anything else.

Wooden or Steel: Wooden and steel shields offer the same basic protection, though they respond differently to special attacks (such as *warp wood* and *heat metal*).

Shield Bash Attacks: You can bash an opponent with a heavy shield, using it as an off-hand weapon. See Table 7–5: Weapons for the damage dealt by a shield bash. Used this way, a heavy shield is a martial bludgeoning weapon. For the purpose of penalties on attack rolls, treat a heavy shield as a one-handed weapon. If you use your shield as a weapon, you lose its AC bonus until your next action (usually until the next round). An enhancement bonus on a shield does not improve the effectiveness of a shield bash made with it, but the shield can be made into a magic weapon in its own right.

Shield, Light, Wooden or Steel: You strap a shield to your forearm and grip it with your hand. A light shield's weight lets you carry other items in that hand, although you cannot use weapons with it.

Wooden or Steel: Wooden and steel shields offer the same basic protection, though they respond differently to special attacks (such as *warp wood* and *heat metal*).

Shield Bash Attacks: You can bash an opponent with a light shield, using it as an off-hand weapon. See Table 7–5: Weapons for the damage dealt by a shield bash. Used this way, a light shield is a martial bludgeoning weapon. For the purpose of penalties on attack rolls, treat a light shield as a light weapon. If you use your shield as a weapon, you lose its AC bonus until your next action (usually until the next round). An enhancement bonus on a shield does not improve the effectiveness of a shield bash made with it, but the shield can be made into a magic weapon in its own right.

Shield, Tower: This massive wooden shield is nearly as tall as you are. In most situations, it provides the indicated shield bonus to your AC. However, you can instead use it as total cover, though you must give up your attacks to do so. The shield does not, however, provide cover against targeted spells; a spellcaster can cast a spell on you by targeting the shield you are holding. You cannot bash with a tower shield, nor can you use your shield hand for anything else.

When employing a tower shield in combat, you take a –2 penalty on attack rolls because of the shield's encumbrance.

Shield Spikes: When added to your shield, these spikes turn it into a martial piercing weapon that increases the damage dealt by a shield bash as if the shield were designed for a creature one size category larger than you (from 1d4 to 1d6, for instance). You can't put spikes on a buckler or a tower shield. Otherwise, attacking with a spiked shield is like making a shield bash attack (see above). An enhancement bonus on a spiked shield does not improve the effectiveness of a shield bash made with it, but a spiked shield can be made into a magic weapon in its own right.

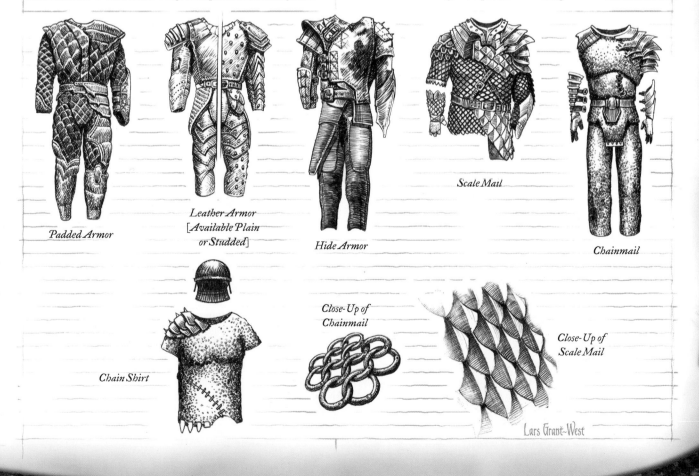

Padded Armor

Leather Armor [Available Plain or Studded]

Hide Armor

Scale Mail

Chainmail

Chain Shirt

Close-Up of Chainmail

Close-Up of Scale Mail

Lars Grant-West

Splint Mail: This armor is made of narrow vertical strips of metal riveted to a backing of leather that is worn over cloth padding. Flexible chainmail protects the joints. The suit includes gauntlets.

Studded Leather: This armor is made from tough but flexible leather (not hardened leather, as with normal leather armor) reinforced with close-set metal rivets.

MASTERWORK ARMOR

Just as with weapons, you can purchase or craft masterwork versions of armor or shields. Such a well-made item functions like the normal version, except that its armor check penalty is lessened by 1. For example, a masterwork chain shirt has an armor check penalty of –1 rather than –2.

A masterwork suit of armor or shield costs an extra 150 gp over and above the normal cost for that type of armor or shield. A masterwork chain shirt would thus cost 250 gp.

The masterwork quality of a suit of armor or shield never provides a bonus on attack or damage rolls, even if the armor or shield is used as a weapon (such as spiked armor or a spiked shield).

All magic armors and shields are automatically considered to be of masterwork quality.

You can't add the masterwork quality to armor or a shield after it is created; it must be crafted as a masterwork item.

GOODS AND SERVICES

Of course, characters need more than just weapons and armor. Table 7–8: Goods and Services provides costs and weights for dozens of other items, and costs for a variety of services that characters can purchase.

ADVENTURING GEAR

Adventurers face all sorts of challenges and difficulties, and the right gear can make the difference between a successful adventure and failure. Most of this gear is basic equipment that might come in handy regardless of a character's skills or class.

A few of the pieces of adventuring gear found on Table 7–8: Goods and Services (page 128) are described below, along with any special benefits they confer on the user ("you"). For objects with hardness and hit points, see Smashing an Object, page 165.

Backpack: A backpack is a leather pack carried on the back, typically with straps to secure it.

Bedroll: You never know where you're going to sleep, and a bedroll helps you get better sleep in a hayloft or on the cold ground. A bedroll consists of bedding and a blanket thin enough to be rolled up and tied. In an emergency, it can double as a stretcher.

Blanket, Winter: A thick, quilted, wool blanket made to keep you warm in cold weather.

Caltrops: A caltrop is a four-pronged iron spike crafted so that one prong faces up no matter how the caltrop comes to rest. You scatter caltrops on the ground in the hope that your enemies step on them or are at least forced to slow down to avoid them. One 2-pound bag of caltrops covers an area 5 feet square.

Each time a creature moves into an area covered by caltrops (or spends a round fighting while standing in such an area), it might step on one. The caltrops make an attack roll (base attack bonus +0) against the creature. For this attack, the creature's shield, armor, and deflection bonuses do not count. (Deflection averts blows as they approach, but it does not prevent a creature from touching something dangerous.) If the creature is wearing shoes or other footwear, it gets a +2 armor bonus to AC. If the caltrops succeed on the attack, the creature has stepped on one. The caltrop deals 1 point of damage, and the creature's speed is reduced by one-half because its foot is wounded. This movement penalty lasts for 24 hours, or until the creature is successfully treated with a DC 15 Heal check, or until it receives at least 1 point of magical curing. A charging or running creature must immediately stop if it steps on a caltrop. Any creature moving at half speed or slower can pick its way through a bed of caltrops with no trouble.

The DM judges the effectiveness of caltrops against unusual opponents. A Small monstrous centipede, for example, can slither through an area containing caltrops with no chance of hurting itself, and a fire giant wearing fire giant-sized boots is immune to normal-size caltrops. (They just get stuck in the soles of his boots.)

Candle: A candle dimly illuminates a 5-foot radius and burns for 1 hour. See page 164 for more rules on illumination.

Case, Map or Scroll: This capped leather or tin tube holds rolled pieces of parchment or paper.

Chain: Chain has hardness 10 and 5 hit points. It can be burst with a DC 26 Strength check.

Crowbar: This iron bar is made for levering closed items open. A crowbar is the perfect tool for prying open doors or chests, shattering chains, and the like, and it grants a +2 circumstance bonus on Strength checks made for such purposes. If used in combat, treat a crowbar as a one-handed improvised weapon (see page 113) that deals bludgeoning damage equal to that of a club of its size.

Flask: This ceramic, glass, or metal container is fitted with a tight stopper and holds 1 pint of liquid.

Flint and Steel: Striking steel and flint together creates sparks. By knocking sparks into tinder, you can create a small flame. Lighting a torch with flint and steel is a full-round action, and lighting any other fire with them takes at least that long.

Grappling Hook: When tied to the end of a rope, a grappling hook can secure the rope to a battlement, window ledge, tree limb, or other protrusion. Throwing a grappling hook successfully requires a Use Rope check (DC 10, +2 per 10 feet of distance thrown).

Hammer: This one-handed hammer with an iron head is useful for pounding pitons into a wall. If a hammer is used in combat, treat it as a one-handed improvised weapon (see page 113) that deals bludgeoning damage equal to that of a spiked gauntlet of its size.

Ink: This is black ink. You can buy ink in other colors, but it costs twice as much.

Inkpen: An inkpen is a wooden stick with a special tip on the end. The tip draws ink in when dipped in a vial and leaves an ink trail when drawn across a surface.

Jug, Clay: This basic ceramic jug is fitted with a stopper and holds 1 gallon of liquid.

Ladder, 10-foot: This item is a straight, simple wooden ladder.

Lamp, Common: A lamp clearly illuminates a 15-foot radius, provides shadowy illumination out to a 30-foot radius, and burns for 6 hours on a pint of oil. It burns with a more even flame than a torch, but, unlike a lantern, it uses an open flame and it can spill easily, a fact that makes it too dangerous for most adventuring. You can carry a lamp in one hand. See page 164 for more rules on illumination.

Lantern, Bullseye: A bullseye lantern has only a single shutter. Its other sides are highly polished inside to reflect the light in a single direction. A bullseye lantern provides clear illumination in a 60-foot cone and shadowy illumination in a 120-foot cone. It burns for 6 hours on a pint of oil. You can carry a bullseye lantern in one hand. See page 164 for more rules on illumination.

Lantern, Hooded: A hooded lantern has shuttered or hinged sides. It clearly illuminates a 30-foot radius and provides shadowy illumination in a 60-foot radius. It burns for 6 hours on a pint of oil. You can carry a hooded lantern in one hand. See page 164 for more rules on illumination.

Lock: A lock is worked with a large, bulky key. The DC to open a lock with the Open Lock skill depends on the lock's quality: simple (DC 20), average (DC 25), good (DC 30), or superior (DC 40).

Manacles and Manacles, Masterwork: The manacles detailed on Table 7–8: Goods and Services can bind a Medium creature. A manacled creature can use the Escape Artist skill to slip free (DC 30, or DC 35 for masterwork manacles). Breaking the manacles requires a Strength check (DC 26, or DC 28 for masterwork manacles). Manacles have hardness 10 and 10 hit points.

Most manacles have locks; add the cost of the lock you want to the cost of the manacles.

For the same cost, you can buy manacles for a Small creature. For a Large creature, manacles cost ten times the indicated amount, and for a Huge creature, one hundred times this amount. Gargantuan, Colossal, Tiny, Diminutive, and Fine creatures can be held only by specially made manacles.

Mirror, Small Steel: A polished steel mirror is handy when you want to look around corners, signal friends with reflected sunlight, keep an eye on a medusa, make sure that you look good enough to present yourself to the queen, or examine wounds that you've received on hard-to-see parts of your body.

Oil: A pint of oil burns for 6 hours in a lantern. You can use a flask of oil as a splash weapon (see Throw Splash Weapon, page 158). Use the rules for alchemist's fire, except that it takes a full-round action to prepare a flask with a fuse. Once it is thrown, there is a 50% chance of the flask igniting successfully.

You can pour a pint of oil on the ground to cover an area 5 feet square, provided that the surface is smooth. If lit, the oil burns for 2 rounds and deals 1d3 points of fire damage to each creature in the area.

Paper: A sheet of standard paper is made from cloth fibers.

Parchment: A sheet of parchment is a piece of goat hide or sheepskin that has been prepared for writing on.

Piton: When a wall doesn't offer handholds and footholds, you can make your own. A piton is a steel spike with an eye through which you can loop a rope. (See the Climb skill, page 69).

Pole, 10-foot: When you suspect a trap, you can put the end of your 10-foot pole through that hole in the wall instead of reaching in with your hand.

Pouch, Belt: This leather pouch straps to your belt. It's good for holding small items.

Ram, Portable: This iron-shod wooden beam is the perfect tool for battering down a door. Not only does it give you a +2 circum-

stance bonus on Strength checks made to break open a door, but it allows a second person to help you without having to roll, increasing your bonus by 2 (see Breaking Items, page 167).

Rations, Trail: Trail rations are compact, dry, high-energy foods suitable for travel, such as jerky, dried fruit, hardtack, and nuts.

Rope, Hempen: This rope has 2 hit points and can be burst with a DC 23 Strength check.

Rope, Silk: This rope has 4 hit points and can be burst with a DC 24 Strength check. It is so supple that it provides a +2 circumstance bonus on Use Rope checks.

Sack: This item is made of burlap or a similar material and has a drawstring so it can be closed.

Signet Ring: Each signet ring has a distinctive design carved into it. When you press this ring into warm sealing wax, you leave an identifying mark.

Sledge: This two-handed, iron-headed hammer is good for smashing open treasure chests.

Spyglass: Objects viewed through a spyglass are magnified to twice their size.

Tent: This simple tent sleeps two.

Torch: A typical torch is a wooden rod capped with twisted flax soaked in tallow. A torch burns for 1 hour, clearly illuminating a 20-foot radius and providing shadowy illumination out to a 40-foot radius. See page 164 for more rules on illumination. If a torch is used in combat, treat it as a one-handed improvised weapon (see page 113) that deals bludgeoning damage equal to that of a gauntlet of its size, plus 1 point of fire damage.

Vial: This ceramic, glass, or metal vial is fitted with a tight stopper and holds 1 ounce of liquid. The stoppered container usually is no more than 1 inch wide and 3 inches high.

Waterskin: A waterskin is a leather pouch with a narrow neck that is used for holding water.

Vial · Antitoxin · Flask · Tindertwigs · Smokesticks · Torch · Belt Pouch · Sunrod · Acid · Signet Ring · Crowbar · Holy Water · Clay Jug · Thieves' Tools · Alchemist's Fire · Spyglass · Tanglefoot Bag · Thunderstone · Steel Mirror · Wizard's spellbook · Ink · Case for Maps or Scrolls · Common Lamp · Bullseye Lantern · Inkpen

Lars Grant-West

SPECIAL SUBSTANCES AND ITEMS

These special substances are prized by adventurers. Any of them except for the everburning torch and holy water can be made by a character with the Craft (alchemy) skill (page 70).

Acid: You can throw a flask of acid as a splash weapon (see Throw Splash Weapon, page 158). Treat this attack as a ranged touch attack with a range increment of 10 feet. A direct hit deals 1d6 points of acid damage. Every creature within 5 feet of the point where the acid hits takes 1 point of acid damage from the splash.

Alchemist's Fire: Alchemist's fire is a sticky, adhesive substance that ignites when exposed to air. You can throw a flask of alchemist's fire as a splash weapon (see Throw Splash Weapon, page 158). Treat this attack as a ranged touch attack with a range increment of 10 feet.

A direct hit deals 1d6 points of fire damage. Every creature within 5 feet of the point where the flask hits takes 1 point of fire damage from the splash. On the round following a direct hit, the target takes an additional 1d6 points of damage. If desired, the target can use a full-round action to attempt to extinguish the flames before taking this additional damage. Extinguishing the flames requires a DC 15 Reflex save. Rolling on the ground provides the target a +2 bonus on the save. Leaping into a lake or magically extinguishing the flames automatically smothers the fire.

Antitoxin: If you drink antitoxin, you get a +5 alchemical bonus on Fortitude saving throws against poison for 1 hour.

Everburning Torch: This otherwise normal torch has a *continual flame* spell cast upon it. An everburning torch clearly illuminates a 20-foot radius and provides shadowy illumination out to a 40-foot radius. See page 164 for more rules on illumination.

Holy Water: Holy water damages undead creatures and evil outsiders almost as if it were acid. A flask of holy water can be thrown as a splash weapon (see Throw Splash Weapon, page 158). Treat this attack as a ranged touch attack with a range increment of 10 feet. A flask breaks if thrown against the body of a corporeal creature, but to use it against an incorporeal creature, you must open the flask and pour the holy water out onto the target. Thus, you can douse an incorporeal creature with holy water only if you are adjacent to it. Doing so is a ranged touch attack that does not provoke attacks of opportunity.

A direct hit by a flask of holy water deals 2d4 points of damage to an undead creature or an evil outsider. Each such creature within 5 feet of the point where the flask hits takes 1 point of damage from the splash.

Temples to good deities sell holy water at cost (making no profit) because the clerics are happy to supply people with what they need to battle evil.

Smokestick: This alchemically treated wooden stick instantly creates thick, opaque smoke when ignited. The smoke fills a 10-foot cube (treat the effect as a *fog cloud* spell, except that a moderate or stronger wind dissipates the smoke in 1 round). The stick is consumed after 1 round, and the smoke dissipates naturally.

Sunrod: This 1-foot-long, gold-tipped, iron rod glows brightly when struck. It clearly illuminates a 30-foot radius and provides shadowy illumination in a 60-foot radius. It glows for 6 hours, after which the gold tip is burned out and worthless. See page 164 for more rules on illumination.

Tanglefoot Bag: This round leather bag is full of alchemical goo. When you throw a tanglefoot bag at a creature (as a ranged touch

TABLE 7–8: GOODS AND SERVICES

ADVENTURING GEAR

Item	Cost	Weight
Backpack (empty)	2 gp	2 lb.[1]
Barrel (empty)	2 gp	30 lb.
Basket (empty)	4 sp	1 lb.
Bedroll	1 sp	5 lb.[1]
Bell	1 gp	—
Blanket, winter	5 sp	3 lb.[1]
Block and tackle	5 gp	5 lb.
Bottle, wine, glass	2 gp	
Bucket (empty)	5 sp	2 lb.
Caltrops	1 gp	2 lb.
Candle	1 cp	—
Canvas (sq. yd.)	1 sp	1 lb.
Case, map or scroll	1 gp	1/2 lb.
Chain (10 ft.)	30 gp	2 lb.
Chalk, 1 piece	1 cp	—
Chest (empty)	2 gp	25 lb.
Crowbar	2 gp	5 lb.
Firewood (per day)	1 cp	20 lb.
Fishhook	1 sp	—
Fishing net, 25 sq. ft.	4 gp	5 lb.
Flask (empty)	3 cp	1-1/2 lb.
Flint and steel	1 gp	—
Grappling hook	1 gp	4 lb.
Hammer	5 sp	2 lb.
Ink (1 oz. vial)	8 gp	—
Inkpen	1 sp	—
Jug, clay	3 cp	9 lb.
Ladder, 10-foot	5 cp	20 lb.
Lamp, common	1 sp	1 lb.
Lantern, bullseye	12 gp	3 lb.
Lantern, hooded	7 gp	2 lb.
Lock		1 lb.
Very simple	20 gp	1 lb.
Average	40 gp	1 lb.
Good	80 gp	1 lb.
Amazing	150 gp	1 lb.
Manacles	15 gp	2 lb.
Manacles, masterwork	50 gp	2 lb.
Mirror, small steel	10 gp	1/2 lb.
Mug/Tankard, clay	2 cp	1 lb.
Oil (1-pint flask)	1 sp	1 lb.
Paper (sheet)	4 sp	—
Parchment (sheet)	2 sp	—
Pick, miner's	3 gp	10 lb.
Pitcher, clay	2 cp	5 lb.
Piton	1 sp	1/2 lb.
Pole, 10-foot	2 sp	8 lb.
Pot, iron	5 sp	10 lb.
Pouch, belt (empty)	1 gp	1/2 lb.[1]
Ram, portable	10 gp	20 lb.
Rations, trail (per day)	5 sp	1 lb.[1]
Rope, hempen (50 ft.)	1 gp	10 lb.
Rope, silk (50 ft.)	10 gp	5 lb.
Sack (empty)	1 sp	1/2 lb.[1]
Sealing wax	1 gp	1 lb.
Sewing needle	5 sp	—
Signal whistle	8 sp	—
Signet ring	5 gp	—
Sledge	1 gp	10 lb.
Soap (per lb.)	5 sp	1 lb.
Spade or shovel	2 gp	8 lb.
Spyglass	1,000 gp	1 lb.
Tent	10 gp	20 lb.[1]
Torch	1 cp	1 lb.
Vial, ink or potion	1 gp	1/10 lb.
Waterskin	1 gp	4 lb.[1]
Whetstone	2 cp	1 lb.

SPECIAL SUBSTANCES AND ITEMS

Item	Cost	Weight
Acid (flask)	10 gp	1 lb.
Alchemist's fire (flask)	20 gp	1 lb.
Antitoxin (vial)	50 gp	—
Everburning torch	110 gp	1 lb.
Holy water (flask)	25 gp	1 lb.
Smokestick	20 gp	1/2 lb.
Sunrod	2 gp	1 lb.
Tanglefoot bag	50 gp	4 lb.
Thunderstone	30 gp	1 lb.
Tindertwig	1 gp	—

TOOLS AND SKILL KITS

Item	Cost	Weight
Alchemist's lab	500 gp	40 lb.
Artisan's tools	5 gp	5 lb.
Artisan's tools, masterwork	55 gp	5 lb.
Climber's kit	80 gp	5 lb.[1]
Disguise kit	50 gp	8 lb.[1]
Healer's kit	50 gp	1 lb.
Holly and mistletoe	—	—
Holy symbol, wooden	1 gp	—
Holy symbol, silver	25 gp	1 lb.
Hourglass	25 gp	1 lb.
Magnifying glass	100 gp	—
Musical instrument, common	5 gp	3 lb.[1]
Musical instrument, masterwork	100 gp	3 lb.[1]
Scale, merchant's	2 gp	1 lb.
Spell component pouch	5 gp	2 lb.
Spellbook, wizard's (blank)	15 gp	3 lb.
Thieves' tools	30 gp	1 lb.

attack with a range increment of 10 feet), the bag comes apart and the goo bursts out, entangling the target and then becoming tough and resilient upon exposure to air. An entangled creature takes a –2 penalty on attack rolls and a –4 penalty to Dexterity and must make a DC 15 Reflex save or be glued to the floor, unable to move. Even on a successful save, it can move only at half speed. Huge or larger creatures are unaffected by a tanglefoot bag. A flying creature is not stuck to the floor, but it must make a DC 15 Reflex save or be unable to fly (assuming it uses its wings to fly) and fall to the ground. A tanglefoot bag does not function underwater.

A creature that is glued to the floor (or unable to fly) can break free by making a DC 17 Strength check or by dealing 15 points of damage to the goo with a slashing weapon. A creature trying to scrape goo off itself, or another creature assisting, does not need to make an attack roll; hitting the goo is automatic, after which the creature that hit makes a damage roll to see how much of the goo was scraped off. Once free, the creature can move (including flying) at half speed. A character capable of spellcasting who is bound by the goo must make a DC 15 Concentration check to cast a spell. The goo becomes brittle and fragile after 2d4 rounds, cracking apart and losing its effectiveness. An application of *universal solvent* (see page 268 of the *Dungeon Master's Guide*) to a stuck creature dissolves the alchemical goo immediately.

Thunderstone: You can throw this stone as a ranged attack with a range increment of 20 feet. When it strikes a hard surface (or is struck hard), it creates a deafening bang that is treated as a sonic attack. Each creature within a 10-foot-radius spread must make a DC 15 Fortitude save or be deafened for 1 hour. A deafened creature, in addition to the obvious effects, takes a –4 penalty on

initiative and has a 20% chance to miscast and lose any spell with a verbal component that it tries to cast.

Since you don't need to hit a specific target, you can simply aim at a particular 5-foot square. Treat the target square as AC 5; if you miss, see Throw Splash Weapon, page 158, to determine where the thunderstone lands.

Tindertwig: The alchemical substance on the end of this small, wooden stick ignites when struck against a rough surface. Creating a flame with a tindertwig is much faster than creating a flame with flint and steel (or a magnifying glass) and tinder. Lighting a torch with a tindertwig is a standard action (rather than a full-round action), and lighting any other fire with one is at least a standard action.

TOOLS AND SKILL KITS

This equipment is particularly useful if you have certain skills or are of a certain class.

Alchemist's Lab: This set of equipment includes beakers, bottles, mixing and measuring containers, and a miscellany of chemicals and substances. An alchemist's lab always has the perfect tool for making alchemical items, so it provides a +2 circumstance bonus on Craft (alchemy) checks. It has no bearing on the costs related to the Craft (alchemy) skill (page 70). Without this lab, a character with the Craft (alchemy) skill is assumed to have enough tools to use the skill but not enough to get the +2 bonus that the lab provides.

Artisan's Tools: These special tools include the items needed to pursue any craft. Without them, you have to use improvised tools (–2 penalty on Craft checks), if you can do the job at all.

Artisan's Tools, Masterwork: These tools serve the same purpose as artisan's tools (above), but masterwork artisan's tools are

Thieves' tools, masterwork	100 gp	2 lb.
Tool, masterwork	50 gp	1 lb.
Water clock	1,000 gp	200 lb.

CLOTHING

Item	Cost	Weight
Artisan's outfit	1 gp	4 lb.[1]
Cleric's vestments	5 gp	6 lb.[1]
Cold weather outfit	8 gp	7 lb.[1]
Courtier's outfit	30 gp	6 lb.[1]
Entertainer's outfit	3 gp	4 lb.[1]
Explorer's outfit	10 gp	8 lb.[1]
Monk's outfit	5 gp	2 lb.[1]
Noble's outfit	75 gp	10 lb.[1]
Peasant's outfit	1 sp	2 lb.[1]
Royal outfit	200 gp	15 lb.[1]
Scholar's outfit	5 gp	6 lb.[1]
Traveler's outfit	1 gp	5 lb.[1]

FOOD, DRINK, AND LODGING

Item	Cost	Weight
Ale		
Gallon	2 sp	8 lb.
Mug	4 cp	1 lb.
Banquet (per person)	10 gp	—
Bread, per loaf	2 cp	1/2 lb.
Cheese, hunk of	1 sp	1/2 lb.
Inn stay (per day)		
Good	2 gp	—
Common	5 sp	—
Poor	2 sp	—
Meals (per day)		
Good	5 sp	—
Common	3 sp	—
Poor	1 sp	—
Meat, chunk of	3 sp	1/2 lb.

Wine		
Common (pitcher)	2 sp	6 lb.
Fine (bottle)	10 gp	1-1/2 lb.

MOUNTS AND RELATED GEAR

Item	Cost	Weight
Barding		
Medium creature	×2	×1
Large creature	×4	×2
Bit and bridle	2 gp	1 lb.
Dog, guard	25 gp	—
Dog, riding	150 gp	—
Donkey or mule	8 gp	—
Feed (per day)	5 cp	10 lb.
Horse		
Horse, heavy	200 gp	—
Horse, light	75 gp	—
Pony	30 gp	—
Warhorse, heavy	400 gp	—
Warhorse, light	150 gp	—
Warpony	100 gp	—
Saddle		
Military	20 gp	30 lb.
Pack	5 gp	15 lb.
Riding	10 gp	25 lb.
Saddle, Exotic		
Military	60 gp	40 lb.
Pack	15 gp	20 lb.
Riding	30 gp	30 lb.
Saddlebags	4 gp	8 lb.
Stabling (per day)	5 sp	—

TRANSPORT

Item	Cost	Weight
Carriage	100 gp	600 lb.
Cart	15 gp	200 lb.
Galley	30,000 gp	—
Keelboat	3,000 gp	—
Longship	10,000 gp	—
Rowboat	50 gp	100 lb.
Oar	2 gp	10 lb.
Sailing ship	10,000 gp	—
Sled	20 gp	300 lb.
Wagon	35 gp	400 lb.
Warship	25,000 gp	—

SPELLCASTING AND SERVICES

Service	Cost
Coach cab	3 cp per mile
Hireling, trained	3 sp per day
Hireling, untrained	1 sp per day
Messenger	2 cp per mile
Road or gate toll	1 cp
Ship's passage	1 sp per mile
Spell, 0-level	Caster level × 5 gp[2]
Spell, 1st-level	Caster level × 10 gp[2]
Spell, 2nd-level	Caster level × 20 gp[2]
Spell, 3rd-level	Caster level × 30 gp[2]
Spell, 4th-level	Caster level × 40 gp[2]
Spell, 5th-level	Caster level × 50 gp[2]
Spell, 6th-level	Caster level × 60 gp[2]
Spell, 7th-level	Caster level × 70 gp[2]
Spell, 8th-level	Caster level × 80 gp[2]
Spell, 9th-level	Caster level × 90 gp[2]

— No weight, or no weight worth noting.

1 These items weigh one-quarter this amount when made for Small characters. Containers for Small characters also carry one-quarter the normal amount.

2 See spell description for additional costs. If the additional costs put the spell's total cost above 3,000 gp, that spell is not generally available except by the DM's permission.

the perfect tools for the job, so you get a +2 circumstance bonus on Craft checks made with them.

Climber's Kit: A climber's kit includes special pitons, boot tips, gloves, and a harness that aids in all sorts of climbing. This is the perfect tool for climbing and gives you a +2 circumstance bonus on Climb checks.

Disguise Kit: This bag contains cosmetics, hair dye, and small physical props. The kit is the perfect tool for disguise and provides a +2 circumstance bonus on Disguise checks. A disguise kit is exhausted after ten uses.

Healer's Kit: This kit is full of herbs, salves, bandages and other useful materials. It is the perfect tool for healing and provides a +2 circumstance bonus on Heal checks. A healer's kit is exhausted after ten uses.

Holly and Mistletoe: Sprigs of holly and mistletoe are used by druids as the default divine focus for druid spells. Druids can easily find these plants in wooded areas and then harvest sprigs from them essentially for free.

Holy Symbol, Silver or Wooden: A holy symbol focuses positive energy. A cleric or paladin uses it as the focus for his spells and as a tool for turning undead. Each religion has its own holy symbol, and a sun symbol is the default holy symbol for clerics not associated with any particular religion.

A silver holy symbol works no better than a wooden one, but it serves as a mark of status for the wielder.

Unholy Symbols: An unholy symbol is like a holy symbol except that it focuses negative energy and is used by evil clerics (or by neutral clerics who want to cast evil spells or command undead). A skull is the default unholy symbol for clerics not associated with any particular religion.

Magnifying Glass: This simple lens allows a closer look at small objects. It is also useful as a substitute for flint and steel when starting fires. Lighting a fire with a magnifying glass requires light as bright as sunlight to focus, tinder to ignite, and at least a full-round action. A magnifying glass grants a +2 circumstance bonus on Appraise checks involving any item that is small or highly detailed, such as a gem.

Musical Instrument, Common or Masterwork: Popular instruments include the fife, recorder, lute, mandolin, and shawm. A masterwork instrument grants a +2 circumstance bonus on Perform checks involving its use and serves as a mark of status.

Scale, Merchant's: This scale includes a small balance and pans, plus a suitable assortment of weights. A scale grants a +2 circumstance bonus on Appraise checks involving items that are valued by weight, including anything made of precious metals.

Spell Component Pouch: This small, watertight leather belt pouch has many compartments. A spellcaster with a spell component pouch is assumed to have all the material components and focuses needed for spellcasting, except for those components that have a specific cost, divine focuses, and focuses that wouldn't fit in a pouch (such as the natural pool that a druid needs to look into to cast *scrying*).

Spellbook, Wizard's (Blank): This large, leatherbound book serves as a wizard's reference. A spellbook has 100 pages of parchment, and each spell takes up one page per spell level (one page each for 0-level spells). See Space in the Spellbook, page 179.

Thieves' Tools: This kit contains the tools you need to use the Disable Device and Open Lock skills. The kit includes one or more skeleton keys, long metal picks and pries, a long-nosed clamp, a small hand saw, and a small wedge and hammer. Without these tools, you must improvise tools, and you take a –2 circumstance penalty on Disable Device and Open Locks checks.

Thieves' Tools, Masterwork: This kit contains extra tools and tools of better make, which grant a +2 circumstance bonus on Disable Device and Open Lock checks.

Tool, Masterwork: This well-made item is the perfect tool for the job. It grants a +2 circumstance bonus on a related skill check (if any). Some examples of this sort of item from on Table 7–8 include masterwork artisan's tools, masterwork thieves' tools, disguise kit, climber's kit, healer's kit, and masterwork musical instrument. This

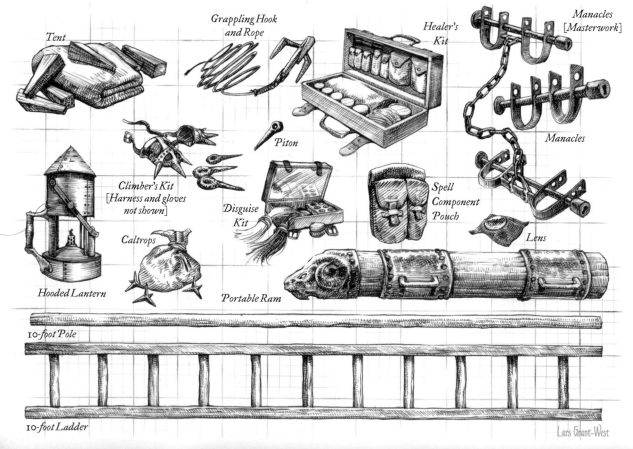

Tent

Grappling Hook and Rope

Healer's Kit

Manacles [Masterwork]

Piton

Manacles

Climber's Kit [Harness and gloves not shown]

Disguise Kit

Spell Component Pouch

Caltrops

Lens

Hooded Lantern

Portable Ram

10-foot Pole

10-foot Ladder

Lars Grant-West

entry covers just about anything else. Bonuses provided by multiple masterwork items used toward the same skill check do not stack, so masterwork pitons and a masterwork climber's kit do not provide a +4 bonus if used together on a Climb check.

Water Clock: This large, bulky contrivance gives the time accurate to within half an hour per day since it was last set. It requires a source of water, and it must be kept still because it marks time by the regulated flow of droplets of water. It is primarily an amusement for the wealthy and a tool for the student of arcane lore. Most people have no way to tell exact time, and there's little point in knowing that it is 2:30 P.M. if nobody else does.

CLOTHING

Different characters may want different outfits for various occasions. A beginning character is assumed to have an artisan's, entertainer's, explorer's, monk's, peasant's, scholar's, or traveler's outfit. This first outfit is free and does not count against the amount of weight a character can carry.

Artisan's Outfit: This outfit includes a shirt with buttons, a skirt or pants with a drawstring, shoes, and perhaps a cap or hat. It may also include a belt or a leather or cloth apron for carrying tools.

Cleric's Vestments: These ecclesiastical clothes are for performing priestly functions, not for adventuring.

Cold Weather Outfit: A cold weather outfit includes a wool coat, linen shirt, wool cap, heavy cloak, thick pants or skirt, and boots. This outfit grants a +5 circumstance bonus on Fortitude saving throws against exposure to cold weather (see the *Dungeon Master's Guide* for information on cold dangers).

Courtier's Outfit: This outfit includes fancy, tailored clothes in whatever fashion happens to be the current style in the courts of the nobles. Anyone trying to influence nobles or courtiers while wearing street dress will have a hard time of it (–2 penalty on Charisma-based skill checks to influence such individuals). If you wear this outfit without jewelry (costing an additional 50 gp), you look like an out-of-place commoner.

Entertainer's Outfit: This set of flashy, perhaps even gaudy, clothes is for entertaining. While the outfit looks whimsical, its practical design lets you tumble, dance, walk a tightrope, or just run (if the audience turns ugly).

Explorer's Outfit: This is a full set of clothes for someone who never knows what to expect. It includes sturdy boots, leather breeches or a skirt, a belt, a shirt (perhaps with a vest or jacket), gloves, and a cloak. Rather than a leather skirt, a leather overtunic may be worn over a cloth skirt. The clothes have plenty of pockets (especially the cloak). The outfit also includes any extra items you might need, such as a scarf or a wide-brimmed hat.

Monk's Outfit: This simple outfit includes sandals, loose breeches, and a loose shirt, and is all bound together with sashes. The outfit is designed to give you maximum mobility, and it's made of high-quality fabric. You can hide small weapons in pockets hidden in the folds, and the sashes are strong enough to serve as short ropes.

Noble's Outfit: This set of clothes is designed specifically to be expensive and to show it. Precious metals and gems are worked into the clothing. To fit into the noble crowd, every would-be noble also needs a signet ring (see Adventuring Gear, above) and jewelry (worth at least 100 gp).

Peasant's Outfit: This set of clothes consists of a loose shirt and baggy breeches, or a loose shirt and skirt or overdress. Cloth wrappings are used for shoes.

Royal Outfit: This is just the clothing, not the royal scepter, crown, ring, and other accoutrements. Royal clothes are ostentatious, with gems, gold, silk, and fur in abundance.

Scholar's Outfit: Perfect for a scholar, this outfit includes a robe, a belt, a cap, soft shoes, and possibly a cloak.

Traveler's Outfit: This set of clothes consists of boots, a wool skirt or breeches, a sturdy belt, a shirt (perhaps with a vest or jacket), and an ample cloak with a hood.

FOOD, DRINK, AND LODGING

Many travelers are lodged by guilds, churches, family, or nobility. Adventurers, however, typically pay for hospitality.

Inn: Poor accommodations at an inn amount to a place on the floor near the hearth, plus the use of a blanket if the innkeeper likes you and you're not worried about fleas. Common accommodations consist of a place on a raised, heated floor, the use of a blanket and a pillow, and the presence of a higher class of company. Good accommodations consist of a small, private room with one bed, some amenities, and a covered chamber pot in the corner.

Meals: Poor meals might be composed of bread, baked turnips, onions, and water. Common meals might consist of bread, chicken stew (easy on the chicken), carrots, and watered-down ale or wine. Good meals might be composed of bread and pastries, beef, peas, and ale or wine.

MOUNTS AND RELATED GEAR

Horses and other mounts let you travel faster and more easily.

Barding, Medium Creature and Large Creature: Barding is a type of armor that covers the head, neck, chest, body, and possibly legs of a horse or other mount. Barding made of medium or heavy armor provides better protection than light barding, but at the expense of speed. Barding can be made of any of the armor types found on Table 7–6: Armor and Shields.

Armor for a horse (a Large nonhumanoid creature) costs four times as much as armor for a human (a Medium humanoid creature) and also weighs twice as much as the armor found on Table 7–6 (see Armor for Unusual Creatures, page 123). If the barding is for a pony or other Medium mount, the cost is only double, and the weight is the same as for Medium armor worn by a humanoid.

Medium or heavy barding slows a mount that wears it, as shown on the table below.

| | Base Speed | | |
Barding	(40 ft.)	(50 ft.)	(60 ft.)
Medium	30 ft.	35 ft.	40 ft.
Heavy	30 ft.[1]	35 ft.[1]	40 ft.[1]

1 A mount wearing heavy armor moves at only triple its normal speed when running instead of quadruple.

Flying mounts can't fly in medium or heavy barding.

Barded animals require special attention. You must take care to prevent chafing and sores caused by the armor. The armor must be removed at night and ideally should not be put on the mount except to prepare for a battle. Removing and fitting barding takes five times as long as the figures given on Table 7–7: Donning Armor. A barded animal cannot be used to carry any load other than the rider and normal saddlebags. Because of this limitation, a mounted warrior often leads a second mount loaded with gear and supplies.

Dog, Riding: This Medium dog is specially trained to carry a Small humanoid rider. It is brave in combat like a warhorse. You take no damage when you fall from a riding dog. (See the *Monster Manual* for more information on riding dogs.)

Donkey or Mule: The best kinds of pack animals around, donkeys and mules are stolid in the face of danger, hardy, surefooted, and capable of carrying heavy loads over vast distances. Unlike a horse, a donkey or a mule is willing (though not eager) to enter dungeons and other strange or threatening places. (See the *Monster Manual* for more information on donkeys and mules.)

Feed: Horses, donkeys, mules, and ponies can graze to sustain themselves, but providing feed for them (such as oats) is much better because it provides a more concentrated form of energy, especially if the animal is exerting itself. If you have a riding dog, you have to feed it at least some meat, which may cost more or less than the given amount.

Horse: The horse is the best all-around work animal and mount in common use. A horse (other than a pony) is suitable as a mount for a human, dwarf, elf, half-elf, or half-orc. A pony is smaller than a horse and is a suitable mount for a gnome or halfling. (See the *Monster Manual* for more information on horses and ponies.)

Warhorses and warponies can be ridden easily into combat. Light horses, ponies, and heavy horses are hard to control in combat (see Mounted Combat, page 157, and the Ride skill, page 80).

Saddle, Exotic: An exotic saddle is like a normal saddle of the same sort except that it is designed for an unusual mount, such as a hippogriff. Exotic saddles come in military, pack, and riding styles.

Saddle, Military: A military saddle braces the rider, providing a +2 circumstance bonus on Ride checks related to staying in the saddle. If you're knocked unconscious while in a military saddle, you have a 75% chance to stay in the saddle (compared to 50% for a riding saddle).

Saddle, Pack: A pack saddle holds gear and supplies, but not a rider. It holds as much gear as the mount can carry. (The *Monster Manual* has notes on how much mounts can carry.)

Saddle, Riding: The standard riding saddle supports a rider.

Stabling: Includes a stable, feed, and grooming.

TRANSPORT

If you can't go where you need to by horse—whether because of excess gear or distance—you'll need some other form of transport.

Carriage: This four-wheeled vehicle can transport as many as four people within an enclosed cab, plus two drivers. In general, two horses (or other beasts of burden) draw it. A carriage comes with the harness needed to pull it.

Cart: This two-wheeled vehicle can be drawn by a single horse (or other beast of burden). It comes with a harness.

Galley: This three-masted ship has seventy oars on either side and requires a total crew of 200. A galley is 130 feet long and 20 feet wide, and it can carry 150 tons of cargo or 250 soldiers. For 8,000 gp more, it can be fitted with a ram and castles with firing platforms fore, aft, and amidships. This ship cannot make sea voyages and sticks to the coast. It moves about 4 miles per hour when being rowed or under sail.

Keelboat: This 50- to 75-foot-long ship is 15 to 20 feet wide and has a few oars to supplement its single mast with a square sail. It has a crew of eight to fifteen and can carry 40 to 50 tons of cargo or 100 soldiers. It can make sea voyages, as well as sail down rivers (thanks to its flat bottom). It moves about 1 mile per hour.

Longship: This 75-foot-long ship with forty oars requires a total crew of 50. It has a single mast and a square sail, and it can carry 50 tons of cargo or 120 soldiers. A longship can make sea voyages. It moves about 3 miles per hour when being rowed or under sail.

Rowboat: This 8- to 12-foot-long boat holds two or three Medium passengers. It moves about 1-1/2 miles per hour.

Sailing Ship: This larger, seaworthy ship is 75 to 90 feet long and 20 feet wide and has a crew of 20. It can carry 150 tons of cargo. It has square sails on its two masts and can make sea voyages. It moves about 2 miles per hour.

Sled: This is a wagon on runners for moving through snow and over ice. In general, two horses (or other beasts of burden) draw it. A sled comes with the harness needed to pull it.

Wagon: This is a four-wheeled, open vehicle for transporting heavy loads. In general, two horses (or other beasts of burden) draw it. A wagon comes with the harness needed to pull it.

Warship: This 100-foot-long ship has a single mast, although oars can also propel it. It has a crew of 60 to 80 rowers. This ship can carry 160 soldiers, but not for long distances, since there isn't room for supplies to support that many people. The warship cannot make sea voyages and sticks to the coast. It is not used for cargo. It moves about 2-1/2 miles per hour when being rowed or under sail.

SPELLCASTING AND SERVICES

Sometimes the best solution for a problem is to hire someone else to take care of it. Since the characters are adventurers, such a solution should be the exception rather than the rule, but there will

come times when the PCs prefer to pay someone else to handle something, whether that something is to deliver a message, cast a spell, or ferry them across the sea.

Coach Cab: The price given is for a ride in a coach that transports people (and light cargo) between towns. For a ride in a cab that transports passengers within a city, 1 copper piece usually takes you anywhere you need to go.

Hireling, Trained: The amount given is the typical daily wage for mercenary warriors, masons, craftsmen, scribes, teamsters, and other trained hirelings. This value represents a minimum wage; many such hirelings require significantly higher pay (see the *Dungeon Master's Guide* for more details).

Hireling, Untrained: The amount shown is the typical daily wage for laborers, porters, cooks, maids, and other menial workers.

Messenger: This entry includes horse-riding messengers and runners. Those willing to carry a message to a place they were going anyway (a crew member on a ship, for example) may ask for only half the indicated amount.

Road or Gate Toll: A toll is sometimes charged to cross a well-trodden, well-kept, and well-guarded road to pay for patrols on it and for its upkeep. Occasionally, a large walled city charges a toll to enter or exit (or sometimes just to enter).

Ship's Passage: Most ships do not specialize in passengers, but many have the capability to take a few along when transporting cargo. Double the given cost for creatures larger than Medium or creatures that are otherwise difficult to bring aboard a ship.

Spell: The indicated amount is how much it costs to get a spellcaster to cast a spell for you. This cost assumes that you can go to the spellcaster and have the spell cast at his or her convenience (generally at least 24 hours later, so that the spellcaster has time to prepare the spell in question). If you want to bring the spellcaster somewhere to cast a spell, such as into a dungeon to cast *knock* on a secret door that you can't open, you need to negotiate with him or her, and the default answer is no.

The cost given is for a spell with no cost for a material component or focus component and no XP cost. If the spell includes a material component, add the cost of that component to the cost of the spell. If the spell has a focus component (other than a divine focus), add 1/10 the cost of that focus to the cost of the spell. If the spell has an XP cost, add 5 gp per XP lost. For instance, to get a 9th-level cleric to cast *commune* for you, you need to pay 450 gp for a 5th-level spell at caster level 9th, plus 500 gp for the 100 XP loss that the caster suffers, plus 25 gp for the holy water, for a total of 975 gp.

Furthermore, if a spell has dangerous consequences (such as *contact other plane*), the spellcaster will certainly require proof that you can and will pay for dealing with any such consequences (that is, assuming that the spellcaster even agrees to cast such a spell, which isn't certain). In the case of spells that transport the caster and characters over a distance (such as *teleport*), you will likely have to pay for two castings of the spell, even if you aren't returning with the caster.

In addition, not every town or village has a spellcaster of sufficient level to cast any spell. In general, you must travel to a small town (or larger settlement) to be reasonably assured of finding a spellcaster capable of casting 1st-level spells, a large town for 2nd-level spells, a small city for 3rd- or 4th-level spells, a large city for 5th- or 6th-level spells, and a metropolis for 7th- or 8th-level spells. Even a metropolis isn't guaranteed to have a local spellcaster able to cast 9th-level spells, so seeking out such a caster may become an adventure itself. (The *Dungeon Master's Guide* has more information on settlement sizes and demographics.)

Because you must get an actual spellcaster to cast a spell for you and can't rely on a neutral broker, money is not always sufficient to get a spell cast. If the spellcaster is opposed to you on religious, moral, or political grounds, you may not be able to get the spell you want for any price. The DM always sets the final price of any spellcasting you want to purchase

WITHIN HUMANOID ANATOMY

Cranial attacks can render an opponent unconscious

Neck blows are well defended. A downward thrust offers the best result.

Shoulder/Arm protection deflects horizontal and downward attacks. Thrusting up may produce a victory.

The mobility required at the wrist may leave it open to attack.

The base of the skull, in conjunction with the frailty of the neck, makes this location a prime target.

The deltoid, shown here in the anterior surrounds the targeted shoulder joint.

A relatively unprotected artery runs along the inside of the arm between the bicep brachii and the tricep brachii.

The inner and outer collateral ligament, if damaged, can destroy the arm's function.

Tendons on the back of the hand, if severed, minimize the hand.

Illus. by A. Swekel

ighty swords clash, arrows hiss through the air, claws rip and tear and rend; these are the thrilling sounds of battle. D&D adventurers constantly find themselves embroiled in combat situations——and they wouldn't have it any other way! Whether the adventurers must fend off a bandit ambush on a deserted road or fight their way out of a bugbear lair in the deepest part of a dungeon, the rules in this chapter provide an exciting way to solve any combat situation.

Many special abilities and forms of damage that affect combat are also covered in the *Dungeon Master's Guide*.

THE BATTLE GRID

To help visualize events in the fictional world of the D&D game, we recommend the use of miniature figures and a battle grid. A battle grid, such as the one provided in the *Dungeon Master's Guide*, consists of a grid of 1-inch squares. Each of these squares represents a 5-foot square in the game world.

You can use the grid, along with miniature figures or some other form of markers or tokens, to show the marching order of your adventuring party (they can walk two abreast down a 10-foot-wide dungeon corridor or single file in a 5-foot-wide tunnel) or the relative location of the characters in any given situation.

As its name implies, however, the best use for a battle grid is when the adventurers charge or stumble into a combat situation. Then the grid helps everyone play out the battle. See the diagram on the following page for some specifics about the battle grid.

HOW COMBAT WORKS

Combat in the D&D game is cyclical; everybody acts in turn in a regular cycle of rounds. Combat follows this sequence:

1. Each combatant starts out flat-footed. Once a combatant acts, he or she is no longer flat-footed.

2. The DM determines which characters are aware of their opponents at the start of the battle. If some but not all of the combatants are aware of their opponents, a surprise round happens before regular rounds of combat begin. The combatants who are aware of the opponents can act in the surprise round, so they roll for initiative. In initiative order (highest to lowest), combatants who started the battle aware of their opponents each take one action (either a standard action or a move action) during the surprise round. Combatants who were unaware do not get to act in the surprise round. If no one or everyone starts the battle aware, there is no surprise round.

3. Combatants who have not yet rolled initiative do so. All combatants are now ready to begin their first regular round of combat.

4. Combatants act in initiative order (highest to lowest).

5. When everyone has had a turn, the combatant with the highest initiative acts again, and steps 4 and 5 repeat until combat ends.

COMBAT STATISTICS

This section summarizes the statistics that determine success in combat, and then details how to use them.

ATTACK ROLL

An attack roll represents your attempt to strike your opponent on your turn in a round. When you make an attack roll, you roll a d20 and add your attack bonus. (Other modifiers may also apply to this roll.) If your result equals or beats the target's Armor Class, you hit and deal damage.

Automatic Misses and Hits: A natural 1 (the d20 comes up 1) on an attack roll is always a miss. A natural 20 (the d20 comes up 20) is always a hit. A natural 20 is also a threat—a possible critical hit (see the Critical Hits sidebar, page 140).

ATTACK BONUS

Your attack bonus with a melee weapon is:

Base attack bonus + Strength modifier + size modifier

With a ranged weapon, your attack bonus is:

Base attack bonus + Dexterity modifier + size modifier + range penalty

Strength Modifier: Strength helps you swing a weapon harder and faster, so your Strength modifier applies to melee attack rolls.

Dexterity Modifier: Dexterity measures coordination and steadiness, so your Dexterity modifier applies to attacks with ranged weapons.

Size Modifier: The smaller you are, the bigger other creatures are relative to you. A human is a big target to a halfling, just as an ogre is a big target to a human. Since this same size modifier applies to Armor Class, two creatures of the same size strike each other normally, regardless of what size they actually are.

TABLE 8–1: SIZE MODIFIERS

Size	Size Modifier	Size	Size Modifier
Colossal	–8	Small	+1
Gargantuan	–4	Tiny	+2
Huge	–2	Diminutive	+4
Large	–1	Fine	+8
Medium	+0		

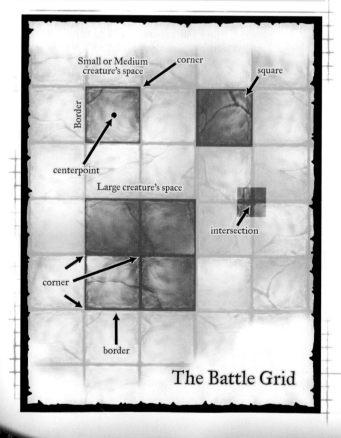

Small or Medium creature's space

corner

square

Border

centerpoint

Large creature's space

intersection

corner

border

The Battle Grid

Range Penalty: The range penalty for a ranged weapon depends on the weapon and the distance to the target. All ranged weapons have a range increment, such as 10 feet for a thrown dart or 100 feet for a longbow (see Table 7–5: Weapons, page 116). Any attack from a distance of less than one range increment is not penalized for range, so an arrow from a shortbow (range increment 60 feet) can strike at enemies up to 59 feet away with no penalty. However, each full range increment causes a cumulative –2 penalty on the attack roll. A shortbow archer firing at a target 200 feet away takes a –6 penalty on his attack roll (because 200 feet is at least three range increments but not four increments).

Thrown weapons, such as throwing axes, have a maximum range of five range increments. Projectile weapons, such as bows, can shoot up to ten increments.

DAMAGE

When your attack succeeds, you deal damage. The type of weapon used (see Table 7–5: Weapons, page 116) determines the amount of damage you deal. Effects that modify weapon damage apply to unarmed strikes and the natural physical attack forms of creatures.

Damage reduces a target's current hit points.

Minimum Damage: If penalties reduce the damage result to less than 1, a hit still deals 1 point of damage.

Strength Bonus: When you hit with a melee or thrown weapon, including a sling, add your Strength modifier to the damage result. A Strength penalty, but not a bonus, applies on attacks made with a bow that is not a composite bow.

Off-Hand Weapon: When you deal damage with a weapon in your off hand, you add only 1/2 your Strength bonus.

Wielding a Weapon Two-Handed: When you deal damage with a weapon that you are wielding two-handed, you add 1-1/2 times your Strength bonus. However, you don't get this higher Strength bonus when using a light weapon with two hands (see Light, One-Handed, and Two-Handed Melee Weapons, page 113).

Multiplying Damage: Sometimes you multiply damage by some factor, such as on a critical hit. Roll the damage (with all modifiers) multiple times and total the results. *Note:* When you multiply damage more than once, each multiplier works off the original, unmultiplied damage (see Multiplying, page 304).

Exception: Extra damage dice over and above a weapon's normal damage, such as that dealt by a sneak attack or the special ability of a flaming sword, are never multiplied.

For example, Krusk the half-orc barbarian has a Strength bonus of +3. That means he gets a +3 bonus on damage rolls when using a longsword, a +4 bonus on damage when using a greataxe (two-handed), and a +1 bonus on damage when using a weapon in his off hand. His critical multiplier with a greataxe is ×3, so if he scores a critical hit with that weapon, he would roll 1d12+4 points of damage three times (the same as rolling 3d12+12).

Ability Damage: Certain creatures and magical effects can cause temporary ability damage (a reduction to an ability score). The *Dungeon Master's Guide* has details on ability damage.

ARMOR CLASS

Your Armor Class (AC) represents how hard it is for opponents to land a solid, damaging blow on you. It's the attack roll result that an opponent needs to achieve to hit you. The average, unarmored peasant has an AC of 10. Your AC is equal to the following:

10 + armor bonus + shield bonus + Dexterity modifier + size modifier

Armor and Shield Bonuses: Your armor and shield each provide a bonus to your AC. This bonus represents their ability to protect you from blows.

Dexterity Modifier: If your Dexterity is high, you are adept at dodging blows. If your Dexterity is low, you are inept at it. That's

COMBAT BASICS

This section summarizes the rules and details concerning combat.

THE BATTLE GRID

Use a battle grid (such as the one in the *Dungeon Master's Guide*) to visualize combat situations. On a battle grid, each 1-inch square represents a 5-foot square in the game world.

ROUNDS

Combat occurs in rounds. In every round, each combatant gets to do something. A round represents 6 seconds in the game world.

INITIATIVE

Before the first round, each player makes an initiative check for his or her character. The DM makes initiative checks for the opponents. An initiative check is a Dexterity check (1d20+Dexterity modifier). Characters act in order from highest initiative result to lowest, with the check applying to all rounds of the combat.

A character is flat-footed until he or she takes an action.

ACTIONS

Every round, on your character's turn, you may take a standard action and a move action (in either order), two move actions, or one full-round action. You may also perform one or more free actions along with any other action, as your DM allows.

ATTACKS

In combat, the most prevalent standard action is an attack. You can move your speed and make an attack in a round (a move action and a standard action). Experienced characters can attack more than once, but only if they don't move (a full-round action). Making a ranged attack provokes attacks of opportunity from opponents that threaten you (see below).

Attack Roll

To score a hit that deals damage on your attack roll, your result must equal or exceed the target's Armor Class (AC).

Melee Attack Roll: 1d20 + base attack bonus + Strength modifier + size modifier.

Ranged Attack Roll: 1d20 + base attack bonus + Dexterity modifier + size modifier + range penalty.

Damage

If you score a hit, roll damage and deduct it from the target's current hit points. Add your Strength modifier on damage rolls involving melee and thrown weapons. If you're using a weapon in your off hand, add one-half your Strength modifier (if it's a bonus). If you're wielding a weapon with both hands, add one and a half times your Strength modifier (if it's a bonus).

Armor Class

A character's Armor Class (AC) is the result you need to get on your attack roll to hit that character in combat.

Armor Class: 10 + armor bonus + shield bonus + Dexterity modifier + size modifier.

Hit Points

Hit points represent how much damage a character can take before falling unconscious or dying.

SPELLS

In most cases, you can move your speed and cast a spell in the same round (a move action and a standard action). Casting a spell provokes attacks of opportunity from opponents that threaten you (see below).

SAVING THROWS

When you are subject to an unusual or magical attack, you generally get a saving throw to negate or reduce its effect. To succeed on a saving throw, you need a result equal to or higher than its Difficulty Class.

Fortitude Saving Throw: 1d20 + base save bonus + Constitution modifier

Reflex Saving Throw: 1d20 + base save bonus + Dexterity modifier

Will Saving Throw: 1d20 + base save bonus + Wisdom modifier

MOVEMENT

Each character has a speed measured in feet. You can move that distance as a move action. You can take a move action before or after a standard action on your turn in a round.

You can instead forego a standard action and take two move actions in a round, which lets you move double your speed. Or you can run, which lets you move quadruple your speed but takes all of your actions for the round.

ATTACKS OF OPPORTUNITY

During combat, you threaten all squares adjacent to yours, even when it's not your turn. An opponent that takes certain actions while in a threatened square provokes an attack of opportunity from you. An attack of opportunity is a free melee attack that does not use up any of your actions. You can make one attack of opportunity per round. Actions that provoke attacks of opportunity include moving (except as noted below), casting a spell, and attacking with a ranged weapon.

You provoke an attack of opportunity when you move out of a threatened square, except:

- If you withdraw (a full-round action), opponents don't get attacks of opportunity when you move from your initial square. If you move into another threatened square, however, opponents get attacks of opportunity when you leave that square.
- If your entire move for the round is 5 feet (a 5-foot step), opponents don't get attacks of opportunity when you move.

DEATH, DYING, AND HEALING

Your hit points represent how much damage you can take before being disabled, knocked unconscious, or killed.

1 or More Hit Points: As long as you have 1 or more hit points, you remain fully functional.

0 Hit Points: If your hit points drop to 0, you are disabled. You can only take one move action or standard action per turn, and you take 1 point of damage after completing an action.

–1 to –9 Hit Points: If your hit points drop to from –1 to –9 hit points, you're unconscious and dying, and you lose 1 hit point per round. Each round, before losing that hit point, you have a 10% chance of becoming stable. While stable, you're still unconscious. Each hour you have a 10% chance to regain consciousness, and if you don't, you lose 1 hit point instead.

–10 Hit Points: If your hit points fall to –10 or lower, you're dead.

Healing: You can stop a dying character's loss of hit points with a DC 15 Heal check or with even 1 point of magical healing. If healing raises a character's hit points to 1 or more, the character can resume acting as normal.

why you apply your Dexterity modifier to your AC.

Note that armor limits your Dexterity bonus, so if you're wearing armor, you might not be able to apply your whole Dexterity bonus to your AC (see Table 7–6: Armor and Shields, page 123).

Sometimes you can't use your Dexterity bonus (if you have one). If you can't react to a blow, you can't use your Dexterity bonus to AC. (If you don't have a Dexterity bonus, nothing happens.) You lose your Dexterity bonus when, for example, an invisible opponent attacks you, you're hanging on to the face of a crumbling cliff high above a river of lava, or you're caught flat-footed at the beginning of a combat.

Size Modifier: The bigger a creature is, the easier it is to hit in combat. The smaller it is, the harder it is to hit. Since this same modifier applies to attack rolls, a halfling, for example, doesn't have a hard time hitting another halfling. See Table 8–1: Size Modifiers, page 134.

Other Modifiers: Many other factors modify your AC.

Enhancement Bonuses: Enhancement effects make your armor better (*+1 chainmail*, *+2 large shield*, etc.).

Deflection Bonus: Magical deflection effects ward off attacks and improve your AC.

Natural Armor: Natural armor improves your AC. (Members of the common races don't have natural armor, which usually consists of scales, fur, or layers of huge muscles.)

Dodge Bonuses: Some other AC bonuses represent actively avoiding blows, such as the dwarf's AC bonus against giants or the AC bonus for fighting defensively. These bonuses are called dodge bonuses. Any situation that denies you your Dexterity bonus also denies you dodge bonuses. (Wearing armor, however, does not limit these bonuses the way it limits a Dexterity bonus to AC.) Unlike most sorts of bonuses, dodge bonuses stack with each other. A dwarf's +4 dodge bonus against giants and his +2 dodge bonus for fighting defensively combine to give him a +6 bonus.

Touch Attacks: Some attacks disregard armor, including shields and natural armor. For example, a wizard's touch with a *shocking grasp* spell hurts you regardless of what armor you're wearing or how thick your skin happens to be. In these cases, the attacker makes a touch attack roll (either ranged or melee). When you are the target of a touch attack, your AC doesn't include any armor bonus, shield bonus, or natural armor bonus. All other modifiers, such as your size modifier, Dexterity modifier, and deflection bonus (if any) apply normally.

For example, if a sorcerer tries to touch Tordek with a *shocking grasp* spell, Tordek gets his +1 Dexterity bonus, but not his +4 armor bonus for his scale mail or his +2 shield bonus for his large wooden shield. His AC is only 11 against a touch attack.

HIT POINTS

Your hit points tell you how much punishment you can take before dropping. Your hit points are based on your class and level, and your Constitution modifier applies. Most monsters' hit points are based on their type, though some monsters have classes and levels, too. (Watch out for medusa sorcerers!)

When your hit point total reaches 0, you're disabled. When it reaches –1, you're dying. When it gets to –10, your problems are over—you're dead (see Injury and Death, page 145).

SPEED

Your speed tells you how far you can move in a round and still do something, such as attack or cast a spell. Your speed depends mostly on your race and what armor you're wearing.

Dwarves, gnomes, and halflings have a speed of 20 feet (4 squares), or 15 feet (3 squares) when wearing medium or heavy armor (except for dwarves, who move 20 feet in any armor).

Humans, elves, half-elves, and half-orcs have a speed of 30 feet (6 squares), or 20 feet (4 squares) in medium or heavy armor.

If you use two move actions in a round (sometimes called a "double move" action), you can move up to double your speed. If you spend the entire round to run all out, you can move up to quadruple your speed (or triple if you are in heavy armor).

SAVING THROWS

As an adventurer, you have more to worry about than taking damage. You also have to face the petrifying gaze of a medusa, a wyvern's lethal venom, and a harpy's captivating song. Luckily, a tough adventurer can survive these threats, too.

Generally, when you are subject to an unusual or magical attack, you get a saving throw to avoid or reduce the effect. Like an attack roll, a saving throw is a d20 roll plus a bonus based on your class, level, and an ability score. Your saving throw modifier is:

Base save bonus + ability modifier

Saving Throw Types: The three different kinds of saving throws are Fortitude, Reflex, and Will:

Fortitude: These saves measure your ability to stand up to physical punishment or attacks against your vitality and health. Apply your Constitution modifier to your Fortitude saving throws. Fortitude saves can be made against attacks or effects such as poison, disease, paralysis, petrification, energy drain, and *disintegrate*.

Reflex: These saves test your ability to dodge area attacks. Apply your Dexterity modifier to your Reflex saving throws. Reflex saves can be made against attacks or effects such as pit traps, catching on fire, *fireball*, *lightning bolt*, and red dragon breath.

Will: These saves reflect your resistance to mental influence as well as many magical effects. Apply your Wisdom modifier to your Will saving throws. Will saves can be made against attacks or effects such as *charm person*, *hold person*, and most illusion spells.

Saving Throw Difficulty Class: The DC for a save is determined by the attack itself. Two examples: A Medium monstrous centipede's poison allows a DC 11 Fortitude save. An ancient red dragon's fiery breath allows a DC 36 Reflex save.

Automatic Failures and Successes: A natural 1 (the d20 comes up 1) on a saving throw is always a failure (and may cause damage to exposed items; see Items Surviving after a Saving Throw, page 177). A natural 20 (the d20 comes up 20) is always a success.

INITIATIVE

Every round, each combatant gets to do something. The combatants' initiative checks, from highest to lowest, determine the order in which they act.

Initiative Checks: At the start of a battle, each combatant makes an initiative check. An initiative check is a Dexterity check. Each character applies his or her Dexterity modifier to the roll. The DM finds out what order characters are acting in, counting down from highest result to lowest, and each character acts in turn. In every round that follows, the characters act in the same order (unless a character takes an action that results in his or her initiative changing; see Special Initiative Actions, page 160). Usually, the DM writes the names of the characters down in initiative order so that on subsequent rounds he can move quickly from one character to the next. If two or more combatants have the same initiative check result, the combatants who are tied act in order of total initiative modifier (highest first). If there is still a tie, the tied characters should roll again to determine which one of them goes before the other.

Monster Initiative: Typically, the DM makes a single initiative check for monsters and other opponents. That way, each player gets a turn each round and the DM also gets one turn. At the DM's option, however, he can make separate initiative checks for different groups of monsters or even for individual creatures. For instance, the DM may make one initiative check for an evil cleric of Nerull and another check for all seven of her zombie guards.

Flat-Footed: At the start of a battle, before you have had a chance to act (specifically, before your first regular turn in the initiative order), you are flat-footed. You can't use your Dexterity bonus to AC (if any) while flat-footed. (This fact can be very bad for you if you're attacked by rogues.) Barbarians and rogues have the uncanny dodge extraordinary ability, which allows them to avoid losing their Dexterity bonus to AC due to being flat-footed. A flat-footed character can't make attacks of opportunity.

Inaction: Even if you can't take actions (for instance, if you become paralyzed or unconscious), you retain your initiative score for the duration of the encounter. For example, when paralyzed by a ghoul, you may miss one or more actions, but once the cleric casts *remove paralysis* on you, you may act again on your next turn.

SURPRISE

When a combat starts, if you are not aware of your opponents and they are aware of you, you're surprised.

Determining Awareness

Sometimes all the combatants on a side are aware of their opponents, sometimes none are, and sometimes only some of them are. Sometimes a few combatants on each side are aware and the other combatants on each side are unaware.

The DM determines who is aware of whom at the start of a battle. He may call for Listen checks, Spot checks, or other checks to see how aware the adventurerers are of their opponents. Some example situations:

- The party (including Tordek, a fighter, and Jozan, a cleric, clanging along in metal armor) comes to a door in a dungeon. The DM knows that the displacer beasts beyond the door hear the party. Lidda listens at the door, hears guttural snarling, and warns the rest of the party. Tordek breaks the door open. Both sides are aware; neither is surprised. The characters and displacer beasts make initiative checks, and the battle begins.

- The party explores a ruined armory, looking through the rusted weapons for anything of value. Kobolds lurk in the nooks and crannies, waiting for the right time to strike. Jozan spots one of the kobolds, and the kobolds shriek and charge. The kobolds and Jozan each get a standard action during the surprise round. Kobolds that are close enough can charge adventurers and attack them. Others can move to try to put themselves in advantageous positions or shoot arrows at the flat-footed party members. Jozan can cast a spell, attack, or take some other action. After the surprise round, the first regular round begins.

- The party advances down a dark corridor, using *light* spells to see where they're going. At the end of the corridor, outside the range of the illumination, a kobold sorcerer doesn't want to be disturbed, and she angrily casts a *lightning bolt*. That's the surprise round. After the *lightning bolt*, the first regular round begins with the party in a tough spot, since they still can't see who attacked them.

The Surprise Round: If some but not all of the combatants are aware of their opponents, a surprise round happens before regular rounds begin. Any combatants aware of the opponents can act in the surprise round, so they roll for initiative. In initiative order (highest to lowest), combatants who started the battle aware of their opponents each take a standard action during the surprise round (see Standard Actions, page 139). You can also take free actions during the surprise round, at the DM's discretion. If no one or everyone is surprised, no surprise round occurs.

Unaware Combatants: Combatants who are unaware at the start of battle don't get to act in the surprise round. Unaware combatants are flat-footed because they have not acted yet, so they lose any Dexterity bonus to AC.

ATTACKS OF OPPORTUNITY

The melee combat rules assume that combatants are actively avoiding attacks. A player doesn't have to declare anything special for her character to be on the defensive. Even if a character's miniature figure is just standing there on the battle grid, you can be sure that if some orc with a falchion attacks the character, she is weaving, dodging, and even threatening the orc with a weapon to keep the orc a little worried for his own hide.

Sometimes, however, a combatant in a melee lets her guard down. In this case, combatants near her can take advantage of her lapse in defense to attack her for free. These free attacks are called attacks of opportunity (see the diagram on the next page).

Threatened Squares: You threaten all squares into which you can make a melee attack, even when it is not your action. Generally, that means everything in all squares adjacent to your space (including diagonally). An enemy that takes certain actions while in a threatened square provokes an attack of opportunity from you. If you're unarmed, you don't normally threaten any squares and thus can't make attacks of opportunity (but see Unarmed Attacks, page 139).

Reach Weapons: Most creatures of Medium or smaller size have a reach of only 5 feet. This means that they can make melee attacks only against creatures up to 5 feet (1 square) away. However, Small and Medium creatures wielding reach weapons (such as a longspear) threaten more squares than a typical creature. For instance, a longspear-wielding human threatens all squares 10 feet (2 squares) away, even diagonally. (This is an exception to the rule that 2 squares of diagonal distance is measured as 15 feet.) In addition, most creatures larger than Medium have a natural reach of 10 feet or more; see Big and Little Creatures in Combat, page 149.

Provoking an Attack of Opportunity: Two kinds of actions can provoke attacks of opportunity: moving out of a threatened square and performing an action within a threatened square.

Moving: Moving out of a threatened square usually provokes an attack of opportunity from the threatening opponent. There are two common methods of avoiding such an attack—the 5-foot-step (see page 144) and the withdraw action (see page 143).

Performing a Distracting Act: Some actions, when performed in a threatened square, provoke attacks of opportunity as you divert your attention from the battle. Casting a spell and attacking with a ranged weapon, for example, are distracting actions. Table 8–2: Actions in Combat notes many of the actions that provoke attacks of opportunity.

Remember that even actions that normally provoke attacks of opportunity may have exceptions to this rule. For instance, a character with the Improved Unarmed Strike feat doesn't incur an attack of opportunity for making an unarmed attack.

Making an Attack of Opportunity: An attack of opportunity is a single melee attack, and you can only make one per round. You don't have to make an attack of opportunity if you don't want to.

An experienced character gets additional regular melee attacks (by using the full attack action), but at a lower attack bonus. You make your attack of opportunity, however, at your normal attack bonus—even if you've already attacked in the round.

An attack of opportunity "interrupts" the normal flow of actions in the round. If an attack of opportunity is provoked, immediately resolve the attack of opportunity, then continue with the next character's turn (or complete the current turn, if the attack of opportunity was provoked in the midst of a character's turn).

Combat Reflexes and Additional Attacks of Opportunity: If you have the Combat Reflexes feat (page 92), you can add your Dexterity modifier to the number of attacks of opportunity you can make in a round. This feat does not let you make more than one attack for a given opportunity, but if the same opponent provokes two attacks of opportunity from you—such as by moving out of a threatened square and then casting a spell in a threatened

Attacks of Opportunity

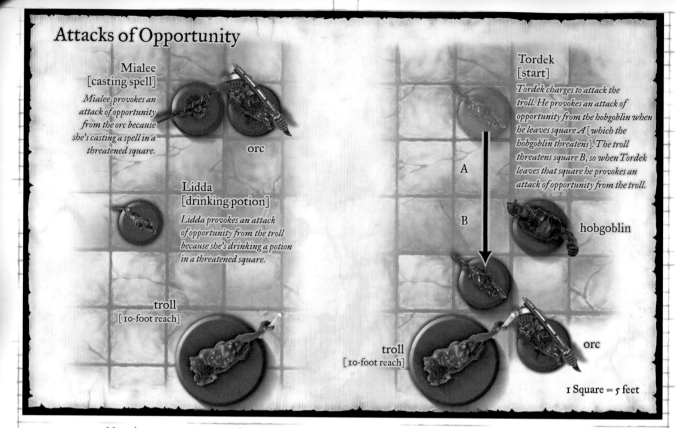

Mialee [casting spell]

Mialee provokes an attack of opportunity from the orc because she's casting a spell in a threatened square.

orc

Lidda [drinking potion]

Lidda provokes an attack of opportunity from the troll because she's drinking a potion in a threatened square.

troll
[10-foot reach]

Tordek [start]

Tordek charges to attack the troll. He provokes an attack of opportunity from the hobgoblin when he leaves square A [which the hobgoblin threatens]. The troll threatens square B, so when Tordek leaves that square he provokes an attack of opportunity from the troll.

A

B

hobgoblin

troll
[10-foot reach]

orc

1 Square = 5 feet

square—you could make two separate attacks of opportunity (since each one represents a different opportunity). Moving out of more than one square threatened by the same opponent in the same round doesn't count as more than one opportunity for that opponent. All these attacks are at your full normal attack bonus.

ACTIONS IN COMBAT

The fundamental actions of moving, attacking, and casting spells cover most of what you want to do in a battle. They're all described here. Other, more specialized options are covered later in Special Attacks, page 154, and Special Initiative Actions, page 160.

THE COMBAT ROUND

Each round represents 6 seconds in the game world. At the table, a round presents an opportunity for each character involved in a combat situation to take an action. Anything a person could reasonably do in 6 seconds, your character can do in 1 round.

Each round's activity begins with the character with the highest initiative result and then proceeds, in order, from there. Each round of a combat uses the same initiative order. When a character's turn comes up in the initiative sequence, that character performs his entire round's worth of actions. (For exceptions, see Attacks of Opportunity, page 137, and Special Initiative Actions, page 160.)

For almost all purposes, there is no relevance to the end of a round or the beginning of a round. The term "round" works like the word "month." A month can mean either a calendar month or a span of time from a day in one month to the same day the next month. In the same way, a round can be a segment of game time starting with the first character to act and ending with the last, but it usually means a span of time from one round to the same initiative count in the next round. Effects that last a certain number of rounds end just before the same initiative count that they began on.

For example, a monk acts on initiative count 15. The monk's stunning attack stuns a creature for 1 round. The stun lasts

through initiative count 16 in the next round, not until the end of the current round. On initiative count 15 in the next round, the stun effect has ended and the previously stunned creature can act.

ACTION TYPES

An action's type essentially tells you how long the action takes to perform (within the framework of the 6-second combat round) and how movement is treated. There are four types of actions: standard actions, move actions, full-round actions, and free actions.

In a normal round, you can perform a standard action and a move action, or you can perform a full-round action. You can also perform as many free actions (see below) as your DM allows. You can always take a move action in place of a standard action.

In some situations (such as in a surprise round), you may be limited to taking only a single move action or standard action.

Standard Action: A standard action allows you to do something. The most common type of standard action is an attack—a single melee or ranged attack. Other common standard actions include casting a spell, concentrating to maintain an active spell, activating a magic item, and using a special ability. See Table 8–2: Actions in Combat for other standard actions.

Move Action: A move action allows you to move your speed or perform an action that takes a similar amount of time. You can move your speed, climb one-quarter of your speed, draw or stow a weapon or other item, stand up, pick up an object, or perform some equivalent action (see Table 8–2: Actions in Combat).

You can take a move action in place of a standard action. For instance, rather than moving your speed and attacking, you could stand up and move your speed (two move actions), put away a weapon and climb one-quarter of your speed (two move actions), or pick up an item and stow it in your backpack (two move actions).

If you move no actual distance in a round (commonly because you have swapped your move for one or more equivalent actions, such as standing up), you can take one 5-foot step either before, during, or after the action. For example, if Tordek is on the ground, he can stand up (a move action), move 5 feet (a 5-foot step), and then attack.

Full-Round Action: A full-round action consumes all your effort during a round. The only movement you can take during a full-round action is a 5-foot step before, during, or after the action. You can also perform free actions (see below) as your DM allows. The most common type of full-round action is a full attack, which allows you to make multiple melee or ranged attacks in a single round.

Some full-round actions do not allow you to take a 5-foot step.

Some full-round actions can be taken as standard actions, but only in situations when you are limited to performing only a standard action during your round (such as in a surprise round). The descriptions of specific actions, below, detail which actions allow this option.

Free Action: Free actions consume a very small amount of time and effort, and over the span of the round, their impact is so minor that they are considered free. You can perform one or more free actions while taking another action normally. However, the DM puts reasonable limits on what you can really do for free. For instance, calling out to your friends for help, dropping an object, and ceasing to concentrate on a spell are all free actions.

Not an Action: Some activities are so minor that they are not even considered free actions. They literally don't take any time at all to do and are considered an inherent part of doing something else. For instance, using the Use Magic Device skill (page 85) while trying to activate a device is not an action, it is part of the standard action to activate a magic item.

Restricted Activity: In some situations (such as when you're *slowed* or during a surprise round), you may be unable to take a full round's worth of actions. In such cases, you are restricted to taking only a single standard action or a single move action (plus free actions as normal). You can't take a full-round action (though you can start or complete a full-round action by using a standard action; see below).

STANDARD ACTIONS

Most standard actions involve making an attack, casting a spell, or activating an item. These are the most common, straightforward actions that a character might take in a combat round. More specialized actions are covered in Special Attacks, page 154.

Attack

Making an attack is a standard action.

Melee Attacks: With a normal melee weapon, you can strike any opponent within 5 feet. (Opponents within 5 feet are considered adjacent to you.) Some melee weapons have reach, as indicated in their descriptions in Chapter 7: Equipment. With a typical reach weapon, you can strike opponents 10 feet away, but you can't strike adjacent foes (those within 5 feet).

Unarmed Attacks: Striking for damage with punches, kicks, and head butts is much like attacking with a melee weapon, except for the following:

Attacks of Opportunity: Attacking unarmed provokes an attack of opportunity from the character you attack, provided she is armed. The attack of opportunity comes before your attack. An unarmed attack does not provoke attacks of opportunity from other foes, as shooting a bow does, nor does it provoke an attack of opportunity from an unarmed foe. You provoke the attack of opportunity because you have to bring your body close to your opponent.

An unarmed character can't take attacks of opportunity (but see "Armed" Unarmed Attacks, below).

"Armed" Unarmed Attacks: Sometimes a character's or creature's unarmed attack counts as an armed attack. A monk, a character with the Improved Unarmed Strike feat (page 96), a spellcaster delivering a touch attack spell, and a creature with claws, fangs, and similar natural physical weapons all count as being armed. Note that being armed counts for both offense and defense. Not

only does a monk not provoke an attack of opportunity when attacking an armed foe, but you provoke an attack of opportunity from a monk if you make an unarmed attack against her.

Unarmed Strike Damage: An unarmed strike from a Medium character deals 1d3 points of damage (plus your Strength modifier, as normal). A Small character's unarmed strike deals 1d2 points of damage, while a Large character's unarmed strike deals 1d4 points of damage. All damage from unarmed strikes is nonlethal damage. Unarmed strikes count as light weapons (for purposes of two-weapon attack penalties and so on).

Dealing Lethal Damage: You can specify that your unarmed strike will deal lethal damage before you make your attack roll, but you take a –4 penalty on your attack roll because you have to strike a particularly vulnerable spot to deal lethal damage. If you have the Improved Unarmed Strike feat, you can deal lethal damage with an unarmed strike without taking a penalty on the attack roll.

Ranged Attacks: With a ranged weapon, you can shoot or throw at any target that is within the weapon's maximum range and in line of sight. The maximum range for a thrown weapon is five range increments. For projectile weapons, it is ten range increments. Some ranged weapons have shorter maximum ranges, as specified in their descriptions.

Attack Rolls: An attack roll represents your attempts to strike your opponent. It does not represent a single swing of the sword, for example. Rather, it indicates whether, over several attempts in the round, you managed to connect solidly.

Your attack roll is 1d20 + your attack bonus with the weapon you're using. If the result is at least as high as the target's AC, you hit and deal damage.

Automatic Misses and Hits: A natural 1 (the d20 comes up 1) on the attack roll is always a miss. A natural 20 (the d20 comes up 20) is always a hit. A natural 20 is also a threat—a possible critical hit (see the Critical Hits sidebar, page 140).

Damage Rolls: If the attack roll result equals or exceeds the target's AC, the attack hits and you deal damage. Roll the

Line of Sight

orc

gnoll

line of sight blocked

line of sight okay

Lidda

Two creatures can see each other if they can trace at least one clear straight line from any part of one creature's space to any part of the other creature's space. The line is clear if it doesn't cross or even touch squares that block line of sight.

appropriate damage for your weapon (see Table 7–5: Weapons, page 116). Damage is deducted from the target's current hit points. If the opponent's hit points drop to 0 or lower, he's in bad shape (see Injury and Death, page 145).

Multiple Attacks: A character who can make more than one attack per round must use the full attack action (see Full-Round Actions, below) in order to get more than one attack.

Shooting or Throwing into a Melee: If you shoot or throw a ranged weapon at a target engaged in melee with a friendly character, you take a –4 penalty on your attack roll because you have to aim carefully to avoid hitting your friend. Two characters are engaged in melee if they are enemies of each other and either threatens the other. (An unconscious or otherwise immobilized character is not considered engaged unless he is actually being attacked.)

If your target (or the part of your target you're aiming at, if it's a big target) is at least 10 feet away from the nearest friendly character, you can avoid the –4 penalty, even if the creature you're aiming at is engaged in melee with a friendly character.

Precise Shot: If you have the Precise Shot feat (page 98), you don't take this penalty.

Fighting Defensively as a Standard Action: You can choose to fight defensively when attacking. If you do so, you take a –4 penalty on all attacks in a round to gain a +2 dodge bonus to AC for the same round. This bonus stacks with the AC bonus granted by the Combat Expertise feat (page 92).

Cast a Spell

Most spells require 1 standard action to cast. You can cast such a spell either before or after you take a move action. See Chapter 10: Magic for details on casting spells, their effects, and so on.

Note: You retain your Dexterity bonus to AC while casting.

Spell Components: To cast a spell with a verbal (V) component, your character must speak in a firm voice. If you're gagged or in the area of a *silence* spell, you can't cast such a spell. A spellcaster who has been deafened has a 20% chance to spoil any spell he tries to cast if that spell has a verbal component.

To cast a spell with a somatic (S) component, you must gesture freely with at least one hand. You can't cast a spell of this type while bound, grappling, or with both your hands full or occupied (swimming, clinging to a cliff, or the like).

To cast a spell with a material (M), focus (F), or divine focus (DF) component, you have to have the proper materials, as described by the spell. Unless these materials are elaborate, such as the 2-foot-by-4-foot mirror that a wizard needs to cast *scrying*, preparing these materials is a free action. For material components and focuses whose costs are not listed, you can assume that you have them if you have your spell component pouch.

Some spells have an experience point (XP) component and entail an experience point cost to you. No spell, not even *restoration*, can restore the lost XP. You cannot spend so much XP that you lose a level, so you cannot cast the spell unless you have enough XP to spare. However, you may, on gaining enough XP to achieve a new level, immediately spend the XP on casting the spell rather than keeping it to advance a level. The XP are expended when you cast the spell, whether or not the casting succeeds.

Concentration: You must concentrate to cast a spell. If you can't concentrate (because you are on the deck of a storm-tossed ship, for instance), you can't cast a spell. If you start casting a spell but something interferes with your concentration, such as an ogre taking the opportunity to hit you with its club (successfully hitting you with his attack of opportunity), you must make a Concentration check or lose the spell. The check's DC depends on what is threatening your concentration (see the Concentration skill, page 69, and Concentration, page 170). If you fail, the spell fizzles with no effect. If you prepare spells (as a wizard, cleric, druid, paladin, or ranger does), it is lost from preparation. If you cast at will (as a sorcerer or bard does), it counts against your daily limit of spells even though you did not cast it successfully.

Concentrating to Maintain a Spell: Some spells require continued concentration to keep them going. Concentrating to maintain a spell is a standard action that doesn't provoke an attack of opportunity. Anything that could break your concentration when casting a spell can keep you from concentrating to maintain a spell. If your concentration breaks, the spell ends.

Casting Time: Most spells have a casting time of 1 standard action. A spell cast in this manner immediately takes effect.

Attacks of Opportunity: Generally, if you cast a spell, you provoke attacks of opportunity from threatening enemies. If you take damage from an attack of opportunity, you must make a Concentration check (DC 10 + points of damage taken + spell level) or lose the spell. Spells that require only a free action to cast (such as *feather fall* or any quickened spell) don't provoke attacks of opportunity.

Casting on the Defensive: You may attempt to cast a spell while paying attention to threats and avoiding blows. In this case, you are no more vulnerable to attack than you would be if you were just standing there, so casting a spell while on the defensive does not provoke an attack of opportunity. It does, however, require a Concentration check (DC 15 + spell level) to pull off. Failure means that you lose the spell.

Touch Spells in Combat: Many spells have a range of touch. To use these spells, you cast the spell and then touch the subject, either in the same round or any time later. In the same round that you cast the spell, you may also touch (or attempt to touch) the target. You may take your move before casting the spell, after touching the

CRITICAL HITS

When you make an attack roll and get a natural 20 (the d20 shows 20), you hit regardless of your target's Armor Class, and you have scored a threat. The hit might be a critical hit (or "crit"). To find out if it's a critical hit, you immediately make a critical roll—another attack roll with all the same modifiers as the attack roll you just made. If the critical roll also results in a hit against the target's AC, your original hit is a critical hit. (The critical roll just needs to hit to give you a crit. It doesn't need to come up 20 again.) If the critical roll is a miss, then your hit is just a regular hit.

A critical hit means that you roll your damage more than once, with all your usual bonuses, and add the rolls together. Unless otherwise specified, the threat range for a critical hit on an attack roll is 20, and the multiplier is ×2.

Exception: Extra damage over and above a weapon's normal dam-

age, such as that dealt by a sneak attack or the special ability of a flaming sword, is not multiplied when you score a critical hit.

Increased Threat Range: Sometimes your threat range is greater than 20. That is, you can score a threat on a lower number. Longswords, for instance, give you a threat on a natural attack roll of 19 or 20. In such cases, a roll of lower than 20 is not an automatic hit. Any attack roll that doesn't result in a hit is not a threat.

Increased Critical Multiplier: Some weapons, such as battleaxes and arrows, deal better than double damage on a critical hit. See Table 7–5: Weapons (page 116) and the Critical section of Weapon Qualities (page 114).

Spells and Critical Hits: A spell that requires an attack roll, such as *shocking grasp* or *Melf's acid arrow,* can score a critical hit. A spell attack that requires no attack roll, such as *lightning bolt,* cannot score a critical hit.

target, or between casting the spell and touching the target. You can automatically touch one friend or use the spell on yourself, but to touch an opponent, you must succeed on an attack roll.

Touch Attacks: Since you need only touch your enemy, you make a touch attack instead of a regular attack. Touching an opponent with a touch spell is considered to be an armed attack and therefore does not provoke attacks of opportunity. The touch spell provides you with a credible threat that the defender is obliged to take into account just as if it were a weapon. However, the act of casting a spell does provoke an attack of opportunity, so you may want to cast the spell and then move to the target instead of vice versa. Touch attacks come in two types: melee touch attacks (for touches made with, say, your hand) and ranged touch attacks (for touches made with magic rays, for example). You can score critical hits with either type of attack. Your opponent's AC against a touch attack does not include any armor bonus, shield bonus, or natural armor bonus. His size modifier, Dexterity modifier, and deflection bonus (if any) all apply normally.

Holding the Charge: If you don't discharge the spell in the round when you cast the spell, you can hold the discharge of the spell (hold the charge) indefinitely. You can continue to make touch attacks round after round. You can touch one friend as a standard action or up to six friends as a full-round action. If you touch anything or anyone while holding a charge, even unintentionally, the spell discharges. If you cast another spell, the touch spell dissipates. Alternatively, you may make a normal

TABLE 8–2: ACTIONS IN COMBAT

Standard Action	Attack of Opportunity[1]
Attack (melee)	No
Attack (ranged)	Yes
Attack (unarmed)	Yes
Activate a magic item other than a potion or oil	No
Aid another (page 154)	Maybe[2]
Bull rush (page 154)	No
Cast a spell (1 standard action casting time)	Yes
Concentrate to maintain an active spell	No
Dismiss a spell	No
Draw a hidden weapon (see Sleight of Hand, page 81)	No
Drink a potion or apply an oil	Yes
Escape a grapple (page 156)	No
Feint (see page 155)	No
Light a torch with a tindertwig (page 129)	Yes
Lower spell resistance	No
Make a dying friend stable (see Heal, page 75)	Yes
Overrun (page 157)	No
Read a scroll	Yes
Ready (triggers a standard action)	No
Sunder a weapon (attack)	Yes
Sunder an object (attack)	Maybe[3]
Total defense	No
Turn or rebuke undead (page 159)	No
Use extraordinary ability	No
Use skill that takes 1 action	Usually
Use spell-like ability	Yes
Use supernatural ability	No

Move Action	Attack of Opportunity[1]
Move	Yes
Control a frightened mount	Yes
Direct or redirect an active spell	No
Draw a weapon[4]	No
Load a hand crossbow or light crossbow	Yes
Open or close a door	No
Mount a horse or dismount	No
Move a heavy object	Yes
Pick up an item	Yes
Sheathe a weapon	Yes
Stand up from prone	Yes
Ready or loose a shield[4]	No
Retrieve a stored item	Yes

Full-Round Action	Attack of Opportunity[1]
Full attack	No
Charge[5] (page 154)	No
Deliver coup de grace (page 153)	Yes
Escape from a net (page 119)	Yes
Extinguish flames	No
Light a torch	Yes
Load a heavy or repeating crossbow	Yes
Lock or unlock weapon in locked gauntlet	Yes
Prepare to throw splash weapon (page 158)	Yes
Run	Yes
Use skill that takes 1 round	Usually
Use touch spell on up to six friends (page 141)	Yes
Withdraw[5]	No

Free Action	Attack of Opportunity[1]
Cast a quickened spell (page 98)	No
Cease concentration on a spell	No
Drop an item	No
Drop to the floor	No
Prepare spell components to cast a spell[6]	No
Speak	No

No Action	Attack of Opportunity[1]
Delay	No
5-foot step	No

Action Type Varies	
Disarm[7] (page 155)	Yes
Grapple[7] (page 155)	Yes
Trip an opponent[7] (page 158)	No
Use feat[8]	Varies

1 Regardless of the action, if you move out of a threatened square, you usually provoke an attack of opportunity. This column indicates whether the action itself, not moving, provokes an attack of opportunity.

2 If you aid someone performing an action that would normally provoke an attack of opportunity, then the act of aiding another provokes an attack of opportunity as well.

3 If the object is being held, carried, or worn by a creature, yes. If not, no.

4 If you have a base attack bonus of +1 or higher, you can combine one of these actions with a regular move. If you have the Two-Weapon Fighting feat, you can draw two light or one-handed weapons in the time it would normally take you to draw one.

5 May be taken as a standard action if you are limited to taking only a single action in a round.

6 Unless the component is an extremely large or awkward item (DM's call).

7 These attack forms substitute for a melee attack, not an action. As melee attacks, they can be used once in an attack or charge action, one or more times in a full attack action, or even as an attack of opportunity.

8 The description of a feat defines its effect.

unarmed attack (or an attack with a natural weapon) while holding a charge. In this case, you aren't considered armed and you provoke attacks of opportunity as normal for the attack. (If your unarmed attack or natural weapon attack doesn't provoke attacks of opportunity, neither does this attack.) If the attack hits, you deal normal damage for your unarmed attack or natural weapon and the spell discharges. If the attack misses, you are still holding the charge.

Dismiss a Spell: Dismissing an active spell (such as *alter self*) is a standard action that doesn't provoke attacks of opportunity.

Activate Magic Item

Many magic items don't need to be activated—magic weapons, magic armor, *gauntlets of Dexterity*, and so forth. However, certain magic items need to be activated, especially potions, scrolls, wands, rods, and staffs. Activating a magic item is a standard action (unless the item description indicates otherwise).

Spell Completion Items: Activating a spell completion item, such as a scroll, is the equivalent of casting a spell. It requires concentration and provokes attacks of opportunity. You lose the spell if your concentration is broken, and you can attempt to activate the item while on the defensive, as with casting a spell (see Casting on the Defensive, above).

Spell Trigger, Command Word, or Use-Activated Items: Activating any of these kinds of items does not require concentration and does not provoke attacks of opportunity. The *Dungeon Master's Guide* has much more information on magic items.

Use Special Ability

Using a special ability is usually a standard action, but whether it is a standard action, a full-round action, or not an action at all is defined by the ability (see Special Abilities, page 180).

Spell-Like Abilities: Using a spell-like ability (such as a paladin calling her special mount) works like casting a spell in that it requires concentration and provokes attacks of opportunity. Spell-like abilities can be disrupted. If your concentration is broken, the attempt to use the ability fails, but the attempt counts as if you had used the ability (for example, it counts against your daily limit if you have one). The casting time of a spell-like ability is 1 standard action, unless the ability description notes otherwise.

Using a Spell-Like Ability on the Defensive: You may attempt to use a spell-like ability on the defensive, just as with casting a spell. If the Concentration check (DC 15 + spell level) fails, you can't use the ability, but the attempt counts as if you had used the ability.

Supernatural Abilities: Using a supernatural ability (such as a cleric's turn or rebuke undead ability) is usually a standard action (unless defined otherwise by the ability's description). Its use cannot be disrupted, does not require concentration, and does not provoke attacks of opportunity.

Extraordinary Abilities: Using an extraordinary ability (such as a barbarian's uncanny dodge ability) is usually not an action because most extraordinary abilities automatically happen in a reactive fashion. Those extraordinary abilities that are actions are usually standard actions that cannot be disrupted, do not require concentration, and do not provoke attacks of opportunity.

Total Defense

You can defend yourself as a standard action. You get a +4 dodge bonus to your AC for 1 round. Your AC improves at the start of this action, so it helps you against any attacks of opportunity you incur during the round. You can't combine total defense with fighting defensively or with the benefit of the Combat Expertise feat (since both of those require you to declare an attack or full attack). You can't make attacks of opportunity while using total defense.

Start/Complete Full-Round Action

The "start full-round action" standard action lets you start undertaking a full-round action, which you can complete in the following round by using another standard action. For instance, if you are limited to taking only a standard action each turn, you can shoot a heavy crossbow every 3 rounds, needing 2 rounds to load it (a full-round action) and 1 round to shoot it. Also, if you want to cast a spell whose casting time is 1 full round, you can start the casting in one round and complete it in the following round, for example. You can't use this action to start or complete a full attack, charge, run, or withdraw.

MOVE ACTIONS

With the exception of specific movement-related skills, most move actions don't require a check.

Move

The simplest move action is moving your speed. If you take this kind of move action during your turn, you can't also take a 5-foot step.

Many nonstandard modes of movement are covered under this category, including climbing (up to one-quarter of your speed) and swimming (up to one-quarter of your speed).

Accelerated Climbing: You can climb one-half your speed as a move action by accepting a –5 penalty on your Climb check.

Crawling: You can crawl 5 feet as a move action. Crawling incurs attacks of opportunity from any attackers who threaten you at any point of your crawl.

Draw or Sheathe a Weapon

Drawing a weapon so that you can use it in combat, or putting it away so that you have a free hand, requires a move action. This action also applies to weaponlike objects carried in easy reach, such as wands. If your weapon or weaponlike object is stored in a pack or otherwise out of easy reach, treat this action as retrieving a stored item.

If you have a base attack bonus of +1 or higher, you may draw a weapon as a free action combined with a regular move. If you have the Two-Weapon Fighting feat (page 102), you can draw two light or one-handed weapons in the time it would normally take you to draw one.

Drawing ammunition for use with a ranged weapon (such as arrows, bolts, sling bullets, or shuriken) is a free action.

Ready or Loose a Shield

Strapping a shield to your arm to gain its shield bonus to your AC, or unstrapping and dropping a shield so you can use your shield hand for another purpose, requires a move action. If you

---

SPEEDING UP COMBAT

You can use a few tricks to make combat run faster.

Attack and Damage: Roll your attack die and damage die (or dice) at the same time. If you miss, you can ignore the damage, but if you hit, your friends don't have to wait for you to make a second roll for damage.

Multiple Attacks: Use dice of different colors so you can make your attack rolls all at once instead of one at a time. Designate which attack is which color before you roll.

Dice as Counters: Use dice to keep track of how many rounds a short-duration magical effect has been active. Each round, turn the die to the next number until the effect ends.

Concealment Rolls: If you know what your chance to miss is because of your target's concealment, you can roll it along with your attack roll. If the concealment roll indicates a miss, just ignore the attack roll.

have a base attack bonus of +1 or higher, you can ready or loose a shield as a free action combined with a regular move.

Dropping a carried (but not worn) shield is a free action.

Manipulate an Item

In most cases, moving or manipulating an item is a move action. This includes retrieving or putting away a stored item, picking up an item, moving a heavy object, and opening a door. Examples of this kind of action, along with whether they incur an attack of opportunity, are given in Table 8–2: Actions in Combat.

Direct or Redirect a Spell

Some spells, such as *flaming sphere* and *spiritual weapon*, allow you to redirect the effect to new targets or areas after you cast the spell. Redirecting a spell requires a move action and does not provoke attacks of opportunity or require concentration (see Cast a Spell under Standard Actions, page 140).

Stand Up

Standing up from a prone position requires a move action and provokes attacks of opportunity.

Mount/Dismount a Steed

Mounting or dismounting from a steed requires a move action.

Fast Mount or Dismount: You can mount or dismount as a free action with a DC 20 Ride check (your armor check penalty, if any, applies to this check). If you fail the check, mounting or dismounting is a move action instead. (You can't attempt a fast mount or fast dismount unless you can perform the mount or dismount as a move action in the current round.)

FULL-ROUND ACTIONS

A full-round action requires an entire round to complete. Thus, it can't be coupled with a standard or a move action, though if it does not involve moving any distance, you can take a 5-foot step.

Full Attack

If you get more than one attack per round because your base attack bonus is high enough, because you fight with two weapons or a double weapon (see Two-Weapon Fighting under Special Attacks, page 160), or for some special reason (such as a feat or a magic item), you must use a full-round action to get your additional attacks. You do not need to specify the targets of your attacks ahead of time. You can see how the earlier attacks turn out before assigning the later ones.

The only movement you can take during a full attack is a 5-foot step. You may take the step before, after, or between your attacks.

If you get multiple attacks because your base attack bonus is high enough, you must make the attacks in order from highest bonus to lowest. If you are using two weapons, you can strike with either weapon first. If you are using a double weapon, you can strike with either part of the weapon first.

Deciding between an Attack or a Full Attack: After your first attack, you can decide to take a move action instead of making your remaining attacks, depending on how the first attack turns out. If you've already taken a 5-foot step, you can't use your move action to move any distance, but you could still use a different kind of move action.

Fighting Defensively as a Full-Round Action: You can choose to fight defensively when taking a full attack action. If you do so, you take a –4 penalty on all attacks in a round to gain a +2 dodge bonus to AC for the same round.

Cleave: The extra attack granted by the Cleave feat (page 92) or Great Cleave feat (page 94) can be taken whenever they apply. This is an exception to the normal limit to the number of attacks you can take when not using a full attack action.

Cast a Spell

A spell that takes 1 round to cast is a full-round action. It comes into effect just before the beginning of your turn in the round after you began casting the spell. You then act normally after the spell is completed.

A spell that takes 1 minute to cast comes into effect just before your turn 1 minute later (and for each of those 10 rounds, you are casting a spell as a full-round action). These actions must be consecutive and uninterrupted, or the spell automatically fails.

When you begin a spell that takes 1 round or longer to cast, you must continue the invocations, gestures, and concentration from one round to just before your turn in the next round (at least). If you lose concentration after starting the spell and before it is complete, you lose the spell.

You only provoke attacks of opportunity when you begin casting a spell, even though you might continue casting for at least one full round. While casting a spell, you don't threaten any squares around you.

This action is otherwise identical to the cast a spell action described under Standard Actions.

Casting a Metamagic Spell: Sorcerers and bards must take more time to cast a metamagic spell (one enhanced by a metamagic feat) than a regular spell. If a spell's normal casting time is 1 standard action, casting a metamagic version of the spell is a full-round action for a sorcerer or bard. Note that this isn't the same as a spell with a 1-round casting time—the spell takes effect in the same round that you begin casting, and you aren't required to continue the invocations, gestures, and concentration until your next turn. For spells with a longer casting time, it takes an extra full-round action to cast the metamagic spell.

Clerics must take more time to spontaneously cast a metamagic version of a *cure* or *inflict* spell. For instance, an 11th-level cleric can swap out a prepared 6th-level spell to cast an empowered *cure critical wounds*. Spontaneously casting a metamagic version of a spell with a casting time of 1 standard action is a full-round action, and spells with longer casting times take an extra full-round action to cast.

Use Special Ability

Using a special ability is usually a standard action, but some may be full-round actions, as defined by the ability. See Special Abilities, page 180, and the Use Special Ability action under Standard Actions, page 142.

Withdraw

Withdrawing from melee combat is a full-round action. When you withdraw, you can move up to double your speed. The square you start out in is not considered threatened by any opponent you can see, and therefore visible enemies do not get attacks of opportunity against you when you move from that square. (Invisible enemies still get attacks of opportunity against you, and you can't withdraw from combat if you're blinded.) You can't take a 5-foot step during the same round in which you withdraw.

If, during the process of withdrawing, you move out of a threatened square (other than the one you started in), enemies get attacks of opportunity as normal.

You may not withdraw using a form of movement for which you don't have a listed speed. For example, a monstrous spider has a listed climb speed, so it can withdraw by climbing away. Your character doesn't normally have a listed climb speed (unless you're under the effect of a *spider climb* spell, for example), so you can't use climbing to withdraw from combat.

Note that despite the name of this action, you don't actually have to leave combat entirely. For instance, you could use a withdraw action to move away from one enemy and toward another.

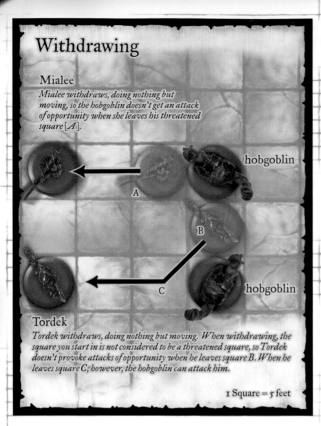

Withdrawing

Mialee

Mialee withdraws, doing nothing but moving, so the hobgoblin doesn't get an attack of opportunity when she leaves his threatened square [A].

hobgoblin

hobgoblin

Tordek

Tordek withdraws, doing nothing but moving. When withdrawing, the square you start in is not considered to be a threatened square, so Tordek doesn't provoke attacks of opportunity when he leaves square B. When he leaves square C, however, the hobgoblin can attack him.

1 Square = 5 feet

Restricted Withdraw: If you are limited to taking only a standard action each round (for instance, if you have been *slowed* or during a surprise round), you can withdraw as a standard action. In this case, you may move up to your speed (rather than up to double your speed).

Run

You can run as a full-round action. (If you do, you do not also get a 5-foot step.) When you run, you can move up to four times your speed in a straight line (or three times your speed if you're in heavy armor). You lose any Dexterity bonus to AC since you can't avoid attacks, unless you have the Run feat (page 99), which allows you to keep your Dexterity bonus to AC when running.

You can run for a number of rounds equal to your Constitution score, but after that you must make a DC 10 Constitution check to continue running. You must check again each round in which you continue to run, and the DC of this check increases by 1 for each check you have made. When you fail this check, you must stop running. A character who has run to his limit must rest for 1 minute (10 rounds) before running again. During a rest period, a character can move no faster than a normal move action.

You can't run across difficult terrain (see page 148), or if you can't see where you're going.

A run represents a speed of about 12 miles per hour for an unencumbered human.

Move 5 Feet through Difficult Terrain

In some situations, your movement may be so hampered that you don't have sufficient speed even to move 5 feet (a single square). In such a case, you may spend a full-round action to move 5 feet (1 square) in any direction, even diagonally. Even though this looks like a 5-foot step, it's not, and thus it provokes attacks of opportunity normally. (You can't take advantage of this rule to move through impassable terrain or to move when all movement is prohibited to you, such as while paralyzed.)

FREE ACTIONS

Free actions don't take any time at all, though your DM may limit the number of free actions you can perform in a turn. Free actions rarely incur attacks of opportunity. Some common free actions are described below.

Drop an Item

Dropping an item in your space or into an adjacent square is a free action.

Drop Prone

Dropping to a prone position in your space is a free action.

Speak

In general, speaking is a free action that you can perform even when it isn't your turn. Some DMs may rule that a character can only speak on his turn, or that a character can't speak while flat-footed (and thus can't warn allies of a surprise threat until he has a chance to act). Speaking more than few sentences is generally beyond the limit of a free action; to communicate more information than that, your DM may require that you take a move action or even a full-round action.

Cease Concentration on Spell

You can stop concentrating on an active spell (such as *detect evil*) as a free action.

Cast a Quickened Spell

You can cast a quickened spell (see the Quicken Spell feat, page 98) or any spell whose casting time is designated as a free action (such as the *feather fall* spell) as a free action. Only one such spell can be cast in any round, and such spells don't count toward your normal limit of one spell per round. Casting a spell with a casting time of a free action doesn't incur an attack of opportunity.

MISCELLANEOUS ACTIONS

Some actions don't fit neatly into the above categories. Some of these options are actions that take the place of or are variations on the actions described under Standard Actions, Move Actions, and Full-Round Actions. For actions not covered below, the DM lets you know how long such an action takes to perform and whether doing so provokes attacks of opportunity from threatening enemies. The variant and special attacks mentioned here are covered under Special Attacks, page 154.

Take 5-Foot Step

You can move 5 feet in any round when you don't perform any other kind of movement. Taking this 5-foot step never provokes an attack of opportunity. You can't take more than one 5-foot step in a round, and you can't take a 5-foot step in the same round when you move any distance.

You can take a 5-foot step before, during, or after your other actions in the round. For example, you could draw a weapon (a move action), take a 5-foot step, and then attack (a standard action), or you could cast *fireball* (a standard action), take a 5-foot step through an open door, then close the door (a move action).

You can only take a 5-foot-step if your movement isn't hampered by difficult terrain (see page 148) or darkness. Any creature with a speed of 5 feet or less can't take a 5-foot step, since moving even 5 feet requires a move action for such a slow creature.

You may not take a 5-foot step using a form of movement for which you do not have a listed speed. For example, if you don't have a climb speed listed, you can't use climbing to make a 5-foot step. Similarly, you can't take a 5-foot step when swimming unless you have a listed swim speed.

5-Foot Step

hobgoblin

Mialee

Mialee takes a 5-foot step away from the hobgoblin and then casts magic missile.

Tordek

Tordek takes a 5-foot step to close with the troll. Both Mialee and Tordek used 5-foot steps to avoid attacks of opportunity.

troll
[10-foot reach]

1 Square = 5 feet

Use Feat

Certain feats, such as Whirlwind Attack, let you take special actions in combat. Other feats do not require actions themselves, but they give you a bonus when attempting something you can already do, such as Improved Disarm. Some feats, such as item creation feats, are not meant to be used within the framework of combat. The individual feat descriptions in Chapter 5 tell you what you need to know about them.

Use Skill

Most skill uses are standard actions, but some might be move actions, full-round actions, free actions, or something else entirely. The individual skill descriptions in Chapter 4 tell you what sorts of actions are required to perform skills.

INJURY AND DEATH

Your hit points measure how hard you are to kill. No matter how many hit points you lose, your character isn't hindered in any way until your hit points drop to 0 or lower.

LOSS OF HIT POINTS

The most common way that your character gets hurt is to take lethal damage and lose hit points, whether from an orc's falchion, a wizard's *lightning bolt* spell, or a fall into molten lava. You record your character's hit point total on your character sheet. As your character takes damage, you subtract that damage from your hit points, leaving you with your current hit points. Current hit points go down when you take damage and go back up when you recover.

What Hit Points Represent: Hit points mean two things in the game world: the ability to take physical punishment and keep going, and the ability to turn a serious blow into a less serious one. For some characters, hit points may represent divine favor or inner power. When a paladin survives a *fireball*, you will be hard pressed to convince bystanders that she doesn't have the favor of some higher power.

Damaging Helpless Defenders: Even if you have lots of hit points, a dagger through the eye is a dagger through the eye. When a character is helpless, meaning that he can't avoid damage or deflect blows somehow, he's in trouble (see Helpless Defenders, page 153).

Effects of Hit Point Damage: Damage gives you scars, bangs up your armor, and gets blood on your tunic, but it doesn't slow you down until your current hit points reach 0 or lower.

At 0 hit points, you're disabled.

At from −1 to −9 hit points, you're dying.

At −10 or lower, you're dead.

Massive Damage: If you ever sustain damage so massive that a single attack deals 50 points of damage or more and it doesn't kill you outright, you must make a DC 15 Fortitude save. If this saving throw fails, you die regardless of your current hit points. This amount of damage represents a single trauma so major that it has a chance to kill even the toughest creature. If you take 50 points of damage or more from multiple attacks, no one of which dealt 50 or more points of damage itself, the massive damage rule does not apply.

DISABLED (0 HIT POINTS)

When your current hit points drop to exactly 0, you're disabled. You're not unconscious, but you're close to it. You can only take a single move or standard action each turn (but not both, nor can you take full-round actions). You can take move actions without further injuring yourself, but if you perform any standard action (or any other action the DM deems as strenuous, including some free actions such as casting a quickened spell) you take 1 point of damage after the completing the act. Unless your activity increased your hit points, you are now at −1 hit points, and you're dying.

Healing that raises your hit points above 0 makes you fully functional again, just as if you'd never been reduced to 0 or fewer hit points. A spellcaster retains the spellcasting capability she had before dropping to 0 hit points.

You can also become disabled when recovering from dying. In this case, it's a step toward recovery, and you can have fewer than 0 hit points (see Stable Characters and Recovery, below).

DYING (−1 TO −9 HIT POINTS)

When your character's current hit points drop to between −1 and −9 inclusive, he's dying.

A dying character immediately falls unconscious and can take no actions.

A dying character loses 1 hit point every round. This continues until the character dies or becomes stable (see below).

DEAD (−10 HIT POINTS OR LOWER)

When your character's current hit points drop to −10 or lower, or if he takes massive damage (see above), he's dead. A character can also die from taking ability damage or suffering an ability drain that reduces his Constitution to 0. When a character dies, his soul immediately departs. Getting it back into the body is a major hassle (see Bringing Back the Dead, page 171).

STABLE CHARACTERS AND RECOVERY

On the next turn after a character is reduced to between −1 and −9 hit points and on all subsequent turns, roll d% to see whether the dying character becomes stable. He has a 10% chance of becoming stable. If he doesn't, he loses 1 hit point. (A character who's unconscious or dying can't use any special action that changes the initiative count on which his action occurs.)

If the character's hit points drop to −10 or lower, he's dead.

You can keep a dying character from losing any more hit points and make him stable with a DC 15 Heal check.

If any sort of healing cures the dying character of even 1 point of damage, he stops losing hit points and becomes stable.

Healing that raises the dying character's hit points to 0 makes him conscious and disabled. Healing that raises his hit points to 1 or more makes him fully functional again, just as if he'd never been reduced to 0 or lower. A spellcaster retains the spellcasting capability she had before dropping below 0 hit points.

A stable character who has been tended by a healer or who has been magically healed eventually regains consciousness and recovers hit points naturally. If the character has no one to tend him, however, his life is still in danger, and he may yet slip away.

Recovering with Help: One hour after a tended, dying character becomes stable, roll d%. He has a 10% chance of becoming conscious, at which point he is disabled (as if he had 0 hit points). If he remains unconscious, he has the same chance to revive and become disabled every hour. Even if unconscious, he recovers hit points naturally. He is back to normal when his hit points rise to 1 or higher.

Recovering without Help: A severely wounded character left alone usually dies. He has a small chance, however, of recovering on his own. Even if he seems as though he's pulling through, he can still finally succumb to his wounds hours or days after originally taking damage.

A character who becomes stable on his own (by making the 10% roll while dying) and who has no one to tend to him still loses hit points, just at a slower rate. He has a 10% chance each hour of becoming conscious. Each time he misses his hourly roll to become conscious, he loses 1 hit point. He also does not recover hit points through natural healing.

Even once he becomes conscious and is disabled, an unaided character still does not recover hit points naturally. Instead, each day he has a 10% chance to start recovering hit points naturally (starting with that day); otherwise, he loses 1 hit point.

Once an unaided character starts recovering hit points naturally, he is no longer in danger of naturally losing hit points (even if his current hit point total is negative).

HEALING

After taking damage, you can recover hit points through natural healing or through magical healing. In any case, you can't regain hit points past your full normal hit point total.

Natural Healing: With a full night's rest (8 hours of sleep or more), you recover 1 hit point per character level. For example, a 5th-level fighter recovers 5 hit points with a night of rest. Any significant interruption (such as combat or the like) during your rest prevents you from healing that night.

If you undergo complete bed rest for an entire day and night, you recover twice your character level in hit points. A 5th-level fighter recovers 10 hit points per 24 hours of bed rest.

Magical Healing: Various abilities and spells, such as a cleric's *cure* spells or a paladin's lay on hands ability, can restore hit points.

Healing Limits: You can never recover more hit points than you lost. Magical healing won't raise your current hit points higher than your full normal hit point total.

Healing Ability Damage: Ability damage is temporary, just as hit point damage is. Ability damage returns at the rate of 1 point per night of rest (8 hours) for each affected ability score. Complete bed rest restores 2 points per day (24 hours) for each affected ability score.

TEMPORARY HIT POINTS

Certain effects, such as the *aid* spell, give a character temporary hit points. When a character gains temporary hit points, note his current hit point total. When the temporary hit points go away, such as at the end of the *aid* spell's duration, the character's hit points drop to his current hit point total. If the character's hit points are below his current hit point total at that time, all the temporary hit points have already been lost and the character's hit point total does not drop further.

When temporary hit points are lost, they cannot be restored as real hit points can be, even by magic.

Increases in Constitution Score and Current Hit Points: An increase in a character's Constitution score, even a temporary one, can give her more hit points (an effective hit point increase), but these are not temporary hit points. They can be restored, such as with *cure light wounds*, and they are not lost first as temporary hit points are. For example, Krusk (now a 3rd-level barbarian) gains +4 to his Constitution score and +6 hit points when he rages, raising his hit points from 31 to 37. If Krusk takes damage dropping him to 32 hit points, Jozan can cure those lost points and get him back to 37. If Krusk is so wounded at the end of his rage that he only has 5 hit points left, then when he loses his 6 extra hit points, he drops to –1 hit points and is dying.

NONLETHAL DAMAGE

Sometimes you get roughed up or weakened, such as by getting clocked in a fistfight or tired out by a forced march. This sort of trauma won't kill you, but it can knock you out or make you faint.

If you take sufficient nonlethal damage, you fall unconscious, but you don't die. Nonlethal damage goes away much faster than lethal damage does.

Dealing Nonlethal Damage: Certain attacks deal nonlethal damage, such as a normal human's unarmed strike (a punch, kick, or head butt). Other effects, such as heat or being exhausted, also deal nonlethal damage. When you take nonlethal damage, keep a running total of how much you've accumulated. *Do not deduct the nonlethal damage number from your current hit points. It is not "real" damage.* Instead, when your nonlethal damage equals your current hit points, you're staggered, and when it exceeds your current hit points, you fall unconscious. It doesn't matter whether the nonlethal damage equals or exceeds your current hit points because the nonlethal damage has gone up or because your current hit points have gone down.

Nonlethal Damage with a Weapon that Deals Lethal Damage: You can use a melee weapon that deals lethal damage to deal nonlethal damage instead, but you take a –4 penalty on your attack roll because you have to use the flat of the blade, strike at nonvital areas, or check your swing.

Lethal Damage with a Weapon that Deals Nonlethal Damage: You can use a weapon that deals nonlethal damage, including an unarmed strike, to deal lethal damage instead, but you take a –4 penalty on your attack roll because you have to strike only in the most vulnerable areas to inflict lethal damage.

Staggered and Unconscious: When your nonlethal damage equals your current hit points, you're staggered. You're so roughed up that you can only take a standard action or a move action in each round. You cease being staggered when your current hit points once again exceed your nonlethal damage.

When your nonlethal damage exceeds your current hit points, you fall unconscious. While unconscious, you are helpless (see Helpless Defenders, page 153).

Spellcasters who fall unconscious retain any spellcasting ability they had before going unconscious.

Healing Nonlethal Damage: You heal nonlethal damage at the rate of 1 hit point per hour per character level. For example, a 7th-level wizard heals 7 points of nonlethal damage each hour until all the nonlethal damage is gone.

When a spell or a magical power cures hit point damage, it also removes an equal amount of nonlethal damage.

MOVEMENT, POSITION, AND DISTANCE

Few characters in a fight stand around motionless. Enemies appear and charge the party. The heroes reply, advancing to take on new foes after they down their first opponents. Wizards remain outside the fight, looking for the best place to use their magic.

Rogues quietly skirt the fracas seeking a straggler or an unwary opponent to strike with a sneak attack. Finally, if the fight is lost, most characters seek to remove themselves from the vicinity. Movement is an important element for gaining the upper hand on the battlefield.

DUNGEONS & DRAGONS miniatures are on the 30mm scale—a miniature figure of a six-foot-tall human is approximately 30mm tall. A square on the battle grid is 1 inch across, representing a 5-foot-by-5-foot area.

TACTICAL MOVEMENT

Where you can move, how long it takes you to get there, and whether you're vulnerable to attacks of opportunity while you're moving are key questions in combat.

How Far Can Your Character Move?

Your speed is determined by your race and your armor (see Table 8–3: Tactical Speed). Your speed while unarmored is your base land speed.

Encumbrance: A character encumbered by carrying a large amount of gear, treasure, or fallen comrades may move slower than normal (see Carrying Capacity, page 161).

Hampered Movement: Difficult terrain, obstacles, or poor visibility can hamper movement (see Terrain and Obstacles, below, and Hampered Movement, page 163).

Movement in Combat: Generally, you can move your speed in a round and still do something, such as swing an axe or cast a spell. If you do nothing but move (that is, if you use both of your actions in a round to move your speed), you can move double your speed. If you spend the entire round running, you can move quadruple your speed. If you do something that requires a full round, such as attacking more than once, you can only take a 5-foot step.

Bonuses to Speed: A barbarian has a +10 foot bonus to his speed (unless he's wearing heavy armor). Experienced monks also have higher speed (unless they're wearing armor of any sort). In addition, many spells and magic items can affect a character's speed. Always apply any modifiers to a character's speed before adjusting the character's speed based on armor or encumbrance, and remember that multiple bonuses of the same type to a character's speed (such as enhancement bonuses) don't stack.

TABLE 8–3: TACTICAL SPEED

Race	No Armor or Light Armor	Medium or Heavy Armor
Human, elf, half-elf, half-orc	30 ft. (6 squares)	20 ft. (4 squares)
Dwarf	20 ft. (4 squares)	20 ft. (4 squares)
Halfling, gnome	20 ft. (4 squares)	15 ft. (3 squares)

Measuring Distance

Diagonals: When measuring distance, the first diagonal counts as 1 square, the second counts as 2 squares, the third counts as 1, the fourth as 2, and so on. (If it helps, you can think of a diagonal as a distance of 1.5 squares.)

You can't move diagonally past a corner (even by taking a 5-foot step). You can move diagonally past a creature, even an opponent. You can also move diagonally past other impassable obstacles, such as pits.

Closest Creature: When it's important to determine the closest square or creature to a location, if two squares or creatures are equally close, randomly determine which one counts as closest by rolling a die.

Moving through a Square

Friend: You can move through a square occupied by a friendly character, unless you are charging (see page 154). When you move through a square occupied by a friendly character, that character doesn't provide you with cover (see page 150).

Diagonal Movement

gnoll

1 square

3 squares

4 squares

gnoll

6 squares

Regdar

If you move or count distance diagonally, the first diagonal counts as 1 square of movement [5 feet], the second as 2 squares [10 feet], the third as 1 square, the fourth as 2 squares, and so on. [If it helps, you can think of a diagonal as a distance of 1.5 squares or 7.5 feet.] The gnoll, with a speed of 6 squares, can move 4 squares diagonally [which counts as 6 squares of movement] and attack Regdar.

Opponent: You can't move through a square occupied by an opponent, unless the opponent is helpless (dead, unconscious, paralyzed, bound, or the like). You can move through a square occupied by a helpless opponent without penalty. (The DM may rule that some creatures, such as an enormous dragon, present an

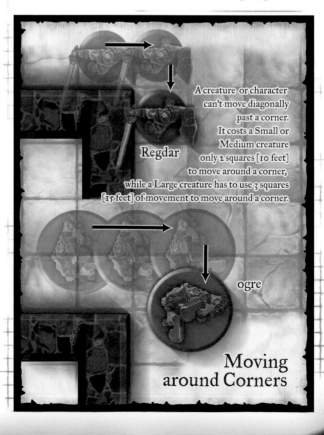

Regdar

A creature or character can't move diagonally past a corner. It costs a Small or Medium creature only 2 squares [10 feet] to move around a corner, while a Large creature has to use 3 squares [15 feet] of movement to move around a corner.

ogre

Moving around Corners

obstacle even when helpless. In such cases, each square you move through counts as 2 squares.)

Ending Your Movement: You can't end your movement in the same square as another creature unless it is helpless.

Overrun: During your movement or as part of a charge, you can attempt to move through a square occupied by an opponent (see Overrun, page 157).

Tumbling: A trained character can attempt to tumble through a square occupied by an opponent (see the Tumble skill, page 84).

Very Small Creature: A Fine, Diminutive, or Tiny creature can move into or through an occupied square. The creature provokes attacks of opportunity when doing so.

Square Occupied by Creature Three Sizes Larger or Smaller: Any creature can move through a square occupied by a creature three size categories larger than it is. A gnome (Small), for example, can run between the legs of a cloud giant (Huge).

A big creature can move through a square occupied by a creature three size categories smaller than it is. A cloud giant, for example, can step over a gnome.

Designated Exceptions: Some creatures break the above rules. For example, a gelatinous cube fills the squares it occupies to a height of 15 feet. A creature can't move through a square occupied by a cube, even with the Tumble skill or similar special abilities.

Terrain and Obstacles

The rules presented so far in this section assume that you're moving through an area clear of obstacles or difficult terrain. However, in dungeons and wilderness areas, that's often not the case.

Difficult Terrain: Difficult terrain, such as rubble, an uneven cave floor, thick undergrowth, and the like, hamper movement. Each square of difficult terrain counts as 2 squares of movement. (Each diagonal move into a difficult terrain square counts as 3 squares.) You can't run or charge across difficult terrain.

If you occupy squares with different kinds of terrain, you can move only as fast as the most difficult terrain you occupy will

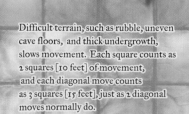

Difficult terrain, such as rubble, uneven cave floors, and thick undergrowth, slows movement. Each square counts as 2 squares [10 feet] of movement, and each diagonal move counts as 3 squares [15 feet], just as 2 diagonal moves normally do.

Difficult Terrain

Moving and Other Creatures

Tordek   Regdar

A character or creature can move through a square occupied by a friendly character or creature, but it can't end its move in an occupied square, and it can't charge through that square, either. You can't move through a square occupied by a nonfriendly or hostile creature.

---

allow. (This is often significant for creatures whose space fills more than one square, such as a giant.)

Flying and incorporeal creatures are not hampered by difficult terrain.

Obstacles: Like difficult terrain, obstacles can hamper movement. If an obstacle hampers movement but doesn't completely block it, such as a low wall or a deadfall of branches, each obstructed square or obstacle between squares counts as 2 squares of movement. You must pay this cost to cross the barrier, in addition to the cost to move into the square on the other side. If you don't have sufficient movement to cross the barrier and move into the square on the other side, you can't cross the barrier. Some obstacles may also require a skill check to cross (such as Climb or Jump).

On the other hand, some obstacles, such as floor-to-ceiling walls, block movement entirely. A character can't move through a blocking obstacle.

Flying and incorporeal creatures can avoid most obstacles, though a floor-to-ceiling wall blocks a flying creature as well as a landbound creature.

Squeezing: In some cases, you may have to squeeze into or through an area that isn't as wide as the space you take up. (This is particularly true for creatures whose space fills more than one square, such as a giant.) You can squeeze through or into a space that is at least half as wide as your normal space. For instance, an ogre (whose space is 10 feet, or 2 squares, wide) can squeeze through or into a space at least 5 feet (1 square) wide. Each move into or through a narrow space counts as if it were 2 squares, and while squeezed in a narrow space you take a –4 penalty on attack rolls and a –4 penalty to AC.

When a Large creature (which normally takes up four squares) squeezes into a space that's one square wide, the creature's miniature figure occupies two squares, centered on the line between the two squares. For a bigger creature, center the creature likewise in the area it squeezes into.

A creature can squeeze past an opponent while moving but it can't end its movement in an occupied square.

To squeeze through or into a space less than half your space's width, you must use the Escape Artist skill (page 73). You can't attack while using Escape Artist to squeeze through or into a narrow space, you take a –4 penalty to AC, and you lose any Dexterity bonus to AC.

Special Movement Rules

These rules cover special movement situations.

Accidentally Ending Movement in an Illegal Space: Sometimes a character ends its movement while moving through a space where it's not allowed to stop. For example, you might incur an attack of opportunity from a monk while moving through a friend's square and become stunned. When that happens, put your miniature in the last legal position you occupied, or the closest legal position, if there's a legal position that's closer.

Squeezing Movement

The ogre can move away from Tordek by squeezing into the 5-foot wide corridor. Each square it moves into while squeezing counts as 2 squares (10 feet) of movement. The ogre can also move through its own ally, the gnoll, but it must move at least 4 squares (20 feet), since it can't end its movement in an occupied square.

The ogre can also move 1 square (5 feet) toward Tordek, or squeeze past Tordek to the open corridor beyond.

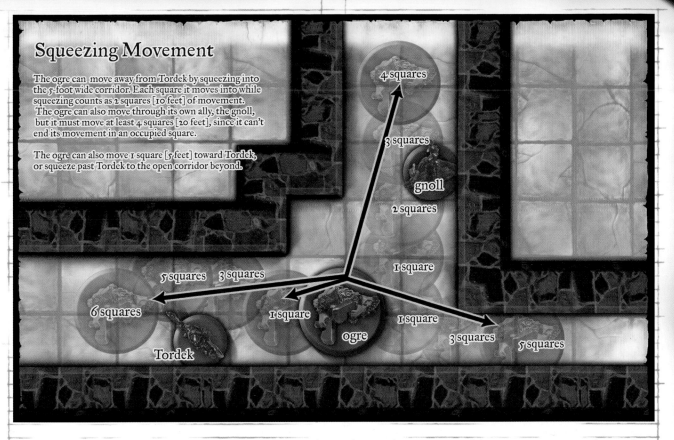

Double Movement Cost: When your movement is hampered in some way, your movement usually costs double. For example, each square of movement through difficult terrain counts as 2 squares, and each diagonal move through such terrain counts as 3 squares (just as two diagonal moves normally do).

If movement cost is doubled twice, then each square counts as 4 squares (or as 6 squares if moving diagonally). If movement cost is doubled three times, then each square counts as 8 squares (12 if diagonal) and so on. This is an exception to the general rule that two doublings are equivalent to a tripling.

Minimum Movement: Despite penalties to movement, you can take a full-round action to move 5 feet (1 square) in any direction, even diagonally. (This rule doesn't allow you to move through impassable terrain or to move when all movement is prohibited, such as while paralyzed.) Such movement provokes attacks of opportunity as normal (despite the distance covered, this move isn't a 5-foot step).

BIG AND LITTLE CREATURES IN COMBAT

Creatures smaller than Small or larger than Medium have special rules relating to position. This section covers the basics; the *Dungeon Master's Guide* has more information on how to handle exceptionally big or small creatures. The illustration on the following page depicts creatures of various size categories.

Tiny, Diminutive, and Fine Creatures: Very small creatures take up less than 1 square of space. This means that more than one such creature can fit into a single square. For example, a Tiny creature (such as a cat) typically occupies a space only 2-1/2 feet across, so four can fit into a single square. Twenty-five Diminutive creatures or 100 Fine creatures can fit into a single square.

Creatures that take up less than 1 square of space typically have a natural reach of 0 feet, meaning they can't reach into adjacent squares. They must enter an opponent's square to attack in melee. This provokes an attack of opportunity from the opponent. You can attack into your own square if you need to, so you can attack such creatures normally. Since they have no natural reach, they do not threaten the squares around them. You can move past them without provoking attacks of opportunity. They also can't flank an enemy.

Large, Huge, Gargantuan, and Colossal Creatures: Very large creatures take up more than 1 square. For instance, an ogre (Large) takes up a space 10 feet on a side (2 squares wide).

Creatures that take up more than 1 square typically have a natural reach of 10 feet or more, meaning that they can reach targets even if they aren't in adjacent squares. For instance, an ogre can attack targets up to 10 feet (2 squares) away from it in any direction, even diagonally. (This is an exception to the rule that 2 squares of diagonal distance is measured as 15 feet.)

Unlike when someone uses a reach weapon, a creature with greater than normal natural reach (more than 5 feet) still threat-

TABLE 8–4: CREATURE SIZE AND SCALE

Creature Size	Example Creature	Space[1]	Natural Reach[1]
Fine	Fly	1/2 ft.	0
Diminutive	Toad	1 ft.	0
Tiny	Cat	2-1/2 ft.	0
Small	Halfling	5 ft.	5 ft.
Medium	Human	5 ft.	5 ft.
Large (tall)	Ogre	10 ft.	10 ft.
Large (long)	Horse	10 ft.	5 ft.
Huge (tall)	Cloud giant	15 ft.	15 ft.
Huge (long)	Bulette	15 ft.	10 ft.
Gargantuan (tall)	50-ft. animated statue	20 ft.	20 ft.
Gargantuan (long)	Kraken	20 ft.	15 ft.
Colossal (tall)	Colossal animated object	30 ft. or more	30 ft. or more
Colossal (long)	Great wyrm red dragon	30 ft. or more	20 ft. or more

1 These values are typical for creatures of the indicated size. Some exceptions exist.

ens squares adjacent to it. A creature with greater than normal natural reach usually gets an attack of opportunity against you if you approach it, because you must enter and move within the range of its reach before you can attack it. (This attack of opportunity is not provoked if you take a 5-foot step.)

Large or larger creatures using reach weapons can strike up to double their natural reach but can't strike at their natural reach or less. For example, an ogre with a Large longspear could strike with the longspear at opponents 15 or 20 feet away, but not at those 5 or 10 feet away.

COMBAT MODIFIERS

Sometimes you just have to go toe-to-toe in a fight, but you can usually gain some advantage by seeking a better position, either offensively or defensively. This section covers the rules for when you can line up a particularly good attack or are forced to make a disadvantageous one.

FAVORABLE AND UNFAVORABLE CONDITIONS

Depending on the situation, you may gain bonuses or take penalties on your attack roll. Generally, any situational modifier created by the attacker's position or tactics applies to the attack roll, while any situational modifier created by the defender's position, state, or tactics applies to the defender's AC. Your DM judges what bonuses and penalties apply, using Table 8–5: Attack Roll Modifiers and Table 8–6: Armor Class Modifiers as guides.

COVER

One of the best defenses available is cover. By taking cover behind a tree, a wall, the side of a wagon, or the battlements of a castle, you can protect yourself from attacks, especially ranged attacks, and also from being spotted.

To determine whether your target has cover from your ranged attack, choose a corner of your square. If any line from this corner to any corner of the target's square passes through a square or border that blocks line of effect or provides cover, or through a square occupied by a creature, the target has cover (+4 to AC).

Creature Size Categories

Lars Grant-West

Colossal *Gargantuan* *Huge* *Large* *Medium* *Small* *Tiny*

TABLE 8–5: ATTACK ROLL MODIFIERS

Attacker is . . .	Melee	Ranged
Dazzled	−1	−1
Entangled	−2[1]	−2[1]
Flanking defender	+2	—
Invisible	+2[2]	+2[2]
On higher ground	+1	+0
Prone	−4	—[3]
Shaken or frightened	−2	−2
Squeezing through a space	−4	−4

1 An entangled character also takes a −4 penalty to Dexterity, which may affect his attack roll.

2 The defender loses any Dexterity bonus to AC. This bonus doesn't apply if the target is blinded.

3 Most ranged weapons can't be used while the attacker is prone, but you can use a crossbow or shuriken while prone at no penalty.

When making a melee attack against an adjacent target, your target has cover if any line from your square to the target's square goes through a wall (including a low wall). When making a melee attack against a target that isn't adjacent to you (such as with a reach weapon), use the rules for determining cover from ranged attacks.

Low Obstacles and Cover: A low obstacle (such as a wall no higher than half your height) provides cover, but only to creatures within 30 feet (6 squares) of it. The attacker can ignore the cover if he's closer to the obstacle than his target.

Cover and Attacks of Opportunity: You can't execute an attack of opportunity against an opponent with cover relative to you.

Cover and Reflex Saves: Cover grants you a +2 bonus on Reflex saves against attacks that originate or burst out from a point on the other side of the cover from you, such as a red dragon's breath weapon or a *lightning bolt*. Note that spread effects (see page 175), such as a *fireball*, can extend around corners and thus negate this cover bonus.

Cover and Hide Checks: You can use cover to make a Hide check. Without cover, you usually need concealment (see below) to make a Hide check.

TABLE 8–6: ARMOR CLASS MODIFIERS

Defender is . . .	Melee	Ranged
Behind cover	+4	+4
Blinded	−2[1]	−2[1]
Concealed or invisible	— See Concealment —	
Cowering	−2[1]	−2[1]
Entangled	+0[2]	+0[2]
Flat-footed (such as surprised, balancing, climbing)	+0[1]	+0[1]
Grappling (but attacker is not)	+0[1]	+0[1, 3]
Helpless (such as paralyzed, sleeping, or bound)	−4[4]	+0[4]
Kneeling or sitting	−2	+2
Pinned	−4[4]	+0[4]
Prone	−4	+4
Squeezing through a space	−4	−4
Stunned	−2[1]	−2[1]

1 The defender loses any Dexterity bonus to AC.

2 An entangled character takes a −4 penalty to Dexterity.

3 Roll randomly to see which grappling combatant you strike. That defender loses any Dexterity bonus to AC.

4 Treat the defender's Dexterity as 0 (−5 modifier). Rogues can sneak attack helpless or pinned defenders. See also Helpless Defenders, page 153.

Soft Cover: Creatures, even your enemies, can provide you with cover against melee attacks, giving you a +4 bonus to AC. However, such soft cover provides no bonus on Reflex saves, nor does soft cover allow you to make a Hide check.

Big Creatures and Cover: Any creature with a space larger than 5 feet (1 square) determines cover against melee attacks slightly differently than smaller creatures do. Such a creature can choose any square that it occupies to determine if an opponent has cover against its melee attacks. Similarly, when making a melee attack against such a creature, you can pick any of the squares it occupies to determine if it has cover against you.

orc
The orc has cover from the wall. [+4 *bonus to AC*]

To determine whether a creature has cover against a ranged attack, the attacker chooses a corner of its square. If any line from this corner to any corner of the defender's square crosses a square or border that blocks line of sight or provides cover, or through a square occupied by another character or creature, the defender has cover [+4 bonus to AC].

Regdar

gnoll
The gnoll receives cover from Regdar [+4 *bonus to AC*], *and Lidda is shooting into melee* [*she receives a* −4 *penalty on her attack roll*].

Lidda
Lidda has line of sight to both the orc and the gnoll.

Cover against Ranged Attacks

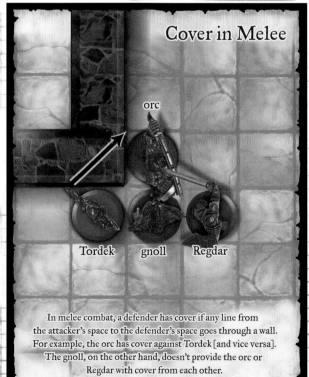

Cover in Melee

orc

Tordek   gnoll   Regdar

In melee combat, a defender has cover if any line from the attacker's space to the defender's space goes through a wall. For example, the orc has cover against Tordek [and vice versa]. The gnoll, on the other hand, doesn't provide the orc or Regdar with cover from each other.

Total Cover: If you don't have line of effect to your target (for instance, if he is completely behind a high wall), he is considered to have total cover from you. You can't make an attack against a target that has total cover.

Varying Degrees of Cover: In some cases, cover may provide a greater bonus to AC and Reflex saves. For instance, a character peering around a corner or through an arrow slit has even better cover than a character standing behind a low wall or an obstacle. In such situations, the DM can double the normal cover bonuses to AC and Reflex saves (to +8 and +4, respectively). A creature with this improved cover effectively gains improved evasion against any attack to which the Reflex save bonus applies (see the improved evasion ability in the rogue class description, page 51). Furthermore, improved cover provides a +10 bonus on Hide checks.

The DM may impose other penalties or restrictions to attacks depending on the details of the cover. For example, to strike effectively through a narrow opening, you need to use a long piercing weapon, such as an arrow or a spear. A battleaxe or a pick just isn't going to get through an arrow slit.

CONCEALMENT

Besides cover, another way to avoid attacks is to make it hard for opponents to know where you are. Concealment encompasses all circumstances where nothing physically blocks a blow or shot but where something interferes with an attacker's accuracy. Concealment gives the subject of a successful attack a chance that the attacker missed because of the concealment.

Typically, concealment is provided by fog, smoke, a shadowy area, darkness, tall grass, foliage, or magical effects that make it difficult to pinpoint a target's location.

To determine whether your target has concealment from your ranged attack, choose a corner of your square. If any line from this corner to any corner of the target's square passes through a square or border that provides concealment, the target has concealment.

When making a melee attack against an adjacent target, your target has concealment if his space is entirely within an effect that grants concealment (such as a cloud of smoke). When making a melee attack against a target that isn't adjacent to you (for instance, with a reach weapon), use the rules for determining concealment from ranged attacks.

In addition, some magical effects (such as the *blur* and *displacement* spells) provide concealment against all attacks, regardless of whether any intervening concealment exists.

Concealment Miss Chance: Concealment gives the subject of a successful attack a 20% chance that the attacker missed because of the concealment. If the attacker hits, the defender must make a miss chance percentile roll to avoid being struck. (To expedite play, make both rolls at the same time.) Multiple concealment conditions (such as a defender in a fog and under the effect of a *blur* spell) do not stack.

Concealment and Hide Checks: You can use concealment to make a Hide check. Without concealment, you usually need cover to make a Hide check.

Total Concealment: If you have line of effect to a target but not line of sight (for instance, if he is in total darkness or invisible, or if you're blinded), he is considered to have total concealment from you. You can't attack an opponent that has total concealment, though you can attack into a square that you think he occupies. A successful attack into a square occupied by an enemy with total concealment has a 50% miss chance (instead of the normal 20% miss chance for an opponent with concealment).

You can't execute an attack of opportunity against an opponent with total concealment, even if you know what square or squares the opponent occupies.

Ignoring Concealment: Concealment isn't always effective. For instance, a shadowy area or darkness doesn't provide any concealment against an opponent with darkvision. Remember also that characters with low-light vision can see clearly for a greater distance with the same light source than other characters. A torch, for example, lets an elf see clearly for 40 feet in all directions from the torch, while a human can see clearly for only 20 feet with the same

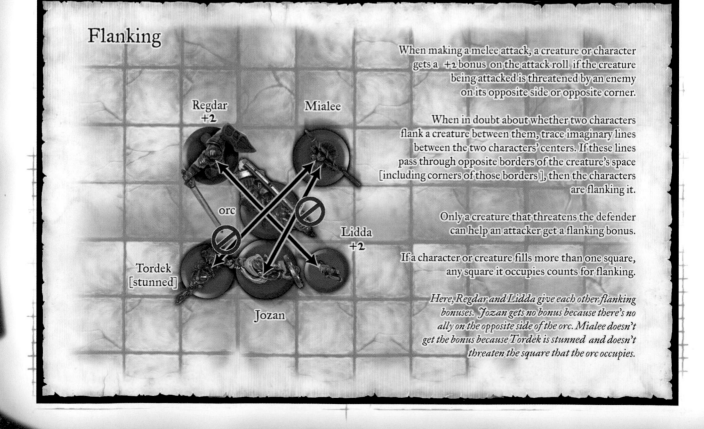

Flanking

When making a melee attack, a creature or character gets a +2 bonus on the attack roll if the creature being attacked is threatened by an enemy on its opposite side or opposite corner.

When in doubt about whether two characters flank a creature between them, trace imaginary lines between the two characters' centers. If these lines pass through opposite borders of the creature's space [including corners of those borders], then the characters are flanking it.

Only a creature that threatens the defender can help an attacker get a flanking bonus.

If a character or creature fills more than one square, any square it occupies counts for flanking.

Here, Regdar and Lidda give each other flanking bonuses. Jozan gets no bonus because there's no ally on the opposite side of the orc. Mialee doesn't get the bonus because Tordek is stunned and doesn't threaten the square that the orc occupies.

Regdar
+2

Mialee

orc

Lidda
+2

Tordek
[stunned]

Jozan

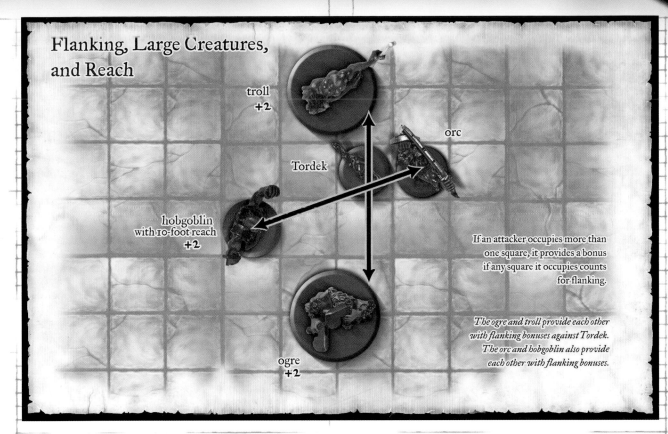

Flanking, Large Creatures, and Reach

troll
+2

orc

Tordek

hobgoblin
with 10-foot reach
+2

ogre
+2

If an attacker occupies more than one square, it provides a bonus if any square it occupies counts for flanking.

The ogre and troll provide each other with flanking bonuses against Tordek. The orc and hobgoblin also provide each other with flanking bonuses.

---

light. (Fog, smoke, foliage, and other visual obstructions work normally against characters with darkvision or low-light vision.)

Although invisibility provides total concealment, sighted opponents may still make Spot checks to notice the location of an invisible character. An invisible character gains a +20 bonus on Hide checks if moving, or a +40 bonus on Hide checks when not moving (even though opponents can't see you, they might be able to figure out where you are from other visual clues).

Varying Degrees of Concealment: As with cover, it's usually not worth diffentiating between more degrees of concealment than described above. However, the DM may rule that certain situations provide more or less than typical concealment, and modify the miss chance accordingly. For instance, a light fog might only provide a 10% miss chance, while near-total darkness could provide a 40% miss chance (and a +10 circumstance bonus on Hide checks).

FLANKING

When making a melee attack, you get a +2 flanking bonus if your opponent is threatened by a character or creature friendly to you on the opponent's opposite border or opposite corner.

When in doubt about whether two friendly characters flank an opponent in the middle, trace an imaginary line between the two friendly characters' centers. If the line passes through opposite borders of the opponent's space (including corners of those borders), then the opponent is flanked.

Exception: If a flanker takes up more than 1 square, it gets the flanking bonus if any square it occupies counts for flanking.

Only a creature or character that threatens the defender can help an attacker get a flanking bonus.

Creatures with a reach of 0 feet can't flank an opponent.

HELPLESS DEFENDERS

A helpless opponent is someone who is bound, sleeping, paralyzed, unconscious, or otherwise at your mercy.

Regular Attack: A helpless character takes a –4 penalty to AC against melee attacks, but no penalty to AC against ranged attacks.

A helpless defender can't use any Dexterity bonus to AC. In fact, his Dexterity score is treated as if it were 0 and his Dexterity modifier to AC as if it were –5 (and a rogue can sneak attack him).

Coup de Grace: As a full-round action, you can use a melee weapon to deliver a coup de grace to a helpless opponent. You can

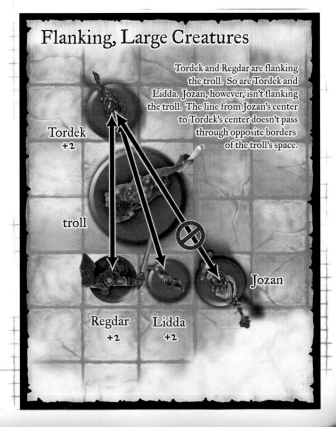

Flanking, Large Creatures

Tordek and Regdar are flanking the troll. So are Tordek and Lidda. Jozan, however, isn't flanking the troll. The line from Jozan's center to Tordek's center doesn't pass through opposite borders of the troll's space.

Tordek
+2

troll

Regdar
+2

Lidda
+2

Jozan

153

also use a bow or crossbow, provided you are adjacent to the target. You automatically hit and score a critical hit. If the defender survives the damage, he must make a Fortitude save (DC 10 + damage dealt) or die. A rogue also gets her extra sneak attack damage against a helpless opponent when delivering a coup de grace.

Delivering a coup de grace provokes attacks of opportunity from threatening opponents because it involves focused concentration and methodical action on the part of the attacker.

You can't deliver a coup de grace against a creature that is immune to critical hits, such as a golem. You can deliver a coup de grace against a creature with total concealment, but doing this requires two consecutive full-round actions (one to "find" the creature once you've determined what square it's in, and one to deliver the coup de grace).

SPECIAL ATTACKS

This section covers grappling, throwing splash weapons (such as acid or holy water), attacking objects (such as trying to hack apart a locked chest), turning or rebuking undead (for clerics and paladins), and an assortment of other special attacks.

TABLE 8–7: SPECIAL ATTACKS

Special Attack	Brief Description
Aid another	Grant an ally a +2 bonus on attacks or AC
Bull rush	Push an opponent back 5 feet or more
Charge	Move up to twice your speed and attack with +2 bonus
Disarm	Knock a weapon from your opponent's hands
Feint	Negate your opponent's Dex bonus to AC
Grapple	Wrestle with an opponent
Overrun	Plow past or over an opponent as you move
Sunder	Strike an opponent's weapon or shield
Throw splash weapon	Throw container of dangerous liquid at target
Trip	Trip an opponent
Turn (rebuke) undead	Channel positive (or negative) energy to turn away (or awe) undead
Two-weapon fighting	Fight with a weapon in each hand

AID ANOTHER

In melee combat, you can help a friend attack or defend by distracting or interfering with an opponent. If you're in position to make a melee attack on an opponent that is engaging a friend in melee combat, you can attempt to aid your friend as a standard action. You make an attack roll against AC 10. If you succeed, your friend gains either a +2 bonus on his next attack roll against that opponent or a +2 bonus to AC against that opponent's next attack (your choice), as long as that attack comes before the beginning of your next turn. Multiple characters can aid the same friend, and similar bonuses stack.

You can also use this standard action to help a friend in other ways, such as when he is affected by a *hypnotism* spell or a *sleep* spell, or to assist another character's skill check (see page 65).

BULL RUSH

You can make a bull rush as a standard action (an attack) or as part of a charge (see Charge, below). When you make a bull rush, you attempt to push an opponent straight back instead of damaging him. You can only bull rush an opponent who is one size category larger than you, the same size, or smaller.

Initiating a Bull Rush: First, you move into the defender's space. Doing this provokes an attack of opportunity from each opponent that threatens you, including the defender. (If you have the Improved Bull Rush feat, you don't provoke an attack of opportunity from the defender.) Any attack of opportunity made by anyone other than the defender against you during a bull rush has a 25% chance of accidentally targeting the defender instead, and

any attack of opportunity by anyone other than you against the defender likewise has a 25% chance of accidentally targeting you. (When someone makes an attack of opportunity, make the attack roll and then roll to see whether the attack went astray.)

Second, you and the defender make opposed Strength checks. You each add a +4 bonus for each size category you are larger than Medium or a –4 penalty for each size category you are smaller than Medium. You get a +2 bonus if you are charging. The defender gets a +4 bonus if he has more than two legs or is otherwise exceptionally stable (such as a dwarf).

Bull Rush Results: If you beat the defender's Strength check result, you push him back 5 feet. If you wish to move with the defender, you can push him back an additional 5 feet for each 5 points by which your check result is greater than the defender's check result. You can't, however, exceed your normal movement limit. (Note: The defender provokes attacks of opportunity if he is moved. So do you, if you move with him. The two of you do not provoke attacks of opportunity from each other, however.)

If you fail to beat the defender's Strength check result, you move 5 feet straight back to where you were before you moved into his space. If that space is occupied, you fall prone in that space.

CHARGE

Charging is a special full-round action that allows you to move up to twice your speed and attack during the action. However, it carries tight restrictions on how you can move.

Movement During a Charge: You must move before your attack, not after. You must move at least 10 feet (2 squares) and may move up to double your speed directly toward the designated opponent. You must have a clear path toward the opponent, and nothing can hinder your movement (such as difficult terrain or obstacles).

Here's what it means to have a clear path. First, you must move to the closest space from which you can attack the opponent. (If this space is occupied or otherwise blocked, you can't charge.) Second, if any line from your starting space to the ending space passes through a square that blocks movement (such as a wall), slows

Regdar

Tordek

orc

When charging, Tordek must move to the nearest square from which he can attack the orc.

When charging, a character or creature moves up to double speed [and at least 2 squares or 10 feet] along the shortest path to the closest space from which it can attack an enemy. If any line drawn between the character's starting space and the ending space passes through a square that slows or prevents movement, or contains an ally, the charge is not allowed.

At the end of a charge, the character makes one melee attack with a +2 bonus against the enemy it charged.

A character can't charge if it doesn't have line of sight to the enemy.

Charging

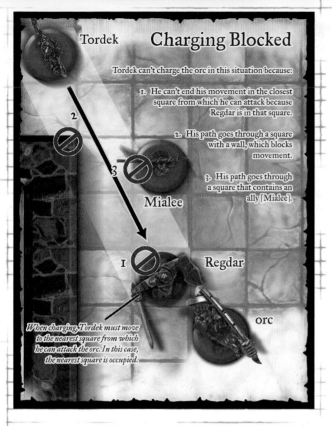

Charging Blocked

Tordek

Tordek can't charge the orc in this situation because:

1. He can't end his movement in the closest square from which he can attack because Regdar is in that square.

2. His path goes through a square with a wall, which blocks movement.

3. His path goes through a square that contains an ally (Mialee).

Mialee

Regdar

orc

When charging, Tordek must move to the nearest square from which he can attack the orc. In this case, the nearest square is occupied.

movement (such as difficult terrain), or contains a creature (even an ally), you can't charge. (Helpless creatures don't stop a charge.)

If you don't have line of sight to the opponent at the start of your turn, you can't charge that opponent.

You can't take a 5-foot step in the same round as a charge.

If you are able to take only a standard action or a move action on your turn, you can still charge, but you are only allowed to move up to your speed (instead of up to double your speed). You can't use this option unless you are restricted to taking only a standard action or move action on your turn (such as during a surprise round).

Attacking on a Charge: After moving, you may make a single melee attack. Since you can use the momentum of the charge in your favor, you get a +2 bonus on the attack roll. Since a charge is a bit reckless, you also take a –2 penalty to your AC until the start of your next turn.

A charging character gets a +2 bonus on the Strength check made to bull rush or overrun an opponent (see Bull Rush, above, and Overrun, below).

Even if you have extra attacks, such as from having a high enough base attack bonus or from using multiple weapons, you only get to make one attack during a charge.

Lances and Charge Attacks: A lance deals double damage if employed by a mounted character in a charge.

Weapons Readied against a Charge: Spears, tridents, and certain other piercing weapons deal double damage when readied (set) and used against a charging character (see Table 7–5: Weapons, page 116, and Ready, page 160).

DISARM

As a melee attack, you may attempt to disarm your opponent. If you do so with a weapon, you knock the opponent's weapon out of his hands and to the ground. If you attempt the disarm while unarmed, you end up with the weapon in your hand.

If you're attempting to disarm a melee weapon, follow the steps outlined here. If the item you are attempting to disarm isn't a melee weapon (for instance, a bow or a wand), the defender may

still oppose you with an attack roll, but takes a penalty and can't attempt to disarm you in return if your attempt fails.

Step 1: Attack of Opportunity. You provoke an attack of opportunity from the target you are trying to disarm. (If you have the Improved Disarm feat, you don't incur an attack of opportunity for making a disarm attempt.) If the defender's attack of opportunity deals any damage, your disarm attempt fails.

Step 2: Opposed Rolls. You and the defender make opposed attack rolls with your respective weapons. The wielder of a two-handed weapon on a disarm attempt gets a +4 bonus on this roll, and the wielder of a light weapon takes a –4 penalty. (An unarmed strike is considered a light weapon, so you always take a penalty when trying to disarm an opponent by using an unarmed strike.) If the combatants are of different sizes, the larger combatant gets a bonus on the attack roll of +4 per difference in size category. If the targeted item isn't a melee weapon, the defender takes a –4 penalty on the roll.

Step Three: Consequences. If you beat the defender, the defender is disarmed. If you attempted the disarm action unarmed, you now have the weapon. If you were armed, the defender's weapon is on the ground in the defender's square.

If you fail on the disarm attempt, the defender may immediately react and attempt to disarm you with the same sort of opposed melee attack roll. His attempt does not provoke an attack of opportunity from you. If he fails his disarm attempt, you do not subsequently get a free disarm attempt against him.

Note: A defender wearing spiked gauntlets (page 118) can't be disarmed. A defender using a weapon attached to a locked gauntlet (page 124) gets a +10 bonus to resist being disarmed.

Grabbing Items

You can use a disarm action to snatch an item worn by the target (such as a necklace or a pair of goggles). If you want to have the item in your hand, the disarm must be made as an unarmed attack. If the item is poorly secured or otherwise easy to snatch or cut away (such as a loose cloak or a brooch pinned to the front of a tunic), the attacker gets a +4 bonus. Unlike on a normal disarm attempt, failing the attempt doesn't allow the defender to attempt to disarm you. This otherwise functions identically to a disarm attempt, as noted above.

You can't snatch an item that is well secured, such as a ring or bracelet, unless you have pinned the wearer (see Grapple). Even then, the defender gains a +4 bonus on his roll to resist the attempt.

FEINT

As a standard action, you can try to mislead an opponent in melee combat so that he can't dodge your next attack effectively. To feint, make a Bluff check opposed by a Sense Motive check by your target. The target may add his base attack bonus to this Sense Motive check. If your Bluff check result exceeds your target's Sense Motive check result, the next melee attack you make against the target does not allow him to use his Dexterity bonus to AC (if any). This attack must be made on or before your next turn.

Feinting in this way against a nonhumanoid is difficult because it's harder to read a strange creature's body language; you take a –4 penalty. Against a creature of animal Intelligence (1 or 2), you take a –8 penalty. Against a nonintelligent creature, it's impossible.

Feinting in combat does not provoke attacks of opportunity.

Feinting as a Move Action: With the Improved Feint feat, you can attempt a feint as a move action instead of as a standard action.

GRAPPLE

Grappling means wrestling and struggling hand-to-hand. It's tricky to perform, but sometimes you want to pin foes instead of killing them, and sometimes you have no choice in the matter. For monsters, grappling can mean trapping you in a toothy maw (the purple worm's favorite tactic) or holding you down so it can claw you to pieces (the dire lion's trick).

Grapple Checks

Repeatedly in a grapple, you need to make opposed grapple checks against an opponent. A grapple check is like a melee attack roll. Your attack bonus on a grapple check is:

Base attack bonus + Strength modifier + special size modifier

Special Size Modifier: The special size modifier for a grapple check is as follows: Colossal +16, Gargantuan +12, Huge +8, Large +4, Medium +0, Small –4, Tiny –8, Diminutive –12, Fine –16. Use this number in place of the normal size modifier you use when making an attack roll.

Starting a Grapple

To start a grapple, you need to grab and hold your target. Starting a grapple requires a successful melee attack roll. If you get multiple attacks, you can attempt to start a grapple multiple times (at successively lower base attack bonuses).

Step 1: Attack of Opportunity. You provoke an attack of opportunity from the target you are trying to grapple. If the attack of opportunity deals damage, the grapple attempt fails. (Certain monsters do not provoke attacks of opportunity when they attempt to grapple, nor do characters with the Improved Grapple feat.) If the attack of opportunity misses or fails to deal damage, proceed to Step 2.

Step 2: Grab. You make a melee touch attack to grab the target. If you fail to hit the target, the grapple attempt fails. If you succeed, proceed to Step 3.

Step 3: Hold. Make an opposed grapple check as a free action. If you succeed, you and your target are now grappling, and you deal damage to the target as if with an unarmed strike.

If you lose, you fail to start the grapple. You automatically lose an attempt to hold if the target is two or more size categories larger than you are.

In case of a tie, the combatant with the higher grapple check modifier wins. If this is a tie, roll again to break the tie.

Step 4: Maintain Grapple. To maintain the grapple for later rounds, you must move into the target's space. (This movement is free and doesn't count as part of your movement in the round.) Moving, as normal, provokes attacks of opportunity from threatening opponents, but not from your target.

If you can't move into your target's space, you can't maintain the grapple and must immediately let go of the target. To grapple again, you must begin at Step 1.

Grappling Consequences

While you're grappling, your ability to attack others and defend yourself is limited.

No Threatened Squares: You don't threaten any squares while grappling.

No Dexterity Bonus: You lose your Dexterity bonus to AC (if you have one) against opponents you aren't grappling. (You can still use it against opponents you are grappling.)

No Movement: You can't move normally while grappling. You may, however, make an opposed grapple check (see below) to move while grappling.

If You're Grappling

When you are grappling (regardless of who started the grapple), you can perform any of the following actions. Some of these actions take the place of an attack (rather than being a standard action or a move action). If your base attack bonus allows you multiple attacks, you can attempt one of these actions in place of each of your attacks, but at successively lower base attack bonuses.

Activate a Magic Item: You can activate a magic item, as long as the item doesn't require a spell completion trigger (such as a scroll does). You don't need to make a grapple check to activate the item.

Attack Your Opponent: You can make an attack with an unarmed strike, natural weapon, or light weapon against another character you are grappling. You take a –4 penalty on such attacks. You can't attack with two weapons while grappling, even if both are light weapons.

Cast a Spell: You can attempt to cast a spell while grappling or even while pinned (see below), provided its casting time is no more than 1 standard action, it has no somatic component, and you have in hand any material components or focuses you might need. Any spell that requires precise and careful action, such as drawing a circle with powdered silver for *protection from evil*, is impossible to cast while grappling or being pinned. If the spell is one that you can cast while grappling, you must make a Concentration check (DC 20 + spell level) or lose the spell. You don't have to make a successful grapple check to cast the spell.

Damage Your Opponent: While grappling, you can deal damage to your opponent equivalent to an unarmed strike. Make an opposed grapple check in place of an attack. If you win, you deal nonlethal damage as normal for your unarmed strike (1d3 points for Medium attackers or 1d2 points for Small attackers, plus Strength modifiers). If you want to deal lethal damage, you take a –4 penalty on your grapple check.

Exception: Monks deal more damage on an unarmed strike than other characters, and the damage is lethal. However, they can choose to deal their damage as nonlethal damage when grappling without taking the usual –4 penalty for changing lethal damage to nonlethal damage (see Dealing Nonlethal Damage, page 146).

Draw a Light Weapon: You can draw a light weapon as a move action with a successful grapple check.

Escape from Grapple: You can escape a grapple by winning an opposed grapple check in place of making an attack. You can make an Escape Artist check in place of your grapple check if you so desire, but this requires a standard action. If more than one opponent is grappling you, your grapple check result has to beat all their individual check results to escape. (Opponents don't have to try to hold you if they don't want to.) If you escape, you finish the action by moving into any space adjacent to your opponent(s).

Move: You can move half your speed (bringing all others engaged in the grapple with you) by winning an opposed grapple check. This requires a standard action, and you must beat all the other individual check results to move the grapple.

Note: You get a +4 bonus on your grapple check to move a pinned opponent, but only if no one else is involved in the grapple.

Retrieve a Spell Component: You can produce a spell component from your pouch while grappling by using a full-round action. Doing so does not require a successful grapple check.

Pin Your Opponent: You can hold your opponent immobile for 1 round by winning an opposed grapple check (made in place of an attack). Once you have an opponent pinned, you have a few options available to you (see below).

Break Another's Pin: If you are grappling an opponent who has another character pinned, you can make an opposed grapple check in place of an attack. If you win, you break the hold that the opponent has over the other character. The character is still grappling, but is no longer pinned.

Use Opponent's Weapon: If your opponent is holding a light weapon, you can use it to attack him. Make an opposed grapple check (in place of an attack). If you win, make an attack roll with the weapon with a –4 penalty (doing this doesn't require another action). You don't gain possession of the weapon by performing this action.

If You're Pinning an Opponent

Once you've pinned your opponent, he's at your mercy. However, you don't have quite the freedom of action that you did while grappling. You can attempt to damage your opponent with an opposed grapple check, you can attempt to use your opponent's weapon against him, or you can attempt to move the grapple (all described above). At your option, you can prevent a pinned opponent from speaking.

You can use a disarm action to remove or grab away a well-secured object worn by a pinned opponent, but he gets a +4 bonus on his roll to resist your attempt (see Disarm, page 155).

You may voluntarily release a pinned character as a free action; if you do so, you are no longer considered to be grappling that character (and vice versa).

You can't draw or use a weapon (against the pinned character or any other character), escape another's grapple, retrieve a spell component, pin another character, or break another's pin while you are pinning an opponent.

If You're Pinned by an Opponent

When an opponent has pinned you, you are held immobile (but not helpless) for 1 round. While you're pinned, you take a –4 penalty to your AC against opponents other than the one pinning you. At your opponent's option, you may also be unable to speak. On your turn, you can try to escape the pin by making an opposed grapple check in place of an attack. You can make an Escape Artist check in place of your grapple check if you want, but this requires a standard action. If you win, you escape the pin, but you're still grappling.

Joining a Grapple

If your target is already grappling someone else, you can use an attack to start a grapple, as above, except that the target doesn't get an attack of opportunity against you, and your grab automatically succeeds. You still have to make a successful opposed grapple check to become part of the grapple.

If there are multiple opponents involved in the grapple, you pick one to make the opposed grapple check against.

Multiple Grapplers

Several combatants can be in a single grapple. Up to four combatants can grapple a single opponent in a given round. Creatures that are one or more size categories smaller than you count for half, creatures that are one size category larger than you count double, and creatures two or more size categories larger count quadruple.

When you are grappling with multiple opponents, you choose one opponent to make an opposed check against. The exception is an attempt to escape from the grapple; to successfully escape, your grapple check must beat the check results of each opponent.

MOUNTED COMBAT

Riding a mount into battle gives you several advantages (see the Ride skill, page 80, and the Mounted Combat feat, page 98).

Horses in Combat: Warhorses and warponies can serve readily as combat steeds. Light horses, ponies, and heavy horses, however, are frightened by combat. If you don't dismount, you must make a DC 20 Ride check each round as a move action to control such a horse. If you succeed, you can perform a standard action after the move action. If you fail, the move action becomes a full-round action and you can't do anything else until your next turn.

Your mount acts on your initiative count as you direct it. You move at its speed, but the mount uses its action to move.

A horse (not a pony) is a Large creature (see Big and Little Creatures in Combat, page 149), and thus takes up a space 10 feet (2 squares) across. For simplicity, assume that you share your mount's space during combat.

Combat while Mounted: With a DC 5 Ride check, you can guide your mount with your knees so as to use both hands to attack or defend yourself. This is a free action.

When you attack a creature smaller than your mount that is on foot, you get the +1 bonus on melee attacks for being on higher ground. If your mount moves more than 5 feet, you can only make a single melee attack. Essentially, you have to wait until the mount gets to your enemy before attacking, so you can't make a full attack. Even at your mount's full speed, you don't take any penalty on melee attacks while mounted.

If your mount charges, you also take the AC penalty associated with a charge. If you make an attack at the end of the charge, you receive the bonus gained from the charge. When charging on horseback, you deal double damage with a lance (see Charge, page 154).

You can use ranged weapons while your mount is taking a double move, but at a –4 penalty on the attack roll. You can use ranged weapons while your mount is running (quadruple speed), at a –8 penalty. In either case, you make the attack roll when your mount has completed half its movement. You can make a full attack with a ranged weapon while your mount is moving. Likewise, you can take move actions normally, so that, for instance, you can load and fire a light crossbow in a round while your mount is moving.

Casting Spells while Mounted: You can cast a spell normally if your mount moves up to a normal move (its speed) either before or after you cast. If you have your mount move both before and after you cast a spell, then you're casting the spell while the mount is moving, and you have to make a Concentration check due to the vigorous motion (DC 10 + spell level) or lose the spell. If the mount is running (quadruple speed), you can cast a spell when your mount has moved up to twice its speed, but your Concentration check is more difficult due to the violent motion (DC 15 + spell level).

If Your Mount Falls in Battle: If your mount falls, you have to succeed on a DC 15 Ride check to make a soft fall and take no damage. If the check fails, you take 1d6 points of damage.

If You Are Dropped: If you are knocked unconscious, you have a 50% chance to stay in the saddle (or 75% if you're in a military saddle). Otherwise you fall and take 1d6 points of damage. Without you to guide it, your mount avoids combat.

OVERRUN

You can attempt an overrun as a standard action taken during your move, or as part of a charge. (In general, you cannot take a standard action during a move; this is an exception.) With an overrun, you attempt to plow past or over your opponent (and move through his square) as you move. You can only overrun an opponent who is one size category larger than you, the same size, or smaller. You can make only one overrun attempt per round.

If you're attempting to overrun an opponent, follow these steps.

Step 1: Attack of Opportunity. Since you begin the overrun by moving into the defender's space, you provoke an attack of opportunity from the defender.

Step 2: Opponent Avoids? The defender has the option to simply avoid you. If he avoids you, he doesn't suffer any ill effect. If you were attempting the overrun as part of a charge, you may keep moving. (You can always move through a square occupied by someone who lets you by.) In either case, the overrun attempt doesn't count against your actions this round (except for any movement required to enter the opponent's square). If your opponent doesn't avoid you, move to Step 3.

Step 3: Opponent Blocks? If your opponent blocks you, make a Strength check opposed by the defender's Dexterity or Strength check (whichever ability score has the higher modifier). A combatant gets a +4 bonus on the check for every size category he is larger than Medium or a –4 penalty for every size category he is smaller than Medium. You gain a +2 bonus on your Strength check if you made the overrun as part of a charge. The defender gets a +4 bonus on his check if he has more than two legs or is otherwise more stable than a normal humanoid (such as a dwarf). If you win, you knock the defender prone. If you lose, the defender may immediately react and make a Strength check opposed by your Dexterity or Strength check (including the size modifiers noted above, but no other modifiers) to try to knock you prone.

Step 4: Consequences. If you succeed in knocking your opponent prone, you can continue your movement as normal. If you fail and are knocked prone in turn, you have to move 5 feet back the way you came and fall prone, ending your movement there. If you fail but are not knocked prone, you have to move 5 feet back the way you came, ending your movement there. If that square is occupied, you fall prone in that square.

Improved Overrun: If you have the Improved Overrun feat, your target may not choose to avoid you.

Mounted Overrun (Trample): If you attempt an overrun while mounted, your mount makes the Strength check to determine the success or failure of the overrun attack (and applies its size modifier, rather than yours). If you have the Trample feat and attempt an overrun while mounted, your target may not choose to avoid you, and if you knock your opponent prone with the overrun, your mount may make one hoof attack against your opponent.

SUNDER

You can use a melee attack with a slashing or bludgeoning weapon to strike a weapon or shield that your opponent is holding. If you're attempting to sunder a weapon or shield, follow the steps outlined here. (Attacking held objects other than weapons or shields is covered below.)

TABLE 8–8: COMMON ARMOR, WEAPON, AND SHIELD HARDNESS AND HIT POINTS

Weapon or Shield	Example	Hardness	HP[1]
Light blade	Short sword	10	2
One-handed blade	Longsword	10	5
Two-handed blade	Greatsword	10	10
Light metal-hafted weapon	Light mace	10	10
One-handed metal-hafted weapon	Heavy mace	10	20
Light hafted weapon	Handaxe	5	2
One-handed hafted weapon	Battleaxe	5	5
Two-handed hafted weapon	Greataxe	5	10
Projectile weapon	Crossbow	5	5
Armor	—	special[2]	armor bonus × 5
Buckler	—	10	5
Light wooden shield	—	5	7
Heavy wooden shield	—	5	15
Light steel shield	—	10	10
Heavy steel shield	—	10	20
Tower shield	—	5	20

1 The hp value given is for Medium armor, weapons, and shields. Divide by 2 for each size category of the item smaller than Medium, or multiply it by 2 for each size category larger than Medium.

2 Varies by material; see Table 9–9, page 166.

Step 1: Attack of Opportunity. You provoke an attack of opportunity from the target whose weapon or shield you are trying to sunder. (If you have the Improved Sunder feat, you don't incur an attack of opportunity for making the attempt.)

Step 2: Opposed Rolls. You and the defender make opposed attack rolls with your respective weapons. The wielder of a two-handed weapon on a sunder attempt gets a +4 bonus on this roll, and the wielder of a light weapon takes a –4 penalty. If the combatants are of different sizes, the larger combatant gets a bonus on the attack roll of +4 per difference in size category.

Step 3: Consequences. If you beat the defender, you have landed a good blow. Roll damage and deal it to the weapon or shield. See Table 8–8: Common Armor, Weapon, and Shield Hardness and Hit Points to determine how much damage you must deal to destroy the weapon or shield.

If you fail the sunder attempt, you don't deal any damage.

Sundering a Carried or Worn Object: You don't use an opposed attack roll to damage a carried or worn object. Instead, just make an attack roll against the object's AC. A carried or worn object's AC is equal to 10 + its size modifier + the Dexterity modifier of the carrying or wearing character. Attacking a carried or worn object provokes an attack of opportunity just as attacking a held object does. To attempt to snatch away an item worn by a defender (such as a cloak or a pair

Missing with a Thrown Weapon

When a thrown weapon misses, roll d8 and refer to this diagram to determine where the weapon lands.

of goggles) rather than damage it, see Disarm, page 155. You can't sunder armor worn by another character.

THROW SPLASH WEAPON

A splash weapon is a ranged weapon that breaks on impact, splashing or scattering its contents over its target and nearby creatures or objects. Most splash weapons consist of liquids, such as acid or holy water, in breakable vials such as glass flasks. (See Special Substances and Items, page 128, for particulars about several different splash weapons.)

To attack with a splash weapon, make a ranged touch attack against the target. Thrown weapons require no weapon proficiency, so you don't take the –4 nonproficiency penalty. A hit deals direct hit damage to the target, and splash damage to all creatures within 5 feet of the target.

You can instead target a specific grid intersection. Treat this as a ranged attack against AC 5. However, if you target a grid intersection, creatures in all adjacent squares are dealt the splash damage, and the direct hit damage is not dealt to any creature. (You can't target a grid intersection occupied by a creature, such as a Large or larger creature; in this case, you're aiming at the creature.)

If you miss the target (whether aiming at a creature or a grid intersection), roll 1d8. This determines the misdirection of the throw, with 1 being straight back at you and 2 through 8 counting clockwise around the grid intersection or target creature. Then, count a number of squares in the indicated direction equal to the range increment of the throw. So, if you miss on a throw out to two range increments and roll a 1 to determine the misdirection of the throw, the splash weapon lands on the intersection that is 2 squares away from the target in the direction toward you. See the accompanying diagram.

After you determine where the weapon landed, it deals splash damage to all creatures in adjacent squares.

TRIP

You can try to trip an opponent as an unarmed melee attack. You can only trip an opponent who is one size category larger than you, the same size, or smaller.

Making a Trip Attack: Make an unarmed melee touch attack against your target. This provokes an attack of opportunity from your target as normal for unarmed attacks.

If your attack succeeds, make a Strength check opposed by the defender's Dexterity or Strength check (whichever ability score has the higher modifier). A combatant gets a +4 bonus for every size category he is larger than Medium or a –4 penalty for every size category he is smaller than Medium. The defender gets a +4 bonus on his check if he has more than two legs or is otherwise more stable than a normal humanoid (such as a dwarf). If you win, you trip the defender. If you lose, the defender may immediately react and make a Strength check opposed by your Dexterity or Strength check to try to trip you.

Avoiding Attacks of Opportunity: If you have the Improved Trip feat, or if you are tripping with a weapon (see below), you don't provoke an attack of opportunity for making a trip attack.

Being Tripped (Prone): A tripped character is prone (see Table 8–6: Armor Class Modifiers). Standing up is a move action.

Tripping a Mounted Opponent: You may make a trip attack against a mounted opponent. The defender may make a Ride check in place of his Dexterity or Strength check. If you succeed, you pull the rider from his mount.

Tripping with a Weapon: Some weapons, including the spiked chain, dire flail, heavy flail, light flail, guisarme, halberd, and whip, can be used to make trip attacks. In this case, you make a melee touch attack with the weapon instead of an unarmed melee touch attack, and you don't provoke an attack of opportunity. If you are tripped during your own trip attempt, you can drop the weapon to avoid being tripped.

TURN OR REBUKE UNDEAD

Good clerics and paladins and some neutral clerics can channel positive energy, which can halt, drive off (rout), or destroy undead. Evil clerics and some neutral clerics can channel negative energy, which can halt, awe (rebuke), control (command), or bolster undead. Regardless of the effect, the general term for the activity is "turning." When attempting to exercise their divine control over these creatures, characters make turning checks.

Turning Checks

Turning undead is a supernatural ability that a character can perform as a standard action. It does not provoke attacks of opportunity. You must present your holy symbol to turn undead. Turning is considered an attack.

Times per Day: You may attempt to turn undead a number of times per day equal to 3 + your Charisma modifier. You can increase this number by taking the Extra Turning feat (page 94).

Range: You turn the closest turnable undead first, and you can't turn undead that are more than 60 feet away or that have total cover relative to you. You don't need line of sight to a target, but you do need line of effect (see page 176).

Turning Check: The first thing you do is roll a turning check to see how powerful an undead creature you can turn. This is a Charisma check (1d20 + your Charisma modifier). Table 8–9: Turning Undead gives you the Hit Dice of the most powerful undead you can affect, relative to your level. On a given turning attempt, you can turn no undead creature whose Hit Dice exceed the result on this table.

Turning Damage: If your roll on Table 8–9: Turning Undead is high enough to let you turn at least some of the undead within 60 feet, roll 2d6 + your cleric level + your Charisma modifier for turning damage. That's how many total Hit Dice of undead you can turn.

If your Charisma score is average or low, it's possible (but unusual) to roll fewer Hit Dice of undead turned than indicated on Table 8–9: Turning Undead. For instance, a 1st-level cleric with an average Charisma score could get a turning check result of 19 (cleric's level +3, or 4 HD), which is enough to turn a wight, but then roll only 3 on his turning damage roll—not enough to turn that wight after all.

You may skip over already turned undead that are still within range, so that you do not waste your turning capacity on them.

Effect and Duration of Turning: Turned undead flee from you by the best and fastest means available to them. They flee for 10 rounds (1 minute). If they cannot flee, they cower (giving any attack rolls against them a +2 bonus). If you approach within 10 feet of them, however, they overcome being turned and act normally. (You can stand within 10 feet without breaking the turning effect—you just can't approach them.) You can attack them with ranged attacks (from at least 10 feet away), and others can attack them in any fashion, without breaking the turning effect.

Destroying Undead: If you have twice as many levels (or more) as the undead have Hit Dice, you destroy any that you would normally turn.

TABLE 8–9: TURNING UNDEAD

Turning Check Result	Most Powerful Undead Affected (Maximum Hit Dice)
0 or lower	Cleric's level – 4
1–3	Cleric's level – 3
4–6	Cleric's level – 2
7–9	Cleric's level – 1
10–12	Cleric's level
13–15	Cleric's level + 1
16–18	Cleric's level + 2
19–21	Cleric's level + 3
22 or higher	Cleric's level + 4

How Turning Works

Jozan, the cleric, and his friends confront seven human zombies led by a wight. Calling on the power of Pelor, Jozan raises his sun disk and attempts to drive the undead away.

First, he makes a turning check (1d20 + Cha modifier) to see what the most powerful undead creature is that he can turn in this action. His result is 9, so he can only turn undead that have fewer Hit Dice than he has levels. Jozan is 3rd level, so on this attempt, he can turn creatures with 2 Hit Dice (such as human zombies) or 1 Hit Die (such as human skeletons) but nothing with more than 2 Hit Dice (such as the wight, which has 4 HD). He does not have twice as many levels as either the zombies or wight, so he will not destroy any of them.

Next, he rolls his turning damage (2d6 + Jozan's level + Cha modifier) to see how many total Hit Dice of creatures he can turn. His result is 11, enough to turn the five closest zombies (accounting for 10 HD out of the maximum of 11). The remaining two zombies and the wight are unaffected.

On Jozan's next turn, he attempts to turn undead again. This time, his turning check result is 21—enough to turn undead creatures of up to 6 HD (his level + 3). His turning damage roll is only 7, though, so he can only turn 7 Hit Dice worth of creatures. He turns the two nearest undead (the remaining 2 HD zombies), but the remaining 3 HD worth of turning isn't enough to turn the 4 HD wight.

Evil Clerics and Undead

Evil clerics channel negative energy to rebuke (awe) or command (control) undead rather than channeling positive energy to turn or destroy them. An evil cleric makes the equivalent of a turning check. Undead that would be turned are rebuked instead, and those that would be destroyed are commanded.

Rebuked: A rebuked undead creature cowers as if in awe (attack rolls against the creature get a +2 bonus). The effect lasts 10 rounds.

Commanded: A commanded undead creature is under the mental control of the evil cleric. The cleric must take a standard action to give mental orders to a commanded undead. At any one time, the cleric may command any number of undead whose total Hit Dice do not exceed his level. He may voluntarily relinquish command on any commanded undead creature or creatures in order to command new ones.

Dispelling Turning: An evil cleric may channel negative energy to dispel a good cleric's turning effect. The evil cleric makes a turning check as if attempting to rebuke the undead. If the turning check result is equal to or greater than the turning check result that the good cleric scored when turning the undead, then the undead are no longer turned. The evil cleric rolls turning damage of 2d6 + cleric level + Charisma modifier to see how many Hit Dice worth of undead he can affect in this way (as if he were rebuking them).

Bolstering Undead: An evil cleric may also bolster undead creatures against turning in advance. He makes a turning check as if attempting to rebuke the undead, but the Hit Dice result on Table 8–9: Turning Undead becomes the undead creatures' effective Hit Dice as far as turning is concerned (provided the result is higher than the creatures' actual Hit Dice). The bolstering lasts 10 rounds. An evil undead cleric can bolster himself in this manner.

Neutral Clerics and Undead

A cleric of neutral alignment can either turn undead but not rebuke them, or rebuke undead but not turn them. See Turn or Rebuke Undead, page 33, for more information.

Even if a cleric is neutral, channeling positive energy is a good act and channeling negative energy is evil.

Paladins and Undead

Beginning at 4th level, paladins can turn undead as if they were clerics of three levels lower than they actually are.

Turning Other Creatures

Some clerics have the ability to turn creatures other than undead. For example, a cleric with the Fire domain can turn or destroy water creatures (as if he were a good cleric turning undead) and rebuke or command fire creatures (as if he were an evil cleric rebuking undead). The turning check result is determined as normal.

Other Uses for Positive or Negative Energy

Positive or negative energy may have uses other than affecting undead. For example, a holy site might be guarded by a magic door that opens for any good cleric who can make a turning check high enough to affect a 3 HD undead and that shatters for an evil cleric who can make a similar check.

TWO-WEAPON FIGHTING

If you wield a second weapon in your off hand, you can get one extra attack per round with that weapon. Fighting in this way is very hard, however, and you suffer a –6 penalty with your regular attack or attacks with your primary hand and a –10 penalty to the attack with your off hand. You can reduce these penalties in two ways:

- If your off-hand weapon is light, the penalties are reduced by 2 each. (An unarmed strike is always considered light.)
- The Two-Weapon Fighting feat lessens the primary hand penalty by 2, and the off-hand penalty by 6.

Table 8–10: Two-Weapon Fighting Penalties summarizes the interaction of all these factors.

TABLE 8–10: TWO-WEAPON FIGHTING PENALTIES

Circumstances	Primary Hand	Off Hand
Normal penalties	–6	–10
Off-hand weapon is light	–4	–8
Two-Weapon Fighting feat	–4	–4
Off-hand weapon is light and Two-Weapon Fighting feat	–2	–2

Double Weapons: You can use a double weapon to make an extra attack with the off-hand end of the weapon as if you were fighting with two weapons. The penalties apply as if the off-hand end of the weapon were a light weapon.

Thrown Weapons: The same rules apply when you throw a weapon from each hand. Treat a dart or shuriken as a light weapon when used in this manner, and treat a bolas, javelin, net, or sling as a one-handed weapon.

SPECIAL INITIATIVE ACTIONS

Here are ways to change when you act during combat by altering your place in the initiative order.

DELAY

By choosing to delay, you take no action and then act normally on whatever initiative count you decide to act. When you delay, you voluntarily reduce your own initiative result for the rest of the combat. When your new, lower initiative count comes up later in the same round, you can act normally. You can specify this new initiative result or just wait until some time later in the round and act then, thus fixing your new initiative count at that point.

Delaying is useful if you need to see what your friends or opponents are going to do before deciding what to do yourself. The price you pay is lost initiative. You never get back the time you spend waiting to see what's going to happen. You can't, however, interrupt anyone else's action (as you can with a readied action).

Initiative Consequences of Delaying: Your initiative result becomes the count on which you took the delayed action. If you come to your next action and have not yet performed an action, you don't get to take a delayed action (though you can delay again). If you take a delayed action in the next round, before your regular turn comes up, your initiative count rises to that new point in the order of battle, and you do not get your regular action that round.

READY

The ready action lets you prepare to take an action later, after your turn is over but before your next one has begun. Readying is a standard action. It does not provoke an attack of opportunity (though the action that you ready might do so).

Readying an Action: You can ready a standard action, a move action, or a free action. To do so, specify the action you will take and the conditions under which you will take it. For example, you might specify that you will shoot an arrow at anyone coming through a nearby doorway. Then, any time before your next action, you may take the readied action in response to that condition. The action occurs just before the action that triggers it. If the triggered action is part of another character's activities, you interrupt the other character. Assuming he is still capable of doing so, he continues his actions once you complete your readied action.

Your initiative result changes. For the rest of the encounter, your initiative result is the count on which you took the readied action, and you act immediately ahead of the character whose action triggered your readied action.

You can take a 5-foot step as part of your readied action, but only if you don't otherwise move any distance during the round. For instance, if you move up to an open door and then ready an action to swing your sword at whatever comes near, you can't take a 5-foot step along with the readied action (since you've already moved in this round).

Initiative Consequences of Readying: Your initiative result becomes the count on which you took the readied action. If you come to your next action and have not yet performed your readied action, you don't get to take the readied action (though you can ready the same action again). If you take your readied action in the next round, before your regular turn comes up, your initiative count rises to that new point in the order of battle, and you do not get your regular action that round.

Distracting Spellcasters: You can ready an attack against a spellcaster with the trigger "if she starts casting a spell." If you damage the spellcaster, she may lose the spell she was trying to cast (as determined by her Concentration check result).

Readying to Counterspell: You may ready a counterspell against a spellcaster (often with the trigger "if she starts casting a spell"). In this case, when the spellcaster starts a spell, you get a chance to identify it with a Spellcraft check (DC 15 + spell level). If you do, and if you can cast that same spell (are able to cast it and have it prepared, if you prepare spells), you can cast the spell as a counterspell and automatically ruin the other spellcaster's spell. Counterspelling works even if one spell is divine and the other arcane.

A spellcaster can use *dispel magic* (page 223) to counterspell another spellcaster, but it doesn't always work.

Readying a Weapon against a Charge: You can ready certain piercing weapons, setting them to receive charges (see Table 7–5: Weapons, page 116). A readied weapon of this type deals double damage if you score a hit with it against a charging character.

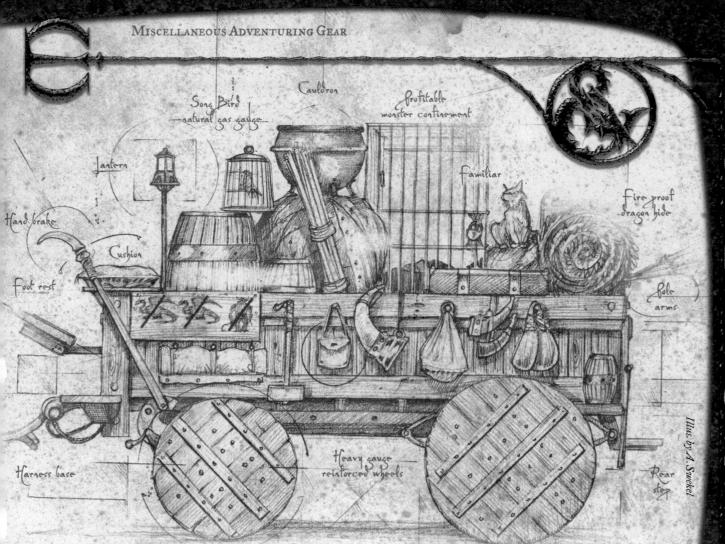

Song Bird
–natural gas gauge

Cauldron

Profitable
monster confinement

Lantern

Familiar

Hand brake

Fire proof
dragon hide

Cushion

Foot rest

Pole
arms

Heavy gauge
reinforced wheels

Harness base

Rear
step

ADVENTURING

CHAPTER NINE

ourneying from place to place is as much a part of the game as combat or magic. This chapter covers carrying capacity and encumbrance, movement overland and through adventure sites, exploration, and treasure.

CARRYING CAPACITY

Encumbrance rules determine how much a character's armor and equipment slow him or her down. Encumbrance comes in two parts: encumbrance by armor and encumbrance by total weight.

Encumbrance by Armor: A character's armor (as described on Table 7–6: Armor and Shields, page 123) defines his or her maximum Dexterity bonus to AC, armor check penalty, speed, and running speed. Unless your character is weak or carrying a lot of gear, that's all you need to know. The extra gear your character carries, such as weapons and rope, won't slow him or her down any more than the armor already does.

If your character is weak or carrying a lot of gear, however, then you'll need to calculate encumbrance by weight. Doing so is most important when your character is trying to carry some heavy object, such as a treasure chest.

Weight: If you want to determine whether your character's gear is heavy enough to slow him or her down more than the armor already does, total the weight of all the character's items, including armor, weapons, and gear. Compare this total to the character's Strength on Table 9–1: Carrying Capacity. Depending on how the weight compares to the character's carrying capacity, he or she may be carrying a light, medium, or heavy load. Like armor, a character's load affects his or her maximum Dexterity bonus to AC, carries a check penalty (which works like an armor check penalty), reduces the character's speed, and affects how fast the character can run, as shown on Table 9–2: Carrying Loads. A medium or heavy load counts as medium or heavy armor for the purpose of abilities or skills that are restricted by armor. Carrying a light load does not encumber a character.

If your character is wearing armor, use the worse figure (from armor or from load) for each category. Do not stack the penalties.

For example, Tordek is wearing scale mail. As shown on Table 7–6: Armor and Shields, this armor cuts his maximum Dex bonus to AC to +3 and gives him a –4 armor check penalty (and would cut his speed to 15 feet, were he not a dwarf and thus able to move normally even when encumbered by armor or a load). The total weight of his gear, including armor, is 71-1/2 pounds. Since Tordek has a Strength of 15, his maximum carrying capacity, or maximum load, is 200 pounds. A medium load for him is 67 pounds or more, and a heavy load is 134 pounds or more, so he is carrying a medium load. Looking at the medium load line on Table 9–2: Carrying Loads, his player sees that these figures are all equal to or less than than the penalties that Tordek is already incurring for wearing scale mail, so he takes no extra penalties.

Mialee has a Strength of 10, and she's carrying 28 pounds of gear. Her light load limit is 33 pounds, so she's carrying a light load (no penalties). She finds 500 gold pieces (weighing 10 pounds) and adds them to her load, so now she's carrying a medium load. Doing so reduces her speed from 30 feet to 20 feet, gives her a –3 check penalty, and sets her maximum Dexterity bonus to AC at +3 (which is okay with her, since that's her Dexterity bonus anyway).

TABLE 9–1: CARRYING CAPACITY

Strength Score	Light Load	Medium Load	Heavy Load
1	3 lb. or less	4–6 lb.	7–10 lb.
2	6 lb. or less	7–13 lb.	14–20 lb.
3	10 lb. or less	11–20 lb.	21–30 lb.
4	13 lb. or less	14–26 lb.	27–40 lb.
5	16 lb. or less	17–33 lb.	34–50 lb.
6	20 lb. or less	21–40 lb.	41–60 lb.
7	23 lb. or less	24–46 lb.	47–70 lb.
8	26 lb. or less	27–53 lb.	54–80 lb.
9	30 lb. or less	31–60 lb.	61–90 lb.
10	33 lb. or less	34–66 lb.	67–100 lb.
11	38 lb. or less	39–76 lb.	77–115 lb.
12	43 lb. or less	44–86 lb.	87–130 lb.
13	50 lb. or less	51–100 lb.	101–150 lb.
14	58 lb. or less	59–116 lb.	117–175 lb.
15	66 lb. or less	67–133 lb.	134–200 lb.
16	76 lb. or less	77–153 lb.	154–230 lb.
17	86 lb. or less	87–173 lb.	174–260 lb.
18	100 lb. or less	101–200 lb.	201–300 lb.
19	116 lb. or less	117–233 lb.	234–350 lb.
20	133 lb. or less	134–266 lb.	267–400 lb.
21	153 lb. or less	154–306 lb.	307–460 lb.
22	173 lb. or less	174–346 lb.	347–520 lb.
23	200 lb. or less	201–400 lb.	401–600 lb.
24	233 lb. or less	234–466 lb.	467–700 lb.
25	266 lb. or less	267–533 lb.	534–800 lb.
26	306 lb. or less	307–613 lb.	614–920 lb.
27	346 lb. or less	347–693 lb.	694–1,040 lb.
28	400 lb. or less	401–800 lb.	801–1,200 lb.
29	466 lb. or less	467–933 lb.	934–1,400 lb.
+10	×4	×4	×4

Then Mialee is knocked unconscious in a fight, and Tordek wants to carry her out of the dungeon. She weighs 104 pounds, and her gear weighs 28 pounds (or 38 pounds with the gold), so Tordek can't quite manage to carry her and her gear, because doing so would put him over his 200-pound maximum load. Fortunately, their companion Jozan is able to carry her gear and the gold, so all Tordek has to worry about is Mialee herself. Tordek hoists Mialee onto his shoulders, and now the dwarf is carrying 175-1/2 pounds. He can manage it, but it's a heavy load. His maximum Dexterity bonus to AC drops to +1, his check penalty worsens from –4 (the armor check penalty for scale mail) to –6 (the check penalty for a heavy load), and now he runs at ×3 speed instead of ×4.

Lifting and Dragging: A character can lift as much as his or her maximum load over his or her head.

A character can lift as much as double his or her maximum load off the ground, but he or she can only stagger around with it. While overloaded in this way, the character loses any Dexterity bonus to AC and can move only 5 feet per round (as a full-round action).

A character can generally push or drag along the ground as much as five times his or her maximum load. Favorable conditions (such as being on smooth ground or dragging a slick object) can double these numbers, and bad circumstances (such as being on broken ground or pushing an object that snags) can reduce them to one-half or less.

Bigger and Smaller Creatures: The figures on Table 9–1: Carrying Capacity are for Medium bipedal creatures. A larger bipedal creature can carry more weight depending on its size category, as follows: Large ×2, Huge ×4, Gargantuan ×8, Colossal ×16. A smaller creature can carry less weight depending on its size category, as follows: Small ×3/4, Tiny ×1/2, Diminutive ×1/4, Fine ×1/8. Thus, a human with a Strength score magically boosted to equal that of a giant would still have a harder time lifting, say, a horse or a boulder than a giant would.

TABLE 9–2: CARRYING LOADS

Load	Max Dex	Check Penalty	Speed (30 ft.)	(20 ft.)	Run
Medium	+3	–3	20 ft.	15 ft.	×4
Heavy	+1	–6	20 ft.	15 ft.	×3

Quadrupeds, such as horses, can carry heavier loads than characters can. Instead of the multipliers given above, multiply the value corresponding to the creature's Strength score from Table 9–1 by the appropriate modifier, as follows: Fine ×1/4, Diminutive ×1/2, Tiny ×3/4, Small ×1, Medium ×1-1/2, Large ×3, Huge ×6, Gargantuan ×12, Colossal ×24.

For example, Mialee, an elf with 10 Strength, can carry as much as 100 pounds. Lidda, a halfling with 10 Strength, can carry only 75 pounds. A donkey, a Medium animal with 10 Strength, can carry as much as 150 pounds.

Tremendous Strength: For Strength scores not shown on Table 9–1, find the Strength score between 20 and 29 that has the same number in the "ones" digit as the creature's Strength score does. Multiply the figures by 4 if the creature's Strength is in the 30s, 16 if it's in the 40s, 64 if it's in the 50s, and so on. For example, a cloud giant with a 35 Strength can carry four times what a creature with a 25 Strength can carry, or 3,200 pounds × 4 because the cloud giant is Huge, for a total of 12,800 pounds.

MOVEMENT

Characters spend a lot of time getting from one place to another. A character who needs to reach the evil tower might choose to walk along the road, hire a boat to row along the river, or cut cross-country on horseback. In addition, a character can climb trees to get a better look at his surroundings, scale mountains, or ford streams.

The DM moderates the pace of a game session, so he or she determines when movement is so important that it's worth measuring. During casual scenes, you usually won't have to worry about movement rates. If your character has come to a new city and takes a stroll to get a feel for the place, no one needs to know exactly how many rounds or minutes the circuit takes.

There are three movement scales in the game, as follows.
- Tactical, for combat, measured in feet (or squares) per round.

TABLE 9–3: MOVEMENT AND DISTANCE

	Speed			
	15 feet	20 feet	30 feet	40 feet
One Round (Tactical)[1]				
Walk	15 ft.	20 ft.	30 ft.	40 ft.
Hustle	30 ft.	40 ft.	60 ft.	80 ft.
Run (×3)	45 ft.	60 ft.	90 ft.	120 ft.
Run (×4)	60 ft.	80 ft.	120 ft.	160 ft.
One Minute (Local)				
Walk	150 ft.	200 ft.	300 ft.	400 ft.
Hustle	300 ft.	400 ft.	600 ft.	800 ft.
Run (×3)	450 ft.	600 ft.	900 ft.	1,200 ft.
Run (×4)	600 ft.	800 ft.	1,200 ft.	1,600 ft.
One Hour (Overland)				
Walk	1-1/2 miles	2 miles	3 miles	4 miles
Hustle	3 miles	4 miles	6 miles	8 miles
Run	—	—	—	—
One Day (Overland)				
Walk	12 miles	16 miles	24 miles	32 miles
Hustle	—	—	—	—
Run	—	—	—	—

1 Tactical movement is often measured in squares on the battle grid (1 square = 5 feet) rather than feet. See page 147 for more information on tactical movement in combat.

TABLE 9–4: HAMPERED MOVEMENT

Condition	Example	Additional Movement Cost
Difficult terrain	Rubble, undergrowth, steep slope, ice, cracked and pitted surface, uneven floor	×2
Obstacle[1]	Low wall, deadfall, broken pillar	×2
Poor visibility	Darkness or fog	×2
Impassable	Floor-to-ceiling wall, closed door, blocked passage	—

1 May require a skill check

- Local, for exploring an area, measured in feet per minute.
- Overland, for getting from place to place, measured in miles per hour or miles per day.

Modes of Movement: While moving at the different movement scales, creatures generally walk, hustle, or run.

Walk: A walk represents unhurried but purposeful movement at 3 miles per hour for an unencumbered human.

Hustle: A hustle is a jog at about 6 miles per hour for an unencumbered human. A character moving his or her speed twice in a single round, or moving that speed in the same round that he or she performs a standard action or another move action is hustling when he or she moves.

Run (×3): Moving three times speed is a running pace for a character in heavy armor. It represents about 9 miles per hour for a human in full plate.

Run (×4): Moving four times speed is a running pace for a character in light, medium, or no armor. It represents about 12 miles per hour for an unencumbered human, or 8 miles per hour for a human in chainmail.

TACTICAL MOVEMENT

Use tactical movement for combat, as detailed on page 147. Characters generally don't walk during combat—they hustle or run. A character who moves his or her speed and takes some action, such as attacking or casting a spell, is hustling for about half the round and doing something else the other half.

Hampered Movement: Difficult terrain, obstacles, or poor visibility can hamper movement. When movement is hampered, each square moved into usually counts as two squares, effectively reducing the distance that a character can cover in a move. For example, a character moving through difficult terrain (such as undergrowth) pays 2 squares of movement per square moved into (double the normal cost).

If more than one condition applies, multiply together all additional costs that apply. (This is a specific exception to the normal rule for doubling; see page 304.) For instance, a character moving through difficult terrain in darkness would pay 4 squares of movement per square moved into (double cost times double cost is quadruple cost).

In some situations, your movement may be so hampered that you don't have sufficient speed even to move 5 feet (1 square). In such a case, you may use a full-round action to move 5 feet (1 square) in any direction, even diagonally. Even though this looks like a 5-foot step, it's not, and thus it provokes attacks of opportunity normally. (You can't take advantage of this rule to move through impassable terrain or to move when all movement is prohibited to you, such as while paralyzed.)

You can't run or charge through any square that would hamper your movement.

LOCAL MOVEMENT

Characters exploring an area use local movement, measured in feet per minute.

Walk: A character can walk without a problem on the local scale.

Hustle: A character can hustle without a problem on the local scale. See Overland Movement, below, for movement measured in miles per hour.

Run: A character with a Constitution score of 9 or higher can run for a minute without a problem. Generally, a character can run for a minute or two before having to rest for a minute (see Run, page 144).

Adventurers prepare for their next challenge.

Illus. by J. Jarvis

TABLE 9–5: TERRAIN AND OVERLAND MOVEMENT

Terrain	Highway	Road or Trail	Trackless
Desert, sandy	×1	×1/2	×1/2
Forest	×1	×1	×1/2
Hills	×1	×3/4	×1/2
Jungle	×1	×3/4	×1/4
Moor	×1	×1	×3/4
Mountains	×3/4	×3/4	×1/2
Plains	×1	×1	×3/4
Swamp	×1	×3/4	×1/2
Tundra, frozen	×1	×3/4	×3/4

TABLE 9–6: MOUNTS AND VEHICLES

Mount/Vehicle	Per Hour	Per Day
Mount (carrying load)		
Light horse or light warhorse	6 miles	48 miles
Light horse (151–450 lb.)[1]	4 miles	32 miles
Light warhorse (231–690 lb.)[1]	4 miles	32 miles
Heavy horse or heavy warhorse	5 miles	40 miles
Heavy horse (201–600 lb.)[1]	3-1/2 miles	28 miles
Heavy warhorse (301–900 lb.)[1]	3-1/2 miles	28 miles
Pony or warpony	4 miles	32 miles
Pony (76–225 lb.)[1]	3 miles	24 miles
Warpony (101–300 lb.)[1]	3 miles	24 miles
Donkey or mule	3 miles	24 miles
Donkey (51–150 lb.)[1]	2 miles	16 miles
Mule (231–690 lb.)[1]	2 miles	16 miles
Dog, riding	4 miles	32 miles
Dog, riding (101–300 lb.)[1]	3 miles	24 miles
Cart or wagon	2 miles	16 miles
Ship		
Raft or barge (poled or towed)[2]	1/2 mile	5 miles
Keelboat (rowed)[2]	1 mile	10 miles
Rowboat (rowed)[2]	1-1/2 miles	15 miles
Sailing ship (sailed)	2 miles	48 miles
Warship (sailed and rowed)	2-1/2 miles	60 miles
Longship (sailed and rowed)	3 miles	72 miles
Galley (rowed and sailed)	4 miles	96 miles

1 Quadrupeds, such as horses, can carry heavier loads than characters can. See Carrying Capacity, above, for more information.

2 Rafts, barges, keelboats, and rowboats are used on lakes and rivers. If going downstream, add the speed of the current (typically 3 miles per hour) to the speed of the vehicle. In addition to 10 hours of being rowed, the vehicle can also float an additional 14 hours, if someone can guide it, so add an additional 42 miles to the daily distance traveled. These vehicles can't be rowed against any significant current, but they can be pulled upstream by draft animals on the shores.

OVERLAND MOVEMENT

Characters covering long distances cross-country use overland movement. Overland movement is measured in miles per hour or miles per day. A day represents 8 hours of actual travel time. For rowed watercraft, a day represents 10 hours of rowing. For a sailing ship, it represents 24 hours.

Walk: A character can walk 8 hours in a day of travel without a problem. Walking for longer than that can wear him or her out (see Forced March, below).

Hustle: A character can hustle for 1 hour without a problem. Hustling for a second hour in between sleep cycles deals 1 point of nonlethal damage, and each additional hour deals twice the damage taken during the previous hour of hustling. A character who takes any nonlethal damage from hustling becomes fatigued. A fatigued character can't run or charge and takes a penalty of –2 to Strength and Dexterity. Eliminating the nonlethal damage also eliminates the fatigue.

Run: A character can't run for an extended period of time. Attempts to run and rest in cycles effectively work out to a hustle.

Terrain: The terrain through which a character travels affects how much distance he or she can cover in an hour or a day (see Table 9–5: Terrain and Overland Movement). Travel is quickest on a highway, not quite as fast on a road or trail, and slowest through trackless terrain. A highway is a straight, major, paved road. A road is typically a dirt track. A trail is like a road, except that it allows only single-file travel and does not benefit a party traveling with vehicles. Trackless terrain is a wild area with no paths.

Forced March: In a day of normal walking, a character walks for 8 hours. The rest of the daylight time is spent making and breaking camp, resting, and eating.

A character can walk for more than 8 hours in a day by making a forced march. For each hour of marching beyond 8 hours, a Constitution check (DC 10, +2 per extra hour) is required. If the check fails, the character takes 1d6 points of nonlethal damage. A character who takes any nonlethal damage from a forced march becomes fatigued. Eliminating the nonlethal damage also eliminates the fatigue. It's possible for a character to march into unconsciousness by pushing himself too hard.

Mounted Movement: A mount bearing a rider can move at a hustle. The damage it takes when doing so, however, is lethal damage, not nonlethal damage. The creature can also be ridden in a forced march, but its Constitution checks automatically fail, and, again, the damage it takes is lethal damage. Mounts also become fatigued when they take any damage from hustling or forced marches.

See Table 9–6: Mounts and Vehicles for mounted speeds and speeds for vehicles pulled by draft animals.

Waterborne Movement: See Table 9–6: Mounts and Vehicles for speeds for water vehicles.

EXPLORATION

Adventurers spend time exploring dark caverns, cursed ruins, catacombs, and other dangerous and forbidding areas. A little careful forethought can help them in their adventures.

PREPARATIONS

Characters should have the supplies they need for their adventures: arrows, food, water, torches, bedrolls, or whatever is needed for the task at hand. Rope, chains, crowbars, and other tools can come in handy, too. Characters should have ranged weapons, if possible, for combats in which they can't close with the enemy (or don't want to). Horses are useful for overland journeys, while sure-footed pack donkeys and mules can be handy for exploring ruins and dungeons.

VISION AND LIGHT

Characters need a way to see in the dark, dangerous places where they often find adventures. Dwarves and half-orcs have darkvision, but everyone else needs light to see by. Typically, adventurers bring along torches or lanterns, and spellcasters have spells that can create light. See Table 9–7: Light Sources and Illumination for the radius that a light source illuminates and how long it lasts.

In an area of bright light, all characters can see clearly. A creature can't hide in an area of bright light unless it is invisible or has cover.

In an area of shadowy illumination, a character can see dimly. Creatures within this area have concealment (see page 152) relative to that character. A creature in an area of shadowy illumination can make a Hide check to conceal itself (see page 76).

In areas of darkness, creatures without darkvision are effectively blinded. In addition to the obvious effects, a blinded creature has a 50% miss chance in combat (all opponents have

TABLE 9–7: LIGHT SOURCES AND ILLUMINATION

Object	Bright	Shadowy	Duration
Candle	n/a[1]	5 ft.	1 hr.
Everburning torch	20 ft.	40 ft.	Permanent
Lamp, common	15 ft.	30 ft.	6 hr./pint
Lantern, bullseye[2]	60-ft. cone	120-ft. cone	6 hr./pint
Lantern, hooded	30 ft.	60 ft.	6 hr./pint
Sunrod	30 ft.	60 ft.	6 hr.
Torch	20 ft.	40 ft.	1 hr.

Spell	Bright	Shadowy	Duration
Continual flame	20 ft.	40 ft.	Permanent
Dancing lights (torches)	20 ft. (each)	40 ft. (each)	1 min.
Daylight	60 ft.	120 ft.	30 min.
Light	20 ft.	40 ft.	10 min.

1 A candle does not provide bright illumination, only shadowy illumination.

2 A bullseye lantern illuminates a cone, not a radius.

total concealment), loses any Dexterity bonus to AC, takes a –2 penalty to AC, moves at half speed, and takes a –4 penalty on Search checks and most Strength and Dexterity-based skill checks.

Characters with low-light vision (elves, gnomes, and half-elves) can see objects twice as far away as the given radius. Double the effective radius of bright light and of shadowy illumination for such characters. For example, a torch provides bright illumination to a radius of 40 feet (rather than 20 feet) for a character with low-light vision, and it provides shadowy illumination to a radius of 80 feet (rather than 40 feet).

Characters with darkvision (dwarves and half-orcs) can see lit areas normally as well as dark areas within 60 feet. A creature can't hide within 60 feet of a character with darkvision unless it is invisible or has cover.

BREAKING AND ENTERING

There inevitably comes a time when a character must break something, whether it's a door, a chain, or a chest full of treasure.

When attempting to break an object, you have two choices: smash it with a weapon or break it with sheer strength.

Smashing an Object

Smashing a weapon or shield with a slashing or bludgeoning weapon is accomplished by the sunder special attack (see Sunder, page 158). Smashing an object is a lot like sundering a weapon or shield, except that your attack roll is opposed by the object's AC. Generally, you can smash an object only with a bludgeoning or slashing weapon.

Armor Class: Objects are easier to hit than creatures because they usually don't move, but many are tough enough to shrug off some damage from each blow. An object's Armor Class is equal to 10 + its size modifier + its Dexterity modifier. An inanimate object has not only a Dexterity of 0 (–5 penalty to AC), but also an additional –2 penalty to its AC. Furthermore, if you take a full-round action to line up a shot, you get an automatic hit with a melee weapon and a +5 bonus on attack rolls with a ranged weapon.

Hardness: Each object has hardness—a number that represents how well it resists damage. Whenever an object takes damage, subtract its hardness from the damage. Only damage in excess of its hardness is deducted from the object's hit points (see Table 9–8: Common Armor, Weapon, and Shield Hardness and Hit Points; Table 9–9: Substance Hardness and Hit Points; and Table 9–11: Object Hardness and Hit Points).

Hit Points: An object's hit point total depends on what it is made of and how big it is (see Table 9–8, Table 9–9, and Table 9–11). When an object's hit points reach 0, it's ruined.

Very large objects have separate hit point totals for different sections. For example, you can attack and ruin a wagon wheel without destroying the whole wagon.

Energy Attacks: Acid and sonic attacks deal damage to most objects just as they do to creatures; roll damage and apply it normally after a successful hit. Electricity and fire attacks deal half damage to most objects; divide the damage dealt by 2 before applying the hardness. Cold attacks deal one-quarter damage to most objects; divide the damage dealt by 4 before applying the hardness.

Ranged Weapon Damage: Objects take half damage from ranged weapons (unless the weapon is a siege engine or something similar). Divide the damage dealt by 2 before applying the object's hardness.

Ineffective Weapons: The DM may determine that certain weapons just can't effectively deal damage to certain objects. For example, you may have a hard time chopping down a door by shooting arrows at it or cutting a rope with a club.

Immunities: Objects are immune to nonlethal damage and to critical hits. Even animated objects, which are otherwise considered creatures, have these immunities because they are constructs.

Magic Armor, Shields, and Weapons: Each +1 of enhancement bonus adds 2 to the hardness of armor, a weapon, or a shield and +10 to the item's hit points. For example, a +1 longsword has hardness 12 and 15 hp, while a +3 heavy steel shield has hardness 16 and 50 hp.

Vulnerability to Certain Attacks: The DM may rule that certain attacks are especially successful against some objects. For example, it's easy to light a curtain on fire, chop down a tree with an ax, or rip up a scroll. In such cases, attacks deal double their normal damage and may (at the DM's discretion) ignore the object's hardness.

Damaged Objects: A damaged object remains fully functional until the item's hit points are reduced to 0, at which point it is destroyed. For instance, the wielder of a damaged weapon takes no penalty due to the weapon's damage, and damaged armor and shields still

Illus. by S. Wood

Eberk

TABLE 9–8: COMMON ARMOR, WEAPON, AND SHIELD HARDNESS AND HIT POINTS

Weapon or Shield	Example	Hardness	HP[1]
Light blade	Short sword	10	2
One-handed blade	Longsword	10	5
Two-handed blade	Greatsword	10	10
Light metal-hafted weapon	Light mace	10	10
One-handed metal-hafted weapon	Heavy mace	10	20
Light hafted weapon	Handaxe	5	2
One-handed hafted weapon	Battleaxe	5	5
Two-handed hafted weapon	Greataxe	5	10
Projectile weapon	Crossbow	5	5
Armor	—	special[2]	armor bonus × 5
Buckler	—	10	5
Light wooden shield	—	5	7
Heavy wooden shield	—	5	15
Light steel shield	—	10	10
Heavy steel shield	—	10	20
Tower shield	—	5	20

1 The hp value given is for Medium armor, weapons, and shields. Divide by 2 for each size category of the item smaller than Medium, or multiply it by 2 for each size category larger than Medium.

2 Varies by material; see Table 9–9.

TABLE 9–9: SUBSTANCE HARDNESS AND HIT POINTS

Substance	Hardness	Hit Points
Paper or cloth	0	2/inch of thickness
Rope	0	2/inch of thickness
Glass	1	1/inch of thickness
Ice	0	3/inch of thickness
Leather or hide	2	5/inch of thickness
Wood	5	10/inch of thickness
Stone	8	15/inch of thickness
Iron or steel	10	30/inch of thickness
Mithral	15	30/inch of thickness
Adamantine	20	40/inch of thickness

provide their full normal bonus to AC. Damaged (but not destroyed) objects can be repaired with the Craft skill (see page 70).

Saving Throws: Nonmagical, unattended items never make saving throws. They are considered to have failed their saving throws, so they always are affected by (for instance) a *disintegrate*

TABLE 9–10: SIZE AND ARMOR CLASS OF OBJECTS

Size (Example)	AC Modifier	Size (Example)	AC Modifier
Colossal (broad side of a barn)	–8	Medium (barrel)	+0
		Small (chair)	+1
Gargantuan (narrow side of a barn)	–4	Tiny (book)	+2
		Diminutive (scroll)	+4
Huge (wagon)	–2	Fine (potion)	+8
Large (big door)	–1		

TABLE 9–11: OBJECT HARDNESS AND HIT POINTS

Object	Hardness	Hit Points	Break DC
Rope (1 inch diam.)	0	2	23
Simple wooden door	5	10	13
Small chest	5	1	17
Good wooden door	5	15	18
Treasure chest	5	15	23
Strong wooden door	5	20	23
Masonry wall (1 ft. thick)	8	90	35
Hewn stone (3 ft. thick)	8	540	50
Chain	10	5	26
Manacles	10	10	26
Masterwork manacles	10	10	28
Iron door (2 in. thick)	10	60	28

TABLE 9–12: DCs TO BREAK OR BURST ITEMS

Strength Check to:	DC
Break down simple door	13
Break down good door	18
Break down strong door	23
Burst rope bonds	23
Bend iron bars	24
Break down barred door	25
Burst chain bonds	26
Break down iron door	28

Condition	DC Adjustment[1]
Hold portal	+5
Arcane lock	+10

1 If both apply, use the larger number.

spell. An item attended by a character (being grasped, touched, or worn) makes saving throws as the character (that is, using the character's saving throw bonus).

HOW PLAYERS CAN HELP

Here are a few ways in which you can help the game go more smoothly.

Mapping: Someone should keep a map of places you explore so that you know where you've been and where you have yet to explore. The responsibility for mapping can be rotated from person to person, if more than one player likes to do this sort of thing, but as a rule the same person should be the mapper throughout a single playing session.

A map is most useful and most important when the characters are in a dungeon setting—an environment with lots of corridors, doors, and rooms that would be almost impossible to navigate through without a record of what parts the characters have already explored.

To make a map, you start with a blank sheet of paper (graph paper is best) and draw the floor plan of the dungeon as you and your group discover it and the Dungeon Master describes what you're seeing. For example, when the characters come to a new, empty room, the DM might say, "The door you have opened leads east into a room 25 feet wide and 30 feet deep. The door is in the middle of the room's west wall, and you can see two other doors: one in the north wall near the corner with the east wall, and one in the east wall about 5 feet south of the middle." Or, if it's easier for you to visualize, the DM

might express the information this way: "From the north edge of the door, the wall goes two squares north, six squares east, five squares south, six squares west, and then north back to the door. There's a door on the sixth square of the north wall and on the fourth square of the east wall."

Party Notes: It often pays to keep notes: names of NPCs the heroes have met, treasure the group has won, secrets the characters have learned, and so forth. The Dungeon Master might keep track of all this information for his or her own benefit, but even so it can be handy for you to jot down facts that might be needed later—at the least, doing this prevents you from having to ask the Dungeon Master, "What was the name of that old man we met in the woods last week?"

Character Notes: You should keep track of hit points, spells, and other characteristics about your character that change during an adventure on scratch paper. Between playing sessions, you might decide to write some of this information directly on your character sheet—but don't worry about updating the sheet constantly. For instance, it would be tedious (and could make a mess of the sheet) if you erased your character's current hit points and wrote in a new number every time he or she took damage.

Magic items always get saving throws. A magic item's Fortitude, Reflex, and Will save bonuses are equal to 2 + one-half its caster level. An attended magic item either makes saving throws as its owner or uses its own saving throw bonus, whichever is better. (Caster levels of magic items are covered in the *Dungeon Master's Guide*.)

Example of Breaking an Object: Lidda, a rogue, can't pick the lock on the big treasure chest that Mialee, the elf, just found behind a secret door, so Krusk, the barbarian, volunteers to open it in a more straightforward manner. He chops at it with his greataxe, dealing 10 points of damage. The chest, made of wood, has hardness 5, so the chest takes only 5 points of damage from his attack. The wood is 1 inch thick, so it had 10 hit points. Now it has 5. Krusk has gouged the wood but not yet broken the chest open. On his second attack, he deals 4 points of damage. That's lower than the chest's hardness, so the chest takes no damage at all—a glancing blow. His third blow, however, deals 12 points of damage (which means the chest takes 7), and the chest breaks open.

Animated Objects: Animated objects (see the *Monster Manual*) count as creatures for purposes of determining their Armor Class (do not treat them as inanimate objects).

Breaking Items

When a character tries to break something with sudden force rather than by dealing damage, use a Strength check (rather than an attack roll and damage roll, as with the sunder special attack) to see whether he or she succeeds. The DC depends more on the construction of the item than on the material. For instance, an iron door with a weak lock can be forced open much more easily than it can be hacked down.

If an item has lost half or more of its hit points, the DC to break it drops by 2.

Larger and smaller creatures get size bonuses and size penalties on Strength checks to break open doors as follows: Fine −16, Diminutive −12, Tiny −8, Small −4, Large +4, Huge +8, Gargantuan +12, Colossal +16.

A crowbar (page 126) or portable ram (page 127) improves a character's chance of breaking open a door.

MARCHING ORDER

The characters in a party need to decide what their marching order is. Marching order is the relative position of the characters to each other while they are moving (who is in front of or next to whom). Arrange your miniature figures on the battle grid to represent the PCs' relative locations. You can change the marching order as the party enters different areas, as characters get wounded, or at other times for any reason.

In a marching order, the sturdiest characters, such as barbarians, fighters, and paladins, usually go in front. Wizards, sorcerers, and bards often find a place in the middle or back of the party, where they are protected from direct attack. Clerics and druids are good choices for rear guard. They're tough enough to withstand a rear attack, and they're important enough as healers that it's risky to put them in the front line. Rogues, rangers, and monks might serve as stealthy scouts, though they have to be careful if they're away from the safety of the party.

If the characters are not far apart, they can protect each other, but they're more vulnerable to many spells when they cluster together, so sometimes it pays to spread out a little.

TREASURE

When characters undertake adventures, they usually end up with some amount of silver, gold, gems, or other treasure. These rewards might be ancient treasures that they have unearthed, the hoards of the villains they have conquered, or pay from a patron who hired them to go on the adventure.

Splitting Treasure: Split treasure evenly among the characters who participated. Some characters may be of higher level than others, or some might happen to have done more on a particular adventure than others did, but the simplest, fastest, and best policy is to split up treasure evenly.

Lidda savors the rewards of opening the treasure chest.

Illus. by J. Foster

Illus. by S. Wood

Gold piece
[exact size]

Special Items: While gems can be cashed in for gold pieces and the coins split evenly among adventurers, some treasures can't be split up so easily. Magic items, for instance, can be sold, but only for half of what they would cost to buy, so it's usually better for characters to keep them. When a character gets a magic item, count half its cost against his or her share of the treasure. For instance, if Jozan, Lidda, Mialee, and Tordek split a treasure of 5,000 gp and a *+1 large steel shield*, the group would count the magic shield as worth 500 gp, roughly half the price someone would have to pay to buy one. Since the treasure is worth 5,500 gp altogether, three characters would each get 1,375 gp, and the fourth character (probably Tordek or Jozan) would get the shield (valued at 500 gp) plus 875 gp in coin.

If more than one character wants a single item, those interested can bid for it. For example, Jozan and Tordek both want the shield, so they bid over how much they're each willing to "pay" for it. Tordek wins the bid at 800 gp. That means the total treasure is 5,800 gp. Mialee, Jozan, and Lidda each get 1,450 gp, and Tordek gets the shield (800 gp) plus 650 gp.

A character can bid only as much as his or her share of the treasure would amount to, unless he or she has extra gold pieces or treasure to back up the bid. For example, if Tordek had no other treasure from earlier adventures, the most he could bid for the magic shield is 1,250 gp—he would get the shield, and the other three characters would split the 5,000 gp.

If no one is willing to take a special item, the party members should sell it (for half its cost, as listed in the *Dungeon Master's Guide*, if they can find a buyer) and split the gold evenly.

Kerwyn

Costs: Sometimes characters incur costs on adventures. A character turned to stone by a basilisk may need a *break enchantment* spell, and it costs at least 450 gp to pay a cleric to cast that spell. (See Table 7–8: Goods and Services, page 128. A cleric must be at least 9th level to cast *break enchantment*, which is a 5th-level spell.) The default policy is to pay these costs out of the treasure found on the adventure, as a sort of "adventurer's insurance," and then split whatever's left.

Party Fund: The party may also want to have a pool of money that its members can use to buy things that benefit the whole group, such as *potions of healing* or holy water.

Amassing Wealth: When you and your friends have split up the treasure among the characters, record your character's share on your character sheet. Soon, he or she will have enough gold to buy better weapons and equipment, even magic items.

OTHER REWARDS

The other rewards that characters can earn, and there are many, depend on the characters' actions and the style of campaign that the DM is running. They bear mention, but the rules cannot define them. These rewards develop naturally in the campaign.

REPUTATION

You can't put it in the bank, but many characters enjoy and even pursue fame and notoriety. Someone who seeks a reputation should wear distinctive clothes or armor, should treat bards well, and might even want to invent a personal symbol for signet rings, surcoats, banners, and other forms of display.

FOLLOWERS

When others hear of the characters, they may offer their services as followers. Followers may be apprentices, admirers, henchmen, students, or sidekicks.

LAND

A character (or a party) might gain land through force of arms or be granted a tract of land by a powerful figure. Land brings in revenue appropriate to its type (such as taxes on harvests in arable land), and it provides a place for a character (or party) to build a stronghold of some kind. In addition to being a base and a safe place, a stronghold can serve as a church, a monastery, a wizards' school, or fulfill some other purpose, as the master of the stronghold wishes.

TITLES AND HONORS

High priests, nobles, and royals often acknowledge the services of powerful characters by granting them honors and titles. These awards are sometimes handed out along with gifts of gold or land, memberships in elite orders, or medals, signet rings, diadems, and other symbolic items.

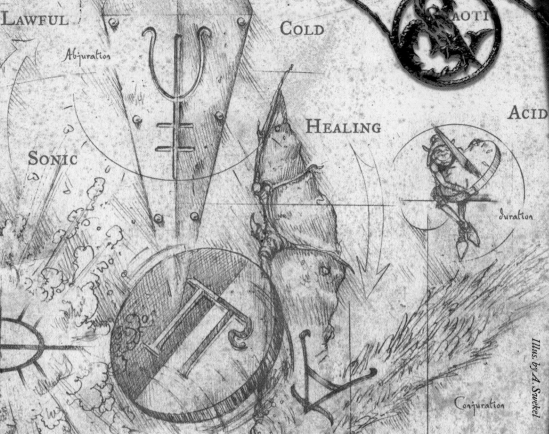

SCHOOLS OF MAGIC

LIGHT

LAWFUL

Abjuration

COLD

CHAOTI

HEALING

ACID

ELECTRICITY

SONIC

Evocation

duration

Transmutation

Conjuration

Illus. by A. Swekel

Before setting out on a dangerous journey with her companions, Mialee sits in her study and opens her spellbook. First she pages through it, selecting the spells that she thinks will be most useful on her adventure. When she has chosen the spells she wants (which could mean choosing the same spell more than once), she meditates on the pages that describe each one. The arcane symbols, which she has penned by hand, would be nonsense to anyone else, but they unlock power from her mind. As she concentrates, she all but finishes casting each spell that she prepares. Each spell now lacks only its final trigger. When she closes the book, her mind is full of spells, each of which she can complete in a brief time.

A spell is a one-time magical effect. Spells come in two types: arcane (cast by bards, sorcerers, and wizards) and divine (cast by clerics, druids, and experienced paladins and rangers). Some spellcasters select their spells from a limited list of spells known, while others have access to a wide variety of options. Most spellcasters prepare their spells in advance—whether from a spellbook or through devout prayers and meditation— while some cast spells spontaneously without preparation. Despite these different ways that characters use to learn or prepare their spells, when it comes to casting them, the spells are very much alike.

Cutting across the categories of arcane and divine spells are the eight schools of magic. These schools represent the different ways that spells take effect. This chapter describes the differences between the eight schools of magic. In addition, it provides an overview of the spell description format, an extensive discussion of how spells work, information about what happens when magical effects combine, and an explanation of the differences between the kinds of special abilities, some of which are magical.

CASTING SPELLS

Whether a spell is arcane or divine, and whether a character prepares spells in advance or chooses them on the spot, casting a spell works the same way.

HOW DOES SPELLCASTING WORK?

Spells operate in different ways depending on the type of spell you're casting. Here are three basic examples.

Charm Person: Tordek is bullying some goblins into revealing the whereabouts of their camp when Mialee casts *charm person* on one of them. The DM rolls a Will saving throw for the goblin against Mialee's save DC of 13 for her 1st-level spells, and the save fails. Mialee is a 1st-level wizard, and the spell lasts 1 hour per caster level, so for the next hour the goblin regards her as his friend, and she gets the information out of him.

Summon Monster I: Lidda is fighting a hobgoblin, and Mialee casts *summon monster I* to conjure a celestial dog. She can have the dog materialize in any location that she can see within 25 feet. She chooses to have it materialize on the opposite side of the hobgoblin from Lidda. One round later, when Mialee is finished casting the spell, the dog appears. It attacks immediately and gets a +2 bonus on its attack roll because it is flanking the hobgoblin. On Lidda's next turn, she makes a sneak attack against the hobgoblin and kills it. The dog disappears at the start of Mialee's next turn because *summon monster I* lasts only 1 round for a 1st-level caster.

Burning Hands: Mialee wants to cast *burning hands* on some Small centipedes, and she wants to hit as many of them as he can. She moves to a spot that puts three centipedes within 15 feet of her, but none next to her, so they can't attack her while she is casting. She chooses a direction and casts her spell. A cone of magical flame shoots out 15 feet, catching the three centipedes in its area. Mialee's player rolls 1d4 to see how much damage each centipede takes and gets a result of 3. The DM makes a Reflex save (DC 13 for one of Mialee's 1st-level spells) for each centipede, and only one succeeds. Two centipedes take 3 points of damage each and drop. The lucky one takes half damage (1 point) and survives.

Casting a spell can be a straightforward process, such as when Jozan casts *cure light wounds* to remove some of the damage that Tordek has taken, or it can be complicated, such as when Jozan is attempting to aim an *insect plague* by ear at a group of nagas who have hidden themselves in a *deeper darkness* spell, all the while avoiding the attacks of the nagas' troglodyte servants.

CHOOSING A SPELL

First you must choose which spell to cast. If you're a cleric, druid, experienced paladin, experienced ranger, or wizard, you select from among spells prepared earlier in the day and not yet cast (see Preparing Wizard Spells, page 177, and Preparing Divine Spells, page 179). If you're a bard or sorcerer, you can select any spell you know, provided you are capable of casting spells of that level or higher.

To cast a spell, you must be able to speak (if the spell has a verbal component), gesture (if it has a somatic component), and manipulate the material components or focus (if any). Additionally, you must concentrate to cast a spell—and it's hard to concentrate in the heat of battle. (See below for details.)

If a spell has multiple versions, you choose which version to use when you cast it. You don't have to prepare (or learn, in the case of a bard or sorcerer) a specific version of the spell. For example, *resist energy* protects a creature from fire, cold, or other energy types. You choose when you cast the spell which energy type it will protect the subject from.

Once you've cast a prepared spell, you can't cast it again until you prepare it again. (If you've prepared multiple copies of a single spell, you can cast each copy once.) If you're a bard or sorcerer, casting a spell counts against your daily limit for spells of that spell level, but you can cast the same spell again if you haven't reached your limit.

CONCENTRATION

To cast a spell, you must concentrate. If something interrupts your concentration while you're casting, you must make a Concentration check or lose the spell. The more distracting the interruption and the higher the level of the spell you are trying to cast, the higher the DC is. (More powerful spells require more mental effort.) If you fail the check, you lose the spell just as if you had cast it to no effect.

Injury: Getting hurt or being affected by hostile magic while trying to cast a spell can break your concentration and ruin the spell. If while trying to cast a spell you take damage, you must make a Concentration check (DC 10 + points of damage taken + the level of the spell you're casting). If you fail the check, you lose the spell without effect. The interrupting event strikes during spellcasting if it comes between when you start and when you complete a spell (for a spell with a casting time of 1 full round or more) or if it comes in response to your casting the spell (such as an attack of opportunity provoked by the spell or a contingent attack, such as a readied action).

If you are taking continuous damage, such as from *Melf's acid arrow*, half the damage is considered to take place while you are casting a spell. You must make a Concentration check (DC 10 + 1/2 the damage that the continuous source last dealt + the level of the spell you're casting). If the last damage dealt was the last damage that the effect could deal (such as the last round of a *Melf's acid arrow*), then the damage is over, and it does not distract you.

Repeated damage, such as from a *spiritual weapon*, does not count as continuous damage.

Spell: If you are affected by a spell while attempting to cast a spell of your own, you must make a Concentration check or lose the spell you are casting. If the spell affecting you deals damage, the DC is 10 + points of damage + the level of the spell you're casting. If the spell interferes with you or distracts you in some other way, the DC is the spell's saving throw DC + the level of the spell you're casting. For a spell with no saving throw, it's the DC that the spell's saving throw would have if a save were allowed.

Grappling or Pinned: The only spells you can cast while grappling or pinned are those without somatic components and whose material components (if any) you have in hand. Even so, you must make a Concentration check (DC 20 + the level of the spell you're casting) or lose the spell.

Vigorous Motion: If you are riding on a moving mount, taking a bouncy ride in a wagon, on a small boat in rough water, belowdecks in a storm-tossed ship, or simply being jostled in a similar fashion, you must make a Concentration check (DC 10 + the level of the spell you're casting) or lose the spell.

Violent Motion: If you are on a galloping horse, taking a very rough ride in a wagon, on a small boat in rapids or in a storm, on deck in a storm-tossed ship, or being tossed roughly about in a similar fashion, you must make a Concentration check (DC 15 + the level of the spell you're casting) or lose the spell.

Violent Weather: You must make a Concentration check if you try to cast a spell in violent weather. If you are in a high wind carrying blinding rain or sleet, the DC is 5 + the level of the spell you're casting. If you are in wind-driven hail, dust, or debris, the DC is 10 + the level of the spell you're casting. In either case, you lose the spell if you fail the Concentration check. If the weather is caused by a spell, use the rules in the Spell subsection above.

Casting Defensively: If you want to cast a spell without provoking any attacks of opportunity, you need to dodge and weave. You must make a Concentration check (DC 15 + the level of the spell you're casting) to succeed. You lose the spell if you fail.

Entangled: If you want to cast a spell while entangled in a net or by a tanglefoot bag (page 128) or while you're affected by a spell with similar effects (such as *entangle*), you must make a DC 15 Concentration check to cast the spell. You lose the spell if you fail.

COUNTERSPELLS

It is possible to cast any spell as a counterspell. By doing so, you are using the spell's energy to disrupt the casting of the same spell by another character. Counterspelling works even if one spell is divine and the other arcane.

How Counterspells Work: To use a counterspell, you must select an opponent as the target of the counterspell. You do this by choosing the ready action (page 160). In doing so, you elect to wait to complete your action until your opponent tries to cast a spell. (You may still move your speed, since ready is a standard action.)

If the target of your counterspell tries to cast a spell, make a Spellcraft check (DC 15 + the spell's level). This check is a free action. If the check succeeds, you correctly identify the opponent's spell and can attempt to counter it. If the check fails, you can't do either of these things.

To complete the action, you must then cast the correct spell. As a general rule, a spell can only counter itself. For example, a *fireball* spell is effective as a counter to another *fireball* spell, but not to any other spell, no matter how similar. *Fireball* cannot counter *delayed blast fireball* or vice versa. If you are able to cast the same spell and you have it prepared (if you prepare spells), you cast it, altering it slightly to create a counterspell effect. If the target is within range, both spells automatically negate each other with no other results.

Counterspelling Metamagic Spells: Metamagic feats are not taken into account when determining whether a spell can be countered. For example, a normal *fireball* can counter a maximized *fireball* (that is, a *fireball* that has been enhanced by the metamagic feat Maximize Spell) and vice versa.

Specific Exceptions: Some spells specifically counter each other, especially when they have diametrically opposed effects. For example, you can counter a *haste* spell with a *slow* spell as well as with another *haste* spell, or you can counter *reduce person* with *enlarge person*.

Dispel Magic **as a Counterspell:** You can use *dispel magic* to counterspell another spellcaster, and you don't need to identify the spell he or she is casting. However, *dispel magic* doesn't always work as a counterspell (see the spell description, page 223).

CASTER LEVEL

A spell's power often depends on its caster level, which for most spellcasting characters is equal to your class level in the class you're using to cast the spell. For example, a *fireball* deals 1d6 points of damage per caster level (to a maximum of 10d6), so a 10th-level wizard can cast a more powerful *fireball* than a 5th-level wizard can.

You can cast a spell at a lower caster level than normal, but the caster level you choose must be high enough for you to cast the spell in question, and all level-dependent features must be based on the same caster level. For example, at 10th level, Mialee can cast a *fireball* to a range of 800 feet for 10d6 points of damage. If she wishes, she can cast a *fireball* that deals less damage by casting the spell at a lower caster level, but she must reduce the range according to the selected caster level, and she can't cast *fireball* with a caster level lower than 5th (the minimum level required for a wizard to cast *fireball*).

In the event that a class feature, domain granted power, or other special ability provides an adjustment to your caster level, that adjustment applies not only to effects based on caster level (such as range, duration, and damage dealt) but also to your caster level check to overcome your target's spell resistance (see Spell Resistance, page 177) and to the caster level used in dispel checks (both the dispel check and the DC of the check). For instance, a 7th-level cleric with the Good domain casts spells with the good descriptor as if he were 8th level. This means that his *holy smite* deals 4d8 points of damage, he rolls 1d20+8 to overcome spell resistance with his good spells, and his *protection from evil* spell resists being dispelled as if it had been cast by an 8th-level spellcaster.

SPELL FAILURE

If you ever try to cast a spell in conditions where the characteristics of the spell (range, area, or the like) cannot be made to conform, the casting fails and the spell is wasted. For example, if you cast *charm person* on a dog, the spell fails because a dog is the wrong sort of target for the spell.

Spells also fail if your concentration is broken and might fail if you're wearing armor while casting a spell with somatic components (see Table 7–6: Armor and Shields, page 123).

THE SPELL'S RESULT

Once you know which creatures (or objects or areas) are affected, and whether those creatures have made successful saving throws (if any were allowed), you can apply whatever results a spell entails.

Many spells affect particular sorts of creatures. *Repel vermin* keeps vermin away, and *calm animals* can calm down animals and magical beasts. These terms, and terms like them, refer to specific creature types defined in the *Monster Manual*.

SPECIAL SPELL EFFECTS

Many special spell effects are handled according to the school of the spells in question. For example, illusory figments all have certain effects in common (see Illusion, page 173). Certain other special spell features are found across spell schools.

Attacks: Some spell descriptions refer to attacking. For instance, *invisibility* is dispelled if you attack anyone or anything while under its effects. All offensive combat actions, even those that don't damage opponents (such as disarm and bull rush) are considered attacks. Attempts to turn or rebuke undead count as attacks. All spells that opponents resist with saving throws, that deal damage, or that otherwise harm or hamper subjects are attacks. *Summon monster I* and similar spells are not attacks because the spells themselves don't harm anyone.

Bonus Types: Many spells give their subjects bonuses to ability scores, Armor Class, attacks, and other attributes. Usually, a bonus has a type that indicates how the spell grants the bonus. For example, *mage armor* grants an armor bonus to AC, indicating that the spell creates a tangible barrier around you. *Shield of faith*, on the other hand, grants a deflection bonus to AC, which makes attacks veer off. (Bonus types are covered in detail in the *Dungeon Master's Guide*.) The important aspect of bonus types is that two bonuses of the same type don't generally stack. With the exception of dodge bonuses, most circumstance bonuses, and racial bonuses, only the better bonus works (see Combining Magical Effects, below). The same principle applies to penalties—a character taking two or more penalties of the same type applies only the worst one.

Bringing Back the Dead: Several spells have the power to restore slain characters to life.

When a living creature dies, its soul departs its body, leaves the Material Plane, travels through the Astral Plane, and goes to abide on the plane where the creature's deity resides. If the creature did not worship a deity, its soul departs to the plane corresponding to its alignment. Bringing someone back from the dead means retrieving his or her soul and returning it to his or her body.

Level Loss: The passage from life to death and back again is a wrenching journey for a being's soul. Consequently, any creature brought back to life usually loses one level of experience. The character's new XP total is midway between the minimum needed for his or her new (reduced) level and the minimum needed for the next one. If the character was 1st level at the time of death, he or she loses 2 points of Constitution instead of losing a level.

This level loss or Constitution loss cannot be repaired by any mortal means, even *wish* or *miracle*. A revived character can regain a lost level by earning XP through further adventuring. A revived character who was 1st level at the time of death can regain lost points of Constitution by improving his or her Constitution score when he or she attains a level that allows an ability score increase.

Preventing Revivification: Enemies can take steps to make it more difficult for a character to be returned from the dead. Keeping the body prevents others from using *raise dead* or *resurrection* to restore the slain character to life. Casting *trap the soul* prevents any sort of revivification unless the soul is first released.

Revivification against One's Will: A soul cannot be returned to life if it does not wish to be. A soul knows the name, alignment, and patron deity (if any) of the character attempting to revive it and may refuse to return on that basis. For example, if Alhandra the paladin is slain and a high priest of Nerull (god of death) grabs her body, Alhandra probably does not wish to be raised from the dead by him. Any attempts he makes to revive her automatically fail. If the evil cleric wants to revive Alhandra to interrogate her, he needs to find some way to trick her soul, such as duping a good cleric into raising her and then capturing her once she is alive again.

COMBINING MAGICAL EFFECTS

Spells or magical effects usually work as described, no matter how many other spells or magical effects happen to be operating in the same area or on the same recipient. Except in special cases, a spell does not affect the way another spell operates. Whenever a spell has a specific effect on other spells, the spell description explains that effect. Several other general rules apply when spells or magical effects operate in the same place:

Stacking Effects: Spells that provide bonuses or penalties on attack rolls, damage rolls, saving throws, and other attributes usually do not stack with themselves. For example, two *bless* spells don't give twice the benefit of one *bless*. Both *bless* spells, however, continue to act simultaneously, and if one ends first, the other one continues to operate for the remainder of its duration. Likewise, two *haste* spells do not make a creature doubly fast.

More generally, two bonuses of the same type don't stack even if they come from different spells (or from effects other than spells; see Bonus Types, above). For example, the enhancement bonus to Strength from a *bull's strength* spell and the enhancement bonus to Strength from a *divine power* spell don't stack. You use whichever bonus gives you the better Strength score. In the same way, a *belt of giant Strength* gives you an enhancement bonus to Strength, which does not stack with the bonus you get from a *bull's strength* spell.

Different Bonus Names: The bonuses or penalties from two different spells stack if the modifiers are of different types. For example, *bless* provides a +1 morale bonus on saves against fear effects, and *protection from evil* provides a +2 resistance bonus on saves against spells cast by evil creatures. A character under the influence of spells gets a +1 bonus against fear effects, a +2 bonus against spells cast by evil beings, and a +3 bonus against *fear* spells cast by evil creatures.

A bonus that isn't named (just a "+2 bonus" rather than a "+2 resistance bonus") stacks with any bonus.

Same Effect More than Once in Different Strengths: In cases when two or more identical spells are operating in the same area or on the same target, but at different strengths, only the best one applies. For example, if a character takes a −4 penalty to Strength from a *ray of enfeeblement* spell and then receives a second *ray of enfeeblement* spell that applies a −6 penalty, he or she takes only the −6 penalty. Both spells are still operating on the character, however. If one *ray of enfeeblement* spell is dispelled or its duration runs out, the other spell remains in effect, assuming that its duration has not yet expired.

Same Effect with Differing Results: The same spell can sometimes produce varying effects if applied to the same recipient more than once. For example, a series of *polymorph* spells might turn a creature into a mouse, a lion, and then a snail. In this case, the last spell in the series trumps the others. None of the previous spells are actually removed or dispelled, but their effects become irrelevant while the final spell in the series lasts.

One Effect Makes Another Irrelevant: Sometimes, one spell can render a later spell irrelevant. For example, if a wizard is using a *shapechange* spell to take the shape of an eagle, a *polymorph* spell could change her into a goldfish. The *shapechange* spell is not negated, however, and since the *polymorph* spell has no effect on the recipient's special abilities, the wizard could use the *shapechange* effect to take any form the spell allows whenever she desires. If a creature using a *shapechange* effect becomes petrified by a *flesh to stone* spell, however, it turns into a mindless, inert statue, and the *shapechange* effect cannot help it escape.

Multiple Mental Control Effects: Sometimes magical effects that establish mental control render each other irrelevant. For example, a *hold person* effect renders any other form of mental control irrelevant because it robs the subject of the ability to move. Mental controls that don't remove the recipient's ability to act usually do not interfere with each other. For example, a person who has received a *geas/quest* spell can also be subjected to a *charm person* spell. The *charmed* person remains committed to fulfilling the quest, however, and resists any order that interferes with that goal. In this case, the *geas/quest* spell doesn't negate *charm person*, but it does reduce its effectiveness, just as nonmagical devotion to a quest would. If a creature is under the mental control of two or more creatures, it tends to obey each to the best of its ability, and to the extent of the control each effect allows. If the controlled creature receives conflicting orders simultaneously, the competing controllers must make opposed Charisma checks to determine which one the creature obeys.

Spells with Opposite Effects: Spells with opposite effects apply normally, with all bonuses, penalties, or changes accruing in the order that they apply. Some spells negate or counter each other. This is a special effect that is noted in a spell's description.

Instantaneous Effects: Two or more spells with instantaneous durations work cumulatively when they affect the same target. For example, when two *fireballs* strike a same creature, the target must attempt a saving throw against each *fireball* and takes damage from each according to the saving throws' results. If a creature receives two *cure light wounds* spells in a single round, both work normally.

SPELL DESCRIPTIONS

The spells available to characters are listed and described in Chapter 11: Spells. The description of each spell is presented in a standard format. Each category of information is explained and defined below.

NAME

The first line of every spell description gives the name by which the spell is generally known.

SCHOOL (SUBSCHOOL)

Beneath the spell name is a line giving the school of magic (and the subschool, if appropriate) that the spell belongs to.

Almost every spell belongs to one of eight schools of magic. A school of magic is a group of related spells that work in similar ways. A small number of spells (*arcane mark, limited wish, permanency, prestidigitation,* and *wish*) are universal, belonging to no school.

Abjuration

Abjurations are protective spells. They create physical or magical barriers, negate magical or physical abilities, harm trespassers, or even banish the subject of the spell to another plane of existence. Representative spells include *protection from evil, dispel magic, antimagic field,* and *banishment.*

If one abjuration spell is active within 10 feet of another for 24 hours or more, the magical fields interfere with each other and create barely visible energy fluctuations. The DC to find such spells with the Search skill drops by 4.

If an abjuration creates a barrier that keeps certain types of creatures at bay, that barrier cannot be used to push away those creatures. If you force the barrier against such a creature, you feel a discernible pressure against the barrier. If you continue to apply pressure, you end the spell.

Conjuration

Each conjuration spell belongs to one of five subschools. Conjurations bring manifestations of objects, creatures, or some form of energy to you (the summoning subschool), actually transport creatures from another plane of existence to your plane (calling), heal (healing), transport creatures or objects over great distances (teleportation), or create objects or effects on the spot (creation). Creatures you conjure usually, but not always, obey your commands. Representative spells include the various *summon monster* spells, *cure light wounds, raise dead, teleport,* and *wall of iron.*

A creature or object brought into being or transported to your location by a conjuration spell cannot appear inside another creature or object, nor can it appear floating in an empty space. It must arrive in an open location on a surface capable of supporting it. The creature or object must appear within the spell's range, but it does not have to remain within the range.

Calling: A calling spell transports a creature from another plane to the plane you are on. The spell grants the creature the one-time ability to return to its plane of origin, although the spell may limit the circumstances under which this is possible. Creatures who are called actually die when they are killed; they do not disappear and reform, as do those brought by a summoning spell (see below). The duration of a calling spell is instantaneous, which means that the called creature can't be dispelled.

Creation: A creation spell manipulates matter to create an object or creature in the place the spellcaster designates (subject to the limits noted above). If the spell has a duration other than instantaneous, magic holds the creation together, and when the spell ends, the conjured creature or object vanishes without a trace. If the spell has an instantaneous duration, the created object or creature is merely assembled through magic. It lasts indefinitely and does not depend on magic for its existence.

Healing: Certain divine conjurations heal creatures or even bring them back to life. These include *cure* spells.

Summoning: A summoning spell instantly brings a creature or object to a place you designate. When the spell ends or is dispelled, a summoned creature is instantly sent back to where it came from, but a summoned object is not sent back unless the spell description specifically indicates this. A summoned creature also goes away if it is killed or if its hit points drop to 0 or lower. It is not really dead. It takes 24 hours for the creature to reform, during which time it can't be summoned again.

When the spell that summoned a creature ends and the creature disappears, all the spells it has cast expire. A summoned creature cannot use any innate summoning abilities it may have, and it refuses to cast any spells that would cost it XP, or to use any spell-like abilities that would cost XP if they were spells.

Teleportation: A teleportation spell transports one or more creatures or objects a great distance. The most powerful of these spells can cross planar boundaries. Unlike summoning spells, the transportation is (unless otherwise noted) one-way and not dispellable. Teleportation is instantaneous travel through the Astral Plane. Anything that blocks astral travel also blocks teleportation.

Divination

Divination spells enable you to learn secrets long forgotten, to predict the future, to find hidden things, and to foil deceptive spells. Representative spells include *identify, detect thoughts, clairaudience/clairvoyance,* and *true seeing.*

Many divination spells have cone-shaped areas (see page 175). These move with you and extend in the direction you look. The cone defines the area that you can sweep each round. If you study the same area for multiple rounds, you can often gain additional information, as noted in the descriptive text for the spell.

Scrying: A scrying spell creates an invisible magical sensor that sends you information. Unless noted otherwise, the sensor has the same powers of sensory acuity that you possess. This level of acuity includes any spells or effects that target you (such as *darkvision* or *see invisibility*), but not spells or effects that emanate from you (such as *detect evil*). However, the sensor is treated as a separate, independent sensory organ of yours, and thus it functions normally even if you have been blinded, deafened, or otherwise suffered sensory impairment. Any creature with an Intelligence score of 12 or higher can notice the sensor by making a DC 20 Intelligence check. The sensor can be dispelled as if it were an active spell.

Lead sheeting or magical protection (such as *antimagic field, mind blank,* or *nondetection*) blocks a scrying spell, and you sense that the spell is so blocked.

Enchantment

Enchantment spells affect the minds of others, influencing or controlling their behavior. Representative spells include *charm person* and *suggestion.*

All enchantments are mind-affecting spells. Two types of enchantment spells grant you influence over a subject creature.

Charm: A charm spell changes how the subject views you, typically making it see you as a good friend.

Compulsion: A compulsion spell forces the subject to act in some manner or changes the way her mind works. Some compulsion spells determine the subject's actions or the effects on the subject, some compulsion spells allow you to determine the subject's actions when you cast the spell, and others give you ongoing control over the subject.

Evocation

Evocation spells manipulate energy or tap an unseen source of power to produce a desired end. In effect, they create something out of nothing. Many of these spells produce spectacular effects, and evocation spells can deal large amounts of damage. Representative spells include *magic missile, fireball,* and *lightning bolt.*

Illusion

Illusion spells deceive the senses or minds of others. They cause people to see things that are not there, not see things that are there, hear phantom noises, or remember things that never happened. Representative illusions include *silent image, invisibility,* and *veil.* Illusions come in five types: figments, glamers, patterns, phantasms, and shadows.

Figment: A figment spell creates a false sensation. Those who perceive the figment perceive the same thing, not their own slightly different versions of the figment. (It is not a personalized mental impression.) Figments cannot make something seem to be something else. A figment that includes audible effects cannot duplicate intelligible speech unless the spell description specifically says it can. If intelligible speech is possible, it must be in a language you can speak. If you try to duplicate a language you cannot speak, the image produces gibberish. Likewise, you cannot make a visual copy of something unless you know what it looks like.

Because figments and glamers (see below) are unreal, they cannot produce real effects the way that other types of illusions can. They cannot cause damage to objects or creatures, support weight, provide nutrition, or provide protection from the elements. Consequently, these spells are useful for confounding or delaying foes, but useless for attacking them directly. For example, it is possible to use a *silent image* spell to create an illusory cottage, but the cottage offers no protection from rain.

A figment's AC is equal to 10 + its size modifier.

Glamer: A glamer spell changes a subject's sensory qualities, making it look, feel, taste, smell, or sound like something else, or even seem to disappear.

Pattern: Like a figment, a pattern spell creates an image that others can see, but a pattern also affects the minds of those who see it or are caught in it. All patterns are mind-affecting spells.

Phantasm: A phantasm spell creates a mental image that usually only the caster and the subject (or subjects) of the spell can perceive. This impression is totally in the minds of the subjects. It is a personalized mental impression. (It's all in their heads and not a fake picture or something that they actually see.) Third parties viewing or studying the scene don't notice the phantasm. All phantasms are mind-affecting spells.

Shadow: A shadow spell creates something that is partially real from extradimensional energy. Such illusions can have real effects. Damage dealt by a shadow illusion is real.

Saving Throws and Illusions (Disbelief): Creatures encountering an illusion usually do not receive saving throws to recognize it as illusory until they study it carefully or interact with it in some fashion. For example, if a party encounters a section of illusory floor, the character in the lead would receive a saving throw if she stopped and studied the floor or if she probed the floor.

A successful saving throw against an illusion reveals it to be false, but a figment or phantasm remains as a translucent outline. For example, a character making a successful saving throw against a figment of an illusory section of floor knows the "floor" isn't safe to walk on and can see what lies below (light permitting), but he or she can still note where the figment lies.

A failed saving throw indicates that a character fails to notice something is amiss. A character faced with proof that an illusion isn't real needs no saving throw. A character who falls through a section of illusory floor into a pit knows something is amiss, as does one who spends a few rounds poking at the same illusion. If any viewer successfully disbelieves an illusion and communicates this fact to others, each such viewer gains a saving throw with a +4 bonus.

Necromancy

Necromancy spells manipulate the power of death, unlife, and the life force. Spells involving undead creatures make up a large part of this school. Representative spells include *cause fear*, *animate dead*, and *finger of death*.

Transmutation

Transmutation spells change the properties of some creature, thing, or condition. Representative spells include *enlarge person*, *reduce person*, *polymorph*, and *shapechange*.

[DESCRIPTOR]

Appearing on the same line as the school and subschool, when applicable, is a descriptor that further categorizes the spell in some way. Some spells have more than one descriptor.

The descriptors are acid, air, chaotic, cold, darkness, death, earth, electricity, evil, fear, fire, force, good, language-dependent, lawful, light, mind-affecting, sonic, and water.

Most of these descriptors have no game effect by themselves, but they govern how the spell interacts with other spells, with special abilities, with unusual creatures, with alignment, and so on.

A language-dependent spell uses intelligible language as a medium for communication. For instance, a cleric's *command* spell fails if the target can't understand what the cleric says, either because it doesn't understand the language he is speaking or because background noise prevents it from hearing what the cleric says.

A mind-affecting spell works only against creatures with an Intelligence score of 1 or higher.

LEVEL

The next line of a spell description gives the spell's level, a number between 0 and 9 that defines the spell's relative power. This number is preceded by an abbreviation for the class whose members can cast the spell. The Level entry also indicates whether a spell is a domain spell and, if so, what its domain and its level as a domain spell are. A spell's level affects the DC for any save allowed against the effect.

For example, the Level entry for *hold person* is "Brd 2, Clr 2, Sor/Wiz 3." That means it is a 2nd-level spell for bards, a 2nd-level spell for clerics, and a 3rd-level spell for sorcerers and wizards. The level entry for *magic vestment* is "Clr 3, Strength 3, War 3." That means it is a 3rd-level spell for clerics, the 3rd-level Strength domain spell, and the 3rd-level War domain spell.

Names of spellcasting classes are abbreviated as follows: bard Brd; cleric Clr; druid Drd; paladin Pal; ranger Rgr; sorcerer Sor; wizard Wiz.

The domains a spell can be associated with include Air, Animal, Chaos, Death, Destruction, Earth, Evil, Fire, Good, Healing, Knowledge, Law, Luck, Magic, Plant, Protection, Strength, Sun, Travel, Trickery, War, and Water.

COMPONENTS

A spell's components are what you must do or possess to cast it. The Components entry in a spell description includes abbreviations that tell you what type of components it has. Specifics for material, focus, and XP components are given at the end of the descriptive text. Usually you don't worry about components, but when you can't use a component for some reason or when a material or focus component is expensive, then the components are important.

Verbal (V): A verbal component is a spoken incantation. To provide a verbal component, you must be able to speak in a strong voice. A *silence* spell or a gag spoils the incantation (and thus the spell). A spellcaster who has been deafened has a 20% chance to spoil any spell with a verbal component that he or she tries to cast.

Somatic (S): A somatic component is a measured and precise movement of the hand. You must have at least one hand free to provide a somatic component.

Material (M): A material component is one or more physical substances or objects that are annihilated by the spell energies in the casting process. Unless a cost is given for a material component, the cost is negligible. Don't bother to keep track of material components with negligible cost. Assume you have all you need as long as you have your spell component pouch.

Focus (F): A focus component is a prop of some sort. Unlike a material component, a focus is not consumed when the spell is cast and can be reused. As with material components, the cost for a focus is negligible unless a price is given. Assume that focus components of negligible cost are in your spell component pouch.

Divine Focus (DF): A divine focus component is an item of spiritual significance. The divine focus for a cleric or a paladin is a holy symbol appropriate to the character's faith. For an evil cleric, the divine focus is an unholy symbol. The default divine focus for a druid or a ranger is a sprig of mistletoe or holly.

If the Components line includes F/DF or M/DF, the arcane version of the spell has a focus component or a material component (the abbreviation before the slash) and the divine version has a divine focus component (the abbreviation after the slash).

XP Cost (XP): Some powerful spells (such as *wish*, *commune*, and *miracle*) entail an experience point cost to you. No spell, not even *restoration*, can restore the XP lost in this manner. You cannot spend so much XP that you lose a level, so you cannot cast the spell unless you have enough XP to spare. However, you may, on gaining enough XP to attain a new level, use those XP for casting a spell rather than keeping them and advancing a level. The XP are treated just like a material component—expended when you cast the spell, whether or not the casting succeeds.

CASTING TIME

Most spells have a casting time of 1 standard action. Others take 1 round or more, while a few require only a free action. Chapter 8: Combat describes the difference between these types of actions.

A spell that takes 1 round to cast is a full-round action. It comes into effect just before the beginning of your turn in the round after you began casting the spell. You then act normally after the spell is completed.

A spell that takes 1 minute to cast comes into effect just before your turn 1 minute later (and for each of those 10 rounds, you are casting a spell as a full-round action, just as noted above for 1-round casting times). These actions must be consecutive and uninterrupted, or the spell automatically fails.

When you begin a spell that takes 1 round or longer to cast, you must continue the concentration from the current round to just before your turn in the next round (at least). If you lose concentration before the casting is complete, you lose the spell.

A spell with a casting time of 1 free action (such as *feather fall*) doesn't count against your normal limit of one spell per round. However, you may cast such a spell only once per round. Casting a spell with a casting time of 1 free action doesn't provoke attacks of opportunity.

You make all pertinent decisions about a spell (range, target, area, effect, version, and so forth) when the spell comes into effect. For example, when casting a *summon monster* spell, you need not decide where you want the monster to appear (or indeed, what monster you are summoning) until the spell comes into effect in the round after you begin casting.

RANGE

A spell's range indicates how far from you it can reach, as defined in the Range entry of the spell description. A spell's range is the maximum distance from you that the spell's effect can occur, as well as the maximum distance at which you can designate the spell's point of origin. If any portion of the spell's area would extend beyond this range, that area is wasted. Standard ranges include the following.

Personal: The spell affects only you.

Touch: You must touch a creature or object to affect it. A touch spell that deals damage can score a critical hit just as a weapon can. A touch spell threatens a critical hit on a natural roll of 20 and deals double damage on a successful critical hit. Some touch spells, such as *teleport* and *water walk,* allow you to touch multiple targets. You can touch as many willing targets as you can reach as part of the casting, but all targets of the spell must be touched in the same round that you finish casting the spell.

Close: The spell reaches as far as 25 feet away from you. The maximum range increases by 5 feet for every two full caster levels (30 feet at 2nd caster level, 35 feet at 4th caster level, and so on).

Medium: The spell reaches as far as 100 feet + 10 feet per caster level.

Long: The spell reaches as far as 400 feet + 40 feet per caster level.

Unlimited: The spell reaches anywhere on the same plane of existence.

Range Expressed in Feet: Some spells have no standard range category, just a range expressed in feet.

AIMING A SPELL

You must make some choice about whom the spell is to affect or where the effect is to originate, depending on the type of spell. The next entry in a spell description defines the spell's target (or targets), its effect, or its area, as appropriate.

Target or Targets: Some spells, such as *charm person,* have a target or targets. You cast these spells on creatures or objects, as defined by the spell itself. You must be able to see or touch the target, and you must specifically choose that target. For example, you can't fire a *magic missile* spell (which always hits its target) into a group of bandits with the instruction to strike "the leader." To strike the leader, you must be able to identify and see the leader (or guess which is the leader and get lucky). However, you do not have to select your target until you finish casting the spell.

If the target of a spell is yourself (the spell description has a line that reads Target: You), you do not receive a saving throw, and spell resistance does not apply. The Saving Throw and Spell Resistance lines are omitted from such spells.

Some spells restrict you to willing targets only. Declaring yourself as a willing target is something that can be done at any time (even if you're flat-footed or it isn't your turn). Unconscious creatures are automatically considered willing, but a character who is conscious but immobile or helpless (such as one who is bound, cowering, grappling, paralyzed, pinned, or stunned) is not automatically willing.

Some spells, such as *flaming sphere* and *spiritual weapon,* allow you to redirect the effect to new targets or areas after you cast the spell. Redirecting a spell is a move action that does not provoke attacks of opportunity.

Effect: Some spells, such as *summon monster* spells, create or summon things rather than affecting things that are already present. You must designate the location where these things are to appear, either by seeing it or defining it (for example, "The *insect plague* will appear 20 feet into the area of darkness that the nagas are hiding in"). Range determines how far away an effect can appear, but if the effect is mobile (a summoned monster, for instance), it can move regardless of the spell's range.

Ray: Some effects are rays (for example, *ray of enfeeblement*). You aim a ray as if using a ranged weapon, though typically you make a ranged touch attack rather than a normal ranged attack. As with a ranged weapon, you can fire into the dark or at an invisible creature and hope you hit something. You don't have to see the creature you're trying to hit, as you do with a targeted spell. Intervening creatures and obstacles, however, can block your line of sight or provide cover for the creature you're aiming at.

If a ray spell has a duration, it's the duration of the effect that the ray causes, not the length of time the ray itself persists.

If a ray spell deals damage, you can score a critical hit just as if it were a weapon. A ray spell threatens a critical hit on a natural roll of 20 and deals double damage on a successful critical hit.

Spread: Some effects, notably clouds and fogs, spread out from a point of origin, which must be a grid intersection. The effect can extend around corners and into areas that you can't see. Figure distance by actual distance traveled, taking into account turns the spell effect takes. When determining distance for spread effects, count around walls, not through them. As with movement, do not trace diagonals across corners. You must designate the point of origin for such an effect, but you need not have line of effect (see below) to all portions of the effect. Example: *obscuring mist.*

Area: Some spells affect an area. Sometimes a spell description specifies a specially defined area, but usually an area falls into one of the categories defined below.

Regardless of the shape of the area, you select the point where the spell originates, but otherwise you don't control which creatures or objects the spell affects. The point of origin of a spell is always a grid intersection. When determining whether a given creature is within the area of a spell, count out the distance from the point of origin in squares just as you do when moving a character or when determining the range for a ranged attack. The only difference is that instead of counting from the center of one square to the center of the next, you count from intersection to intersection. You can count diagonally across a square, but remember that every second diagonal counts as 2 squares of distance. If the far edge of a square is within the spell's area, anything within that square is within the spell's area. If the spell's area only touches the near edge of a square, however, anything within that square is unaffected by the spell.

Burst, Emanation, or Spread: Most spells that affect an area function as a burst, an emanation, or a spread. In each case, you select the spell's point of origin and measure its effect from that point.

A burst spell affects whatever it catches in its area, even including creatures that you can't see. For instance, if you designate a four-way intersection of corridors to be the point of origin of a *dispel magic* spell, the spell bursts in all four directions, possibly catching creatures that you can't see because they're around the corner from you but not from the point of origin. It can't affect creatures with total cover from its point of origin (in other words, its effects don't extend around corners). The default shape for a burst effect is a sphere, but some burst spells are specifically described as cone-shaped. A burst's area defines how far from the point of origin the spell's effect extends. Example: *holy smite.*

An emanation spell functions like a burst spell, except that the effect continues to radiate from the point of origin for the duration of the spell. Most emanations are cones or spheres. Example: *detect magic.*

A spread spell spreads out like a burst but can turn corners. You select the point of origin, and the spell spreads out a given distance in all directions. Figure the area the spell effect fills by taking into account any turns the spell effect takes. Example: *fireball.*

Cone, Cylinder, Line, or Sphere: Most spells that affect an area have a particular shape, such as a cone, cylinder, line, or sphere.

A cone-shaped spell shoots away from you in a quarter-circle in the direction you designate. It starts from any corner of your square and widens out as it goes. Most cones are either bursts or emanations (see above), and thus won't go around corners. Example: *cone of cold.*

When casting a cylinder-shaped spell, you select the spell's point of origin. This point is the center of a horizontal circle, and the spell shoots down from the circle, filling a cylinder. A cylinder-shaped spell ignores any obstructions within its area. Example: *flame strike.*

A line-shaped spell shoots away from you in a line in the direction you designate. It starts from any corner of your square and extends

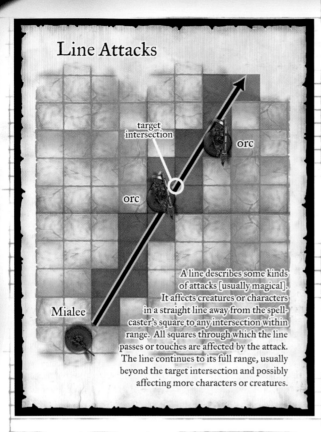

Line Attacks

target
intersection

orc

orc

Mialee

A line describes some kinds
of attacks [usually magical].
It affects creatures or characters
in a straight line away from the spellcaster's square to any intersection within
range. All squares through which the line
passes or touches are affected by the attack.
The line continues to its full range, usually
beyond the target intersection and possibly
affecting more characters or creatures.

to the limit of its range or until it strikes a barrier that blocks line of effect. A line-shaped spell affects all creatures in squares that the line passes through. Example: *lightning bolt*.

A sphere-shaped spell expands from its point of origin to fill a spherical area. Spheres may be bursts, emanations, or spreads. Example: *globe of invulnerability*.

Creatures: A spell with this kind of area affects creatures directly (like a targeted spell), but it affects all creatures in an area of some kind rather than individual creatures you select. The area might be a spherical burst (such as *sleep*), a cone-shaped burst (such as *fear*), or some other shape.

Many spells affect "living creatures," which means all creatures other than constructs and undead. The *sleep* spell, for instance, affects only living creatures. If you cast *sleep* in the midst of gnolls and skeletons, the *sleep* spell ignores the skeletons and affects the gnolls. The skeletons do not count against the creatures affected.

Objects: A spell with this kind of area affects objects within an area you select (as Creatures, but affecting objects instead).

Other: A spell can have a unique area, as defined in its description.

(S) Shapeable: If an Area or Effect entry ends with "(S)," you can shape the spell. A shaped effect or area can have no dimension smaller than 10 feet. Many effects or areas are given as cubes to make it easy to model irregular shapes. Three-dimensional volumes are most often needed to define aerial or underwater effects and areas.

Line of Effect: A line of effect is a straight, unblocked path that indicates what a spell can affect. A line of effect is canceled by a solid barrier. It's like line of sight for ranged weapons, except that it's not blocked by fog, darkness, and other factors that limit normal sight.

You must have a clear line of effect to any target that you cast a spell on or to any space in which you wish to create an effect (such as conjuring a monster). You must have a clear line of effect to the point of origin of any spell you cast, such as the center of a *fireball*. A burst, cone, cylinder, or emanation spell affects only an area, creatures, or objects to which it has line of effect from its origin (a spherical burst's center point, a cone-shaped burst's starting point, a cylinder's circle, or an emanation's point of origin).

An otherwise solid barrier with a hole of at least 1 square foot through it does not block a spell's line of effect. Such an opening means that the 5-foot length of wall containing the hole is no longer considered a barrier for purposes of a spell's line of effect.

DURATION

A spell's Duration entry tells you how long the magical energy of the spell lasts.

Timed Durations: Many durations are measured in rounds, minutes, hours, or some other increment. When the time is up, the magic goes away and the spell ends. If a spell's duration is variable (*power word stun*, for example), the DM rolls it secretly.

Instantaneous: The spell energy comes and goes the instant the spell is cast, though the consequences might be long-lasting. For example, a *cure light wounds* spell lasts only an instant, but the healing it bestows never runs out or goes away.

Permanent: The energy remains as long as the effect does. This means the spell is vulnerable to *dispel magic*. Example: *secret page*.

Concentration: The spell lasts as long as you concentrate on it. Concentrating to maintain a spell is a standard action that does not provoke attacks of opportunity. Anything that could break your concentration when casting a spell can also break your concentration while you're maintaining one, causing the spell to end. You can't cast a spell while concentrating on another one. Sometimes a spell lasts for a short time after you cease concentrating. For example, the spell *hypnotic pattern* has a duration of concentration + 2 rounds. In such a case, the spell keeps going for the given length of time after you stop concentrating, but no longer. Otherwise, you must concentrate to maintain the spell, but you can't maintain it for more than a stated duration in any event. If a target moves out of range, the spell reacts as if your concentration had been broken.

Subjects, Effects, and Areas: If the spell affects creatures directly (for example, *charm person*), the result travels with the subjects for the spell's duration. If the spell creates an effect, the effect lasts for the duration. The effect might move (for example, a summoned monster might chase your enemies) or remain still. Such an effect can be destroyed prior to when its duration ends (for example, *fog cloud* can be dispersed by wind). If the spell affects an area, as *silence* does, then the spell stays with that area for its duration. Creatures become subject to the spell when they enter the area and are no longer subject to it when they leave.

Touch Spells and Holding the Charge: In most cases, if you don't discharge a touch spell on the round you cast it, you can hold the charge (postpone the discharge of the spell) indefinitely. You can make touch attacks round after round. If you cast another spell, the touch spell dissipates.

Some touch spells, such as *teleport* and *water walk*, allow you to touch multiple targets as part of the spell. You can't hold the charge of such a spell; you must touch all targets of the spell in the same round that you finish casting the spell.

Discharge: Occasionally a spells lasts for a set duration or until triggered or discharged. For instance, *magic mouth* waits until triggered, and the spell ends once the mouth has said its message.

(D) Dismissible: If the Duration line ends with "(D)," you can dismiss the spell at will. You must be within range of the spell's effect and must speak words of dismissal, which are usually a modified form of the spell's verbal component. If the spell has no verbal component, you can dismiss the effect with a gesture. Dismissing a spell is a standard action that does not provoke attacks of opportunity. A spell that depends on concentration is dismissible by its very nature, and dismissing it does not take an action, since all you have to do to end the spell is to stop concentrating on your turn.

SAVING THROW

Usually a harmful spell allows a target to make a saving throw to avoid some or all of the effect. The Saving Throw entry in a spell description defines which type of saving throw the spell allows and describes how saving throws against the spell work.

Negates: The spell has no effect on a subject that makes a successful saving throw.

Partial: The spell causes an effect on its subject, such as death. A successful saving throw means that some lesser effect occurs (such as being dealt damage rather than being killed).

Half: The spell deals damage, and a successful saving throw halves the damage taken (round down).

None: No saving throw is allowed.

Disbelief: A successful save lets the subject ignore the effect.

(object): The spell can be cast on objects, which receive saving throws only if they are magical or if they are attended (held, worn, grasped, or the like) by a creature resisting the spell, in which case the object uses the creature's saving throw bonus unless its own bonus is greater. (This notation does not mean that a spell can be cast only on objects. Some spells of this sort can be cast on creatures or objects.) A magic item's saving throw bonuses are each equal to 2 + one-half the item's caster level.

(harmless): The spell is usually beneficial, not harmful, but a targeted creature can attempt a saving throw if it desires.

Saving Throw Difficulty Class: A saving throw against your spell has a DC of 10 + the level of the spell + your bonus for the relevant ability (Intelligence for a wizard, Charisma for a sorcerer or bard, or Wisdom for a cleric, druid, paladin, or ranger). A spell's level can vary depending on your class. For example, *fire trap* is a 2nd-level spell for a druid but a 4th-level spell for a sorcerer or wizard. Always use the spell level applicable to your class.

Succeeding on a Saving Throw: A creature that successfully saves against a spell that has no obvious physical effects feels a hostile force or a tingle, but cannot deduce the exact nature of the attack. For example, if you secretly cast *charm person* on a creature and its saving throw succeeds, it knows that someone used magic against it, but it can't tell what you were trying to do. Likewise, if a creature's saving throw succeeds against a targeted spell, such as *charm person*, you sense that the spell has failed. You do not sense when creatures succeed on saves against effect and area spells.

Automatic Failures and Successes: A natural 1 (the d20 comes up 1) on a saving throw is always a failure, and the spell may cause damage to exposed items (see Items Surviving after a Saving Throw, below). A natural 20 (the d20 comes up 20) is always a success.

Voluntarily Giving up a Saving Throw: A creature can voluntarily forego a saving throw and willingly accept a spell's result. Even a character with a special resistance to magic (for example, an elf's resistance to *sleep* effects) can suppress this quality.

TABLE 10–1: ITEMS AFFECTED BY MAGICAL ATTACKS

Order[1]	Item
1st	Shield
2nd	Armor
3rd	Magic helmet, hat, or headband
4th	Item in hand (including weapon, wand, or the like)
5th	Magic cloak
6th	Stowed or sheathed weapon
7th	Magic bracers
8th	Magic clothing
9th	Magic jewelry (including rings)
10th	Anything else

1 In order of most likely to least likely to be affected.

Items Surviving after a Saving Throw: Unless the descriptive text for the spell specifies otherwise, all items carried or worn by a creature are assumed to survive a magical attack. If a creature rolls a natural 1 on its saving throw against the effect, however, an exposed item is harmed (if the attack can harm objects). Refer to Table 10–1: Items Affected by Magical Attacks. Determine which four objects carried or worn by the creature are most likely to be affected and roll randomly among them. The randomly determined item must make a saving throw against the attack form and take whatever damage the attack deals (see Smashing an Object, page 165). For instance, Tordek is hit by a *lightning bolt* and gets a natural 1 on his saving throw. The items of his most likely to have been affected are his shield, his armor, his waraxe (in his hand), and his shortbow (stowed). (He doesn't have magic headgear or a magic cloak, so those entries are skipped.)

If an item is not carried or worn and is not magical, it does not get a saving throw. It simply is dealt the appropriate damage.

SPELL RESISTANCE

Spell resistance is a special defensive ability. If your spell is being resisted by a creature with spell resistance, you must make a caster level check (1d20 + caster level) at least equal to the creature's spell resistance for the spell to affect that creature. The defender's spell resistance is like an Armor Class against magical attacks. The *Dungeon Master's Guide* has more details on spell resistance. Include any adjustments to your caster level (such as from domain granted powers) to this caster level check.

The Spell Resistance entry and the descriptive text of a spell description tell you whether spell resistance protects creatures from the spell. In many cases, spell resistance applies only when a resistant creature is targeted by the spell, not when a resistant creature encounters a spell that is already in place.

The terms "object" and "harmless" mean the same thing for spell resistance as they do for saving throws. A creature with spell resistance must voluntarily lower the resistance (a standard action) in order to be affected by a spell noted as harmless. In such a case, you do not need to make the caster level check described above.

DESCRIPTIVE TEXT

This portion of a spell description details what the spell does and how it works. If one of the previous entries in the description included "see text," this is where the explanation is found. If the spell you're reading about is based on another spell (see Spell Chains, page 181), you might have to refer to a different spell for the "see text" information.

ARCANE SPELLS

Wizards, sorcerers, and bards cast arcane spells, which involve the direct manipulation of mystic energies. These manipulations require natural talent (in the case of sorcerers), long study (in the case of wizards), or both (in the case of bards). Compared to divine spells, arcane spells are more likely to produce dramatic results, such as flight, explosions, or transformations.

PREPARING WIZARD SPELLS

Before setting out on an adventure with her companions, Mialee pores over her spellbook and prepares two 1st-level spells (one for being a 1st-level wizard and an additional one as her 1st-level bonus spell for Intelligence 15) and three 0-level spells. (Arcane spellcasters often call their 0-level spells "cantrips.") From the spells in her spellbook, she chooses *charm person*, *sleep*, *detect magic* (twice), and *light*. While traveling, she and her party are attacked by gnoll raiders, and she casts her *sleep* spell. After she and her companions have dispatched the gnolls, she casts *detect magic* to see whether any of the gnolls' items are enchanted. (They're not.) The party then camps for the night in the wilderness. Come morning, Mialee can once again prepare spells from her spellbook. She already has *charm person*, *detect magic* (once), and *light* prepared from the day before. She chooses to abandon her *light* spell and then prepare *sleep*, *detect magic*, and *ghost sound*. It takes her a little over half an hour to prepare these spells because they represent a little over half of her daily capacity.

A wizard's level limits the number of spells she can prepare and cast (see Table 3–18: The Wizard, page 55). Her high Intelligence score (see Table 1–1: Ability Modifiers and Bonus Spells, page 8) might allow her to prepare a few extra spells. She can prepare the same spell more than once, but each preparation counts as one spell toward her daily limit. Preparing an arcane spell is an arduous mental task. To do so, the wizard must have an Intelligence score of at least 10 + the spell's level.

Rest: To prepare her daily spells, a wizard must have a clear mind. To clear her mind, she must first sleep for 8 hours. The wizard does not have to slumber for every minute of the time, but she must refrain from movement, combat, spellcasting, skill use, conversation, or any other fairly demanding physical or mental task during the rest period. If her rest is interrupted, each interruption adds 1 hour to the total amount of time she has to rest in order to clear her mind, and she must have at least 1 hour of uninterrupted rest immediately prior to preparing her spells. If the character does not need to sleep for some reason, she still must have 8 hours of restful calm before preparing any spells. For example, elf wizards need 8 hours of rest to clear their minds, even though they need only 4 hours of trance to refresh their bodies. Thus, an elf wizard could trance for 4 hours and rest for 4 hours, then prepare spells.

Recent Casting Limit/Rest Interruptions: If a wizard has cast spells recently, the drain on her resources reduces her capacity to prepare new spells. When she prepares spells for the coming day, all the spells she has cast within the last 8 hours count against her daily limit. If Mialee can normally cast two 1st-level spells per day, but she had to cast *magic missile* during the night, she can prepare only one 1st-level spell the next day.

Preparation Environment: To prepare any spell, a wizard must have enough peace, quiet, and comfort to allow for proper concentration. The wizard's surroundings need not be luxurious, but they must be free from overt distractions, such as combat raging nearby or other loud noises. Exposure to inclement weather prevents the necessary concentration, as does any injury or failed saving throw the character might experience while studying. Wizards also must have access to their spellbooks to study from and sufficient light to read them by. There is one major exception: A wizard can prepare a *read magic* spell even without a spellbook. A great portion of her initial training goes into mastering this minor but vital feat of magic.

Spell Preparation Time: After resting, a wizard must study her spellbook to prepare any spells that day. If she wants to prepare all her spells, the process takes 1 hour. Preparing some smaller portion of her daily capacity takes a proportionally smaller amount of time, but always at least 15 minutes, the minimum time required to achieve the proper mental state.

Spell Selection and Preparation: Until she prepares spells from her spellbook, the only spells a wizard has available to cast are the ones that she already had prepared from the previous day and has not yet used. During the study period, she chooses which spells to prepare. The act of preparing a spell is actually the first step in casting it. A spell is designed in such a way that it has an interruption point near its end. This allows a wizard to cast most of the spell ahead of time and finish when it's needed, even if she is under considerable pressure. Her spellbook serves as a guide to the mental exercises she must perform to create the spell's effect. If a wizard already has spells prepared (from the previous day) that she has not cast, she can abandon some or all of them to make room for new spells.

When preparing spells for the day, a wizard can leave some of these spell slots open. Later during that day, she can repeat the preparation process as often as she likes, time and circumstances permitting. During these extra sessions of preparation, the wizard can fill these unused spell slots. She cannot, however, abandon a previously prepared spell to replace it with another one or fill a slot that is empty because she has cast a spell in the meantime. That sort of preparation requires a mind fresh from rest. Like the first session

of the day, this preparation takes at least 15 minutes, and it takes longer if the wizard prepares more than one-quarter of her spells.

Spell Slots: The various character class tables in Chapter 3: Classes show how many spells of each level a character can cast per day. These openings for daily spells are called spell slots. A spellcaster always has the option to fill a higher-level spell slot with a lower-level spell. For example, a 7th-level wizard has at least one 4th-level spell slot and two 3rd-level spell slots (see Table 3–18: The Wizard, page 55). However, the character could choose to prepare three 3rd-level spells instead, filling the 4th-level slot with a 3rd-level spell. A spellcaster who lacks a high enough ability score to cast spells that would otherwise be his or her due still gets the slots but must fill them with spells of lower level.

Prepared Spell Retention: Once a wizard prepares a spell, it remains in her mind as a nearly cast spell until she uses the prescribed components to complete and trigger it or until she abandons it. Upon the casting of a spell, the spell's energy is expended and purged from the character, leaving her feeling a little tired. Certain other events, such as the effects of magic items or special attacks from monsters, can wipe a prepared spell from a character's mind.

Death and Prepared Spell Retention: If a spellcaster dies, all prepared spells stored in his or her mind are wiped away. Potent magic (such as *raise dead*, *resurrection*, or *true resurrection*) can recover the lost energy when it recovers the character.

ARCANE MAGICAL WRITINGS

To record an arcane spell in written form, a character uses complex notation that describes the magical forces involved in the spell. The notation constitutes a universal arcane language that wizards have discovered, not invented. The writer uses the same system no matter what her native language or culture. However, each character uses the system in her own way. Another person's magical writing remains incomprehensible to even the most powerful wizard until she takes time to study and decipher it.

To decipher an arcane magical writing (such as a single spell in written form in another's spellbook or on a scroll), a character must make a Spellcraft check (DC 20 + the spell's level). If the skill check fails, the character cannot attempt to read that particular spell again until the next day. A *read magic* spell automatically deciphers a magical writing without a skill check. If the person who created the magical writing is on hand to help the reader, success is also automatic.

Once a character deciphers a particular magical writing, she does not need to decipher it again. Deciphering a magical writing allows the reader to identify the spell and gives some idea of its effects (as explained in the spell description). If the magical writing was a scroll and the reader can cast arcane spells, she can attempt to use the scroll (see the information on scrolls in the *Dungeon Master's Guide*).

Wizard Spells and Borrowed Spellbooks

A wizard can use a borrowed spellbook to prepare a spell she already knows and has recorded in her own spellbook, but preparation success is not assured. First, the wizard must decipher the writing in the book (see Arcane Magical Writings, above). Once a spell from another spellcaster's book is deciphered, the reader must make a Spellcraft check (DC 15 + spell's level) to prepare the spell. If the check succeeds, the wizard can prepare the spell. She must repeat the check to prepare the spell again, no matter how many times she has prepared it before. If the check fails, she cannot try to prepare the spell from the same source again until the next day. (However, as explained above, she does not need to repeat a check to decipher the writing.)

Adding Spells to a Wizard's Spellbook

Wizards can add new spells to their spellbooks through several methods. If a wizard has chosen to specialize in a school of magic, she can learn spells only from schools whose spells she can cast.

Spells Gained at a New Level: Wizards perform a certain

amount of spell research between adventures. Each time a character attains a new wizard level, she gains two spells of her choice to add to her spellbook. These spells represent the results of her research. The two free spells must be of spell levels she can cast. If she has chosen to specialize in a school of magic, one of the two free spells must be from her specialty school.

Spells Copied from Another's Spellbook or a Scroll: A wizard can also add a spell to her book whenever she encounters one on a magic scroll or in another wizard's spellbook. No matter what the spell's source, the wizard must first decipher the magical writing (see Arcane Magical Writings, above). Next, she must spend a day studying the spell. At the end of the day, she must make a Spellcraft check (DC 15 + spell's level). A wizard who has specialized in a school of spells gains a +2 bonus on the Spellcraft check if the new spell is from her specialty school. She cannot, however, learn any spells from her prohibited schools.

If the check succeeds, the wizard understands the spell and can copy it into her spellbook (see Writing a New Spell into a Spellbook, below). The process leaves a spellbook that was copied from unharmed, but a spell successfully copied from a magic scroll disappears from the parchment.

If the check fails, the wizard cannot understand or copy the spell. She cannot attempt to learn or copy that spell again until she gains another rank in Spellcraft. A spell that was being copied from a scroll does not vanish from the scroll.

In most cases, wizards charge a fee for the privilege of copying spells from their spellbooks. This fee is usually equal to the spell's level × 50 gp, though many wizards jealously guard their higher-level spells and may charge much more, or even deny access to them altogether. Wizards friendly to one another often trade access to equal-level spells from each other's spellbooks at no cost.

Independent Research: A wizard also can research a spell independently, duplicating an existing spell or creating an entirely new one. The *Dungeon Master's Guide* has information on this topic under Creating New Spells in Chapter 2.

Writing a New Spell into a Spellbook

Once a wizard understands a new spell, she can record it into her spellbook.

Time: The process takes 24 hours, regardless of the spell's level.

Space in the Spellbook: A spell takes up one page of the spellbook per spell level, so a 2nd-level spell takes two pages, a 5th-level spell takes five pages, and so forth. Even a 0-level spell (cantrip) takes one page. A spellbook has one hundred pages.

Materials and Costs: Materials for writing the spell (special quills, inks, and other supplies) cost 100 gp per page.

Note that a wizard does not have to pay these costs in time or gold for the spells she gains for free at each new level. She simply adds these to her spellbook as part of her ongoing research.

Replacing and Copying Spellbooks

A wizard can use the procedure for learning a spell to reconstruct a lost spellbook. If she already has a particular spell prepared, she can write it directly into a new book at a cost of 100 gp per page (as noted in Writing a New Spell into a Spellbook, above). The process wipes the prepared spell from her mind, just as casting it would. If she does not have the spell prepared, she can prepare it from a borrowed spellbook and then write it into a new book.

Duplicating an existing spellbook uses the same procedure as replacing it, but the task is much easier. The time requirement and cost per page are halved.

Selling a Spellbook

Captured spellbooks can be sold for a gp amount equal to one-half the cost of purchasing and inscribing the spells within (that is, one-half of 100 gp per page of spells). A spellbook entirely filled with spells (that is, with one hundred pages of spells inscribed in it) is worth 5,000 gp.

SORCERERS AND BARDS

Sorcerers and bards cast arcane spells, but they do not have spellbooks and do not prepare their spells. A sorcerer's or bard's class level limits the number of spells he can cast (see these class descriptions in Chapter 3: Classes). His high Charisma score (see Table 1–1: Ability Modifiers and Bonus Spells, page 8) might allow him to cast a few extra spells. A member of either class must have a Charisma score of at least 10 + a spell's level to cast the spell.

Daily Readying of Spells: Each day, sorcerers and bards must focus their minds on the task of casting their spells. A sorcerer or bard needs 8 hours of rest (just like a wizard), after which he spends 15 minutes concentrating. (A bard must sing, recite, or play an instrument of some kind while concentrating.) During this period, the sorcerer or bard readies his mind to cast his daily allotment of spells. Without such a period to refresh himself, the character does not regain the spell slots he used up the day before.

For example, at 7th level, Gimble the bard can cast one 3rd-level spell (a bonus spell due to his 16 Charisma). If he casts a 3rd-level spell, he can't use his 3rd-level spell slot again until the next day—after he readies his spells for the day.

Recent Casting Limit: As with wizards, any spells cast within the last 8 hours count against the sorcerer's or bard's daily limit.

Adding Spells to a Sorcerer's or Bard's Repertoire: A sorcerer or bard gains spells each time he attains a new level in his class and never gains spells any other way. When your sorcerer or bard gains a new level, consult Table 3–5: Bard Spells Known or Table 3–17: Sorcerer Spells Known to learn how many spells from the appropriate spell list in Chapter 11: Spells he now knows. With the DM's permission, sorcerers and bards can also select the spells they gain from new and unusual spells that they have gained some understanding of (see Spells in the sorcerer description, page 54).

For instance, when Hennet the sorcerer becomes 2nd level, he gains an additional 0-level spell. He can pick that spell from the 0-level spells on the sorcerer and wizard spell list, or he might have learned an unusual spell from an arcane scroll or spellbook.

DIVINE SPELLS

Clerics, druids, experienced paladins, and experienced rangers can cast divine spells. Unlike arcane spells, divine spells draw power from a divine source. Clerics gain spell power from deities or from divine forces. The divine force of nature powers druid and ranger spells. The divine forces of law and good power paladin spells. Divine spells tend to focus on healing and protection and are less flashy, destructive, and disruptive than arcane spells.

PREPARING DIVINE SPELLS

Divine spellcasters prepare their spells in largely the same manner as wizards do, but with a few differences. The relevant ability for divine spells is Wisdom. To prepare a divine spell, a character must have a Wisdom score of 10 + the spell's level. For example, a cleric or druid must have a Wisdom score of at least 10 to prepare a 0-level spell and a Wisdom score of 11 to prepare a 1st-level spell. (Divine spellcasters often call their 0-level spells "orisons.") Likewise, bonus spells are based on Wisdom.

Time of Day: A divine spellcaster chooses and prepares spells ahead of time, just as a wizard does. However, a divine spellcaster does not require a period of rest to prepare spells. Instead, the character chooses a particular part of the day to pray and receive spells. The time is usually associated with some daily event. Dawn, dusk, noon, and midnight are common choices. Some deities set the time or impose other special conditions for granting spells to their clerics. If some event prevents a character from praying at the proper time, he must do so as soon as possible. If the character does not stop to pray for spells at the first opportunity, he must wait until the next day to prepare spells.

Spell Selection and Preparation: A divine spellcaster selects and prepares spells ahead of time through prayer and meditation at a particular time of day. The time required to prepare spells is the same as it is for a wizard (1 hour), as is the requirement for a relatively peaceful environment. A divine spellcaster does not have to prepare all his spells at once. However, the character's mind is considered fresh only during his or her first daily spell preparation, so a divine spellcaster cannot fill a slot that is empty because he or she has cast a spell or abandoned a previously prepared spell.

Divine spellcasters do not require spellbooks. However, such a character's spell selection is limited to the spells on the list for his or her class (see Chapter 11: Spells). Clerics, druids, paladins, and rangers have separate spell lists. A cleric also has access to two domains determined during his character creation. Each domain gives him access to a domain spell at each spell level from 1st to 9th, as well as a special granted power. With access to two domain spells at each spell level—one from each of his two domains—a cleric must prepare, as an extra domain spell, one or the other each day for each level of spell he can cast. (The extra domain spell is the "+1" that appears as part of the cleric's Spells per Day figure on Table 3–6: The Cleric, page 31.) If a domain spell is not on the cleric spell list, it can be prepared only in a domain spell slot.

Spell Slots: The character class tables in Chapter 3: Classes show how many spells of each level a character can cast per day. These openings for daily spells are called spell slots. A spellcaster always has the option to fill a higher-level spell slot with a lower-level spell. For example, a 7th-level cleric has at least one 4th-level spell slot and two 3rd-level spell slots. However, he could choose to prepare three 3rd-level spells instead, filling the 4th-level slot with a lower-level spell. Similarly, he could fill his 4th-level domain spell slot with a lower-level domain spell. A spellcaster who lacks a high enough ability score to cast spells that would otherwise be his or her due still gets the slots but must fill them with spells of lower level. For example, a 9th-level cleric who has a Wisdom score of only 14 cannot cast a 5th-level spell but can prepare an extra lower-level spell in its place and store it in the 5th-level spell slot.

Recent Casting Limit: As with arcane spells, at the time of preparation any spells cast within the previous 8 hours count against the number of spells that can be prepared.

Spontaneous Casting of _Cure_ and _Inflict_ Spells: A good cleric (or a cleric of a good deity) can spontaneously cast a _cure_ spell in place of a prepared spell of the same level or higher, but not in place of a domain spell. An evil cleric (or a cleric of an evil deity) can spontaneously cast an _inflict_ spell in place of a prepared spell (one that is not a domain spell) of the same level or higher. Each neutral cleric of a neutral deity either spontaneously casts _cure_ spells like a good cleric or _inflict_ spells like an evil one, depending on which option the player chooses when creating the character. The divine energy of the spell that the _cure_ or _inflict_ spell substitutes for is converted into the _cure_ or _inflict_ spell as if that spell had been prepared all along.

Spontaneous Casting of _Summon Nature's Ally_ Spells: A druid can spontaneously cast a _summon nature's ally_ spell in place of a prepared spell of the same level or higher. The divine energy of the spell that the _summon nature's ally_ spell substitutes for is converted into the _summon_ spell as if that spell had been prepared all along.

DIVINE MAGICAL WRITINGS

Divine spells can be written down and deciphered just as arcane spells can (see Arcane Magical Writings, above). Any character with the Spellcraft skill can attempt to decipher the divine magical writing and identify it. However, only characters who have the spell in question (in its divine form) on their class spell list can cast a divine spell from a scroll.

NEW DIVINE SPELLS

Divine spellcasters most frequently gain new spells in one of the following two ways.

Spells Gained at a New Level: Characters who can cast divine spells undertake a certain amount of study between adventures. Each time such a character receives a new level of divine spells, he or she learns new spells from that level automatically.

Independent Research: A divine spellcaster also can research a spell independently, much as an arcane spellcaster can. (The _Dungeon Master's Guide_ has information on this topic under Creating New Spells in Chapter 2.) Only the creator of such a spell can prepare and cast it, unless he decides to share it with others. Some such creators share their research with their churches, but others do not. The character can create a magic scroll (provided that he or she has the Scribe Scroll feat) or write a special text similar to a spellbook to contain spells he or she has independently researched. Other divine spellcasters who find the spell in written form can learn to cast it, provided they are of sufficient level to do so and are of the same class as the creator. The process requires deciphering the writing (see Arcane Magical Writings, above).

SPECIAL ABILITIES

Medusas, dryads, harpies, and other magical creatures can create magical effects without being spellcasters. Characters using magic wands, rods, and other enchanted items, as well as certain class features, can also create magical effects. These effects come in two types: spell-like and supernatural. Additionally, members of certain classes and certain creatures can use special abilities that aren't magical. These abilities are called extraordinary or natural.

Spell-Like Abilities: A dryad's _charm person_ effect and the _greater teleport_ ability of many devils are spell-like abilities. Usually, a spell-like ability works just like the spell of that name. A few spell-like abilities are unique; these are explained in the text where they are described.

A spell-like ability has no verbal, somatic, or material component, nor does it require a focus or have an XP cost. The user activates it mentally. Armor never affects a spell-like ability's use, even if the ability resembles an arcane spell with a somatic component. A spell-like ability has a casting time of 1 standard action unless noted otherwise in the ability or spell description. In all other ways, a spell-like ability functions just like a spell.

Spell-like abilities are subject to spell resistance and to being dispelled by _dispel magic_. They do not function in areas where magic is suppressed or negated, such as an _antimagic field_. Spell-like abilities cannot be used to counterspell, nor can they be counterspelled.

Some creatures are actually sorcerers of a sort. They cast arcane spells as sorcerers do, using components when required. In fact, an individual creature (such as some dragons) could have some spell-like abilities and also cast other spells as a sorcerer.

Supernatural Abilities: A dragon's fiery breath, a medusa's petrifying gaze, a spectre's energy drain, and a cleric's use of positive or negative energy to turn or rebuke undead are supernatural abilities. These abilities cannot be disrupted in combat, as spells can, and they generally do not provoke attacks of opportunity. Supernatural abilities are not subject to spell resistance, counterspells, or to being dispelled by _dispel magic_, and do not function in areas where magic is suppressed or negated (such as an _antimagic field_).

Extraordinary Abilities: A rogue's evasion ability and a troll's ability to regenerate are extraordinary abilities. These abilities cannot be disrupted in combat, as spells can, and they generally do not provoke attacks of opportunity. Effects or areas that negate or disrupt magic have no effect on extraordinary abilities. They are not subject to dispelling, and they function normally in an _antimagic field_. Indeed, extraordinary abilities do not qualify as magical, though they may break the laws of physics.

Natural Abilities: This category includes abilities a creature has because of its physical nature, such as a bird's ability to fly. Natural abilities are those not otherwise designated as extraordinary, supernatural, or spell-like.

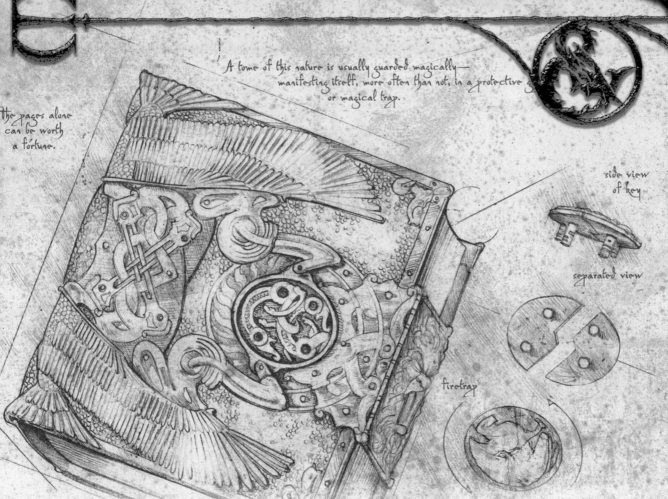

A tome of this nature is usually guarded magically— manifesting itself, more often than not, in a protective [glyph] or magical trap.

the pages alone can be worth a fortune.

side view of key

separated view

Illus. by A. Swekel

firetrap

FIG. A

FIG. B

View of Spine

This chapter begins with the spell lists of the spellcasting classes and the list of cleric domains and the spells associated with each domain. An ᴹ or ᶠ appearing at the end of a spell's name in the spell lists denotes a spell with a material or focus component, respectively, that is not normally included in a spell component pouch. An ˣ denotes a spell with an XP component paid by the caster.

The remainder of the chapter contains spell descriptions in alphabetical order by spell name.

Spell Chains: Some spells reference other spells that they are based upon. (For instance, *cure light wounds* is the spell upon which all other *cure* spells are based, and *lesser planar ally* is the spell upon which *planar ally* and *greater planar ally* are based.) Only information about a spell elsewhere in the spell chain that is different from the base spell is covered in the spell being described. Spell description entries and descriptive text that are the same as the base spell are not repeated.

Order of Presentation: In the spell lists and the spell descriptions that follow them, the spells are presented in alphabetical order by name except for those belonging to certain spell chains. When a spell's name begins with "lesser," "greater," or "mass," the spell description is alphabetized under the second word of the spell name instead. For instance, the spell *mass suggestion* is entered in the lists as "Suggestion, Mass," and its description can be found immediately following the description for *suggestion*.

Hit Dice: The term "Hit Dice" is used synonymously with "character levels" for effects that affect a number of Hit Dice of creatures. Creatures with Hit Dice only from their race, not from classes, have character levels equal to their Hit Dice.

Caster Level: A spell's power often depends on caster level, which is defined as the caster's class level for the purpose of cast-

ing a particular spell. A creature with no classes has a caster level equal to its Hit Dice unless otherwise specified. The word "level" in the spell lists that follow always refers to caster level.

Spell Effects and Conditions: If a spell causes its subject or subjects to be affected by one or more conditions (such as blinded, incorporeal, invisible, or stunned), refer to the glossary for details of how that condition affects the subject. Chapter 8 of the *Dungeon Master's Guide* has more information on the various conditions.

Creatures and Characters: The words "creature" and "character" are used synonymously in the spell descriptions.

BARD SPELLS

O-LEVEL BARD SPELLS (CANTRIPS)

Dancing Lights: Creates torches or other lights.

Daze: Humanoid creature of 4 HD or less loses next action.

Detect Magic: Detects spells and magic items within 60 ft.

Flare: Dazzles one creature (–1 on attack rolls).

Ghost Sound: Figment sounds.

Know Direction: You discern north.

Light: Object shines like a torch.

Lullaby: Makes subject drowsy; –5 on Spot and Listen checks, –2 on Will saves against *sleep*.

Mage Hand: 5-pound telekinesis.

Mending: Makes minor repairs on an object.

Opened properly, the book can be a library unto itself— as well as a vast archive of archaic knowledge.

Message: Whispered conversation at distance.

Open/Close: Opens or closes small or light things.

Prestidigitation: Performs minor tricks.

Read Magic: Read scrolls and spellbooks.

Resistance: Subject gains +1 on saving throws.

Summon Instrument: Summons one instrument of the caster's choice.

1ST-LEVEL BARD SPELLS

Alarm: Wards an area for 2 hours/level.

Animate Rope: Makes a rope move at your command.

Cause Fear: One creature of 5 HD or less flees for 1d4 rounds.

Charm Person: Makes one person your friend.

Comprehend Languages: You understand all spoken and written languages.

Cure Light Wounds: Cures 1d8 damage +1/level (max +5).

Detect Secret Doors: Reveals hidden doors within 60 ft.

Disguise Self: Changes your appearance.

Erase: Mundane or magical writing vanishes.

Expeditious Retreat: Your speed increases by 30 ft.

Feather Fall: Objects or creatures fall slowly.

Grease: Makes 10-ft. square or one object slippery.

Hypnotism: Fascinates 2d4 HD of creatures.

Identifyᴹ: Determines properties of magic item.

Lesser Confusion: One creature is *confused* for 1 round.

Magic Mouthᴹ: Speaks once when triggered.

Nystul's Magic Aura: Alters object's magic aura.

Obscure Object: Masks object against scrying.

Remove Fear: Suppresses fear or gives +4 on saves against fear for one subject + one per four levels.

Silent Image: Creates minor illusion of your design.

Sleep: Puts 4 HD of creatures into magical slumber.

Summon Monster I: Calls extraplanar creature to fight for you.

Tasha's Hideous Laughter: Subject loses actions for 1 round/level.

Undetectable Alignment: Conceals alignment for 24 hours.

Unseen Servant: Invisible force obeys your commands.

Ventriloquism: Throws voice for 1 min./level.

2ND-LEVEL BARD SPELLS

Alter Self: Assume form of a similar creature.

Animal Messenger: Sends a Tiny animal to a specific place.

Animal Trance: Fascinates 2d6 HD of animals.

Blindness/Deafness: Makes subject blind or deaf.

Blur: Attacks miss subject 20% of the time.

Calm Emotions: Calms creatures, negating emotion effects.

Cat's Grace: Subject gains +4 to Dex for 1 min./level.

Cure Moderate Wounds: Cures 2d8 damage +1/level (max +10).

Darkness: 20-ft. radius of supernatural shadow.

Daze Monster: Living creature of 6 HD or less loses next action.

Delay Poison: Stops poison from harming subject for 1 hour/level.

Detect Thoughts: Allows "listening" to surface thoughts.

Eagle's Splendor: Subject gains +4 to Cha for 1 min./level.

Enthrall: Captivates all within 100 ft. + 10 ft./level.

Fox's Cunning: Subject gains +4 to Int for 1 min./level.

Glitterdust: Blinds creatures, outlines invisible creatures.

Heroism: Gives +2 on attack rolls, saves, skill checks.

Hold Person: Paralyzes one humanoid for 1 round/level.

Hypnotic Pattern: Fascinates (2d4 + level) HD of creatures.

Invisibility: Subject is invisible for 1 min./level or until it attacks.

Locate Object: Senses direction toward object (specific or type).

Minor Image: As *silent image*, plus some sound.

Mirror Image: Creates decoy duplicates of you (1d4 +1 per three levels, max 8).

Misdirection: Misleads divinations for one creature or object.

Pyrotechnics: Turns fire into blinding light or choking smoke.

Rage: Gives +2 to Str and Con, +1 on Will saves, −2 to AC.

Scare: Panics creatures of less than 6 HD.

Shatter: Sonic vibration damages objects or crystalline creatures.

Silence: Negates sound in 15-ft. radius.

Sound Burst: Deals 1d8 sonic damage to subjects; may stun them.

Suggestion: Compels subject to follow stated course of action.

Summon Monster II: Calls extraplanar creature to fight for you.

Summon Swarm: Summons swarm of bats, rats, or spiders.

Tongues: Speak any language.

Whispering Wind: Sends a short message 1 mile/level.

3RD-LEVEL BARD SPELLS

Blink: You randomly vanish and reappear for 1 round/level.

Charm Monster: Makes monster believe it is your ally.

Clairaudience/Clairvoyance: Hear or see at a distance for 1 min./level.

Confusion: Subjects behave oddly for 1 round/level.

Crushing Despair: Subjects take −2 on attack rolls, damage rolls, saves, and checks.

Cure Serious Wounds: Cures 3d8 damage +1/level (max +15).

Daylight: 60-ft. radius of bright light.

Deep Slumber: Puts 10 HD of creatures to sleep.

Dispel Magic: Cancels magical spells and effects.

Displacement: Attacks miss subject 50%.

Fear: Subjects within cone flee for 1 round/level.

Gaseous Form: Subject becomes insubstantial and can fly slowly.

Geas, Lesser: Commands subject of 7 HD or less.

Glibness: You gain +30 bonus on Bluff checks, and your lies can escape magical discernment.

Good Hope: Subjects gain +2 on attack rolls, damage rolls, saves, and checks.

Haste: One creature/level moves faster, +1 on attack rolls, AC, and Reflex saves.

Illusory Scriptᴹ: Only intended reader can decipher.

Invisibility Sphere: Makes everyone within 10 ft. invisible.

Leomund's Tiny Hut: Creates shelter for ten creatures.

Major Image: As *silent image*, plus sound, smell and thermal effects.

Phantom Steed: Magic horse appears for 1 hour/level.

Remove Curse: Frees object or person from curse.

Scryingᶠ: Spies on subject from a distance.

Sculpt Sound: Creates new sounds or changes existing ones.

Secret Page: Changes one page to hide its real content.

See Invisibility: Reveals invisible creatures or objects.

Sepia Snake Sigilᴹ: Creates text symbol that immobilizes reader.

Slow: One subject/level takes only one action/round, −2 to AC and attack rolls.

Speak with Animals: You can communicate with animals.

Summon Monster III: Calls extraplanar creature to fight for you.

4TH-LEVEL BARD SPELLS

Break Enchantment: Frees subjects from enchantments, alterations, curses, and petrification.

Cure Critical Wounds: Cures 4d8 damage +1/level (max +20).

Detect Scrying: Alerts you of magical eavesdropping.

Dimension Door: Teleports you short distance.

Dominate Person: Controls humanoid telepathically.

Freedom of Movement: Subject moves normally despite impediments.

Hallucinatory Terrain: Makes one type of terrain appear like another (field into forest, or the like).

Hold Monster: As *hold person*, but any creature.

Invisibility, Greater: As *invisibility*, but subject can attack and stay invisible.

Legend Lore [M F]: Lets you learn tales about a person, place, or thing.

Leomund's Secure Shelter: Creates sturdy cottage.

Locate Creature: Indicates direction to familiar creature.

Modify Memory: Changes 5 minutes of subject's memories.

Neutralize Poison: Immunizes subject against poison, detoxifies venom in or on subject.

Rainbow Pattern: Lights fascinate 24 HD of creatures.

Repel Vermin: Insects, spiders, and other vermin stay 10 ft. away.

Shadow Conjuration: Mimics conjuring below 4th level, but only 20% real.

Shout: Deafens all within cone and deals 5d6 sonic damage.

Speak with Plants: You can talk to normal plants and plant creatures.

Summon Monster IV: Calls extraplanar creature to fight for you.

Zone of Silence: Keeps eavesdroppers from overhearing conversations.

5TH-LEVEL BARD SPELLS

Cure Light Wounds, Mass: Cures 1d8 damage +1/level for many creatures.

Dispel Magic, Greater: As *dispel magic*, but +20 on check.

Dream: Sends message to anyone sleeping.

False Vision [M]: Fools scrying with an illusion.

Heroism, Greater: Gives +4 bonus on attack rolls, saves, skill checks; immunity to fear; temporary hp.

Mind Fog: Subjects in fog get –10 to Wis and Will checks.

Mirage Arcana: As *hallucinatory terrain*, plus structures.

Mislead: Turns you invisible and creates illusory double.

Nightmare: Sends vision dealing 1d10 damage, fatigue.

Persistent Image: As *major image*, but no concentration required.

Seeming: Changes appearance of one person per two levels.

Shadow Evocation: Mimics evocation of lower than 5th level, but only 20% real.

Shadow Walk: Step into shadow to travel rapidly.

Song of Discord: Forces targets to attack each other.

Suggestion, Mass: As *suggestion*, plus one subject/level.

Summon Monster V: Calls extraplanar creature to fight for you.

6TH-LEVEL BARD SPELLS

Analyze Dweomer [F]: Reveals magical aspects of subject.

Animate Objects: Objects attack your foes.

Cat's Grace, Mass: As *cat's grace*, affects one subject/level.

Charm Monster, Mass: As *charm monster*, but all within 30 ft.

Cure Moderate Wounds, Mass: Cures 2d8 damage +1/level for many creatures.

Eagle's Splendor, Mass: As *eagle's splendor*, affects one subject/level.

Eyebite: Target becomes panicked, sickened, and comatose.

Find the Path: Shows most direct way to a location.

Fox's Cunning, Mass: As *fox's cunning*, affects one subject/level.

Geas/Quest: As *lesser geas*, plus it affects any creature.

Heroes' Feast: Food for one creature/level cures and grants combat bonuses.

Otto's Irresistible Dance: Forces subject to dance.

Permanent Image: Includes sight, sound, and smell.

Programmed Image [M]: As *major image*, plus triggered by event.

Project Image: Illusory double can talk and cast spells.

Scrying, Greater: As *scrying*, but faster and longer.

Shout, Greater: Devastating yell deals 10d6 sonic damage; stuns creatures, damages objects.

Summon Monster VI: Calls extraplanar creature to fight for you.

Sympathetic Vibration: Deals 2d10 damage/round to freestanding structure.

Veil: Changes appearance of group of creatures.

CLERIC SPELLS

0-LEVEL CLERIC SPELLS (ORISONS)

Create Water: Creates 2 gallons/level of pure water.

Cure Minor Wounds: Cures 1 point of damage.

Detect Magic: Detects spells and magic items within 60 ft.

Detect Poison: Detects poison in one creature or object.

Guidance: +1 on one attack roll, saving throw, or skill check.

Inflict Minor Wounds: Touch attack, 1 point of damage.

Light: Object shines like a torch.

Mending: Makes minor repairs on an object.

Purify Food and Drink: Purifies 1 cu. ft./level of food or water.

Read Magic: Read scrolls and spellbooks.

Resistance: Subject gains +1 on saving throws.

Virtue: Subject gains 1 temporary hp.

1ST-LEVEL CLERIC SPELLS

Bane: Enemies take –1 on attack rolls and saves against fear.

Bless: Allies gain +1 on attack rolls and saves against fear.

Bless Water [M]: Makes holy water.

Cause Fear: One creature of 5 HD or less flees for 1d4 rounds.

Command: One subject obeys selected command for 1 round.

Comprehend Languages: You understand all spoken and written languages.

Cure Light Wounds: Cures 1d8 damage +1/level (max +5).

Curse Water [M]: Makes unholy water.

Deathwatch: Reveals how near death subjects within 30 ft. are.

Detect Chaos/Evil/Good/Law: Reveals creatures, spells, or objects of selected alignment.

Detect Undead: Reveals undead within 60 ft.

Divine Favor: You gain +1 per three levels on attack and damage rolls.

Doom: One subject takes –2 on attack rolls, damage rolls, saves, and checks.

Endure Elements: Exist comfortably in hot or cold environments.

Entropic Shield: Ranged attacks against you have 20% miss chance.

Hide from Undead: Undead can't perceive one subject/level.

Inflict Light Wounds: Touch deals 1d8 damage +1/level (max +5).

Magic Stone: Three stones gain +1 on attack, deal 1d6 +1 damage.

Magic Weapon: Weapon gains +1 bonus.

Obscuring Mist: Fog surrounds you.

Protection from Chaos/Evil/Good/Law: +2 to AC and saves, counter mind control, hedge out elementals and outsiders.

Remove Fear: Suppresses fear or gives +4 on saves against fear for one subject + one per four levels.

Sanctuary: Opponents can't attack you, and you can't attack.

Shield of Faith: Aura grants +2 or higher deflection bonus.

Summon Monster I: Calls extraplanar creature to fight for you.

2ND-LEVEL CLERIC SPELLS

Aid: +1 on attack rolls and saves against fear, 1d8 temporary hp +1/level (max +10).

Align Weapon: Weapon becomes good, evil, lawful, or chaotic.

Augury [M F]: Learns whether an action will be good or bad.

Bear's Endurance: Subject gains +4 to Con for 1 min./level.

Bull's Strength: Subject gains +4 to Str for 1 min./level.

Calm Emotions: Calms creatures, negating emotion effects.

Consecrate [M]: Fills area with positive energy, making undead weaker.

Cure Moderate Wounds: Cures 2d8 damage +1/level (max +10).

Darkness: 20-ft. radius of supernatural shadow.

Death Knell: Kills dying creature; you gain 1d8 temporary hp, +2 to Str, and +1 level.

Delay Poison: Stops poison from harming subject for 1 hour/level.

Desecrate M: Fills area with negative energy, making undead stronger.

Eagle's Splendor: Subject gains +4 to Cha for 1 min./level.

Enthrall: Captivates all within 100 ft. + 10 ft./level.

Find Traps: Notice traps as a rogue does.

Gentle Repose: Preserves one corpse.

Hold Person: Paralyzes one humanoid for 1 round/level.

Inflict Moderate Wounds: Touch attack, 2d8 damage +1/level (max +10).

Make Whole: Repairs an object.

Owl's Wisdom: Subject gains +4 to Wis for 1 min./level.

Remove Paralysis: Frees one or more creatures from paralysis or *slow* effect.

Resist Energy: Ignores 10 (or more) points of damage/attack from specified energy type.

Restoration, Lesser: Dispels magical ability penalty or repairs 1d4 ability damage.

Shatter: Sonic vibration damages objects or crystalline creatures.

Shield Other F: You take half of subject's damage.

Silence: Negates sound in 15-ft. radius.

Sound Burst: Deals 1d8 sonic damage to subjects; may stun them.

Spiritual Weapon: Magic weapon attacks on its own.

Status: Monitors condition, position of allies.

Summon Monster II: Calls extraplanar creature to fight for you.

Undetectable Alignment: Conceals alignment for 24 hours.

Zone of Truth: Subjects within range cannot lie.

3RD-LEVEL CLERIC SPELLS

Animate Dead M: Creates undead skeletons and zombies.

Bestow Curse: −6 to an ability score; −4 on attack rolls, saves, and checks; or 50% chance of losing each action.

Blindness/Deafness: Makes subject blinded or deafened.

Contagion: Infects subject with chosen disease.

Continual Flame M: Makes a permanent, heatless torch.

Create Food and Water: Feeds three humans (or one horse)/level.

Cure Serious Wounds: Cures 3d8 damage +1/level (max +15).

Daylight: 60-ft. radius of bright light.

Deeper Darkness: Object sheds supernatural shadow in 60-ft. radius.

Dispel Magic: Cancels spells and magical effects.

Glyph of Warding M: Inscription harms those who pass it.

Helping Hand: Ghostly hand leads subject to you.

Inflict Serious Wounds: Touch attack, 3d8 damage +1/level (max +15).

Invisibility Purge: Dispels invisibility within 5 ft./level.

Locate Object: Senses direction toward object (specific or type).

Magic Circle against Chaos/Evil/Good/Law: As *protection* spells, but 10-ft. radius and 10 min./level.

Magic Vestment: Armor or shield gains +1 enhancement per four levels.

Meld into Stone: You and your gear merge with stone.

Obscure Object: Masks object against scrying.

Prayer: Allies +1 bonus on most rolls, enemies −1 penalty.

Protection from Energy: Absorb 12 points/level of damage from one kind of energy.

Remove Blindness/Deafness: Cures normal or magical conditions.

Remove Curse: Frees object or person from curse.

Remove Disease: Cures all diseases affecting subject.

Searing Light: Ray deals 1d8/two levels damage, more against undead.

Speak with Dead: Corpse answers one question/two levels.

Stone Shape: Sculpts stone into any shape.

Summon Monster III: Calls extraplanar creature to fight for you.

Water Breathing: Subjects can breathe underwater.

Water Walk: Subject treads on water as if solid.

Wind Wall: Deflects arrows, smaller creatures, and gases.

4TH-LEVEL CLERIC SPELLS

Air Walk: Subject treads on air as if solid (climb at 45-degree angle).

Control Water: Raises or lowers bodies of water.

Cure Critical Wounds: Cures 4d8 damage +1/level (max +20).

Death Ward: Grants immunity to death spells and negative energy effects.

Dimensional Anchor: Bars extradimensional movement.

Discern Lies: Reveals deliberate falsehoods.

Dismissal: Forces a creature to return to native plane.

Divination M: Provides useful advice for specific proposed actions.

Divine Power: You gain attack bonus, +6 to Str, and 1 hp/level.

Freedom of Movement: Subject moves normally despite impediments.

Giant Vermin: Turns centipedes, scorpions, or spiders into giant vermin.

Imbue with Spell Ability: Transfer spells to subject.

Inflict Critical Wounds: Touch attack, 4d8 damage +1/level (max +20).

Magic Weapon, Greater: +1 bonus/four levels (max +5).

Neutralize Poison: Immunizes subject against poison, detoxifies venom in or on subject.

Planar Ally, Lesser X: Exchange services with a 6 HD extraplanar creature.

Poison: Touch deals 1d10 Con damage, repeats in 1 min.

Repel Vermin: Insects, spiders, and other vermin stay 10 ft. away.

Restoration M: Restores level and ability score drains.

Sending: Delivers short message anywhere, instantly.

Spell Immunity: Subject is immune to one spell per four levels.

Summon Monster IV: Calls extraplanar creature to fight for you.

Tongues: Speak any language.

5TH-LEVEL CLERIC SPELLS

Atonement F X: Removes burden of misdeeds from subject.

Break Enchantment: Frees subjects from enchantments, alterations, curses, and petrification.

Command, Greater: As *command*, but affects one subject/level.

Commune X: Deity answers one yes-or-no question/level.

Cure Light Wounds, Mass: Cures 1d8 damage +1/level for many creatures.

Dispel Chaos/Evil/Good/Law: +4 bonus against attacks.

Disrupting Weapon: Melee weapon destroys undead.

Flame Strike: Smite foes with divine fire (1d6/level damage).

Hallow M: Designates location as holy.

Inflict Light Wounds, Mass: Deals 1d8 damage +1/level to many creatures.

Insect Plague: Locust swarms attack creatures.

Mark of Justice: Designates action that will trigger *curse* on subject.

Plane Shift F: As many as eight subjects travel to another plane.

Raise Dead M: Restores life to subject who died as long as one day/level ago.

Righteous Might: Your size increases, and you gain combat bonuses.

Scrying F: Spies on subject from a distance.

Slay Living: Touch attack kills subject.

Spell Resistance: Subject gains SR 12 + level.

Summon Monster V: Calls extraplanar creature to fight for you.

Symbol of Pain M: Triggered rune wracks nearby creatures with pain.

Symbol of Sleep M: Triggered rune puts nearby creatures into catatonic slumber.

True Seeing [M]: Lets you see all things as they really are.

Unhallow [M]: Designates location as unholy.

Wall of Stone: Creates a stone wall that can be shaped.

6TH-LEVEL CLERIC SPELLS

Animate Objects: Objects attack your foes.

Antilife Shell: 10-ft. field hedges out living creatures.

Banishment: Banishes 2 HD/level of extraplanar creatures.

Bear's Endurance, Mass: As *bear's endurance*, affects one subject/level.

Blade Barrier: Wall of blades deals 1d6/level damage.

Bull's Strength, Mass: As *bull's strength*, affects one subject/level.

Create Undead: Create ghouls, ghasts, mummies, or mohrgs.

Cure Moderate Wounds, Mass: Cures 2d8 damage +1/level for many creatures.

Dispel Magic, Greater: As *dispel magic*, but up to +20 on check.

Eagle's Splendor, Mass: As *eagle's splendor*, affects one subject/level.

Find the Path: Shows most direct way to a location.

Forbiddance [M]: Blocks planar travel, damages creatures of different alignment.

Geas/Quest: As *lesser geas*, plus it affects any creature.

Glyph of Warding, Greater: As *glyph of warding*, but up to 10d8 damage or 6th-level spell.

Harm: Deals 10 points/level damage to target.

Heal: Cures 10 points/level of damage, all diseases and mental conditions.

Heroes' Feast: Food for one creature/level cures and grants combat bonuses.

Inflict Moderate Wounds, Mass: Deals 2d8 damage +1/level to many creatures.

Owl's Wisdom, Mass: As *owl's wisdom*, affects one subject/level.

Planar Ally [X]: As *lesser planar ally*, but up to 12 HD.

Summon Monster VI: Calls extraplanar creature to fight for you.

Symbol of Fear [M]: Triggered rune panics nearby creatures.

Symbol of Persuasion [M]: Triggered rune charms nearby creatures.

Undeath to Death [M]: Destroys 1d4 HD/level undead (max 20d4).

Wind Walk: You and your allies turn vaporous and travel fast.

Word of Recall: Teleports you back to designated place.

7TH-LEVEL CLERIC SPELLS

Blasphemy: Kills, paralyzes, weakens, or dazes nonevil subjects.

Control Weather: Changes weather in local area.

Cure Serious Wounds, Mass: Cures 3d8 damage +1/level for many creatures.

Destruction [F]: Kills subject and destroys remains.

Dictum: Kills, paralyzes, slows, or deafens nonlawful subjects.

Ethereal Jaunt: You become ethereal for 1 round/level.

Holy Word: Kills, paralyzes, blinds, or deafens nongood subjects.

Inflict Serious Wounds, Mass: Deals 3d8 damage +1/level to many creatures.

Refuge [M]: Alters item to transport its possessor to you.

Regenerate: Subject's severed limbs grow back, cures 4d8 damage +1/level (max +35).

Repulsion: Creatures can't approach you.

Restoration, Greater [X]: As *restoration*, plus restores all levels and ability scores.

Resurrection [M]: Fully restore dead subject.

Scrying, Greater: As *scrying*, but faster and longer.

Summon Monster VII: Calls extraplanar creature to fight for you.

Symbol of Stunning [M]: Triggered rune stuns nearby creatures.

Symbol of Weakness [M]: Triggered rune weakens nearby creatures.

Word of Chaos: Kills, *confuses*, stuns, or deafens nonchaotic subjects.

8TH-LEVEL CLERIC SPELLS

Antimagic Field: Negates magic within 10 ft.

Cloak of Chaos [F]: +4 to AC, +4 resistance, and SR 25 against lawful spells.

Create Greater Undead [M]: Create shadows, wraiths, spectres, or devourers.

Cure Critical Wounds, Mass: Cures 4d8 damage +1/level for many creatures.

Dimensional Lock: Teleportation and interplanar travel blocked for one day/level.

Discern Location: Reveals exact location of creature or object.

Earthquake: Intense tremor shakes 5-ft./level radius.

Fire Storm: Deals 1d6/level fire damage.

Holy Aura [F]: +4 to AC, +4 resistance, and SR 25 against evil spells.

Planar Ally, Greater [X]: As *lesser planar ally*, but up to 18 HD.

Inflict Critical Wounds, Mass: Deals 4d8 damage +1/level to many creatures.

Shield of Law [F]: +4 to AC, +4 resistance, and SR 25 against chaotic spells.

Spell Immunity, Greater: As *spell immunity*, but up to 8th-level spells.

Summon Monster VIII: Calls extraplanar creature to fight for you.

Symbol of Death [M]: Triggered rune slays nearby creatures.

Symbol of Insanity [M]: Triggered rune renders nearby creatures insane.

Unholy Aura [F]: +4 to AC, +4 resistance, and SR 25 against good spells.

9TH-LEVEL CLERIC SPELLS

Astral Projection [M]: Projects you and companions onto Astral Plane.

Energy Drain: Subject gains 2d4 negative levels.

Etherealness: Travel to Ethereal Plane with companions.

Gate [X]: Connects two planes for travel or summoning.

Heal, Mass: As *heal*, but with several subjects.

Implosion: Kills one creature/round.

Miracle [X]: Requests a deity's intercession.

Soul Bind [F]: Traps newly dead soul to prevent *resurrection*.

Storm of Vengeance: Storm rains acid, lightning, and hail.

Summon Monster IX: Calls extraplanar creature to fight for you.

True Resurrection [M]: As *resurrection*, plus remains aren't needed.

CLERIC DOMAINS

AIR DOMAIN

Deities: Obad-Hai.

Granted Powers: Turn or destroy earth creatures as a good cleric turns undead. Rebuke, command, or bolster air creatures as an evil cleric rebukes undead. Use these abilities a total number of times per day equal to 3 + your Charisma modifier. This granted power is a supernatural ability.

Air Domain Spells

1 **Obscuring Mist:** Fog surrounds you.
2 **Wind Wall:** Deflects arrows, smaller creatures, and gases.
3 **Gaseous Form:** Subject becomes insubstantial and can fly slowly.
4 **Air Walk:** Subject treads on air as if solid (climb at 45-degree angle).
5 **Control Winds:** Change wind direction and speed.
6 **Chain Lightning:** 1d6/level damage; 1 secondary bolt/level each deals half damage.
7 **Control Weather:** Changes weather in local area.
8 **Whirlwind:** Cyclone deals damage and can pick up creatures.
9 **Elemental Swarm**[*]: Summons multiple elementals.

[*]Cast as an air spell only.

ANIMAL DOMAIN

Deities: Ehlonna, Obad-Hai.

Granted Powers: You can use *speak with animals* once per day as a spell-like ability.

Add Knowledge (nature) to your list of cleric class skills.

Animal Domain Spells

1 **Calm Animals:** Calms (2d4 + level) HD of animals.
2 **Hold Animal:** Paralyzes one animal for 1 round/level.
3 **Dominate Animal:** Subject animal obeys silent mental commands.
4 **Summon Nature's Ally IV*:** Calls creature to fight.
5 **Commune with Nature:** Learn about terrain for 1 mile/level.
6 **Antilife Shell:** 10-ft. field hedges out living creatures.
7 **Animal Shapes:** One ally/level polymorphs into chosen animal.
8 **Summon Nature's Ally VIII*:** Calls creature to fight.
9 **Shapechange**F: Transforms you into any creature, and change forms once per round.

*Can only summon animals.

CHAOS DOMAIN

Deities: Corellon Larethian, Erythnul, Gruumsh, Kord, Olidammara.

Granted Power: You cast chaos spells at +1 caster level.

Chaos Domain Spells

1 **Protection from Law:** +2 to AC and saves, counter mind control, hedge out elementals and outsiders.
2 **Shatter:** Sonic vibration damages objects or crystalline creatures.
3 **Magic Circle against Law:** As *protection* spells, but 10-ft. radius and 10 min./level.
4 **Chaos Hammer:** Damages and staggers lawful creatures.
5 **Dispel Law:** +4 bonus against attacks by lawful creatures.
6 **Animate Objects:** Objects attack your foes.
7 **Word of Chaos:** Kills, *confuses*, stuns, or deafens nonchaotic subjects.
8 **Cloak of Chaos**F: +4 to AC, +4 resistance, SR 25 against lawful spells.
9 **Summon Monster IX*:** Calls extraplanar creature to fight for you.

*Cast as a chaos spell only.

DEATH DOMAIN

Deities: Nerull, Wee Jas.

Granted Power: You may use a death touch once per day. Your death touch is a supernatural ability that produces a death effect. You must succeed on a melee touch attack against a living creature (using the rules for touch spells). When you touch, roll 1d6 per cleric level you possess. If the total at least equals the creature's current hit points, it dies (no save).

Death Domain Spells

1 **Cause Fear:** One creature of 5 HD or less flees for 1d4 rounds.
2 **Death Knell:** Kill dying creature and gain 1d8 temporary hp, +2 to Str, and +1 caster level.
3 **Animate Dead**M: Creates undead skeletons and zombies.
4 **Death Ward:** Grants immunity to death spells and negative energy effects.
5 **Slay Living:** Touch attack kills subject.
6 **Create Undead**M: Create ghouls, ghasts, mummies, or mohrgs.
7 **Destruction**F: Kills subject and destroys remains.
8 **Create Greater Undead**M: Create shadows, wraiths, spectres, or devourers.
9 **Wail of the Banshee:** Kills one creature/level.

DESTRUCTION DOMAIN

Deities: St. Cuthbert, Hextor.

Granted Power: You gain the smite power, the supernatural ability to make a single melee attack with a +4 bonus on attack rolls and a bonus on damage rolls equal to your cleric level (if you hit). You must declare the smite before making the attack. This ability is usable once per day.

Destruction Domain Spells

1 **Inflict Light Wounds:** Touch attack, 1d8 damage +1/level (max +5).
2 **Shatter:** Sonic vibration damages objects or crystalline creatures.
3 **Contagion:** Infects subject with chosen disease.
4 **Inflict Critical Wounds:** Touch attack, 4d8 damage +1/level (max +20).
5 **Inflict Light Wounds, Mass:** Deals 1d8 damage +1/level to many creatures.
6 **Harm:** Deals 10 points/level damage to target.
7 **Disintegrate:** Makes one creature or object vanish.
8 **Earthquake:** Intense tremor shakes 5-ft./level radius.
9 **Implosion:** Kills one creature/round.

EARTH DOMAIN

Deities: Moradin, Obad-Hai.

Granted Power: Turn or destroy air creatures as a good cleric turns undead. Rebuke, command, or bolster earth creatures as an evil cleric rebukes undead. Use these abilities a total number of times per day equal to 3 + your Charisma modifier. This granted power is a supernatural ability.

Earth Domain Spells

1 **Magic Stone:** Three stones become +1 projectiles, 1d6 +1 damage.
2 **Soften Earth and Stone:** Turns stone to clay or dirt to sand or mud.
3 **Stone Shape:** Sculpts stone into any shape.
4 **Spike Stones:** Creatures in area take 1d8 damage, may be *slowed*.
5 **Wall of Stone:** Creates a stone wall that can be shaped.
6 **Stoneskin**M: Ignore 10 points of damage per attack.
7 **Earthquake:** Intense tremor shakes 5-ft./level radius.
8 **Iron Body:** Your body becomes living iron.
9 **Elemental Swarm*:** Summons multiple elementals.

*Cast as an earth spell only.

EVIL DOMAIN

Deities: Erythnul, Gruumsh, Hextor, Nerull, Vecna.

Granted Power: You cast evil spells at +1 caster level.

Evil Domain Spells

1 **Protection from Good:** +2 to AC and saves, counter mind control, hedge out elementals and outsiders.
2 **Desecrate**M: Fills area with negative energy, making undead stronger.
3 **Magic Circle against Good:** As *protection* spells, but 10-ft. radius and 10 min./level.
4 **Unholy Blight:** Damages and sickens good creatures.
5 **Dispel Good:** +4 bonus against attacks by good creatures.
6 **Create Undead**M: Create ghouls, ghasts, mummies, or mohrgs.
7 **Blasphemy:** Kills, paralyzes, weakens, or dazes nonevil subjects.
8 **Unholy Aura**F: +4 to AC, +4 resistance, SR 25 against good spells.
9 **Summon Monster IX*:** Calls extraplanar creature to fight for you.

*Cast as an evil spell only.

FIRE DOMAIN

Deity: Obad-Hai.

Granted Power: Turn or destroy water creatures as a good cleric turns undead. Rebuke, command, or bolster fire creatures as an evil cleric rebukes undead. Use these abilities a total number of times per day equal to 3 + your Charisma modifier. This granted power is a supernatural ability.

Fire Domain Spells

1 **Burning Hands:** 1d4/level fire damage (max 5d4).
2 **Produce Flame:** 1d6 damage +1/ level, touch or thrown.
3 **Resist Energy***: Ignores 10 (or more) points of damage/attack from specified energy type.
4 **Wall of Fire:** Deals 2d4 fire damage out to 10 ft. and 1d4 out to 20 ft. Passing through wall deals 2d6 damage +1/level.
5 **Fire Shield:** Creatures attacking you take fire damage; you're protected from heat or cold.
6 **Fire Seeds:** Acorns and berries become grenades and bombs.
7 **Fire Storm:** Deals 1d6/level fire damage.
8 **Incendiary Cloud:** Cloud deals 4d6 fire damage/round.
9 **Elemental Swarm****: Summons multiple elementals.

*Resist cold or fire only.
**Cast as a fire spell only.

GOOD DOMAIN

Deities: Corellon Larethian, Ehlonna, Garl Glittergold, Heironeous, Kord, Moradin, Pelor, Yondalla.

Granted Power: You cast good spells at +1 caster level.

Good Domain Spells

1 **Protection from Evil:** +2 to AC and saves, counter mind control, hedge out elementals and outsiders.
2 **Aid:** +1 on attack rolls, +1 on saves against fear, 1d8 temporary hp +1/level (max +10).
3 **Magic Circle against Evil:** As *protection* spells, but 10-ft. radius and 10 min./level.
4 **Holy Smite:** Damages and blinds evil creatures.
5 **Dispel Evil:** +4 bonus against attacks by evil creatures.
6 **Blade Barrier:** Wall of blades deals 1d6/level damage.
7 **Holy Word** F: Kills, paralyzes, slows, or deafens nongood subjects.
8 **Holy Aura:** +4 to AC, +4 resistance, and SR 25 against evil spells.
9 **Summon Monster IX***: Calls extraplanar creature to fight for you.

*Cast as a good spell only.

HEALING DOMAIN

Deity: Pelor.

Granted Power: You cast healing spells at +1 caster level.

Healing Domain Spells

1 **Cure Light Wounds:** Cures 1d8 damage +1/level (max +5).
2 **Cure Moderate Wounds:** Cures 2d8 damage +1/level (max +10).
3 **Cure Serious Wounds:** Cures 3d8 damage +1/level (max +15).
4 **Cure Critical Wounds:** Cures 4d8 damage +1/level (max +20).
5 **Cure Light Wounds, Mass:** Cures 1d8 damage +1/level (max +25) for many creatures.
6 **Heal:** Cures 10 points/level of damage, all diseases and mental conditions.
7 **Regenerate:** Subject's severed limbs grow back, cures 4d8 damage +1/level (max +35).
8 **Cure Critical Wounds, Mass:** Cures 4d8 damage +1/level (max +40) for many creatures.
9 **Heal, Mass:** As *heal*, but with several subjects.

KNOWLEDGE DOMAIN

Deities: Boccob, Vecna.

Granted Power: Add all Knowledge skills to your list of cleric class skills.

You cast divination spells at +1 caster level.

Knowledge Domain Spells

1 **Detect Secret Doors:** Reveals hidden doors within 60 ft.
2 **Detect Thoughts:** Allows "listening" to surface thoughts.
3 **Clairaudience/Clairvoyance:** Hear or see at a distance for 1 min./level.
4 **Divination** M: Provides useful advice for specific proposed actions.
5 **True Seeing** M: Lets you see all things as they really are.
6 **Find the Path:** Shows most direct way to a location.
7 **Legend Lore** M F: Lets you learn tales about a person, place, or thing.
8 **Discern Location:** Reveals exact location of creature or object.
9 **Foresight:** "Sixth sense" warns of impending danger.

LAW DOMAIN

Deities: St. Cuthbert, Heironeous, Hextor, Moradin, Wee Jas, Yondalla.

Granted Power: You cast law spells at +1 caster level.

Law Domain Spells

1 **Protection from Chaos:** +2 to AC and saves, counter mind control, hedge out elementals and outsiders.
2 **Calm Emotions:** Calms creatures, negating emotion effects.
3 **Magic Circle against Chaos:** As *protection* spells, but 10-ft. radius and 10 min./level.
4 **Order's Wrath:** Damages and dazes chaotic creatures.
5 **Dispel Chaos:** +4 bonus against attacks by chaotic creatures.
6 **Hold Monster:** As *hold person*, but any creature.
7 **Dictum:** Kills, paralyzes, slows, or deafens nonlawful subjects.
8 **Shield of Law** F: +4 to AC, +4 resistance, and SR 25 against chaotic spells.
9 **Summon Monster IX***: Calls extraplanar creature to fight for you.

*Cast as a law spell only.

LUCK DOMAIN

Deities: Fharlanghn, Kord, Olidammara.

Granted Power: You gain the power of good fortune, which is usable once per day. This extraordinary ability allows you to reroll one roll that you have just made before the DM declares whether the roll results in success or failure. You must take the result of the reroll, even if it's worse than the original roll.

Luck Domain Spells

1 **Entropic Shield:** Ranged attacks against you have 20% miss chance.
2 **Aid:** +1 on attack rolls, +1 against fear, 1d8 temporary hp +1/level (max +10).
3 **Protection from Energy:** Absorb 12 points/level of damage from one kind of energy.
4 **Freedom of Movement:** Subject moves normally despite impediments.
5 **Break Enchantment:** Frees subjects from enchantments, alterations, curses, and petrification.
6 **Mislead:** Turns you invisible and creates illusory double.
7 **Spell Turning:** Reflect 1d4+6 spell levels back at caster.
8 **Moment of Prescience:** You gain insight bonus on single attack roll, check, or save.
9 **Miracle** X: Requests a deity's intercession.

MAGIC DOMAIN

Deities: Boccob, Vecna, Wee Jas.

Granted Power: Use scrolls, wands, and other devices with spell completion or spell trigger activation as a wizard of one-half your cleric level (at least 1st level). For the purpose of using a scroll or other magic device, if you are also a wizard, actual wizard levels and these effective wizard levels stack.

Magic Domain Spells

1. **Nystul's Magic Aura:** Alters object's magic aura.
2. **Identify:** Determines properties of magic item.
3. **Dispel Magic:** Cancels magical spells and effects.
4. **Imbue with Spell Ability:** Transfer spells to subject.
5. **Spell Resistance:** Subject gains SR 12 + level.
6. **Antimagic Field:** Negates magic within 10 ft.
7. **Spell Turning:** Reflect 1d4+6 spell levels back at caster.
8. **Protection from Spells** M F: Confers +8 resistance bonus.
9. **Mordenkainen's Disjunction:** Dispels magic, disenchants magic items.

PLANT DOMAIN

Deities: Ehlonna, Obad-Hai.

Granted Powers: Rebuke or command plant creatures as an evil cleric rebukes or commands undead. Use this ability a total number of times per day equal to 3 + your Charisma modifier. This granted power is a supernatural ability.

Add Knowledge (nature) to your list of cleric class skills.

Plant Domain Spells

1. **Entangle:** Plants entangle everyone in 40-ft.-radius.
2. **Barkskin:** Grants +2 (or higher) enhancement to natural armor.
3. **Plant Growth:** Grows vegetation, improves crops.
4. **Command Plants:** Sway the actions of one or more plant creatures.
5. **Wall of Thorns:** Thorns damage anyone who tries to pass.
6. **Repel Wood:** Pushes away wooden objects.
7. **Animate Plants:** One or more trees animate and fight for you.
8. **Control Plants:** Control actions of one or more plant creatures.
9. **Shambler:** Summons 1d4+2 shambling mounds to fight for you.

PROTECTION DOMAIN

Deities: Corellon Larethian, St. Cuthbert, Fharlanghn, Garl Glittergold, Moradin, Yondalla.

Granted Power: You can generate a *protective ward* as a supernatural ability. Grant someone you touch a resistance bonus equal to your cleric level on his or her next saving throw. Activating this power is a standard action. The *protective ward* is an abjuration effect with a duration of 1 hour that is usable once per day.

Protection Domain Spells

1. **Sanctuary:** Opponents can't attack you, and you can't attack.
2. **Shield Other** F: You take half of subject's damage.
3. **Protection from Energy:** Absorb 12 points/level of damage from one kind of energy.
4. **Spell Immunity:** Subject is immune to one spell per four levels.
5. **Spell Resistance:** Subject gains SR 12 + level.
6. **Antimagic Field:** Negates magic within 10 ft.
7. **Repulsion:** Creatures can't approach you.
8. **Mind Blank:** Subject is immune to mental/emotional magic and scrying.
9. **Prismatic Sphere:** As *prismatic wall*, but surrounds on all sides.

STRENGTH DOMAIN

Deities: St. Cuthbert, Gruumsh, Kord, Pelor.

Granted Power: You can perform a feat of strength as a supernatural ability. You gain an enhancement bonus to Strength equal to your cleric level. Activating the power is a free action, the power lasts 1 round, and it is usable once per day.

Strength Domain Spells

1. **Enlarge Person:** Humanoid creature doubles in size.
2. **Bull's Strength:** Subject gains +4 to Str for 1 min./level.
3. **Magic Vestment:** Armor or shield gains +1 enhancement per four levels.
4. **Spell Immunity:** Subject is immune to one spell per four levels.
5. **Righteous Might:** Your size increases, and you gain combat bonuses.
6. **Stoneskin** M: Ignore 10 points of damage per attack.
7. **Bigby's Grasping Hand:** Large hand provides cover, pushes, or grapples.
8. **Bigby's Clenched Fist:** Large hand provides cover, pushes, or attacks your foes.
9. **Bigby's Crushing Hand:** Large hand provides cover, pushes, or crushes your foes.

SUN DOMAIN

Deities: Ehlonna, Pelor.

Granted Power: Once per day, you can perform a greater turning against undead in place of a regular turning. The greater turning is like a normal turning except that the undead creatures that would be turned are destroyed instead.

Sun Domain Spells

1. **Endure Elements:** Exist comfortably in hot or cold environments.
2. **Heat Metal:** Make metal so hot it damages those who touch it.
3. **Searing Light:** Ray deals 1d8/two levels, more against undead.
4. **Fire Shield:** Creatures attacking you take fire damage; you're protected from heat or cold.
5. **Flame Strike:** Smite foes with divine fire (1d6/level damage).
6. **Fire Seeds:** Acorns and berries become grenades and bombs.
7. **Sunbeam:** Beam blinds and deals 4d6 damage.
8. **Sunburst:** Blinds all within 10 ft., deals 6d6 damage.
9. **Prismatic Sphere:** As *prismatic wall*, but surrounds on all sides.

TRAVEL DOMAIN

Deities: Fharlanghn.

Granted Powers: For a total time per day of 1 round per cleric level you possess, you can act normally regardless of magical effects that impede movement as if you were affected by the spell *freedom of movement*. This effect occurs automatically as soon as it applies, lasts until it runs out or is no longer needed, and can operate multiple times per day (up to the total daily limit of rounds). This granted power is a supernatural ability.

Add Survival to your list of cleric class skills.

Travel Domain Spells

1. **Longstrider:** Increases your speed.
2. **Locate Object:** Senses direction toward object (specific or type).
3. **Fly:** Subject flies at speed of 60 ft.
4. **Dimension Door:** Teleports you short distance.
5. **Teleport:** Instantly transports you as far as 100 miles/level.
6. **Find the Path:** Shows most direct way to a location.
7. **Teleport, Greater:** As *teleport*, but no range limit and no off-target arrival.

8 **Phase Door:** Creates an invisible passage through wood or stone.
9 **Astral Projection** [M]: Projects you and companions onto Astral Plane.

TRICKERY DOMAIN

Deities: Boccob, Erythnul, Garl Glittergold, Olidammara, Nerull.

Granted Power: Add Bluff, Disguise, and Hide to your list of cleric class skills.

Trickery Domain Spells

1 **Disguise Self:** Disguise own appearance.
2 **Invisibility:** Subject invisible 1 min./level or until it attacks.
3 **Nondetection** [M]: Hides subject from divination, scrying.
4 **Confusion:** Subjects behave oddly for 1 round/level.
5 **False Vision** [M]: Fools scrying with an illusion.
6 **Mislead:** Turns you invisible and creates illusory double.
7 **Screen:** Illusion hides area from vision, scrying.
8 **Polymorph Any Object:** Changes any subject into anything else.
9 **Time Stop:** You act freely for 1d4+1 rounds.

WAR DOMAIN

Deities: Corellon Larethian, Erythnul, Gruumsh, Heironeous, Hextor.

Granted Power: Free Martial Weapon Proficiency with deity's favored weapon (if necessary) and Weapon Focus with the deity's favored weapon.

The favored weapons of the war deities are as follows: Corellon, longsword; Erythnul, morningstar; Gruumsh, spear (or longspear); Heironeous, longsword; Hextor, flail (light or heavy).

War Domain Spells

1 **Magic Weapon:** Weapon gains +1 bonus.
2 **Spiritual Weapon:** Magical weapon attacks on its own.
3 **Magic Vestment:** Armor or shield gains +1 enhancement per four levels.
4 **Divine Power:** You gain attack bonus, +6 to Str, and 1 hp/level.
5 **Flame Strike:** Smite foes with divine fire (1d6/level damage).
6 **Blade Barrier:** Wall of blades deals 1d6/level damage.
7 **Power Word Blind:** Blinds creature with 200 hp or less.
8 **Power Word Stun:** Stuns creature with 150 hp or less.
9 **Power Word Kill:** Kills creature with 100 hp or less.

WATER DOMAIN

Deity: Obad-Hai.

Granted Power: Turn or destroy fire creatures as a good cleric turns undead. Rebuke, command, or bolster water creatures as an evil cleric rebukes undead. Use these abilities a total number of times per day equal to 3 + your Charisma modifier. This granted power is a supernatural ability.

Water Domain Spells

1 **Obscuring Mist:** Fog surrounds you.
2 **Fog Cloud:** Fog obscures vision.
3 **Water Breathing:** Subjects can breathe underwater.
4 **Control Water:** Raises or lowers bodies of water.
5 **Ice Storm:** Hail deals 5d6 damage in cylinder 40 ft. across.
6 **Cone of Cold:** 1d6/level cold damage.
7 **Acid Fog:** Fog deals acid damage.
8 **Horrid Wilting:** Deals 1d6/level damage within 30 ft.
9 **Elemental Swarm***: Summons multiple elementals.
*Cast as a water spell only.

DRUID SPELLS

0-LEVEL DRUID SPELLS (ORISONS)

Create Water: Creates 2 gallons/level of pure water.
Cure Minor Wounds: Cures 1 point of damage.
Detect Magic: Detects spells and magic items within 60 ft.
Detect Poison: Detects poison in one creature or object.
Flare: Dazzles one creature (–1 penalty on attack rolls).
Guidance: +1 on one attack roll, saving throw, or skill check.
Know Direction: You discern north.
Light: Object shines like a torch.
Mending: Makes minor repairs on an object.
Purify Food and Drink: Purifies 1 cu. ft./level of food or water.
Read Magic: Read scrolls and spellbooks.
Resistance: Subject gains +1 bonus on saving throws.
Virtue: Subject gains 1 temporary hp.

1ST-LEVEL DRUID SPELLS

Calm Animals: Calms (2d4 + level) HD of animals.
Charm Animal: Makes one animal your friend.
Cure Light Wounds: Cures 1d8 damage +1/level (max +5).
Detect Animals or Plants: Detects kinds of animals or plants.
Detect Snares and Pits: Reveals natural or primitive traps.
Endure Elements: Exist comfortably in hot or cold environments.
Entangle: Plants entangle everyone in 40-ft.-radius.
Faerie Fire: Outlines subjects with light, canceling *blur*, concealment, and the like.
Goodberry: 2d4 berries each cure 1 hp (max 8 hp/24 hours).
Hide from Animals: Animals can't perceive one subject/level.
Jump: Subject gets bonus on Jump checks.
Longstrider: Your speed increases by 10 ft.
Magic Fang: One natural weapon of subject creature gets +1 on attack and damage rolls.
Magic Stone: Three stones gain +1 on attack rolls, deal 1d6+1 damage.
Obscuring Mist: Fog surrounds you.
Pass without Trace: One subject/level leaves no tracks.
Produce Flame: 1d6 damage +1/level, touch or thrown.
Shillelagh: Cudgel or quarterstaff becomes +1 weapon (1d10 damage) for 1 min./level.
Speak with Animals: You can communicate with animals.
Summon Nature's Ally I: Calls creature to fight.

2ND-LEVEL DRUID SPELLS

Animal Messenger: Sends a Tiny animal to a specific place.
Animal Trance: Fascinates 2d6 HD of animals.
Barkskin: Grants +2 (or higher) enhancement to natural armor.
Bear's Endurance: Subject gains +4 to Con for 1 min./level.
Bull's Strength: Subject gains +4 to Str for 1 min./level.
Cat's Grace: Subject gains +4 to Dex for 1 min./level.
Chill Metal: Cold metal damages those who touch it.
Delay Poison: Stops poison from harming subject for 1 hour/level.
Fire Trap [M]: Opened object deals 1d4 +1/level damage.
Flame Blade: Touch attack deals 1d8 +1/two levels damage.
Flaming Sphere: Creates rolling ball of fire, 2d6 damage, lasts 1 round/level.
Fog Cloud: Fog obscures vision.
Gust of Wind: Blows away or knocks down smaller creatures.
Heat Metal: Make metal so hot it damages those who touch it.
Hold Animal: Paralyzes one animal for 1 round/level.
Owl's Wisdom: Subject gains +4 to Wis for 1 min./level.
Reduce Animal: Shrinks one willing animal.

Resist Energy: Ignores 10 (or more) points of damage/attack from specified energy type.

Restoration, Lesser: Dispels magical ability penalty or repairs 1d4 ability damage.

Soften Earth and Stone: Turns stone to clay or dirt to sand or mud.

Spider Climb: Grants ability to walk on walls and ceilings.

Summon Nature's Ally II: Calls creature to fight.

Summon Swarm: Summons swarm of bats, rats, or spiders.

Tree Shape: You look exactly like a tree for 1 hour/level.

Warp Wood: Bends wood (shaft, handle, door, plank).

Wood Shape: Rearranges wooden objects to suit you.

3RD-LEVEL DRUID SPELLS

Call Lightning: Calls down lightning bolts (3d6 per bolt) from sky.

Contagion: Infects subject with chosen disease.

Cure Moderate Wounds: Cures 2d8 damage +1/level (max +10).

Daylight: 60-ft. radius of bright light.

Diminish Plants: Reduces size or blights growth of normal plants.

Dominate Animal: Subject animal obeys silent mental commands.

Magic Fang, Greater: One natural weapon of subject creature gets +1/three levels on attack and damage rolls (max +5).

Meld into Stone: You and your gear merge with stone.

Neutralize Poison: Immunizes subject against poison, detoxifies venom in or on subject.

Plant Growth: Grows vegetation, improves crops.

Poison: Touch deals 1d10 Con damage, repeats in 1 min.

Protection from Energy: Absorb 12 points/level of damage from one kind of energy.

Quench: Extinguishes nonmagical fires or one magic item.

Remove Disease: Cures all diseases affecting subject.

Sleet Storm: Hampers vision and movement.

Snare: Creates a magic booby trap.

Speak with Plants: You can talk to normal plants and plant creatures.

Spike Growth: Creatures in area take 1d4 damage, may be *slowed*.

Stone Shape: Sculpts stone into any shape.

Summon Nature's Ally III: Calls creature to fight.

Water Breathing: Subjects can breathe underwater.

Wind Wall: Deflects arrows, smaller creatures, and gases.

4TH-LEVEL DRUID SPELLS

Air Walk: Subject treads on air as if solid (climb at 45-degree angle).

Antiplant Shell: Keeps animated plants at bay.

Blight: Withers one plant or deals 1d6/level damage to plant creature.

Command Plants: Sway the actions of one or more plant creatures.

Control Water: Raises or lowers bodies of water.

Cure Serious Wounds: Cures 3d8 damage +1/level (max +15).

Dispel Magic: Cancels spells and magical effects.

Flame Strike: Smite foes with divine fire (1d6/level damage).

Freedom of Movement: Subject moves normally despite impediments.

Giant Vermin: Turns centipedes, scorpions, or spiders into giant vermin.

Ice Storm: Hail deals 5d6 damage in cylinder 40 ft. across.

Reincarnate: Brings dead subject back in a random body.

Repel Vermin: Insects, spiders, and other vermin stay 10 ft. away.

Rusting Grasp: Your touch corrodes iron and alloys.

Scrying^F: Spies on subject from a distance.

Spike Stones: Creatures in area take 1d8 damage, may be *slowed*.

Summon Nature's Ally IV: Calls creature to fight.

5TH-LEVEL DRUID SPELLS

Animal Growth: One animal/two levels doubles in size.

Atonement: Removes burden of misdeeds from subject.

Awaken^X: Animal or tree gains human intellect.

Baleful Polymorph: Transforms subject into harmless animal.

Call Lightning Storm: As *call lightning*, but 5d6 damage per bolt.

Commune with Nature: Learn about terrain for 1 mile/level.

Control Winds: Change wind direction and speed.

Cure Critical Wounds: Cures 4d8 damage +1/level (max +20).

Death Ward: Grants immunity to all death spells and negative energy effects.

Hallow^M: Designates location as holy.

Insect Plague: Locust swarms attack creatures.

Stoneskin^M: Ignore 10 points of damage per attack.

Summon Nature's Ally V: Calls creature to fight.

Transmute Mud to Rock: Transforms two 10-ft. cubes per level.

Transmute Rock to Mud: Transforms two 10-ft. cubes per level.

Tree Stride: Step from one tree to another far away.

Unhallow^M: Designates location as unholy.

Wall of Fire: Deals 2d4 fire damage out to 10 ft. and 1d4 out to 20 ft. Passing through wall deals 2d6 damage +1/level.

Wall of Thorns: Thorns damage anyone who tries to pass.

6TH-LEVEL DRUID SPELLS

Antilife Shell: 10-ft.-radius field hedges out living creatures.

Bear's Endurance, Mass: As *bear's endurance*, affects one subject/level.

Bull's Strength, Mass: As *bull's strength*, affects one subject/level.

Cat's Grace, Mass: As *cat's grace*, affects one subject/level.

Cure Light Wounds, Mass: Cures 1d8 damage +1/level for many creatures.

Dispel Magic, Greater: As *dispel magic*, but +20 on check.

Find the Path: Shows most direct way to a location.

Fire Seeds: Acorns and berries become grenades and bombs.

Ironwood: Magic wood is strong as steel.

Liveoak: Oak becomes treant guardian.

Move Earth: Digs trenches and builds hills.

Owl's Wisdom, Mass: As *owl's wisdom*, affects one subject/level.

Repel Wood: Pushes away wooden objects.

Spellstaff: Stores one spell in wooden quarterstaff.

Stone Tell: Talk to natural or worked stone.

Summon Nature's Ally VI: Calls creature to fight.

Transport via Plants: Move instantly from one plant to another of the same kind.

Wall of Stone: Creates a stone wall that can be shaped.

7TH-LEVEL DRUID SPELLS

Animate Plants: One or more plants animate and fight for you.

Changestaff: Your staff becomes a treant on command.

Control Weather: Changes weather in local area.

Creeping Doom: Swarms of centipedes attack at your command.

Cure Moderate Wounds, Mass: Cures 2d8 damage +1/level for many creatures.

Fire Storm: Deals 1d6/level fire damage.

Heal: Cures 10 points/level of damage, all diseases and mental conditions.

Scrying, Greater: As *scrying*, but faster and longer.

Summon Nature's Ally VII: Calls creature to fight.

Sunbeam: Beam blinds and deals 4d6 damage.

Transmute Metal to Wood: Metal within 40 ft. becomes wood.

True Seeing^M: Lets you see all things as they really are.

Wind Walk: You and your allies turn vaporous and travel fast.

8TH-LEVEL DRUID SPELLS

Animal Shapes: One ally/level polymorphs into chosen animal.
Control Plants: Control actions of one or more plant creatures.
Cure Serious Wounds, Mass: Cures 3d8 damage +1/level for many creatures.
Earthquake: Intense tremor shakes 5-ft./level radius.
Finger of Death: Kills one subject.
Repel Metal or Stone: Pushes away metal and stone.
Reverse Gravity: Objects and creatures fall upward.
Summon Nature's Ally VIII: Calls creature to fight.
Sunburst: Blinds all within 10 ft., deals 6d6 damage.
Whirlwind: Cyclone deals damage and can pick up creatures.
Word of Recall: Teleports you back to designated place.

9TH-LEVEL DRUID SPELLS

Antipathy: Object or location affected by spell repels certain creatures.
Cure Critical Wounds, Mass: Cures 4d8 damage +1/level for many creatures.
Elemental Swarm: Summons multiple elementals.
Foresight: "Sixth sense" warns of impending danger.
Regenerate: Subject's severed limbs grow back, cures 4d8 damage +1/level (max +35).
Shambler: Summons 1d4+2 shambling mounds to fight for you.
Shapechange F: Transforms you into any creature, and change forms once per round.
Storm of Vengeance: Storm rains acid, lightning, and hail.
Summon Nature's Ally IX: Calls creature to fight.
Sympathy M: Object or location attracts certain creatures.

PALADIN SPELLS

1ST-LEVEL PALADIN SPELLS

Bless: Allies gain +1 on attack rolls and +1 on saves against fear.
Bless Water: Makes holy water.
Bless Weapon: Weapon strikes true against evil foes.
Create Water: Creates 2 gallons/level of pure water.
Cure Light Wounds: Cures 1d8 damage +1/level (max +5).
Detect Poison: Detects poison in one creature or small object.
Detect Undead: Reveals undead within 60 ft.
Divine Favor: You gain +1 per three levels on attack and damage rolls.
Endure Elements: Exist comfortably in hot or cold environments.
Magic Weapon: Weapon gains +1 bonus.
Protection from Chaos/Evil: +2 to AC and saves, counter mind control, hedge out elementals and outsiders.
Read Magic: Read scrolls and spellbooks.
Resistance: Subject gains +1 on saving throws.
Restoration, Lesser: Dispels magical ability penalty or repairs 1d4 ability damage.
Virtue: Subject gains 1 temporary hp.

2ND-LEVEL PALADIN SPELLS

Bull's Strength: Subject gains +4 to Str for 1 min./level.
Delay Poison: Stops poison from harming subject for 1 hour/level.
Eagle's Splendor: Subject gains +4 to Cha for 1 min./level.
Owl's Wisdom: Subject gains +4 to Wis for 1 min./level.
Remove Paralysis: Frees one or more creatures from paralysis or slow effect.
Resist Energy: Ignores 10 (or more) points of damage/attack from specified energy type.
Shield Other F: You take half of subject's damage.
Undetectable Alignment: Conceals alignment for 24 hours.
Zone of Truth: Subjects within range cannot lie.

3RD-LEVEL PALADIN SPELLS

Cure Moderate Wounds: Cures 2d8 damage +1/level (max +10).
Daylight: 60-ft. radius of bright light.
Discern Lies: Reveals deliberate falsehoods.
Dispel Magic: Cancels spells and magical effects.
Heal Mount: As *heal* on warhorse or other special mount.
Magic Circle against Chaos: As *protection from chaos*, but 10-ft. radius and 10 min./level.
Magic Circle against Evil: As *protection from evil*, but 10-ft. radius and 10 min./level.
Magic Weapon, Greater: +1 bonus/four levels (max +5).
Prayer: Allies +1 bonus on most rolls, enemies –1 penalty.
Remove Blindness/Deafness: Cures normal or magical conditions.
Remove Curse: Frees object or person from curse.

4TH-LEVEL PALADIN SPELLS

Break Enchantment: Frees subjects from enchantments, alterations, curses, and petrification.
Cure Serious Wounds: Cures 3d8 damage +1/level (max +15).
Death Ward: Grants immunity to death spells and negative energy effects.
Dispel Chaos: +4 bonus against attacks by chaotic creatures.
Dispel Evil: +4 bonus against attacks by evil creatures.
Holy Sword: Weapon becomes +5, deals +2d6 damage against evil.
Mark of Justice: Designates action that will trigger *curse* on subject.
Neutralize Poison: Immunizes subject against poison, detoxifies venom in or on subject.
Restoration M: Restores level and ability score drains.

RANGER SPELLS

1ST-LEVEL RANGER SPELLS

Alarm: Wards an area for 2 hours/level.
Animal Messenger: Sends a Tiny animal to a specific place.
Calm Animals: Calms (2d4 + level) HD of animals.
Charm Animal: Makes one animal your friend.
Delay Poison: Stops poison from harming subject for 1 hour/level.
Detect Animals or Plants: Detects kinds of animals or plants.
Detect Poison: Detects poison in one creature or object.
Detect Snares and Pits: Reveals natural or primitive traps.
Endure Elements: Exist comfortably in hot or cold environments.
Entangle: Plants entangle everyone in 40-ft.-radius circle.
Hide from Animals: Animals can't perceive one subject/level.
Jump: Subject gets bonus on Jump checks.
Longstrider: Increases your speed.
Magic Fang: One natural weapon of subject creature gets +1 on attack and damage rolls.
Pass without Trace: One subject/level leaves no tracks.
Read Magic: Read scrolls and spellbooks.
Resist Energy: Ignores 10 (or more) points of damage/attack from specified energy type.
Speak with Animals: You can communicate with animals.
Summon Nature's Ally I: Calls animal to fight for you.

2ND-LEVEL RANGER SPELLS

Barkskin: Grants +2 (or higher) enhancement to natural armor.
Bear's Endurance: Subject gains +4 to Con for 1 min./level.
Cat's Grace: Subject gains +4 to Dex for 1 min./level.
Cure Light Wounds: Cures 1d8 damage +1/level (max +5).
Hold Animal: Paralyzes one animal for 1 round/level.
Owl's Wisdom: Subject gains +4 to Wis for 1 min./level.

Protection from Energy: Absorb 12 points/level of damage from one kind of energy.

Snare: Creates a magic booby trap.

Speak with Plants: You can talk to normal plants and plant creatures.

Spike Growth: Creatures in area take 1d4 damage, may be *slowed*.

Summon Nature's Ally II: Calls animal to fight for you.

Wind Wall: Deflects arrows, smaller creatures, and gases.

3RD-LEVEL RANGER SPELLS

Command Plants: Sway the actions of one or more plant creatures.

Cure Moderate Wounds: Cures 2d8 damage +1/level (max +10).

Darkvision: See 60 ft. in total darkness.

Diminish Plants: Reduces size or blights growth of normal plants.

Magic Fang, Greater: One natural weapon of subject creature gets +1/three caster levels on attack and damage rolls (max +5).

Neutralize Poison: Immunizes subject against poison, detoxifies venom in or on subject.

Plant Growth: Grows vegetation, improves crops.

Reduce Animal: Shrinks one willing animal.

Remove Disease: Cures all diseases affecting subject.

Repel Vermin: Insects, spiders, and other vermin stay 10 ft. away.

Summon Nature's Ally III: Calls animal to fight for you.

Tree Shape: You look exactly like a tree for 1 hour/level.

Water Walk: Subject treads on water as if solid.

4TH-LEVEL RANGER SPELLS

Animal Growth: One animal/two levels doubles in size.

Commune with Nature: Learn about terrain for 1 mile/level.

Cure Serious Wounds: Cures 3d8 damage +1/level (max +15).

Freedom of Movement: Subject moves normally despite impediments.

Nondetection M: Hides subject from divination, scrying.

Summon Nature's Ally IV: Calls animal to fight for you.

Tree Stride: Step from one tree to another far away.

SORCERER/WIZARD SPELLS

0-LEVEL SORCERER/WIZARD SPELLS (CANTRIPS)

Abjur **Resistance:** Subject gains +1 on saving throws.

Conj **Acid Splash:** Orb deals 1d3 acid damage.

Div **Detect Poison:** Detects poison in one creature or small object.

Detect Magic: Detects spells and magic items within 60 ft.

Read Magic: Read scrolls and spellbooks.

Ench **Daze:** Humanoid creature of 4 HD or less loses next action.

Evoc **Dancing Lights:** Creates torches or other lights.

Flare: Dazzles one creature (–1 on attack rolls).

Light: Object shines like a torch.

Ray of Frost: Ray deals 1d3 cold damage.

Illus **Ghost Sound:** Figment sounds.

Necro **Disrupt Undead:** Deals 1d6 damage to one undead.

Touch of Fatigue: Touch attack fatigues target.

Trans **Mage Hand:** 5-pound telekinesis.

Mending: Makes minor repairs on an object.

Message: Whispered conversation at distance.

Open/Close: Opens or closes small or light things.

Univ **Arcane Mark:** Inscribes a personal rune (visible or invisible).

Prestidigitation: Performs minor tricks.

1ST-LEVEL SORCERER/WIZARD SPELLS

Abjur **Alarm:** Wards an area for 2 hours/level.

Endure Elements: Exist comfortably in hot or cold environments.

Hold Portal: Holds door shut.

Protection from Chaos/Evil/Good/Law: +2 to AC and saves, counter mind control, hedge out elementals and outsiders.

Shield: Invisible disc gives +4 to AC, blocks *magic missiles*.

Conj **Grease:** Makes 10-ft. square or one object slippery.

Mage Armor: Gives subject +4 armor bonus.

Mount: Summons riding horse for 2 hours/level.

Obscuring Mist: Fog surrounds you.

Summon Monster I: Calls extraplanar creature to fight for you.

Unseen Servant: Invisible force obeys your commands.

Div **Comprehend Languages:** You understand all spoken and written languages.

Detect Secret Doors: Reveals hidden doors within 60 ft.

Detect Undead: Reveals undead within 60 ft.

Identify M: Determines properties of magic item.

True Strike: +20 on your next attack roll.

Ench **Charm Person:** Makes one person your friend.

Hypnotism: Fascinates 2d4 HD of creatures.

Sleep: Puts 4 HD of creatures into magical slumber.

Evoc **Burning Hands:** 1d4/level fire damage (max 5d4).

Magic Missile: 1d4+1 damage; +1 missile per two levels above 1st (max 5).

Shocking Grasp: Touch delivers 1d6/level electricity damage (max 5d6).

Tenser's Floating Disk: Creates 3-ft.-diameter horizontal disk that holds 100 lb./level.

Illus **Color Spray:** Knocks unconscious, blinds, and/or stuns 1d6 weak creatures.

Disguise Self: Changes your appearance.

Nystul's Magic Aura: Alters object's magic aura.

Silent Image: Creates minor illusion of your design.

Ventriloquism: Throws voice for 1 min./level.

Necro **Cause Fear:** One creature of 5 HD or less flees for 1d4 rounds.

Chill Touch: One touch/level deals 1d6 damage and possibly 1 Str damage.

Ray of Enfeeblement: Ray deals 1d6 +1 per two levels Str damage.

Trans **Animate Rope:** Makes a rope move at your command.

Enlarge Person: Humanoid creature doubles in size.

Erase: Mundane or magical writing vanishes.

Expeditious Retreat: Your speed increases by 30 ft.

Feather Fall: Objects or creatures fall slowly.

Jump: Subject gets bonus on Jump checks.

Magic Weapon: Weapon gains +1 bonus.

Reduce Person: Humanoid creature halves in size.

2ND-LEVEL SORCERER/WIZARD SPELLS

Abjur **Arcane Lock** M: Magically locks a portal or chest.

Obscure Object: Masks object against scrying.

Protection from Arrows: Subject immune to most ranged attacks.

Resist Energy: Ignores first 10 (or more) points of damage/attack from specified energy type.

Conj **Fog Cloud:** Fog obscures vision.

Glitterdust: Blinds creatures, outlines invisible creatures.

Melf's Acid Arrow: Ranged touch attack; 2d4 damage for 1 round +1 round/three levels.

Summon Monster II: Calls extraplanar creature to fight for you.

Summon Swarm: Summons swarm of bats, rats, or spiders.

Web: Fills 20-ft.-radius spread with sticky spiderwebs.

Div **Detect Thoughts:** Allows "listening" to surface thoughts.

Locate Object: Senses direction toward object (specific or type).

See Invisibility: Reveals invisible creatures or objects.

Ench **Daze Monster:** Living creature of 6 HD or less loses next action.

Tasha's Hideous Laughter: Subject loses actions for 1 round/level.

Touch of Idiocy: Subject takes 1d6 points of Int, Wis, and Cha damage.

Evoc **Continual Flame** ^{M}: Makes a permanent, heatless torch.

Darkness: 20-ft. radius of supernatural shadow.

Flaming Sphere: Creates rolling ball of fire, 2d6 damage, lasts 1 round/level.

Gust of Wind: Blows away or knocks down smaller creatures.

Scorching Ray: Ranged touch attack deals 4d6 fire damage, +1 ray/four levels (max 3).

Shatter: Sonic vibration damages objects or crystalline creatures.

Illus **Blur:** Attacks miss subject 20% of the time.

Hypnotic Pattern: Fascinates (2d4 + level) HD of creatures.

Invisibility: Subject is invisible for 1 min./level or until it attacks.

Leomund's Trap ^{M}: Makes item seem trapped.

Magic Mouth ^{M}: Speaks once when triggered.

Minor Image: As *silent image*, plus some sound.

Mirror Image: Creates decoy duplicates of you (1d4 +1 per three levels, max 8).

Misdirection: Misleads divinations for one creature or object.

Necro **Blindness/Deafness:** Makes subject blinded or deafened.

Command Undead: Undead creature obeys your commands.

False Life: Gain 1d10 temporary hp +1/level (max +10).

Ghoul Touch: Paralyzes one subject, which exudes stench that makes those nearby sickened.

Scare: Panics creatures of less than 6 HD.

Spectral Hand: Creates disembodied glowing hand to deliver touch attacks.

Trans **Alter Self:** Assume form of a similar creature.

Bear's Endurance: Subject gains +4 to Con for 1 min./level.

Bull's Strength: Subject gains +4 to Str for 1 min./level.

Cat's Grace: Subject gains +4 to Dex for 1 min./level.

Darkvision: See 60 ft. in total darkness.

Eagle's Splendor: Subject gains +4 to Cha for 1 min./level.

Fox's Cunning: Subject gains +4 Int for 1 min./level.

Knock: Opens locked or magically sealed door.

Levitate: Subject moves up and down at your direction.

Owl's Wisdom: Subject gains +4 to Wis for 1 min./level.

Pyrotechnics: Turns fire into blinding light or choking smoke.

Rope Trick: As many as eight creatures hide in extradimensional space.

Spider Climb: Grants ability to walk on walls and ceilings.

Whispering Wind: Sends a short message 1 mile/level.

3RD-LEVEL SORCERER/WIZARD SPELLS

Abjur **Dispel Magic:** Cancels magical spells and effects.

Explosive Runes: Deals 6d6 damage when read.

Magic Circle against Chaos/Evil/Good/Law: As *protection* spells, but 10-ft. radius and 10 min./level.

Nondetection ^{M}: Hides subject from divination, scrying.

Protection from Energy: Absorb 12 points/level of damage from one kind of energy.

Conj **Phantom Steed:** Magic horse appears for 1 hour/level.

Sepia Snake Sigil ^{M}: Creates text symbol that immobilizes reader.

Sleet Storm: Hampers vision and movement.

Stinking Cloud: Nauseating vapors, 1 round/level.

Summon Monster III: Calls extraplanar creature to fight for you.

Div **Arcane Sight:** Magical auras become visible to you.

Clairaudience/Clairvoyance: Hear or see at a distance for 1 min./level.

Tongues: Speak any language.

Ench **Deep Slumber:** Puts 10 HD of creatures to sleep.

Heroism: Gives +2 bonus on attack rolls, saves, skill checks.

Hold Person: Paralyzes one humanoid for 1 round/level.

Rage: Subjects gains +2 to Str and Con, +1 on Will saves, −2 to AC.

Suggestion: Compels subject to follow stated course of action.

Evoc **Daylight:** 60-ft. radius of bright light.

Fireball: 1d6 damage per level, 20-ft. radius.

Leomund's Tiny Hut: Creates shelter for ten creatures.

Lightning Bolt: Electricity deals 1d6/level damage.

Wind Wall: Deflects arrows, smaller creatures, and gases.

Illus **Displacement:** Attacks miss subject 50%.

Illusory Script ^{M}: Only intended reader can decipher.

Invisibility Sphere: Makes everyone within 10 ft. invisible.

Major Image: As *silent image*, plus sound, smell and thermal effects.

Necro **Gentle Repose:** Preserves one corpse.

Halt Undead: Immobilizes undead for 1 round/level.

Ray of Exhaustion: Ray makes subject exhausted.

Vampiric Touch: Touch deals 1d6/two levels damage; caster gains damage as hp.

Trans **Blink:** You randomly vanish and reappear for 1 round/level.

Flame Arrow: Arrows deal +1d6 fire damage.

Fly: Subject flies at speed of 60 ft.

Gaseous Form: Subject becomes insubstantial and can fly slowly.

Haste: One creature/level moves faster, +1 on attack rolls, AC, and Reflex saves.

Keen Edge: Doubles normal weapon's threat range.

Magic Weapon, Greater: +1/four levels (max +5).

Secret Page: Changes one page to hide its real content.

Shrink Item: Object shrinks to one-sixteenth size.

Slow: One subject/level takes only one action/round, −2 to AC, −2 on attack rolls.

Water Breathing: Subjects can breathe underwater.

4TH-LEVEL SORCERER/WIZARD SPELLS

Abjur **Dimensional Anchor:** Bars extradimensional movement.

Fire Trap ^{M}: Opened object deals 1d4 damage +1/level.

Globe of Invulnerability, Lesser: Stops 1st- through 3rd-level spell effects.

Remove Curse: Frees object or person from curse.

Conj **Stoneskin** ^M: Ignore 10 points of damage per attack.

Dimension Door: Teleports you short distance.

Evard's Black Tentacles: Tentacles grapple all within 15 ft. spread.

Leomund's Secure Shelter: Creates sturdy cottage.

Minor Creation: Creates one cloth or wood object.

Solid Fog: Blocks vision and slows movement.

Summon Monster IV: Calls extraplanar creature to fight for you.

Div **Arcane Eye:** Invisible floating eye moves 30 ft./round.

Detect Scrying: Alerts you of magical eavesdropping.

Locate Creature: Indicates direction to familiar creature.

Scrying ^F: Spies on subject from a distance.

Ench **Charm Monster:** Makes monster believe it is your ally.

Confusion: Subjects behave oddly for 1 round/level.

Crushing Despair: Subjects take −2 on attack rolls, damage rolls, saves, and checks.

Geas, Lesser: Commands subject of 7 HD or less.

Evoc **Fire Shield:** Creatures attacking you take fire damage; you're protected from heat or cold.

Ice Storm: Hail deals 5d6 damage in cylinder 40 ft. across.

Otiluke's Resilient Sphere: Force globe protects but traps one subject.

Shout: Deafens all within cone and deals 5d6 sonic damage.

Wall of Fire: Deals 2d4 fire damage out to 10 ft. and 1d4 out to 20 ft. Passing through wall deals 2d6 damage +1/level.

Wall of Ice: *Ice plane* creates wall with 15 hp +1/level, or *hemisphere* can trap creatures inside.

Illus **Hallucinatory Terrain:** Makes one type of terrain appear like another (field into forest, or the like).

Illusory Wall: Wall, floor, or ceiling looks real, but anything can pass through.

Invisibility, Greater: As *invisibility,* but subject can attack and stay invisible.

Phantasmal Killer: Fearsome illusion kills subject or deals 3d6 damage.

Rainbow Pattern: Lights fascinate 24 HD of creatures.

Shadow Conjuration: Mimics conjuration below 4th level, but only 20% real.

Necro **Animate Dead** ^M: Creates undead skeletons and zombies.

Bestow Curse: −6 to an ability score; −4 on attack rolls, saves, and checks; or 50% chance of losing each action.

Contagion: Infects subject with chosen disease.

Enervation: Subject gains 1d4 negative levels.

Fear: Subjects within cone flee for 1 round/level.

Trans **Enlarge Person, Mass:** Enlarges several creatures.

Polymorph: Gives one willing subject a new form.

Rary's Mnemonic Enhancer ^F: *Wizard only.* Prepares extra spells or retains one just cast.

Reduce Person, Mass: Reduces several creatures.

Stone Shape: Sculpts stone into any shape.

5TH-LEVEL SORCERER/WIZARD SPELLS

Abjur **Break Enchantment:** Frees subjects from enchantments, alterations, curses, and petrification.

Dismissal: Forces a creature to return to native plane.

Mordenkainen's Private Sanctum: Prevents anyone from viewing or scrying an area for 24 hours.

Conj **Cloudkill:** Kills 3 HD or less; 4–6 HD save or die, 6+ HD take Con damage.

Leomund's Secret Chest ^F: Hides expensive chest on Ethereal Plane; you retrieve it at will.

Major Creation: As *minor creation,* plus stone and metal.

Mordenkainen's Faithful Hound: Phantom dog can guard, attack.

Planar Binding, Lesser: Traps extraplanar creature of 6 HD or less until it performs a task.

Summon Monster V: Calls extraplanar creature to fight for you.

Teleport: Instantly transports you as far as 100 miles/level.

Wall of Stone: Creates a stone wall that can be shaped.

Div **Contact Other Plane:** Lets you ask question of extraplanar entity.

Prying Eyes: 1d4 +1/level floating eyes scout for you.

Rary's Telepathic Bond: Link lets allies communicate.

Ench **Dominate Person:** Controls humanoid telepathically.

Feeblemind: Subject's Int and Cha drop to 1.

Hold Monster: As *hold person,* but any creature.

Mind Fog: Subjects in fog get −10 to Wis and Will checks.

Symbol of Sleep ^M: Triggered rune puts nearby creatures into catatonic slumber.

Evoc **Bigby's Interposing Hand:** Hand provides cover against one opponent.

Cone of Cold: 1d6/level cold damage.

Sending: Delivers short message anywhere, instantly.

Wall of Force: Wall is immune to damage.

Illus **Dream:** Sends message to anyone sleeping.

False Vision ^M: Fools scrying with an illusion.

Mirage Arcana: As *hallucinatory terrain,* plus structures.

Nightmare: Sends vision dealing 1d10 damage, fatigue.

Persistent Image: As *major image,* but no concentration required.

Seeming: Changes appearance of one person per two levels.

Shadow Evocation: Mimics evocation below 5th level, but only 20% real.

Necro **Blight:** Withers one plant or deals 1d6/level damage to plant creature.

Magic Jar ^F: Enables possession of another creature.

Symbol of Pain ^M: Triggered rune wracks nearby creatures with pain.

Waves of Fatigue: Several targets become fatigued.

Trans **Animal Growth:** One animal/two levels doubles in size.

Baleful Polymorph: Transforms subject into harmless animal.

Fabricate: Transforms raw materials into finished items.

Overland Flight: You fly at a speed of 40 ft. and can hustle over long distances.

Passwall: Creates passage through wood or stone wall.

Telekinesis: Moves object, attacks creature, or hurls object or creature.

Transmute Mud to Rock: Transforms two 10-ft. cubes per level.

Transmute Rock to Mud: Transforms two 10-ft. cubes per level.

Univ **Permanency** ^X: Makes certain spells permanent.

6TH-LEVEL SORCERER/WIZARD SPELLS

Abjur **Antimagic Field:** Negates magic within 10 ft.

Dispel Magic, Greater: As *dispel magic,* but +20 on check.

Globe of Invulnerability: As *lesser globe of invulnerability,* plus 4th-level spell effects.

Guards and Wards: Array of magic effects protect area.

Repulsion: Creatures can't approach you.

Conj **Acid Fog:** Fog deals acid damage.

Planar Binding: As *lesser planar binding,* but up to 12 HD.

Summon Monster VI: Calls extraplanar creature to fight for you.

Wall of Iron ^M: 30 hp/four levels; can topple onto foes.

Div **Analyze Dweomer** ^F: Reveals magical aspects of subject.

Legend Lore ^{M F}: Lets you learn tales about a person, place, or thing.

True Seeing [M]: Lets you see all things as they really are.

Ench **Geas/Quest**: As *lesser geas*, plus it affects any creature.

Heroism, Greater: Gives +4 bonus on attack rolls, saves, skill checks; immunity to fear; temporary hp.

Suggestion, Mass: As *suggestion*, plus one subject/level.

Symbol of Persuasion [M]: Triggered rune charms nearby creatures.

Evoc **Bigby's Forceful Hand**: Hand pushes creatures away.

Chain Lightning: 1d6/level damage; 1 secondary bolt/level each deals half damage.

Contingency [F]: Sets trigger condition for another spell.

Otiluke's Freezing Sphere: Freezes water or deals cold damage.

Illus **Mislead**: Turns you invisible and creates illusory double.

Permanent Image: Includes sight, sound, and smell.

Programmed Image [M]: As *major image*, plus triggered by event.

Shadow Walk: Step into shadow to travel rapidly.

Veil: Changes appearance of group of creatures.

Necro **Circle of Death** [M]: Kills 1d4/level HD of creatures.

Create Undead [M]: Creates ghouls, ghasts, mummies, or mohrgs.

Eyebite: Target becomes panicked, sickened, and comatose.

Symbol of Fear [M]: Triggered rune panics nearby creatures.

Undeath to Death [M]: Destroys 1d4/level HD of undead (max 20d4).

Trans **Bear's Endurance, Mass**: As *bear's endurance*, affects one subject/level.

Bull's Strength, Mass: As *bull's strength*, affects one subject/level.

Cat's Grace, Mass: As *cat's grace*, affects one subject/level.

Control Water: Raises or lowers bodies of water.

Disintegrate: Makes one creature or object vanish.

Eagle's Splendor, Mass: As *eagle's splendor*, affects one subject/level.

Flesh to Stone: Turns subject creature into statue.

Fox's Cunning, Mass: As *fox's cunning*, affects one subject/level.

Mordenkainen's Lucubration: *Wizard only*. Recalls spell of 5th level or lower.

Move Earth: Digs trenches and build hills.

Owl's Wisdom, Mass: As *owl's wisdom*, affects one subject/level.

Stone to Flesh: Restores petrified creature.

Tenser's Transformation [M]: You gain combat bonuses.

7TH-LEVEL SORCERER/WIZARD SPELLS

Abjur **Banishment**: Banishes 2 HD/level of extraplanar creatures.

Sequester: Subject is invisible to sight and scrying; renders creature comatose.

Spell Turning: Reflect 1d4+6 spell levels back at caster.

Conj **Drawmij's Instant Summons** [M]: Prepared object appears in your hand.

Mordenkainen's Magnificent Mansion [F]: Door leads to extradimensional mansion.

Phase Door: Creates an invisible passage through wood or stone.

Plane Shift [F]: As many as eight subjects travel to another plane.

Summon Monster VII: Calls extraplanar creature to fight for you.

Teleport, Greater: As *teleport*, but no range limit and no off-target arrival.

Teleport Object: As *teleport*, but affects a touched object.

Div **Arcane Sight, Greater**: As *arcane sight*, but also reveals magic effects on creatures and objects.

Scrying, Greater: As *scrying*, but faster and longer.

Vision [M][X]: As *legend lore*, but quicker and strenuous.

Ench **Hold Person, Mass**: As *hold person*, but all within 30 ft.

Insanity: Subject suffers continuous *confusion*.

Power Word Blind: Blinds creature with 200 hp or less.

Symbol of Stunning [M]: Triggered rune stuns nearby creatures.

Evoc **Bigby's Grasping Hand**: Hand provides cover, pushes, or grapples.

Delayed Blast Fireball: 1d6/level fire damage; you can postpone blast for 5 rounds.

Forcecage [M]: Cube or cage of force imprisons all inside.

Mordenkainen's Sword [F]: Floating magic blade strikes opponents.

Prismatic Spray: Rays hit subjects with variety of effects.

Illus **Invisibility, Mass**: As *invisibility*, but affects all in range.

Project Image: Illusory double can talk and cast spells.

Shadow Conjuration, Greater: As *shadow conjuration*, but up to 6th level and 60% real.

Simulacrum [M][X]: Creates partially real double of a creature.

Necro **Control Undead**: Undead don't attack you while under your command.

Finger of Death: Kills one subject.

Symbol of Weakness [M]: Triggered rune weakens nearby creatures.

Waves of Exhaustion: Several targets become exhausted.

Trans **Control Weather**: Changes weather in local area.

Ethereal Jaunt: You become ethereal for 1 round/level.

Reverse Gravity: Objects and creatures fall upward.

Statue: Subject can become a statue at will.

Univ **Limited Wish** [X]: Alters reality—within spell limits.

8TH-LEVEL SORCERER/WIZARD SPELLS

Abjur **Dimensional Lock**: Teleportation and interplanar travel blocked for one day/level.

Mind Blank: Subject is immune to mental/emotional magic and scrying.

Prismatic Wall: Wall's colors have array of effects.

Protection from Spells [M][F]: Confers +8 resistance bonus.

Conj **Incendiary Cloud**: Cloud deals 4d6 fire damage/round.

Maze: Traps subject in extradimensional maze.

Planar Binding, Greater: As *lesser planar binding*, but up to 18 HD.

Summon Monster VIII: Calls extraplanar creature to fight for you.

Trap the Soul [M][F]: Imprisons subject within gem.

Div **Discern Location**: Reveals exact location of creature or object.

Moment of Prescience: You gain insight bonus on single attack roll, check, or save.

Prying Eyes, Greater: As *prying eyes*, but eyes have *true seeing*.

Ench **Antipathy**: Object or location affected by spell repels certain creatures.

Binding [M]: Utilizes an array of techniques to imprison a creature.

Charm Monster, Mass: As *charm monster*, but all within 30 ft.

Demand: As *sending*, plus you can send *suggestion*.

Otto's Irresistible Dance: Forces subject to dance.

Power Word Stun: Stuns creature with 150 hp or less.

Symbol of Insanity [M]: Triggered rune renders nearby creatures insane.

Sympathy [F]: Object or location attracts certain creatures.

Evoc **Bigby's Clenched Fist:** Large hand provides cover, pushes, or attacks your foes.

Otiluke's Telekinetic Sphere: As *Otiluke's resilient sphere*, but you move sphere telekinetically.

Polar Ray: Ranged touch attack deals 1d6/level cold damage.

Shout, Greater: Devastating yell deals 10d6 sonic damage; stuns creatures, damages objects.

Sunburst: Blinds all within 10 ft., deals 6d6 damage.

Illus **Scintillating Pattern:** Twisting colors *confuse*, stun, or render unconscious.

Screen: Illusion hides area from vision, scrying.

Shadow Evocation, Greater: As *shadow evocation*, but up to 7th level and 60% real.

Necro **Clone** ^M F: Duplicate awakens when original dies.

Create Greater Undead ^M: Create shadows, wraiths, spectres, or devourers.

Horrid Wilting: Deals 1d6/level damage within 30 ft.

Symbol of Death ^M: Triggered rune slays nearby creatures.

Trans **Iron Body:** Your body becomes living iron.

Polymorph Any Object: Changes any subject into anything else.

Temporal Stasis ^M: Puts subject into suspended animation.

9TH-LEVEL SORCERER/WIZARD SPELLS

Abjur **Freedom:** Releases creature from *imprisonment*.

Imprisonment: Entombs subject beneath the earth.

Mordenkainen's Disjunction: Dispels magic, disenchants magic items.

Prismatic Sphere: As *prismatic wall*, but surrounds on all sides.

Conj **Gate** ^X: Connects two planes for travel or summoning.

Refuge ^M: Alters item to transport its possessor to you.

Summon Monster IX: Calls extraplanar creature to fight for you.

Teleportation Circle ^M: Circle teleports any creature inside to designated spot.

Div **Foresight:** "Sixth sense" warns of impending danger.

Ench **Dominate Monster:** As *dominate person*, but any creature.

Hold Monster, Mass: As *hold monster*, but all within 30 ft.

Power Word Kill: Kills one creature with 100 hp or less.

Evoc **Bigby's Crushing Hand:** Large hand provides cover, pushes, or crushes your foes.

Meteor Swarm: Four exploding spheres each deal 6d6 fire damage.

Illus **Shades:** As *shadow conjuration*, but up to 8th level and 80% real.

Weird: As *phantasmal killer*, but affects all within 30 ft.

Necro **Astral Projection** ^M: Projects you and companions onto Astral Plane.

Energy Drain: Subject gains 2d4 negative levels.

Soul Bind ^F: Traps newly dead soul to prevent *resurrection*.

Wail of the Banshee: Kills one creature/level.

Trans **Ethereality:** Travel to Ethereal Plane with companions.

Shapechange ^F: Transforms you into any creature, and change forms once per round.

Time Stop: You act freely for 1d4+1 rounds.

Univ **Wish** ^X: As *limited wish*, but with fewer limits.

SPELLS

The spells herein are presented in alphabetical order (with the exception of those whose names begin with "greater," "lesser," or "mass"; see Order of Presentation, page 181).

Acid Fog

Conjuration (Creation) [Acid]
Level: Sor/Wiz 6, Water 7
Components: V, S, M/DF
Casting Time: 1 standard action
Range: Medium (100 ft. + 10 ft./level)
Effect: Fog spreads in 20-ft. radius, 20 ft. high
Duration: 1 round/level
Saving Throw: None
Spell Resistance: No

Acid fog creates a billowing mass of misty vapors similar to that produced by a *solid fog* spell (page 281). In addition to slowing creatures down and obscuring sight, this spell's vapors are highly acidic. Each round on your turn, starting when you cast the spell, the fog deals 2d6 points of acid damage to each creature and object within it.

Arcane Material Component: A pinch of dried, powdered peas combined with powdered animal hoof.

Acid Splash

Conjuration (Creation) [Acid]
Level: Sor/Wiz 0
Components: V, S
Casting Time: 1 standard action
Range: Close (25 ft. + 5 ft./2 levels)
Effect: One missile of acid
Duration: Instantaneous
Saving Throw: None
Spell Resistance: No

You fire a small orb of acid at the target. You must succeed on a ranged touch attack to hit your target. The orb deals 1d3 points of acid damage.

Aid

Enchantment (Compulsion) [Mind-Affecting]
Level: Clr 2, Good 2, Luck 2
Components: V, S, DF
Casting Time: 1 standard action
Range: Touch
Target: Living creature touched
Duration: 1 min./level
Saving Throw: None
Spell Resistance: Yes (harmless)

Aid grants the target a +1 morale bonus on attack rolls and saves against fear effects, plus temporary hit points equal to 1d8 + caster level (to a maximum of 1d8+10 temporary hit points at caster level 10th).

Air Walk

Transmutation [Air]
Level: Air 4, Clr 4, Drd 4
Components: V, S, DF
Casting Time: 1 standard action
Range: Touch
Target: Creature (Gargantuan or smaller) touched
Duration: 10 min./level
Saving Throw: None
Spell Resistance: Yes (harmless)

The subject can tread on air as if walking on solid ground. Moving upward is similar to walking up a hill. The maximum upward or downward angle possible is 45 degrees, at a rate equal to one-half the air walker's normal speed.

A strong wind (21+ mph) can push the subject along or hold it back. At the end of its turn each round, the wind blows the air walker 5 feet for each 5 miles per hour of wind speed. The creature can, at the DM's option, be subject to additional penalties in exceptionally strong or turbulent winds, such as loss of control over movement or physical damage from being buffeted about.

Should the spell duration expire while the subject is still aloft, the magic fails slowly. The subject floats downward 60 feet per round for 1d6 rounds. If it reaches the ground in that amount of time, it lands safely. If not, it falls the rest of the distance, taking 1d6 points of damage per 10 feet of fall. Since dispelling a spell effectively ends it, the subject also descends in this way if the *air walk* spell is dispelled, but not if it is negated by an *antimagic field*.

You can cast *air walk* on a specially trained mount so it can be ridden through the air. You can train a mount to move with the aid of *air walk* (counts as a trick; see page 74) with one week of work and a DC 25 Handle Animal check.

Alarm
Abjuration
Level: Brd 1, Rgr 1, Sor/Wiz 1
Components: V, S, F/DF
Casting Time: 1 standard action
Range: Close (25 ft. + 5 ft./2 levels)
Area: 20-ft.-radius emanation centered on a point in space
Duration: 2 hours/level (D)
Saving Throw: None
Spell Resistance: No

Alarm sounds a mental or audible alarm each time a creature of Tiny or larger size enters the warded area or touches it. A creature that speaks the password (determined by you at the time of casting) does not set off the *alarm*. You decide at the time of casting whether the *alarm* will be mental or audible.

Mental Alarm: A mental *alarm* alerts you (and only you) so long as you remain within 1 mile of the warded area. You note a single mental "ping" that awakens you from normal sleep but does not otherwise disturb concentration. A *silence* spell has no effect on a mental *alarm*.

Audible Alarm: An audible *alarm* produces the sound of a hand bell, and anyone within 60 feet of the warded area can hear it clearly. Reduce the distance by 10 feet for each interposing closed door and by 20 feet for each substantial interposing wall. In quiet conditions, the ringing can be heard faintly as far as 180 feet away. The sound lasts for 1 round. Creatures within a *silence* spell cannot hear the ringing.

Ethereal or astral creatures do not trigger the *alarm*.

Alarm can be made permanent with a *permanency* spell.

Arcane Focus: A tiny bell and a piece of very fine silver wire.

Align Weapon
Transmutation [see text]
Level: Clr 2
Components: V, S, DF
Casting Time: 1 standard action
Range: Touch
Target: Weapon touched or fifty projectiles (all of which must be in contact with each other at the time of casting)
Duration: 1 min./level
Saving Throw: Will negates (harmless, object)
Spell Resistance: Yes (harmless, object)

Align weapon makes a weapon good, evil, lawful, or chaotic, as you choose. A weapon that is aligned can bypass the damage reduction of certain creatures, usually outsiders of the opposite alignment. This spell has no effect on a weapon that already has an alignment, such as a holy sword.

You can't cast this spell on a natural weapon, such as an unarmed strike.

When you make a weapon good, evil, lawful, or chaotic, *align weapon* is a good, evil, lawful, or chaotic spell, respectively.

Alter Self
Transmutation
Level: Brd 2, Sor/Wiz 2
Components: V, S
Casting Time: 1 standard action
Range: Personal
Target: You
Duration: 10 min./level (D)

You assume the form of a creature of the same type as your normal form (such as humanoid or magical beast). The new form must be within one size category of your normal size. The maximum HD of an assumed form is equal to your caster level, to a maximum of 5 HD at 5th level. You can change into a member of your own kind or even into yourself.

You retain your own ability scores. Your class and level, hit points, alignment, base attack bonus, and base save bonuses all remain the same. You retain all supernatural and spell-like special attacks and qualities of your normal form, except for those requiring a body part that the new form does not have (such as a mouth for a breath weapon or eyes for a gaze attack). You keep all extraordinary special attacks and qualities derived from class levels (such as a barbarian's rage ability), but you lose any from your normal form that are not derived from class levels (such as a dragon's frightful presence ability).

If the new form is capable of speech, you can communicate normally. You retain any spellcasting ability you had in your original form, but the new form must be able to speak intelligibly (that is, speak a language) to use verbal components and must have limbs capable of fine manipulation to use somatic or material components.

You acquire the physical qualities of the new form while retaining your own mind. Physical qualities include natural size, mundane movement capabilities (such as burrowing, climbing, walking, swimming, and flight with wings, to a maximum speed of 120 feet for flying or 60 feet for nonflying movement), natural armor bonus, natural weapons (such as claws, bite, and so on), racial skill bonuses, racial bonus feats, and any gross physical qualities (presence or absence of wings, number of extremities, and so forth). A body with extra limbs does not allow you to make more attacks (or more advantageous two-weapon attacks) than normal.

You do not gain any extraordinary special attacks or special qualities not noted above under physical qualities, such as darkvision, low-light vision, blindsense, blindsight, fast healing, regeneration, scent, and so forth.

You do not gain any supernatural special attacks, special qualities, or spell-like abilities of the new form. Your creature type and subtype (if any) remain the same regardless of your new form. You cannot take the form of any creature with a template, even if that template doesn't change the creature type or subtype.

You can freely designate the new form's minor physical qualities (such as hair color, hair texture, and skin color) within the normal ranges for a creature of that kind. The new form's significant physical qualities (such as height, weight, and gender) are also under your control, but they must fall within the norms for the new form's kind. You are effectively disguised as an average member of the new form's race. If you use this spell to create a disguise, you get a +10 bonus on your Disguise check.

When the change occurs, your equipment, if any, either remains worn or held by the new form (if it is capable of wearing or holding the item), or melds into the new form and becomes nonfunctional. When you revert to your true form, any objects previously melded into the new form reappear in the same location on your body they previously occupied and are once again functional. Any new items you wore in the assumed form and can't wear in your normal form fall off and land at your feet; any that you could wear in either form or carry in a body part common to both forms (mouth, hands, or the like) at the time of reversion are still held in the same way. Any part of the body or piece of equipment that is separated from the whole reverts to its true form.

Analyze Dweomer
Divination
Level: Brd 6, Sor/Wiz 6
Components: V, S, F
Casting Time: 1 standard action
Range: Close (25 ft. + 5 ft./2 levels)
Targets: One object or creature per caster level
Duration: 1 round/level (D)
Saving Throw: None or Will negates; see text
Spell Resistance: No

You discern all spells and magical properties present in a number of creatures or objects. Each round, you may examine a single creature or object that you can see as a free action. In the case of a magic item, you learn its functions, how to activate its functions (if appropriate), and how many charges are left (if it uses charges). In the case of an object or creature with active spells cast upon it, you learn each spell, its effect, and its caster level.

An attended object may attempt a Will save to resist this effect if its holder so desires. If the save succeeds, you learn nothing about the object except what you can discern by looking at it. An object that makes its save cannot be affected by any other *analyze dweomer* spells for 24 hours.

Analyze dweomer does not function when used on an artifact (see the *Dungeon Master's Guide* for details on artifacts).

Focus: A tiny lens of ruby or sapphire set in a small golden loop. The gemstone must be worth at least 1,500 gp.

Animal Growth

Transmutation
Level: Drd 5, Rgr 4, Sor/Wiz 5
Components: V, S
Casting Time: 1 standard action
Range: Medium (100 ft. + 10 ft./level)
Targets: Up to one animal (Gargantuan or smaller) per two levels, no two of which can be more than 30 ft. apart
Duration: 1 min./level
Saving Throw: Fortitude negates
Spell Resistance: Yes

A number of animals grow to twice their normal size and eight times their normal weight. This alteration changes each animal's size category to the next largest (from Large to Huge, for example), grants it a +8 size bonus to Strength and a +4 size bonus to Constitution (and thus an extra 2 hit points per HD), and imposes a −2 size penalty to Dexterity. The creature's existing natural armor bonus increases by 2. The size change also affects the animal's modifier to AC and attack rolls and its base damage, as detailed on Table 2–2 in the *Dungeon Master's Guide*. The animal's space and reach change as indicated on Table 8–4: Creature Size and Scale (page 149), but its speed does not change.

The spell also grants each subject damage reduction 10/magic and a +4 resistance bonus on saving throws.

If insufficient room is available for the desired growth, the creature attains the maximum possible size and may make a Strength check (using its increased Strength) to burst any enclosures in the process. If it fails, it is constrained without harm by the materials enclosing it—the spell cannot be used to crush a creature by increasing its size.

All equipment worn or carried by an animal is similarly enlarged by the spell, though this change has no effect on the magical properties of any such equipment. Any enlarged item that leaves the enlarged creature's possession instantly returns to its normal size.

The spell gives no means of command or influence over the enlarged animals.

Multiple magical effects that increase size do not stack, which means (among other things) that you can't use a second casting of this spell to further increase the size of an animal that's still under the effect of the first casting.

Animal Messenger

Enchantment (Compulsion) [Mind-Affecting]
Level: Brd 2, Drd 2, Rgr 1
Components: V, S, M
Casting Time: 1 standard action
Range: Close (25 ft. + 5 ft./2 levels)
Target: One Tiny animal
Duration: One day/level
Saving Throw: None; see text
Spell Resistance: Yes

You compel a Tiny animal to go to a spot you designate. The most common use for this spell is to get an animal to carry a message to your allies. The animal cannot be one tamed or trained by someone else, including such creatures as familiars and animal companions.

Using some type of food desirable to the animal as a lure, you call the animal to you. It advances and awaits your bidding. You can mentally impress on the animal a certain place well known to you or an obvious landmark (such as the peak of a distant mountain). The directions must be simple, because the animal depends on your knowledge and can't find a destination on its own. You can attach some small item or note to the messenger. The animal then goes to the designated location and waits there until the duration of the spell expires, whereupon it resumes its normal activities.

During this period of waiting, the messenger allows others to approach it and remove any scroll or token it carries. Unless the intended recipient of a message is expecting a messenger in the form of a bird or other small animal, the carrier may be ignored. The intended recipient gains no special ability to communicate with the animal or read any attached message (if it's written in a language he or she doesn't know, for example).

Material Component: A morsel of food the animal likes.

Animal Shapes

Transmutation
Level: Animal 7, Drd 8
Components: V, S, DF

Casting Time: 1 standard action
Range: Close (25 ft. + 5 ft./2 levels)
Targets: Up to one willing creature per level, all within 30 ft. of each other
Duration: 1 hour/level (D)
Saving Throw: None; see text
Spell Resistance: Yes (harmless)

As *polymorph*, except you polymorph up to one willing creature per caster level into an animal of your choice; the spell has no effect on unwilling creatures. All creatures must take the same kind of animal form; for example, you can't turn one subject into a hawk and another into a dire wolf. Recipients remain in the animal form until the spell expires or until you dismiss it for all recipients. In addition, an individual subject may choose to resume its normal form as a full-round action; doing so ends the spell for that subject alone. The maximum HD of an assumed form is equal to the subject's HD or your caster level, whichever is lower, to a maximum of 20 HD at 20th level.

Animal Trance

Enchantment (Compulsion) [Mind-Affecting, Sonic]
Level: Brd 2, Drd 2
Components: V, S
Casting Time: 1 standard action
Range: Close (25 ft. + 5 ft./2 levels)
Targets: Animals or magical beasts with Intelligence 1 or 2
Duration: Concentration
Saving Throw: Will negates; see text
Spell Resistance: Yes

Your swaying motions and music (or singing, or chanting) compel animals and magical beasts to do nothing but watch you. Only a creature with an Intelligence score of 1 or 2 can be fascinated by this spell. Roll 2d6 to determine the total number of HD worth of creatures that you fascinate. The closest targets are selected first until no more targets within range can be affected. For example, if Vadania affects 7 HD worth of animals and there are several 2 HD wolves within close range, only the three closest wolves are affected.

A magical beast, a dire animal, or an animal trained to attack or guard is allowed a saving throw; an animal not trained to attack or guard is not.

Animate Dead

Necromancy [Evil]
Level: Clr 3, Death 3, Sor/Wiz 4
Components: V, S, M
Casting Time: 1 standard action
Range: Touch
Targets: One or more corpses touched
Duration: Instantaneous
Saving Throw: None
Spell Resistance: No

This spell turns the bones or bodies of dead creatures into undead skeletons or zombies that follow your spoken commands. The undead can follow you, or they can remain in an area and attack any creature (or just a specific kind of creature) entering the place. They remain animated until they are destroyed. (A destroyed skeleton or zombie can't be animated again.)

Regardless of the type of undead you create with this spell, you can't create more HD of undead than twice your caster level with a single casting of *animate dead*. (The *desecrate* spell doubles this limit; see page 218.)

The undead you create remain under your control indefinitely. No matter how many times you use this spell, however, you can control only 4 HD worth of undead creatures per caster level. If you exceed this number, all the newly created creatures fall under your control, and any excess undead from previous castings become uncontrolled. (You choose which creatures are released.) If you are a cleric, any undead you might command by virtue of your power to command or rebuke undead do not count toward the limit.

Skeletons: A skeleton can be created only from a mostly intact corpse or skeleton. The corpse must have bones, so creating a skeleton from a purple worm, for example, is not possible. If a skeleton is made from a corpse, the flesh falls off the bones. The statistics for a skeleton depend on its size; they do not depend on what abilities the creature may have had while alive. The *Monster Manual* has game statistics for skeletons.

Zombies: A zombie can be created only from a mostly intact corpse. The corpse must be that of a creature with a true anatomy, so a dead gelatinous cube, for example, cannot be animated as a zombie. The statistics for a zombie depend on its size, not on what abilities the creature may have had while alive. The *Monster Manual* has game statistics for zombies.

Material Component: You must place a black onyx gem worth at least 25 gp per Hit Die of the undead into the mouth or eye socket of each corpse you intend to animate. The magic of the spell turns these gems into worthless, burned-out shells.

Animate Objects

Transmutation
Level: Brd 6, Chaos 6, Clr 6
Components: V, S
Casting Time: 1 standard action
Range: Medium (100 ft. + 10 ft./level)
Targets: One Small object per caster level; see text
Duration: 1 round/level
Saving Throw: None
Spell Resistance: No

You imbue inanimate objects with mobility and a semblance of life. Each such animated object then immediately attacks whomever or whatever you initially designate. An animated object can be of any nonmagical material—wood, metal, stone, fabric, leather, ceramic, glass, or the like You may animate one Small or smaller object (such as a chair) or an equivalent number of larger objects per caster level. A Medium object (such as a coat rack) counts as two Small or smaller objects, a Large object (such as a table) as four, a Huge object as eight, a Gargantuan object as sixteen, and a Colossal object as thirty-two. You can change the designated target or targets as a move action, as if directing an active spell.

The *Monster Manual* has game statistics for animated objects.

This spell cannot animate objects carried or worn by a creature.

Animate objects can be made permanent with a *permanency* spell.

Animate Plants

Transmutation
Level: Drd 7, Plant 7
Components: V
Casting Time: 1 standard action
Range: Close (25 ft. + 5 ft./2 levels)
Targets: One Large plant per three caster levels or all plants within range; see text
Duration: 1 round/level or 1 hour/level; see text
Saving Throw: None
Spell Resistance: No

You imbue inanimate plants with mobility and a semblance of life. Each animated plant then immediately attacks whomever or whatever you initially designate as though it were an animated object of the appropriate size category. You may animate one Large or smaller plant (such as a tree), or an equivalent number of larger plants, per three caster levels. A Huge plant counts as two Large or smaller plants, a Gargantuan plant as four, and a Colossal plant as eight. You can change the designated target or targets as a move action, as if directing an active spell.

Use the statistics for animated objects found in the *Monster Manual,* except that plants smaller than Large don't have hardness unless the DM rules otherwise for a given case.

Animate plants cannot affect plant creatures (such as treants), nor does it affect nonliving vegetable material (such as a cotton tunic or hempen rope).

Entangle: Alternatively, you may imbue all plants within range with a degree of mobility, which allows them to entwine around creatures in the area. This usage of the spell duplicates the effect of an *entangle* spell. Spell resistance does not keep creatures from being entangled. This effect lasts 1 hour per caster level.

Animate Rope

Transmutation
Level: Brd 1, Sor/Wiz 1
Components: V, S
Casting Time: 1 standard action
Range: Medium (100 ft. + 10 ft./level)
Target: One ropelike object, length up to 50 ft. + 5 ft./level; see text
Duration: 1 round/level
Saving Throw: None
Spell Resistance: No

You can animate a nonliving ropelike object, such as string, yarn, cord, line, rope, or even a cable. The maximum length assumes a rope with a 1-inch diameter. Reduce the maximum length by 50% for every additional inch of thickness, and increase it by 50% for each reduction of the rope's diameter by half.

The possible commands are "coil" (form a neat, coiled stack), "coil and knot," "loop," "loop and knot," "tie and knot," and the opposites of all of the above ("uncoil," and so forth). You can give one command each round as a move action, as if directing an active spell.

The rope can enwrap only a creature or an object within 1 foot of it—it does not snake outward—so it must be thrown near the intended target. Doing so requires a successful ranged touch attack roll (range increment 10 feet). A typical 1-inch-diameter hempen rope has 2 hit points, AC 10, and requires a DC 23 Strength check to burst it. The rope does not deal damage, but it can be used as a trip line or to cause a single opponent that fails a Reflex saving throw to become entangled. A creature capable of spellcasting that is bound by this spell must make a DC 15 Concentration check to cast a spell. An entangled creature can slip free with a DC 20 Escape Artist check.

The rope itself and any knots tied in it are not magical.

This spell grants a +2 bonus on any Use Rope checks you make when using the transmuted rope.

The spell cannot animate objects carried or worn by a creature.

Antilife Shell

Abjuration
Level: Animal 6, Clr 6, Drd 6
Components: V, S, DF
Casting Time: 1 round
Range: 10 ft.
Area: 10-ft.-radius emanation, centered on you
Duration: 10 min./level (D)
Saving Throw: None
Spell Resistance: Yes

You bring into being a mobile, hemispherical energy field that prevents the entrance of most types of living creatures. The effect hedges out animals, aberrations, dragons, fey, giants, humanoids, magical beasts, monstrous humanoids, oozes, plants, and vermin, but not constructs, elementals, outsiders, or undead. See the *Monster Manual* for more about creature types.

This spell may be used only defensively, not aggressively. Forcing an abjuration barrier against creatures that the spell keeps at bay collapses the barrier (see Abjuration, page 172).

Antimagic Field

Abjuration

Level: Clr 8, Magic 6, Protection 6, Sor/Wiz 6

Components: V, S, M/DF

Casting Time: 1 standard action

Range: 10 ft.

Area: 10-ft.-radius emanation, centered on you

Duration: 10 min./level (D)

Saving Throw: None

Spell Resistance: See text

An invisible barrier surrounds you and moves with you. The space within this barrier is impervious to most magical effects, including spells, spell-like abilities, and supernatural abilities. Likewise, it prevents the functioning of any magic items or spells within its confines.

An *antimagic field* suppresses any spell or magical effect used within, brought into, or cast into the area, but does not dispel it. A *hasted* creature, for example, is not *hasted* while inside the field, but the spell resumes functioning when the creature leaves the field. Time spent within an *antimagic field* counts against the suppressed spell's duration.

Summoned creatures of any type and incorporeal undead wink out if they enter an *antimagic field*. They reappear in the same spot once the field goes away. Time spent winked out counts normally against the duration of the conjuration that is maintaining the creature. If you cast *antimagic field* in an area occupied by a summoned creature that has spell resistance, you must make a caster level check (1d20 + caster level) against the creature's spell resistance to make it wink out. (The effects of instantaneous conjurations, such as *create water*, are not affected by an *antimagic field* because the conjuration itself is no longer in effect, only its result.)

A normal creature (a normally encountered griffon rather than a conjured one, for instance) can enter the area, as can normal missiles. Furthermore, while a magic sword does not function magically within the area, it is still a sword (and a masterwork sword at that). The spell has no effect on golems and other constructs that are imbued with magic during their creation process and are thereafter self-supporting (unless they have been summoned, in which case they are treated like any other summoned creatures). Elementals, corporeal undead, and outsiders are likewise unaffected unless summoned. These creatures' spell-like or supernatural abilities, however, may be temporarily nullified by the field.

Dispel magic does not remove the field. Two or more *antimagic fields* sharing any of the same space have no effect on each other. Certain spells, such as *wall of force*, *prismatic sphere*, and *prismatic wall*, remain unaffected by *antimagic field* (see the individual spell descriptions). Artifacts and deities are unaffected by mortal magic such as this. (See the *Dungeon Master's Guide* for more about artifacts.)

Should a creature be larger than the area enclosed by the barrier, any part of it that lies outside the barrier is unaffected by the field.

Arcane Material Component: A pinch of powdered iron or iron filings.

Antipathy

Enchantment (Compulsion) [Mind-Affecting]

Level: Drd 9, Sor/Wiz 8

Components: V, S, M/DF

Casting Time: 1 hour

Range: Close (25 ft. + 5 ft./2 levels)

Target: One location (up to a 10-ft. cube/level) or one object

Duration: 2 hours/level (D)

Saving Throw: Will partial

Spell Resistance: Yes

You cause an object or location to emanate magical vibrations that repel either a specific kind of intelligent creature or creatures of a particular alignment, as defined by you. The kind of creature to be affected must be named specifically—for example, red dragons, hill giants, wererats, lammasus, cloakers, or vampires. A creature subtype (such as goblinoid) is not specific enough. Likewise, the specific alignment to be repelled must be named—for example, chaotic evil, chaotic good, lawful neutral, or neutral.

Creatures of the designated kind or alignment feel an overpowering urge to leave the area or to avoid the affected item. A compulsion forces them to abandon the area or item, shunning it and never willingly returning to it while the spell is in effect. A creature that makes a successful saving throw can stay in the area or touch the item but feels uncomfortable doing so. This distracting discomfort reduces the creature's Dexterity score by 4 points.

Antipathy counters and dispels *sympathy*.

Arcane Material Component: A lump of alum soaked in vinegar.

Antiplant Shell

Abjuration

Level: Drd 4

Components: V, S, DF

Casting Time: 1 standard action

Range: 10 ft.

Area: 10-ft.-radius emanation, centered on you

Duration: 10 min./level (D)

Saving Throw: None

Spell Resistance: Yes

The *antiplant shell* spell creates an invisible, mobile barrier that keeps all creatures within the shell protected from attacks by plant creatures or animated plants. As with many abjuration spells, forcing the barrier against creatures that the spell keeps at bay strains and collapses the field (see Abjuration, page 172).

Arcane Eye

Divination (Scrying)

Level: Sor/Wiz 4

Components: V, S, M

Casting Time: 10 minutes

Range: Unlimited

Effect: Magical sensor

Duration: 1 min./level (D)

Saving Throw: None

Spell Resistance: No

You create an invisible magical sensor that sends you visual information. You can create the *arcane eye* at any point you can see, but it can then travel outside your line of sight without hindrance. An *arcane eye* travels at 30 feet per round (300 feet per minute) if viewing an area ahead as a human would (primarily looking at the floor) or 10 feet per round (100 feet per minute) if examining the ceiling and walls as well as the floor ahead. It sees exactly as you would see if you were there. The eye can travel in any direction as long as the spell lasts. Solid barriers block its passage, but it can pass through a hole or space as small as 1 inch in diameter. The eye can't enter another plane of existence, even through a *gate* or similar magical portal.

You must concentrate to use an *arcane eye*. If you do not concentrate, the eye is inert until you again concentrate.

Material Component: A bit of bat fur.

Arcane Lock

Abjuration

Level: Sor/Wiz 2

Components: V, S, M

Casting Time: 1 standard action

Range: Touch

Target: The door, chest, or portal touched, up to 30 sq. ft./level in size

Duration: Permanent
Saving Throw: None
Spell Resistance: No

An *arcane lock* spell cast upon a door, chest, or portal magically locks it. You can freely pass your own *arcane lock* without affecting it; otherwise, a door or object secured with this spell can be opened only by breaking in or with a successful *dispel magic* or *knock* spell. Add 10 to the normal DC to break open a door or portal affected by this spell. (A *knock* spell does not remove an *arcane lock*; it only suppresses the effect for 10 minutes.)

Material Component: Gold dust worth 25 gp.

Arcane Mark
Universal
Level: Sor/Wiz 0
Components: V, S
Casting Time: 1 standard action
Range: 0 ft.
Effect: One personal rune or mark, all of which must fit within 1 sq. ft.
Duration: Permanent
Saving Throw: None
Spell Resistance: No

This spell allows you to inscribe your personal rune or mark, which can consist of no more than six characters. The writing can be visible or invisible. An *arcane mark* spell enables you to etch the rune upon any substance (even stone or metal) without harm to the material upon which it is placed. If an invisible mark is made, a *detect magic* spell causes it to glow and be visible, though not necessarily understandable. *See invisibility, true seeing, a gem of seeing,* or a *robe of eyes* likewise allows the user to see an invisible *arcane mark.* A *read magic* spell reveals the words, if any. The mark cannot be dispelled, but it can be removed by the caster or by an *erase* spell. If an *arcane mark* is placed on a living being, normal wear gradually causes the effect to fade in about a month.

Arcane mark must be cast on an object prior to casting *Drawmij's instant summons* on the same object (see that spell description for details).

Arcane Sight
Divination
Level: Sor/Wiz 3
Components: V, S
Casting Time: 1 standard action
Range: Personal
Target: You
Duration: 1 min./level (D)

This spell makes your eyes glow blue and allows you to see magical auras within 120 feet of you. The effect is similar to that of a *detect magic* spell, but *arcane sight* does not require concentration and discerns aura location and power more quickly.

You know the location and power of all magical auras within your sight. An aura's power depends on a spell's functioning level or an item's caster level, as noted in the description of the *detect magic* spell (page 219). If the items or creatures bearing the auras are in line of sight, you can make Spellcraft skill checks to determine the school of magic involved in each. (Make one check per aura; DC 15 + spell level, or 15 + one-half caster level for a nonspell effect.)

If you concentrate on a specific creature within 120 feet of you as a standard action, you can determine whether it has any spellcasting or spell-like abilities, whether these are arcane or divine (spell-like abilities register as arcane), and the strength of the most powerful spell or spell-like ability the creature currently has available for use. In some cases, *arcane sight* may give a deceptively low reading—for example, when you use it on a spellcaster who has used up most of his or her daily spell allotment.

Arcane sight can be made permanent with a *permanency* spell.

Arcane Sight, Greater
Divination
Level: Sor/Wiz 7

This spell functions like *arcane sight,* except that you automatically know which spells or magical effects are active upon any individual or object you see.

Greater arcane sight doesn't let you identify magic items.

Unlike *arcane sight,* this spell cannot be made permanent with a *permanency* spell.

Astral Projection
Necromancy
Level: Clr 9, Sor/Wiz 9, Travel 9
Components: V, S, M
Casting Time: 30 minutes
Range: Touch
Targets: You plus one additional willing creature touched per two caster levels
Duration: See text
Saving Throw: None
Spell Resistance: Yes

By freeing your spirit from your physical body, this spell allows you to project an astral body onto another plane altogether. You can bring the astral forms of other willing creatures with you, provided that these subjects are linked in a circle with you at the time of the casting. These fellow travelers are dependent upon you and must accompany you at all times. If something happens to you during the journey, your companions are stranded wherever you left them.

You project your astral self onto the Astral Plane, leaving your physical body behind on the Material Plane in a state of suspended animation. The spell projects an astral copy of you and all you wear or carry onto the Astral Plane. Since the Astral Plane touches upon other planes, you can travel astrally to any of these other planes as you will. To enter one, you leave the Astral Plane, forming a new physical body (and equipment) on the plane of existence you have chosen to enter.

While you are on the Astral Plane, your astral body is connected at all times to your physical body by a silvery cord. If the cord is broken, you are killed, astrally and physically. Luckily, very few things can destroy a silver cord (see the *Dungeon Master's Guide* for more information). When a second body is formed on a different plane, the incorporeal silvery cord remains invisibly attached to the new body. If the second body or the astral form is slain, the cord simply returns to your body where it rests on the Material Plane, thereby reviving it from its state of suspended animation. Although astral projections are able to function on the Astral Plane, their actions affect only creatures existing on the Astral Plane; a physical body must be materialized on other planes.

You and your companions may travel through the Astral Plane indefinitely. Your bodies simply wait behind in a state of suspended animation until you choose to return your spirits to them. The spell lasts until you desire to end it, or until it is terminated by some outside means, such as *dispel magic* cast upon either the physical body or the astral form, the breaking of the silver cord, or the destruction of your body back on the Material Plane (which kills you).

Material Component: A jacinth worth at least 1,000 gp, plus a silver bar worth 5 gp for each person to be affected.

Atonement
Abjuration
Level: Clr 5, Drd 5
Components: V, S, M, F, DF, XP
Casting Time: 1 hour
Range: Touch
Target: Living creature touched
Duration: Instantaneous
Saving Throw: None
Spell Resistance: Yes

This spell removes the burden of evil acts or misdeeds from the subject. The creature seeking atonement must be truly repentant and desirous of setting right its misdeeds. If the atoning creature committed the evil act unwittingly or under some form of compulsion, *atonement* operates normally at no cost to you. However, in the case of a creature atoning for deliberate misdeeds and acts of a knowing and willful nature, you must intercede with your deity (requiring you to expend 500 XP) in order to expunge the subject's burden. Many casters first assign a subject of this sort a quest (see *geas/quest*) or similar penance to determine whether the creature is truly contrite before casting the *atonement* spell on its behalf.

Atonement may be cast for one of several purposes, depending on the version selected.

Reverse Magical Alignment Change: If a creature has had its alignment magically changed, *atonement* returns its alignment to its original status at no cost in experience points.

Restore Class: A paladin who has lost her class features due to committing an evil act may have her paladinhood restored to her by this spell.

Restore Cleric or Druid Spell Powers: A cleric or druid who has lost the ability to cast spells by incurring the anger of his or her deity may regain that ability by seeking *atonement* from another cleric of the same deity or another druid. If the transgression was intentional, the casting cleric loses 500 XP for his intercession. If the transgression was unintentional, he does not lose XP.

Redemption or Temptation: You may cast this spell upon a creature of an opposing alignment in order to offer it a chance to change its alignment to match yours. The prospective subject must be present for the entire casting process. Upon completion of the spell, the subject freely chooses whether it retains its original alignment or acquiesces to your offer and changes to your alignment. No duress, compulsion, or magical influence can force the subject to take advantage of the opportunity offered if it is unwilling to abandon its old alignment. This use of the spell does not work on outsiders or any creature incapable of changing its alignment naturally.

Though the spell description refers to evil acts, *atonement* can also be used on any creature that has performed acts against its alignment, whether those acts are evil, good, chaotic, or lawful.

Note: Normally, changing alignment is up to the player (for PCs) or the DM (for NPCs). This use of *atonement* simply offers a believable way for a character to change his or her alignment drastically, suddenly, and definitively.

Material Component: Burning incense.

Focus: In addition to your holy symbol or normal divine focus, you need a set of prayer beads (or other prayer device, such as a prayer wheel or prayer book) worth at least 500 gp.

XP Cost: When cast for the benefit of a creature whose guilt was the result of deliberate acts, the cost to you is 500 XP per casting (see above).

Augury
Divination
Level: Clr 2
Components: V, S, M, F
Casting Time: 1 minute
Range: Personal
Target: You
Duration: Instantaneous

An *augury* can tell you whether a particular action will bring good or bad results for you in the immediate future. For example, if a character is considering destroying a weird seal that closes a portal, an *augury* might determine whether that act is a good idea.

The base chance for receiving a meaningful reply is 70% + 1% per caster level, to a maximum of 90%; the DM makes the roll secretly. The DM may determine that a question is so straightforward that a successful result is automatic, or so vague as to have no chance of success. If the *augury* succeeds, you get one of four results:
* Weal (if the action will probably bring good results).
* Woe (for bad results).
* Weal and woe (for both).
* Nothing (for actions that don't have especially good or bad results).

If the spell fails, you get the "nothing" result. A cleric who gets the "nothing" result has no way to tell whether it was the consequence of a failed or successful *augury*.

The *augury* can see into the future only about half an hour, so anything that might happen after that does not affect the result. Thus, the result might not take into account the long-term consequences of a contemplated action. All *auguries* cast by the same person about the same topic use the same dice result as the first casting.

Material Component: Incense worth at least 25 gp.

Focus: A set of marked sticks, bones, or similar tokens of at least 25 gp value.

Awaken
Transmutation
Level: Drd 5
Components: V, S, DF, XP
Casting Time: 24 hours
Range: Touch
Target: Animal or tree touched
Duration: Instantaneous
Saving Throw: Will negates
Spell Resistance: Yes

You awaken a tree or animal to humanlike sentience. To succeed, you must make a Will save (DC 10 + the animal's current HD, or the HD the tree will have once awakened).

The *awakened* animal or tree is friendly toward you. You have no special empathy or connection with a creature you awaken, although it serves you in specific tasks or endeavors if you communicate your desires to it.

An *awakened* tree has characteristics as if it were an animated object (see the *Monster Manual*), except that it gains the plant type and its Intelligence, Wisdom, and Charisma scores are each 3d6. An *awakened* plant gains the ability to move its limbs, roots, vines, creepers, and so forth, and it has senses similar to a human's.

An *awakened* animal gets 3d6 Intelligence, +1d3 Charisma, and +2 HD. Its type becomes magical beast (augmented animal). An awakened animal can't serve as an animal companion, familiar, or special mount.

An *awakened* tree or animal can speak one language that you know, plus one additional language that you know per point of Intelligence bonus (if any).

XP Cost: 250 XP.

Baleful Polymorph
Transmutation
Level: Drd 5, Sor/Wiz 5
Components: V, S
Casting Time: 1 standard action
Range: Close (25 ft. + 5 ft./2 levels)
Target: One creature
Duration: Permanent
Saving Throw: Fortitude negates, Will partial; see text
Spell Resistance: Yes

As *polymorph*, except that you change the subject into a Small or smaller animal of no more than 1 HD (such as a dog, lizard, monkey, or toad). If the new form would prove fatal to the creature (for example, if you polymorphed a landbound target into a fish, or a flying target into a toad), the subject gets a +4 bonus on the save.

If the spell succeeds, the subject must also make a Will save. If this second save fails, the creature loses its extraordinary, supernatural, and spell-like abilities, loses its ability to cast spells (if it had the ability), and gains the alignment, special abilities, and Intelligence, Wisdom, and Charisma scores of its new form in place of its own. It still retains its class and level (or HD), as well as all benefits deriving therefrom (such as base attack bonus, base save bonuses, and hit points). It retains any class features (other than spellcasting) that aren't extraordinary, supernatural, or spell-like abilities.

Incorporeal or gaseous creatures are immune to being *polymorphed*, and a creature with the shapechanger subtype (such as a lycanthrope or a doppelganger) can revert to its natural form as a standard action.

Bane

Enchantment (Compulsion) [Fear, Mind-Affecting]
Level: Clr 1
Components: V, S, DF
Casting Time: 1 standard action
Range: 50 ft.
Area: All enemies within 50 ft.
Duration: 1 min./level
Saving Throw: Will negates
Spell Resistance: Yes

Bane fills your enemies with fear and doubt. Each affected creature takes a –1 penalty on attack rolls and a –1 penalty on saving throws against fear effects.

Bane counters and dispels *bless*.

Banishment

Abjuration
Level: Clr 6, Sor/Wiz 7
Components: V, S, F
Casting Time: 1 standard action
Range: Close (25 ft. + 5 ft./2 levels)
Targets: One or more extraplanar creatures, no two of which can be more than 30 ft. apart
Duration: Instantaneous
Saving Throw: Will negates
Spell Resistance: Yes

A *banishment* spell is a more powerful version of the *dismissal* spell. It enables you to force extraplanar creatures out of your home plane. As many as 2 Hit Dice of creatures per caster level can be banished. You can improve the spell's chance of success by presenting at least one object or substance that the target hates, fears, or otherwise opposes. For each such object or substance, you gain a +1 bonus on your caster level check to overcome the target's spell resistance (if any), the saving throw DC increases by 2. For example, if this spell were cast on a demon that hated light and was vulnerable to holy water and cold iron weapons, you might use iron, holy water, and a torch in the spell. The three items would give you a +3 bonus on your check to overcome the demon's spell resistance and add 6 to the spell's save DC.

At the DM's option, certain rare items might work twice as well as a normal item for the purpose of the bonuses (each providing a +2 bonus on the caster level check against spell resistance and increasing the save DC by 4).

Arcane Focus: Any item that is distasteful to the subject (optional, see above).

Barkskin

Transmutation
Level: Drd 2, Rgr 2, Plant 2
Components: V, S, DF
Casting Time: 1 standard action
Range: Touch
Target: Living creature touched
Duration: 10 min./level
Saving Throw: None
Spell Resistance: Yes (harmless)

Barkskin toughens a creature's skin. The effect grants a +2 enhancement bonus to the creature's existing natural armor bonus. This enhancement bonus increases by 1 for every three caster levels above 3rd, to a maximum of +5 at caster level 12th.

The enhancement bonus provided by *barkskin* stacks with the target's natural armor bonus, but not with other enhancement bonuses to natural armor. A creature without natural armor has an effective natural armor bonus of +0, much as a character wearing only normal clothing has an armor bonus of +0.

Bear's Endurance

Transmutation
Level: Clr 2, Drd 2, Rgr 2, Sor/Wiz 2
Components: V, S, DF
Casting Time: 1 standard action
Range: Touch
Target: Creature touched
Duration: 1 min./level
Saving Throw: Will negates (harmless)
Spell Resistance: Yes

The affected creature gains greater vitality and stamina. The spell grants the subject a +4 enhancement bonus to Constitution, which adds the usual benefits to hit points, Fortitude saves, Constitution checks, and so forth.

Hit points gained by a temporary increase in Constitution score are not temporary hit points. They go away when the subject's Constitution drops back to normal. They are not lost first as temporary hit points are (see page 146).

Bear's Endurance, Mass

Transmutation
Level: Clr 6, Drd 6, Sor/Wiz 6
Range: Close (25 ft. + 5 ft./2 levels)
Targets: One creature/level, no two of which can be more than 30 ft. apart

Mass bear's endurance works like *bear's endurance*, except that it affects multiple creatures.

Bestow Curse

Necromancy
Level: Clr 3, Sor/Wiz 4
Components: V, S

Casting Time: 1 standard action
Range: Touch
Target: Creature touched
Duration: Permanent
Saving Throw: Will negates
Spell Resistance: Yes

You place a curse on the subject. Choose one of the following three effects.
- –6 decrease to an ability score (minimum 1).
- –4 penalty on attack rolls, saves, ability checks, and skill checks.
- Each turn, the target has a 50% chance to act normally; otherwise, it takes no action.

You may also invent your own curse, but it should be no more powerful than those described above, and the DM has final say on the curse's effect.

The *curse* bestowed by this spell cannot be dispelled, but it can be removed with a *break enchantment, limited wish, miracle, remove curse,* or *wish* spell.

Bestow curse counters *remove curse.*

Bigby's Clenched Fist

Evocation [Force]
Level: Sor/Wiz 8, Strength 8
Components: V, S, F/DF

This spell functions like *Bigby's interposing hand,* except that the hand can interpose itself, push, or strike one opponent that you select. The floating hand can move as far as 60 feet and can attack in the same round. Since this hand is directed by you, its ability to notice or attack invisible or concealed creatures is no better than yours.

The hand attacks once per round, and its attack bonus equals your caster level + your Intelligence, Wisdom, or Charisma modifier (for a wizard, cleric, or sorcerer, respectively), +11 for the hand's Strength score (33), –1 for being Large. The hand deals 1d8+11 points of damage on each attack, and any creature struck must make a Fortitude save (against this spell's save DC) or be stunned for 1 round. Directing the spell to a new target is a move action.

The *clenched fist* can also interpose itself as *Bigby's interposing hand* does, or it can bull rush an opponent as *Bigby's forceful hand* does, but at a +15 bonus on the Strength check.

Clerics who cast this spell name it for their deities—*Pelor's clenched fist,* for example.

Arcane Focus: A leather glove.

Bigby's Crushing Hand

Evocation [Force]
Level: Sor/Wiz 9, Strength 9
Components: V, S, M, F/DF

This spell functions like *Bigby's interposing hand*, except that the hand can interpose itself, push, or crush one opponent that you select.

The *crushing hand* can grapple an opponent like *Bigby's grasping hand* does. Its grapple bonus equals your caster level + your Intelligence, Wisdom, or Charisma modifier (for a wizard, cleric, or sorcerer, respectively), +12 for the hand's Strength score (35), +4 for being Large. The hand deals 2d6+12 points of damage (lethal, not nonlethal) on each successful grapple check against an opponent.

The *crushing hand* can also interpose itself as *Bigby's interposing hand* does, or it can bull rush an opponent as *Bigby's forceful hand* does, but at a +18 bonus.

Directing the spell to a new target is a move action.

Clerics who cast this spell name it for their deities—*St. Cuthbert's crushing hand,* for example.

Arcane Material Component: The shell of an egg.

Arcane Focus: A glove of snakeskin.

Bigby's Forceful Hand

Evocation [Force]
Level: Sor/Wiz 6
Components: V, S, F

This spell functions like *Bigby's interposing hand*, except that the *forceful hand* pursues and pushes away the opponent that you designate. Treat this attack as a bull rush with a +14 bonus on the Strength check (+8 for Strength 27, +4 for being Large, and a +2 bonus for charging, which it always gets). The hand always moves with the opponent to push that target back the full distance allowed, and it has no speed limit. Directing the spell to a new target is a move action.

A very strong creature could not push the hand out of its way because the latter would instantly reposition itself between the creature and you, but an opponent could push the hand up against you by successfully bull rushing it.

Focus: A sturdy glove made of leather or heavy cloth.

Bigby's Grasping Hand

Evocation [Force]
Level: Sor/Wiz 7, Strength 7
Components: V, S, F/DF

This spell functions like *Bigby's interposing hand*, except the hand can also grapple one opponent that you select. The *grasping hand* gets one grapple attack per round. Its attack bonus to make contact equals your caster level + your Intelligence, Wisdom, or Charisma modifier (for wizards, clerics, and sorcerers, respectively), +10 for the hand's Strength score (31), −1

for being Large. Its grapple bonus is this same figure, except with a +4 modifier for being Large instead of −1. The hand holds but does not harm creatures it grapples. Directing the spell to a new target is a move action.

The *grasping hand* can also bull rush an opponent as *Bigby's forceful hand* does, but at a +16 bonus on the Strength check (+10 for Strength 35, +4 for being Large, and a +2 bonus for charging, which it always gets), or interpose itself as *Bigby's interposing hand* does.

Clerics who cast this spell name it for their deities—*Kord's grasping hand,* for example.

Arcane Focus: A leather glove.

Bigby's Interposing Hand

Evocation [Force]
Level: Sor/Wiz 5
Components: V, S, F
Casting Time: 1 standard action
Range: Medium (100 ft. + 10 ft./level)
Effect: 10-ft. hand
Duration: 1 round/level (D)
Saving Throw: None
Spell Resistance: Yes

Bigby's interposing hand creates a Large magic hand that appears between you and one opponent. This floating, disembodied hand then moves to remain between the two of you, regardless of where you move or how the opponent tries to get around it, providing cover (+4 AC) for you against that opponent. Nothing can fool the hand—it sticks with the selected opponent in spite of darkness, invisibility, polymorphing, or any other attempt at hiding or disguise. The hand does not pursue an opponent, however.

A *Bigby's hand* is 10 feet long and about that wide with its fingers outstretched. It has as many hit points as you do when you're undamaged, and its AC is 20 (−1 size, +11 natural). It takes damage as a normal creature, but most magical effects that don't cause damage do not affect it. The hand never provokes attacks of opportunity from opponents. It cannot push through a *wall of force* or enter an *antimagic field*, but it suffers the full effect of a *prismatic wall* or *prismatic sphere*. The hand makes saving throws as its caster. *Disintegrate* or a successful *dispel magic* destroys it.

Any creature weighing 2,000 pounds or less that tries to push past the hand is slowed to half its normal speed. The hand cannot reduce the speed of a creature weighing more than 2,000 pounds, but it still affects the creature's attacks.

Directing the spell to a new target is a move action.

Focus: A soft glove.

Binding

Enchantment (Compulsion) [Mind-Affecting]
Level: Sor/Wiz 8
Components: V, S, M
Casting Time: One minute
Range: Close (25 ft. + 5 ft./2 levels)
Target: One living creature
Duration: See text (D)
Saving Throw: Will negates; see text
Spell Resistance: Yes

A *binding* spell creates a magical restraint to hold a creature. The target gets an initial saving throw only if its Hit Dice equal at least one-half your caster level.

You may have as many as six assistants help you with the spell. For each assistant who casts *suggestion*, your caster level for this casting of *binding* increases by 1. For each assistant who casts *dominate animal, dominate person,* or *dominate monster,* your caster level for this casting of *binding* increases by a number equal to one-third of that assistant's level, provided that the spell's target is appropriate for a *binding* spell. Since the assistants' spells are cast simply to improve your caster level for the purpose of the *binding* spell, saving throws and spell resistance against the assistants' spells are irrelevant. Your caster level determines whether the target gets an initial Will saving throw and how long the *binding* lasts. All *binding* spells are dismissible.

Regardless of the version of *binding* you cast, you can specify triggering conditions that end the spell and release the creature whenever they occur. These triggers can be as simple or elaborate as you desire, but the DM must agree that the condition is reasonable and has a likelihood of coming to pass. The conditions can be based on a creature's name, identity, or alignment but otherwise must be based on observable actions or qualities. Intangibles such as level, class, Hit Dice, or hit points don't qualify. For example, a *bound* creature can be released when a lawful good creature approaches, but not when a paladin approaches. Once the spell is cast, its triggering conditions cannot be changed. Setting a release condition increases the save DC (assuming a saving throw is allowed) by 2.

If you are casting any of the first three versions of *binding* (those with limited durations), you may cast additional *binding* spells to prolong the effect, since the durations overlap. If you do so, the target gets a saving throw at the end of the first spell's duration, even if your caster level was high enough to disallow an initial saving throw. If the creature succeeds on this save, all the *binding* spells it has received are broken.

The *binding* spell has six versions. Choose one of the following versions when you cast the spell.

Chaining: The subject is confined by restraints that generate an *antipathy* spell affecting all creatures who approach the subject, except you. The duration is one year per caster level. The subject of this form of *binding* is confined to the spot it occupied when it received the spell.

Slumber: This version causes the subject to become comatose for as long as one year per caster level. The subject does not need to eat or drink while *slumbering*, nor does it age. This form of *binding* is more difficult to cast than *chaining*, making it slightly easier to resist. Reduce the spell's save DC by 1.

Bound Slumber: This combination of *chaining* and *slumber* lasts for as long as one month per caster level. Reduce the save DC by 2.

Hedged Prison: The subject is transported to or otherwise brought within a confined area (such as a labyrinth) from which it cannot wander by any means. The effect is permanent. Reduce the save DC by 3.

Metamorphosis: The subject assumes gaseous form, except for its head or face. It is held harmless in a jar or other container, which may be transparent if you so choose. The creature remains aware of its surroundings and can speak, but it cannot leave the container, attack, or use any of its powers or abilities. The *binding* is permanent. The subject does not need to breathe, eat, or drink while *metamorphosed*, nor does it age. Reduce the save DC by 4.

Minimus Containment: The subject is shrunk to a height of 1 inch or even less and held within some gem, jar, or similar object. The *binding* is permanent. The subject does not need to breathe, eat, or drink while *contained*, nor does it age. Reduce the save DC by 4.

You can't dispel a *binding* spell with *dispel magic* or a similar effect, though an *antimagic field* or *Mordenkainen's disjunction* affects it normally. A bound extraplanar creature cannot be sent back to its home plane due to *dismissal, banishment,* or a similar effect.

Components: The components for a *binding* spell vary according to the version of the spell, but they always include a continuous chanting utterance read from the scroll or spellbook page containing the spell, somatic gestures, and materials appropriate to the form of *binding* used. These components can include such items as miniature chains of special metals (silver for lycanthropes, cold iron for demons, and so forth), soporific herbs of the rarest sort (for *slumber* bindings), a bell jar of the finest crystal, and the like.

In addition to the specially made props suited to the specific type of *binding* (cost 500 gp), the spell requires opals worth at least 500 gp for each HD of the target and a vellum depiction or carved statuette of the subject to be captured.

Blade Barrier
Evocation [Force]
Level: Clr 6, Good 6, War 6
Components: V, S
Casting Time: 1 standard action
Range: Medium (100 ft. + 10 ft./level)
Effect: Wall of whirling blades up to 20 ft. long/ level, or a ringed wall of whirling blades with a radius of up to 5 ft. per two levels; either form 20 ft. high
Duration: 1 min./level (D)
Saving Throw: Reflex half or Reflex negates; see text
Spell Resistance: Yes

An immobile, vertical curtain of whirling blades shaped of pure force springs into existence. Any creature passing through the wall takes 1d6 points of damage per caster level (maximum 15d6), with a Reflex save for half damage.

If you evoke the barrier so that it appears where creatures are, each creature takes damage as if passing through the wall. Each such creature can avoid the wall (ending up on the side of its choice) and thus take no damage by making a successful Reflex save.

A *blade barrier* provides cover (+4 bonus to AC, +2 bonus on Reflex saves) against attacks made through it.

Blasphemy
Evocation [Evil, Sonic]
Level: Clr 7, Evil 7
Components: V
Casting Time: 1 standard action
Range: 30 ft.
Area: Nonevil creatures in a 40-ft.-radius spread centered on you
Duration: Instantaneous
Saving Throw: None or Will negates; see text
Spell Resistance: Yes

Any nonevil creature within the area of a *blasphemy* spell suffers the following ill effects.

HD	Effect
Equal to caster level	Dazed
Up to caster level –1	Weakened, dazed
Up to caster level –5	Paralyzed, weakened, dazed
Up to caster level –10	Killed, paralyzed, weakened, dazed

The effects are cumulative and concurrent. No saving throw is allowed against these effects.

Dazed: The creature can take no actions for 1 round, though it defends itself normally.

Weakened: The creature's Strength score decreases by 2d6 points for 2d4 rounds.

Paralyzed: The creature is paralyzed and helpless for 1d10 minutes.

Killed: Living creatures die. Undead creatures are destroyed.

Furthermore, if you are on your home plane when you cast this spell, nonevil extraplanar creatures within the area are instantly banished back to their home planes. Creatures so banished cannot return for at least 24 hours. This effect takes place regardless of whether the creatures hear the *blasphemy.* The banishment effect allows a Will save (at a –4 penalty) to negate.

Creatures whose Hit Dice exceed your caster level are unaffected by *blasphemy.*

Bless
Enchantment (Compulsion) [Mind-Affecting]
Level: Clr 1, Pal 1
Components: V, S, DF
Casting Time: 1 standard action
Range: 50 ft.
Area: The caster and all allies within a 50-ft. burst, centered on the caster
Duration: 1 min./level
Saving Throw: None
Spell Resistance: Yes (harmless)

Bless fills your allies with courage. Each ally gains a +1 morale bonus on attack rolls and on saving throws against fear effects.

Bless counters and dispels *bane.*

Bless Water
Transmutation [Good]
Level: Clr 1, Pal 1
Components: V, S, M
Casting Time: 1 minute
Range: Touch
Target: Flask of water touched
Duration: Instantaneous
Saving Throw: Will negates (object)
Spell Resistance: Yes (object)

This transmutation imbues a flask (1 pint) of water with positive energy, turning it into holy water (page 128).

Material Component: 5 pounds of powdered silver (worth 25 gp).

Bless Weapon
Transmutation
Level: Pal 1
Components: V, S
Casting Time: 1 standard action
Range: Touch
Target: Weapon touched
Duration: 1 min./level
Saving Throw: None
Spell Resistance: No

This transmutation makes a weapon strike true against evil foes. The weapon is treated as having a +1 enhancement bonus for the purpose of bypassing the damage reduction of evil creatures or striking evil incorporeal creatures (though the spell doesn't grant an actual enhancement bonus). The weapon also becomes good, which means it can bypass the damage reduction of certain creatures, particularly evil outsiders. (This effect overrides and suppresses any other alignment the weapon might have.) Individual arrows or bolts can be transmuted, but affected projectile weapons (such as bows) don't confer the benefit to the projectiles they shoot.

In addition, all critical hit rolls against evil foes are automatically successful, so every threat is a critical hit. This last effect does not apply to any weapon that already has a magical effect related to critical hits, such as a keen weapon or a vorpal sword.

Blight

Necromancy
Level: Drd 4, Sor/Wiz 5
Components: V, S, DF
Casting Time: 1 standard action
Range: Touch
Duration: Instantaneous
Saving Throw: Fortitude half; see text
Spell Resistance: Yes

This spell withers a single plant of any size. An affected plant creature takes 1d6 points of damage per level (maximum 15d6) and may attempt a Fortitude saving throw for half damage. A plant that isn't a creature (such as a tree or shrub) doesn't receive a save and immediately withers and dies.

This spell has no effect on the soil or surrounding plant life.

Blindness/Deafness

Necromancy
Level: Brd 2, Clr 3, Sor/Wiz 2
Components: V
Casting Time: 1 standard action
Range: Medium (100 ft. + 10 ft./level)
Target: One living creature
Duration: Permanent (D)
Saving Throw: Fortitude negates
Spell Resistance: Yes

You call upon the powers of unlife to render the subject blinded or deafened, as you choose.

Blink

Transmutation
Level: Brd 3, Sor/Wiz 3
Components: V, S
Casting Time: 1 standard action
Range: Personal
Target: You
Duration: 1 round/level (D)

Like a blink dog (see the *Monster Manual*), you "blink" back and forth between the Material Plane and the Ethereal Plane. You look as though you're winking in and out of reality very quickly and at random.

Blinking has several effects, as follows.

Physical attacks against you have a 50% miss chance, and the Blind-Fight feat doesn't help opponents, since you're ethereal and not merely invisible. If the attack is capable of striking ethereal creatures, the miss chance is only 20% (for concealment). If the attacker can see invisible creatures, the miss chance is also only 20%. (For an attacker who can both see and strike ethereal creatures, there is no miss chance.) Likewise, your own attacks have a 20% miss chance, since you sometimes go ethereal just as you are about to strike.

Any individually targeted spell has a 50% chance to fail against you while you're *blinking* unless your attacker can target invisible, ethereal creatures. Your own spells have a 20% chance to activate just as you go ethereal, in which case they typically do not affect the Material Plane.

While *blinking*, you take only half damage from area attacks (but full damage from those that extend onto the Ethereal Plane). You strike as an invisible creature (with a +2 bonus on attack rolls), denying your target any Dexterity bonus to AC. You take only half damage from falling, since you fall only while you are material.

While *blinking*, you can step through (but not see through) solid objects. For each 5 feet of solid material you walk through, there is a 50% chance that you become material. If this occurs, you are shunted off to the nearest open space and take 1d6 points of damage per 5 feet so traveled. You can move at only three-quarters speed (because movement on the Ethereal Plane is at half speed, and you spend about half your time there and half your time material.)

Since you spend about half your time on the Ethereal Plane, you can see and even attack ethereal creatures. You interact with ethereal creatures roughly the same way you interact with material ones. For instance, your spells against ethereal creatures are 20% likely to activate just as you go material and be lost.

An ethereal creature is invisible, incorporeal, and capable of moving in any direction, even up or down. As an incorporeal creature, you can move through solid objects, including living creatures. An ethereal creature can see and hear the Material Plane, but everything looks gray and insubstantial. Sight and hearing on the Material Plane are limited to 60 feet. Force effects (such as *magic missile* and *wall of force*) and abjurations affect you

normally. Their effects extend onto the Ethereal Plane from the Material Plane, but not vice versa. An ethereal creature can't attack material creatures, and spells you cast while ethereal affect only other ethereal things. Certain material creatures or objects have attacks or effects that work on the Ethereal Plane (such as the basilisk and its gaze attack). Treat other ethereal creatures and objects as material.

Blur

Illusion (Glamer)
Level: Brd 2, Sor/Wiz 2
Components: V
Casting Time: 1 standard action
Range: Touch
Target: Creature touched
Duration: 1 min./level (D)
Saving Throw: Will negates (harmless)
Spell Resistance: Yes (harmless)

The subject's outline appears blurred, shifting and wavering. This distortion grants the subject concealment (20% miss chance).

A *see invisibility* spell does not counteract the *blur* effect, but a *true seeing* spell does.

Opponents that cannot see the subject ignore the spell's effect (though fighting an unseen opponent carries penalties of its own; see page 151).

The subject of a blur spell.

Break Enchantment

Abjuration
Level: Brd 4, Clr 5, Luck 5, Pal 4, Sor/Wiz 5
Components: V, S
Casting Time: 1 minute
Range: Close (25 ft. + 5 ft./2 levels)
Targets: Up to one creature per level, all within 30 ft. of each other
Duration: Instantaneous
Saving Throw: See text
Spell Resistance: No

This spell frees victims from enchantments, transmutations, and curses. *Break enchantment* can reverse even an instantaneous effect, such as *flesh to stone.* For each such effect, you make a caster level check (1d20 + caster level, maximum +15) against a DC of 11 + caster level of the effect. Success means that the creature is free of the spell, curse, or effect. For a cursed magic item, the DC is 25.

If the spell is one that cannot be dispelled by *dispel magic, break enchantment* works only if that spell is 5th level or lower. For instance, *bestow curse* cannot be dispelled by *dispel magic,* but *break enchantment* can dispel it.

If the effect comes from some permanent magic item, such as a cursed sword, *break enchantment* does not remove the curse from the item, but it does frees the victim from the item's effects. For example, a cursed item can change the alignment of its user. *Break enchantment* allows the victim to be rid of the item and negates the alignment change, but the item's curse is intact and affects the next creature to pick up the item—even if it's the recent recipient of the *break enchantment* spell.

Bull's Strength

Transmutation
Level: Clr 2, Drd 2, Pal 2, Sor/Wiz 2, Strength 2
Components: V, S, M/DF
Casting Time: 1 standard action
Range: Touch
Target: Creature touched
Duration: 1 min./level
Saving Throw: Will negates (harmless)
Spell Resistance: Yes (harmless)

The subject becomes stronger. The spell grants a +4 enhancement bonus to Strength, adding the usual benefits to melee attack rolls, melee damage rolls, and other uses of the Strength modifier.

Arcane Material Component: A few hairs, or a pinch of dung, from a bull.

Bull's Strength, Mass

Transmutation
Level: Clr 6, Drd 6, Sor/Wiz 6
Range: Close (25 ft. + 5 ft./2 levels)
Targets: One creature/level, no two of which can be more than 30 ft. apart

This spell functions like *bull's strength,* except that it affects multiple creatures.

Burning Hands

Evocation [Fire]
Level: Fire 1, Sor/Wiz 1
Components: V, S
Casting Time: 1 standard action
Range: 15 ft.
Area: Cone-shaped burst
Duration: Instantaneous
Saving Throw: Reflex half
Spell Resistance: Yes

A cone of searing flame shoots from your fingertips. Any creature in the area of the flames takes 1d4 points of fire damage per caster level (maximum 5d4). Flammable materials such as cloth, paper, parchment, and thin wood burn if the flames touch them. A character can extinguish burning items as a full-round action.

Call Lightning

Evocation [Electricity]
Level: Drd 3
Components: V, S
Casting Time: 1 round
Range: Medium (100 ft. + 10 ft./level)
Effect: One or more 30-ft.-long vertical lines of lightning
Duration: 1 min./level
Saving Throw: Reflex half
Spell Resistance: Yes

Immediately upon completion of the spell, and once per round thereafter, you may call down a 5-foot-wide, 30-foot-long, vertical bolt of lightning that deals 3d6 points of electricity damage. The bolt of lightning flashes down in a vertical stroke at whatever target point you choose within the spell's range (measured from your position at the time). Any creature in the target square or in the path of the bolt is affected.

You need not call a bolt of lightning immediately; other actions, even spellcasting, can be performed. However, each round after the first you may use a standard action (concentrating on the spell) to call a bolt. You may call a total number of bolts equal to your caster level (maximum 10 bolts).

If you are outdoors and in a stormy area—a rain shower, clouds and wind, hot and cloudy conditions, or even a tornado (including a whirlwind formed by a djinni or an air elemental of at least Large size; see the *Monster Manual*)—each bolt deals 3d10 points of electricity damage instead of 3d6.

This spell functions indoors or underground but not underwater.

Call Lightning Storm

Evocation [Electricity]
Level: Drd 5
Range: Long (400 ft. + 40 ft./level)

This spell functions like *call lightning,* except that each bolt deals 5d6 points of electricity damage (or 5d10 if created outdoors in a stormy area), and you may call a maximum of 15 bolts.

Calm Animals

Enchantment (Compulsion) [Mind-Affecting]
Level: Animal 1, Drd 1, Rgr 1
Components: V, S
Casting Time: 1 standard action
Range: Close (25 ft. + 5 ft./2 levels)
Targets: Animals within 30 ft. of each other
Duration: 1 min./level
Saving Throw: Will negates; see text
Spell Resistance: Yes

This spell soothes and quiets animals, rendering them docile and harmless. Only ordinary animals (those with Intelligence scores of 1 or 2) can be affected by this spell. All the subjects must be of the same kind, and no two may be more than 30 feet apart. The maximum number of Hit Dice of animals you can affect is equal to 2d4 + caster level. A dire animal or an animal trained to attack or guard is allowed a saving throw; other animals are not. (A druid could calm a normal bear or wolf with little trouble, but it's more difficult to affect a trained guard dog.)

The affected creatures remain where they are and do not attack or flee. They are not helpless and defend themselves normally if attacked. Any threat (such as fire, a hungry predator, or an imminent attack) breaks the spell on the threatened creatures.

Calm Emotions

Enchantment (Compulsion) [Mind-Affecting]
Level: Brd 2, Clr 2, Law 2
Components: V, S, DF
Casting Time: 1 standard action
Range: Medium (100 ft. + 10 ft./level)
Area: Creatures in a 20-ft.-radius spread
Duration: Concentration, up to 1 round/level (D)
Saving Throw: Will negates
Spell Resistance: Yes

This spell calms agitated creatures. You have no control over the affected creatures, but *calm emotions* can stop raging creatures from fighting or joyous ones from reveling. Creatures so affected cannot take violent actions (although they can defend themselves) or do anything destructive. Any aggressive action against or damage dealt to a calmed creature immediately breaks the spell on all calmed creatures.

This spell automatically suppresses (but does not dispel) any morale bonuses granted by spells such as *bless*, *good hope*, and *rage*, as well as negating a bard's ability to inspire courage or a barbarian's rage ability. It also suppresses any fear effects and removes the *confused* condition from all targets. While the spell lasts, a suppressed spell or effect has no effect. When the *calm emotions* spell ends, the original spell or effect takes hold of the creature again, provided that its duration has not expired in the meantime.

Cat's Grace

Transmutation
Level: Brd 2, Drd 2, Rgr 2, Sor/Wiz 2
Components: V, S, M
Casting Time: 1 standard action
Range: Touch
Target: Creature touched
Duration: 1 min./level
Saving Throw: Will negates (harmless)
Spell Resistance: Yes

The transmuted creature becomes more graceful, agile, and coordinated. The spell grants a +4 enhancement bonus to Dexterity, adding the usual benefits to AC, Reflex saves, and other uses of the Dexterity modifier.

Material Component: A pinch of cat fur.

Cat's Grace, Mass

Transmutation
Level: Brd 6, Drd 6, Sor/Wiz 6
Range: Close (25 ft. + 5 ft./2 levels)
Targets: One creature/level, no two of which can be more than 30 ft. apart

This spell functions like *cat's grace*, except that it affects multiple creatures.

Cause Fear

Necromancy [Fear, Mind-Affecting]
Level: Brd 1, Clr 1, Death 1, Sor/Wiz 1
Components: V, S
Casting Time: 1 standard action
Range: Close (25 ft. + 5 ft./2 levels)
Target: One living creature with 5 or fewer HD
Duration: 1d4 rounds or 1 round; see text
Saving Throw: Will partial
Spell Resistance: Yes

The affected creature becomes frightened. If the subject succeeds on a Will save, it is shaken for 1 round. Creatures with 6 or more Hit Dice are immune to this effect.

Cause fear counters and dispels *remove fear*.

Chain Lightning

Evocation [Electricity]
Level: Air 6, Sor/Wiz 6
Components: V, S, F
Casting Time: 1 standard action
Range: Long (400 ft. + 40 ft./level)
Targets: One primary target, plus one secondary target/level (each of which must be within 30 ft. of the primary target)
Duration: Instantaneous
Saving Throw: Reflex half
Spell Resistance: Yes

This spell creates an electrical discharge that begins as a single stroke commencing from your fingertips. Unlike *lightning bolt*, *chain lightning* strikes one object or creature initially, then arcs to other targets.

The bolt deals 1d6 points of electricity damage per caster level (maximum 20d6) to the primary target. After it strikes, lightning can arc to a number of secondary targets equal to your caster level (maximum 20). The secondary bolts each strike one target and deal half as much damage as the primary one did (rounded down). For example, a 19th-level sorcerer generates a primary bolt (19d6 points of damage) and as many as nineteen secondary bolts (each of which deals half as much damage as the primary bolt dealt). Each target can attempt a Reflex saving throw for half damage. You choose secondary targets as you like, but they must all be within 30 feet of the primary target, and no target can be struck more than once. You can choose to affect fewer secondary targets than the maximum (to avoid allies in the area, for example).

Focus: A bit of fur; a piece of amber, glass, or a crystal rod; plus one silver pin for each of your caster levels.

Changestaff

Transmutation
Level: Drd 7
Components: V, S, F
Casting Time: 1 round
Range: Touch
Target: Your touched staff
Duration: 1 hour/level (D)
Saving Throw: None
Spell Resistance: No

You change a specially prepared quarterstaff into a Huge treantlike creature, about 24 feet tall. When you plant the end of the staff in the ground and speak a special command to conclude the casting of the spell, your staff turns into a creature that looks and fights just like a treant (see the *Monster Manual*). The staff-treant defends you and obeys any spoken commands. However, it is by no means a true treant; it cannot converse with actual tre-

ants or control trees. If the staff-treant is reduced to 0 or fewer hit points, it crumbles to powder and the staff is destroyed. Otherwise, the staff returns to its normal form when the spell duration expires (or when the spell is dismissed), and it can be used as the focus for another casting of the spell. The staff-treant is always at full strength when created, despite any wounds it may have incurred the last time it appeared.

Focus: The quarterstaff, which must be specially prepared. The staff must be a sound limb cut from an ash, oak, or yew, then cured, shaped, carved, and polished (a process requiring twenty-eight days). You cannot adventure or engage in other strenuous activity during the shaping and carving of the staff.

Chaos Hammer

Evocation [Chaotic]
Level: Chaos 4
Components: V, S
Casting Time: 1 standard action
Range: Medium (100 ft. + 10 ft./level)
Area: 20-ft.-radius burst
Duration: Instantaneous (1d6 rounds); see text
Saving Throw: Will partial; see text
Spell Resistance: Yes

You unleash chaotic power to smite your enemies. The power takes the form of a multicolored explosion of leaping, ricocheting energy. Only lawful and neutral (not chaotic) creatures are harmed by the spell.

The spell deals 1d8 points of damage per two caster levels (maximum 5d8) to lawful creatures (or 1d6 points of damage per caster level, maximum 10d6, to lawful outsiders) and slows them for 1d6 rounds. A slowed creature can take only a single standard action or move action on each of its turns, plus free actions as normal. In addition, it takes a –2 penalty to AC, attack rolls, damage rolls, and Reflex saves. A successful Will save reduces the damage by half and negates the slow effect.

The spell deals only half damage against creatures who are neither lawful nor chaotic, and they are not slowed. Such a creature can reduce the damage by half again (down to one-quarter) with a successful Will save.

Charm Animal

Enchantment (Charm) [Mind-Affecting]
Level: Drd 1, Rgr 1
Target: One animal

This spell functions like *charm person*, except that it affects a creature of the animal type. See the *Monster Manual* for more information on creature types.

Charm Monster

Enchantment (Charm) [Mind-Affecting]
Level: Brd 3, Sor/Wiz 4
Target: One living creature
Duration: One day/level

This spell functions like *charm person*, except that the effect is not restricted by creature type or size.

Charm Monster, Mass

Enchantment (Charm) [Mind-Affecting]
Level: Brd 6, Sor/Wiz 8
Components: V
Targets: One or more creatures, no two of which can be more than 30 ft. apart
Duration: One day/level

This spell functions like *charm monster*, except that *mass charm monster* affects a number of creatures whose combined HD do not exceed twice your level, or at least one creature regardless of HD. If there are more potential targets than you can affect, you choose them one at a time until you choose a creature with too many HD.

Charm Person

Enchantment (Charm) [Mind-Affecting]
Level: Brd 1, Sor/Wiz 1
Components: V, S
Casting Time: 1 standard action
Range: Close (25 ft. + 5 ft./2 levels)
Target: One humanoid creature
Duration: 1 hour/level
Saving Throw: Will negates
Spell Resistance: Yes

This charm makes a humanoid creature regard you as its trusted friend and ally (treat the target's attitude as friendly; see Influencing NPC Attitudes, page 72). If the creature is currently being threatened or attacked by you or your allies, however, it receives a +5 bonus on its saving throw.

The spell does not enable you to control the *charmed* person as if it were an automaton, but it perceives your words and actions in the most favorable way. You can try to give the subject orders, but you must win an opposed Charisma check to convince it to do anything it wouldn't ordinarily do. (Retries are not allowed.) An affected creature never obeys suicidal or obviously harmful orders, but a *charmed* fighter, for example, might believe you if you assured him that the only chance to save your life is for him to hold back an onrushing red dragon for "just a few seconds." Any act by you or your apparent allies that threatens the *charmed* person breaks the spell. You must speak the person's language to communicate your commands, or else be good at pantomiming.

Chill Metal

Transmutation [Cold]
Level: Drd 2
Components: V, S, DF
Casting Time: 1 standard action
Range: Close (25 ft. + 5 ft./2 levels)
Target: Metal equipment of one creature per two levels, no two of which can be more than 30 ft. apart; or 25 lb. of metal/level, none of which can be more than 30 ft. away from any of the rest
Duration: 7 rounds
Saving Throw: Will negates (object)
Spell Resistance: Yes (object)

Chill metal makes metal extremely cold. Unattended, nonmagical metal gets no saving throw. Magical metal is allowed a saving throw against the spell. (Magic items' saving throws are covered in the *Dungeon Master's Guide*.) An item in a creature's possession uses the creature's saving throw bonus unless its own is higher.

A creature takes cold damage if its equipment is chilled. It takes full damage if its armor is affected or if it is holding, touching, wearing, or carrying metal weighing one-fifth of its weight. The creature takes minimum damage (1 point or 2 points; see the table) if it's not wearing metal armor and the metal that it's carrying weighs less than one-fifth of its weight.

On the first round of the spell, the metal becomes chilly and uncomfortable to touch but deals no damage. The same effect also occurs on the last round of the spell's duration. During the second (and also the next-to-last) round, icy coldness causes pain and damage. In the third, fourth, and fifth rounds, the metal is freezing cold, causing more damage, as shown on the table below.

	Metal	
Round	Temperature	Damage
1	Cold	None
2	Icy	1d4 points
3–5	Freezing	2d4 points
6	Icy	1d4 points
7	Cold	None

Any heat intense enough to damage the creature negates cold damage from the spell (and vice versa) on a point-for-point basis. For example, if the damage roll from a *chill metal* spell indicates 5 points of cold damage and the subject plunges through a *wall of fire* in the same round and takes 8 points of fire damage, it winds up taking no cold damage and only 3 points of fire damage. Underwater, *chill metal* deals no damage, but ice immediately forms around the affected metal, making it more buoyant.

Chill metal counters and dispels *heat metal*.

Chill Touch

Necromancy
Level: Sor/Wiz 1
Components: V, S
Casting Time: 1 standard action
Range: Touch
Targets: Creature or creatures touched (up to one/level)
Duration: Instantaneous
Saving Throw: Fortitude partial or Will negates; see text
Spell Resistance: Yes

A touch from your hand, which glows with blue energy, disrupts the life force of living creatures. Each touch channels negative energy that deals 1d6 points of damage. The touched creature also takes 1 point of Strength damage unless it makes a successful Fortitude saving throw. You can use this melee touch attack up to one time per level.

An undead creature you touch takes no damage of either sort, but it must make a successful Will saving throw or flee as if panicked for 1d4 rounds +1 round per caster level.

Circle of Death

Necromancy [Death]
Level: Sor/Wiz 6
Components: V, S, M
Casting Time: 1 standard action
Range: Medium (100 ft. + 10 ft./level)
Area: Several living creatures within a 40-ft.-radius burst
Duration: Instantaneous
Saving Throw: Fortitude negates
Spell Resistance: Yes

A *circle of death* snuffs out the life force of living creatures, killing them instantly.

The spell slays 1d4 HD worth of living creatures per caster level (maximum 20d4). Creatures with the fewest HD are affected first; among creatures with equal HD, those who are closest to the burst's point of origin are affected first. No creature of 9 or more HD can be affected, and Hit Dice that are not sufficient to affect a creature are wasted.

Material Component: The powder of a crushed black pearl with a minimum value of 500 gp.

Clairaudience/Clairvoyance

Divination (Scrying)
Level: Brd 3, Knowledge 3, Sor/Wiz 3
Components: V, S, F/DF
Casting Time: 10 minutes
Range: Long (400 ft. + 40 ft./level)
Effect: Magical sensor
Duration: 1 min./level (D)
Saving Throw: None
Spell Resistance: No

Clairaudience/clairvoyance creates an invisible magical sensor at a specific location that enables you to hear or see (your choice) almost as if you were there. You don't need line of sight or line of effect, but the locale must be known—a place familiar to you or an obvious one, such as behind a door, around a corner, or in a grove of trees. Once you have selected the locale, the sensor doesn't move, but you can rotate it in all directions to view the area as desired. Unlike other scrying spells, this spell does not allow magically or supernaturally enhanced senses to work through it. If the chosen locale is magically dark, you see nothing. If it is naturally pitch black, you can see in a 10-foot radius around the center of the spell's effect. *Clairaudience/clairvoyance* functions only on the plane of existence you are currently occupying.

Arcane Focus: A small horn (for hearing) or a glass eye (for seeing).

Cloak of Chaos

Abjuration [Chaotic]
Level: Chaos 8, Clr 8
Components: V, S, F
Casting Time: 1 standard action
Range: 20 ft.
Targets: One creature/level in a 20-ft.-radius burst centered on you
Duration: 1 round/level (D)
Saving Throw: See text
Spell Resistance: Yes (harmless)

A random pattern of color surrounds the subjects, protecting them from attacks, granting them resistance to spells cast by lawful creatures, and causing lawful creatures that strike the subjects to become *confused.* This abjuration has four effects.

First, each warded creature gains a +4 deflection bonus to AC and a +4 resistance bonus on saves. Unlike *protection from law,* the benefit of this spell applies against all attacks, not just against attacks by lawful creatures.

Second, each warded creature gains spell resistance 25 against lawful spells and spells cast by lawful creatures.

Third, the abjuration blocks possession and mental influence, just as *protection from law* does.

Finally, if a lawful creature succeeds on a melee attack against a warded creature, the offending attacker is *confused* for 1 round (Will save negates, as with the *confusion* spell, but against the save DC of *cloak of chaos*).

Focus: A tiny reliquary containing some sacred relic, such as a scrap of parchment from a chaotic text. The reliquary costs at least 500 gp.

Clone

Necromancy
Level: Sor/Wiz 8
Components: V, S, M, F

Casting Time: 10 minutes
Range: 0 ft.
Effect: One clone
Duration: Instantaneous
Saving Throw: None
Spell Resistance: No

This spell makes an inert duplicate of a creature. If the original individual has been slain, its soul immediately transfers to the clone, creating a replacement (provided that the soul is free and willing to return; see Bringing Back the Dead, page 171). The original's physical remains, should they still exist, become inert and cannot thereafter be restored to life. If the original creature has reached the end of its natural life span (that is, it has died of natural causes), any cloning attempt fails.

To create the duplicate, you must have a piece of flesh (not hair, nails, scales, or the like) with a volume of at least 1 cubic inch that was taken from the original creature's living body. The piece of flesh need not be fresh, but it must be kept from rotting (for example, by the *gentle repose* spell). Once the spell is cast, the duplicate must be grown in a laboratory for 2d4 months.

When the clone is completed, the original's soul enters it immediately, if that creature is already dead. The clone is physically identical with the original and possesses the same personality and memories as the original. In other respects, treat the clone as if it were the original character raised from the dead, including the loss of one level or 2 points of Constitution (if the original was a 1st-level character). If this Constitution adjustment would give the clone a Constitution score of 0, the spell fails. If the original creature has lost levels since the flesh sample was taken and died at a lower level than the clone would otherwise be, the clone is one level below the level at which the original died.

The spell duplicates only the original's body and mind, not its equipment.

A duplicate can be grown while the original still lives, or when the original soul is unavailable, but the resulting body is merely a soulless bit of inert flesh, which rots if not preserved.

Material Component: The piece of flesh and various laboratory supplies (cost 1,000 gp).

Focus: Special laboratory equipment (cost 500 gp).

Cloudkill

Conjuration (Creation)
Level: Sor/Wiz 5
Components: V, S
Casting Time: 1 standard action
Range: Medium (100 ft. + 10 ft./level)
Effect: Cloud spreads in 20-ft. radius, 20 ft. high

Duration: 1 min./level
Saving Throw: Fortitude partial; see text
Spell Resistance: No

This spell generates a bank of fog, similar to a *fog cloud,* except that its vapors are yellowish green and poisonous. These vapors automatically kill any living creature with 3 or fewer HD (no save). A living creature with 4 to 6 HD is slain unless it succeeds on a Fortitude save (in which case it takes 1d4 points of Constitution damage on your turn each round while in the cloud). A living creature with 6 or more HD takes 1d4 points of Constitution damage on your turn each round while in the cloud (a successful Fortitude save halves this damage). Holding one's breath doesn't help, but creatures immune to poison are unaffected by the spell.

Unlike a *fog cloud,* the *cloudkill* moves away from you at 10 feet per round, rolling along the surface of the ground. Figure out the cloud's new spread each round based on its new point of origin, which is 10 feet farther away from the point of origin where you cast the spell.

Because the vapors are heavier than air, they sink to the lowest level of the land, even pouring down den or sinkhole openings; thus, the spell is ideal for slaying hives of giant ants, for example. It cannot penetrate liquids, nor can it be cast underwater.

Color Spray

Illusion (Pattern) [Mind-Affecting]
Level: Sor/Wiz 1
Components: V, S, M
Casting Time: 1 standard action
Range: 15 ft.
Area: Cone-shaped burst
Duration: Instantaneous; see text
Saving Throw: Will negates
Spell Resistance: Yes

A vivid cone of clashing colors springs forth from your hand, causing creatures to become stunned, perhaps also blinded, and possibly knocking them unconscious. Each creature within the cone is affected according to its Hit Dice.

2 HD or less: The creature is unconscious, blinded, and stunned for 2d4 rounds, then blinded and stunned for 1d4 rounds, and then stunned for 1 round. (Only living creatures are knocked unconscious.)

3 or 4 HD: The creature is blinded and stunned for 1d4 rounds, then stunned for 1 round.

5 or more HD: The creature is stunned for 1 round.

Sightless creatures are not affected by *color spray.*

Material Component: A pinch each of powder or sand that is colored red, yellow, and blue.

Command

Enchantment (Compulsion) [Language-Dependent, Mind-Affecting]
Level: Clr 1
Components: V
Casting Time: 1 standard action
Range: Close (25 ft. + 5 ft./2 levels)
Target: One living creature
Duration: 1 round
Saving Throw: Will negates
Spell Resistance: Yes

You give the subject a single command, which it obeys to the best of its ability at its earliest opportunity. You may select from the following options.

Approach: On its turn, the subject moves toward you as quickly and directly as possible for 1 round. The creature may do nothing but move during its turn, and it provokes attacks of opportunity for this movement as normal.

Drop: On its turn, the subject drops whatever it is holding. It can't pick up any dropped item until its next turn.

Fall: On its turn, the subject falls to the ground and remains prone for 1 round. It may act normally while prone but takes any appropriate penalties.

Flee: On its turn, the subject moves away from you as quickly as possible for 1 round. It may do nothing but move during its turn, and it provokes attacks of opportunity for this movement as normal.

Halt: The subject stands in place for 1 round. It may not take any actions but is not considered helpless.

If the subject can't carry out your command on its next turn, the spell automatically fails.

Command, Greater

Enchantment (Compulsion) [Language-Dependent, Mind-Affecting]
Level: Clr 5
Targets: One creature/level, no two of which can be more than 30 ft. apart
Duration: 1 round/level

This spell functions like *command*, except that up to one creature per level may be affected, and the activities continue beyond 1 round. At the start of each commanded creature's action after the first, it gets another Will save to attempt to break free from the spell. Each creature must receive the same command.

Command Plants

Transmutation
Level: Drd 4, Plant 4, Rgr 3
Components: V
Casting Time: 1 standard action
Range: Close (25 ft. + 5 ft./2 levels)
Targets: Up to 2 HD/level of plant creatures, no two of which can be more than 30 ft. apart

Duration: One day/level
Saving Throw: Will negates
Spell Resistance: Yes

This spell allows you some degree of control over one or more plant creatures. Affected plant creatures can understand you, and they perceive your words and actions in the most favorable way (treat their attitude as friendly). They will not attack you while the spell lasts. You can try to give a subject orders, but you must win an opposed Charisma check to convince it to do anything it wouldn't ordinarily do. (Retries are not allowed.) A commanded plant never obeys suicidal or obviously harmful orders, but it might be convinced that something very dangerous is worth doing (see *charm person*).

You can affect a number of plant creatures whose combined level or HD do not exceed twice your level.

Command Undead

Necromancy
Level: Sor/Wiz 2
Components: V, S, M
Casting Time: 1 standard action
Range: Close (25 ft. + 5 ft./2 levels)
Targets: One undead creature
Duration: One day/level
Saving Throw: Will negates; see text
Spell Resistance: Yes

This spell allows you some degree of control over an undead creature. Assuming the subject is intelligent, it perceives your words and actions in the most favorable way (treat its attitude as friendly). It will not attack you while the spell lasts. You can try to give the subject orders, but you must win an opposed Charisma check to convince it to do anything it wouldn't ordinarily do. (Retries are not allowed.) An intelligent commanded undead never obeys suicidal or obviously harmful orders, but it might be convinced that something very dangerous is worth doing (see *charm person*).

A nonintelligent undead creature (such as a skeleton or zombie) gets no saving throw against this spell. When you control a mindless being, you can communicate only basic commands, such as "come here," "go there," "fight," "stand still," and so on. Nonintelligent undead won't resist suicidal or obviously harmful orders.

Any act by you or your apparent allies that threatens the commanded undead (regardless of its Intelligence) breaks the spell.

Your commands are not telepathic. The undead creature must be able to hear you.

Material Component: A shred of raw meat and a splinter of bone.

Commune

Divination
Level: Clr 5
Components: V, S, M, DF, XP
Casting Time: 10 minutes
Range: Personal
Target: You
Duration: 1 round/level

You contact your deity—or agents thereof—and ask questions that can be answered by a simple yes or no. (A cleric of no particular deity contacts a philosophically allied deity.) You are allowed one such question per caster level. The answers given are correct within the limits of the entity's knowledge. "Unclear" is a legitimate answer, because powerful beings of the Outer Planes are not necessarily omniscient. In cases where a one-word answer would be misleading or contrary to the deity's interests, the DM should give a short phrase (five words or less) as an answer instead.

The spell, at best, provides information to aid character decisions. The entities contacted structure their answers to further their own purposes. If you lag, discuss the answers, or go off to do anything else, the spell ends.

Material Component: Holy (or unholy) water and incense.

XP Cost: 100 XP.

Commune with Nature

Divination
Level: Animal 5, Drd 5, Rgr 4
Components: V, S
Casting Time: 10 minutes
Range: Personal
Target: You
Duration: Instantaneous

You become one with nature, attaining knowledge of the surrounding territory. You instantly gain knowledge of as many as three facts from among the following subjects: the ground or terrain, plants, minerals, bodies of water, people, general animal population, presence of woodland creatures, presence of powerful unnatural creatures, or even the general state of the natural setting. For example, you could determine the location of any powerful undead creatures, the location of all major sources of safe drinking water, and the location of any buildings (which register as blind spots).

In outdoor settings, the spell operates in a radius of 1 mile per caster level. In natural underground settings—caves, caverns, and the like—the radius is limited to 100 feet per caster level. The spell does not function where nature has been replaced by construction or settlement, such as in dungeons and towns.

Comprehend Languages

Divination
Level: Brd 1, Clr 1, Sor/Wiz 1
Components: V, S, M/DF
Casting Time: 1 standard action
Range: Personal
Target: You
Duration: 10 min./level

You can understand the spoken words of creatures or read otherwise incomprehensible written messages. In either case, you must touch the creature or the writing. The ability to read does not necessarily impart insight into the material, merely its literal meaning. The spell enables you to understand or read an unknown language, not speak or write it.

Written material can be read at the rate of one page (250 words) per minute. Magical writing cannot be read, though the spell reveals that it is magical, but *comprehend languages* is often useful when deciphering treasure maps. This spell can be foiled by certain warding magic (such as the *secret page* and *illusory script* spells). It does not decipher codes or reveal messages concealed in otherwise normal text.

Comprehend languages can be made permanent with a *permanency* spell.

Arcane Material Component: A pinch of soot and a few grains of salt.

Cone of Cold

Evocation [Cold]
Level: Sor/Wiz 5, Water 6
Components: V, S, M/DF
Casting Time: 1 standard action
Range: 60 ft.
Area: Cone-shaped burst
Duration: Instantaneous
Saving Throw: Reflex half
Spell Resistance: Yes

Cone of cold creates an area of extreme cold, originating at your hand and extending outward in a cone. It drains heat, dealing 1d6 points of cold damage per caster level (maximum 15d6).

Arcane Material Component: A very small crystal or glass cone.

Confusion

Enchantment (Compulsion) [Mind-Affecting]
Level: Brd 3, Sor/Wiz 4, Trickery 4
Components: V, S, M/DF
Casting Time: 1 standard action
Range: Medium (100 ft. + 10 ft./level)
Targets: All creatures in a 15-ft. radius burst
Duration: 1 round/level
Saving Throw: Will negates
Spell Resistance: Yes

This spell causes the targets to become *confused*, making them unable to independently determine what they will do. Roll on the following table at the beginning of each subject's turn each round to see what the subject does in that round.

d%	Behavior
01–10	Attack caster with melee or ranged weapons (or close with caster if attack is not possible).
11–20	Act normally.
21–50	Do nothing but babble incoherently.
51–70	Flee away from caster at top possible speed.
71–100	Attack nearest creature (for this purpose, a familiar counts as part of the subject's self).

A *confused* character who can't carry out the indicated action does nothing but babble incoherently. Attackers are not at any special advantage when attacking a *confused* character. Any *confused* character who is attacked automatically attacks its attackers on its next turn, as long as it is still *confused* when its turn comes. Note that a *confused* character will not make attacks of opportunity against any creature that it is not already devoted to attacking (either because of its most recent action or because it has just been attacked).

Arcane Material Component: A set of three nut shells.

Confusion, Lesser

Enchantment (Compulsion) [Mind-Affecting]
Level: Brd 1
Components: V, S, DF
Range: Close (25 ft. + 5 ft./2 levels)
Target: One living creature
Duration: 1 round

This spell causes a single creature to become *confused* for 1 round. See the *confusion* spell, above, to determine the exact effect on the subject.

Consecrate

Evocation [Good]
Level: Clr 2
Components: V, S, M, DF
Casting Time: 1 standard action
Range: Close (25 ft. + 5 ft./2 levels)
Area: 20-ft.-radius emanation
Duration: 2 hours/level
Saving Throw: None
Spell Resistance: No

This spell blesses an area with positive energy. Each Charisma check made to turn undead within this area gains a +3 sacred bonus. Every undead creature entering a *consecrated* area suffers minor disruption, giving it a –1 penalty on attack rolls, damage rolls, and saves. Undead cannot be created within or summoned into a *consecrated* area.

If the *consecrated* area contains an altar, shrine, or other permanent fixture dedicated to your deity, pantheon, or aligned higher power, the modifiers given above are doubled (+6 sacred bonus on turning checks, –2 penalties for undead in the area). You cannot consecrate an area with a similar fixture of a deity other than your own patron.

If the area does contain an altar, shrine, or other permanent fixture of a deity, pantheon, or higher power other than your patron, the *consecrate* spell instead curses the area, cutting off its connection with the associated deity or power. This secondary function, if used, does not also grant the bonuses and penalties relating to undead, as given above.

Consecrate counters and dispels *desecrate*.

Material Component: A vial of holy water and 25 gp worth (5 pounds) of silver dust, all of which must be sprinkled around the area.

Contact Other Plane

Divination
Level: Sor/Wiz 5
Components: V
Casting Time: 10 minutes
Range: Personal
Target: You
Duration: Concentration

You send your mind to another plane of existence (an Elemental Plane or some plane farther removed) in order to receive advice and information from powers there. (See the accompanying table for possible consequences and results of the attempt.) The powers reply in a language you understand, but they resent such contact and give only brief answers to your questions. (The DM answers all questions with "yes," "no," "maybe," "never," "irrelevant," or some other one-word answer.) You must concentrate on maintaining the spell (a standard action) in order to ask questions at the rate of one per round. A question is answered by the power during the same round. For every two caster levels, you may ask one question.

Contact with minds far removed from your home plane increases the probability that you will incur a decrease to Intelligence and Charisma, but the chance of the power knowing the answer, as well as the probability of the entity answering correctly, are likewise increased by moving to distant planes. Once the Outer Planes are reached, the power of the deity contacted determines the effects. (Random results obtained from the table are subject to DM

CONTACT OTHER PLANE

Plane Contacted	Avoid Int/Cha Decrease	True Answer	Don't Know	Lie	Random Answer
Elemental Plane	DC 7/1 week	01–34	35–62	63–83	84–100
(appropriate)	(DC 7/1 week)	(01–68)	(69–75)	(76–98)	(99–100)
Positive/Negative Energy Plane	DC 8/1 week	01–39	40–65	66–86	87–100
Astral Plane	DC 9/1 week	01–44	45–67	68–88	89–100
Outer Plane, demideity	DC 10/2 weeks	01–49	50–70	71–91	92–100
Outer Plane, lesser deity	DC 12/3 weeks	01–60	61–75	76–95	96–100
Outer Plane, intermediate deity	DC 14/4 weeks	01–73	74–81	82–98	99–100
Outer Plane, greater deity	DC 16/5 weeks	01–88	89–90	91–99	100

Avoid Int/Cha Decrease: You must succeed on an Intelligence check against this DC to avoid a decrease in Intelligence and Charisma. If the check fails, your Intelligence and Charisma scores each fall to 8 for the stated duration, and you become unable to cast arcane spells. If you lose Intelligence and Charisma, the effect strikes as soon as the first question is asked, and no answer is received. (The entries in parentheses are for questions that pertain to the appropriate Elemental Plane.)

Results of a Successful Contact: The DM rolls d% for the result shown on the table:

True Answer: You get a true, one-word answer. Questions that cannot be answered in this way are answered randomly.

Don't Know: The entity tells you that it doesn't know.

Lie: The entity intentionally lies to you.

Random Answer: The entity tries to lie but doesn't know the answer, so it makes one up.

changes, the personalities of individual deities, and so on.)

On rare occasions, this divination may be blocked by an act of certain deities or forces.

Contagion

Necromancy [Evil]
Level: Clr 3, Destruction 3, Drd 3, Sor/Wiz 4
Components: V, S
Casting Time: 1 standard action
Range: Touch
Target: Living creature touched
Duration: Instantaneous
Saving Throw: Fortitude negates
Spell Resistance: Yes

The subject contracts a disease selected from the table below, which strikes immediately (no incubation period). The DC noted is for the subsequent saves (use *contagion's* normal save DC for the initial saving throw).

Disease	DC	Damage
Blinding sickness	16	1d4 Str[1]
Cackle fever	16	1d6 Wis
Filth fever	12	1d3 Dex and 1d3 Con
Mindfire	12	1d4 Int
Red ache	15	1d6 Str
Shakes	13	1d8 Dex
Slimy doom	14	1d4 Con

1 Each time a victim takes 2 or more points of Strength damage from blinding sickness, he or she must make another Fortitude save (using the disease's save DC) or be permanently blinded.

See the *Dungeon Master's Guide* for descriptions of each disease, as well as for the general effects of disease.

Contingency

Evocation
Level: Sor/Wiz 6
Components: V, S, M, F
Casting Time: At least 10 minutes; see text
Range: Personal
Target: You
Duration: One day/level (D) or until discharged

You can place another spell upon your person so that it comes into effect under some condition you dictate when casting *contingency.* The *contingency* spell and the companion spell are cast at the same time. The 10-minute casting time is the minimum total for both castings; if the companion spell has a casting time longer than 10 minutes, use that instead.

The spell to be brought into effect by the *contingency* must be one that affects your person (*feather fall, levitate, fly, teleport,* and so forth) and be of a spell level no higher than one-third your caster level (rounded down, maximum 6th level).

The conditions needed to bring the spell into effect must be clear, although they can be general. For example, a *contingency* cast with *water breathing* might prescribe that any time you are plunged into or otherwise engulfed in water or similar liquid, the *water breathing* spell instantly comes into effect. Or a *contingency* could bring a *feather fall* spell into effect any time you fall more than 4 feet. In all cases, the *contingency* immediately brings into effect the companion spell, the latter being "cast" instantaneously when the prescribed circumstances occur. If complicated or convoluted conditions are prescribed, the whole spell combination (*contingency* and the companion magic) may fail when

called on. The companion spell occurs based solely on the stated conditions, regardless of whether you want it to.

You can use only one *contingency* spell at a time; if a second is cast, the first one (if still active) is dispelled.

Material Component: That of the companion spell, plus quicksilver and an eyelash of an ogre mage, rakshasa, or similar spell-using creature.

Focus: A statuette of you carved from elephant ivory and decorated with gems (worth at least 1,500 gp). You must carry the focus for the *contingency* to work.

Continual Flame

Evocation [Light]
Level: Clr 3, Sor/Wiz 2
Components: V, S, M
Casting Time: 1 standard action
Range: Touch
Target: Object touched
Effect: Magical, heatless flame
Duration: Permanent
Saving Throw: None
Spell Resistance: No

A flame, equivalent in brightness to a torch, springs forth from an object that you touch. The effect looks like a regular flame, but it creates no heat and doesn't use oxygen. A *continual flame* can be covered and hidden but not smothered or quenched.

Light spells counter and dispel darkness spells of an equal or lower level.

Material Component: You sprinkle ruby dust (worth 50 gp) on the item that is to carry the flame.

Control Plants

Transmutation
Level: Drd 8, Plant 8
Components: V, S, DF
Casting Time: 1 standard action
Range: Close (25 ft. + 5 ft./2 levels)
Targets: Up to 2 HD/level of plant creatures, no two of which can be more than 30 ft. apart
Duration: 1 min./level
Saving Throw: Will negates
Spell Resistance: No

This spell enables you to control the actions of one or more plant creatures for a short period of time. You command the creatures by voice and they understand you, no matter what language you speak. Even if vocal communication is impossible (in the area of a *silence* spell, for instance), the controlled plants do not attack you. At the end of the spell, the subjects revert to their normal behavior.

Suicidal or self-destructive commands are simply ignored.

Control Undead

Necromancy
Level: Sor/Wiz 7
Components: V, S, M
Casting Time: 1 standard action
Range: Close (25 ft. + 5 ft./2 levels)
Targets: Up to 2 HD/level of undead creatures, no two of which can be more than 30 ft. apart
Duration: 1 min./level
Saving Throw: Will negates
Spell Resistance: Yes

This spell enables you to command undead creatures for a short period of time. You command them by voice and they understand you, no matter what language you speak. Even if vocal communication is impossible (in the area of a *silence* spell, for instance), the controlled undead do not attack you. At the end of the spell, the subjects revert to their normal behavior. Intelligent undead creatures remember that you controlled them.

Material Component: A small piece of bone and a small piece of raw meat.

Control Water

Transmutation [Water]
Level: Clr 4, Drd 4, Sor/Wiz 6, Water 4
Components: V, S, M/DF
Casting Time: 1 standard action
Range: Long (400 ft. + 40 ft./level)
Area: Water in a volume of 10 ft./level by 10 ft./level by 2 ft./level (S)
Duration: 10 min./level (D)
Saving Throw: None; see text
Spell Resistance: No

Depending on the version you choose, the *control water* spell raises or lowers water.

Lower Water: This causes water or similar liquid to reduce its depth by as much as 2 feet per caster level (to a minimum depth of 1 inch). The water is lowered within a squarish depression whose sides are up to caster level × 10 feet long. In extremely large and deep bodies of water, such as a deep ocean, the spell creates a whirlpool that sweeps ships and similar craft downward, putting them at risk and rendering them unable to leave by normal movement for the duration of the spell. When cast on water elementals and other water-based creatures, this spell acts as a *slow* spell (Will negates). The spell has no effect on other creatures.

Raise Water: This causes water or similar liquid to rise in height, just as the *lower water* version causes it to lower. Boats raised in this way slide down the sides of the hump that the spell creates. If the area affected by the spell includes riverbanks, a beach, or other land nearby, the water can spill over onto dry land.

With either version, you may reduce one horizontal dimension by half and double the other horizontal dimension.

Arcane Material Component: A drop of water (for *raise water*) or a pinch of dust (for *lower water*).

Control Weather

Transmutation
Level: Air 7, Clr 7, Drd 7, Sor/Wiz 7
Components: V, S
Casting Time: 10 minutes; see text
Range: 2 miles
Area: 2-mile-radius circle, centered on you; see text
Duration: 4d12 hours; see text
Saving Throw: None
Spell Resistance: No

You change the weather in the local area. It takes 10 minutes to cast the spell and an additional 10 minutes for the effects to manifest. The current, natural weather conditions are determined by the DM. You can call forth weather appropriate to the climate and season of the area you are in.

Season	Possible Weather
Spring	Tornado, thunderstorm, sleet storm, or hot weather
Summer	Torrential rain, heat wave, or hailstorm
Autumn	Hot or cold weather, fog, or sleet
Winter	Frigid cold, blizzard, or thaw
Late winter	Hurricane-force winds or early spring (coastal area)

You control the general tendencies of the weather, such as the direction and intensity of the wind. You cannot control specific applications of the weather—where lightning strikes, for example, or the exact path of a tornado. When you select a certain weather condition to occur, the weather assumes that condition 10 minutes later (changing gradually, not abruptly). The weather continues as you left it for the duration, or until you use a standard action to designate a new kind of weather (which fully manifests itself 10 minutes later). Contradictory conditions are not possible simultaneously—fog and strong wind, for example.

Control weather can do away with atmospheric phenomena (naturally occurring or otherwise) as well as create them.

A druid casting this spell doubles the duration and affects a circle with a 3-mile radius.

Control Winds

Transmutation [Air]
Level: Air 5, Drd 5
Components: V, S
Casting Time: 1 standard action
Range: 40 ft./level

Area: 40 ft./level radius cylinder 40 ft. high
Duration: 10 min./level
Saving Throw: Fortitude negates
Spell Resistance: No

You alter wind force in the area surrounding you. You can make the wind blow in a certain direction or manner, increase its strength, or decrease its strength. The new wind direction and strength persist until the spell ends or until you choose to alter your handiwork, which requires concentration. You may create an "eye" of calm air up to 80 feet in diameter at the center of the area if you so desire, and you may choose to limit the area to any cylindrical area less than your full limit (for example, a 20-foot-diameter tornado centered 100 feet away).

Wind Direction: You may choose one of four basic wind patterns to function over the spell's area.

- A downdraft blows from the center outward in equal strength in all directions.
- An updraft blows from the outer edges in toward the center in equal strength from all directions, veering upward before impinging on the eye in the center.
- A rotation causes the winds to circle the center in clockwise or counterclockwise fashion.
- A blast simply causes the winds to blow in one direction across the entire area from one side to the other.

Wind Strength: For every three caster levels, you can increase or decrease wind strength by one level. (The categories of wind strength are briefly described below, with more detail to be found in the *Dungeon Master's Guide*.) Each round on your turn, a creature in the wind must make a Fortitude save or suffer the effect of being in the windy area.

Strong winds (21+ mph) make sailing difficult.

A severe wind (31+ mph) causes minor ship and building damage.

A windstorm (51+ mph) drives most flying creatures from the skies, uproots small trees, knocks down light wooden structures, tears off roofs, and endangers ships.

Hurricane force winds (75+ mph) destroy wooden buildings, sometimes uproot even large trees, and cause most ships to founder.

A tornado (175+ mph) destroys all non-fortified buildings and often uproots large trees.

Create Food and Water

Conjuration (Creation)
Level: Clr 3
Components: V, S

Casting Time: 10 minutes
Range: Close (25 ft. + 5 ft./2 levels)
Effect: Food and water to sustain three humans or one horse/level for 24 hours
Duration: 24 hours; see text
Saving Throw: None
Spell Resistance: No

The food that this spell creates is simple fare of your choice—highly nourishing, if rather bland. Food so created decays and becomes inedible within 24 hours, although it can be kept fresh for another 24 hours by casting a *purify food and water* spell on it. The water created by this spell is just like clean rain water, and it doesn't go bad as the food does.

Create Greater Undead
Necromancy [Evil]
Level: Clr 8, Death 8, Sor/Wiz 8

This spell functions like *create undead*, except that you can create more powerful and intelligent sorts of undead: shadows, wraiths, spectres, and devourers (see the *Monster Manual* for more information on all types of undead). The type or types of undead you can create is based on your caster level, as shown on the table below.

Caster Level	Undead Created
15th or lower	Shadow
16th–17th	Wraith
18th–19th	Spectre
20th or higher	Devourer

Create Undead
Necromancy [Evil]
Level: Clr 6, Death 6, Evil 6, Sor/Wiz 6
Components: V, S, M
Casting Time: 1 hour
Range: Close (25 ft. + 5 ft./2 levels)
Target: One corpse
Duration: Instantaneous
Saving Throw: None
Spell Resistance: No

A much more potent spell than *animate dead*, this evil spell allows you to create more powerful sorts of undead: ghouls, ghasts, mummies, and mohrgs (see the *Monster Manual* for more information on all types of undead). The type or types of undead you can create is based on your caster level, as shown on the table below.

Caster Level	Undead Created
11th or lower	Ghoul
12th–14th	Ghast
15th–17th	Mummy
18th or higher	Mohrg

You may create less powerful undead than your level would allow if you choose. For example, at 16th level you could decide to create a ghoul or a ghast instead of a mummy. Doing this may be a good idea, because created undead are not automatically under the control of their animator. If you are capable of commanding undead, you may attempt to command the undead creature as it forms (see Turn or Rebuke Undead, page 159).

This spell must be cast at night.

Material Component: A clay pot filled with grave dirt and another filled with brackish water. The spell must be cast on a dead body. You must place a black onyx gem worth at least 50 gp per HD of the undead to be created into the mouth or eye socket of each corpse. The magic of the spell turns these gems into worthless shells.

Create Water
Conjuration (Creation) [Water]
Level: Clr 0, Drd 0, Pal 1
Components: V, S
Casting Time: 1 standard action
Range: Close (25 ft. + 5 ft./2 levels)
Effect: Up to 2 gallons of water/level
Duration: Instantaneous
Saving Throw: None
Spell Resistance: No

This spell generates wholesome, drinkable water, just like clean rain water. Water can be created in an area as small as will actually contain the liquid, or in an area three times as large—possibly creating a downpour or filling many small receptacles.

Note: Conjuration spells can't create substances or objects within a creature. Water weighs about 8 pounds per gallon. One cubic foot of water contains roughly 8 gallons and weighs about 60 pounds.

Creeping Doom
Conjuration (Summoning)
Level: Drd 7
Components: V, S
Casting Time: 1 round
Range: Close (25 ft. + 5 ft./2 levels)/ 100 ft.; see text
Effect: One swarm of centipedes per two levels
Duration: 1 min./level
Saving Throw: None
Spell Resistance: No

When you utter the spell of *creeping doom*, you call forth a mass of centipede swarms (one per two caster levels, to a maximum of ten swarms at 20th level), which need not appear adjacent to one another. (See the *Monster Manual* for details on centipede swarms.)

You may summon the centipede swarms so that they share the area of other creatures. The swarms remain stationary, attacking any creatures in their area, unless you command the creeping doom to move (a standard action). As a standard action, you can command any number of the swarms to move toward any prey within 100 feet of you. You cannot command any swarm to move more than 100 feet away from you, and if you move more than 100 feet from any swarm, that swarm remains stationary, attacking any creatures in its area (but it can be commanded again if you move within 100 feet).

Crushing Despair
Enchantment (Compulsion) [Mind-Affecting]
Level: Brd 3, Sor/Wiz 4
Components: V, S, M
Casting Time: 1 standard action
Range: 30 ft.
Area: Cone-shaped burst
Duration: 1 min./level
Saving Throw: Will negates
Spell Resistance: Yes

An invisible cone of despair causes great sadness in the subjects. Each affected creature takes a –2 penalty on attack rolls, saving throws, ability checks, skill checks, and weapon damage rolls.

Crushing despair counters and dispels *good hope*.

Material Component: A vial of tears.

Cure Critical Wounds
Conjuration (Healing)
Level: Brd 4, Clr 4, Drd 5, Healing 4

This spell functions like *cure light wounds*, except that it cures 4d8 points of damage +1 point per caster level (maximum +20).

Cure Critical Wounds, Mass
Conjuration (Healing)
Level: Clr 8, Drd 9, Healing 8

This spell functions like *mass cure light wounds*, except that it cures 4d8 points of damage +1 point per caster level (maximum +40).

Cure Light Wounds
Conjuration (Healing)
Level: Brd 1, Clr 1, Drd 1, Healing 1, Pal 1, Rgr 2
Components: V, S
Casting Time: 1 standard action
Range: Touch
Target: Creature touched
Duration: Instantaneous
Saving Throw: Will half (harmless); see text
Spell Resistance: Yes (harmless); see text

When laying your hand upon a living creature, you channel positive energy that cures 1d8 points of damage +1 point per caster level (maximum +5).

Since undead are powered by negative energy, this spell deals damage to them instead of curing their wounds. An undead creature can apply spell resistance, and can attempt a Will save to take half damage.

Cure Light Wounds, Mass

Conjuration (Healing)
Level: Brd 5, Clr 5, Drd 6, Healing 5
Components: V, S
Casting Time: 1 standard action
Range: Close (25 ft. + 5 ft./2 levels)
Target: One creature/level, no two of which can be more than 30 ft. apart
Duration: Instantaneous
Saving Throw: Will half (harmless) or Will half; see text
Spell Resistance: Yes (harmless) or Yes; see text

You channel positive energy to cure 1d8 points of damage +1 point per caster level (maximum +25) in each selected creature.

Like other *cure spells*, *mass cure light wounds* deals damage to undead in its area rather than curing them. Each affected undead may attempt a Will save for half damage.

Cure Minor Wounds

Conjuration (Healing)
Level: Clr 0, Drd 0

This spell functions like *cure light wounds*, except that it cures only 1 point of damage.

Cure Moderate Wounds

Conjuration (Healing)
Level: Brd 2, Clr 2, Drd 3, Healing 2, Pal 3, Rgr 3

This spell functions like *cure light wounds*, except that it cures 2d8 points of damage +1 point per caster level (maximum +10).

Cure Moderate Wounds, Mass

Conjuration (Healing)
Level: Brd 6, Clr 6, Drd 7

This spell functions like *mass cure light wounds*, except that it cures 2d8 points of damage +1 point per caster level (maximum +30).

Cure Serious Wounds

Conjuration (Healing)
Level: Brd 3, Clr 3, Drd 4, Pal 4, Rgr 4, Healing 3

This spell functions like *cure light wounds*, except that it cures 3d8 points of damage +1 point per caster level (maximum +15).

Cure Serious Wounds, Mass

Conjuration (Healing)
Level: Clr 7, Drd 8

This spell functions like *mass cure light wounds*, except that it cures 3d8 points of damage +1 point per caster level (maximum +35).

Curse Water

Necromancy [Evil]
Level: Clr 1
Components: V, S, M
Casting Time: 1 minute
Range: Touch
Target: Flask of water touched
Duration: Instantaneous
Saving Throw: Will negates (object)
Spell Resistance: Yes (object)

This spell imbues a flask (1 pint) of water with negative energy, turning it into unholy water. Unholy water damages good outsiders the way holy water damages undead and evil outsiders.

Material Component: 5 pounds of powdered silver (worth 25 gp).

Dancing Lights

Evocation [Light]
Level: Brd 0, Sor/Wiz 0
Components: V, S
Casting Time: 1 standard action
Range: Medium (100 ft. + 10 ft./level)
Effect: Up to four lights, all within a 10-ft.-radius area
Duration: 1 minute (D)
Saving Throw: None
Spell Resistance: No

Depending on the version selected, you create up to four lights that resemble lanterns or torches (and cast that amount of light), or up to four glowing spheres of light (which look like will-o'-wisps), or one faintly glowing, vaguely humanoid shape. The *dancing lights* must stay within a 10-foot-radius area in relation to each other but otherwise move as you desire (no concentration required): forward or back, up or down, straight or turning corners, or the like. The lights can move up to 100 feet per round. A light winks out if the distance between you and it exceeds the spell's range.

Dancing lights can be made permanent with a *permanency* spell.

Darkness

Evocation [Darkness]
Level: Brd 2, Clr 2, Sor/Wiz 2
Components: V, M/DF
Casting Time: 1 standard action
Range: Touch
Target: Object touched
Duration: 10 min./level (D)
Saving Throw: None
Spell Resistance: No

This spell causes an object to radiate shadowy illumination out to a 20-foot radius. All creatures in the area gain concealment (20% miss chance). Even creatures that can normally see in such conditions (such as with darkvision or low-light vision) have the miss chance in an area shrouded in magical *darkness*. Normal lights (torches, candles, lanterns, and so forth) are incapable of brightening the area, as are light spells of lower level (such as *light* or *dancing lights*). Higher-level light spells (such as *daylight*) are not affected by *darkness*.

If *darkness* is cast on a small object that is placed inside or under a lightproof covering, the spell's effect is blocked until the covering is removed.

Darkness counters or dispels any light spell of equal or lower spell level.

Arcane Material Component: A bit of bat fur and either a drop of pitch or a piece of coal.

Darkvision

Transmutation
Level: Rgr 3, Sor/Wiz 2
Components: V, S, M
Casting Time: 1 standard action
Range: Touch
Target: Creature touched
Duration: 1 hour/level
Saving Throw: Will negates (harmless)
Saving Throw: None
Spell Resistance: Yes (harmless)

The subject gains the ability to see 60 feet even in total darkness. Darkvision is black and white only but otherwise like normal sight. *Darkvision* does not grant one the ability to see in magical darkness.

Darkvision can be made permanent with a *permanency* spell.

Material Component: Either a pinch of dried carrot or an agate.

Daylight

Evocation [Light]
Level: Brd 3, Clr 3, Drd 3, Pal 3, Sor/Wiz 3
Components: V, S
Casting Time: 1 standard action
Range: Touch
Target: Object touched
Duration: 10 min./level (D)
Saving Throw: None
Spell Resistance: No

The object touched sheds light as bright as full daylight in a 60-foot radius, and dim light for an additional 60 feet beyond that. Creatures that take penalties in bright light also take them while within the radius of this magical light. Despite its name, this spell is not the equivalent of daylight for the purposes of creatures that are damaged or destroyed by bright light (such as vampires). If *daylight* is cast on a small object that is then placed inside or under a lightproof covering, the spell's effects are blocked until the covering is removed.

Daylight brought into an area of magical darkness (or vice versa) is temporarily negated, so that the otherwise prevailing light conditions exist in the overlapping areas of effect.

Daylight counters or dispels any darkness spell of equal or lower level, such as *darkness*.

Daze

Enchantment (Compulsion) [Mind-Affecting]
Level: Brd 0, Sor/Wiz 0
Components: V, S, M
Casting Time: 1 standard action
Range: Close (25 ft. + 5 ft./2 levels)
Target: One humanoid creature of 4 HD or less
Duration: 1 round
Saving Throw: Will negates
Spell Resistance: Yes

This enchantment clouds the mind of a humanoid creature with 4 or fewer Hit Dice so that it takes no actions. Humanoids of 5 or more HD are not affected. A dazed subject is not stunned, so attackers get no special advantage against it.

Material Component: A pinch of wool or similar substance.

Daze Monster

Enchantment (Compulsion) [Mind-Affecting]
Level: Brd 2, Sor/Wiz 2
Range: Medium (100 ft. + 10 ft./level)
Target: One living creature of 6 HD or less

This spell functions like *daze*, but *daze monster* can affect any one living creature of any type. Creatures of 7 or more HD are not affected.

Death Knell

Necromancy [Death, Evil]
Level: Clr 2, Death 2
Components: V, S
Casting Time: 1 standard action
Range: Touch
Target: Living creature touched
Duration: Instantaneous/10 minutes per HD of subject; see text
Saving Throw: Will negates
Spell Resistance: Yes

You draw forth the ebbing life force of a creature and use it to fuel your own power. Upon casting this spell, you touch a living creature that has –1 or fewer hit points. If the subject fails its saving throw, it dies, and you gain 1d8 temporary hit points and a +2 bonus to Strength. Additionally, your effective caster level goes up by +1, improving spell effects dependent on caster level. (This increase in effective

caster level does not grant you access to more spells.) These effects last for 10 minutes per HD of the subject creature.

Death Ward

Necromancy
Level: Clr 4, Death 4, Drd 5, Pal 4
Components: V, S, DF
Casting Time: 1 standard action
Range: Touch
Target: Living creature touched
Duration: 1 min./level
Saving Throw: Will negates (harmless)
Spell Resistance: Yes (harmless)

The subject is immune to all death spells, magical death effects, energy drain, and any negative energy effects (such as from *inflict* spells or *chill touch*).

This spell doesn't remove negative levels that the subject has already gained, nor does it affect the saving throw necessary 24 hours after gaining a negative level.

Death ward does not protect against other sorts of attacks, such as hit point loss, poison, or petrification, even if those attacks might be lethal.

Deathwatch

Necromancy [Evil]
Level: Clr 1
Components: V, S
Casting Time: 1 standard action
Range: 30 ft.
Area: Cone-shaped emanation
Duration: 10 min./level
Saving Throw: None
Spell Resistance: No

Using the foul sight granted by the powers of unlife, you can determine the condition of creatures near death within the spell's range. You instantly know whether each creature within the area is dead, fragile (alive and wounded, with 3 or fewer hit points left), fighting off death (alive with 4 or more hit points), undead, or neither alive nor dead (such as a construct). *Deathwatch* sees through any spell or ability that allows creatures to feign death.

Deep Slumber

Enchantment (Compulsion) [Mind-Affecting]
Level: Brd 3, Sor/Wiz 3
Range: Close (25 ft. + 5 ft./2 levels)

This spell functions like *sleep*, except that it affects 10 HD of creatures.

Deeper Darkness

Evocation [Darkness]
Level: Clr 3
Duration: One day/level (D)

This spell functions like *darkness*, except that the object radiates shadowy illumination in a 60-foot radius and the *darkness* lasts longer.

Daylight brought into an area of *deeper darkness* (or vice versa) is temporarily negated, so that the otherwise prevailing light conditions exist in the overlapping areas of effect.

Deeper darkness counters and dispels any light spell of equal or lower level, including *daylight* and *light*.

Delay Poison

Conjuration (Healing)
Level: Brd 2, Clr 2, Drd 2, Pal 2, Rgr 1
Components: V, S, DF
Casting Time: 1 standard action
Range: Touch
Target: Creature touched
Duration: 1 hour/level
Saving Throw: Fortitude negates (harmless)
Spell Resistance: Yes (harmless)

The subject becomes temporarily immune to poison. Any poison in its system or any poison to which it is exposed during the spell's duration does not affect the subject until the spell's duration has expired. *Delay poison* does not cure any damage that poison may have already done.

Delayed Blast Fireball

Evocation [Fire]
Level: Sor/Wiz 7
Duration: 5 rounds or less; see text

This spell functions like *fireball*, except that it is more powerful and can detonate up to 5 rounds after the spell is cast. The burst of flame deals 1d6 points of fire damage per caster level (maximum 20d6).

The glowing bead created by *delayed blast fireball* can detonate immediately if you desire, or you can choose to delay the burst for as many as 5 rounds. You select the amount of delay upon completing the spell, and that time cannot change once it has been set unless someone touches the bead (see below). If you choose a delay, the glowing bead sits at its destination until it detonates. A creature can pick up and hurl the bead as a thrown weapon (range increment 10 feet). If a creature handles and moves the bead within 1 round of its detonation, there is a 25% chance that the bead detonates while being handled.

Demand

Enchantment (Compulsion) [Mind-Affecting]
Level: Sor/Wiz 8
Saving Throw: Will partial
Spell Resistance: Yes

This spell functions like *sending*, but the message can also contain a *suggestion* (see the *suggestion* spell), which the subject does its best to carry out. A successful Will save negates the *suggestion* effect but not the contact itself. The *demand*, if received, is understood even if the subject's Intelligence score is as low as 1. If the message is impossible or meaningless according to the circumstances that exist for the subject at the time the *demand* is issued, the message is understood but the *suggestion* is ineffective.

The *demand*'s message to the creature must be twenty-five words or less, including the *suggestion*. The creature can also give a short reply immediately.

Material Component: A short piece of copper wire and some small part of the subject—a hair, a bit of nail, or the like.

Desecrate

Evocation [Evil]
Level: Clr 2, Evil 2
Components: V, S, M, DF
Casting Time: 1 standard action
Range: Close (25 ft. + 5 ft./2 levels)
Area: 20-ft.-radius emanation
Duration: 2 hours/level
Saving Throw: None
Spell Resistance: Yes

This spell imbues an area with negative energy. Each Charisma check made to turn undead within this area takes a –3 profane penalty, and every undead creature entering a *desecrated* area gains a +1 profane bonus on attack rolls, damage rolls, and saving throws. An undead creature created within or summoned into such an area gains +1 hit points per HD.

If the *desecrated* area contains an altar, shrine, or other permanent fixture dedicated to your deity or aligned higher power, the modifiers given above are doubled (–6 profane penalty on turning checks, +2 profane bonus and +2 hit points per HD for undead in the area). Furthermore, anyone who casts *animate dead* within this area may create as many as double the normal amount of undead (that is, 4 HD per caster level rather than 2 HD per caster level).

If the area contains an altar, shrine, or other permanent fixture of a deity, pantheon, or higher power other than your patron, the *desecrate* spell instead curses the area, cutting off its connection with the associated deity or power. This secondary function, if used, does not also grant the bonuses and penalties relating to undead, as given above.

Desecrate counters and dispels *consecrate*.

Material Component: A vial of unholy water and 25 gp worth (5 pounds) of silver dust, all of which must be sprinkled around the area.

Destruction

Necromancy [Death]
Level: Clr 7, Death 7
Components: V, S, F
Casting Time: 1 standard action
Range: Close (25 ft. + 5 ft./2 levels)
Target: One creature
Duration: Instantaneous
Saving Throw: Fortitude partial
Spell Resistance: Yes

This spell instantly slays the subject and consumes its remains (but not its equipment and possessions) utterly. If the target's Fortitude saving throw succeeds, it instead takes 10d6 points of damage. The only way to restore life to a character who has failed to save against this spell is to use *true resurrection*, a carefully worded *wish* spell followed by *resurrection*, or *miracle*.

Focus: A special holy (or unholy) symbol of silver marked with verses of anathema (cost 500 gp).

Detect Animals or Plants

Divination
Level: Drd 1, Rgr 1
Components: V, S
Casting Time: 1 standard action
Range: Long (400 ft. + 40 ft./level)
Area: Cone-shaped emanation
Duration: Concentration, up to 10 min./level (D)
Saving Throw: None
Spell Resistance: No

You can detect a particular kind of animal or plant in a cone emanating out from you in whatever direction you face. You must think of a kind of animal or plant when using the spell, but you can change the animal or plant kind each round. The amount of information revealed depends on how long you search a particular area or focus on a specific kind of animal or plant.

1st Round: Presence or absence of that kind of animal or plant in the area.

2nd Round: Number of individuals of the specified kind in the area, and the condition of the healthiest specimen.

3rd Round: The condition (see below) and location of each individual present. If an animal or plant is outside your line of sight, then you discern its direction but not its exact location.

Conditions: For purposes of this spell, the categories of condition are as follows:

Normal: Has at least 90% of full normal hit points, free of disease.

Fair: 30% to 90% of full normal hit points remaining.

Poor: Less than 30% of full normal hit points remaining, afflicted with a disease, or suffering from a debilitating injury.

Weak: 0 or fewer hit points remaining, afflicted with a disease in the terminal stage, or crippled.

If a creature falls into more than one category, the spell indicates the weaker of the two.

Each round you can turn to detect a kind of animal or plant in a new area. The spell can penetrate barriers, but 1 foot of stone, 1 inch of common metal, a thin sheet of lead, or 3 feet of wood or dirt blocks it.

The DM decides if a specific kind of animal or plant is present.

Detect Chaos

Divination
Level: Clr 1

This spell functions like *detect evil*, except that it detects the auras of chaotic creatures, clerics of chaotic deities, chaotic spells, and chaotic magic items, and you are vulnerable to an overwhelming chaotic aura if you are lawful.

Detect Evil

Divination
Level: Clr 1
Components: V, S, DF
Casting Time: 1 standard action
Range: 60 ft.
Area: Cone-shaped emanation
Duration: Concentration, up to 10 min./ level (D)
Saving Throw: None
Spell Resistance: No

You can sense the presence of evil. The amount of information revealed depends on how long you study a particular area or subject.

1st Round: Presence or absence of evil.

2nd Round: Number of evil auras (creatures, objects, or spells) in the area and the power of the most potent evil aura present. If you are of good alignment, and the strongest evil aura's power is overwhelming (see below), and the HD or level of the aura's source is at least twice your character level, you are stunned for 1 round and the spell ends.

3rd Round: The power and location of each aura. If an aura is outside your line of sight, then you discern its direction but not its exact location.

Aura Power: An evil aura's power depends on the type of evil creature or object that you're detecting and its HD, caster level, or (in the case of a cleric) class level; see the accompanying table. If an aura falls into more than one strength category, the spell indicates the stronger of the two.

For example, as indicated on the table, an evil outsider with 12 HD has an overwhelming aura of evil. A good cleric who casts this spell and directs it at the location of such a creature for longer than 1 round loses the spell and is stunned for 1

DETECT EVIL

Creature/Object	Faint	Moderate	Strong	Overwhelming
		Aura Power		
Evil creature[1] (HD)	10 or lower	11–25	26–50	51 or higher
Undead (HD)	2 or lower	3–8	9–20	21 or higher
Evil outsider (HD)	1 or lower	2–4	5–10	11 or higher
Cleric of an evil deity[2] (class levels)	1	2–4	5–10	11 or higher
Evil magic item or spell (caster level)	2nd or lower	3rd–8th	9th–20th	21st or higher

1 Except for undead and outsiders, which have their own entries on the table.
2 Some characters who are not clerics may radiate an aura of equivalent power. The class description will indicate whether this applies.

round if his character level is 6th or lower.

Lingering Aura: An evil aura lingers after its original source dissipates (in the case of a spell) or is destroyed (in the case of a creature or magic item). If *detect evil* is cast and directed at such a location, the spell indicates an aura strength of dim (even weaker than a faint aura). How long the aura lingers at this dim level depends on its original power:

Original Strength	Duration of Lingering Aura
Faint	1d6 rounds
Moderate	1d6 minutes
Strong	1d6×10 minutes
Overwhelming	1d6 days

Animals, traps, poisons, and other potential perils are not evil, and as such this spell does not detect them.

Each round, you can turn to detect evil in a new area. The spell can penetrate barriers, but 1 foot of stone, 1 inch of common metal, a thin sheet of lead, or 3 feet of wood or dirt blocks it.

Detect Good

Divination
Level: Clr 1

This spell functions like *detect evil*, except that it detects the auras of good creatures, clerics or paladins of good deities, good spells, and good magic items, and you are vulnerable to an overwhelming good aura if you are evil. Healing potions, antidotes, and similar beneficial items are not good.

Detect Law

Divination
Level: Clr 1

This spell functions like *detect evil*, except that it detects the auras of lawful creatures, clerics of lawful deities, lawful spells, and lawful magic items, and you are vulnerable to an overwhelming lawful aura if you are chaotic.

Detect Magic

Divination
Level: Brd 0, Clr 0, Drd 0, Sor/Wiz 0
Components: V, S
Casting Time: 1 standard action

Range: 60 ft.
Area: Cone-shaped emanation
Duration: Concentration, up to 1 min./level (D)
Saving Throw: None
Spell Resistance: No

You detect magical auras. The amount of information revealed depends on how long you study a particular area or subject.

1st Round: Presence or absence of magical auras.

2nd Round: Number of different magical auras and the power of the most potent aura.

3rd Round: The strength and location of each aura. If the items or creatures bearing the auras are in line of sight, you can make Spellcraft skill checks to determine the school of magic involved in each. (Make one check per aura; DC 15 + spell level, or 15 + half caster level for a nonspell effect.)

Magical areas, multiple types of magic, or strong local magical emanations may distort or conceal weaker auras.

Aura Strength: An aura's power depends on a spell's functioning spell level or an item's caster level. If an aura falls into more than one category, *detect magic* indicates the stronger of the two.

Lingering Aura: A magical aura lingers after its original source dissipates (in the case of a spell) or is destroyed (in the case of a magic item). If *detect magic* is cast and directed at such a location, the spell indicates an aura strength of dim (even weaker than a faint aura). How long the aura lingers at this dim level depends on its original power:

Original Strength	Duration of Lingering Aura
Faint	1d6 rounds
Moderate	1d6 minutes
Strong	1d6×10 minutes
Overwhelming	1d6 days

Outsiders and elementals are not magical in themselves, but if they are summoned, the conjuration spell registers.

Each round, you can turn to detect magic in a new area. The spell can penetrate barriers, but 1 foot of stone, 1 inch of common metal, a thin sheet of lead, or 3 feet of wood or dirt blocks it.

Detect magic can be made permanent with a *permanency* spell.

Detect Poison

Divination
Level: Clr 0, Drd 0, Pal 1, Rgr 1, Sor/Wiz 0
Components: V, S
Casting Time: 1 standard action
Range: Close (25 ft. + 5 ft./2 levels)
Target or Area: One creature, one object, or a 5-ft. cube
Duration: Instantaneous
Saving Throw: None
Spell Resistance: No

You determine whether a creature, object, or area has been poisoned or is poisonous. You can determine the exact type of poison with a DC 20 Wisdom check. A character with the Craft (alchemy) skill may try a DC 20 Craft (alchemy) check if the Wisdom check fails, or may try the Craft (alchemy) check prior to the Wisdom check.

The spell can penetrate barriers, but 1 foot of stone, 1 inch of common metal, a thin sheet of lead, or 3 feet of wood or dirt blocks it.

Detect Scrying

Divination
Level: Brd 4, Sor/Wiz 4
Components: V, S, M
Casting Time: 1 standard action
Range: 40 ft.
Area: 40-ft.-radius emanation centered on you
Duration: 24 hours
Saving Throw: None
Spell Resistance: No

You immediately become aware of any attempt to observe you by means of a divination (scrying) spell or effect. The spell's area radiates from you and moves as you move. You know the location of every magical sensor within the spell's area.

If the scrying attempt originates within the area, you also know its location; otherwise, you and the scrier immediately make opposed caster level checks (1d20 + caster level). If you at least match the scrier's result, you get a visual image of the scrier and an accurate sense of his

DETECT MAGIC

Spell or Object	Faint	Moderate	Strong	Overwhelming
		Aura Power		
Functioning spell (spell level)	3rd or lower	4th–6th	7th–9th	10th+ (deity-level)
Magic item (caster level)	5th or lower	6th–11th	12th–20th	21st+ (artifact)

or her direction and distance from you.

Material Component: A small piece of mirror and a miniature brass hearing trumpet.

Detect Secret Doors

Divination
Level: Brd 1, Knowledge 1, Sor/Wiz 1
Components: V, S
Casting Time: 1 standard action
Range: 60 ft.
Area: Cone-shaped emanation
Duration: Concentration, up to 1 min./level (D)
Saving Throw: None
Spell Resistance: No

You can detect secret doors, compartments, caches, and so forth. Only passages, doors, or openings that have been specifically constructed to escape detection are detected by this spell—an ordinary trapdoor underneath a pile of crates would not be detected. The amount of information revealed depends on how long you study a particular area or subject.

1st Round: Presence or absence of secret doors.

2nd Round: Number of secret doors and the location of each. If an aura is outside your line of sight, then you discern its direction but not its exact location.

Each Additional Round: The mechanism or trigger for one particular secret portal closely examined by you.

Each round, you can turn to detect secret doors in a new area. The spell can penetrate barriers, but 1 foot of stone, 1 inch of common metal, a thin sheet of lead, or 3 feet of wood or dirt blocks it.

Detect Snares and Pits

Divination
Level: Drd 1, Rgr 1
Components: V, S
Casting Time: 1 standard action
Range: 60 ft.
Area: Cone-shaped emanation
Duration: Concentration, up to 10 min./level (D)
Saving Throw: None
Spell Resistance: No

You can detect simple pits, deadfalls, and snares as well as mechanical traps constructed of natural materials. The spell does not detect complex traps, including trapdoor traps.

Detect snares and pits does detect certain natural hazards—quicksand (a snare), a sinkhole (a pit), or unsafe walls of natural rock (a deadfall). However, it does not reveal other potentially dangerous conditions, such as a cavern that floods during rain, an unsafe construction, or a naturally poisonous plant. The spell does not detect magic traps (except those that

operate by pit, deadfall, or snaring; see the spell *snare*), nor mechanically complex ones, nor those that have been rendered safe or inactive.

The amount of information revealed depends on how long you study a particular area.

1st Round: Presence or absence of hazards.

2nd Round: Number of hazards and the location of each. If a hazard is outside your line of sight, then you discern its direction but not its exact location.

Each Additional Round: The general type and trigger for one particular hazard closely examined by you.

Each round, you can turn to detect snares and pits in a new area. The spell can penetrate barriers, but 1 foot of stone, 1 inch of common metal, a thin sheet of lead, or 3 feet of wood or dirt blocks it.

Detect Thoughts

Divination [Mind-Affecting]
Level: Brd 2, Knowledge 2, Sor/Wiz 2
Components: V, S, F/DF
Casting Time: 1 standard action
Range: 60 ft.
Area: Cone-shaped emanation
Duration: Concentration, up to 1 min./level (D)
Saving Throw: Will negates; see text
Spell Resistance: No

You detect surface thoughts. The amount of information revealed depends on how long you study a particular area or subject.

1st Round: Presence or absence of thoughts (from conscious creatures with Intelligence scores of 1 or higher).

2nd Round: Number of thinking minds and the Intelligence score of each. If the highest Intelligence is 26 or higher (and at least 10 points higher than your own Intelligence score), you are stunned for 1 round and the spell ends. This spell does not let you determine the location of the thinking minds if you can't see the creatures whose thoughts you are detecting.

3rd Round: Surface thoughts of any mind in the area. A target's Will save prevents you from reading its thoughts, and you must cast *detect thoughts* again to have another chance. Creatures of animal intelligence (Int 1 or 2) have simple, instinctual thoughts that you can pick up.

Each round, you can turn to detect thoughts in a new area. The spell can penetrate barriers, but 1 foot of stone, 1 inch of common metal, a thin sheet of lead, or 3 feet of wood or dirt blocks it.

Arcane Focus: A copper piece.

Detect Undead

Divination
Level: Clr 1, Pal 1, Sor/Wiz 1
Components: V, S, M/DF

Casting Time: 1 standard action
Range: 60 ft.
Area: Cone-shaped emanation
Duration: Concentration, up to 1 minute/ level (D)
Saving Throw: None
Spell Resistance: No

You can detect the aura that surrounds undead creatures. The amount of information revealed depends on how long you study a particular area.

1st Round: Presence or absence of undead auras.

2nd Round: Number of undead auras in the area and the strength of the strongest undead aura present. If you are of good alignment, and the strongest undead aura's strength is overwhelming (see below), and the creature has HD of at least twice your character level, you are stunned for 1 round and the spell ends.

3rd Round: The strength and location of each undead aura. If an aura is outside your line of sight, then you discern its direction but not its exact location.

Aura Strength: The strength of an undead aura is determined by the HD of the undead creature, as given on the following table:

HD	Strength
1 or lower	Faint
2–4	Moderate
5–10	Strong
11 or higher	Overwhelming

Lingering Aura: An undead aura lingers after its original source is destroyed. If *detect undead* is cast and directed at such a location, the spell indicates an aura strength of dim (even weaker than a faint aura). How long the aura lingers at this dim level depends on its original power:

Original Strength	Duration of Lingering Aura
Faint	1d6 rounds
Moderate	1d6 minutes
Strong	1d6×10 minutes
Overwhelming	1d6 days

Each round, you can turn to detect undead in a new area. The spell can penetrate barriers, but 1 foot of stone, 1 inch of common metal, a thin sheet of lead, or 3 feet of wood or dirt blocks it.

Arcane Material Component: A bit of earth from a grave.

Dictum

Evocation [Lawful, Sonic]
Level: Clr 7, Law 7
Components: V
Casting Time: 1 standard action
Range: 40 ft.

Area: Nonlawful creatures in a 40-ft.-radius spread centered on you
Duration: Instantaneous
Saving Throw: None or Will negates; see text
Spell Resistance: Yes

Any nonlawful creature within the area of a *dictum* spell suffers the following ill effects.

HD	Effect
Equal to caster level	Deafened
Up to caster level −1	*Slowed*, deafened
Up to caster level −5	Paralyzed, *slowed*, deafened
Up to caster level −10	Killed, paralyzed, *slowed*, deafened

The effects are cumulative and concurrent. No saving throw is allowed against these effects.

Deafened: The creature is deafened for 1d4 rounds.

Slowed: The creature is *slowed*, as by the *slow* spell, for 2d4 rounds.

Paralyzed: The creature is paralyzed and helpless for 1d10 minutes.

Killed: Living creatures die. Undead creatures are destroyed.

Furthermore, if you are on your home plane when you cast this spell, nonlawful extraplanar creatures within the area are instantly banished back to their home planes. Creatures so banished cannot return for at least 24 hours. This effect takes place regardless of whether the creatures hear the *dictum*. The banishment effect allows a Will save (at a −4 penalty) to negate.

Creatures whose HD exceed your caster level are unaffected by *dictum*.

Dimension Door

Conjuration (Teleportation)
Level: Brd 4, Sor/Wiz 4, Travel 4
Components: V
Casting Time: 1 standard action
Range: Long (400 ft. + 40 ft./level)
Target: You and touched objects or other touched willing creatures
Duration: Instantaneous
Saving Throw: None and Will negates (object)
Spell Resistance: No and Yes (object)

You instantly transfer yourself from your current location to any other spot within range. You always arrive at exactly the spot desired—whether by simply visualizing the area or by stating direction, such as "900 feet straight downward," or "upward to the northwest, 45-degree angle, 1,200 feet." After using this spell, you can't take any other actions until your next turn. You can bring along objects as long as their weight doesn't exceed your maxi-mum load. You may also bring one addi-tional willing Medium or smaller creature (carrying gear or objects up to its maxi-mum load) or its equivalent per three caster levels. A Large creature counts as two Medium creatures, a Huge creature counts as two Large creatures, and so forth. All creatures to be transported must be in contact with one another, and at least one of those creatures must be in contact with you.

If you arrive in a place that is already occupied by a solid body, you and each creature traveling with you take 1d6 points of damage and are shunted to a random open space on a suitable surface within 100 feet of the intended location. If there is no free space within 100 feet, you and each creature traveling with you take an additional 2d6 points of damage and are shunted to a free space within 1,000 feet. If there is no free space within 1,000 feet, you and each creature travel-ling with you take an additional 4d6 points of damage and the spell simply fails.

Dimensional Anchor

Abjuration
Level: Clr 4, Sor/Wiz 4
Components: V, S
Casting Time: 1 standard action
Range: Medium (100 ft. + 10 ft./level)
Effect: Ray
Duration: 1 min./level
Saving Throw: None
Spell Resistance: Yes (object)

A green ray springs from your out-stretched hand. You must make a ranged touch attack to hit the target. Any crea-ture or object struck by the ray is covered with a shimmering emerald field that completely blocks extradimensional travel. Forms of movement barred by a *dimensional anchor* include *astral projection*, *blink*, *dimension door*, *ethereal jaunt*, *ethereal-ness*, *gate*, *maze*, *plane shift*, *shadow walk*, *tele-port*, and similar spell-like or psionic abili-ties. The spell also prevents the use of a *gate* or *teleportation circle* for the duration of the spell.

A *dimensional anchor* does not interfere with the movement of creatures already in ethereal or astral form when the spell is cast, nor does it block extradimensional perception or attack forms such as a basilisk's gaze. Also, *dimensional anchor* does not prevent summoned creatures from disappearing at the end of a sum-moning spell.

Dimensional Lock

Abjuration
Level: Clr 8, Sor/Wiz 8
Components: V, S
Casting Time: 1 standard action
Range: Medium (100 ft. + 10 ft./level)
Area: 20-ft.-radius emanation centered on a point in space
Duration: One day/level
Saving Throw: None
Spell Resistance: Yes

You create a shimmering emerald barrier that completely blocks extradimensional travel. Forms of movement barred in-clude *astral projection*, *blink*, *dimension door*, *ethereal jaunt*, *etherealness*, *gate*, *maze*, *plane shift*, *shadow walk*, *teleport*, and similar spell-like or psionic abilities. Once *dimen-sional lock* is in place, extradimensional travel into or out of the area is not possible.

A *dimensional lock* does not interfere with the movement of creatures already in ethereal or astral form when the spell is cast, nor does it block extradimensional perception or attack forms, such as a basilisk's gaze. Also, the spell does not pre-vent summoned creatures from disap-pearing at the end of a summoning spell.

Diminish Plants

Transmutation
Level: Drd 3, Rgr 3
Components: V, S, DF
Casting Time: 1 standard action
Range: See text
Target or Area: See text
Duration: Instantaneous
Saving Throw: None
Spell Resistance: No

This spell has two versions.

Prune Growth: This version causes nor-mal vegetation (grasses, briars, bushes, creepers, hedges, thistles, trees, vines, and so forth) within long range (400 feet + 40 feet per level) to shrink to about one-third of their normal size, becoming untangled and less bushy. The affected vegetation appears to have been carefully pruned and trimmed.

At your option, the area can be a 100-foot-radius circle, a 150-foot-radius semi-circle, or a 200-foot-radius quarter-circle. You may also designate portions of the area that are not affected.

Stunt Growth: This version targets nor-mal plants within a range of 1/2 mile, reducing their potential productivity over the course of the following year to one-third below normal.

Diminish plants counters *plant growth*.

This spell has no effect on plant crea-tures.

Discern Lies

Divination
Level: Clr 4, Pal 3
Components: V, S, DF
Casting Time: 1 standard action
Range: Close (25 ft. + 5 ft./2 levels)

Targets: One creature/level, no two of which can be more than 30 ft. apart
Duration: Concentration, up to 1 round/level
Saving Throw: Will negates
Spell Resistance: No

Each round, you concentrate on one subject, who must be within range. You know if the subject deliberately and knowingly speaks a lie by discerning disturbances in its aura caused by lying. The spell does not reveal the truth, uncover unintentional inaccuracies, or necessarily reveal evasions. Each round, you may concentrate on a different subject.

Discern Location

Divination
Level: Clr 8, Knowledge 8, Sor/Wiz 8
Components: V, S, DF
Casting Time: 10 minutes
Range: Unlimited
Target: One creature or object
Duration: Instantaneous
Saving Throw: None
Spell Resistance: No

A *discern location* spell is among the most powerful means of locating creatures or objects. Nothing short of a *mind blank* spell or the direct intervention of a deity keeps you from learning the exact location of a single individual or object. *Discern location* circumvents normal means of protection from scrying or location. The spell reveals the name of the creature or object's location (place, name, business name, building name, or the like), community, county (or similar political division), country, continent, and the plane of existence where the target lies.

To find a creature with the spell, you must have seen the creature or have some item that once belonged to it. To find an object, you must have touched it at least once.

Disguise Self

Illusion (Glamer)
Level: Brd 1, Sor/Wiz 1, Trickery 1
Components: V, S
Casting Time: 1 standard action
Range: Personal
Target: You
Duration: 10 min./level (D)

You make yourself—including clothing, armor, weapons, and equipment—look different. You can seem 1 foot shorter or taller, thin, fat, or in between. You cannot change your body type. For example, a human caster could look human, humanoid, or like any other human-shaped bipedal creature. Otherwise, the extent of the apparent change is up to you. You could add or obscure a minor feature, such as a mole or a beard, or look like an entirely different person.

The spell does not provide the abilities or mannerisms of the chosen form, nor does it alter the perceived tactile (touch) or audible (sound) properties of you or your equipment. A battleaxe made to look like a dagger still functions as a battleaxe.

If you use this spell to create a disguise, you get a +10 bonus on the Disguise check.

A creature that interacts with the glamer gets a Will save to recognize it as an illusion. For example, a creature that touched you and realized that the tactile sensation did not match the visual one would be entitled to such a save.

Disintegrate

Transmutation
Level: Destruction 7, Sor/Wiz 6
Components: V, S, M/DF
Casting Time: 1 standard action
Range: Medium (100 ft. + 10 ft./level)
Effect: Ray
Duration: Instantaneous
Saving Throw: Fortitude partial (object)
Spell Resistance: Yes

A thin, green ray springs from your pointing finger. You must make a successful ranged touch attack to hit. Any creature struck by the ray takes 2d6 points of damage per caster level (to a maximum of 40d6). Any creature reduced to 0 or fewer hit points by this spell is entirely disintegrated, leaving behind only a trace of fine dust. A disintegrated creature's equipment is unaffected.

When used against an object, the ray simply disintegrates as much as one 10-foot cube of nonliving matter. Thus, the spell disintegrates only part of any very large object or structure targeted. The ray affects even objects constructed entirely of force, such as *Bigby's forceful hand* or a *wall of force*, but not magical effects such as a *globe of invulnerability* or an *antimagic field*.

A creature or object that makes a successful Fortitude save is partially affected, taking only 5d6 points of damage. If this damage reduces the creature or object to 0 or fewer hit points, it is entirely disintegrated.

Only the first creature or object struck can be affected; that is, the ray affects only one target per casting.

Arcane Material Component: A lodestone and a pinch of dust.

Dismissal

Abjuration
Level: Clr 4, Sor/Wiz 5
Components: V, S, DF
Casting Time: 1 standard action
Range: Close (25 ft. + 5 ft./2 levels)
Target: One extraplanar creature
Duration: Instantaneous
Saving Throw: Will negates; see text
Spell Resistance: Yes

This spell forces an extraplanar creature back to its proper plane if it fails a special Will save (DC = spell's save DC – creature's HD + your caster level). If the spell is successful, the creature is instantly whisked away, but there is a 20% chance of actually sending the subject to a plane other than its own.

Dispel Chaos

Abjuration [Lawful]
Level: Clr 5, Law 5, Pal 4

This spell functions like *dispel evil*, except that you are surrounded by constant, blue, lawful energy, and the spell affects chaotic creatures and spells rather than evil ones.

Dispel Evil

Abjuration [Good]
Level: Clr 5, Good 5, Pal 4
Components: V, S, DF
Casting Time: 1 standard action
Range: Touch
Target or Targets: You and a touched evil creature from another plane; or you and an enchantment or evil spell on a touched creature or object
Duration: 1 round/level or until discharged, whichever comes first
Saving Throw: See text
Spell Resistance: See text

Shimmering, white, holy energy surrounds you. This power has three effects.

First, you gain a +4 deflection bonus to AC against attacks by evil creatures.

Second, on making a successful melee touch attack against an evil creature from another plane, you can choose to drive that creature back to its home plane. The creature can negate the effects with a successful Will save (spell resistance applies). This use discharges and ends the spell.

Third, with a touch you can automatically dispel any one enchantment spell cast by an evil creature or any one evil spell. *Exception:* Spells that can't be dispelled by *dispel magic* also can't be dispelled by *dispel evil.* Saving throws and spell resistance do not apply to this effect. This use discharges and ends the spell.

Dispel Good

Abjuration [Evil]
Level: Clr 5, Evil 5

This spell functions like *dispel evil*, except that you are surrounded by dark, wavering, unholy energy, and the spell affects good creatures and spells rather than evil ones.

Dispel Law
Abjuration [Chaotic]
Level: Chaos 5, Clr 5

This spell functions like *dispel evil*, except that you are surrounded by flickering, yellow, chaotic energy, and the spell affects lawful creatures and spells rather than evil ones.

Dispel Magic
Abjuration
Level: Brd 3, Clr 3, Drd 4, Magic 3, Pal 3, Sor/Wiz 3
Components: V, S
Casting Time: 1 standard action
Range: Medium (100 ft. + 10 ft./level)
Target or Area: One spellcaster, creature, or object; or 20-ft.-radius burst
Duration: Instantaneous
Saving Throw: None
Spell Resistance: No

Because magic is powerful, so too is the ability to dispel magic. You can use *dispel magic* to end ongoing spells that have been cast on a creature or object, to temporarily suppress the magical abilities of a magic item, to end ongoing spells (or at least their effects) within an area, or to counter another spellcaster's spell. A dispelled spell ends as if its duration had expired. Some spells, as detailed in their descriptions, can't be defeated by *dispel magic*. *Dispel magic* can dispel (but not counter) spell-like effects just as it does spells.

Note: The effect of a spell with an instantaneous duration can't be dispelled, because the magical effect is already over before the *dispel magic* can take effect. Thus, you can't use *dispel magic* to repair fire damage caused by a *fireball* or to turn a petrified character back to flesh. In these cases, the magic has departed, leaving only burned flesh or perfectly normal stone in its wake.

You choose to use *dispel magic* in one of three ways: a targeted dispel, an area dispel, or a counterspell:

Targeted Dispel: One object, creature, or spell is the target of the *dispel magic* spell. You make a dispel check (1d20 + your caster level, maximum +10) against the spell or against each ongoing spell currently in effect on the object or creature. The DC for this dispel check is 11 + the spell's caster level.

For example, Mialee, at 5th level, targets *dispel magic* on a drow who is under the effects of *haste*, *mage armor*, and *bull's strength*. All three spells were cast on the drow by a 7th-level wizard. Mialee makes a dispel check (1d20 + 5 against DC 18) three times, once each for the *haste*, *mage armor*, and *bull's strength* effects. If she succeeds on a particular check, that spell is dispelled (the drow's spell resistance doesn't help him); if she fails, that spell remains in effect.

If you target an object or creature that is the effect of an ongoing spell (such as a monster summoned by *monster summoning*), you make a dispel check to end the spell that conjured the object or creature.

If the object that you target is a magic item, you make a dispel check against the item's caster level. If you succeed, all the item's magical properties are suppressed for 1d4 rounds, after which the item recovers on its own. A suppressed item becomes nonmagical for the duration of the effect. An interdimensional interface (such as a *bag of holding*) is temporarily closed. A magic item's physical properties are unchanged: A suppressed magic sword is still a sword (a masterwork sword, in fact). Artifacts and deities are unaffected by mortal magic such as this.

You automatically succeed on your dispel check against any spell that you cast yourself.

Area Dispel: When *dispel magic* is used in this way, the spell affects everything within a 30-foot radius.

For each creature within the area that is the subject of one or more spells, you make a dispel check against the spell with the highest caster level. If that check fails, you make dispel checks against progressively weaker spells until you dispel one spell (which discharges the *dispel magic* spell so far as that target is concerned) or until you fail all your checks. The creature's magic items are not affected.

For each object within the area that is the target of one or more spells, you make dispel checks as with creatures. Magic items are not affected by an area dispel.

For each ongoing area or effect spell whose point of origin is within the area of the *dispel magic* spell, you can make a dispel check to dispel the spell.

For each ongoing spell whose area overlaps that of the *dispel magic* spell, you can make a dispel check to end the effect, but only within the overlapping area.

If an object or creature that is the effect of an ongoing spell (such as a monster summoned by *monster summoning*) is in the area, you can make a dispel check to end the spell that conjured that object or creature (returning it whence it came) in addition to attempting to dispel spells targeting the creature or object.

You may choose to automatically succeed on dispel checks against any spell that you have cast.

Counterspell: When *dispel magic* is used in this way, the spell targets a spellcaster and is cast as a counterspell (page 170). Unlike a true counterspell, however, *dispel magic* may not work; you must make a dispel check to counter the other spellcaster's spell.

Dispel Magic, Greater
Abjuration
Level: Brd 5, Clr 6, Drd 6, Sor/Wiz 6

This spell functions like *dispel magic*, except that the maximum caster level on your dispel check is +20 instead of +10. Additionally, *greater dispel magic* has a chance to dispel any effect that *remove curse* can remove, even if *dispel magic* can't dispel that effect.

Displacement
Illusion (Glamer)
Level: Brd 3, Sor/Wiz 3
Components: V, M
Casting Time: 1 standard action
Range: Touch
Target: Creature touched
Duration: 1 round/level (D)
Saving Throw: Will negates (harmless)
Spell Resistance: Yes (harmless)

Emulating the natural ability of the displacer beast (see the *Monster Manual*), the subject of this spell appears to be about 2 feet away from its true location. The creature benefits from a 50% miss chance as if it had total concealment. However, unlike actual total concealment, *displacement* does not prevent enemies from targeting the creature normally. *True seeing* reveals its true location.

Material Component: A small strip of leather made from displacer beast hide, twisted into a loop.

Disrupt Undead
Necromancy
Level: Sor/Wiz 0
Components: V, S
Casting Time: 1 standard action
Range: Close (25 ft. + 5 ft./2 levels)
Effect: Ray
Duration: Instantaneous
Saving Throw: None
Spell Resistance: Yes

You direct a ray of positive energy. You must make a ranged touch attack to hit, and if the ray hits an undead creature, it deals 1d6 points of damage to it.

Disrupting Weapon
Transmutation
Level: Clr 5
Components: V, S
Casting Time: 1 standard action
Range: Touch
Targets: One melee weapon
Duration: 1 round/level
Saving Throw: Will negates (harmless, object); see text
Spell Resistance: Yes (harmless, object)

This spell makes a melee weapon deadly to undead. Any undead creature with HD equal to or less than your caster level must succeed on a Will save or be destroyed utterly if struck in combat with this weapon. Spell resistance does not apply against the destruction effect.

Divination

Divination
Level: Clr 4, Knowledge 4
Components: V, S, M
Casting Time: 10 minutes
Range: Personal
Target: You
Duration: Instantaneous

Similar to *augury* but more powerful, a *divination* spell can provide you with a useful piece of advice in reply to a question concerning a specific goal, event, or activity that is to occur within one week. The advice can be as simple as a short phrase, or it might take the form of a cryptic rhyme or omen.

For example, suppose the question is "Will we do well if we venture into the ruined temple of Erythnul?" The DM knows that a terrible troll guarding 10,000 gp and a *+1 shield* lurks near the entrance but estimates that your party could beat the troll after a hard fight. Therefore the divination response might be: "Ready oil and open flame light your way to wealth." In all cases, the DM controls what information you receive. If your party doesn't act on the information, the conditions may change so that the information is no longer useful. (For example, the troll could move away and take the treasure with it.)

The base chance for a correct *divination* is 70% + 1% per caster level, to a maximum of 90%. The DM adjusts the chance if unusual circumstances require it (if, for example, unusual precautions against divination spells have been taken). If the dice roll fails, you know the spell failed, unless specific magic yielding false information is at work.

As with *augury*, multiple *divinations* about the same topic by the same caster use the same dice result as the first *divination* spell and yield the same answer each time.

Material Component: Incense and a sacrificial offering appropriate to your religion, together worth at least 25 gp.

Divine Favor

Evocation
Level: Clr 1, Pal 1
Components: V, S, DF
Casting Time: 1 standard action
Range: Personal
Target: You
Duration: 1 minute

Calling upon the strength and wisdom of a deity, you gain a +1 luck bonus on attack and weapon damage rolls for every three caster levels you have (at least +1, maximum +6). The bonus doesn't apply to spell damage.

Divine Power

Evocation
Level: Clr 4, War 4
Components: V, S, DF
Casting Time: 1 standard action
Range: Personal
Target: You
Duration: 1 round/level

Calling upon the divine power of your patron, you imbue yourself with strength and skill in combat. Your base attack bonus becomes equal to your character level (which may give you additional attacks), you gain a +6 enhancement bonus to Strength, and you gain 1 temporary hit point per caster level.

Dominate Animal

Enchantment (Compulsion) [Mind-Affecting]
Level: Animal 3, Drd 3
Components: V, S
Casting Time: 1 round
Range: Close (25 ft. + 5 ft./2 levels)
Target: One animal
Duration: 1 round/level
Saving Throw: Will negates
Spell Resistance: Yes

You can enchant an animal and direct it with simple commands such as "Attack," "Run," and "Fetch." Suicidal or self-destructive commands (including an order to attack a creature two or more size categories larger than the *dominated* animal) are simply ignored.

Dominate animal establishes a mental link between you and the subject creature. The animal can be directed by silent mental command as long as it remains in range. You need not see the creature to control it. You do not receive direct sensory input from the creature, but you know what it is experiencing. Because you are directing the animal with your own intelligence, it may be able to undertake actions normally beyond its own comprehension, such as manipulating objects with its paws and mouth. You need not concentrate exclusively on controlling the creature unless you are trying to direct it to do something it normally couldn't do. Changing your instructions or giving a *dominated* creature a new command is the equivalent of redirecting a spell, so it is a move action.

Dominate Monster

Enchantment (Compulsion) [Mind-Affecting]
Level: Sor/Wiz 9
Target: One creature

This spell functions like *dominate person*, except that the spell is not restricted by creature type.

Dominate Person

Enchantment (Compulsion) [Mind-Affecting]
Level: Brd 4, Sor/Wiz 5
Components: V, S
Casting Time: 1 round
Range: Close (25 ft. + 5 ft./2 levels)
Target: One humanoid
Duration: One day/level
Saving Throw: Will negates
Spell Resistance: Yes

You can control the actions of any humanoid creature through a telepathic link that you establish with the subject's mind. If you and the subject have a common language, you can generally force the subject to perform as you desire, within the limits of its abilities. If no common language exists, you can communicate only basic commands, such as "Come here," "Go there," "Fight," and "Stand still." You know what the subject is experiencing, but you do not receive direct sensory input from it, nor can it communicate with you telepathically.

Once you have given a *dominated* creature a command, it continues to attempt to carry out that command to the exclusion of all other activities except those necessary for day-to-day survival (such as sleeping, eating, and so forth). Because of this limited range of activity, a Sense Motive check against DC 15 (rather than DC 25) can determine that the subject's behavior is being influenced by an enchantment effect (see the Sense Motive skill description, page 81).

Changing your instructions or giving a *dominated* creature a new command is the equivalent of redirecting a spell, so it is a move action.

By concentrating fully on the spell (a standard action), you can receive full sensory input as interpreted by the mind of the subject, though it still can't communicate with you. You can't actually see through the subject's eyes, so it's not as good as being there yourself, but you still get a good idea of what's going on (the subject is walking through a smelly courtyard, the subject is talking to a guard, the guard looks suspicious, and so forth).

Subjects resist this control, and any subject forced to take actions against its nature receives a new saving throw with a +2 bonus. Obviously self-destructive orders are not carried out. Once control is established, the range at which it can be exercised is unlimited, as long as you and the subject are on the same plane. You need not see the subject to control it.

If you don't spend at least 1 round concentrating on the spell each day, the subject receives a new saving throw to throw off the domination.

Protection from evil or a similar spell can prevent you from exercising control or using the telepathic link while the subject is so warded, but such an effect neither prevents the establishment of domination nor dispels it.

Doom

Necromancy [Fear, Mind-Affecting]
Level: Clr 1
Components: V, S, DF
Casting Time: 1 standard action
Range: Medium (100 ft. + 10 ft./level)
Target: One living creature
Duration: 1 min./level
Saving Throw: Will negates
Spell Resistance: Yes

This spell fills a single subject with a feeling of horrible dread that causes it to become shaken.

Drawmij's Instant Summons

Conjuration (Summoning)
Level: Sor/Wiz 7
Components: V, S, M
Casting Time: 1 standard action
Range: See text
Target: One object weighing 10 lb. or less whose longest dimension is 6 ft. or less
Duration: Permanent until discharged
Saving Throw: None
Spell Resistance: No

You call some nonliving item from virtually any location directly to your hand.

First, you must place your *arcane mark* (page 201) on the item. Then you cast this spell, which magically and invisibly inscribes the name of the item on a sapphire worth at least 1,000 gp. Thereafter, you can summon the item by speaking a special word (set by you when the spell is cast) and crushing the gem. The item appears instantly in your hand. Only you can use the gem in this way.

If the item is in the possession of another creature, the spell does not work, but you know who the possessor is and roughly where that creature is located when the summons occurs.

The inscription on the gem is invisible. It is also unreadable, except by means of a *read magic* spell, to anyone but you.

The item can be summoned from another plane, but only if no other creature has claimed ownership of it.

Material Component: A sapphire worth at least 1,000 gp.

Dream

Illusion (Phantasm) [Mind-Affecting]
Level: Brd 5, Sor/Wiz 5
Components: V, S
Casting Time: 1 minute
Range: Unlimited
Target: One living creature touched
Duration: See text
Saving Throw: None
Spell Resistance: Yes

You, or a messenger touched by you, sends a phantasmal message to others in the form of a dream. At the beginning of the spell, you must name the recipient or identify him or her by some title that leaves no doubt as to identity. The messenger then enters a trance, appears in the intended recipient's dream, and delivers the message. The message can be of any length, and the recipient remembers it perfectly upon waking. The communication is one-way. The recipient cannot ask questions or offer information, nor can the messenger gain any information by observing the dreams of the recipient. Once the message is delivered, the messenger's mind returns instantly to its body. The duration of the spell is the time required for the messenger to enter the recipient's dream and deliver the message.

If the recipient is awake when the spell begins, the messenger can choose to wake up (ending the spell) or remain in the trance. The messenger can remain in the trance until the recipient goes to sleep, then enter the recipient's dream and deliver the message as normal. A messenger that is disturbed during the trance comes awake, ending the spell.

Creatures who don't sleep (such as elves, but not half-elves) or don't dream cannot be contacted by this spell.

The messenger is unaware of its own surroundings or of the activities around it while in the trance. It is defenseless both physically and mentally (always fails any saving throw, for example) while in the trance.

Eagle's Splendor

Transmutation
Level: Brd 2, Clr 2, Pal 2, Sor/Wiz 2
Components: V, S, M/DF
Casting Time: 1 standard action
Range: Touch
Target: Creature touched
Duration: 1 min./level
Saving Throw: Will negates (harmless)
Spell Resistance: Yes

The transmuted creature becomes more poised, articulate, and personally forceful. The spell grants a +4 enhancement bonus to Charisma, adding the usual benefits to Charisma-based skill checks and other uses of the Charisma modifier. Sorcerers and bards (and other spellcasters who rely on Charisma) affected by this spell do not gain any additional bonus spells for the increased Charisma, but the save DCs for spells they cast while under this spell's effect do increase.

Arcane Material Component: A few feathers or a pinch of droppings from an eagle.

Eagle's Splendor, Mass

Transmutation
Level: Brd 6, Clr 6, Sor/Wiz 6
Range: Close (25 ft. + 5 ft./2 levels)
Target: One creature/level, no two of which can be more than 30 ft. apart

This spell functions like *eagle's splendor*, except that it affects multiple creatures.

Earthquake

Evocation [Earth]
Level: Clr 8, Destruction 8, Drd 8, Earth 7
Components: V, S, DF
Casting Time: 1 standard action
Range: Long (400 ft. + 40 ft./level)
Area: 80-ft.-radius spread (S)
Duration: 1 round
Saving Throw: See text
Spell Resistance: No

When you cast *earthquake*, an intense but highly localized tremor rips the ground. The shock knocks creatures down, collapses structures, opens cracks in the ground, and more. The effect lasts for 1 round, during which time creatures on the ground can't move or attack. A spellcaster on the ground must make a Concentration check (DC 20 + spell level) or lose any spell he or she tries to cast. The earthquake affects all terrain, vegetation, structures, and creatures in the area. The specific effect of an *earthquake* spell depends on the nature of the terrain where it is cast.

Cave, Cavern, or Tunnel: The spell collapses the roof, dealing 8d6 points of bludgeoning damage to any creature caught under the cave-in (Reflex DC 15 half) and pinning that creature beneath the rubble (see below). An *earthquake* cast on the roof of a very large cavern could also endanger those outside the actual area but below the falling debris.

Cliffs: Earthquake causes a cliff to crumble, creating a landslide that travels horizontally as far as it fell vertically. An *earthquake* cast at the top of a 100-foot cliff would sweep debris 100 feet outward from the base of the cliff. Any creature in the path takes 8d6 points of bludgeoning damage (Reflex DC 15 half) and is pinned beneath the rubble (see below).

Open Ground: Each creature standing in the area must make a DC 15 Reflex save or fall down. Fissures open in the earth, and every creature on the ground has a 25% chance to fall into one (Reflex DC 20 to avoid a fissure). At the end of the spell, all fissures grind shut, killing any creatures still trapped within.

Structure: Any structure standing on open ground takes 100 points of damage, enough to collapse a typical wooden or masonry building, but not a structure built of stone or reinforced masonry. Hardness does not reduce this damage, nor is it halved as damage dealt to objects normally is. (See the *Dungeon Master's Guide* for information on hit points for walls and the like.) Any creature caught inside a collapsing structure takes 8d6 points of bludgeoning damage (Reflex DC 15 half) and is pinned beneath the rubble (see below).

River, Lake, or Marsh: Fissures open underneath the water, draining away the water from that area and forming muddy ground. Soggy marsh or swampland becomes quicksand for the duration of the spell, sucking down creatures and structures. Each creature in the area must make a DC 15 Reflex save or sink down in the mud and quicksand. At the end of the spell, the rest of the body of water rushes in to replace the drained water, possibly drowning those caught in the mud.

Pinned beneath Rubble: Any creature pinned beneath rubble takes 1d6 points of nonlethal damage per minute while pinned. If a pinned character falls unconscious, he or she must make a DC 15 Constitution check or take 1d6 points of lethal damage each minute thereafter until freed or dead.

Elemental Swarm

Conjuration (Summoning) [see text]
Level: Air 9, Drd 9, Earth 9, Fire 9, Water 9
Components: V, S
Casting Time: 10 minutes
Range: Medium (100 ft. + 10 ft./level)
Effect: Two or more summoned creatures, no two of which can be more than 30 ft. apart
Duration: 10 min./level (D)
Saving Throw: None
Spell Resistance: No

This spell opens a portal to an Elemental Plane and summons elementals from it. A druid can choose the plane (Air, Earth, Fire, or Water); a cleric opens a portal to the plane matching his domain.

When the spell is complete, 2d4 Large elementals appear. Ten minutes later, 1d4 Huge elementals appear. Ten minutes after that, one greater elemental appears. Each elemental has maximum hit points per HD. Once these creatures appear, they serve you for the duration of the spell.

The elementals obey you explicitly and never attack you, even if someone else manages to gain control over them. You do not need to concentrate to maintain control over the elementals. You can dismiss them singly or in groups at any time.

When you use a summoning spell to summon an air, earth, fire, or water creature, it is a spell of that type. For example, *elemental swarm* is a fire spell when you cast it to summon fire elementals and a water spell when you use it to summon water elementals.

Endure Elements

Abjuration
Level: Clr 1, Drd 1, Pal 1, Rgr 1, Sor/Wiz 1, Sun 1
Components: V, S
Casting Time: 1 standard action
Range: Touch
Target: Creature touched
Duration: 24 hours
Saving Throw: Will negates (harmless)
Spell Resistance: Yes (harmless)

A creature protected by *endure elements* suffers no harm from being in a hot or cold environment. It can exist comfortably in conditions between −50 and 140 degrees Fahrenheit without having to make Fortitude saves (as described in the *Dungeon Master's Guide*). The creature's equipment is likewise protected.

Endure elements doesn't provide any protection from fire or cold damage, nor does it protect against other environmental hazards such as smoke, lack of air, and so forth.

Energy Drain

Necromancy
Level: Clr 9, Sor/Wiz 9
Saving Throw: Fortitude partial; see text for *enervation*

This spell functions like *enervation*, except that the creature struck gains 2d4 negative levels, and the negative levels last longer.

There is no saving throw to avoid gaining the negative levels, but 24 hours after gaining them, the subject must make a Fortitude saving throw (DC = *energy drain* spell's save DC) for each negative level. If the save succeeds, that negative level is removed. If it fails, the negative level also goes away, but one of the subject's character levels is permanently drained.

An undead creature struck by the ray gains 2d4×5 temporary hit points for 1 hour.

Enervation

Necromancy
Level: Sor/Wiz 4
Components: V, S

Casting Time: 1 standard action
Range: Close (25 ft. + 5 ft./2 levels)
Effect: Ray of negative energy
Duration: Instantaneous
Saving Throw: None
Spell Resistance: Yes

You point your finger and utter the incantation, releasing a black ray of crackling negative energy that suppresses the life force of any living creature it strikes. You must make a ranged touch attack to hit. If the attack succeeds, the subject gains 1d4 negative levels.

If the subject has at least as many negative levels as HD, it dies. Each negative level gives a creature a −1 penalty on attack rolls, saving throws, skill checks, ability checks, and effective level (for determining the power, duration, DC, and other details of spells or special abilities). Additionally, a spellcaster loses one spell or spell slot from his or her highest available level. Negative levels stack.

Assuming the subject survives, it regains lost levels after a number of hours equal to your caster level (maximum 15 hours). Usually, negative levels have a chance of permanently draining the victim's levels, but the negative levels from *enervation* don't last long enough to do so.

An undead creature struck by the ray gains 1d4×5 temporary hit points for 1 hour.

Enlarge Person

Transmutation
Level: Sor/Wiz 1, Strength 1
Components: V, S, M
Casting Time: 1 round
Range: Close (25 ft. + 5 ft./2 levels)
Target: One humanoid creature
Duration: 1 min./level (D)
Saving Throw: Fortitude negates
Spell Resistance: Yes

This spell causes instant growth of a humanoid creature, doubling its height and multiplying its weight by 8. This increase changes the creature's size category to the next larger one. The target gains a +2 size bonus to Strength, a −2 size penalty to Dexterity (to a minimum of 1), and a −1 penalty on attack rolls and AC due to its increased size.

A humanoid creature whose size increases to Large has a space of 10 feet and a natural reach of 10 feet. This spell does not change the target's speed.

If insufficient room is available for the desired growth, the creature attains the maximum possible size and may make a Strength check (using its increased Strength) to burst any enclosures in the process. If it fails, it is constrained without harm by the materials enclosing it—

the spell cannot be used to crush a creature by increasing its size.

All equipment worn or carried by a creature is similarly enlarged by the spell. Melee and projectile weapons affected by this spell deal more damage (see Table 2–2 in the *Dungeon Master's Guide*). Other magical properties are not affected by this spell. Any *enlarged* item that leaves an *enlarged* creature's possession (including a projectile or thrown weapon) instantly returns to its normal size. This means that thrown weapons deal their normal damage, and projectiles deal damage based on the size of the weapon that fired them. Magical properties of *enlarged* items are not increased by this spell—an *enlarged +1 sword* still has only a +1 enhancement bonus, a staff-sized wand is still only capable of its normal functions, a giant-sized potion merely requires a greater fluid intake to make its magical effects operate, and so on.

Multiple magical effects that increase size do not stack, which means (among other things) that you can't use a second casting of this spell to further increase the size of a humanoid that's still under the effect of the first casting.

Enlarge person counters and dispels *reduce person*.

Enlarge person can be made permanent with a *permanency* spell.

Material Component: A pinch of powdered iron.

Enlarge Person, Mass

Transmutation
Level: Sor/Wiz 4
Target: One humanoid creature/level, no two of which can be more than 30 ft. apart

This spell functions like *enlarge person*, except that it affects multiple creatures.

Entangle

Transmutation
Level: Drd 1, Plant 1, Rgr 1
Components: V, S, DF
Casting Time: 1 standard action
Range: Long (400 ft. + 40 ft./level)
Area: Plants in a 40-ft.-radius spread
Duration: 1 min./level (D)
Saving Throw: Reflex partial; see text
Spell Resistance: No

Grasses, weeds, bushes, and even trees wrap, twist, and entwine about creatures in the area or those that enter the area, holding them fast and causing them to become entangled. The creature can break free and move half its normal speed by using a full-round action to make a DC 20 Strength check or a DC 20 Escape Artist check. A creature that succeeds on a Reflex save is not entangled but can still

move at only half speed through the area. Each round on your turn, the plants once again attempt to entangle all creatures that have avoided or escaped entanglement.

Note: The DM may alter the effects of the spell somewhat, based on the nature of the entangling plants.

Enthrall

Enchantment (Charm) [Language Dependent, Mind-Affecting, Sonic]
Level: Brd 2, Clr 2
Components: V, S
Casting Time: 1 round
Range: Medium (100 ft. + 10 ft./level)
Targets: Any number of creatures
Duration: 1 hour or less
Saving Throw: Will negates; see text
Spell Resistance: Yes

If you have the attention of a group of creatures, you can use this spell to hold them spellbound. To cast the spell, you must speak or sing without interruption for 1 full round. Thereafter, those affected give you their undivided attention, ignoring their surroundings. They are considered to have an attitude of friendly while under the effect of the spell (see the *Dungeon Master's Guide* for information about NPC attitudes). Any potentially affected creature of a race or religion unfriendly to yours gets a +4 bonus on the saving throw.

A creature with 4 or more HD or with a Wisdom score of 16 or higher remains aware of its surroundings and has an attitude of indifferent. It gains a new saving throw if it witnesses actions that it opposes.

The effect lasts as long as you speak or sing, to a maximum of 1 hour. Those *enthralled* by your words take no action while you speak or sing and for 1d3 rounds thereafter while they discuss the topic or performance. Those entering the area during the performance must also successfully save or become *enthralled*. The speech ends (but the 1d3-round delay still applies) if you lose concentration or do anything other than speak or sing.

If those not *enthralled* have unfriendly or hostile attitudes toward you, they can collectively make a Charisma check to try to end the spell by jeering and heckling. For this check, use the Charisma bonus of the creature with the highest Charisma in the group; others may make Charisma checks to assist (as described in Aid Another, page 65). The heckling ends the spell if this check result beats your Charisma check result. Only one such challenge is allowed per use of the spell.

If any member of the audience is attacked or subjected to some other overtly hostile act, the spell ends and the previously *enthralled* members become imme-

diately unfriendly toward you. Each creature with 4 or more HD or with a Wisdom score of 16 or higher becomes hostile.

Entropic Shield

Abjuration
Level: Clr 1, Luck 1
Components: V, S
Casting Time: 1 standard action
Range: Personal
Target: You
Duration: 1 min./level (D)

A magical field appears around you, glowing with a chaotic blast of multicolored hues. This field deflects incoming arrows, rays, and other ranged attacks. Each ranged attack directed at you for which the attacker must make an attack roll (including arrows, magic arrows, *Melf's acid arrow*, *ray of enfeeblement*, and so forth) has a 20% miss chance (similar to the effects of concealment). Other attacks that simply work at a distance, such as a dragon's breath weapon, are not affected.

Erase

Transmutation
Level: Brd 1, Sor/Wiz 1
Components: V, S
Casting Time: 1 standard action
Range: Close (25 ft. + 5 ft./2 levels)
Target: One scroll or two pages
Duration: Instantaneous
Saving Throw: See text
Spell Resistance: No

Erase removes writings of either magical or mundane nature from a scroll or from one or two pages of paper, parchment, or similar surfaces. With this spell, you can remove *explosive runes*, a *glyph of warding*, a *sepia snake sigil*, or an *arcane mark*, but not *illusory script* or a *symbol* spell. Nonmagical writing is automatically erased if you touch it and no one else is holding it. Otherwise, the chance of erasing nonmagical writing is 90%.

Magic writing must be touched to be erased, and you also must succeed on a caster level check (1d20 + caster level) against DC 15. (A natural 1 or 2 is always a failure on this check.) If you fail to erase *explosive runes*, a *glyph of warding*, or a *sepia snake sigil*, you accidentally activate that writing instead.

Ethereal Jaunt

Transmutation
Level: Clr 7, Sor/Wiz 7
Components: V, S
Casting Time: 1 standard action
Range: Personal
Target: You
Duration: 1 round/level (D)

You become ethereal, along with your equipment. For the duration of the spell, you are in a place called the Ethereal Plane, which overlaps the normal, physical, Material Plane. When the spell expires, you return to material existence.

An ethereal creature is invisible, insubstantial, and capable of moving in any direction, even up or down, albeit at half normal speed. As an insubstantial creature, you can move through solid objects, including living creatures. An ethereal creature can see and hear on the Material Plane, but everything looks gray and ephemeral. Sight and hearing onto the Material Plane are limited to 60 feet. Force effects (such as *magic missile* and *wall of force*) and abjurations affect an ethereal creature normally. Their effects extend onto the Ethereal Plane from the Material Plane, but not vice versa. An ethereal creature can't attack material creatures, and spells you cast while ethereal affect only other ethereal things. Certain material creatures or objects have attacks or effects that work on the Ethereal Plane (such as a basilisk's gaze attack). Treat other ethereal creatures and ethereal objects as if they were material.

If you end the spell and become material while inside a material object (such as a solid wall), you are shunted off to the nearest open space and take 1d6 points of damage per 5 feet that you so travel.

Etherealness

Transmutation
Level: Clr 9, Sor/Wiz 9
Range: Touch; see text
Targets: You and one other touched creature per three levels
Duration: 1 min./level (D)
Spell Resistance: Yes

This spell functions like *ethereal jaunt*, except that you and other willing creatures joined by linked hands (along with their equipment) become ethereal. Besides yourself, you can bring one creature per three caster levels to the Ethereal Plane. Once ethereal, the subjects need not stay together.

When the spell expires, all affected creatures on the Ethereal Plane return to material existence.

Evard's Black Tentacles

Conjuration (Creation)
Level: Sor/Wiz 4
Components: V, S, M
Casting Time: 1 standard action
Range: Medium (100 ft. + 10 ft./level)
Area: 20-ft.-radius spread
Duration: 1 round/level (D)
Saving Throw: None
Spell Resistance: No

This spell conjures a field of rubbery black tentacles, each 10 feet long. These waving members seem to spring forth from the earth, floor, or whatever surface is underfoot—including water. They grasp and entwine around creatures that enter the area, holding them fast and crushing them with great strength.

Every creature within the area of the spell must make a grapple check, opposed by the grapple check of the tentacles. Treat the tentacles attacking a particular target as a Large creature with a base attack bonus equal to your caster level and a Strength score of 19. Thus, its grapple check modifier is equal to your caster level +8. The tentacles are immune to all types of damage.

Once the tentacles grapple an opponent, they may make a grapple check each round on your turn to deal 1d6+4 points of bludgeoning damage. The tentacles continue to crush the opponent until the spell ends or the opponent escapes.

Any creature that enters the area of the spell is immediately attacked by the tentacles. Even creatures who aren't grappling with the tentacles may move through the area at only half normal speed.

Material Component: A piece of tentacle from a giant octopus or a giant squid.

Expeditious Retreat

Transmutation
Level: Brd 1, Sor/Wiz 1
Components: V, S
Casting Time: 1 standard action
Range: Personal
Target: You
Duration: 1 min./level (D)

This spell increases your base land speed by 30 feet. (This adjustment is treated as an enhancement bonus.) There is no effect on other modes of movement, such as burrow, climb, fly, or swim. As with any effect that increases your speed, this spell affects your jumping distance (see the Jump skill, page 77).

This spell need not be used as part of a retreat; the name of the spell merely hints at the typical wizard's attitude toward combat.

Explosive Runes

Abjuration [Force]
Level: Sor/Wiz 3
Components: V, S
Casting Time: 1 standard action
Range: Touch
Target: One touched object weighing no more than 10 lb.
Duration: Permanent until discharged (D)
Saving Throw: See text
Spell Resistance: Yes

You trace these mystic runes upon a book, map, scroll, or similar object bearing written information. The *runes* detonate when read, dealing 6d6 points of force damage. Anyone next to the *runes* (close enough to read them) takes the full damage with no saving throw; any other creature within 10 feet of the *runes* is entitled to a Reflex save for half damage. The object on which the *runes* were written also takes full damage (no saving throw).

You and any characters you specifically instruct can read the protected writing without triggering the *runes*. Likewise, you can remove the *runes* whenever desired. Another creature can remove them with a successful *dispel magic* or *erase* spell, but attempting to dispel or erase the *runes* and failing to do so triggers the explosion.

Note: Magic traps such as *explosive runes* are hard to detect and disable. A rogue (only) can use the Search skill to find the *runes* and Disable Device to thwart them. The DC in each case is 25 + spell level, or 28 for *explosive runes*.

Eyebite

Necromancy [Evil]
Level: Brd 6, Sor/Wiz 6
Components: V, S
Casting Time: 1 standard action
Range: Close (25 ft. + 5 ft./2 levels)
Target: One living creature
Duration: 1 round per three levels; see text
Saving Throw: Fortitude negates
Spell Resistance: Yes

Each round, you may target a single living creature, striking it with waves of evil power. Depending on the target's HD, this attack has as many as three effects.

HD	Effect
10 or more	Sickened
5–9	Panicked, sickened
4 or less	Comatose, panicked, sickened

The effects are cumulative and concurrent.

Sickened: Sudden pain and fever sweeps over the subject's body. A sickened creature takes a –2 penalty on attack rolls, weapon damage rolls, saving throws, skill checks, and ability checks. A creature affected by this spell remains sickened for 10 minutes per caster level. The effects cannot be negated by a *remove disease* or *heal* spell, but a *remove curse* is effective.

Panicked: The subject becomes panicked for 1d4 rounds. Even after the panic ends, the creature remains shaken for 10 minutes per caster level, and it automatically becomes panicked again if it comes within sight of you during that time. This is a fear effect.

Comatose: The subject falls into a catatonic coma for 10 minutes per caster level. During this time, it cannot be awakened by any means short of dispelling the effect. This is not a *sleep* effect, and thus elves are not immune to it.

The spell lasts for 1 round per three caster levels. You must spend a move action each round after the first to target a foe.

Fabricate
Transmutation
Level: Sor/Wiz 5
Components: V, S, M
Casting Time: See text
Range: Close (25 ft. + 5 ft./2 levels)
Target: Up to 10 cu. ft./level; see text
Duration: Instantaneous
Saving Throw: None
Spell Resistance: No

You convert material of one sort into a product that is of the same material. Thus, you can fabricate a wooden bridge from a clump of trees, a rope from a patch of hemp, clothes from flax or wool, and so forth. Creatures or magic items cannot be created or transmuted by the *fabricate* spell. The quality of items made by this spell is commensurate with the quality of material used as the basis for the new fabrication. If you work with a mineral, the target is reduced to 1 cubic foot per level instead of 10 cubic feet.

You must make an appropriate Craft check to fabricate articles requiring a high degree of craftsmanship (jewelry, swords, glass, crystal, and the like).

Casting requires 1 round per 10 cubic feet (or 1 cubic foot) of material to be affected by the spell.

Material Component: The original material, which costs the same amount as the raw materials required to craft the item to be created.

Faerie Fire
Evocation [Light]
Level: Drd 1
Components: V, S, DF
Casting Time: 1 standard action
Range: Long (400 ft. + 40 ft./level)
Area: Creatures and objects within a 5-ft.-radius burst
Duration: 1 min./level (D)
Saving Throw: None
Spell Resistance: Yes

A pale glow surrounds and outlines the subjects. Outlined subjects shed light as candles. Outlined creatures do not benefit from the concealment normally provided by darkness (though a 2nd-level or higher magical *darkness* effect functions normally), *blur*, displacement, invisibility, or similar effects. The light is too dim to have any special effect on undead or dark-dwelling creatures vulnerable to light. The *faerie fire* can be blue, green, or violet, according to your choice at the

time of casting. The *faerie fire* does not cause any harm to the objects or creatures thus outlined.

False Life
Necromancy
Level: Sor/Wiz 2
Components: V, S, M
Casting Time: 1 standard action
Range: Personal
Target: You
Duration: 1 hour/level or until discharged; see text

You harness the power of unlife to grant yourself a limited ability to avoid death. While this spell is in effect, you gain temporary hit points equal to 1d10 +1 per caster level (maximum +10).

Material Component: A small amount of alcohol or distilled spirits, which you use to trace certain sigils on your body during casting. These sigils cannot be seen once the alcohol or spirits evaporate.

False Vision
Illusion (Glamer)
Level: Brd 5, Sor/Wiz 5, Trickery 5
Components: V, S, M
Casting Time: 1 standard action
Range: Touch
Area: 40-ft.-radius emanation
Duration: 1 hour/level (D)
Saving Throw: None
Spell Resistance: No

Any divination (scrying) spell used to view anything within the area of this spell instead receives a false image (as the *major image* spell), as defined by you at the time of casting. As long as the duration lasts, you can concentrate to change the image as desired. While you aren't concentrating, the image remains static.

Arcane Material Component: The ground dust of a piece of jade worth at least 250 gp, which is sprinkled into the air when the spell is cast.

Fear
Necromancy [Fear, Mind-Affecting]
Level: Brd 3, Sor/Wiz 4
Components: V, S, M
Casting Time: 1 standard action
Range: 30 ft.
Area: Cone-shaped burst
Duration: 1 round/level or 1 round; see text
Saving Throw: Will partial
Spell Resistance: Yes

An invisible cone of terror causes each living creature in the area to become panicked unless it succeeds on a Will save. If cornered, a panicked creature begins cowering. (See the *Dungeon Master's Guide* for more information on fear-panicked crea-

tures.) If the Will save succeeds, the creature is shaken for 1 round.

Material Component: Either the heart of a hen or a white feather.

Feather Fall
Transmutation
Level: Brd 1, Sor/Wiz 1
Components: V
Casting Time: 1 free action
Range: Close (25 ft. + 5 ft./2 levels)
Targets: One Medium or smaller free-falling object or creature/level, no two of which may be more than 20 ft. apart
Duration: Until landing or 1 round/level
Saving Throw: Will negates (harmless) or Will negates (object)
Spell Resistance: Yes (object)

The affected creatures or objects fall slowly, though faster than feathers typically do. *Feather fall* instantly changes the rate at which the targets fall to a mere 60 feet per round (equivalent to the end of a fall from a few feet), and the subjects take no damage upon landing while the spell is in effect. However, when the spell duration expires, a normal rate of falling resumes.

The spell affects one or more Medium or smaller creatures (including gear and carried objects up to each creature's maximum load) or objects, or the equivalent in larger creatures: A Large creature or object counts as two Medium creatures or objects, a Huge creature or object counts as two Large creatures or objects, and so forth.

You can cast this spell with an instant utterance, quickly enough to save yourself if you unexpectedly fall. Casting the spell is a free action, like casting a quickened spell, and it counts toward the normal limit of one quickened spell per round. You may even cast this spell when it isn't your turn.

This spell has no special effect on ranged weapons unless they are falling quite a distance. If the spell is cast on a falling item, such as a boulder dropped from the top of a castle wall, the object does half normal damage based on its weight, with no bonus for the height of the drop. (See the *Dungeon Master's Guide* for information on falling objects.)

Feather fall works only upon free-falling objects. It does not affect a sword blow or a charging or flying creature.

Feeblemind
Enchantment (Compulsion) [Mind-Affecting]
Level: Sor/Wiz 5
Components: V, S, M
Casting Time: 1 standard action
Range: Medium (100 ft. + 10 ft./level)
Target: One creature
Duration: Instantaneous

Saving Throw: Will negates; see text
Spell Resistance: Yes

If the target creature fails a Will saving throw, its Intelligence and Charisma scores each drop to 1, giving it roughly the intellect of a lizard. The affected creature is unable to use Intelligence- or Charisma-based skills, cast spells, understand language, or communicate coherently. Still, it knows who its friends are and can follow them and even protect them. The subject remains in this state until a *heal*, *limited wish*, *miracle*, or *wish* spell is used to cancel the effect of the *feeblemind*. A creature that can cast arcane spells, such as a sorcerer or a wizard, takes a –4 penalty on its saving throw.

Material Component: A handful of clay, crystal, glass, or mineral spheres.

Find the Path

Divination
Level: Brd 6, Clr 6, Drd 6, Knowledge 6, Travel 6
Components: V, S, F
Casting Time: 3 rounds
Range: Personal or touch
Target: You or creature touched
Duration: 10 min./level
Saving Throw: None or Will negates (harmless)
Spell Resistance: No or Yes (harmless)

The recipient of this spell can find the shortest, most direct physical route to a specified destination, be it the way into or out of a locale. The locale can be outdoors, underground, or even inside a *maze* spell. *Find the path* works with respect to locations, not objects or creatures at a locale. Thus, the subject could not find the way to "a forest where a green dragon lives" or "a hoard of platinum pieces," but it could find the exit to a labyrinth. The location must be on the same plane as you are at the time of casting.

The spell enables the subject to sense the correct direction that will eventually lead it to its destination, indicating at appropriate times the exact path to follow or physical actions to take. For example, the spell enables the subject to sense trip wires or the proper word to bypass a *glyph of warding*. The spell ends when the destination is reached or the duration expires, whichever comes first. *Find the path* can be used to remove the subject and its companions from the effect of a *maze* spell in a single round.

This divination is keyed to the recipient, not its companions, and its effect does not predict or allow for the actions of creatures (including guardians).

Focus: A set of divination counters of the sort you favor—bones, ivory counters, sticks, carved runes, or the like

Find Traps

Divination
Level: Clr 2
Components: V, S
Casting Time: 1 standard action
Range: Personal
Target: You
Duration: 1 min./level

You gain intuitive insight into the workings of traps. You can use the Search skill to detect traps just as a rogue can. In addition, you gain an insight bonus equal to one-half your caster level (maximum +10) on Search checks made to find traps while the spell is in effect.

Note that *find traps* grants no ability to disable the traps that you may find.

Finger of Death

Necromancy [Death]
Level: Drd 8, Sor/Wiz 7
Components: V, S
Casting Time: 1 standard action
Range: Close (25 ft. + 5 ft./2 levels)
Target: One living creature
Duration: Instantaneous
Saving Throw: Fortitude partial
Spell Resistance: Yes

You can slay any one living creature within range. The target is entitled to a Fortitude saving throw to survive the attack. If the save is successful, the creature instead takes 3d6 points of damage +1 point per caster level (maximum +25). The subject might die from damage even if it succeeds on its saving throw.

Fire Seeds

Conjuration (Creation) [Fire]
Level: Drd 6, Fire 6, Sun 6
Components: V, S, M
Casting Time: 1 standard action
Range: Touch
Targets: Up to four touched acorns or up to eight touched holly berries
Duration: 10 min./level or until used
Saving Throw: None or Reflex half; see text
Spell Resistance: No

Depending on the version of *fire seeds* you choose, you turn acorns into splash weapons that you or another character can throw, or you turn holly berries into bombs that you can detonate on command.

Acorn Grenades: As many as four acorns turn into special splash weapons that can be hurled as far as 100 feet. A ranged touch attack roll is required to strike the intended target. Together, the acorns are capable of dealing 1d6 points of fire damage per caster level (maximum 20d6), divided up among the acorns as you wish. For example, a 20th-level druid could create one 20d6 missile, two 10d6 mis-siles, one 11d6 and three 3d6 missiles, or any other combination totaling up to four acorns and 20d6 points of damage.

Each acorn explodes upon striking any hard surface. In addition to its regular fire damage, it deals 1 point of splash damage per die, and it ignites any combustible materials within 10 feet. A creature within this area that makes a successful Reflex saving throw takes only half damage; a creature struck directly is not allowed a saving throw.

Holly Berry Bombs: You turn as many as eight holly berries into special bombs. The holly berries are usually placed by hand, since they are too light to make effective thrown weapons (they can be tossed only 5 feet). If you are within 200 feet and speak a word of command, each berry instantly bursts into flame, causing 1d8 points of fire damage +1 point per caster level to every creature in a 5-foot-radius burst and igniting any combustible materials within 5 feet. A creature in the area that makes a successful Reflex saving throw takes only half damage.

Material Component: The acorns or holly berries.

Fire Shield

Evocation [Fire or Cold]
Level: Fire 5, Sor/Wiz 4, Sun 4
Components: V, S, M/DF
Casting Time: 1 standard action
Range: Personal
Target: You
Duration: 1 round/level (D)

This spell wreathes you in flame and causes damage to each creature that attacks you in melee. The flames also protect you from either cold-based or fire-based attacks (your choice).

Any creature striking you with its body or a handheld weapon deals normal damage, but at the same time the attacker takes 1d6 points of damage +1 point per caster level (maximum +15). This damage is either cold damage (if the *shield* protects against fire-based attacks) or fire damage (if the *shield* protects against cold-based attacks). If the attacker has spell resistance, it applies to this effect. Creatures wielding weapons with exceptional reach, such as longspears, are not subject to this damage if they attack you.

When casting this spell, you appear to immolate yourself, but the flames are thin and wispy, giving off light equal to only half the illumination of a normal torch (10 feet). The color of the flames is determined randomly (50% chance of either color)—blue or green if the *chill shield* is cast, violet or blue if the *warm shield* is employed. The special powers of each version are as follows.

Warm Shield: The flames are warm to the touch. You take only half damage from cold-based attacks. If such an attack allows a Reflex save for half damage, you take no damage on a successful save.

Chill Shield: The flames are cool to the touch. You take only half damage from fire-based attacks. If such an attack allows a Reflex save for half damage, you take no damage on a successful save.

Arcane Material Component: A bit of phosphorus for the *warm shield;* a live firefly or glowworm or the tail portions of four dead ones for the *chill shield.*

Fire Storm

Evocation [Fire]
Level: Clr 8, Drd 7, Fire 7
Components: V, S
Casting Time: 1 round
Range: Medium (100 ft. + 10 ft./level)
Area: Two 10-ft. cubes per level (S)
Duration: Instantaneous
Saving Throw: Reflex half
Spell Resistance: Yes

When a *fire storm* spell is cast, the whole area is shot through with sheets of roaring flame. The raging flames do not harm natural vegetation, ground cover, and any plant creatures in the area that you wish to exclude from damage. Any other creature within the area takes 1d6 points of fire damage per caster level (maximum 20d6).

Fire Trap

Abjuration [Fire]
Level: Drd 2, Sor/Wiz 4
Components: V, S, M
Casting Time: 10 minutes
Range: Touch
Target: Object touched
Duration: Permanent until discharged (D)
Saving Throw: Reflex half; see text
Spell Resistance: Yes

Fire trap creates a fiery explosion when an intruder opens the item that the trap protects. A *fire trap* can ward any object that can be opened and closed (book, box, bottle, chest, coffer, coffin, door, drawer, and so forth).

When casting *fire trap,* you select a point on the object as the spell's center. When someone other than you opens the object, a fiery explosion fills the area within a 5-foot radius around the spell's center. The flames deal 1d4 points of fire damage +1 point per caster level (maximum +20). The item protected by the trap is not harmed by this explosion.

A *fire trapped* item cannot have a second closure or warding spell placed on it.

A *knock* spell does not bypass a *fire trap.* An unsuccessful *dispel magic* spell does not detonate the spell.

Underwater, this ward deals half damage and creates a large cloud of steam.

You can use the *fire trapped* object without discharging it, as can any individual to whom the object was specifically attuned when cast. Attuning a *fire trapped* object to an individual usually involves setting a password that you can share with friends.

Note: Magic traps such as *fire trap* are hard to detect and disable. A rogue (only) can use the Search skill to find a *fire trap* and Disable Device to thwart it. The DC in each case is 25 + spell level (DC 27 for a druid's *fire trap* or DC 29 for the arcane version).

Material Component: A half-pound of gold dust (cost 25 gp) sprinkled on the warded object.

Fireball

Evocation [Fire]
Level: Sor/Wiz 3
Components: V, S, M
Casting Time: 1 standard action
Range: Long (400 ft. + 40 ft./level)
Area: 20-ft.-radius spread
Duration: Instantaneous
Saving Throw: Reflex half
Spell Resistance: Yes

A *fireball* spell is an explosion of flame that detonates with a low roar and deals 1d6 points of fire damage per caster level (maximum 10d6) to every creature within the area. Unattended objects also take this damage. The explosion creates almost no pressure.

You point your finger and determine the range (distance and height) at which the *fireball* is to burst. A glowing, pea-sized bead streaks from the pointing digit and, unless it impacts upon a material body or solid barrier prior to attaining the prescribed range, blossoms into the *fireball* at that point. (An early impact results in an early detonation.) If you attempt to send the bead through a narrow passage, such as through an arrow slit, you must "hit" the opening with a ranged touch attack, or else the bead strikes the barrier and detonates prematurely.

The *fireball* sets fire to combustibles and damages objects in the area. It can melt metals with low melting points, such as lead, gold, copper, silver, and bronze. If the damage caused to an interposing barrier shatters or breaks through it, the *fireball* may continue beyond the barrier if the area permits; otherwise it stops at the barrier just as any other spell effect does.

Material Component: A tiny ball of bat guano and sulfur.

Flame Arrow

Transmutation [Fire]
Level: Sor/Wiz 3
Components: V, S, M

Casting Time: 1 standard action
Range: Close (25 ft. + 5 ft./2 levels)
Target: Fifty projectiles, all of which must be in contact with each other at the time of casting
Duration: 10 min./level
Saving Throw: None
Spell Resistance: No

You turn ammunition (such as arrows, bolts, shuriken, and stones) into fiery projectiles. Each piece of ammunition deals an extra 1d6 points of fire damage to any target it hits. A flaming projectile can easily ignite a flammable object or structure, but it won't ignite a creature it strikes.

Material Component: A drop of oil and a small piece of flint.

Flame Blade

Evocation [Fire]
Level: Drd 2
Components: V, S, DF
Casting Time: 1 standard action
Range: 0 ft.
Effect: Swordlike beam
Duration: 1 min./level (D)
Saving Throw: None
Spell Resistance: Yes

A 3-foot-long, blazing beam of red-hot fire springs forth from your hand. You wield this bladelike beam as if it were a scimitar. Attacks with the *flame blade* are melee touch attacks. The blade deals 1d8 points of fire damage +1 point per two caster levels (maximum +10). Since the blade is immaterial, your Strength modifier does not apply to the damage. A *flame blade* can ignite combustible materials such as parchment, straw, dry sticks, and cloth.

The spell does not function underwater.

Flame Strike

Evocation [Fire]
Level: Clr 5, Drd 4, Sun 5, War 5
Components: V, S, DF
Casting Time: 1 standard action
Range: Medium (100 ft. + 10 ft./level)
Area: Cylinder (10-ft. radius, 40 ft. high)
Duration: Instantaneous
Saving Throw: Reflex half
Spell Resistance: Yes

A *flame strike* produces a vertical column of divine fire roaring downward. The spell deals 1d6 points of damage per caster level (maximum 15d6). Half the damage is fire damage, but the other half results directly from divine power and is therefore not subject to being reduced by resistance to fire-based attacks, such as that granted by *protection from energy* (fire), *fire shield* (*chill shield*), and similar magic.

Flaming Sphere

Evocation [Fire]

Level: Drd 2, Sor/Wiz 2
Components: V, S, M/DF
Casting Time: 1 standard action
Range: Medium (100 ft. + 10 ft./level)
Effect: 5-ft.-diameter sphere
Duration: 1 round/level
Saving Throw: Reflex negates
Spell Resistance: Yes

A burning globe of fire rolls in whichever direction you point and burns those it strikes. It moves 30 feet per round. As part of this movement, it can ascend or jump up to 30 feet to strike a target. If it enters a space with a creature, it stops moving for the round and deals 2d6 points of fire damage to that creature, though a successful Reflex save negates that damage. A *flaming sphere* rolls over barriers less than 4 feet tall, such as furniture and low walls. It ignites flammable substances it touches and illuminates the same area as a torch would.

The sphere moves as long as you actively direct it (a move action for you); otherwise, it merely stays at rest and burns. It can be extinguished by any means that would put out a normal fire of its size. The surface of the sphere has a spongy, yielding consistency and so does not cause damage except by its flame. It cannot push aside unwilling creatures or batter down large obstacles. A *flaming sphere* winks out if it exceeds the spell's range.

Arcane Material Component: A bit of tallow, a pinch of brimstone, and a dusting of powdered iron.

Flare

Evocation [Light]

Level: Brd 0, Drd 0, Sor/Wiz 0
Components: V
Casting Time: 1 standard action
Range: Close (25 ft. + 5 ft./2 levels)
Effect: Burst of light
Duration: Instantaneous
Saving Throw: Fortitude negates
Spell Resistance: Yes

This cantrip creates a burst of light. If you cause the light to burst directly in front of a single creature, that creature is dazzled for 1 minute unless it makes a successful Fortitude save. Sightless creatures, as well as creatures already dazzled, are not affected by *flare*.

Flesh to Stone

Transmutation

Level: Sor/Wiz 6
Components: V, S, M
Casting Time: 1 standard action
Range: Medium (100 ft. + 10 ft./level)
Target: One creature
Duration: Instantaneous
Saving Throw: Fortitude negates
Spell Resistance: Yes

The subject, along with all its carried gear, turns into a mindless, inert statue. If the statue resulting from this spell is broken or damaged, the subject (if ever returned to its original state) has similar damage or deformities. The creature is not dead, but it does not seem to be alive either when viewed with spells such as *deathwatch*. Only creatures made of flesh are affected by this spell.

Material Component: Lime, water, and earth.

Fly

Transmutation

Level: Sor/Wiz 3, Travel 3
Components: V, S, F/DF
Casting Time: 1 standard action
Range: Touch
Target: Creature touched
Duration: 1 min./level
Saving Throw: Will negates (harmless)
Spell Resistance: Yes (harmless)

The subject can fly at a speed of 60 feet (or 40 feet if it wears medium or heavy armor, or if it carries a medium or heavy load). It can ascend at half speed and descend at double speed, and its maneuverability is good. Using a *fly* spell requires only as much concentration as walking, so the subject can attack or cast spells normally. The subject of a *fly* spell can charge but not run, and it cannot carry aloft more weight than its maximum load, plus any armor it wears.

Should the spell duration expire while the subject is still aloft, the magic fails slowly. The subject floats downward 60 feet per round for 1d6 rounds. If it reaches the ground in that amount of time, it lands safely. If not, it falls the rest of the distance, taking 1d6 points of damage per 10 feet of fall. Since dispelling a spell effectively ends it, the subject also descends in this way if the *fly* spell is dispelled, but not if it is negated by an *antimagic field*.

Arcane Focus: A wing feather from any bird.

Fog Cloud

Conjuration (Creation)

Level: Drd 2, Sor/Wiz 2, Water 2
Components: V, S
Casting Time: 1 standard action
Range: Medium (100 ft. + 10 ft. level)
Effect: Fog spreads in 20-ft. radius, 20 ft. high
Duration: 10 min./level
Saving Throw: None
Spell Resistance: No

A bank of fog billows out from the point you designate. The fog obscures all sight, including darkvision, beyond 5 feet. A creature within 5 feet has concealment (attacks have a 20% miss chance). Creatures farther away have total concealment (50% miss chance, and the attacker can't use sight to locate the target).

A moderate wind (11+ mph) disperses the fog in 4 rounds; a strong wind (21+ mph) disperses the fog in 1 round.

The spell does not function underwater.

Forbiddance

Abjuration

Level: Clr 6
Components: V, S, M, DF
Casting Time: 6 rounds
Range: Medium (100 ft. + 10 ft./level)
Area: 60-ft. cube/level (S)
Duration: Permanent
Saving Throw: See text
Spell Resistance: Yes

Forbiddance seals an area against all planar travel into or within it. This includes all teleportation spells (such as *dimension door* and *teleport*), *plane shifting*, astral travel, ethereal travel, and all summoning spells. Such effects simply fail automatically.

In addition, it damages entering creatures whose alignments are different from yours. The effect on those attempting to enter the warded area is based on their alignment relative to yours (see below). A creature inside the area when the spell is cast takes no damage unless it exits the area and attempts to reenter, at which time it is affected as normal.

Alignments identical: No effect. The creature may enter the area freely (although not by planar travel).

Alignments different with respect to either law/chaos or good/evil: The creature takes 6d6 points of damage. A successful Will save halves the damage, and spell resistance applies.

Alignments different with respect to both law/chaos and good/evil: The creature takes 12d6 points of damage. A successful Will save halves the damage, and spell resistance applies.

At your option, the abjuration can include a password, in which case creatures of alignments different from yours can avoid the damage by speaking the password as they enter the area. You must select this option (and the password) at the time of casting.

Dispel magic does not dispel a *forbiddance* effect unless the dispeller's level is at least as high as your caster level.

You can't have multiple overlapping *forbiddance* effects. In such a case, the more recent effect stops at the boundary of the older effect.

Material Component: A sprinkling of holy water and rare incenses worth at least 1,500 gp, plus 1,500 gp per 60-foot cube. If a password is desired, this requires the burning of additional rare incenses worth at least 1,000 gp, plus 1,000 gp per 60-foot cube.

Forcecage

Evocation [Force]
Level: Sor/Wiz 7
Components: V, S, M
Casting Time: 1 standard action
Range: Close (25 ft. + 5 ft./2 levels)
Area: Barred cage (20-ft. cube) or windowless cell (10-ft. cube)
Duration: 2 hours/level (D)
Saving Throw: None
Spell Resistance: No

This powerful spell brings into being an immobile, invisible cubical prison composed of either bars of force or solid walls of force (your choice).

Creatures within the area are caught and contained unless they are too big to fit inside, in which case the spell automatically fails. Teleportation and other forms of astral travel provide a means of escape, but the force walls or bars extend into the Ethereal Plane, blocking ethereal travel.

Like a *wall of force* spell, a *forcecage* resists *dispel magic*, but it is vulnerable to a *disintegrate* spell, and it can be destroyed by a *sphere of annihilation* or a *rod of cancellation*.

Barred Cage: This version of the spell produces a 20-foot cube made of bands of force (similar to a *wall of force* spell) for bars. The bands are a half-inch wide, with half-inch gaps between them. Any creature capable of passing through such a small space can escape; others are confined. You can't attack a creature in a barred cage with a weapon unless the weapon can fit between the gaps. Even against such weapons (including arrows and similar ranged attacks), a creature in the barred cage has cover. All spells and breath weapons can pass through the gaps in the bars.

Windowless Cell: This version of the spell produces a 10-foot cube with no way in and no way out. Solid walls of force form its six sides.

Material Component: Ruby dust worth 1,500 gp, which is tossed into the air and disappears when you cast the spell.

Foresight

Divination
Level: Drd 9, Knowledge 9, Sor/Wiz 9
Components: V, S, M/DF
Casting Time: 1 standard action
Range: Personal or touch
Target: See text
Duration: 10 min./level
Saving Throw: None or Will negates (harmless)
Spell Resistance: No or Yes (harmless)

This spell grants you a powerful sixth sense in relation to yourself or another. Once *foresight* is cast, you receive instantaneous warnings of impending danger or harm to the subject of the spell. Thus, if you are the subject of the spell, you would be warned in advance if a rogue were about to attempt a sneak attack on you, or if a creature were about to leap out from a hiding place, or if an attacker were specifically targeting you with a spell or ranged weapon. You are never surprised or flat-footed. In addition, the spell gives you a general idea of what action you might take to best protect yourself—duck, jump right, close your eyes, and so on—and gives you a +2 insight bonus to AC and Reflex saves. This insight bonus is lost whenever you would lose a Dexterity bonus to AC.

When another creature is the subject of the spell, you receive warnings about that creature. You must communicate what you learn to the other creature for the warning to be useful, and the creature can be caught unprepared in the absence of such a warning. Shouting a warning, yanking a person back, and even telepathically communicating (via an appropriate spell) can all be accomplished before some danger befalls the subject, provided you act on the warning without delay. The subject, however, does not gain the insight bonus to AC and Reflex saves.

Arcane Material Component: A hummingbird's feather.

Fox's Cunning

Transmutation
Level: Brd 2, Sor/Wiz 2
Components: V, S, M/DF
Casting Time: 1 standard action
Range: Touch
Target: Creature touched
Duration: 1 min./level
Saving Throw: Will negates (harmless)
Spell Resistance: Yes

The transmuted creature becomes smarter. The spell grants a +4 enhancement bonus to Intelligence, adding the usual benefits to Intelligence-based skill checks and other uses of the Intelligence modifier. Wizards (and other spellcasters who rely on Intelligence) affected by this spell do not gain any additional bonus spells for the increased Intelligence, but the save DCs for spells they cast while under this spell's effect do increase. This spell doesn't grant extra skill points.

Arcane Material Component: A few hairs, or a pinch of dung, from a fox.

Fox's Cunning, Mass

Transmutation
Level: Brd 6, Sor/Wiz 6
Range: Close (25 ft. + 5 ft./2 levels)
Target: One creature/level, no two of which can be more than 30 ft. apart

This spell functions like *fox's cunning*, except that it affects multiple creatures.

Freedom

Abjuration
Level: Sor/Wiz 9
Components: V, S
Casting Time: 1 standard action
Range: Close (25 ft. + 5 ft./2 levels) or see text
Target: One creature
Duration: Instantaneous
Saving Throw: Will negates (harmless)
Spell Resistance: Yes

The subject is freed from spells and effects that restrict its movement, including *binding*, *entangle*, grappling, *imprisonment*, *maze*, paralysis, *petrification*, pinning, *sleep*, *slow*, stunning, *temporal stasis*, and *web*. To free a creature from *imprisonment* or *maze*, you must know its name and background, and you must cast this spell at the spot where it was entombed or banished into the *maze*.

Freedom of Movement

Abjuration
Level: Brd 4, Clr 4, Drd 4, Luck 4, Rgr 4
Components: V, S, M, DF
Casting Time: 1 standard action
Range: Personal or touch
Target: You or creature touched
Duration: 10 min./level
Saving Throw: Will negates (harmless)
Spell Resistance: Yes (harmless)

This spell enables you or a creature you touch to move and attack normally for the duration of the spell, even under the influence of magic that usually impedes movement, such as paralysis, *solid fog*, *slow*, and *web*. The subject automatically succeeds on any grapple check made to resist a grapple attempt, as well as on grapple checks or Escape Artist checks made to escape a grapple or a pin.

The spell also allows the subject to move and attack normally while underwater, even with slashing weapons such as axes and swords or with bludgeoning weapons such as flails, hammers, and maces, provided that the weapon is wielded in the hand rather than hurled. The *freedom of movement* spell does not, however, allow water breathing.

Material Component: A leather thong, bound around the arm or a similar appendage.

Gaseous Form

Transmutation
Level: Air 3, Brd 3, Sor/Wiz 3
Components: S, M/DF
Casting Time: 1 standard action
Range: Touch
Target: Willing corporeal creature touched
Duration: 2 min./level (D)
Saving Throw: None
Spell Resistance: No

The subject and all its gear become insubstantial, misty, and translucent. Its material armor (including natural armor) becomes worthless, though its size, Dexterity, deflection bonuses, and armor bonuses from force effects (for example, from the *mage armor* spell) still apply. The subject gains damage reduction 10/magic and becomes immune to poison and critical hits. It can't attack or cast spells with verbal, somatic, material, or focus components while in gaseous form. (This does not rule out the use of certain spells that the subject may have prepared using the feats Silent Spell, Still Spell, and Eschew Materials.) The subject also loses supernatural abilities while in gaseous form. If it has a touch spell ready to use, that spell is discharged harmlessly when the *gaseous form* spell takes effect.

A gaseous creature can't run, but it can fly at a speed of 10 feet (maneuverability perfect). It can pass through small holes or narrow openings, even mere cracks, with all it was wearing or holding in its hands, as long as the spell persists. The creature is subject to the effects of wind, and it can't enter water or other liquid. It also can't manipulate objects or activate items, even those carried along with its gaseous form. Continuously active items remain active, though in some cases their effects may be moot (such as those that supply armor or natural armor bonuses).

Arcane Material Component: A bit of gauze and a wisp of smoke.

Gate

Conjuration (Creation or Calling)
Level: Clr 9, Sor/Wiz 9
Components: V, S, XP; see text
Casting Time: 1 standard action
Range: Medium (100 ft. + 10 ft./level)
Effect: See text
Duration: Instantaneous or concentration (up to 1 round/level); see text
Saving Throw: None
Spell Resistance: No

Casting a *gate* spell has two effects. First, it creates an interdimensional connection between your plane of existence and a plane you specify, allowing travel between those two planes in either direction.

Second, you may then call a particular individual or kind of being through the *gate*.

The *gate* itself is a circular hoop or disk from 5 to 20 feet in diameter (caster's choice), oriented in the direction you desire when it comes into existence (typically vertical and facing you). It is a two-dimensional window looking into the plane you specified when casting the spell, and anyone or anything that moves through is shunted instantly to the other side.

A *gate* has a front and a back. Creatures moving through the *gate* from the front are transported to the other plane; creatures moving through it from the back are not.

Planar Travel: As a mode of planar travel, a *gate* spell functions much like a *plane shift* spell, except that the *gate* opens precisely at the point you desire (a creation effect). Deities and other beings who rule a planar realm can prevent a *gate* from opening in their presence or personal demesnes if they so desire. Travelers need not join hands with you—anyone who chooses to step through the portal is transported. A *gate* cannot be opened to another point on the same plane; the spell works only for interplanar travel.

You could position a *gate* in a hallway in order to absorb any attack or force coming at you by shunting it to another plane. Whether the denizens of that plane appreciate this tactic is, of course, another matter.

You may hold the *gate* open only for a brief time (no more than 1 round per caster level), and you must concentrate on doing so, or else the interplanar connection is severed.

Calling Creatures: The second effect of the *gate* spell is to call an extraplanar creature to your aid (a calling effect). By naming a particular being or kind of being as you cast the spell, you cause the *gate* to open in the immediate vicinity of the desired creature and pull the subject through, willing or unwilling. Deities and unique beings are under no compulsion to come through the *gate*, although they may choose to do so of their own accord. This use of the spell creates a *gate* that remains open just long enough to transport the called creatures. This use of the spell has an XP cost (see below).

If you choose to call a kind of creature instead of a known individual—for instance, a bearded devil or a ghaele eladrin—you may call either a single creature (of any HD) or several creatures. You can call and control several creatures as long as their HD total does not exceed your caster level. In the case of a single creature, you can control it if its HD do not exceed twice your caster level. A single creature with more HD than twice your caster level can't be controlled. Deities and unique beings cannot be controlled in any event. An uncontrolled being acts as it pleases, making the calling of such

creatures rather dangerous. An uncontrolled being may return to its home plane at any time.

A controlled creature can be commanded to perform a service for you. Such services fall into two categories: immediate tasks and contractual service. Fighting for you in a single battle or taking any other actions that can be accomplished within 1 round per caster level counts as an immediate task; you need not make any agreement or pay any reward for the creature's help. The creature departs at the end of the spell.

If you choose to exact a longer or more involved form of service from a called creature, you must offer some fair trade in return for that service. The service exacted must be reasonable with respect to the promised favor or reward; see the *lesser planar ally* spell for appropriate rewards. (Some creatures may want their payment in "livestock" rather than in coin, which could involve complications.) Immediately upon completion of the service, the being is transported to your vicinity, and you must then and there turn over the promised reward. After this is done, the creature is instantly freed to return to its own plane.

Failure to fulfill the promise to the letter results in your being subjected to service by the creature or by its liege and master, at the very least. At worst, the creature or its kin may attack you.

Note: When you use a calling spell such as *gate* to call an air, chaotic, earth, evil, fire, good, lawful, or water creature, it becomes a spell of that type. For example, *gate* is a chaotic and evil spell when you cast it to call a demon.

XP Cost: 1,000 XP (only for the *calling creatures* function).

Geas/Quest

Enchantment (Compulsion) [Language-Dependent, Mind-Affecting]
Level: Brd 6, Clr 6, Sor/Wiz 6
Casting Time: 10 minutes
Target: One living creature
Saving Throw: None

This spell functions similarly to *lesser geas*, except that it affects a creature of any HD and allows no saving throw.

Instead of taking penalties to ability scores (as with *lesser geas*), the subject takes 3d6 points of damage each day it does not attempt to follow the *geas/quest*. Additionally, each day it must make a Fortitude saving throw or become sickened. These effects end 24 hours after the creature attempts to resume the *geas/quest*.

A *remove curse* spell ends a *geas/quest* spell only if its caster level is at least two higher than your caster level. *Break en-*

chantment does not end a *geas/quest*, but *limited wish*, *miracle*, and *wish* do.

Bards, sorcerers, and wizards usually refer to this spell as *geas*, while clerics call the same spell *quest*.

Geas, Lesser

Enchantment (Compulsion) [Language-Dependent, Mind-Affecting]
Level: Brd 3, Sor/Wiz 4
Components: V
Casting Time: 1 round
Range: Close (25 ft. + 5 ft./2 levels)
Target: One living creature with 7 HD or less
Duration: One day/level or until discharged (D)
Saving Throw: Will negates
Spell Resistance: Yes

A *lesser geas* places a magical command on a creature to carry out some service or to refrain from some action or course of activity, as desired by you. The creature must have 7 or fewer Hit Dice and be able to understand you. While a *geas* cannot compel a creature to kill itself or perform acts that would result in certain death, it can cause almost any other course of activity. The *geased* creature must follow the given instructions until the *geas* is completed, no matter how long it takes.

If the instructions involve some open-ended task that the recipient cannot complete through his own actions (such as "Wait here" or "Defend this area against attack"), the spell remains in effect for a maximum of one day per caster level. A clever recipient can subvert some instructions: For example, if you order the recipient to protect you from all harm, it might place you in a nice, safe dungeon for the duration of the spell.

If the subject is prevented from obeying the *lesser geas* for 24 hours, it takes a −2 penalty to each of its ability scores. Each day, another −2 penalty accumulates, up to a total of −8. No ability score can be reduced to less than 1 by this effect. The ability score penalties are removed 24 hours after the subject resumes obeying the *lesser geas*.

A *lesser geas* (and all ability score penalties) can be ended by *break enchantment*, *limited wish*, *remove curse*, *miracle*, or *wish*. *Dispel magic* does not affect a *lesser geas*.

Gentle Repose

Necromancy
Level: Clr 2, Sor/Wiz 3
Components: V, S, M/DF
Casting Time: 1 standard action
Range: Touch
Target: Corpse touched
Duration: One day/level
Saving Throw: Will negates (object)
Spell Resistance: Yes (object)

You preserve the remains of a dead creature so that they do not decay. Doing so effectively extends the time limit on raising that creature from the dead (see *raise dead*). Days spent under the influence of this spell don't count against the time limit. Additionally, this spell makes transporting a fallen comrade more pleasant.

The spell also works on severed body parts and the like.

Arcane Material Component: A pinch of salt, and a copper piece for each eye the corpse has (or had).

Ghost Sound

Illusion (Figment)
Level: Brd 0, Sor/Wiz 0
Components: V, S, M
Casting Time: 1 standard action
Range: Close (25 ft. + 5 ft./2 levels)
Effect: Illusory sounds
Duration: 1 round/level (D)
Saving Throw: Will disbelief (if interacted with)
Spell Resistance: No

Ghost sound allows you to create a volume of sound that rises, recedes, approaches, or remains at a fixed place. You choose what type of sound *ghost sound* creates when casting it and cannot thereafter change the sound's basic character.

The volume of sound created depends on your level. You can produce as much noise as four normal humans per caster level (maximum twenty humans). Thus, talking, singing, shouting, walking, marching, or running sounds can be created. The noise a *ghost sound* spell produces can be virtually any type of sound within the volume limit. A horde of rats running and squeaking is about the same volume as eight humans running and shouting. A roaring lion is equal to the noise from sixteen humans, while a roaring dire tiger is equal to the noise from twenty humans.

Ghost sound can enhance the effectiveness of a *silent image* spell.

Ghost sound can be made permanent with a *permanency* spell.

Material Component: A bit of wool or a small lump of wax.

Ghoul Touch

Necromancy
Level: Sor/Wiz 2
Components: V, S, M
Casting Time: 1 standard action
Range: Touch
Target: Living humanoid touched
Duration: 1d6+2 rounds
Saving Throw: Fortitude negates
Spell Resistance: Yes

Imbuing you with negative energy, this spell allows you to paralyze a single living

humanoid for the duration of the spell with a successful melee touch attack.

Additionally, the paralyzed subject exudes a carrion stench that causes all living creatures (except you) in a 10-foot-radius spread to become sickened (Fortitude negates). A *neutralize poison* spell removes the effect from a sickened creature, and creatures immune to poison are unaffected by the stench.

Material Component: A small scrap of cloth taken from clothing worn by a ghoul, or a pinch of earth from a ghoul's lair.

Giant Vermin

Transmutation
Level: Clr 4, Drd 4
Components: V, S, DF
Casting Time: 1 standard action
Range: Close (25 ft. + 5 ft./2 levels)
Targets: Up to three vermin, no two of which can be more than 30 ft. apart
Duration: 1 min./level
Saving Throw: None
Spell Resistance: Yes

You turn three normal-sized centipedes, two normal-sized spiders, or a single normal-sized scorpion into larger forms. Only one type of vermin can be transmuted (so a single casting cannot affect both a centipede and a spider), and all must be grown to the same size. The size to which the vermin can be grown depends on your level; see the table below. The *Monster Manual* has game statistics for centipedes, spiders, and scorpions, as well as other kinds of vermin.

Any giant vermin created by this spell do not attempt to harm you, but your control of such creatures is limited to simple commands ("Attack," "Defend," "Stop," and so forth). Orders to attack a certain creature when it appears or guard against a particular occurrence are too complex for the vermin to understand. Unless commanded to do otherwise, the giant vermin attack whoever or whatever is near them.

The DM can extend this spell's effects to other kinds of insects, arachnids, or other vermin, such as ants, bees, beetles, praying mantises, and wasps, if he so chooses.

Caster Level	Vermin Size
9th or lower	Medium
10th–13th	Large
14th–17th	Huge
18th–19th	Gargantuan
20th or higher	Colossal

Glibness

Transmutation
Level: Brd 3
Components: S
Casting Time: 1 standard action
Range: Personal

Target: You
Duration: 10 min./level (D)

Your speech becomes fluent and more believable. You gain a +30 bonus on Bluff checks made to convince another of the truth of your words. (This bonus doesn't apply to other uses of the Bluff skill, such as feinting in combat, creating a diversion to hide, or communicating a hidden message via innuendo.)

If a divination is attempted against you that would detect your lies or force you to speak the truth (such as *discern lies* or *zone of truth*), the caster of the divination must succeed on a caster level check (1d20 + caster level) against a DC of 15 + your caster level to succeed. Failure means the divination does not detect your lies or force you to speak only the truth.

Glitterdust

Conjuration (Creation)
Level: Brd 2, Sor/Wiz 2
Components: V, S, M
Casting Time: 1 standard action
Range: Medium (100 ft. + 10 ft./level)
Area: Creatures and objects within 10-ft.-radius spread
Duration: 1 round/level
Saving Throw: Will negates (blinding only)
Spell Resistance: No

A cloud of golden particles covers everyone and everything in the area, causing creatures to become blinded and visibly outlining invisible things for the duration of the spell. All within the area are covered by the dust, which cannot be removed and continues to sparkle until it fades.

Any creature covered by the dust takes a –40 penalty on Hide checks.

Material Component: Ground mica.

Globe of Invulnerability

Abjuration
Level: Sor/Wiz 6

This spell functions like *lesser globe of invulnerability*, except that it also excludes 4th-level spells and spell-like effects.

Globe of Invulnerability, Lesser

Abjuration
Level: Sor/Wiz 4
Components: V, S, M
Casting Time: 1 standard action
Range: 10 ft.
Area: 10-ft.-radius spherical emanation, centered on you
Duration: 1 round/level (D)
Saving Throw: None
Spell Resistance: No

An immobile, faintly shimmering magical sphere surrounds you and excludes all spell effects of 3rd level or lower. The area or effect of any such spells does not include the area of the *lesser globe of invulnerability*. Such spells fail to affect any target located within the globe. Excluded effects include spell-like abilities and spells or spell-like effects from items. However, any type of spell can be cast through or out of the magical globe. Spells of 4th level and higher are not affected by the globe, nor are spells already in effect when the globe is cast. The globe can be brought down by a targeted *dispel magic* spell, but not by an area *dispel magic*. You can leave and return to the globe without penalty.

Note that spell effects are not disrupted unless their effects enter the globe, and even then they are merely suppressed, not dispelled. For example, creatures inside the globe would still see a *mirror image* created by a caster outside the globe. If that caster then entered the globe, the images would wink out, to reappear when the caster exited the globe. Likewise, a caster standing in the area of a *light* spell would still receive sufficient illumination for vision, even though that part of the *light* spell's area that lies within the globe would not be luminous.

If a given spell has more than one level depending on which character class is casting it, use the level appropriate to the caster to determine whether *lesser globe of invulnerability* stops it.

Material Component: A glass or crystal bead that shatters at the expiration of the spell.

Glyph of Warding

Abjuration
Level: Clr 3
Components: V, S, M
Casting Time: 10 minutes
Range: Touch
Target or Area: Object touched or up to 5 sq. ft./level
Duration: Permanent until discharged (D)
Saving Throw: See text
Spell Resistance: No (object) and Yes; see text

This powerful inscription harms those who enter, pass, or open the warded area or object. A *glyph of warding* can guard a bridge or passage, ward a portal, trap a chest or box, and so on.

You set the conditions of the ward. Typically, any creature entering the warded area or opening the warded object without speaking a password (which you set when casting the spell) is subject to the magic it stores. Alternatively or in addition to a password trigger, *glyphs* can be set according to physical characteristics (such as height or weight) or creature type, subtype, or kind (such as aberration, drow, or red dragon). *Glyphs* can also be set with respect to good, evil, law, or chaos, or to pass those of your religion. They cannot be set according to class, Hit Dice, or level. *Glyphs* respond to invisible creatures normally but are not triggered by those who travel past them ethereally. Multiple *glyphs* cannot be cast on the same area. However, if a cabinet has three drawers, each can be separately warded.

When casting the spell, you weave a tracery of faintly glowing lines around the warding sigil. A *glyph* can be placed to conform to any shape up to the limitations of your total square footage. When the spell is completed, the *glyph* and tracery become nearly invisible.

Glyphs cannot be affected or bypassed by such means as physical or magical probing, though they can be dispelled. *Mislead, polymorph,* and *nondetection* (and similar magical effects) can fool a *glyph*, though nonmagical disguises and the like can't.

Read magic allows you to identify a *glyph of warding* with a DC 13 Spellcraft check. Identifying the *glyph* does not discharge it and allows you to know the basic nature of the *glyph* (version, type of damage caused, what spell is stored).

The DM may decide that the exact *glyphs* available to you depend on your deity. He or she might also make new *glyphs* available according to the magical research rules in the *Dungeon Master's Guide*.

Note: Magic traps such as *glyph of warding* are hard to detect and disable. A rogue (only) can use the Search skill to find the *glyph* and Disable Device to thwart it. The DC in each case is 25 + spell level, or 28 for *glyph of warding*.

Depending on the version selected, a *glyph* either blasts the intruder or activates a spell.

Blast Glyph: A *blast glyph* deals 1d8 points of damage per two caster levels (maximum 5d8) to the intruder and to all within 5 feet of him or her. This damage is acid, cold, fire, electricity, or sonic (caster's choice, made at time of casting). Each creature affected can attempt a Reflex save to take half damage. Spell resistance applies against this effect.

Spell Glyph: You can store any harmful spell of 3rd level or lower that you know. All level-dependent features of the spell are based on your caster level at the time of casting the *glyph*. If the spell has a target, it targets the intruder. If the spell has an area or an amorphous effect (such as a cloud), the area or effect is centered on the intruder. If the spell summons creatures, they appear as close as possible to the intruder and attack. Saving throws and spell resistance operate as normal, except that the DC is based on the level of the spell stored in the *glyph*.

Material Component: You trace the *glyph* with incense, which must first be sprinkled with powdered diamond worth at least 200 gp.

Glyph of Warding, Greater
Abjuration
Level: Clr 6

This spell functions like *glyph of warding*, except that a *greater blast glyph* deals up to 10d8 points of damage, and a *greater spell glyph* can store a spell of 6th level or lower.
Material Component: You trace the *glyph* with incense, which must first be sprinkled with powdered diamond worth at least 400 gp.

Goodberry
Transmutation
Level: Drd 1
Components: V, S, DF
Casting Time: 1 standard action
Range: Touch
Targets: 2d4 fresh berries touched
Duration: One day/level
Saving Throw: None
Spell Resistance: Yes

Casting *goodberry* upon a handful of freshly picked berries makes 2d4 of them magical. You (as well as any other druid of 3rd or higher level) can immediately discern which berries are affected. Each transmuted berry provides nourishment as if it were a normal meal for a Medium creature. The berry also cures 1 point of damage when eaten, subject to a maximum of 8 points of such curing in any 24-hour period.

Good Hope
Enchantment (Compulsion) [Mind-Affecting]
Level: Brd 3
Components: V, S
Casting Time: 1 standard action
Range: Medium (100 ft. + 10 ft./level)
Targets: One living creature/level, no two of which may be more than 30 ft. apart
Duration: 1 min./level
Saving Throw: Will negates (harmless)
Spell Resistance: Yes (harmless)

This spell instills powerful hope in the subjects. Each affected creature gains a +2 morale bonus on saving throws, attack rolls, ability checks, skill checks, and weapon damage rolls.
Good hope counters and dispels *crushing despair*.

Grease
Conjuration (Creation)
Level: Brd 1, Sor/Wiz 1
Components: V, S, M
Casting Time: 1 standard action
Range: Close (25 ft. + 5 ft./2 levels)
Target or Area: One object or a 10-ft. square
Duration: 1 round/level (D)
Saving Throw: See text
Spell Resistance: No

A *grease* spell covers a solid surface with a layer of slippery grease. Any creature in the area when the spell is cast must make a successful Reflex save or fall. This save is repeated on your turn each round that the creature remains within the area. A creature can walk within or through the area of grease at half normal speed with a DC 10 Balance check. Failure means it can't move that round (and must then make a Reflex save or fall), while failure by 5 or more means it falls (see the Balance skill for details).

The DM should adjust saving throws by circumstance. For example, a creature charging down an incline that is suddenly *greased* has little chance to avoid the effect, but its ability to exit the affected area is almost assured (whether it wants to or not).

The spell can also be used to create a greasy coating on an item—a rope, ladder rungs, or a weapon handle, for instance. Material objects not in use are always affected by this spell, while an object wielded or employed by a creature receives a Reflex saving throw to avoid the effect. If the initial saving throw fails, the creature immediately drops the item. A saving throw must be made in each round that the creature attempts to pick up or use the *greased* item. A creature wearing *greased* armor or clothing gains a +10 circumstance bonus on Escape Artist checks and on grapple checks made to resist or escape a grapple or to escape a pin.
Material Component: A bit of pork rind or butter.

Greater (Spell Name)
Any spell whose name begins with *greater* is alphabetized in this chapter according to the second word of the spell name. Thus, the description of a *greater* spell appears near the description of the spell on which it is based. Spell chains that have *greater* spells in them include those based on the spells *arcane sight, command, dispel magic, glyph of warding, invisibility, magic fang, magic weapon, planar ally, planar binding, prying eyes, restoration, scrying, shadow conjuration, shadow evocation, shout,* and *teleport.*

Guards and Wards
Abjuration
Level: Sor/Wiz 6
Components: V, S, M, F
Casting Time: 30 minutes
Range: Anywhere within the area to be warded
Area: Up to 200 sq. ft./level (S)
Duration: 2 hours/level (D)
Saving Throw: See text
Spell Resistance: See text

This powerful spell is primarily used to defend your stronghold. The ward protects 200 square feet per caster level. The warded area can be as much as 20 feet high, and shaped as you desire. You can ward several stories of a stronghold by dividing the area among them; you must be somewhere within the area to be warded to cast the spell. The spell creates the following magical effects within the warded area.

Fog: Fog fills all corridors, obscuring all sight, including darkvision, beyond 5 feet. A creature within 5 feet has concealment (attacks have a 20% miss chance). Creatures farther away have total concealment (50% miss chance, and the attacker cannot use sight to locate the target). Saving Throw: None. Spell Resistance: No.

Arcane Locks: All doors in the warded area are *arcane locked.* Saving Throw: None. Spell Resistance: No.

Webs: Webs fill all stairs from top to bottom. These strands are identical with those created by the *web* spell, except that they regrow in 10 minutes if they are burned or torn away while the *guards and wards* spell lasts. Saving Throw: Reflex negates; see text for *web.* Spell Resistance: No.

Confusion: Where there are choices in direction—such as a corridor intersection or side passage—a minor *confusion*-type effect functions so as to make it 50% probable that intruders believe they are going in the opposite direction from the one they actually chose. This is an enchantment, mind-affecting effect. Saving Throw: None. Spell Resistance: Yes.

Lost Doors: One door per caster level is covered by a *silent image* to appear as if it were a plain wall. Saving Throw: Will disbelief (if interacted with). Spell Resistance: No.

In addition, you can place your choice of one of the following five magical effects.

1. *Dancing lights* in four corridors. You can designate a simple program that causes the lights to repeat as long as the *guards and wards* spell lasts. Saving Throw: None. Spell Resistance: No.

2. A *magic mouth* in two places. Saving Throw: None. Spell Resistance: No.

3. A *stinking cloud* in two places. The vapors appear in the places you designate; they return within 10 minutes if dispersed by wind while the *guards and wards* spell lasts. Saving Throw: Fortitude negates; see text for *stinking cloud.* Spell Resistance: No.

4. A *gust of wind* in one corridor or room. Saving Throw: Fortitude negates. Spell Resistance: Yes.

5. A *suggestion* in one place. You select an area of up to 5 feet square, and any creature who enters or passes through the area receives the *suggestion* mentally. Saving Throw: Will negates. Spell Resistance: Yes.

The whole warded area radiates strong magic of the abjuration school. A *dispel magic* cast on a specific effect, if successful, removes only that effect. A successful *Mordenkainen's disjunction* destroys the entire *guards and wards* effect.

Material Component: Burning incense, a small measure of brimstone and oil, a knotted string, and a small amount of umber hulk blood.

Focus: A small silver rod.

Guidance
Divination
Level: Clr 0, Drd 0
Components: V, S
Casting Time: 1 standard action
Range: Touch
Target: Creature touched
Duration: 1 minute or until discharged
Saving Throw: Will negates (harmless)
Spell Resistance: Yes

This spell imbues the subject with a touch of divine guidance. The creature gets a +1 competence bonus on a single attack roll, saving throw, or skill check. It must choose to use the bonus before making the roll to which it applies.

Gust of Wind
Evocation [Air]
Level: Drd 2, Sor/Wiz 2
Components: V, S
Casting Time: 1 standard action
Range: 60 ft.
Effect: Line-shaped gust of severe wind emanating out from you to the extreme of the range
Duration: 1 round
Saving Throw: Fortitude negates
Spell Resistance: Yes

This spell creates a severe blast of air (approximately 50 mph) that originates from you, affecting all creatures in its path.

A Tiny or smaller creature on the ground is knocked down and rolled 1d4×10 feet, taking 1d4 points of nonlethal damage per 10 feet. If flying, a Tiny or smaller creature is blown back 2d6×10 feet and takes 2d6 points of nonlethal damage due to battering and buffeting.

Small creatures are knocked prone by the force of the wind, or if flying are blown back 1d6×10 feet.

Medium creatures are unable to move forward against the force of the wind, or if flying are blown back 1d6×5 feet.

Large or larger creatures may move normally within a *gust of wind* effect.

A *gust of wind* can't move a creature beyond the limit of its range.

Any creature, regardless of size, takes a –4 penalty on ranged attacks and Listen checks in the area of a *gust of wind*.

The force of the *gust* automatically extinguishes candles, torches, and similar unprotected flames. It causes protected flames, such as those of lanterns, to dance wildly and has a 50% chance to extinguish those lights.

In addition to the effects noted, a *gust of wind* can do anything that a sudden blast of wind would be expected to do. It can create a stinging spray of sand or dust, fan a large fire, overturn delicate awnings or hangings, heel over a small boat, and blow gases or vapors to the edge of its range.

Gust of wind can be made permanent with a *permanency* spell.

Hallow
Evocation [Good]
Level: Clr 5, Drd 5
Components: V, S, M, DF
Casting Time: 24 hours
Range: Touch
Area: 40-ft. radius emanating from the touched point
Duration: Instantaneous
Saving Throw: See text
Spell Resistance: See text

Hallow makes a particular site, building, or structure a holy site. This has four major effects.

First, the site or structure is guarded by a *magic circle against evil* effect.

Second, all Charisma checks made to turn undead gain a +4 sacred bonus, and Charisma checks to command undead take a –4 penalty. Spell resistance does not apply to this effect. (This provision does not apply to the druid version of the spell.)

Third, any dead body interred in a *hallowed* site cannot be turned into an undead creature.

Finally, you may choose to fix a single spell effect to the *hallowed* site. The spell effect lasts for one year and functions throughout the entire site, regardless of the normal duration and area or effect. You may designate whether the effect applies to all creatures, creatures who share your faith or alignment, or creatures who adhere to another faith or alignment. For example, you may create a *bless* effect that aids all creatures of your alignment or faith in the area, or a *bane* effect that hinders creatures of the opposed alignment or an enemy faith. At the end of the year, the chosen effect lapses, but it can be renewed or replaced simply by casting *hallow* again.

Spell effects that may be tied to a *hallowed* site include *aid, bane, bless, cause fear, darkness, daylight, death ward, deeper darkness, detect evil, detect magic, dimensional anchor, discern lies, dispel magic, endure elements, freedom of movement, invisibility purge, protection from energy, remove fear, resist energy, silence, tongues,* and *zone of truth.* Saving throws and spell resistance might apply to these spells' effects. (See the individual spell descriptions for details.)

An area can receive only one *hallow* spell (and its associated spell effect) at a time.

Hallow counters but does not dispel *unhallow.*

Material Component: Herbs, oils, and incense worth at least 1,000 gp, plus 1,000 gp per level of the spell to be included in the *hallowed* area.

Hallucinatory Terrain
Illusion (Glamer)
Level: Brd 4, Sor/Wiz 4
Components: V, S, M
Casting Time: 10 minutes
Range: Long (400 ft. + 40 ft./level)
Area: One 30-ft. cube/level (S)
Duration: 2 hours/level (D)
Saving Throw: Will disbelief (if interacted with)
Spell Resistance: No

You make natural terrain look, sound, and smell like some other sort of natural terrain. Thus, open fields or a road can be made to resemble a swamp, hill, crevasse, or some other difficult or impassable terrain. A pond can be made to seem like a grassy meadow, a precipice like a gentle slope, or a rock-strewn gully like a wide and smooth road. Structures, equipment, and creatures within the area are not hidden or changed in appearance.

Material Component: A stone, a twig, and a bit of green plant.

Halt Undead
Necromancy
Level: Sor/Wiz 3
Components: V, S, M
Casting Time: 1 standard action
Range: Medium (100 ft. + 10 ft./level)
Targets: Up to three undead creatures, no two of which can be more than 30 ft. apart
Duration: 1 round/level
Saving Throw: Will negates (see text)
Spell Resistance: Yes

This spell renders as many as three undead creatures immobile. A nonintelligent undead creature (such as a skeleton or zombie) gets no saving throw; an intelligent undead creature does. If the spell is successful, it renders the undead creature immobile for the duration of the spell (similar to the effect of *hold person* on a living creature). The effect is broken if the *halted* creatures are attacked or take damage.

Material Component: A pinch of sulfur and powdered garlic.

Harm

Necromancy
Level: Clr 6, Destruction 6
Components: V, S
Casting Time: 1 standard action
Range: Touch
Target: Creature touched
Duration: Instantaneous
Saving Throw: Will half; see text
Spell Resistance: Yes

Harm charges a subject with negative energy that deals 10 points of damage per caster level (to a maximum of 150 points at 15th level). If the creature successfully saves, *harm* deals half this amount, but it cannot reduce the target's hit points to less than 1.

If used on an undead creature, *harm* acts like *heal*.

Haste

Transmutation
Level: Brd 3, Sor/Wiz 3
Components: V, S, M
Casting Time: 1 standard action
Range: Close (25 ft. + 5 ft./2 levels)
Targets: One creature/level, no two of which can be more than 30 ft. apart
Duration: 1 round/level
Saving Throw: Fortitude negates (harmless)
Spell Resistance: Yes (harmless)

The transmuted creatures move and act more quickly than normal. This extra speed has several effects.

When making a full attack action, a hasted creature may make one extra attack with any weapon he is holding. The attack is made using the creature's full base attack bonus, plus any modifiers appropriate to the situation. (This effect is not cumulative with similar effects, such as that provided by a weapon of speed, nor does it actually grant an extra action, so you can't use it to cast a second spell or otherwise take an extra action in the round.)

A *hasted* creature gains a +1 bonus on attack rolls and a +1 dodge bonus to AC and Reflex saves. Any condition that makes you lose your Dexterity bonus to Armor Class (if any) also makes you lose dodge bonuses.

All of the *hasted* creature's modes of movement (including land movement, burrow, climb, fly, and swim) increase by 30 feet, to a maximum of twice the subject's normal speed using that form of movement. This increase counts as an enhancement bonus, and it affects the creature's jumping distance as normal for increased speed.

Multiple *haste* effects don't stack. *Haste* dispels and counters *slow*.

Material Component: A shaving of licorice root.

Heal

Conjuration (Healing)
Level: Clr 6, Drd 7, Healing 6
Components: V, S
Casting Time: 1 standard action
Range: Touch
Target: Creature touched
Duration: Instantaneous
Saving Throw: Will negates (harmless)
Spell Resistance: Yes (harmless)

Heal enables you to channel positive energy into a creature to wipe away injury and afflictions. It immediately ends any and all of the following adverse conditions affecting the target: ability damage, blinded, *confused*, dazed, dazzled, deafened, diseased, exhausted, fatigued, *feebleminded*, insanity, nauseated, sickened, stunned, and poisoned. It also cures 10 hit points of damage per level of the caster, to a maximum of 150 points at 15th level.

Heal does not remove negative levels, restore permanently drained levels, or restore permanently drained ability score points.

If used against an undead creature, *heal* instead acts like *harm*.

Heal, Mass

Conjuration (Healing)
Level: Clr 9, Healing 9
Range: Close (25 ft. + 5 ft./2 levels)
Targets: One or more creatures, no two of which can be more than 30 ft. apart

This spell functions like *heal,* except as noted above. The maximum number of hit points restored to each creature is 250.

Heal Mount

Conjuration (Healing)
Level: Pal 3
Components: V, S
Casting Time: 1 standard action
Range: Touch
Target: Your mount touched
Duration: Instantaneous
Saving Throw: Will negates (harmless)
Spell Resistance: Yes (harmless)

This spell functions like *heal,* but it affects only the paladin's special mount (typically a warhorse).

Heat Metal

Transmutation [Fire]
Level: Drd 2, Sun 2
Components: V, S, DF
Casting Time: 1 standard action
Range: Close (25 ft. + 5 ft./2 levels)
Target: Metal equipment of one creature per two levels, no two of which can be more than 30 ft. apart; or 25 lb. of metal/level, all of which must be within a 30-ft. circle
Duration: 7 rounds

Saving Throw: Will negates (object)
Spell Resistance: Yes (object)

Heat metal makes metal extremely warm. Unattended, nonmagical metal gets no saving throw. Magical metal is allowed a saving throw against the spell. (Magic items' saving throws are covered in the *Dungeon Master's Guide.*) An item in a creature's possession uses the creature's saving throw bonus unless its own is higher.

A creature takes fire damage if its equipment is heated. It takes full damage if its armor is affected or if it is holding, touching, wearing, or carrying metal weighing one-fifth of its weight. The creature takes minimum damage (1 point or 2 points; see the table) if it's not wearing metal armor and the metal that it's carrying weighs less than one-fifth of its weight.

On the first round of the spell, the metal becomes warm and uncomfortable to touch but deals no damage. The same effect also occurs on the last round of the spell's duration. During the second (and also the next-to-last) round, intense heat causes pain and damage. In the third, fourth, and fifth rounds, the metal is searing hot, causing more damage, as shown on the table below.

Round	Metal Temperature	Damage
1	Warm	None
2	Hot	1d4 points
3–5	Searing	2d4 points
6	Hot	1d4 points
7	Warm	None

Any cold intense enough to damage the creature negates fire damage from the spell (and vice versa) on a point-for-point basis. For example, if the damage roll from a *heat metal* spell indicates 2 points of fire damage and the subject is hit by a *ray of frost* in the same round and takes 3 points of cold damage, it winds up taking no fire damage and only 1 point of cold damage. If cast underwater, *heat metal* deals half damage and boils the surrounding water.

Heat metal counters and dispels *chill metal.*

Helping Hand

Evocation
Level: Clr 3
Components: V, S, DF
Casting Time: 1 standard action
Range: 5 miles
Effect: Ghostly hand
Duration: 1 hour/level
Saving Throw: None
Spell Resistance: No

You create the ghostly image of a hand, which you can send to find a creature within 5 miles. The hand then beckons to that creature and leads it to you if the creature is willing to follow.

When the spell is cast, the hand appears in front of you. You then specify a person (or any creature) by physical description, which can include race, gender, and appearance but not ambiguous factors such as level, alignment, or class. When the description is complete, the hand streaks off in search of a subject that fits the description. The amount of time it takes to find the subject depends on how far away she is.

Distance	Time to Locate
100 ft. or less	1 round
1,000 ft.	1 minute
1 mile	10 minutes
2 miles	1 hour
3 miles	2 hours
4 miles	3 hours
5 miles	4 hours

Once the hand locates the subject, it beckons the creature to follow it. If the subject does so, the hand points in your direction, indicating the most direct feasible route. The hand hovers 10 feet in front of the subject, moving before it at a speed of as much as 240 feet per round. Once the hand leads the subject back to you, it disappears.

The subject is not compelled to follow the hand or act in any particular way toward you. If the subject chooses not to follow, the hand continues to beckon for the duration of the spell, then disappears. If the spell expires while the subject is en route to you, the hand disappears; the subject must then rely on her own devices to locate you.

If more than one subject in a 5-mile radius

meets the description, the hand locates the closest creature. If that creature refuses to follow the hand, the hand does not seek out a second subject.

If, at the end of 4 hours of searching, the hand has found no subject that matches the description within 5 miles, it returns to you, displays an outstretched palm (indicating that no such creature was found), and disappears.

The ghostly hand has no physical form. It is invisible to anyone except you and a potential subject. It cannot engage in combat or execute any other task aside from locating a subject and leading it back to you. The hand can't pass through solid objects but can ooze through small cracks and slits. The hand cannot travel more than 5 miles from the spot it appeared when you cast the spell.

Heroes' Feast

Conjuration [Creation]
Level: Brd 6, Clr 6
Components: V, S, DF
Casting Time: 10 minutes
Range: Close (25 ft. + 5 ft./2 levels)
Effect: Feast for one creature/level
Duration: 1 hour plus 12 hours; see text
Saving Throw: None
Spell Resistance: No

You bring forth a great feast, including a magnificent table, chairs, service, and food and drink. The feast

takes 1 hour to consume, and the beneficial effects do not set in until this hour is over. Every creature partaking of the feast is cured of all diseases, sickness, and nausea; becomes immune to poison for 12 hours; and gains 1d8 temporary hit points +1 point per two caster levels (maximum +10) after imbibing the nectarlike beverage that is part of the feast. The ambrosial food that is consumed grants each creature that partakes a +1 morale bonus on attack rolls and Will saves and immunity to fear effects for 12 hours.

If the feast is interrupted for any reason, the spell is ruined and all effects of the spell are negated.

Heroism

Enchantment (Compulsion) [Mind-Affecting]
Level: Brd 2, Sor/Wiz 3
Components: V, S
Casting Time: 1 standard action
Range: Touch
Target: Creature touched
Duration: 10 min./level
Saving Throw: Will negates (harmless)
Spell Resistance: Yes (harmless)

This spell imbues a single creature with great bravery and morale in battle. The target gains a +2 morale bonus on attack rolls, saves, and skill checks.

Heroism, Greater

Enchantment (Compulsion) [Mind-Affecting]
Level: Brd 5, Sor/Wiz 6
Duration: 1 min./level

This spell functions like *heroism*, except the creature gains a +4 morale bonus on attack rolls, saves, and skill checks, immunity to fear effects, and temporary hit points equal to your caster level (maximum 20).

Jozan casts holy smite against a succubus.

Hide from Animals

Abjuration
Level: Drd 1, Rgr 1
Components: S, DF
Casting Time: 1 standard action
Range: Touch
Targets: One creature touched/level
Duration: 10 min./level (D)
Saving Throw: Will negates (harmless)
Spell Resistance: Yes

Animals cannot see, hear, or smell the warded creatures. Even extraordinary or supernatural sensory capabilities, such as blindsense, blindsight, scent, and tremorsense, cannot detect or locate warded creatures. Animals simply act as though the warded creatures are not there. Warded creatures could stand before the hungriest of lions and not be molested or even noticed. If a warded character touches an animal or attacks any creature, even with a spell, the spell ends for all recipients.

Hide from Undead

Abjuration
Level: Clr 1
Components: V, S, DF
Casting Time: 1 standard action
Range: Touch
Targets: One touched creature/level
Duration: 10 min./level (D)
Saving Throw: Will negates (harmless); see text
Spell Resistance: Yes

Undead cannot see, hear, or smell the warded creatures. Even extraordinary or supernatural sensory capabilities, such as blindsense, blindsight, scent, and tremorsense, cannot detect or locate warded creatures. Nonintelligent undead creatures are automatically affected and act as though the warded creatures are not there. An intelligent undead creature gets a single Will saving throw. If it fails, the subject can't see any of the warded creatures. However, if it has reason to believe unseen opponents are present, it can attempt to find or strike them.

If a warded creature attempts to turn or command undead, touches an undead creature, or attacks any creature (even with a spell), the spell ends for all recipients.

Hold Animal

Enchantment (Compulsion) [Mind-Affecting]
Level: Animal 2, Drd 2, Rgr 2
Components: V, S
Target: One animal

This spell functions like *hold person*, except that it affects an animal instead of a humanoid.

Hold Monster

Enchantment (Compulsion) [Mind-Affecting]
Level: Brd 4, Law 6, Sor/Wiz 5
Components: V, S, M/DF
Target: One living creature

This spell functions like *hold person*, except that it affects any living creature that fails its Will save.

Arcane Material Component: One hard metal bar or rod, which can be as small as a three-penny nail.

Hold Monster, Mass

Enchantment (Compulsion) [Mind-Affecting]
Level: Sor/Wiz 9
Targets: One or more creatures, no two of which can be more than 30 ft. apart

This spell functions like *hold person*, except that it affects multiple creatures and holds any living creature that fails its Will save.

Hold Person

Enchantment (Compulsion) [Mind-Affecting]
Level: Brd 2, Clr 2, Sor/Wiz 3
Components: V, S, F/DF
Casting Time: 1 standard action
Range: Medium (100 ft. + 10 ft./level)
Target: One humanoid creature
Duration: 1 round/level (D); see text
Saving Throw: Will negates; see text
Spell Resistance: Yes

The subject becomes paralyzed and freezes in place. It is aware and breathes normally but cannot take any actions, even speech. Each round on its turn, the subject may attempt a new saving throw to end the effect. (This is a full-round action that does not provoke attacks of opportunity.)

A winged creature who is paralyzed cannot flap its wings and falls. A swimmer can't swim and may drown.

Arcane Focus: A small, straight piece of iron.

Hold Person, Mass

Enchantment (Compulsion) [Mind-Affecting]
Level: Sor/Wiz 7
Targets: One or more humanoid creatures, no two of which can be more than 30 ft. apart

This spell functions like *hold person*, except as noted above.

Hold Portal

Abjuration
Level: Sor/Wiz 1
Component: V

Casting Time: 1 standard action
Range: Medium (100 ft. + 10 ft./level)
Target: One portal, up to 20 sq. ft./level
Duration: 1 min./level (D)
Saving Throw: None
Spell Resistance: No

This spell magically holds shut a door, gate, window, or shutter of wood, metal, or stone. The magic affects the portal just as if it were securely closed and normally locked. A *knock* spell or a successful *dispel magic* spell can negate a *hold portal* spell. For a portal affected by this spell, add 5 to the normal DC for forcing open the portal.

Holy Aura

Abjuration [Good]
Level: Clr 8, Good 8
Components: V, S, F
Casting Time: 1 standard action
Range: 20 ft.
Targets: One creature/level in a 20-ft.-radius burst centered on you
Duration: 1 round/level (D)
Saving Throw: See text
Spell Resistance: Yes (harmless)

A brilliant divine radiance surrounds the subjects, protecting them from attacks, granting them resistance to spells cast by evil creatures, and causing evil creatures to become blinded when they strike the subjects. This abjuration has four effects.

First, each warded creature gains a +4 deflection bonus to AC and a +4 resistance bonus on saves. Unlike *protection from evil*, this benefit applies against all attacks, not just against attacks by evil creatures.

Second, each warded creature gains spell resistance 25 against evil spells and spells cast by evil creatures.

Third, the abjuration blocks possession and mental influence, just as *protection from evil* does.

Finally, if an evil creature succeeds on a melee attack against a warded creature, the offending attacker is blinded (Fortitude save negates, as *blindness/deafness*, but against *holy aura's* save DC).

Focus: A tiny reliquary containing some sacred relic, such as a scrap of cloth from a saint's robe or a piece of parchment from a holy text. The reliquary costs at least 500 gp.

Holy Smite

Evocation [Good]
Level: Good 4
Components: V, S
Casting Time: 1 standard action
Range: Medium (100 ft. + 10 ft./level)
Area: 20-ft.-radius burst
Duration: Instantaneous (1 round); see text
Saving Throw: Will partial; see text
Spell Resistance: Yes

You draw down holy power to smite your enemies. Only evil and neutral creatures are harmed by the spell; good creatures are unaffected.

The spell deals 1d8 points of damage per two caster levels (maximum 5d8) to each evil creature in the area (or 1d6 points of damage per caster level, maximum 10d6, to an evil outsider) and causes it to become blinded for 1 round. A successful Will saving throw reduces damage to half and negates the blinded effect.

The spell deals only half damage to creatures who are neither good nor evil, and they are not blinded. Such a creature can reduce that damage by half (down to one-quarter of the roll) with a successful Will save.

Holy Sword

Evocation [Good]
Level: Pal 4
Components: V, S
Casting Time: 1 standard action
Range: Touch
Target: Melee weapon touched
Duration: 1 round/level
Saving Throw: None
Spell Resistance: No

This spell allows you to channel holy power into your sword, or any other melee weapon you choose. The weapon acts as a +5 *holy weapon* (+5 enhancement bonus on attack and damage rolls, extra 2d6 damage against evil opponents). It also emits a *magic circle against evil* effect (as the spell). If the *magic circle* ends, the sword creates a new one on your turn as a free action. The spell is automatically canceled 1 round after the weapon leaves your hand. You cannot have more than one *holy sword* at a time.

If this spell is cast on a magic weapon, the powers of the spell supersede any that the weapon normally has, rendering the normal enhancement bonus and powers of the weapon inoperative for the duration of the spell. This spell is not cumulative with *bless weapon* or any other spell that might modify the weapon in any way.

This spell does not work on artifacts.

Note: A masterwork weapon's bonus to attack does not stack with an enhancement bonus to attack.

Holy Word

Evocation [Good, Sonic]
Level: Clr 7, Good 7
Components: V
Casting Time: 1 standard action
Range: 40 ft.
Area: Nongood creatures in a 40-ft.-radius spread centered on you
Duration: Instantaneous
Saving Throw: None or Will negates; see text
Spell Resistance: Yes

Any nongood creature within the area that hears the *holy word* suffers the following ill effects.

HD	Effect
Equal to caster level	Deafened
Up to caster level −1	Blinded, deafened
Up to caster level −5	Paralyzed, blinded, deafened
Up to caster level −10	Killed, paralyzed, blinded, deafened

The effects are cumulative and concurrent. No saving throw is allowed against these effects.

Deafened: The creature is deafened for 1d4 rounds.

Blinded: The creature is blinded for 2d4 rounds.

Paralyzed: The creature is paralyzed and helpless for 1d10 minutes.

Killed: Living creatures die. Undead creatures are destroyed.

Furthermore, if you are on your home plane when you cast this spell, nongood extraplanar creatures within the area are instantly banished back to their home planes. Creatures so banished cannot return for at least 24 hours. This effect takes place regardless of whether the creatures hear the *holy word*. The banishment effect allows a Will save (at a −4 penalty) to negate.

Creatures whose HD exceed your caster level are unaffected by *holy word*.

Horrid Wilting

Necromancy
Level: Sor/Wiz 8, Water 8
Components: V, S, M/DF
Casting Time: 1 standard action
Range: Long (400 ft. + 40 ft./level)
Targets: Living creatures, no two of which can be more than 60 ft. apart
Duration: Instantaneous
Saving Throw: Fortitude half
Spell Resistance: Yes

This spell evaporates moisture from the body of each subject living creature, dealing 1d6 points of damage per caster level (maximum 20d6). This spell is especially devastating to water elementals and plant creatures, which instead take 1d8 points of damage per caster level (maximum 20d8).

Arcane Material Component: A bit of sponge.

Hypnotic Pattern

Illusion (Pattern) [Mind-Affecting]
Level: Brd 2, Sor/Wiz 2
Components: V (Brd only), S, M; see text
Casting Time: 1 standard action
Range: Medium (100 ft. + 10 ft./level)
Effect: Colorful lights in a 10-ft.-radius spread
Duration: Concentration + 2 rounds
Saving Throw: Will negates
Spell Resistance: Yes

A twisting pattern of subtle, shifting colors weaves through the air, fascinating creatures within it. Roll 2d4 and add your caster level (maximum 10) to determine the total number of Hit Dice of creatures affected. Creatures with the fewest HD are affected first; and, among creatures with equal HD, those who are closest to the spell's point of origin are affected first. Hit Dice that are not sufficient to affect a creature are wasted. Affected creatures become fascinated by the pattern of colors. Sightless creatures are not affected.

A wizard or sorcerer need not utter a sound to cast this spell, but a bard must sing, play music, or recite a rhyme as a verbal component.

Material Component: A glowing stick of incense or a crystal rod filled with phosphorescent material.

Hypnotism

Enchantment (Compulsion) [Mind-Affecting]
Level: Brd 1, Sor/Wiz 1
Components: V, S
Casting Time: 1 round
Range: Close (25 ft. + 5 ft./2 levels)
Area: Several living creatures, no two of which may be more than 30 ft. apart
Duration: 2d4 rounds (D)
Saving Throw: Will negates
Spell Resistance: Yes

Your gestures and droning incantation fascinate nearby creatures, causing them to stop and stare blankly at you. In addition, you can use their rapt attention to make your suggestions and requests seem more plausible. Roll 2d4 to see how many total Hit Dice of creatures you affect. Creatures with fewer HD are affected before creatures with more HD. Only creatures that can see or hear you are affected, but they do not need to understand you to be fascinated.

If you use this spell in combat, each target gains a +2 bonus on its saving throw. If the spell affects only a single creature not in combat at the time, the saving throw has a penalty of −2.

While the subject is fascinated by this spell, it reacts as though it were two steps more friendly in attitude (see Influencing NPC Attitudes, page 72). This allows you to make a single request of the affected creature (provided you can communicate with it). The request must be brief and reasonable. Even after the spell ends, the creature retains its new attitude toward you, but only with respect to that particular request.

A creature that fails its saving throw does not remember that you enspelled it.

Ice Storm
Evocation [Cold]
Level: Drd 4, Sor/Wiz 4, Water 5
Components: V, S, M/DF
Casting Time: 1 standard action
Range: Long (400 ft. + 40 ft./level)
Area: Cylinder (20-ft. radius, 40 ft. high)
Duration: 1 full round
Saving Throw: None
Spell Resistance: Yes

Great magical hailstones pound down for 1 full round, dealing 3d6 points of bludgeoning damage and 2d6 points of cold damage to every creature in the area. A –4 penalty applies to each Listen check made within the *ice storm*'s effect, and all land movement within its area is at half speed. At the end of the duration, the hail disappears, leaving no aftereffects (other than the damage dealt).

Arcane Material Component: A pinch of dust and a few drops of water.

Identify
Divination
Level: Brd 1, Magic 2, Sor/Wiz 1
Components: V, S, M/DF
Casting Time: 1 hour
Range: Touch
Targets: One touched object
Duration: Instantaneous
Saving Throw: None
Spell Resistance: No

The spell determines all magic properties of a single magic item, including how to activate those functions (if appropriate), and how many charges are left (if any).

Identify does not function when used on an artifact (see the *Dungeon Master's Guide* for details on artifacts).

Arcane Material Component: A pearl of at least 100 gp value, crushed and stirred into wine with an owl feather; the infusion must be drunk prior to spellcasting.

Illusory Script
Illusion (Phantasm) [Mind-Affecting]
Level: Brd 3, Sor/Wiz 3
Components: V, S, M
Casting Time: 1 minute or longer; see text
Range: Touch
Target: One touched object weighing no more than 10 lb.
Duration: One day/level (D)
Saving Throw: Will negates; see text
Spell Resistance: Yes

You write instructions or other information on parchment, paper, or any suitable writing material. The *illusory script* appears to be some form of foreign or magical writing. Only the person (or people) designated by you at the time of the casting are able to read the writing; it's unintelligible to any other character, although an illusionist recognizes it as *illusory script*.

Any unauthorized creature attempting to read the script triggers a potent illusory effect and must make a saving throw. A successful saving throw means the creature can look away with only a mild sense of disorientation. Failure means the creature is subject to a suggestion implanted in the script by you at the time the illusory script spell was cast. The suggestion lasts only 30 minutes. Typical suggestions include "Close the book and leave," "Forget the existence of the book," and so forth. If successfully dispelled by *dispel magic*, the *illusory script* and its secret message disappear. The hidden message can be read by a combination of the *true seeing* spell with the *read magic* or *comprehend languages* spell.

The casting time depends on how long a message you wish to write, but it is always at least 1 minute.

Material Component: A lead-based ink (cost of not less than 50 gp).

Illusory Wall
Illusion (Figment)
Level: Sor/Wiz 4
Components: V, S
Casting Time: 1 standard action
Range: Close (25 ft. + 5 ft./2 levels)
Effect: Image 1 ft. by 10 ft. by 10 ft.
Duration: Permanent
Saving Throw: Will disbelief (if interacted with)
Spell Resistance: No

This spell creates the illusion of a wall, floor, ceiling, or similar surface. It appears absolutely real when viewed, but physical objects can pass through it without difficulty. When the spell is used to hide pits, traps, or normal doors, any detection abilities that do not require sight work normally. Touch or a probing search reveals the true nature of the surface, though such measures do not cause the illusion to disappear.

Imbue with Spell Ability
Evocation
Level: Clr 4, Magic 4
Components: V, S, DF
Casting Time: 10 minutes
Range: Touch
Target: Creature touched; see text
Duration: Permanent until discharged (D)
Saving Throw: Will negates (harmless)
Spell Resistance: Yes (harmless)

You transfer some of your currently prepared spells, and the ability to cast them, to another creature. Only a creature with an Intelligence score of at least 5 and a Wisdom score of at least 9 can receive this bestowal. Only cleric spells from the schools of abjuration, divination, and conjuration (healing) can be transferred. The number and level of spells that the subject can be granted depends on its Hit Dice; even multiple castings of *imbue with spell ability* can't exceed this limit.

HD of Recipient	Spells Imbued
2 or lower	One 1st-level spell
3–4	One or two 1st-level spells
5 or higher	One or two 1st-level spells and one 2nd-level spell

The transferred spell's variable characteristics (range, duration, area, and the like) function according to your level, not the level of the recipient.

Once you cast *imbue with spell ability*, you cannot prepare a new 4th-level spell to replace it until the recipient uses the imbued spells or is slain, or until you dismiss the *imbue with spell ability* spell. In the meantime, you remain responsible to your deity or your principles for the use to which the spell is put. If the number of 4th-level spells you can cast decreases, and that number drops below your current number of active *imbue with spell ability* spells, the more recently cast imbued spells are dispelled.

To cast a spell with a verbal component, the subject must be able to speak. To cast a spell with a somatic component, it must have humanlike hands. To cast a spell with a material component or focus, it must have the materials or focus.

Implosion
Evocation
Level: Clr 9, Destruction 9
Components: V, S
Casting Time: 1 standard action
Range: Close (25 ft. + 5 ft./2 levels)
Targets: One corporeal creature/round
Duration: Concentration (up to 4 rounds)
Saving Throw: Fortitude negates
Spell Resistance: Yes

You create a destructive resonance in a corporeal creature's body. For each round you concentrate, you cause one creature to collapse in on itself, killing it. (This effect, being instantaneous, cannot be dispelled.)

You can target a particular creature only once with each casting of the spell.

Implosion has no effect on creatures in gaseous form or on incorporeal creatures.

Imprisonment

Abjuration
Level: Sor/Wiz 9
Components: V, S
Casting Time: 1 standard action
Range: Touch
Target: Creature touched
Duration: Instantaneous
Saving Throw: Will negates; see text
Spell Resistance: Yes

When you cast *imprisonment* and touch a creature, it is entombed in a state of sus-pended animation (see the *temporal stasis* spell) in a small sphere far beneath the surface of the earth. The subject remains there unless a *freedom* spell is cast at the locale where the imprisonment took place. Magical search by a *crystal ball*, a *locate object* spell, or some other similar divination does not reveal the fact that a creature is imprisoned, but *discern location* does. A *wish* or *miracle* spell will not free the recipient, but will reveal where it is entombed. If you know the target's name and some facts about its life, the target takes a –4 penalty on its save.

Incendiary Cloud

Conjuration (Creation) [Fire]
Level: Fire 8, Sor/Wiz 8
Components: V, S
Casting Time: 1 standard action
Range: Medium (100 ft. + 10 ft./level)
Effect: Cloud spreads in 20-ft. radius, 20 ft. high
Duration: 1 round/level
Saving Throw: Reflex half; see text
Spell Resistance: No

An *incendiary cloud* spell creates a cloud of roiling smoke shot through with white-hot embers. The smoke obscures all sight as a *fog cloud* does. In addition, the white-hot embers within the cloud deal 4d6 points of fire damage to everything with-in the cloud on your turn each round. All targets can make Reflex saves each round to take half damage.

As with a *cloudkill* spell, the smoke moves away from you at 10 feet per round. Figure out the smoke's new spread each round based on its new point of origin, which is 10 feet farther away from where you were when you cast the spell. By con-centrating, you can make the cloud (actu-ally its point of origin) move as much as 60 feet each round. Any portion of the cloud that would extend beyond your maximum range dissipates harmlessly, reducing the remainder's spread there-after.

As with *fog cloud*, wind disperses the smoke, and the spell can't be cast under-water.

Inflict Critical Wounds

Necromancy
Level: Clr 4, Destruction 4

This spell functions like *inflict light wounds*, except that you deal 4d8 points of damage +1 point per caster level (maxi-mum +20).

Inflict Critical Wounds, Mass

Necromancy
Level: Clr 8

This spell functions like *mass inflict light wounds*, except that it deals 4d8 points of damage +1 point per caster level (maxi-mum +40).

Inflict Light Wounds

Necromancy
Level: Clr 1, Destruction 1
Components: V, S
Casting Time: 1 standard action
Range: Touch
Target: Creature touched
Duration: Instantaneous
Saving Throw: Will half
Spell Resistance: Yes

When laying your hand upon a creature, you channel negative energy that deals 1d8 points of damage +1 point per caster level (maximum +5).

Since undead are powered by negative energy, this spell cures such a creature of a like amount of damage, rather than harm-ing it.

Inflict Light Wounds, Mass

Necromancy
Level: Clr 5, Destruction 5
Components: V, S
Casting Time: 1 standard action
Range: Close (25 ft. + 5 ft./2 levels)
Target: One creature/level, no two of which can be more than 30 ft. apart
Duration: Instantaneous
Saving Throw: Will half
Spell Resistance: Yes

Negative energy spreads out in all direc-tions from the point of origin, dealing 1d8 points of damage +1 point per caster level (maximum +25) to nearby living enemies.

Like other *inflict* spells, *mass inflict light wounds* cures undead in its area rather than damaging them. A cleric capable of spontaneously casting *inflict* spells can also spontaneously cast *mass inflict* spells.

Inflict Minor Wounds

Necromancy
Level: Clr 0
Saving Throw: Will negates

This spell functions like *inflict light wounds*, except that you deal 1 point of

damage and a Will save negates the damage instead of halving it.

Inflict Moderate Wounds

Necromancy
Level: Clr 2

This spell functions like *inflict light wounds*, except that you deal 2d8 points of damage +1 point per caster level (maxi-mum +10).

Inflict Moderate Wounds, Mass

Necromancy
Level: Clr 6

This spell functions like *mass inflict light wounds*, except that it deals 2d8 points of damage +1 point per caster level (maxi-mum +30).

Inflict Serious Wounds

Necromancy
Level: Clr 3

This spell functions like *inflict light wounds*, except that you deal 3d8 points of damage +1 point per caster level (maxi-mum +15).

Inflict Serious Wounds, Mass

Necromancy
Level: Clr 7

This spell functions like *mass inflict light wounds*, except that it deals 3d8 points of damage +1 point per caster level (maxi-mum +35).

Insanity

Enchantment (Compulsion) [Mind-Affecting]
Level: Sor/Wiz 7
Components: V, S
Casting Time: 1 standard action
Range: Medium (100 ft. + 10 ft./level)
Target: One living creature
Duration: Instantaneous
Saving Throw: Will negates
Spell Resistance: Yes

The affected creature suffers from a con-tinuous *confusion* effect, as the spell.

Remove curse does not remove *insanity*. *Greater restoration, heal, limited wish, mira-cle,* or *wish* can restore the creature.

Insect Plague

Conjuration (Summoning)
Level: Clr 5, Drd 5
Components: V, S, DF
Casting Time: 1 round
Range: Long (400 ft. + 40 ft./level)
Effect: One swarm of locusts per three levels, each of which must be adjacent to at least one other swarm
Duration: 1 min./level

Saving Throw: None
Spell Resistance: No

You summon a number of swarms of locusts (one per three levels, to a maximum of six swarms at 18th level). The swarms must be summoned so that each one is adjacent to at least one other swarm (that is, the swarms must fill one contiguous area). You may summon the locust swarms so that they share the area of other creatures. Each swarm attacks any creatures occupying its area. The swarms are stationary after being summoned, and won't pursue creatures that flee.

See the *Monster Manual* for details on locust swarms.

Invisibility
Illusion (Glamer)
Level: Brd 2, Sor/Wiz 2, Trickery 2
Components: V, S, M/DF
Casting Time: 1 standard action
Range: Personal or touch
Target: You or a creature or object weighing no more than 100 lb./level
Duration: 1 min./level (D)
Saving Throw: Will negates (harmless) or Will negates (harmless, object)
Spell Resistance: Yes (harmless) or Yes (harmless, object)

The creature or object touched becomes invisible, vanishing from sight, even from darkvision. If the recipient is a creature carrying gear, that vanishes, too. If you cast the spell on someone else, neither you nor your allies can see the subject, unless you can normally see invisible things or you employ magic to do so.

Items dropped or put down by an invisible creature become visible; items picked up disappear if tucked into the clothing or pouches worn by the creature. Light, however, never becomes invisible, although a source of light can become so (thus, the effect is that of a light with no visible source). Any part of an item that the subject carries but that extends more than 10 feet from it becomes visible, such as a trailing rope.

Of course, the subject is not magically *silenced*, and certain other conditions can render the recipient detectable (such as stepping in a puddle). The spell ends if the subject attacks any creature. For purposes of this spell, an attack includes any spell targeting a foe or whose area or effect includes a foe. (Exactly who is a foe depends on the invisible character's perceptions.) Actions directed at unattended objects do not break the spell. Causing harm indirectly is not an attack. Thus, an invisible being can open doors, talk, eat, climb stairs, summon monsters and have them attack, cut the ropes holding a rope bridge while enemies are on the bridge,

remotely trigger traps, open a portcullis to release attack dogs, and so forth. If the subject attacks directly, however, it immediately becomes visible along with all its gear. Spells such as *bless* that specifically affect allies but not foes are not attacks for this purpose, even when they include foes in their area.

See Table 8–5: Attack Roll Modifiers and Table 8–6: Armor Class Modifiers, page 151, for the effects of invisibility on combat.

Invisibility can be made permanent (on objects only) with a *permanency* spell.

Arcane Material Component: An eyelash encased in a bit of gum arabic.

Invisibility, Greater
Illusion (Glamer)
Level: Brd 4, Sor/Wiz 4
Components: V, S
Target: You or creature touched
Duration: 1 round/level (D)
Saving Throw: Will negates (harmless)

This spell functions like *invisibility,* except that it doesn't end if the subject attacks.

Invisibility, Mass
Illusion (Glamer)
Level: Sor/Wiz 7
Components: V, S, M
Range: Long (400 ft. + 40 ft./level)
Targets: Any number of creatures, no two of which can be more than 180 ft. apart

This spell functions like *invisibility,* except that the effect is mobile with the group and is broken when anyone in the group attacks. Individuals in the group cannot see each other. The spell is broken for any individual who moves more than 180 feet from the nearest member of the group. (If only two individuals are affected, the one moving away from the other one loses its invisibility. If both are moving away from each other, they both become visible when the distance between them exceeds 180 feet.)

Material Component: An eyelash encased in a bit of gum arabic.

Invisibility Purge
Evocation
Level: Clr 3
Components: V, S
Casting Time: 1 standard action
Range: Personal
Target: You
Duration: 1 min./level (D)

You surround yourself with a sphere of power with a radius of 5 feet per caster level that negates all forms of invisibility. Anything invisible becomes visible while in the area.

Invisibility Sphere
Illusion (Glamer)
Level: Brd 3, Sor/Wiz 3
Components: V, S, M
Area: 10-ft.-radius emanation around the creature or object touched

This spell functions like *invisibility,* except that this spell confers invisibility upon all creatures within 10 feet of the recipient. The center of the effect is mobile with the recipient.

Those affected by this spell can see each other and themselves as if unaffected by the spell. Any affected creature moving out of the area becomes visible, but creatures moving into the area after the spell is cast do not become invisible. Affected creatures (other than the recipient) who attack negate the invisibility only for themselves. If the spell recipient attacks, the *invisibility sphere* ends.

Iron Body
Transmutation
Level: Earth 8, Sor/Wiz 8
Components: V, S, M/DF
Casting Time: 1 standard action
Range: Personal
Target: You
Duration: 1 min./level (D)

This spell transforms your body into living iron, which grants you several powerful resistances and abilities.

You gain damage reduction 15/adamantine. You are immune to blindness, critical hits, ability score damage, deafness, disease, drowning, electricity, poison, stunning, and all spells or attacks that affect your physiology or respiration, because you have no physiology or respiration while this spell is in effect. You take only half damage from acid and fire of all kinds. However, you also become vulnerable to all special attacks that affect iron golems.

You gain a +6 enhancement bonus to your Strength score, but you take a –6 penalty to Dexterity as well (to a minimum Dexterity score of 1), and your speed is reduced to half normal. You have an arcane spell failure chance of 50% and a –8 armor check penalty, just as if you were clad in full plate armor. You cannot drink (and thus can't use potions) or play wind instruments.

Your unarmed attacks deal damage equal to a club sized for you (1d4 for Small characters or 1d6 for Medium characters), and you are considered armed when making unarmed attacks.

Your weight increases by a factor of ten, causing you to sink in water like a stone. However, you could survive the crushing pressure and lack of air at the bottom of the ocean—at least until the spell duration expires.

Arcane Material Component: A small piece of iron that was once part of either an iron golem, a hero's armor, or a war machine.

Ironwood

Transmutation
Level: Drd 6
Components: V, S, M
Casting Time: 1 minute/lb. created
Range: 0 ft.
Effect: An *ironwood* object weighing up to 5 lb./level
Duration: One day/level (D)
Saving Throw: None
Spell Resistance: No

Ironwood is a magical substance created by druids from normal wood. While remaining natural wood in almost every way, *ironwood* is as strong, heavy, and resistant to fire as steel. Spells that affect metal or iron (such as *heat metal*) do not function on *ironwood*. Spells that affect wood (such as *wood shape*) do affect *ironwood*, although *ironwood* does not burn. Using this spell with *wood shape* or a wood-related Craft check, you can fashion wooden items that function as steel items. Thus, wooden plate armor and wooden swords can be created that are as durable as their normal steel counterparts. These items are freely usable by druids.

Further, if you make only half as much *ironwood* as the spell would normally allow, any weapon, shield, or suit of armor so created is treated as a magic item with a +1 enhancement bonus.

Material Component: Wood shaped into the form of the intended *ironwood* object.

Jump

Transmutation
Level: Drd 1, Rgr 1, Sor/Wiz 1
Components: V, S, M
Casting Time: 1 standard action
Range: Touch
Target: Creature touched
Duration: 1 min./level (D)
Saving Throw: Will negates (harmless)
Spell Resistance: Yes

The subject gets a +10 enhancement bonus on Jump checks. The enhancement bonus increases to +20 at caster level 5th, and to +30 (the maximum) at caster level 9th.

Material Component: A grasshopper's hind leg, which you break when the spell is cast.

Keen Edge

Transmutation
Level: Sor/Wiz 3
Components: V, S
Casting Time: 1 standard action
Range: Close (25 ft. + 5 ft./2 levels)

Targets: One weapon or fifty projectiles, all of which must be in contact with each other at the time of casting
Duration: 10 min./level
Saving Throw: Will negates (harmless, object)
Spell Resistance: Yes (harmless, object)

This spell makes a weapon magically keen, improving its ability to deal telling blows. This transmutation doubles the threat range of the weapon. A threat range of 20 becomes 19–20, a threat range of 19–20 becomes 17–20, and a threat range of 18–20 becomes 15–20. The spell can be cast only on piercing or slashing weapons. If cast on arrows or crossbow bolts, the *keen edge* on a particular projectile ends after one use, whether or not the missile strikes its intended target. (Treat shuriken as arrows, rather than as thrown weapons, for the purpose of this spell.)

Multiple effects that increase a weapon's threat range (such as the *keen edge* spell and the Improved Critical feat) don't stack. You can't cast this spell on a natural weapon, such as a claw.

Knock

Transmutation
Level: Sor/Wiz 2
Components: V
Casting Time: 1 standard action
Range: Medium (100 ft. + 10 ft./level)
Target: One door, box, or chest with an area of up to 10 sq. ft./level
Duration: Instantaneous; see text
Saving Throw: None
Spell Resistance: No

The *knock* spell opens stuck, barred, locked, *held,* or *arcane locked* doors. It opens secret doors, as well as locked or trick-opening boxes or chests. It also loosens welds, shackles, or chains (provided they serve to hold closures shut). If used to open a *arcane locked* door, the spell does not remove the *arcane lock* but simply suspends its functioning for 10 minutes. In all other cases, the door does not relock itself or become stuck again on its own. *Knock* does not raise barred gates or similar impediments (such as a portcullis), nor does it affect ropes, vines, and the like. The effect is limited by the area. A 3rd-level caster can cast a *knock* spell on a door of 30 square feet or less (for example, a standard 4-foot-by-7-foot door). Each spell can undo as many as two means of preventing egress. Thus if a door is locked, barred, and *held,* or quadruple locked, opening it requires two *knock* spells.

Know Direction

Divination
Level: Brd 0, Drd 0
Components: V, S

Casting Time: 1 standard action
Range: Personal
Target: You
Duration: Instantaneous

You instantly know the direction of north from your current position. The spell is effective in any environment in which "north" exists, but it may not work in extraplanar settings. Your knowledge of north is correct at the moment of casting, but you can get lost again within moments if you don't find some external reference point to help you keep track of direction.

Legend Lore

Divination
Level: Brd 4, Knowledge 7, Sor/Wiz 6
Components: V, S, M, F
Casting Time: See text
Range: Personal
Target: You
Duration: See text

Legend lore brings to your mind legends about an important person, place, or thing. If the person or thing is at hand, or if you are in the place in question, the casting time is only 1d4×10 minutes. If you have only detailed information on the person, place, or thing, the casting time is 1d10 days, and the resulting lore is less complete and specific (though it often provides enough information to help you find the person, place, or thing, thus allowing a better *legend lore* result next time). If you know only rumors, the casting time is 2d6 weeks, and the resulting lore is vague and incomplete (though it often directs you to more detailed information, thus allowing a better *legend lore* result next time).

During the casting, you cannot engage in other than routine activities: eating, sleeping, and so forth. When completed, the divination brings legends (if any) about the person, place, or things to your mind. These may be legends that are still current, legends that have been forgotten, or even information that has never been generally known. If the person, place, or thing is not of legendary importance, you gain no information. As a rule of thumb, characters who are 11th level and higher are "legendary," as are the sorts of creatures they contend with, the major magic items they wield, and the places where they perform their key deeds.

Examples of *legend lore* results include the following.

A divination about a mysterious magic axe you have at hand: "Woe to the evildoer whose hand touches the axe, for even the haft chops the hand of the evil ones. Only a true Son or Daughter of Stone, one who loves Moradin and whom Moradin loves, may awaken the true powers of the axe, and only with the sacred word 'Rudnogg' on the lips."

A divination about a legendary paladin about whom you know many details: "Vanashon has been denied the glory of death and the duty of life. He waits patiently beneath the Forbidden Mountain." (The paladin has been turned to stone in the caverns under the mountain.)

A divination about ancient ruins about which you have only a passing reference in a partially damaged tome: "The sorcerer who called herself Ryth built a library without words and a temple without gods. Those who read and those who pray tore it down in a night and a day." (These clues may be enough for you to find out more and get the details you need to cast a better *legend lore*.)

Material Component: Incense worth at least 250 gp.

Focus: Four strips of ivory (worth 50 gp each) formed into a rectangle.

Leomund's Secret Chest

Conjuration (Summoning)
Level: Sor/Wiz 5
Components: V, S, F
Casting Time: 10 minutes
Range: See text
Target: One chest and up to 1 cu. ft. of goods/caster level
Duration: Sixty days or until discharged
Saving Throw: None
Spell Resistance: No

You hide a chest on the Ethereal Plane for as long as sixty days and can retrieve it at will. The chest can contain up to 1 cubic foot of material per caster level (regardless of the chest's actual size, which is about 3 feet by 2 feet by 2 feet). If any living creatures are in the chest, there is a 75% chance that the spell simply fails. Once the chest is hidden, you can retrieve it by concentrating (a standard action), and it appears next to you.

The chest must be exceptionally well crafted and expensive, constructed for you by master crafters. If made principally of wood, it must be ebony, rosewood, sandalwood, teak, or the like, and all of its corner fittings, nails, and hardware must be platinum. If constructed of ivory, the metal fittings of the chest must be gold. If the chest is fashioned from bronze, copper, or silver, its fittings must be silver or electrum (a valuable metal). The cost of such a chest is never less than 5,000 gp. Once it is constructed, you must make a tiny replica (of the same materials and perfect in every detail), so that the miniature of the chest appears to be a perfect copy. (The replica costs 50 gp.) You can have but one pair of these chests at any given time—even a *wish* spell does not allow more. The chests are nonmagi-

cal and can be fitted with locks, wards, and so on, just as any normal chest can be.

To hide the chest, you cast the spell while touching both the chest and the replica. The chest vanishes into the Ethereal Plane. You need the replica to recall the chest. After sixty days, there is a cumulative chance of 5% per day that the chest is irretrievably lost. If the miniature of the chest is lost or destroyed, there is no way, not even with a *wish* spell, that the large chest can be summoned back, although an extraplanar expedition might be mounted to find it.

Living things in the chest eat, sleep, and age normally, and they die if they run out of food, air, water, or whatever they need to survive.

Focus: The chest and its replica.

Leomund's Secure Shelter

Conjuration (Creation)
Level: Brd 4, Sor/Wiz 4
Components: V, S, M, F; see text
Casting Time: 10 minutes
Range: Close (25 ft. + 5 ft./2 levels)
Effect: 20-ft.-square structure
Duration: 2 hours/level (D)
Saving Throw: None
Spell Resistance: No

You conjure a sturdy cottage or lodge made of material that is common in the area where the spell is cast—stone, timber, or (at worst) sod. The floor is level, clean, and dry. In all respects the lodging resembles a normal cottage, with a sturdy door, two shuttered windows, and a small fireplace.

The shelter has no heating or cooling source (other than natural insulation qualities). Therefore, it must be heated as a normal dwelling, and extreme heat adversely affects it and its occupants. The dwelling does, however, provide considerable security otherwise—it is as strong as a normal stone building, regardless of its material composition. The dwelling resists flames and fire as if it were stone. It is impervious to normal missiles (but not the sort cast by siege engines or giants).

The door, shutters, and even chimney are secure against intrusion, the former two being *arcane locked* and the latter secured by an iron grate at the top and a narrow flue. In addition, these three areas are protected by an *alarm* spell. Finally, an *unseen servant* is conjured to provide service to you for the duration of the shelter.

The *secure shelter* contains rude furnishings—eight bunks, a trestle table, eight stools, and a writing desk.

Material Component: A square chip of stone, crushed lime, a few grains of sand, a sprinkling of water, and several splinters of wood. These must be augmented by the components of the *unseen servant* spell

(string and a bit of wood) if this benefit is to be included.

Focus: The focus of the *alarm* spell (silver wire and a tiny bell) if this benefit is to be included.

Leomund's Tiny Hut

Evocation [Force]
Level: Brd 3, Sor/Wiz 3
Components: V, S, M
Casting Time: 1 standard action
Range: 20 ft.
Effect: 20-ft.-radius sphere centered on your location
Duration: 2 hours/level (D)
Saving Throw: None
Spell Resistance: No

You create an unmoving, opaque sphere of force of any color you desire around yourself. Half the sphere projects above the ground, and the lower hemisphere passes through the ground. As many as nine other Medium creatures can fit into the field with you; they can freely pass into and out of the hut without harming it. However, if you remove yourself from the hut, the spell ends.

The temperature inside the hut is 70° F if the exterior temperature is between 0° and 100° F. An exterior temperature below 0° or above 100° lowers or raises the interior temperature on a 1-degree-for-1 basis (thus, if it's –20° outside, inside the hut it's 50°). The hut also provides protection against the elements, such as rain, dust, and sandstorms. The hut withstands any wind of less than hurricane force, but a hurricane (75+ mph wind speed) or greater force destroys it.

The interior of the hut is a hemisphere. You can illuminate it dimly upon command or extinguish the light as desired. Although the force field is opaque from the outside, it is transparent from within. Missiles, weapons, and most spell effects can pass through the hut without affecting it, although the occupants cannot be seen from outside the hut (they have total concealment).

Material Component: A small crystal bead that shatters when the spell duration expires or the *hut* is dispelled.

Leomund's Trap

Illusion (Glamer)
Level: Sor/Wiz 2
Components: V, S, M
Casting Time: 1 standard action
Range: Touch
Target: Object touched
Duration: Permanent (D)
Saving Throw: None
Spell Resistance: No

This spell makes a lock or other small mechanism seem to be trapped to anyone who can detect traps. You place the spell upon any small mechanism or device, such as a lock, hinge, hasp, cork, cap, or ratchet. Any character able to detect traps, or who uses any spell or device enabling trap detection, is 100% certain a real trap exists. Of course, the effect is illusory and nothing happens if the trap is "sprung"; its primary purpose is to frighten away thieves or make them waste precious time.

If another *Leomund's trap* is active within 50 feet when the spell is cast, the casting fails.

Material Component: A piece of iron pyrite touched to the object to be trapped while the object is sprinkled with a special dust requiring 50 gp to prepare.

Lesser (Spell Name)

Any spell whose name begins with *lesser* is alphabetized in this chapter according to the second word of the spell name. Thus, the description of a *lesser* spell appears near the description of the spell on which it is based. Spell chains that have *lesser* spells in them include those based on the spells *confusion, geas, globe of invulnerability, planar ally, planar binding,* and *restoration.*

Levitate

Transmutation
Level: Sor/Wiz 2
Components: V, S, F
Casting Time: 1 standard action
Range: Personal or close (25 ft. + 5 ft./2 levels)
Target: You or one willing creature or one object (total weight up to 100 lb./level)
Duration: 1 min./level (D)
Saving Throw: None
Spell Resistance: No

Levitate allows you to move yourself, another creature, or an object up and down as you wish. A creature must be willing to be *levitated,* and an object must be unattended or possessed by a willing creature. You can mentally direct the recipient to move up or down as much as 20 feet each round; doing so is a move action. You cannot move the recipient horizontally, but the recipient could clamber along the face of a cliff, for example, or push against a ceiling to move laterally (generally at half its base land speed).

A *levitating* creature that attacks with a melee or ranged weapon finds itself increasingly unstable; the first attack has a –1 penalty on attack rolls, the second –2, and so on, to a maximum penalty of –5. A full round spent stabilizing allows the creature to begin again at –1.

Focus: Either a small leather loop or a piece of golden wire bent into a cup shape with a long shank on one end.

Light

Evocation [Light]
Level: Brd 0, Clr 0, Drd 0, Sor/Wiz 0
Components: V, M/DF
Casting Time: 1 standard action
Range: Touch
Target: Object touched
Duration: 10 min./level (D)
Saving Throw: None
Spell Resistance: No

This spell causes an object to glow like a torch, shedding bright light in a 20-foot-radius (and dim light for an additional 20 feet) from the point you touch. The effect is immobile, but it can be cast on a movable object. Light taken into an area of magical *darkness* does not function.

A *light* spell (one with the light descriptor) counters and dispels a darkness spell (one with the darkness descriptor) of an equal or lower level.

Arcane Material Component: A firefly or a piece of phosphorescent moss.

Lightning Bolt

Evocation [Electricity]
Level: Sor/Wiz 3
Components: V, S, M
Casting Time: 1 standard action
Range: 120 ft.
Area: 120-ft. line
Duration: Instantaneous
Saving Throw: Reflex half
Spell Resistance: Yes

You release a powerful stroke of electrical energy that deals 1d6 points of electricity damage per caster level (maximum 10d6) to each creature within its area. The bolt begins at your fingertips.

The *lightning bolt* sets fire to combustibles and damages objects in its path. It can melt metals with a low melting point, such as lead, gold, copper, silver, or bronze. If the damage caused to an interposing barrier shatters or breaks through it, the bolt may continue beyond the barrier if the spell's range permits; otherwise, it stops at the barrier just as any other spell effect does.

Material Component: A bit of fur and an amber, crystal, or glass rod.

Limited Wish

Universal
Level: Sor/Wiz 7
Components: V, S, XP
Casting Time: 1 standard action
Range: See text
Target, Effect, or Area: See text
Duration: See text
Saving Throw: None; see text
Spell Resistance: Yes

A *limited wish* lets you create nearly any type of effect. For example, a *limited wish* can do any of the following things.

- Duplicate any sorcerer/wizard spell of 6th level or lower, provided the spell is not of a school prohibited to you.
- Duplicate any other spell of 5th level or lower, provided the spell is not of a school prohibited to you.
- Duplicate any sorcerer/wizard spell of 5th level or lower, even if it's of a prohibited school.
- Duplicate any other spell of 4th level or lower, even if it's of a prohibited school.
- Undo the harmful effects of many spells, such as *geas/quest* or *insanity.*
- Produce any other effect whose power level is in line with the above effects, such as a single creature automatically hitting on its next attack or taking a –7 penalty on its next saving throw.

A duplicated spell allows saving throws and spell resistance as normal (but the save DC is for a 7th-level spell). When a *limited wish* duplicates a spell that has an XP cost, you must pay that cost or 300 XP, whichever is more. When a *limited wish* spell duplicates a spell with a material component that costs more than 1,000 gp, you must provide that component.

XP Cost: 300 XP or more (see above).

Liveoak

Transmutation
Level: Drd 6
Components: V, S
Casting Time: 10 minutes
Range: Touch
Target: Tree touched
Duration: One day/level (D)
Saving Throw: None
Spell Resistance: No

This spell turns an oak tree into a protector or guardian. The spell can be cast on only a single tree at a time; while *liveoak* is in effect, you can't cast it again on another tree. The tree on which the spell is cast must be within 10 feet of your dwelling place, within a place sacred to you, or within 300 feet of something that you wish to guard or protect.

Liveoak must be cast on a healthy, Huge oak. A triggering phrase of up to one word per caster level is placed on the targeted oak. For instance, "Attack any persons who come near without first saying 'sacred mistletoe'" is an eleven-word trigger phrase that you could use at 11th level or higher. The *liveoak* spell triggers the tree into animating as a treant (see the *Monster Manual*). At the DM's option, you can extrapolate statistics for a smaller tree from the treant statistics if you cast *liveoak* on a smaller oak.

If *liveoak* is dispelled, the tree takes root immediately, wherever it happens to be. If released by you, the tree tries to return to its original location before taking root.

Locate Creature

Divination
Level: Brd 4, Sor/Wiz 4
Components: V, S, M
Duration: 10 min./level

This spell functions like *locate object*, except this spell locates a known or familiar creature.

You slowly turn and sense when you are facing in the direction of the creature to be located, provided it is within range. You also know in which direction the creature is moving, if any.

The spell can locate a creature of a specific kind (such as a human or a unicorn) or a specific creature known to you. It cannot find a creature of a certain type (such as humanoid or animal). To find a kind of creature, you must have seen such a creature up close (within 30 feet) at least once.

Running water blocks the spell. It cannot detect objects. It can be fooled by *mislead*, *nondetection*, and *polymorph* spells.

Material Component: A bit of fur from a bloodhound.

Locate Object

Divination
Level: Brd 2, Clr 3, Sor/Wiz 2, Travel 2
Components: V, S, F/DF
Casting Time: 1 standard action
Range: Long (400 ft. + 40 ft./level)
Area: Circle, centered on you, with a radius of 400 ft. + 40 ft./level
Duration: 1 min./level
Saving Throw: None
Spell Resistance: No

You sense the direction of a well-known or clearly visualized object. The spell locates such objects as apparel, jewelry, furniture, tools, weapons, or even a ladder. You can search for general items such as a stairway, a sword, or a jewel, in which case you locate the nearest one of its kind if more than one is within range. Attempting to find a certain item, such as a particular piece of jewelry, requires a specific and accurate mental image; if the image is not close enough to the actual object, the spell fails. You cannot specify a unique item (such as "Baron Vulden's signet ring") unless you have observed that particular item firsthand (not through divination).

The spell is blocked by even a thin sheet of lead. Creatures cannot be found by this spell. *Polymorph any object* fools it.

Arcane Focus: A forked twig.

Longstrider

Transmutation
Level: Drd 1, Rgr 1, Travel 1
Components: V, S, M
Casting Time: 1 standard action
Range: Personal
Target: You
Duration: 1 hour/level (D)

This spell increases your base land speed by 10 feet. (This adjustment counts as an enhancement bonus.) It has no effect on other modes of movement, such as burrow, climb, fly, or swim.

Material Component: A pinch of dirt.

Lullaby

Enchantment (Compulsion) [Mind-Affecting]
Level: Brd 0
Components: V, S
Casting Time: 1 standard action
Range: Medium (100 ft. + 10 ft./level)
Area: Living creatures within a 10-ft.-radius burst
Duration: Concentration + 1 round/level (D)
Saving Throw: Will negates
Spell Resistance: Yes

Any creature within the area that fails a Will save becomes drowsy and inattentive, taking a –5 penalty on Listen and Spot checks and a –2 penalty on Will saves against *sleep* effects while the *lullaby* is in effect. *Lullaby* lasts for as long as the caster concentrates, plus up to 1 round per caster level thereafter.

Mage Armor

Conjuration (Creation) [Force]
Level: Sor/Wiz 1
Components: V, S, F
Casting Time: 1 standard action
Range: Touch
Target: Creature touched
Duration: 1 hour/level (D)
Saving Throw: Will negates (harmless)
Spell Resistance: No

An invisible but tangible field of force surrounds the subject of a *mage armor* spell, providing a +4 armor bonus to AC. Unlike mundane armor, *mage armor* entails no armor check penalty, arcane spell failure chance, or speed reduction. Since *mage armor* is made of force, incorporeal creatures can't bypass it the way they do normal armor.

Focus: A piece of cured leather.

Mage Hand

Transmutation
Level: Brd 0, Sor/Wiz 0
Components: V, S
Casting Time: 1 standard action
Range: Close (25 ft. + 5 ft./2 levels)
Target: One nonmagical, unattended object weighing up to 5 lb.
Duration: Concentration
Saving Throw: None
Spell Resistance: No

You point your finger at an object and can lift it and move it at will from a distance. As a move action, you can propel the object as far as 15 feet in any direction, though the spell ends if the distance between you and the object ever exceeds the spell's range.

Magic Circle against Chaos

Abjuration [Lawful]
Level: Clr 3, Law 3, Pal 3, Sor/Wiz 3

This spell functions like *magic circle against evil*, except that it is similar to *protection from chaos* instead of *protection from evil*, and it can imprison a nonlawful called creature.

Magic Circle against Evil

Abjuration [Good]
Level: Clr 3, Good 3, Pal 3, Sor/Wiz 3
Components: V, S, M/DF
Casting Time: 1 standard action
Range: Touch
Area: 10-ft.-radius emanation from touched creature
Duration: 10 min./level
Saving Throw: Will negates (harmless)
Spell Resistance: No; see text

All creatures within the area gain the effects of a *protection from evil* spell, and no nongood summoned creatures can enter the area either. You must overcome a creature's spell resistance in order to keep it at bay (as in the third function of *protection from evil*), but the deflection and resistance bonuses and the protection from mental control apply regardless of enemies' spell resistance.

This spell has an alternative version that you may choose when casting it. A *magic circle against evil* can be focused inward rather than outward. When focused inward, the spell binds a nongood called creature (such as those called by the *lesser planar binding*, *planar binding*, and *greater planar binding* spells) for a maximum of 24 hours per caster level, provided that you cast the spell that calls the creature within 1 round of casting the *magic circle*. The creature cannot cross the circle's boundaries. If a creature too large to fit into the spell's area is the subject of the spell, the spell acts as a normal *protection from evil* spell for that creature only.

A *magic circle* leaves much to be desired as a trap. If the circle of powdered silver laid down in the process of spellcasting is broken, the effect immediately ends. The trapped creature can do nothing that disturbs the circle, directly or indirectly, but other creatures can. If the called creature has spell resistance, it can test the trap once a day. If you fail to overcome its spell resistance, the creature breaks free, destroying the circle. A creature capable of any form of dimensional travel (*astral projection, blink, dimension door, etherealness, gate, plane shift, shadow walk, teleport,* and similar abilities) can simply leave the circle through that means. You can prevent the creature's extradimensional escape by casting a *dimensional anchor* spell on it, but you must cast the spell before the creature acts. If you are successful, the *anchor* effect lasts as long as the *magic circle* does. The creature cannot reach across the *magic circle*, but its ranged attacks (ranged weapons, spells, magical abilities, and the like) can. The creature can attack any target it can reach with its ranged attacks except for the circle itself.

You can add a special diagram (a two-dimensional bounded figure with no gaps along its circumference, augmented with various magical sigils) to make the *magic circle* more secure. Drawing the diagram by hand takes 10 minutes and requires a DC 20 Spellcraft check. The DM makes this check secretly. If the check fails, the diagram is ineffective. You can take 10 (see page 65) when drawing the diagram if you are under no particular time pressure to complete the task. This task also takes 10 full minutes. If time is no factor at all, and you devote 3 hours and 20 minutes to the task, you can take 20.

A successful diagram allows you to cast a *dimensional anchor* spell on the *magic circle* during the round before casting any summoning spell. The *anchor* holds any called creatures in the *magic circle* for 24 hours per caster level. A creature cannot use its spell resistance against a *magic circle* prepared with a diagram, and none of its abilities or attacks can cross the diagram. If the creature tries a Charisma check to break free of the trap (see the *lesser planar binding* spell), the DC increases by 5. The creature is immediately released if anything disturbs the diagram—even a straw laid across it. However, the creature itself cannot disturb the diagram either directly or indirectly, as noted above.

This spell is not cumulative with *protection from evil* and vice versa.

Arcane Material Component: A little powdered silver with which you trace a 3-foot-diameter circle on the floor (or ground) around the creature to be warded.

Magic Circle against Good

Abjuration [Evil]
Level: Clr 3, Evil 3, Sor/Wiz 3

This spell functions like *magic circle against evil*, except that it is similar to *protection from good* instead of *protection from evil*, and it can imprison a nonevil called creature.

Magic Circle against Law

Abjuration [Chaotic]
Level: Chaos 3, Clr 3, Sor/Wiz 3

This spell functions like *magic circle against evil*, except that it is similar to *protection from law* instead of *protection from evil*, and it can imprison a nonchaotic called creature.

Magic Fang

Transmutation
Level: Drd 1, Rgr 1
Components: V, S, DF
Casting Time: 1 standard action
Range: Touch
Target: Living creature touched
Duration: 1 min./level
Saving Throw: Will negates (harmless)
Spell Resistance: Yes (harmless)

Magic fang gives one natural weapon of the subject a +1 enhancement bonus on attack and damage rolls. The spell can affect a slam attack, fist, bite, or other natural weapon. (The spell does not change an unarmed strike's damage from nonlethal damage to lethal damage.)

Magic fang can be made permanent with a *permanency* spell.

Magic Fang, Greater

Transmutation
Level: Drd 3, Rgr 3
Range: Close (25 ft. + 5 ft./2 levels)
Target: One living creature
Duration: 1 hour/level

This spell functions like *magic fang*, except that the enhancement bonus on attack and damage rolls is +1 per four caster levels (maximum +5).

Alternatively, you may imbue all of the creature's natural weapons with a +1 enhancement bonus (regardless of your caster level).

Greater magic fang can be made permanent with a *permanency* spell.

Magic Jar

Necromancy
Level: Sor/Wiz 5
Components: V, S, F
Casting Time: 1 standard action
Range: Medium (100 ft. + 10 ft./level)
Target: One creature
Duration: 1 hour/level or until you return to your body
Saving Throw: Will negates; see text
Spell Resistance: Yes

By casting *magic jar*, you place your soul in a gem or large crystal (known as the *magic jar*), leaving your body lifeless. Then you can attempt to take control of a nearby body, forcing its soul into the *magic jar*. You may move back to the jar (thereby returning the trapped soul to its body) and attempt to possess another body. The spell ends when you send your soul back to your own body, leaving the receptacle empty.

To cast the spell, the *magic jar* must be within spell range and you must know where it is, though you do not need line of sight or line of effect to it. When you transfer your soul upon casting, your body is, as near as anyone can tell, dead.

While in the *magic jar*, you can sense and attack any life force within 10 feet per caster level (and on the same plane of existence). You do need line of effect from the jar to the creatures. You cannot determine the exact creature types or positions of these creatures. In a group of life forces, you can sense a difference of 4 or more Hit Dice between one creature and another and can determine whether a life force is powered by positive or negative energy. (Undead creatures are powered by negative energy. Only sentient undead creatures have, or are, souls.)

For example, if two 10th-level characters are attacking a hill giant (12 HD) and four ogres (4 HD), you could determine that there are three stronger and four weaker life forces within range, all powered by positive energy. You could choose to take over either a stronger or a weaker creature, but which particular stronger or weaker creature you attempt to possess is determined randomly.

Attempting to possess a body is a full-round action. It is blocked by *protection from evil* or a similar ward. You possess the body and force the creature's soul into the *magic jar* unless the subject succeeds on a Will save. Failure to take over the host leaves your life force in the *magic jar*, and the target automatically succeeds on further saving throws if you attempt to possess its body again.

If you are successful, your life force occupies the host body, and the host's life force is imprisoned in the *magic jar*. You keep your Intelligence, Wisdom, Charisma, level, class, base attack bonus, base save bonuses, alignment, and mental abilities. The body retains its Strength, Dexterity, Constitution, hit points, natural abilities, and automatic abilities. For example, a fish's body breathes water and a troll's body regenerates. A body with extra limbs does not allow you to make more attacks (or more advantageous two-weapon attacks) than normal. You can't choose to activate the body's extraordinary or supernatural abilities. The creature's spells and spell-like abilities do not stay with the body.

As a standard action, you can shift freely from a host to the *magic jar* if within range, sending the trapped soul back to its body. The spell ends when you shift from the jar to your own body.

If the host body is slain, you return to the *magic jar*, if within range, and the life force of the host departs (it is dead). If the host body is slain beyond the range of the spell, both you and the host die. Any life force with nowhere to go is treated as slain.

If the spell ends while you are in the *magic jar*, you return to your body (or die if your body is out of range or destroyed). If the spell ends while you are in a host, you return to your body (or die, if it is out of range of your current position), and the soul in the *magic jar* returns to its body (or dies if it is out of range). Destroying the receptacle ends the spell, and the spell can be dispelled at either the *magic jar* or at the host's location.

Focus: A gem or crystal worth at least 100 gp.

Magic Missile

Evocation [Force]
Level: Sor/Wiz 1
Components: V, S
Casting Time: 1 standard action
Range: Medium (100 ft. + 10 ft./level)
Targets: Up to five creatures, no two of which can be more than 15 ft. apart
Duration: Instantaneous
Saving Throw: None
Spell Resistance: Yes

A missile of magical energy darts forth from your fingertip and strikes its target, dealing 1d4+1 points of force damage.

The missile strikes unerringly, even if the target is in melee combat or has less than total cover or total concealment. Specific parts of a creature can't be singled out. Inanimate objects are not damaged by the spell.

For every two caster levels beyond 1st, you gain an additional missile—two at 3rd level, three at 5th, four at 7th, and the maximum of five missiles at 9th level or higher. If you shoot multiple missiles, you can have them strike a single creature or several creatures. A single missile can strike only one creature. You must designate targets before you check for spell resistance or roll damage.

Magic Mouth

Illusion (Glamer)
Level: Brd 1, Sor/Wiz 2
Components: V, S, M
Casting Time: 1 standard action
Range: Close (25 ft. + 5 ft./2 levels)
Target: One creature or object
Duration: Permanent until discharged
Saving Throw: Will negates (object)
Spell Resistance: Yes (object)

This spell imbues the chosen object or creature with an enchanted mouth that suddenly appears and speaks its message the next time a specified event occurs. The message, which must be twenty-five or fewer words long, can be in any language known by you and can be delivered over a period of 10 minutes. The mouth

cannot utter verbal components, use command words, or activate magical effects. It does, however, move according to the words articulated; if it were placed upon a statue, the mouth of the statue would move and appear to speak. Of course, *magic mouth* can be placed upon a tree, rock, or any other object or creature.

The spell functions when specific conditions are fulfilled according to your command as set in the spell. Commands can be as general or as detailed as desired, although only visual and audible triggers can be used, such as the following: "Speak only when a venerable female human carrying a sack sits cross-legged within a distance of one foot." Triggers react to what appears to be the case. Disguises and illusions can fool them. Normal darkness does not defeat a visual trigger, but magical *darkness* or *invisibility* does. Silent movement or magical *silence* defeats audible triggers. Audible triggers can be keyed to general types of noises (footsteps, metal clanking) or to a specific noise or spoken word (when a pin drops, or when anyone says "Boo"). Actions can serve as triggers if they are visible or audible. For example, "Speak when any creature touches the statue" is an acceptable command if the creature is visible. A *magic mouth* cannot distinguish alignment, level, Hit Dice, or class except by external garb.

The range limit of a trigger is 15 feet per caster level, so a 6th-level caster can command a *magic mouth* to respond to triggers as far as 90 feet away. Regardless of range, the mouth can respond only to visible or audible triggers and actions in line of sight or within hearing distance.

Magic mouth can be made permanent with a *permanency* spell.

Material Component: A small bit of honeycomb and jade dust worth 10 gp.

Magic Stone

Transmutation
Level: Clr 1, Drd 1, Earth 1
Components: V, S, DF
Casting Time: 1 standard action
Range: Touch
Targets: Up to three pebbles touched
Duration: 30 minutes or until discharged
Saving Throw: Will negates (harmless, object)
Spell Resistance: Yes (harmless, object)

You transmute as many as three pebbles, which can be no larger than sling bullets, so that they strike with great force when thrown or slung. If hurled, they have a range increment of 20 feet. If slung, treat them as sling bullets (range increment 50 feet). The spell gives them a +1 enhancement bonus on attack and damage rolls.

The user of the stones makes a normal ranged attack. Each stone that hits deals 1d6+1 points of damage (including the spell's enhancement bonus), or 2d6+2 points against undead.

Magic Vestment

Transmutation
Level: Clr 3, Strength 3, War 3
Components: V, S, DF
Casting Time: 1 standard action
Range: Touch
Target: Armor or shield touched
Duration: 1 hour/level
Saving Throw: Will negates (harmless, object)
Spell Resistance: Yes (harmless, object)

You imbue a suit of armor or a shield with an enhancement bonus of +1 per four caster levels (maximum +5 at 20th level). An outfit of regular clothing counts as armor that grants no AC bonus for the purpose of this spell.

Magic Weapon

Transmutation
Level: Clr 1, Pal 1, Sor/Wiz 1, War 1
Components: V, S, DF
Casting Time: 1 standard action
Range: Touch
Target: Weapon touched
Duration: 1 min./level
Saving Throw: Will negates (harmless, object)
Spell Resistance: Yes (harmless, object)

Magic weapon gives a weapon a +1 enhancement bonus on attack and damage rolls. (An enhancement bonus does not stack with a masterwork weapon's +1 bonus on attack rolls.)

You can't cast this spell on a natural weapon, such as an unarmed strike (instead, see *magic fang*). A monk's unarmed strike is considered a weapon, and thus it can be enhanced by this spell.

Magic Weapon, Greater

Transmutation
Level: Clr 4, Pal 3, Sor/Wiz 3
Components: V, S, M/DF
Casting Time: 1 standard action
Range: Close (25 ft. + 5 ft./2 levels)
Target: One weapon or fifty projectiles (all of which must be in contact with each other at the time of casting)
Duration: 1 hour/level
Saving Throw: Will negates (harmless, object)
Spell Resistance: Yes (harmless, object)

This spell functions like *magic weapon*, except that it gives a weapon an enhancement bonus on attack and damage rolls of +1 per four caster levels (maximum +5).

Alternatively, you can affect as many as

fifty arrows, bolts, or bullets. The projectiles must be of the same kind, and they have to be together (in the same quiver or other container). Projectiles, but not thrown weapons, lose their transmutation when used. (Treat shuriken as projectiles, rather than as thrown weapons, for the purpose of this spell.)

Arcane Material Component: Powdered lime and carbon.

Major Creation

Conjuration (Creation)
Level: Sor/Wiz 5
Casting Time: 10 minutes
Range: Close (25 ft. + 5 ft./2 levels)
Duration: See text

This spell functions like *minor creation,* except that you can also create an object of mineral nature: stone, crystal, metal, or the like. The duration of the created item varies with its relative hardness and rarity, as indicated on the following table.

Hardness and Rarity Examples	Duration
Vegetable matter	2 hr./level
Stone, crystal, base metals	1 hr./level
Precious metals	20 min./level
Gems	10 min./level
Rare metal[1]	1 round/level

1 Includes adamantine, alchemical silver, and mithral. You can't use major creation to create a cold iron item. See the *Dungeon Master's Guide* for details.

Major Image

Illusion (Figment)
Level: Brd 3, Sor/Wiz 3
Duration: Concentration + 3 rounds

This spell functions like *silent image,* except that sound, smell, and thermal illusions are included in the spell effect. While concentrating, you can move the image within the range.

The image disappears when struck by an opponent unless you cause the illusion to react appropriately.

Make Whole

Transmutation
Level: Clr 2
Casting Time: 1 standard action
Range: Close (25 ft. + 5 ft./2 levels)
Target: One object of up to 10 cu. ft./ level

This spell functions like *mending,* except that *make whole* completely repairs an object made of any substance, even one with multiple breaks, to be as strong as new. The spell does not restore the magical abilities of a broken magic item made whole, and it cannot mend broken magic rods, staffs, or wands. The spell does not

repair items that have been warped, burned, disintegrated, ground to powder, melted, or vaporized, nor does it affect creatures (including constructs).

Mark of Justice

Necromancy
Level: Clr 5, Pal 4
Components: V, S, DF
Casting Time: 10 minutes
Range: Touch
Target: Creature touched
Duration: Permanent; see text
Saving Throw: None
Spell Resistance: Yes

When moral persuasion fails to win a criminal over to right conduct, you can use *mark of justice* to encourage the miscreant to walk the straight and narrow path.

You draw an indelible mark on the subject and state some behavior on the part of the subject that will activate the mark. When activated, the mark curses the subject. Typically, you designate some sort of criminal behavior that activates the mark, but you can pick any act you please. The effect of the mark is identical with the effect of *bestow curse.*

Since this spell takes 10 minutes to cast and involves writing on the target, you can cast it only on a creature that is willing or restrained.

Like the effect of *bestow curse,* a *mark of justice* cannot be dispelled, but it can be removed with a *break enchantment, limited wish, miracle, remove curse,* or *wish* spell. *Remove curse* works only if its caster level is equal to or higher than your *mark of justice* caster level. These restrictions apply regardless of whether the mark has activated.

Mass (Spell Name)

Any spell whose name begins with *mass* is alphabetized in this chapter according to the second word of the spell name. Thus, the description of a *mass* spell appears near the description of the spell on which it is based. Spell chains that have *mass* spells in them include those based on the spells *bear's endurance, bull's strength, cat's grace, charm monster, cure critical wounds, cure light wounds, cure moderate wounds, cure serious wounds, eagle's splendor, enlarge person, fox's cunning, heal, hold monster, hold person, inflict critical wounds, inflict light wounds, inflict moderate wounds, inflict serious wounds, invisibility, owl's wisdom, reduce person,* and *suggestion.*

Maze

Conjuration (Teleportation)
Level: Sor/Wiz 8
Components: V, S
Casting Time: 1 standard action
Range: Close (25 ft. + 5 ft./2 levels)

Target: One creature
Duration: See text
Saving Throw: None
Spell Resistance: Yes

You banish the subject into an extradimensional labyrinth of force planes. Each round on its turn, it may attempt a DC 20 Intelligence check to escape the labyrinth as a full-round action. If the subject doesn't escape, the maze disappears after 10 minutes, forcing the subject to leave.

On escaping or leaving the maze, the subject reappears where it had been when the *maze* spell was cast. If this location is filled with a solid object, the subject appears in the nearest open space.

Spells and abilities that move a creature within a plane, such as *teleport* and *dimension door,* do not help a creature escape a *maze* spell, although a *plane shift* spell allows it to exit to whatever plane is designated in that spell. Minotaurs are not affected by this spell.

Meld into Stone

Transmutation [Earth]
Level: Clr 3, Drd 3
Components: V, S, DF
Casting Time: 1 standard action
Range: Personal
Target: You
Duration: 10 min./level

Meld into stone enables you to meld your body and possessions into a single block of stone. The stone must be large enough to accommodate your body in all three dimensions. When the casting is complete, you and not more than 100 pounds of nonliving gear merge with the stone. If either condition is violated, the spell fails and is wasted.

While in the stone, you remain in contact, however tenuous, with the face of the stone through which you melded. You remain aware of the passage of time and can cast spells on yourself while hiding in the stone. Nothing that goes on outside the stone can be seen, but you can still hear what happens around you. Minor physical damage to the stone does not harm you, but its partial destruction (to the extent that you no longer fit within it) expels you and deals you 5d6 points of damage. The stone's complete destruction expels you and slays you instantly unless you make a DC 18 Fortitude save.

Any time before the duration expires, you can step out of the stone through the surface that you entered. If the spell's duration expires or the effect is dispelled before you voluntarily exit the stone, you are violently expelled and take 5d6 points of damage.

The following spells harm you if cast upon the stone that you are occupying: *Stone to flesh* expels you and deals you 5d6 points of damage. *Stone shape* deals you 3d6 points of damage but does not expel you. *Transmute rock to mud* expels you and then slays you instantly unless you make a DC 18 Fortitude save, in which case you are merely expelled. Finally, *passwall* expels you without damage.

Melf's Acid Arrow

Conjuration (Creation) [Acid]
Level: Sor/Wiz 2
Components: V, S, M, F
Casting Time: 1 standard action
Range: Long (400 ft. + 40 ft./level)
Effect: One arrow of acid
Duration: 1 round + 1 round per three
  levels
Saving Throw: None
Spell Resistance: No

A magical arrow of acid springs from your hand and speeds to its target. You must succeed on a ranged touch attack to hit your target. The arrow deals 2d4 points of acid damage with no splash damage. For every three caster levels (to a maximum of 18th), the acid, unless somehow neutralized, lasts for another round, dealing another 2d4 points of damage in that round.

Material Component: Powdered rhubarb leaf and an adder's stomach.

Focus: A dart.

Mending

Transmutation
Level: Brd 0, Clr 0, Drd 0, Sor/Wiz 0
Components: V, S
Casting Time: 1 standard action
Range: 10 ft.
Target: One object of up to 1 lb.
Duration: Instantaneous
Saving Throw: Will negates (harmless,
  object)
Spell Resistance: Yes (harmless, object)

Mending repairs small breaks or tears in objects (but not warps, such as might be caused by a *warp wood* spell). It will weld broken metallic objects such as a ring, a chain link, a medallion, or a slender dagger, providing but one break exists. Ceramic or wooden objects with multiple breaks can be invisibly rejoined to be as strong as new. A hole in a leather sack or a wineskin is completely healed over by *mending*. The spell can repair a magic item, but the item's magical abilities are not restored. (For restoring a broken magic item's abilities, see the item creation feats in Chapter 5: Feats.) The spell cannot mend broken magic rods, staffs, or wands, nor does it affect creatures (including constructs).

Message

Transmutation [Language-Dependent]
Level: Brd 0, Sor/Wiz 0

Components: V, S, F
Casting Time: 1 standard action
Range: Medium (100 ft. + 10 ft./level)
Targets: One creature/level
Duration: 10 min./level
Saving Throw: None
Spell Resistance: No

You can whisper messages and receive whispered replies with little chance of being overheard. You point your finger at each creature you want to receive the message. When you whisper, the whispered message is audible to all targeted creatures within range. Magical *silence*, 1 foot of stone, 1 inch of common metal (or a thin sheet of lead), or 3 feet of wood or dirt blocks the spell. The message does not have to travel in a straight line. It can circumvent a barrier if there is an open path between you and the subject, and the path's entire length lies within the spell's range. The creatures that receive the message can whisper a reply that you hear. The spell transmits sound, not meaning. It doesn't transcend language barriers.

Note: To speak a message, you must mouth the words and whisper, possibly allowing observers the opportunity to read your lips.

Focus: A short piece of copper wire.

Meteor Swarm

Evocation [Fire]
Level: Sor/Wiz 9
Components: V, S
Casting Time: 1 standard action
Range: Long (400 ft. + 40 ft./level)
Area: Four 40-ft.-radius spreads; see text
Duration: Instantaneous
Saving Throw: None or Reflex half; see
  text
Spell Resistance: Yes

Meteor swarm is a very powerful and spectacular spell that is similar to *fireball* in many aspects. When you cast it, four 2-foot-diameter spheres spring from your outstretched hand and streak in straight lines to the spots you select. The meteor spheres leave a fiery trail of sparks.

If you aim a sphere at a specific creature, you may make a ranged touch attack to strike the target with the meteor. Any creature struck by one of these spheres takes 2d6 points of bludgeoning damage (no save) and receives no saving throw against the sphere's fire damage (see below). If a targeted sphere misses its target, it simply explodes at the nearest corner of the target's space. You may aim more than one meteor at the same target.

Once a sphere reaches its destination, it explodes in a 40-foot-radius spread, dealing 6d6 points of fire damage to each creature in the area. If a creature is within the area of more than one sphere, it must save separately against each. (Fire resistance applies to each sphere's damage individually.)

Mind Blank

Abjuration
Level: Protection 8, Sor/Wiz 8
Components: V, S
Casting Time: 1 standard action
Range: Close (25 ft. + 5 ft./2 levels)
Target: One creature
Duration: 24 hours
Saving Throw: Will negates (harmless)
Spell Resistance: Yes (harmless)

The subject is protected from all devices and spells that detect, influence, or read emotions or thoughts. This spell protects against all mind-affecting spells and effects as well as information gathering by divination spells or effects. *Mind blank* even foils *limited wish*, *miracle*, and *wish* spells when they are used in such a way as to affect the subject's mind or to gain information about it. In the case of scrying that scans an area the creature is in, such as *arcane eye*, the spell works but the creature simply isn't detected. Scrying attempts that are targeted specifically at the subject do not work at all.

Mind Fog

Enchantment (Compulsion) [Mind-
  Affecting]
Level: Brd 5, Sor/Wiz 5
Components: V, S
Casting Time: 1 standard action
Range: Medium (100 ft. + 10 ft./level)
Effect: Fog spreads in 20-ft. radius, 20 ft.
  high
Duration: 30 minutes and 2d6 rounds;
  see text
Saving Throw: Will negates
Spell Resistance: Yes

Mind fog produces a bank of thin mist that weakens the mental resistance of those caught in it. Creatures in the *mind fog* take a –10 competence penalty on Wisdom checks and Will saves. (A creature that successfully saves against the fog is not affected and need not make further saves even if it remains in the fog.) Affected creatures take the penalty as long as they remain in the fog and for 2d6 rounds thereafter. The fog is stationary and lasts for 30 minutes (or until dispersed by wind).

A moderate wind (11+ mph) disperses the fog in four rounds; a strong wind (21+ mph) disperses the fog in 1 round.

The fog is thin and does not significantly hamper vision.

Minor Creation

Conjuration (Creation)
Level: Sor/Wiz 4
Components: V, S, M
Casting Time: 1 minute

Range: 0 ft.
Effect: Unattended, nonmagical object
  of nonliving plant matter, up to
  1 cu. ft./level
Duration: 1 hour/level (D)
Saving Throw: None
Spell Resistance: No

You create a nonmagical, unattended object of nonliving, vegetable matter—linen clothes, a hemp rope, a wooden ladder, and so forth. The volume of the item created cannot exceed 1 cubic foot per caster level. You must succeed on an appropriate skill check to make a complex item, such as a Craft (bowmaking) check to make straight arrow shafts.

Attempting to use any created object as a material component causes the spell to fail.

Material Component: A tiny piece of matter of the same sort of item you plan to create with *minor creation*—a bit of twisted hemp to create rope, and so forth.

Minor Image

Illusion (Figment)
Level: Brd 2, Sor/Wiz 2
Duration: Concentration +2 rounds

This spell functions like *silent image*, except that *minor image* includes some minor sounds but not understandable speech.

Miracle

Evocation
Level: Clr 9, Luck 9
Components: V, S, XP; see text
Casting Time: 1 standard action
Range: See text
Target, Effect, or Area: See text
Duration: See text
Saving Throw: See text
Spell Resistance: Yes

You don't so much cast a *miracle* as request one. You state what you would like to have happen and request that your deity (or the power you pray to for spells) intercede. The DM then determines the particular effect of the *miracle*.

A *miracle* can do any of the following things.
- Duplicate any cleric spell of 8th level or lower (including spells to which you have access because of your domains).
- Duplicate any other spell of 7th level or lower.
- Undo the harmful effects of certain spells, such as *feeblemind* or *insanity*.
- Have any effect whose power level is in line with the above effects.

If the *miracle* has any of the above effects, casting it has no experience point cost.

Alternatively, a cleric can make a very powerful request. Casting such a *miracle* costs the cleric 5,000 XP because of the powerful divine energies involved. Examples of especially powerful *miracles* of this sort could include the following.
- Swinging the tide of a battle in your favor by raising fallen allies to continue fighting.
- Moving you and your allies, with all your and their gear, from one plane to another through planar barriers to a specific locale with no chance of error.
- Protecting a city from an earthquake, volcanic eruption, flood, or other major natural disaster.

In any event, a request that is out of line with the deity's (or alignment's) nature is refused.

A duplicated spell allows saving throws and spell resistance as normal, but the save DCs are as for a 9th-level spell. When a *miracle* duplicates a spell that has an XP cost, you must pay that cost. When a *miracle* spell duplicates a spell with a material component that costs more than 100 gp, you must provide that component.

XP Cost: 5,000 XP (for some uses of the *miracle* spell; see above).

Mirage Arcana

Illusion (Glamer)
Level: Brd 5, Sor/Wiz 5
Components: V, S
Casting Time: 1 standard action
Area: One 20-ft. cube/level (S)
Duration: Concentration +1 hour/
  level (D)

This spell functions like *hallucinatory terrain*, except that it enables you to make any area appear to be something other than it is. The illusion includes audible, visual, tactile, and olfactory elements. Unlike *hallucinatory terrain*, the spell can alter the appearance of structures (or add them where none are present). Still, it can't disguise, conceal, or add creatures (though creatures within the area might hide themselves within the illusion just as they can hide themselves within a real location).

Mirror Image

Illusion (Figment)
Level: Brd 2, Sor/Wiz 2
Components: V, S
Casting Time: 1 standard action
Range: Personal; see text
Target: You
Duration: 1 min./level (D)

Several illusory duplicates of you pop into being, making it difficult for enemies to know which target to attack. The figments stay near you and disappear when struck.

Mirror image creates 1d4 images plus one image per three caster levels (maximum eight images total). These figments separate from you and remain in a cluster, each within 5 feet of at least one other figment or you. You can move into and through a *mirror image*. When you and the *mirror image* separate, observers can't use vision or hearing to tell which one is you and which is the image. The figments may also move through each other. The figments mimic your actions, pretending to cast spells when you cast a spell, drink potions when you drink a potion, levitate when you levitate, and so on.

Enemies attempting to attack you or cast spells at you must select from among indistinguishable targets. Generally, roll randomly to see whether the selected target is real or a figment. Any successful attack against an image destroys it. An image's AC is 10 + your size modifier + your Dex modifier. Figments seem to react normally to area spells (such as looking like they're burned or dead after being hit by a *fireball*).

While moving, you can merge with and split off from figments so that enemies who have learned which image is real are again confounded.

An attacker must be able to see the images to be fooled. If you are invisible or an attacker shuts his or her eyes, the spell has no effect. (Being unable to see carries the same penalties as being blinded.)

Misdirection

Illusion (Glamer)
Level: Brd 2, Sor/Wiz 2
Components: V, S
Casting Time: 1 standard action
Range: Close (25 ft. + 5 ft./2 levels)
Target: One creature or object, up to a
  10-ft. cube in size
Duration: 1 hour/level
Saving Throw: None or Will negates;
  see text
Spell Resistance: No

By means of this spell, you misdirect the information from divination spells that reveal auras (*detect evil*, *detect magic*, *discern lies*, and the like). On casting the spell, you choose another object within range. For the duration of the spell, the subject of *misdirection* is detected as if it were the other object. (Neither the subject nor the other object gets a saving throw against this effect.) Detection spells provide information based on the second object rather than on the actual target of the detection unless the caster of the detection succeeds on a Will save. For instance, you could make yourself detect as a tree if one were within range at casting: not evil, not lying, not magical, neutral in alignment, and so forth. This spell does not affect other types of divination magic (*augury*, *detect thoughts*, *clairaudience/clairvoyance*, and the like).

Mislead

Illusion (Figment, Glamer)
Level: Brd 5, Luck 6, Sor/Wiz 6, Trickery 6
Components: S
Casting Time: 1 standard action
Range: Close (25 ft. + 5 ft./2 levels)
Target/Effect: You/one illusory double
Duration: 1 round/level (D) and concentration + 3 rounds; see text
Saving Throw: None or Will disbelief (if interacted with); see text
Spell Resistance: No

You become invisible (as *improved invisibility*, a glamer), and at the same time, an illusory double of you (as *major image*, a figment) appears. You are then free to go elsewhere while your double moves away. The double appears within range but thereafter moves as you direct it (which requires concentration beginning on the first round after the casting). You can make the figment appear superimposed perfectly over your own body so that observers don't notice an image appearing and you turning invisible. You and the figment can then move in different directions. The double moves at your speed and can talk and gesture as if it were real, but it cannot attack or cast spells, though it can pretend to do so.

The illusory double lasts as long as you concentrate upon it, plus 3 additional rounds. After you cease concentration, the illusory double continues to carry out the same activity (for instance, fleeing down a hallway) until the duration expires. The *improved invisibility* lasts for 1 round per level, regardless of concentration.

Modify Memory

Enchantment (Compulsion) [Mind-Affecting]
Level: Brd 4
Components: V, S
Casting Time: 1 round; see text
Range: Close (25 ft. + 5 ft./2 levels)
Target: One living creature
Duration: Permanent
Saving Throw: Will negates
Spell Resistance: Yes

You reach into the subject's mind and modify as many as 5 minutes of its memories in one of the following ways.
- Eliminate all memory of an event the subject actually experienced. This spell cannot negate *charm*, *geas/quest*, *suggestion*, or similar spells.

- Allow the subject to recall with perfect clarity an event it actually experienced. For instance, it could recall every word from a 5-minute conversation or every detail from a passage in a book.
- Change the details of an event the subject actually experienced.
- Implant a memory of an event the subject never experienced.

Casting the spell takes 1 round. If the subject fails to save, you proceed with the spell by spending as much as 5 minutes (a period of time equal to the amount of memory time you want to modify) visualizing the memory you wish to modify in the subject. If your concentration is disturbed before the visualization is complete, or if the subject is ever beyond the spell's range during this time, the spell is lost.

A modified memory does not necessarily affect the subject's actions, particularly if it contradicts the creature's natural inclinations. An illogical modified memory, such as the subject recalling how much it enjoyed drinking poison, is dismissed by the creature as a bad dream or a memory muddied by too much wine. More useful applications of *modify memory* include implanting memories of friendly encounters with you (inclining the subject to act favorably toward you), changing the details of orders given to the subject by a superior, or causing the subject to forget that it ever saw you or your party. The DM reserves the right to decide whether a modified memory is too nonsensical to significantly affect the subject.

Moment of Prescience

Divination
Level: Luck 8, Sor/Wiz 8
Components: V, S
Casting Time: 1 standard action
Range: Personal
Target: You
Duration: 1 hour/level or until discharged

This spell grants you a powerful sixth sense in relation to yourself. Once during the spell's duration, you may choose to use its effect. This spell grants you an insight bonus equal to your caster level (maximum +25) on any single attack roll, opposed ability or skill check, or saving throw. Alternatively, you can apply the insight bonus to your AC against a single attack (even if flat-footed). Activating the effect doesn't take an action; you can even activate it on another character's turn if needed. You must choose to use the *moment of prescience* before you make the roll it is to modify. Once used, the spell ends.

You can't have more than one *moment of prescience* active on you at the same time.

Mordenkainen's Disjunction

Abjuration
Level: Magic 9, Sor/Wiz 9
Components: V
Casting Time: 1 standard action
Range: Close (25 ft. + 5 ft./2 levels)
Area: All magical effects and magic items within a 40-ft.-radius burst
Duration: Instantaneous
Saving Throw: Will negates (object)
Spell Resistance: No

All magical effects and magic items within the radius of the spell, except for those that you carry or touch, are disjoined. That is, spells and spell-like effects are separated into their individual components (ending the effect as a *dispel magic* spell does), and each permanent magic item must make a successful Will save or be turned into a normal item. An item in a creature's possession uses its own Will save bonus or its possessor's Will save bonus, whichever is higher.

You also have a 1% chance per caster level of destroying an *antimagic field*. If the *antimagic field* survives the *disjunction*, no items within it are disjoined.

Even artifacts are subject to *disjunction*, though there is only a 1% chance per caster level of actually affecting such powerful items. Additionally, if an artifact is destroyed, you must make a DC 25 Will save or permanently lose all spellcasting abilities. (These abilities cannot be recovered by mortal magic, not even *miracle* or *wish*.)

Note: Destroying artifacts is a dangerous business, and it is 95% likely to attract the attention of some powerful being who has an interest in or connection with the device.

Mordenkainen's Faithful Hound

Conjuration (Creation)
Level: Sor/Wiz 5
Components: V, S, M
Casting Time: 1 standard action
Range: Close (25 ft. + 5 ft./2 levels)
Effect: Phantom watchdog
Duration: 1 hour/caster level or until discharged, then 1 round/caster level; see text
Saving Throw: None
Spell Resistance: No

You conjure up a phantom watchdog that is invisible to everyone but yourself. It then guards the area where it was conjured (it does not move). The hound immediately starts barking loudly if any Small or larger creature approaches within 30 feet of it. (Those within 30 feet of the hound when it is conjured may move about in the area, but if they leave and return, they activate the barking.) The hound sees invisible and ethereal creatures. It does not react to figments, but it does react to shadow illusions.

If an intruder approaches to within 5 feet of the hound, the dog stops barking and delivers a vicious bite (+10 attack bonus, 2d6+3 points of piercing damage) once per round. The dog also gets the bonuses appropriate to an invisible creature. The dog is considered ready to bite intruders, so it delivers its first bite on the intruder's turn. Its bite is the equivalent of a magic weapon for the purpose of damage reduction. The hound cannot be attacked, but it can be dispelled.

The spell lasts for 1 hour per caster level, but once the hound begins barking, it lasts only 1 round per caster level. If you are ever more than 100 feet distant from the hound, the spell ends.

Material Component: A tiny silver whistle, a piece of bone, and a thread.

Mordenkainen's Lucubration

Transmutation
Level: Wiz 6
Components: V, S
Casting Time: 1 standard action
Range: Personal
Target: You
Duration: Instantaneous

You instantly recall any one spell of 5th level or lower that you have used during the past 24 hours. The spell must have been actually cast during that period. The recalled spell is stored in your mind as through prepared in the normal fashion. If the recalled spell requires material components, you must provide them. The recovered spell is not usable until the material components are available.

Mordenkainen's Magnificent Mansion

Conjuration (Creation)
Level: Sor/Wiz 7
Components: V, S, F
Casting Time: 1 standard action
Range: Close (25 ft. + 5 ft./2 levels)
Effect: Extradimensional mansion, up to three 10-ft. cubes/level (S)
Duration: 2 hours/level (D)
Saving Throw: None
Spell Resistance: No

You conjure up an extradimensional dwelling that has a single entrance on the plane from which the spell was cast. The entry point looks like a faint shimmering in the air that is 4 feet wide and 8 feet high. Only those you designate may enter the mansion, and the portal is shut and made invisible behind you when you enter. You may open it again from your own side at will. Once observers have passed beyond the entrance, they are in a magnificent foyer with numerous chambers beyond. The atmosphere is clean, fresh, and warm.

You can create any floor plan you desire to the limit of the spell's effect. The place is furnished and contains sufficient foodstuffs to serve a nine-course banquet to a dozen people per caster level. A staff of near-transparent servants (as many as two per caster level), liveried and obedient, wait upon all who enter. The servants function as *unseen servant* spells except that they are visible and can go anywhere in the mansion.

Since the place can be entered only through its special portal, outside conditions do not affect the mansion, nor do conditions inside it pass to the plane beyond.

Focus: A miniature portal carved from ivory, a small piece of polished marble, and a tiny silver spoon (each item worth 5 gp).

Mordenkainen's Private Sanctum

Abjuration
Level: Sor/Wiz 5
Components: V, S, M
Casting Time: 10 minutes
Range: Close (25 ft. + 5 ft./2 levels)
Area: 30-ft. cube/level (S)
Duration: 24 hours (D)
Saving Throw: None
Spell Resistance: No

This spell ensures privacy. Anyone looking into the area from outside sees only a dark, foggy mass. Darkvision cannot penetrate it. No sounds, no matter how loud, can escape the area, so nobody can eavesdrop from outside. Those inside can see out normally.

Divination (scrying) spells cannot perceive anything within the area, and those within are immune to *detect thoughts*. The ward prevents speech between those inside and those outside (because it blocks sound), but it does not prevent other communication, such as a *sending* or *message* spell, or telepathic communication, such as that between a wizard and her familiar.

The spell does not prevent creatures or objects from moving into and out of the area.

Mordenkainen's private sanctum can be made permanent with a *permanency* spell.

Material Component: A thin sheet of lead, a piece of opaque glass, a wad of cotton or cloth, and powdered chrysolite.

Mordenkainen's Sword

Evocation [Force]
Level: Sor/Wiz 7
Components: V, S, F
Casting Time: 1 standard action
Range: Close (25 ft. + 5 ft./2 levels)
Effect: One sword
Duration: 1 round/level (D)
Saving Throw: None
Spell Resistance: Yes

This spell brings into being a shimmering, swordlike plane of force. The sword strikes at any opponent within its range, as you desire, starting in the round that you cast the spell. The sword attacks its designated target once each round on your turn. Its attack bonus is equal to your caster level + your Int bonus or your Cha bonus (for wizards or sorcerers, respectively) with an additional +3 enhancement bonus. As a force effect, it can strike ethereal and incorporeal creatures. It deals 4d6+3 points of force damage, with a threat range of 19–20 and a critical multiplier of ×2.

The sword always strikes from your direction. It does not get a bonus for flanking or help a combatant get one. If the sword goes beyond the spell range from you, if it goes out of your sight, or if you are not directing it, the sword returns to you and hovers.

Each round after the first, you can use a standard action to switch the sword to a new target. If you do not, the sword continues to attack the previous round's target. The sword cannot be attacked or harmed by physical attacks, but *dispel magic*, *disintegrate*, a *sphere of annihilation*, or a *rod of cancellation* affects it. The sword's AC is 13 (10, +0 size bonus for Medium object, +3 deflection bonus).

If an attacked creature has spell resistance, the resistance is checked the first time *Mordenkainen's sword* strikes it. If the sword is successfully resisted, the spell is dispelled. If not, the sword has its normal full effect on that creature for the duration of the spell.

Focus: A miniature platinum sword with a grip and pommel of copper and zinc. It costs 250 gp to construct.

Mount

Conjuration (Summoning)
Level: Sor/Wiz 1
Components: V, S, M
Casting Time: 1 round
Range: Close (25 ft. + 5 ft./2 levels)
Effect: One mount
Duration: 2 hours/level (D)
Saving Throw: None
Spell Resistance: No

You summon a light horse or a pony (your choice) to serve you as a mount. The steed serves willingly and well. The mount comes with a bit and bridle and a riding saddle.

Material Component: A bit of horse hair.

Move Earth

Transmutation [Earth]
Level: Drd 6, Sor/Wiz 6
Components: V, S, M
Casting Time: See text
Range: Long (400 ft. + 40 ft./level)
Area: Dirt in an area up to 750 ft. square and up to 10 ft. deep (S)
Duration: Instantaneous
Saving Throw: None
Spell Resistance: No

Move earth moves dirt (clay, loam, sand), possibly collapsing embankments, moving hillocks, shifting dunes, and so forth. However, in no event can rock formations be collapsed or moved. The area to be affected determines the casting time. For every 150-foot square (up to 10 feet deep), casting takes 10 minutes. The maximum area, 750 feet by 750 feet, takes 4 hours and 10 minutes to move.

This spell does not violently break the surface of the ground. Instead, it creates wavelike crests and troughs, with the earth reacting with glacierlike fluidity until the desired result is achieved. Trees, structures, rock formations, and such are mostly unaffected except for changes in elevation and relative topography.

The spell cannot be used for tunneling and is generally too slow to trap or bury creatures. Its primary use is for digging or filling moats or for adjusting terrain contours before a battle.

This spell has no effect on earth creatures.

Material Component: A mixture of soils (clay, loam, and sand) in a small bag, and an iron blade.

Neutralize Poison

Conjuration (Healing)
Level: Brd 4, Clr 4, Drd 3, Pal 4, Rgr 3
Components: V, S, M/DF
Casting Time: 1 standard action
Range: Touch
Target: Creature or object of up to 1 cu. ft./level touched
Duration: 10 min./level
Saving Throw: Will negates (harmless, object)
Spell Resistance: Yes (harmless, object)

You detoxify any sort of venom in the creature or object touched. A poisoned creature suffers no additional effects from the poison, and any temporary effects are ended, but the spell does not reverse instantaneous effects, such as hit point damage, temporary ability damage, or effects that don't go away on their own. For example, if a poison has dealt 3 points of Constitution damage to a character and threatens to deal more damage later, this spell prevents the future damage but does not repair the damage already done.

The creature is immune to any poison it is exposed to during the duration of the spell. Unlike with *delay poison*, such effects aren't postponed until after the duration—the creature need not make any saves against poison effects applied to it during the length of the spell.

This spell can instead neutralize the poison in a poisonous creature or object for the duration of the spell, at the caster's option.

Arcane Material Component: A bit of charcoal.

Nightmare

Illusion (Phantasm) [Mind-Affecting, Evil]
Level: Brd 5, Sor/Wiz 5
Components: V, S
Casting Time: 10 minutes
Range: Unlimited
Target: One living creature
Duration: Instantaneous
Saving Throw: Will negates; see text
Spell Resistance: Yes

You send a hideous and unsettling phantasmal vision to a specific creature that you name or otherwise specifically designate. The *nightmare* prevents restful sleep and causes 1d10 points of damage. The *nightmare* leaves the subject fatigued and unable to regain arcane spells for the next 24 hours.

The difficulty of the save depends on how well you know the subject and what sort of physical connection (if any) you have to that creature.

Knowledge	Will Save Modifier
None[1]	+10
Secondhand (you have heard of the subject)	+5
Firsthand (you have met the subject)	+0
Familiar (you know the subject well)	–5
1 You must have some sort of connection to a creature you have no knowledge of.	

Connection	Will Save Modifier
Likeness or picture	–2
Possession or garment	–4
Body part, lock of hair, bit of nail, etc.	–10

Dispel evil cast on the subject while you are casting the spell dispels the *nightmare* and causes you to be stunned for 10 minutes per caster level of the *dispel evil*.

If the recipient is awake when the spell begins, you can choose to cease casting (ending the spell) or to enter a trance until the recipient goes to sleep, whereupon you become alert again and complete the casting. If you are disturbed during the trance, you must succeed on a Concentration check as if you were in the midst of casting a spell (see page 69) or the spell ends.

If you choose to enter a trance, you are not aware of your surroundings or the activities around you while in the trance. You are defenseless, both physically and mentally, while in the trance. (You always fail any saving throw, for example.)

Creatures who don't sleep (such as elves, but not half-elves) or dream are immune to this spell.

Nondetection

Abjuration
Level: Rgr 4, Sor/Wiz 3, Trickery 3
Components: V, S, M
Casting Time: 1 standard action
Range: Touch
Target: Creature or object touched
Duration: 1 hour/level
Saving Throw: Will negates (harmless, object)
Spell Resistance: Yes (harmless, object)

The warded creature or object becomes difficult to detect by divination spells such as *clairaudience/clairvoyance*, *locate object*, and *detect* spells. *Nondetection* also prevents location by such magic items as *crystal balls*. If a divination is attempted against the warded creature or item, the caster of the divination must succeed on a caster level check (1d20 + caster level) against a DC of 11 + the caster level of the spellcaster who cast *nondetection*. If you cast *nondetection* on yourself or on an item currently in your possession, the DC is 15 + your caster level.

If cast on a creature, *nondetection* wards the creature's gear as well as the creature itself.

Material Component: A pinch of diamond dust worth 50 gp.

Nystul's Magic Aura

Illusion (Glamer)
Level: Brd 1, Magic 1, Sor/Wiz 1
Components: V, S, F
Casting Time: 1 standard action
Range: Touch
Target: One touched object weighing up to 5 lb./level
Duration: One day/level (D)
Saving Throw: None; see text
Spell Resistance: No

You alter an item's aura so that it registers to *detect* spells (and spells with similar capabilities) as though it were nonmagical, or a magic item of a kind you specify, or the subject of a spell you specify. You could make an ordinary sword register as a *+2 vorpal sword* as far as magical detection is concerned or make a *+2 vorpal sword* register as if it were a *+1 sword* or even a nonmagical sword.

If the object bearing *Nystul's magic aura* has *identify* cast on it or is similarly examined, the examiner recognizes that the aura is false and detects the object's actual qualities if he succeeds on a Will save.

Otherwise, he believes the aura and no amount of testing reveals what the true magic is.

If the targeted item's own aura is exceptionally powerful (if it is an artifact, for instance), *Nystul's magic aura* doesn't work.

Note: A magic weapon, shield, or suit of armor must be a masterwork item, so a sword of average make, for example, looks suspicious if it has a magical aura.

Focus: A small square of silk that must be passed over the object that receives the aura.

Obscure Object

Abjuration
Level: Brd 1, Clr 3, Sor/Wiz 2
Components: V, S, M/DF
Casting Time: 1 standard action
Range: Touch
Target: One object touched of up to 100 lb./level
Duration: 8 hours (D)
Saving Throw: Will negates (object)
Spell Resistance: Yes (object)

This spell hides an object from location by divination (scrying) effects, such as the *scrying* spell or a *crystal ball*. Such an attempt automatically fails (if the divination is targeted on the object) or fails to perceive the object (if the divination is targeted on a nearby location, object, or person).

Arcane Material Component: A piece of chameleon skin.

Obscuring Mist

Conjuration (Creation)
Level: Air 1, Clr 1, Drd 1, Sor/Wiz 1, Water 1
Components: V, S
Casting Time: 1 standard action
Range: 20 ft.
Effect: Cloud spreads in 20-ft. radius from you, 20 ft. high
Duration: 1 min./level
Saving Throw: None
Spell Resistance: No

A misty vapor arises around you. It is stationary once created. The vapor obscures all sight, including darkvision, beyond 5 feet. A creature 5 feet away has concealment (attacks have a 20% miss chance). Creatures farther away have total concealment (50% miss chance, and the attacker cannot use sight to locate the target).

A moderate wind (11+ mph), such as from a *gust of wind* spell, disperses the fog in 4 rounds. A strong wind (21+ mph) disperses the fog in 1 round. A *fireball, flame strike,* or similar spell burns away the fog in the explosive or fiery spell's area. A *wall of fire* burns away the fog in the area into which it deals damage.

This spell does not function underwater.

Open/Close

Transmutation
Level: Brd 0, Sor/Wiz 0
Components: V, S, F
Casting Time: 1 standard action
Range: Close (25 ft. + 5 ft./2 levels)
Target: Object weighing up to 30 lb. or portal that can be opened or closed
Duration: Instantaneous
Saving Throw: Will negates (object)
Spell Resistance: Yes (object)

You can open or close (your choice) a door, chest, box, window, bag, pouch, bottle, barrel, or other container. If anything resists this activity (such as a bar on a door or a lock on a chest), the spell fails. In addition, the spell can only open and close things weighing 30 pounds or less. Thus, doors, chests, and similar objects sized for enormous creatures may be beyond this spell's ability to affect.

Focus: A brass key.

Order's Wrath

Evocation [Lawful]
Level: Law 4
Components: V, S
Casting Time: 1 standard action
Range: Medium (100 ft. + 10 ft./level)
Area: Nonlawful creatures within a burst that fills a 30-ft. cube
Duration: Instantaneous (1 round); see text
Saving Throw: Will partial; see text
Spell Resistance: Yes

You channel lawful power to smite enemies. The power takes the form of a three-dimensional grid of energy. Only chaotic and neutral (not lawful) creatures are harmed by the spell.

The spell deals 1d8 points of damage per two caster levels (maximum 5d8) to chaotic creatures (or 1d6 points of damage per caster level, maximum 10d6, to chaotic outsiders) and causes them to be dazed for 1 round. A successful Will save reduces the damage to half and negates the daze effect.

The spell deals only half damage to creatures who are neither chaotic nor lawful, and they are not dazed. They can reduce the damage in half again (down to one-quarter of the roll) with a successful Will save.

Otiluke's Freezing Sphere

Evocation [Cold]
Level: Sor/Wiz 6
Components: V, S, F
Casting Time: 1 standard action
Range: Long (400 ft. + 40 ft./level)
Target, Effect, or Area: See text
Duration: Instantaneous or 1 round/level; see text
Saving Throw: Reflex half; see text
Spell Resistance: Yes

Otiluke's freezing sphere creates a frigid globe of cold energy that streaks from your fingertips to the location you select, where it explodes in a 10-foot-radius burst, dealing 1d6 points of cold damage per caster level (maximum 15d6) to each creature in the area. An elemental (water) creature instead takes 1d8 points of cold damage per caster level (maximum 15d8).

If the *freezing sphere* strikes a body of water or a liquid that is principally water (not including water-based creatures), it freezes the liquid to a depth of 6 inches over an area equal to 100 square feet (a 10-foot square) per caster level (maximum 1,500 square feet). This ice lasts for 1 round per caster level. Creatures that were swimming on the surface of frozen water become trapped in the ice. Attempting to break free is a full-round action. A trapped creature must make a DC 25 Strength check or a DC 25 Escape Artist check to do so.

You can refrain from firing the globe after completing the spell, if you wish. Treat this as a touch spell for which you are holding the charge (see page 176). You can hold the charge for as long as 1 round per level, at the end of which time the *freezing sphere* bursts centered on you (and you receive no saving throw to resist its effect). Firing the globe in a later round is a standard action.

Focus: A small crystal sphere.

Otiluke's Resilient Sphere

Evocation [Force]
Level: Sor/Wiz 4
Components: V, S, M
Casting Time: 1 standard action
Range: Close (25 ft. + 5 ft./2 levels)
Effect: 1-ft.-diameter/level sphere, centered around a creature
Duration: 1 min./level (D)
Saving Throw: Reflex negates
Spell Resistance: Yes

A globe of shimmering force encloses a creature, provided the creature is small enough to fit within the diameter of the sphere. The sphere contains its subject for the spell's duration. The sphere is not subject to damage of any sort except from a *rod of cancellation,* a *rod of negation,* a *disintegrate* spell, or a targeted *dispel magic* spell. These effects destroy the sphere without harm to the subject. Nothing can pass through the sphere, inside or out, though the subject can breathe normally. The subject may struggle, but the sphere cannot be physically moved either by people outside it or by the struggles of those within.

Material Component: A hemispherical piece of clear crystal and a matching hemispherical piece of gum arabic.

Otiluke's Telekinetic Sphere
Evocation [Force]
Level: Sor/Wiz 8
Components: V, S, M
Casting Time: 1 standard action
Range: Close (25 ft. + 5 ft./2 levels)
Effect: 1-ft.-diameter/level sphere, centered around creatures or objects
Duration: 1 min./level (D)
Saving Throw: Reflex negates (object)
Spell Resistance: Yes (object)

This spell functions like *Otiluke's resilient sphere*, with the addition that the creatures or objects inside the globe are nearly weightless. Anything contained within an *Otiluke's telekinetic sphere* weighs only one-sixteenth of its normal weight. You can telekinetically lift anything in the sphere that normally weighs 5,000 pounds or less. The telekinetic control extends from you out to medium range (100 feet + 10 feet per caster level) after the sphere has succeeded in encapsulating its contents.

You can move objects or creatures in the sphere that weigh a total of 5,000 pounds or less by concentrating on the sphere. You can begin moving a sphere in the round after casting the spell. If you concentrate on doing so (a standard action), you can move the sphere as much as 30 feet in a round. If you cease concentrating, the sphere does not move in that round (if on a level surface) or descends at its falling rate (if aloft) until it reaches a level surface, or the spell's duration expires, or you begin concentrating again. If you cease concentrating (voluntarily or due to failing a Concentration check), you can resume concentrating on your next turn or any later turn during the spell's duration.

The sphere falls at a rate of only 60 feet per round, which is not fast enough to cause damage to the contents of the sphere.

You can move the sphere telekinetically even if you are in it.

Material Component: A hemispherical piece of clear crystal, a matching hemispherical piece of gum arabic, and a pair of small bar magnets.

Otto's Irresistible Dance
Enchantment (Compulsion) [Mind-Affecting]
Level: Brd 6, Sor/Wiz 8
Components: V
Casting Time: 1 standard action
Range: Touch
Target: Living creature touched
Duration: 1d4+1 rounds
Saving Throw: None
Spell Resistance: Yes

The subject feels an undeniable urge to dance and begins doing so, complete with foot shuffling and tapping. The spell effect makes it impossible for the subject to do anything other than caper and prance in place. The effect imposes a –4 penalty to Armor Class and a –10 penalty on Reflex saves, and it negates any AC bonus granted by a shield the target holds. The dancing subject provokes attacks of opportunity each round on its turn.

Overland Flight
Transmutation
Level: Sor/Wiz 5
Components: V, S
Range: Personal
Target: You
Duration: 1 hour/level

This spell functions like a *fly* spell, except you can fly at a speed of 40 feet (30 feet if wearing medium or heavy armor, or if carrying a medium or heavy load) with average maneuverability. When using this spell for long-distance movement, you can hustle without taking nonlethal damage (a forced march still requires Constitution checks). This means you can cover 64 miles in an eight-hour period of flight (or 48 miles at a speed of 30 feet). See page 164 for more on overland movement.

Owl's Wisdom
Transmutation
Level: Clr 2, Drd 2, Pal 2, Rgr 2, Sor/Wiz 2
Components: V, S, M/DF
Casting Time: 1 standard action
Range: Touch
Target: Creature touched
Duration: 1 min./level
Saving Throw: Will negates (harmless)
Spell Resistance: Yes

The transmuted creature becomes wiser. The spell grants a +4 enhancement bonus to Wisdom, adding the usual benefit to Wisdom-related skills. Clerics, druids, paladins, and rangers (and other Wisdom-based spellcasters) who receive *owl's wisdom* do not gain any additional bonus spells for the increased Wisdom, but the save DCs for their spells increase.

Arcane Material Component: A few feathers, or a pinch of droppings, from an owl.

Owl's Wisdom, Mass
Transmutation
Level: Clr 6, Drd 6, Sor/Wiz 6
Range: Close (25 ft. + 5 ft./2 levels)
Target: One creature/level, no two of which can be more than 30 ft. apart

This spell functions like *owl's wisdom*, except that it affects multiple creatures.

Passwall
Transmutation
Level: Sor/Wiz 5
Components: V, S, M
Casting Time: 1 standard action
Range: Touch
Effect: 5 ft. by 8 ft. opening, 10 ft. deep plus 5 ft. deep per three additional levels
Duration: 1 hour/level (D)
Saving Throw: None
Spell Resistance: No

You create a passage through wooden, plaster, or stone walls, but not through metal or other harder materials. The passage is 10 feet deep plus an additional 5 feet deep per three caster levels above 9th (15 feet at 12th, 20 feet at 15th, and a maximum of 25 feet deep at 18th level). If the wall's thickness is more than the depth of the passage created, then a single *passwall* simply makes a niche or short tunnel. Several *passwall* spells can then form a continuing passage to breach very thick walls. When *passwall* ends, creatures within the passage are ejected out the nearest exit. If someone dispels the *passwall* or you dismiss it, creatures in the passage are ejected out the far exit, if there is one, or out the sole exit if there is only one.

Material Component: A pinch of sesame seeds.

Pass without Trace
Transmutation
Level: Drd 1, Rgr 1
Components: V, S, DF
Casting Time: 1 standard action
Range: Touch
Targets: One creature/level touched
Duration: 1 hour/level (D)
Saving Throw: Will negates (harmless)
Spell Resistance: Yes (harmless)

The subject or subjects can move through any type of terrain—mud, snow, dust, or the like—and leave neither footprints nor scent. Tracking the subjects is impossible by nonmagical means.

Permanency
Universal
Level: Sor/Wiz 5
Components: V, S, XP
Casting Time: 2 rounds
Range: See text
Target, Effect, or Area: See text
Duration: Permanent; see text
Saving Throw: None
Spell Resistance: No

This spell makes certain other spells permanent. Depending on the spell, you must be of a minimum caster level and must expend a number of XP.

You can make the following spells permanent in regard to yourself.

Spell	Minimum Caster Level	XP Cost
Arcane sight	11th	1,500 XP
Comprehend languages	9th	500 XP
Darkvision	10th	1,000 XP
Detect magic	9th	500 XP
Read magic	9th	500 XP
See invisibility	10th	1,000 XP
Tongues	11th	1,500 XP

You cast the desired spell and then follow it with the *permanency* spell. You cannot cast these spells on other creatures. This application of *permanency* can be dispelled only by a caster of higher level than you were when you cast the spell.

In addition to personal use, *permanency* can be used to make the following spells permanent on yourself, another creature, or an object (as appropriate).

Spell	Minimum Caster Level	XP Cost
Enlarge person	9th	500 XP
Magic fang	9th	500 XP
Magic fang, greater	11th	1,500 XP
Rary's telepathic bond[1]	13th	2,500 XP
Reduce person	9th	500 XP
Resistance	9th	500 XP

1 Only bonds two creatures per casting of *permanency*.

Additionally, the following spells can be cast upon objects or areas only and rendered permanent.

Spell	Minimum Caster Level	XP Cost
Alarm	9th	500 XP
Animate objects	14th	3,000 XP
Dancing lights	9th	500 XP
Ghost sound	9th	500 XP
Gust of wind	11th	1,500 XP
Invisibility	10th	1,000 XP
Magic mouth	10th	1,000 XP
Mordenkainen's private sanctum	13th	2,500 XP
Phase door	15th	3,500 XP
Prismatic sphere	17th	4,500 XP
Prismatic wall	16th	4,000 XP
Shrink item	11th	1,500 XP
Solid fog	12th	2,000 XP
Stinking cloud	11th	1,500 XP
Symbol of death	16th	4,000 XP
Symbol of fear	14th	3,000 XP
Symbol of insanity	16th	4,000 XP
Symbol of pain	13th	2,500 XP
Symbol of persuasion	14th	3,000 XP
Symbol of sleep	16th	4,000 XP
Symbol of stunning	15th	3,500 XP
Symbol of weakness	15th	3,500 XP
Teleportation circle	17th	4,500 XP
Wall of fire	12th	2,000 XP
Wall of force	13th	2,500 XP
Web	10th	1,000 XP

Spells cast on other creatures, objects, or locations (not on you) are vulnerable to *dispel magic* as normal.

The DM may allow other selected spells to be made permanent. Researching this possible application of a spell costs as much time and money as independently researching the selected spell (see the *Dungeon Master's Guide* for details). If the DM has already determined that the application is not possible, the research automatically fails. Note that you never learn what is possible except by the success or failure of your research.

XP Cost: See tables above.

Permanent Image
Illusion (Figment)
Level: Brd 6, Sor/Wiz 6
Effect: Figment that cannot extend beyond a 20-ft. cube + one 10-ft. cube/level (S)
Duration: Permanent (D)

This spell functions like *silent image*, except that the figment includes visual, auditory, olfactory, and thermal elements, and the spell is permanent. By concentrating, you can move the image within the limits of the range, but it is static while you are not concentrating.

Material Component: A bit of fleece plus powdered jade worth 100 gp.

Persistent Image
Illusion (Figment)
Level: Brd 5, Sor/Wiz 5
Duration: 1 min./level (D)

This spell functions like *silent image*, except that the figment includes visual, auditory, olfactory, and thermal components, and the figment follows a script determined by you. The figment follows that script without your having to concentrate on it. The illusion can include intelligible speech if you wish. For instance, you could create the illusion of several orcs playing cards and arguing, culminating in a fistfight.

Material Component: A bit of fleece and several grains of sand.

Phantasmal Killer
Illusion (Phantasm) [Fear, Mind-Affecting]
Level: Sor/Wiz 4
Components: V, S
Casting Time: 1 standard action
Range: Medium (100 ft. + 10 ft./level)
Target: One living creature
Duration: Instantaneous
Saving Throw: Will disbelief (if interacted with), then Fortitude partial; see text
Spell Resistance: Yes

You create a phantasmal image of the most fearsome creature imaginable to the subject simply by forming the fears of the subject's subconscious mind into something that its conscious mind can visualize: this most horrible beast. Only the spell's subject can see the phantasmal killer. You see only a vague shape. The target first gets a Will save to recognize the image as unreal. If that save fails, the phantasm touches the subject, and the subject must succeed on a Fortitude save or die from fear. Even if the Fortitude save is successful, the subject takes 3d6 points of damage.

If the subject of a *phantasmal killer* attack succeeds in disbelieving and is wearing a *helm of telepathy*, the beast can be turned upon you. You must then disbelieve it or become subject to its deadly fear attack.

Phantom Steed
Conjuration (Creation)
Level: Brd 3, Sor/Wiz 3
Components: V, S
Casting Time: 10 minutes
Range: 0 ft.
Effect: One quasi-real, horselike creature
Duration: 1 hour/level (D)
Saving Throw: None
Spell Resistance: No

You conjure a Large, quasi-real, horselike creature. The steed can be ridden only by you or by the one person for whom you specifically created the mount. A phantom steed has a black head and body, gray mane and tail, and smoke-colored, insubstantial hooves that make no sound. It has what seems to be a saddle, bit, and bridle. It does not fight, but animals shun it and refuse to attack it.

The mount has an AC of 18 (−1 size, +4 natural armor, +5 Dex) and 7 hit points +1 hit point per caster level. If it loses all its hit points, the phantom steed disappears. A phantom steed has a speed of 20 feet per caster level, to a maximum of 240 feet. It can bear its rider's weight plus up to 10 pounds per caster level.

These mounts gain certain powers according to caster level. A mount's abilities include those of mounts of lower caster levels. Thus, a mount created by a 12th-level caster has the 8th, 10th, and 12th caster level abilities.

8th Level: The mount can ride over sandy, muddy, or even swampy ground without difficulty or decrease in speed.

10th Level: The mount can use *water walk* at will (as the spell, no action required to activate this ability).

12th Level: The mount can use *air walk* at will (as the spell, no action required to activate this ability) for up to 1 round at a time, after which it falls to the ground.

14th Level: The mount can fly at its speed (average maneuverability).

Phase Door
Conjuration (Creation)
Level: Sor/Wiz 7, Travel 8
Components: V
Casting Time: 1 standard action
Range: 0 ft.
Effect: Ethereal 5 ft. by 8 ft. opening, 10 ft. deep + 5 ft. deep per three levels
Duration: One usage per two levels
Saving Throw: None
Spell Resistance: No

This spell creates an ethereal passage through wooden, plaster, or stone walls, but not other materials. The *phase door* is invisible and inaccessible to all creatures except you, and only you can use the passage. You disappear when you enter the *phase door* and appear when you exit. If you desire, you can take one other creature (Medium or smaller) through the door. This counts as two uses of the door. The door does not allow light, sound, or spell effects through it, nor can you see through it without using it. Thus, the spell can provide an escape route, though certain creatures, such as phase spiders, can follow with ease. A *gem of true seeing* or similar magic reveals the presence of a *phase door* but does not allow its use.

A *phase door* is subject to *dispel magic.* If anyone is within the passage when it is dispelled, he is harmlessly ejected just as if he were inside a *passwall* effect.

You can allow other creatures to use the *phase door* by setting some triggering condition for the door. Such conditions can be as simple or elaborate as you desire. They can be based on a creature's name, identity, or alignment, but otherwise must be based on observable actions or qualities. Intangibles such as level, class, Hit Dice, and hit points don't qualify.

Phase door can be made permanent with a *permanency* spell.

Planar Ally
Conjuration (Calling) [see text for *lesser planar ally*]
Level: Clr 6
Effect: One or two called elementals or outsiders, totaling no more than 12 HD, which cannot be more than 30 ft. apart when they appear

This spell functions like *lesser planar ally,* except you may call a single creature of 12 HD or less, or two creatures of the same kind whose Hit Dice total no more than 12. The creatures agree to help you and request your return payment together.
XP Cost: 250 XP.

Planar Ally, Greater
Conjuration (Calling) [see text for *lesser planar ally*]
Level: Clr 8
Effect: Up to three called elementals or outsiders, totaling no more than 18 HD, no two of which can be more than 30 ft. apart when they appear.

This spell functions like *lesser planar ally,* except that you may call a single creature of 18 HD or less, or up to three creatures of the same kind whose Hit Dice total no more than 18. The creatures agree to help you and request your return payment together.
XP Cost: 500 XP.

Planar Ally, Lesser
Conjuration (Calling) [see text]
Level: Clr 4
Components: V, S, DF, XP
Casting Time: 10 minutes
Range: Close (25 ft. + 5 ft./2 levels)
Effect: One called elemental or outsider of 6 HD or less
Duration: Instantaneous
Saving Throw: None
Spell Resistance: No

By casting this spell, you request your deity to send you an elemental or outsider (of 6 HD or less) of the deity's choice. If you serve no particular deity, the spell is a general plea answered by a creature sharing your philosophical alignment. If you know an individual creature's name, you may request that individual by speaking the name during the spell (though you might get a different creature anyway).

You may ask the creature to perform one task in exchange for a payment from you. Tasks might range from the simple (fly us across the chasm, help us fight a battle) to the complex (spy on our enemies, protect us on our foray into the dungeon). You must be able to communicate with the creature called in order to bargain for its services.

The creature called requires a payment for its services. This payment can take a variety of forms, from donating gold or magic items to an allied temple, to a gift given directly to the creature, to some other action on your part that matches the creature's alignment and goals. Regardless, this payment must be made before the creature agrees to perform any services. The bargaining takes at least 1 round, so any actions by the creature begin in the round after it arrives.

A task taking up to 1 minute per caster level requires a payment of 100 gp per HD of the creature called. For a task taking up to 1 hour per caster level, the creature requires a payment of 500 gp per HD. A long-term task, one requiring up to one

day per caster level, requires a payment of 1,000 gp per HD.

A nonhazardous task requires only half the indicated payment, while an especially hazardous task might require a greater gift. Few if any creatures will accept a task that seems suicidal (remember, a called creature actually dies when it is killed, unlike a summoned creature). However, if the task is strongly aligned with the creature's ethos, the DM may halve or even waive the payment. For instance, a celestial creature called to battle demons might require a gift of only half the normal value.

At the end of its task, or when the duration bargained for expires, the creature returns to its home plane (after reporting back to you, if appropriate and possible).

Note: When you use a calling spell that calls an air, chaotic, earth, evil, fire, good, lawful, or water creature, it is a spell of that type. For example, *lesser planar ally* is a fire spell when it calls a fire elemental.
XP Cost: 100 XP.

Planar Binding
Conjuration (Calling) [see text for *lesser planar binding*]
Level: Sor/Wiz 6
Components: V, S
Targets: Up to three elementals or outsiders, totaling no more than 12 HD, no two of which can be more than 30 ft. apart when they appear

This spell functions like *lesser planar binding,* except that you may call a single creature of 12 HD or less, or up to three creatures of the same kind whose Hit Dice total no more than 12. Each creature gets a save, makes an independent attempt to escape, and must be individually persuaded to aid you.

Planar Binding, Greater
Conjuration (Calling) [see text for *lesser planar binding*]
Level: Sor/Wiz 8
Components: V, S
Targets: Up to three elementals or outsiders, totaling no more than 18 HD, no two of which can be more than 30 ft. apart when they appear.

This spell functions like *lesser planar binding,* except that you may call a single creature of 18 HD or less, or up to three creatures of the same kind whose Hit Dice total no more than 18. Each creature gets a saving throw, makes independent attempts to escape, and must be persuaded to aid you individually.

Planar Binding, Lesser
Conjuration (Calling) [see text]
Level: Sor/Wiz 5
Components: V, S

Casting Time: 10 minutes
Range: Close (25 ft. + 5 ft./2 levels);
see text
Target: One elemental or outsider with 6
HD or less
Duration: Instantaneous
Saving Throw: Will negates
Spell Resistance: No and Yes; see text

Casting this spell attempts a dangerous act: to lure a creature from another plane to a specifically prepared trap, which must lie within the spell's range. The called creature is held in the trap until it agrees to perform one service in return for its freedom.

To create the trap, you must use a *magic circle* spell, focused inward. The kind of creature to be bound must be known and stated. If you wish to call a specific individual, you must use that individual's proper name in casting the spell.

The target creature is allowed a Will saving throw. If the saving throw succeeds, the creature resists the spell. If the saving throw fails, the creature is immediately drawn to the trap (spell resistance does not keep it from being called). The creature can escape from the trap with by successfully pitting its spell resistance against your caster level check, by dimensional travel, or with a successful Charisma check (DC 15 + 1/2 your caster level + your Cha modifier). It can try each method once per day. If it breaks loose, it can flee or attack you. A *dimensional anchor* cast on the creature prevents its escape via dimensional travel. You can also employ a calling diagram (see *magic circle against evil*, page 249) to make the trap more secure.

If the creature does not break free of the trap, you can keep it bound for as long as you dare. You can attempt to compel the creature to perform a service by describing the service and perhaps offering some sort of reward. You make a Charisma check opposed by the creature's Charisma check. The DM assigns your check a bonus of +0 to +6 based on the nature of the service and the reward. If the creature wins the opposed check, it refuses service. New offers, bribes, and the like can be made or the old ones reoffered every 24 hours. This process can be repeated until the creature promises to serve, until it breaks free, or until you decide to get rid of it by means of some other spell. Impossible demands or unreasonable commands are never agreed to. If you roll a 1 on the Charisma check, the creature breaks free of the binding and can escape or attack you.

Once the requested service is completed, the creature need only so inform you to be instantly sent back whence it came. The creature might later seek re-venge. If you assign some open-ended task that the creature cannot complete though its own actions (such as "Wait here" or "Defend this area against attack"), the spell remains in effect for a maximum of one day per caster level, and the creature gains an immediate chance to break free. Note that a clever recipient can subvert some instructions.

When you use a calling spell to call an air, chaotic, earth, evil, fire, good, lawful, or water creature, it is a spell of that type. For example, *lesser planar binding* is a water spell when you cast it to call a water elemental.

Plane Shift

Conjuration (Teleportation)
Level: Clr 5, Sor/Wiz 7
Components: V, S, F
Casting Time: 1 standard action
Range: Touch
Target: Creature touched, or up to eight willing creatures joining hands
Duration: Instantaneous
Saving Throw: Will negates
Spell Resistance: Yes

You move yourself or some other creature to another plane of existence or alternate dimension. If several willing persons link hands in a circle, as many as eight can be affected by the *plane shift* at the same time. Precise accuracy as to a particular arrival location on the intended plane is nigh impossible. From the Material Plane, you can reach any other plane, though you appear 5 to 500 miles (5d%) from your intended destination.

Note: Plane shift transports creatures instantaneously and then ends. The creatures need to find other means if they are to travel back.

Focus: A small, forked metal rod. The size and metal type dictates to which plane of existence or alternate dimension the spell sends the affected creatures. Forked rods keyed to certain planes or dimensions may be difficult to come by, as decided by the DM.

Plant Growth

Transmutation
Level: Drd 3, Plant 3, Rgr 3
Components: V, S, DF
Casting Time: 1 standard action
Range: See text
Target or Area: See text
Duration: Instantaneous
Saving Throw: None
Spell Resistance: No

Plant growth has different effects depending on the version chosen.

Overgrowth: This effect causes normal vegetation (grasses, briars, bushes, creepers, thistles, trees, vines) within long range (400 feet + 40 feet per caster level) to become thick and overgrown. The plants entwine to form a thicket or jungle that creatures must hack or force a way through. Speed drops to 5 feet, or 10 feet for Large or larger creatures. (The DM may allow faster movement for very small or very large creatures.) The area must have brush and trees in it for this spell to take effect.

At your option, the area can be a 100-foot-radius circle, a 150-foot-radius semicircle, or a 200-foot-radius quarter circle. You may designate places within the area that are not affected.

Enrichment: This effect targets plants within a range of one-half mile, raising their potential productivity over the course of the next year to one-third above normal.

In many farming communities, clerics or druids cast this spell at planting time as part of the spring festivals.

Plant growth counters *diminish plants*.

This spell has no effect on plant creatures.

Poison

Necromancy
Level: Clr 4, Drd 3
Components: V, S, DF
Casting Time: 1 standard action
Range: Touch
Target: Living creature touched
Duration: Instantaneous; see text
Saving Throw: Fortitude negates; see text
Spell Resistance: Yes

Calling upon the venomous powers of natural predators, you infect the subject with a horrible poison by making a successful melee touch attack. The poison deals 1d10 points of temporary Constitution damage immediately and another 1d10 points of temporary Constitution damage 1 minute later. Each instance of damage can be negated by a Fortitude save (DC 10 + 1/2 your caster level + your Wis modifier).

Polar Ray

Evocation [Cold]
Level: Sor/Wiz 8
Components: V, S, F
Casting Time: 1 standard action
Range: Close (25 ft. + 5 ft./2 levels)
Effect: Ray
Duration: Instantaneous
Saving Throw: None
Spell Resistance: Yes

A blue-white ray of freezing air and ice springs from your hand. You must succeed on a ranged touch attack with the ray to deal damage to a target. The ray deals 1d6 points of cold damage per caster level (maximum 25d6).

Focus: A small, white ceramic cone or prism.

Polymorph

Transmutation
Level: Sor/Wiz 4
Components: V, S, M
Casting Time: 1 standard action
Range: Touch
Target: Willing living creature touched
Duration: 1 min./level (D)
Saving Throw: None
Spell Resistance: No

This spell functions like *alter self,* except that you change the willing subject into another form of living creature. The new form may be of the same type as the subject or any of the following types: aberration, animal, dragon, fey, giant, humanoid, magical beast, monstrous humanoid, ooze, plant, or vermin. The assumed form can't have more Hit Dice than your caster level (or the subject's HD, whichever is lower), to a maximum of 15 HD at 15th level. You can't cause a subject to assume a form smaller than Fine, nor can you cause a subject to assume an incorporeal or gaseous form. The subject's creature type and subtype (if any) change to match the new form (see the *Monster Manual* for more information).

Upon changing, the subject regains lost hit points as if it had rested for a night (though this healing does not restore temporary ability damage and provide other benefits of resting; and changing back does not heal the subject further). If slain, the subject reverts to its original form, though it remains dead.

The subject gains the Strength, Dexterity, and Constitution scores of the new form but retains its own Intelligence, Wisdom, and Charisma scores. It also gains all extraordinary special attacks possessed by the form (such as constrict, improved grab, and poison) but does not gain the extraordinary special qualities possessed by the new form (such as blindsense, fast healing, regeneration, and scent) or any supernatural or spell-like abilities.

Incorporeal or gaseous creatures are immune to being *polymorphed,* and a creature with the shapechanger subtype (such as a lycanthrope or a doppelganger) can revert to its natural form as a standard action.

Material Component: An empty cocoon.

Polymorph Any Object

Transmutation
Level: Sor/Wiz 8, Trickery 8
Components: V, S, M/DF
Casting Time: 1 standard action
Range: Close (25 ft. + 5 ft./2 levels)
Target: One creature, or one nonmagical object of up to 100 cu. ft./level
Duration: See text
Saving Throw: Fortitude negates (object); see text
Spell Resistance: Yes (object)

This spell functions like *polymorph,* except that it changes one object or creature into another. The duration of the spell depends on how radical a change is made from the original state to its enchanted state. The DM determines the duration by using the following guidelines.

Changed Subject Is:	Increase to Duration Factor1
Same kingdom (animal, vegetable, mineral)	+5
Same class (mammals, fungi, metals, etc.)	+2
Same size	+2
Related (twig is to tree, wolf fur is to wolf, etc.)	+2
Same or lower Intelligence	+2

1 Add all that apply. Look up the total on the next table.

Duration

Factor	Duration	Example
0	20 minutes	Pebble to human
2	1 hour	Marionette to human
4	3 hours	Human to marionette
5	12 hours	Lizard to manticore
6	2 days	Sheep to wool coat
7	1 week	Shrew to manticore
9+	Permanent	Manticore to shrew

Unlike *polymorph, polymorph any object* does grant the creature the Intelligence score of its new form. If the original form didn't have a Wisdom or Charisma score, it gains those scores as appropriate for the new form.

Damage taken by the new form can result in the injury or death of the polymorphed creature. For example, it is possible to polymorph a creature into rock and then grind it to dust, causing damage, perhaps even death. If the creature was changed to dust to start with, more creative methods to damage it would be needed. Perhaps you could use a *gust of wind* spell to scatter the dust far and wide. In general, damage occurs when the new form is changed through physical force, although the DM must adjudicate many of these situations.

A nonmagical object cannot be made into a magic item with this spell. Magic items aren't affected by this spell.

This spell cannot create material of great intrinsic value, such as copper, silver, gems, silk, gold, platinum, mithral, or adamantine. It also cannot reproduce the special properties of cold iron in order to overcome the damage reduction of certain creatures.

This spell can also be used to duplicate the effects of *polymorph, flesh to stone, stone to flesh, transmute mud to rock, transmute water to dust,* or *transmute rock to mud.*

Arcane Material Component: Mercury, gum arabic, and smoke.

Power Word Blind

Enchantment (Compulsion) [Mind-Affecting]
Level: Sor/Wiz 7, War 7
Components: V
Casting Time: 1 standard action
Range: Close (25 ft. + 5 ft./2 levels)
Target: One creature with 200 hp or less
Duration: See text
Saving Throw: None
Spell Resistance: Yes

You utter a single word of power that causes one creature of your choice to become blinded, whether the creature can hear the word or not. The duration of the spell depends on the target's current hit point total. Any creature that currently has 201 or more hit points is unaffected by *power word blind.*

Hit Points	Duration
50 or less	Permanent
51–100	1d4+1 minutes
101–200	1d4+1 rounds

Power Word Kill

Enchantment (Compulsion) [Death, Mind-Affecting]
Level: Sor/Wiz 9, War 9
Components: V
Casting Time: 1 standard action
Range: Close (25 ft. + 5 ft./2 levels)
Target: One living creature with 100 hp or less
Duration: Instantaneous
Saving Throw: None
Spell Resistance: Yes

You utter a single word of power that instantly kills one creature of your choice, whether the creature can hear the word or not. Any creature that currently has 101 or more hit points is unaffected by *power word kill.*

Power Word Stun

Enchantment (Compulsion) [Mind-Affecting]
Level: Sor/Wiz 8, War 8
Components: V
Casting Time: 1 standard action
Range: Close (25 ft. + 5 ft./2 levels)
Target: One creature with 150 hp or less
Duration: See text
Saving Throw: None
Spell Resistance: Yes

You utter a single word of power that instantly causes one creature of your choice to become stunned, whether the creature can hear the word or not. The duration of the spell depends on the target's current hit point total. Any creature that currently has 151 or more hit points is unaffected by *power word stun*.

Hit Points	Duration
50 or less	4d4 rounds
51–100	2d4 rounds
101–150	1d4 rounds

Prayer

Enchantment (Compulsion) [Mind-Affecting]
Level: Clr 3, Pal 3
Components: V, S, DF
Casting Time: 1 standard action
Range: 40 ft.
Area: All allies and foes within a 40-ft.-radius burst centered on you
Duration: 1 round/level
Saving Throw: None
Spell Resistance: Yes

You bring special favor upon yourself and your allies while bringing disfavor to your enemies. You and your each of your allies gain a +1 luck bonus on attack rolls, weapon damage rolls, saves, and skill checks, while each of your foes takes a –1 penalty on such rolls.

Prestidigitation

Universal
Level: Brd 0, Sor/Wiz 0
Components: V, S
Casting Time: 1 standard action
Range: 10 ft.
Target, Effect, or Area: See text
Duration: 1 hour
Saving Throw: See text
Spell Resistance: No

Prestidigitations are minor tricks that novice spellcasters use for practice. Once cast, a *prestidigitation* spell enables you to perform simple magical effects for 1 hour. The effects are minor and have severe limitations. A prestidigitation can slowly lift 1 pound of material. It can color, clean, or soil items in a 1-foot cube each round. It can chill, warm, or flavor 1 pound of nonliving material. It cannot deal damage or affect the concentration of spellcasters. *Prestidigitation* can create small objects, but they look crude and artificial. The materials created by a *prestidigitation* spell are extremely fragile, and they cannot be used as tools, weapons, or spell components. Finally, a *prestidigitation* lacks the power to duplicate any other spell effects. Any actual change to an object (beyond just moving, cleaning, or soiling it) persists only 1 hour.

Characters typically use *prestidigitation* spells to impress common folk, amuse children, and brighten dreary lives. Common tricks with *prestidigitations* include producing tinklings of ethereal music, brightening faded flowers, creating glowing balls that float over your hand, generating puffs of wind to flicker candles, spicing up aromas and flavors of bland food, and making little whirlwinds to sweep dust under rugs.

Prismatic Sphere

Abjuration
Level: Protection 9, Sor/Wiz 9, Sun 9
Components: V
Range: 10 ft.
Effect: 10-ft.-radius sphere centered on you

This spell functions like *prismatic wall*, except you conjure up an immobile, opaque globe of shimmering, multicolored light that surrounds you and protects you from all forms of attack. The sphere flashes in all colors of the visible spectrum.

The sphere's *blindness* effect on creatures with less than 8 HD lasts 2d4×10 minutes.

You can pass into and out of the *prismatic sphere* and remain near it without harm. However, when you're inside it, the sphere blocks any attempt to project something through the sphere (including spells). Other creatures that attempt to attack you or pass through suffer the effects of each color, one at a time.

Typically, only the upper hemisphere of the globe will exist, since you are at the center of the sphere, so the lower half is usually excluded by the floor surface you are standing on.

The colors of the sphere have the same effects as the colors of a *prismatic wall*.

Prismatic sphere can be made permanent with a *permanency* spell.

Prismatic Spray

Evocation
Level: Sor/Wiz 7
Components: V, S
Casting Time: 1 standard action
Range: 60 ft.
Area: Cone-shaped burst
Duration: Instantaneous
Saving Throw: See text
Spell Resistance: Yes

This spell causes seven shimmering, intertwined, multicolored beams of light to spray from your hand. Each beam has a different power. Creatures in the area of the spell with 8 HD or less are automatically blinded for 2d4 rounds. Every creature in the area is randomly struck by one or more beams, which have additional effects.

	Color	
1d8	of Beam	Effect
1	Red	20 points fire damage (Reflex half)
2	Orange	40 points acid damage (Reflex half)
3	Yellow	80 points electricity damage (Reflex half)
4	Green	Poison (Kills; Fortitude partial, take 1d6 points of Con damage instead)
5	Blue	Turned to stone (Fortitude negates)
6	Indigo	Insane, as *insanity* spell (Will negates)
7	Violet	Sent to another plane (Will negates)
8		Struck by two rays; roll twice more, ignoring any "8" results.

Prismatic Wall

Abjuration
Level: Sor/Wiz 8
Components: V, S
Casting Time: 1 standard action
Range: Close (25 ft. + 5 ft./2 levels)
Effect: Wall 4 ft./level wide, 2 ft./level high
Duration: 10 min./level (D)
Saving Throw: See text
Spell Resistance: See text

Prismatic wall creates a vertical, opaque wall—a shimmering, multicolored plane of light that protects you from all forms of attack. The wall flashes with seven colors, each of which has a distinct power and purpose. The wall is immobile, and you can pass through and remain near the wall without harm. However, any other creature with less than 8 HD that is within 20 feet of the wall is blinded for 2d4 rounds by the colors if it looks at the wall.

The wall's maximum proportions are 4 feet wide per caster level and 2 feet high per caster level. A *prismatic wall* spell cast to materialize in a space occupied by a creature is disrupted, and the spell is wasted.

Each color in the wall has a special effect. The accompanying table shows the seven colors of the wall, the order in which they appear, their effects on creatures trying to attack you or pass through the wall, and the magic needed to negate each color.

The wall can be destroyed, color by color, in consecutive order, by various magical effects; however, the first color must be brought down before the second can be affected, and so on. A *rod of cancellation* or a *Mordenkainen's disjunction* spell destroys a *prismatic wall*, but an *antimagic field* fails to penetrate it. *Dispel magic* and *greater dispel magic* cannot dispel the wall or anything beyond it. Spell resistance is

Prismatic wall makes an effective barrier.

enemies. You can strike an opponent with a melee touch attack, dealing fire damage equal to 1d6 +1 point per caster level (maximum +5). Alternatively, you can hurl the flames up to 120 feet as a thrown weapon. When doing so, you attack with a ranged touch attack (with no range penalty) and deal the same damage as with the melee attack. No sooner do you hurl the flames than a new set appears in your hand. Each attack you make reduces the remaining duration by 1 minute. If an attack reduces the remaining duration to 0 minutes or less, the spell ends after the attack resolves.

This spell does not function underwater.

Programmed Image
Illusion (Figment)
Level: Brd 6, Sor/Wiz 6
Effect: Visual figment that cannot extend beyond a 20-ft. cube + one 10-ft. cube/level (S)
Duration: Permanent until triggered, then 1 round/level

This spell functions like *silent image*, except that this spell's figment activates when a specific condition occurs. The figment includes visual, auditory, olfactory, and thermal elements, including intelligible speech.

You set the triggering condition (which may be a special word) when casting the spell. The event that triggers the illusion can be as general or as specific and detailed as desired but must be based on an audible, tactile, olfactory, or visual trigger. The trigger cannot be based on some quality not normally obvious to the senses, such as alignment. (See *magic mouth* for more details about such triggers.)

Material Component: A bit of fleece and jade dust worth 25 gp.

Project Image
Illusion (Shadow)
Level: Brd 6, Sor/Wiz 7
Components: V, S, M
Casting Time: 1 standard action
Range: Medium (100 ft. + 10 ft./level)
Effect: One shadow duplicate
Duration: 1 round/level (D)
Saving Throw: Will disbelief (if interacted with)
Spell Resistance: No

You tap energy from the Plane of Shadow to create a quasi-real, illusory version of yourself. The projected image looks, sounds, and smells like you but is intangible. The projected image mimics your actions (including speech) unless you direct it to act differently (which is a move action).

PRISMATIC WALL

Color	Order	Effect of Color	Negated By
Red	1st	Stops nonmagical ranged weapons. Deals 20 points of fire damage (Reflex half).	*Cone of cold*
Orange	2nd	Stops magical ranged weapons. Deals 40 points of acid damage (Reflex half).	*Gust of wind*
Yellow	3rd	Stops poisons, gases, and petrification. Deals 80 points of electricity damage (Reflex half).	*Disintegrate*
Green	4th	Stops breath weapons. Poison (Kills; Fortitude partial for 1d6 points of Con damage instead).	*Passwall*
Blue	5th	Stops divination and mental attacks. Turned to stone (Fortitude negates).	*Magic missile*
Indigo	6th	Stops all spells. Will save or become insane (as *insanity* spell).	*Daylight*
Violet	7th	Energy field destroys all objects and effects.[1] Creatures sent to another plane (Will negates).	*Dispel magic*

1 The violet effect makes the special effects of the other six colors redundant, but these six effects are included here because certain magic items can create prismatic effects one color at a time, and spell resistance might render some colors ineffective (see above).

effective against a *prismatic wall*, but the caster level check must be repeated for each color present.

Prismatic wall can be made permanent with a *permanency* spell.

Produce Flame
Evocation [Fire]
Level: Drd 1, Fire 2
Components: V, S
Casting Time: 1 standard action
Range: 0 ft.
Effect: Flame in your palm
Duration: 1 min./level (D)
Saving Throw: None
Spell Resistance: Yes

Flames as bright as a torch appear in your open hand. The flames harm neither you nor your equipment.

In addition to providing illumination, the flames can be hurled or used to touch

Illus. by D. Martin

You can see through its eyes and hear through its ears as if you were standing where it is, and during your turn you can switch from using its senses to using your own, or back again, as a free action. While you are using its senses, your body is considered blinded and deafened.

If you desire, any spell you cast whose range is touch or greater can originate from the projected image instead of from you. The projected image can't cast any spells on itself except for illusion spells. The spells affect other targets normally, despite originating from the projected image.

Objects are affected by the projected image as if they had succeeded on their Will save.

You must maintain line of effect to the projected image at all times. If your line of effect is obstructed, the spell ends. If you use *dimension door, teleport, plane shift,* or a similar spell that breaks your line of effect, even momentarily, the spell ends.

Material Component: A small replica of you (a doll), which costs 5 gp to create.

Protection from Arrows

Abjuration
Level: Sor/Wiz 2
Components: V, S, F
Casting Time: 1 standard action
Range: Touch
Target: Creature touched
Duration: 1 hour/level or until discharged
Saving Throw: Will negates (harmless)
Spell Resistance: Yes (harmless)

The warded creature gains resistance to ranged weapons. The subject gains damage reduction 10/magic against ranged weapons. (This spell doesn't grant you the ability to damage creatures with similar damage reduction.) Once the spell has prevented a total of 10 points of damage per caster level (maximum 100 points), it is discharged.

Focus: A piece of shell from a tortoise or a turtle.

Protection from Chaos

Abjuration [Lawful]
Level: Clr 1, Law 1, Pal 1, Sor/Wiz 1

This spell functions like *protection from evil,* except that the deflection and resistance bonuses apply to attacks from chaotic creatures, and chaotic summoned creatures cannot touch the subject.

Protection from Energy

Abjuration
Level: Clr 3, Drd 3, Luck 3, Protection 3, Rgr 2, Sor/Wiz 3
Components: V, S, DF
Casting Time: 1 standard action
Range: Touch
Target: Creature touched
Duration: 10 min./level or until discharged
Saving Throw: Fortitude negates (harmless)
Spell Resistance: Yes (harmless)

Protection from energy grants temporary immunity to the type of energy you specify when you cast it (acid, cold, electricity, fire, or sonic). When the spell absorbs 12 points per caster level of energy damage (to a maximum of 120 points at 10th level), it is discharged.

Note: Protection from energy overlaps (and does not stack with) *resist energy.* If a character is warded by *protection from energy* and *resist energy,* the *protection* spell absorbs damage until its power is exhausted.

Protection from Evil

Abjuration [Good]
Level: Clr 1, Good 1, Pal 1, Sor/Wiz 1
Components: V, S, M/DF
Casting Time: 1 standard action
Range: Touch
Target: Creature touched
Duration: 1 min./level (D)
Saving Throw: Will negates (harmless)
Spell Resistance: No; see text

This spell wards a creature from attacks by evil creatures, from mental control, and from summoned creatures. It creates a magical barrier around the subject at a distance of 1 foot. The barrier moves with the subject and has three major effects.

First, the subject gains a +2 deflection bonus to AC and a +2 resistance bonus on saves. Both these bonuses apply against attacks made or effects created by evil creatures.

Second, the barrier blocks any attempt to possess the warded creature (by a *magic jar* attack, for example) or to exercise mental control over the creature (including enchantment (charm) effects and enchantment (compulsion) effects that grant the caster ongoing control over the subject, such as *dominate person*). The protection does not prevent such effects from targeting the protected creature, but it suppresses the effect for the duration of the *protection from evil* effect. If the *protection from evil* effect ends before the effect granting mental control does, the would-be controller would then be able to mentally command the controlled creature. Likewise, the barrier keeps out a possessing life force but does not expel one if it is in place before the spell is cast. This second effect works regardless of alignment.

Third, the spell prevents bodily contact by summoned creatures. This causes the natural weapon attacks of such creatures to fail and the creatures to recoil if such attacks require touching the warded creature. Good summoned creatures are immune to this effect. The protection against contact by summoned creatures ends if the warded creature makes an attack against or tries to force the barrier against the blocked creature. Spell resistance can allow a creature to overcome this protection and touch the warded creature.

Arcane Material Component: A little powdered silver with which you trace a 3-foot-diameter circle on the floor (or ground) around the creature to be warded.

Protection from Good

Abjuration [Evil]
Level: Clr 1, Evil 1, Sor/Wiz 1

This spell functions like *protection from evil,* except that the deflection and resistance bonuses apply to attacks from good creatures, and good summoned creatures cannot touch the subject.

Protection from Law

Abjuration [Chaotic]
Level: Chaos 1, Clr 1, Sor/Wiz 1

This spell functions like *protection from evil,* except that the deflection and resistance bonuses apply to attacks from lawful creatures, and lawful summoned creatures cannot touch the subject.

Protection from Spells

Abjuration
Level: Magic 8, Sor/Wiz 8
Components: V, S, M, F
Casting Time: 1 standard action
Range: Touch
Targets: Up to one creature touched per four levels
Duration: 10 min./level
Saving Throw: Will negates (harmless)
Spell Resistance: Yes (harmless)

The subject gains a +8 resistance bonus on saving throws against spells and spell-like abilities (but not against supernatural and extraordinary abilities).

Material Component: A diamond of at least 500 gp value, which must be crushed and sprinkled over the targets.

Focus: One 1,000 gp diamond per creature to be granted the protection. Each subject must carry one such gem for the duration of the spell. If a subject loses the gem, the spell ceases to affect him.

Prying Eyes

Divination
Level: Sor/Wiz 5
Components: V, S, M
Casting Time: 1 minute
Range: One mile
Effect: Ten or more levitating eyes

Duration: 1 hour/level; see text (D)
Saving Throw: None
Spell Resistance: No

You create a number of semitangible, visible magical orbs (called "eyes") equal to 1d4 + your caster level. These eyes move out, scout around, and return as you direct them when casting the spell. Each eye can see 120 feet (normal vision only) in all directions.

While the individual eyes are quite fragile, they're small and difficult to spot. Each eye is a Fine construct, about the size of a small apple, that has 1 hit point, AC 18 (+8 bonus for its size), flies at a speed of 30 feet with perfect maneuverability, and has a +16 Hide modifier. It has a Spot modifier equal to your caster level (maximum +15) and is subject to illusions, darkness, fog, and any other factors that would affect your ability to receive visual information about your surroundings. An eye traveling through darkness must find its way by touch.

When you create the eyes, you specify instructions you want them to follow in a command of no more than twenty-five words. Any knowledge you possess is known by the eyes as well, so if you know, for example, what a typical merchant looks like, the eyes do as well.

A sample command: "Surround me at a range of four hundred feet and return if you spot any dangerous creatures." The phrase "Surround me" directs the eyes to form an equally spaced, horizontal ring at whatever range you indicate, and then move with you. As eyes return or are destroyed, the rest automatically space themselves to compensate. In the case of this sample command, an eye returns only if it spots a creature you would regard as dangerous. A "peasant" that is actually a *shapechanged* dragon wouldn't trigger an eye's return. Ten eyes can form a ring with a radius of 400 feet and between themselves see everything that crosses the ring.

Another sample command: "Spread out and search the town for Arweth. Follow him for three minutes, staying out of sight, and then return." The phrase "Spread out" directs the eyes to move away from you in all directions. In this case, each eye would separately follow Arweth for three minutes once it spots him.

Other commands that might be useful include having the eyes form a line in a certain manner, making them move at random within a certain range, or having them follow a certain type of creature. The DM is the final judge of the suitability of your directions.

In order to report their findings, the eyes must return to your hand. Each replays in your mind all it has seen during its existence. It takes an eye 1 round to replay 1 hour of recorded images. After relaying its findings, an eye disappears.

If an eye ever gets more than 1 mile away from you, it instantly ceases to exist. However, your link with the eye is such that you won't know if the eye was destroyed because it wandered out of range or because of some other event.

The eyes exist for up to 1 hour per caster level or until they return to you. *Dispel magic* can destroy eyes. Roll separately for each eye caught in an area dispel. Of course, if an eye is sent into darkness, it could hit a wall or similar obstacle and destroy itself.

Material Component: A handful of crystal marbles.

Prying Eyes, Greater
Divination
Level: Sor/Wiz 8

This spell functions like *prying eyes*, except that the eyes can see all things as they actually are, just as if they had *true seeing* with a range of 120 feet. Thus, they can navigate darkened areas at full normal speed. Also, a *greater prying eye's* maximum Spot modifier is +25 instead of +15.

Purify Food and Drink
Transmutation
Level: Clr 0, Drd 0
Components: V, S
Casting Time: 1 standard action
Range: 10 ft.
Target: 1 cu. ft./level of contaminated food and water
Duration: Instantaneous
Saving Throw: Will negates (object)
Spell Resistance: Yes (object)

This spell makes spoiled, rotten, poisonous, or otherwise contaminated food and water pure and suitable for eating and drinking. This spell does not prevent subsequent natural decay or spoilage. Unholy water and similar food and drink of significance is spoiled by *purify food and drink*, but the spell has no effect on creatures of any type nor upon magic potions.

Note: Water weighs about 8 pounds per gallon. One cubic foot of water contains roughly 8 gallons and weighs about 60 pounds.

Pyrotechnics
Transmutation
Level: Brd 2, Sor/Wiz 2
Components: V, S, M
Casting Time: 1 standard action
Range: Long (400 ft. + 40 ft./level)
Target: One fire source, up to a 20-ft. cube
Duration: 1d4+1 rounds, or 1d4+1 rounds after creatures leave the smoke cloud; see text
Saving Throw: Will negates or Fortitude negates; see text
Spell Resistance: Yes or No; see text

Pyrotechnics turns a fire into either a burst of blinding fireworks or a thick cloud of choking smoke, depending on the version you choose.

Fireworks: The fireworks are a flashing, fiery, momentary burst of glowing, colored aerial lights. This effect causes creatures within 120 feet of the fire source to become blinded for 1d4+1 rounds (Will negates). These creatures must have line of sight to the fire to be affected. Spell resistance can prevent blindness.

Smoke Cloud: A writhing stream of smoke billows out from the source, forming a choking cloud. The cloud spreads 20 feet in all directions and lasts for 1 round per caster level. All sight, even darkvision, is ineffective in or through the cloud. All within the cloud take −4 penalties to Strength and Dexterity (Fortitude negates). These effects last for 1d4+1 rounds after the cloud dissipates or after the creature leaves the area of the cloud. Spell resistance does not apply.

Material Component: The spell uses one fire source, which is immediately extinguished. A fire so large that it exceeds a 20-foot cube is only partly extinguished. Magical fires are not extinguished, although a fire-based creature (such as a fire elemental) used as a source takes 1 point of damage per caster level.

Quench
Transmutation
Level: Drd 3
Components: V, S, DF
Casting Time: 1 standard action
Range: Medium (100 ft. + 10 ft./level)
Area or Target: One 20-ft. cube/level (S) or one fire-based magic item
Duration: Instantaneous
Saving Throw: None or Will negates (object)
Spell Resistance: No or Yes (object)

Quench is often used to put out forest fires and other conflagrations. It extinguishes all nonmagical fires in its area. The spell also dispels any fire spells in its area, though you must succeed on a dispel check (1d20 +1 per caster level, maximum +15) against each spell to dispel it. The DC to dispel such spells is 11 + the caster level of the fire spell.

Each elemental (fire) creature within the area of a *quench* spell takes 1d6 points of damage per caster level (maximum 15d6, no save allowed).

Alternatively, you can target the spell on a single magic item that creates or controls flame, such as a *wand of fireball* or a *flaming burst sword*. The item loses all its fire-based magical abilities for 1d4 hours unless it succeeds on a Will save. (Artifacts are immune to this effect.)

Rage

Enchantment (Compulsion) [Mind-Affecting]
Level: Brd 2, Sor/Wiz 3
Components: V, S
Casting Time: 1 standard action
Range: Medium (100 ft. + 10 ft./level)
Targets: One willing living creature per three levels, no two of which may be more than 30 ft. apart
Duration: Concentration + 1 round/level (D)
Saving Throw: None
Spell Resistance: Yes

Each affected creature gains a +2 morale bonus to Strength and Constitution, a +1 morale bonus on Will saves, and a −2 penalty to AC. The effect is otherwise identical with a barbarian's rage (see page 25), except that the subjects aren't fatigued at the end of the rage.

Rainbow Pattern

Illusion (Pattern) [Mind-Affecting]
Level: Brd 4, Sor/Wiz 4
Components: V (Brd only), S, M, F; see text
Casting Time: 1 standard action
Range: Medium (100 ft. + 10 ft./level)
Effect: Colorful lights with a 20-ft.-radius spread
Duration: Concentration +1 round/level (D)
Saving Throw: Will negates
Spell Resistance: Yes

A glowing, rainbow-hued pattern of interweaving colors fascinates those within it. *Rainbow pattern* fascinates a maximum of 24 Hit Dice of creatures. Creatures with the fewest HD are affected first. Among creatures with equal HD, those who are closest to the spell's point of origin are affected first. An affected creature that fails its saves is fascinated by the pattern.

With a simple gesture (a free action), you can make the rainbow pattern move up to 30 feet per round (moving its effective point of origin). All fascinated creatures follow the moving rainbow of light, trying to get or remain within the effect. Fascinated creatures who are restrained and removed from the pattern still try to follow it. If the pattern leads its subjects into a dangerous area (through flame, off a cliff, or the like), each fascinated creature gets a second save. If the view of the lights is completely blocked (by an *obscuring mist* spell, for instance), creatures who can't see them are no longer affected.

The spell does not affect sightless creatures.

Verbal Component: A wizard or sorcerer need not utter a sound to cast this spell, but a bard must sing, play music, or recite a rhyme as a verbal component.

Material Component: A piece of phosphor.

Focus: A crystal prism.

Raise Dead

Conjuration (Healing)
Level: Clr 5
Components: V, S, M, DF
Casting Time: 1 minute
Range: Touch
Target: Dead creature touched
Duration: Instantaneous
Saving Throw: None; see text
Spell Resistance: Yes (harmless)

You restore life to a deceased creature. You can raise a creature that has been dead for no longer than one day per caster level. In addition, the subject's soul must be free and willing to return (see Bringing Back the Dead, page 171). If the subject's soul is not willing to return, the spell does not work; therefore, a subject that wants to return receives no saving throw.

Coming back from the dead is an ordeal. The subject of the spell loses one level (or 1 Hit Die) when it is raised, just as if it had lost a level or a Hit Die to an energy-draining creature. If the subject is 1st level, it loses 2 points of Constitution instead (if this would reduce its Con to 0 or less, it can't be raised). This level/HD loss or Constitution loss cannot be repaired by any means. A character who died with spells prepared has a 50% chance of losing any given spell upon being raised, in addition to losing spells for losing a level. A spellcasting creature that doesn't prepare spells (such as a sorcerer) has a 50% chance of losing any given unused spell slot as if it had been used to cast a spell, in addition to losing spell slots for losing a level.

A raised creature has a number of hit points equal to its current Hit Dice. Any ability scores damaged to 0 are raised to 1. Normal poison and normal disease are cured in the process of raising the subject, but magical diseases and curses are not undone. While the spell closes mortal wounds and repairs lethal damage of most kinds, the body of the creature to be raised must be whole. Otherwise, missing parts are still missing when the creature is brought back to life. None of the dead creature's equipment or possessions are affected in any way by this spell.

A creature who has been turned into an undead creature or killed by a death effect can't be raised by this spell. Constructs, elementals, outsiders, and undead creatures can't be raised. The spell cannot bring back a creature that has died of old age.

Material Component: Diamonds worth a total of at least 5,000 gp.

Rary's Mnemonic Enhancer

Transmutation
Level: Wiz 4
Components: V, S, M, F
Casting Time: 10 minutes
Range: Personal
Target: You
Duration: Instantaneous

Casting this spell allows you to prepare additional spells or retain spells recently cast. Pick one of these two versions when the spell is cast.

Prepare: You prepare up to three additional levels of spells (such as three 1st-level spells, a 2nd- and a 1st-level spell, or a 3rd-level spell). A cantrip counts as 1/2 level for this purpose. You prepare and cast these spells normally.

Retain: You retain any spell of 3rd level or lower that you had cast up to 1 round before you started casting the *mnemonic enhancer*. This restores the previously cast spell to your mind.

In either event, the spell or spells prepared or retained fade after 24 hours (if not cast).

Material Component: A piece of string, and ink consisting of squid secretion with black dragon's blood.

Focus: An ivory plaque of at least 50 gp value.

Rary's Telepathic Bond

Divination
Level: Sor/Wiz 5
Components: V, S, M
Casting Time: 1 standard action
Range: Close (25 ft. + 5 ft./2 levels)
Targets: You plus one willing creature per three levels, no two of which can be more than 30 ft. apart
Duration: 10 min./level (D)
Saving Throw: None
Spell Resistance: No

You forge a telepathic bond among yourself and a number of willing creatures, each of which must have an Intelligence score of 3 or higher. Each creature included in the link is linked to all the others. The creatures can communicate telepathically through the bond regardless of language. No special power or influence is established as a result of the bond. Once the bond is formed, it works over any distance (although not from one plane to another).

If desired, you may leave yourself out of the telepathic bond forged. This decision must be made at the time of casting.

Rary's telepathic bond can be made permanent with a *permanency* spell, though it only bonds two creatures per casting of *permanency*.

Material Component: Pieces of eggshell from two different kinds of creatures.

Ray of Enfeeblement

Necromancy
Level: Sor/Wiz 1
Components: V, S
Casting Time: 1 standard action
Range: Close (25 ft. + 5 ft./2 levels)
Effect: Ray
Duration: 1 min./level
Saving Throw: None
Spell Resistance: Yes

A coruscating ray springs from your hand. You must succeed on a ranged touch attack to strike a target. The subject takes a penalty to Strength equal to 1d6+1 per two caster levels (maximum 1d6+5). The subject's Strength score cannot drop below 1.

Ray of Exhaustion

Necromancy
Level: Sor/Wiz 3
Components: V, S, M
Casting Time: 1 standard action
Range: Close (25 ft. + 5 ft./2 levels)
Effect: Ray
Duration: 1 min./level
Saving Throw: Fortitude partial; see text
Spell Resistance: Yes

A black ray projects from your pointing finger. You must succeed on a ranged touch attack with the ray to strike a target. The subject is immediately exhausted for the spell's duration. A successful Fortitude save means the creature is only fatigued. A character that is already fatigued instead becomes exhausted.

This spell has no effect on a creature that is already exhausted. Unlike normal exhaustion or fatigue, the effect ends as soon as the spell's duration expires.

Material Component: A drop of sweat.

Ray of Frost

Evocation [Cold]
Level: Sor/Wiz 0
Components: V, S
Casting Time: 1 standard action
Range: Close (25 ft. + 5 ft./2 levels)
Effect: Ray
Duration: Instantaneous
Saving Throw: None
Spell Resistance: Yes

A ray of freezing air and ice projects from your pointing finger. You must succeed on a ranged touch attack with the ray to deal damage to a target. The ray deals 1d3 points of cold damage.

Read Magic

Divination
Level: Brd 0, Clr 0, Drd 0, Pal 1, Rgr 1, Sor/Wiz 0
Components: V, S, F
Casting Time: 1 standard action
Range: Personal
Target: You
Duration: 10 min./level

By means of *read magic,* you can decipher magical inscriptions on objects—books, scrolls, weapons, and the like—that would otherwise be unintelligible. This deciphering does not normally invoke the magic contained in the writing, although it may do so in the case of a cursed scroll. Furthermore, once the spell is cast and you have read the magical inscription, you are thereafter able to read that particular writing without recourse to the use of *read magic.* You can read at the rate of one page (250 words) per minute. The spell allows you to identify a *glyph of warding* with a DC 13 Spellcraft check, a *greater glyph of warding* with a DC 16 Spellcraft check, or any *symbol* spell with a Spellcraft check (DC 10 + spell level).

Read magic can be made permanent with a *permanency* spell.

Focus: A clear crystal or mineral prism.

Reduce Animal

Transmutation
Level: Drd 2, Rgr 3
Components: V, S
Casting Time: 1 standard action
Range: Touch
Target: One willing animal of Small, Medium, Large, or Huge size
Duration: 1 hour/level (D)
Saving Throw: None
Spell Resistance: No

This spell functions like *reduce person,* except that it affects a single willing animal (not one with which you are engaged in combat, for instance). This decrease in size allows the animal to fit better into tight spaces, such as the typical dungeon room or subterranean passage. Reduce the damage dealt by the animal's natural attacks as shown on Table 2–3 in the *Dungeon Master's Guide.*

Reduce Person

Transmutation
Level: Sor/Wiz 1
Components: V, S, M
Casting Time: 1 round
Range: Close (25 ft. + 5 ft./2 levels)
Target: One humanoid creature
Duration: 1 min./level (D)
Saving Throw: Fortitude negates
Spell Resistance: Yes

This spell causes instant diminution of a humanoid creature, halving its height, length, and width and dividing its weight by 8. This decrease changes the creature's size category to the next smaller one. The target gains a +2 size bonus to Dexterity, a –2 size penalty to Strength (to a minimum of 1), and a +1 bonus on attack rolls and AC due to its reduced size.

A Small humanoid creature whose size decreases to Tiny has a space of 2-1/2 feet and a natural reach of 0 feet (meaning that it must enter an opponent's square to attack). A Large humanoid creature whose size decreases to Medium has a space of 5 feet and a natural reach of 5 feet. This spell doesn't change the target's speed.

All equipment worn or carried by a creature is similarly reduced by the spell. Melee and projectile weapons deal less damage (see Table 2–3 in the *Dungeon Master's Guide*). Other magical properties are not affected by this spell. Any *reduced* item that leaves the *reduced* creature's possession (including a projectile or thrown weapon) instantly returns to its normal size. This means that thrown weapons deal their normal damage (projectiles deal damage based on the size of the weapon that fired them).

Multiple magical effects that reduce size do not stack, which means (among other things) that you can't use a second casting of this spell to further reduce the size of a humanoid that's still under the effect of the first casting.

Reduce person counters and dispels *enlarge person.*

Reduce person can be made permanent with a *permanency* spell.

Material Component: A pinch of powdered iron.

Reduce Person, Mass

Transmutation
Level: Sor/Wiz 4
Target: One humanoid creature/level, no two of which can be more than 30 ft. apart

This spell functions like *reduce person,* except that it affects multiple creatures.

Refuge

Conjuration (Teleportation)
Level: Clr 7, Sor/Wiz 9
Components: V, S, M
Casting Time: 1 standard action
Range: Touch
Target: Object touched
Duration: Permanent until discharged
Saving Throw: None
Spell Resistance: No

You create powerful magic in some specially prepared object—a statuette, a jeweled rod, a gem, or the like. This object contains the power to instantly transport its possessor across any distance within the same plane to your abode. Once the item is transmuted, you must give it willingly to a creature and at the same time inform it of a command word to be spoken when the item is used. To make use of the item, the subject speaks the command word at the same time that it rends or breaks the item (a standard action). When this is done, the individual and all objects it is wearing and carrying (to a maximum of the character's heavy load) are instantly transported to your abode. No other creatures are affected (aside from a familiar that is touching the subject).

You can alter the spell when casting it so that it transports you to within 10 feet of the possessor of the item when it is broken and the command word spoken. You will have a general idea of the location and situation of the item possessor at the time the *refuge* spell is discharged, but once you decide to alter the spell in this fashion, you have no choice whether or not to be transported.

Material Component: The specially prepared object, whose construction requires gems worth 1,500 gp.

Regenerate

Conjuration (Healing)
Level: Clr 7, Drd 9, Healing 7
Components: V, S, DF
Casting Time: 3 full rounds
Range: Touch
Target: Living creature touched
Duration: Instantaneous
Saving Throw: Fortitude negates (harmless)
Spell Resistance: Yes (harmless)

The subject's severed body members (fingers, toes, hands, feet, arms, legs, tails, or even heads of multiheaded creatures), broken bones, and ruined organs grow back. After the spell is cast, the physical regeneration is complete in 1 round if the severed members are present and touching the creature. It takes 2d10 rounds otherwise.

Regenerate also cures 4d8 points of damage +1 point per caster level (maximum +35), rids the subject of exhaustion and/or fatigue, and eliminates all nonlethal damage the subject has taken. It has no effect on nonliving creatures (including undead).

Reincarnate

Transmutation
Level: Drd 4
Components: V, S, M, DF
Casting Time: 10 minutes
Range: Touch

Target: Dead creature touched
Duration: Instantaneous
Saving Throw: None; see text
Spell Resistance: Yes (harmless)

With this spell, you bring back a dead creature in another body, provided that its death occurred no more than one week before the casting of the spell and the subject's soul is free and willing to return (see Bringing Back the Dead, page 171). If the subject's soul is not willing to return, the spell does not work; therefore, a subject that wants to return receives no saving throw.

Since the dead creature is returning in a new body, all physical ills and afflictions are repaired. The condition of the remains is not a factor. So long as some small portion of the creature's body still exists, it can be reincarnated, but the portion receiving the spell must have been part of the creature's body at the time of death. The magic of the spell creates an entirely new young adult body for the soul to inhabit from the natural elements at hand. This process takes 1 hour to complete. When the body is ready, the subject is reincarnated.

A reincarnated creature recalls the majority of its former life and form. It retains any class abilities, feats, or skill ranks it formerly possessed. Its class, base attack bonus, base save bonuses, and hit points are unchanged. Strength, Dexterity, and Constitution scores depend partly on the new body. First eliminate the subject's racial adjustments (since it is no longer of his previous race) and then apply the adjustments found below to the its remaining ability scores. The subject's level (or Hit Dice) is reduced by 1. If the subject was 1st level, its new Constitution score is reduced by 2. (If this reduction would put its Con at 0 or lower, it can't be reincarnated). This level/HD loss or Constitution loss cannot be repaired by any means.

It's possible for the change in the subject's ability scores to make it difficult for it to pursue its previous character class. If this is the case, the subject is well advised to become a multiclass character.

For a humanoid creature, the new incarnation is determined using the following table. For nonhumanoid creatures, the DM should create a similar table of creatures of the same type or simply choose the new form.

A creature that has been turned into an undead creature or killed by a death effect can't be returned to life by this spell. Constructs, elementals, outsiders, and undead creatures can't be reincarnated. The spell cannot bring back a creature who has died of old age.

d%	Incarnation	Str	Dex	Con
01	Bugbear	+4	+2	+2
02–13	Dwarf	+0	+0	+2
14–25	Elf	+0	+2	–2
26	Gnoll	+4	+0	+2
27–38	Gnome	–2	+0	+2
39–42	Goblin	–2	+2	+0
43–52	Half-elf	+0	+0	+0
53–62	Half-orc	+2	+0	+0
63–74	Halfling	–2	+2	+0
75–89	Human	+0	+0	+0
90–93	Kobold	–4	+2	–2
94	Lizardfolk	+2	+0	+2
95–98	Orc	+4	+0	+0
99	Troglodyte	+0	–2	+4
100	Other (DM's choice)	?	?	?

The reincarnated creature gains all abilities associated with its new form, including forms of movement and speeds, natural armor, natural attacks, extraordinary abilities, and the like, but it doesn't automatically speak the language of the new form. Refer to the *Monster Manual* for details.

A *wish* or a *miracle* spell can restore a reincarnated character to his or her original form.

Material Component: Rare oils and unguents worth a total of least 1,000 gp, spread over the remains.

Remove Blindness/Deafness

Conjuration (Healing)
Level: Clr 3, Pal 3
Components: V, S
Casting Time: 1 standard action
Range: Touch
Target: Creature touched
Duration: Instantaneous
Saving Throw: Fortitude negates (harmless)
Spell Resistance: Yes (harmless)

Remove blindness/deafness cures blindness or deafness (your choice), whether the effect is normal or magical in nature. The spell does not restore ears or eyes that have been lost, but it repairs them if they are damaged.

Remove blindness/deafness counters and dispels *blindness/deafness*.

Remove Curse

Abjuration
Level: Brd 3, Clr 3, Pal 3, Sor/Wiz 4
Components: V, S
Casting Time: 1 standard action
Range: Touch
Target: Creature or item touched
Duration: Instantaneous
Saving Throw: Will negates (harmless)
Spell Resistance: Yes (harmless)

Remove curse instantaneously removes all curses on an object or a creature. *Remove curse* does not remove the curse from a cursed shield, weapon, or suit of armor, although the spell typically enables the creature afflicted with any such cursed item to remove and get rid of it. Certain special curses may not be countered by this spell or may be countered only by a caster of a certain level or higher.

Remove curse counters and dispels *bestow curse*.

Remove Disease
Conjuration (Healing)
Level: Clr 3, Drd 3, Rgr 3
Components: V, S
Casting Time: 1 standard action
Range: Touch
Target: Creature touched
Duration: Instantaneous
Saving Throw: Fortitude negates (harmless)
Spell Resistance: Yes (harmless)

Remove disease cures all diseases that the subject is suffering from. The spell also kills parasites, including green slime and others. Certain special diseases may not be countered by this spell or may be countered only by a caster of a certain level or higher.

Note: Since the spell's duration is instantaneous, it does not prevent reinfection after a new exposure to the same disease at a later date.

Remove Fear
Abjuration
Level: Brd 1, Clr 1
Components: V, S
Casting Time: 1 standard action
Range: Close (25 ft. + 5 ft./2 levels)
Targets: One creature plus one additional creature per four levels, no two of which can be more than 30 ft. apart
Duration: 10 minutes; see text
Saving Throw: Will negates (harmless)
Spell Resistance: Yes (harmless)

You instill courage in the subject, granting it a +4 morale bonus against *fear* effects for 10 minutes. If the subject is under the influence of a *fear* effect when receiving the spell, that effect is suppressed for the duration of the spell.

Remove fear counters and dispels *cause fear*.

Remove Paralysis
Conjuration (Healing)
Level: Clr 2, Pal 2
Components: V, S
Casting Time: 1 standard action
Range: Close (25 ft. + 5 ft./2 levels)
Targets: Up to four creatures, no two of which can be more than 30 ft. apart
Duration: Instantaneous
Saving Throw: Will negates (harmless)
Spell Resistance: Yes (harmless)

You can free one or more creatures from the effects of any temporary paralysis or related magic, including a ghoul's touch or a *slow* spell. If the spell is cast on one creature, the paralysis is negated. If cast on two creatures, each receives another save with a +4 resistance bonus against the effect that afflicts it. If cast on three or four creatures, each receives another save with a +2 resistance bonus.

The spell does not restore ability scores reduced by penalties, damage, or drain.

Repel Metal or Stone
Abjuration [Earth]
Level: Drd 8
Components: V, S
Casting Time: 1 standard action
Range: 60 ft.
Area: 60-ft. line from you
Duration: 1 round/level (D)
Saving Throw: None
Spell Resistance: No

Like *repel wood*, this spell creates waves of invisible and intangible energy that roll forth from you. All metal or stone objects in the path of the spell are pushed away from you to the limit of the range. Fixed metal or stone objects larger than 3 inches in diameter and loose objects weighing more than 500 pounds are not affected. Anything else, including animated objects, small boulders, and creatures in metal armor, moves back. Fixed objects 3 inches in diameter or smaller bend or break, and the pieces move with the wave of energy. Objects affected by the spell are repelled at the rate of 40 feet per round.

Objects such as metal armor, swords, and the like are pushed back, dragging their bearers with them. Even magic items with metal components are repelled, although an *antimagic field* blocks the effects.

The waves of energy continue to sweep down the set path for the spell's duration. After you cast the spell, the path is set, and you can then do other things or go elsewhere without affecting the spell's power.

Repel Vermin
Abjuration
Level: Brd 4, Clr 4, Drd 4, Rgr 3
Components: V, S, DF
Casting Time: 1 standard action
Range: 10 ft.
Area: 10-ft.-radius emanation centered on you
Duration: 10 min./level (D)
Saving Throw: None or Will negates; see text
Spell Resistance: Yes

An invisible barrier holds back vermin. A vermin with Hit Dice of less than one-third your level cannot penetrate the barrier. A vermin with Hit Dice of one-third your level or more can penetrate the barrier if it succeeds on a Will save. Even so, crossing the barrier deals the vermin 2d6 points of damage, and pressing against the barrier causes pain, which deters most vermin.

Repel Wood
Transmutation
Level: Drd 6, Plant 6
Components: V, S
Casting Time: 1 standard action
Range: 60 ft.
Area: 60-ft. line-shaped emanation from you
Duration: 1 min./level (D)
Saving Throw: None
Spell Resistance: No

Waves of energy roll forth from you, moving in the direction that you determine, causing all wooden objects in the path of the spell to be pushed away from you to the limit of the range. Wooden objects larger than 3 inches in diameter that are fixed firmly are not affected, but loose objects are. Objects 3 inches in diameter or smaller that are fixed in place splinter and break, and the pieces move with the wave of energy. Objects affected by the spell are repelled at the rate of 40 feet per round.

Objects such as wooden shields, spears, wooden weapon shafts and hafts, and arrows and bolts are pushed back, dragging those carrying them along. (A creature being dragged by an item it is carrying can let go. A creature being dragged by a shield can loose it as a move action and drop it as a free action.) If a spear is planted (set) to prevent this forced movement, it splinters. Even magic items with wooden sections are repelled, although an *antimagic field* blocks the effects.

The waves of energy continue to sweep down the set path for the spell's duration. After you cast the spell, the path is set, and you can then do other things or go elsewhere without affecting the spell's power.

Repulsion
Abjuration
Level: Clr 7, Protection 7, Sor/Wiz 6
Components: V, S, F/DF
Casting Time: 1 standard action
Range: Up to 10 ft./level
Area: Up to 10-ft.-radius/level emanation centered on you
Duration: 1 round/level (D)
Saving Throw: Will negates
Spell Resistance: Yes

An invisible, mobile field surrounds you and prevents creatures from approaching you. You decide how big the field is at the time of casting (to the limit your level allows). Any creature within or entering the field must attempt a save. If it fails, it becomes unable to move toward you for the duration of the spell. Repelled creatures' actions are not otherwise restricted. They can fight other creatures and can cast spells and attack you with ranged weapons. If you move closer to an affected creature, nothing happens. (The creature is not forced back.) The creature is free to make melee attacks against you if you come within reach. If a repelled creature moves away from you and then tries to turn back toward you, it cannot move any closer if it is still within the spell's area.

Arcane Focus: A pair of small iron bars attached to two small canine statuettes, one black and one white, the whole array worth 50 gp.

Resistance

Abjuration
Level: Brd 0, Clr 0, Drd 0, Pal 1, Sor/Wiz 0
Components: V, S, M/DF
Casting Time: 1 standard action
Range: Touch
Target: Creature touched
Duration: 1 minute
Saving Throw: Will negates (harmless)
Spell Resistance: Yes (harmless)

You imbue the subject with magical energy that protects it from harm, granting it a +1 resistance bonus on saves.

Resistance can be made permanent with a *permanency* spell.

Arcane Material Component: A miniature cloak.

Resist Energy

Abjuration
Level: Clr 2, Drd 2, Fire 3, Pal 2, Rgr 1, Sor/Wiz 2
Components: V, S, DF
Casting Time: 1 standard action
Range: Touch
Target: Creature touched
Duration: 10 min./level
Saving Throw: Fortitude negates (harmless)
Spell Resistance: Yes (harmless)

This abjuration grants a creature limited protection from damage of whichever one of five energy types you select: acid, cold, electricity, fire, or sonic. The subject gains energy resistance 10 against the energy type chosen, meaning that each time the creature is subjected to such damage (whether from a natural or magical source), that damage is reduced by 10 points before being applied to the creature's hit points. The value of the energy resistance granted increases to 20 points at 7th level and to a maximum of 30 points at 11th level. The spell protects the recipient's equipment as well.

Resist energy absorbs only damage. The subject could still suffer unfortunate side effects, such as drowning in acid (since drowning damage comes from lack of oxygen) or becoming encased in ice.

Note: Resist energy overlaps (and does not stack with) *protection from energy*. If a character is warded by *protection from energy* and *resist energy*, the *protection* spell absorbs damage until its power is exhausted.

Restoration

Conjuration (Healing)
Level: Clr 4, Pal 4
Components: V, S, M

This spell functions like *lesser restoration,* except that it also dispels negative levels and restores one experience level to a creature who has had a level drained. The drained level is restored only if the time since the creature lost the level is equal to or less than one day per caster level. Thus, if a 10th-level character has been struck by a wight and drained to 9th level, *restoration* brings the character up to exactly the minimum number of experience points necessary to restore him to 10th level (45,000 XP), gaining him an additional Hit Die and level functions accordingly.

Restoration cures all temporary ability damage, and it restores all points permanently drained from a single ability score (your choice if more than one is drained). It also eliminates any fatigue or exhaustion suffered by the target.

Restoration does not restore levels or Constitution points lost due to death.

Material Component: Diamond dust worth 100 gp that is sprinkled over the target.

Restoration, Greater

Conjuration (Healing)
Level: Clr 7
Components: V, S, XP
Casting Time: 10 minutes

This spell functions like *lesser restoration,* except that it dispels all negative levels afflicting the healed creature. This effect also reverses level drains by a force or creature, restoring the creature to the highest level it had previously attained. The drained levels are restored only if the time since the creature lost the level is no more than one week per caster level.

Greater restoration also dispels all magical effects penalizing the creature's abilities, cures all temporary ability damage, and restores all points permanently drained from all ability scores. It also eliminates fatigue and exhaustion, and removes all forms of insanity, *confusion,* and similar mental effects. *Greater restoration* does not restore levels or Constitution points lost due to death.

XP Cost: 500 XP.

Restoration, Lesser

Conjuration (Healing)
Level: Clr 2, Drd 2, Pal 1
Components: V, S
Casting Time: 3 rounds
Range: Touch
Target: Creature touched
Duration: Instantaneous
Saving Throw: Will negates (harmless)
Spell Resistance: Yes (harmless)

Lesser restoration dispels any magical effects reducing one of the subject's ability scores (such as *ray of enfeeblement*) or cures 1d4 points of temporary ability damage to one of the subject's ability scores (such as from a shadow's touch or from poison). It also eliminates any fatigue suffered by the character, and improves an exhausted condition to fatigued. It does not restore permanent ability drain.

Resurrection

Conjuration (Healing)
Level: Clr 7
Casting Time: 10 minutes

This spell functions like *raise dead,* except that you are able to restore life and complete strength to any deceased creature. The condition of the remains is not a factor. So long as some small portion of the creature's body still exists, it can be resurrected, but the portion receiving the spell must have been part of the creature's body at the time of death. (The remains of a creature hit by a *disintegrate* spell count as a small portion of its body.) The creature can have been dead no longer than 10 years per caster level.

Upon completion of the spell, the creature is immediately restored to full hit points, vigor, and health, with no loss of prepared spells. However, the subject loses one level, or 2 points of Constitution if the subject was 1st level. (If this reduction would bring its Con to 0 or lower, it can't be resurrected). This level loss or Constitution loss cannot be repaired by any means.

You can resurrect someone killed by a death effect or someone who has been turned into an undead creature and then destroyed. You cannot resurrect someone who has died of old age. Constructs, elementals, outsiders, and undead creatures can't be resurrected.

Material Component: A sprinkle of holy water and diamonds worth a total of at least 10,000 gp.

Reverse Gravity
Transmutation
Level: Drd 8, Sor/Wiz 7
Components: V, S, M/DF
Casting Time: 1 standard action
Range: Medium (100 ft. + 10 ft./level)
Area: Up to one 10-ft. cube per two levels (S)
Duration: 1 round/level (D)
Saving Throw: None; see text
Spell Resistance: No

This spell reverses gravity in an area, causing all unattached objects and creatures within that area to fall upward and reach the top of the area in 1 round. If some solid object (such as a ceiling) is encountered in this fall, falling objects and creatures strike it in the same manner as they would during a normal downward fall. If an object or creature reaches the top of the area without striking anything, it remains there, oscillating slightly, until the spell ends. At the end of the spell duration, affected objects and creatures fall downward.

Provided it has something to hold onto, a creature caught in the area can attempt a Reflex save to secure itself when the spell strikes. Creatures who can fly or levitate can keep themselves from falling.

Arcane Material Component: A lodestone and iron filings.

Righteous Might
Transmutation
Level: Clr 5, Strength 5
Components: V, S, DF
Casting Time: 1 standard action
Range: Personal
Target: You
Duration: 1 round/level (D)

Your height immediately doubles, and your weight increases by a factor of eight. This increase changes your size category to the next larger one, and you gain a +8 size bonus to Strength and a +4 size bonus to Constitution. You gain a +4 enhancement bonus to your natural armor. You gain damage reduction 5/evil (if you normally channel positive energy) or damage reduction 5/good (if you normally channel negative energy). At 12th level this damage reduction becomes 10/evil or 10/good, and at 15th level it becomes 15/evil or 15/good (the maximum). Your size modifier for AC and attacks changes as appropriate to your new size category (if your original size was Diminutive, Tiny, Small, Medium, or Large, the modifier decreases by 1; otherwise see Size Modifier, page 134).

Use Table 8–4: Creature Size and Scale to determine your new space and reach. This spell doesn't change your speed.

If insufficient room is available for the desired growth, you attain the maximum possible size and may make a Strength check (using your increased Strength) to burst any enclosures in the process. If you fail, you are constrained without harm by the materials enclosing you—the spell cannot crush you by increasing your size.

All equipment you wear or carry is similarly enlarged by the spell. Melee and projectile weapons deal more damage (see Table 2–2 in the *Dungeon Master's Guide.*). Other magical properties are not affected by this spell. Any enlarged item that leaves your possession (including a projectile or thrown weapon) instantly returns to its normal size. This means that thrown weapons deal their normal damage (projectiles deal damage based on the size of the weapon that fired them).

Multiple magical effects that increase size do not stack, which means (among other things) that you can't use a second casting of this spell to further increase your size while you are still under the effect of the first casting.

Rope Trick
Transmutation
Level: Sor/Wiz 2
Components: V, S, M
Casting Time: 1 standard action
Range: Touch
Target: One touched piece of rope from 5 ft. to 30 ft. long
Duration: 1 hour/level (D)
Saving Throw: None
Spell Resistance: No

When this spell is cast upon a piece of rope from 5 to 30 feet long, one end of the rope rises into the air until the whole rope hangs perpendicular to the ground, as if affixed at the upper end. The upper end is, in fact, fastened to an extradimensional space that is outside the multiverse of extradimensional spaces ("planes"). Creatures in the extradimensional space are hidden, beyond the reach of spells (including divinations), unless those spells work across planes. The space holds as many as eight creatures (of any size). Creatures in the space can pull the rope up into the space, making the rope "disappear." In that case, the rope counts as one of the eight creatures that can fit in the space. The rope can support up to 16,000 pounds. A weight greater than that can pull the rope free.

Spells cannot be cast across the extradimensional interface, nor can area effects cross it. Those in the extradimen-

sional space can see out of it as if a 3-foot-by-5-foot window were centered on the rope. The window is present on the Material Plane, but it's invisible, and even creatures that can see the window can't see through it. Anything inside the extradimensional space drops out when the spell ends. The rope can be climbed by only one person at a time. The *rope trick* spell enables climbers to reach a normal place if they do not climb all the way to the extradimensional space.

Note: It is hazardous to create an extradimensional space within an existing extradimensional space or to take an extradimensional space into an existing one.

Material Component: Powdered corn extract and a twisted loop of parchment.

Rusting Grasp
Transmutation
Level: Drd 4
Components: V, S, DF
Casting Time: 1 standard action
Range: Touch
Target: One nonmagical ferrous object (or the volume of the object within 3 ft. of the touched point) or one ferrous creature
Duration: See text
Saving Throw: None
Spell Resistance: No

Any iron or iron alloy item you touch becomes instantaneously rusted, pitted, and worthless, effectively destroyed. If the item is so large that it cannot fit within a 3-foot radius (a large iron door or a *wall of iron*), a 3-foot-radius volume of the metal is rusted and destroyed. Magic items made of metal are immune to this spell.

You may employ *rusting grasp* in combat with a successful melee touch attack. *Rusting grasp* used in this way instantaneously destroys 1d6 points of Armor Class gained from metal armor (to the maximum amount of protection the armor offered) through corrosion. For example, full plate armor (AC +8) could be reduced to +7 or as low as +2 in protection, depending on the die roll.

Weapons in use by an opponent targeted by the spell are more difficult to grasp. You must succeed on a melee touch attack against the weapon. A metal weapon that is hit is destroyed.

Note: Striking at an opponent's weapon provokes an attack of opportunity. Also, you must touch the weapon and not the other way around.

Against a ferrous creature, *rusting grasp* instantaneously deals 3d6 points of damage +1 per caster level (maximum +15) per successful attack. The spell lasts for 1 round per level, and you can make one melee touch attack per round.

Sanctuary

Abjuration
Level: Clr 1, Protection 1
Components: V, S, DF
Casting Time: 1 standard action
Range: Touch
Target: Creature touched
Duration: 1 round/level
Saving Throw: Will negates
Spell Resistance: No

Any opponent attempting to strike or otherwise directly attack the warded creature, even with a targeted spell, must attempt a Will save. If the save succeeds, the opponent can attack normally and is unaffected by that casting of the spell. If the save fails, the opponent can't follow through with the attack, that part of its action is lost, and it can't directly attack the warded creature for the duration of the spell. Those not attempting to attack the subject remain unaffected. This spell does not prevent the warded creature from being attacked or affected by area or effect spells. The subject cannot attack without breaking the spell but may use nonattack spells or otherwise act. This allows a warded cleric to heal wounds, for example, or to cast a *bless* spell, perform an *augury,* summon creatures, and so on.

Scare

Necromancy [Fear, Mind-Affecting]
Level: Brd 2, Sor/Wiz 2
Components: V, S, M
Casting Time: 1 standard action
Range: Medium (100 ft. + 10 ft./level)
Targets: One living creature per three
  levels, no two of which can be more
  than 30 ft. apart
Duration: 1 round/level or 1 round; see
  text for *cause fear*
Saving Throw: Will partial
Spell Resistance: Yes

This spell functions like *cause fear,* except that it causes all targeted creatures of less than 6 HD to become frightened.

Material Component: A bit of bone from an undead skeleton, zombie, ghoul, ghast, or mummy.

Scintillating Pattern

Illusion (Pattern) [Mind-Affecting]
Level: Sor/Wiz 8
Components: V, S, M
Casting Time: 1 standard action
Range: Close (25 ft. + 5 ft./2 levels)
Effect: Colorful lights in a 20-ft.-radius
  spread
Duration: Concentration + 2 rounds
Saving Throw: None
Spell Resistance: Yes

A twisting pattern of discordant, coruscating colors weaves through the air, affecting creatures within it. The spell affects a total number of Hit Dice of creatures equal to your caster level (maximum 20). Creatures with the fewest HD are affected first; and, among creatures with equal HD, those who are closest to the spell's point of origin are affected first. Hit Dice that are not sufficient to affect a creature are wasted. The spell affects each subject according to its Hit Dice.

6 or less: Unconscious for 1d4 rounds, then stunned for 1d4 rounds, and then *confused* for 1d4 rounds. (Treat an unconscious result as stunned for nonliving creatures.)

7 to 12: Stunned for 1d4 rounds, then *confused* for 1d4 rounds.

13 or more: Confused for 1d4 rounds.

Sightless creatures are not affected by *scintillating pattern.*

Material Component: A small crystal prism.

Scorching Ray

Evocation [Fire]
Level: Sor/Wiz 2
Components: V, S
Casting Time: 1 standard action
Range: Close (25 ft. + 5 ft./2 levels)
Effect: One or more rays
Duration: Instantaneous
Saving Throw: None
Spell Resistance: Yes

You blast your enemies with fiery rays. You may fire one ray, plus one additional ray for every four levels beyond 3rd (to a maximum of three rays at 11th level). Each ray requires a ranged touch attack to hit and deals 4d6 points of fire damage. The rays may be fired at the same or different targets, but all bolts must be aimed at targets within 30 feet of each other and fired simultaneously.

Screen

Illusion (Glamer)
Level: Sor/Wiz 8, Trickery 7
Components: V, S
Casting Time: 10 minutes
Range: Close (25 ft. + 5 ft./2 levels)
Area: 30-ft. cube/level (S)
Duration: 24 hours
Saving Throw: None or Will disbelief (if
  interacted with); see text
Spell Resistance: No

This spell combines several elements to create a powerful protection from scrying and direct observation. When casting the spell, you dictate what will and will not be observed in the spell's area. The illusion created must be stated in general terms. Thus, you could specify the illusion of yourself and another character playing chess for the duration of the spell, but you could not have the illusory chess players take a break, make dinner, and then resume their game. You could have a crossroads appear quiet and empty even while an army is actually passing through the area. You could specify that no one be seen (including passing strangers), that your troops be undetected, or even that every fifth person or unit should be visible. Once the conditions are set, they cannot be changed.

Attempts to scry the area automatically detect the image stated by you with no save allowed. Sight and sound are appropriate to the illusion created. A band of people standing in a meadow could be concealed as an empty meadow with birds chirping, for instance.

Direct observation may allow a save (as per a normal illusion), if there is cause to disbelieve what is seen. Certainly onlookers in the area would become suspicious if a marching army disappeared at one point to reappear at another. Even entering the area does not cancel the illusion or necessarily allow a save, assuming that hidden beings take care to stay out of the way of those affected by the illusion.

Scrying

Divination (Scrying)
Level: Brd 3, Clr 5, Drd 4, Sor/Wiz 4
Components: V, S, M/DF, F
Casting Time: 1 hour
Range: See text
Effect: Magical sensor
Duration: 1 min./level
Saving Throw: Will negates
Spell Resistance: Yes

You can see and hear some creature, which may be at any distance. If the subject succeeds on a Will save, the scrying attempt simply fails. The difficulty of the save depends on how well you know the subject and what sort of physical connection (if any) you have to that creature. Furthermore, if the subject is on another plane, it gets a +5 bonus on its Will save.

Knowledge	Will Save Modifier
None[1]	+10
Secondhand (you have heard of the subject)	+5
Firsthand (you have met the subject)	+0
Familiar (you know the subject well)	–5
1 You must have some sort of connection to a creature you have no knowledge of.	

Connection	Will Save Modifier
Likeness or picture	–2
Possession or garment	–4
Body part, lock of hair, bit of nail, etc.	–10

If the save fails, you can see (but not hear) the subject and the subject's immediate surroundings (approximately 10 feet in all directions of the subject). If the subject moves, the sensor follows at a speed of up to 150 feet.

As with all divination (scrying) spells, the sensor has your full visual acuity, including any magical effects. In addition, the following spells have a 5% chance per caster level of operating through the sensor: *detect chaos, detect evil, detect good, detect law, detect magic,* and *message.*

If the save succeeds, you can't attempt to scry on that subject again for at least 24 hours.

Arcane Material Component: The eye of a hawk, an eagle, or a roc, plus nitric acid, copper, and zinc.

Wizard, Sorcerer, or Bard Focus: A mirror of finely wrought and highly polished silver costing not less than 1,000 gp. The mirror must be at least 2 feet by 4 feet.

Cleric Focus: A holy water font costing not less than 100 gp.

Druid Focus: A natural pool of water.

Scrying, Greater
Divination (Scrying)
Level: Brd 6, Clr 7, Drd 7, Sor/Wiz 7
Components: V, S
Casting Time: 1 standard action
Duration: 1 hour/level

This spell functions like *scrying,* except as noted above. Additionally, all of the following spells function reliably through the sensor: *detect chaos, detect evil, detect good, detect law, detect magic, message, read magic,* and *tongues.*

Sculpt Sound
Transmutation
Level: Brd 3
Components: V, S
Casting Time: 1 standard action
Range: Close (25 ft. + 5 ft./2 levels)
Targets: One creature or object/level, no two of which can be more than 30 ft. apart
Duration: 1 hour/level (D)
Saving Throw: Will negates (object)
Spell Resistance: Yes (object)

You change the sounds that creatures or objects make. You can create sounds where none exist (such as making trees sing), deaden sounds (such as making a party of adventurers silent), or transform sounds into other sounds (such as making a caster's voice sound like a pig snorting). All affected creatures or objects must be transmuted in the same way. Once the transmutation is made, you cannot change it.

You can change the qualities of sounds but cannot create words with which you are unfamiliar yourself. For instance, you can't change your voice so that it sounds as though you are giving the command word to activate a magic item unless you know that command word.

A spellcaster whose voice is changed dramatically (such as into that of the aforementioned snorting pig) is unable to cast spells with verbal components.

Searing Light
Evocation
Level: Clr 3, Sun 3
Components: V, S
Casting Time: 1 standard action
Range: Medium (100 ft. + 10 ft./level)
Effect: Ray
Duration: Instantaneous
Saving Throw: None
Spell Resistance: Yes

Focusing divine power like a ray of the sun, you project a blast of light from your open palm. You must succeed on a ranged touch attack to strike your target. A creature struck by this ray of light takes 1d8 points of damage per two caster levels (maximum 5d8). An undead creature takes 1d6 points of damage per caster level (maximum 10d6), and an undead creature particularly vulnerable to bright light, such as a vampire, takes 1d8 points of damage per caster level (maximum 10d8). A construct or inanimate object takes only 1d6 points of damage per two caster levels (maximum 5d6).

Secret Page
Transmutation
Level: Brd 3, Sor/Wiz 3
Components: V, S, M
Casting Time: 10 minutes
Range: Touch
Target: Page touched, up to 3 sq. ft. in size
Duration: Permanent
Saving Throw: None
Spell Resistance: No

Secret page alters the contents of a page so that they appear to be something entirely different. Thus, a map can be changed to become a treatise on burnishing ebony walking sticks. The text of a spell can be changed to show a ledger page or even another spell. *Explosive runes* or *sepia snake sigil* can be cast upon the *secret page.*

A *comprehend languages* spell alone cannot reveal a *secret page*'s contents. You are able to reveal the original contents by speaking a special word. You can then peruse the actual page, and return it to its *secret page* form at will. You can also remove the spell by double repetition of the special word. A *detect magic* spell reveals dim magic on the page in question but does not reveal its true contents. *True seeing* reveals the presence of the hidden material but does not reveal the contents unless cast in combination with *comprehend languages.* A *secret page* spell can be dispelled, and the hidden writings can be

destroyed by means of an *erase* spell.

Material Component: Powdered herring scales and will-o'-wisp essence.

See Invisibility
Divination
Level: Brd 3, Sor/Wiz 2
Components: V, S, M
Casting Time: 1 standard action
Range: Personal
Target: You
Duration: 10 min./level (D)

You can see any objects or beings that are invisible within your range of vision, as well as any that are ethereal, as if they were normally visible. Such creatures are visible to you as translucent shapes, allowing you easily to discern the difference between visible, invisible, and ethereal creatures.

The spell does not reveal the method used to obtain invisibility. It does not reveal illusions or enable you to see through opaque objects. It does not reveal creatures who are simply hiding, concealed, or otherwise hard to see.

See invisibility can be made permanent with a *permanency* spell.

Material Component: A pinch of talc and a small sprinkling of powdered silver.

Seeming
Illusion (Glamer)
Level: Brd 5, Sor/Wiz 5
Components: V, S
Casting Time: 1 standard action
Range: Close (25 ft. + 5 ft./2 levels)
Targets: One creature per two levels, no two of which can be more than 30 ft. apart
Duration: 12 hours (D)
Saving Throw: Will negates or Will disbelief (if interacted with)
Spell Resistance: Yes or No; see text

This spell functions like *disguise self,* except that you can change the appearance of other people as well. Affected creatures resume their normal appearances if slain.

Unwilling targets can negate the spell's effect on them by making Will saves or with spell resistance.

Sending
Evocation
Level: Clr 4, Sor/Wiz 5
Components: V, S, M/DF
Casting Time: 10 minutes
Range: See text
Target: One creature
Duration: 1 round; see text
Saving Throw: None
Spell Resistance: No

You contact a particular creature with which you are familiar and send a short message of twenty-five words or less to the subject. The subject recognizes you if it knows you. It can answer in like manner immediately. A creature with an Intelligence score as low as 1 can understand the *sending*, though the subject's ability to react is limited as normal by its Intelligence score. Even if the *sending* is received, the subject is not obligated to act upon it in any manner.

If the creature in question is not on the same plane of existence as you are, there is a 5% chance that the *sending* does not arrive. (Local conditions on other planes may worsen this chance considerably, at the option of the DM.)

Arcane Material Component: A short piece of fine copper wire.

Sepia Snake Sigil

Conjuration (Creation) [Force]
Level: Brd 3, Sor/Wiz 3
Components: V, S, M
Casting Time: 10 minutes
Range: Touch
Target: One touched book or written work
Duration: Permanent or until discharged; until released or 1d4 days + one day/level; see text
Saving Throw: Reflex negates
Spell Resistance: No

When you cast *sepia snake sigil*, a small symbol appears in the text of one written work such as a book, scroll, or map. The text containing the symbol must be at least twenty-five words long. When anyone reads the text containing the symbol, the *sepia snake* springs into being and strikes the reader, provided there is line of effect between the symbol and the reader. Simply seeing the enspelled text is not sufficient to trigger the spell; the subject must deliberately read it. The target is entitled to a save to evade the snake's strike. If it succeeds, the *sepia snake* dissipates in a flash of brown light accompanied by a puff of dun-colored smoke and a loud noise. If the target fails its save, it is engulfed in a shimmering amber field of force and immobilized until released, either at your command or when 1d4 days + one day per caster level have elapsed.

While trapped in the amber field of force, the subject does not age, breathe, grow hungry, sleep, or regain spells. It is preserved in a state of suspended animation, unaware of its surroundings. It can be damaged by outside forces (and perhaps even killed), since the field provides no protection against physical injury. However, a dying subject does not lose hit points or become stable until the spell ends.

The hidden sigil cannot be detected by normal observation, and *detect magic* reveals only that the entire text is magical. A *dispel magic* can remove the sigil. An *erase* spell destroys the entire page of text. *Sepia snake sigil* can be cast in combination with other spells that hide or garble text, such as *secret page*.

Material Component: 500 gp worth of powdered amber, a scale from any snake, and a pinch of mushroom spores.

Sequester

Abjuration
Level: Sor/Wiz 7
Components: V, S, M
Casting Time: 1 standard action
Range: Touch
Target: One willing creature or object (up to a 2-ft. cube/level) touched
Duration: One day/level (D)
Saving Throw: None or Will negates (object)
Spell Resistance: No or Yes (object)

When cast, this spell not only prevents divination spells from working to detect or locate the creature or object affected by *sequester*, it also renders the affected creature or object invisible to any form of sight or seeing (as the *invisibility* spell). Thus, *sequester* can mask a secret door, a treasure vault, or anything similar. The spell does not prevent the subject from being discovered through tactile means or through the use of devices (such as a *robe of eyes* or a *gem of seeing*). Creatures affected by *sequester* become comatose and are effectively in a state of suspended animation until the spell wears off or is dispelled.

Note: The Will save prevents an attended or magical object from being *sequestered*. There is no save to see the *sequestered* creature or object or to detect it with a divination spell.

Material Component: A basilisk eyelash, gum arabic, and a dram of whitewash.

Shades

Illusion (Shadow)
Level: Sor/Wiz 9

This spell functions like *shadow conjuration*, except that it mimics sorcerer and wizard conjuration spells of 8th level or lower. The illusory conjurations created deal four-fifths (80%) damage to nonbelievers, and nondamaging effects are 80% likely to work against nonbelievers.

Shadow Conjuration

Illusion (Shadow)
Level: Brd 4, Sor/Wiz 4
Components: V, S
Casting Time: 1 standard action
Range: See text
Effect: See text
Duration: See text
Saving Throw: Will disbelief (if interacted with); varies; see text
Spell Resistance: Yes; see text

You use material from the Plane of Shadow to shape quasi-real illusions of one or more creatures, objects, or forces. *Shadow conjuration* can mimic any sorcerer or wizard conjuration (summoning) or conjuration (creation) spell of 3rd level or lower. *Shadow conjurations* are actually one-fifth (20%) as strong as the real things, though creatures who believe the *shadow conjurations* to be real are affected by them at full strength.

Any creature that interacts with the conjured object, force, or creature can make a Will save to recognize its true nature.

Spells that deal damage, such as *Melf's acid arrow*, have normal effects unless the affected creature succeeds on a Will save. Each disbelieving creature takes only one-fifth (20%) damage from the attack. If the disbelieved attack has a special effect other than damage, that effect is only 20% likely to occur. Regardless of the result of the save to disbelieve, an affected creature is also allowed any save that the spell being simulated allows, but the save DC is set according to *shadow conjuration's* level (5th) rather than the spell's normal level. In addition, any effect created by *shadow conjuration* allows spell resistance, even if the spell it is simulating does not.

Shadow objects or substances, such as *obscuring mist*, have normal effects except against those who disbelieve them. Against disbelievers, they are 20% likely to work.

A shadow creature has one-fifth the hit points of a normal creature of its kind (regardless of whether it's recognized as shadowy). It deals normal damage and has all normal abilities and weaknesses. Against a creature that recognizes it as a shadow creature, however, the shadow creature's damage is one-fifth (20%) normal, and all special abilities that do not deal lethal damage are only 20% likely to work. (Roll for each use and each affected character separately.) Furthermore, the shadow creature's AC bonuses are one-fifth as large (so a +7 bonus resulting in AC 17 would change to a +1 total bonus for a new AC of 11).

A creature that succeeds on its save sees the *shadow conjurations* as transparent images superimposed on vague, shadowy forms.

Objects automatically succeed on their Will saves against this spell.

Shadow Conjuration, Greater

Illusion (Shadow)
Level: Sor/Wiz 7

This spell functions like *shadow conjuration*, except that it can duplicate any sorcerer or wizard conjuration (summoning) or conjuration (creation) spell of 6th level or lower. The illusory conjurations created deal three-fifths (60%) damage to nonbelievers, and nondamaging effects are 60% likely to work against nonbelievers.

Shadow Evocation
Illusion (Shadow)
Level: Brd 5, Sor/Wiz 5
Components: V, S
Casting Time: 1 standard action
Range: See text
Effect: See text
Duration: See text
Saving Throw: Will disbelief (if interacted with)
Spell Resistance: Yes

You tap energy from the Plane of Shadow to cast a quasi-real, illusory version of a sorcerer or wizard evocation spell of 4th level or lower. (For a spell with more than one level, use the best one applicable to you.)

Spells that deal damage, such as *lightning bolt*, have normal effects unless an affected creature succeeds on a Will save. Each disbelieving creature takes only one-fifth damage from the attack. If the disbelieved attack has a special effect other than damage, that effect is one-fifth as strong (if applicable) or only 20% likely to occur. If recognized as a *shadow evocation*, a damaging spell deals only one-fifth (20%) damage. Regardless of the result of the save to disbelieve, an affected creature is also allowed any save (or spell resistance) that the spell being simulated allows, but the save DC is set according to *shadow evocation*'s level (5th) rather than the spell's normal level.

Nondamaging effects, such as *gust of wind*, have normal effects except against those who disbelieve them. Against disbelievers, they have no effect.

Objects automatically succeed on their Will saves against this spell.

Shadow Evocation, Greater
Illusion (Shadow)
Level: Sor/Wiz 8

This spell functions like *shadow evocation*, except that it enables you to create partially real, illusory versions of sorcerer or wizard evocation spells of 7th level or lower. If recognized as a *greater shadow evocation*, a damaging spell deals only three-fifths (60%) damage.

Shadow Walk
Illusion (Shadow)
Level: Brd 5, Sor/Wiz 6
Components: V, S
Casting Time: 1 standard action
Range: Touch

Targets: Up to one touched creature/level
Duration: 1 hour/level (D)
Saving Throw: Will negates
Spell Resistance: Yes

To use the *shadow walk* spell, you must be in an area of shadowy illumination. You and any creature you touch are then transported along a coiling path of shadowstuff to the edge of the Material Plane where it borders the Plane of Shadow. The effect is largely illusory, but the path is quasi-real. You can take more than one creature along with you (subject to your level limit), but all must be touching each other.

In the region of shadow, you move at a rate of 50 miles per hour, moving normally on the borders of the Plane of Shadow but much more rapidly relative to the Material Plane. Thus, you can use this spell to travel rapidly by stepping onto the Plane of Shadow, moving the desired distance, and then stepping back onto the Material Plane.

Because of the blurring of reality between the Plane of Shadow and the Material Plane, you can't make out details of the terrain or areas you pass over during transit, nor can you predict perfectly where your travel will end. It's impossible to judge distances accurately, making the spell virtually useless for scouting or spying. Furthermore, when the spell effect ends, you are shunted 1d10×100 feet in a random horizontal direction from your desired endpoint. If this would place you within a solid object, you are shunted 1d10×1,000 feet in the same direction. If this would still place you within a solid object, you (and any creatures with you) are shunted to the nearest empty space available, but the strain of this activity renders each creature fatigued (no save).

Shadow walk can also be used to travel to other planes that border on the Plane of Shadow, but this usage requires the transit of the Plane of Shadow to arrive at a border with another plane of reality. The transit of the Plane of Shadow requires 1d4 hours.

Any creatures touched by you when *shadow walk* is cast also make the transition to the borders of the Plane of Shadow. They may opt to follow you, wander off through the plane, or stumble back into the Material Plane (50% chance for either of the latter results if they are lost or abandoned by you). Creatures unwilling to accompany you into the Plane of Shadow receive a Will saving throw, negating the effect if successful.

Shambler
Conjuration (Creation)
Level: Drd 9, Plant 9
Components: V, S

Casting Time: 1 standard action
Range: Medium (100 ft. + 10 ft./level)
Effect: Three or more shambling mounds, no two of which can be more than 30 ft. apart; see text
Duration: Seven days or seven months (D); see text
Saving Throw: None
Spell Resistance: No

The *shambler* spell creates 1d4+2 shambling mounds with 11 HD each. (See the *Monster Manual* for details about shambling mounds.) The creatures willingly aid you in combat or battle, perform a specific mission, or serve as bodyguards. The creatures remain with you for seven days unless you dismiss them. If the shamblers are created only for guard duty, however, the duration of the spell is seven months. In this case, the shamblers can only be ordered to guard a specific site or location. Shamblers summoned to guard duty cannot move outside the spell's range, which is measured from the point where each first appeared.

The shamblers have resistance to fire as normal shambling mounds do only if the terrain is rainy, marshy, or damp.

Shapechange
Transmutation
Level: Animal 9, Drd 9, Sor/Wiz 9
Components: V, S, F
Casting Time: 1 standard action
Range: Personal
Target: You
Duration: 10 min./level (D)

This spell functions like *polymorph*, except that it enables you to assume the form of any single nonunique creature (of any type) from Fine to Colossal size. The assumed form cannot have more than twice your caster level in Hit Dice (to a maximum of 50 HD). Unlike *polymorph*, this spell allows incorporeal or gaseous forms to be assumed.

You gain all extraordinary and supernatural abilities (both attacks and qualities) of the assumed form, but you lose your own supernatural abilities. You also gain the type of the new form (for example, dragon or magical beast) in place of your own. The new form does not disorient you. Parts of your body or pieces of equipment that are separated from you do not revert to their original forms.

You can become just about anything you are familiar with. You can change form once each round as a free action. The change takes place either immediately before your regular action or immediately after it, but not during the action. For example, you are in combat and assume the form of a will-o'-wisp. When this form is no longer useful, you change into a stone golem and walk away. When pursued, you change into a flea, which hides on a horse until it can hop off. From there, you can become a dragon, an orc, or just about anything else you are familiar with.

If you use this spell to create a disguise, you get a +10 bonus on your Disguise check.

Focus: A jade circlet worth no less than 1,500 gp, which you must place on your head when casting the spell. (The focus melds into your new form when you change shape.)

Shatter

Evocation [Sonic]
Level: Brd 2, Chaos 2, Clr 2, Destruction 2, Sor/Wiz 2
Components: V, S, M/DF
Casting Time: 1 standard action
Range: Close (25 ft. + 5 ft./2 levels)
Area or Target: 5-ft.-radius spread; or one solid object or one crystalline creature
Duration: Instantaneous
Saving Throw: Will negates (object); Will negates (object) or Fortitude half; see text
Spell Resistance: Yes (object)

Shatter creates a loud, ringing noise that breaks brittle, nonmagical objects; sunders a single solid, nonmagical object; or damages a crystalline creature.

Used as an area attack, *shatter* destroys nonmagical objects of crystal, glass, ceramic, or porcelain, such as vials, bottles, flasks, jugs, windows, mirrors, and so forth. All such objects within a 5-foot radius of the point of origin are smashed into dozens of pieces by the spell. Objects weighing more than 1 pound per your level are not affected, but all other objects of the appropriate composition are shattered.

Alternatively, you can target *shatter* against a single solid object, regardless of composition, weighing up to 10 pounds per caster level.

Targeted against a crystalline creature (of any weight), *shatter* deals 1d6 points of sonic damage per caster level (maximum 10d6), with a Fortitude save for half damage.

Arcane Material Component: A chip of mica.

Shield

Abjuration [Force]
Level: Sor/Wiz 1
Components: V, S
Casting Time: 1 standard action
Range: Personal
Target: You
Duration: 1 min./level (D)

Shield creates an invisible, tower shield-sized mobile disk of force that hovers in front of you. It negates *magic missile* attacks directed at you. The disk also provides a +4 shield bonus to AC. This bonus applies against incorporeal touch attacks, since it is a force effect. The *shield* has no armor check penalty or arcane spell failure chance. Unlike with a normal tower shield, you can't use the *shield* spell for cover.

Shield of Faith

Abjuration
Level: Clr 1
Components: V, S, M
Casting Time: 1 standard action
Range: Touch
Target: Creature touched
Duration: 1 min./level
Saving Throw: Will negates (harmless)
Spell Resistance: Yes (harmless)

This spell creates a shimmering, magical field around the touched creature that averts attacks. The spell grants the subject a +2 deflection bonus to AC, with an additional +1 to the bonus for every six levels you have (maximum +5 deflection bonus at 18th level).

Material Component: A small parchment with a bit of holy text written upon it.

Shield of Law

Abjuration [Lawful]
Level: Clr 8, Law 8
Components: V, S, F
Casting Time: 1 standard action
Range: 20 ft.
Targets: One creature/level in a 20-ft.-radius burst centered on you
Duration: 1 round/level (D)
Saving Throw: See text
Spell Resistance: Yes (harmless)

A dim, blue glow surrounds the subjects, protecting them from attacks, granting them resistance to spells cast by chaotic creatures, and *slowing* chaotic creatures when they strike the subjects. This abjuration has four effects.

First, each warded creature gains a +4 deflection bonus to AC and a +4 resistance bonus on saves. Unlike *protection from chaos*, this benefit applies against all attacks, not just against attacks by chaotic creatures.

Second, a warded creature gains spell resistance 25 against chaotic spells and spells cast by chaotic creatures.

Third, the abjuration blocks possession and mental influence, just as *protection from chaos* does.

Finally, if a chaotic creature succeeds on a melee attack against a warded creature, the attacker is *slowed* (Will save negates, as the *slow* spell, but against *shield of law's* save DC).

Focus: A tiny reliquary containing some sacred relic, such as a scrap of parchment from a lawful text. The reliquary costs at least 500 gp.

Shield Other

Abjuration
Level: Clr 2, Pal 2, Protection 2
Components: V, S, F
Casting Time: 1 standard action
Range: Close (25 ft. + 5 ft./2 levels)
Target: One creature
Duration: 1 hour/level (D)
Saving Throw: Will negates (harmless)
Spell Resistance: Yes (harmless)

This spell wards the subject and creates a mystic connection between you and the subject so that some of its wounds are transferred to you. The subject gains a +1 deflection bonus to AC and a +1 resistance bonus on saves. Additionally, the subject takes only half damage from all wounds and attacks (including that dealt by special abilities) that deal hit point damage. The amount of damage not taken by the warded creature is taken by you. Forms of harm that do not involve hit points, such as *charm* effects, temporary ability damage, level draining, and death effects, are not affected. If the subject suffers a reduction of hit points from a lowered Constitution score, the reduction is not split with you because it is not hit point damage. When the spell ends, subsequent damage is no longer divided between the subject and you, but damage already split is not reassigned to the subject.

If you and the subject of the spell move out of range of each other, the spell ends.

Focus: A pair of platinum rings (worth at least 50 gp each) worn by both you and the warded creature.

Shillelagh

Transmutation
Level: Drd 1
Components: V, S, DF
Casting Time: 1 standard action
Range: Touch
Target: One touched nonmagical oak club or quarterstaff
Duration: 1 min./level
Saving Throw: Will negates (object)
Spell Resistance: Yes (object)

Your own nonmagical club or quarterstaff becomes a weapon with a +1 enhancement bonus on attack and damage rolls. (A quarterstaff gains this enhancement for both ends of the weapon.) It deals damage as if it were two size categories larger (a Small club or quarterstaff so transmuted deals 1d8 points of damage, a Medium 2d6, and a Large 3d6), +1 for its enhancement bonus. These effects only occur when the weapon is wielded by you. If you do not wield it, the weapon behaves as if unaffected by this spell.

Shocking Grasp

Evocation [Electricity]
Level: Sor/Wiz 1
Components: V, S
Casting Time: 1 standard action
Range: Touch
Target: Creature or object touched
Duration: Instantaneous
Saving Throw: None
Spell Resistance: Yes

Your successful melee touch attack deals 1d6 points of electricity damage per caster level (maximum 5d6). When delivering the jolt, you gain a +3 bonus on attack rolls if the opponent is wearing metal armor (or made out of metal, carrying a lot of metal, or the like).

Shout

Evocation [Sonic]
Level: Brd 4, Sor/Wiz 4
Components: V
Casting Time: 1 standard action
Range: 30 ft.
Area: Cone-shaped burst
Duration: Instantaneous
Saving Throw: Fortitude partial or Reflex negates (object); see text
Spell Resistance: Yes (object)

You emit an ear-splitting yell that deafens and damages creatures in its path. Any creature within the area is deafened for 2d6 rounds and takes 5d6 points of sonic damage. A successful save negates the deafness and reduces the damage by half. Any exposed brittle or crystalline object or crystalline creature takes 1d6 points of sonic damage per caster level (maximum 15d6). An affected creature is allowed a Fortitude save to reduce the damage by half, and a creature holding fragile objects can negate damage to them with a successful Reflex save.

A *shout* spell cannot penetrate a *silence* spell.

Shout, Greater

Evocation [Sonic]
Level: Brd 6, Sor/Wiz 8
Components: V, S, F
Range: 60 ft.
Saving Throw: Fortitude partial or Reflex negates (object); see text

This spell functions like *shout*, except that the cone deals 10d6 points of sonic damage (or 1d6 points of sonic damage per caster level, maximum 20d6, against exposed brittle or crystalline objects or crystalline creatures). It also causes creatures to be stunned for 1 round and deafened for 4d6 rounds. A creature in the area of the cone can negate the stunning and halve both the damage and the duration of the deafness with a successful Fort-

itude save. A creature holding vulnerable objects can attempt a Reflex save to negate the damage to those objects.

Arcane Focus: A small metal or ivory horn.

Shrink Item

Transmutation
Level: Sor/Wiz 3
Components: V, S
Casting Time: 1 standard action
Range: Touch
Target: One touched object of up to 2 cu. ft./level
Duration: One day/level; see text
Saving Throw: Will negates (object)
Spell Resistance: Yes (object)

You are able to shrink one nonmagical item (if it is within the size limit) to 1/16 of its normal size in each dimension (to about 1/4,000 the original volume and mass). This change effectively reduces the object's size by four categories (for instance, from Large to Diminutive). Optionally, you can also change its now-shrunken composition to a clothlike one. Objects changed by a *shrink item* spell can be returned to normal composition and size merely by tossing them onto any solid surface or by a word of command from the original caster. Even a burning fire and its fuel can be shrunk by this spell. Restoring the shrunken object to its normal size and composition ends the spell.

Shrink item can be made permanent with a *permanency* spell, in which case the affected object can be shrunk and expanded an indefinite number of times, but only by the original caster.

Silence

Illusion (Glamer)
Level: Brd 2, Clr 2
Components: V, S
Casting Time: 1 standard action
Range: Long (400 ft. + 40 ft./level)
Area: 20-ft.-radius emanation centered on a creature, object, or point in space
Duration: 1 min./level (D)
Saving Throw: Will negates; see text or none (object)
Spell Resistance: Yes; see text or no (object)

Upon the casting of this spell, complete silence prevails in the affected area. All sound is stopped: Conversation is impossible, spells with verbal components cannot be cast, and no noise whatsoever issues from, enters, or passes through the area. The spell can be cast on a point in space, but the effect is stationary unless cast on a mobile object. The spell can be centered on a creature, and the effect then radiates from the creature and moves as it moves. An unwilling creature can attempt

a Will save to negate the spell and can use spell resistance, if any. Items in a creature's possession or magic items that emit sound receive the benefits of saves and spell resistance, but unattended objects and points in space do not. This spell provides a defense against sonic or language-based attacks, such as *command*, a harpy's captivating song, a *horn of blasting*, and the like.

Silent Image

Illusion (Figment)
Level: Brd 1, Sor/Wiz 1
Components: V, S, F
Casting Time: 1 standard action
Range: Long (400 ft. + 40 ft./level)
Effect: Visual figment that cannot extend beyond four 10-ft. cubes + one 10-ft. cube/level (S)
Duration: Concentration
Saving Throw: Will disbelief (if interacted with)
Spell Resistance: No

This spell creates the visual illusion of an object, creature, or force, as visualized by you. The illusion does not create sound, smell, texture, or temperature. You can move the image within the limits of the size of the effect.

Focus: A bit of fleece.

Simulacrum

Illusion (Shadow)
Level: Sor/Wiz 7
Components: V, S, M, XP
Casting Time: 12 hours
Range: 0 ft.
Effect: One duplicate creature
Duration: Instantaneous
Saving Throw: None
Spell Resistance: No

Simulacrum creates an illusory duplicate of any creature. The duplicate creature is partially real and formed from ice or snow. It appears to be the same as the original, but it has only one-half of the real creature's levels or Hit Dice (and the appropriate hit points, feats, skill ranks, and special abilities for a creature of that level or HD). You can't create a simulacrum of a creature whose Hit Dice or levels exceed twice your caster level. You must make a Disguise check when you cast the spell to determine how good the likeness is. A creature familiar with the original might detect the ruse with a successful Spot check (opposed by the caster's Disguise check) or a DC 20 Sense Motive check.

At all times the simulacrum remains under your absolute command. No special telepathic link exists, so command must be exercised in some other manner. A simulacrum has no ability to become more powerful. It cannot increase its level or abilities. If reduced to 0 hit points or otherwise destroyed, it reverts to snow and melts instantly into nothingness. A complex process requiring at least 24 hours, 100 gp per hit point, and a fully equipped magical laboratory can repair damage to a simulacrum.

Material Component: The spell is cast over the rough snow or ice form, and some piece of the creature to be duplicated (hair, nail, or the like) must be placed inside the snow or ice. Additionally, the spell requires powdered ruby worth 100 gp per HD of the simulacrum to be created.

XP Cost: 100 XP per HD of the simulacrum to be created (minimum 1,000 XP).

Slay Living

Necromancy [Death]
Level: Clr 5, Death 5
Components: V, S
Casting Time: 1 standard action
Range: Touch
Target: Living creature touched
Duration: Instantaneous
Saving Throw: Fortitude partial
Spell Resistance: Yes

You can slay any one living creature. You must succeed on a melee touch attack to touch the subject, and it can avoid death with a successful Fortitude save. If it succeeds, it instead takes 3d6 points of damage +1 point per caster level. (Of course, the subject might die from damage even if it succeeds on its save.)

Sleep

Enchantment (Compulsion) [Mind-Affecting]
Level: Brd 1, Sor/Wiz 1
Components: V, S, M
Casting Time: 1 round
Range: Medium (100 ft. + 10 ft./level)
Area: One or more living creatures within a 10-ft.-radius burst
Duration: 1 min./level
Saving Throw: Will negates
Spell Resistance: Yes

A *sleep* spell causes a magical slumber to come upon 4 Hit Dice of creatures. Creatures with the fewest HD are affected first. Among creatures with equal HD, those who are closest to the spell's point of origin are affected first. Hit Dice that are not sufficient to affect a creature are wasted.

For example, Mialee casts *sleep* at one rat (1/4 HD), one kobold (1 HD), two gnolls (2 HD), and an ogre (4 HD). The rat, the kobold, and one gnoll are affected (1/4 + 1 + 2 = 3-1/4 HD). The remaining 3/4 HD is not enough to affect the last gnoll or the ogre. Mialee can't choose to have *sleep* affect the ogre or the two gnolls.

Sleeping creatures are helpless. Slap-ping or wounding awakens an affected creature, but normal noise does not. Awakening a creature is a standard action (an application of the aid another action).

Sleep does not target unconscious creatures, constructs, or undead creatures.

Material Component: A pinch of fine sand, rose petals, or a live cricket.

Sleet Storm

Conjuration (Creation) [Cold]
Level: Drd 3, Sor/Wiz 3
Components: V, S, M/DF
Casting Time: 1 standard action
Range: Long (400 ft. + 40 ft./level)
Area: Cylinder (40-ft. radius, 20 ft. high)
Duration: 1 round/level
Saving Throw: None
Spell Resistance: No

Driving sleet blocks all sight (even darkvision) within it and causes the ground in the area to be icy. A creature can walk within or through the area of sleet at half normal speed with a DC 10 Balance check. Failure means it can't move in that round, while failure by 5 or more means it falls (see the Balance skill for details).

The sleet extinguishes torches and small fires.

Arcane Material Component: A pinch of dust and a few drops of water.

Slow

Transmutation
Level: Brd 3, Sor/Wiz 3
Components: V, S, M
Casting Time: 1 standard action
Range: Close (25 ft. + 5 ft./2 levels)
Targets: One creature/level, no two of which can be more than 30 ft. apart
Duration: 1 round/level
Saving Throw: Will negates
Spell Resistance: Yes

An affected creature moves and attacks at a drastically slowed rate. A *slowed* creature can take only a single move action or standard action each turn, but not both (nor may it take full-round actions). Additionally, it takes a –1 penalty on attack rolls, AC, and Reflex saves. A *slowed* creature moves at half its normal speed (round down to the next 5-foot increment), which affects the creature's jumping distance as normal for decreased speed.

Multiple *slow* effects don't stack. *Slow* counters and dispels *haste*.

Material Component: A drop of molasses.

Snare

Transmutation
Level: Rgr 2, Drd 3
Components: V, S, DF
Casting Time: 3 rounds
Range: Touch
Target: Touched nonmagical circle of vine, rope, or thong with a 2 ft. diameter + 2 ft./level
Duration: Until triggered or broken
Saving Throw: None
Spell Resistance: No

This spell enables you to make a snare that functions as a magic trap. The snare can be made from any supple vine, a thong, or a rope. When you cast *snare* upon it, the cordlike object blends with its surroundings (Search DC 23 for a character with the trapfinding ability to locate). One end of the snare is tied in a loop that contracts around one or more of the limbs of any creature stepping inside the circle. (The head of a worm or a snake could be thus ensnared, for example.)

If a strong and supple tree is nearby, the snare can be fastened to it. The spell causes the tree to bend and then straighten when the loop is triggered, dealing 1d6 points of damage to the creature trapped and lifting it off the ground by the trapped limb or limbs. If no such tree is available, the cordlike object tightens around the creature, dealing no damage but causing it to be entangled.

The snare is magical. To escape, a trapped creature must make a DC 23 Escape Artist check or a DC 23 Strength check that is a full-round action. The snare has AC 7 and 5 hit points. A successful escape from the snare breaks the loop and ends the spell.

Soften Earth and Stone

Transmutation [Earth]
Level: Drd 2, Earth 2
Components: V, S, DF
Casting Time: 1 standard action
Range: Close (25 ft. + 5 ft./2 levels)
Area: 10-ft. square/level; see text
Duration: Instantaneous
Saving Throw: None
Spell Resistance: No

When this spell is cast, all natural, undressed earth or stone in the spell's area is softened. Wet earth becomes thick mud, dry earth becomes loose sand or dirt, and stone becomes soft clay that is easily molded or chopped. You affect a 10-foot-square area to a depth of 1 to 4 feet, depending on the toughness or resilience of the ground at that spot (DM's option). Magical, enchanted, dressed, or worked stone cannot be affected. Earth or stone creatures are not affected.

A creature in mud must succeed on a Reflex save or be caught for 1d2 rounds and unable to move, attack, or cast spells. A creature that succeeds on its save can move through the mud at half speed, and it can't run or charge.

Loose dirt is not as troublesome as mud, but all creatures in the area can move at only half their normal speed and can't run or charge over the surface.

Stone softened into clay does not hinder movement, but it does allow characters to cut, shape, or excavate areas they may not have been able to affect before. For example, a party of adventurers trying to break out of a cavern might use this spell to soften a wall. While *soften earth and stone* does not affect dressed or worked stone, cavern ceilings or vertical surfaces such as cliff faces can be affected. Usually, this causes a moderate collapse or landslide as the loosened material peels away from the face of the wall or roof and falls.

A moderate amount of structural damage can be dealt to a manufactured structure (such as a wall or a tower) by softening the ground beneath it, causing it to settle. However, most well-built structures will only be damaged by this spell, not destroyed.

Solid Fog

Conjuration (Creation)
Level: Sor/Wiz 4
Components: V, S, M
Duration: 1 min./level
Spell Resistance: No

This spell functions like *fog cloud*, but in addition to obscuring sight, the *solid fog* is so thick that any creature attempting to move through it progresses at a speed of 5 feet, regardless of its normal speed, and it takes a −2 penalty on all melee attack and melee damage rolls. The vapors prevent effective ranged weapon attacks (except for magic rays and the like). A creature or object that falls into *solid fog* is slowed, so that each 10 feet of vapor that it passes through reduces falling damage by 1d6. A creature can't take a 5-foot step while in *solid fog*.

However, unlike normal fog, only a severe wind (31+ mph) disperses these vapors, and it does so in 1 round.

Solid fog can be made permanent with a *permanency* spell. A permanent *solid fog* dispersed by wind reforms in 10 minutes.

Material Component: A pinch of dried, powdered peas combined with powdered animal hoof.

Song of Discord

Enchantment (Compulsion) [Mind-
    Affecting, Sonic]
Level: Brd 5
Components: V, S
Casting Time: 1 standard action
Range: Medium (100 ft. + 10 ft./level)
Area: Creatures within a 20-ft.-radius
    spread
Duration: 1 round/level
Saving Throw: Will negates
Spell Resistance: Yes

This spell causes those within the area to turn on each other rather than attack their foes. Each affected creature has a 50% chance to attack the nearest target each round. (Roll to determine each creature's behavior every round at the beginning of its turn.) A creature that does not attack its nearest neighbor is free to act normally for that round.

Creatures forced by a *song of discord* to attack their fellows employ all methods at their disposal, choosing their deadliest spells and most advantageous combat tactics. They do not, however, harm targets that have fallen unconscious.

Soul Bind

Necromancy
Level: Clr 9, Sor/Wiz 9
Components: V, S, F
Casting Time: 1 standard action
Range: Close (25 ft. + 5 ft./2 levels)
Target: Corpse
Duration: Permanent
Saving Throw: Will negates
Spell Resistance: No

You draw the soul from a newly dead body and imprison it in a black sapphire gem. The subject must have been dead no more than 1 round per caster level. The soul, once trapped in the gem, cannot be returned through *clone, raise dead, reincarnation, resurrection, true resurrection,* or even a *miracle* or a *wish*. Only by destroying the gem or dispelling the spell on the gem can one free the soul (which is then still dead).

Focus: A black sapphire of at least 1,000 gp value for every Hit Die possessed by the creature whose soul is to be bound. If the gem is not valuable enough, it shatters when the binding is attempted. (While creatures have no concept of level or Hit Dice as such, the value of the gem needed to trap an individual can be researched. Remember that this value can change over time as creatures gain more Hit Dice.)

Sound Burst

Evocation [Sonic]
Level: Brd 2, Clr 2
Components: V, S, F/DF
Casting Time: 1 standard action
Range: Close (25 ft. + 5 ft./2 levels)
Area: 10-ft.-radius spread
Duration: Instantaneous
Saving Throw: Fortitude partial
Spell Resistance: Yes

You blast an area with a tremendous cacophony. Every creature in the area takes 1d8 points of sonic damage and must succeed on a Fortitude save to avoid being stunned for 1 round.

Creatures that cannot hear are not stunned but are still damaged.

Arcane Focus: A musical instrument.

Speak with Animals

Divination
Level: Brd 3, Drd 1, Rgr 1
Components: V, S
Casting Time: 1 standard action
Range: Personal
Target: You
Duration: 1 min./level

You can comprehend and communicate with animals. You are able to ask questions of and receive answers from animals, although the spell doesn't make them any more friendly or cooperative than normal. Furthermore, wary and cunning animals are likely to be terse and evasive, while the more stupid ones make inane comments. If an animal is friendly toward you, it may do some favor or service for you (as determined by the DM).

Speak with Dead

Necromancy [Language-Dependent]
Level: Clr 3
Components: V, S, DF
Casting Time: 10 minutes
Range: 10 ft.
Target: One dead creature
Duration: 1 min./level
Saving Throw: Will negates; see text
Spell Resistance: No

You grant the semblance of life and intellect to a corpse, allowing it to answer several questions that you put to it. You may ask one question per two caster levels. Unasked questions are wasted if the duration expires. The corpse's knowledge is limited to what the creature knew during life, including the languages it spoke (if any). Answers are usually brief, cryptic, or repetitive. If the creature's alignment was different from yours, the corpse gets a Will save to resist the spell as if it were alive.

If the corpse has been subject to *speak with dead* within the past week, the new spell fails. You can cast this spell on a corpse that has been deceased for any amount of time, but the body must be mostly intact to be able to respond. A damaged corpse may be able to give partial answers or partially correct answers, but it must at least have a mouth in order to speak at all.

This spell does not let you actually speak to the person (whose soul has departed). It instead draws on the imprinted knowledge stored in the corpse. The partially animated body retains the imprint of the soul that once inhabited it, and thus it can speak with all the knowledge that the creature had while alive. The corpse, however, cannot learn new information. Indeed, it can't even remember being questioned.

This spell does not affect a corpse that has been turned into an undead creature.

Speak with Plants

Divination
Level: Brd 4, Drd 3, Rgr 2
Components: V, S
Casting Time: 1 standard action
Range: Personal
Target: You
Duration: 1 min./level

You can comprehend and communicate with plants, including both normal plants and plant creatures. You are able to ask questions of and receive answers from plants. A regular plant's sense of its surroundings is limited, so it won't be able to give (or recognize) detailed descriptions of creatures or answer questions about events outside its immediate vicinity.

The spell doesn't make plant creatures any more friendly or cooperative than normal. Furthermore, wary and cunning plant creatures are likely to be terse and evasive, while the more stupid ones may make inane comments. If a plant creature is friendly toward you, it may do some favor or service for you (as determined by the DM).

Spectral Hand

Necromancy
Level: Sor/Wiz 2
Components: V, S
Casting Time: 1 standard action
Range: Medium (100 ft. + 10 ft./level)
Effect: One spectral hand
Duration: 1 min./level (D)
Saving Throw: None
Spell Resistance: No

A ghostly, glowing hand shaped from your life force materializes and moves as you desire, allowing you to deliver low-level, touch range spells at a distance. On casting the spell, you lose 1d4 hit points that return when the spell ends (even if it is dispelled), but not if the hand is destroyed. (The hit points can be healed as normal.) For as long as the spell lasts, any touch range spell of 4th level or lower that you cast can be delivered by the *spectral hand*. The spell gives you a +2 bonus on your melee touch attack roll, and attacking with the hand counts normally as an attack. The hand always strikes from your direction. The hand cannot flank targets like a creature can. After it delivers a spell, or if the hand goes beyond the spell range, goes out of your sight, the hand returns to you and hovers.

The hand is incorporeal and thus cannot be harmed by normal weapons. It has improved evasion (half damage on a failed Reflex save and no damage on a successful save), your save bonuses, and an AC of at least 22. Your Intelligence modifier applies to the hand's AC as if it were the hand's Dexterity modifier. The hand has 1

to 4 hit points, the same number that you lost in creating it.

Spell Immunity

Abjuration
Level: Clr 4, Protection 4, Strength 4
Components: V, S, DF
Casting Time: 1 standard action
Range: Touch
Target: Creature touched
Duration: 10 min./level
Saving Throw: Will negates (harmless)
Spell Resistance: Yes (harmless)

The warded creature is immune to the effects of one specified spell for every four levels you have. The spells must be of 4th level or lower. The warded creature effectively has unbeatable spell resistance regarding the specified spell or spells. Naturally, that immunity doesn't protect a creature from spells for which spell resistance doesn't apply. *Spell immunity* protects against spells, spell-like effects of magic items, and innate spell-like abilities of creatures. It does not protect against supernatural or extraordinary abilities, such as breath weapons or gaze attacks. Only a particular spell can be protected against, not a certain domain or school of spells or a group of spells that are similar in effect. Thus, a creature given immunity to *lightning bolt* is still vulnerable to *shocking grasp* or *chain lightning*.

A creature can have only one *spell immunity* or *greater spell immunity* spell in effect on it at a time.

Spell Immunity, Greater

Abjuration
Level: Clr 8

This spell functions like *spell immunity*, except the immunity applies to spells of 8th level or lower.

A creature can have only one *spell immunity* or *greater spell immunity* spell in effect on it at a time.

Spell Resistance

Abjuration
Level: Clr 5, Magic 5, Protection 5
Components: V, S, DF
Casting Time: 1 standard action
Range: Touch
Target: Creature touched
Duration: 1 min./level
Saving Throw: Will negates (harmless)
Spell Resistance: Yes (harmless)

The creature gains spell resistance equal to 12 + your caster level.

Spellstaff

Transmutation
Level: Drd 6
Components: V, S, F

Casting Time: 10 minutes
Range: Touch
Target: Wooden quarterstaff touched
Duration: Permanent until discharged (D)
Saving Throw: Will negates (object)
Spell Resistance: Yes (object)

You store one spell that you can normally cast in a wooden quarterstaff. Only one such spell can be stored in a staff at a given time, and you cannot have more than one *spellstaff* at any given time. You can cast a spell stored within a staff just as though it were among those you had prepared, but it does not count against your normal allotment for a given day. You use up any applicable material components required to cast the spell when you store it in the *spellstaff*.

Focus: The staff that stores the spell.

Spell Turning

Abjuration
Level: Luck 7, Magic 7, Sor/Wiz 7
Components: V, S, M/DF
Casting Time: 1 standard action
Range: Personal
Target: You
Duration: Until expended or 10 min./level

Spells and spell-like effects targeted on you are turned back upon the original caster. The abjuration turns only spells that have you as a target. Effect and area spells are not affected. *Spell turning* also fails to stop touch range spells. Thus, a *charm person* spell cast at you could be turned back upon the caster and possibly enable you to use the *charm* effect on that individual, but a *fireball* could not be turned back, and neither could *inflict critical wounds*.

From seven to ten (1d4+6) spell levels are affected by the turning. The DM secretly rolls the exact number. When a spell is turned, the DM subtracts its level from the amount of spell turning left.

When you are targeted by a spell of higher level than the amount of spell turning you have left, that spell is partially turned. The DM subtracts the amount of spell turning left from the spell level of the incoming spell, then divides the result by the spell level of the incoming spell to see what fraction of the effect gets through. For damaging spells, you and the caster each take a fraction of the damage. For nondamaging spells, each of you has a proportional chance to be affected.

For example, if you had three levels of spell turning left and were targeted by an *inflict critical wounds* spell (a 4th-level spell), you would turn three-fourths of the spell back at the caster. You would take one-fourth of the damage, while the caster takes three-fourths of the damage. If you were targeted by a wizard's *fear* spell (also a 4th-level spell) in the same situation, you would have a one in four (25%) chance to be affected by the spell, while the caster would have a three in four (75%) chance to be affected.

If you and a spellcasting attacker are both warded by *spell turning* effects in operation, a resonating field is created. Roll randomly to determine the result.

d%	Effect
01–70	Spell drains away without effect.
71–80	Spell affects both of you equally at full effect.
81–97	Both turning effects are rendered nonfunctional for 1d4 minutes.
98–100	Both of you go through a rift into another plane.

Arcane Material Component: A small silver mirror.

Spider Climb

Transmutation
Level: Drd 2, Sor/Wiz 2
Components: V, S, M
Casting Time: 1 standard action
Range: Touch
Target: Creature touched
Duration: 10 min./level
Saving Throw: Will negates (harmless)
Spell Resistance: Yes (harmless)

The subject can climb and travel on vertical surfaces or even traverse ceilings as well as a spider does. The affected creature must have its hands free to climb in this manner. The subject gains a climb speed of 20 feet; furthermore, it need not make Climb checks to traverse a vertical or horizontal surface (even upside down). A *spider climbing* creature retains its Dexterity bonus to Armor Class (if any) while climbing, and opponents get no special bonus to their attacks against it. It cannot, however, use the run action while climbing.

Material Component: A drop of bitumen and a live spider, both of which must be eaten by the subject.

Spike Growth

Transmutation
Level: Drd 3, Rgr 2
Components: V, S, DF
Casting Time: 1 standard action
Range: Medium (100 ft. + 10 ft./level)
Area: One 20-ft. square/level
Duration: 1 hour/level (D)
Saving Throw: Reflex partial
Spell Resistance: Yes

Any ground-covering vegetation in the spell's area becomes very hard and sharply pointed without changing its appearance. In areas of bare earth, roots and rootlets

act in the same way. Typically, *spike growth* can be cast in any outdoor setting except open water, ice, heavy snow, sandy desert, or bare stone. Any creature moving on foot into or through the spell's area takes 1d4 points of piercing damage for each 5 feet of movement through the spiked area.

Any creature that takes damage from this spell must also succeed on a Reflex save or suffer injuries to its feet and legs that slow its land speed by one-half. This speed penalty lasts for 24 hours or until the injured creature receives a *cure* spell (which also restores lost hit points). Another character can remove the penalty by taking 10 minutes to dress the injuries and succeeding on a Heal check against the spell's save DC.

Spike growth can't be disabled with the Disable Device skill.

Note: Magic traps such as *spike growth* are hard to detect. A rogue (only) can use the Search skill to find a *spike growth*. The DC is 25 + spell level, or DC 28 for *spike growth* (or DC 27 for *spike growth* cast by a ranger).

Spike Stones

Transmutation [Earth]
Level: Drd 4, Earth 4
Components: V, S, DF
Casting Time: 1 standard action
Range: Medium (100 ft. + 10 ft./level)
Area: One 20-ft. square/level
Duration: 1 hour/level (D)
Saving Throw: Reflex partial
Spell Resistance: Yes

Rocky ground, stone floors, and similar surfaces shape themselves into long, sharp points that blend into the background. *Spike stones* impede progress through an area and deal damage. Any creature moving on foot into or through the spell's area moves at half speed.

In addition, each creature moving through the area takes 1d8 points of piercing damage for each 5 feet of movement through the spiked area.

Any creature that takes damage from this spell must also succeed on a Reflex save to avoid injuries to its feet and legs. A failed save causes the creature's speed to be reduced to half normal for 24 hours or until the injured creature receives a *cure* spell (which also restores lost hit points). Another character can remove the penalty by taking 10 minutes to dress the injuries and succeeding on a Heal check against the spell's save DC.

Spike stones is a magic trap that can't be disabled with the Disable Device skill.

Note: Magic traps such as *spike stones* are hard to detect. A rogue (only) can use the Search skill to find *spike stones*. The DC is 25 + spell level, or DC 29 for *spike stones*.

Spiritual Weapon

Evocation [Force]
Level: Clr 2, War 2
Components: V, S, DF
Casting Time: 1 standard action
Range: Medium (100 ft. + 10 ft./level)
Effect: Magic weapon of force
Duration: 1 round/level (D)
Saving Throw: None
Spell Resistance: Yes

A weapon made of pure force springs into existence and attacks opponents at a distance, as you direct it, dealing 1d8 force damage per hit, +1 point per three caster levels (maximum +5 at 15th level). The weapon takes the shape of a weapon favored by your deity or a weapon with some spiritual significance or symbolism to you (see below) and has the same threat range and critical multipliers as a real weapon of its form. It strikes the opponent you designate, starting with one attack in the round the spell is cast and continuing each round thereafter on your turn. It uses your base attack bonus (possibly allowing it multiple attacks per round in subsequent rounds) plus your Wisdom modifier as its attack bonus. It strikes as a spell, not as a weapon, so, for example, it can damage creatures that have damage reduction. As a force effect, it can strike incorporeal creatures without the normal miss chance associated with incorporeality. The weapon always strikes from your direction. It does not get a flanking bonus or help a combatant get one. Your feats (such as Weapon Focus) or combat actions (such as charge) do not affect the weapon. If the weapon goes beyond the spell range, if it goes out of your sight, or if you are not directing it, the weapon returns to you and hovers.

Each round after the first, you can use a move action to redirect the weapon to a new target. If you do not, the weapon continues to attack the previous round's target. On any round that the weapon switches targets, it gets one attack. Subsequent rounds of attacking that target allow the weapon to make multiple attacks if your base attack bonus would allow it to. Even if the *spiritual weapon* is a ranged weapon, use the spell's range, not the weapon's normal range increment, and switching targets still is a move action.

A *spiritual weapon* cannot be attacked or harmed by physical attacks, but *dispel magic*, *disintegrate*, a *sphere of annihilation*, or a *rod of cancellation* affects it. A *spiritual weapon's* AC against touch attacks is 12 (10 + size bonus for Tiny object).

If an attacked creature has spell resistance, you make a caster level check (1d20 + caster level) against that spell resistance the first time the *spiritual weapon* strikes it. If the weapon is successfully resisted, the spell is dispelled. If not, the weapon has its normal full effect on that creature for the duration of the spell.

The weapon that you get is often a force replica of your deity's own personal weapon, many of which have individual names. A cleric without a deity gets a weapon based on his alignment. A neutral cleric without a deity can create a *spiritual weapon* of any alignment, provided he is acting at least generally in accord with that alignment at the time. The weapons associated with each deity or alignment are as follows.

Boccob: Quarterstaff, "Staff of Boccob"

Corellon Larethian: Longsword, "Sahandrian"

Ehlonna: Longbow, "Jenevier"

Erythnul: Morningstar, "Agony"

Fharlanghn: Quarterstaff, "Traveler's Friend"

Garl Glittergold: Battleaxe, "Arumdina"

Gruumsh: Spear, "Bloodspear"

Heironeous: Longsword, "Justicebringer"

Hextor: Flail, "Executioner"

Kord: Greatsword, "Kelmar"

Moradin: Warhammer, "Soulhammer"

Nerull: Scythe, "Lifecutter"

Obad-Hai: Quarterstaff, "Stormstouch"

Olidammara: Rapier, "Swiftstrike"

Pelor: Heavy mace, "Sunscepter"

St. Cuthbert: Heavy mace, "The Mace of Cuthbert"

Vecna: Dagger, "Afterthought"

Wee Jas: Dagger, "Discretion"

Yondalla: Short sword, "Hornblade"

Chaos: Battleaxe, "The Blade of Change"

Evil: Light flail, "The Scourge of Souls"

Good: Warhammer, "The Hammer of Justice"

Law: Longsword, "The Sword of Truth"

Statue

Transmutation
Level: Sor/Wiz 7
Components: V, S, M
Casting Time: 1 round
Range: Touch
Target: Creature touched
Duration: 1 hour/level (D)
Saving Throw: Will negates (harmless)
Spell Resistance: Yes (harmless)

A *statue* spell turns the subject to solid stone, along with any garments and equipment worn or carried. In statue form, the subject gains hardness 8. The subject retains its own hit points.

The subject can see, hear, and smell normally, but it does not need to eat or breathe. Feeling is limited to those sensations that can affect the granite-hard substance of the individual's body. Chipping is equal to a mere scratch, but breaking off one of the statue's arms constitutes serious damage.

The subject of a *statue* spell can return to its normal state, act, and then return instantly to the statue state (a free action) if it so desires, as long as the spell duration is in effect.

Material Component: Lime, sand, and a drop of water stirred by an iron bar, such as a nail or spike.

Status

Divination
Level: Clr 2
Components: V, S
Casting Time: 1 standard action
Range: Touch
Targets: One living creature touched per three levels
Duration: 1 hour/level
Saving Throw: Will negates (harmless)
Spell Resistance: Yes (harmless)

When you need to keep track of comrades who may get separated, *status* allows you to mentally monitor their relative positions and general condition. You are aware of direction and distance to the creatures and any conditions affecting them: unharmed, wounded, disabled, staggered, unconscious, dying, nauseated, panicked, stunned, poisoned, diseased, *confused*, or the like. Once the spell has been cast upon the subjects, the distance between them and the caster does not affect the spell as long as they are on the same plane of existence. If a subject leaves the plane, or if it dies, the spell ceases to function for it.

Stinking Cloud

Conjuration (Creation)
Level: Sor/Wiz 3
Components: V, S, M
Casting Time: 1 standard action
Range: Medium (100 ft. + 10 ft./level)
Effect: Cloud spreads in 20-ft. radius, 20 ft. high
Duration: 1 round/level
Saving Throw: Fortitude negates; see text
Spell Resistance: No

Stinking cloud creates a bank of fog like that created by *fog cloud*, except that the vapors are nauseating. Living creatures in the cloud become nauseated. This condition lasts as long as the creature is in the cloud and for 1d4+1 rounds after it leaves. (Roll separately for each nauseated character.) Any creature that succeeds on its save but remains in the cloud must continue to save each round on your turn.

Stinking cloud can be made permanent with a *permanency* spell. A permanent *stinking cloud* dispersed by wind reforms in 10 minutes.

Material Component: A rotten egg or several skunk cabbage leaves.

Stone Shape

Transmutation [Earth]
Level: Clr 3, Drd 3, Earth 3, Sor/Wiz 5
Components: V, S, M/DF
Casting Time: 1 standard action
Range: Touch
Target: Stone or stone object touched, up to 10 cu. ft. + 1 cu. ft./level
Duration: Instantaneous
Saving Throw: None
Spell Resistance: No

You can form an existing piece of stone into any shape that suits your purpose. For example, you can make a stone weapon, a special trapdoor, or a crude idol. *Stone shape* also permits you to reshape a stone door to make an exit where one didn't exist or to seal a door shut. While it's possible to make crude coffers, doors, and so forth with *stone shape*, fine detail isn't possible. There is a 30% chance that any shape including moving parts simply doesn't work.

Arcane Material Component: Soft clay, which must be worked into roughly the desired shape of the stone object and then touched to the stone while the verbal component is uttered.

Stoneskin

Abjuration
Level: Drd 5, Earth 6, Sor/Wiz 4, Strength 6
Components: V, S, M
Casting Time: 1 standard action
Range: Touch
Target: Creature touched
Duration: 10 min./level or until discharged
Saving Throw: Will negates (harmless)
Spell Resistance: Yes (harmless)

The warded creature gains resistance to blows, cuts, stabs, and slashes. The subject gains damage reduction 10/adamantine. (It ignores the first 10 points of damage each time it takes damage from a weapon, though an adamantine weapon bypasses the reduction.) Once the spell has prevented a total of 10 points of damage per caster level (maximum 150 points), it is discharged.

Material Component: Granite and 250 gp worth of diamond dust sprinkled on the target's skin.

Stone Tell

Divination
Level: Drd 6
Components: V, S, DF
Casting Time: 10 minutes
Range: Personal
Target: You
Duration: 1 min./level

You gain the ability to speak with stones, which relate to you who or what has touched them as well as revealing what is covered or concealed behind or under them. The stones relate complete descriptions if asked. A stone's perspective, perception, and knowledge may prevent the stone from providing the details you are looking for (as determined by the DM). You can speak with natural or worked stone.

Stone to Flesh

Transmutation
Level: Sor/Wiz 6
Components: V, S, M
Casting Time: 1 standard action
Range: Medium (100 ft. + 10 ft./level)
Target: One petrified creature or a cylinder of stone from 1 ft. to 3 ft. in diameter and up to 10 ft. long
Duration: Instantaneous
Saving Throw: Fortitude negates (object); see text
Spell Resistance: Yes

This spell restores a petrified creature to its normal state, restoring life and goods. The creature must make a DC 15 Fortitude save to survive the process. Any petrified creature, regardless of size, can be restored.

The spell also can convert a mass of stone into a fleshy substance. Such flesh is inert and lacking a vital life force unless a life force or magical energy is available. (For example, this spell would turn a stone golem into a flesh golem, but an ordinary statue would become a corpse.) You can affect an object that fits within a cylinder from 1 foot to 3 feet in diameter and up to 10 feet long or a cylinder of up to those dimensions in a larger mass of stone.

Material Component: A pinch of earth and a drop of blood.

Storm of Vengeance

Conjuration (Summoning)
Level: Drd 9, Clr 9
Components: V, S
Casting Time: 1 round
Range: Long (400 ft. + 40 ft./level)
Effect: 360-ft.-radius storm cloud
Duration: Concentration (maximum 10 rounds) (D)
Saving Throw: See text
Spell Resistance: Yes

This spell creates an enormous black storm cloud. Lightning and crashing claps of thunder appear within the storm. Each creature beneath the cloud must succeed on a Fortitude save or be deafened for 1d4×10 minutes.

If you do not maintain concentration on the spell after casting it, the spell ends. If you continue to concentrate, the spell generates additional effects in each fol-

lowing round, as noted below. Each effect occurs during your turn.

2nd Round: Acid rains down in the area, dealing 1d6 points of acid damage (no save).

3rd Round: You call six bolts of lightning down from the cloud. You decide where the bolts strike. No two bolts may be directed at the same target. Each bolt deals 10d6 points of electricity damage. A creature struck can attempt a Reflex save for half damage.

4th Round: Hailstones rain down in the area, dealing 5d6 points of bludgeoning damage (no save).

5th through 10th Rounds: Violent rain and wind gusts reduce visibility. The rain obscures all sight, including darkvision, beyond 5 feet. A creature 5 feet away has concealment (attacks have a 20% miss chance). Creatures farther away have total concealment (50% miss chance, and the attacker cannot use sight to locate the target). Speed is reduced by three-quarters. Ranged attacks within the area of the storm are impossible. Spells cast within the area are disrupted unless the caster succeeds on a Concentration check against a DC equal to the *storm of vengeance*'s save DC + the level of the spell the caster is trying to cast.

Suggestion

Enchantment (Compulsion) [Language-Dependent, Mind-Affecting]
Level: Brd 2, Sor/Wiz 3
Components: V, M
Casting Time: 1 standard action
Range: Close (25 ft. + 5 ft./2 levels)
Target: One living creature
Duration: 1 hour/level or until completed
Saving Throw: Will negates
Spell Resistance: Yes

You influence the actions of the target creature by suggesting a course of activity (limited to a sentence or two). The *suggestion* must be worded in such a manner as to make the activity sound reasonable. Asking the creature to stab itself, throw itself onto a spear, immolate itself, or do some other obviously harmful act automatically negates the effect of the spell. However, a *suggestion* that a pool of acid is actually pure water and that a quick dip would be refreshing is another matter. Urging a red dragon to stop attacking your party so that the dragon and party could jointly loot a rich treasure elsewhere is likewise a reasonable use of the spell's power.

The suggested course of activity can continue for the entire duration, such as in the case of the red dragon mentioned above. If the suggested activity can be completed in a shorter time, the spell

ends when the subject finishes what it was asked to do. You can instead specify conditions that will trigger a special activity during the duration. For example, you might suggest that a noble knight give her warhorse to the first beggar she meets. If the condition is not met before the spell duration expires, the activity is not performed.

A very reasonable *suggestion* causes the save to be made with a penalty (such as −1 or −2) at the discretion of the DM.

Material Component: A snake's tongue and either a bit of honeycomb or a drop of sweet oil.

Suggestion, Mass

Enchantment (Compulsion) [Language-Dependent, Mind-Affecting]
Level: Brd 5, Sor/Wiz 6
Range: Medium (100 ft. + 10 ft./level)
Targets: One creature/level, no two of which can be more than 30 ft. apart

This spell functions like *suggestion*, except that it can affect more creatures. The same *suggestion* applies to all these creatures.

Summon Instrument

Conjuration (Summoning)
Level: Brd 0
Components: V, S
Casting Time: 1 round
Range: 0 ft.
Effect: One summoned handheld musical instrument
Duration: 1 min./level (D)
Saving Throw: None
Spell Resistance: No

This spell summons one handheld musical instrument of your choice. This instrument appears in your hands or at your feet (your choice). The instrument is typical for its type. Only one instrument appears per casting, and it will play only for you. You can't summon an instrument too large to be held in two hands (such as a harp, piano, harpsichord, alphorn, or pipe organ).

Summon Monster I

Conjuration (Summoning) [see text]
Level: Brd 1, Clr 1, Sor/Wiz 1
Components: V, S, F/DF
Casting Time: 1 round
Range: Close (25 ft. + 5 ft./2 levels)
Effect: One summoned creature
Duration: 1 round/level (D)
Saving Throw: None
Spell Resistance: No

This spell summons an extraplanar creature (typically an outsider, elemental, or magical beast native to another plane). It appears where you designate and acts immediately, on your turn. It attacks your

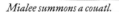

Mialee summons a couatl.

opponents to the best of its ability. If you can communicate with the creature, you can direct it not to attack, to attack particular enemies, or to perform other actions.

The spell conjures one of the creatures from the 1st-level list on the accompanying Summon Monster table. You choose which kind of creature to summon, and you can change that choice each time you cast the spell. Information on these creatures can be found in the *Monster Manual*.

A summoned monster cannot summon or otherwise conjure another creature, nor can it use any teleportation or planar travel abilities. Creatures cannot be summoned into an environment that cannot support them. For instance, a celestial porpoise may only be summoned in an aquatic environment.

When you use a summoning spell to summon an air, chaotic, earth, evil, fire, good, lawful, or water creature, it is a spell of that type. For example, *summon monster I* is a lawful and evil spell when cast to summon a fiendish dire rat.

Arcane Focus: A tiny bag and a small (not necessarily lit) candle.

Summon Monster II

Conjuration (Summoning) [see text for *summon monster I*]

Level: Brd 2, Clr 2, Sor/Wiz 2

Effect: One or more summoned creatures, no two of which can be more than 30 ft. apart

This spell functions like *summon monster I*, except that you can summon one creature from the 2nd-level list or 1d3 creatures of the same kind from the 1st-level list.

Summon Monster III

Conjuration (Summoning) [see text for *summon monster I*]

Level: Brd 3, Clr 3, Sor/Wiz 3

Effect: One or more summoned creatures, no two of which can be more than 30 ft. apart

This spell functions like *summon monster I*, except that you can summon one creature from the 3rd-level list, 1d3 creatures of the same kind from the 2nd-level list, or 1d4+1 creatures of the same kind from the 1st-level list.

Summon Monster IV

Conjuration (Summoning) [see text for *summon monster I*]

Level: Brd 4, Clr 4, Sor/Wiz 4

Effect: One or more summoned creatures, no two of which can be more than 30 ft. apart

This spell functions like *summon monster I*, except that you can summon one creature from the 4th-level list, 1d3 creatures of the same kind from the 3rd-level list, or 1d4+1 creatures of the same kind from a lower-level list.

Summon Monster V

Conjuration (Summoning) [see text for *summon monster I*]

Level: Brd 5, Clr 5, Sor/Wiz 5

Effect: One or more summoned creatures, no two of which can be more than 30 ft. apart

This spell functions like *summon monster I*, except that you can summon one creature from the 5th-level list, 1d3 creatures of the same kind from the 4th-level list, or 1d4+1 creatures of the same kind from a lower-level list.

Summon Monster VI

Conjuration (Summoning) [see text for *summon monster I*]

Level: Brd 6, Clr 6, Sor/Wiz 6

Effect: One or more summoned creatures, no two of which can be more than 30 ft. apart

This spell functions like *summon monster I*, except you can summon one creature from the 6th-level list, 1d3 creatures of the same kind from the 5th-level list, or 1d4+1 creatures of the same kind from a lower-level list.

Summon Monster VII

Conjuration (Summoning) [see text for *summon monster I*]

Level: Clr 7, Sor/Wiz 7

This spell functions like *summon monster I*, except that you can summon one creature from the 7th-level list, 1d3 creatures of the same kind from the 6th-level list, or 1d4+1 creatures of the same kind from a lower-level list.

Summon Monster VIII

Conjuration (Summoning) [see text for *summon monster I*]

Level: Clr 8, Sor/Wiz 8

This spell functions like *summon monster I*, except that you can summon one creature from the 8th-level list, 1d3 creatures of the same kind from the 7th-level list, or 1d4+1 creatures of the same kind from a lower-level list.

Summon Monster

1st Level

Celestial dog	LG
Celestial owl	LG
Celestial giant fire beetle	NG
Celestial porpoise[1]	NG
Celestial badger	CG
Celestial monkey	CG
Fiendish dire rat	LE
Fiendish raven	LE
Fiendish monstrous centipede, Medium	NE
Fiendish monstrous scorpion, Small	NE
Fiendish hawk	CE
Fiendish monstrous spider, Small	CE
Fiendish octopus[1]	CE
Fiendish snake, Small viper	CE

2nd Level

Celestial giant bee	LG
Celestial giant bombardier beetle	NG
Celestial riding dog	NG
Celestial eagle	CG
Lemure (devil)	LE
Fiendish squid[1]	LE
Fiendish wolf	LE
Fiendish monstrous centipede, Large	NE
Fiendish monstrous scorpion, Medium	NE
Fiendish shark, Medium[1]	NE
Fiendish monstrous spider, Medium	CE
Fiendish snake, Medium viper	CE

3rd Level

Celestial black bear	LG
Celestial bison	NG
Celestial dire badger	CG
Celestial hippogriff	CG
Elemental, Small (any)	N
Fiendish ape	LE
Fiendish dire weasel	LE
Hell hound	LE
Fiendish snake, constrictor	LE
Fiendish boar	NE
Fiendish dire bat	NE
Fiendish monstrous centipede, Huge	NE
Fiendish crocodile	CE
Dretch (demon)	CE
Fiendish snake, Large viper	CE
Fiendish wolverine	CE

4th Level

Archon, lantern	LG
Celestial giant owl	LG
Celestial giant eagle	CG
Celestial lion	CG
Mephit (any)	N
Fiendish dire wolf	LE
Fiendish giant wasp	LE
Fiendish giant praying mantis	NE
Fiendish shark, Large[1]	NE
Yeth hound	NE
Fiendish monstrous spider, Large	CE
Fiendish snake, Huge viper	CE
Howler	CE

5th Level

Archon, hound	LG
Celestial brown bear	LG
Celestial giant stag beetle	NG
Celestial sea cat[1]	NG
Celestial griffon	CG
Elemental, Medium (any)	N
Achaierai	LE
Devil, bearded	LE
Fiendish deinonychus	LE
Fiendish dire ape	LE
Fiendish dire boar	NE
Fiendish shark, Huge	NE
Fiendish monstrous scorpion, Large	NE
Shadow mastiff	NE
Fiendish dire wolverine	CE
Fiendish giant crocodile	CE
Fiendish tiger	CE

6th Level

Celestial polar bear	LG
Celestial orca whale[1]	NG
Bralani (eladrin)	CG
Celestial dire lion	CG
Elemental, Large (any)	N
Janni (genie)	N
Chaos beast	CN
Devil, chain	LE
Xill	LE
Fiendish monstrous centipede, Gargantuan	NE
Fiendish rhinoceros	NE
Fiendish elasmosaurus[1]	CE
Fiendish monstrous spider, Huge	CE
Fiendish snake, giant constrictor	CE

7th Level

Celestial elephant	LG
Avoral (guardinal)	NG
Celestial baleen whale[1]	NG
Djinni (genie)	CG
Elemental, Huge (any)	N
Invisible stalker	N
Slaad, red	CN
Devil, bone	LE
Fiendish megaraptor	LE
Fiendish monstrous scorpion, Huge	NE
Babau (demon)	CE
Fiendish giant octopus[1]	CE
Fiendish girallon	CE

8th Level

Celestial dire bear	LG
Celestial cachalot whale[1]	NG
Celestial triceratops	NG
Lillend	CG
Elemental, greater (any)	N
Slaad, blue	CN
Fiendish giant squid[1]	LE
Hellcat	LE
Fiendish monstrous centipede, Colossal	NE
Fiendish dire tiger	CE
Fiendish monstrous spider, Gargantuan	CE
Fiendish tyrannosaurus	CE
Vrock (demon)	CE

9th Level

Couatl	LG
Leonal (guardinal)	NG
Celestial roc	CG
Elemental, elder (any)	N
Slaad, green	CN
Devil, barbed	LE
Fiendish dire shark[1]	NE
Fiendish monstrous scorpion, Gargantuan	NE
Night hag	NE
Bebilith (demon)	CE
Fiendish monstrous spider, Colossal	CE
Hezrou (demon)	CE

1 May be summoned only into an aquatic or watery environment.

Summon Monster IX

Conjuration (Summoning) [see text for *summon monster I*]
Level: Chaos 9, Clr 9, Evil 9, Good 9, Law 9, Sor/Wiz 9

This spell functions like *summon monster I*, except that you can summon one creature from the 9th-level list, 1d3 creatures of the same kind from the 8th-level list, or 1d4+1 creatures of the same kind from a lower-level list.

Summon Nature's Ally I

Conjuration (Summoning)
Level: Drd 1, Rgr 1
Components: V, S, DF
Casting Time: 1 round
Range: Close (25 ft. + 5 ft./2 levels)
Effect: One summoned creature
Duration: 1 round/level (D)
Saving Throw: None
Spell Resistance: No

This spell summons a natural creature. It appears where you designate and acts immediately, on your turn. It attacks your opponents to the best of its ability. If you can communicate with the creature, you can direct it not to attack, to attack particular enemies, or to perform other actions.

A summoned monster cannot summon or otherwise conjure another creature, nor can it use any teleportation or planar travel abilities. Creatures cannot be summoned into an environment that cannot support them. For instance, a porpoise may only be summoned in an aquatic environment.

The spell conjures one of the creatures from the 1st-level list on the accompanying Summon Nature's Ally table. You choose which kind of creature to summon, and you can change that choice each time you cast the spell. All the creatures on the table are neutral unless otherwise noted.

Summon Nature's Ally II

Conjuration (Summoning)
Level: Drd 2, Rgr 2
Effect: One or more creatures, no two of which can be more than 30 ft. apart

This spell functions like *summon nature's ally I*, except that you can summon one 2nd-level creature or 1d3 1st-level creatures of the same kind.

Summon Nature's Ally III

Conjuration (Summoning) [see text]
Level: Drd 3, Rgr 3
Effect: One or more creatures, no two of which can be more than 30 ft. apart

This spell functions like *summon nature's ally I*, except that you can summon one 3rd-level creature, 1d3 2nd-level creatures of the same kind, or 1d4+1 1st-level creatures of the same kind.

When you use a summoning spell to summon an air, chaotic, earth, evil, fire, good, lawful, or water creature, it is a spell of that type. For example, *summon nature's ally III* is an evil and fire spell when you cast it to summon a salamander.

SUMMON NATURE'S ALLY

1st Level
Dire rat
Eagle (animal)
Monkey (animal)
Octopus[1] (animal)
Owl (animal)
Porpoise[1] (animal)
Snake, Small viper (animal)
Wolf (animal)

2nd Level
Bear, black (animal)
Crocodile (animal)
Dire badger
Dire bat
Elemental, Small (any)
Hippogriff
Shark, Medium[1] (animal)
Snake, Medium viper (animal)
Squid[1] (animal)
Wolverine (animal)

3rd Level
Ape (animal)
Dire weasel
Dire wolf
Eagle, giant [NG]
Lion
Owl, giant [NG]
Satyr [CN; without pipes]
Shark, Large[1] (animal)
Snake, constrictor (animal)
Snake, Large viper (animal)
Thoqqua

4th Level
Arrowhawk, juvenile
Bear, brown (animal)
Crocodile, giant (animal)
Deinonychus (dinosaur)
Dire ape
Dire boar
Dire wolverine
Elemental, Medium (any)
Salamander, flamebrother [NE]
Sea cat[1]
Shark, Huge[1] (animal)
Snake, Huge viper (animal)
Tiger (animal)
Tojanida, juvenile[1]
Unicorn [CG]
Xorn, minor

Summon Nature's Ally IV

Conjuration (Summoning) [see text]
Level: Animal 4, Drd 4, Rgr 4
Effect: One or more creatures, no two of which can be more than 30 ft. apart

This spell functions like *summon nature's ally I*, except that you can summon one 4th-level creature, 1d3 3rd-level creatures

5th Level
Arrowhawk, adult
Bear, polar (animal)
Dire lion
Elasmosaurus[1] (dinosaur)
Elemental, Large (any)
Griffon
Janni (genie)
Rhinoceros (animal)
Satyr [CN; with pipes]
Snake, giant constrictor (animal)
Nixie (sprite)
Tojanida, adult[1]
Whale, orca[1] (animal)

6th Level
Dire bear
Elemental, Huge (any)
Elephant (animal)
Girallon
Megaraptor (dinosaur)
Octopus, giant[1] (animal)
Pixie* (sprite) [NG; no special arrows]
Salamander, average [NE]
Whale, baleen[1]
Xorn, average
*Can't cast *Otto's irresistible dance*

7th Level
Arrowhawk, elder
Dire tiger
Elemental, greater (any)
Djinni (genie) [NG]
Invisible stalker
Pixie* (sprite) [NG; with sleep arrows]
Squid, giant[1] (animal)
Triceratops (dinosaur)
Tyrannosaurus (dinosaur)
Whale, cachalot[1] (animal)
Xorn, elder
*Can't cast *Otto's irresistible dance*

8th Level
Dire shark[1]
Roc
Salamander, noble [NE]
Tojanida, elder

9th Level
Elemental, elder
Grig [NG; with fiddle] (sprite)
Pixie* (sprite) [NG; with sleep and memory loss arrows]
Unicorn, celestial charger
*Can cast *Otto's irresistible dance*

1 May be summoned only into an aquatic or watery environment.

of the same kind, or 1d4+1 lower-level creatures of the same kind.

When you use a summoning spell to summon an air, chaotic, earth, evil, fire, good, lawful, or water creature, it is a spell of that type.

Summon Nature's Ally V

Conjuration (Summoning) [see text]
Level: Drd 5
Effect: One or more creatures, no two of which can be more than 30 ft. apart

This spell functions like *summon nature's ally I*, except that you can summon one 5th-level creature, 1d3 4th-level creatures of the same kind, or 1d4+1 lower-level creatures of the same kind.

When you use a summoning spell to summon an air, chaotic, earth, evil, fire, good, lawful, or water creature, it is a spell of that type.

Summon Nature's Ally VI

Conjuration (Summoning) [see text]
Level: Drd 6
Effect: One or more creatures, no two of which can be more than 30 ft. apart

This spell functions like *summon nature's ally I*, except that you can summon one 6th-level creature, 1d3 5th-level creatures of the same kind, or 1d4+1 lower-level creatures of the same kind.

When you use a summoning spell to summon an air, chaotic, earth, evil, fire, good, lawful, or water creature, it is a spell of that type.

Summon Nature's Ally VII

Conjuration (Summoning) [see text]
Level: Drd 7
Effect: One or more creatures, no two of which can be more than 30 ft. apart

This spell functions like *summon nature's ally I*, except that you can summon one 7th-level creature, 1d3 6th-level creatures of the same kind, or 1d4+1 lower-level creatures of the same kind.

When you use a summoning spell to summon an air, chaotic, earth, evil, fire, good, lawful, or water creature, it is a spell of that type.

Summon Nature's Ally VIII

Conjuration (Summoning) [see text]
Level: Animal 8, Drd 8
Effect: One or more creatures, no two of which can be more than 30 ft. apart

This spell functions like *summon nature's ally I*, except that you can summon one 8th-level creature, 1d3 7th-level creatures of the same kind, or 1d4+1 lower-level creatures of the same kind.

When you use a summoning spell to

summon an air, chaotic, earth, evil, fire, good, lawful, or water creature, it is a spell of that type.

Summon Nature's Ally IX

Conjuration (Summoning) [see text]
Level: Drd 9
Effect: One or more creatures, no two of which can be more than 30 ft. apart

This spell functions like *summon nature's ally I*, except that you can summon one 9th-level creature, 1d3 8th-level creatures of the same kind, or 1d4+1 lower-level creatures of the same kind.

When you use a summoning spell to summon an air, chaotic, earth, evil, fire, good, lawful, or water creature, it is a spell of that type.

Summon Swarm

Conjuration (Summoning)
Level: Brd 2, Drd 2, Sor/Wiz 2
Components: V, S, M/DF
Casting Time: 1 round
Range: Close (25 ft. + 5 ft./2 levels)
Effect: One swarm of bats, rats, or spiders
Duration: Concentration + 2 rounds
Saving Throw: None
Spell Resistance: No

You summon a swarm of bats, rats, or spiders (your choice), which attacks all other creatures within its area. (You may summon the swarm so that it shares the area of other creatures.) If no living creatures are within its area, the swarm attacks or pursues the nearest creature as best it can. The caster has no control over its target or direction of travel.

See the *Monster Manual* for details of bat, rat, and spider swarms.

Arcane Material Component: A square of red cloth.

Sunbeam

Evocation [Light]
Level: Drd 7, Sun 7
Components: V, S, DF
Casting Time: 1 standard action
Range: 60 ft.
Area: Line from your hand
Duration: 1 round/level or until all beams are exhausted
Saving Throw: Reflex negates and Reflex half; see text
Spell Resistance: Yes

For the duration of this spell, you can use a standard action to evoke a dazzling beam of intense light each round. You can call forth one beam per three caster levels (maximum six beams at 18th level). The spell ends when its duration runs out or your allotment of beams is exhausted.

Each creature in the beam is blinded

and takes 4d6 points of damage. Any creatures to which sunlight is harmful or unnatural take double damage. A successful Reflex save negates the blindness and reduces the damage by half.

An undead creature caught within the beam takes 1d6 points of damage per caster level (maximum 20d6), or half damage if a Reflex save is successful. In addition, the beam results in the destruction of any undead creature specifically harmed by bright light (such as a vampire) if it fails its save.

The ultraviolet light generated by the spell deals damage to fungi, mold, oozes, and slimes just as if they were undead creatures.

Sunburst

Evocation [Light]
Level: Drd 8, Sor/Wiz 8, Sun 8
Components: V, S, M/DF
Casting Time: 1 standard action
Range: Long (400 ft. + 40 ft./level)
Area: 80-ft.-radius burst
Duration: Instantaneous
Saving Throw: Reflex partial; see text
Spell Resistance: Yes

Sunburst causes a globe of searing radiance to explode silently from a point you select. All creatures in the globe are blinded and take 6d6 points of damage. A creature to which sunlight is harmful or unnatural takes double damage. A successful Reflex save negates the blindness and reduces the damage by half.

An undead creature caught within the globe takes 1d6 points of damage per caster level (maximum 25d6), or half damage if a Reflex save is successful. In addition, the burst results in the destruction of any undead creature specifically harmed by bright light (such as a vampire) if it fail its save.

The ultraviolet light generated by the spell deals damage to fungi, mold, oozes, and slimes just as if they were undead creatures.

Sunburst dispels any darkness spells of lower than 9th level within its area.

Arcane Material Component: A piece of sunstone and a naked flame.

Symbol of Death

Necromancy [Death]
Level: Clr 8, Sor/Wiz 8
Components: V, S, M
Casting Time: 10 minutes
Range: 0 ft.; see text
Effect: One symbol
Duration: See text
Saving Throw: Fortitude negates
Spell Resistance: Yes

This spell allows you to scribe a potent rune of power upon a surface. When triggered, a *symbol of death* slays one or more creatures within 60 feet of the symbol (treat as a burst) whose combined total current hit points do not exceed 150. The *symbol of death* affects the closest creatures first, skipping creatures with too many hit points to affect. Once triggered, the *symbol* becomes active and glows, lasting for 10 minutes per caster level or until it has affected 150 hit points' worth of creatures, whichever comes first. Any creature that enters the area while the *symbol of death* is active is subject to its effect, whether or not that creature was in the area when it was triggered. A creature need save against the *symbol* only once as long as it remains within the area, though if it leaves the area and returns while the *symbol* is still active, it must save again.

Until it is triggered, the *symbol of death* is inactive (though visible and legible at a distance of 60 feet). To be effective, a *symbol of death* must always be placed in plain sight and in a prominent location. Covering or hiding the rune renders the *symbol of death* ineffective, unless a creature removes the covering, in which case the *symbol of death* works normally.

As a default, a *symbol of death* is triggered whenever a creature does one or more of the following, as you select: looks at the rune; reads the rune; touches the rune; passes over the rune; or passes through a portal bearing the rune. Regardless of the trigger method or methods chosen, a creature more than 60 feet from a symbol of death can't trigger it (even if it meets one or more of the triggering conditions, such as reading the rune). Once the spell is cast, a *symbol of death*'s triggering conditions cannot be changed.

In this case, "reading" the rune means any attempt to study it, identify it, or fathom its meaning. Throwing a cover over a *symbol of death* to render it inoperative triggers it if the symbol reacts to touch. You can't use a *symbol of death* offensively; for instance, a touch-triggered symbol of death remains untriggered if an item bearing the *symbol of death* is used to touch a creature. Likewise, a *symbol of death* cannot be placed on a weapon and set to activate when the weapon strikes a foe.

You can also set special triggering limitations of your own. These can be as simple or elaborate as you desire. Special conditions for triggering a *symbol of death* can be based on a creature's name, identity, or alignment, but otherwise must be based on observable actions or qualities. Intangibles such as level, class, Hit Dice, and hit points don't qualify. For example, a *symbol of death* can be set to activate when a lawful good creature approaches, but not when a paladin approaches.

When scribing a *symbol of death*, you can specify a password or phrase that prevents a creature using it from triggering the effect. Anyone using the password remains immune to that particular rune's effects so long as the creature remains within 60 feet of the rune. If the creature leaves the radius and returns later, it must use the password again.

You also can attune any number of creatures to the *symbol of death*, but doing this can extend the casting time. Attuning one or two creatures takes negligible time, and attuning a small group (as many as ten creatures) extends the casting time to 1 hour. Attuning a large group (as many as twenty-five creatures) takes 24 hours. Attuning larger groups takes proportionately longer, as the DM sees fit. Any creature attuned to a *symbol of death* cannot trigger it and is immune to its effects, even if within its radius when triggered. You are automatically considered attuned to your own *symbols of death*, and thus always ignore the effects and cannot inadvertently trigger them.

Read magic allows you to identify a *symbol of death* with a DC 19 Spellcraft check. Of course, if the *symbol of death* is set to be triggered by reading it, this will trigger the symbol.

A *symbol of death* can be removed by a successful *dispel magic* targeted solely on the rune. An *erase* spell has no effect on a *symbol of death*. Destruction of the surface where a *symbol of death* is inscribed destroys the *symbol* but also triggers it.

Symbol of death can be made permanent with a *permanency* spell. A permanent *symbol of death* that is disabled or that has affected its maximum number of hit points becomes inactive for 10 minutes, then can be triggered again as normal.

Note: Magic traps such as *symbol of death* are hard to detect and disable. A rogue (only) can use the Search skill to find a *symbol of death* and Disable Device to thwart it. The DC in each case is 25 + spell level, or 33 for *symbol of death*.

Material Component: Mercury and phosphorus, plus powdered diamond and opal with a total value of at least 5,000 gp each.

Symbol of Fear

Necromancy [Fear, Mind-Affecting]
Level: Clr 6, Sor/Wiz 6
Saving Throw: Will negates

This spell functions like *symbol of death*, except that all creatures within 60 feet of the *symbol of fear* instead become panicked for 1 round per caster level.

Note: Magic traps such as *symbol of fear* are hard to detect and disable. A rogue (only) can use the Search skill to find a *symbol of fear* and Disable Device to thwart it. The DC in each case is 25 + spell level, or 31 for *symbol of fear*.

Material Component: Mercury and phosphorus, plus powdered diamond and opal with a total value of at least 1,000 gp.

Symbol of Insanity

Enchantment (Compulsion) [Mind-Affecting]
Level: Clr 8, Sor/Wiz 8
Saving Throw: Will negates

This spell functions like *symbol of death*, except that all creatures within the radius of the *symbol of insanity* instead become permanently insane (as the *insanity* spell).

Unlike *symbol of death*, symbol of insanity has no hit point limit; once triggered, a *symbol of insanity* simply remains active for 10 minutes per caster level.

Note: Magic traps such as *symbol of insanity* are hard to detect and disable. A rogue (only) can use the Search skill to find a *symbol of insanity* and Disable Device to thwart it. The DC in each case is 25 + spell level, or 33 for *symbol of insanity*.

Material Component: Mercury and phosphorus, plus powdered diamond and opal with a total value of at least 5,000 gp.

Symbol of Pain

Necromancy [Evil]
Level: Clr 5, Sor/Wiz 5

This spell functions like *symbol of death*, except that each creature within the radius of a *symbol of pain* instead suffers wracking pains that impose a –4 penalty on attack rolls, skill checks, and ability checks. These effects last for 1 hour after the creature moves farther than 60 feet from the symbol.

Unlike *symbol of death*, symbol of pain has no hit point limit; once triggered, a *symbol of pain* simply remains active for 10 minutes per caster level.

Note: Magic traps such as *symbol of pain* are hard to detect and disable. A rogue (only) can use the Search skill to find a *symbol of pain* and Disable Device to thwart it. The DC in each case is 25 + spell level, or 30 for *symbol of pain*.

Material Component: Mercury and phosphorus, plus powdered diamond and opal with a total value of at least 1,000 gp.

Symbol of Persuasion

Enchantment (Charm) [Mind-Affecting]
Level: Clr 6, Sor/Wiz 6
Saving Throw: Will negates

This spell functions like *symbol of death*, except that all creatures within the radius of a *symbol of persuasion* instead become charmed by the caster (as the *charm monster* spell) for 1 hour per caster level.

Unlike *symbol of death*, symbol of persuasion has no hit point limit; once triggered, a *symbol of persuasion* simply remains active for 10 minutes per caster level.

Note: Magic traps such as *symbol of persuasion* are hard to detect and disable. A rogue (only) can use the Search skill to find a *symbol of persuasion* and Disable Device to thwart it. The DC in each case is 25 + spell level, or 31 for *symbol of persuasion*.

Material Component: Mercury and phosphorus, plus powdered diamond and opal with a total value of at least 5,000 gp.

Symbol of Sleep
Enchantment (Compulsion) [Mind-Affecting]
Level: Clr 5, Sor/Wiz 5
Saving Throw: Will negates

This spell functions like *symbol of death*, except that all creatures of 10 HD or less within 60 feet of the *symbol of sleep* instead fall into a catatonic slumber for 3d6×10 minutes. Unlike with the *sleep* spell, sleeping creatures cannot be awakened by nonmagical means before this time expires.

Unlike *symbol of death*, *symbol of sleep* has no hit point limit; once triggered, a *symbol of sleep* simply remains active for 10 minutes per caster level.

Note: Magic traps such as *symbol of sleep* are hard to detect and disable. A rogue (only) can use the Search skill to find a *symbol of sleep* and Disable Device to thwart it. The DC in each case is 25 + spell level, or 30 for *symbol of sleep*.

Material Component: Mercury and phosphorus, plus powdered diamond and opal with a total value of at least 1,000 gp.

Symbol of Stunning
Enchantment (Compulsion) [Mind-Affecting]
Level: Clr 7, Sor/Wiz 7
Saving Throw: Will negates

This spell functions like *symbol of death*, except that all creatures within 60 feet of a *symbol of stunning* instead become stunned for 1d6 rounds.

Note: Magic traps such as *symbol of stunning* are hard to detect and disable. A rogue (only) can use the Search skill to find a *symbol of stunning* and Disable Device to thwart it. The DC in each case is

Jozan casts symbol of pain.

25 + spell level, or 32 for *symbol of stunning*.

Material Component: Mercury and phosphorus, plus powdered diamond and opal with a total value of at least 5,000 gp.

Symbol of Weakness
Necromancy
Level: Clr 7, Sor/Wiz 7

This spell functions like *symbol of death*, except that every creature within 60 feet of a *symbol of weakness* instead suffers crippling weakness that deals 3d6 points of Strength damage.

Unlike *symbol of death*, *symbol of weakness* has no hit point limit; once triggered, a *symbol of weakness* simply remains active for 10 minutes per caster level.

Note: Magic traps such as *symbol of weakness* are hard to detect and disable. A rogue (only) can use the Search skill to find a *symbol of weakness* and Disable Device to thwart it. The DC in each case is 25 + spell level, or 32 for *symbol of weakness*.

Material Component: Mercury and phosphorus, plus powdered diamond and opal with a total value of at least 5,000 gp.

Sympathetic Vibration
Evocation [Sonic]
Level: Brd 6
Components: V, S, F
Casting Time: 10 minutes
Range: Touch
Target: One freestanding structure
Duration: Up to 1 round/level
Saving Throw: None; see text
Spell Resistance: Yes

By attuning yourself to a freestanding structure such as a building, bridge, or dam, you can create a damaging vibration within it. Once it begins, the vibration deals 2d10 points of damage per round to the target structure. (Hardness has no effect on the spell's damage.) You can choose at the time of casting to limit the duration of the spell; otherwise it lasts for 1 round/level. If the spell is cast upon a target that is not freestanding, such as a hillside, the surrounding stone dissipates the effect and no damage occurs.

Sympathetic vibration cannot affect creatures (including constructs). Since a structure is an unattended object, it gets no saving throw to resist the effect.

Focus: A tuning fork.

Sympathy

Enchantment (Compulsion) [Mind-Affecting]
Level: Drd 9, Sor/Wiz 8
Components: V, S, M
Casting Time: 1 hour
Range: Close (25 ft. + 5 ft./2 levels)
Target: One location (up to a 10-ft. cube/level) or one object
Duration: 2 hours/level (D)
Saving Throw: Will negates; see text
Spell Resistance: Yes

You cause an object or location to emanate magical vibrations that attract either a specific kind of intelligent creature or creatures of a particular alignment, as defined by you. The particular kind of creature to be affected must be named specifically—for example, red dragons, hill giants, wererats, lammasus, or vampires. A creature subtype (such as goblinoid) is not specific enough. Likewise, the specific alignment must be named—for example, chaotic evil, chaotic good, lawful neutral, or neutral.

Creatures of the specified kind or alignment feel elated and pleased to be in the area or desire to touch or to possess the object. The compulsion to stay in the area or touch the object is overpowering. If the save is successful, the creature is released from the enchantment, but a subsequent save must be made 1d6×10 minutes later. If this save fails, the affected creature attempts to return to the area or object.

Sympathy counters and dispels *antipathy*.

Material Component: 1,500 gp worth of crushed pearls and a drop of honey.

Tasha's Hideous Laughter

Enchantment (Compulsion) [Mind-Affecting]
Level: Brd 1, Sor/Wiz 2
Components: V, S, M
Casting Time: 1 standard action
Range: Close (25 ft. + 5 ft./2 levels)
Target: One creature; see text
Duration: 1 round/level
Saving Throw: Will negates
Spell Resistance: Yes

This spell afflicts the subject with uncontrollable laughter. It collapses into gales of manic laughter, falling prone. The subject can take no actions while laughing, but is not considered helpless. After the spell ends, it can act normally.

A creature with an Intelligence score of 2 or lower is not affected. A creature whose type (such as humanoid or dragon) is different from the caster's receives a +4 bonus on its saving throw, because humor doesn't "translate" well.

Material Component: Tiny tarts that are thrown at the target and a feather that is waved in the air.

Telekinesis

Transmutation
Level: Sor/Wiz 5
Components: V, S
Casting Time: 1 standard action
Range: Long (400 ft. + 40 ft./level)
Target or Targets: See text
Duration: Concentration (up to 1 round/ level) or instantaneous; see text
Saving Throw: Will negates (object) or None; see text
Spell Resistance: Yes (object); see text

You move objects or creatures by concentrating on them. Depending on the version selected, the spell can provide a gentle, sustained force, perform a variety of combat maneuvers, or exert a single short, violent thrust.

Sustained Force: A sustained force moves an object weighing no more than 25 pounds per caster level (maximum 375 pounds at 15th level) up to 20 feet per round. A creature can negate the effect on an object it possesses with a successful Will save or with spell resistance.

This version of the spell can last 1 round per caster level, but it ends if you cease concentration. The weight can be moved vertically, horizontally, or in both directions. An object cannot be moved beyond your range. The spell ends if the object is forced beyond the range. If you cease concentration for any reason, the object falls or stops.

An object can be telekinetically manipulated as if with one hand. For example, a lever or rope can be pulled, a key can be turned, an object rotated, and so on, if the force required is within the weight limitation. You might even be able to untie simple knots, though delicate activities such as these require Intelligence checks against a DC set by the DM.

Combat Maneuver: Alternatively, once per round, you can use *telekinesis* to perform a bull rush, disarm, grapple (including pin), or trip. Resolve these attempts as normal, except that they don't provoke attacks of opportunity, you use your caster level in place of your base attack bonus (for disarm and grapple), you use your Intelligence modifier (if a wizard) or Charisma modifier (if a sorcerer) in place of your Strength or Dexterity modifier, and a failed attempt doesn't allow a reactive attempt by the target (such as for disarm or trip). No save is allowed against these attempts, but spell resistance applies normally. This version of the spell can last 1 round per caster level, but it ends if you cease concentration.

Violent Thrust: Alternatively, the spell energy can be spent in a single round. You can hurl one object or creature per caster level (maximum 15) that are within range and all within 10 feet of each other toward any target within 10 feet per level of all the objects. You can hurl up to a total weight of 25 pounds per caster level (maximum 375 pounds at 15th level).

You must succeed on attack rolls (one per creature or object thrown) to hit the target with the items, using your base attack bonus + your Intelligence modifier (if a wizard) or Charisma modifier (if a sorcerer). Weapons cause standard damage (with no Strength bonus; note that arrows or bolts deal damage as daggers of their size when used in this manner). Other objects cause damage ranging from 1 point per 25 pounds (for less dangerous objects such as a barrel) to 1d6 points of damage per 25 pounds (for hard, dense objects such as a boulder).

Creatures who fall within the weight capacity of the spell can be hurled, but they are allowed Will saves (and spell resistance) to negate the effect, as are those whose held possessions are targeted by the spell. If a telekinesed creature is hurled against a solid surface, it takes damage as if it had fallen 10 feet (1d6 points).

Teleport

Conjuration (Teleportation)
Level: Sor/Wiz 5, Travel 5
Components: V
Casting Time: 1 standard action
Range: Personal and touch
Target: You and touched objects or other touched willing creatures
Duration: Instantaneous
Saving Throw: None and Will negates (object)
Spell Resistance: No and Yes (object)

This spell instantly transports you to a designated destination, which may be as distant as 100 miles per caster level. Interplanar travel is not possible. You can bring along objects as long as their weight doesn't exceed your maximum load. You may also bring one additional willing Medium or smaller creature (carrying gear or objects up to its maximum load) or its equivalent (see below) per three caster levels. A Large creature counts as two Medium creatures, a Huge creature counts as two Large creatures, and so forth. All creatures to be transported must be in contact with one another, and at least one of those creatures must be in contact with you. As with all spells where the range is personal and the target is you, you need not make a saving throw, nor is spell resistance applicable to you. Only objects held or in use (attended) by another person receive saving throws and spell resistance.

You must have some clear idea of the location and layout of the destination.

You can't simply teleport to the warlord's tent if you don't know where that tent is, what it looks like, or what's in it. The clearer your mental image, the more likely the teleportation works. Areas of strong physical or magical energy may make teleportation more hazardous or even impossible.

To see how well the teleportation works, roll d% and consult the Teleport table. Refer to the following information for definitions of the terms on the table.

Familiarity: "Very familiar" is a place where you have been very often and where you feel at home. "Studied carefully" is a place you know well, either because you can currently see it, you've been there often, or you have used other means (such as *scrying*) to study the place for at least one hour. "Seen casually" is a place that you have seen more than once but with which you are not very familiar. "Viewed once" is a place that you have seen once, possibly using magic.

"False destination" is a place that does not truly exist, such as if you scryed on an enemy's sanctum but instead viewed a *false vision,* or if you are teleporting to an otherwise familiar location that no longer exists as such or has been so completely altered as to no longer be familiar to you (for instance, a home that has burned to the ground). When traveling to a false destination, roll 1d20+80 to obtain results on the table, rather than rolling d%, since there is no real destination for you to hope to arrive at or even be off target from.

On Target: You appear where you want to be.

Off Target: You appear safely a random distance away from the destination in a random direction. Distance off target is 1d10×1d10% of the distance that was to be traveled. For example, if you tried to travel 120 miles, landed off target, and rolled 5 and 3 on the two d10s, then you would be 15% off target. That's 18 miles, in this case. The DM determines the direction off target randomly, such as by rolling 1d8 and designating 1 as north, 2 as northeast, and so forth. If you were teleporting to a coastal city and wound up 18 miles out at sea, you could be in trouble.

Similar Area: You wind up in an area that's visually or thematically similar to the target area. A wizard heading for her home laboratory might wind up in another wizard's laboratory or in an alchemy supply shop that has many of the same tools and implements as in her laboratory. Generally, you appear in the closest similar place within range. If the DM determines no such area exists within the spell's range, the spell simply fails instead.

Mishap: You and anyone else teleporting with you have gotten "scrambled." You each take 1d10 points of damage, and you reroll on the chart to see where you wind up. For these rerolls, roll 1d20+80. Each time "Mishap" comes up, the characters take more damage and must reroll.

Teleport Object

Conjuration (Teleportation)
Level: Sor/Wiz 7
Range: Touch
Target: One touched object of up to 50 lb./level and 3 cu. ft./level
Saving Throw: Will negates (object)
Spell Resistance: Yes (object)

This spell functions like *teleport,* except that it teleports an object, not you. Creatures and magical forces (such as a *delayed blast fireball* bead) cannot be teleported.

If desired, the target object can be sent to a distant location on the Ethereal Plane. In this case, the point from which the object was teleported remains faintly magical until the item is retrieved. A successful targeted *dispel magic* spell cast on that point brings the vanished item back from the Ethereal Plane.

Teleport, Greater

Conjuration (Teleportation)
Level: Sor/Wiz 7, Travel 7

This spell functions like *teleport,* except that there is no range limit and there is no chance you arrive off target. In addition, you need not have seen the destination, but in that case you must have at least a reliable description of the place to which you are teleporting (such as a detailed description from someone else or a particularly precise map). If you attempt to teleport with insufficient information (or with misleading information), you disappear and simply reappear in your original location. Interplanar travel is not possible.

Teleportation Circle

Conjuration (Teleportation)
Level: Sor/Wiz 9
Components: V, M
Casting Time: 10 minutes
Range: 0 ft.
Effect: 5-ft.-radius circle that teleports those who activate it
Duration: 10 min./level (D)
Saving Throw: None
Spell Resistance: Yes

You create a circle on the floor or other horizontal surface that teleports, as *greater teleport,* any creature who stands on it to a designated spot. Once you designate the destination for the circle, you can't change it. The spell fails if you attempt to set the circle to teleport creatures into a solid object, to a place with which you are not familiar and have no clear description, or to another plane.

The circle itself is subtle and nearly impossible to notice. If you intend to keep creatures from activating it accidentally, you need to mark the circle in some way, such as by placing it on a raised platform.

Teleportation circle can be made permanent with a *permanency* spell. A permanent *teleportation circle* that is disabled becomes inactive for 10 minutes, then can be triggered again as normal.

Note: Magic traps such as *teleportation circle* are hard to detect and disable. A rogue (only) can use the Search skill to find the circle and Disable Device to thwart it. The DC in each case is 25 + spell level, or 34 in the case of *teleportation circle.*

Material Component: Amber dust to cover the area of the circle (cost 1,000 gp).

Temporal Stasis

Transmutation
Level: Sor/Wiz 8
Components: V, S, M
Casting Time: 1 standard action
Range: Touch
Target: Creature touched
Duration: Permanent
Saving Throw: Fortitude negates
Spell Resistance: Yes

You must succeed on a melee touch attack. You place the subject into a state of suspended animation. For the creature, time ceases to flow and its condition becomes fixed. The creature does not grow older. Its body functions virtually cease, and no force or effect can harm it. This state persists until the magic is removed (such as by a successful *dispel magic* spell or a *freedom* spell).

Material Component: A powder composed of diamond, emerald, ruby, and sapphire dust with a total value of at least 5,000 gp.

TELEPORT

Familiarity	On Target	Off Target	Similar Area	Mishap
Very familiar	01–97	98–99	100	—
Studied carefully	01–94	95–97	98–99	100
Seen casually	01–88	89–94	95–98	99–100
Viewed once	01–76	77–88	89–96	97–100
False destination (1d20+80)	—	—	81–92	93–100

Tenser's Floating Disk

Evocation [Force]
Level: Sor/Wiz 1
Components: V, S, M
Casting Time: 1 standard action
Range: Close (25 ft. + 5 ft./2 levels)
Effect: 3-ft.-diameter disk of force
Duration: 1 hour/level
Saving Throw: None
Spell Resistance: No

You create a slightly concave, circular plane of force that follows you about and carries loads for you. The disk is 3 feet in diameter and 1 inch deep at its center. It can hold 100 pounds of weight per caster level. (If used to transport a liquid, its capacity is 2 gallons.) The disk floats approximately 3 feet above the ground at all times and remains level. It floats along horizontally within spell range and will accompany you at a rate of no more than your normal speed each round. If not otherwise directed, it maintains a constant interval of 5 feet between itself and you. The disk winks out of existence when the spell duration expires. The disk also winks out if you move beyond range (by moving too fast or by such means as a *teleport* spell) or try to take the disk more than 3 feet away from the surface beneath it. When the disk winks out, whatever it was supporting falls to the surface beneath it.

Material Component: A drop of mercury.

Tenser's Transformation

Transmutation
Level: Sor/Wiz 6
Components: V, S, M
Casting Time: 1 standard action
Range: Personal
Target: You
Duration: 1 round/level

You become a virtual fighting machine—stronger, tougher, faster, and more skilled in combat. Your mind-set changes so that you relish combat and you can't cast spells, even from magic items.

You gain a +4 enhancement bonus to Strength, Dexterity, and Constitution, a +4 natural armor bonus to AC, a +5 competence bonus on Fortitude saves, and proficiency with all simple and martial weapons. Your base attack bonus equals your character level (which may give you multiple attacks).

You lose your spellcasting ability, including your ability to use spell activation or spell completion magic items, just as if the spells were no longer on your class list.

Material Component: A *potion of bull's strength,* which you drink (and whose effects are subsumed by the spell effects).

Time Stop

Transmutation
Level: Sor/Wiz 9, Trickery 9
Components: V
Casting Time: 1 standard action
Range: Personal
Target: You
Duration: 1d4+1 rounds (apparent time); see text

This spell seems to make time cease to flow for everyone but you. In fact, you speed up so greatly that all other creatures seem frozen, though they are actually still moving at their normal speeds. You are free to act for 1d4+1 rounds of apparent time. Normal and magical fire, cold, gas, and the like can still harm you. While the *time stop* is in effect, other creatures are invulnerable to your attacks and spells; you cannot target such creatures with any attack or spell. A spell that affects an area and has a duration longer than the remaining duration of the *time stop* (such as *cloudkill*) have their normal effects on other creatures once the *time stop* ends. Most spellcasters use the additional time to improve their defenses, summon allies, or flee from combat.

You cannot move or harm items held, carried, or worn by a creature stuck in normal time, but you can affect any item that is not in another creature's possession.

You are undetectable while *time stop* lasts. You cannot enter an area protected by an *antimagic field* while under the effect of *time stop.*

Tongues

Divination
Level: Brd 2, Clr 4, Sor/Wiz 3
Components: V, M/DF
Casting Time: 1 standard action
Range: Touch
Target: Creature touched
Duration: 10 min./level
Saving Throw: Will negates (harmless)
Spell Resistance: No

This spell grants the creature touched the ability to speak and understand the language of any intelligent creature, whether it is a racial tongue or a regional dialect. The subject can speak only one language at a time, although it may be able to understand several languages. *Tongues* does not enable the subject to speak with creatures who don't speak. The subject can make itself understood as far as its voice carries. This spell does not predispose any creature addressed toward the subject in any way.

Tongues can be made permanent with a *permanency* spell.

Arcane Material Component: A small clay model of a ziggurat, which shatters when the verbal component is pronounced.

Touch of Fatigue

Necromancy
Level: Sor/Wiz 0
Components: V, S, M
Casting Time: 1 standard action
Range: Touch
Target: Creature touched
Duration: 1 round/level
Saving Throw: Fortitude negates
Spell Resistance: Yes

You channel negative energy through your touch, fatiguing the target. You must succeed on a touch attack to strike a target. The subject is immediately fatigued for the spell's duration.

This spell has no effect on a creature that is already fatigued. Unlike with normal fatigue, the effect ends as soon as the spell's duration expires.

Material Component: A drop of sweat.

Touch of Idiocy

Enchantment (Compulsion) [Mind-Affecting]
Level: Sor/Wiz 2
Components: V, S
Casting Time: 1 standard action
Range: Touch
Target: Living creature touched
Duration: 10 min./level
Saving Throw: No
Spell Resistance: Yes

With a touch, you reduce the target's mental faculties. Your successful melee touch attack applies a 1d6 penalty to the target's Intelligence, Wisdom, and Charisma scores. This penalty can't reduce any of these scores below 1.

This spell's effect may make it impossible for the target to cast some or all of its spells, if the requisite ability score drops below the minimum required to cast spells of that level.

Transmute Metal to Wood

Transmutation
Level: Drd 7
Components: V, S, DF
Casting Time: 1 standard action
Range: Long (400 ft. + 40 ft./level)
Area: All metal objects within a 40-ft.-radius burst
Duration: Instantaneous
Saving Throw: None
Spell Resistance: Yes (object; see text)

This spell enables you to change all metal objects within its area to wood. Weapons, armor, and other metal objects carried by creatures are affected as well. A magic object made of metal effectively has spell resistance equal to 20 + its caster level against this spell. Artifacts cannot be transmuted. Weapons converted from metal to wood take a –2 penalty on attack and damage rolls. The armor bonus of any armor converted from metal to wood is reduced by 2. Weapons changed by this spell splinter and break on any natural attack roll of 1 or 2, and armor changed by this spell loses an additional point of armor bonus every time it is struck with a natural attack roll of 19 or 20.

Only *limited wish*, *miracle*, *wish*, or similar magic can restore a transmuted object to its metallic state. Otherwise, for example, a metal door changed to wood is forevermore a wooden door.

Transmute Mud to Rock
Transmutation [Earth]
Level: Drd 5, Sor/Wiz 5
Components: V, S, M/DF
Casting Time: 1 standard action
Range: Medium (100 ft. + 10 ft./level)
Area: Up to two 10-ft. cubes/level (S)
Duration: Permanent
Saving Throw: See text
Spell Resistance: No

This spell transforms normal mud or quicksand of any depth into soft stone (sandstone or a similar mineral) permanently. Any creature in the mud is allowed a Reflex save to escape before the area is hardened to stone.

Transmute mud to rock counters and dispels *transmute rock to mud*.

Arcane Material Component: Sand, lime, and water.

Transmute Rock to Mud
Transmutation [Earth]
Level: Drd 5, Sor/Wiz 5
Components: V, S, M/DF
Casting Time: 1 standard action
Range: Medium (100 ft. + 10 ft./level)
Area: Up to two 10-ft. cubes/level (S)
Duration: Permanent; see text
Saving Throw: See text
Spell Resistance: No

This spell turns natural, uncut or unworked rock of any sort into an equal volume of mud. If the spell is cast upon a boulder, for example, the boulder collapses into mud. Magical stone is not affected by the spell. The depth of the mud created cannot exceed 10 feet. A creature unable to levitate, fly, or otherwise free itself from the mud sinks until hip- or chest-deep, reducing its speed to 5 feet and causing a –2 penalty on attack rolls and AC. Brush thrown atop the mud can support creatures able to climb on top of it. Creatures large enough to walk on the bottom can wade through the area at a speed of 5 feet.

If *transmute rock to mud* is cast upon the ceiling of a cavern or tunnel, the mud falls to the floor and spreads out in a pool at a depth of 5 feet. For example, a 10th-level caster could convert twenty 10-foot cubes into mud. Pooling on the floor, this mud would cover an area of forty 10-foot squares to a depth of 5 feet. The falling mud and the ensuing cave-in deal 8d6 points of bludgeoning damage to anyone caught directly beneath the area, or half damage to those who succeed on Reflex saves.

Castles and large stone buildings are generally immune to the effect of the spell, since *transmute rock to mud* can't affect worked stone and doesn't reach deep enough to undermine such buildings' foundations. However, small buildings or structures often rest upon foundations shallow enough to be damaged or even partially toppled by this spell.

The mud remains until a successful *dispel magic* or *transmute mud to rock* spell restores its substance—but not necessarily its form. Evaporation turns the mud to normal dirt over a period of days. The exact time depends on exposure to the sun, wind, and normal drainage.

Arcane Material Component: Clay and water.

Transport via Plants
Transmutation
Level: Drd 6
Components: V, S
Casting Time: 1 standard action
Range: Unlimited
Target: You and touched objects or other touched willing creatures
Duration: 1 round
Saving Throw: None
Spell Resistance: No

You can enter any normal plant (Medium or larger) and pass any distance to a plant of the same kind in a single round, regardless of the distance separating the two. The entry plant must be alive. The destination plant need not be familiar to you, but it also must be alive. If you are uncertain of the location of a particular kind of destination plant, you need merely designate direction and distance ("an oak tree one hundred miles due north of here"), and the *transport via plants* spell moves you as close as possible to the desired location. If a particular destination plant is desired (the oak tree outside your druid grove, for instance), but the plant is not living, the spell fails and you are ejected from the entry plant.

You can bring along objects as long as their weight doesn't exceed your maximum load. You may also bring one additional willing Medium or smaller creature (carrying gear or objects up to its maxi-

mum load) or its equivalent per three caster levels. Use the following equivalents to determine the maximum number of larger creatures you can bring along: A Large creature counts as two Medium creatures, a Huge creature counts as two Large creatures, and so forth. All creatures to be transported must be in contact with one another, and at least one of those creatures must be in contact with you.

You can't use this spell to travel through plant creatures such as shambling mounds and treants.

The destruction of an occupied plant slays you and any creatures you have brought along, and ejects the bodies and all carried objects from the tree.

Trap the Soul
Conjuration (Summoning)
Level: Sor/Wiz 8
Components: V, S, M, (F); see text
Casting Time: 1 standard action or see text
Range: Close (25 ft. + 5 ft./2 levels)
Target: One creature
Duration: Permanent; see text
Saving Throw: See text
Spell Resistance: Yes; see text

Trap the soul forces a creature's life force (and its material body) into a gem.

The gem holds the trapped entity indefinitely or until the gem is broken and the life force is released, which allows the material body to reform. If the trapped creature is a powerful creature from another plane (which could mean a character trapped by an inhabitant of another plane when the character is not on the Material Plane), it can be required to perform a service immediately upon being freed. Otherwise, the creature can go free once the gem imprisoning it is broken.

Depending on the version selected, the spell can be triggered in one of two ways.

Spell Completion: First, the spell can be completed by speaking its final word as a standard action as if you were casting a regular spell at the subject. This allows spell resistance (if any) and a Will save to avoid the effect. If the creature's name is spoken as well, any spell resistance is ignored and the save DC increases by 2. If the save or spell resistance is successful, the gem shatters.

Trigger Object: The second method is far more insidious, for it tricks the subject into accepting a trigger object inscribed with the final spell word, automatically placing the creature's soul in the trap. To use this method, both the creature's name and the trigger word must be inscribed on the trigger object when the gem is enspelled. A *sympathy* spell can also be placed on the trigger object. As soon as the subject picks up or accepts the trigger object, its life force is automatically transferred to the gem without the benefit of spell resistance or a save.

Material Component: Before the actual casting of *trap the soul,* you must procure a gem of at least 1,000 gp value for every Hit Die possessed by the creature to be trapped (for example, it requires a gem of 10,000 gp value to trap a 10 HD creature). If the gem is not valuable enough, it shatters when the entrapment is attempted. (While creatures have no concept of level or Hit Dice as such, the value of the gem needed to trap an individual can be researched. Remember that this value can change over time as creatures gain more Hit Dice.)

Focus (Trigger Object Only): If the trigger object method is used, a special trigger object, prepared as described above, is needed.

Tree Shape

Transmutation
Level: Drd 2, Rgr 3
Components: V, S, DF
Casting Time: 1 standard action
Range: Personal
Target: You
Duration: 1 hour/level (D)

By means of this spell, you are able to assume the form of a Large living tree or shrub or a Large dead tree trunk with a small number of limbs. The closest inspection cannot reveal that the tree in question is actually a magically concealed creature. To all normal tests you are, in fact, a tree or shrub, although a *detect magic* spell reveals a faint transmutation on the tree. While in tree form, you can observe all that transpires around you just as if you were in your normal form, and your hit points and save bonuses remain unaffected. You gain a +10 natural armor bonus to AC but have an effective Dexterity score of 0 and a speed of 0 feet. You are immune to critical hits while in tree form. All clothing and gear carried or worn changes with you.

You can dismiss *tree shape* as a free action (instead of as a standard action).

Tree Stride

Conjuration (Teleportation)
Level: Drd 5, Rgr 4
Components: V, S, DF
Casting Time: 1 standard action
Range: Personal
Target: You
Duration: 1 hour/level or until expended; see text

You gain the ability to enter trees and move from inside one tree to inside another tree. The first tree you enter and all others you enter must be of the same kind, must be living, and must have girth at least equal to yours. By moving into an oak tree (for example), you instantly know the location of all other oak trees within transport range (see below) and may choose whether you want to pass into one or simply step back out of the tree you moved into. You may choose to pass to any tree of the appropriate kind within the transport range as shown on the following table.

Type of Tree	Transport Range
Oak, ash, yew	3,000 feet
Elm, linden	2,000 feet
Other deciduous	1,500 feet
Any coniferous	1,000 feet
All other trees	500 feet

You may move into a tree up to one time per caster level (passing from one tree to another counts only as moving into one tree). The spell lasts until the duration expires or you exit a tree. This means that in a thick oak forest, a 10th-level druid could make ten transports over the course of 10 rounds, traveling as far as 30,000 feet (about 6 miles) in doing so. Each transport is a full-round action.

You can, at your option, remain within a tree without transporting yourself, but you are forced out when the spell ends. If the tree in which you are concealed is chopped down or burned, you are slain if you do not exit before the process is complete.

True Resurrection

Conjuration (Healing)
Level: Clr 9
Casting Time: 10 minutes

This spell functions like *raise dead,* except that you can resurrect a creature that has been dead for as long as 10 years per caster level. This spell can even bring back creatures whose bodies have been destroyed, provided that you unambiguously identify the deceased in some fashion (reciting the deceased's time and place of birth or death is the most common method).

Upon completion of the spell, the creature is immediately restored to full hit points, vigor, and health, with no loss of level (or Constitution points) or prepared spells.

You can revive someone killed by a death effect or someone who has been turned into an undead creature and then destroyed. This spell can also resurrect elementals or outsiders, but it can't resurrect constructs or undead creatures.

Even *true resurrection* can't restore to life a creature who has died of old age.

Material Component: A sprinkle of holy water and diamonds worth a total of at least 25,000 gp.

True Seeing

Divination
Level: Clr 5, Drd 7, Knowledge 5, Sor/Wiz 6
Components: V, S, M
Casting Time: 1 standard action
Range: Touch
Target: Creature touched
Duration: 1 min./level
Saving Throw: Will negates (harmless)
Spell Resistance: Yes (harmless)

You confer on the subject the ability to see all things as they actually are. The subject sees through normal and magical darkness, notices secret doors hidden by magic, sees the exact locations of creatures or objects under *blur* or *displacement* effects, sees invisible creatures or objects normally, sees through illusions, and sees the true form of polymorphed, changed, or transmuted things. Further, the subject can focus its vision to see into the Ethereal Plane (but not into extradimensional spaces). The range of *true seeing* conferred is 120 feet.

True seeing, however, does not penetrate solid objects. It in no way confers X-ray vision or its equivalent. It does not negate concealment, including that caused by fog and the like. *True seeing* does not help the viewer see through mundane disguises, spot creatures who are simply hiding, or notice secret doors hidden by mundane means. In addition, the spell effects cannot be further enhanced with known magic, so one cannot use *true seeing* through a *crystal ball* or in conjunction with *clairaudience/clairvoyance.*

Material Component: An ointment for the eyes that costs 250 gp and is made from mushroom powder, saffron, and fat.

True Strike

Divination
Level: Sor/Wiz 1
Components: V, F
Casting Time: 1 standard action
Range: Personal
Target: You
Duration: See text

You gain temporary, intuitive insight into the immediate future during your next attack. Your next single attack roll (if it is made before the end of the next round) gains a +20 insight bonus. Additionally, you are not affected by the miss chance that applies to attackers trying to strike a concealed target.

Focus: A small wooden replica of an archery target.

Undeath to Death

Necromancy
Level: Clr 6, Sor/Wiz 6
Components: V, S, M/DF
Area: Several undead creatures within a 40-ft.-radius burst
Saving Throw: Will negates

This spell functions like *circle of death*, except that it destroys undead creatures as noted above.

Material Component: The powder of a crushed diamond worth at least 500 gp.

Undetectable Alignment

Abjuration
Level: Brd 1, Clr 2, Pal 2
Components: V, S
Casting Time: 1 standard action
Range: Close (25 ft. + 5 ft./2 levels)
Target: One creature or object
Duration: 24 hours
Saving Throw: Will negates (object)
Spell Resistance: Yes (object)

An *undetectable alignment* spell conceals the alignment of an object or a creature from all forms of divination.

Unhallow

Evocation [Evil]
Level: Clr 5, Drd 5
Components: V, S, M
Casting Time: 24 hours
Range: Touch
Area: 40-ft. radius emanating from the touched point
Duration: Instantaneous
Saving Throw: See text
Spell Resistance: See text

Unhallow makes a particular site, building, or structure an unholy site. This has three major effects.

First, the site or structure is guarded by a *magic circle against good* effect.

Second, all turning checks made to turn undead take a −4 penalty, and turning checks to rebuke undead gain a +4 profane bonus. Spell resistance does not apply to this effect. (This provision does not apply to the druid version of the spell.)

Finally, you may choose to fix a single spell effect to the *unhallowed* site. The spell effect lasts for one year and functions throughout the entire site, regardless of its normal duration and area or effect. You may designate whether the effect applies to all creatures, creatures that share your faith or alignment, or creatures that adhere to another faith or alignment. For example, you may create a *bless* effect that aids all creatures of like alignment or faith in the area, or a *bane* effect that hinders creatures of the opposite alignment or an enemy faith. At the end

of the year, the chosen effect lapses, but it can be renewed or replaced simply by casting *unhallow* again.

Spell effects that may be tied to an *unhallowed* site include *aid, bane, bless, cause fear, darkness, daylight, death ward, deeper darkness, detect magic, detect good, dimensional anchor, discern lies, dispel magic, endure elements, freedom of movement, invisibility purge, protection from energy, remove fear, resist energy, silence, tongues,* and *zone of truth.* Saving throws and spell resistance might apply to these spells' effects. (See the individual spell descriptions for details.)

An area can receive only one *unhallow* spell (and its associated spell effect) at a time.

Unhallow counters but does not dispel *hallow.*

Material Component: Herbs, oils, and incense worth at least 1,000 gp, plus 1,000 gp per level of the spell to be tied to the *unhallowed* area.

Unholy Aura

Abjuration [Evil]
Level: Clr 8, Evil 8
Components: V, S, F
Casting Time: 1 standard action
Range: 20 ft.
Targets: One creature/level in a 20-ft.-radius burst centered on you
Duration: 1 round/level (D)
Saving Throw: See text
Spell Resistance: Yes (harmless)

A malevolent darkness surrounds the subjects, protecting them from attacks, granting them resistance to spells cast by good creatures, and weakening good creatures when they strike the subjects. This abjuration has four effects.

First, each warded creature gains a +4 deflection bonus to AC and a +4 resistance bonus on saves. Unlike the effect of *protection from good,* this benefit applies against all attacks, not just against attacks by good creatures.

Second, a warded creature gains spell resistance 25 against good spells and spells cast by good creatures.

Third, the abjuration blocks possession and mental influence, just as *protection from good* does.

Finally, if a good creature succeeds on a melee attack against a warded creature, the offending attacker takes 1d6 points of temporary Strength damage (Fortitude negates).

Focus: A tiny reliquary containing some sacred relic, such as a piece of parchment from an unholy text. The reliquary costs at least 500 gp.

Unholy Blight

Evocation [Evil]
Level: Evil 4
Components: V, S
Casting Time: 1 standard action
Range: Medium (100 ft. + 10 ft./level)
Area: 20-ft.-radius spread
Duration: Instantaneous (1d4 rounds); see text
Saving Throw: Will partial
Spell Resistance: Yes

You call up unholy power to smite your enemies. The power takes the form of a cold, cloying miasma of greasy darkness. Only good and neutral (not evil) creatures are harmed by the spell.

The spell deals 1d8 points of damage per two caster levels (maximum 5d8) to a good creature (or 1d6 per caster level, maximum 10d6, to a good outsider) and causes it to be sickened for 1d4 rounds. A successful Will save reduces damage to half and negates the sickened effect. The effects cannot be negated by *remove disease* or *heal,* but *remove curse* is effective.

The spell deals only half damage to creatures who are neither evil nor good, and they are not sickened. Such a creature can reduce the damage in half again (down to one-quarter) with a successful Will save.

Unseen Servant

Conjuration (Creation)
Level: Brd 1, Sor/Wiz 1
Components: V, S, M
Casting Time: 1 standard action
Range: Close (25 ft. + 5 ft./2 levels)
Effect: One invisible, mindless, shapeless servant
Duration: 1 hour/level
Saving Throw: None
Spell Resistance: No

An *unseen servant* is an invisible, mindless, shapeless force that performs simple tasks at your command. It can run and fetch things, open unstuck doors, and hold chairs, as well as clean and mend. The servant can perform only one activity at a time, but it repeats the same activity over and over again if told to do so, thus allowing you to command it to clean the floor and then turn your attention elsewhere as long as you remain within range. It can open only normal doors, drawers, lids, and the like. It has an effective Strength score of 2 (so it can lift 20 pounds or drag 100 pounds). It can trigger traps and such, but it can exert only 20 pounds of force, which is not enough to activate certain pressure plates and other devices. It can't perform any task that requires a skill check with a DC higher than 10 or that requires a check using a skill that can't be used untrained. Its speed is 15 feet.

The servant cannot attack in any way; it is never allowed an attack roll. It cannot be killed, but it dissipates if it takes 6 points of damage from area attacks. (It gets no saves against attacks.) If you attempt to send it beyond the spell's range (measured from your current position), the servant ceases to exist.

Material Component: A piece of string and a bit of wood.

Vampiric Touch

Necromancy
Level: Sor/Wiz 3
Components: V, S
Casting Time: 1 standard action
Range: Touch
Target: Living creature touched
Duration: Instantaneous/1 hour; see text
Saving Throw: None
Spell Resistance: Yes

You must succeed on a melee touch attack. Your touch deals 1d6 points of damage per two caster levels (maximum 10d6). You gain temporary hit points equal to the damage you deal. However, you can't gain more than the subject's current hit points +10, which is enough to kill the subject. The temporary hit points disappear 1 hour later.

Veil

Illusion (Glamer)
Level: Brd 6, Sor/Wiz 6
Components: V, S
Casting Time: 1 standard action
Range: Long (400 ft. + 40 ft./level)
Targets: One or more creatures, no two of which can be more than 30 ft. apart
Duration: Concentration + 1 hour/level (D)
Saving Throw: Will negates; see text
Spell Resistance: Yes; see text

You instantly change the appearance of the subjects and then maintain that appearance for the spell's duration. You can make the subjects appear to be anything you wish. A party might be made to resemble a mixed band of sprites led by a treant. The subjects look, feel, and smell just like the creatures the spell makes them resemble. Affected creatures resume their normal appearances if slain. You must succeed on a Disguise check to duplicate the appearance of a specific individual. This spell gives you a +10 bonus on the check.

Unwilling targets can negate the spell's effect on them by making Will saves or with spell resistance. Those who interact with the subjects can attempt Will disbelief saves to see through the glamer, but spell resistance doesn't help.

Ventriloquism

Illusion (Figment)
Level: Brd 1, Sor/Wiz 1
Components: V, F
Casting Time: 1 standard action
Range: Close (25 ft. + 5 ft./2 levels)
Effect: Intelligible sound, usually speech
Duration: 1 min./level (D)
Saving Throw: Will disbelief (if interacted with)
Spell Resistance: No

You can make your voice (or any sound that you can normally make vocally) seem to issue from someplace else, such as from another creature, a statue, from behind a door, down a passage, etc. You can speak in any language you know. With respect to such voices and sounds, anyone who hears the sound and rolls a successful save recognizes it as illusory (but still hears it).

Focus: A parchment rolled up into a small cone.

Virtue

Transmutation
Level: Clr 0, Drd 0, Pal 1
Components: V, S, DF
Casting Time: 1 standard action
Range: Touch
Target: Creature touched
Duration: 1 min.
Saving Throw: Fortitude negates (harmless)
Spell Resistance: Yes (harmless)

The subject gains 1 temporary hit point.

Vision

Divination
Level: Sor/Wiz 7
Components: V, S, M, XP
Casting Time: 1 standard action

This spell functions like *legend lore*, except that it works more quickly but produces some strain on you. You pose a question about some person, place, or object, then cast the spell. If the person or object is at hand or if you are in the place in question, you receive a vision about it by succeeding on a caster level check (1d20 +1 per caster level; maximum +25) against DC 20. If only detailed information on the person, place, or object is known, the DC is 25, and the information gained is incomplete. If only rumors are known, the DC is 30, and the information gained is vague.

XP Cost: 100 XP.

Wail of the Banshee

Necromancy [Death, Sonic]
Level: Death 9, Sor/Wiz 9
Components: V
Casting Time: 1 standard action

Range: Close (25 ft. + 5 ft./2 levels)
Area: One living creature/level within a 40-ft.-radius spread
Duration: Instantaneous
Saving Throw: Fortitude negates
Spell Resistance: Yes

You emit a terrible scream that kills creatures that hear it (except for yourself). Creatures closest to the point of origin are affected first.

Wall of Fire

Evocation [Fire]
Level: Drd 5, Fire 4, Sor/Wiz 4
Components: V, S, M/DF
Casting Time: 1 standard action
Range: Medium (100 ft. + 10 ft./level)
Effect: Opaque sheet of flame up to 20 ft. long/level or a ring of fire with a radius of up to 5 ft. per two levels; either form 20 ft. high
Duration: Concentration + 1 round/level
Saving Throw: None
Spell Resistance: Yes

An immobile, blazing curtain of shimmering violet fire springs into existence. One side of the wall, selected by you, sends forth waves of heat, dealing 2d4 points of fire damage to creatures within 10 feet and 1d4 points of fire damage to those past 10 feet but within 20 feet. The wall deals this damage when it appears and on your turn each round to all creatures in the area. In addition, the wall deals 2d6 points of fire damage +1 point of fire damage per caster level (maximum +20) to any creature passing through it. The wall deals double damage to undead creatures.

If you evoke the wall so that it appears where creatures are, each creature takes damage as if passing through the wall.

If any 5-foot length of wall takes 20 points of cold damage or more in 1 round, that length goes out. (Do not divide cold damage by 4, as normal for objects.)

Wall of fire can be made permanent with a *permanency* spell. A permanent *wall of fire* that is extinguished by cold damage becomes inactive for 10 minutes, then reforms at normal strength.

Arcane Material Component: A small piece of phosphorus.

Wall of Force

Evocation [Force]
Level: Sor/Wiz 5
Components: V, S, M
Casting Time: 1 standard action
Range: Close (25 ft. + 5 ft./2 levels)
Effect: Wall whose area is up to one 10-ft. square/level
Duration: 1 round /level (D)
Saving Throw: None
Spell Resistance: No

A *wall of force* spell creates an invisible wall of force. The wall cannot move, it is immune to damage of all kinds, and it is unaffected by most spells, including *dispel magic*. However, *disintegrate* immediately destroys it, as does a *rod of cancellation*, a *sphere of annihilation*, or a *Mordenkainen's disjunction* spell. Breath weapons and spells cannot pass through the wall in either direction, although *dimension door*, *teleport*, and similar effects can bypass the barrier. It blocks ethereal creatures as well as material ones (though ethereal creatures can usually get around the wall by floating under or over it through material floors and ceilings). Gaze attacks can operate through a *wall of force*.

The caster can form the wall into a flat, vertical plane whose area is up to one 10-foot square per level. The wall must be continuous and unbroken when formed. If its surface is broken by any object or creature, the spell fails.

Wall of force can be made permanent with a *permanency* spell.

Material Component: A pinch of powder made from a clear gem.

Wall of Ice

Evocation [Cold]
Level: Sor/Wiz 4
Components: V, S, M
Casting Time: 1 standard action
Range: Medium (100 ft. + 10 ft./level)
Effect: Anchored plane of ice, up to one 10-ft. square/level, or hemisphere of ice with a radius of up to 3 ft. + 1 ft./level
Duration: 1 min./level
Saving Throw: Reflex negates; see text
Spell Resistance: Yes

This spell creates an anchored plane of ice or a hemisphere of ice, depending on the version selected. A *wall of ice* cannot form in an area occupied by physical objects or creatures. Its surface must be smooth and unbroken when created. Any creature adjacent to the wall when it is created may attempt a Reflex save to disrupt the wall as it is being formed. A successful save indicates that the spell automatically fails. Fire, including a *fireball* spell and red dragon breath, can melt a *wall of ice*, and it deals full damage to the wall (instead of the normal half damage taken by objects). Suddenly melting a *wall of ice* creates a great cloud of steamy fog that lasts for 10 minutes.

Ice Plane: A sheet of strong, hard ice appears. The wall is 1 inch thick per caster level. It covers up to a 10-foot-square area per caster level (so a 10th-level wizard can create a wall of ice 100 feet long and 10 feet high, a wall 50 feet long and 20 feet high, or some other combination of

length and height that does not exceed 1,000 square feet). The plane can be oriented in any fashion as long as it is anchored. A vertical wall need only be anchored on the floor, while a horizontal or slanting wall must be anchored on two opposite sides.

The wall is primarily defensive in nature and is used to stop pursuers from following you and the like. Each 10-foot square of wall has 3 hit points per inch of thickness. Creatures can hit the wall automatically. A section of wall whose hit points drop to 0 is breached. If a creature tries to break through the wall with a single attack, the DC for the Strength check is 15 + caster level.

Even when the ice has been broken through, a sheet of frigid air remains. Any creature stepping through it (including the one who broke through the wall) takes 1d6 points of cold damage +1 point per caster level (no save).

Hemisphere: The wall takes the form of a hemisphere whose maximum radius is 3 feet + 1 foot per caster level. Thus, a 7th-level caster can create a hemisphere 10 feet in radius. The *hemisphere* is as hard to break through as the *ice plane* form, but it does not deal damage to those who go through a breach.

Material Component: A small piece of quartz or similar rock crystal.

Wall of Iron

Conjuration (Creation)
Level: Sor/Wiz 6
Components: V, S, M
Casting Time: 1 standard action
Range: Medium (100 ft. + 10 ft./level)
Effect: Iron wall whose area is up to one 5-ft. square/level; see text
Duration: Instantaneous
Saving Throw: See text
Spell Resistance: No

You cause a flat, vertical iron wall to spring into being. This wall can be used to seal off a passage or close a breach, for the wall inserts itself into any surrounding nonliving material if its area is sufficient to do so. The wall cannot be conjured so that it occupies the same space as a creature or another object. It must always be a flat plane, though you can shape its edges to fit the available space.

A *wall of iron* is 1 inch thick per four caster levels. You can double the wall's area by halving its thickness. Each 5-foot square of the wall has 30 hit points per inch of thickness and hardness 10. A section of wall whose hit points drop to 0 is breached. If a creature tries to break through the wall with a single attack, the DC for the Strength check is 25 + 2 per inch of thickness.

If you desire, the wall can be created vertically resting on a flat surface but not attached to the surface, so that it can be tipped over to fall on and crush creatures beneath it. The wall is 50% likely to tip in either direction if left unpushed. Creatures can push the wall in one direction rather than letting it fall randomly. A creature must make a DC 40 Strength check to push the wall over. Creatures with room to flee the falling wall may do so by making successful Reflex saves. Any Large or smaller creature that fails takes 10d6 points of damage. The wall cannot crush Huge and larger creatures.

Like any iron wall, this wall is subject to rust, perforation, and other natural phenomena.

Material Component: A small piece of sheet iron plus gold dust worth 50 gp (1 pound of gold dust).

Wall of Stone

Conjuration (Creation) [Earth]
Level: Clr 5, Drd 6, Earth 5, Sor/Wiz 5
Components: V, S, M/DF
Casting Time: 1 standard action
Range: Medium (100 ft. + 10 ft./level)
Effect: Stone wall whose area is up to one 5-ft. square/level (S)
Duration: Instantaneous
Saving Throw: See text
Spell Resistance: No

This spell creates a wall of rock that merges into adjoining rock surfaces. It is typically employed to close passages, portals, and breaches against opponents. A *wall of stone* is 1 inch thick per four caster levels and composed of up to one 5-foot square per level. You can double the wall's

area by halving its thickness. The wall cannot be conjured so that it occupies the same space as a creature or another object.

Unlike a *wall of iron*, you can create a *wall of stone* in almost any shape you desire. The wall created need not be vertical, nor rest upon any firm foundation; however, it must merge with and be solidly supported by existing stone. It can be used to bridge a chasm, for instance, or as a ramp. For this use, if the span is more than 20 feet, the wall must be arched and buttressed. This requirement reduces the spell's area by half. Thus, a 20th-level caster can create a span with a surface area of ten 5-foot squares. The wall can be crudely shaped to allow crenellations, battlements, and so forth by likewise reducing the area.

Like any other stone wall, this one can be destroyed by a *disintegrate* spell or by normal means such as breaking and chipping. Each 5-foot square of the wall has 15 hit points per inch of thickness and hardness 8. A section of wall whose hit points drop to 0 is breached. If a creature tries to break through the wall with a single attack, the DC for the Strength check is 20 + 2 per inch of thickness.

It is possible, but difficult, to trap mobile opponents within or under a *wall of stone*, provided the wall is shaped so it can hold the creatures. Creatures can avoid entrapment with successful Reflex saves.

Arcane Material Component: A small block of granite.

Wall of Thorns

Conjuration (Creation)
Level: Drd 5, Plant 5
Components: V, S
Casting Time: 1 standard action
Range: Medium (100 ft. + 10 ft./level)
Effect: Wall of thorny brush, up to one 10-ft. cube/level (S)
Duration: 10 min./level (D)
Saving Throw: None
Spell Resistance: No

A *wall of thorns* spell creates a barrier of very tough, pliable, tangled brush bearing needle-sharp thorns as long as a human's finger. Any creature forced into or attempting to move through a *wall of thorns* takes slashing damage per round of movement equal to 25 minus the creature's AC. Dexterity and dodge bonuses to AC do not count for this calculation. (Creatures with an Armor Class of 25 or higher, without considering Dexterity and dodge bonuses, take no damage from contact with the wall.)

You can make the wall as thin as 5 feet thick, which allows you to shape the wall as a number of 10-by-10-by-5-foot blocks equal to twice your caster level. This has no effect on the damage dealt by the thorns, but any creature attempting to break through takes that much less time to force its way through the barrier.

Creatures can force their way slowly through the wall by making a Strength check as a full-round action. For every 5 points by which the check exceeds 20, a creature moves 5 feet (up to a maximum distance equal to its normal land speed). For example, a creature that rolled 25 on its Strength check could move 5 ft in a round. Of course, moving or attempting to move through the thorns incurs damage as described above. A creature trapped in the thorns can choose to remain motionless in order to avoid taking any more damage.

Any creature within the area of the spell when it is cast takes damage as if it had moved into the wall and is caught inside. In order to escape, it must attempt to push its way free, or it can wait until the spell ends. Creatures with the ability to pass through overgrown areas unhindered can pass through a *wall of thorns* at normal speed without taking damage.

A *wall of thorns* can be breached by slow work with edged weapons. Chopping away at the wall creates a safe passage 1 foot deep for every 10 minutes of work. Normal fire cannot harm the barrier, but magical fire burns it away in 10 minutes.

Despite its appearance, a *wall of thorns* is not actually a living plant, and thus is unaffected by spells that affect plants.

Warp Wood

Transmutation
Level: Drd 2
Components: V, S
Casting Time: 1 standard action
Range: Close (25 ft. + 5 ft./2 levels)
Target: 1 Small wooden object/level, all within a 20-ft. radius
Duration: Instantaneous
Saving Throw: Will negates (object)
Spell Resistance: Yes (object)

You cause wood to bend and warp, permanently destroying its straightness, form, and strength. A warped door springs open (or becomes stuck, requiring a Strength check to open, at your option). A boat or ship springs a leak. Warped ranged weapons are useless. A warped melee weapon causes a −4 penalty on attack rolls.

You may warp one Small or smaller object (such as a wagon wheel or a human's crossbow) or its equivalent per caster level. A Medium object (such as an oar or a human's spear) counts as two Small objects, a Large object (such as a rowboat or a hill giant's greatclub) as four, a Huge object (such as a wagon or a cloud giant's morningstar) as eight, a Gargantuan object (such as a keelboat) as sixteen, and a Colossal object (such as a sailing ship) as thirty-two.

Alternatively, you can unwarp wood (effectively warping it back to normal) with this spell, straightening wood that has been warped by this spell or by other means. *Make whole*, on the other hand, does no good in repairing a warped item.

You can combine multiple consecutive *warp wood* spells to warp (or unwarp) an object that is too large for you to warp with a single spell. For instance, an 8th-level druid could cast two *warp wood* spells to warp a Gargantuan object, or four *warp wood* spells to warp a Colossal object. Until the object is completely warped, it suffers no ill effects.

Water Breathing

Transmutation
Level: Clr 3, Drd 3, Sor/Wiz 3, Water 3
Components: V, S, M/DF
Casting Time: 1 standard action
Range: Touch
Target: Living creatures touched
Duration: 2 hours/level; see text
Saving Throw: Will negates (harmless)
Spell Resistance: Yes (harmless)

The transmuted creatures can breathe water freely. Divide the duration evenly among all the creatures you touch.

The spell does not make creatures unable to breathe air.

Arcane Material Component: A short reed or piece of straw.

Water Walk

Transmutation [Water]
Level: Clr 3, Rgr 3
Components: V, S, DF
Casting Time: 1 standard action
Range: Touch
Targets: One touched creature/level
Duration: 10 min./level (D)
Saving Throw: Will negates (harmless)
Spell Resistance: Yes (harmless)

The transmuted creatures can tread on any liquid as if it were firm ground. Mud, oil, snow, quicksand, running water, ice, and even lava can be traversed easily, since the subjects' feet hover an inch or two above the surface. (Creatures crossing molten lava still take damage from the heat because they are near it.) The subjects can walk, run, charge, or otherwise move across the surface as if it were normal ground.

If the spell is cast underwater (or while the subjects are partially or wholly submerged in whatever liquid they are in), the subjects are borne toward the surface at 60 feet per round until they can stand on it.

Waves of Exhaustion

Necromancy
Level: Sor/Wiz 7
Components: V, S
Casting Time: 1 standard action
Range: 60 ft.
Area: Cone-shaped burst
Duration: Instantaneous
Saving Throw: No
Spell Resistance: Yes

Waves of negative energy cause all living creatures in the spell's area to become exhausted. This spell has no effect on a creature that is already exhausted.

Waves of Fatigue

Necromancy
Level: Sor/Wiz 5
Components: V, S
Casting Time: 1 standard action
Range: 30 ft.
Area: Cone-shaped burst
Duration: Instantaneous
Saving Throw: No
Spell Resistance: Yes

Waves of negative energy render all living creatures in the spell's area fatigued. This spell has no effect on a creature that is already fatigued.

Web

Conjuration (Creation)
Level: Sor/Wiz 2
Components: V, S, M
Casting Time: 1 standard action
Range: Medium (100 ft. + 10 ft./level)
Effect: Webs in a 20-ft.-radius spread
Duration: 10 min./level (D)
Saving Throw: Reflex negates; see text
Spell Resistance: No

Web creates a many-layered mass of strong, sticky strands. These strands trap those caught in them. The strands are similar to spider webs but far larger and tougher. These masses must be anchored to two or more solid and diametrically opposed points—floor and ceiling, opposite walls, or the like—or else the web collapses upon itself and disappears. Creatures caught within a *web* become entangled among the gluey fibers. Attacking a creature in a web won't cause you to become entangled.

Anyone in the effect's area when the spell is cast must make a Reflex save. If this save succeeds, the creature is entangled, but not prevented from moving, though moving is more difficult than normal for being entangled (see below). If the save fails, the creature is entangled and can't move from its space, but can break loose by spending 1 round and making a DC 20 Strength check or a DC 25 Escape Artist check. Once loose (either

by making the initial Reflex save or a later Strength check or Escape Artist check), a creature remains entangled, but may move through the *web* very slowly. Each round devoted to moving allows the creature to make a new Strength check or Escape Artist check. The creature moves 5 feet for each full 5 points by which the check result exceeds 10.

If you have at least 5 feet of web between you and an opponent, it provides cover. If you have at least 20 feet of web between you, it provides total cover (see Cover, page 150).

The strands of a *web* spell are flammable. A magic *flaming sword* can slash them away as easily as a hand brushes away cobwebs. Any fire—a torch, burning oil, a flaming sword, and so forth—can set the webs alight and burn away 5 square feet in 1 round. All creatures within flaming webs take 2d4 points of fire damage from the flames.

Web can be made permanent with a *permanency* spell. A permanent *web* that is damaged (but not destroyed) regrows in 10 minutes.

Material Component: A bit of spider web.

Weird

Illusion (Phantasm) [Fear, Mind-Affecting]
Level: Sor/Wiz 9
Targets: Any number of creatures, no two of which can be more than 30 ft. apart

This spell functions like *phantasmal killer*, except it can affect more than one creature. Only the affected creatures see the phantasmal creatures attacking them, though you see the attackers as shadowy shapes.

If a subject's Fortitude save succeeds, it still takes 3d6 points of damage and is stunned for 1 round. The subject also takes 1d4 points of temporary Strength damage.

Whirlwind

Evocation [Air]
Level: Air 8, Drd 8
Components: V, S, DF
Casting Time: 1 standard action
Range: Long (400 ft. + 40 ft./level)
Effect: Cyclone 10 ft. wide at base, 30 ft. wide at top, and 30 ft. tall
Duration: 1 round/level (D)
Saving Throw: Reflex negates; see text
Spell Resistance: Yes

This spell creates a powerful cyclone of raging wind that moves through the air, along the ground, or over water at a speed of 60 feet per round. You can concentrate on controlling the cyclone's every movement or specify a simple pro-

gram, such as move straight ahead, zigzag, circle, or the like. Directing the cyclone's movement or changing its programmed movement is a standard action for you. The cyclone always moves during your turn. If the cyclone exceeds the spell's range, it moves in a random, uncontrolled fashion for 1d3 rounds—possibly endangering you or your allies—and then dissipates. (You can't regain control of the cyclone, even if comes back within range.)

Any Large or smaller creature that comes in contact with the spell effect must succeed on a Reflex save or take 3d6 points of damage. A Medium or smaller creature that fails its first save must succeed on a second one or be picked up bodily by the cyclone and held suspended in its powerful winds, taking 1d8 points of damage each round on your turn with no save allowed. You may direct the cyclone to eject any carried creatures whenever you wish, depositing the hapless souls wherever the cyclone happens to be when they are released.

Whispering Wind

Transmutation [Air]
Level: Brd 2, Sor/Wiz 2
Components: V, S
Casting Time: 1 standard action
Range: 1 mile/level
Area: 10-ft.-radius spread
Duration: No more than 1 hour/level or until discharged (destination is reached)
Saving Throw: None
Spell Resistance: No

You send a message or sound on the wind to a designated spot. The *whispering wind* travels to a specific location within range that is familiar to you, provided that it can find a way to the location. (It can't pass through walls, for instance.) A *whispering wind* is as gentle and unnoticed as a zephyr until it reaches the location. It then delivers its whisper-quiet message or other sound. Note that the message is delivered regardless of whether anyone is present to hear it. The wind then dissipates. You can prepare the spell to bear a message of no more than twenty-five words, cause the spell to deliver other sounds for 1 round, or merely have the *whispering wind* seem to be a faint stirring of the air. You can likewise cause the *whispering wind* to move as slowly as 1 mile per hour or as quickly as 1 mile per 10 minutes. When the spell reaches its objective, it swirls and remains in place until the message is delivered. As with *magic mouth*, *whispering wind* cannot speak verbal components, use command words, or activate magical effects.

Wind Walk

Transmutation [Air]
Level: Clr 6, Drd 7
Components: V, S, DF
Casting Time: 1 standard action
Range: Touch
Targets: You and one touched creature per three levels
Duration: 1 hour/level (D); see text
Saving Throw: No and Will negates (harmless)
Spell Resistance: No and Yes (harmless)

You alter the substance of your body to a cloudlike vapor (as the *gaseous form* spell) and move through the air, possibly at great speed. You can take other creatures with you, each of which acts independently.

Normally, a *wind walker* flies at a speed of 10 feet with perfect maneuverability. If desired by the subject, a magical wind wafts a *wind walker* along at up to 600 feet per round (60 mph) with poor maneuverability. *Wind walkers* are not invisible but rather appear misty and translucent. If fully clothed in white, they are 80% likely to be mistaken for clouds, fog, vapors, or the like.

A *wind walker* can regain its physical form as desired and later resume the cloud form. Each change to and from vaporous form takes 5 rounds, which counts toward the duration of the spell (as does any time spent in physical form). As noted above, you can dismiss the spell, and you can even dismiss it for individual wind walkers and not others.

For the last minute of the spell's duration, a *wind walker* in cloud form automatically descends 60 feet per round (for a total of 600 feet), though it may descend faster if it wishes. This descent serves as a warning that the spell is about to end.

Wind Wall

Evocation [Air]
Level: Air 2, Clr 3, Drd 3, Rgr 2, Sor/Wiz 3
Components: V, S, M/DF
Casting Time: 1 standard action
Range: Medium (100 ft. + 10 ft./level)
Effect: Wall up to 10 ft./level long and 5 ft./level high (S)
Duration: 1 round/level
Saving Throw: None; see text
Spell Resistance: Yes

An invisible vertical curtain of wind appears. It is 2 feet thick and of considerable strength. It is a roaring blast sufficient to blow away any bird smaller than an eagle, or tear papers and similar materials from unsuspecting hands. (A Reflex save allows a creature to maintain its grasp on an object.) Tiny and Small flying creatures cannot pass through the barrier. Loose materials and cloth garments fly upward when caught in a *wind wall*. Arrows and bolts are deflected upward and miss, while any other normal ranged weapon passing through the wall has a 30% miss chance. (A giant-thrown boulder, a siege engine projectile, and other massive ranged weapons are not affected.) Gases, most gaseous breath weapons, and creatures in gaseous form cannot pass through the wall (although it is no barrier to incorporeal creatures).

While the wall must be vertical, you can shape it in any continuous path along the ground that you like. It is possible to create cylindrical or square wind walls to enclose specific points. A 5th-level caster can create a wall up to 50 feet long and up to 25 feet high, sufficient to form a cylinder of wind 15 feet in diameter.

Arcane Material Component: A tiny fan and a feather of exotic origin.

Wish

Universal
Level: Sor/Wiz 9
Components: V, XP
Casting Time: 1 standard action
Range: See text
Target, Effect, or Area: See text
Duration: See text
Saving Throw: See text
Spell Resistance: Yes

Wish is the mightiest spell a wizard or sorcerer can cast. By simply speaking aloud, you can alter reality to better suit you. Even *wish*, however, has its limits.

A *wish* can produce any one of the following effects.

- Duplicate any wizard or sorcerer spell of 8th level or lower, provided the spell is not of a school prohibited to you.
- Duplicate any other spell of 6th level or lower, provided the spell is not of a school prohibited to you.
- Duplicate any wizard or sorcerer spell of 7th level or lower even if it's of a prohibited school.
- Duplicate any other spell of 5th level or lower even if it's of a prohibited school.
- Undo the harmful effects of many other spells, such as *geas/quest* or *insanity*.
- Create a nonmagical item of up to 25,000 gp in value.
- Create a magic item, or add to the powers of an existing magic item.
- Grant a creature a +1 inherent bonus to an ability score. Two to five *wish* spells cast in immediate succession can grant a creature a +2 to +5 inherent bonus to an ability score (two wishes for a +2 inherent bonus, three for a +3 inherent

bonus, and so on). Inherent bonuses are instantaneous, so they cannot be dispelled. *Note:* An inherent bonus may not exceed +5 for a single ability score, and inherent bonuses to a particular ability score do not stack, so only the best one applies.
- Remove injuries and afflictions. A single *wish* can aid one creature per caster level, and all subjects are cured of the same kind of affliction. For example, you could heal all the damage you and your companions have taken, or remove all poison effects from everyone in the party, but not do both with the same *wish*. A *wish* can never restore the experience point loss from casting a spell or the level or Constitution loss from being raised from the dead.
- Revive the dead. A *wish* can bring a dead creature back to life by duplicating a *resurrection* spell. A *wish* can revive a dead creature whose body has been destroyed, but the task takes two *wishes*, one to recreate the body and another to infuse the body with life again. A *wish* cannot prevent a character who was brought back to life from losing an experience level.
- Transport travelers. A *wish* can lift one creature per caster level from anywhere on any plane and place those creatures anywhere else on any plane regardless of local conditions. An unwilling target gets a Will save to negate the effect, and spell resistance (if any) applies.
- Undo misfortune. A *wish* can undo a single recent event. The *wish* forces a reroll of any roll made within the last round (including your last turn). Reality reshapes itself to accommodate the new result. For example, a *wish* could undo an opponent's successful save, a foe's successful critical hit (either the attack roll or the critical roll), a friend's failed save, and so on. The reroll, however, may be as bad as or worse than the original roll. An unwilling target gets a Will save to negate the effect, and spell resistance (if any) applies.

You may try to use a *wish* to produce greater effects than these, but doing so is dangerous. Such a *wish* gives the DM the opportunity to fulfill your request without fulfilling it completely. (The *wish* may pervert your intent into a literal but undesirable fulfillment or only a partial fulfillment.) For example, wishing for a *staff of the magi* might get you instantly transported to the presence of the staff's current owner. Wishing to be immortal could get you imprisoned in a hidden extradimensional space (as by an *imprison-*

ment spell), where you could "live" indefinitely.

Duplicated spells allow saves and spell resistance as normal (but save DCs are for 9th-level spells).

Material Component: When a *wish* duplicates a spell with a material component that costs more than 10,000 gp, you must provide that component.

XP Cost: The minimum XP cost for casting *wish* is 5,000 XP. When a *wish* duplicates a spell that has an XP cost, you must pay 5,000 XP or that cost, whichever is more. When a *wish* creates or improves a magic item, you must pay twice the normal XP cost for crafting or improving the item, plus an additional 5,000 XP.

Wood Shape

Transmutation
Level: Drd 2
Components: V, S, DF
Casting Time: 1 standard action
Range: Touch
Target: One touched piece of wood no larger than 10 cu. ft. + 1 cu. ft./level
Duration: Instantaneous
Saving Throw: Will negates (object)
Spell Resistance: Yes (object)

Wood shape enables you to form one existing piece of wood into any shape that suits your purpose. For example, you can make a wooden weapon, fashion a special trapdoor, or sculpt a crude idol. This spell also permits you to reshape a wood door to make an exit where one didn't exist or to seal a door shut. While it is possible to make crude coffers, doors, and so forth, fine detail isn't possible. There is a 30% chance that any shape that includes moving parts simply doesn't work.

Word of Chaos

Evocation [Chaotic, Sonic]
Level: Chaos 7, Clr 7
Components: V
Casting Time: 1 standard action
Range: 40 ft.
Area: Nonchaotic creatures in a 40-ft.-radius spread centered on you
Duration: Instantaneous
Saving Throw: None or Will negates; see text
Spell Resistance: Yes

Any nonchaotic creature within the area who hears the *word of chaos* suffers the following ill effects.

The effects are cumulative and concurrent. No saving throw is allowed against these effects.

Deafened: The creature is deafened for 1d4 rounds.

Stunned: The creature is stunned for 1 round.

Confused: The creature is *confused*, as by the *confusion* spell, for 1d10 minutes. This is a mind-affecting enchantment effect.

Killed: Living creatures die. Undead creatures are destroyed.

HD	Effect
Equal to caster level	Deafened
Up to caster level –1	Stunned, deafened
Up to caster level –5	*Confused*, stunned, deafened
Up to caster level –10	Killed, *confused*, stunned, deafened

Furthermore, if you are on your home plane when you cast this spell, nonchaotic extraplanar creatures within the area are instantly banished back to their home planes. Creatures so banished cannot return for at least 24 hours. This effect takes place regardless of whether the creatures hear the *word of chaos*. The banishment effect allows a Will save (at a –4 penalty) to negate.

Creatures whose HD exceed your caster level are unaffected by *word of chaos*.

Word of Recall

Conjuration (Teleportation)
Level: Clr 6, Drd 8
Components: V
Casting Time: 1 standard action
Range: Unlimited
Target: You and touched objects or other willing creatures
Duration: Instantaneous
Saving Throw: None or Will negates (harmless, object)
Spell Resistance: No or Yes (harmless, object)

Word of recall teleports you instantly back to your sanctuary when the word is uttered. You must designate the sanctuary when you prepare the spell, and it must be a very familiar place. The actual point of arrival is a designated area no larger than 10 feet by 10 feet. You can be transported any distance within a plane but cannot travel between planes. You can transport, in addition to yourself, any objects you carry, as long as their weight doesn't exceed your maximum load. You may also bring one additional willing Medium or smaller creature (carrying gear or objects up to its maximum load) or its equivalent per three caster levels. A Large creature counts as two Medium creatures, a Huge creature counts as two Large creatures, and so forth. All creatures to be transported must be in contact with one another, and at least one of those creatures must be in contact with you. Exceeding this limit causes the spell to fail.

An unwilling creature can't be teleported by *word of recall*. Likewise, a creature's Will save (or spell resistance) prevents items in its possession from being teleported. Unattended, nonmagical objects receive no saving throw.

Zone of Silence

Illusion (Glamer)
Level: Brd 4
Components: V, S
Casting Time: 1 round
Range: Personal
Area: 5-ft.-radius emanation centered on you
Duration: 1 hour/level (D)

By casting *zone of silence*, you manipulate sound waves in your immediate vicinity so that you and those within the spell's area can converse normally, yet no one outside can hear your voices or any other noises from within, including language-dependent or sonic spell effects (such as *command* or *shout*).This effect is centered on you and moves with you. Anyone who enters the zone immediately becomes subject to its effects, but those who leave are no longer affected. Note, however, that a successful Spot check to read lips can still reveal what's said inside a *zone of silence*.

Zone of Truth

Enchantment (Compulsion) [Mind-Affecting]
Level: Clr 2, Pal 2
Components: V, S, DF
Casting Time: 1 standard action
Range: Close (25 ft. + 5 ft./2 levels)
Area: 20-ft.-radius emanation
Duration: 1 min./level
Saving Throw: Will negates
Spell Resistance: Yes

Creatures within the emanation area (or those who enter it) can't speak any deliberate and intentional lies. Each potentially affected creature is allowed a save to avoid the effects when the spell is cast or when the creature first enters the emanation area. Affected creatures are aware of this enchantment. Therefore, they may avoid answering questions to which they would normally respond with a lie, or they may be evasive as long as they remain within the boundaries of the truth. Creatures who leave the area are free to speak as they choose.

General Guidelines and Glossary

The general rules for what to do when rounding fractions and when several multipliers apply to a die roll (often encountered as what to do when doubling something that is already doubled) are provided below, followed by a glossary of game terms.

ROUNDING FRACTIONS

In general, if you wind up with a fraction, round down, even if the fraction is one-half or larger. For example, if a *fireball* deals you 17 points of damage, but you succeed on your saving throw and only take half damage, you take 8 points of damage.

Exception: Certain rolls, such as damage and hit points, have a minimum of 1.

MULTIPLYING

Sometimes a special rule makes you multiply a number or a die roll. As long as you're applying a single multiplier, multiply the number normally. When two or more multipliers apply to any abstract value (such as a modifier or a die roll), however, combine them into a single multiple, with each extra multiple adding 1 less than its value to the first multiple. Thus, a double (×2) and a double (×2) applied to the same number results in a triple (×3, because 2 + 1 = 3).

For example, Tordek, a high-level dwarf fighter, deals 1d8+6 points of damage with a warhammer. On a critical hit, a warhammer deals triple damage, so that's 3d8+18 damage for Tordek. A magic *dwarven thrower* warhammer deals double damage (2d8+12 for Tordek) when thrown. If Tordek scores a critical hit while throwing the *dwarven thrower*, his player rolls quadruple damage (4d8+24) because 3 + 1 = 4.

Another way to think of it is to convert the multiples into additions. Tordek's critical hit increases his damage by 2d8+12, and the *dwarven thrower*'s doubling of damage increases his damage by 1d8+6, so both of them together increase his damage by 3d8+18 for a grand total of 4d8+24.

When applying multipliers to real-world values (such as weight or distance), normal rules of math apply instead. A creature whose size doubles (thus multiplying its weight by 8) and then is turned to stone (which would multiply its weight by a factor of roughly 3) now weighs about 24 times normal, not 10 times normal. Similarly, a blinded creature attempting to negotiate difficult terrain would count each square as 4 squares (doubling the cost twice, for a total multiplier of ×4), rather than as 3 squares (adding 100% twice).

GLOSSARY

0-level spell: A spell of the lowest possible level. Arcane spellcasters often call their 0-level spells "cantrips," and divine spellcasters often call them "orisons."

5-foot step: A small position adjustment that does not count as an action. Usually (but not always), a 5-foot step is permitted at any point in the round (such as before or after a full-round action, between attacks in a full attack, between a standard action and a move action, or between two move actions). You can't take a 5-foot step in the same round that you move any distance. You can't take a 5-foot step if your movement is hampered, such as into a square of difficult terrain, in darkness, or when blinded. Taking a 5-foot step does not provoke an attack of opportunity, even if you move out of a threatened square.

ability: One of the six basic character qualities: Strength (Str), Dexterity (Dex), Constitution (Con), Intelligence (Int), Wisdom (Wis), and Charisma (Cha). See ability score.

ability check: A check of 1d20 + the appropriate ability modifier.

ability damage: A temporary loss of 1 or more ability score points. Lost points return at a rate of 1 point per day unless otherwise noted by the condition dealing the damage. A character with Strength 0 falls to the ground and is helpless. A character with Dexterity 0 is paralyzed. A character with Constitution 0 is dead. A character with Intelligence, Wisdom, or Charisma 0 is unconscious.

ability decrease: A decrease in an ability score that ends when the condition causing it does.

ability drain: A permanent loss of 1 or more ability score points. The character can only regain these points through magical means. A character with Strength 0 falls to the ground and is helpless. A character with Dexterity 0 is paralyzed. A character with Constitution 0 is dead. A character with Intelligence, Wisdom, or Charisma 0 is unconscious.

ability modifier: The bonus or penalty associated with a particular ability score. Ability modifiers apply to die rolls for character actions involving the corresponding abilities.

ability score: The numeric rating of one of the six character abilities (see ability). Some creatures lack certain ability scores; others cannot be rated in particular abilities.

action: A character activity. Actions are divided into the following categories, according to the time required to perform them (from most time required to least): full-round actions, standard actions, move actions, and free actions.

adjacent: In a square that shares a border or a corner with a designated square. Each square is adjacent to eight other squares on the board.

adventuring party: A group of characters who adventure together. An adventuring party is composed of player characters plus any followers, familiars, animal companions, associates, cohorts, or hirelings they might have.

alignment: One of the nine descriptors of morality for intelligent creatures: lawful good (LG), neutral good (NG), chaotic good (CG), lawful neutral (LN), neutral (N), chaotic neutral (CN), lawful evil (LE), neutral evil (NE), and chaotic evil (CE).

ally: A creature friendly to you. In most cases, references to "allies" include yourself.

animal: A type of creature that includes all natural animals, dire animals, giant animals, and some other nonmagical vertebrate creatures (see the *Monster Manual*). Animals always have an Intelligence score of 1 or 2.

arcane spell failure: The chance that a spell fails and is cast to no effect because the caster's ability to use a somatic component was hampered by armor. Bards can ignore the arcane spell failure chance for light armor when casting bard spells.

Lidda surprises…

arcane spells: Arcane spells involve the direct manipulation of mystic energies. Bards, sorcerers, and wizards cast arcane spells.

armor bonus: A bonus to Armor Class granted by armor or by a spell or magical effect that mimics armor. Armor bonuses stack with all other bonuses to Armor Class (even with natural armor bonuses) except other armor bonuses. Magic armor typically grants an enhancement bonus to the armor's armor bonus, which has the effect of increasing the armor's overall bonus. An armor bonus granted by a spell or magic item typically takes the form of an invisible, tangible field of force around the recipient. An armor bonus doesn't apply against touch attacks, except for armor bonuses granted by force effects (such as the *mage armor* spell) which apply against incorporeal touch attacks, such as that of a shadow.

Armor Class (AC): A number representing a creature's ability to avoid being hit in combat. An opponent's attack roll must equal or exceed the target creature's Armor Class to hit it. Armor Class = 10 + all modifiers that apply (typically armor bonus, shield bonus, Dexterity modifier, and size modifier).

artifact: A magic item of incredible power. Some spells do not function when targeted on an artifact.

Astral Plane: An open, weightless plane that connects with all other planes of existence and is used for transportation among them (and is thus described as a transitive plane, like the Ethereal Plane and the Plane of Shadow). Certain spells (such as *astral projection*) allow access to this plane.

attack: Any of numerous actions intended to harm, disable, or neutralize an opponent. The outcome of an attack is determined by an attack roll.

attack of opportunity: A single extra melee attack per round that a combatant can make when an opponent within reach takes an action that provokes attacks of opportunity. Cover prevents attacks of opportunity.

attack roll: A roll to determine whether an attack hits. To make an attack roll, roll 1d20 and add the appropriate modifiers for the attack type, as follows: melee attack roll = 1d20 + base attack bonus + Strength modifier + size modifier; ranged attack roll = 1d20 + base attack bonus + Dexterity modifier + size modifier + range penalty. In either case, the attack hits if the result is at least as high as the target's Armor Class.

automatic hit: An attack that hits regardless of target AC. Automatic hits occur on an attack roll of natural 20 or as a result of certain spells. A natural 20 attack roll is also a threat—a possible critical hit.

automatic miss: An attack that misses regardless of target AC. Automatic misses occur on an attack roll of natural 1.

barbarian (Bbn): A class made up of ferocious warriors who use inborn fury and instinct to bring down foes.

bard (Brd): A class made up of performers whose music and poetics produce magical effects.

base attack bonus: An attack roll bonus derived from character class and level. Base attack bonuses increase at different rates for different character classes. A character gains a second attack when his or her base attack bonus reaches +6, a third with a base attack bonus of +11 or higher, and a fourth with a base attack bonus of +16 or higher. Base attack bonuses gained from different classes, such as when a character is a multiclass character, stack.

base land speed: The speed a character can move while unarmored. Base land speed is derived from character race.

base save bonus: A saving throw modifier derived from character class and level. Base save bonuses increase at different rates for different character classes. Base save bonuses gained from different classes, such as when a character is a multiclass character, stack.

battle grid: A play surface marked off in 1-inch squares, which is used to keep track of the locations of creatures and characters (represented by miniature figures) during combat and other tactical situations.

blinded: Unable to see. A blinded character takes a −2 penalty to Armor Class, loses his Dexterity bonus to AC (if any), moves at half speed, and takes a −4 penalty on Search checks and on most Strength- and Dexterity-based skill checks. All checks and activities that rely on vision (such as reading and Spot checks) automatically fail. All opponents are considered to have total concealment (50% miss chance) relative to the blinded character.

bolster undead: A supernatural ability of evil clerics (and some neutral ones). Bolstering undead increases the resistance of those undead creatures to turning attempts.

bonus: A positive modifier to a die roll. In most cases, multiple bonuses from the same source or of the same type in effect on the same character or object do not stack; only the highest bonus of that type applies. Bonuses that don't have a specific type always stack with all bonuses.

...and sneak attacks a troll.

cantrip: An arcane 0-level spell.

cast a spell: Trigger the magical or divine energy of a spell by means of words, gestures, focuses, and/or special materials. Spellcasting requires the uninterrupted concentration of the caster during the requisite casting time. Disruption of this concentration forces the caster to make a successful Concentration check or lose the spell. Successful casting brings about the spell's listed effect or effects.

caster level: A measure of the power with which a spellcaster casts a spell. Generally, a spell's caster level is the spellcaster's class level.

caster level check: A roll of 1d20 + the caster level (in the relevant class). If the result equals or exceeds the DC (or the spell resistance, in the case of caster level checks made for spell resistance), the check succeeds.

casting time: The time required to cast a spell, usually either 1 standard action, 1 round, or 1 free action. Spells with casting times longer than 1 round require full-round actions for all the rounds encompassed in the casting time.

Charisma (Cha): The ability that measures a character's force of personality, persuasiveness, personal magnetism, ability to lead, and physical attractiveness.

character: A fictional individual within the confines of a fantasy game setting. The words "character" and "creature" are often used synonymously within these rules, since almost any creature could be a character within the game, and every character is a creature (as opposed to an object).

character class: One of the eleven player character types—barbarian, bard, cleric, druid, fighter, monk, paladin, ranger, rogue, sorcerer, or wizard. Class defines a character's predominant talents and general function within an adventuring party. Character class may also refer to a nonplayer character class or a prestige class (see the *Dungeon Master's Guide*).

character level: A character's total level. For a character with levels in only one class, class level and character level are the same thing.

check: A method of determining the result when a character attempts an action (other than an attack or a saving throw) that has a chance of failure. Checks are based on a relevant character ability, skill, or other characteristic. Most checks are either ability checks or skill checks, though special types such as turning checks, caster level checks, dispel checks, and initiative checks also exist. The specific name of the check usually corresponds to the skill or ability used. To make a check, roll 1d20 and add any relevant modifiers. (Higher results are always better.) If this check result equals or exceeds the Difficulty Class number assigned by the DM (or the opponent's check, if the action is opposed), the check succeeds.

checked: Prevented from achieving forward motion by an applied force, such as wind. Checked creatures on the ground merely stop. Checked flying creatures move back a distance specified in the description of the effect.

circumstance bonus: A bonus granted because of specific conditional factors favorable to the success of the task at hand. Circumstance bonuses stack with all other bonuses, including other circumstance bonuses, unless they arise from essentially the same benefit. For instance, a magnifying glass gives a +2 circumstance bonus on Appraise checks involving any item that is small or highly detailed, such as a gem. If you had a second tool that also granted a circumstance bonus from improved visual acuity (such as a jeweler's loupe), the circumstance bonuses wouldn't stack.

class: See character class.

class feature: Any special characteristic derived from a character class.

class level: A character's level in a single class. Class features generally depend on class level rather than character level.

class skill: A skill to which characters of a particular class have easier access than characters of other classes. Characters may buy class skills at a rate of 1 rank per skill point, as opposed to 1/2 rank per skill point for cross-class skills. The maximum rank for a class skill is 3 + character level.

cleric (Clr): A class made up of characters who cast divine spells and are also capable in combat.

Colossal: A Colossal creature is typically 64 feet or more in height or length and weighs 250,000 pounds or more.

comatose: Effectively in a state of suspended animation. A comatose creature is helpless.

command word item: A magic item that activates when the user speaks a particular word or phrase. Activating a command word item does not require concentration and does not provoke attacks of opportunity.

command undead: The supernatural ability of evil clerics and some neutral clerics to control undead creatures by channeling negative energy.

competence bonus: A bonus that improves a character's performance of a particular task, such as from the bardic ability to inspire competence. Such a bonus may apply on attack rolls, saving throws, skill checks, caster level checks, or any other checks to which a bonus relating to level or skill ranks would normally apply. It does not apply on ability checks, damage rolls, initiative checks, or other rolls that aren't related to a character's level or skill ranks. Multiple competence bonuses don't stack; only the highest bonus applies.

concealment: Something that prevents an attacker from clearly seeing his or her target. Concealment creates a chance that an otherwise successful attack misses (a miss chance).

concentrate on a spell: Concentrate to maintain an active spell's effect. Concentrating on a spell is a standard action and provokes an attack of opportunity.

confused: Befuddled and unable to determine a course of action due to a spell or magical effect. A *confused* character's actions are determined by rolling d% at the beginning of his turn: 01–10, attack caster with melee or ranged weapons (or close with caster if attacking is not possible); 11–20, act normally; 21–50, do nothing but babble incoherently; 51–70, flee away from caster at top possible speed; 71–100, attack nearest creature (for this purpose, a familiar counts as part of the subject's self). A *confused* character who can't carry out the indicated action does nothing but babble incoherently. Attackers are not at any special advantage when attacking a *confused* character. Any *confused* character who is attacked automatically attacks its attackers on its next turn, as long as it is still *confused* when its turn comes. A *confused* character does not make attacks of opportunity against any creature that it is not already devoted to attacking (either because of its most recent action or because it has just been attacked).

Constitution (Con): The ability that represents a character's health and stamina.

continuous damage: Damage from a single attack that continues to deal damage every round without the need for additional attack rolls.

copper piece (cp): The most prevalent form of currency among beggars and laborers. Ten copper pieces are equivalent to 1 silver piece.

coup de grace: A full-round action that allows an attacker to attempt a killing blow against a helpless opponent. A coup de grace can be administered with a melee weapon, or with a bow or crossbow if the attacker is adjacent to the opponent. An attacker delivering a coup de grace automatically scores a critical hit, after which the defender must make a Fortitude save (DC 10 + damage dealt) or die. Rogues also gain their extra sneak attack damage for this attack. Delivering a coup de grace provokes attacks of opportunity from threatening foes. A coup de grace is not possible against a creature immune to critical hits.

cover: Any barrier between an attacker and defender. Such a barrier can be an object, a creature, or a magical force. Cover grants the defender a bonus to Armor Class.

cowering: Frozen in fear and unable to take actions. A cowering character takes a –2 penalty to Armor Class and loses her Dexterity bonus (if any).

creature: A living or otherwise active being, not an object. The terms "creature" and "character" are sometimes used interchangeably.

creature type: One of several broad categories of creatures. The creature types are aberration, animal, construct, dragon, elemental, fey, giant, humanoid, magical beast, monstrous humanoid, ooze, outsider, plant, undead, and vermin. (See the *Monster Manual* for full descriptions.)

critical hit (crit): A hit that strikes a vital area and therefore deals double damage or more. To score a critical hit, an attacker must first score a threat (usually a natural 20 on an attack roll) and then succeed on a critical roll (just like another attack roll). Critical hit damage is usually double damage, which means rolling damage twice, just as if the attacker had actually hit the defender two times. (Any extra damage dice, such as from a rogue's sneak attack, are not rolled multiple times, but are added to the total at the end of the calculation.)

critical roll: A special second attack roll made in the event of a threat to determine whether a critical hit has been scored. If the critical roll is a hit against the target creature's AC, then the original attack is a critical hit. Otherwise, the original attack is a regular hit.

cross-class (cc) skill: A skill that is not a class skill for a character. Characters may buy cross-class skills at the rate of a half rank per skill point, as opposed to 1 rank per skill point for class skills. The most ranks a character can have in a cross-class skill is one-half of the class skill maximum (3 + the character's level), rounded neither up nor down.

cure **spell:** Any spell with the word "cure" in its name, such as *cure minor wounds*, *cure light wounds*, or *mass cure critical wounds*.

current hit points: A character's hit points at a given moment in the game. Current hit points go down when the character takes damage and go back up upon recovery.

damage: A decrease in hit points, an ability score, or other aspects of a character caused by an injury, illness, or magical effect. The three main categories of damage are lethal damage, nonlethal damage, and ability damage. In addition, wherever it is relevant, the type of damage an attack deals is specified, since natural abilities, magic items, or spell effects may grant immunity to certain types of damage. Damage types include weapon damage (subdivided into bludgeoning, slashing, and piercing) and energy damage (positive, negative, acid, cold, electricity, fire, and sonic). Modifiers to melee damage rolls apply to both subcategories of weapon damage (melee and unarmed). Some modifiers apply to both weapon and spell damage, but only if so stated. Damage points are deducted from whatever character attribute has been harmed—lethal and nonlethal damage from current hit points, and ability damage from the relevant ability score). Damage heals naturally over time, but can also be negated wholly or partially by curative magic.

damage reduction (DR): A special defense that allows a creature to ignore a set amount of damage from most weapons, unarmed attacks, or natural weapons, but not from energy attacks, spells, spell-like abilities, and supernatural abilities. The number in a creature's damage reduction is the amount of hit points of damage the creature ignores. The information after the slash indicates the type of weapon (such as magic, silver, or evil) that overcomes the damage reduction. Some damage reduction, such as that of a barbarian, is not overcome by any type of weapon.

darkvision: An extraordinary ability possessed by some creatures that enables them to see in the dark.

dazed: Unable to act normally. A dazed character can take no actions, but has no penalty to AC.

dazzled: Unable to see well because of overstimulation of the eyes. A dazzled creature takes a −1 penalty on attack rolls, Spot checks, and Search checks.

dead: A character dies when his or her hit points drop to −10 or lower. A character also dies when his or her Constitution drops to 0, and certain spells or effects (such as failing a Fortitude save against massive damage) can also kill a character outright. Death causes the character's soul to leave the body and journey to an Outer Plane. Dead characters cannot benefit from normal or magical healing, but they can be restored to life via magic. A dead body decays normally unless magically preserved, but magic that restores a dead character to life also restores the body either to full health or to its condition at the time of death (depending on the spell or device).

deafened: Unable to hear. A deafened character takes a −4 penalty on initiative checks, automatically fails Listen checks, and has a 20% chance of spell failure when casting spells with verbal components.

deal damage: Cause damage to a target with a successful attack. How much damage is dealt is usually expressed in terms of dice (for example, 2d6+4) and may have a situational modifier as well. However, damage dealt by a weapon or spell does not necessarily equal damage taken by the target, because the target may have special defenses that negate some or all of the damage.

death attack: A spell or special ability that instantly slays the target, such as *finger of death*. Neither *raise dead* nor *reincarnation* can grant life to a creature slain by a death attack, though *resurrection* and more powerful effects can.

deflection bonus: A bonus to Armor Class granted by a spell or magic effect that makes attacks veer off harmlessly. Deflection bonuses stack with all other bonuses to AC except other deflection bonuses. A deflection bonus applies against touch attacks.

Dexterity (Dex): The ability that measures a character's hand-eye coordination, agility, reflexes, and balance.

difficult terrain: An area containing one or more features (such as rubble or undergrowth) that costs 2 squares instead of 1 square to move through.

Difficulty Class (DC): The target number that a player must meet or beat for a check or saving throw to succeed. Difficulty Classes other than those given in specific spell or item descriptions are set by the DM using the skill rules as a guideline.

Diminutive: A Diminutive creature is typically between 6 inches and 1 foot in height or length and weighs between 1/8 pound and 1 pound.

direct a spell: Direct an active spell's effect at a specific target or targets. Directing a spell is a move action and does not provoke an attack of opportunity.

disabled: At exactly 0 current hit points, or in negative hit points but stable and conscious. A disabled character may take a single move action or standard action each round (but not both, nor can she take full-round actions). She moves at half speed. Taking move actions doesn't risk further injury, but performing any standard action (or any other action the DM deems strenuous, including some free actions such as casting a quickened spell) deals 1 point of damage after the completion of the act. Unless the action increased the disabled character's hit points, she is now in negative hit points and dying.

dispel: Negate, suppress, or remove one or more existing spells or other effects on a creature, item, or area. Dispel usually refers to a *dispel magic* spell, though other forms of dispelling are possible. Certain spells cannot be dispelled, as noted in the individual spell descriptions.

dispel check: A roll of 1d20 + caster level of the character making the attempt to dispel (usually used with *dispel magic*). The DC is 11 plus the level of the spellcaster who initiated the effect being dispelled.

dispel turning: Channel negative energy to negate a successful turning undead attempt by a good cleric or a paladin.

divine spells: Spells of religious origin powered by faith or by a deity. Clerics, druids, paladins, and rangers cast divine spells.

dodge bonus: A bonus to Armor Class (and sometimes Reflex saves) resulting from physical skill at avoiding blows and other ill effects. Dodge bonuses are never granted by spells or magic items. Any situation or effect (except wearing armor) that negates a character's Dexterity bonus also negates any dodge bonuses the character may have (for instance, you lose any dodge bonuses to AC when you're flat-footed). Dodge bonuses stack with all other bonuses to AC, even other dodge bonuses. Dodge bonuses apply against touch attacks.

domain: A granted power and a set of nine divine spells (one each of 1st through 9th level) themed around a particular concept and associated with one or more deities. The available domains are: Air, Animal, Chaos, Death, Destruction, Earth, Evil, Fire, Good, Healing, Knowledge, Law, Luck, Magic, Plant, Protection, Strength, Sun, Travel, Trickery, War, and Water.

domain spell: A divine spell belonging to a domain. Each domain offers one spell of each spell level. In addition to their normal daily complement of spells, clerics can cast one domain spell per day for each spell level that their caster levels allow. This spell may be from either of their domains. Domain spells cannot be exchanged for *cure* or *inflict* spells.

double weapon: A weapon with two ends, blades, or heads that are both intended for use in combat. Any weapon for which two damage ranges are listed is a double weapon. Double weapons can be used to make an extra attack as if the wielder were fighting with two weapons (light weapon in the off hand).

druid (Drd): A class made up of characters who draw energy from the natural world to cast divine spells and gain special magical powers.

Dungeon Master (DM): The player who portrays nonplayer characters, makes up the story setting for the other players, and serves as a referee.

dying: Unconscious and near death. A dying character has –1 to –9 current hit points, can take no actions, and is unconscious. Each round on her turn, a dying character rolls d% to see whether she becomes stable. She has a 10% chance of becoming stable. If she does not, she loses 1 hit point. If a dying character reaches –10 hit points, she is dead.

effective hit point increase: Hit points gained through temporary increases in Constitution score. Unlike temporary hit points, points gained in this manner are not lost first, and must be subtracted from the character's current hit points at the time the Constitution increase ends.

electrum: A naturally occurring alloy of gold and silver.

Elemental Plane: One of the Inner Planes consisting almost entirely of one type of element: air, earth, fire, or water.

end of round: The point in a combat round when all the participants have completed all their allowed actions. End of round occurs when no one else involved in the combat has an action pending for that round.

enemy: A creature unfriendly to you.

energy damage: Damage caused by one of five types of energy (not counting positive and negative energy): acid, cold, electricity, fire, and sonic.

energy drain: An attack that saps a creature's vital energy giving it negative levels, which might permanently drain the creature's levels.

Energy Plane: An Inner Plane, either the Positive Energy Plane or the Negative Energy Plane.

engaged: Threatening or being threatened by an enemy. (Unconscious or otherwise immobilized characters are not considered engaged unless they are actually being attacked.)

enhancement bonus: A bonus that represents an increase in the sturdiness and/or effectiveness of armor or natural armor, or the effectiveness of a weapon, or a general bonus to an ability score. Multiple enhancement bonuses on the same object (in the case of armor and weapons), creature (in the case of natural armor), or ability score do not stack. Only the highest enhancement bonus applies. Since enhancement bonuses to armor or natural armor effectively increase the armor or natural armor's bonus to AC, they don't apply against touch attacks.

entangled: Ensnared. Being entangled impedes movement, but does not entirely prevent it unless the bonds are anchored to an immobile object or tethered by an opposing force. An entangled creature moves at half speed, cannot run or charge, and takes a –2 penalty on attack rolls and a –4 penalty to its effective Dexterity score. An entangled character who attempts to cast a spell must make a Concentration check (DC 15 + the spell's level) or lose the spell.

ethereal: On the Ethereal Plane. An ethereal creature is invisible and intangible to creatures on the Material Plane, but visible and corporeal to creatures on the Ethereal Plane. As such, such a creature is capable of moving through solid objects on the Material Plane and in any direction (even up or down), though all movement is at half speed. Ethereal beings can see and hear what is happening in the same area of the Material Plane to a distance of 60 feet, but everything looks gray and insubstantial. Force effects originating on the Material Plane can affect items and creatures that are ethereal, but the reverse is not true.

Ethereal Plane: A gray, foggy plane parallel to the Material Plane at all points. Creatures within the Ethereal Plane can see and hear into the Material Plane to a distance of 60 feet, though the reverse is not usually true. Force effects originating on the Material Plane can affect items and creatures on the Ethereal Plane, but the reverse is not true. Because the Ethereal Plane is often used for travel, it is also considered a transitive plane (like the Astral Plane and the Plane of Shadow).

exhausted: Tired to the point of significant impairment. An exhausted character moves at half speed and takes a –6 penalty to Strength and Dexterity. After 1 hour of complete rest, an exhausted character becomes fatigued. A fatigued character becomes exhausted by doing something else that would normally cause fatigue.

experience points (XP): A numerical measure of a character's personal achievement and advancement. Characters earn experience points by defeating opponents and overcoming challenges. At the end of each adventure, the DM assigns experience to the characters based on what they have accomplished. Characters continue to accumulate experience points throughout their adventuring careers, gaining new levels in their character classes at certain experience point totals.

extraordinary ability (Ex): A nonmagical special ability (as opposed to a spell-like or supernatural ability).

extraplanar: Native to a plane of existence other than the plane on which a creature is present. On the Material Plane, an outsider is an extraplanar creature. On an outsider's home plane, a native of the Material Plane is an extraplanar creature.

failure: An unsuccessful result on a check, saving throw, or other determination involving a die roll.

fascinated: Entranced by a supernatural or spell effect. A fascinated creature stands or sits quietly, taking no actions other than to pay attention to the fascinating effect, for as long as the effect lasts. It takes a –4 penalty on skill checks made as reactions, such as Listen and Spot checks. Any potential threat, such as a hostile creature approaching, allows the fascinated creature a new saving throw against the fascinating effect. Any obvious threat, such as someone drawing a weapon, casting a spell, or aiming a ranged weapon at the fascinated creature, automatically breaks the effect. A fascinated creature's ally may shake it free of the effect as a standard action.

fatigued: Tired to the point of impairment. A fatigued character can neither run nor charge and takes a –2 penalty to Strength and Dexterity. Doing anything that would normally cause fatigue causes the fatigued character to become exhausted. After 8 hours of complete rest, fatigued characters are no longer fatigued.

fear effect: Any spell or magical effect that causes the victim to become shaken, frightened, or panicked, or to suffer from some other fear-based effect defined in the description of the specific spell or item in question.

fighter (Ftr): A class made up of characters who have exceptional combat capability and unequaled skill with weapons.

Fine: A Fine creature is typically 6 inches or less in height or length and weighs 1/8 pound or less.

flank: To be directly on the other side of a character who is being threatened by another character. A flanking attacker gains a +2 flanking bonus on attack rolls against the defender. A rogue can sneak attack a defender that she is flanking.

flat-footed: Especially vulnerable to attacks at the beginning of a battle. Characters are flat-footed until their first turns in the initiative cycle. A flat-footed creature loses its Dexterity bonus to Armor Class (if any) and cannot make attacks of opportunity.

force damage: A special type of damage dealt by force effects, such as a *magic missile* spell. A force effect can strike incorporeal creatures without the normal miss chance associated with incorporeality.

Fortitude save: A type of saving throw, related to a character's ability to withstand damage thanks to his physical stamina.

free action: Free actions consume a negligible amount of time, and one or more such actions can be performed in conjunction with actions of other types.

frightened: Fearful of a creature, situation, or object. A frightened creature flees from the source of its fear as best it can. If unable to flee, it may fight. A frightened creature takes a –2 penalty on all attack rolls, saving throws, skill checks, and ability checks. A frightened creature can use special abilities, including spells, to flee; indeed, the creature must use such means if they are the only way to escape.

full normal hit points: An individual character's maximum hit points when undamaged.

full-round action: Full-round actions consume all of a character's effort during a round. The only movement possible in conjunction with a full-round action is a 5-foot step, which can occur before, after, or during the action. Some full-round actions (as specified in their descriptions) do not allow even this much movement. When using a full-round action to cast a spell whose casting time is 1 round, the spell is not completed until the beginning of the caster's next turn.

Gargantuan: A Gargantuan creature is typically between 32 and 64 feet in height or length and weighs between 32,000 and 250,000 pounds.

gold piece (gp): The primary unit of currency used by adventurers.

grab: The initial attack required to start a grapple. To grab a target, the character must make a successful melee touch attack.

granted power: The special ability a cleric gains from each of his selected domains.

grapple check: An opposed check that determines a character's ability to struggle in a grapple. Grapple check = 1d20 + base attack modifier + Strength modifier + special size modifier (+4 for every size category larger than Medium or –4 for every size category smaller than Medium).

grappling: Engaged in wrestling or some other form of hand-to-hand struggle with one or more attackers. A grappling character can undertake only a limited number of actions. He does not threaten any squares, and loses his Dexterity bonus to AC (if any) against opponents he isn't grappling. For creatures, grappling can also mean trapping opponents in any number of ways (in a toothy maw, under a huge paw, and so on).

half speed: When restricted to moving at half speed, count each square moved into as 2 squares, and every square of diagonal movement as 3 squares. If you are restricted to half speed, you can't run or charge, nor can you take a 5-foot step.

hardness: A measure of an object's ability to resist damage. Only damage in excess of the object's hardness is actually deducted from the object's hit points upon a successful attack.

helpless: Paralyzed, *held*, bound, sleeping, unconscious, or otherwise completely at an opponent's mercy. A helpless target is treated as having a Dexterity of 0 (–5 modifier). Melee attacks against a helpless target get a +4 bonus. An attacker can use a coup de grace against a helpless target.

hit: Make a successful attack roll.

Hit Die/Dice (HD): In the singular form, a die rolled to generate hit points. In the plural form, a measure of relative power that is synonymous with character level for the sake of spells, magic items, and magical effects that affect a certain number of Hit Dice of creatures.

hit points (hp): A measure of a character's health or an object's integrity. Damage decreases current hit points, and lost hit points return with healing or natural recovery. A character's hit point total increases permanently with additional experience

and/or permanent increases in Constitution, or temporarily through the use of various special abilities, spells, magic items, or magical effects (see temporary hit points and effective hit point increase).

Huge: A Huge creature is typically between 16 and 32 feet in height or length and weighs between 4,000 and 32,000 pounds.

incorporeal: Having no physical body. Incorporeal creatures are immune to all nonmagical attack forms. They can be harmed only by other incorporeal creatures, +1 or better magic weapons, spells, spell-like effects, or supernatural effects. Even when struck by spells, magical effects, or magic weapons, however, they have a 50% chance to ignore any damage from a corporeal source. In addition, rogues cannot employ sneak attacks against incorporeal beings, since such opponents have no vital areas to target. An incorporeal creature has no armor or natural armor bonus (or loses any armor or natural armor bonus it may have when corporeal), but it gains a deflection bonus equal to its Charisma modifier or +1, whichever is greater. Such creatures can move in any direction and even pass through solid objects at will, but not through force effects. Therefore, their attacks negate the bonuses provided by natural armor, armor, and shields, but deflection bonuses and force effects (such as *mage armor*) work normally against them. Incorporeal creatures have no weight, do not leave footprints, have no scent, and make no noise, so they cannot be heard with Listen checks unless they wish it. Incorporeal creatures cannot fall or take falling damage.

inflict spell: A spell with the word "inflict" in its name, such as *inflict light wounds*, *inflict moderate wounds*, or *mass inflict critical wounds*.

inherent bonus: A bonus to an ability score resulting from powerful magic, such as a *wish*. Inherent bonuses cannot be dispelled. A character is limited to a total inherent bonus of +5 to any ability score. Multiple inherent bonuses to a particular ability score do not stack, so only the best one applies.

initiative: A system of determining the order of actions in battle. Before the first round of combat, each combatant makes a single initiative check. Each round, the participants act in order from the highest initiative result to the lowest.

initiative check: A check used to determine a creature's place in the initiative order for a combat. An initiative check is 1d20 + Dex modifier + other modifiers.

initiative count: The result of an initiative check, expressed as a number that indicates when a character's turn comes up.

initiative modifier: A bonus or penalty on initiative checks.

Inner Plane: One of several portions of the planar landscape that contain the primal forces—those energies and elements that make up the building blocks of reality. The Elemental Planes and the Energy Planes are Inner Planes.

insight bonus: An insight bonus improves performance of a given activity by granting the character an almost precognitive knowledge of what might occur. Multiple insight bonuses on the same character or object do not stack. Only the highest insight bonus applies.

Intelligence (Int): The ability that determines how well a character learns and reasons.

invisible: Visually undetectable. An invisible creature gains a +2 bonus on attack rolls against sighted opponents, and ignores its opponents' Dexterity bonuses to AC (if any). (Invisibility has no effect against blinded or otherwise nonsighted creatures.) An invisible creature's location cannot be pinpointed by visual means. It has total concealment; even if an attacker correctly guesses the invisible creature's location, the attacker has a 50% miss chance in combat.

An invisible creature gains a +40 bonus on Hide checks if immobile, or a +20 bonus on Hide checks if moving. Locating the square an invisible creature occupies requires a Spot check (DC 40 if the creature is immobile, DC 20 if the creature moved during its last turn), modified by appropriate factors (such as an armor check penalty or a penalty for movement).

kind: A subcategory of creature type. For example, giant is a creature type, and hill giant is a kind of giant.

known spell: A spell that an arcane spellcaster has learned and can prepare. For wizards, knowing a spell means having it in their spellbooks. For sorcerers and bards, knowing a spell means having selected it when acquiring new spells as a benefit of level advancement.

Large: A Large creature is typically between 8 and 16 feet in height or length and weighs between 500 and 4,000 pounds.

lethal damage: Damage that reduces a creature's hit points.

level: A measure of advancement or power applied to several areas of the game. See caster level, character level, class level, and spell level.

light weapon: A weapon suitable for use in the wielder's off hand, such as a dagger. A light weapon is considered to be an object two size categories smaller than its designated wielder (for example, a Medium dagger is a Tiny object).

line of effect: Line of effect tells you whether an effect (such as an explosion) can reach a creature. Line of effect is just like line of sight, except line of effect ignores restrictions on visual ability. For instance, a *fireball*'s explosion doesn't care if a creature is invisible or hiding in darkness.

line of sight: Two creatures can see each other if they have line of sight to each other. To determine line of sight, draw an imaginary line between your space and the target's space. If any such line is clear (not blocked), then you have line of sight to the creature (and it has line of sight to you). The line is clear if it doesn't intersect or even touch squares that block line of sight. If you can't see the target (for instance, if you're blind or the target is invisible), you can't have line of sight to it even if you could draw an unblocked line between your space and the target's.

low-light vision: The ability to see in conditions of dim illumination as if the illumination were actually as bright as daylight.

luck bonus: A modifier that represents good fortune. Multiple luck bonuses on the same character or object do not stack. Only the highest luck bonus applies.

massive damage: At least 50 points of damage resulting from a single attack.

masterwork: Exceptionally well-made, generally providing a +1 enhancement bonus on attack rolls (if the item is a weapon or ammunition), reducing the armor check penalty by 1 (if the item is armor or a shield), or adding +2 to relevant skill checks (if the item is a tool).

Material Plane: The "normal" plane of existence.

Medium: A Medium creature is typically between 4 and 8 feet in height or length and weighs between 60 and 500 pounds.

melee: Melee combat consists of physical blows exchanged by opponents close enough to threaten one another's space, as opposed to ranged combat.

melee attack: A physical attack suitable for close combat.

melee attack bonus: A modifier applied to a melee attack roll.

melee attack roll: An attack roll during melee combat, as opposed to a ranged attack roll. See attack roll.

melee touch attack: A touch attack made in melee, as opposed to a ranged touch attack. See touch attack.

melee weapon: A handheld weapon designed for close combat.

miniature figure: The physical representation of a creature or character on the battle grid; a three-dimensional figurine.

miss chance: The possibility that a successful attack roll misses anyway because of the attacker's uncertainty about the target's location. See concealment.

miss chance roll: A d% roll to determine the success of an attack roll to which a miss chance applies.

modifier: Any bonus or penalty applying to a die roll. A positive modifier is a bonus, and a negative modifier is a penalty. Modifiers from the same source do not stack, and modifiers with specific descriptors generally do not stack with others of the same type. If more than one modifier of a type is present, only the best bonus or worst penalty in that grouping applies. Bonuses or penalties that do not have descriptors stack with those that do.

monk (Mnk): A class made up of characters who are masters of the martial arts and have a number of exotic powers.

morale bonus: A bonus representing the effects of greater hope, courage, and determination. Multiple morale bonuses on the same character do not stack. Only the highest morale bonus applies. Nonintelligent creatures (creatures with an Intelligence of 0 or no Intelligence at all) cannot benefit from morale bonuses.

move action: An action that is the equivalent of the character moving his speed. Move actions include standing up from prone, drawing or sheathing a weapon, opening a door, loading a light crossbow, and moving your speed. In a typical round, a character can take a move action and a standard action, or he can take a second move action in place of his standard action.

mundane: Normal, commonplace, or everyday. Also used as a synonym for "nonmagical."

natural: A natural result on a roll or check is the actual number appearing on the die, not the modified result obtained by adding bonuses or subtracting penalties.

natural ability: A nonmagical capability, such as walking, swimming (for aquatic creatures), and flight (for winged creatures).

natural armor bonus: A bonus to Armor Class resulting from a creature's naturally tough hide. Natural armor bonuses stack with all other bonuses to Armor Class (even with armor bonuses) except other natural armor bonuses. Some magical effects (such as the *barkskin* spell) grant an enhancement bonus to the creature's existing natural armor bonus, which has the effect of increasing the natural armor's overall bonus to Armor Class. A natural armor bonus doesn't apply against touch attacks.

natural reach: The distance from which a creature can make a melee attack. The creature threatens all squares within that distance from its space.

natural weapon: A creature's body part that deals damage in combat. Natural weapons include teeth, claws, horns, tails, and other appendages.

nauseated: Experiencing stomach distress. Nauseated creatures are unable to attack, cast spells, concentrate on spells, or do anything else requiring attention. The only action such a character can take is a single move action per turn, plus free actions (except for casting quickened spells).

negate: Invalidate, prevent, or end an effect with respect to a designated area or target.

negative energy: A black, crackling energy that originates on the Negative Material Plane. In general, negative energy heals undead creatures and hurts the living.

Negative Energy Plane: The Inner Plane from which negative energy originates.

negative level: A loss of vital energy resulting from energy drain, spells, magic items, or magical effects. For each negative level gained, a creature takes a –1 penalty on all attack rolls, saving throws, skill checks, and ability checks, loses 5 hit points, and takes a –1 penalty to effective level. (That is, whenever the creature's level is used in a die roll or calculation, reduce its value by 1 for each negative level.) In addition, a spellcaster loses one spell or spell slot from the highest spell level castable. If two or more spells fit this criterion, the caster decides which one becomes inaccessible. The lost spell becomes available again as soon as the negative level is removed, providing the caster would be capable of using it at that time. Negative levels remain in place for 24 hours after acquisition or until removed. After that period, the negative level goes away, but the afflicted creature must make a

Fortitude save (DC 10 + 1/2 the attacker's Hit Dice + the attacker's Cha modifier) to determine whether there is a lasting effect. If the saving throw succeeds, there is no harm to the character. Otherwise, the creature's character level drops by one and any benefits acquired with that level are lost. The afflicted creature must make a separate saving throw for each negative level possessed.

nonintelligent: Lacking an Intelligence score. Mind-affecting spells do not affect nonintelligent creatures, nor can nonintelligent creatures benefit from morale bonuses.

nonlethal damage: Damage typically resulting from an unarmed attack, an armed attack delivered with intent to subdue, a forced march, or a debilitating condition such as heat or starvation.

nonplayer character (NPC): A character controlled by the Dungeon Master rather than by one of the other players in a game session, as opposed to a player character.

off hand: A character's weaker or less dexterous hand (usually the left). An attack made with the off hand incurs a –4 penalty on the attack roll. In addition, only one-half of a character's Strength bonus may be added to damage dealt with a weapon held in the off hand.

one-handed weapon: A weapon designed for use in one hand, such as a longsword, often either along with a shield or a light weapon in the other hand. A one-handed weapon is considered to be an object one size category smaller than its designated wielder (for example, a Medium longsword is a Small object).

orison: A divine 0-level spell.

Outer Plane: One of several planes of existence where spirits of mortal beings go after death. These planes are the homes of powerful beings, such as demons, devils, and deities. Individual Outer Planes typically exhibit the traits of one or two specific alignments associated with the beings who control them.

overlap: Coexist with another effect or modifier in the same area or on the same target. Bonuses that do not stack with each other overlap instead, such that only the largest bonus provides its benefit.

paladin (Pal): A class made up of characters who are champions of justice and destroyers of evil, with an array of divine powers.

panicked: A panicked creature must drop anything it holds and flee at top speed from the source of its fear, as well as any other dangers it encounters, along a random path. It can't take any other actions. In addition, the creature takes a –2 penalty on saving throws, skill checks, and ability checks. If cornered, a panicked creature cowers and does not attack, typically using the total defense action in combat. A panicked creature can use special abilities, including spells, to flee; indeed, the creature must use such means if they are the only way to escape.

paralyzed: Frozen in place and unable to move or act, such as by the *hold person* spell. A paralyzed character has effective Dexterity and Strength scores of 0 and is helpless, but can take purely mental actions. A winged creature flying in the air at the time that it becomes paralyzed cannot flap its wings and falls. A paralyzed swimmer can't swim and may drown. A creature can move through a space occupied by a paralyzed creature—ally or not. Each square occupied by a paralyzed creature, however, counts as 2 squares.

party: A group of adventurers.

penalty: A negative modifier to a die roll. Penalties do not usually have a type, and always stack with other penalties (except those from the same source) unless otherwise stated.

petrified: Turned to stone. Petrified characters are considered unconscious. If a petrified character cracks or breaks, but the broken pieces are joined with the body as it returns to flesh, he is unharmed. Otherwise, the DM must assign some amount of permanent hit point loss and/or debilitation.

pinned: Held immobile (but not helpless) in a grapple.

plane of existence: One of many dimensions that may be accessed by spells, spell-like abilities, magic items, or specific creatures. These planes include (but are not limited to) the Astral Plane, the Ethereal Plane, the Inner Planes, the Outer Planes, the Plane of Shadow, and various other realities. The "normal" world is part of the Material Plane.

Plane of Shadow: A plane of existence that pervades the Material Plane. The Plane of Shadow may be accessed and manipulated from the Material Plane through shadows. Shadow spells make use of the substance of this plane in their casting. Since some creatures use the Plane of Shadow to travel from place to place, it is often described as a transitive plane (like the Astral Plane and Ethereal Plane).

platinum piece (pp): A form of currency not in common circulation but occasionally found as treasure. One platinum piece is equivalent to 10 gold pieces.

player character (PC): A character controlled by a player other than the Dungeon Master, as opposed to a nonplayer character.

point of origin: The location in space where a spell or magical effect begins. The caster designates the point of origin for any spells in which it is variable.

points of damage: A number by which an attack reduces a character's current hit points.

positive energy: A white, luminous energy that originates on the Positive Material Plane. In general, positive energy heals the living and hurts undead creatures.

Positive Energy Plane: The Inner Plane from which positive energy originates.

prerequisite: A requirement that must be met before a given benefit can be gained.

profane bonus: A bonus that stems from the power of evil. Multiple profane bonuses on the same character or object do not stack. Only the highest profane bonus applies.

projectile weapon: A device, such as a bow, that uses mechanical force to propel a projectile toward a target.

prone: Lying on the ground. An attacker who is prone has a –4 penalty on melee attack rolls and cannot use a ranged weapon (except for a crossbow). A defender who is prone gains a +4 bonus to Armor Class against ranged attacks, but takes a –4 penalty to AC against melee attacks.

racial bonus: A bonus granted because of the culture a particular creature was brought up in or because of innate characteristics of that type of creature. If a creature's race changes (for instance, if it dies and is reincarnated), it loses all racial bonuses it had in its previous form.

range increment: Each full range increment of distance between an attacker using a ranged weapon and a target gives the attacker a cumulative –2 penalty on the ranged attack roll. Thrown weapons have a maximum range of five range increments. Projectile weapons have a maximum range of ten range increments.

range penalty: A penalty applied to a ranged attack roll based on distance. See range increment.

ranged attack: Any attack made at a distance with a ranged weapon, as opposed to a melee attack.

ranged attack roll: An attack roll made with a ranged weapon. See attack roll.

ranged touch attack: A touch attack made at range, as opposed to a melee touch attack. See touch attack.

ranged weapon: A thrown or projectile weapon designed for ranged attacks.

ranger (Rgr): A class made up of characters who are particularly skilled at adventuring in the wilderness.

ray: A beam created by a spell. The caster must succeed on a ranged touch attack to hit with a ray.

reach weapon: A long melee weapon, or one that has a long haft. Reach weapons allow the user to threaten or strike at opponents 10 feet away with a melee attack roll. Most such weapons cannot be used to attack adjacent foes, however.

reaction: Acting in response to a situation or circumstance beyond one's control. For example, the DM may call for a Listen check as a reaction to see if you hear something you weren't specifically trying to hear.

rebuke undead: A supernatural ability to make undead cower by channeling negative energy.

redirect a spell: Redirect an active spell's effect at a specific target or targets. Redirecting a spell is a move action and does not provoke an attack of opportunity.

Reflex save: A type of saving throw, related to a character's ability to withstand damage thanks to his agility or quick reactions.

regeneration: The ability of some creatures to regrow severed body parts and ruined organs, repair broken bones, and heal other damage. Severed body parts that are not reattached simply die, and the regenerating creature grows replacements at a rate specified in the individual spell or monster description. Most damage dealt to a naturally regenerating creature is treated as nonlethal damage, which heals at a fixed rate. However, certain attack forms (typically fire and acid) deal damage that does not convert to nonlethal damage. Such damage is not regenerated. Regeneration does not alter conditions that do not deal damage in hit points, such as poison and disintegration.

resistance bonus: A bonus on saving throws that provides extra protection against harm. Multiple resistance bonuses on the same character or object do not stack. Only the highest resistance bonus applies.

resistance to energy: A creature with resistance to an energy type ignores a certain amount of damage dealt by that energy type each time it is dealt. For instance, a creature with fire resistance 10 ignores the first 10 points of fire damage dealt by each attack. Resistance to energy doesn't affect the saving throw made against the attack (if any). Multiple sources of resistance to a certain energy type (such as a spell and a special quality of a monster) don't stack with each other; only the highest value applies to any given attack.

result: The numerical outcome of a check, attack roll, saving throw, or other 1d20 roll. The result is the sum of the natural die roll and all applicable modifiers.

rogue (Rog): A class made up of characters who primarily rely on stealth rather than brute force or magical ability.

round: A 6-second unit of game time used to manage combat. Every combatant may take at least one action every round.

sacred bonus: A bonus that stems from the power of good. Multiple sacred bonuses on the same character or object do not stack. Only the highest sacred bonus applies.

saving throw (save): A roll made to avoid (at least partially) damage or harm. The three types of saving throws are Fortitude, Reflex, and Will.

school of magic: A group of related spells that work in similar ways. The eight schools of magic available to spellcasters are abjuration, conjuration, divination, enchantment, evocation, illusion, necromancy, and transmutation.

scribe: Write a spell onto a scroll.

scry: See and hear events from afar through the use of a spell or a magic item.

shaken: Mildly fearful. A shaken character takes a −2 penalty on attack rolls, saving throws, skill checks, and ability checks.

shield bonus: A bonus to Armor Class granted by a shield or by a spell or magic effect that mimics a shield. Shield bonuses stack with all other bonuses to AC except other shield bonuses. A magic shield typically grants an enhancement bonus to the shield's shield bonus, which has the effect of increasing the shield's overall bonus to AC. A shield bonus granted by a spell or magic item typically takes the form of an invisible, tangible field of force that protects the recipient. A shield bonus doesn't apply against touch attacks.

sickened: Mildly ill. A sickened character takes a −2 penalty on all attack rolls, weapon damage rolls, saving throws, skill checks, and ability checks.

silver piece (sp): The most prevalent form of currency among commoners. Ten silver pieces are equivalent to 1 gold piece.

size: The physical dimensions and/or weight of a creature or object. The sizes, from smallest to largest, are Fine, Diminutive, Tiny, Small, Medium, Large, Huge, Gargantuan, and Colossal.

size modifier: The bonus or penalty derived from a creature's size category. Size modifiers of different kinds apply to Armor Class, attack rolls, Hide checks, grapple checks, and various other checks.

skill: A talent that a character acquires and improves through training.

skill check: A check relating to use of a skill. The basic skill check = 1d20 + skill rank + the relevant ability modifier (or simply 1d20 + skill modifier).

skill modifier: The bonus or penalty associated with a particular skill. Skill modifier = skill rank + ability modifier + miscellaneous modifiers. (Miscellaneous modifiers include racial bonuses, armor check penalty, situational modifiers, and so forth.) Skill modifiers apply to skill checks made by characters in the course of using the corresponding skills.

skill points: A measure of a character's ability to gain and improve skills. At each level, a character gains skill points and spends them to buy skill ranks. Each skill point buys 1 rank in a class skill or 1/2 rank in a cross-class skill.

skill rank: A number indicating how much training or experience a character has with a given skill. Skill rank is incorporated into the skill modifier, which in turn improves the chance of success for skill checks with that skill.

Small: A Small creature is typically between 2 feet and 4 feet in height or length and weighs between 8 pounds and 60 pounds.

sorcerer (Sor): A class made up of characters who have inborn magical ability.

space: The amount of floor space a creature requires to fight effectively, expressed as one dimension of a square area (for example, a creature with a space of 10 feet occupies a 10-foot-by-10-foot area on the battle grid). Space determines how many creatures can fight side by side in a corridor, as well as how many creatures can attack a single opponent at once. A creature's space depends upon both its size and its body shape. Sometimes also called fighting space.

special qualities: Characteristics possessed by certain monsters (and sometimes characters) that are distinctive in some way. The *Monster Manual* has detailed information on all special qualities.

speed: The number of feet a creature can move when taking a move action.

spell: A one-time magical effect. The two primary categories of spells are arcane and divine. Clerics, druids, paladins, and rangers cast divine spells, while wizards, sorcerers, and bards cast arcane spells. Spells are further grouped into eight schools of magic.

spell completion item: A magic item (typically a scroll) that contains a partially cast spell. Since the spell preparation step has already been completed, all the user need do to cast the spell is complete the final gestures or words normally required to trigger it. To use a spell completion item safely, the caster must be high enough level in the appropriate class to cast the spell already, though it need not be a known spell. A caster who does not fit this criterion has a chance of spell failure. Activating a spell completion item is a standard action and provokes attacks of opportunity just as casting a spell does.

spell failure: The chance that a spell fails and is ruined when cast under less than ideal conditions; when a spell is cast to no effect.

spell level: A number from 0 to 9 that indicates the general power of a spell.

spell-like ability (Sp): A special ability with effects that resemble those of a spell. In most cases, a spell-like ability works just like the spell of the same name.

spell preparation: Part of the spellcasting process for wizards, clerics, paladins, rangers, and druids. Preparing a spell requires careful reading from a spellbook (for wizards) or devout prayers or meditation (for divine spellcasters). The character actually casts the first and lengthiest part of the spell during the preparation phase, leaving only the very end for completion at another time. To use a prepared spell, the character finishes the casting with the appropriate spell components—a few special words, some complex gestures, a specific item, or a combination of the three. A prepared spell is used up once cast and cannot be cast again until the spellcaster prepares it again. Sorcerers and bards need not prepare their spells.

spell resistance (SR): A special defensive ability that allows a creature or item to resist the effects of spells and spell-like abilities. Supernatural abilities are not subject to spell resistance. To overcome a creature's spell resistance, the caster of the spell or spell-like ability must equal or exceed the creature's spell resistance with a caster level check.

spell slot: The "space" in a spellcaster's mind dedicated to holding a spell of a particular spell level. A spellcaster has enough spell slots to accommodate an entire day's allotment of spells. Spellcasters who must prepare their spells in advance generally fill their spell slots during the preparation period, though a few slots can be left open for spells prepared later in the day. A spellcaster can always opt to fill a higher-level spell slot with a lower-level spell, if desired.

spell trigger item: A magic item (such as a wand) that produces a particular spell effect. Any spellcaster whose class spell list includes a particular spell knows how to use a spell trigger item that duplicates it, regardless of whether the character knows (or could know) that spell at the time. The user must determine what the spell stored in the item is before trying to use it. To activate the item, the user must speak a word, but no gesture or spell finishing is required. Activating a spell trigger item is a standard action and does not provoke attacks of opportunity.

spell version: One of several variations of the same spell. The caster must select the desired version of the spell at the time of casting. *Lesser restoration, dispel*

magic, and *create undead* are examples of spells with multiple versions.

spellcaster: A character capable of casting spells.

splash weapon: A ranged weapon that splashes on impact, dealing damage to creatures who are within 5 feet of the spot where it lands as well as to targets it actually hits. Attacks with splash weapons are ranged touch attacks.

spontaneous casting: The special ability of a cleric to drop a prepared spell (but not a domain spell) to gain a *cure* or *inflict* spell of the same level or lower, or of a druid to drop a prepared spell to gain a *summon nature's ally* spell of the same level or lower. Since the substitution of spells occurs on the spur of the moment, clerics need not prepare their *cure* or *inflict* spells in advance, nor do druids need to prepare their *summon nature's ally* spells in advance.

square: A square on the battle grid. A square is 1 inch on a side and represents a 5-foot-by-5-foot area. The terms "1 square" and "5 feet" are generally interchangeable.

stable: Unconscious and having a current hit point total between –1 and –9, but not dying. A dying character who is stable regains no hit points, but stops losing them at a rate of 1 per round.

stack: Combine for a cumulative effect. In most cases, modifiers to a given check or roll stack if they come from different sources and have different descriptors (or no descriptors at all), but do not stack if they have the same descriptors or come from the same source (such as the same spell cast twice in succession). If the modifiers to a particular roll do not stack, only the best bonus or worst penalty applies. Dodge bonuses and circumstance bonuses however, do stack with one another unless otherwise specified. Spell effects that do not stack may overlap, coexist independently, or render one another irrelevant, depending on their exact effects.

staggered: Having nonlethal damage exactly equal to current hit points. A staggered character may take a single move action or standard action each round (but not both, nor can she take full-round actions).

standard action: The most basic type of action. Common standard actions including making a melee or ranged attack, casting a spell, and using a magic item. In a typical round, a character can take a standard action and a move action, but he can't take a second standard action in place of his move action.

Strength (Str): The ability that measures a character's muscle and physical power.

stunned: A stunned creature drops everything held, can't take actions, takes a –2 penalty to AC, and loses his Dexterity bonus to AC (if any).

subject: A creature affected by a spell.

subschool: A category of spells within a school of magic. For example, charm and compulsion are subschools within the school of enchantment.

subtype: A subdivision of creature type. For example, humans and elves are both of the humanoid type, but each of those races also constitutes its own subtype of humanoid.

Jozan brings a friend back from the dead

313

supernatural ability (Su): A magical power that produces a particular effect, as opposed to a natural, extraordinary, or spell-like ability. Using a supernatural ability generally does not provoke an attack of opportunity. Supernatural abilities are not subject to dispelling, disruption, or spell resistance. However, they do not function in areas where magic is suppressed or negated, such as inside an *antimagic field*.

suppress: Cause a magical effect to cease functioning without actually ending it. When the suppression ends, the spell effect returns, provided it has not expired in the meantime.

surprise: A special situation that occurs at the beginning of a battle if some (but not all) combatants are unaware of their opponents' presence. In this case, a surprise round happens before regular rounds begin. In initiative order (highest to lowest), those combatants who started the battle aware of their opponents each take a partial action during the surprise round. Creatures unaware of opponents are flat-footed through the entire surprise round and do not enter the initiative cycle until the first regular combat round.

take damage: Be affected by damage (either lethal or non-lethal) from a successful attack. Damage dealt by an opponent does not necessarily equal damage taken, since various special defenses may reduce or negate damage from certain kinds of attacks.

take 10: To reduce the chances of failure on certain skill checks by assuming an average die roll result (10 on a d20 roll). You can't take 10 if distracted or threatened, such as during combat.

take 20: To assume that a character makes sufficient retries to obtain the maximum possible check result (as if a 20 were rolled on d20). Taking 20 takes as much time as making twenty separate skill checks (usually at least 2 minutes). Taking 20 assumes that the character fails many times before succeeding, and thus can't be used if failure carries negative consequences.

target: The intended recipient of an attack, spell, supernatural ability, extraordinary ability, or magical effect. If a targeted spell is successful, its recipient is known as the subject of the spell.

temporary hit points: Hit points gained for a limited time through certain spells (such as *aid*) and magical effects. When a character with temporary hit points is dealt damage, deduct the damage from temporary hit points first, then deduct any remaining damage (if any) to the character's actual (nontemporary) hit points. Temporary hit points can cause a character's hit point total to exceed its normal maximum.

threat: A possible critical hit.

threat range: All natural die roll results that constitute a threat when rolled for an attack roll. For most weapons, the threat range is 20, but some weapons have threat ranges of 19–20 or 18–20. Any attack roll that does not result in a hit is not a threat, whether or not it lies within the weapon's threat range.

threaten: To be able to attack in melee without moving from your current space. A creature typically threatens all squares within its natural reach, even when it is not its turn to take an action. For a Medium or Small creature this usually includes all squares adjacent to its space. Larger creatures threaten more squares, while smaller creatures may not threaten any squares except their own.

threatened square: A square within an opponent's reach. Generally, characters threaten all adjacent squares, though reach weapons can alter this range. Certain actions provoke attacks of opportunity when taken within a threatened square.

thrown weapon: A ranged weapon that a character hurls at an enemy, such as a spear, as opposed to a projectile weapon.

Tiny: A Tiny creature is typically between 1 and 2 feet in height or length and weighs between 1 and 8 pounds.

total concealment: Attacks against a target with total concealment have a 50% miss chance. Total concealment blocks line of sight. See concealment.

total cover: Attacks against a target that has total cover automatically fail. Total cover blocks line of sight and line of effect. See cover.

touch attack: An attack in which the attacker must connect with an opponent but does not need to penetrate armor. Touch attacks may be either melee or ranged. The target's armor bonus, shield bonus, and natural armor bonus (including any enhancement bonuses to those values) do not apply to AC against a touch attack.

touch spell: A spell that delivers its effect when the caster touches a target creature or object. Touch spells are delivered to unwilling targets by touch attacks.

trained: Having at least 1 rank in a skill. Many skills can be used untrained by making a successful skill check using 0 skill ranks. Others, such as Spellcraft, can be used only by characters who are trained in that skill.

transitive plane: A plane of existence often used to travel from one place (or plane) to another. The Astral Plane, the Ethereal Plane, and the Plane of Shadow are all transitive planes.

turn: The point in the round at which you take your action(s). On your turn, you may perform one or more actions, as dictated by your current circumstances.

turn undead: The supernatural ability to drive off or destroy undead by channeling positive energy.

turned: Affected by a turn undead attempt. Turned undead flee for 10 rounds (1 minute) by the best and fastest means available to them. If they cannot flee, they cower.

turning check: A roll of 1d20 + Charisma modifier to determine how much positive or negative energy is able to be channeled when attempting to turn or rebuke undead.

turning damage: The number of Hit Dice of undead that are turned or rebuked with a particular turning check. Turning damage = 2d6 + cleric level + Charisma modifier.

two-handed weapon: A weapon designed for use in two hands, such as a greatsword. A two-handed weapon is considered to be an object of the same size as its designated wielder (for example, a Medium greatsword is a Medium object).

type: See creature type.

unarmed attack: A melee attack made with no weapon in hand.

unarmed strike: A successful blow, typically dealing non-lethal damage, from a character attacking without weapons. A monk can deal lethal damage with an unarmed strike, but others deal nonlethal damage.

unconscious: Knocked out and helpless. Unconsciousness can result from having current hit points between –1 and –9, or from nonlethal damage in excess of current hit points. A character who is unconscious as a result of having current hit points between –1 and –9 who becomes stable has a 10% chance every hour to become conscious. A character who is unconscious as a result of having nonlethal damage in excess of current hit points has a 10% chance every minute to wake up and be staggered.

untrained: Having no ranks in a skill. Many skills can be used untrained by making a successful skill check using 0 ranks and including all other modifiers as normal. Other skills can be used only by characters who are trained in that skill.

use-activated item: A magic item that activates upon typical usage for a normal item of its type. For example, a character can activate a potion by drinking it, a magic sword by swinging it, a lens by looking through it, or a cloak by wearing it. Characters do not learn what a use-activated item does just by wearing or using it unless the benefit occurs automatically with use.

Will save: A type of saving throw, related to a character's ability to withstand damage thanks to his mental toughness.

Wisdom (Wis): The ability that describes a character's will-power, common sense, perception, and intuition.

wizard (Wiz): A class made up of characters who are schooled in the arcane arts.

Index

Note: Page references in this index point to significant locations in Chapters 1–11 where these topics are discussed. For definitions of game terms and concepts, refer to the Glossary beginning on page 304.

DUNGEONS & DRAGONS®

CHARACTER RECORD SHEET

CHARACTER NAME _____ PLAYER _____

CLASS AND LEVEL _____ RACE _____ ALIGNMENT _____ DEITY _____

SIZE _____ AGE _____ GENDER _____ HEIGHT _____ WEIGHT _____ EYES _____ HAIR _____ SKIN _____

ABILITY NAME	ABILITY SCORE	ABILITY MODIFIER	TEMPORARY SCORE	TEMPORARY MODIFIER
STR STRENGTH				
DEX DEXTERITY				
CON CONSTITUTION				
INT INTELLIGENCE				
WIS WISDOM				
CHA CHARISMA				

HP HIT POINTS — TOTAL / WOUNDS/CURRENT HP — NONLETHAL DAMAGE — **SPEED**

AC ARMOR CLASS — TOTAL = 10+ ARMOR BONUS + SHIELD BONUS + DEX MODIFIER + SIZE MODIFIER + NATURAL ARMOR + DEFLECTION MODIFIER + MISC MODIFIER

DAMAGE REDUCTION

TOUCH ARMOR CLASS   **FLAT-FOOTED** ARMOR CLASS

INITIATIVE MODIFIER = TOTAL DEX MODIFIER + MISC MODIFIER

SAVING THROWS

	TOTAL	BASE SAVE	ABILITY MODIFIER	MAGIC MODIFIER	MISC. MODIFIER	TEMPORARY MODIFIER	CONDITIONAL MODIFIERS
FORTITUDE (CONSTITUTION)	=	+	+	+		
REFLEX (DEXTERITY)	=	+	+	+		
WILL (WISDOM)	=	+	+	+		

BASE ATTACK BONUS _____   **SPELL RESISTANCE** _____

GRAPPLE MODIFIER = TOTAL BASE ATTACK BONUS + STRENGTH MODIFIER + SIZE MODIFIER + MISC MODIFIER

ATTACK	ATTACK BONUS	DAMAGE	CRITICAL
RANGE / **TYPE**		**NOTES**	

AMMUNITION _____ ▢▢▢▢ ▢▢▢▢ ▢▢▢▢ ▢▢▢▢ ▢▢▢▢ ▢▢▢▢

ATTACK	ATTACK BONUS	DAMAGE	CRITICAL
RANGE / **TYPE**		**NOTES**	

AMMUNITION _____ ▢▢▢▢ ▢▢▢▢ ▢▢▢▢ ▢▢▢▢ ▢▢▢▢ ▢▢▢▢

ATTACK	ATTACK BONUS	DAMAGE	CRITICAL
RANGE / **TYPE**		**NOTES**	

AMMUNITION _____ ▢▢▢▢ ▢▢▢▢ ▢▢▢▢ ▢▢▢▢ ▢▢▢▢ ▢▢▢▢

ATTACK	ATTACK BONUS	DAMAGE	CRITICAL
RANGE / **TYPE**		**NOTES**	

AMMUNITION _____ ▢▢▢▢ ▢▢▢▢ ▢▢▢▢ ▢▢▢▢ ▢▢▢▢ ▢▢▢▢

ATTACK	ATTACK BONUS	DAMAGE	CRITICAL
RANGE / **TYPE**		**NOTES**	

AMMUNITION _____ ▢▢▢▢ ▢▢▢▢ ▢▢▢▢ ▢▢▢▢ ▢▢▢▢ ▢▢▢▢

SKILLS (CLASS/CROSS-CLASS) MAX RANKS ___ / ___

CLASS SKILL?	SKILL NAME	KEY ABILITY	SKILL MODIFIER		ABILITY MODIFIER	RANKS	MISC MODIFIER
▢	Appraise ■	INT		=	+	+	
▢	Balance ■	DEX*		=	+	+	
▢	Bluff ■	CHA		=	+	+	
▢	Climb ■	STR*		=	+	+	
▢	Concentration ■	CON		=	+	+	
▢	Craft ■ (_____)	INT		=	+	+	
▢	Craft ■ (_____)	INT		=	+	+	
▢	Craft ■ (_____)	INT		=	+	+	
▢	Decipher Script	INT		=	+	+	
▢	Diplomacy ■	CHA		=	+	+	
▢	Disable Device	INT		=	+	+	
▢	Disguise ■	CHA		=	+	+	
▢	Escape Artist ■	DEX*		=	+	+	
▢	Forgery ■	INT		=	+	+	
▢	Gather Information ■	CHA		=	+	+	
▢	Handle Animal	CHA		=	+	+	
▢	Heal ■	WIS		=	+	+	
▢	Hide ■	DEX*		=	+	+	
▢	Intimidate ■	CHA		=	+	+	
▢	Jump ■	STR*		=	+	+	
▢	Knowledge (_____)	INT		=	+	+	
▢	Knowledge (_____)	INT		=	+	+	
▢	Knowledge (_____)	INT		=	+	+	
▢	Knowledge (_____)	INT		=	+	+	
▢	Knowledge (_____)	INT		=	+	+	
▢	Listen ■	WIS		=	+	+	
▢	Move Silently ■	DEX*		=	+	+	
▢	Open Lock	DEX		=	+	+	
▢	Perform (_____)	CHA		=	+	+	
▢	Perform (_____)	CHA		=	+	+	
▢	Perform (_____)	CHA		=	+	+	
▢	Profession (_____)	WIS		=	+	+	
▢	Profession (_____)	WIS		=	+	+	
▢	Ride ■	DEX		=	+	+	
▢	Search ■	INT		=	+	+	
▢	Sense Motive ■	WIS		=	+	+	
▢	Sleight of Hand	DEX*		=	+	+	
▢	Spellcraft	INT		=	+	+	
▢	Spot ■	WIS		=	+	+	
▢	Survival ■	WIS		=	+	+	
▢	Swim ■	STR*		=	+	+	
▢	Tumble	DEX*		=	+	+	
▢	Use Magic Device	CHA		=	+	+	
▢	Use Rope ■	DEX		=	+	+	
▢	_____	___		=	+	+	
▢	_____	___		=	+	+	
▢	_____	___		=	+	+	

■ Denotes a skill that can be used untrained.
▢ Mark this box with an X if the skill is a class skill for the character.
* Armor check penalty, if any, applies. (Double penalty for Swim.)

CAMPAIGN

EXPERIENCE POINTS

GEAR

ARMOR/PROTECTIVE ITEM

	TYPE	AC BONUS	MAX DEX

CHECK PENALTY	SPELL FAILURE	SPEED	WEIGHT	SPECIAL PROPERTIES

SHIELD/PROTECTIVE ITEM

	AC BONUS	WEIGHT	CHECK PENALTY

SPELL FAILURE	SPECIAL PROPERTIES

PROTECTIVE ITEM

	AC BONUS	WEIGHT	SPECIAL PROPERTIES

PROTECTIVE ITEM

	AC BONUS	WEIGHT	SPECIAL PROPERTIES

OTHER POSSESSIONS

ITEM	PG.	WT.	ITEM	PG.	WT.
				TOTAL WEIGHT CARRIED	

LIGHT LOAD	MEDIUM LOAD	HEAVY LOAD	LIFT OVER HEAD EQUALS MAX LOAD	LIFT OFF GROUND 2 × MAX LOAD	PUSH OR DRAG 5 × MAX LOAD

MONEY

CP —

SP —

GP —

PP —

FEATS
PG.

SPECIAL ABILITIES
PG.

LANGUAGES

Initial languages = Common + racial languages + one per point of Int bonus

SPELLS

DOMAINS/SPECIALTY SCHOOL:

0:

1ST:

2ND:

3RD:

4TH:

5TH:

6TH:

7TH:

8TH:

9TH:

SPELL SAVE
DC MOD

ARCANE SPELL FAILURE %

CONDITIONAL MODIFIERS

SPELLS KNOWN	SPELL SAVE DC	LEVEL	SPELLS PER DAY	BONUS SPELLS
		0		0
		1ST		
		2ND		
		3RD		
		4TH		
		5TH		
		6TH		
		7TH		
		8TH		
		9TH		

find adventure
WITHOUT A
Dungeon Master

Leave your dice bag behind. For this trek into the exciting **Dungeons & Dragons**® world, all you need is your imagination. Join Regdar, Lidda, Jozan, Mialee, and other familiar characters as they burst out of the core rulebooks and onto the pages of this action-packed novel series. So, pick up a **Dungeons & Dragons** novel at your favorite hobby or bookstore. And enjoy keeping all the experience for yourself.

DUNGEONS & DRAGONS NOVELS

www.wizards.com/books